Oxford

COLOUR SPANISH

Dictionary Plus

Third edition

SPANISH–ENGLISH
ENGLISH–SPANISH

ESPAÑOL–INGLÉS
INGLÉS–ESPAÑOL

OXFORD
UNIVERSITY PRESS

OXFORD
UNIVERSITY PRESS

Great Clarendon Street, Oxford OX2 6DP

Oxford University Press is a department of the University of Oxford.
It furthers the University's objective of excellence in research, scholarship,
and education by publishing worldwide in

Oxford New York

Auckland Cape Town Dar es Salaam Hong Kong Karachi
Kuala Lumpur Madrid Melbourne Mexico City Nairobi
New Delhi Shanghai Taipei Toronto

With offices in

Argentina Austria Brazil Chile Czech Republic France Greece
Guatemala Hungary Italy Japan Poland Portugal Singapore
South Korea Switzerland Thailand Turkey Ukraine Vietnam

Oxford is a registered trade mark of Oxford University Press
in the UK and in certain other countries

Published in the United States
by Oxford University Press Inc., New York

First published as the Oxford Spanish Minidictionary 2005
Supplementary material first published by OUP in 2001, 2005, and 2006
This edition published 2007

British Library Cataloguing in Publication Data
Data available

Library of Congress Cataloging in Publication Data
Data available

Typeset by Interactive Sciences Ltd, Gloucester
Printed in Italy
by Legoprint S.p.A

ISBN 978–0–19–921470–9
ISBN 978–0–19–921894–3 (US edition)

10 9 8 7 6 5 4 3 2 1

Contents

Preface

This dictionary is designed primarily for students of Spanish. The clear presentation and use of color make it easily accessible. This new edition contains new material, not found in the previous edition, on texting. In addition, the notes on Spanish life and culture have been expanded. It also contains a list of the Spanish words you must know, making it even more useful for students who wish to improve their vocabulary.

Contributors

Third Edition

Editors:
Nicholas Rollin
Carol Styles Carvajal

Supplementary Material:
Ana Cristina Llompart
John Butt
Michael Britton
Valerie Grundy
Josephine Grundy
Jane Horwood

Second Edition

Editors:
Carol Styles Carvajal
Michael Britton
Jane Horwood

First Edition

Editors:
Christine Lea

Introduction

The word list for this dictionary has been comprehensively revised to reflect recent additions to both languages.

Another valuable feature of the dictionary is the special status given to more complex grammatical words which provide the basic structure of both languages. Boxed entries in the text for these *function words* provide extended treatment, including notes to warn of possible pitfalls.

The dictionary has an easy-to-use, streamlined layout. A new feature for this edition is the list of Spanish words you must know, which can be found in the centre section of the dictionary. A 🔲 symbol next to a headword means that there is more information on this subject in the A–Z of Spanish life and culture found in the centre section. Round bullets ● separate each new part of speech within an entry. Nuances of sense or usage are pinpointed by indicators or by typical collocates with which the word frequently occurs. Extra help is given in the form of symbols to mark the register of words and phrases. An exclamation mark 🔲 indicates colloquial language, and a cross 🔲 indicates slang.

The swung dash (∼) is used to replace a headword or that part of a headword preceding the vertical bar (|). Square bullets ■ indicate phrasal verbs.

In both English and Spanish only irregular plurals are given. Normally Spanish nouns and adjectives ending in an unstressed vowel form the plural by adding s (e.g. *libro*, *libros*). Nouns and adjectives ending in a stressed vowel or a consonant add es (e.g. *rubí*, *rubíes*, *pared*, *paredes*). An accent on the final syllable is not required when *es* is added (e.g. *nación*, *naciones*). Final z becomes *ces* (e.g. *vez*, *veces*).

Spanish nouns and adjectives ending in o form the feminine by changing the final o to a (e.g. *hermano*, *hermana*). Most Spanish nouns and adjectives ending in anything other than final o do not have a separate feminine form, with the exception of those denoting nationality etc.; these add a to the masculine singular form (e.g. *español, española*). An accent on the final syllable is then not required (e.g. *inglés, inglesa*). Adjectives ending in án, ón, or or behave like those denoting nationality, with the following exceptions: inferior, mayor, mejor, menor, peor, superior, where the feminine has the same form as the masculine. Spanish verb tables will be found at the back of the book.

The Spanish alphabet

In Spanish ñ is considered a separate letter and in the Spanish–English section, therefore, is alphabetized after *ny*.

Proprietary terms

This dictionary includes some words which have, or are asserted to have, proprietary status as trademarks. Their inclusion does not imply that they have acquired for legal purposes a non-proprietary or general significance, nor any other judgement concerning their legal status. In cases where the editorial staff have some evidence that a word has proprietary status this is indicated in the entry for that word by the symbol ®, but no judgement concerning the legal status of such words is made or implied thereby.

Pronunciation of Spanish

Vowels

a between pronunciation of *a* in English *cat* and *arm*

e like *e* in English *bed*

i like *ee* in English *see* but a little shorter

o like *o* in English *hot* but a little longer

u like *oo* in English *too*

y when a vowel is as Spanish **i**

Consonants

b (1) in initial position or after a nasal consonant is like English *b*

(2) in other positions is between English *b* and English *v*

c (1) before **e** or **i** is like *th* in English *thin*. In Latin American Spanish is like English *s*.

(2) in other positions is like *c* in English *cat*

ch like *ch* in English *chip*

d (1) in initial position, after nasal consonants, and after /is like English *d*

(2) in other positions is like *th* in English *this*

f like English *f*

g (1) before **e** or **i** is like *ch* in Scottish *loch*

(2) in initial position is like *g* in English *get*

(3) in other positions is like (2) but a little softer

h silent in Spanish but see also **ch**

j like *ch* in Scottish *loch*

k like English *k*

Pronunciation of Spanish

- **l**   like English *l* but see also **ll**
- **ll**   like *lli* in English *million*
- **m**   like English *m*
- **n**   like English *n*
- **ñ**   like *ni* in English *opinion*
- **p**   like English *p*
- **q**   like English *k*
- **r**   rolled or trilled
- **s**   like *s* in English *sit*
- **t**   like English *t*
- **v**   (1) in initial position or after a nasal consonant is like English *b*
  (2) in other positions is between English *b* and English *v*
- **w**   like Spanish **b** or **v**
- **x**   like English *x*
- **y**   like English *y*
- **z**   like *th* in English *thin*

Glossary of grammatical terms

Abbreviation
A shortened form of a word or phrase: **Mr** = Sr.

Active
In the active form the subject of the verb performs the action: **Pedro kisses Ana** = Pedro *besa* a Ana

Adjective
A word describing a noun: **a *red* pencil** = un lápiz *rojo*; ***my* house** = *mi* casa

Adverb
A word that describes or changes the meaning of a verb, an adjective, or another adverb: **he ran *quickly*** = corrió *rápidamente*; ***very* pretty** = *muy* bonito; **she sings *very* badly** = canta *muy* mal

Apocope
The omission of the final sound of a word, as in Spanish *algún* (alguno), *tan* (tanto)

Article
The definite article, **the** = el/la/los/las, and indefinite article, **a/an** = un/una

Attributive
An adjective or noun is attributive when it is used directly before a noun: **a *good* wine** = un *buen* vino; ***business* hours** = horas *de oficina*

Auxiliary verb
A verb used with another verb to form compound tenses, as English **be, do,** and **have**: **I *have* eaten** = *he* comido; **he *was* sleeping** = *estaba* durmiendo

Cardinal number A whole number representing a quantity: **one/two/three** = uno/dos/tres

Clause
A self-contained section of a sentence that contains a subject and a verb

Collective noun
A noun that is singular in form but refers to a group of individual persons or things, e.g. **royalty, government**

Collocate
A word that regularly occurs with another; in Spanish, libro is a typical collocate of the verb leer

Comparative
The form of an adjective or adverb that makes it "more": **smaller** = más pequeño; **better** = mejor

Compound
An adjective, noun, or verb formed from two or more separate words: **self-confident (self + confident)** = seguro de sí mismo; **airmail (air + mail)** = correo aéreo; **outdo (out + do)** = superar

Conditional tense
A tense of a verb that expresses what would happen if something else occurred: **he would go** = iría

Conjugation
Variation of the form of a verb to show tense, person, mood, etc

Conjunction
A word used to join clauses together: **and** = y; **because** = porque

Glossary of grammatical terms

Countable noun
A noun that can form a plural and, in the singular, can be used with the indefinite article, e.g. **a book, two books**

Definite article:
the = el/la/los/las

Demonstrative adjective An adjective indicating the person or thing referred to: *this* **table** = *esta* mesa

Demonstrative pronoun
A pronoun indicating the person or thing referred to: *this* **is my sister** = *ésta* es mi hermana

Direct object
The noun or pronoun directly affected by the verb: **I bought** *a book* = compré *un libro*

Direct speech
A speaker's actual words or the use of these in writing: **he said:** *be quiet!* = dijo: *¡cállense!*

Ending
Letters added to the stem of verbs to show tense, and to nouns to show plurality

Feminine
One of the genders in Spanish, applied to nouns, pronouns, adjectives, and articles: **la casa blanca** = **the white house**; **ella** = **she**

Future tense
The tense of a verb that refers to something that will happen in the future: **he** *will arrive* **late** = *llegará* tarde

Gender Spanish nouns, pronouns, adjectives, and articles almost all fall into two genders, masculine and feminine; in addition, Spanish uses the neuter pronouns **esto, eso,** and **aquello,** and the neuter article **lo**

Gerund
The part of a verb used in Spanish to form continuous tenses: **muriendo = dying**; **cantando = singing**

Imperative
A form of a verb that expresses a command: **come here! = ¡ven aquí!**

Imperfect tense
The tense of a verb that refers to an uncompleted or a habitual action in the past: **the children** *were playing* = los niños *jugaban*; **I** *went/used to go* **there every Monday** = *iba* allí todos los lunes

Impersonal verb
A verb in English used only with **it**: **it is raining** = está lloviendo

Indefinite article
a/an = un/una

Indefinite pronoun
A pronoun that does not identify a specific person or object: **one, something**

Indicative form
The form of a verb used when making a statement of fact or asking questions of fact: **I'm not hungry** = no tengo hambre

Indirect object
The noun or pronoun indirectly affected by the verb, at which the direct object is aimed: **I wrote a letter** *to my mother* = *le* escribí una carta *a mi madre*

Indirect speech
A report of what someone has said which does not reproduce the exact words: **she said that they had gone**

out = dijo que habían salido; **he told me to be quiet** = me dijo que me callara

Infinitive
The basic part of a verb: **to sing** = cantar

Inflect
To change the ending or form of a word to show its tense or its grammatical relation to other words: **gone** and **went** are inflected forms of **to go**

Interjection
A sound, word, or remark expressing a strong feeling such as anger, fear, or joy, or attracting attention: **ouch!** = ¡ay!; **good heavens!** = ¡Dios mío!

Interrogative
An adjective, adverb, or pronoun that asks a question: **what?** = ¿qué?; **how much?** = ¿cuánto?; **who?** = ¿quién?

Intransitive verb
A verb that does not have a direct object: **he died suddenly** = murió repentinamente

Invariable noun
A noun that has the same form in the plural as the singular: **sheep, species**

Irregular verb
A verb that does not follow one of the set patterns and has its own individual forms, e.g. English **to be**, Spanish **ser**

Masculine
One of the genders in Spanish applied to nouns, pronouns, adjectives, and articles: **el perro negro** = **the black dog**; **él** = **he**

Modal verb A verb that is used with another verb to express necessity or possibility, e.g. **might, should, will**

Mood
A category of verb use, expressing fact (indicative), command (imperative), or wish or conditionality (subjunctive)

Negative
Expressing refusal or denial

Neuter
One of the genders in Spanish, used only in the pronouns **esto, eso**, and **aquello**, and the article **lo**

Noun
A word that names a person or a thing

Number
The state of being either singular or plural

Object
The word or words naming the person or thing acted upon by a verb or preposition: **John studies geography** = John estudia geografía

Ordinal number
A number that shows a person's or thing's position in a series: **first** = primero

Part of speech
A grammatical term for the function of a word; noun, verb, adjective, etc, are parts of speech

Passive
In the passive form the subject of the verb experiences the action rather than performs it – common in English, but not in Spanish: **Ana is kissed by Pedro** = Ana es besada por Pedro

Past participle
The part of a verb used to form past tenses: **she had gone** = había ido

Perfect tense
The tense of the verb that refers to an event that has taken place in a period of time that includes the present: **I have eaten** = he comido

Person
Any of the three groups of personal pronouns and forms taken by verbs; the **first person** (e.g. I/yo) refers to the person(s) speaking, the **second person** (e.g. **you/tú**) refers to the person(s) spoken to; the **third person** (e.g. **he/él**) refers to the persons spoken about

Personal pronoun
A pronoun that refers to a person or thing: **I/he/she** = yo/él/ella

Phrasal verb
A verb in English combined with a preposition or an adverb to have a particular meaning: **run away** = huir; **go past** = pasar

Phrase A self-contained section of a sentence that does not contain a full verb

Pluperfect tense
The tense of a verb that refers to something that happened before a particular point in the past: **he had left** = había salido

Plural
Of nouns etc, referring to more than one: **the houses** = las casas

Possessive adjective
An adjective that shows possession, belonging to someone or something: **my/your** = mi/tu

Possessive pronoun
A pronoun that shows possession, belonging to someone or something: **mine/yours** = mío/tuyo

Predicative
An adjective is predicative when it comes after a verb such as **be** or **become: she is beautiful** = es hermosa

Prefix
A letter or group of letters added to the beginning of a word to change its meaning: ***im*possible** = *im*posible, **unlucky** = *desa*fortunado

Preposition
A word that stands in front of a noun or pronoun, relating it to the rest of the sentence: **with** = con; **without** = sin

Present participle
The part of a verb that in English ends in **-ing**, and is used in forming continuous tenses: **doing** = haciendo

Present tense
The tense of a verb that refers to something happening now: **I *open* the door** = *abro* la puerta

Preterite tense
A simple tense referring to a completed action in the past: **I *did* it yesterday** = lo *hice* ayer

Pronominal verb
A Spanish verb conjugated using the pronouns me, te, se, nos, and os, in which the pronoun refers to the subject of the verb: **(yo) me equivoqué** = I was wrong. A subgroup of these verbs are REFLEXIVE VERBS

Pronoun A word that stands instead of a noun: **he/she** = él/ella; **someone** = alguien; **mine** = el mío/ la mía

Glossary of grammatical terms

Proper noun
A name of a person, place, institution, etc, in English written with a capital letter at the start: **Spain, the Atlantic, London, Juan, Madrid** are all proper nouns

Reflexive pronoun
A pronoun that refers back to the subject of the clause in which it is used: **myself = me; themselves = se**

Reflexive verb
A verb whose object is the same as its subject; in Spanish, it is used with a reflexive pronoun: **he washed himself = se lavó**

Regular verb
A verb that follows a set pattern in its different forms

Relative pronoun
A pronoun that introduces a subordinate clause, relating to a person or thing mentioned in the main clause: **the man *who* visited us = el hombre *que* nos visitó**

Reported speech
Another name for INDIRECT SPEECH

Sentence
A sequence of words, with a subject and a verb, that can stand on their own to make a statement, ask a question, or give a command

Singular
Of nouns etc, referring to just one: **the house = la casa**

Stem
The part of a word to which endings are added: **care** is the stem of **careful** and **careless**; in Spanish **cuidado** is the stem of **cuidadoso**

Subject
In a clause or sentence, the noun or pronoun that causes the action of the verb: ***John* studies geography = *John* estudia geografía**

Subjunctive
A verb form that is used to express wishes or conditionality: **long *live* the King! = ¡*viva* el Rey!; if it *was* or *were* possible = si *fuera* posible**

Subordinate clause
A clause which adds information to the main clause of a sentence but cannot be used as a sentence by itself, e.g. **she answered the phone *when it rang***

Suffix
A letter or group of letters joined to the end of a word to make another word, e.g. **quick*ly* = rápida*mente***

Superlative
The form of an adjective or adverb that makes it "most": **the smallest = la más pequeña; the best = el mejor**

Tense
The form of a verb that tells when the action takes place: present, future, imperfect, perfect, pluperfect are all tenses

Transitive verb
A verb that is used with a direct object: **she *read* the book = *leyó* el libro**

Uncountable noun
A noun that cannot form a plural in ordinary usage and is not used with the indefinite article: **china, luggage**

Verb
A word or group of words that describes an action: **the children *are playing* = los niños *están jugando***

Abbreviations / Abreviaturas

adjective	*adj*	adjetivo
abbreviation	*abbr/abrev*	abreviatura
adverb	*adv*	adverbio
American	*Amer*	americano
motoring	*Auto*	automóvil
British	*Brit*	británico
commerce	*Com*	comercio
computing	*Comp*	informática
conjunction	*conj*	conjunción
cookery	*Culin*	cocina
electricity	*Elec*	electricidad
Spain	*Esp*	España
feminine	*f*	femenino
familiar	*fam*	familiar
figurative	*fig*	figurado
philosophy	*Fil*	filosofía
photography	*Foto*	fotografía
grammar	*Gram*	gramática
interjection	*int*	interjección
invariable	*invar*	invariable
legal, law	*Jurid*	jurídico
Latin American	*LAm*	latinoamericano
masculine	*m*	masculino
mathematics	*Mat(h)*	matemáticas
mechanics	*Mec*	mecánica
medicine	*Med*	medicina
Mexico	*Mex*	México
military	*Mil*	militar
music	*Mus*	música
noun	*n*	nombre
nautical	*Naut*	náutica
oneself	*o. s.*	uno mismo, se

Abbreviations/Abreviaturas

pejorative	*pej*	peyorativo
photography	*Photo*	fotografía
plural	*pl*	plural
politics	*Pol*	política
possessive	*poss*	posesivo
past participle	*pp*	participio pasado
preposition	*prep*	preposición
present participle	*pres p*	participio de presente
pronoun	*pron*	pronombre
past tense	*pt*	tiempo pasado
railroad	*Rail*	ferrocarril
religion	*Relig*	religión
school	*Schol*	enseñanza
singular	*sing*	singular
someone	*s. o.*	alguien
something	*sth*	algo
technical	*Tec*	técnico
university	*Univ*	universidad
verb	*vb*	verbo
intransitive verb	*vi*	verbo intransitivo
pronominal verb	*vpr*	verbo pronominal
transitive verb	*vt*	verbo transitivo
transitive & intransitive verb	*vti*	verbo transitivo e intransitivo
colloquial	🔳	lenguaje coloquial
slang	🔳	argot
proprietary term	®	marca registrada
see A–Z of Spanish life and culture	🔳	
Spanish verb table number	**6**	

a preposición

Note that **a** followed by **el** becomes **al**, e.g. **vamos al cine**

····➤ (*dirección*) to. **fui a México** I went to Mexico. **muévete a la derecha** move to the right

····➤ (*posición*) **se sentaron a la mesa** they sat at the table. **al lado del banco** next to the bank. **a orillas del río** on the banks of the river

····➤ (*distancia*) **queda a 5 km** it's 5 km away. **a pocos metros de aquí** a few meters from here

····➤ (*fecha*) **hoy estamos a 5** today is the 5th. **¿a cuánto estamos?**, (LAm) **¿a cómo estamos?** what's the date?

····➤ (*hora, momento*) at. **a las 2** at 2 o'clock. **a fin de mes** at the end of the month. **a los 21 años** at the age of 21; (*después de*) after 21 years

····➤ (*precio*) **¿a cómo están las peras?** how much are the pears? **están a 3 euros el kilo** they're 3 euros a kilo. **salen a 15 euros cada uno** they work out at 15 euros each.

····➤ (*medio, modo*) **fuimos a pie** we went on foot. **hecho a mano** hand made. **pollo al horno** (LAm) roast chicken

····➤ (*cuando precede al objeto directo de persona*) no se traduce. **conocí a Juan** I met Juan. **quieren mucho a sus hijos** they love their children very much

····➤ (*con objeto indirecto*) to. **se lo di a Juan** I gave it to Juan. **le vendí el coche a mi amigo** I sold my friend the car, I sold the car to my friend. **se lo compré a mi madre** I bought it from my mother; (*para*) I bought it for my mother

▶ Cuando la preposición **a** se emplea precedida de ciertos verbos como **empezar, faltar, ir, llegar** etc., ver bajo el respectivo verbo

ábaco m abacus

abadejo m pollack

abadía f abbey

abajo adv (*down*) below; (*dirección*) down(wards); (*en casa*) downstairs. •int down with. ~ **de** (LAm) under(neath). **calle** ~ down the street. **el** ~ **firmante** the undersigned. **escaleras** ~ down the stairs. **la parte de** ~ the bottom (part). **más** ~ further down

abalanzarse 10 vpr rush (**hacia** towards)

abanderado m standard-bearer; (Mex, en fútbol) linesman

abandon|ado adj abandoned; (*descuidado*) neglected; (*persona*) untidy. ~**ar** vt leave (*un lugar*); abandon (*persona, cosa*). •vi give up. ~**arse** vpr give in; (*descuidarse*) let o.s. go. ~**o** m abandonment; (*estado*) neglect

abani|car 7 vt fan. ~**co** m fan

abaratar vt reduce

abarcar 7 vt put one's arms around, embrace; (*comprender*) embrace

abarrotar vt overfill, pack full

abarrotes mpl (LAm) groceries; (*tienda*) grocer's shop

abast|ecer 11 vt supply. ~**ecimiento** m supply; (*acción*) supplying. ~**o** m supply. **no dar** ~**o** be unable to cope (**con** with)

a

abati|do adj depressed. **~miento** m depression

abdicar 🗗 vt give up. •vi abdicate

abdom|en m abdomen. **~inal** adj abdominal

abec|é m 🗓 alphabet, ABC. **~edario** m alphabet

abedul m birch (tree)

abej|a f bee. **~orro** m bumble-bee

aberración f aberration

abertura f opening

abeto m fir (tree)

abierto pp véase ABRIR. •adj open

abism|al adj abysmal; (profundo) deep. **~ar** vt throw into an abyss; (fig, abatir) humble. **~arse** vpr be absorbed (**en** in), be lost (**en** in). **~o** m abyss; (fig, diferencia) world of difference

ablandar vt soften. **~se** vpr soften

abnega|ción f self-sacrifice. **~do** adj self-sacrificing

abochornar vt embarrass. **~se** vpr feel embarrassed

abofetear vt slap

aboga|cía f law. **~do** m lawyer, solicitor; (ante tribunal superior) barrister (Brit), attorney (Amer).

abolengo m ancestry

aboli|ción f abolition. **~cionismo** m abolitionism. **~cionista** m & f abolitionist. **~r** 🗓 vt abolish

abolla|dura f dent. **~r** vt dent

abolsado adj baggy

abomba|do adj convex; (LAm, atontado) dopey. **~r** vt make convex. **~rse** vpr (LAm, descomponerse) go bad

abominable adj abominable

abona|ble adj payable. **~do** adj paid. •m subscriber. **~r** vt pay; (en agricultura) fertilize. **~rse** vpr subscribe.

abono m payment; (estiércol) fertilizer; (a un periódico) subscription

aborda|ble adj reasonable;

(persona) approachable. **~je** m boarding. **~r** vt tackle (un asunto); approach (una persona); (Naut) come alongside; (Mex, Aviac) board

aborigen adj & m native

aborrec|er 🗓 vt loathe. **~ible** adj loathsome. **~ido** adj loathed. **~imiento** m loathing

abort|ar vi have a miscarriage. **~ivo** adj abortive. **~o** m miscarriage; (voluntario) abortion. **hacerse un ~o** have an abortion

abotonar vt button (up). **~se** vpr button (up)

abovedado adj vaulted

abrasa|dor adj burning. **~r** vt burn. **~rse** vpr burn

abraz|ar vt 🗓 embrace. **~arse** vpr embrace. **~o** m hug. **un fuerte ~o de** (en una carta) with best wishes from

abre|botellas m invar bottle-opener. **~cartas** m invar paper-knife. **~latas** m invar tin opener (Brit), can opener

abrevia|ción f abbreviation; (texto abreviado) abridged text. **~do** adj brief; (texto) abridged. **~r** vt abbreviate; abridge (texto); cut short (viaje etc). •vi be brief. **~tura** f abbreviation

abrig|ado adj (lugar) sheltered; (persona) well wrapped up. **~ador** adj (Mex, ropa) warm. **~ar** 🗓 vt shelter; cherish (esperanza); harbour (duda, sospecha). **~arse** vpr (take) shelter; (con ropa) wrap up. **~o** m (over)coat; (lugar) shelter

abril m April. **~eño** adj April

abrillantar vt polish

abrir (pp **abierto**) vt/i open. **~se** vpr open; (extenderse) open out; (el tiempo) clear

abrochar vt do up; (con botones) button up

abruma|dor adj overwhelming. **~r** vt overwhelm

abrupto adj steep; (áspero) harsh

abrutado adj brutish

absentismo m absenteeism

absolución f (Relig) absolution; (Jurid) acquittal

absolut|amente adv absolutely, completely. ~o adj absolute. **en ~o** (not) at all. ~**orio** adj of acquittal

absolver 2 (pp **absuelto**) vt (Relig) absolve; (Jurid) acquit

absor|bente adj absorbent; (fig, interesante) absorbing. ~**ber** vt absorb. ~**ción** f absorption. ~**to** adj absorbed

abstemio adj teetotal. ●m teetotaller

absten|ción f abstention. ~**erse** 40 vpr abstain, refrain (**de** from)

abstinencia f abstinence

abstra|cción f abstraction. ~**cto** adj abstract. ~**er** 41 vt abstract. ~**erse** vpr be lost in thought. ~**ído** adj absent-minded

absuelto adj (Relig) absolved; (Jurid) acquitted

absurdo adj absurd. ●m absurd thing

abuche|ar vt boo. ~o m booing

abuel|a f grandmother. ~o m grandfather. ~**os** mpl grandparents

ab|ulia f apathy. ~**úlico** adj apathetic

abulta|do adj bulky. ~r vt (fig, exagerar) exaggerate. ●vi be bulky

abunda|ncia f abundance. **nadar en la ~ncia** be rolling in money. ~**nte** adj abundant, plentiful. ~r vi be plentiful

aburguesarse vpr become middle-class

aburri|do adj (con estar) bored; (con ser) boring. ~**dor** adj (LAm) boring. ~**miento** m boredom. (cosa pesada) bore. ~r vt bore. ~**rse** vpr get bored

abus|ar vi take advantage. ~**ar de la bebida** drink too much. ~**ivo** adj excessive. ~o m abuse

acá adv here. ~ **y allá** here and there. **de ~ para allá** to and fro. **de ~ ayer** since yesterday. **más ~** nearer

acaba|do adj finished; (perfecto) perfect. ●m finish. ~r vt/i finish. ~**rse** vpr finish; (agotarse) run out; (morirse) die. ~**r con** put an end to. ~**r de** (+ infinitivo) have just (+ pp). ~ **de llegar** he has just arrived. ~**r por** (+ infinitivo) end up (+ gerundio). **¡se acabó!** that's it!

acabóse m. **ser el ~** be the end, be the limit

acad|emia f academy. ~**émico** adj academic

acallar vt silence

acalora|do adj heated; (persona) hot. ~**rse** vpr get hot; (fig, excitarse) get excited

acampar vi camp

acantilado m cliff

acapara|r vt hoard, (monopolizar) monopolize. ~**miento** m hoarding; (monopolio) monopolizing

acariciar vt caress; (animal) stroke; (idea) nurture

ácaro m mite

acarre|ar vt transport; (desgracias etc) cause. ~o m transport

acartona|do adj (piel) wizened. ~**rse** vpr (ponerse rígido) go stiff; (piel) become wizened

acaso adv maybe, perhaps. ●m chance. ~ **llueva mañana** perhaps it will rain tomorrow. **por si ~** (just) in case

acata|miento m compliance (**de** with). ~r vt comply with

acatarrarse vpr catch a cold, get a cold

acaudalado adj well off

acceder vi agree; (tener acceso) have access

acces|ible adj accessible; (persona) approachable. ~o m access, entry; (Med, ataque) attack

accesorio adj & m accessory

a

accident|ado adj (terreno) uneven; (agitado) troubled; (persona) injured. **~al** adj accidental. **~arse** vpr have an accident. **~e** m accident

acci|ón f (incl Jurid) action; (hecho) deed; (Com) share. **~onar** vt work. ●vi gesticulate. **~onista** m & f shareholder

acebo m holly (tree)

acech|ar vt lie in wait for. **~o** m spying. **al ~o** on the look-out

aceit|ar vt oil; (Culin) add oil to. **~e** m oil. **~e de oliva** olive oil. **~te de ricino** castor oil. **~era** f cruet; (para engrasar) oilcan. **~ero** adj oil. **~oso** adj oily

aceitun|a f olive. **~ado** adj olive. **~o** m olive tree

acelera|dor m accelerator. **~r** vt accelerate; (fig) speed up, quicken

acelga f chard

acent|o m accent; (énfasis) stress. **~uación** f accentuation. **~uar** 21 vt stress; (fig) emphasize. **~uarse** vpr become noticeable

acepción f meaning, sense

acepta|ble adj acceptable. **~ción** f acceptance; (éxito) success. **~r** vt accept

acequia f irrigation channel

acera f pavement (Brit), sidewalk (Amer)

acerca de prep about

acerca|miento m approach; (fig) reconciliation. **~r** 7 vt bring near. **~rse** vpr approach

acero m steel. **~ inoxidable** stainless steel

acérrimo adj (fig) staunch

acert|ado adj right, correct; (apropiado) appropriate. **~ar** 1 vt (adivinar) get right, guess. ●vi get right; (en el blanco) hit. **~ar a** happen to. **~ar con** hit on. **~ijo** m riddle

achacar 7 vt attribute

achacoso adj sickly

achaque m ailment

achatar vt flatten

achicar 7 vt make smaller; (fig, fam, empequeñecer) belittle; (Naut) bale out. **~rse** vpr become smaller; (humillarse) be intimidated

achicharra|r vt burn; (fig) pester. **~rse** vpr burn

achichincle m & f (Mex) hanger-on

achicopalado adj (Mex) depressed

achicoria f chicory

achiote m (LAm) annatto

achispa|do adj tipsy. **~rse** vpr get tipsy

achulado adj cocky

acicala|do adj dressed up. **~r** vt dress up. **~rse** vpr get dressed up

acicate m spur

acidez f acidity; (Med) heartburn

ácido adj sour. ●m acid

acierto m success; (idea) good idea; (habilidad) skill

aclama|ción f acclaim; (aplausos) applause. **~r** vt acclaim; (aplaudir) applaud

aclara|ción f explanation. **~r** vt lighten (colores); (explicar) clarify; (enjuagar) rinse. ●vi (el tiempo) brighten up. **~rse** vpr become clear. **~torio** adj explanatory

aclimata|ción f acclimatization, acclimation (Amer). **~r** vt acclimatize, acclimate (Amer). **~rse** vpr become acclimatized, become acclimated (Amer)

acné m acne

acobardar vt intimidate. **~se** vpr lose one's nerve

acocil m (Mex) freshwater shrimp

acog|edor adj welcoming; (ambiente) friendly. **~er** 14 vt welcome; (proteger) shelter; (recibir) receive. **~erse** vpr take refuge. **~ida** f welcome; (refugio) refuge

acolcha|do adj quilted. **~r** vt quilt, pad

acomedido adj (Mex) obliging

acomet|er vt attack; (emprender) undertake. ~**ida** f attack

acomod|ado adj well off. ~**ador** m usher. ~**adora** f usherette. ~**ar** vt arrange; (adaptar) adjust. •vi be suitable. ~**arse** vpr settle down; (adaptarse) conform

acompaña|miento m accompaniment. ~**nte** m & f companion; (Mus) accompanist. ~**r** vt go with; (hacer compañía) keep company; (adjuntar) enclose

acondicionar vt fit out; (preparar) prepare

aconseja|ble adj advisable. ~**do** adj advised. ~**r** vt advise. ~**rse** vpr. ~**rse con** consult

acontec|er 🔟 vi happen. ~**imiento** m event

acopla|miento m coupling; (Elec) connection. ~**r** vt fit; (Elec) connect; (Rail) couple

acorazado adj armour plated. •m battleship

acord|ar 🔟 vt agree (upon); (decidir) decide; (recordar) remind. ~**arse** vpr remember. ~**e** adj in agreement; (Mus) harmonious. •m chord

acorde|ón m accordion. ~**onista** m & f accordionist

acordona|do adj (lugar) cordoned off; (zapatos) lace-up. ~**r** vt lace (up); (rodear) cordon off

acorralar vt round up (animales); corner (personas)

acortar vt shorten; cut short (permanencia). ~**se** vpr get shorter

acos|ar vt hound; (fig) pester. ~**o** m pursuit; (fig) pestering

acostar 🔟 vt put to bed; (Naut) bring alongside. •vi (Naut) reach land. ~**se** vpr go to bed; (echarse) lie down. ~**se con** (fig) sleep with

acostumbra|do adj (habitual) usual. ~**do a** used to. ~**r** vt get used. **me ha** ~**do a levantarme por la noche** he's got me used to

getting up at night. •vi. ~**r** be accustomed to. **acostumbro a comer a la una** I usually have lunch at one o'clock. ~**rse** vpr become accustomed, get used

acota|ción f (nota) margin note (en el teatro) stage direction; (cota) elevation mark. ~**miento** m (Mex) hard shoulder

acrecentar 🔟 vt increase. ~**se** vpr increase

acredita|do adj reputable; (Pol) accredited. ~**r** vt prove; accredit (diplomático); (garantizar) guarantee; (autorizar) authorize. ~**rse** vpr make one's name

acreedor adj worthy (**de** of). •m creditor

acribillar vt (a balazos) riddle (**a** with); (a picotazos) cover (**a** with); (fig, a preguntas etc) bombard (**a** with)

acr|obacia f acrobatics. ~**obacias aéreas** aerobatics. ~**obata** m & f acrobat. ~**obático** adj acrobatic

acta f minutes; (certificado) certificate

actitud f posture, position; (fig) attitude, position

activ|ar vt activate; (acelerar) speed up. ~**idad** f activity. ~**o** adj active. •m assets

acto m act; (ceremonia) ceremony. **en el** ~ immediately

act|or m actor. ~**riz** f actress

actuación f action; (conducta) behaviour; (Theat) performance

actual adj present; (asunto) topical. ~**idad** f present; (de asunto) topicality. **en la** ~**idad** (en este momento) currently; (hoy en día) nowadays. ~**idades** fpl current affairs. ~**ización** f modernization. ~**izar** 🔟 vt modernize. ~**mente** adv now, at the present time

actuar 🔟 vi act. ~ **de** act as

acuarel|a f watercolour. ~**ista** m & f watercolourist

acuario m aquarium. **A**~ Aquarius

acuartelar vt quarter, billet; (mantener en cuartel) confine to barracks

acuático adj aquatic

acuchillar vt slash; stab (persona)

acuci|ante adj urgent. ~ar vt urge on; (dar prisa a) hasten. ~oso adj keen

acudir vi. ~ a go to; (asistir) attend; turn up for (a una cita); (en auxilio) go to help

acueducto m aqueduct

acuerdo m agreement. ●vb véase ACORDAR. ¡de ~! OK! de ~ con in accordance with. estar de ~ agree. ponerse de ~ agree

acuesto vb véase ACOSTAR

acumula|dor m accumulator. ~r vt accumulate. ~rse vpr accumulate

acunar vt rock

acuñar vt mint, coin

acupuntura f acupuncture

acurrucarse 7 vpr curl up

acusa|do adj accused; (destacado) marked. ●m accused. ~r vt accuse; (mostrar) show; (denunciar) denounce; acknowledge (recibo)

acuse m. ~ de recibo acknowledgement of receipt

acus|ica m & f 1 telltale. ~ón m 1 telltale

acústic|a f acoustics. ~o adj acoustic

adapta|ble adj adaptable. ~ción f adaptation. ~dor m adapter. ~r vt adapt; (ajustar) fit. ~rse vpr adapt o.s.

adecua|do adj suitable. ~r vt adapt, make suitable

adelant|ado adj advanced; (niño) precocious; (reloj) fast. por ~ado in advance.. ~amiento m advance(ment); (Auto) overtaking. ~r vt advance, move forward; (acelerar) speed up; put forward (reloj); (Auto) overtake. ●vi advance, go forward; (reloj) gain, be fast. ~arse vpr advance, move forward; (reloj) gain; (Auto) overtake. ~e adv forward. ●int come in!; (¡siga!) carry on! más ~e (lugar) further on; (tiempo) later on. ~o m advance; (progreso) progress

adelgaza|miento m slimming. ~r 10 vt make thin; lose (kilos). ●vi lose weight; (adrede) slim. ~rse vpr lose weight; (adrede) slim

ademán m gesture. en ~ de as if to. ademanes mpl (modales) manners.

además adv besides; (también) also; (lo que es más) what's more. ~ de besides

adentr|arse vpr. ~arse en penetrate into; study thoroughly (tema etc). ~o adv in(side). ~o de (LAm) in(side). mar ~o out at sea. tierra ~o inland

adepto m supporter

aderez|ar 10 vt flavour (bebidas); (condimentar) season; dress (ensalada). ~o m flavouring; (con condimentos) seasoning; (para ensalada) dressing

adeud|ar vt owe. ~o m debit

adhe|rir 4 vt/i stick. ~rirse vpr stick; (fig) follow. ~sión f adhesion; (fig) support. ~sivo adj & m adhesive

adici|ón f addition. ~onal adj additional. ~onar vt add

adicto adj addicted. ●m addict; (seguidor) follower

adiestra|do adj trained. ~miento m training. ~r vt train. ~rse vpr practise

adinerado adj wealthy

adiós int goodbye!; (al cruzarse con alguien) hello!

adit|amento m addition; (accesorio) accessory. ~ivo m additive

adivin|anza f riddle. ~ar vt foretell; (acertar) guess. ~o m fortune-teller

adjetivo adj adjectival. ●m adjective

adjudica|ción f award. **~r** 🔟 vt award. **~rse** vpr appropriate. **~tario** m winner of an award

adjunt|ar vt enclose. **~o** adj enclosed; (auxiliar) assistant. ● m assistant

administra|ción f administration; (gestión) management. **~dor** m administrator; (gerente) manager. **~dora** f administrator; manageress. **~r** vt administer. **~tivo** adj administrative

admira|ble adj admirable. **~ción** f admiration. **~dor** m admirer. **~r** vt admire; (sorprender) amaze. **~rse** vpr be amazed

admi|sibilidad f admissibility. **~sible** adj acceptable. **~sión** f admission; (aceptación) acceptance. **~tir** vt admit; (aceptar) accept

adobar vt (Culin) pickle; (condimentar) marinade

adobe m sun-dried brick

adobo m pickle; (condimento) marinade

adoctrinar vt indoctrinate

adolecer 🔟 vi. **~ de** suffer from

adolescen|cia f adolescence. **~te** adj adolescent. ● m & f teenager, adolescent

adonde adv where

adónde adv where?

adop|ción f adoption. **~tar** vt adopt. **~tivo** adj adoptive; (hijo) adopted; (patria) of adoption

adoquín m paving stone; (imbécil) idiot. **~inado** m paving. **~inar** vt pave

adora|ción f adoration. **~r** vt adore

adormec|er 🔟 vt send to sleep; (fig, calmar) calm, soothe. **~erse** vpr fall asleep; (un miembro) go to sleep. **~ido** adj sleepy; (un miembro) numb

adormilarse vpr doze

adorn|ar vt adorn (**con, de** with). **~o** m decoration

adosar vt lean (**a** against); (Mex, adjuntar) to enclose

adqui|rir 🔟 vt acquire; (comprar) purchase. **~sición** f acquisition; (compra) purchase. **~sitivo** adj purchasing

adrede adv on purpose

adrenalina f adrenalin

aduan|a f customs. **~ero** adj customs. ● m customs officer

aducir 🔟 vt allege

adueñarse vpr take possession

adul|ación f flattery. **~ador** adj flattering. ● m flatterer. **~ar** vt flatter

ad|ulterar vt adulterate. **~ulterio** m adultery

adulto adj & m adult, grown-up

advenedizo adj & m upstart

advenimiento m advent, arrival; (subida al trono) accession

adverbio m adverb

advers|ario m adversary. **~idad** f adversity. **~o** adj adverse, unfavourable

advert|encia f warning. **~ir** 🔟 vt warn; (notar) notice

adviento m Advent

adyacente adj adjacent

aéreo adj air; (foto) aerial; (ferrocarril) overhead

aeróbico adj aerobic

aerodeslizador m hovercraft

aero|ligero m microlight. **~lito** m meteorite. **~moza** f (LAm) flight attendant. **~puerto** m airport. **~sol** m aerosol

afab|ilidad f affability. **~le** adj affable

afamado adj famous

af|án m hard work; (deseo) desire. **~anador** m (Mex) cleaner. **~anar** vt 🔀 pinch 🔟. **~anarse** vpr strive (**en, por** to)

afear vt disfigure, make ugly; (censurar) censure

a

afecta|ción f affectation. **~do** adj
affected. **~r** vt affect

afect|ivo adj sensitive. **~o** m
(cariño) affection. • a. **~o a**
attached to. **~uoso** adj
affectionate. **con un ~uoso
saludo** (en cartas) with kind
regards. **suyo ~ísimo** (en cartas)
yours sincerely

afeita|do m shave. **~dora** f
electric razor. **~r** vt shave. **~rse**
vpr shave, have a shave

afeminado adj effeminate. • m
effeminate person

aferrar vt grasp. **~se** vpr to cling (**a**
to)

afianza|miento m (refuerzo)
strengthening; (garantía) guarantee.
~rse vpr become established

afiche m (LAm) poster

afici|ón f liking; (conjunto de
aficionados) fans. **por ~ón** as a
hobby. **~onado** adj keen (**a** on),
fond (**a** of). • m fan. **~onar** vt
make fond. **~onarse** vpr take a
liking to

afila|do adj sharp. **~dor** m
knifegrinder. **~r** vt sharpen

afilia|ción f affiliation. **~do** adj
affiliated. **~rse** vpr become a
member (**a** of)

afín adj similar; (contiguo) adjacent;
(personas) related

afina|ción f (Auto, Mus) tuning.
~do adj (Mus) in tune. **~dor** m
tuner. **~r** vt (afilar) sharpen; (Auto,
Mus) tune. **~rse** vpr become
thinner

afincarse 🟦 vpr settle

afinidad f affinity; (parentesco)
relationship by marriage

afirma|ción f affirmation. **~r** vt
make firm; (asentir) affirm. **~rse**
vpr steady o.s. **~tivo** adj
affirmative

aflicción f affliction

afligi|do adj distressed. **~r** 🟦 vt
distress. **~rse** vpr distress o.s.

aflojar vt loosen; (relajar) ease. • vi
let up. **~se** vpr loosen

aflu|encia f flow. **~ente** adj
flowing. • m tributary. **~ir** 🟦 vi
flow (**a** into)

afónico adj hoarse

aforismo m aphorism

aforo m capacity

afortunado adj fortunate, lucky

afrancesado adj Frenchified

afrenta f insult; (vergüenza) disgrace

África f Africa. **~ del Sur** South
Africa

africano adj & m African

afrodisíaco adj & m aphrodisiac

afrontar vt bring face to face;
(enfrentar) face, confront

afuera adv out(side) **¡~!** out of
the way! **~ de** (LAm) outside. **~s**
fpl outskirts

agachar vt lower. **~se** vpr bend
over

agalla f (de los peces) gill. **~s** fpl (fig)
guts

agarradera f (LAm) handle

agarr|ado adj (fig, fam) mean. **~ar**
vt grasp; (esp LAm) take; (LAm, pillar)
catch. **~arse** vpr hold on; (fam,
reñirse) have a fight. **~ón** m tug;
(LAm, riña) row

agarrotar vt tie tightly; (el frío)
stiffen; garotte (un reo). **~se** vpr go
stiff; (Auto) seize up

agasaj|ado m guest of honour.
~ar vt look after well. **~o** m good
treatment

agazaparse vpr crouch

agencia f agency. **~ de viajes**
travel agency. **~ inmobiliaria**
estate agency (Brit), real estate
agency (Amer). **~rse** vpr find (out)
for o.s.

agenda f diary (Brit), appointment
book (Amer); (programa) agenda

agente m agent; (de policía)
policeman. • f agent; (de policía)
policewoman. **~ de aduanas**

customs officer. **~ de bolsa** stockbroker

ágil adj agile

agili|dad f agility. **~zación** f speeding up. **~zar** vt speed up

agita|ción f waving; (de un líquido) stirring; (intranquilidad) agitation. **~do** adj (el mar) rough; (fig) agitated. **~dor** m (Pol) agitator

agitar vt wave; shake (botellas etc); stir (líquidos); (fig) stir up. **~se** vpr wave; (el mar) get rough; (fig) get excited

aglomera|ción f agglomeration; (de tráfico) traffic jam. **~r** vt amass. **~rse** vpr form a crowd

agnóstico adj & m agnostic

agobi|ante adj (trabajo) exhausting; (calor) oppressive. **~ar** vt weigh down; (fig, abrumar) overwhelm. **~o** m weight; (cansancio) exhaustion; (opresión) oppression

agolparse vpr crowd together

agon|ía f death throes; (fig) agony. **~izante** adj dying; (luz) failing. **~izar** 10 vi be dying

agosto m August. **hacer su ~** feather one's nest

agota|do adj exhausted; (todo vendido) sold out; (libro) out of print. **~dor** adj exhausting. **~miento** m exhaustion. **~r** vt exhaust. **~rse** vpr be exhausted; (existencias) sell out; (libro) go out of print

agracia|do adj attractive; (que tiene suerte) lucky. **~r** vt make attractive

agrada|ble adj pleasant, nice. **~r** vt/i please. **esto me ~** I like this

agradec|er 11 vt thank (persona); be grateful for (cosa). **~ido** adj grateful. **¡muy ~ido!** thanks a lot! **~imiento** m gratitude

agrado m pleasure; (amabilidad) friendliness

agrandar vt enlarge; (fig) exaggerate. **~se** vpr get bigger

agrario adj agrarian, land; (política) agricultural

agrava|nte adj aggravating. • f additional problem. **~r** vt aggravate; (aumentar el peso) make heavier. **~rse** vpr get worse

agravi|ar vt offend; (perjudicar) wrong. **~o** m offence

agredir 24 vt attack. **~ de palabra** insult

agrega|do m aggregate; (diplomático) attaché. **~r** 12 vt add; appoint (persona). **~rse** vpr to join

agres|ión f aggression; (ataque) attack. **~ividad** f aggressiveness. **~ivo** adj aggressive. **~or** m aggressor

agreste adj country; (terreno) rough

agriar regular, o raramente 20 vt sour. **~se** vpr turn sour; (fig) become embittered

agr|ícola adj agricultural. **~icultor** m farmer. **~icultura** f agriculture, farming

agridulce adj bitter-sweet; (Culin) sweet-and-sour

agrietar vt crack. **~se** vpr crack; (piel) chap

agrio adj sour. **~s** mpl citrus fruits

agro|nomía f agronomy. **~pecuario** adj farming

agrupa|ción f group; (acción) grouping. **~r** vt group. **~rse** vpr form a group

agruras fpl (Mex) heartburn

agua f water; (lluvia) rain; (marea) tide; (vertiente del tejado) slope. **~ abajo** downstream. **~ arriba** upstream. **~ bendita** holy water. **~ corriente** running water. **~ de colonia** eau de cologne. **~ dulce** fresh water. **~ mineral con gas** fizzy mineral water. **~ mineral sin gas** still mineral water. **~ potable** drinking water. **~ salada** salt water. **hacer ~** (Naut) leak. **se me hizo ~ la boca** (LAm) my mouth watered

aguacate m avocado pear; (árbol) avocado pear tree

aguacero m downpour, heavy shower

aguado adj watery; (Mex, aburrido) boring

agua|fiestas m & f invar spoilsport, wet blanket. ~**mala** f (Mex), ~**mar** m jellyfish. ~**marina** f aquamarine

aguant|ar vt put up with, bear; (sostener) support. ●vi hold out. ~**arse** vpr restrain o.s. ~**e** m patience; (resistencia) endurance

aguar vt water down

aguardar vt wait for. ●vi wait

agua|rdiente m (cheap) brandy. ~**rrás** m turpentine, turps

agud|eza f sharpness; (fig, perspicacia) insight; (fig, ingenio) wit. ~**izar** vt sharpen. ~**izarse** vpr (enfermedad) get worse. ~**o** adj sharp; (ángulo, enfermedad) acute; (voz) high-pitched

agüero m omen. **ser de mal** ~ be a bad omen

aguijón m sting; (vara) goad

águila f eagle; (persona perspicaz) astute person; (Mex, de moneda) heads. **¿**~ **o sol?** heads or tails?

aguileño adj aquiline

aguinaldo m Christmas box; (LAm, paga) Christmas bonus

aguja f needle; (del reloj) hand; (de torre) steeple. ~**s** fpl (Rail) points

agujer|ear vt make holes in. ~**o** m hole

agujetas fpl stiffness; (Mex, de zapatos) shoe laces. **tener** ~ be stiff

aguzado adj sharp

ah int ah!, oh!

ahí adv there. ~ **nomás** (LAm) just there. **de** ~ **que** that is why. **por** ~ that way; (aproximadamente) thereabouts

ahija|da f god-daughter, godchild. ~**do** m godson, godchild. ~**dos** mpl godchildren

ahínco m enthusiasm; (empeño) insistence

ahog|ado adj (en el agua) drowned; (asfixiado) suffocated. ~**ar** vt (en el agua) drown; (asfixiar) suffocate; put out (fuego). ~**arse** vpr (en el agua) drown; (asfixiarse) suffocate. ~**o** m breathlessness; (fig, angustia) distress

ahondar vt deepen. ●vi go deep. ~ **en** (fig) examine in depth. ~**se** vpr get deeper

ahora adv now; (hace muy poco) just now; (dentro de poco) very soon. ~ **bien** however. ~ **mismo** right now. **de** ~ **en adelante** from now on, in future. **por** ~ for the time being

ahorcar vt hang. ~**se** vpr hang o.s.

ahorita adv (esp LAm fam) now. ~ **mismo** right now

ahorr|ador adj thrifty. ~**ar** vt save. ~**arse** vpr save o.s. ~**o** m saving. ~**os** mpl savings

ahuecar vt hollow; fluff up (colchón); deepen (la voz)

ahuizote m (Mex) scourge

ahuma|do adj (Culin) smoked; (de colores) smoky. ~**r** vt (Culin) smoke; (llenar de humo) fill with smoke. ●vi smoke. ~**rse** vpr become smoky; (comida) acquire a smoky taste

ahuyentar vt drive away; banish (pensamientos etc)

aimará adj & m Aymara. ●m & f Aymara indian

airado adj annoyed

aire m air; (viento) breeze; (corriente) draught; (aspecto) appearance; (Mus) tune, air. ~ **acondicionado** air-conditioning. **al** ~ **libre** outdoors. **darse** ~**s** give o.s. airs. ~**ar** vt air; (ventilar) ventilate; (fig, publicar) make public. ~**arse** vpr. **salir para** ~**arse** go out for some fresh air

airoso adj graceful; (exitoso) successful

aisla|do adj isolated; (Elec) insulated. **~dor** adj (Elec) insulating. **~nte** adj insulating. **~r** 28 vt isolate; (Elec) insulate

ajar vt crumple; (estropear) spoil

ajedre|cista m & f chess-player. **~z** m chess

ajeno adj (de otro) someone else's; (de otros) other people's; (extraño) alien

ajetre|ado adj hectic, busy. **~o** m bustle

ají m (LAm) chilli; (salsa) chilli sauce

aj|illo m garlic. **al ~illo** cooked with garlic. **~o** m garlic. **~onjolí** m sesame

ajuar m furnishings; (de novia) trousseau; (de bebé) layette

ajust|ado adj right; (vestido) tight. **~ar** vt fit; (adaptar) adapt; (acordar) agree; settle (una cuenta); (apretar) tighten. ●vi fit. **~arse** vpr fit; (adaptarse) adapt o.s.; (acordarse) come to an agreement. **~e** m fitting; (adaptación) adjustment; (acuerdo) agreement; (de una cuenta) settlement

al = a + el

ala f wing; (de sombrero) brim. ●m & f (deportes) winger

alaba|nza f praise. **~r** vt praise

alacena f cupboard (Brit), closet (Amer)

alacrán m scorpion

alambr|ada f wire fence. **~ado** m (LAm) wire fence. **~e** m wire. **~e de púas** barbed wire

alameda f avenue; (plantío de álamos) poplar grove

álamo m poplar. **~ temblón** aspen

alarde m show. **hacer ~ de** boast of

alarga|do adj long. **~dor** m extension. **~r** 12 vt lengthen; stretch out (mano etc); (dar) give, pass. **~rse** vpr get longer

alarido m shriek

alarm|a f alarm. **~ante** adj alarming. **~ar** vt alarm, frighten. **~arse** vpr be alarmed. **~ista** m & f alarmist

alba f dawn

albacea m & f executor

albahaca f basil

albanés adj & m Albanian

Albania f Albania

albañil m builder; (que coloca ladrillos) bricklayer

albarán m delivery note

albaricoque m apricot. **~ro** m apricot tree

albedrío m will. **libre ~** free will

alberca f tank, reservoir; (Mex, piscina) swimming pool

alberg|ar 12 vt (alojar) put up; (vivienda) house; (dar refugio) shelter. **~arse** vpr stay; (refugiarse) shelter. **~ue** m accommodation; (refugio) shelter. **~ue de juventud** youth hostel

albino adj & m albino

albóndiga f meatball, rissole

albornoz m bathrobe

alborot|ado adj excited; (aturdido) hasty. **~ador** adj rowdy. ●m trouble-maker. **~ar** vt disturb, upset. ●vi make a racket. **~arse** vpr get excited; (el mar) get rough. **~o** m row, uproar

álbum m (pl **~es** o **~s**) album

alcachofa f artichoke

🄰**alcald|e** m mayor. **~esa** f mayoress. **~ía** f mayoralty; (oficina) mayor's office

alcance m reach; (de arma, telescopio etc) range; (déficit) deficit

alcancía f money-box; (LAm, de niño) piggy bank

alcantarilla f sewer; (boca) drain

alcanzar 10 vt (llegar a) catch up; (coger) reach; catch (un autobús);

🄰 *see* A-Z of Spanish life and culture

a

(bala etc) strike, hit. • vi reach; (ser suficiente) be enough. **~ a** manage

alcaparra f caper

alcázar m fortress

alcoba f bedroom

alcoh|ol m alcohol. **~ol desnaturalizado** methylated spirits, meths. **~ólico** adj & m alcoholic. **~olímetro** m Breathalyser . **~olismo** m alcoholism

alcornoque m cork-oak; (persona torpe) idiot

aldaba f door-knocker

aldea f village. **~no** adj village. • m villager

alea|ción f alloy. **~r** vt alloy

aleatorio adj uncertain

aleccionar vt instruct

aledaños mpl outskirts

alega|ción f allegation; (LAm, disputa) argument. **~r** 12 vt claim; (Jurid) plead. • vi (LAm) argue. **~ta** f (Mex) argument. **~to** m plea

alegoría f allegory

alegr|ar vt make happy; (avivar) brighten up. **~arse** vpr be happy; (emborracharse) get merry; **~e** adj happy; (achispado) merry, tight. **~ía** f happiness

aleja|do adj distant. **~miento** m removal; (entre personas) estrangement; (distancia) distance. **~r** vt remove; (ahuyentar) get rid of; (fig, apartar) separate. **~rse** vpr move away

alemán adj & m German

Alemania f Germany. **~ Occidental** (historia) West Germany. **~ Oriental** (historia) East Germany

alenta|dor adj encouraging. **~r** 1 vt encourage. • vi breathe

alerce m larch

al|ergia f allergy. **~érgico** adj allergic

alero m (del tejado) eaves

alerta adj alert. **¡~!** look out! **estar ~** be alert; (en guardia) be on the alert. **~r** vt alert

aleta f wing; (de pez) fin

aletarga|do adj lethargic. **~r** 12 vt make lethargic. **~rse** vpr become lethargic

alet|azo m (de un ave) flap of the wings; (de un pez) flick of the fin. **~ear** vi flap its wings, flutter

alevosía f treachery

alfab|ético adj alphabetical. **~etizar** 10 vt alphabetize; teach to read and write. **~eto** m alphabet. **~eto Morse** Morse code

alfalfa f alfalfa

alfar|ería m pottery. **~ero** m potter

alféizar m (window)sill

alférez m second lieutenant

alfil m (en ajedrez) bishop

alfile|r m pin. **~tero** m pincushion; (estuche) pin-case

alfombr|a f (grande) carpet; (pequeña) rug, mat. **~ado** adj (LAm) carpeted. **~ar** vt carpet. **~illa** f rug, mat; (Med) type of measles

alforja f saddle-bag

algarabía f hubbub

algas fpl seaweed

álgebra f algebra

álgido adj (fig) decisive

algo pron something; (en frases interrogativas, condicionales) anything. • adv rather. **¿~ más?** anything else? **¿quieres tomar ~?** would you like a drink?; (de comer) would you like something to eat?

algod|ón m cotton. **~ón de azúcar** candy floss (Brit), cotton candy (Amer). **~ón hidrófilo** cotton wool. **~onero** adj cotton. • m cotton plant

alguacil m bailiff

alguien pron someone, somebody; (en frases interrogativas, condicionales) anyone, anybody

algún véase **ALGUNO**

alguno adj (delante de nombres masculinos en singular **algún**) some; (en frases interrogativas, condicionales) any; (pospuesto al nombre en frases negativas) at all. **no tiene idea alguna** he hasn't any idea at all. **alguna que otra vez** from time to time. **algunas veces, alguna vez** sometimes. ● pron one; (en plural) some; (alguien) someone

alhaja f piece of jewellery; (fig) treasure. ~**s** fpl jewellery

alharaca f fuss

alhelí m wallflower

alia|do adj allied. ● m ally. ~**nza** f alliance; (anillo) wedding ring. ~**r** 20 vt combine. ~**rse** vpr be combined; (formar una alianza) form an alliance

alias adv & m alias

alicaído adj (fig, débil) weak; (fig, abatido) depressed

alicates mpl pliers

aliciente m incentive; (de un lugar) attraction

alienado adj mentally ill

aliento m breath; (ánimo) courage

aligerar vt make lighter; (aliviar) alleviate, ease; (apresurar) quicken

alijo m (de contrabando) consignment

alimaña f pest. ~**s** fpl vermin

aliment|ación f diet; (acción) feeding. ~**ar** vt feed; (nutrir) nourish. ● vi be nourishing. ~**arse** vpr feed (**con, de** on). ~**icio** adj nourishing. **productos** mpl ~**icios** foodstuffs. ~**o** m food. ~**os** mpl (Jurid) alimony

alinea|ción f alignment; (en deportes) line-up. ~**r** vt align, line up

aliñ|ar vt (Culin) season; dress (ensalada). ~**o** m seasoning; (para ensalada) dressing

alioli m garlic mayonnaise

alisar vt smooth

alistar vt put on a list; (Mil) enlist. ~**se** vpr enrol; (Mil) enlist; (LAm, prepararse) get ready

alivi|ar vt lighten; relieve (dolor, etc); (arg, hurtar) steal, pinch 🔲. ~**arse** vpr (dolor) diminish; (persona) get better. ~**o** m relief

aljibe m tank

allá adv (over) there. **¡~ él!** that's his business! ~ **fuera** out there. ~ **por 1970** back in 1970. **el más** ~ the beyond. **más** ~ further on. **más** ~ **de** beyond. **por** ~ that way

allana|miento m. ~**miento (de morada)** breaking and entering; (LAm, por la autoridad) raid. ~**r** vt level; remove (obstáculos); (fig) iron out (dificultades etc); break into (una casa); (LAm, por la autoridad) raid

allega|do adj close. ● m close friend; (pariente) close relative. ~**r** 12 vt collect

allí adv there; (tiempo) then. ~ **fuera** out there. **por** ~ that way

alma f soul; (habitante) inhabitant

almac|én m warehouse; (LAm, tienda) grocer's shop; (de un arma) magazine. ~**enes** mpl department store. ~**enaje** m storage; (derechos) storage charges. ~**enar** vt store; stock up with (provisiones)

almanaque m almanac

almeja f clam

almendr|a f almond. ~**ado** adj almond-shaped. ~**o** m almond tree

alm|íbar m syrup. ~**ibarar** vt cover in syrup

almid|ón m starch. ~**onado** adj starched; (fig, estirado) starchy

almirante m admiral

almizcle m musk. ~**ra** f muskrat

almohad|a f pillow. **consultar con la** ~**a** sleep on it. ~**illa** f small cushion. ~**ón** m large pillow, bolster

almorranas fpl haemorrhoids, piles

a

alm|orzar 2 & 10 vt (a mediodía) have for lunch; (desayunar) have for breakfast. • vi (a mediodía) have lunch; (desayunar) have breakfast. **~uerzo** m (a mediodía) lunch; (desayuno) breakfast

alocado adj scatter-brained

aloja|miento m accommodation. **~r** vt put up. **~rse** vpr stay

alondra f lark

alpaca f alpaca

alpargata f canvas shoe, espadrille

alpin|ismo m mountaineering, climbing. **~ista** m & f mountaineer, climber. **~o** adj Alpine

alpiste m birdseed

alquil|ar vt (tomar en alquiler) hire (vehículo), rent (piso, casa); (dar en alquiler) hire (out) (vehículo), rent (out) (piso, casa). **se alquila** to let (Brit), for rent (Amer). **~er** m (acción — de alquilar un piso etc) renting; (— de alquilar un vehículo) hiring; (precio — por el que se alquila un piso etc) rent; (— por el que se alquila un vehículo) hire charge. **de ~er** for hire

alquimi|a f alchemy. **~sta** m alchemist

alquitrán m tar

alrededor adv around. **~ de** around; (con números) about. **~es** mpl surroundings; (de una ciudad) outskirts

alta f discharge

altaner|ía f (arrogancia) arrogance. **~o** adj arrogant, haughty

altar m altar

altavoz m loudspeaker

altera|ble adj changeable. **~ción** f change, alteration. **~r** vt change, alter; (perturbar) disturb; (enfadar) anger, irritate. **~rse** vpr change, alter; (agitarse) get upset; (enfadarse) get angry; (comida) go off

altercado m argument

altern|ar vt/i alternate. **~arse** vpr take turns. **~ativa** f alternative. **~ativo** adj alternating. **~o** adj alternate; (Elec) alternating

Alteza f (título) Highness

altibajos mpl (de terreno) unevenness; (fig) ups and downs

altiplanicie f, **altiplano** m high plateau

altisonante adj pompous

altitud f altitude

altiv|ez f arrogance. **~o** adj arrogant

alto adj high; (persona, edificio) tall; (voz) loud; (fig, elevado) lofty; (Mus) (nota) high(-pitched); (Mus) (voz, instrumento) alto; (horas) early. • adv high; (de sonidos) loud(ly). • m height; (de un edificio) top floor; (viola) viola; (voz) alto; (parada) stop. • int halt!, stop! **en lo ~ de** on the top of. **tiene 3 metros de ~** it is 3 metres high

altoparlante m (esp LAm) loudspeaker

altruis|mo m altruism. **~ta** adj altruistic. • m & f altruist

altura f height; (Aviac, Geog) altitude; (de agua) depth; (fig, cielo) sky. **a estas ~s** at this stage. **tiene 3 metros de ~** it is 3 metres high

alubia f (haricot) bean

alucinación f hallucination

alud m avalanche

aludi|do adj in question. **darse por ~do** take it personally. **no darse por ~do** turn a deaf ear. **~r** vi mention

alumbra|do adj lit. • m lighting. **~miento** m lighting; (parto) childbirth. **~r** vt light

aluminio m aluminium (Brit), aluminum (Amer)

alumno m pupil; (Univ) student

aluniza|je m landing on the moon. **~r** 10 vi land on the moon

alusi|ón f allusion. **~vo** adj allusive

alza f rise. ~**da** f (de caballo) height; (Jurid) appeal. ~**do** adj raised; (Mex, soberbio) vain; (precio) fixed. ~**miento** m (Pol) uprising. ~**r** 🔟 vt raise, lift (up); raise (precios). ~**rse** vpr (Pol) rise up

ama f lady of the house. ~ **de casa** housewife. ~ **de cría** wet-nurse. ~ **de llaves** housekeeper

amab|ilidad f kindness. ~**le** adj kind; (simpático) nice

amaestra|do adj trained. ~**r** vt train

amag|ar 🔢 vt (mostrar intención de) make as if to; (Mex, amenazar) threaten. ●vi threaten; (algo bueno) be in the offing. ~**o** m threat; (señal) sign; (Med) symptom

amainar vi let up

amalgama f amalgam. ~**r** vt amalgamate

amamantar vt/i breast-feed; (animal) to suckle

amanecer m dawn. ●vi dawn; (persona) wake up. **al** ~ at dawn, at daybreak. ~**se** vpr (Mex) stay up all night

amanera|do adj affected. ~**rse** vpr become affected

amansar vt tame; break in (un caballo); soothe (dolor etc), ~**se** vpr calm down

amante adj fond. ●m & f lover

amapola f poppy

amar vt love

amara|je m landing on water; (de astronave) splash-down. ~**r** vi land on water; (astronave) splash down

amarg|ado adj embittered. ~**ar** 🔢 vt make bitter; embitter (persona). ~**arse** vpr become bitter. ~**o** adj bitter. ~**ura** f bitterness

amariconado adj 🔟 effeminate

amarill|ento adj yellowish; (tez) sallow. ~**o** adj & m yellow

amarra|s fpl. **soltar las** ~**s** cast off. ~**do** adj (LAm) mean. ~**r** vt

moor; (esp LAm, atar) tie. ~**rse** vpr LAm tie up

amas|ar vt knead; (acumular) to amass. ~**ijo** m dough; (acción) kneading; (fig, fam, mezcla) hotchpotch

amate m (Mex) fig tree

amateur adj & m & f amateur

amazona f Amazon; (jinete) horsewoman

ámbar m amber

ambici|ón f ambition. ~**onar** vt aspire to. ~**onar ser** have an ambition to be. ~**oso** adj ambitious. ●m ambitious person

ambidextro adj ambidextrous. ●m ambidextrous person

ambient|ar vt give an atmosphere to. ~**arse** vpr adapt o.s. ~**e** m atmosphere; (entorno) environment

ambig|üedad f ambiguity. ~**uo** adj ambiguous

ámbito m sphere; (alcance) scope

ambos adj & pron both

ambulancia f ambulance

ambulante adj travelling

🗔**ambulatorio** m out-patients' department

amedrentar vt frighten, scare. ~**se** vpr be frightened

amén ●m amen. ●int amen! **en un decir** ~ in an instant

amenaza f threat. ~**r** 🔟 vt threaten

amen|idad f pleasantness. ~**izar** 🔟 vt brighten up. ~**o** adj pleasant

América f America. ~ **Central** Central America. ~ **del Norte** North America. ~ **del Sur** South America. ~ **Latina** Latin America

american|a f jacket. ~**ismo** m Americanism. ~**o** adj American

amerita|do adj (LAm) meritorious. ~**r** vt (LAm) deserve

amerizaje m véase **AMARAJE**

....

🗔 *see A-Z of Spanish life and culture*

ametralla|dora f machine-gun. **∼r** vt machine-gun

amianto m asbestos

amig|a f friend; (novia) girl-friend; (amante) lover. **∼able** adj friendly. **∼ablemente** adv amicably

am|ígdala f tonsil. **∼igdalitis** f tonsillitis

amigo adj friendly. ●m friend; (novio) boyfriend; (amante) lover. **ser ∼ de** be fond of. **ser muy ∼s** be close friends

amilanar vt daunt. **∼se** vpr be daunted

aminorar vt lessen; reduce (velocidad)

amist|ad f friendship. **∼ades** fpl friends. **∼oso** adj friendly

amn|esia f amnesia. **∼ésico** adj amnesiac

amnist|ía f amnesty. **∼iar** 20 vt grant an amnesty to

amo m master; (dueño) owner

amodorrarse vpr feel sleepy

amoldar vt mould; (adaptar) adapt; (acomodar) fit. **∼se** vpr adapt

amonestar vt rebuke, reprimand; (anunciar la boda) publish the banns

amoniaco, amoníaco m ammonia

amontonar vt pile up; (fig, acumular) accumulate. **∼se** vpr pile up; (gente) crowd together

amor m love. **∼es** mpl (relaciones amorosas) love affairs. **∼ propio** pride. **con mil ∼es, de mil ∼es** with (the greatest of) pleasure. **hacer el ∼** make love. **por (el) ∼ de Dios** for God's sake

amoratado adj purple; (de frío) blue

amordazar 10 vt gag; (fig) silence

amorfo adj amorphous, shapeless

amor|ío m affair. **∼oso** adj loving; (cartas) love; (LAm, encantador) cute

amortajar vt shroud

amortigua|dor adj deadening. ●m

(Auto) shock absorber. **∼r** 15 vt deaden (ruido); dim (luz); cushion (golpe); tone down (color)

amortiza|ble adj redeemable. **∼ción** f (de una deuda) repayment; (de bono etc) redemption. **∼r** 10 vt repay (una deuda)

amotinar vt incite to riot. **∼se** vpr rebel; (Mil) mutiny

ampar|ar vt help; (proteger) protect. **∼arse** vpr seek protection; (de la lluvia) shelter. **∼o** m protection; (de la lluvia) shelter. **al ∼o de** under the protection of

amperio m ampere, amp 1

amplia|ción f extension; (photo) enlargement. **∼r** 20 vt enlarge, extend; (photo) enlarge

amplifica|ción f amplification. **∼dor** m amplifier. **∼r** 7 amplify

ampli|o adj wide; (espacioso) spacious; (ropa) loose-fitting. **∼tud** f extent; (espaciosidad) spaciousness; (espacio) space

ampolla f (Med) blister; (de medicamento) ampoule, phial

ampuloso adj pompous

amputar vt amputate; (fig) delete

amueblar vt furnish

amuleto m charm, amulet

amuralla|do adj walled. **∼r** vt build a wall around

anacr|ónico adj anachronistic. **∼onismo** m anachronism

anales mpl annals

analfabet|ismo m illiteracy. **∼o** adj & m illiterate

analgésico adj analgesic. ●m painkiller

an|álisis m invar analysis. **∼álisis de sangre** blood test. **∼alista** m & f analyst. **∼alítico** adj analytical. **∼alizar** 10 vt analyze

an|alogía f analogy. **∼álogo** adj analogous

anaranjado adj orangey

an|arquía f anarchy. **∼árquico** adj

anarchic. ~arquismo m anarchism. **~arquista** adj anarchistic. ● m & f anarchist

anat|omía f anatomy. **~ómico** adj anatomical

anca f haunch; (parte superior) rump; (fam, nalgas) bottom. **en ~s** (LAm) on the crupper

ancestro m ancestor

ancho adj wide; (ropa) loose-fitting; (fig) relieved; (demasiado grande) too big; (ufano) smug. ● m width; (Rail) gauge. **~ de banda** bandwidth. **tiene 3 metros de ~** it is 3 metres wide

anchoa f anchovy

anchura f width; (medida) measurement

ancian|o adj elderly, old. ● m elderly man, old man. **~a** f elderly woman, old woman. **los ~os** old people

ancla f anchor. **echar ~s** drop anchor. **levar ~s** weigh anchor. **~r** vi anchor

andad|eras fpl (Mex) baby-walker. **~or** m baby-walker

Andalucía f Andalusia

andaluz adj & m Andalusian

andamio m platform. **~s** mpl scaffolding

and|anzas fpl adventures. **~ar** 25 vt (recorrer) cover, go. ● vi walk; (máquina) go, work; (estar) be; (moverse) move. **~ar a caballo** (LAm) ride a horse. **~ar en bicicleta** (LAm) ride a bicycle. **¡anda!** go on!, come on! **~ar por** be about. **~arse** vpr (LAm, en imperativo) **¡andate!** go away! ● m walk. **~ariego** adj fond of walking

andén m platform

Andes mpl. **los ~** the Andes

andin|o adj Andean. **~ismo** m (LAm) mountaineering, climbing. **~ista** m & f (LAm) mountaineer, climber

andrajo m rag. **~so** adj ragged

anduve vb véase ANDAR

anécdota f anecdote

anecdótico adj anecdotal

anegar 12 vt flood. **~se** vpr be flooded, flood

anejo adj véase ANEXO

an|emia f anaemia. **~émico** adj anaemic

anest|esia f anaesthesia; (droga) anaesthetic. **~esiar** vt anaesthetize. **~ésico** adj & m anaesthetic. **~esista** m & f anaesthetist

anex|ar vt annex. **~o** adj attached. ● m annexe

anfibio adj amphibious. ● m amphibian

anfiteatro m amphitheatre; (en un teatro) upper circle

anfitri|ón m host. **~ona** f hostess

ángel m angel; (encanto) charm

angelical adj, **angélico** adj angelic

angina f. **~ de pecho** angina (pectoris). **tener ~s** have tonsillitis

anglicano adj & m Anglican

angl|icismo m Anglicism. **~ófilo** adj & m Anglophile. **~ohispánico** adj Anglo-Spanish. **~osajón** adj & m Anglo Saxon

angosto adj narrow

angu|ila f eel. **~la** f elver, baby eel

ángulo m angle; (rincón, esquina) corner; (curva) bend

angusti|a f anguish. **~ar** vt distress; (inquietar) worry. **~arse** vpr get distressed; (inquietarse) get worried. **~oso** adj anguished; (que causa angustia) distressing

anhel|ar vt (+ nombre) long for; (+ verbo) long to. **~o** m (fig) yearning

anidar vi nest

anill|a f ring. **~o** m ring. **~o de boda** wedding ring

ánima f soul

anima|ción f (de personas) life; (de

cosas) liveliness; (bullicio) bustle; (en el cine) animation. **~do** adj lively; (sitio etc) busy. **~dor** m host. **~dora** f hostess; (de un equipo) cheerleader

animadversión f ill will

animal adj animal; (fig, fam, torpe) stupid. ●m animal; (fig, fam, idiota) idiot; (fig, fam, bruto) brute

animar vt give life to; (dar ánimo) encourage; (dar vivacidad) liven up. **~se** vpr (decidirse) decide; (ponerse alegre) cheer up. **¿te animas a ir al cine?** do you feel like going to the cinema?

ánimo m soul; (mente) mind; (valor) courage; (intención) intention. **¡~!** come on!, cheer up! **dar ~s** encourage

animos|idad f animosity. **~o** adj brave; (resuelto) determined

aniquilar vt annihilate; (acabar con) ruin

anís m aniseed; (licor) anisette

aniversario m anniversary

anoche adv last night, yesterday evening

anochecer 11 vi get dark. **anochecí en Madrid** I was in Madrid at dusk. ●m nightfall, dusk. **al ~** at nightfall

anodino adj bland

an|omalía f anomaly. **~ómalo** adj anomalous

an|onimato m anonymity. **~ónimo** adj anonymous; (sociedad) limited. ●m (carta) anonymous letter

anormal adj abnormal. ●m & f 🗓 idiot. **~idad** f abnormality

anota|ción f (nota) note; (acción de poner notas) annotation. **~r** vt (poner nota) annotate; (apuntar) make a note of; (LAm) score (un gol)

anquilosa|miento m (fig) paralysis. **~rse** vpr become paralyzed

ansi|a f anxiety, worry; (anhelo)

yearning. **~ar** 20 vt long for. **~edad** f anxiety. **~oso** adj anxious; (deseoso) eager

antag|ónico adj antagonistic. **~onismo** m antagonism. **~onista** m & f antagonist

antaño adv in days gone by

antártico adj & m Antarctic

ante prep in front of, before; (frente a) in the face of; (en vista de) in view of. ●m elk; (piel) suede. **~anoche** adv the night before last. **~ayer** adv the day before yesterday. **~brazo** m forearm

antece|dente adj previous. ●m antecedent. **~dentes** mpl history, background. **~dentes penales** criminal record. **~der** vt precede. **~sor** m predecessor; (antepasado) ancestor

antelación f (advance) notice. **con ~** in advance

antemano adv. **de ~** beforehand

antena f antenna; (radio, TV) aerial

antenoche adv (LAm) the night before last

anteoj|eras fpl blinkers. **~o** m telescope. **~os** mpl binoculars; (LAm, gafas) glasses, spectacles. **~os de sol** sunglasses

ante|pasados mpl forebears, ancestors. **~poner** 34 vt put in front (**a** of); (fig) put before, prefer. **~proyecto** m preliminary sketch; (fig) blueprint

anterior adj previous; (delantero) front. **~idad** f. **con ~idad** previously. **con ~idad a** prior to

antes adv before; (antiguamente) in the past; (mejor) rather; (primero) first. **~ de** before. **~ de ayer** the day before yesterday. **~ de que** + subjuntivo before. **~ de que llegue** before he arrives. **cuanto ~, lo ~ posible** as soon as possible

anti|aéreo adj anti-aircraft. **~biótico** adj & m antibiotic. **~ciclón** m anticyclone

anticip|ación f. **con ~ación** in

advance. **con media hora de ~ación** half an hour early. **~ado** adj advance. **por ~ado** in advance. **~ar** vt bring forward; advance (dinero). **~arse** vpr be early. **~o** m (dinero) advance; (fig) foretaste

anti|conceptivo adj & m contraceptive. **~ de emergencia** morning-after pill. **~congelante** m antifreeze

anticua|do adj old-fashioned. **~rio** m antique dealer

anticuerpo m antibody

antídoto m antidote

anti|estético adj ugly. **~faz** m mask

antig|ualla f old relic. **~uamente** adv formerly; (hace mucho tiempo) long ago. **~üedad** f antiquity; (objeto) antique; (en un empleo) length of service. **~uo** adj old; (ruinas) ancient; (mueble) antique

Antillas fpl. **las ~** the West Indies

antílope m antelope

antinatural adj unnatural

antip|atía f dislike; (cualidad de antipático) unpleasantness. **~ático** adj unpleasant, unfriendly

anti|semita m & f anti-Semite. **~séptico** adj & m antiseptic. **~social** adj antisocial

antítesis f invar antithesis

antoj|adizo adj capricious. **~arse** vpr fancy. **se le ~a un caramelo** he fancies a sweet. **~itos** mpl (Mex) snacks bought at street stands. **~o** m whim; (de embarazada) craving

antología f anthology

antorcha f torch

ántrax m anthrax

antro m (fig) dump, hole. **~ de perversión** den of iniquity

antrop|ología f anthropology. **~ólogo** m anthropologist

anua|l adj annual. **~lidad** f

annuity. **~lmente** adv yearly. **~rio** m yearbook

anudar vt tie, knot. **~se** vpr tie

anula|ción f annulment, cancellation. **~r** vt annul, cancel. ●adj (dedo) ring. ●m ring finger

anunci|ante m & f advertiser. **~ar** vt announce; advertise (producto comercial); (presagiar) be a sign of. **~o** m announcement; (para vender algo) advertisement, advert 🅣; (cartel) poster

anzuelo m (fish)hook; (fig) bait. **tragar el ~** swallow the bait

añadi|dura f addition. **por ~dura** in addition. **~r** vt add

añejo adj (vino) mature

añicos mpl. **hacer(se) ~** smash to pieces

año m year. **~ bisiesto** leap year. **~ nuevo** new year. **al ~** per year, a year. **¿cuántos ~s tiene?** how old is he? **tiene 5 ~s** he's 5 (years old). **el ~ pasado** last year. **el ~ que viene** next year. **entrado en ~s** elderly. **los ~s 60** the sixties

añora|nza f nostalgia. **~r** vt miss

apabulla|nte adj overwhelming. **~r** vt overwhelm

apacible adj gentle; (clima) mild

apacigua|r 🅘 vt pacify; (calmar) calm; relieve (dolor etc). **~rse** vpr calm down

apadrinar vt sponsor; be godfather to (a un niño)

apag|ado adj extinguished; (color) dull; (aparato eléctrico, luz) off; (persona) lifeless; (sonido) muffled. **~ar** 🅘 vt put out (fuego, incendio); turn off, switch off (aparato eléctrico, luz); quench (sed); muffle (sonido). **~arse** vpr (fuego, luz) go out; (sonido) die away. **~ón** m blackout

apalabrar vt make a verbal agreement; (contratar) engage

apalear vt winnow (grano); beat (alfombra, frutos, persona)

apantallar vt (Mex) impress

apañar vt (arreglar) fix; (remendar) mend; (agarrar) grasp, take hold of. **~se** vpr get along, manage

apapachar vt (Mex) cuddle

aparador m sideboard; (Mex, de tienda) shop window

aparato m apparatus; (máquina) machine; (doméstico) appliance; (teléfono) telephone; (radio, TV) set; (ostentación) show, pomp. **~so** adj showy, ostentatious; (caída) spectacular

aparca|miento m car park (Brit), parking lot (Amer). **~r** 🈁 vt/i park

aparear vt mate (animales).**~se** vpr mate

aparecer 🈁 vi appear. **~se** vpr appear

aparej|ado adj. **llevar ~ado**, **traer ~ado** mean, entail. **~o** m (avíos) equipment; (de caballo) tack; (de pesca) tackle

aparent|ar vt (afectar) feign; (parecer) look. • vi show off. **~a 20 años** she looks like she's 20. **~e** adj apparent

apari|ción f appearance; (visión) apparition. **~encia** f appearance; (fig) show. **guardar las ~encias** keep up appearances

apartado adj separated; (aislado) isolated. • m (de un texto) section. **~ (de correos)** post-office box, PO box

apartamento m apartment, flat (Brit)

apart|ar vt separate; (alejar) move away; (quitar) remove; (guardar) set aside. **~arse** vpr leave; (quitarse de en medio) get out of the way; (aislarse) cut o.s. off. **~e** adv apart; (por separado) separately; (además) besides. • m aside; (párrafo) new paragraph. **~e de** apart from. **dejar ~e** leave aside. **eso ~e** apart from that

apasiona|do adj passionate; (entusiasta) enthusiastic; (falto de objetividad) biased. • m. **~do de** lover. **~miento** m passion. **~r** vt

excite. **~rse** vpr be mad (**por** about); (ser parcial) become biased

ap|atía f apathy. **~ático** adj apathetic

apea|dero m (Rail) halt. **~rse** vpr get off

apechugar 🈁 vi. 🈁 **~ con** put up with

apedrear vt stone

apeg|ado adj attached (**a** to). **~o** m 🈁 attachment. **tener ~o a** be fond of

apela|ción f appeal. **~r** vi appeal; (recurrir) resort (**a** to). • vt (apodar) call. **~tivo** m (nick)name

apellid|ar vt call. **~arse** vpr be called. **¿cómo te apellidas?** what's your surname? **~o** m surname

apelmazarse vpr (lana) get matted

apenar vt sadden; (LAm, avergonzar) embarrass. **~se** vpr be sad; (LAm, avergonzarse) be embarrassed

apenas adv hardly, scarcely; (Mex, sólo) only. • conj (esp LAm, en cuanto) as soon as. **~ si** 🈁 hardly

ap|éndice m appendix. **~endicitis** f appendicitis

aperitivo m (bebida) aperitif; (comida) appetizer

aperos mpl implements; (de labranza) agricultural equipment; (LAm, de un caballo) tack

apertura f opening

apesadumbrar vt upset. **~se** vpr sadden

apestar vt infect. • vi stink (**a** of)

apet|ecer 🈁 vi. **¿te ~ece una copa?** do you fancy a drink? do you feel like a drink?. **no me ~ece** I don't feel like it. **~ecible** adj attractive. **~ito** m appetite; (fig) desire. **~itoso** adj appetizing

apiadarse vpr feel sorry (**de** for)

ápice m (nada, en frases negativas) anything. **no ceder un ~** not give an inch

apilar vt pile up

apiñar vt pack in. **~se** vpr (personas) crowd together; (cosas) be packed tight

apio m celery

aplacar 7 vt placate; soothe (dolor)

aplanar vt level. **~ calles** (LAm fam) loaf around

aplasta|nte adj overwhelming. **~r** vt crush. **~rse** vpr flatten o.s.

aplau|dir vt clap, applaud; (fig) applaud. **~so** m applause; (fig) praise

aplaza|miento m postponement. **~r** 10 vt postpone; defer (pago)

aplica|ble adj applicable. **~ción** f application. **~do** adj (persona) diligent. **~r** 7 vt apply. • vi (LAm, a un puesto) apply (for). **~rse** vpr apply o.s.

aplom|ado adj composed. **~o** m composure

apocado adj timid

apocar 7 vt belittle (persona). **~se** vpr feel small

apodar vt nickname

apodera|do m representative. **~rse** vpr seize

apodo m nickname

apogeo m (fig) height

apolilla|do adj moth-eaten. **~rse** vpr get moth-eaten

apolítico adj non-political

apología f defence

apoltronarse vpr settle o.s. down

apoplejía f stroke

aporrear vt hit, thump; beat up (persona)

aport|ación f contribution. **~ar** vt contribute. **~e** m (LAm) contribution

aposta adv on purpose

apostar[1] vt/i bet

apostar[2] vt station. **~se** vpr station o.s.

apóstol m apostle

apóstrofo m apostrophe

apoy|ar vt lean (**en** against); (descansar) rest; (asentar) base; (reforzar) support. **~arse** vpr lean, rest. **~o** m support

apreci|able adj appreciable; (digno de estima) worthy. **~ación** f appreciation; (valoración) appraisal. **~ar** vt value; (estimar) appreciate. **~o** m appraisal; (fig) esteem

apremi|ante adj urgent, pressing. **~ar** vt urge; (obligar) compel; (dar prisa a) hurry up. • vi be urgent. **~o** m urgency; (obligación) obligation

aprender vt/i learn. **~se** vpr learn

aprendiz m apprentice. **~aje** m learning; (período) apprenticeship

aprensi|ón f apprehension; (miedo) fear. **~vo** adj apprehensive, fearful

apresar vt seize; (capturar) capture

aprestar vt prepare. **~se** vpr prepare

apresura|do adj in a hurry; (hecho con prisa) hurried. **~r** vt hurry. **~rse** vpr hurry up

apret|ado adj tight; (difícil) difficult; (tacaño) stingy, mean. **~ar** 1 vt tighten; press (botón); squeeze (persona); (comprimir) press down. • vi be too tight. **~arse** vpr crowd together. **~ón** m squeeze. **~ón de manos** handshake

aprieto m difficulty. **verse en un ~** be in a tight spot

aprisa adv quickly

aprisionar vt trap

aproba|ción f approval. **~r** 2 vt approve (of); pass (examen). • vi pass

apropia|ción f appropriation. **~do** adj appropriate. **~rse** vpr. **~rse de** appropriate, take

aprovecha|ble adj usable. **~do** adj (aplicado) diligent; (ingenioso) resourceful; (oportunista) opportunist. **bien ~do** well

a

spent. ~**miento** m advantage;
(uso) use. ~**r** vt take advantage of;
(utilizar) make use of. •vi make the
most of it. **¡que aproveche!**
enjoy your meal! ~**rse** vpr. ~**rse
de** take advantage of

aprovisionar vt provision (**con**,
de with). ~**se** vpr stock up

aproxima|ción f approximation;
(proximidad) closeness; (en la lotería)
consolation prize. ~**damente** adv
roughly, approximately. ~**do** adj
approximate, rough. ~**r** vt bring
near; (fig) bring together (personas).
~**rse** vpr come closer, approach

apt|itud f suitability; (capacidad)
ability. ~**o** adj (capaz) capable;
(adecuado) suitable

apuesta f bet

apuesto m handsome. •vb véase
APOSTAR ¹

apuntalar vt shore up

apunt|ar vt aim (arma); (señalar)
point at; (anotar) make a note of,
note down; (inscribir) enrol; (en el
teatro) prompt. •vi (con un arma) to
aim (**a** at). ~**arse** vpr put one's
name down; score (triunfo, tanto etc).
~**e** m note; (bosquejo) sketch.
tomar ~**s** take notes

apuñalar vt stab

apur|ado adj difficult; (sin dinero)
hard up; (LAm, con prisa) in a hurry.
~**ar** vt (acabar) finish; drain (vaso
etc); (causar vergüenza) embarrass;
(LAm, apresurar) hurry. ~**arse** vpr
worry; (LAm, apresurarse) hurry up.
~**o** m tight spot, difficult
situation; (vergüenza)
embarrassment; (estrechez)
hardship, want; (LAm, prisa) hurry

aquejar vt afflict

aquel adj (f **aquella**, mpl **aquellos**, fpl
aquellas) that; (en plural) those

aquél pron (f **aquélla**, mpl **aquéllos**,
fpl **aquéllas**) that one; (en plural)
those

aquello pron that; (asunto) that
business

aquí adv here. **de** ~ from here. **de**

~ **a 15 días** in a fortnight's time.
~ **mismo** right here. **de** ~ **para
allá** to and fro. **de** ~ **que** that is
why. **hasta** ~ until now. **por** ~
around here

aquietar vt calm (down)

árabe adj & m & f Arab; (lengua)
Arabic

Arabia f Arabia. ~ **Saudita**, ~
Saudí Saudi Arabia

arado m plough. ~**r** m ploughman

arancel m tariff; (impuesto) duty.
~**ario** adj tariff

arándano m blueberry

arandela f washer

araña f spider; (lámpara) chandelier.
~**r** vt scratch

arar vt plough

arbitra|je m arbitration; (en
deportes) refereeing. ~**r** vt/i
arbitrate; (en fútbol etc) referee; (en
tenis etc) umpire

arbitr|ariedad f arbitrariness.
~**ario** adj arbitrary. ~**io** m (free)
will

árbitro m arbitrator; (en fútbol etc)
referee; (en tenis etc) umpire

árbol m tree; (eje) axle; (palo) mast.
~ **genealógico** family tree. ~ **de
Navidad** Christmas tree

arbol|ado m trees. ~**eda** f wood

arbusto m bush

arca f (caja) chest. ~ **de Noé**
Noah's ark

arcada f arcade; (de un puente) arch;
(náuseas) retching

arcaico adj archaic

arce m maple (tree)

arcén m (de autopista) hard shoulder;
(de carretera) verge

archipiélago m archipelago

archiv|ador m filing cabinet. ~**ar**
vt file (away). ~**o** m file; (de
documentos históricos) archives

arcilla f clay

arco m arch; (Elec, Mat) arc; (Mus,

arma) bow; (LAm, en fútbol) goal. ~ **iris** rainbow

arder vi burn; (LAm, escocer) sting; (fig, de ira) seethe. **estar que arde** be very tense

ardid m trick, scheme

ardiente adj burning

ardilla f squirrel

ardor m heat; (fig) ardour; (LAm, escozor) smarting. ~ **de estómago** heartburn

arduo adj arduous

área f area

arena f sand; (en deportes) arena; (en los toros) (bull)ring. ~ **movediza** quicksand

arenoso adj sandy

arenque m herring. ~ **ahumado** kipper

arete m (Mex) earring

Argel m Algiers. ~**ia** f Algeria

Argentina f Argentina

argentino adj Argentinian, Argentine. ●m Argentinian

argolla f ring. ~ **de matrimonio** (LAm) wedding ring

arg|ot m slang. ~**ótico** adj slang

argucia f cunning argument

argüir 19 vt (probar) prove, show; (argumentar) argue. ●vi argue

argument|ación f argument. ~**ar** vt/i argue. ~**o** m argument; (de libro, película etc) story, plot

aria f aria

aridez f aridity, dryness

árido adj arid, dry. ~**s** mpl dry goods

Aries m Aries

arisco adj unfriendly

arist|ocracia f aristocracy. ~**ócrata** m & f aristocrat. ~**ocrático** adj aristocratic

aritmética f arithmetic

arma f arm, weapon; (sección) section. ~ **de fuego** firearm, ~**s de destrucción masiva** weapons of mass destruction. ~**da** f navy; (flota) fleet. ~**do** adj armed (**de** with). ~**dura** f armour; (de gafas etc) frame; (Tec) framework. ~**mentismo** m build up of arms. ~**mento** m arms, armaments; (acción de armar) armament. ~**r** vt arm (**de** with); (montar) put together. ~**r un lío** kick up a fuss

armario m cupboard; (para ropa) wardrobe (Brit), closet (Amer)

armatoste m huge great thing

armazón m & f frame(work)

armiño m ermine

armisticio m armistice

armonía f harmony

armónica f harmonica, mouth organ

armoni|oso adj harmonious. ~**zar** 10 vt harmonize. ●vi harmonize; (personas) get on well (**con** with); (colores) go well (**con** with)

arn|és m armour. ~**eses** mpl harness

aro m ring, hoop

arom|a m aroma; (de flores) scent; (de vino) bouquet. ~**ático** adj aromatic

arpa f harp

arpía f harpy; (fig) hag

arpillera f sackcloth, sacking

arpón m harpoon

arquear vt arch, bend. ~**se** vpr arch, bend

arque|ología f archaeology. ~**ológico** adj archaeological. ~**ólogo** m archaeologist

arquero m archer; (LAm, en fútbol) goalkeeper

arquitect|o m architect. ~**ónico** adj architectural. ~**ura** f architecture

arrabal m suburb; (barrio pobre) poor area. ~**es** mpl outskirts. ~**ero** adj suburban; (de modales groseros) common

arraiga|do adj deeply rooted. ~r
12 vi take root. ~rse vpr take root;
(fig) settle

arran|car 7 vt pull up (planta); pull
out (diente); (arrebatar) snatch; (Auto)
start. •vi start. ~carse vpr pull
out. ~que m sudden start; (Auto)
start; (fig) outburst

arras fpl security; (en boda) coins

arrasar vt level, smooth; raze to
the ground (edificio etc); (llenar) fill
to the brim. •vi (en deportes) sweep
to victory; (en política) win a
landslide victory

arrastr|ar vt pull; (por el suelo) drag
(along); give rise to (consecuencias).
•vi trail on the ground. ~arse vpr
crawl; (humillarse) grovel. ~e m
dragging; (transporte) haulage.
estar para el ~e 1 be done in

arre int gee up! ~ar vt urge on

arrebat|ado adj (irreflexivo)
impetuous. ~ar vt snatch (away);
(fig) win (over); captivate (corazón
etc). ~arse vpr get carried away.
~o m (de cólera etc) fit; (éxtasis)
ecstasy

arrech|ar vt (LAm fam, enfurecer) to
infuriate. ~arse vpr get furious.
~o adj furious

arrecife m reef

arregl|ado adj neat; (bien vestido)
well-dressed; (LAm, amañado) fixed.
~ar vt arrange; (poner en orden) tidy
up; sort out (asunto, problema etc);
(reparar) mend. ~arse vpr
(solucionarse) get sorted out;
(prepararse) get ready; (apañarse)
manage, make do; (ponerse de
acuerdo) come to an agreement.
~árselas manage, get by. ~o m
(incl Mus) arrangement; (acción de
reparar) repair; (acuerdo) agreement;
(solución) solution. **con ~o a**
according to

arrellanarse vpr settle o.s. (**en**
into)

arremangar 12 vt roll up (mangas);
tuck up (falda). ~se vpr roll up
one's sleeves

arremeter vi charge (**contra** at);
(atacar) attack

arremolinarse vpr mill about; (el
agua) to swirl

arrenda|dor m landlord. ~dora f
landlady. ~miento m renting;
(contrato) lease; (precio) rent. ~r 1
vt (dar casa en alquiler) let; (dar cosa en
alquiler) hire out; (tomar en alquiler)
rent. ~tario m tenant

arreos mpl tack

arrepenti|miento m repentance,
regret. ~rse 4 vpr (retractarse) to
change one's mind; (lamentarse) be
sorry. ~rse de regret; repent of
(pecados)

arrest|ar vt arrest, detain;
(encarcelar) imprison. ~o m arrest;
(encarcelamiento) imprisonment

arriar 20 vt lower (bandera, vela)

arriba adv up; (dirección) up(wards);
(en casa) upstairs. •int up with;
(¡levántate!) up you get!; (¡ánimo!)
come on! **¡~ España!** long live
Spain! **~ de** (LAm) on top of. **~
mencionado** aforementioned.
calle ~ up the street. **de ~
abajo** from top to bottom. **de 10
euros para ~** over 10 euros.
escaleras ~ upstairs. **la parte de
~** the top part. **los de ~** those at
the top. **más ~** higher up

arrib|ar vi (barco) reach port; (esp
LAm, llegar) arrive. ~ista m & f social
climber. ~o m (esp LAm) arrival

arriero m muleteer

arriesga|do adj risky; (person)
daring. ~r 12 vt risk; (aventurar)
venture. ~rse vpr take a risk

arrim|ar vt bring close(r). ~arse
vpr come closer, approach

arrincona|do adj forgotten;
(acorralado) cornered. ~r vt put in a
corner; (perseguir) corner; (arrumbar)
put aside. ~rse vpr become a
recluse

arroba f (Internet) at (@); measure
of weight

arrocero adj rice

arrodillarse vpr kneel (down)

arrogan|cia f arrogance; (orgullo) pride. **~te** adj arrogant; (orgulloso) proud

arroj|ar vt throw; (emitir) give off, throw out; (producir) produce. • vi (esp LAm, vomitar) throw up. **~arse** vpr throw o.s. **~o** m courage

arrollar vt roll (up); (atropellar) run over; (vencer) crush

arropar vt wrap up; (en la cama) tuck up. **~se** vpr wrap (o.s.) up

arroy|o m stream; (de una calle) gutter. **~uelo** m small stream

arroz m rice. **~ con leche** rice pudding. **~al** m rice field

arruga f (en la piel) wrinkle, line; (en tela) crease. **~r** 🔢 vt wrinkle; crumple (papel); crease (tela). **~rse** vpr (la piel) become wrinkled; (tela) crease, get creased

arruinar vt ruin; (destruir) destroy. **~se** vpr (persona) be ruined

arrullar vt lull to sleep. • vi (palomas) coo

arrumbar vt put aside

arsenal m (astillero) shipyard; (de armas) arsenal; (fig) mine

arsénico m arsenic

arte m (f en plural) art; (habilidad) skill; (astucia) cunning. **bellas ~s** fine arts. **con ~** skilfully. **malas ~s** trickery. **por amor al ~** for the fun of it

artefacto m device

arteria f artery; (fig, calle) main road

artesan|al adj craft. **~ía** f handicrafts. **objeto** m **de ~ía** traditional craft object. **~o** m artisan, craftsman

ártico adj Arctic. **Á~** m. **el Á~** the Arctic

articula|ción f joint; (pronunciación) articulation. **~do** adj articulated; (lenguaje) articulate. **~r** vt articulate

artículo m article. **~s** mpl (géneros)

goods. **~ de exportación** export product. **~ de fondo** editorial, leader

artífice m & f artist; (creador) architect

artifici|al adj artificial. **~o** m (habilidad) skill; (dispositivo) device; (engaño) trick

artiller|ía f artillery. **~o** m artilleryman, gunner

artilugio m gadget

artimaña f trick

art|ista m & f artist. **~ístico** adj artistic

artritis f arthritis

arveja f (LAm) pea

arzobispo m archbishop

as m ace

asa f handle

asado adj roast(ed) • m roast (meat), joint; (LAm, reunión) barbecue. **~o a la parrilla** grilled meat; (LAm) barbecued meat

asalariado adj salaried. • m employee

asalt|ante m attacker; (de un banco) robber. **~ar** vt storm (fortaleza); attack (persona); raid (banco etc); (fig) (duda) assail; (fig) (idea etc) cross one's mind. **~o** m attack; (robo) robbery; (en boxeo) round

asamblea f assembly; (reunión) meeting

asar vt roast. **~se** vpr be very hot. **~ a la parrilla** (LAm) barbecue. **~ al horno** (sin grasa) bake; (con grasa) roast

asbesto m asbestos

ascend|encia f descent; (LAm, influencia) influence. **~ente** adj ascending. **~er** 🔢 vt promote. • vi go up, ascend; (cuenta etc) come to, amount to; (ser ascendido) be promoted. **~iente** m & f ancestor; (influencia) influence

ascens|ión f ascent; (de grado) promotion. **día** m **de la A~ión**

a

Ascension Day. ~**o** m ascent; (de grado) promotion

ascensor m lift (Brit), elevator (Amer). ~**ista** m & f lift attendant (Brit), elevator operator (Amer)

asco m disgust. **dar** ~ be disgusting; (fig, causar enfado) be infuriating. **estar hecho un** ~ be disgusting. **me da** ~ it makes me feel sick. **¡qué** ~! how disgusting! **ser un** ~ be disgusting

ascua f ember. **estar en** ~**s** be on tenterhooks

asea|do adj clean; (arreglado) neat. ~**r** vt (lavar) wash; (limpiar) clean; (arreglar) tidy up

asedi|ar vt besiege; (fig) pester. ~**o** m siege

asegura|do adj & m insured. ~**dor** m insurer. ~**r** vt secure, make safe; (decir) assure; (concertar un seguro) insure; (preservar) safeguard. ~**rse** vpr make sure

asemejarse vpr be alike

asenta|do adj situated; (arraigado) established. ~**r** 🔢 vt place; (asegurar) settle; (anotar) note down; (Mex, afirmar) state. ~**rse** vpr settle; (estar situado) be situated; (esp LAm, sentar cabeza) settle down

asentir 🔢 vi agree (**a** to). ~ **con la cabeza** nod

aseo m cleanliness. ~**s** mpl toilets

asequible adj obtainable; (precio) reasonable; (persona) approachable

asesin|ar vt murder; (Pol) assassinate. ~**ato** m murder; (Pol) assassination. ~**o** m murderer; (Pol) assassin

asesor m adviser, consultant. ~**ar** vt advise. ~**arse** vpr. ~**arse con** consult. ~**ía** f consultancy; (oficina) consultant's office

asfalt|ado adj asphalt. ~**ar** vt asphalt. ~**o** m asphalt

asfixia f suffocation. ~**nte** adj suffocating. ~**r** vt suffocate. ~**rse** vpr suffocate

así adv (de esta manera) like this, like that. ●adj such. ~ ~ so-so. **como** just as. ~ ~ **como** ~, (LAm) ~ **nomás** just like that. ~ ... **como** both ... and. ~ **pues** so. ~ **que** so; (en cuanto) as soon as. ~ **sea** so be it. ~ **y todo** even so. **aun** ~ even so. **¿no es** ~? isn't that right? **si es** ~ if that is the case. **y** ~ (**sucesivamente**) and so on

Asia f Asia

asiático adj & m Asian

asidero m handle; (fig, pretexto) excuse

asidu|amente adv regularly. ~**o** adj & m regular

asiento m seat; (en contabilidad) entry. ~ **delantero** front seat. ~ **trasero** back seat

asignar vt assign; allot (porción, tiempo etc)

asignatura f subject. ~ **pendiente** (en enseñanza) failed subject; (fig) matter still to be resolved

asil|ado m inmate; (Pol) refugee. ~**o** m asylum; (fig) shelter; (de ancianos etc) home. **pedir** ~**o político** ask for political asylum

asimétrico adj asymmetrical

asimila|ción f assimilation. ~**r** vt assimilate

asimismo adv also; (igualmente) in the same way, likewise

asir 🔢 vt grasp

asist|encia f attendance; (gente) people (present); (en un teatro etc) audience; (ayuda) assistance. ~**encia médica** medical care. ~**enta** f (mujer de la limpieza) charwoman. ~**ente** m & f assistant. ~**ente social** social worker. ~**ido** adj assisted. ~**ir** vt assist, help. ●vi. ~**ir a** attend, be present at

asm|a f asthma. ~**ático** adj & m asthmatic

asno m donkey; (fig) ass

asocia|ción f association; (Com) partnership. **~do** adj associated; (socio) associate. • m associate. **~r** vt associate; (Com) take into partnership. **~rse** vpr associate; (Com) become a partner

asolar ▯ vt devastate

asomar vt show. • vi appear, show. **~se** vpr (persona) lean out (**a, por** of); (cosa) appear

asombr|ar vt (pasmar) amaze; (sorprender) surprise. **~arse** vpr be amazed; (sorprenderse) be surprised. **~o** m amazement, surprise. **~oso** adj amazing, astonishing

asomo m sign. **ni por ~** by no means

aspa f cross, X-shape; (de molino) (windmill) sail. **en ~** X-shaped

aspaviento m show, fuss. **~s** mpl gestures. **hacer ~s** make a big fuss

aspecto m look, appearance; (fig) aspect

aspereza f roughness; (de sabor etc) sourness

áspero adj rough; (sabor etc) bitter

aspersión f sprinkling

aspiración f breath; (deseo) ambition

aspirador m, **aspiradora** f vacuum cleaner

aspira|nte m & f candidate. **~r** vt breathe in; (máquina) suck up. • vi breathe in; (máquina) suck. **~r a** aspire to

aspirina f aspirin

asquear vt sicken. • vi be sickening. **~se** vpr be disgusted

asqueroso adj disgusting

asta f spear; (de la bandera) flagpole; (cuerno) horn. **a media ~** at half-mast. **~bandera** f (Mex) flagpole

asterisco m asterisk

astilla f splinter. **~s** fpl firewood

astillero m shipyard

astringente adj & m astringent

astr|o m star. **~ología** f astrology. **~ólogo** m astrologer. **~onauta** m & f astronaut. **~onave** f spaceship. **~onomía** f astronomy. **~ónomo** m astronomer

astu|cia f cleverness; (ardid) cunning trick. **~to** adj astute; (taimado) cunning

asumir vt assume

asunción f assumption. **la A~** the Assumption

asunto m (cuestión) matter; (de una novela) plot; (negocio) business. **~s** mpl **exteriores** foreign affairs. **el ~ es que** the fact is that

asusta|dizo adj easily frightened. **~r** vt frighten. **~rse** vpr be frightened

ataca|nte m & f attacker. **~r** ▯ vt attack

atad|o adj tied. • m bundle. **~ura** f tie

ataj|ar vi take a short cut; (Mex, en tenis) pick up the balls. • vt (LAm, agarrar) catch. **~o** m short cut

atañer ▯ vt concern

ataque m attack; (Med) fit, attack. **~ al corazón** heart attack. **~ de nervios** fit of hysterics

atar vt tie. **~se** vpr tie up

atarantar vt (LAm) fluster. **~se** vpr (LAm) get flustered

atardecer ▯ vi get dark. • m dusk. **al ~** at dusk

atareado adj busy

atasc|ar ▯ vt block; (fig) hinder. **~arse** vpr get stuck; (tubo etc) block. **~o** m blockage; (Auto) traffic jam

ataúd m coffin

atav|iar ▯ vt dress up. **~iarse** vpr dress up, get dressed up. **~ío** m dress, attire

atemorizar ▯ vt frighten. **~se** vpr be frightened

atención f attention; (cortesía) courtesy, kindness; (interés) interest. **¡∼!** look out!. **llamar la ∼** attract attention, catch the eye; **prestar ∼** pay attention

atender 1 vt attend to; (cuidar) look after. ●vi pay attention

atenerse 40 vpr abide (**a** by)

atentado m (ataque) attack; (afrenta) affront (**contra** to). **∼ contra la vida de uno** attempt on s.o.'s life

atentamente adv attentively; (con cortesía) politely; (con amabilidad) kindly. **lo saluda ∼** (en cartas) yours faithfully

atentar vi. **∼ contra** threaten. **∼ contra la vida de uno** make an attempt on s.o.'s life

atento adj attentive; (cortés) polite; (amable) kind

atenua|nte adj extenuating. ●f extenuating circumstance. **∼r 21** vt attenuate; (hacer menor) diminish, lessen

ateo adj atheistic. ●m atheist

aterciopelado adj velvety

aterra|dor adj terrifying. **∼r** vt terrify

aterriza|je m landing. **∼je forzoso** emergency landing. **∼r 10** vt land

aterrorizar 10 vt terrify

atesorar vt hoard; amass (fortuna)

atesta|do adj packed, full up. ●m sworn statement. **∼r** vt fill up, pack; (Jurid) testify

atestiguar 15 vt testify to; (fig) prove

atiborrar vt fill, stuff. **∼se** vpr stuff o.s.

ático m attic

atina|do adj right; (juicioso) wise, sensible. **∼r** vt/i hit upon; (acertar) guess right

atizar 10 vt poke; (fig) stir up

atlántico adj Atlantic. **el (océano) A∼** the Atlantic (Ocean)

atlas m atlas

atl|eta m & f athlete. **∼ético** adj athletic. **∼etismo** m athletics

atmósfera f atmosphere

atole m (LAm) boiled maize drink

atolladero m bog; (fig) tight corner

atolondra|do adj scatter-brained; (aturdido) stunned. **∼r** vt fluster; (pasmar) stun. **∼rse** vpr get flustered

at|ómico adj atomic. **∼omizador** m spray, atomizer

átomo m atom

atónito m amazed

atonta|do adj stunned; (tonto) stupid. **∼r** vt stun. **∼rse** vpr get confused

atorar vt (esp LAm) to block; (Mex, sujetar) secure. **∼se** vpr (esp LAm, atragantarse) choke; (atascarse) get blocked; (puerta) get jammed

atormentar vt torture. **∼se** vpr worry, torment o.s.

atornillar vt screw on

atosigar 12 vt pester

atraca|dor m mugger; (de banco) bank robber. **∼r 7** vt dock; (arrimar) bring alongside; hold up (banco); mug (persona). ●vi (barco) dock

atracci|ón f attraction. **∼ones** fpl entertainment, amusements

atrac|o m hold-up, robbery. **∼ón** m. **darse un ∼ón** stuff o.s. (**de** with)

atractivo adj attractive. ●m attraction; (encanto) charm

atraer 41 vt attract

atragantarse vpr choke (**con** on). **la historia se me atraganta** I can't stand history

atrancar 7 vt bolt (puerta). **∼se** vpr get stuck

atrapar vt catch; (encerrar) trap

atrás adv back; (tiempo) previously, before. **años ∼** years ago. **∼ de** (LAm) behind. **dar un paso ∼** step

backwards. **hacia** ~, **para** ~
backwards

atras|ado adj behind; (reloj) slow;
(con deudas) in arrears; (país)
backward. **llegar ~ado** (esp LAm)
arrive late. ~**ar** vt put back (reloj);
(demorar) delay, postpone. • vi (reloj)
be slow. ~**arse** vpr be late; (reloj)
be slow; (quedarse atrás) fall behind.
~**o** m delay; (de un reloj) slowness;
(de un país) backwardness. ~**os** mpl
(Com) arrears

atravesa|do adj lying across. ~**r**
1 vt cross; (traspasar) go through
(poner transversalmente) lay across.
~**rse** vpr lie across; (en la garganta)
get stuck, stick

atrayente adj attractive

atrev|erse vpr dare. ~**erse con**
tackle. ~**ido** adj daring; (insolente)
insolent. ~**imiento** m daring;
(descaro) insolence

atribu|ción f attribution.
~**ciones** fpl authority. ~**uir** **17** vt
attribute; confer (función). ~**irse**
vpr claim

atribulado adj afflicted

atributo m attribute

atril m lectern; (Mus) music stand

atrocidad f atrocity. **¡qué ~!** how
awful!

atrofiarse vpr atrophy

atropell|ado adj hasty. ~**ar** vt
knock down; (por encima) run over;
(empujar) push aside; (fig) outrage,
insult. ~**arse** vpr rush. ~**o** m
(Auto) accident; (fig) outrage

atroz adj appalling; (fig) atrocious

atuendo m dress, attire

atún m tuna (fish)

aturdi|do adj bewildered; (por
golpe) stunned. ~**r** vt bewilder;
(golpe) stun; (ruido) deafen

auda|cia f boldness, audacity. ~**z**
adj bold

audi|ble adj audible. ~**ción** f
hearing; (prueba) audition. ~**encia** f
audience; (tribunal) court; (sesión)
hearing

auditor m auditor. ~**io** m
audience; (sala) auditorium

auge m peak; (Com) boom

augur|ar vt predict; (cosas) augur.
~**io** m prediction. **con nuestros
mejores ~ios para** with our best
wishes for. **mal ~** bad omen

aula f class-room; (Univ) lecture
room

aull|ar **23** vi howl. ~**ido** m howl

aument|ar vt increase; magnify
(imagen). • vi increase. ~**o** m
increase; (de sueldo) rise

aun adv even. ~ **así** even so. ~
cuando although. **más ~** even
more. **ni ~** not even

aún adv still, yet. ~ **no ha llegado**
it still hasn't arrived, it hasn't
arrived yet

aunar **23** vt join. ~**se** vpr join
together

aunque conj although, (even)
though

aúpa int up! **de ~** wonderful

aureola f halo

auricular m (de teléfono) receiver.
~**es** mpl headphones

aurora f dawn

ausen|cia f absence. **en ~cia de**
in the absence of. ~**tarse** vpr
leave. ~**te** adj absent. • m & f
absentee; (Jurid) missing person.
~**tismo** m (LAm) absenteeism

auspici|ador m sponsor. ~**ar** vt
sponsor. ~**o** m sponsorship; (signo)
omen. **bajo los ~s de**
sponsored by

auster|idad f austerity. ~**o** adj
austere

austral adj southern

Australia m Australia

australiano adj & m Australian

Austria f Austria

austriaco, **austríaco** adj & m
Austrian

aut|enticar **7** authenticate.

~enticidad f authenticity.
~éntico adj authentic

auto m (Jurid) decision; (orden) order; (Auto, fam) car. ~s mpl proceedings

auto|abastecimiento m self-sufficiency. ~biografía f autobiography

autobús m bus. **en** ~ by bus

autocar m (long-distance) bus, coach (Brit)

autocontrol m self-control

autóctono adj indigenous

auto|determinación f self-determination. ~didacta adj self-taught. ●m & f self-taught person. ~escuela f driving school. ~financiamiento m self-financing

autógrafo m autograph

autómata m robot

autom|ático adj automatic. ●m press-stud. ~atización f automation

automotor m diesel train

autom|óvil adj motor. ●m car. ~ovilismo m motoring. ~ovilista m & f driver, motorist

⏏aut|onomía f autonomy. ~onómico adj, ~ónomo adj autonomous

autopista f motorway (Brit), freeway (Amer)

autopsia f autopsy

autor m author. ~a f author(ess)

autori|dad f authority. ~tario adj authoritarian

autoriza|ción f authorization. ~do adj authorized, official; (opinión etc) authoritative. ~r 10 vt authorize

auto|rretrato m self-portrait. ~servicio m self-service restaurant. ~stop m hitch-hiking. **hacer** ~**stop** hitch-hike

autosuficiente adj self-sufficient

⏏ see A-Z of Spanish life and culture

autovía f dual carriageway

auxili|ar adj auxiliary; (profesor) assistant. ●m & f assistant. ●vt help. ~o m help. ¡~o! help! **en** ~**o de** in aid of. **pedir** ~**o** shout for help. **primeros** ~**os** first aid

Av. abrev (**Avenida**) Ave

aval m guarantee

avalancha f avalanche

avalar vt guarantee

aval|uar vt 21 (LAm) value. ~úo m valuation

avance m advance; (en el cine) trailer. **avances** mpl (Mex) trailer

avanzar 10 vt move forward. ~ **la pantalla** scroll up. ●vi advance

avar|icia f avarice. ~icioso adj, ~iento adj greedy; (tacaño) miserly. ~o adj miserly. ●m miser

avasallar vt dominate

Avda. abrev (**Avenida**) Ave

ave f bird. ~ **de paso** (incl fig) bird of passage. ~ **de rapiña** bird of prey

avecinarse vpr approach

avejentar vt age

avellan|a f hazelnut. ~o m hazel (tree)

avemaría f Hail Mary

avena f oats

avenida f (calle) avenue

avenir 53 vt reconcile. ~**se** vpr come to an agreement; (entenderse) get on well (**con** with)

aventaja|do adj outstanding. ~r vt be ahead of; (superar) surpass

avent|ar 1 vt fan; winnow (grano etc); (Mex, lanzar) throw; (Mex, empujar) push. ~**arse** vpr (Mex) throw o.s.; (atreverse) dare. ~**ón** m (Mex) ride, lift (Brit)

aventur|a f adventure. ~**a amorosa** love affair. ~**ado** adj risky. ~**ero** adj adventurous. ●m adventurer

avergonzar 10 & 16 vt shame;

(abochornar) embarrass. **~se** vpr be ashamed; (abochornarse) be embarrassed

aver|ía f (Auto) breakdown; (en máquina) failure. **~iado** adj broken down. **~iarse** 20 vpr break down

averigua|ción f inquiry; (Mex, disputa) argument. **~r** 15 vt find out. ●vi (Mex) argue

aversión f aversion (**a, hacia, por** to)

avestruz m ostrich

avia|ción f aviation; (Mil) air force. **~dor** m (piloto) pilot

av|ícola adj poultry. **~icultura** f poultry farming

avidez f eagerness, greed

ávido adj eager, greedy

avinagra|do adj sour. **~rse** vpr go sour; (fig) become embittered

avi|ón m aeroplane (Brit), airplane (Amer); (Mex, juego) hopscotch. **~onazo** m (Mex) plane crash

avis|ar vt warn; (informar) notify, inform; call (médico etc). **~o** m warning; (comunicación) notice; (LAm, anuncio, cartel) advertisement; (en televisión) commercial. **estar sobre ~o** be on the alert. **sin previo ~o** without prior warning

avisp|a f wasp. **~ado** adj sharp. **~ero** m wasps' nest; (fig) mess. **~ón** m hornet

avistar vt catch sight of

avivar vt stoke up (fuego); brighten up (color); arouse (interés, pasión); intensify (dolor). **~se** vpr revive; (animarse) cheer up; (LAm, despabilarse) wise up

axila f armpit, axilla

axioma m axiom

ay int (de dolor) ouch!; (de susto) oh!; (de pena) oh dear! **¡~ de ti!** poor you!

aya f governess, child's nurse

ayer adv yesterday. ●m past. **antes de ~** the day before yesterday. **~**

por la mañana, (LAm) **~ en la mañana** yesterday morning

ayuda f help, aid. **~ de cámara** valet. **~nta** f, **~nte** m assistant; (Mil) adjutant. **~r** vt help

ayun|ar vi fast. **~as** fpl. **estar en ~as** have had nothing to eat or drink; (fig, fam) be in the dark. **~o** m fasting

🔲**ayuntamiento** m town council, city council; (edificio) town hall

azabache m jet

azad|a f hoe. **~ón** m (large) hoe

azafata f air hostess

azafate m (LAm) tray

azafrán m saffron

azahar m orange blossom; (del limonero) lemon blossom

azar m chance; (desgracia) misfortune. **al ~** at random. **por ~** by chance. **~es** mpl ups and downs

azaros|amente adv hazardously. **~o** adj hazardous, risky; (vida) eventful

azorar vt embarrass. **~rse** vpr be embarrassed

Azores fpl. **las ~** the Azores

azotador m (Mex) caterpillar

azot|ar vt whip, beat; (Mex, puerta) slam. **~e** m whip; (golpe) smack; (fig, calamidad) calamity

azotea f flat roof

🔲**azteca** adj & m & f Aztec

az|úcar m & f sugar. **~ucarado** adj sweet, sugary. **~ucarar** vt sweeten. **~ucarero** m sugar bowl

azucena f (white) lily

azufre m sulphur

azul adj & m blue. **~ado** adj bluish. **~ marino** navy blue

azulejo m tile

azuzar 10 vt urge on, incite

....

🔲 *see* A-Z of Spanish life and culture

Bb

bab|a f spittle. **~ear** vi drool, slobber; (niño) dribble. **caérsele la ~a a uno** be delighted. **~eo** m drooling; (de un niño) dribbling. **~ero** m bib

babor m port. **a ~** to port, on the port side

babosa f slug

babosada f (Mex) drivel

babos|ear vt slobber over; (niño) dribble over. •vi (Mex) day dream. **~o** adj slimy; (LAm, tonto) silly

babucha f slipper

baca f luggage rack

bacalao m cod

bache m pothole; (fig) bad patch

▣ bachillerato m school-leaving examination

bacteria f bacterium

bagaje m. **~ cultural** cultural knowledge; (de un pueblo) cultural heritage

bahía f bay

bail|able adj dance. **~aor** m Flamenco dancer. **~ar** vt/i dance. **ir a ~ar** go dancing. **~arín** m dancer. **~arina** f dancer; (de ballet) ballerina. **~e** m dance; (actividad) dancing. **~e de etiqueta** ball

baja f drop, fall; (Mil) casualty. **~ por maternidad** maternity leave. **darse de ~** take sick leave. **~da** f slope; (acto de bajar) descent; (camino) way down. **~r** vt lower; (llevar abajo) get down; go down (escalera); bow (la cabeza). •vi go down; (temperatura, precio) fall. **~rse** vpr pull down (pantalones). **~r(se) de** get out of (coche); get off (autobús, caballo, tren, bicicleta)

··
▣ see A-Z of Spanish life and culture

bajeza f vile deed

bajío m shallows; (de arena) sandbank; (LAm, terreno bajo) low-lying area

bajo adj low; (de estatura) short, small; (cabeza, ojos) lowered; (humilde) humble, low; (vil) vile, low; (voz) low; (Mus) deep. •m lowland; (Mus) bass. •adv quietly; (volar) low. •prep under. **~ cero** below zero. **~ la lluvia** in the rain. **los ~s** (LAm) ground floor (Brit), first floor (Amer); **los ~s fondos** the underworld

bajón m sharp drop; (de salud) sudden decline

bala f bullet; (de algodón etc) bale. (LAm, en atletismo) shot. **como una ~** like a shot. **lanzamiento de ~** (LAm) shot put

balada f ballad

balan|ce m balance; (documento) balance sheet; (resultado) outcome. **~cear** vt balance. **~cearse** vpr swing. **~ceo** m swinging. **~cín** m rocking chair; (de niños) seesaw. **~za** f scales; (Com) balance

balar vi bleat

balazo m (disparo) shot; (herida) bullet wound

balboa f (unidad monetaria panameña) balboa

balbuc|ear vt/i stammer; (niño) babble. **~eo** m stammering; (de niño) babbling. **~ir** 24 vt/i stammer; (niño) babble

balcón m balcony

balda f shelf

balde m bucket. **de ~** free (of charge). **en ~** in vain

baldío adj (terreno) waste

baldosa f (floor) tile; (losa) flagstone

bale|ar adj Balearic. ●**las (Islas) B~ares** the Balearics, the Balearic Islands. ●vt (LAm) to shoot. **~o** m (LAm, tiroteo) shooting

balero m (Mex) cup and ball toy; (rodamiento) bearing

balido m bleat; (varios sonidos) bleating

balística f ballistics

baliza f (Naut) buoy; (Aviac) beacon

ballena f whale

ballet /ba'le/ (pl **~s**) m ballet

balneario m spa; (con playa) seaside resort

balompié m soccer, football (Brit)

bal|ón m ball. **~oncesto** m basketball. **~onmano** m handball. **~onvolea** m volleyball

balotaje m (LAm) voting

balsa f (de agua) pool; (plataforma flotante) raft

bálsamo m balsam; (fig) balm

baluarte m (incl fig) bastion

bambalina f drop curtain. **entre ~s** behind the scenes

bambole|ar vi sway. **~arse** vpr sway; (mesa etc) wobble; (barco) rock. **~o** m swaying; (de mesa etc) wobbling; (de barco) rocking

bambú m (pl **~es**) bamboo

banal adj banal. **~idad** f banality

banan|a f (esp LAm) banana. **~ero** adj banana. **~o** m (LAm) banana tree

banc|a f banking; (conjunto de bancos) banks; (en juegos) bank; (LAm, asiento) bench. **~ario** adj bank, banking. **~arrota** f bankruptcy. **hacer ~arrota, ir a la ~arrota** go bankrupt. **~o** m (asiento) bench; (Com) bank; (bajío) sandbank; (de peces) shoal

banda f (incl Mus, Radio) band; (Mex, para el pelo) hair band; (raya ancha) stripe; (cinta ancha) sash; (grupo) gang, group. **~ sonora** soundtrack. **~da** f (de pájaros) flock; (de peces) shoal

bandeja f tray

bandejón m (Mex) central reservation (Brit), median strip (Amer)

bander|a f flag. **~illa** f banderilla. **~ear** vt stick the banderillas in. **~ero** m banderillero. **~ín** m pennant, small flag

bandido m bandit

bando m edict, proclamation; (facción) camp, side. **~s** mpl banns. **pasarse al otro ~** go over to the other side

bandolero m bandit

bandoneón m large accordion

banjo m banjo

banquero m banker

banquete m banquet; (de boda) wedding reception

banquillo m bench; (Jurid) dock; (taburete) footstool

bañ|ador m (de mujer) swimming costume; (de hombre) swimming trunks. **~ar** vt bath (niño); (Culin, recubrir) coat. **~arse** vpr go swimming, have a swim; (en casa) have a bath. **~era** f bath (tub). **~ista** m & f bather. **~o** m bath; (en piscina, mar etc) swim; (cuarto) bathroom; (LAm, wáter) toilet; (bañera) bath(tub); (capa) coat(ing)

baqueano (LAm), **baquiano** m guide

🅱 **bar** m bar

baraja f pack of cards. **~r** vt shuffle; (cifras etc) consider; (posibilidades); (Mex, explicar) explain

baranda, barandilla f rail; (de escalera) banisters

barat|a f (Mex) sale. **~ija** f trinket. **~illo** m junk shop; (géneros) cheap goods. **~o** adj cheap. ●adv cheap(ly)

🅱 *see* A-Z of Spanish life and culture

barba f chin; (pelo) beard

barbacoa f barbecue; (carne) barbecued meat

barbari|dad f atrocity; (fam, mucho) awful lot ⓘ. **¡qué ~dad!** how awful! **~e** f barbarity; (fig) ignorance. **~smo** m barbarism

bárbaro adj barbaric, cruel; (bruto) uncouth; (fam, estupendo) terrific ⓘ ●m barbarian. **¡qué ~!** how marvellous!

barbear vt (Mex, lisonjear) suck up to

barbecho m. **en ~** fallow

barber|ía f barber's (shop). **~o** m barber; (Mex, adulador) creep

barbilla f chin

barbitúrico m barbiturate

barbudo adj bearded

barca f (small) boat. **~ de pasaje** ferry. **~za** f barge

barcelonés adj of Barcelona, from Barcelona. ●m native of Barcelona

barco m boat; (navío) ship. **~ cisterna** tanker. **~ de vapor** steamer. **~ de vela** sailing boat. **ir en ~** go by boat

barda f (Mex) wall; (de madera) fence

barítono adj & m baritone

barman m (pl **~s**) barman

barniz m varnish; (para loza etc) glaze; (fig) veneer. **~ar** 🔟 vt varnish; glaze (loza etc)

barómetro m barometer

bar|ón m baron. **~onesa** f baroness

barquero m boatman

barquillo m wafer; (Mex, de helado) ice-cream cone

barra f bar; (pan) loaf of French bread; (palanca) lever; (de arena) sandbank; (LAm, de hinchas) supporters. **~ de labios** lipstick

barrabasada f mischief, prank

🔁 see A-Z of Spanish life and culture

barraca f hut; (vivienda pobre) shack, shanty

barranco m ravine, gully; (despeñadero) cliff, precipice

barrer vt sweep; thrash (rival)

barrera f barrier. **~ del sonido** sound barrier

barriada f district; (LAm, barrio marginal) slum

barrial m (LAm) quagmire

barrida f sweep; (LAm, redada) police raid

barrig|a f belly. **~ón** adj, **~udo** adj pot-bellied

barril m barrel

🔁**barrio** m district, area. **~s bajos** poor quarter, poor area. **el otro ~** (fig, fam) the other world. **~bajero** adj vulgar, common

barro m mud; (arcilla) clay; (arcilla cocida) earthenware

barroco adj Baroque. ●m Baroque style

barrote m bar

bartola f. **tirarse a la ~** take it easy

bártulos mpl things. **liar los ~** pack one's bags

barullo m racket; (confusión) confusion. **a ~** galore

basar vt base. **~se** vpr. **~se en** be based on

báscula f scales

base f base; (fig) basis, foundation. **a ~ de** thanks to; (mediante) by means of; (en una receta) mainly consisting of. **~ de datos** database. **partiendo de la ~ de, tomando como ~** on the basis of

básico adj basic

basílica f basilica

básquetbol, basquetbol m (LAm) basketball

bastante

● adjetivo/pronombre

····▸ (suficiente) enough. ¿hay ∼s sillas? are there enough chairs? ya tengo ∼ I have enough already

····▸ (mucho) quite a lot. vino ∼ gente quite a lot of people came. tiene ∼s amigos he has quite a lot of friends ¿te gusta?- sí, ∼ do you like it? — yes, quite a lot

● adverbio

····▸ (suficientemente) enough. no has estudiado ∼ you haven't studied enough. no es lo ∼ inteligente he's not clever enough (como para to)

····▸ bastante + adjetivo/adverbio (modificando la intensidad) quite, fairly. parece ∼ simpático he looks quite friendly. es ∼ fácil de hacer it's quite easy to do. canta ∼ bien he sings quite well

····▸ bastante con verbo (considerablemente) quite a lot. el lugar ha cambiado ∼ the place has changed quite a lot

bastar vi be enough. ¡basta! that's enough! basta con decir que suffice it to say that. basta y sobra that's more than enough

bastardilla f italics

bastardo adj & m bastard

bastidor m frame; (Auto) chassis. ∼es mpl (en el teatro) wings. entre ∼es behind the scenes

basto adj coarse. ∼s mpl (naipes) clubs

bast|ón m walking stick; (de esquí) ski pole. ∼onazo m blow with a stick; (de mando) staff of office

basur|a f rubbish, garbage (Amer); (en la calle) litter. ∼al m (LAm, lugar) rubbish dump. ∼ero m dustman (Brit), garbage collector (Amer); (sitio) rubbish dump; (Mex, recipiente) dustbin (Brit), garbage can (Amer)

bata f dressing-gown; (de médico etc)

white coat; (esp LAm, de baño) bathrobe

batahola f (LAm) pandemonium

batall|a f battle. ∼a campal pitched battle. de ∼a everyday. ∼ador adj fighting. ● m fighter. ∼ar vi battle, fight. ∼ón m battalion.

batata f sweet potato

bate m bat. ∼ador m batter; (cricket) batsman. ∼ar vi bat

batería f battery; (Mus) drums. ● m & f drummer. ∼ de cocina kitchen utensils, pots and pans

baterista m & f drummer

batido adj beaten; (nata) whipped. ● m batter; (bebida) milk shake. ∼ra f (food) mixer

batir vt beat; break (récord); whip (nata). ∼ palmas clap. ∼se vpr fight

batuta f baton. llevar la ∼ be in command, be the boss

baúl m trunk

bauti|smal adj baptismal. ∼smo m baptism, christening. ∼zar **10** vt baptize, christen. ∼zo m christening

baya f berry

bayeta f cloth

bayoneta f bayonet

baza f (naipes) trick; (fig) advantage. meter ∼ interfere

bazar m bazaar

bazofia f revolting food; (fig) rubbish

beato adj blessed; (piadoso) devout; (pey) overpious

bebé m baby

beb|edero m drinking trough; (sitio) watering place. ∼edizo m potion; (veneno) poison. ∼edor m heavy drinker. ∼er vt/i drink. ∼ida f drink. ∼ido adj drunk

beca f grant, scholarship. ∼do m (LAm) scholarship holder, scholar. ∼r **7** vt give a scholarship to.

b

~**rio** m scholarship holder, scholar

beige /beis, beʒ/ adj & m beige

béisbol m, (Mex) **beisbol** m baseball

belén m crib, nativity scene

belga adj & m & f Belgian

Bélgica f Belgium

bélico adj, **belicoso** adj warlike

bell|eza f beauty. ~**o** adj beautiful. ~**as artes** fpl fine arts

bellota f acorn

bemol m flat. **tener (muchos) ~es** be difficult

bend|ecir 46 (pero imperativo **bendice**, futuro, condicional y pp regulares) vt bless. ~**ición** f blessing. ~**ito** adj blessed; (que tiene suerte) lucky; (feliz) happy

benefactor m benefactor

benefic|encia f charity. **de ~encia** charitable. ~**iar** vt benefit. ~**iarse** vpr benefit. ~**iario** m beneficiary; (de un cheque etc) payee. ~**io** m benefit; (ventaja) advantage; (ganancia) profit, gain. ~**ioso** adj beneficial

benéfico adj beneficial; (de beneficencia) charitable

ben|evolencia f benevolence. ~**évolo** adj benevolent

bengala f flare. **luz** f **de ~** flare

benigno adj kind; (moderado) gentle, mild; (tumor) benign

berberecho m cockle

berenjena f aubergine (Brit), eggplant (Amer)

berr|ear vi (animales) bellow; (niño) bawl. ~**ido** m bellow; (de niño) bawling

berrinche m temper; (de un niño) tantrum

berro m watercress

besamel(a) f white sauce

bes|ar vt kiss. ~**arse** vpr kiss (each other). ~**o** m kiss

bestia f beast; (bruto) brute; (idiota) idiot. ~ **de carga** beast of burden. ~**l** adj bestial, animal; (fig, fam) terrific. ~**lidad** f (acción brutal) horrid thing; (insensatez) stupidity

besugo m red bream

besuquear vt cover with kisses

betabel f (Mex) beetroot

betún m (para el calzado) shoe polish

biberón m feeding-bottle

Biblia f Bible

bibliografía f bibliography

biblioteca f library; (mueble) bookcase. ~ **de consulta** reference library. ~**rio** m librarian

bicarbonato m bicarbonate

bicho m insect, bug; (animal) small animal, creature. ~ **raro** odd sort

bici f 🚲 bike. ~**cleta** f bicycle. **ir en ~cleta** cycle. ~**moto** (LAm) moped

bidé, **bidet** /bi'ðeɪ/ m bidet

bidón m drum, can

bien adv well; (muy) very, quite; (correctamente) right; (de buena gana) willingly. ● m good; (efectos) property. ¡~! fine!, OK!, good! ~... (o) ~ either... or. ¡está ~! fine!, alright!; (basta) that is enough! **más** ~ rather. ¡**muy** ~! good! **no** ~ as soon as. ¡**qué** ~! marvellous!, great! 🔲. **si** ~ although

bienal adj biennial

bien|aventurado adj fortunate. ~**estar** m well-being. ~**hablado** adj well-spoken. ~**hechor** m benefactor. ~**intencionado** adj well-meaning

bienio m two year-period

bienvenid|a f welcome. **dar la ~a a uno** welcome s.o. ~**o** adj welcome. ¡~**o**! welcome!

bifurca|ción f junction. ~**rse** 7 vpr fork; (rail) branch off

b|igamia f bigamy. ~**ígamo** adj bigamous. ● m bigamist

bigot|e m moustache. **~ón** adj (Mex), **~udo** adj with a big moustache

bikini m bikini

bilingüe adj bilingual

billar m billiards

billete m ticket; (de banco) (bank) note (Brit), bill (Amer). **~ de ida y vuelta** return ticket (Brit), round-trip ticket (Amer). **~ sencillo** single ticket (Brit), one-way ticket (Amer). **~ra** f, **~ro** m wallet, billfold (Amer)

billón m billion (Brit), trillion (Amer)

bi|mensual adj fortnightly, twice-monthly. **~mestral** adj two-monthly. **~mestre** two-month period. **~motor** adj twin-engined. • m twin-engined plane

binoculares mpl binoculars

bi|ografía f biography. **~ográfico** adj biographical

bi|ología f biology. **~ológico** adj biological. **~ólogo** m biologist

biombo m folding screen

biopsia f biopsy

bioterrorismo m bioterrorism

biplaza m two-seater

biquini m bikini

birlar vt 🗈 steal, pinch 🗈

bis m encore. **¡~!** encore! **vivo en el 3 ~** I live at 3A

bisabuel|a f great-grandmother. **~o** m great-grandfather. **~os** mpl great-grandparents

bisagra f hinge

bisiesto adj. **año m ~** leap year

bisniet|a f great-granddaughter. **~o** m great-grandson. **~os** mpl great-grandchildren

bisonte m bison

bisoño adj inexperienced

bisté, bistec m steak

bisturí m scalpel

bisutería f imitation jewellery, costume jewellery

bitácora f binnacle

bizco adj cross-eyed

bizcocho m sponge (cake)

bizquear vi squint

blanc|a f white woman; (Mus) minim. **~o** adj white; (tez) fair. • m white; (persona) white man; (espacio) blank; (objetivo) target. **dar en el ~o** hit the mark. **dejar en ~o** leave blank. **pasar la noche en ~o** have a sleepless night. **~ura** f whiteness

blandir 🗷 vt brandish

bland|o adj soft; (carácter) weak; (cobarde) cowardly; (carne) tender. **~ura** f softness; (de la carne) tenderness

blanque|ar vt whiten; whitewash (paredes); bleach (tela); launder (dinero). • vi turn white. **~o** m whitening; (de dinero) laundering

blasón m coat of arms

bledo m. **me importa un ~** I couldn't care less

blinda|je m armour (plating). **~r** vt armour(-plate)

bloc m (pl **~s**) pad

bloque m block; (Pol) bloc. **en ~** en bloc. **~ar** vt block, (Mil) blockade; (Com) freeze. **~o** m blockade; (Com) freezing

blusa f blouse

bob|ada f silly thing. **decir ~adas** talk nonsense. **~ería** f silly thing

bobina f reel; (Elec) coil

bobo adj silly, stupid. • m idiot, fool

boca f mouth; (fig, entrada) entrance; (de buzón) slot; (de cañón) muzzle. **~ abajo** face down. **~ arriba** face up

bocacalle f junction. **la primera ~ a la derecha** the first turning on the right

bocad|illo m (filled) roll; (fam, comida ligera) snack. **~o** m mouthful; (mordisco) bite; (de caballo) bit

boca|jarro: a ~jarro point-blank. **~manga** f cuff

bocanada f puff; (de vino etc) mouthful; (ráfaga) gust

bocata f sandwich

bocatería f sandwich bar

bocaza m & f invar big-mouth

boceto m sketch; (de proyecto) outline

bochinche m row; (alboroto) racket. **~ro** adj (LAm) rowdy

bochorno m sultry weather; (fig, vergüenza) embarrassment. **¡qué ~!** how embarrassing!. **~so** adj oppressive; (fig) embarrassing

bocina f horn; (LAm, auricular) receiver. **tocar la ~** sound one's horn. **~zo** m toot

boda f wedding

bodeg|a f cellar; (de vino) wine cellar; (LAm, almacén) warehouse; (de un barco) hold. **~ón** m cheap restaurant; (pintura) still life

bodoque m & f (fam, tonto) thickhead; (Mex, niño) kid

bofes mpl lights. **echar los ~** slog away

bofet|ada f slap; (fig) blow. **~ón** m punch

boga f (moda) fashion. **estar en ~** be in fashion, be in vogue. **~r** 12 vt row. **~vante** m (crustáceo) lobster

Bogotá f Bogotá

bogotano adj from Bogotá. •m native of Bogotá

bohemio adj & m Bohemian

bohío m (LAm) hut

boicot m (pl **~s**) boycott. **~ear** vt boycott. **~eo** m boycott. **hacer un ~** boycott

boina f beret

bola f ball; (canica) marble; (mentira) fib; (Mex, reunión desordenada) rowdy party; (Mex, montón) rowdy. **una ~ de** a

bunch of; (Mex, revolución) revolution; (Mex, brillo) shine

boleadoras (LAm) fpl bolas

bolear vt (Mex) polish, shine

bolera f bowling alley

bolero m (baile, chaqueta) bolero; (fig, fam, mentiroso) liar; (Mex, limpiabotas) bootblack

bole|ta f (LAm, de rifa) ticket; (Mex, de notas) (school) report; (Mex, electoral) ballot paper. **~taje** m (Mex) tickets. **~tería** f (LAm) ticket office; (de teatro, cine) box office. **~tero** m (LAm) ticket-seller

boletín m bulletin; (publicación periódica) journal; (de notas) report

boleto m (esp LAm) ticket; (Mex, de avión) (air) ticket. **~ de ida y vuelta**, (Mex) **~ redondo** return ticket (Brit), round-trip ticket (Amer). **~ sencillo** single ticket (Brit), one-way ticket (Amer)

boli m 🡒 Biro ®, ball-point pen

boliche m (juego) bowls; (bolera) bowling alley

bolígrafo m Biro ®, ball-point pen

bolillo m bobbin; (Mex, pan) (bread) roll

bolívar m (unidad monetaria venezolana) bolívar

Bolivia f Bolivia

boliviano adj Bolivian. •m Bolivian; (unidad monetaria de Bolivia) boliviano

boll|ería f baker's shop. **~o** m roll; (con azúcar) bun

bolo m skittle; (Mex, en bautizo) coins. **~s** mpl (juego) bowling

bols|a f bag; (Mex, bolsillo) pocket; (Mex, de mujer) handbag; (Com) stock exchange; (cavidad) cavity. **~a de agua caliente** hot-water bottle. **~illo** m pocket. **de ~illo** pocket. **~o** m (de mujer) handbag. **~o de mano**, **~o de viaje** (overnight) bag

bomba f bomb; (máquina) pump;

(noticia) bombshell. **~ de aceite** (Auto) oil pump. **~ de agua** (Auto) water pump. **pasarlo ~** have a marvellous time

bombachos mpl baggy trousers, baggy pants (Amer)

bombarde|ar vt bombard; (desde avión) bomb. **~o** m bombardment; (desde avión) bombing. **~ro** m (avión) bomber

bombazo m explosion

bombear vt pump

bombero m fireman. **cuerpo m de ~s** fire brigade (Brit), fire department (Amer)

bombilla f (light) bulb; (LAm, para mate) pipe for drinking maté

bombín m pump; (fam, sombrero) bowler (hat) (Brit), derby (Amer)

bombo m (tambor) bass drum. **a ~ y platillos** with a lot of fuss

bomb|ón m chocolate; (Mex, malvavisco) marshmallow. **~ona** f gas cylinder

bonachón adj easygoing; (bueno) good-natured

bonaerense adj from Buenos Aires. ●m native of Buenos Aires

bondad f goodness; (amabilidad) kindness; (del clima) mildness. **tenga la ~ de** would you be kind enough to. **~oso** adj kind

boniato m sweet potato

bonito adj nice; (mono) pretty. **¡muy ~!, ¡qué ~!** that's nice!, very nice!. ●m bonito

bono m voucher; (título) bond. **~ del Tesoro** government bond

boñiga f dung

boqueada f gasp. **dar la última ~** be dying

boquerón m anchovy

boquete m hole; (brecha) breach

boquiabierto adj open-mouthed; (fig) amazed, dumbfounded. **quedarse ~** be amazed

boquilla f mouthpiece; (para

cigarillos) cigarette-holder; (filtro de cigarillo) tip

borbotón m. **hablar a borbotones** gabble. **salir a borbotones** gush out

borda|do adj embroidered. ●m embroidery. **~r** vt embroider

bord|e m edge; (de carretera) side; (de plato etc) rim; (de un vestido) hem. **al ~e de** on the edge of; (fig) on the brink of. ●adj (Esp fam) stroppy. **~ear** vt go round; (fig) border on. **~illo** m kerb (Brit), curb (esp Amer)

bordo: a ~ on board

borla f tassel

borrach|era f drunkenness. **pegarse una ~era** get drunk. **~ín** m drunk; (habitual) drunkard. **~o** adj drunk. ●m drunkard. **estar ~o** be drunk. **ser ~o** be a drunkard

borrador m rough draft; (de contrato) draft; (para la pizarra) (black)board rubber; (goma) eraser

borrar vt rub out; (tachar) cross out; delete (información)

borrasc|a f depression, (tormenta) storm. **~oso** adj stormy

borrego m year-old lamb; (Mex, noticia falsa) canard

borrico m donkey; (fig, fam) ass

borrón m smudge; (de tinta) inkblot. **~ y cuenta nueva** let's forget about it!

borroso adj blurred; (fig) vague

bos|coso adj wooded. **~que** m wood, forest

bosquej|ar vt sketch; outline (plan). **~o** m sketch; (de plan) outline

bosta f dung

bostez|ar 10 vi yawn. **~o** m yawn

bota f boot; (recipiente) wineskin

botana f (Mex) snack, appetizer

botánic|a f botany. **~o** adj botanical. ●m botanist

botar vt launch; bounce (pelota);

b

(esp LAm, tirar) throw away. •vi bounce

botarate m irresponsible person; (esp LAm, derrochador) spendthrift

bote m boat; (de una pelota) bounce; (lata) tin, can; (vasija) jar. ~ **de la basura** (Mex) rubbish bin (Brit), trash can (Amer). ~ **salvavidas** lifeboat. **de** ~ **en** ~ packed

botella f bottle

botica f chemist's (shop) (Brit), drugstore (Amer). ~**rio** m chemist (Brit), druggist (Amer)

botijo m earthenware jug

botín m half boot; (de guerra) booty; (de ladrones) haul

botiquín m medicine chest; (de primeros auxilios) first aid kit

bot|ón m button; (yema) bud; (LAm, insignia) badge. ~**ones** m invar bellboy (Brit), bellhop (Amer)

bóveda f vault

boxe|ador m boxer. ~**ar** vi box. ~**o** m boxing

boya f buoy; (corcho) float. ~**nte** adj buoyant

bozal m (de perro etc) muzzle; (de caballo) halter

bracear vi wave one's arms; (nadar) swim, crawl

bracero m seasonal farm labourer

braga(s) f(pl) panties, knickers (Brit)

bragueta f flies

bram|ar vi bellow. ~**ido** m bellowing

branquia f gill

bras|a f ember. **a la** ~**a** grilled. ~**ero** m brazier

brasier m (Mex) bra

Brasil m. **(el)** ~ Brazil

brasile|ño adj & m Brazilian. ~**ro** adj & m (LAm) Brazilian

bravío adj wild

brav|o adj fierce; (valeroso) brave;

(mar) rough. **¡~!** int well done! bravo! ~**ura** f ferocity; (valor) bravery

braz|a f fathom. **nadar a** ~**a** swim breast-stroke. ~**ada** f (en natación) stroke. ~**alete** m bracelet; (brazal) arm-band. ~**o** m arm; (de caballo) foreleg; (rama) branch. ~**o derecho** right-hand man. **del** ~**o** arm in arm

brea f tar, pitch

brebaje m potion; (pej) concoction

brecha f opening; (Mil) breach; (Med) gash. ~ **generacional** generation gap. **estar en la** ~ be in the thick of it

brega f struggle. **andar a la** ~ work hard

breva f early fig

breve adj short. **en** ~ soon, shortly. **en** ~**s momentos** soon. ~**dad** f shortness

brib|ón m rogue, rascal. ~**onada** f dirty trick

brida f bridle

brigad|a f squad; (Mil) brigade. ~**ier** m brigadier (Brit), brigadier-general (Amer)

brill|ante adj bright; (lustroso) shiny; (persona) brilliant. •m diamond. ~**ar** vi shine; (centellear) sparkle. ~**o** m shine; (brillantez) brilliance; (centelleo) sparkle. **sacar** ~**o** polish. ~**oso** adj (LAm) shiny

brinc|ar 7 vi jump up and down. ~**o** m jump. **dar un** ~**o, pegar un** ~**o** jump

brind|ar vt offer. •vi. ~**ar por** toast, drink a toast to. ~**is** m toast

br|ío m energy; (decisión) determination. ~**ioso** adj spirited; (garboso) elegant

brisa f breeze

británico adj British. •m Briton, British person

brocha f paintbrush; (para afeitarse) shaving-brush

broche m clasp, fastener; (joya)

b

brooch; (Mex, para el pelo) hairslide (Brit), barrete (Amer)

brocheta f skewer; (plato) kebab

brócoli m broccoli

brom|a f joke. ~**a pesada** practical joke. **en** ~**a** in fun. **ni de** ~**a** no way. ~**ear** vi joke. ~**ista** adj fond of joking. ● m & f joker

bronca f row; (represión) telling-off; (LAm, rabia) foul mood. **dar** ~ **a uno** bug s.o.

bronce m bronze; (LAm) brass. ~**ado** adj bronze; (por el sol) tanned. ~**ar** vt tan (piel). ~**arse** vpr get a suntan

bronquitis f bronchitis

brot|ar vi (plantas) sprout; (Med) break out; (líquido) gush forth; (lágrimas) well up. ~**e** m shoot; (Med) outbreak

bruces: **de** ~ face down(wards). **caer de** ~ fall flat on one's face

bruj|a f witch. ~**ería** f witchcraft. ~**o** m wizard, magician. ● adj (Mex) broke

brújula f compass

brum|a f mist; (fig) confusion. ~**oso** adj misty, foggy

brusco adj (repentino) sudden; (persona) brusque

Bruselas f Brussels

brusquedad f roughness; (de movimiento) abruptness

brut|al adj brutal. ~**alidad** f brutality; (estupidez) stupidity. ~**o** adj ignorant; (tosco) rough; (peso, sueldo) gross

bucal adj oral; (lesión) mouth

buce|ar vi dive; (nadar) swim under water. ~**o** m diving; (natación) underwater swimming

bucle m ringlet

budín m pudding

budis|mo m Buddhism. ~**ta** m & f Buddhist

buen véase BUENO

buenaventura f good luck; (adivinación) fortune

bueno adj (delante de nombre masculino en singular **buen**) good; (agradable) nice; (tiempo) fine. ● int well!; (de acuerdo) OK!, very well! **¡buena la has hecho!** you've gone and done it now! **¡buenas noches!** good night! **¡buenas tardes!** (antes del atardecer) good afternoon!; (después del atardecer) good evening! **¡~s días!** good morning! **estar de buenas** be in a good mood. **por las buenas** willingly. **¡qué bueno!** (LAm) great!

Buenos Aires m Buenos Aires

buey m ox

búfalo m buffalo

bufanda f scarf

bufar vi snort

bufete m (mesa) writing-desk; (despacho) lawyer's office

buf|o adj comic. ~**ón** adj comical. ● m buffoon; (Historia) jester

buhardilla f attic; (ventana) dormer window

búho m owl

buhonero m pedlar

buitre m vulture

bujía f (Auto) spark plug

bulbo m bulb

bulevar m avenue, boulevard

Bulgaria f Bulgaria

búlgaro adj & m Bulgarian

bull|a f noise. ~**icio** m hubbub; (movimiento) bustle. ~**icioso** adj bustling; (ruidoso) noisy

bullir 22 vi boil; (burbujear) bubble; (fig) bustle

bulto m (volumen) bulk; (forma) shape; (paquete) package; (maleta etc) piece of luggage; (protuberancia) lump

buñuelo m fritter

BUP abrev (**Bachillerato Unificado**

⬛ see A-Z of Spanish life and culture

Polivalente) secondary school education

buque m ship, boat

burbuj|a f bubble. **~ear** vi bubble; (vino) sparkle

burdel m brothel

burdo adj rough, coarse; (excusa) clumsy

burgu|és adj middle-class, bourgeois. ●m middle-class person. **~esía** f middle class, bourgeoisie

burla f taunt; (broma) joke; (engaño) trick. **~r** vt evade. **~rse** vpr. **~rse de** mock, make fun of

burlesco adj (en literatura) burlesque

burlón adj mocking

bur|ocracia f bureaucracy; (Mex, funcionariado) civil service. **~ócrata** m & f bureaucrat; (Mex, funcionario) civil servant. **~ocrático** adj

bureaucratic; (Mex) (empleado) government

burro adj stupid; (obstinado) pigheaded. ●m donkey; (fig) ass

bursátil adj stock-exchange

bus m bus

busca f search. **a la ~ de** in search of. ●m beeper

buscador m search engine

buscapleitos m & f invar (LAm) trouble-maker

buscar 7 vt look for. ●vi look. **buscársela** ask for it; **ir a ~ a uno** fetch s.o.

búsqueda f search

busto m bust

butaca f armchair; (en el teatro etc) seat

buzo m diver

buzón m postbox (Brit), mailbox (Amer)

Cc

C/ abrev (**Calle**) St, Rd

cabal adj exact; (completo) complete. **no estar en sus ~es** not be in one's right mind

cabalga|dura f mount, horse. **~r** 12 vt ride. ●vi ride, go riding. **~ta** f ride; (desfile) procession

caballa f mackerel

caballerango m (Mex) groom

caballeresco adj gentlemanly. **literatura f caballeresca** books of chivalry

caballer|ía f mount, horse. **~iza** f stable. **~izo** m groom

caballero m gentleman; (de orden de caballería) knight; (tratamiento) sir. **~so** adj gentlemanly

caballete m (del tejado) ridge; (para

mesa) trestle; (de pintor) easel

caballito m pony. **~ del diablo** dragonfly. **~ de mar** sea-horse. **~s** mpl (carrusel) merry-go-round

caballo m horse; (del ajedrez) knight; (de la baraja española) queen. **~ de fuerza** horsepower. **a ~** on horseback

cabaña f hut

cabaret /kaba're/ m (pl **~s**) night-club

cabecear vi nod off; (en fútbol) head the ball; (caballo) toss its head

cabecera f (de la cama) headboard; (de la mesa) head; (en un impreso) heading

cabecilla m ringleader

cabello m hair. **~s** mpl hair

caber 🔲 vi fit (**en** into). **no cabe duda** there's no doubt

cabestr|illo m sling. ~**o** m halter

cabeza f head; (fig, inteligencia) intelligence. **andar de** ~ have a lot to do. ~**da** f nod. **dar una** ~**da** nod off. ~**zo** m butt; (en fútbol) header

cabida f capacity; (extensión) area; (espacio) room. **dar** ~ **a** have room for, accommodate

cabina f (de pasajeros) cabin; (de pilotos) cockpit; (electoral) booth; (de camión) cab. ~ **telefónica** telephone box (Brit), telephone booth (Amer)

cabizbajo adj crestfallen

cable m cable

cabo m end; (trozo) bit; (Mil) corporal; (mango) handle; (en geografía) cape; (Naut) rope. **al** ~ **de** after. **de** ~ **a rabo** from beginning to end. **llevar a** ~ carry out

cabr|a f goat. ~**iola** f jump, skip. ~**itilla** f kid. ~**ito** m kid

cábula f (Mex) crook

cacahuate, (Mex) cacahuete m peanut

cacalote m (Mex) crow

cacao m (planta y semillas) cacao; (polvo) cocoa; (fig) confusion

cacarear vt boast about. ●vi (gallo) crow; (gallina) cluck

cacería f hunt. **ir de** ~ go hunting

cacerola f saucepan, casserole

cacharro m (earthenware) pot; (coche estropeado) wreck; (cosa inútil) piece of junk; (chisme) thing. ~**s** mpl pots and pans

cachear vt frisk

cachemir m, **cachemira** f cashmere

cacheo m frisking

cachetada f (LAm) slap

cache|te m slap; (esp LAm, mejilla) cheek. ~**tear** vt (LAm) slap. ~**tón** adj (LAm) chubby-cheeked

cachimba f pipe

cachiporra f club, truncheon

cachivache m piece of junk. ~**s** mpl junk

cacho m bit, piece; (LAm, cuerno) horn

cachondeo m 🔳 joking, joke

cachorro m (perrito) puppy; (de león, tigre) cub

cachucha f (Mex) cup

caciqu|e m cacique, chief; (Pol) local political boss; (hombre poderoso) tyrant. ~**il** adj despotic. ~**ismo** m despotism

caco m thief

cacofonía f cacophony

cacto m, **cactus** m invar cactus

cada adj invar each, every. ~ **uno** each one, everyone. **uno de** ~ **cinco** one in five. ~ **vez más** more and more

cadáver m corpse

cadena f chain; (TV) channel. ~ **de fabricación** production line. ~ **de montañas** mountain range. ~ **perpetua** life imprisonment

cadera f hip

cadete m cadet

caduc|ar 🔳 vi expire. ~**idad** f. **fecha** f **de** ~**idad** sell-by date. ~**o** adj outdated

cae|r 🔲 vi fall. **dejar** ~**r** drop. **este vestido no me** ~ **bien** this dress doesn't suit me. **hacer** ~**r** knock over. **Juan me** ~ **bien** I like Juan. **su cumpleaños cayó en martes** his birthday fell on a Tuesday. ~**rse** vpr fall (over). **se le cayó** he dropped it

café m coffee; (📗cafetería) café; (Mex, marrón) brown. ●adj. **color** ~ coffee-coloured. ~ **con leche** white coffee. ~ **cortado** coffee with a little milk. ~ **negro** (LAm) expresso. ~ **solo** black coffee

cafeína f caffeine. ~**tal** m coffee

....
📗 see A-Z of Spanish life and culture

plantation. ~tera f coffee-pot.
~tería f café. ~tero adj coffee

caíd|a f fall; (disminución) drop;
(pendiente) slope. ~o adj fallen

caigo vb véase CAER

caimán m cayman, alligator

caj|a f box; (de botellas) case; (ataúd)
coffin; (en tienda) cash desk; (en
supermercado) check-out; (en banco)
cashier's desk. ~a de ahorros
savings bank. ~a de cambios
gearbox. ~a de caudales, ~a
fuerte safe. ~a negra black box.
~a registradora till. ~ero m
cashier. ~ero automático cash
dispenser. ~etilla f packet. ~ita f
small box. ~ón m (de mueble)
drawer; (caja grande) crate; (LAm,
ataúd) coffin; (Mex, en estacionamiento)
parking space. ser de ~ón be
obvious. ~uela f (Mex) boot (Brit),
trunk (Amer)

cal m lime

cala f cove

calaba|cín m, calabacita f (Mex)
courgette (Brit), zucchini (Amer).
~za f pumpkin; (fig, fam, idiota)
idiot. dar ~zas a uno give s.o.
the brush-off

calabozo m prison; (celda) cell

calado adj soaked. estar ~ hasta
los huesos be soaked to the skin.
● m (Naut) draught

calamar m squid

calambre m cramp

calami|dad f calamity, disaster.
~toso adj calamitous

calaña f sort

calar vt soak; (penetrar) pierce; (fig,
penetrar) see through; rumble
(persona); sample (fruta). ~se vpr get
soaked; (zapatos) leak; (Auto) stall

calavera f skull; (Mex, Auto) tail
light

calcar 🔳 vt trace; (fig) copy

calcet|a f. hacer ~ knit. ~ín m
sock

calcinar vt burn

calcio m calcium

calcomanía f transfer

calcula|dor adj calculating. ~dora
f calculator. ~r vt calculate;
(suponer) reckon, think; (imaginar)
imagine

cálculo m calculation; (Med) stone

caldear vt heat, warm. ~se vpr get
hot

caldera f boiler

calderilla f small change

caldo m stock; (sopa) clear soup,
broth

calefacción f heating. ~ central
central heating

caleidoscopio m kaleidoscope

calendario m calendar; (programa)
schedule

calent|ador m heater. ~amiento
m warming; (en deportes) warm-up.
~ar 🔳 vt heat; (templar) warm.
~arse vpr get hot; (templarse) warm
up; (LAm, enojarse) get mad. ~ura f
fever, (high) temperature.
~uriento adj feverish

calibr|ar vt calibrate; (fig) weigh
up. ~e m calibre; (diámetro)
diameter; (fig) importance

calidad f quality; (condición)
capacity. en ~ de as

calidez f (LAm) warmth

cálido adj warm

caliente adj hot; (habitación, ropa)
warm; (LAm, enojado) angry

califica|ción f qualification;
(evaluación) assessment; (nota) mark.
~do adj (esp LAm) qualified; (mano
de obra) skilled. ~r 🔳 vt qualify;
(evaluar) assess; mark (examen etc).
~r de describe as, label

cáliz m chalice; (en botánica) calyx

caliz|a f limestone. ~o adj lime

calla|do adj quiet. ~r vt silence;
keep (secreto); hush up (asunto). ● vi
be quiet, keep quiet, shut up 🔳.
~rse vpr be quiet, keep quiet,

shut up ▣ ¡**cállate!** be quiet!, shut up! ▣

calle f street, road; (en deportes, autopista) lane. **~ de dirección única** one-way street. **~ mayor** high street, main street. **de ~** everyday. **~ja** f narrow street. **~jear** vi hang out on the streets. **~jero** adj street. • m street plan. **~jón** m alley. **~ón sin salida** dead end. **~juela** † back street, side street

call|ista m & f chiropodist. **~o** m corn, callus. **~os** mpl tripe. **~osidad** f callus

calm|a f calm. ¡**~a!** calm down!. **en ~a** calm. **perder la ~a** lose one's composure. **~ante** m tranquilizer; (para el dolor) painkiller. **~ar** vt calm; (aliviar) soothe. • vi (viento) abate. **~arse** vpr calm down; (viento) abate. **~o** adj calm. **~oso** adj calm; (fam, flemático) slow

calor m heat; (afecto) warmth. **hace ~** it's hot. **tener ~** be hot. **~ía** f calorie. **~ífero** adj heat-producing. **~ífico** adj calorific

calumni|a f calumny; (oral) slander; (escrita) libel. **~ar** vt slander; (por escrito) libel. **~oso** adj slanderous; (cosa escrita) libellous

caluroso adj warm; (clima) hot

calv|a f bald head; (parte sin pelo) bald patch. **~icie** f baldness. **~o** adj bald

calza f wedge

calzada f road; (en autopista) carriageway

calza|do adj wearing shoes. • m footwear, shoe. **~dor** m shoehorn. **~r** ▣ vt put shoes on; (llevar) wear. **¿qué número calza Vd?** what size shoe do you take? • vi wear shoes. **~rse** vpr put on

calz|ón m shorts. **~ones** mpl shorts; (LAm, ropa interior) panties. **~oncillos** mpl underpants

cama f bed. **~ de matrimonio** double bed. **~ individual** single bed. **guardar ~** stay in bed

camada f litter

camafeo m cameo

camaleón m chameleon

cámara f (aposento) chamber; (fotográfica) camera. **~ fotográfica** camera. **a ~ lenta** in slow motion

camarad|a m & f colleague; (de colegio) schoolfriend; (Pol) comrade. **~ería** f camaraderie

camarer|a f chambermaid; (de restaurante etc) waitress. **~o** m waiter

camarógrafo m cameraman

camarón m shrimp

camarote m cabin

cambi|able adj changeable; (Com etc) exchangeable. **~ante** adj variable; (persona) moody. **~ar** vt change; (trocar) exchange. • vi change. **~ar de idea** change one's mind. **~arse** vpr change. **~o** m change; (Com) exchange rate; (moneda menuda) (small) change; (Auto) gear. **en ~o** on the other hand

camello m camel

camellón m (Mex) traffic island

camerino m dressing room

camilla f stretcher

camin|ante m traveller. **~ar** vt/i walk. **~ata** f long walk. **~o** m road; (sendero) path, track; (dirección, ruta) way. **~o de** towards, on the way to. **abrir ~o** make way. **a medio ~o, a la mitad del ~o** half-way. **de ~o** on the way

cami|ón m truck, lorry; (Mex, autobús) bus. **~onero** m lorry-driver; (Mex, de autobús) bus driver. **~oneta** f van; (LAm, coche familiar) estate car

camis|a f shirt. **~a de fuerza** strait-jacket. **~ería** f shirtmaker's. **~eta** f T-shirt; (ropa interior) vest. **~ón** m nightdress

camorra f ▣ row. **buscar ~** look for a fight

C

camote m (LAm) sweet potato

campamento m camp. **de ~** adj camping

campan|a f bell. **~ada** f stroke. **~ario** m bell tower, belfry. **~illa** f bell

campaña f campaign

campe|ón adj & m champion. **~onato** m championship

campes|ino adj country. ●m peasant. **~tre** adj country

camping /'kampin/ m (pl **~s**) camping; (lugar) campsite. **hacer ~** go camping

camp|iña f countryside. **~o** m country; (agricultura, fig) field; (de fútbol) pitch; (de golf) course. **~osanto** m cemetery

camufla|je m camouflage. **~r** vt camouflage

cana f grey hair, white hair. **peinar ~s** be getting old

Canadá m. **el ~** Canada

canadiense adj & m & f Canadian

canal m (incl TV) channel; (artificial) canal; (del tejado) gutter. **~ de la Mancha** English Channel. **~ de Panamá** Panama Canal. **~ón** m (horizontal) gutter; (vertical) drain-pipe

canalla f rabble. ●m (fig, fam) swine. **~da** f dirty trick

canapé m sofa, couch; (Culin) canapé

Canarias fpl. **las (islas) ~** the Canary Islands, the Canaries

canario adj of the Canary Islands. ●m native of the Canary Islands; (pájaro) canary

canast|a f (large) basket **~illa** f small basket; (para un bebé) layette. **~illo** m small basket. **~o** m (large) basket

cancela|ción f cancellation. **~r** vt cancel; write off (deuda)

cáncer m cancer. **C~** Cancer

⋯⋯⋯⋯⋯⋯⋯⋯⋯⋯⋯⋯⋯⋯⋯⋯⋯⋯⋯⋯

🖪 *see A-Z of Spanish life and culture*

cancha f court; (LAm, de fútbol, rugby) pitch, ground

canciller m chancellor; (LAm, ministro) Minister of Foreign Affairs

canci|ón f song. **~ón de cuna** lullaby. **~onero** m song-book

candado m padlock

candel|a f candle. **~abro** m candelabra. **~ero** m candlestick

candente adj (rojo) red-hot; (fig) burning

candidato m candidate

candidez f innocence; (ingenuidad) naivety

cándido adj naive

candil m oil lamp. **~ejas** fpl footlights

candor m innocence; (ingenuidad) naivety

canela f cinnamon

cangrejo m crab. **~ de río** crayfish

canguro m kangaroo. ●m & f (persona) baby-sitter

caníbal adj & m & f cannibal

canica f marble

canijo adj weak; (Mex, terco) stubborn; (Mex, intenso) incredible

canilla f (LAm) shinbone

canino adj canine. ●m canine (tooth)

canje m exchange. **~ar** vt exchange

cano adj grey. **de pelo ~** grey-haired

canoa f canoe

can|ónigo m canon. **~onizar** 🔟 vt canonize

canoso adj grey-haired

cansa|do adj tired; (que cansa) tiring. **~dor** (LAm) tiring. **~ncio** m tiredness. **~r** vt tire; (aburrir) bore. ●vi be tiring; (aburrir) get boring. **~rse** vpr get tired

canta|nte adj singing. ●m & f

singer. **~or** m Flamenco singer.
~r vt/i sing. **~rlas claras** speak
frankly. ●m singing; (poema) poem

cántaro m pitcher. **llover a ~s**
pour down

cante m folk song. **~ flamenco**, **~
jondo** Flamenco singing

cantera f quarry

cantidad f quantity; (número)
number; (de dinero) sum. **una ~ de**
lots of

cantimplora f water-bottle

cantina f canteen; (Rail) buffet;
(LAm, bar) bar

cant|inela f song. **~o** m singing;
(canción) chant; (borde) edge; (de un
cuchillo) blunt edge. **~o rodado**
boulder; (guijarro) pebble. **de ~o**
on edge

canturre|ar vt/i hum. **~o** m
humming

canuto m tube

caña f (planta) reed; (del trigo) stalk;
(del bambú) cane; (de pescar) rod; (de
la bota) leg; (vaso) glass. **~ de
azúcar** sugar-cane. **~da** f ravine;
(camino) track; (LAm, arroyo) stream

cáñamo m hemp. **~ indio**
cannabis

cañ|ería f pipe; (tubería) piping. **~o**
m pipe, tube; (de fuente) jet. **~ón** m
(de pluma) quill; (de artillería) cannon;
(de arma de fuego) barrel; (desfiladero)
canyon. **~onera** f gunboat

caoba f mahogany

ca|os m chaos. **~ótico** adj chaotic

capa f layer; (de pintura) coat; (Culin)
coating; (prenda) cloak; (más corta)
cape; (en geología) stratum

capaci|dad f capacity; (fig) ability.
~tar vt qualify, enable; (instruir)
train

caparazón m shell

capataz m foreman

capaz adj capable, able

capcioso adj sly, insidious

capellán m chaplain

caperuza f hood; (de bolígrafo) cap

capilla f chapel

capital adj capital, very important.
●m (dinero) capital. ●f (ciudad)
capital. **~ de provincia** county
town. **~ino** adj (LAm) of/from the
capital. **~ismo** m capitalism.
~ista adj & m & f capitalist. **~izar**
[10] vt capitalize

capit|án m captain; (de pesquero)
skipper. **~anear** vt lead,
command; skipper (pesquero);
captain (un equipo)

capitel m (de columna) capital

capitulaci|ón f surrender. **~ones**
fpl marriage contract

capítulo m chapter; (de serie)
episode

capó m bonnet (Brit), hood (Amer)

capón m (pollo) capon

caporal m (Mex) foreman

capot|a f (de mujer) bonnet; (Auto)
folding top; (de cochecito) hood. **~e**
m cape; (Mex, de coche) bonnet (Brit),
hood (Amer)

capricho m whim. **~so** adj
capricious, whimsical

Capricornio m Capricorn

cápsula f capsule

captar vt harness (agua); grasp
(sentido); capture (atención); win
(confianza); (radio) pick up

captura f capture. **~r** vt capture

capucha f hood

capullo m bud; (de insecto) cocoon

caqui m khaki

cara f face; (de una moneda) heads;
(de un objeto) side; (aspecto) look,
appearance; (descaro) cheek. **~ a**
facing. **~ a ~** face to face. **~
dura** véase CARADURA. **~ o cruz**
heads or tails. **dar la ~ a** face up
to. **hacer ~ a** face. **tener mala
~** look ill. **volver la ~** look the
other way

carabela f caravel

carabina f carbine; (fig, fam, señora) chaperone

caracol m snail; (de mar) winkle; (LAm, concha) conch; (de pelo) curl. **¡~es!** Good Heavens!. **~a** f conch

carácter m (pl **caracteres**) character; (indole) nature. **con ~ de** as

característic|a f characteristic. **~o** adj characteristic, typical

caracteriza|do adj characterized; (prestigioso) distinguished. **~r** 🔟 vt characterize

caradura f cheek, nerve. ●m & f cheeky person

caramba int good heavens!

carambola f (en billar) cannon; (Mex, choque múltiple) pile-up. **de ~** by pure chance

caramelo m sweet (Brit), candy (Amer); (azúcar fundido) caramel

caraqueño adj from Caracas

carátula f (de disco) sleeve (Brit), jacket (Amer); (de video) case; (de libro) cover; (Mex, del reloj) face

caravana f caravan; (de vehículos) convoy; (Auto) long line, traffic jam; (remolque) caravan (Brit), trailer (Amer); (Mex, reverencia) bow

caray int 🔟 good heavens!

carb|ón m coal; (para dibujar) charcoal. **~ de leña** charcoal. **~oncillo** m charcoal. **~onero** adj coal. ●m coal-merchant. **~onizar** 🔟 vt (fig) burn (to a cinder). **~ono** m carbon

carbura|dor m carburettor. **~nte** m fuel

carcajada f guffaw. **reírse a ~s** roar with laughter. **soltar una ~** burst out laughing

cárcel f prison, jail

carcelero m jailer

carcom|er vt eat away; (fig) undermine. **~erse** vpr be eaten away; (fig) waste away

cardenal m cardinal; (contusión) bruise

cardiaco, cardíaco adj cardiac, heart

cardinal adj cardinal

cardo m thistle

carear vt bring face to face (personas); compare (cosas)

care|cer 🔟 vi. **~cer de** lack. **~cer de sentido** not to make sense. **~ncia** f lack. **~nte** adj lacking

care|ro adj pricey. **~stía** f (elevado) high cost

careta f mask

carey m tortoiseshell

carga f load; (fig) burden; (acción) loading; (de barco, avión) cargo; (de tren) freight; (de arma) charge; (Elec, ataque) charge; (obligación) obligation. **llevar la ~ de algo** be responsible for sth. **~da** f (Mex, Pol) supporters. **~do** adj loaded; (fig) burdened; (atmósfera) heavy; (café) strong; (pila) charged. **~mento** m load; (acción) loading; (de un barco) cargo. **~r** 🔟 vt load; (fig) burden; (Elec, atacar) charge; fill (pluma etc). ●vi load. **~r con** carry. **~rse** vpr (pila) charge. **~rse de** to load s.o. down with

cargo m (puesto) post; (acusación) charge. **a ~ de** in the charge of. **hacerse ~ de** take responsibility for. **tener a su ~** be in charge of

carguero m (Naut) cargo ship

caria|do adj decayed. **~rse** vpr decay

caribeño adj Caribbean

caricatura f caricature

caricia f caress; (a animal) stroke

caridad f charity. **¡por ~!** for goodness sake!

caries f invar tooth decay; (lesión) cavity

cariño m affection; (caricia) caress. **~ mío** my darling. **con mucho ~** (en carta) with love from. **tener ~ a** be fond of. **tomar ~ a** become fond of. **~so** adj affectionate

carisma m charisma

caritativo adj charitable

cariz m look

carmesí adj & m crimson

carmín m (de labios) lipstick; (color) red

carnal adj carnal. **primo ~** first cousin

🔲**carnaval** m carnival. **~esco** adj carnival

carne f meat; (Anat, de frutos, pescado) flesh. **~ de cerdo** pork. **~ de cordero** lamb. **~ de gallina** goose pimples. **~ molida** (LAm), **~ picada** (Brit), ground beef (Amer). **~ de ternera** veal. **~ de vaca** beef. **me pone la ~ de gallina** it gives me the creeps. **ser de ~ y hueso** be only human

carné, carnet m card. 🔲**~ de conducir** driving licence (Brit), driver's license (Amer) 🔲**~ de identidad** identity card. **~ de manejar** (LAm) driving license (Brit), driver's license (Amer). **~ de socio** membership card

carnero m ram

carnicer|ía f butcher's (shop); (fig) massacre. **~o** adj carnivorous. ●m butcher

carnívoro adj carnivorous. ●m carnivore

carnoso adj fleshy; (pollo) meaty

caro adj expensive. ●adv dear, dearly. **costar ~ a uno** cost s.o. dear.

carpa f carp; (LAm, tienda) tent

carpeta f folder, file. **~zo** m. **dar ~zo a** shelve

carpinter|ía f carpentry. **~o** m carpenter, joiner

carraspe|ar vi clear one's throat. **~ra** f. **tener ~ra** have a frog in one's throat

carrera f run; (prisa) rush; (concurso) race; (estudios) degree course; (profesión) career; (de taxi) journey

carreta f cart. **~da** f cartload

carrete m reel; (película) film

carretear vi (LAm) taxi

carretera f road. **~ de circunvalación** bypass, ring road. **~ nacional** A road (Brit), highway (Amer)

carretilla f wheelbarrow

carril m lane; (Rail) rail

carrito m (en supermercado, para equipaje) trolley (Brit), cart (Amer)

carro m cart; (LAm, coche) car; (Mex, vagón) coach. **~ de combate** tank. **~cería** f (Auto) bodywork

carroña f carrion

carroza f coach, carriage; (en desfile de fiesta) float

carruaje m carriage

carrusel m merry-go-round

cart|a f letter; (lista de platos) menu; (lista de vinos) list; (mapa) map; (naipe) card. **~a blanca** free hand. **~a de crédito** letter of credit. **~a verde** green card. **~earse** vpr correspond

cartel m poster; (letrero) sign. **~era** f hoarding; (en periódico) listings; (LAm en escuela, oficina) notice board (Brit), bulletin board (Amer). **de ~** celebrated

carter|a f wallet; (de colegial) satchel; (para documentos) briefcase; (LAm, de mujer) handbag (Brit), purse (Amer). **~ista** m & f pickpocket

cartero m postman, mailman (Amer)

cartílago m cartilage

cartilla f first reading book. **~ de ahorros** savings book. **leerle la ~ a uno** tell s.o. off

cartón m cardboard

cartucho m cartridge

cartulina f card

casa f house; (hogar) home; (empresa) firm. **~ de huéspedes** boarding-house. **~ de socorro** first aid post. **ir a ~** go home. **salir de ~** go out

....

🔲 see A-Z of Spanish life and culture

casaca f jacket

casado adj married. **los recién ~s** the newly-weds

casa|mentero m matchmaker. **~miento** m marriage; (ceremonia) wedding. **~r** vt marry. **~rse** vpr get married

cascabel m small bell; (de serpiente) rattle

cascada f waterfall

casca|nueces m invar nutcrackers. **~r** 7 vt crack (nuez, huevo); (pegar) beat. **~rse** vpr crack

cáscara f (de huevo, nuez) shell; (de naranja) peel; (de plátano) skin

cascarrabias adj invar grumpy

casco m helmet; (de cerámica etc) piece, fragment; (cabeza) scalp; (de barco) hull; (envase) empty bottle; (de caballo) hoof; (de una ciudad) part, area

cascote m piece of rubble. **~s** mpl rubble

caserío m country house; (poblado) hamlet

casero adj home-made; (doméstico) domestic; (amante del hogar) home-loving; (reunión) family. ●m owner; (vigilante) caretaker

caseta f hut; (puesto) stand. **~ de baño** bathing hut

casete m & f cassette

casi adv almost, nearly; (en frases negativas) hardly. **~ ~** very nearly. **~ nada** hardly any. **¡~ nada!** is that all? **~ nunca** hardly ever

casill|a f hut; (en ajedrez etc) square; (en formulario) box; (compartimiento) pigeonhole. **~ electrónica** e-mail address. **~ero** m pigeonholes; (compartimiento) pigeonhole

casino m casino; (club social) club

caso m case. **el ~ es que** the fact is that. **en ~ de** in the event of. **en cualquier ~** in any case, whatever happens. **en ese ~** in

that case. **en todo ~** in any case. **en último ~** as a last resort. **hacer ~ de** take notice of. **poner por ~** suppose

caspa f dandruff

casquivana f flirt

cassette m & f cassette

casta f (de animal) breed; (de persona) descent; (grupo social) caste

castaña f chestnut

castañetear vi (dientes) chatter

castaño adj chestnut; (ojos) brown. ●m chestnut (tree)

castañuela f castanet

castellano adj Castilian. ●m (persona) Castilian; (lengua) Castilian, Spanish. **~parlante** adj Castilian-speaking, Spanish-speaking. **¿habla Vd ~?** do you speak Spanish?

castidad f chastity

castig|ar 12 vt punish; (en deportes) penalize. **~o** m punishment; (en deportes) penalty

castillo m castle

cast|izo adj traditional; (puro) pure. **~o** adj chaste

castor m beaver

castrar vt castrate

castrense m military

casual adj chance, accidental. **~idad** f chance, coincidence. **dar la ~idad** happen. **de ~idad, por ~idad** by chance. **¡qué ~idad!** what a coincidence!. **~mente** adv by chance; (precisamente) actually

cataclismo m cataclysm

catador m taster

catalán adj & m Catalan

catalizador m catalyst

cat|alogar 12 vt catalogue; (fig) classify. **~álogo** m catalogue

Cataluña f Catalonia

catamarán m catamaran

catapulta f catapult

see A-Z of Spanish life and culture

catar vt taste, try

catarata f waterfall, falls; (Med) cataract

catarro m cold

cat|ástrofe m catastrophe. **~astrófico** adj catastrophic

catecismo m catechism

cátedra f (en universidad) professorship, chair; (en colegio) post of head of department

catedral f cathedral

catedrático m professor; (de colegio) teacher, head of department

categ|oría f category; (clase) class. **de ~oría** important. **de primera ~oría** first-class. **~órico** adj categorical

cat|olicismo m catholicism. **~ólico** adj (Roman) Catholic ●m (Roman) Catholic

catorce adj & m fourteen

cauce m river bed; (fig, artificial) channel

caucho m rubber

caudal m (de río) volume of flow; (riqueza) wealth. **~oso** adj (río) large

caudillo m leader

causa f cause; (motivo) reason, (Jurid) trial. **a ~ de, por ~ de** because of. **~r** vt cause

cautel|a f caution. **~oso** adj cautious, wary

cauterizar 10 vt cauterize

cautiv|ar vt capture; (fig, fascinar) captivate. **~erio** m, **~idad** f captivity. **~o** adj & m captive

cauto adj cautious

cavar vt/i dig

caverna f cave, cavern

caviar m caviare

cavidad f cavity

caza f hunting; (con fusil) shooting; (animales) game. ●m fighter. **andar**

a (la) ~ de be in search of. **~ mayor** game hunting. **dar ~** chase, go after. **ir de ~** go hunting/shooting. **~dor** m hunter. **~dora** f jacket. **~r** 10 vt hunt; (con fusil) shoot; (fig) track down; (obtener) catch, get

caz|o m saucepan; (cucharón) ladle. **~oleta** f (small) saucepan. **~uela** f casserole

cebada f barley

ceb|ar vt fatten (up); bait (anzuelo); prime (arma de fuego). **~o** m bait; (de arma de fuego) charge

ceboll|a f onion. **~eta** f spring onion (Brit), scallion (Amer). **~ino** m chive

cebra f zebra

cece|ar vi lisp. **~o** m lisp

cedazo m sieve

ceder vt give up; (transferir) transfer. ●vi give in; (disminuir) ease off; (romperse) give way, collapse. **ceda el paso** give way (Brit), yield (Amer)

cedro m cedar

cédula f bond. **~ de identidad** identity card

CE(E) abrev (**Comunidad (Económica) Europea**) E(E)C

ceg|ador adj blinding. **~ar** 1 & 12 vt blind; (tapar) block up. **~arse** vpr be blinded (**de** by). **~uera** f blindness

ceja f eyebrow

cejar vi give way

celada f ambush; (fig) trap

cela|dor m (de cárcel) prison warder; (de museo etc) security guard. **~r** vt watch

celda f cell

celebra|ción f celebration. **~r** vt celebrate; (alabar) praise. **~rse** vpr take place

célebre adj famous

celebridad f fame; (persona) celebrity

celest|e adj heavenly; (vestido) pale blue. **azul ~e** sky-blue. **~ial** adj heavenly

celibato m celibacy

célibe adj celibate

celo m zeal; (de las hembras) heat; (de los machos) rut; (cinta adhesiva) Sellotape ® (Brit), Scotch ® tape (Amer). **~s** mpl jealousy. **dar ~s** make jealous. **tener ~s** be jealous

celofán m cellophane

celoso adj conscientious; (que tiene celos) jealous

celta adj & m (lengua) Celtic. •m & f Celt

célula f cell

celular adj cellular. •m (LAm) mobile, cellphone

celulosa f cellulose

cementerio m cemetery

cemento m cement; (hormigón) concrete; (LAm, cola) glue

cena f dinner; (comida ligera) supper

cenag|al m marsh, bog; (fig) tight spot. **~oso** adj boggy

cenar vt have for dinner; (en cena ligera) have for supper. •vi have dinner; (tomar cena ligera) have supper

cenicero m ashtray

ceniza f ash

censo m census. **~ electoral** electoral roll

censura f censure; (de prensa etc) censorship. **~r** vt censure; censor (prensa etc)

centavo adj & m hundredth; (moneda) centavo

centell|a f flash; (chispa) spark. **~ar**, **~ear** vi sparkle

centena f hundred. **~r** m hundred. **a ~res** by the hundred. **~rio** adj centenarian. •m centenary; (persona) centenarian

centeno m rye

centésim|a f hundredth. **~o** adj hundredth

cent|ígrado adj centigrade, Celsius. •m centigrade. **~igramo** m centigram. **~ilitro** m centilitre. **~ímetro** m centimetre

céntimo adj hundredth. •m cent

centinela f sentry

centolla f, **centollo** m spider crab

central adj central. •f head office. **~ de correos** general post office. **~ eléctrica** power station. **~ nuclear** nuclear power station. **~ telefónica** telephone exchange. **~ita** f switchboard

centraliza|ción f centralization. **~r** 10 vt centralize

centrar vt centre

céntrico adj central

centrífugo adj centrifugal

centro m centre. **~ comercial** shopping centre (Brit), shopping mall (Amer). **~ de llamadas** call centre

Centroamérica f Central America

centroamericano adj & m Central American

ceñi|do adj tight. **~r** 5 & 22 vt take (corona); (vestido) cling to. **~rse** vpr limit o.s. (**a** to)

ceñ|o m frown. **fruncir el ~o** frown. **~udo** adj frowning

cepill|ar vt brush; (en carpintería) plane. **~o** m brush; (en carpintería) plane. **~o de dientes** toothbrush

cera f wax

cerámic|a f ceramics; (materia) pottery; (objeto) piece of pottery. **~o** adj ceramic

cerca f fence; (de piedra) wall.• adv near, close. **~ de** prep close to, close up, closely

cercan|ía f nearness, proximity. **~ías** fpl vicinity. **tren** m **de ~ías** local train. **~o** adj near, close.

cercar 7 vt fence in, enclose;

(gente) surround; (asediar) besiege

cerciorar vt convince. **~se** vpr make sure

cerco m (asedio) siege; (círculo) ring; (LAm, valla) fence; (LAm, seto) hedge

cerdo m pig; (carne) pork

cereal m cereal

cerebr|al adj cerebral. **~o** m brain; (persona) brains

ceremoni|a f ceremony. **~al** adj ceremonial. **~oso** adj ceremonious

cerez|a f cherry. **~o** m cherry tree

cerill|a f match. **~o** m (Mex) match

cern|er 1 vt sieve. **~erse** vpr hover. **~idor** m sieve

cero m nought, zero; (fútbol) nil (Brit), zero (Amer); (tenis) love; (persona) nonentity

cerquillo m (LAm, flequillo) fringe (Brit), bangs (Amer)

cerra|do adj shut, closed; (espacio) shut in, enclosed; (cielo) overcast; (curva) sharp. **~dura** f lock; (acción de cerrar) shutting, closing. **~jero** m locksmith. **~r** 1 vt shut, close; (con llave) lock; (cercar) enclose; turn off (grifo); block up (agujero etc). ●vi shut, close. **~rse** vpr shut, close; (herida) heal. **~r con llave** lock

cerro m hill

cerrojo m bolt. **echar el ~** bolt

certamen m competition, contest

certero adj accurate

certeza, certidumbre f certainty

certifica|do adj (carta etc) registered. ●m certificate. **~r** 7 vt certify

certitud f certainty

cervatillo, cervato m fawn

cerve|cería f beerhouse, bar; (fábrica) brewery. **~za** f beer. **~za de barril** draught beer. **~za rubia** lager

cesa|ción f cessation, suspension. **~nte** adj redundant. **~r** vt stop. ●vi stop, cease; (dejar un empleo) resign. **sin ~r** incessantly

cesárea f caesarian (section)

cese m cessation; (de un empleo) dismissal. **~ del fuego** (LAm) ceasefire

césped m grass, lawn

cest|a f basket. **~o** m basket. **~o de los papeles** waste-paper basket

chabacano adj common; (chiste etc) vulgar. ●m (Mex, albaricoque) apricot

chabola f shack. **~s** fpl shanty town

cháchara f 🔲 chatter; (Mex, objetos sin valor) junk

chacharear vt (Mex) sell. ●vi 🔲 chatter

chacra f (LAm) farm

chal m shawl

chalado adj 🔲 crazy

chalé m house (with a garden), villa

chaleco m waistcoat, vest (Amer). **~ salvavidas** life-jacket

chalet m (pl **~s**) house (with a garden), villa

chalote m shallot

chamac|a f (esp Mex) girl. **~o** m (esp Mex) boy

chamarra f sheepskin jacket; (Mex, chaqueta corta) jacket

chamb|a f (Mex, trabajo) work. **por ~a** by fluke. **~ear** vi (Mex, fam) work

champán m, **champaña** m & f champagne

champiñón m mushroom

champú m (pl **~es** o **~s**) shampoo

chamuscar 7 vt scorch

chance m (esp LAm) chance

chancho m (LAm) pig

chanchullo m 🔲 swindle, fiddle 🔲

chanclo m clog; (de caucho) rubber overshoe

chándal m (pl ~s) tracksuit

chantaje m blackmail. ~ar vt blackmail

chanza f joke

chapa f plate, sheet; (de madera) plywood; (de botella) metal top; (carrocería) bodywork; (LAm cerradura) lock. ~do adj plated. ~do a la antigua old-fashioned. ~do en oro gold-plated

chaparro adj (LAm) short, squat

chaparrón m downpour

chapopote m (Mex) tar

chapotear vi splash

chapucero adj (persona) slapdash; (trabajo) shoddy

chapulín m (Mex) locust; (saltamontes) grasshopper

chapurrar, chapurrear vt have a smattering of, speak a little

chapuza f botched job; (trabajo ocasional) odd job

chaquet|a f jacket. **cambiar de ~a** change sides. ~ón m three-quarter length coat

charc|a f pond, pool. ~o m puddle, pool

charcutería f delicatessen

charla f chat; (conferencia) talk. ~dor adj talkative. ~r vi 🔢 chat. ~tán adj talkative. ●m chatterbox; (vendedor) cunning hawker; (curandero) charlatan

charol m varnish; (cuero) patent leather. ~a f (Mex) tray

charr|a f (Mex) horsewoman, cowgirl. ~o m (Mex) horseman, cowboy

chascar 🔢 vt crack (látigo); click (lengua); snap (dedos). ●vi (madera) creak. ~ con la lengua click one's tongue

chasco m disappointment

chasis m (Auto) chassis

chasqu|ear vt crack (látigo); click

(lengua); snap (dedos). ●vi (madera) creak. ~ con la lengua click one's tongue. ~ido m crack; (de la lengua) click; (de los dedos) snap

chatarra f scrap iron; (fig) scrap

chato adj (nariz) snub; (objetos) flat. ●m wine glass

chav|a f (Mex) girl, lass. ~al m 🔢 boy, lad. ~o m (Mex) boy, lad.

checa|da f (Mex) check; (Mex, Med) checkup. ~r 🔢 vt (Mex) check; (vigilar) check up on. ~r tarjeta clock in

checo adj & m Czech. ~slovaco adj & m (History) Czechoslovak

chelín m shilling

chelo m cello

cheque m cheque. ~ de viaje traveller's cheque. ~ar vt check; (LAm) check in (equipaje). ~o m check; (Med) checkup. ~ra f cheque-book

chévere adj (LAm) great

chica f girl; (criada) maid, servant

chicano adj & m Chicano, Mexican-American

chícharo m (Mex) pea

chicharra f cicada; (timbre) buzzer

chichón m bump

chicle m chewing-gum

chico adj 🔢 small; (esp LAm, de edad) young. ●m boy. ~s mpl children

chicoria f chicory

chifla|do adj 🔢 crazy, daft. ~r vt whistle at, boo. ●vi (LAm) whistle; (🔢, gustar mucho) **me chifla el chocolate** I'm mad about chocolate. ~rse vpr be mad (por about)

chilango adj (Mex) from Mexico City

chile m chilli

Chile m Chile

chileno adj & m Chilean

chill|ar vi scream, shriek; (ratón) squeak; (cerdo) squeal. ~ido m scream, screech. ~**ón** adj noisy; (colores) loud; (sonido) shrill

chimenea f chimney; (hogar) fireplace

chimpancé m chimpanzee

china f Chinese (woman)

China f China

chinche m drawing-pin (Brit), thumbtack (Amer); (insecto) bedbug; (fig) nuisance. ~**ta** f drawing-pin (Brit), thumbtack (Amer)

chinela f slipper

chino adj Chinese; (Mex rizado) curly. ●m Chinese (man); (Mex, de pelo rizado) curly-haired person

chipriota adj & m & f Cypriot

chiquero m pen; (LAm, pocilga) pigsty (Brit), pigpen (Amer)

chiquillo adj childish. ●m child, kid 🔢

chirimoya f custard apple

chiripa f fluke

chirri|ar 🔢 vi creak; (frenos) screech; (pájaro) chirp. ~**do** m creaking; (de frenos) screech; (de pájaros) chirping

chis int sh!, hush!; (fam, para llamar a uno) hey!, psst!

chism|e m gadget, thingumajig 🔢; (chismorreo) piece of gossip. ~**es** mpl things, bits and pieces. ~**orreo** m gossip. ~**oso** adj gossipy.● m gossip

chisp|a f spark; (pizca) drop; (gracia) wit; (fig) sparkle. **estar que echa** ~**a(s)** be furious. ~**eante** adj sparkling. ~**ear** vi spark; (lloviznar) drizzle; (fig) sparkle. ~**orrotear** vt throw out sparks; (fuego) crackle; (aceite) spit

chistar vi. **ni chistó** he didn't say a word. **sin** ~ without saying a word

chiste m joke, funny story. **tener** ~ be funny

chistera f top hat

chistoso adj funny

chiva|rse vpr tip-off; (niño) tell.

~**tazo** m tip-off. ~**to** m informer; (niño) telltale

chivo m kid; (LAm, macho cabrío) billy goat

choca|nte adj shocking; (Mex desagradable) unpleasant. ~**r** 🔢 vt clink (vasos); (LAm) crash (vehículo). **¡chócala!** give me five! ●vi collide, hit. ~**r con**, ~**r contra** crash into

choch|ear vi be gaga. ~**o** adj gaga; (fig) soft

choclo m (LAm) corn on the cob

chocolate m chocolate. **tableta** f **de** ~ bar of chocolate

chófer, (LAm) **chofer** m chauffeur; (conductor) driver

cholo adj & m (LAm) half-breed

chopo m poplar

choque m collision; (fig) clash; (eléctrico) shock; (Auto, Rail etc) crash, accident; (sacudida) jolt

chorizo m chorizo

chorro m jet, stream; (caudal pequeño) trickle; (fig) stream. **a** ~ (avión) jet. **a** ~**s** (fig) in abundance

chovinista adj chauvinistic. ● m & f chauvinist

choza f hut

chuba|sco m shower. ~**quero** m raincoat, anorak

chuchería f trinket

chueco adj (LAm) crooked

chufa f tiger nut

chuleta f chop

chulo adj cocky; (bonito) lovely (Brit), neat (Amer); (Mex, atractivo) cute. ● m tough guy; (proxeneta) pimp

chup|ada f suck; (al helado) lick; (al cigarro) puff. ~**ado** adj skinny; (fam, fácil) very easy. ~**ar** vt suck; puff at (cigarro etc); (absorber) absorb. ~**ete** m dummy (Brit), pacifier (Amer). ~**ón** m sucker; (LAm) dummy (Brit), pacifier (Amer); (Mex, del biberón) teat

churrasco m barbecued steak

churro m fritter; 🔢 mess

chut|ar vi shoot. **~e** m shot

cianuro m cyanide

cibernética f cibernetics

cicatriz f scar. **~ar** 🔟 vt/i heal. **~arse** vpr heal

cíclico adj cyclic(al)

ciclis|mo m cycling. **~ta** adj cycle. •m & f cyclist

ciclo m cycle; (de películas, conciertos) season; (de conferencias) series

ciclomotor m moped

ciclón m cyclone

ciego adj blind. •m blind man, blind person. **a ciegas** in the dark

cielo m sky; (Relig) heaven; (persona) darling. **¡~!** good heavens!, goodness me!

ciempiés m invar centipede

cien adj a hundred. **~ por ~** one hundred per cent

ciénaga f bog, swamp

ciencia f science; (fig) knowledge. **~s** fpl (Univ etc) science. **~s empresariales** business studies. **a ~ cierta** for certain

cieno m mud

científico adj scientific. •m scientist

ciento adj & m a hundred, one hundred. **~s de** hundreds of. **por ~** per cent

cierre m fastener; (acción de cerrar) shutting, closing; (LAm, cremallera) zip, zipper (Amer)

cierto adj certain; (verdad) true. **estar en lo ~** be right. **lo ~ es que** the fact is that. **no es ~** that's not true. **¿no es ~?** isn't that right? **por ~** by the way. **si bien es ~ que** although

ciervo m deer

cifra f figure, number; (cantidad) sum. **en ~** coded, in code. **~do** adj coded. **~r** vt code; place (esperanzas)

cigala f crayfish

cigarra f cicada

cigarr|illera f cigarette box; (de bolsillo) cigarette case. **~illo** m cigarette. **~o** m (cigarrillo) cigarette; (puro) cigar

cigüeña f stork

cilantro m coriander

cil|índrico adj cylindrical. **~indro** m cylinder

cima f top; (fig) summit

cimbr|ear vt shake. **~earse** vpr sway. **~onada** f, **~onazo** m (LAm) jolt; (de explosión) blast

cimentar 🔳 vt lay the foundations of; (fig, reforzar) strengthen

cimientos mpl foundations

cinc m zinc

cincel m chisel. **~ar** vt chisel

cinco adj & m five; (en fechas) fifth

cincuent|a adj & m fifty; (quincuagésimo) fiftieth. **~ón** adj in his fifties

cine m cinema; (local) cinema (Brit), movie theater (Amer). **~asta** m & f film maker (Brit), movie maker (Amer). **~matográfico** adj film (Brit), movie (Amer)

cínico adj cynical. •m cynic

cinismo m cynicism

cinta f ribbon; (película) film (Brit), movie (Amer); (para grabar, en carreras) tape. **~ aislante** insulating tape. **~ métrica** tape measure. **~ virgen** blank tape

cintur|a f waist. **~ón** m belt. **~ón de seguridad** safety belt. **~ón salvavidas** lifebelt

ciprés m cypress (tree)

circo m circus

circuito m circuit; (viaje) tour. **~ cerrado** closed circuit. **corto ~** short circuit

circula|ción f circulation; (vehículos) traffic. **~r** adj circular. •vi circulate; (líquidos) flow; (conducir) drive; (caminar) walk; (autobús) run

círculo m circle. **~ vicioso** vicious

circle. **en ~** in a circle

circunci|dar vt circumcise. **~sión** f circumcision

circunferencia f circumference

circunflejo m circumflex

circunscri|bir (pp **circunscrito**) vt confine. **~birse** vpr confine o.s. (**a** to). **~pción** f (distrito) district. **~pción electoral** constituency

circunspecto adj circumspect

circunstancia f circumstance

circunv|alar vt bypass. **~olar** vt ② circle

cirio m candle

ciruela f plum. **~ pasa** prune

ciru|gía f surgery. **~jano** m surgeon

cisne m swan

cisterna f tank, cistern

cita f appointment; (entre chico y chica) date; (referencia) quotation. **~ a ciegas** blind date. **~ flash** speed dating. **~ción** f quotation; (Jurid) summons. **~do** adj aforementioned. **~r** vt make an appointment with; (mencionar) quote, (Jurid) summons. **~rse** vpr arrange to meet

cítara f zither

ciudad f town; (grande) city. **~ balneario** (LAm) coastal resort. **~ perdida** (Mex) shanty town. **~ universitaria** university campus. **~anía** f citizenship; (habitantes) citizens. **~ano** adj civic. ● m citizen, inhabitant

cívico adj civic

civil adj civil. ● m & f civil guard; (persona no militar) civilian

civiliza|ción f civilization. **~r** ⑩ vt civilize. **~rse** vpr become civilized

civismo m community spirit

clam|ar vi cry out, clamour. **~or** m clamour; (protesta) outcry. **~oroso** adj noisy; (éxito) resounding

clandestino adj clandestine, secret; (periódico) underground

clara f (de huevo) egg white

claraboya f skylight

clarear vi dawn; (aclarar) brighten up

clarete m rosé

claridad f clarity; (luz) light

clarifica|ción f clarification. **~r** ⑦ vt clarify

clar|ín m bugle. **~inete** m clarinet. **~inetista** m & f clarinettist

clarividen|cia f clairvoyance; (fig) far-sightedness. **~te** adj clairvoyant; (fig) far-sighted

claro adj clear; (luminoso) bright; (colores) light; (líquido) thin. ● m (en bosque etc) clearing; (espacio) gap. ● adv clearly. ● int of course! **¡~ que sí!** yes, of course! **¡~ que no!** of course not!

clase f class; (tipo) kind, sort; (aula) classroom. **~ media** middle class. **~ obrera** working class. **~ social** social class. **dar ~s** teach

clásico adj classical; (típico) classic. ● m classic

clasifica|ción f classification; (deportes) league. **~r** ⑦ vt classify

claustro m cloister; (Univ) staff

claustrof|obia f claustrophobia. **~óbico** adj claustrophobic

cláusula f clause

clausura f closure

clava|do adj fixed; (con clavo) nailed. **es ~do a su padre** he's the spitting image of his father. ● m (LAm) dive. **~r** vt knock in (clavo); stick in (cuchillo); (fijar) fix; (juntar) nail together

clave f key; (Mus) clef; (instrumento) harpsichord. **~cín** m harpsichord

clavel m carnation

clavícula f collarbone, clavicle

clav|ija f peg; (Elec) plug. **~o** m nail; (Culin) clove

claxon /'klakson/ m (pl **~s**) horn

clemencia f clemency, mercy

clementina f tangerine

cleptómano m kleptomaniac

clerical adj clerical

clérigo m priest

clero m clergy

clic m: **hacer ~ en** to click on

cliché m cliché; (Foto) negative

cliente m customer; (de médico) patient; (de abogado) client. **~la** f clientele, customers; (de médico) patients

clim|a m climate; (ambiente) atmosphere. **~ático** adj climatic. **~atizado** adj air-conditioned

clínic|a f clinic. **~o** adj clinical

cloaca f drain, sewer

clon m clone

cloro m chlorine

club m (pl ~s o ~es) club

coacci|ón f coercion. **~onar** vt coerce

coagular vt coagulate; clot (sangre); curdle (leche). **~se** vpr coagulate; (sangre) clot; (leche) curdle

coalición f coalition

coarta|da f alibi. **~r** vt hinder; restrict (libertad etc)

cobard|e adj cowardly. • m coward. **~ía** f cowardice

cobert|izo m shed. **~ura** f covering; (en radio, TV) coverage

cobij|a f (Mex, manta) blanket. **~as** fpl (LAm, ropa de cama) bedclothes. **~ar** vt shelter. **~arse** vpr (take) shelter. **~o** m shelter

cobra f cobra

cobra|dor m collector; (de autobús) conductor. **~r** vt collect; (ganar) earn; charge (precio); cash (cheque); (recuperar) recover. • vi be paid

cobr|e m copper. **~izo** adj coppery

cobro m collection; (de cheque) cashing; (pago) payment. **presentar al ~** cash

coca|ína f cocaine. **~lero** adj (of)

coca farming. • m coca farmer

cocción f cooking; (Tec) firing

coc|er 2 & 9 vt/i cook; (hervir) boil; (Tec) fire. **~ido** m stew

coche m car, automobile (Amer); (de tren) coach, carriage; (de bebé) pram (Brit), baby carriage (Amer). **~-cama** sleeper. **~ fúnebre** hearse. **~ restaurante** dining-car. **~s de choque** dodgems. **~ra** f garage; (de autobuses) depot

cochin|ada f dirty thing. **~o** adj dirty, filthy. • m pig

cociente m quotient. **~ intelectual** intelligence quotient, IQ

cocin|a f kitchen; (arte) cookery, cuisine; (aparato) cooker. **~a de gas** gas cooker. **~a eléctrica** electric cooker. **~ar** vt/i cook. **~ero** m cook

coco m coconut; (árbol) coconut palm; (cabeza) head; (que mete miedo) bogeyman. **comerse el ~** think hard

cocoa f (LAm) cocoa

cocodrilo m crocodile

cocotero m coconut palm

cóctel m (pl ~s or ~es) cocktail

cod|azo m nudge (with one's elbow). **~ear** vt/i elbow, nudge. **~earse** vpr rub shoulders (**con** with)

codici|a f greed. **~ado** adj coveted, sought after. **~ar** vt covet. **~oso** adj greedy

código m code. **~ de la circulación** Highway Code

codo m elbow; (dobladura) bend. **~ a ~** side by side. **hablar (hasta) por los ~s** talk too much

codorniz m quail

coeficiente m coefficient. **~ intelectual** intelligence quotient, IQ

coerción f constraint

coetáneo adj & m contemporary

coexist|encia f coexistence. **∼ir** vi coexist

cofradía f brotherhood

cofre m chest; (Mex, capó) bonnet (Brit), hood (Amer)

coger 14 vt (esp Esp) take; catch (tren, autobús, pelota, catarro); (agarrar) take hold of; (del suelo) pick up; pick (frutos etc); (LAm, vulgar) to screw. **∼se** vpr trap, catch; (agarrarse) hold on

cogollo m (de lechuga etc) heart; (brote) bud

cogote m nape; (LAm, cuello) neck

cohech|ar vt bribe. **∼o** m bribery

cohe|rente adj coherent. **∼sión** f cohesion

cohete m rocket

cohibi|do adj shy; (inhibido) awkward; (incómodo) awkward. **∼r** vt inhibit; (incomodar) make s.o. feel embarrassed. **∼rse** vpr feel inhibited

coima f (LAm) bribe

coincid|encia f coincidence. **dar la ∼encia** happen. **∼ir** vt coincide

coje|ar vt limp; (mueble) wobble. **∼ra** f lameness

cojín m cushion. **∼inete** m small cushion

cojo adj lame; (mueble) wobbly. • m lame person

col f cabbage. **∼es de Bruselas** Brussel sprouts

cola f tail; (fila) queue; (para pegar) glue. **a la ∼** at the end. **hacer ∼** queue (up) (Brit), line up (Amer)

colabora|ción f collaboration. **∼dor** m collaborator. **∼r** vi collaborate

colada f washing. **hacer la ∼** do the washing

colador m strainer

colapso m collapse; (fig) standstill

colar 2 vt strain; pass (moneda falsa etc). • vi (líquido) seep through; (fig) be believed. **∼se** vpr slip; (en una

cola) jump the queue; (en fiesta) gatecrash

colch|a f bedspread. **∼ón** m mattress. **∼oneta** f air bed; (en gimnasio) mat

colear vi wag its tail; (asunto) not be resolved. **vivito y coleando** alive and kicking

colecci|ón f collection. **∼onar** vt collect. **∼onista** m & f collector

colecta f collection

colectivo adj collective

colega m & f colleague

colegi|al m schoolboy. **∼ala** f schoolgirl. **∼o** m school; (de ciertas profesiones) college. **∼o mayor** hall of residence

cólera m cholera. • f anger, fury. **montar en ∼** fly into a rage

colérico adj furious, irate

colesterol m cholesterol

coleta f pigtail

colga|nte adj hanging. • m pendant. **∼r** 2 & 12 vt hang; hang out (ropa lavada); hang up (abrigo etc); put down (teléfono). • vi hang; (teléfono) hang up. **∼rse** vpr hang o.s. **dejar a uno ∼do** let s.o. down

colibrí m hummingbird

cólico m colic

coliflor f cauliflower

colilla f cigarette end

colina f hill

colinda|nte adj adjoining. **∼r** vt border (**con** on)

colisión f collision, crash; (fig) clash

collar m necklace; (de perro) collar

colmar vt fill to the brim; try (paciencia); (fig) fulfill. **∼ a uno de atenciones** lavish attention on s.o.

colmena f beehive, hive

colmillo m eye tooth, canine (tooth); (de elefante) tusk; (de carnívoro) fang

colmo m height. **ser el ~** be the limit, be the last straw

coloca|ción f positioning; (empleo) job, position. **~r** ⁊ vt put, place; (buscar empleo) find work for. **~rse** vpr find a job

Colombia f Colombia

colombiano adj & m Colombian

colon m colon

colón m (unidad monetaria de Costa Rica y El Salvador) colon

colon|ia f colony; (comunidad) community; (agua de colonia) cologne; (Mex, barrio) residential suburb. **~ia de verano** holiday camp. **~iaje** m (LAm) colonial period. **~ial** adj colonial. **~ialista** m & f colonialist. **~ización** f colonization. **~izar** ⑩ colonize. **~o** m colonist, settler; (labrador) tenant farmer

coloqui|al adj colloquial. **~o** m conversation; (congreso) conference

color m colour. **de ~** colour. **en ~(es)** (fotos, película) colour. **~ado** adj (rojo) red. **~ante** m colouring. **~ear** vt/i colour. **~ete** m blusher. **~ido** m colour

colosal adj colossal; (fig, fam, magnífico) terrific

columna f column; (en anatomía) spine. **~ vertebral** spinal column; (fig) backbone

columpi|ar vt swing. **~arse** vpr swing. **~o** m swing

coma f comma; (Mat) point. ● m (Med) coma

comadre f (madrina) godmother; (amiga) friend. **~ar** vi gossip

comadreja f weasel

comadrona f midwife

comal m (Mex) griddle

comand|ancia f command. **~ante** m & f commander. **~o** m command; (Mil, soldado) commando; (de terroristas) cell

comarca f area, region

comba f bend; (juguete) skipping-rope; (de viga) sag. **saltar a la ~** skip. **~rse** vpr bend; (viga) sag

combat|e m combat; (pelea) fight. **~iente** m fighter. **~ir** vt/i fight

combina|ción f combination; (enlace) connection; (prenda) slip. **~r** vt combine; put together (colores)

combustible m fuel

comedia f comedy; (cualquier obra de teatro) play; (LAm, telenovela) soap (opera)

comedi|do adj restrained; (LAm, atento) obliging. **~rse** ⑤ vpr show restraint

comedor m dining-room; (restaurante) restaurant

comensal m companion at table, fellow diner

comentar vt comment on; discuss (tema); (mencionar) mention. **~io** m commentary; (observación) comment. **~ios** mpl gossip. **~ista** m & f commentator

comenzar ① & ⑩ vt/i begin, start

comer vt eat; (a mediodía) have for lunch; (esp LAm, cenar) have for dinner; (corroer) eat away; (en ajedrez) take. ● vi eat; (a mediodía) have lunch; (esp LAm, cenar) have dinner. **dar de ~ a** feed. **~se** vpr eat (up)

comerci|al adj commercial; (ruta) trade; (nombre, trato) business. ● m (LAm) commercial, ad. **~ante** m trader; (de tienda) shopkeeper. **~ar** vi trade (**con** with, **en** in); (con otra persona) do business. **~o** m commerce; (actividad) trade; (tienda) shop; (negocios) business

comestible adj edible. **~s** mpl food. **tienda de ~s** grocer's (shop) (Brit), grocery (Amer)

cometa m comet. ● f kite

comet|er vt commit; make (falta). **~ido** m task

comezón m itch

comicios mpl elections

cómico adj comic; (gracioso) funny.

●m comic actor; (humorista) comedian

comida f food; (a mediodía) lunch; (esp LAm, cena) dinner; (acto) meal

comidilla f. **ser la ~ del pueblo** be the talk of the town

comienzo m beginning, start

comillas fpl inverted commas

comil|ón adj greedy. **~ona** f feast

comino m cumin. **(no) me importa un ~** I couldn't care less

comisar|ia f police station. **~io** m commissioner; (deportes) steward

comisión f assignment; (organismo) commission, committee; (Com) commission

comisura f corner. **~ de los labios** corner of the mouth

comité m committee

como prep as; (comparación) like. ● adv about. ● conj as. **~ quieras** as you like. **~ si** as if

cómo adverbio

····▸ how. ¿**~ se llega?** how do you get there? ¿**~ es de alto?** how tall is it? **sé ~ pasó** I know how it happened

! Cuando **cómo** va seguido del ■ verbo **llamar** se traduce por *what*, p. ej. ¿**~ te llamas?** *what's your name?*

····▸ **cómo** + ser (*sugiriendo descripción*) ¿**~ es su marido?** what's her husband like?; (*físicamente*) what does her husband look like? **no sé ~ es la comida** I don't know what the food's like

····▸ (*por qué*) why. ¿**~ no actuaron antes?** why didn't they act sooner?

····▸ (*pidiendo que se repita*) sorry?, pardon? ¿**~?** no te escuché sorry? I didn't hear you

····▸ (*en exclamaciones*) ¡**~ llueve!**

it's really pouring! ¡**~!** ¿**que no lo sabes?** what! you mean you don't know? ¡**~ no!** of course!

cómoda f chest of drawers

comodidad f comfort. **a su ~** at your convenience

cómodo adj comfortable; (conveniente) convenient

comoquiera conj. **~ que sea** however it may be

compacto adj compact; (denso) dense; (líneas etc) close

compadecer 11 vt feel sorry for. **~se** vpr. **~se de** feel sorry for

compadre m godfather; (amigo) friend

compañ|ero m companion; (de trabajo) colleague; (de clase) classmate; (pareja) partner. **~ía** f company. **en ~ía de** with

compara|ble adj comparable. **~ción** f comparison. **~r** vt compare. **~tivo** adj & m comparative

comparecer 11 vi appear

comparsa f group. ● m & f (en el teatro) extra

compartim(i)ento m compartment

compartir vt share

compás m (instrumento) (pair of) compasses; (ritmo) rhythm; (división) bar (Brit), measure (Amer); (Naut) compass. **a ~** in time

compasi|ón f compassion, pity. **tener ~ón de** feel sorry for. **~vo** adj compassionate

compatib|ilidad f compatibility. **~le** adj compatible

compatriota m & f compatriot

compendio m summary

compensa|ción f compensation. **~ción por despido** redundancy payment. **~r** vt compensate

competen|cia f competition; (capacidad) competence; (poder)

authority; (incumbencia) jurisdiction.
~**te** adj competent

competi|ción f competition.
~**dor** m competitor. ~**r 5** vi
compete

compinche m accomplice; (fam,
amigo) friend, mate 𝕋

complac|er 32 vt please. ~**erse** vpr
be pleased. ~**iente** adj obliging;
(marido) complaisant

complej|idad f complexity. ~**o** adj
& m complex

complement|ario adj
complementary. ~**o** m
complement; (Gram) object,
complement

complet|ar vt complete. ~**o** adj
complete; (lleno) full; (exhaustivo)
comprehensive

complexión f build

complica|ción f complication; (esp
LAm, implicación) involvement. ~**r 7**
vt complicate; involve (persona).
~**rse** vpr become complicated;
(implicarse) get involved

cómplice m & f accomplice

complot m (pl ~**s**) plot

compon|ente adj component. ●m
component; (miembro) member.
~**er 34** vt make up; (Mus, Literatura
etc) write, compose; (esp LAm,
reparar) mend; (LAm) set (hueso);
settle (estómago). ~**erse** vpr be
made up; (arreglarse) get better.
~**érselas** manage

comporta|miento m behaviour.
~**rse** vpr behave. ~**rse mal**
misbehave

composi|ción f composition.
~**tor** m composer

compostura f composure; (LAm,
arreglo) repair

compota f stewed fruit

compra f purchase. ~ **a plazos**
hire purchase. **hacer la(s) ~(s)**
do the shopping. **ir de ~s** go
shopping. ~**dor** m buyer. ~**r** vt

....
𝕔 *see* A-Z of Spanish life and culture

buy. ~**venta** f buying and selling;
(Jurid) sale and purchase contract.
negocio m **de ~venta** second-
hand shop

compren|der vt understand;
(incluir) include. ~**sión** f
understanding. ~**sivo** adj
understanding

compresa f compress; (de mujer)
sanitary towel

compr|esión f compression.
~**imido** adj compressed. ●m pill,
tablet. ~**imir** vt compress

comproba|nte m proof; (recibo)
receipt. ~**r** vt check; (demostrar)
prove

comprom|eter vt compromise;
(arriesgar) jeopardize. ~**eterse** vpr
compromise o.s.; (obligarse) agree
to; (novios) get engaged. ~**etido** adj
(situación) awkward, delicate; (autor)
politically committed. ~**iso** m
obligation; (apuro) predicament;
(cita) appointment; (acuerdo)
agreement. **sin ~iso** without
obligation

compuesto adj compound;
(persona) smart. ●m compound

computa|ción f (esp LAm)
computing. **curso** m **de ~ción**
computer course. ~**dor** m,
computadora f computer. ~**r** vt
calculate. ~**rizar, computerizar**
10 vt computerize

cómputo m calculation

comulgar 12 vi take Communion

común adj common; (compartido)
joint. **en ~** in common. **por lo ~**
generally. ●m **el ~ de** most

comunal adj communal

comunica|ción f communication.
~**do** m communiqué. ~**do de**
prensa press release. ~**r 7** vt
communicate; (informar) inform;
(LAm, por teléfono) put through. **está**
~**ndo** (teléfono) it's engaged. ~**rse**
vpr communicate; (ponerse en
contacto) get in touch. ~**tivo** adj
communicative

comunidad f community. 𝕔~ **de**

63 comunión | condominio

vecinos residents' association. **C~ (Económica) Europea** European (Economic) Community. **en ~** together

comunión f communion; (Relig) (Holy) Communion

comunis|mo m communism. **~ta** adj & m & f communist

con prep with; (+ infinitivo) by. **~ decir la verdad** by telling the truth. **~ que** so. **~ tal que** as long as

concebir 5 vt/i conceive

conceder vt concede, grant; award (premio); (admitir) admit

concej|al m councillor. **~ero** m (LAm) councillor. **~o** m council

concentra|ción f concentration; (Pol) rally. **~r** vt concentrate; assemble (personas). **~rse** vpr concentrate

concep|ción f conception. **~to** m concept; (opinión) opinion. **bajo ningún ~to** in no way

concerniente adj. **en lo ~ a** with regard to

concertar 1 vt arrange; agree (upon) (plan)

concesión f concession

concha f shell; (carey) tortoiseshell

conciencia f conscience; (conocimiento) awareness. **~ limpia** clear conscience. **~ sucia** guilty conscience. **a ~ de que** fully aware that. **en ~** honestly. **tener ~ de** be aware of. **tomar ~ de** become aware of. **~r** vt make aware. **~rse** vpr become aware

concientizar 10 vt (esp LAm) make aware. **~se** vpr become aware

concienzudo adj conscientious

concierto m concert; (acuerdo) agreement; (Mus, composición) concerto

concilia|ción f reconciliation. **~r** vt reconcile. **~r el sueño** get to sleep. **~rse** vpr gain

concilio m council

conciso m concise

conclu|ir 17 vt finish; (deducir) conclude. •vi finish, end. **~sión** f conclusion. **~yente** adj conclusive

concord|ancia f agreement. **~ar** 2 vt reconcile. •vi agree. **~e** adj in agreement. **~ia** f harmony

concret|amente adv specifically, to be exact. **~ar** vt make specific. **~arse** vpr become definite; (limitarse) confine o.s. **~o** adj concrete; (determinado) specific, particular. **en ~o** definite; (concretamente) to be exact; (en resumen) in short. •m (LAm, hormigón) concrete

concurr|encia f concurrence; (reunión) audience. **~ido** adj crowded, busy. **~ir** vi meet; ; (coincidir) agree. **~ a** (asistir a) attend

concurs|ante m & f competitor, contestant. **~ar** vi compete, take part. **~o** m competition; (ayuda) help

cond|ado m county. **~e** m earl, count

condena f sentence. **~ción** f condemnation. **~do** m convicted person. **~r** vt condemn; (Jurid) convict

condensa|ción f condensation. **~r** vt condense

condesa f countess

condescende|ncia f condescension; (tolerancia) indulgence. **~r** 1 vi agree; (dignarse) condescend

condici|ón f condition. **a ~ón de (que)** on condition that. **~onal** adj conditional. **~onar** vt condition

condiment|ar vt season. **~o** m seasoning

condolencia f condolence

condominio m joint ownership; (LAm, edificio) block of flats (Brit), condominium (esp Amer)

see A-Z of Spanish life and culture

condón m condom

condonar vt (perdonar) reprieve; cancel (deuda)

conducir ⁴⁷ vt drive (vehículo); carry (electricidad, gas, agua). •vi drive; (fig, llevar) lead. **¿a qué conduce?** what's the point? **~se** vpr behave

conducta f behaviour

conducto m pipe, tube; (en anatomía) duct. **por ~ de** through. **~r** m driver; (jefe) leader; (Elec) conductor

conduzco vb véase CONDUCIR

conectar vt/i connect

conejo m rabbit

conexión f connection

confabularse vpr plot

confección f (de trajes) tailoring; (de vestidos) dressmaking. **~ones** fpl clothing, clothes. **de ~ón** ready-to-wear. **~onar** vt make

confederación f confederation

conferencia f conference; (al teléfono) long-distance call; (Univ) lecture. **~ en la cima, ~ (en la) cumbre** summit conference. **~nte** m & f lecturer

conferir ⁴ vt confer; award (premio)

confes|ar ■ vt/i confess. **~arse** vpr confess. **~ión** f confession. **~ionario** m confessional. **~or** m confessor

confeti m confetti

confia|do adj trusting; (seguro de sí mismo) confident. **~nza** f trust; (en sí mismo) confidence; (intimidad) familiarity. **~r** ²⁰ vt entrust. •vi. **~r en** trust

confiden|cia f confidence, secret. **~cial** adj confidential. **~te** m confidant. •f confidante

configur|ación f configuration. **~ar** vt to configure

conf|ín m border. **~ines** mpl outermost parts. **~inar** vt confine; (desterrar) banish

confirma|ción f confirmation. **~r** vt confirm

confiscar ⁷ vt confiscate

confit|ería f sweet-shop (Brit), candy store (Amer). **~ura** f jam

conflict|ivo adj difficult; (época) troubled; (polémico) controversial. **~o** m conflict

confluencia f confluence

conform|ación f conformation, shape. **~ar** vt (acomodar) adjust. •vi agree. **~arse** vpr conform. **~e** adj in agreement; (contento) happy, satisfied; (según) according (**con** to). **~e a** in accordance with, according to. •conj as. •int OK!. **~idad** f agreement; (tolerancia) resignation. **~ista** m & f conformist

conforta|ble adj comfortable. **~nte** adj comforting. **~r** vt comfort

confronta|ción f confrontation. **~r** vt confront

confu|ndir vt (equivocar) mistake, confuse; (mezclar) mix up, confuse; (turbar) embarrass. **~ndirse** vpr become confused; (equivocarse) make a mistake. **~sión** f confusion; (vergüenza) embarrassment. **~so** adj confused; (borroso) blurred

congela|do adj frozen. **~dor** m freezer. **~r** vt freeze

congeniar vi get on

congesti|ón f congestion. **~onado** adj congested. **~onarse** vpr become congested

congoja f distress; (pena) grief

congraciarse vpr ingratiate o.s.

congratular vt congratulate

congrega|ción f gathering; (Relig) congregation. **~rse** ¹² vpr gather, assemble

congres|ista m & f delegate, member of a congress. **~o** m congress, conference. **C~o Parliament. C~o de los Diputados** Chamber of Deputies

cónico | consiguiente

cónico adj conical

conífer|a f conifer. **~o** adj coniferous

conjetura f conjecture, guess. **~r** vt conjecture, guess

conjuga|ción f conjugation. **~r** 12 vt conjugate

conjunción f conjunction

conjunto adj joint. •m collection; (Mus) band; (ropa) suit, outfit. **en ~** altogether

conjurar vt exorcise; avert (peligro). •vi plot, conspire

conllevar vt to entail

conmemora|ción f commemoration. **~r** vt commemorate

conmigo pron with me

conmo|ción f shock; (tumulto) upheaval. **~ cerebral** concussion. **~cionar** vt shock. **~ver** 2 vt shake; (emocionar) move

conmuta|dor m switch; (LAm, de teléfonos) switchboard. **~r** vt exchange

connota|ción f connotation. **~do** adj (LAm, destacado) distinguished. **~r** vt connote

cono m cone

conoc|edor adj & m expert. **~er** 11 vt know; (por primera vez) meet; (reconocer) recognize, know. **se conoce que** apparently. **dar a ~er** make known. **~erse** vpr know o.s.; (dos personas) know each other; (notarse) be obvious. **~ido** adj well-known. •m acquaintance. **~imiento** m knowledge; (sentido) consciousness. **sin ~imiento** unconscious. **tener ~imiento de** know about

conozco vb véase CONOCER

conque conj so

conquista f conquest. **~dor** adj conquering. •m conqueror; (de América) ▆conquistador. **~r** vt conquer, win

consabido adj usual, habitual

consagra|ción f consecration. **~r** vt consecrate; (fig) devote. **~rse** vpr devote o.s.

consanguíneo m blood relation

consciente adj conscious

consecuen|cia f consequence; (coherencia) consistency. **a ~cia de** as a result of. **~te** adj consistent

consecutivo adj consecutive

conseguir 5 & 13 vt get, obtain; (lograr) manage; achieve (objetivo)

consej|ero m adviser; (miembro de consejo) member. **~o** m piece of advice; (Pol) council. **~o de ministros** cabinet

consenso m assent, consent

consenti|do adj (niño) spoilt. **~miento** m consent. **~r** 4 vt allow; spoil (niño). •vi consent

conserje m porter, caretaker. **~ría** f porter's office

conserva f (mermelada) preserve; (en lata) tinned food. **en ~** tinned (Brit), canned. **~ción** f conservation; (de alimentos) preservation

conservador adj & m (Pol) conservative

conservar vt keep; preserve (alimentos). **~se** vpr keep; (costumbre) survive

conservatorio m conservatory

considera|ble adj considerable. **~ción** f consideration; (respeto) respect. **de mi ~ción** serious. **de mi ~ción** (LAm, en cartas) Dear Sir. **~do** adj considerate; (respetado) respected. **~r** vt consider; (respetar) respect

consigna f order; (para equipaje) left luggage office (Brit), baggage room (Amer); (eslogan) slogan

consigo pron (él) with him; (ella) with her; (Ud, Uds) with you; (uno mismo) with o.s.

consiguiente adj consequent. **por ~** consequently

▆ *see* A-Z of Spanish life and culture

consist|encia f consistency. **~ente** adj consisting (**en** of); (firme) solid; (LAm, congruente) consistent. **~ir** vi. **~ en** consist of; (radicar en) be due to

consola|ción f consolation. **~r** 2 vt console, comfort. **~rse** vpr console o.s.

consolidar vt consolidate. **~se** vpr consolidate

consomé m clear soup, consommé

consonante adj consonant. •f consonant

consorcio m consortium

conspira|ción f conspiracy. **~dor** m conspirator. **~r** vi conspire

consta|ncia f constancy; (prueba) proof; (LAm, documento) written evidence. **~nte** adj constant. **~r** vi be clear; (figurar) appear, figure; (componerse) consist. **hacer ~r** state; (por escrito) put on record. **me ~ que** I'm sure that. **que conste que** believe me

constatar vt check; (confirmar) confirm

constipa|do m cold. •adj. **estar ~do** have a cold; (LAm, estreñido) be constipated. **~rse** vpr catch a cold

constitu|ción f constitution; (establecimiento) setting up. **~cional** adj constitutional. **~ir** 17 vt constitute; (formar) form; (crear) set up, establish. **~irse** vpr set o.s. up (**en** as). **~tivo** adj, **~yente** adj constituent

constru|cción f construction. **~ctor** m builder. **~ir** 17 vt construct; build (edificio)

consuelo m consolation

consuetudinario adj customary

cónsul m & f consul

consulado m consulate

consult|a f consultation. **horas fpl de ~a** surgery hours. **obra f de ~a** reference book. **~ar** vt consult. **~orio** m surgery

consumar vt complete; commit

(crimen); carry out (robo); consummate (matrimonio)

consum|ición f consumption; (bebida) drink; (comida) food. **~ición mínima** minimum charge. **~ido** adj skinny, wasted. **~idor** m consumer. **~ir** vt consume. **~irse** vpr (persona) waste away; (vela, cigarillo) burn down; (líquido) dry up. **~ismo** m consumerism. **~o** m consumption; (LAm, en restaurante etc) (bebida) drink; (comida) food. **~o mínimo** minimum charge

contab|ilidad f book-keeping; (profesión) accountancy. **~le** m & f accountant

contacto m contact. **ponerse en ~ con** get in touch with

conta|do adj. **al ~** cash. **~dos** adj pl few. **tiene los días ~dos** his days are numbered. **~dor** m meter; (LAm, persona) accountant

contagi|ar vt infect (persona); pass on (enfermedad); (fig) contaminate. **~o** m infection; (directo) contagion. **~oso** adj infectious; (por contacto directo) contagious

contamina|ción f contamination, pollution. **~r** vt contaminate, pollute

contante adj. **dinero m ~** cash

contar 2 vt count; tell (relato). **se cuenta que** it's said that. •vi count. **~ con** rely on, count on. **~se** vpr be included (**entre** among)

contempla|ción f contemplation. **sin ~ciones** unceremoniously. **~r** vt look at; (fig) contemplate

contemporáneo adj & m contemporary

conten|er 40 vt contain; hold (respiración). **~erse** vpr contain o.s. **~ido** adj contained. •m contents

content|ar vt please. **~arse** vpr. **~arse con** be satisfied with, be pleased with. **~o** adj (alegre) happy; (satisfecho) pleased

contesta|ción f answer. **~dor** m.

~**dorautomático** answering machine. ~r vt/i answer; (replicar) answer back

contexto m context

contienda f conflict; (lucha) contest

contigo pron with you

contiguo adj adjacent

continen|tal adj continental. ~te m continent

continu|ación f continuation. a ~ación immediately after. ~ar [21] vt continue, resume. •vi continue. ~idad f continuity. ~o adj continuous; (frecuente) continual. **corriente f** ~**a** direct current

contorno m outline; (de árbol) girth; (de caderas) measurement. ~s mpl surrounding area

contorsión f contortion

contra prep against. **en** ~ against. •m cons. •f snag. **llevar la** ~ contradict

contraata|car [7] vt/i counter-attack. ~**que** m counter-attack

contrabaj|ista m & f double-bass player. ~o m double-bass; (persona) double bass player

contraband|ista m & f smuggler. ~o m contraband

contracción f contraction

contrad|ecir [46] vt contradict. ~**icción** f contradiction. ~**ictorio** adj contradictory

contraer [41] vt contract. ~ **matrimonio** marry. ~**se** vpr contract

contralto m counter tenor. •f contralto

contra|mano. a ~ in the wrong direction. ~**partida** f compensation. ~**pelo. a** ~ the wrong way

contrapes|ar vt counterweight. ~o m counterweight

contraproducente adj counter-productive

contrari|a f. **llevar la** ~**a** contradict. ~**ado** adj upset; (enojado) annoyed; ~**ar** [20] vt upset; (enojar) annoy. ~**edad** f setback; (disgusto) annoyance. ~o adj contrary (**a** to); (dirección) opposite. **al** ~**o** on the contrary. **al** ~**o de** contrary to. **de lo** ~**o** otherwise. **por el** ~**o** on the contrary. **ser** ~**o a** be opposed to, be against

contrarrestar vt counteract

contrasentido m contradiction

contraseña f (palabra) password; (en cine) stub

contrast|ar vt check, verify. •vi contrast. ~e m contrast; (en oro, plata) hallmark

contratar vt contract (servicio); hire, take on (empleados); sign up (jugador)

contratiempo m setback; (accidente) mishap

contrat|ista m & f contractor. ~o m contract

contraven|ción f contravention. ~**ir** [53] vt contravene

contraventana f shutter

contribu|ción f contribution; (tributo) tax. ~ **ir** [17] vt/i contribute. ~**yente** m & f contributor; (que paga impuestos) taxpayer

contrincante m rival, opponent

control m control; (vigilancia) check; (lugar) checkpoint. ~**ar** vt control; (vigilar) check. ~**arse** vpr control s.o.

controversia f controversy

contundente adj (arma) blunt; (argumento) convincing

contusión f bruise

convalec|encia f convalescence. ~**er** [11] vi convalesce. ~**iente** adj & m & f convalescent

convalidar vt recognize (título)

convenc|er [9] vt convince. ~**imiento** m conviction

convenci|ón f convention. ~**onal** adj conventional

conveni|encia f convenience; (aptitud) suitability. **~ente** adj suitable; (aconsejable) advisable; (provechoso) useful. **~o** m agreement. **~r** 53 vt agree. ●vi agree (**en** on); (ser conveniente) be convenient for, suit; (ser aconsejable) be advisable

convento m (de monjes) monastery; (de monjas) convent

conversa|ción f conversation. **~ciones** fpl talks. **~r** vi converse, talk

conver|sión f conversion. **~so** adj converted. **~tible** adj convertible. ●m (LAm) convertible. **~tir** 4 vt convert. **~tirse** vpr. **~tirse en** turn into; (Relig) convert

convic|ción f conviction. **~to** adj convicted

convida|do m guest. **~r** vt invite

convincente adj convincing

conviv|encia f coexistence; (de parejas) life together. **~ir** vi live together; (coexistir) coexist

convocar 7 vt call (huelga, elecciones); convene (reunión); summon (personas)

convulsión f convulsion

conyugal adj marital, conjugal; (vida) married

cónyuge m spouse. **~s** mpl married couple

coñac m (pl **~s**) brandy

coopera|ción f cooperation. **~r** vi cooperate. **~nte** m & f voluntary aid worker. **~tiva** f cooperative. **~tivo** adj cooperative

coordinar vt coordinate

copa f glass; (deportes, fig) cup; (de árbol) top. **~s** fpl (naipes) hearts. **tomar una ~** have a drink

copia f copy. **~ en limpio** fair copy. **sacar una ~** make a copy. **~r** vt copy

copioso adj copious; (lluvia, nevada etc) heavy

copla f verse; (canción) folksong

copo m flake. **~ de nieve** snowflake. **~s de maíz** cornflakes

coquet|a f flirt; (mueble) dressing-table. **~ear** vi flirt. **~o** adj flirtatious

coraje m courage; (rabia) anger

coral adj choral. ●m coral; (Mus) chorale

coraza f cuirass; (Naut) armour-plating; (de tortuga) shell

coraz|ón m heart; (persona) darling. **sin ~ón** heartless. **tener buen ~ón** be good-hearted. **~onada** f hunch; (impulso) impulse

corbata f tie, necktie (esp Amer). **~ de lazo** bow tie

corche|a f quaver. **~te** m fastener, hook and eye; (gancho) hook; (paréntesis) square bracket

corcho m cork. **~lata** f (Mex) (crown) cap

corcova f hump

cordel m cord, string

cordero m lamb

cordial adj cordial, friendly. ●m tonic. **~idad** f cordiality, warmth

cordillera f mountain range

córdoba m (unidad monetaria de Nicaragua) córdoba

cordón m string; (de zapatos) lace; (cable) cord; (fig) cordon. **~ umbilical** umbilical cord

coreografía f choreography

corista f (bailarina) chorus girl

cornet|a f bugle; (Mex, de coche) horn. **~ín** m cornet

coro m (Mus) choir; (en teatro) chorus

corona f crown; (de flores) wreath, garland. **~ción** f coronation. **~r** vt crown

coronel m colonel

coronilla f crown. **estar hasta la ~** be fed up

corpora|ción f corporation. **~l** adj

(castigo) corporal; (trabajo) physical

corpulento adj stout

corral m farmyard. **aves** fpl **de ~** poultry

correa f strap; (de perro) lead; (cinturón) belt

correc|ción f correction; (cortesía) good manners. **~to** adj correct; (cortés) polite

corrector ortográfico m spell checker

corre|dizo adj running. **nudo** m **~dizo** slip knot. **puerta** f **~diza** sliding door. **~dor** m runner; (pasillo) corridor; (agente) agent, broker. **~dor de coches** racing driver

corregir 5 & 14 vt correct

correlación f correlation

correo m post, mail; (persona) courier; (LAm, oficina) post office. ⬛**~s** mpl post office. **~ electrónico** e-mail. **echar al ~** post

correr vt run; (mover) move; draw (cortinas). ● vi run; (agua, electricidad etc) flow; (tiempo) pass. **~se** vpr (apartarse) move along; (colores) run

correspond|encia f correspondence. **~er** vi correspond; (ser adecuado) be fitting; (contestar) reply; (pertenecer) belong; (incumbir) fall to. **~erse** vpr (amarse) love one another. **~iente** adj corresponding

corresponsal m correspondent

⬛**corrid|a** f run. **~a de toros** bullfight. **de ~a** from memory. **~o** adj (continuo) continuous

corriente adj (agua) running; (monedas, publicación, cuenta, año) current; (ordinario) ordinary. ● f current; (de aire) draught; (fig) tendency. ● m current month. **al ~** (al día) up-to-date; (enterado) aware

corr|illo m small group. **~o** m circle

corroborar vt corroborate

corroer 24 & 37 vt corrode; (en

geología) erode; (fig) eat away

corromper vt corrupt, rot (materia). **~se** vpr become corrupted; (materia) rot; (alimentos) go bad

corrosi|ón f corrosion. **~vo** adj corrosive

corrupción f corruption; (de materia etc) rot

corsé m corset

corta|do adj cut; (carretera) closed; (leche) curdled; (avergonzado) embarrassed; (confuso) confused. ● m coffee with a little milk. **~dura** f cut. **~nte** adj sharp; (viento) biting; (frío) bitter. **~r** vt cut; (recortar) cut out; (aislar, separar, interrumpir) cut off. ● vi cut; (novios) break up. **~rse** vpr cut o.s.; (leche etc) curdle; (fig) be embarrassed. **~rse el pelo** have one's hair cut. **~rse las uñas** cut one's nails. **~uñas** m invar nail-clippers

corte m cut; (de tela) length. **~ de luz** power cut. **~ y confección** dressmaking. ● f court; (LAm, tribunal) Court of Appeal. **hacer la ~** court. **las C~s** the Spanish parliament. **la C~ Suprema** the Supreme Court

corlej|ar vt court. **~o** m (de rey etc) entourage. **~o fúnebre** cortège, funeral procession

cortés adj polite

cortesía f courtesy

corteza f bark; (de queso) rind; (de pan) crust

cortijo m farm; (casa) farmhouse

cortina f curtain

corto adj short; (apocado) shy. **~ de** short of. **~ de alcances** dim, thick. **~ de vista** short-sighted. **a la corta o a la larga** sooner or later. **quedarse ~** (subestimar) underestimate. **~circuito** m short circuit.

Coruña f. **La ~** Corunna

cosa f thing; (asunto) business; (idea)

⬛ *see* A-Z of Spanish life and culture

idea. **como si tal** ~ just like that; (como si no hubiera pasado nada) as if nothing had happened. **decirle a uno cuatro** ~**s** tell s.o. a thing or two

cosecha f harvest; (de vino) vintage. ~**r** vt harvest

coser vt sew; sew on (botón); stitch (herida). • vi sew. ~**se** vpr stick to s.o.

cosmético adj & m cosmetic

cósmico adj cosmic

cosmo|polita adj & m & f cosmopolitan. ~**s** m cosmos

cosquillas fpl. **dar** ~ tickle. **hacer** ~ tickle. **tener** ~ be ticklish

costa f coast. **a** ~ **de** at the expense of. **a toda** ~ at any cost

costado m side

costal m sack

costar [2] vt cost. • vi cost; (resultar difícil) to be hard. ~ **caro** be expensive. **cueste lo que cueste** at any cost

costarricense adj & m, **costarriqueño** adj & m Costa Rican

cost|as fpl (Jurid) costs. ~**e** m cost. ~**ear** vt pay for; (Naut) sail along the coast

costero adj coastal

costilla f rib; (chuleta) chop

costo m cost. ~**so** adj expensive

costumbre f custom; (de persona) habit. **de** ~ usual; (como adv) usually

costur|a f sewing; (línea) seam; (confección) dressmaking. ~**era** f dressmaker. ~**ero** m sewing box

cotejar vt compare

cotidiano adj daily

cotille|ar vt gossip. ~**o** m gossip

cotiza|ción f quotation, price. ~**r** [10] vt (en la bolsa) quote. • vi pay contributions. ~**rse** vpr fetch; (en la bolsa) stand at; (fig) be valued

....
see A-Z of Spanish life and culture

coto m enclosure; (de caza) preserve. ~ **de caza** game preserve

cotorr|a f parrot; (fig) chatterbox. ~**ear** vi chatter

coyuntura f joint

coz f kick

cráneo m skull

cráter m crater

crea|ción f creation. ~**dor** adj creative. • m creator. ~**r** vt create

crec|er [11] vi grow; (aumentar) increase; (río) rise. ~**ida** f (de río) flood. ~**ido** adj (persona) grown-up; (número) large, considerable; (plantas) fully-grown. ~**iente** adj growing; (luna) crescent. ~**imiento** m growth

credencial f document. • adj. **cartas** fpl ~**es** credentials

credibilidad f credibility

crédito m credit; (préstamo) loan. **digno de** ~ reliable

credo m creed

crédulo adj credulous

cre|encia f belief. ~**er** [18] vt/i believe; (pensar) think. ~**o que no** I don't think so, I think not. ~**o que sí** I think so. **no** ~**o** I don't think so. **¡ya lo** ~**o!** I should think so!. ~**erse** vpr consider o.s. **no me lo** ~**o** I don't believe it. ~**íble** adj credible

crema f cream; (Culin) custard; (LAm, de la leche) cream. ~ **batida** (LAm) whipped cream. ~ **bronceadora** sun-tan cream

cremallera f zip (Brit), zipper (Amer)

crematorio m crematorium

crepitar vi crackle

crepúsculo m twilight

crespo adj frizzy; (LAm, rizado) curly. • m (LAm) curl

cresta f crest; (de gallo) comb

creyente m believer

cría f breeding; (animal) baby

animal. **las ~s** the young

cria|da f maid, servant. **~dero** m (de pollos etc) farm; (de ostras) bed; (de plantas) nursery. **•~do** m servant. **~dor** m breeder. **~nza** f breeding. **~r 20** vt suckle; grow (plantas); breed (animales); (educar) bring up (Brit), raise (esp Amer). **~rse** vpr grow up

criatura f creature; (niño) baby

crim|en m (serious) crime; (asesinato) murder; (fig) crime. **~inal** adj & m & f criminal

crin f mane

crío m child

criollo adj Creole; (LAm, música, comida) traditional. **•** m Creole; (LAm, nativo) Peruvian, Chilean etc

crisantemo m chrysanthemum

crisis f invar crisis

crispar vt twitch; (fam, irritar) annoy. **~le los nervios a uno** get on s.o.'s nerves

cristal m crystal; (Esp, vidrio) glass; (Esp, de una ventana) pane of glass. **limpiar los ~es** (Esp) clean the windows. **~ino** adj crystalline; (fig) crystal-clear. **~izar 10** crystallize. **~izarse** vpr crystallize

cristian|dad f Christendom. **~ismo** m Christianity. **~o** adj Christian. **ser ~o** be a Christian. **•** m Christian

cristo m crucifix

Cristo m Christ

criterio m criterion; (discernimiento) judgement; (opinión) opinion

crític|a f criticism; (reseña) review. **~iticar 7** vt criticize. **~ítico** adj critical. **•** m critic

croar vi croak

crom|ado adj chromium-plated. **~o** m chromium, chrome

crónic|a f chronicle; (de radio, TV) report; (de periódico) feature. **~ deportiva** sport section. **~o** adj chronic

cronista m & f reporter

crono|grama m schedule, timetable. **~logía** f chronology

cron|ometrar vt time. **~ómetro** m (en deportes) stop-watch

croqueta f croquette

cruce m crossing; (de calles, carreteras) crossroads; (de peatones) (pedestrian) crossing

crucial adj crucial

crucifi|car 7 vt crucify. **~jo** m crucifix

crucigrama m crossword (puzzle)

crudo adj raw; (fig) harsh. **•** m crude (oil)

cruel adj cruel. **~dad** f cruelty

cruji|do m (de seda, de hojas secas) rustle; (de muebles) creak. **~r** vi (seda, hojas secas) rustle; (muebles) creak

cruz f cross; (de moneda) tails. **~ gamada** swastika. **la C~ Roja** the Red Cross

cruza|da f crusade. **~r 10** vt cross; exchange (palabras). **~rse** vpr cross; (pasar en la calle) pass each other. **~rse con** pass

cuaderno m exercise book; (para apuntes) notebook

cuadra f (caballeriza) stable; (LAm, distancia) block

cuadrado adj & m square

cuadragésimo adj fortieth

cuadr|ar vt square. **•** vi suit; (cuentas) tally. **~arse** vpr (Mil) stand to attention; (fig) dig one's heels in. **~ilátero** m quadrilateral; (Boxeo) ring

cuadrilla f group; (pandilla) gang

cuadro m square; (pintura) painting; (Teatro) scene; (de números) table; (de mando etc) panel; (conjunto del personal) staff. **~ de distribución** switchboard. **a ~s, de ~s** check. **¡qué ~!, ¡vaya un ~!** what a sight!

cuadrúpedo m quadruped

cuádruple adj & m quadruple

cuajar vt congeal (sangre); curdle (leche); (llenar) fill up. • vi (nieve) settle; (fig, fam) work out. **cuajado de** full of. **~se** vpr coagulate; (sangre) clot; (leche) curdle

cual pron. **el ~, la ~** etc (animales o cosas) that, which; (personas, sujeto) who, that; (personas, objeto) whom. • adj (LAm, qué) what. **~ si** as if. **cada ~** everyone. **lo ~** which. **por lo ~** because of which. **sea ~ sea** whatever

cuál pron which; (LAm, qué) what

cualidad f quality

cualquiera adj (delante de nombres **cualquier**, pl **cualesquiera**) any. • pron (pl **cualesquiera**) anyone, anybody; (cosas) whatever, whichever. **un ~** a nobody. **una ~** a slut

cuando adv when. • conj when; (si) if. **~ más** at the most. **~ menos** at the least. **aun ~** even if. **de ~ en ~** from time to time

cuándo adv & conj when. **¿de ~ acá?, ¿desde ~?** since when? **¡~ no!** (LAm) as usual!, typical!

cuant|ía f quantity; (extensión) extent. **~ioso** adj abundant. **~o** adj as much ... as, as many ... as. • pron as much as, as many as. • adv as much as. **~o antes** as soon as possible. **~o más, mejor** the more the merrier. **en ~o** as soon as. **en ~o a** as for. **por ~o** since. **unos ~os** a few, some

cuánto adj (interrogativo) how much?; (interrogativo en plural) how many?; (exclamativo) what a lot of! • pron how much?; (en plural) how many? • adv how much. **¿~ mides?** how tall are you? **¿~ tiempo?** how long? **¡~ tiempo sin verte!** it's been a long time! **¿a ~s estamos?** what's the date today? **un Sr. no sé ~s** Mr So-and-So

cuáquero m Quaker

cuarent|a adj & m forty; (cuadragésimo) fortieth. **~ena** f (Med) quarantine. **~ón** adj about forty

cuaresma f Lent

cuarta f (palmo) span

cuartel m (Mil) barracks. **~ general** headquarters

cuarteto m quartet

cuarto adj fourth. • m quarter; (habitación) room. **~ de baño** bathroom. **~ de estar** living room. **~ de hora** quarter of an hour. **estar sin un ~** be broke. **y ~** (a) quarter past

cuarzo m quartz

cuate m (Mex) twin; (amigo) friend; (🔲, tipo) guy

cuatro adj & m four. **~cientos** adj & m four hundred

Cuba f Cuba

cuba|libre m rum and Coke ®. **~no** adj & m Cuban

cúbico adj cubic

cubículo m cubicle

cubiert|a f cover; (neumático) tyre; (Naut) deck. **~o** adj covered; (cielo) overcast. • m place setting, piece of cutlery; (en restaurante) cover charge. **a ~o** under cover

cubilete m bowl; (molde) mould; (para los dados) cup

cubis|mo m cubism. **~ta** adj & m & f cubist

cubo m bucket; (Mat) cube

cubrecama m bedspread

cubrir (pp **cubierto**) vt cover; fill (vacante). **~se** vpr cover o.s.; (ponerse el sombrero) put on one's hat; (el cielo) cloud over, become overcast

cucaracha f cockroach

cuchar|a f spoon. **~ada** f spoonful. **~adita** f teaspoonful. **~illa, ~ita** f teaspoon. **~ón** m ladle

cuchichear vi whisper

cuchill|a f large knife; (de carnicero) cleaver; (hoja de afeitar) razor blade. **~ada** f stab; (herida) knife wound. **~o** m knife

cuchitril m (fig) hovel

cuclillas: en ~ adv squatting

cuco adj shrewd; (mono) pretty, nice. • m cuckoo

cucurucho m cornet

cuello m neck; (de camisa) collar. **cortar(le) el ~ a uno** cut s.o.'s throat

cuenc|a f (del ojo) (eye) socket; (de río) basin. ~**o** m hollow; (vasija) bowl

cuenta f count; (acción de contar) counting; (cálculo) calculation; (factura) bill; (en banco, relato) account; (de collar) bead. ~ **corriente** current account, checking account (Amer). **dar ~ de** give an account of. **darse ~ de** realize. **en resumidas ~s** in short. **por mi propia ~** on my own account. **tener en ~** bear in mind

cuentakilómetros m invar milometer

cuent|ista m & f story-writer; (de mentiras) fibber. ~**o** m story; (mentira) fib, tall story. ~ **de hadas** fairy tale. • vb véase CONTAR

cuerda f rope; (más fina) string; (Mus) string. ~ **floja** tightrope. **dar ~ a** wind up (un reloj)

cuerdo adj (persona) sane; (acción) sensible

cuerno m horn

cuero m leather; (piel) skin; (del grifo) washer. ~ **cabelludo** scalp. **en ~s (vivos)** stark naked

cuerpo m body

cuervo m crow

cuesta f slope, hill. ~ **abajo** downhill. ~ **arriba** uphill. **a ~s** on one's back

cuestión f matter; (problema) problem; (cosa) thing

cueva f cave

cuida|do m care; (preocupación) worry. **i~do!** watch out!. **tener ~do** be careful. ~**doso** adj careful. ~**r** vt look after. • vi. ~**r**

de look after. ~**rse** vpr look after o.s. ~**rse de** be careful to

culata f (de revólver, fusil) butt. ~**zo** m recoil

culebr|a f snake. ~**ón** m soap opera

culinario adj culinary

culminar vi culminate

culo m 🄸 bottom; (LAm vulg) arse (Brit vulg), ass (Amer vulg)

culpa f fault. **echar la ~** blame. **por ~ de** because of. **tener la ~** be to blame (**de** for). ~**bilidad** f guilt. ~**ble** adj guilty. • m & f culprit. ~**r** vt blame (**de** for)

cultiv|ar vt farm; grow (plantas); (fig) cultivate. ~**o** m farming; (de plantas) growing

cult|o adj (persona) educated. • m cult; (homenaje) worship. ~**ura** f culture. ~**ural** adj cultural

culturismo m body-building

cumbre f summit

cumpleaños m invar birthday

cumplido adj perfect; (cortés) polite. • m compliment. **de ~** courtesy. **por ~** out of a sense of duty. ~**r** adj reliable

cumpli|miento m fulfilment; (de ley) observance; (de orden) carrying out. ~**r** vt carry out; observe (ley); serve (condena); reach (años); keep (promesa). **hoy cumple 3 años** he's 3 (years old) today. • vi do one's duty. **por ~r** as a mere formality. ~**rse** vpr expire; (realizarse) be fulfilled

cuna f cradle; (fig, nacimiento) birthplace

cundir vi spread; (rendir) go a long way

cuneta f ditch

cuña f wedge

cuñad|a f sister-in-law. ~**o** m brother-in-law

cuño m stamp. **de nuevo ~** new

cuota f quota; (de sociedad etc)

membership, fee; (LAm, plazo) instalment; (Mex, peaje) toll

cupe vb véase CABER

cupo m cuota; (LAm, capacidad) room; (Mex, plaza) place

cupón m coupon

cúpula f dome

cura f cure; (tratamiento) treatment. • m priest. ~**ción** f healing. ~**ndero** m faith-healer. ~**r** vt (incl Culin) cure; dress (herida); (tratar) treat; (fig) remedy; tan (pieles). ~**rse** vpr get better

curios|ear vi pry; (mirar) browse. ~**idad** f curiosity. ~**o** adj curious; (raro) odd, unusual • m onlooker; (fisgón) busybody

curita f (LAm) (sticking) plaster

curriculum (vitae) m curriculum vitae, CV

cursar vt issue; (estudiar) study

cursi adj pretentious, showy

cursillo m short course

cursiva f italics

curso m course; (Univ etc) year. **en** ~ under way; (año etc) current

cursor m cursor

curtir vt tan; (fig) harden. ~**se** vpr become tanned; (fig) become hardened

curv|a f curve; (de carretera) bend. ~**ar** vt bend; bow (estante). ~**arse** vpr bend; (estante) bow; (madera) warp. ~**ilíneo** adj curvilinear; (mujer) curvaceous. ~**o** adj curved

cúspide f top; (fig) pinnacle

custodi|a f safe-keeping; (Jurid) custody. ~**ar** vt guard; (guardar) look after. ~**o** m guardian

cutáneo adj skin

cutis m skin, complexion

cuyo pron (de persona) whose, of whom; (de cosa) whose, of which. **en** ~ **caso** in which case

Dd

dactilógrafo m typist

dado m dice. • adj given. ~ **que** since, given that

daltónico adj colour-blind

dama f lady. ~ **de honor** bridesmaid. ~**s** fpl draughts (Brit), checkers (Amer)

damasco m damask; (LAm, fruta) apricot

danés adj Danish. • m Dane; (idioma) Danish

danza f dance; (acción) dancing. ~**r** 10 vt/i dance

dañ|ar vt damage. ~**se** vpr get damaged. ~**ino** adj harmful. ~**o** m damage; (a una persona) harm. ~**os**

y perjuicios damages. **hacer** ~**o a** harm, hurt. **hacerse** ~**o** hurt o.s.

dar 26 vt give; bear (frutos); give out (calor); strike (la hora). • vi give. **da igual** it doesn't matter. **¡dale!** go on! **da lo mismo** it doesn't matter. ~ **a** (ventana) look on to; (edificio) face. ~ **a luz** give birth. ~ **con** meet (persona); find (cosa). **¿qué más da?** it doesn't matter! ~**se** vpr have (baño). **dárselas de** make o.s. out to be. ~**se por** consider o.s.

dardo m dart

datar vi. ~ **de** date from

dátil m date

dato m piece of information. **~s**
mpl data, information. **~s**
personales personal details

de preposición

Note that **de** before **el** becomes
del, e.g. **es del norte**

••••➤ (contenido, material) of. **un**
vaso de agua a glass of water.
es de madera it's made of
wood (pertenencia) **el coche de**
Juan Juan's car. **es de ella** it's
hers. **es de María** it's María's.
las llaves del coche the car keys
(procedencia, origen, época) from.
soy de Madrid I'm from Madrid.
una llamada de Lima a call
from Lima. **es del siglo V** it's
from the 5th century (causa,
modo) **se murió de cáncer** he
died of cancer. **temblar de**
miedo to tremble with fear. **de**
dos en dos two by two

••••➤ (parte del día, hora) **de noche**
at night. **de madrugada** early in
the morning. **las diez de la**
mañana ten (o'clock) in the
morning. **de 9 a 12** from 9 to 12

••••➤ (en oraciones pasivas) by.
rodeado de agua surrounded
by water. **va seguido de coma**
it's followed by a comma. **es de**
Mozart it's by Mozart

••••➤ (al especificar) **el cajón de**
arriba the top drawer. **la clase**
de inglés the English lesson. **la**
chica de verde the girl in green.
el de debajo the one
underneath

••••➤ (en calidad de) as. **trabaja de**
oficinista he works as a clerk.
vino de chaperón he came as a
chaperon

••••➤ (en comparaciones) than. **pesa**
más de un kilo it weighs more
than a kilo

••••➤ (con superlativo) **el más alto**
del mundo the tallest in the
world. **el mejor de todos** the
best of all

••••➤ (sentido condicional) if. **de**

haberlo sabido if I had known. **de**
continuar así if this goes on

▶ Cuando la preposición **de** se
emplea como parte de
expresiones como **de prisa, de**
acuerdo etc., y de nombres
compuestos como **hombre de**
negocios, saco de dormir etc.,
ver bajo el respectivo nombre

deambular vi roam (**por** about)

debajo adv underneath. **~ de**
under(neath). **el de ~** the one
underneath. **por ~** underneath.
por ~ de below

debat|e m debate. **~ir** vt debate

deber vt owe. • verbo auxiliar have to,
must; (en condicional) should. **debo**
marcharme I must go, I have to
go. • m duty. **~es** mpl homework.
~se vpr. **~se a** be due to

debido adj due; (correcto) proper. **~**
a due to. **como es ~** as is proper

débil adj weak; (sonido) faint; (luz)
dim

debili|dad f weakness. **~tar** vt
weaken. **~tarse** vpr weaken, get
weak

débito m debit. **~ bancario** (LAm)
direct debit

debut m debut

debutar vi make one's debut

década f decade

deca|dencia f decline. **~dente** adj
decadent. **~er** 29 vi decline;
(debilitarse) weaken. **~ído** adj in low
spirits. **~imiento** m decline,
weakening

decano m dean; (miembro más antiguo)
senior member

decapitar vt behead

decena f ten. **una ~ de** about ten

decencia f decency

decenio m decade

decente adj decent; (decoroso)
respectable; (limpio) clean, tidy

decepci|ón f disappointment.
~**onar** vt disappoint

decidi|do adj decided; (persona)
determined, resolute. ~**r** vt
decide; settle (cuestión etc). ● vi
decide. ~**rse** vpr make up one's
mind

decimal adj & m decimal

décimo adj & m tenth. ● m (de lotería)
tenth part of a lottery ticket

decir 46 vt say; (contar) tell. ● m
saying. ~ **que no** say no. ~ **que
sí** say yes. **dicho de otro modo**
in other words. **dicho y hecho** no
sooner said than done. **¿dígame?**
can I help you? **¡dígame!** (al
teléfono) hello! **digamos** let's say.
es ~ that is to say. **mejor dicho**
rather. **¡no me digas!** you don't
say!, really! **por así ~, por ~lo
así** so to speak, as it were. **querer
~** mean. **se dice que** it is said
that, they say that

decisi|ón f decision. ~**vo** adj
decisive

declara|ción f declaration; (a
autoridad, prensa) statement. ~**ción
de renta** income tax return. ~**r**
vt/i declare. ~**rse** vpr declare o.s.;
(epidemia etc) break out

declinar vt turn down; (Gram)
decline

declive m slope; (fig) decline. **en ~**
sloping

decola|je m (LAm) take-off. ~**r** vi
(LAm) take off

decolorarse vpr become
discoloured, fade

decora|ción f decoration. ~**do** m
(en el teatro) set. ~**r** vt decorate.
~**tivo** adj decorative

decoro m decorum. ~**so** adj
decent, respectable

decrépito adj decrepit

decret|ar vt decree. ~**o** m decree

dedal m thimble

dedica|ción f dedication. ~**r** 7 vt
dedicate; devote (tiempo). ~**rse** vpr.
~**rse a** devote o.s. to. **¿a qué se**

dedica? what does he do? ~**toria**
f dedication

dedo m finger; (del pie) toe. ~
anular ring finger. ~ **corazón**
middle finger. ~ **gordo** thumb;
(del pie) big toe. ~ **índice** index
finger. ~ **meñique** little finger.
~ **pulgar** thumb

deduc|ción f deduction. ~**ir** 47 vt
deduce; (descontar) deduct

defect|o m fault, defect. ~**uoso**
adj defective

defen|der 1 vt defend. ~**sa** f
defence. ~**derse** vpr defend o.s.
~**sivo** adj defensive. ~**sor** m
defender. **abogado** m ~**sor**
defence counsel

defeño m (Mex) person from the
Federal District

deficien|cia f deficiency. ~**cia
mental** mental handicap. ~**te** adj
poor, deficient. ● m & f ~**te
mental** mentally handicapped
person

déficit m invar deficit

defini|ción f definition. ~**do** adj
defined. ~**r** vt define. ~**tivo** adj
definitive. **en ~tiva** all in all

deform|ación f deformation; (de
imagen etc) distortion. ~**ar** vt
deform; distort (imagen, metal).
~**arse** vpr go out of shape. ~**e** adj
deformed

defraudar vt defraud; (decepcionar)
disappoint

defunción f death

degenera|ción f degeneration;
(cualidad) degeneracy. ~**do** adj
degenerate. ~**r** vi degenerate

degollar 16 vt cut s.o.'s throat

degradar vt degrade; (Mil) demote.
~**se** vpr demean o.s..

degusta|ción f tasting. ~**r** vt taste

dehesa f pasture

deja|dez f slovenliness; (pereza)
laziness. ~**do** adj slovenly;
(descuidado) slack, negligent. ~**r** vt
leave; (abandonar) abandon; give up

(estudios); (prestar) lend; (permitir) let. **~r a un lado** leave aside. **~r de** stop

dejo m aftertaste; (tonillo) slight accent; (toque) touch

del = **de + el**

delantal m apron

delante adv in front. **~ de** in front of. **de ~** front. **~ra** f front; (de teatro etc) front row; (ventaja) lead; (de equipo) forward line. **llevar la ~ra** be in the lead. **~ro** adj front. • m forward

delat|ar vt denounce. **~or** m informer

delega|ción f delegation; (oficina) regional office; (Mex, comisaría) police station. **~do** m delegate; (Com) agent, representative. **~r** 12 vt delegate

deleit|ar vt delight. **~e** m delight

deletrear vt spell (out)

delfín m dolphin

delgad|ez f thinness. **~o** adj thin; (esbelto) slim. **~ucho** adj skinny

delibera|ción f deliberation. **~do** adj deliberate. **~r** vi deliberate (**sobre** on)

delicad|eza f gentleness; (fragilidad) frailty; (tacto) tact. **falta de ~eza** tactlessness. **tener la ~ de** have the courtesy to. **~o** adj delicate; (refinado) refined; (sensible) sensitive

delici|a f delight. **~oso** adj delightful; (sabor etc) delicious

delimitar vt delimit

delincuen|cia f delinquency. **~te** m & f criminal, delinquent

delinquir 8 vi commit a criminal offence

delir|ante adj delirious. **~ar** vi be delirious; (fig) talk nonsense. **~io** m delirium; (fig) frenzy

delito m crime, offence

demacrado adj haggard

demagogo m demagogue

demanda f demand; (Jurid)

lawsuit. **~do** m defendant. **~nte** m & f (Jurid) plaintiff. **~r** vt (Jurid) sue; (LAm, requerir) require

demarcación f demarcation

demás adj rest of the, other. • pron rest, others. **lo ~** the rest. **por ~** extremely. **por lo ~** otherwise

demas|ía f. **en ~ía** in excess. **~iado** adj too much; (en plural) too many. • adv too much; (con adjetivo) too

demen|cia f madness. **~te** adj demented, mad

dem|ocracia f democracy. **~ócrata** m & f democrat. **~ocrático** adj democratic

demol|er 2 vt demolish. **~ición** f demolition

demonio m devil, demon. **¡~!** hell! **¿cómo ~s?** how the hell? **¡qué ~s!** what the hell!

demora f delay. **~r** vt delay. • vi stay on. **~rse** vpr be too long; (LAm, cierto tiempo). **se ~ una hora en llegar** it takes him an hour to get there

demostra|ción f demonstration, show. **~r** 2 vt demonstrate; (mostrar) show, (probar) prove. **~tivo** adj demonstrative

dengue m dengue fever

denigrar vt denigrate

denominado adj named; (supuesto) so-called

dens|idad f density. **~o** adj dense, thick

denta|dura f teeth. **~dura postiza** dentures, false teeth. **~l** adj dental

dent|era f. **darle ~era a uno** set s.o.'s teeth on edge. **~ífrico** m toothpaste. **~ista** m & f dentist

dentro adv inside; (de un edificio) indoors. **~ de** in. **~ de poco** soon. **por ~** inside

denuncia f report; (acusación) accusation. **~r** vt report; (periódico etc) denounce

departamento m department; (LAm, apartamento) flat (Brit), apartment (Amer)

depend|encia f dependence; (sección) section; (oficina) office. **~encias** fpl buildings. **~er** vi depend (**de** on). **~ienta** f shop assistant. **~iente** adj dependent (**de** on). •m shop assistant

depila|r vt depilate. **~torio** adj depilatory

deplora|ble adj deplorable. **~r** vt deplore, regret

deponer 34 vt remove from office; depose (rey); lay down (armas). •vi give evidence

deporta|ción f deportation. **~r** vt deport

deport|e m sport. **hacer ~e** take part in sports. **~ista** m sportsman. •f sportswoman. **~ivo** adj sports. •m sports car

dep|ositante m & f depositor. **~ositar** vt deposit; (poner) put, place. **~ósito** m deposit; (almacén) warehouse; (Mil) depot; (de líquidos) tank

depravado adj depraved

deprecia|ción f depreciation. **~r** vt depreciate. **~rse** vpr depreciate

depr|esión f depression. **~imido** adj depressed. **~imir** vt depress. **~imirse** vpr get depressed

depura|ción f purification. **~do** adj refined. **~r** vt purify; (Pol) purge; refine (estilo)

derech|a f (mano) right hand; (lado) right. **a la ~a** on the right; (hacia el lado derecho) to the right. **~ista** adj right-wing. •m & f right-winger. **~o** adj right; (vertical) upright; (recto) straight. •adv straight. **todo ~o** straight on. •m right; (Jurid) law; (lado) right side. **~os** mpl dues. **~os de autor** royalties

deriva f drift. **a la ~** drifting, adrift

deriva|do adj derived. •m derivative, by-product. **~r** vt divert. •vi. **~r de** derive from, be

derived from. **~rse** vpr. **~rse de** be derived from

derram|amiento m spilling. **~amiento de sangre** bloodshed. **~ar** vt spill; shed (lágrimas). **~arse** vpr spill. **~e** m spilling; (pérdida) leakage; (Med) discharge; (Med, de sangre) haemorrhage

derretir 5 vt melt

derribar vt knock down; bring down, overthrow (gobierno etc)

derrocar 7 vt bring down, overthrow (gobierno etc)

derroch|ar vt squander. **~e** m waste

derrot|a f defeat. **~ar** vt defeat. **~ado** adj defeated. **~ero** m course

derrumba|r vt knock down. **~rse** vpr collapse; (persona) go to pieces

desabotonar vt unbutton, undo. **~se** vpr come undone; (persona) undo

desabrido adj tasteless; (persona) surly; (LAm) dull

desabrochar vt undo. **~se** vpr come undone; (persona) undo

desacato m defiance; (Jurid) contempt of court

desac|ertado adj ill-advised; (erróneo) wrong. **~ierto** m mistake

desacreditar vt discredit

desactivar vt defuse

desacuerdo m disagreement

desafiar 20 vt challenge; (afrontar) defy

desafina|do adj out of tune. **~r** vi be out of tune. **~rse** vpr go out of tune

desafío m challenge; (a la muerte) defiance; (combate) duel

desafortunad|amente adv unfortunately. **~o** adj unfortunate

desagrada|ble adj unpleasant. **~r** vt displease. •vi be unpleasant. **me ~ el sabor** I don't like the taste

desagradecido adj ungrateful

desagrado m displeasure. **con ~** unwillingly

desagüe m drain; (acción) drainage. **tubo** m **de ~** drain-pipe

desahog|ado adj roomy; (acomodado) comfortable. **~ar** 12 vt vent. **~arse** vpr let off steam. **~o** m comfort; (alivio) relief

desahuci|ar vt declare terminally ill (enfermo); evict (inquilino). **~o** m eviction

desair|ar vt snub. **~e** m snub

desajuste m maladjustment; (desequilibrio) imbalance

desala|dora f desalination plant. **~r** vt to desalinate

desal|entador adj disheartening. **~entar** 1 vt discourage. **~iento** m discouragement

desaliñado adj slovenly

desalmado adj heartless

desalojar vt (ocupantes) evacuate; (policía) to clear; (LAm) evict (inquilino)

desampar|ado adj helpless; (lugar) unprotected. **~ar** vt abandon. **~o** m helplessness; (abandono) lack of protection

desangrar vt bleed. **~se** vpr bleed

desanima|do adj down-hearted. **~r** vt discourage. **~rse** vpr lose heart

desapar|ecer 11 vi disappear; (efecto) wear off. **~ecido** adj missing. ●m missing person. **~ición** f disappearance

desapego m indifference

desapercibido adj. **pasar ~** go unnoticed

desaprobar 2 vt disapprove of

desarm|able adj collapsible; (estante) easy to dismantle. **~ar** vt disarm; (desmontar) dismantle; take apart; (LAm) take down (carpa). **~e** m disarmament

desarraig|ado adj rootless. **~ar** 12 vt uproot. **~o** m uprooting

desarregl|ar vt mess up; (alterar) disrupt. **~o** m disorder

desarroll|ar vt develop. **~arse** vpr (incl Foto) develop; (suceso) take place. **~o** m development

desaseado adj dirty; (desordenado) untidy

desasosiego m anxiety; (intranquilidad) restlessness

desastr|ado adj scruffy. **~e** m disaster. **~oso** adj disastrous

desatar vt untie; (fig, soltar) unleash. **~se** vpr come undone; to undo (zapatos)

desatascar 7 vt unblock

desaten|der 1 vt not pay attention to; neglect (deber etc). **~to** adj inattentive; (descortés) discourteous

desatin|ado adj silly. **~o** m silliness; (error) mistake

desatornillar vt unscrew

desautorizar 10 vt declare unauthorized; discredit (persona); (desmentir) deny

desavenencia f disagreement

desayun|ar vt have for breakfast. ●vi have breakfast. **~o** m breakfast

desazón m (fig) unease

desbandarse vpr (Mil) disband; (dispersarse) disperse

desbarajust|ar vt mess up. **~e** m mess

desbaratar vt spoil; (Mex) mess up (papeles)

desbloquear vt clear; release (mecanismo); unfreeze (cuenta)

desbocado adj (caballo) runaway; (escote) wide

desbordarse vpr overflow; (río) burst its banks

descabellado adj crazy

descafeinado adj decaffeinated. ●m decaffeinated coffee

descalabro m disaster

descalificar 7 vt disqualify; (desacreditar) discredit

descalz|ar 10 vt take off (zapatos). **~o** adj barefoot

descampado m open ground. **al ~** (LAm) in the open air

descans|ado adj rested; (trabajo) easy. **~ar** vt/i rest. **~illo** m landing. **~o** m rest; (del trabajo) break; (LAm, rellano) landing; (en deportes) half-time; (en el teatro etc) interval

descapotable adj convertible

descarado adj cheeky; (sin vergüenza) shameless

descarg|a f unloading; (Mil, Elec) discharge. **~ar** 12 vt unload; (Mil, Elec) discharge; (Informática) download. **~o** m (recibo) receipt; (Jurid) evidence

descaro m cheek, nerve

descarriarse 20 vpr go the wrong way; (res) stray; (fig) go astray

descarrila|miento m derailment. **~r** vi be derailed. **~rse** vpr (LAm) be derailed

descartar vt rule out

descascararse vpr (pintura) peel; (taza) chip

descen|dencia f descent; (personas) descendants. **~der** 1 vt go down (escalera etc). • vi go down; (temperatura) fall, drop; (provenir) be descended (**de** from). **~diente** m & f descendant. **~so** m descent; (de temperatura, fiebre etc) fall, drop

descifrar vt decipher; decode (clave)

descolgar 2 & 12 vt take down; pick up (el teléfono). **~se** vpr lower o.s.

descolor|ar vt discolour, fade. **~ido** adj discoloured, faded; (persona) pale

descomp|oner 34 vt break down; decompose (materia); upset (estómago); (esp LAm, estropear) break; (esp LAm, desarreglar) mess up. **~onerse** vpr decompose; (esp LAm,

estropearse) break down; (persona) feel sick. **~ostura** f (esp LAm, de máquina) breakdown; (esp LAm, náuseas) sickness; (esp LAm, diarrea) diarrhoea; (LAm, falla) fault. **~uesto** adj decomposed; (encolerizado) angry; (esp LAm, estropeado) broken. **estar ~uesto** (del estómago) have diarrhoea

descomunal adj enormous

desconc|ertante adj disconcerting. **~ertar** 1 vt disconcert; (dejar perplejo) puzzle. **~ertarse** vpr be put out, be disconcerted

desconectar vt disconnect

desconfia|do adj distrustful. **~nza** f distrust, suspicion. **~r** 20 vi. **~r de** mistrust; (no creer) doubt

descongelar vt defrost; (Com) unfreeze

desconoc|er 11 vt not know, not recognize. **~ido** adj unknown; (cambiado) unrecognizable. •m stranger. **~imiento** m ignorance

desconsidera|ción f lack of consideration. **~do** adj inconsiderate

descons|olado adj distressed. **~uelo** m distress; (tristeza) sadness

desconta|do adj. **dar por ~do (que)** take for granted (that). **~r** 2 vt discount; deduct (impuestos etc)

descontento adj unhappy (**con** with), dissatisfied (**con** with). •m discontent

descorazonar vt discourage. **~se** vpr lose heart

descorchar vt uncork

descorrer vt draw (cortina). **~ el cerrojo** unbolt the door

descort|és adj rude, discourteous. **~esía** f rudeness

descos|er vt unpick. **~erse** vpr come undone. **~ido** adj unstitched

descrédito m disrepute. **ir en ~ de** damage the reputation of

descremado adj skimmed

descri|bir (pp **descrito**) vt describe.
~**pción** f description

descuartizar ⑩ vt cut up

descubierto adj discovered; (no
cubierto) uncovered; (vehículo) open-
top; (piscina) open-air; (cielo) clear;
(cabeza) bare. ●m overdraft. **poner
al** ~ expose

descubri|miento m discovery. ~**r**
(pp **descubierto**) vt discover;
(destapar) uncover; (revelar) reveal;
unveil (estatua). ~**rse** vpr (quitarse el
sombrero) take off one's hat

descuento m discount; (del sueldo)
deduction; (en deportes) injury time

descuid|ado adj careless; (aspecto
etc) untidy; (desprevenido)
unprepared. ~**ar** vt neglect. ●vi
not worry. **¡~a!** don't worry!.
~**arse** vpr be careless ~**o** m
carelessness; (negligencia)
negligence

desde prep (lugar etc) from; (tiempo)
since, from. ~ **ahora** from now
on. ~ **hace un mes** for a month.
~ **luego** of course. ~ **Madrid
hasta Barcelona** from Madrid to
Barcelona. ~ **niño** since
childhood

desdecirse ㊻ vpr. ~ **de** take back
(palabras etc); go back on (promesa)

desd|én m scorn. ~**eñable** adj
insignificant. **nada** ~**eñable**
significant. ~**eñar** vt scorn

desdicha f misfortune. **por** ~
unfortunately. ~**do** adj
unfortunate

desdoblar vt (desplegar) unfold

desear vt want; wish (suerte etc). **le
deseo un buen viaje** I hope you
have a good journey. **¿qué desea
Vd?** can I help you?

desech|able adj disposable. ~**ar** vt
throw out; (rechazar) reject. ~**o** m
waste

desembalar vt unpack

desembarcar ⑦ vt unload. ●vi
disembark

desemboca|dura f (de río) mouth;

(de calle) opening. ~**r** ⑦ vi. ~**r en**
(río) flow into; (calle) lead to

desembolso m payment

desembragar ⑫ vi declutch

desempaquetar vt unwrap

desempat|ar vi break a tie. ~**e** m
tie-breaker

desempeñ|ar vt redeem; play
(papel); hold (cargo); perform, carry
out (deber etc). ~**arse** vpr (LAm)
perform. ~**arse bien** manage
well. ~**o** m redemption; (de un
deber, una función) discharge; (LAm,
actuación) performance

desemple|ado adj unemployed.
●m unemployed person. **los
~ados** the unemployed. ~**o** m
unemployment

desencadenar vt unchain (preso);
unleash (perro); (causar) trigger.
~**se** vpr be triggered off; (guerra etc)
break out

desencajar vt dislocate;
(desconectar) disconnect. ~**se** vpr
become dislocated

desenchufar vt unplug

desenfad|ado adj uninhibited;
(desenvuelto) self assured. ●**o** m
lack of inhibition; (desenvoltura)
self-assurance

desenfocado adj out of focus

desenfren|ado adj unrestrained.
~**o** m licentiousness

desenganchar vt unhook;
uncouple (vagón)

desengañ|ar vt disillusion. ~**arse**
vpr become disillusioned; (darse
cuenta) realize. ~**o** m
disillusionment, disappointment

desenlace m outcome

desenmascarar vt unmask

desenredar vt untangle. ~**se** vpr
untangle

desenro|llar vt unroll, unwind.
~**scar** ⑦ vt unscrew

desentend|erse ① vpr want
nothing to do with. ~**ido** m.

hacerse el ~ido (fingir no oír) pretend not to hear; (fingir ignorancia) pretend not to know

desenterrar ∎ vt exhume; (fig) unearth

desentonar vi be out of tune; (colores) clash

desenvoltura f ease; (falta de timidez) confidence

desenvolver ∎ (pp **desenvuelto**) vt unwrap; expound (idea etc). **~se** vpr perform; (manejarse) manage

deseo m wish, desire. **~so** adj eager. **estar ~so de** be eager to

desequilibr|ado adj unbalanced. **~io** m imbalance

des|ertar vt desert; (Pol) defect. **~értico** adj desert-like. **~ertor** m deserter; (Pol) defector

desespera|ción f despair. **~do** adj desperate. **~nte** adj infuriating. **~r** vt drive to despair. **~rse** vpr despair

desestimar vt (rechazar) reject

desfachat|ado adj brazen, shameless. **~ez** f nerve, cheek

desfallec|er ∎ vt weaken. ●vi become weak; (desmayarse) faint. **~imiento** m weakness; (desmayo) faint

desfasado adj out of phase; (idea) outdated; (persona) out of touch

desfavorable adj unfavourable

desfil|adero m narrow mountain pass; (cañón) narrow gorge. **~ar** vi march (past). **~e** m procession, parade. **~e de modelos** fashion show

desgana f, (LAm) **desgano** m (falta de apetito) lack of appetite; (Med) weakness, faintness; (fig) unwillingness

desgarr|ador adj heart-rending. **~ar** vt tear; (fig) break (corazón). **~o** m tear, rip

desgast|ar vt wear away; wear out (ropa). **~arse** vpr wear away; (ropa) be worn out; (persona) wear o.s. out. **~e** m wear

desgracia f misfortune; (accidente) accident; **por ~** unfortunately. **¡qué ~!** what a shame!. **~do** adj unlucky; (pobre) poor. ●m unfortunate person, poor devil ∎

desgranar vt shell (habas etc)

desgreñado adj ruffled, dishevelled

deshabitado adj uninhabited; (edificio) unoccupied

deshacer ∎ vt undo; strip (cama); unpack (maleta); (desmontar) take to pieces; break (trato); (derretir) melt; (disolver) dissolve. **~se** vpr come undone; (disolverse) dissolve; (derretirse) melt. **~se de algo** get rid of sth. **~se en lágrimas** dissolve into tears. **~se por hacer algo** go out of one's way to do sth

desheredar vt disinherit

deshidratarse vpr become dehydrated

deshielo m thaw

deshilachado adj frayed

deshincha|do adj (neumático) flat. **~r** vt deflate; (Med) reduce the swelling in. **~rse** vpr go down

deshollinador m chimney sweep

deshon|esto adj dishonest; (obsceno) indecent. **~ra** f disgrace. **~rar** vt dishonour

deshora f. **a ~** out of hours. **comer a ~s** eat between meals

deshuesar vt bone (carne); stone (fruta)

desidia f slackness; (pereza) laziness

desierto adj deserted. ●m desert

designar vt designate; (fijar) fix

desigual adj unequal; (terreno) uneven; (distinto) different. **~dad** f inequality

desilusi|ón f disappointment; (pérdida de ilusiones) disillusionment. **~onar** vt disappoint; (quitar las ilusiones) disillusion. **~onarse** vpr be disappointed; (perder las ilusiones) become disillusioned

desinfecta|nte m disinfectant. ~**r** vt disinfect

desinflar vt deflate. ~**se** vpr go down

desinhibido adj uninhibited

desintegrar vt disintegrate. ~**se** vpr disintegrate

desinter|és m lack of interest; (generosidad) unselfishness. ~**esado** adj uninterested; (liberal) unselfish

desistir vi. ~ **de** give up

desleal adj disloyal. ~**tad** f disloyalty

desligar 12 vt untie; (separar) separate; (fig, librar) free. ~**se** vpr break away; (de un compromiso) free o.s. (**de** from)

desliza|dor m (Mex) hang glider. ~**r** 10 vt slide, slip. ~**se** vpr slide, slip; (patinador) glide; (tiempo) slip by, pass; (fluir) flow

deslucido adj tarnished; (gastado) worn out; (fig) undistinguished

deslumbrar vt dazzle

desmadr|arse vpr get out of control. ~**e** m excess

desmán m outrage

desmanchar vt (LAm) remove the stains from

desmantelar vt dismantle; (despojar) strip

desmaquillador m make-up remover

desmay|ado adj unconscious. ~**arse** vpr faint. ~**o** m faint

desmedido adj excessive

desmemoriado adj forgetful

desmenti|do m denial. ~**r** 4 vt deny; (contradecir) contradict

desmenuzar 10 vt crumble; shred (carne etc)

desmerecer 11 vi. **no** ~ **de** compare favourably with

desmesurado adj excessive;

(enorme) enormous

desmonta|ble adj collapsible; (armario) easy to dismantle; (separable) removable. ~**r** vt (quitar) remove; (desarmar) dismantle, take apart. ●vi dismount

desmoralizar 10 vt demoralize

desmoronarse vpr crumble; (edificio) collapse

desnatado adj skimmed

desnivel m unevenness; (fig) difference, inequality

desnud|ar vt strip; undress, strip (persona). ~**arse** vpr undress. ~**ez** f nudity. ~**o** adj naked; (fig) bare. ●m nude

desnutri|ción f malnutrition. ~**do** adj undernourished

desobed|ecer 11 vt disobey. ~**iencia** f disobedience

desocupa|do adj (asiento etc) vacant, free; (sin trabajo) unemployed; (ocioso) idle. ~**r** vt vacate; (vaciar) empty; (desalojar) clear

desodorante m deodorant

desolado adj desolate; (persona) sorry, sad

desorbitante adj excessive

desorden m disorder, untidiness; (confusión) confusion. ~**ado** adj untidy. ~**ar** vt disarrange, make a mess of

desorganizar 10 vt disorganize; (trastornar) disturb

desorienta|do adj confused. ~**r** vt disorientate. ~**rse** vpr lose one's bearings

despabila|do adj wide awake; (listo) quick. ~**r** vt (despertar) wake up; (avivar) wise up. ~**rse** vpr wake up; (avivarse) wise up

despach|ar vt finish; (tratar con) deal with; (atender) serve; (vender) sell; (enviar) send; (despedir) fire. ~**o** m dispatch; (oficina) office; (venta) sale; (de localidades) box office

despacio adv slowly

despampanante adj stunning

desparpajo m confidence; (descaro) impudence

desparramar vt scatter; spill (líquidos)

despavorido adj terrified

despecho m spite. **a ~ de** in spite of. **por ~** out of spite

despectivo adj contemptuous; (sentido etc) pejorative

despedazar 10 vt tear to pieces

despedi|da f goodbye, farewell. **~da de soltero** stag-party. **~r** 5 vt say goodbye to, see off; dismiss (empleado); evict (inquilino); (arrojar) throw; give off (olor etc). **~rse** vpr say goodbye (**de** to)

despeg|ar 12 vt unstick. •vi (avión) take off. **~ue** m take-off

despeinar vt ruffle the hair of

despeja|do adj clear; (persona) wide awake. **~r** vt clear; (aclarar) clarify. •vi clear. **~rse** vpr (aclararse) become clear; (tiempo) clear up

despellejar vt skin

despenalizar vt decriminalize

despensa f pantry, larder

despeñadero m cliff

desperdici|ar vt waste. **~o** m waste. **~os** mpl rubbish

desperta|dor m alarm clock. **~r** 1 vt wake (up); (fig) awaken. **~rse** vpr wake up

despiadado adj merciless

despido m dismissal

despierto adj awake; (listo) bright

despilfarr|ar vt waste. **~o** m squandering

despintarse vpr (Mex) run

despista|do adj (con estar) confused; (con ser) absent-minded. **~r** vt throw off the scent; (fig) mislead. **~rse** vpr (fig) get confused

despiste m mistake; (confusión) muddle

desplaza|miento m displacement; (de opinión etc) swing, shift. **~r** 10 vt displace. **~rse** vpr travel

desplegar 1 & 12 vt open out; spread (alas); (fig) show

desplomarse vpr collapse

despoblado m deserted area

despoj|ar vt deprive (persona); strip (cosa). **~os** mpl remains; (de res) offal; (de ave) giblets

depreci|able adj despicable; (cantidad) negligible. **~ar** vt despise; (rechazar) scorn. **~o** m contempt; (desaire) snub

desprender vt remove; give off (olor). **~se** vpr fall off; (fig) part with; (deducirse) follow

despreocupa|do adj unconcerned; (descuidado) careless. **~rse** vpr not worry

desprestigiar vt discredit

desprevenido adj unprepared. **pillar a uno ~** catch s.o. unawares

desproporcionado adj disproportionate

desprovisto adj. **~ de** lacking in, without

después adv after, afterwards; (más tarde) later; (a continuación) then. **~ de** after. **~ de comer** after eating. **~ de todo** after all. **~ (de) que** after. **poco ~** soon after

desquit|arse vpr get even (**de** with). **~e** m revenge

destaca|do adj outstanding. **~r** 7 vt emphasize. •vi stand out. **~rse** vpr stand out. **~rse en** excel at

destajo m. **trabajar a ~** do piece-work

destap|ar vt uncover; open (botella). **~arse** vpr reveal one's true self. **~e** m (fig) permissiveness

destartalado adj (coche) clapped-out; (casa) ramshackle

destello m sparkle; (de estrella) twinkle; (fig) glimmer

destemplado adj discordant; (nervios) frayed

desteñir 5 & 22 vt fade. •vi fade; (color) run. ~**se** vpr fade; (color) run

desterra|do m exile. ~**r** 1 vt banish

destetar vt wean

destiempo m. **a** ~ at the wrong moment; (Mus) out of time

destierro m exile

destil|ar vt distil. ~**ería** f distillery

destin|ar vt destine; (nombrar) post. ~**atario** m addressee. ~**o** m (uso) use, function; (lugar) destination; (suerte) destiny. **con** ~**o a** (going) to

destituir 17 vt dismiss

destornilla|dor m screwdriver. ~**r** vt unscrew

destreza f skill

destroz|ar 10 vt destroy; (fig) shatter. ~**os** mpl destruction, damage

destru|cción f destruction. ~**ir** 17 vt destroy

desus|ado adj old-fashioned; (insólito) unusual. ~**o** m disuse. **caer en** ~**o** fall into disuse

desvalido adj needy, destitute

desvalijar vt rob; ransack (casa)

desvalorizar 10 vt devalue

desván m loft

desvanec|er 11 vt make disappear; (borrar) blur; (fig) dispel. ~**erse** vpr disappear; (desmayarse) faint. ~**imiento** m (Med) faint

desvariar 20 vi be delirious; (fig) talk nonsense

desvel|ar vt keep awake. ~**arse** vpr stay awake, have a sleepless night. ~**o** m sleeplessness

desvencijado adj (mueble) rickety

desventaja f disadvantage

desventura f misfortune. ~**do** adj unfortunate

desverg|onzado adj impudent, cheeky. ~**üenza** f impudence, cheek

desvestirse 5 vpr undress

desv|iación f deviation; (Auto) diversion. ~**iar** 20 vt divert; deflect (pelota). ~**iarse** vpr (carretera) branch off; (del camino) make a detour; (del tema) stray. ~**ío** m diversion

desvivirse vpr. ~**se por** be completely devoted to; (esforzarse) go out of one's way to

detall|ar vt relate in detail. ~**e** m detail; (fig) gesture. **al** ~**e** retail. **entrar en** ~**es** go into detail. **¡qué** ~**e!** how thoughtful! ~**ista** m & f retailer

detect|ar vt detect. ~**ive** m & f detective

deten|ción f stopping; (Jurid) arrest; (en la cárcel) detention. ~**er** 40 vt stop; (Jurid) arrest; (encarcelar) detain; (retrasar) delay. ~**erse** vpr stop; (entretenerse) spend a lot of time. ~**idamente** adv at length. ~**ido** adj (Jurid) under arrest. •m prisoner

detergente adj & m detergent

deterior|ar vt damage, spoil. ~**arse** vpr deteriorate. ~**o** m deterioration

determina|ción f determination; (decisión) decison. ~**nte** adj decisive. ~**r** vt determine; (decidir) decide

detestar vt detest

detrás adv behind; (en la parte posterior) on the back. ~**de** behind. **por** ~ at the back; (por la espalda) from behind

detrimento m detriment. **en** ~ **de** to the detriment of

deud|a f debt. ~**or** m debtor

devalua|ción f devaluation. ~**r** 21 vt devalue. ~**se** vpr depreciate

devastador adj devastating

devoción f devotion

devol|ución f return; (Com) repayment, refund. ~**ver** 5 (pp **devuelto**) vt return; (Com) repay, refund. ●vi be sick

devorar vt devour

devoto adj devout; (amigo etc) devoted. ●m admirer

di vb véase DAR, DECIR

día m day. ~ **de fiesta** (public) holiday. ~ **del santo** saint's day. ~ **feriado** (LAm), ~ **festivo** (public) holiday. **al** ~ up to date. **al** ~ **siguiente** (on) the following day. **¡buenos** ~**s!** good morning! **de** ~ by day. **el** ~ **de hoy** today. **el** ~ **de mañana** tomorrow. **un** ~ **sí y otro no** every other day. **vivir al** ~ live from hand to mouth

diab|etes f diabetes. ~**ético** adj diabetic

diab|lo m devil. ~**lura** f mischief. ~**ólico** adj diabolical

diadema f diadem

diáfano adj diaphanous; (cielo) clear

diafragma m diaphragm

diagn|osis f diagnosis. ~**osticar** 7 vt diagnose. ~**óstico** m diagnosis

diagonal adj & f diagonal

diagrama m diagram

dialecto m dialect

di|alogar 12 vi talk. ~**álogo** m dialogue; (Pol) talks

diamante m diamond

diámetro m diameter

diana f reveille; (blanco) bull's-eye

diapositiva f slide, transparency

diario adj daily. ●m newspaper; (libro) diary. **a** ~**o** daily. **de** ~**o** everyday, ordinary

diarrea f diarrhoea

dibuj|ante m draughtsman. ●f draughtswoman. ~**ar** vt draw. ~**o**
m drawing. ~**os animados** cartoons

diccionario m dictionary

dich|a f happiness. **por** ~**a** fortunately. ~**o** adj said; (tal) such. ●m saying. ~**o y hecho** no sooner said than done. **mejor** ~**o** rather. **propiamente** ~**o** strictly speaking. ~**oso** adj happy; (afortunado) fortunate

diciembre m December

dicta|do m dictation. ~**dor** m dictator. ~**dura** f dictatorship. ~**men** m opinion; (informe) report. ~**r** vt dictate; pronounce (sentencia etc); (LAm) give (clase)

didáctico adj didactic

dieci|nueve adj & m nineteen. ~**ocho** adj & m eighteen. ~**séis** adj & m sixteen. ~**siete** adj & m seventeen

diente m tooth; (de tenedor) prong; (de ajo) clove. ~ **de león** dandelion. **hablar entre** ~**s** mumble

diestro adj right-handed; (hábil) skillful

dieta f diet

diez adj & m ten

diezmar vt decimate

difamación f (con palabras) slander; (por escrito) libel

diferen|cia f difference; (desacuerdo) disagreement. ~**ciar** vt differentiate between. ~**ciarse** vpr differ. ~**te** adj different; (diversos) various

diferido adj (TV etc) **en** ~ recorded

dif|ícil adj difficult; (poco probable) unlikely. ~**icultad** f difficulty. ~**icultar** vt make difficult

difteria f diphtheria

difundir vt spread; (TV etc) broadcast

difunto adj late, deceased. ●m deceased

difusión f spreading

dige|rir 4 vt digest. ~**stión** f digestion. ~**stivo** adj digestive

digital adj digital; (de los dedos) finger

dign|arse vpr deign to. ~**atario** m dignitary. ~**idad** f dignity. ~**o** adj honourable; (decoroso) decent; (merecedor) worthy (**de** of). ~ **de elogio** praiseworthy

digo vb véase DECIR

dije vb véase DECIR

dilatar vt expand; (Med) dilate; (prolongar) prolong. ~**se** vpr expand; (Med) dilate; (extenderse) extend; (Mex, demorarse) be late

dilema m dilemma

diligen|cia f diligence; (gestión) job; (carruaje) stagecoach. ~**te** adj diligent

dilucidar vt clarify; solve (misterio)

diluir 17 vt dilute

diluvio m flood

dimensión f dimension; (tamaño) size

diminut|ivo adj & m diminutive. ~**o** adj minute

dimitir vt/i resign

Dinamarca f Denmark

dinamarqués adj Danish. ●m Dane

dinámic|a f dynamics. ~**o** adj dynamic

dinamita f dynamite

dínamo m dynamo

dinastía f dynasty

diner|al m fortune. ~**o** m money. ~**o efectivo** cash. ~**o suelto** change

dinosaurio m dinosaur

dios m god. ~**a** f goddess. **¡D~ mío!** good heavens! **¡gracias a D~!** thank God!

diplom|a m diploma. ~**acia** f diplomacy. ~**ado** adj qualified. ~**arse** vpr (LAm) graduate. ~**ático** adj diplomatic. ●m diplomat

diptongo m diphthong

diputa|ción f delegation. ~**ción provincial** county council. ~**do** m deputy; (Pol, en España) member of the Cortes; (Pol, en Inglaterra) Member of Parliament; (Pol, en Estados Unidos) congressman

dique m dike

direc|ción f direction; (señas) address; (los que dirigen) management; (Pol) leadership; (Auto) steering. ~**ción prohibida** no entry. ~**ción única** one-way. ~**ta** f (Auto) top gear. ~**tiva** f board; (Pol) executive committee. ~**tivas** fpl guidelines. ~**to** adj direct; (línea) straight; (tren) through. **en** ~**to** (TV etc) live. ~**tor** m director; (Mus) conductor; (de escuela) headmaster; (de periódico) editor; (gerente) manager. ~**tora** f (de escuela etc) headmistress. ~**torio** m board of directors; (LAm, de teléfonos) telephone directory

dirig|ente adj ruling. ●m & f leader; (de empresa) manager. ~**ir** 14 vt direct; (Mus) conduct; run (empresa etc); address (carta etc). ~**irse** vpr make one's way; (hablar) address

disciplina f discipline. ~**r** vt discipline. ~**rio** adj disciplinary

discípulo m disciple; (alumno) pupil

disco m disc; (Mus) record; (deportes) discus; (de teléfono) dial; (de tráfico) sign; (Rail) signal. ~ **duro** hard disk. ~ **flexible** floppy disk

disconforme adj not in agreement

discord|e adj discordant. ~**ia** f discord

discoteca f discothèque, disco 🔳; (colección de discos) record collection

discreción f discretion

discrepa|ncia f discrepancy; (desacuerdo) disagreement. ~**r** vi differ

discreto adj discreet; (moderado) moderate

discrimina|ción f discrimination. ~**r** vt (distinguir) discriminate between; (tratar injustamente) discriminate against

disculpa f apology; (excusa) excuse. **pedir ~s** apologize. **~r** vt excuse, forgive. **~rse** vpr apologize

discurs|ar vi speak (**sobre** about). **~o** m speech

discusión f discussion; (riña) argument

discuti|ble adj debatable. **~r** vt discuss; (contradecir) contradict. •vi argue (**por** about)

disecar 🗷 vt stuff; (cortar) dissect

diseminar vt disseminate, spread

disentir 🗗 vi disagree (**de** with, **en** on)

diseñ|ador m designer. **~ar** vt design. **~o** m design; (fig) sketch

disertación f dissertation

disfraz m fancy dress; (para engañar) disguise. **~ar** 🔟 vt dress up; (para engañar) disguise. **~arse** vpr. **~arse de** dress up as; (para engañar) disguise o.s. as.

disfrutar vt enjoy. •vi enjoy o.s. **~ de** enjoy

disgust|ar vt displease; (molestar) annoy. **~arse** vpr get annoyed, get upset; (dos personas) fall out. **~o** m annoyance; (problema) trouble; (riña) quarrel; (dolor) sorrow, grief

disidente adj & m & f dissident

disimular vt conceal. •vi pretend

disipar vt dissipate; (derrochar) squander

dislocarse 🗷 vpr dislocate

disminu|ción f decrease. **~ir** 🗓 vi diminish

disolver 🖸 (pp **disuelto**) vt dissolve. **~se** vpr dissolve

dispar adj different

disparar vt fire; (Mex, pagar) buy. •vi shoot (**contra** at)

disparate m silly thing; (error) mistake. **decir ~s** talk nonsense. **¡qué ~!** how ridiculous!

disparidad f disparity

disparo m (acción) firing; (tiro) shot

dispensar vt give; (eximir) exempt. •vi. **¡Vd dispense!** forgive me

dispers|ar vt scatter, disperse. **~arse** vpr scatter, disperse. **~ión** f dispersion. **~o** adj scattered

dispon|er 🗷 vt arrange; (Jurid) order. •vi. **~er de** have; (vender etc) dispose of. **~erse** vpr prepare (**a** to). **~ibilidad** f availability. **~ible** adj available

disposición f arrangement; (aptitud) talent; (disponibilidad) disposal; (Jurid) order, decree. **~ de ánimo** frame of mind. **a la ~ de** at the disposal of. **a su ~** at your service

dispositivo m device

dispuesto adj ready; (persona) disposed (**a** to); (servicial) helpful

disputa f dispute; (pelea) argument

disquete m diskette, floppy disk

dista|ncia f distance. **a ~ncia** from a distance. **guardar las ~ncias** keep one's distance. **~nciar** vt space out; distance (amigos). **~nciarse** vpr (dos personas) fall out. **~nte** adj distant. **~r** vi be away; (fig) be far. **~ 5 kilómetros** it's 5 kilometres away

distin|ción f distinction; (honor) award. **~guido** adj distinguished. **~guir** 🗓 vt/i distinguish. **~guirse** vpr distinguish o.s.; (diferenciarse) differ. **~tivo** adj distinctive. •m badge. **~to** adj different, distinct

distra|cción f amusement; (descuido) absent-mindedness, inattention. **~er** 🗓 vt distract; (divertir) amuse. **~erse** vpr amuse o.s.; (descuidarse) not pay attention. **~ído** adj (desatento) absent-minded

distribu|ción f distribution. **~idor** m distributor. **~ir** 🗓 vt distribute

distrito m district

disturbio m disturbance

disuadir vt deter, dissuade

diurno adj daytime

divagar 🔢 vi digress; (hablar sin sentido) ramble

diván m settee, sofa

diversi|dad f diversity. **~ficar** 🔢 vt diversify

diversión f amusement, entertainment; (pasatiempo) pastime

diverso adj different

diverti|do adj amusing; (que tiene gracia) funny. **~r** 🔢 vt amuse, entertain. **~rse** vpr enjoy o.s.

dividir vt divide; (repartir) share out

divino adj divine

divisa f emblem. **~s** fpl currency

divisar vt make out

división f division

divorci|ado adj divorced. ● m divorcee. **~ar** vt divorce. **~arse** vpr get divorced. **~o** m divorce

divulgar 🔢 vt spread; divulge (secreto)

dizque adv (LAm) apparently; (supuestamente) supposedly

do m C; (solfa) doh

dobl|adillo m hem; (de pantalón) turn-up (Brit), cuff (Amer). **~ar** vt double; (plegar) fold; (torcer) bend; turn (esquina); dub (película). ● vi turn; (campana) toll. **~arse** vpr double; (curvarse) bend. **~e** adj double. ● m double. **el ~e** twice as much (**de, que** as). **~egar** 🔢 vt (fig) force to give in. **~egarse** vpr give in

doce adj & m twelve. **~na** f dozen

docente adj teaching. ● m & f teacher

dócil adj obedient

doctor m doctor. **~ado** m doctorate

doctrina f doctrine

document|ación f documentation, papers. **~al** adj & m documentary. **~o** m document. **🔳D~o Nacional de Identidad** identity card

dólar m dollar

dolarizar vt dollarize

dol|er 🔢 vi hurt, ache; (fig) grieve. **me duele la cabeza** I have a headache. **le duele el estómago** he has (a) stomach-ache. **~or** m pain; (sordo) ache; (fig) sorrow. **~or de cabeza** headache. **~or de muelas** toothache. **~oroso** adj painful

domar vt tame; break in (caballo)

dom|esticar 🔢 vt domesticate. **~éstico** adj domestic

domicili|ar vt. **~ar los pagos** pay by direct debit. **~o** m address. **~o particular** home address. **reparto a ~** home delivery service

domina|nte adj dominant; (persona) domineering. **~r** vt dominate; (contener) control; (fig) have a good command of. ● vi dominate. **~rse** vpr control o.s.

domingo m Sunday

dominio m authority; (territorio) domain; (fig) command

dominó m (pl **~s**) dominoes; (ficha) domino

don m talent, gift; (en un sobre) Mr. **~ Pedro** Pedro

donación f donation

donaire m grace, charm

dona|nte m & f (de sangre) donor. **~r** vt donate

doncella f maiden; (criada) maid

donde adv where

dónde adv where?; (LAm, cómo) how; **¿hasta ~?** how far? **¿por ~?** whereabouts?; (¿por qué camino?) which way? **¿a ~ vas?** where are you going? **¿de ~ eres?** where are you from?

dondequiera adv. **~ que** wherever. **por ~** everywhere

doña f (en un sobre) Mrs. **~ María** María

dora|do adj golden; (cubierto de oro)

🔳 see A-Z of Spanish life and culture

gilt. ~r vt gilt; (Culin) brown

dormi|do adj asleep. **quedarse ~do** fall asleep; (no despertar) oversleep. ~r 🔲 vt send to sleep. • vi sleep. ~rse vpr fall asleep. ~r **la siesta** have an afternoon nap, have a siesta. ~tar vi doze. ~torio m bedroom

dors|al adj back. • m (en deportes) number. ~o m back. **nadar de ~** (Mex) do (the) backstroke

dos adj & m two. **de ~ en ~** in twos, in pairs. **los ~, las ~** both (of them). ~cientos adj & m two hundred

dosi|ficar 🔲 vt dose; (fig) measure out. ~s f invar dose

dot|ado adj gifted. ~ar vt give a dowry; (proveer) provide (**de** with). ~e m dowry

doy vb véase DAR

dragar 🔲 vt dredge

drama m drama; (obra de teatro) play. ~turgo m playwright

drástico adj drastic

droga f drug. ~dicto m drug addict. ~do m drug addict. ~r 🔲 vt drug. ~rse vpr take drugs

droguería f hardware store

ducha f shower. ~rse vpr have a shower

dud|a f doubt. **poner en ~a**

question. **sin ~a (alguna)** without a doubt. ~ar vt/i doubt. ~oso adj doubtful; (sospechoso) dubious

duelo m duel; (luto) mourning

duende m imp

dueñ|a f owner, proprietress; (de una pensión) landlady. ~o m owner, proprietor; (de una pensión) landlord

duermo vb véase DORMIR

dul|ce adj sweet; (agua) fresh; (suave) soft, gentle. • m (LAm) sweet. ~zura f sweetness; (fig) gentleness

duna f dune

dúo m duet, duo

duplica|do adj duplicated. **por ~** in duplicate. • m duplicate. ~r 🔲 vt duplicate. ~rse vpr double

duque m duke. ~sa f duchess

dura|ción f duration, length. ~dero adj lasting. ~nte prep during; (medida de tiempo) for. ~ **todo el año** all year round. ~r vi last

durazno m (LAm, fruta) peach

dureza f hardness; (Culin) toughness; (fig) harshness

duro adj hard; (Culin) tough; (fig) harsh. • adv (esp LAm) hard

DVD m (**Disco Versátil Digital**) DVD. ~teca f DVD library

Ee

e conj and

Ébola m ebola

ebrio adj drunk

ebullición f boiling

eccema m eczema

....

echar vt throw; post (carta); give off (olor); pour (líquido); (expulsar) expel; (de recinto) throw out; fire (empleado); (poner) put on; get (gasolina); put out (raíces); show (película). ~ **a** start. ~ **a perder** spoil. ~ **de menos** miss. ~se **atrás** (fig) back down. **echárselas de** feign. ~se vpr throw o.s.;

(tumbarse) lie down

eclesiástico adj ecclesiastical

eclipse m eclipse

eco m echo. **hacerse ~ de** echo

ecolog|ía f ecology. **~ista** m & f ecologist

economato m cooperative store

econ|omía f economy; (ciencia) economics. **~ómico** adj economic; (no caro) inexpensive. **~omista** m & f economist. **~omizar** 10 vt/i economize

ecoturismo m ecotourism

ecuación f equation

ecuador m equator. **el E~** the Equator. **E~** (país) Ecuador

ecuánime adj level-headed; (imparcial) impartial

ecuatoriano adj & m Ecuadorian

ecuestre adj equestrian

edad f age. **~ avanzada** old age. **E~ de Piedra** Stone Age. **E~ Media** Middle Ages. **¿qué ~ tiene?** how old is he?

edición f edition; (publicación) publication

edicto m edict

edific|ación f building. **~ante** adj edifying. **~ar** 7 vt build; (fig) edify. **~io** m building; (fig) structure

edit|ar vt edit; (publicar) publish. **~or** adj publishing. ●m editor; (que publica) publisher. **~orial** adj editorial. ●m leading article. ●f publishing house

edredón m duvet

educa|ción f upbringing; (modales) (good) manners; (enseñanza) education. **falta de ~ción** rudeness, bad manners. **~do** adj polite. **bien ~do** polite. **mal ~do** rude. **~r** 7 vt bring up; (enseñar) educate. **~tivo** adj educational

edulcorante m sweetener

EE.UU. abrev (**Estados Unidos**) USA

efect|ivamente adv really; (por supuesto) indeed. **~ivo** adj effective; (auténtico) real. ●m cash. **~o** m effect; (impresión) impression. **en ~o** really; (como respuesta) indeed. **~os** mpl belongings; (Com) goods. **~uar** 21 vt carry out; make (viaje, compras etc)

efervescente adj effervescent; (bebidas) fizzy

efica|cia f effectiveness; (de persona) efficiency. **~z** adj effective; (persona) efficient

eficien|cia f efficiency. **~te** adj efficient

efímero adj ephemeral

efusi|vidad f effusiveness. **~vo** adj effusive; (persona) demonstrative

egipcio adj & m Egyptian

Egipto m Egypt

ego|ísmo m selfishness, egotism. **~ísta** adj selfish

egresar vi (LAm) graduate; (de colegio) leave school, graduate (Amer)

eje m axis; (Tec) axle

ejecu|ción f execution; (Mus) performance. **~tar** vt carry out; (Mus) perform; (matar) execute. **~tivo** m executive

ejempl|ar adj exemplary; (ideal) model. ●m specimen; (libro) copy; (revista) issue, number. **~ificar** 7 vt exemplify. **~o** m example. **dar (el) ~o** set an example. **por ~o** for example

ejerc|er 9 vt exercise; practise (profesión); exert (influencia). ●vi practise. **~icio** m exercise; (de profesión) practice. **hacer ~icios** take exercise. **~itar** vt exercise

ejército m army

ejido m (Mex) cooperative

ejote m (Mex) green bean

el artículo definido masculino (pl **los**)

The masculine article **el** is also used before feminine nouns which begin with stressed **a** or **ha**, e.g. **el ala derecha, el hada madrina.** Also, **de** followed by **el** becomes **del** and **el** preceded by **a** becomes **al**

⋯▸ the. **el tren de las seis** the six o'clock train. **el vecino de al lado** the next-door neighbour. **cerca del hospital** near the hospital

⋯▸ No se traduce en los siguientes casos: (con *nombre abstracto, genérico*) **el tiempo vuela** time flies. **odio el queso** I hate cheese. **el hilo es muy durable** linen is very durable

⋯▸ (con *colores, días de la semana*) **el rojo está de moda** red is in fashion. **el lunes es fiesta** Monday is a holiday

⋯▸ (con *algunas instituciones*) **termino el colegio mañana** I finish school tomorrow. **lo ingresaron en el hospital** he was admitted to hospital

⋯▸ (con *nombres propios*) **el Sr. Díaz** Mr Díaz. **el doctor Lara** Doctor Lara

⋯▸ (antes de infinitivo) **es muy cuidadosa en el vestir** she takes great care in the way she dresses. **me di cuenta al verlo** I realized when I saw him

⋯▸ (con *partes del cuerpo, artículos personales*) se traduce por un posesivo. **apretó el puño** he clenched his fist. **tienes el zapato desatado** your shoe is undone

⋯▸ **el + de. es de Pedro** it's Pedro's. **el del sombrero** the one with the hat

⋯▸ **el + que** (*persona*) **el que me atendió** the one who served me. (*cosa*) **el que se rompió** the one that broke.

⋯▸ **el + que** + subjuntivo

⚑ see A-Z of Spanish life and culture

(*quienquiera*) whoever. **el que gane la lotería** whoever wins the lottery. (*cualquiera*) whichever. **compra el que sea más barato** buy whichever is cheaper

él pron (*persona*) he; (*persona con prep*) him; (*cosa*) it. **es de** ~ it's his

elabora|ción f elaboration; (*fabricación*) manufacture. ~**r** vt elaborate; manufacture (*producto*); (*producir*) produce

el|asticidad f elasticity. ~**ástico** adj & m elastic

⚑ **elec|ción** f choice; (*de político etc*) election. ~**ciones** fpl (Pol) election. ~**tor** m voter. ~**torado** m electorate. ~**toral** adj electoral; (*campaña*) election

electrici|dad f electricity. ~**sta** m & f electrician

eléctrico adj electric; (*aparato*) electrical

electri|ficar 🛈 vt electrify. ~**zar** 🛈 vt electrify

electrocutar vt electrocute. ~**se** vpr be electrocuted

electrodoméstico adj electrical appliance

electrónic|a f electronics. ~**o** adj electronic

elefante m elephant

elegan|cia f elegance. ~**te** adj elegant

elegía f elegy

elegi|ble adj eligible. ~**do** adj chosen. ~**r** 🛈 & 🛈 vt choose; (*por votación*) elect

element|al adj elementary; (*esencial*) fundamental. ~**o** m element; (*persona*) person, bloke (Brit, fam). ~**os** mpl (*nociones*) basic principles

elenco m (*en el teatro*) cast

eleva|ción f elevation; (*de precios*) rise, increase; (*acción*) raising. ~**dor** m (Mex) lift (Brit), elevator

(Amer). ~r vt raise; (promover) promote

elimina|ción f elimination. ~r vt eliminate; (Informática) delete. ~**toria** f preliminary heat

élite /e'lit, e'lite/ f elite

ella pron (persona) she; (persona con prep) her; (cosa) it. **es de ~s** it's theirs. ~**s** pron pl they; (con prep) them. **es de ~** it's hers

ello pron it

ellos pron pl they; (con prep) them. **es de ~** it's theirs

elocuen|cia f eloquence. ~**te** adj eloquent

elogi|ar vt praise. ~**o** m praise

elote m (Mex) corncob; (Culin) corn on the cob

eludir vt avoid, elude

emanar vi emanate (**de** from); (originarse) originate (**de** from, in)

emancipa|ción f emancipation. ~r vt emancipate. ~**rse** vpr become emancipated

embadurnar vt smear

embajad|a f embassy. ~**or** m ambassador

embalar vt pack

embaldosar vt tile

embalsamar vt embalm

embalse m reservoir

embaraz|ada adj pregnant. • f pregnant woman. ~**ar** 10 vt get pregnant. ~**o** m pregnancy; (apuro) embarrassment; (estorbo) hindrance. ~**oso** adj awkward, embarrassing

embar|cación f vessel. ~**cadero** m jetty, pier. ~**car** 7 vt load (mercancías etc). ~**carse** vpr board. ~**carse en** (fig) embark upon

embargo m embargo; (Jurid) seizure. **sin ~** however

embarque m loading; (de pasajeros) boarding

embaucar 7 vt trick

embelesar vt captivate

embellecer 11 vt make beautiful

embesti|da f charge. ~r 5 vt/i charge

emblema m emblem

embolsarse vpr pocket

embonar vt (Mex) fit

emborrachar vt get drunk. ~**se** vpr get drunk

emboscada f ambush

embotar vt dull

embotella|miento m (de vehículos) traffic jam. ~r vt bottle

embrague m clutch

embriag|arse 12 vpr get drunk. ~**uez** f drunkenness

embrión m embryo

embroll|ar vt mix up; involve (persona). ~**arse** vpr get into a muddle; (en un asunto) get involved. ~**o** m tangle; (fig) muddle

embruj|ado adj bewitched; (casa) haunted. ~**ar** vt bewitch. ~**o** m spell

embrutecer 11 vt brutalize

embudo m funnel

embuste m lie. ~**ro** adj deceitful. • m liar

embuti|do m (Culin) sausage. ~r vt stuff

emergencia f emergency

emerger 14 vi appear, emerge

emigra|ción f emigration. ~**nte** adj & m & f emigrant. ~r vi emigrate

eminen|cia f eminence. ~**te** adj eminent

emisario m emissary

emi|sión f emission; (de dinero) issue; (TV etc) broadcast. ~**sor** adj issuing; (TV etc) broadcasting. ~**sora** f radio station. ~**tir** vt emit, give out; (TV etc) broadcast; cast (voto); (poner en circulación) issue

emoci|ón f emotion; (excitación) excitement. **¡qué ~ón!** how

exciting!. ~onado adj moved.
~onante adj exciting; (conmovedor)
moving. ~onar vt move. ~onarse
vpr get excited; (conmoverse) be
moved

emotivo adj emotional; (conmovedor)
moving

empacar 7 vt (LAm) pack

empacho m indigestion

empadronar vt register. ~se vpr
register

empalagoso adj sickly; (persona)
cloying

empalizada f fence

empalm|ar vt connect, join. •vi
meet. ~e m junction; (de trenes)
connection

empan|ada f (savoury) pie; (LAm,
individual) pasty. ~adilla f pasty

empantanarse vpr become
swamped; (coche) get bogged down

empañar vt steam up; (fig) tarnish.
~se vpr steam up

empapar vt soak. ~se vpr get
soaked

empapela|do m wallpaper. ~r vt
wallpaper

empaquetar vt package

emparedado m sandwich

emparentado adj related

empast|ar vt fill (muela). ~e m
filling

empat|ar vi draw. ~e m draw

empedernido adj confirmed;
(bebedor) inveterate

empedrar 1 vt pave

empeine m instep

empeñ|ado adj in debt; (decidido)
determined (**en** to). ~ar vt pawn;
pledge (palabra). ~arse vpr get into
debt; (estar decidido a) be
determined (**en** to). ~o m pledge;
(resolución) determination. **casa** f
de ~s pawnshop. ~oso adj (LAm)
hardworking

empeorar vt make worse. •vi get

worse. ~se vpr get worse

empequeñecer 11 vt become
smaller; (fig) belittle

empera|dor m emperor. ~triz f
empress

empezar 1 & 10 vt/i start, begin.
para ~ to begin with

empina|do adj (cuesta) steep. ~r vt
raise. ~rse vpr (persona) stand on
tiptoe

empírico adj empirical

emplasto m plaster

emplaza|miento m (Jurid)
summons; (lugar) site. ~r 10 vt
summon; (situar) site

emple|ada f employee; (doméstica)
maid. ~ado m employee. ~ar vt
use; employ (persona); spend
(tiempo). ~arse vpr get a job. ~o m
use; (trabajo) employment; (puesto)
job

empobrecer 11 vt impoverish.
~se vpr become poor

empoll|ar vt incubate (huevos); (arg,
estudiar) cram 1. •vi (ave) sit;
(estudiante) ⊠ cram. ~ón m ⊠ swot
(Brit, fam), grind (Amer, fam)

empolvarse vpr powder

empotra|do adj built-in, fitted.
~r vt fit

emprende|dor adj enterprising.
~r vt undertake; set out on (viaje).
~rla con uno pick a fight with
s.o.

empresa f undertaking; (Com)
company, firm. ~ **puntocom** dot-
com company. ~rio m
businessman; (patrón) employer;
(de teatro etc) impresario

empuj|ar vt push. ~e m (fig) drive.
~ón m push, shove

empuña|dura f handle

emular vt emulate

en prep in; (sobre) on; (dentro) inside,
in; (medio de transporte) by. ~ **casa** at
home. ~ **coche** by car. ~ **10 días**
in 10 days. **de pueblo ~ pueblo**
from town to town

enagua f petticoat

enajena|ción f alienation. **~ción mental** insanity. **~r** vt alienate; (volver loco) derange

enamora|do adj in love. ●m lover. **~r** vt win the love of. **~rse** vpr fall in love (**de** with)

enano adj & m dwarf

enardecer 11 vt inflame. **~se** vpr get excited (**por** about)

encabeza|do m (Mex) headline. **~miento** m heading; (de periódico) headline. **~r** 10 vt head; lead (revolución etc)

encabritarse vpr rear up

encadenar vt chain; (fig) tie down

encaj|ar vt fit; fit together (varias piezas). ●vi fit; (cuadrar) tally. **~arse** vpr put on. **~e** m lace; (Com) reserve

encaminar vt direct. **~se** vpr make one's way

encandilar vt dazzle; (estimular) stimulate

encant|ado adj enchanted; (persona) delighted. **¡~ado!** pleased to meet you! **~ador** adj charming. **~amiento** m spell. **~ar** vt bewitch; (fig) charm, delight. **me ~a la leche** I love milk. **~o** m spell; (fig) delight

encapricharse vpr. **~ con** take a fancy to

encarar vt face; (LAm) stand up to (persona). **~se** vpr. **~se con** stand up to

encarcelar vt imprison

encarecer 11 vt put up the price of. **~se** vpr become more expensive

encarg|ado adj in charge. ●m manager, person in charge. **~ar** 12 vt entrust; (pedir) order. **~arse** vpr take charge (**de** of). **~o** m job; (Com) order; (recado) errand. **hecho de ~o** made to measure

encariñarse vpr. **~ con** take to, become fond of

encarna|ción f incarnation. **~do** adj incarnate; (rojo) red; (uña) ingrowing. ●m red

encarnizado adj bitter

encarpetar vt file; (LAm, dar carpetazo) shelve

encarrilar vt put back on the rails; (fig) direct, put on the right track

encasillar vt classify; (fig) pigeonhole

encauzar 10 vt channel

enceguecer vt 11 (LAm) blind

encend|edor m lighter. **~er** 1 vt light; switch on, turn on (aparato eléctrico); start (motor); (fig) arouse. **~erse** vpr light; (aparato eléctrico) come on; (excitarse) get excited; (ruborizarse) blush. **~ido** adj lit; (aparato eléctrico) on; (rojo) bright red. ●m (Auto) ignition

encera|do adj waxed. ●m (pizarra) blackboard. **~r** vt wax

encerr|ar 1 vt shut in; (con llave) lock up; (fig, contener) contain. **~ona** f trap

enchilar vt (Mex) add chili to

enchinar vt (Mex) perm

enchuf|ado adj switched on. **~ar** vt plug in; fit together (tubos etc). **~e** m socket; (clavija) plug; (de tubos etc) joint; (fam, influencia) contact. **tener ~e** have friends in the right places

encía f gum

enciclopedia f encyclopaedia

encierro m confinement; (cárcel) prison

encim|a adv on top; (arriba) above. **~ de** on, on top of; (sobre) over; (además de) besides, as well as. **por ~** on top; (adj la ligera) superficially. **por ~ de todo** above all. **~ar** vt (Mex) stack up. **~era** f worktop

encina f holm oak

encinta adj pregnant

enclenque adj weak; (enfermizo) sickly

encoger 14 vt shrink; (contraer) contract. **~se** vpr shrink. **~erse de hombros** shrug one's shoulders

encolar vt glue; (pegar) stick

encolerizar 10 vt make angry. **~se** vpr get furious

encomendar 1 vt entrust

encomi|ar vt praise. **~o** m praise. **~oso** adj (LAm) complimentary

encono m bitterness, ill will

encontra|do adj contrary, conflicting. **~r** 2 vt find; (tropezar con) meet. **~rse** vpr meet; (hallarse) be. **no ~rse** feel uncomfortable

encorvar vt hunch. **~se** vpr stoop

encrespa|do adj (pelo) curly; (mar) rough. **~r** vt curl (pelo); make rough (mar)

encrucijada f crossroads

encuaderna|ción f binding. **~dor** m bookbinder. **~r** vt bind

encub|ierto adj hidden. **~rir** (pp **encubierto**) vt hide, conceal; cover up (delito); shelter (delincuente)

encuentro m meeting; (en deportes) match; (Mil) encounter

encuesta f survey; (investigación) inquiry

encumbrado adj eminent; (alto) high

encurtidos mpl pickles

endeble adj weak

endemoniado adj possessed; (muy malo) wretched

enderezar 10 vt straighten out; (poner vertical) put upright; (fig, arreglar) put right, sort out; (dirigir) direct. **~se** vpr straighten out

endeudarse vpr get into debt

endiablado adj possessed; (malo) terrible; (difícil) difficult

endosar vt endorse (cheque)

endulzar 10 vt sweeten; (fig) soften

endurecer 11 vt harden. **~se** vpr harden

enemi|go adj enemy. **•**m enemy. **~stad** f enmity. **~star** vt make an enemy of. **~starse** vpr fall out (con with)

en|ergía f energy. **~érgico** adj (persona) lively; (decisión) forceful

energúmeno m madman

enero m January

enésimo adj nth, umpteenth 1

enfad|ado adj angry; (molesto) annoyed. **~ar** vt make cross, anger; (molestar) annoy. **~arse** vpr get angry; (molestarse) get annoyed. **~o** m anger; (molestia) annoyance

énfasis m invar emphasis, stress. **poner ~** stress, emphasize

enfático adj emphatic

enferm|ar vi fall ill. **~arse** vpr (LAm) fall ill. **~edad** f illness. **~era** f nurse. **~ería** f sick bay; (carrera) nursing. **~ero** m (male) nurse **~izo** adj sickly. **~o** adj ill. **•**m patient

enflaquecer 11 vt make thin. **•**vi lose weight

enfo|car 7 vt shine on; focus (lente); (fig) approach. **~que** m focus; (fig) approach

enfrentar vt face, confront; (poner frente a frente) bring face to face. **~se** vpr. **~se con** confront; (en deportes) meet

enfrente adv opposite. **~ de** opposite. **de ~** opposite

enfria|miento m cooling; (catarro) cold. **~r** 20 vt cool (down); (fig) cool down. **~rse** vpr go cold; (fig) cool off

enfurecer 11 vt infuriate. **~se** vpr get furious

engalanar vt adorn. **~se** vpr dress up

enganchar vt hook; hang up (ropa). **~se** vpr get caught; (Mil) enlist

engañ|ar vt deceive, trick; (ser infiel) be unfaithful. **~arse** vpr be wrong, be mistaken; (no admitir la verdad) deceive o.s. **~o** m deceit, trickery; (error) mistake. **~oso** adj deceptive; (persona) deceitful

engarzar ⑩ vt string (cuentas); set (joyas)

engatusar vt ① coax

engendr|ar vt father; (fig) breed. **~o** m (monstruo) monster; (fig) brainchild

englobar vt include

engomar vt glue

engordar vt fatten, gain (kilo). ●vi get fatter, put on weight

engorro m nuisance

engranaje m (Auto) gear

engrandecer ⑪ vt (enaltecer) exalt, raise

engrasar vt grease; (con aceite) oil; (ensuciar) get grease on

engreído adj arrogant

engullir ㉒ vt gulp down

enhebrar vt thread

enhorabuena f congratulations. **dar la ~** congratulate

enigm|a m enigma. **~ático** adj enigmatic

enjabonar vt soap. **~se** vpr to soap o.s.

enjambre m swarm

enjaular vt put in a cage

enjuag|ar ⑫ vt rinse. **~ue** m rinsing; (para la boca) mouthwash

enjugar ⑫ vt wipe (away)

enjuiciar vt pass judgement on

enjuto adj (persona) skinny

enlace m connection; (matrimonial) wedding

enlatar vt tin, can

enlazar ⑩ vt link; tie together (cintas); (Mex, casar) marry

enlodar vt, **enlodazar** ⑩ vt cover in mud

enloquecer ⑪ vt drive mad. ●vi go mad. **~se** vpr go mad

enlosar vt (con losas) pave; (con baldosas) tile

enmarañar vt tangle (up), entangle; (confundir) confuse. **~se** vpr get into a tangle; (confundirse) get confused

enmarcar ⑦ vt frame

enm|endar vt correct. **~endarse** vpr mend one's way. **~ienda** f correction; (de ley etc) amendment

enmohecerse ⑪ vpr (con óxido) go rusty; (con hongos) go mouldy

enmudecer ⑪ vi be dumbstruck; (callar) fall silent

ennegrecer ⑪ vt blacken

ennoblecer ⑪ vt ennoble; (fig) add style to

enoj|adizo adj irritable. **~ado** adj angry; (molesto) annoyed. **~ar** vt anger; (molestar) annoy. **~arse** vpr get angry; (molestarse) get annoyed. **~o** m anger; (molestia) annoyance. **~oso** adj annoying

enorgullecerse ⑪ vpr be proud

enorm|e adj huge, enormous. **~emente** adv enormously. **~idad** f immensity; (de crimen) enormity

enraizado adj deeply rooted

enrarecido adj rarefied

enred|adera f creeper. **~ar** vt tangle (up), entangle; (confundir) confuse; (involucrar) involve. **~arse** vpr get tangled; (confundirse) get confused; (persona) get involved (**con** with). **~o** m tangle; (fig) muddle, mess

enrejado m bars

enriquecer ⑪ vt make rich; (fig) enrich. **~se** vpr get rich

enrojecerse ⑪ vpr (persona) go red, blush

enrolar vt enlist

enrollar vt roll (up), wind (hilo etc)

enroscar ⑦ vt coil; (atornillar) screw in

ensalad|a f salad. **armar una ~a** make a mess. **~era** f salad bowl.

e

~illa f Russian salad

ensalzar 10 vt praise; (enaltecer) exalt

ensambla|dura f, **ensamblaje** m (acción) assembling; (efecto) joint. ~r vt join

ensanch|ar vt widen; (agrandar) enlarge. ~**arse** vpr get wider. ~**e** m widening

ensangrentar 1 vt stain with blood

ensañarse vpr. ~ **con** treat cruelly

ensartar vt string (cuentas etc)

ensay|ar vt test; rehearse (obra de teatro etc). ~**o** m test, trial; (composición literaria) essay

enseguida adv at once, immediately

ensenada f inlet, cove

enseña|nza f education; (acción de enseñar) teaching. ~**nza media** secondary education. ~**r** vt teach; (mostrar) show

enseres mpl equipment

ensillar vt saddle

ensimismarse vpr be lost in thought

ensombrecer 11 vt darken

ensordecer 11 vt deafen. ●vi go deaf

ensuciar vt dirty. ~**se** vpr get dirty

ensueño m dream

entablar vt (empezar) start

entablillar vt put in a splint

entallar vt tailor (un vestido). ●vi fit

entarimado m parquet; (plataforma) platform

ente m entity, being; (fam, persona rara) weirdo; (Com) firm, company

entend|er 1 vt understand; (opinar) believe, think. ●vi understand. ~**er de** know about. **a mi** ~**er** in my opinion. **dar a** ~**er** hint. **darse a** ~**er** make o.s. understood. ~**erse** vpr make o.s. understood;

(comprenderse) be understood. ~**erse con** get on with. ~**ido** adj understood; (enterado) well-informed. **no darse por** ~**ido** pretend not to understand. ●interj agreed!, OK! 🇹. ~**imiento** m understanding

entera|do adj well-informed; (que sabe) aware. **darse por** ~**do** take the hint. ~**r** vt inform (**de** of). ~**rse** vpr. ~**rse de** find out about, hear of. **¡entérate!** listen! **¿te** ~**s?** do you understand?

entereza f (carácter) strength of character

enternecer 11 vt (fig) move, touch. ~**se** vpr be moved, be touched

entero adj entire, whole. **por** ~ entirely, completely

enterra|dor m gravedigger. ~**r** 1 vt bury

entibiar vt (enfriar) cool; (calentar) warm (up). ~**se** vpr (enfriarse) cool down; (fig) cool; (calentarse) get warm

entidad f entity; (organización) organization; (Com) company; (importancia) significance

entierro m burial; (ceremonia) funeral

entona|ción f intonation. ~**r** vt intone; sing (nota). ●vi (Mus) be in tune; (colores) match. ~**rse** vpr (emborracharse) get tipsy

entonces adv then. **en aquel** ~ at that time, then

entorn|ado adj (puerta) ajar; (ventana) slightly open. ~**o** m environment; (en literatura) setting

entorpecer 11 vt dull; slow down (tráfico); (dificultar) hinder

entra|da f entrance; (incorporación) admission, entry; (para cine etc) ticket; (de datos, Tec) input; (de una comida) starter. **de** ~**da** right away. ~**do** adj. ~**do en años** elderly. **ya** ~**da la noche** late at night. ~**nte** adj next, coming

entraña f (fig) heart. ~**s** fpl entrails; (fig) heart. ~**ble** adj (cariño) deep; (amigo) close. ~r vt involve

entrar vt (traer) bring in; (llevar) take in. •vi go in, enter; (venir) come in, enter; (empezar) start, begin; (incorporarse) join. ~ **en**, (LAm) ~ **a** go into

entre prep (dos personas o cosas) between; (más de dos) among(st)

entre|abierto adj half-open. ~**abrir** (pp **entreabierto**) vt half open. ~**acto** m interval. ~**cejo** m forehead. **fruncir el ~cejo** frown. ~**cerrar** ① vt (LAm) half close. ~**cortado** adj (voz) faltering; (respiración) laboured. ~**cruzar** ⑩ vt intertwine

entrega f handing over; (de mercancías etc) delivery; (de novela etc) instalment; (dedicación) commitment. ~**r** ⑫ vt deliver; (dar) give; hand in (deberes); hand over (poder). ~**rse** vpr surrender, give o.s. up; (dedicarse) devote o.s. (**a** to)

entre|lazar ⑩ vt intertwine. ~**més** m hors-d'oeuvre; (en el teatro) short comedy. ~**mezclar** vt intermingle

entrena|dor m trainer ~**miento** m training. ~**r** vt train. ~**rse** vpr train

entre|pierna f crotch; medida inside leg measurement. ~**piso** m (LAm) mezzanine. ~**sacar** ⑦ vt pick out; (peluquería) thin out ~**suelo** m mezzanine; (de cine) dress circle ~**tanto** adv meanwhile, in the meantime ~**tejer** vt weave; (entrelazar) interweave

entreten|ción f (LAm) entertainment. ~**er** ⑩ vt entertain, amuse; (detener) delay, keep. ~**erse** vpr amuse o.s.; (tardar) delay, linger. ~**ido** adj (con ser) entertaining; (con estar) busy. ~**imiento** m entertainment

entrever ⑭ vt make out, glimpse

entrevista f interview; (reunión)

meeting. ~**rse** vpr have an interview

entristecer ⑪ vt sadden, make sad. ~**se** vpr grow sad

entromet|erse vpr interfere. ~**ido** adj interfering

entumec|erse ⑪ vpr go numb. ~**ido** adj numb

enturbiar vt cloud

entusi|asmar vt fill with enthusiasm; (gustar mucho) delight. ~**asmarse** vpr. ~**asmarse con** get enthusiastic about. ~**asmo** m enthusiasm. ~**asta** adj enthusiastic. •m & f enthusiast

enumerar vt enumerate

envalentonar vt encourage. ~**se** vpr become bolder

envas|ado m packaging; (en latas) canning; (en botellas) bottling. ~**ar** vt package; (en latas) tin, can; (en botellas) bottle. ~**e** m packaging; (lata) tin, can; (botella) bottle

envejec|er ⑪ vt make (look) older. •vi age, grow old. ~**erse** vpr age, grow old

envenenar vt poison

envergadura f importance

envia|do m envoy; (de la prensa) correspondent. ~**r** ⑳ vt send

enviciarse vpr become addicted (**con** to)

envidi|a f envy; (celos) jealousy. ~**ar** vt envy, be envious of. ~**oso** adj envious; (celoso) jealous. **tener ~a a** envy

envío m sending, dispatch; (de mercancías) consignment; (de dinero) remittance. ~ **contra reembolso** cash on delivery. **gastos** mpl **de ~** postage and packing (costs)

enviudar vi be widowed

env|oltura f wrapping. ~**olver** ② (pp **envuelto**) vt wrap; (cubrir) cover; (rodear) surround; (fig, enredar) involve. ~**uelto** adj wrapped (up)

enyesar vt plaster; (Med) put in plaster

épica f epic

épico adj epic

epid|emia f epidemic. ~**émico** adj epidemic

epil|epsia f epilepsy. ~**éptico** adj epileptic

epílogo m epilogue

episodio m episode

epístola f epistle

epitafio m epitaph

época f age; (período) period. **hacer ~** make history, be epoch-making

equidad f equity

equilibr|ado adj (well-)balanced. ~**ar** vt balance. ~**io** m balance; (de balanza) equilibrium. ~**ista** m & f tightrope walker

equinoccio m equinox

equipaje m luggage (esp Brit), baggage (esp Amer)

equipar vt equip; (de ropa) fit out

equiparar vt make equal; (comparar) compare

equipo m equipment; (de personas) team

equitación f riding

equivale|nte adj equivalent. ~**r** 42 vi be equivalent; (significar) mean

equivoca|ción f mistake, error. ~**do** wrong. ~**rse** vpr make a mistake; (estar en error) be wrong, be mistaken. ~**rse de** be wrong about. ~**rse de número** dial the wrong number. **si no me equivoco** if I'm not mistaken

equívoco adj equivocal; (sospechoso) suspicious ● m misunderstanding; (error) mistake

era f era. ● vb véase **SER**

erario m treasury

erección f erection

eres vb véase **SER**

erguir 48 vt raise. ~**se** vpr raise

erigir 14 vt erect. ~**se** vpr. ~**se en** set o.s. up as; (llegar a ser) become

eriza|do adj prickly. ~**rse** 10 vpr stand on end; (LAm) (persona) get goose pimples

erizo m hedgehog; (de mar) sea urchin. ~ **de mar** sea urchin

ermita f hermitage. ~**ño** m hermit

erosi|ón f erosion. ~**onar** vt erode

er|ótico adj erotic. ~**otismo** m eroticism

err|ar 1 (la i inicial pasa a ser **y**) vt miss. ● vi wander; (equivocarse) make a mistake, be wrong. ~**ata** f misprint. ~**óneo** adj erroneous, wrong. ~**or** m error, mistake. **estar en un ~or** be wrong, be mistaken

eruct|ar vi belch. ~**o** m belch

erudi|ción f learning, erudition. ~**to** adj learned; (palabra) erudite

erupción f eruption; (Med) rash

es vb véase **SER**

esa adj véase **ESE**

ésa pron véase **ÉSE**

esbelto adj slender, slim

esboz|ar 10 vt sketch, outline. ~**o** m sketch, outline

escabeche m brine. **en ~** pickled

escabroso adj (terreno) rough; (asunto) difficult; (atrevido) crude

escabullirse 22 vpr slip away

escafandra f diving-suit

escala f scale; (escalera de mano) ladder; (Aviac) stopover. **hacer ~ en** stop at. **vuelo sin ~s** non-stop flight. ~**da** f climbing; (Pol) escalation. ~**r** vt climb; break into (una casa). ● vi climb, go climbing

escaldar vt scald

escalera f staircase, stairs; (de mano) ladder. ~ **de caracol** spiral staircase. ~ **de incendios** fire escape. ~ **de tijera** step-ladder. ~ **mecánica** escalator

escalfa|do adj poached. ~**r** vt poach

escalinata f flight of steps

escalofrío m shiver. **tener ~s** be shivering

escalón m step, stair; (de escala) rung

escalope m escalope

escam|a f scale; (de jabón, de la piel) flake. **~oso** adj scaly; (piel) flaky

escamotear vt make disappear; (robar) steal, pinch

escampar vi stop raining

escandal|izar ⑩ vt scandalize, shock. **~andalizarse** vpr be shocked. **~ándalo** m scandal; (alboroto) commotion, racket. **armar un ~** make a scene. **~andaloso** adj scandalous; (alborotador) noisy

escandinavo adj & m Scandinavian

escaño m bench; (Pol) seat

escapa|da f escape; (visita) flying visit. **~r** vi escape. **dejar ~r** let out **~rse** vpr escape; (líquido, gas) leak

escaparate m (shop) window

escap|atoria f (fig) way out. **~e** m (de gas, de líquido) leak; (fuga) escape; (Auto) exhaust

escarabajo m beetle

escaramuza f skirmish

escarbar vt scratch; pick (dientes, herida); (fig, escudriñar) pry (**en** into). **~se** vpr pick

escarcha f frost. **~do** adj (fruta) crystallized

escarlat|a adj invar scarlet. **~ina** f scarlet fever

escarm|entar ① vt teach a lesson to. •vi learn one's lesson. **~iento** m punishment; (lección) lesson

escarola f endive

escarpado adj steep

escas|ear vi be scarce. **~ez** f scarcity, shortage; (pobreza) poverty. **~o** adj scarce; (poco) little; (muy justo) barely. **~o de** short of

escatimar vt be sparing with

escayola f plaster

esc|ena f scene; (escenario) stage. **~enario** m stage; (fig) scene. **~énico** adj stage. **~enografía** f set design

esc|epticismo m scepticism. **~éptico** adj sceptical. •m sceptic

esclarecer ⑪ vt (fig) throw light on, clarify

esclav|itud f slavery. **~izar** ⑩ vt enslave. **~o** m slave

esclusa f lock; (de presa) floodgate

escoba f broom

escocer ② & ⑨ vi sting

escocés adj Scottish. •m Scot

Escocia f Scotland

escog|er ⑭ vt choose. **~ido** adj chosen; (mercancía) choice; (clientela) select

escolar adj school. •m schoolboy. •f schoolgirl

escolta f escort

escombros mpl rubble

escond|er vt hide. **~erse** vpr hide. **~idas** fpl (LAm, juego) hide-and-seek. **a ~idas** secretly. **~ite** m hiding place; (juego) hide-and-seek. **~rijo** m hiding place

escopeta f shotgun

escoria f slag; (fig) dregs

escorpión m scorpion

Escorpión m Scorpio

escot|ado adj low-cut. **~e** m low neckline. **pagar a ~e** share the expenses

escozor m stinging

escri|bano m clerk. **~bir** (pp **escrito**) vt/i write. **~bir a máquina** type. **¿cómo se escribe...?** how do you spell...? **~birse** vpr write to each other. **~to** adj written. **por ~to** in writing. •m document. **~tor** m writer. **~torio** m desk; (oficina) office; (LAm, en una casa) study. **~tura** f (hand)writing; (Jurid) deed

escrúpulo | esparadrapo

escr|úpulo m scruple. **~upuloso** adj scrupulous

escrut|ar vt scrutinize; count (votos). **~inio** m count

escuadr|a f (instrumento) square; (Mil) squad; (Naut) fleet. **~ón** m squadron

escuálido adj skinny

escuchar vt listen to; (esp LAm, oír) hear. ●vi listen

escudo m shield. **~ de armas** coat of arms

escudriñar vt examine

escuela f school. **~ normal** teachers' training college

escueto adj simple

escuincle m (Mex fam) kid 🔟

escul|pir vt sculpture. **~tor** m sculptor. **~tora** f sculptress. **~tura** f sculpture

escupir vt/i spit

escurr|eplatos m invar plate rack. **~idizo** adj slippery. **~ir** vt drain; wring out (ropa). ●vi drain; (ropa) drip. **~irse** vpr slip

ese adj (f **esa**) that; (mpl **esos**, fpl **esas**) those

ése pron (f **ésa**) that one; (mpl **ésos**, fpl **ésas**) those; (primero de dos) the former

esencia f essence. **~l** adj essential. **lo ~l** the main thing

esf|era f sphere; (de reloj) face. **~érico** adj spherical

esf|orzarse 2 & 🔟 vpr make an effort. **~uerzo** m effort

esfumarse vpr fade away; (persona) vanish

esgrim|a f fencing. **~ir** vt brandish; (fig) use

esguince m sprain

eslabón m link

eslavo adj Slavic, Slavonic

eslogan m slogan

esmalt|ar vt enamel. **~e** m enamel. **~e de uñas** nail polish

esmerado adj careful; (persona) painstaking

esmeralda f emerald

esmer|arse vpr take care (**en** over).

esmero m care

esmoquin (pl **esmóquines**) m dinner jacket, tuxedo (Amer)

esnob adj invar snobbish. ●m & f (pl **~s**) snob. **~ismo** m snobbery

esnórkel m snorkel

eso pron that. **¡~ es!** that's it! **~ mismo** exactly. **a ~ de** about. **en ~** at that moment. **¿no es ~?** isn't that right? **por ~** that's why. **y ~ que** even though

esos adj pl véase **ESE**

ésos pron pl véase **ÉSE**

espabila|do adj bright; (despierto) awake. **~r** vt (avivar) brighten up; (despertar) wake up. **~rse** vpr wake up; (avivarse) wise up; (apresurarse) hurry up

espaci|al adj space. **~ar** vt space out. **~o** m space. **~oso** adj spacious

espada f sword. **~s** fpl (en naipes) spades

espaguetis mpl spaghetti

espald|a f back. **a ~as de uno** behind s.o.'s back. **volver la(s) ~a(s) a uno** give s.o. the cold shoulder. **~ mojada** wetback. **~illa** f shoulder-blade

espant|ajo m, **~apájaros** m invar scarecrow. **~ar** vt frighten; (ahuyentar) frighten away. **~arse** vpr be frightened; (ahuyentarse) be frightened away. **~o** m terror; (horror) horror. **¡qué ~o!** how awful! **~oso** adj horrific; (terrible) terrible

España f Spain

español adj Spanish. ●m (persona) Spaniard; (lengua) Spanish. **los ~es** the Spanish

esparadrapo m (sticking) plaster

esparcir [9] vt scatter; (difundir) spread. **~rse** vpr be scattered; (difundirse) spread; (divertirse) enjoy o.s.

espárrago m asparagus

espasm|o m spasm. **~ódico** adj spasmodic

espátula f spatula; (en pintura) palette knife

especia † spice

especial adj special. **en ~** especially. **~idad** f speciality (Brit), specialty (Amer). **~ista** adj & m & f specialist **~ización** f specialization. **~izarse** [10] vpr specialize. **~mente** adv especially

especie f kind, sort; (en biología) species. **en ~** in kind

especifica|ción f specification. **~r** [7] vt specify

específico adj specific

espect|áculo m sight; (de circo etc) show. **~acular** adj spectacular. **~ador** m & f spectator

espectro m spectre; (en física) spectrum

especula|dor m speculator. **~r** vi speculate

espej|ismo m mirage. **~o** m mirror. **~o retrovisor** (Auto) rear-view mirror

espeluznante adj horrifying

espera f wait. **a la ~** waiting (**de** for). **~nza** f hope. **~r** vt hope; (aguardar) wait for; expect (vista, carta, bebé). **espero que no** I hope not. **espero que sí** I hope so. ●vi (aguardar) wait. **~rse** vpr hang on; (prever) expect

esperma f sperm

esperpento m fright

espes|ar vt/i thicken. **~arse** vpr thicken. **~o** adj thick. **~or** m thickness

espetón m spit

esp|ía f spy. **~iar** [20] vt spy on. ●vi spy

espiga f (de trigo etc) ear

espina f thorn; (de pez) bone; (en anatomía) spine. **~ dorsal** spine

espinaca f spinach

espinazo m spine

espinilla f shin; (Med) blackhead; (LAm, grano) spot

espino m hawthorn. **~so** adj thorny; (fig) difficult

espionaje m espionage

espiral adj & f spiral

esp|iritista m & f spiritualist. **~íritu** m spirit; (mente) mind. **~iritual** adj spiritual

espl|éndido adj splendid; (persona) generous. **~endor** m splendour

espolear vt spur (on)

espolvorear vt sprinkle

esponj|a f sponge. **~oso** adj spongy

espont|aneidad f spontaneity. **~áneo** adj spontaneous

esporádico adj sporadic

espos|a f wife. **~as** fpl handcuffs. **~ar** vt handcuff. **~o** m husband

espuela f spur; (fig) incentive

espum|a f foam; (en bebidas) froth; (de jabón) lather; (de las olas) surf. **echar ~a** foam, froth. **~oso** adj (vino) sparkling

esqueleto m skeleton; (estructura) framework

esquema m outline

esqu|í m (pl **~is**, **~íes**) ski; (deporte) skiing. **~iar** [20] vi ski

esquilar vt shear

esquimal adj & m Eskimo

esquina f corner

esquiv|ar vt avoid; dodge (golpe). **~o** adj elusive

esquizofrénico adj & m schizophrenic

esta adj véase ESTE

ésta pron véase ÉSTE

estab|ilidad f stability. **~le** adj stable

establec|er 11 vt establish. **~erse** vpr settle; (Com) set up. **~imiento** m establishment

establo m cattleshed

estaca f stake

estación f station; (del año) season. **~ de invierno** winter (sports) resort. **~ de servicio** service station

estaciona|miento m parking; (LAm, lugar) car park (Brit), parking lot (Amer). **~r** vt station; (Auto) park. **~rio** adj stationary

estadía f (LAm) stay

estadio m stadium; (fase) stage

estadista m statesman. • f stateswoman

estadístic|a f statistics; (cifra) statistic. **~o** adj statistical

estado m state; (Med) condition. **~ civil** marital status. **~ de ánimo** frame of mind. **~ de cuenta** bank statement. **~ mayor** (Mil) staff. **en buen ~** in good condition

Estados Unidos mpl United States

estadounidense adj American, United States. • m & f American

estafa f swindle. **~r** vt swindle

estafeta f (oficina de correos) (sub‑)post office

estala|ctita f stalactite. **~gmita** f stalagmite

estall|ar vi explode; (olas) break; (guerra etc) break out; (fig) burst. **~ar en llanto** burst into tears. **~ar de risa** burst out laughing. **~ido** m explosion; (de guerra etc) outbreak

estamp|a f print; (aspecto) appearance. **~ado** adj printed. • m printing; (motivo) pattern; (tela) cotton print. **~ar** vt stamp; (imprimir) print

---

⊞ see A‑Z of Spanish life and culture

estampido m bang

estampilla f (LAm, de correos) (postage) stamp

estanca|do adj stagnant. **~r** 7 vt stem. **~rse** vpr stagnate

estancia f stay; (cuarto) large room

⊞ estanco adj watertight. • m tobacconist's (shop)

estandarte m standard, banner

estanque m pond; (depósito de agua) (water) tank

estanquero m tobacconist

estante m shelf. **~ría** f shelves; (para libros) bookcase

estaño m tin

---

estar 27

● verbo intransitivo

‥‥▶ to be ¿**cómo estás?** how are you?. **estoy enfermo** I'm ill. **está muy cerca** it's very near. ¿**está Pedro?** is Pedro in? ¿**cómo está el tiempo?** what's the weather like? **ya estamos en invierno** it's winter already

‥‥▶ (quedarse) to stay. **sólo ~é una semana** I'll only be staying for a week. **estoy en un hotel** I'm staying in a hotel

‥‥▶ (con fecha) ¿**a cuánto estamos?** what's the date today? **estamos a 8 de mayo** it's the 8th of May.

‥‥▶ (en locuciones) ¿**estamos?** all right? **¡ahí está!** that's it! **~ por** (apoyar a) to support; (LAm, encontrarse a punto de) to be about to; (quedar por) **eso está por verse** that remains to be seen. **son cuentas que están por pagar** they're bills still to be paid

● verbo auxiliar

‥‥▶ (con gerundio) **estaba estudiando** I was studying

‥‥▶ (con participio) **está condenado a muerte** he's been sentenced to death. **está mal traducido** it's wrongly translated. **estarse** verbo pronominal to stay. **no se está quieto** he won't stay still

▶ Cuando el verbo **estar** forma parte de expresiones como **estar de acuerdo, estar a la vista, estar constipado,** etc., ver bajo el respectivo nombre o adjetivo

estatal adj state

estático adj static

estatua f statue

estatura f height

estatuto m statute; (norma) rule

este adj (región) eastern; (viento, lado) east. •m east. •adj (f **esta**) this; (mpl **estos**, fpl **estas**) these. •int (LAm) well, er

éste pron (f **ésta**) this one; (mpl **éstos**, fpl **éstas**) these; (segundo de dos) the latter

estela f wake; (de avión) trail; (lápida) carved stone

estera f mat; (tejido) matting

est|éreo adj stereo. **~ereofónico** adj stereo, stereophonic

estereotipo m stereotype

estéril adj sterile; (terreno) barren

esterilla f mat

esterlina adj. **libra** f **~** pound sterling

estético adj aesthetic

estiércol m dung; (abono) manure

estigma m stigma. **~s** mpl (Relig) stigmata

estil|arse vpr be used. **~o** m style; (en natación) stroke. **~ mariposa** butterfly. **~ pecho** (LAm) breaststroke. **por el ~o** of that sort

estilográfica f fountain pen

estima f esteem. **~do** adj (amigo, colega) valued. **~do señor** (en cartas) Dear Sir. **~r** vt esteem; have great respect for (persona); (valorar)

value; (juzgar) consider

est|imulante adj stimulating. •m stimulant. **~imular** vt stimulate; (incitar) incite. **~ímulo** m stimulus

estir|ado adj stretched; (persona) haughty. **~ar** vt stretch; (fig) stretch out. **~ón** m pull, tug; (crecimiento) sudden growth

estirpe m stock

esto pron neutro this; (este asunto) this business. **en ~** at this point. **en ~ de** in this business of. **por ~** therefore

estofa|do adj stewed. •m stew. **~r** vt stew

estómago m stomach. **dolor** m **de ~** stomach ache

estorb|ar vt obstruct; (molestar) bother. •vi be in the way. **~o** m hindrance; (molestia) nuisance

estornud|ar vi sneeze. **~o** m sneeze

estos adj mpl véase ESTE

éstos pron mpl véase ÉSTE

estoy vb véase ESTAR

estrabismo m squint

estrado m stage; (Mus) bandstand

estrafalario adj eccentric; (ropa) outlandish

estrago m devastation. **hacer ~os** devastate

estragón m tarragon

estrambótico adj eccentric; (ropa) outlandish

estrangula|dor m strangler; (Auto) choke. **~r** vt strangle

estratagema f stratagem

estrat|ega m & f strategist. **~egia** f strategy. **~égico** adj strategic

estrato m stratum

estrech|ar vt make narrower; take in (vestido); embrace (persona). **~ar la mano a uno** shake hands with s.o. **~arse** vpr become narrower; (abrazarse) embrace. **~ez** f narrowness. **~eces** fpl financial difficulties. ~o adj narrow; (vestido etc) tight; (fig, íntimo) close. ~o de **miras** narrow-minded. ●m strait(s)

estrella f star. ~ de mar starfish. ~do adj starry

estrellar vt smash; crash (coche). ~se vpr crash (**contra** into)

estremec|er ⑪ vt shake. ~erse vpr shake; (de emoción etc) tremble (**de** with). ~imiento m shaking

estren|ar vt wear for the first time (vestido etc); show for the first time (película). ~arse vpr make one's début. ~o m (de película) première; (de obra de teatro) first night; (de persona) debut

estreñi|do adj constipated. ~miento m constipation

estrés m stress

estría f groove; (de la piel) stretch mark

estribillo m (incl Mus) refrain

estribo m stirrup; (de coche) step. **perder los** ~s lose one's temper

estribor m starboard

estricto adj strict

estridente adj strident, raucous

estrofa f stanza, verse

estropajo m scourer

estropear vt damage; (plan) spoil; ruin (ropa). ~se vpr be damaged; (averiarse) break down; (ropa) get ruined; (fruta etc) go bad; (fracasar) fail

estructura f structure. ~l adj structural

estruendo m roar; (de mucha gente) uproar

estrujar vt squeeze; wring (out) (ropa); (fig) drain

estuario m estuary

estuche m case

estudi|ante m & f student. ~antil adj student. ~ar vt study. ~o m study; (de artista) studio. ~oso adj studious

estufa f heater; (Mex, cocina) cooker

estupefac|iente m narcotic. ~to adj astonished

estupendo adj marvellous; (persona) fantastic; ¡~! that's great!

est|upidez f stupidity; (acto) stupid thing. ~úpido adj stupid

estupor m amazement

estuve vb véase ESTAR

etapa f stage. **por** ~s in stages

etéreo adj ethereal

etern|idad f eternity. ~o adj eternal

étic|a f ethics. ~o adj ethical

etimología f etymology

etiqueta f ticket, tag; (ceremonial) etiquette. **de** ~ formal

étnico adj ethnic

eucalipto m eucalyptus

eufemismo m euphemism

euforia f euphoria

euro m euro. ~escéptico adj & m Eurosceptic

Europa f Europe

euro|peo adj & m European. ~zona f eurozone

eutanasia f euthanasia

evacua|ción f evacuation. ~r ㉑ vt evacuate

evadir vt avoid; evade (impuestos). ~se vpr escape

evalua|ción f evaluation. ~r ㉑ vt assess; evaluate (datos)

evangeli|o m gospel. ~sta m & f evangelist; (Mex, escribiente) scribe

evapora|ción f evaporation. ~rse vpr evaporate; (fig) disappear

evasi|ón f evasion; (fuga) escape. ~vo adj evasive

evento m event; (caso) case

eventual adj possible. ~idad f eventuality

eviden|cia f evidence. **poner en**

~**cia a uno** show s.o. up. ~**ciar** vt show. ~**ciarse** vpr be obvious. ~**te** adj obvious. ~**temente** adv obviously

evitar vt avoid; (ahorrar) spare; (prevenir) prevent

evocar 🔢 vt evoke

evoluci|ón f evolution. ~**onar** vi evolve; (Mil) manoeuvre

ex prefijo ex-, former

exacerbar vt exacerbate

exact|amente adv exactly. ~**itud** f exactness. ~**o** adj exact; (preciso) accurate; (puntual) punctual. ¡~**!** exactly!

exagera|ción f exaggeration. ~**do** adj exaggerated. ~**r** vt/i exaggerate

exalta|do adj exalted; (excitado) (over)excited; (fanático) hot-headed. ~**r** vt exalt. ~**rse** vpr get excited

exam|en m exam, examination. ~**inar** vt examine. ~**inarse** vpr take an exam

exasperar vt exasperate. ~**se** vpr get exasperated

excarcela|ción f release (from prison). ~**r** vt release

excava|ción f excavation. ~**dora** f digger. ~**r** vt excavate

excede|ncia f leave of absence. ~**nte** adj & m surplus. ~**r** vi exceed. ~**rse** vpr go too far

excelen|cia f excellence; (tratamiento) Excellency. ~**te** adj excellent

exc|entricidad f eccentricity. ~**éntrico** adj & m eccentric

excepci|ón f exception. ~**onal** adj exceptional. **a** ~**ón de, con** ~**ón de** except (for)

except|o prep except (for). ~**uar** 🔢 vt except

exces|ivo adj excessive. ~**o** m excess. ~**o de equipaje** excess luggage (esp Brit), excess baggage (esp Amer)

excita|ción f excitement. ~**r** vt excite; (incitar) incite. ~**rse** vpr get excited

exclama|ción f exclamation. ~**r** vi exclaim

exclu|ir 🔢 vt exclude. ~**sión** f exclusion. ~**siva** f sole right; (reportaje) exclusive (story). ~**sivo** adj exclusive

excomu|lgar 🔢 vt excommunicate. ~**nión** f excommunication

excremento m excrement

excursi|ón f excursion, outing. ~**onista** m & f day-tripper

excusa f excuse; (disculpa) apology. **presentar sus** ~**s** apologize. ~**r** vt excuse

exento adj exempt; (libre) free

exhalar vt exhale, breath out; give off (olor etc)

exhaust|ivo adj exhaustive. ~**o** adj exhausted

exhibi|ción f exhibition; (demostración) display. ~**cionista** m & f exhibitionist. ~**r** vt exhibit ~**rse** vpr show o.s.; (hacerse notar) draw attention to o.s.

exhumar vt exhume; (fig) dig up

exig|encia f demand ~**ente** adj demanding. ~**ir** 🔢 vt demand

exiguo adj meagre

exil|(i)ado adj exiled. •m exile. ~**(i)arse** vpr go into exile. ~**io** m exile

exim|ente m reason for exemption; (Jurid) grounds for acquittal. ~**ir** vt exempt

existencia f existence. ~**s** fpl stock. ~**lismo** m existentialism

exist|ente adj existing. ~**ir** vi exist

éxito m success. **no tener** ~ fail. **tener** ~ be successful

exitoso adj successful

éxodo m exodus

exonerar vt exonerate

exorbitante adj exorbitant

exorci|smo m exorcism. **~zar** 10 vt exorcise

exótico adj exotic

expan|dir vt expand; (fig) spread. **~dirse** vpr expand. **~sión** f expansion. **~sivo** adj expansive

expatria|do adj & m expatriate. **~rse** vpr emigrate; (exiliarse) go into exile

expectativa f prospect; (esperanza) expectation. **estar a la ~** be waiting

expedi|ción f expedition; (de documento) issue; (de mercancías) dispatch. **~ente** m record, file; (Jurid) proceedings. **~r** 5 vt issue; (enviar) dispatch, send. **~to** adj clear; (LAm, fácil) easy

expeler vt expel

expend|edor m dealer. **~edor automático** vending machine. **~io** m (LAm) shop; (venta) sale

expensas fpl (Jurid) costs. **a ~ de** at the expense of. **a mis ~** at my expense

experiencia f experience

experiment|al adj experimental. **~ar** vt test, experiment with; (sentir) experience. **~o** m experiment

experto adj & m expert

expiar 20 vt atone for

expirar vi expire

explanada f levelled area; (paseo) esplanade

explayarse vpr speak at length; (desahogarse) unburden o.s. (**con** to)

explica|ción f explanation. **~r** 7 vt explain. **~rse** vpr understand; (hacerse comprender) explain o.s. **no me lo explico** I can't understand it

explícito adj explicit

explora|ción f exploration. **~dor** m explorer; (muchacho) boy scout. **~r** vt explore

explosi|ón f explosion; (fig) outburst. **~onar** vt blow up. **~vo** adj & m explosive

explota|ción f working; (abuso) exploitation. **~r** vt work (mina); farm (tierra); (abusar) exploit. ●vi explode

expone|nte m exponent. **~r** 34 vt expose; display (mercancías); present (tema); set out (hechos); exhibit (cuadros etc); (arriesgar) risk. ●vi exhibit. **~rse** vpr. **~se a que** run the risk of

exporta|ción f export. **~dor** m exporter. **~r** vt export

exposición f exposure; (de cuadros etc) exhibition; (de hechos) exposition

expres|ar vt express. **~arse** vpr express o.s. **~ión** f expression. **~ivo** adj expressive; (cariñoso) affectionate

expreso adj express. ●m express; (café) expresso

exprimi|dor m squeezer. **~r** vt squeeze

expropiar vt expropriate

expuesto adj on display; (lugar etc) exposed; (peligroso) dangerous. **estar ~ a** be exposed to

expuls|ar vt expel; throw out (persona); send off (jugador). **~ión** f expulsion

exquisito adj exquisite; (de sabor) delicious

éxtasis m invar ecstasy

extend|er 1 vt spread (out); (ampliar) extend; issue (documento). **~erse** vpr spread; (paisaje etc) extend, stretch. **~ido** adj spread out; (generalizado) widespread; (brazos) outstretched

extens|amente adv widely; (detalladamente) in full. **~ión** f extension; (área) expanse; (largo) length. **~o** adj extensive

extenuar 21 vt exhaust

exterior adj external, exterior; (del

extranjero) foreign; (aspecto etc) outward. • m outside, exterior; (países extranjeros) abroad

extermin|ación f extermination. **~ar** vt exterminate. **~io** m extermination

externo adj external; (signo etc) outward. • m day pupil

extin|ción f extinction. **~guidor** m (LAm) fire extinguisher. **~guir** 🔢 vt extinguish. **~guirse** vpr die out; (fuego) go out. **~to** adj (raza etc) extinct. **~tor** m fire extinguisher

extirpar vt eradicate; remove (tumor)

extorsión f extortion

extra adj invar extra; (de buena calidad) good-quality; (huevos) large. **paga** f **~** bonus

extracto m extract

extradición f extradition

extraer 🔢 vt extract

extranjer|ía f (Esp) **la ley de ~** immigration law. **~o** adj foreign. • m foreigner; (países) foreign countries. **del ~** from abroad. **en el ~, por el ~** abroad

extrañ|ar vt surprise; (encontrar extraño) find strange; (LAm, echar de menos) miss. **~arse** vpr be surprised (**de** at). **~eza** f strangeness; (asombro) surprise. **~o** adj strange. • m stranger

extraoficial adj unofficial

extraordinario adj extraordinary

extrarradio m outlying districts

extraterrestre adj extraterrestrial. • m alien

extravagan|cia f oddness, eccentricity. **~te** adj odd, eccentric

extrav|iado adj lost. **~iar** 🔢 vt lose. **~iarse** vpr get lost; (objetos) go missing. **~ío** m loss

extremar vt take extra (precauciones); tighten up (vigilancia). **~se** vpr make every effort

extremeño adj from Extremadura

extrem|idad f end. **~idades** fpl extremities. **~ista** adj & m & f extremist. **~o** adj extreme. • m end; (colmo) extreme. **en ~o** extremely. **en último ~o** as a last resort

extrovertido adj & m extrovert

exuberan|cia f exuberance. **~te** adj exuberant

eyacular vt/i ejaculate

Ff

fa m F; (solfa) fah

fabada f bean and pork stew

fábrica f factory. **marca** f **de ~** trade mark

fabrica|ción f manufacture. **~ción en serie** mass production. **~nte** m & f manufacturer. **~r** 🔢 vt manufacture

fábula f fable; (mentira) fabrication

fabuloso adj fabulous

facci|ón f faction. **~ones** fpl (de la cara) features

faceta f facet

facha f (fam, aspecto) look. **~da** f façade

fácil adj easy; (probable) likely

facili|dad f ease; (disposición) aptitude. **~dades** fpl facilities.

~**tar** vt facilitate; (proporcionar) provide

factible adj feasible

factor m factor

factura f bill, invoice. ~**r** vt (hacer la factura) invoice; (al embarcar) check in

faculta|d f faculty; (capacidad) ability; (poder) power. ~**tivo** adj optional

faena f job. ~**s domésticas** housework

faisán m pheasant

faja f (de tierra) strip; (corsé) corset; (Mil etc) sash

fajo m bundle; (de billetes) wad

falda f skirt; (de montaña) side

falla f fault; (defecto) flaw. ~ **humana** (LAm) human error. ~**r** vi fail. **me falló** he let me down. **sin** ~**r** without fail. ●vt (errar) miss

fallec|er vi die. ~**ido** m deceased

fallido adj vain; (fracasado) unsuccessful

fallo m (defecto) fault; (error) mistake. ~ **humano** human error; (en certamen) decision; (Jurid) ruling

falluca f (Mex) smuggled goods

fals|ear vt falsify, distort. ~**ificación** f forgery. ~**ificador** m forger. ~**ificar** vt forge. ~**o** adj false; (falsificado) forged; (joya) fake

falt|a f lack; (ausencia) absence; (escasez) shortage; (defecto) fault, defect; (culpa) fault; (error) mistake; (en fútbol etc) foul; (en tenis) fault. **a** ~**a de** for lack of. **echar en** ~**a** miss. **hacer** ~**a** be necessary. **me hace** ~**a** I need. **sacar** ~**as** find fault. ~**o** adj lacking (**de** in)

see A-Z of Spanish life and culture

faltar verbo intransitivo

! cuando el verbo **faltar** va precedido del complemento indirecto **le** (o **les, nos**) el sujeto en español pasa a ser el objeto en inglés p.ej: **les falta experiencia** they lack experience

····▸ (no estar) to be missing **¿quién falta?** who's missing? **falta una de las chicas** one of the girls is missing. **al abrigo le faltan 3 botones** the coat has three buttons missing. ~ **a algo** (no asistir) to be absent from sth; (no acudir) to miss sth

····▸ (no haber suficiente) **va a** ~ **leche** there won't be enough milk. **nos faltó tiempo** we didn't have enough time

····▸ (no tener) **le falta cariño** he lacks affection

····▸ (hacer falta) **le falta sal** it needs more salt. **¡es lo que nos faltaba!** that's all we needed!

····▸ (quedar) **¿te falta mucho?** are you going to be much longer? **falta poco para Navidad** it's not long until Christmas. **aún falta mucho** (distancia) there's a long way to go yet **¡no faltaba más!** of course!

fama f fame; (reputación) reputation

famélico adj starving

familia f family; (hijos) children. ~ **numerosa** large family. ~**r** adj familiar; (de la familia) family; (sin ceremonia) informal; (lenguaje) colloquial. ●m & f relative. ~**ridad** f familiarity. ~**rizarse** vpr become familiar (**con** with)

famoso adj famous

fanático adj fanatical. ●m fanatic

fanfarr|ón adj boastful. ●m braggart. ~**onear** vi show off

fango m mud. ~**so** adj muddy

fantasía f fantasy. **de** ~ fancy; (joya) imitation

fantasma m ghost

fantástico adj fantastic

fardo m bundle

faringe f pharynx

farmac|éutico m chemist (Brit), pharmacist, druggist (Amer). ▣~**ia** f (ciencia) pharmacy; (tienda) chemist's (shop) (Brit), pharmacy

faro m lighthouse; (Aviac) beacon; (Auto) headlight

farol m lantern; (de la calle) street lamp. ~**a** f street lamp

farr|a f partying. ~**ear** vi (LAm) go out partying

farsa f farce. ~**nte** m & f fraud

fascículo m instalment

fascinar vt fascinate

fascis|mo m fascism

fase f phase

fastidi|ar vt annoy; (estropear) spoil. ~**arse** vpr (máquina) break down; hurt (pierna), (LAm, molestarse) get annoyed. **¡para que te ~es!** so there!. ~**o** m nuisance; (aburrimiento) boredom. ~**oso** adj annoying

fatal adj fateful; (mortal) fatal; (fam, pésimo) terrible. ~**idad** f fate; (desgracia) misfortune

fatig|a f fatigue. ~**ar** [12] vt tire. ~**arse** vpr get tired. ~**oso** adj tiring

fauna f fauna

favor m favour. **a ~ de, en ~ de** in favour of. **haga el ~ de** would you be so kind as to, please. **por ~** please

favorec|er [11] vt favour; (vestido, peinado etc) suit. ~**ido** adj favoured

favorito adj & m favourite

fax m fax

faxear vt fax

faz f face

fe f faith. **dar ~ de** certify. **de buena ~** in good faith

febrero m February

febril adj feverish

fecha f date. **a estas ~s** now; (todavía) still. **hasta la ~** so far. **poner la ~** date. ~**r** vt date

fecund|ación f fertilization. ~**ación artificial** artificial insemination. ~**ar** vt fertilize. ~**o** adj fertile; (fig) prolific

federa|ción f federation. ~**l** adj federal

felici|dad f happiness. ~**dades** fpl best wishes; (congratulaciones) congratulations. ~**tación** f letter of congratulation. **¡felicitaciones!** (LAm) congratulations! ~**tar** vt congratulate

feligrés m parishioner

feliz adj happy; (afortunado) lucky. **¡Felices Pascuas!** Happy Christmas! **¡F~ Año Nuevo!** Happy New Year!

felpudo m doormat

fem|enil adj (Mex) women's. ~**enino** adj feminine; (equipo) women's; (en biología) female. ●m feminine. ~**inista** adj & m & f feminist

fen|omenal adj phenomenal. ~**ómeno** m phenomenon; (monstruo) freak

feo adj ugly; (desagradable) nasty. ●adv (LAm) (mal) had

feria f fair; (verbena) carnival; (Mex, cambio) small change. ~**do** m (LAm) public holiday

ferment|ar vt/i ferment. ~**o** m ferment

fero|cidad f ferocity. ~**z** adj fierce

férreo adj iron; (disciplina) strict

ferreter|ía f hardware store, ironmonger's (Brit). ~**o** m hardware dealer, ironmonger (Brit)

ferro|carril m railway (Brit), railroad (Amer). ~**viario** adj rail. ●m railwayman (Brit), railroader (Amer)

fértil adj fertile

fertili|dad f fertility. ~**zante** m

....

▣ *see* A-Z of Spanish life and culture

fertilizer. **~zar** 🔟 vt fertilize

ferv|iente adj fervent. **~or** m fervour

festej|ar vt celebrate; entertain (persona). **~o** m celebration

festiv|al m festival. **~idad** f festivity. **~o** adj festive. ●m public holiday

fétido adj stinking

feto m foetus

fiable adj reliable

fiado m. **al ~** on credit. **~r** m (Jurid) guarantor

fiambre m cold meat. **~ría** f (LAm) delicatessen

fianza f (dinero) deposit; (objeto) surety. **bajo ~** on bail

fiar 🔟 vt (vender) sell on credit; (confiar) confide. ●vi give credit. **~se** vpr. **~se de** trust

fibra f fibre. **~ de vidrio** fibreglass

ficción f fiction

fich|a f token; (tarjeta) index card; (en juegos) counter. **~ar** vt open a file on. **estar ~ado** have a (police) record. **~ero** m card index; (en informática) file

fidedigno adj reliable

fidelidad f faithfulness

fideos mpl noodles

fiebre f fever. **~ aftosa** foot-and-mouth disease. **~ del heno** hay fever. **~ porcina** swine fever. **tener ~** have a temperature

fiel adj faithful; (memoria, relato etc) reliable. ●m believer

fieltro m felt

fier|a f wild animal. **~o** adj fierce

fierro m (LAm) metal bar; (hierro) iron

🔳**fiesta** f party; (día festivo) holiday. **~s** fpl celebrations

figura f figure; (forma) shape. **~r** vi

🔳 see A-Z of Spanish life and culture

appear; (destacar) show off. **~rse** vpr imagine. **¡figúrate!** just imagine!

fij|ación f fixing; (obsesión) fixation. **~ar** vt fix; establish (residencia). **~arse** vpr (poner atención) pay attention; (percatarse) notice. **¡fíjate!** just imagine! **~o** adj fixed; (firme) stable; (permanente) permanent. ●adv. **mirar ~o** stare

fila f line; (de soldados etc) file; (en el teatro, cine etc) row; (cola) queue. **ponerse en ~** line up

filántropo m philanthropist

filat|elia f stamp collecting, philately. **~élico** adj philatelic. ●m stamp collector, philatelist

filete m fillet

filial adj filial. ●f subsidiary

Filipinas fpl. **las (islas) ~** the Philippines

filipino adj Philippine, Filipino

filmar vt film; shoot (película)

filo m edge; (de hoja) cutting edge. **al ~ de las doce** at exactly twelve o'clock. **sacar ~ a** sharpen

filología f philology

filón m vein; (fig) gold-mine

fil|osofía f philosophy. **~ósofo** m philosopher

filtr|ar vt filter. **~arse** vpr filter; (dinero) disappear; (noticia) leak. **~o** m filter; (bebida) philtre. **~ solar** sunscreen

fin m end; (objetivo) aim. **~ de semana** weekend. **a ~ de** in order to. **a ~ de cuentas** at the end of the day. **a ~ de que** in order that. **a ~es de** at the end of. **al ~** finally. **al ~ y al cabo** after all. **dar ~ a** end. **en ~** in short. **por ~** finally. **sin ~** endless

final adj final. ●m end. ●f final. **~idad** f aim. **~ista** m & f finalist. **~izar** 🔟 vt finish. ●vi end

financi|ación f financing; (fondos) funds; (facilidades) credit facilities.

∼ar vt finance. **∼ero** adj financial. ●m financier

finca f property; (tierras) estate; (rural) farm; (de recreo) country house

fingir ⓭ vt feign; (simular) simulate. ●vi pretend. **∼se** vpr pretend to be

finlandés adj Finnish. ●m (persona) Finn; (lengua) Finnish

Finlandia f Finland

fino adj fine; (delgado) thin; (oído) acute; (de modales) refined; (sutil) subtle

firma f signature; (acto) signing; (empresa) firm

firmar vt/i sign

firme adj firm; (estable) stable, steady; (color) fast. ●m (pavimento) (road) surface. ●adv hard. **∼za** f firmness

fisc|al adj fiscal, tax. ●m & f public prosecutor. **∼o** m treasury

fisg|ar ⓬ vi snoop (around). **∼ón** adj nosy. ●m snooper

físic|a f physics. **∼o** adj physical. ●m physique; (persona) physicist

fisonomista m & f. **ser buen ∼** be good at remembering faces

fistol m (Mex) tiepin

flaco adj thin, skinny; (débil) weak

flagelo m scourge

flagrante adj flagrant. **en ∼** redhanded

flama f (Mex) flame

flamante adj splendid; (nuevo) brand-new

flamear vi flame; (bandera etc) flap

🔲**flamenco** adj flamenco; (de Flandes) Flemish. ●m (ave) flamingo; (música etc) flamenco; (idioma) Flemish

flan m crème caramel

flaqueza f thinness; (debilidad) weakness

flauta f flute

flecha f arrow. **∼zo** m love at first sight

fleco m fringe; (Mex, en el pelo) fringe (Brit), bangs (Amer)

flem|a f phlegm. **∼ático** adj phlegmatic

flequillo m fringe (Brit), bangs (Amer)

fletar vt charter; (LAm, transportar) transport

flexible adj flexible

flirte|ar vi flirt. **∼o** m flirting

floj|ear vi flag; (holgazanear) laze around. **∼o** adj loose; (poco fuerte) weak; (perezoso) lazy

flor f flower. **la ∼ y nata** the cream. **∼a** f flora. **∼ecer** ⓫ vi flower, bloom; (fig) flourish. **∼eciente** adj (fig) flourishing. **∼ero** m flower vase. **∼ista** m & f florist

flot|a f fleet. **∼ador** m float; (de niño) rubber band. **∼ar** vi float **∼e. a ∼e** afloat

fluctua|ción f fluctuation. **∼r** ㉑ vi fluctuate

flu|idez f fluidity; (fig) fluency. **∼ido** adj fluid; (fig) fluent. ●m fluid. **∼ir** ⓱ vi flow

fluoruro m fluoride

fluvial adj river

fobia f phobia

foca f seal

foco m focus; (lámpara) floodlight; (LAm, de coche) (head)light; (Mex, bombilla) light bulb

fogón m cooker; (LAm, fogata) bonfire

folio m sheet

folklórico adj folk

follaje m foliage

follet|ín m newspaper serial. **∼o** m pamphlet

follón m ⓵ mess; (alboroto) row; (problema) trouble

fomentar vt promote; boost

🔲 *see* A-Z of Spanish life and culture

fonda | franquear

(ahorro); stir up (odio)

fonda f (pensión) boarding-house; (LAm, restaurant) cheap restaurant

fondo m bottom; (de calle, pasillo) end; (de sala etc) back; (de escenario, pintura etc) background. ~ **de reptiles** slush fund. ~s mpl funds, money. **a** ~ thoroughly

fonétic|a f phonetics. ~**o** adj phonetic

fontanero m plumber

footing /'futin/ m jogging

forastero m stranger

forcejear vi struggle

forense adj forensic. ●m & f forensic scientist

forjar vt forge. ~**se** vpr forge; build up (ilusiones)

forma f form; (contorno) shape; (modo) way; (Mex, formulario) form. ~s fpl conventions. **de todas** ~s anyway. **estar en** ~ be in good form. ~**ción** f formation; (educación) training. ~**l** adj formal; (de fiar) reliable; (serio) serious. ~**lidad** f formality; (fiabilidad) reliability; (seriedad) seriousness. ~**r** vt form; (componer) make up; (enseñar) train. ~**rse** vpr form; (desarrollarse) develop; (educarse) to be educated. ~**to** m format

formidable adj formidable; (muy grande) enormous

fórmula f formula; (sistema) way. ~ **de cortesía** polite expression

formular vt formulate; make (queja etc). ~**io** m form

fornido adj well-built

forr|ar vt (en el interior) line; (en el exterior) cover. ~**o** m lining; (cubierta) cover

fortale|cer vt strengthen. ~**za** f strength; (Mil) fortress; (fuerza moral) fortitude

fortuito adj fortuitous; (encuentro) chance

fortuna f fortune; (suerte) luck

forz|ar vt force; strain

(vista). ~**osamente** adv necessarily. ~**oso** adj necessary

fosa f ditch; (tumba) grave. ~s fpl **nasales** nostrils

fósforo m phosphorus; (cerilla) match

fósil adj & m fossil

foso m ditch; (en castillo) moat; (de teatro) pit

foto f photo. **sacar** ~s take photos

fotocopia f photocopy. ~**dora** f photocopier. ~**r** vt photocopy

fotogénico adj photogenic

fot|ografía f photography; (Foto) photograph. ~**ografiar** vt photograph. ~**ógrafo** m photographer

foul /faʊl/ m (pl ~s) (LAm) foul

frac m (pl ~s o **fraques**) tails

fracas|ar vi fail. ~**o** m failure

fracción f fraction; (Pol) faction

fractura f fracture. ~**r** vt fracture. ~**rse** vpr fracture

fragan|cia f fragrance. ~**te** adj fragrant

frágil adj fragile

fragmento m fragment; (de canción etc) extract

fragua f forge. ~**r** vt forge; (fig) concoct. ●vi set

fraile m friar; (monje) monk

frambuesa f raspberry

franc|és adj French. ●m (persona) Frenchman; (lengua) French. ~**esa** f Frenchwoman

Francia f France

franco adj frank; (evidente) marked; (Com) free. ●m (moneda) franc

francotirador m sniper

franela f flannel

franja f border; (banda) stripe; (de terreno) strip

franque|ar vt clear; (atravesar) cross; pay the postage on (carta). ~**o** m postage

franqueza f frankness

frasco m bottle; (de mermelada etc) jar

frase f phrase; (oración) sentence. **~ hecha** set phrase

fratern|al adj fraternal. **~idad** f fraternity

fraud|e m fraud. **~ulento** adj fraudulent

fray m brother, friar

frecuen|cia f frequency. **con ~cia** frequently. **~tar** vt frequent. **~te** adj frequent

frega|dero m sink. **~r 1** & **12** vt scrub; wash (los platos); mop (el suelo); (LAm, fam, molestar) annoy

freír 51 (pp **frito**) vt fry. **~se** vpr fry; (persona) roast

frenar vt brake; (fig) check

frenético adj frenzied; (furioso) furious

freno m (de caballería) bit; (Auto) brake, (fig) check

frente m front. **~ a** opposite. **~ a ~** face to face. **al ~** at the head; (hacia delante) forward. **chocar de ~** crash head on. **de ~ a** (LAm) facing. **hacer ~ a** face (cosa); stand up to (persona). ● f forehead. **arrugar la ~** frown

fresa f strawberry

fresc|o adj (frío) cool; (reciente) fresh; (descarado) cheeky. ● m fresh air; (frescor) coolness; (mural) fresco; (persona) impudent person. **al ~o** in the open air. **hacer ~o** be cool. **tomar el ~o** get some fresh air. **~or** m coolness. **~ura** f freshness; (frío) coolness; (descaro) cheek

frialdad f coldness; (fig) indifference

fricci|ón f rubbing; (fig, Tec) friction; (masaje) massage. **~onar** vt rub

frigidez f frigidity

frígido adj frigid

frigorífico m fridge, refrigerator

frijol m (LAm) bean. **~es refritos** (Mex) fried purée of beans

frío adj & m cold. **tomar ~** catch cold. **hacer ~** be cold. **tener ~** be cold

frito adj fried; (fam, harto) fed up. **me tiene ~** I'm sick of him

fr|ivolidad f frivolity. **~ívolo** adj frivolous

fronter|a f border, frontier. **~izo** adj border; (país) bordering

frontón m pelota court; (pared) fronton

frotar vt rub; strike (cerilla)

fructífero adj fruitful

fruncir 9 vt gather (tela). **~ el ceño** frown

frustra|ción f frustration. **~r** vt frustrate. **~rse** vpr (fracasar) fail. **quedar ~do** be disappointed

frut|a f fruit. **~al** adj fruit. **~ería** f fruit shop. **~ero** m fruit seller; (recipiente) fruit bowl. **~icultura** f fruit-growing. **~o** m fruit

fucsia f fuchsia. ● m fuchsia

fuego m fire. **~s artificiales** fireworks. **a ~ lento** on a low heat. **tener ~** have a light

fuente f fountain; (manantial) spring; (plato) serving dish; (fig) source

fuera adv out; (al exterior) outside; (en otra parte) away; (en el extranjero) abroad. **~ de** outside; (excepto) except for, besides. **por ~** on the outside. ● vb véase IR y SER

fuerte adj strong; (color) bright; (sonido) loud; (dolor) severe; (duro) hard; (grande) large; (lluvia, nevada) heavy. ● m fort; (fig) strong point. ● adv hard; (con hablar etc) loudly; (llover) heavily; (mucho) a lot

fuerza f strength; (poder) power; (en física) force; (Mil) forces. **~ de voluntad** will-power. **a ~ de** by (dint of). **a la ~** by necessity. **por ~** by force; (por necesidad) by necessity. **tener ~s para** have the strength to

fuese vb véase IR y SER

fug|a f flight, escape; (de gas etc) leak; (Mus) fugue. **~arse** 12 vpr flee, escape. **~az** adj fleeting. **~itivo** adj & m fugitive

fui vb véase IR, SER

fulano m so-and-so. **~, mengano y zutano** every Tom, Dick and Harry

fulminar vt (fig, con mirada) look daggers at

fuma|dor adj smoking. ●m smoker. **~r** vt/i smoke. **~r en pipa** smoke a pipe. **~rse** vpr smoke. **~rada** f puff of smoke

funci|ón f function; (de un cargo etc) duty; (de teatro) show, performance. **~onal** adj functional. **~onar** vi work, function. **no ~ona** out of order. **~onario** m civil servant

funda f cover. **~ de almohada** pillowcase

funda|ción f foundation. **~mental** adj fundamental. **~mentar** vt base (**en** on). **~mento** m foundation. **~r** vt found; (fig) base. **~rse** vpr be based

fundi|ción f melting; (de metales) smelting; (taller) foundry. **~r** vt melt; smelt (metales); cast (objeto); blend (colores); (fusionar) merge; (Elec) blow; (LAm) seize up (motor). **~rse** vpr melt; (unirse) merge

fúnebre adj funeral; (sombrío) gloomy

funeral adj funeral. ●m funeral. **~es** mpl funeral

funicular adj & m funicular

furg|ón m van. **~oneta** f van

fur|ia f fury; (violencia) violence. **~ibundo** adj furious. **~ioso** adj furious. **~or** m fury

furtivo adj furtive. **cazador ~** poacher

furúnculo m boil

fusible m fuse

fusil m rifle. **~ar** vt shoot

fusión f melting; (unión) fusion; (Com) merger

fútbol m, (Mex) **futbol** m football

futbolista m & f footballer

futur|ista adj futuristic. ●m & f futurist. **~o** adj & m future

Gg

gabardina f raincoat

gabinete m (Pol) cabinet; (en museo etc) room; (de dentista, médico etc) consulting room

gaceta f gazette

gafa f hook. **~s** fpl glasses, spectacles. **~s de sol** sunglasses

gaf|ar vt 1 bring bad luck to. **~e** m jinx

gaita f bagpipes

gajo m segment

gala f gala. **~s** fpl finery, best clothes. **estar de ~** be dressed

up. **hacer ~ de** show off

galán m (en el teatro) (romantic) hero; (enamorado) lover

galante adj gallant. **~ar** vt court. **~ría** f gallantry

galápago m turtle

galardón m award

galaxia f galaxy

galera f galley

galer|ía f gallery. **~ía comercial** (shopping) arcade. **~ón** m (Mex) hall

Gales m Wales. **país de** ~ Wales

gal|és adj Welsh. ●m Welshman; (lengua) Welsh. **~esa** f Welshwoman

galgo m greyhound

Galicia f Galicia

galimatías m invar gibberish

gallard|ía f elegance. **~o** adj elegant

🔲 **gallego** adj & m Galician

galleta f biscuit (Brit), cookie (Amer)

gall|ina f hen, chicken; (fig, fam) coward. **~o** m cock

galón m gallon; (cinta) braid; (Mil) stripe

galop|ar vi gallop. **~e** m gallop

gama f scale; (fig) range

gamba f prawn (Brit), shrimp (Amer)

gamberro m hooligan

gamuza f (piel) chamois leather; (de otro animal) suede

gana f wish, desire; (apetito) appetite. **de buena** ~ willingly. **de mala** ~ reluctantly. **no me da la** ~ I don't feel like it. **tener ~s de** (+ infinitivo) feel like (+ gerundio)

ganad|ería f cattle raising; (ganado) livestock. **~o** m livestock. **~o lanar** sheep. **~o porcino** pigs. **~o vacuno** cattle

gana|dor adj winning. ●m winner. **~ncia** f gain; (Com) profit. **~r** vt earn; (en concurso, juego etc) win; (alcanzar) reach. ●vi (vencer) win; (mejorar) improve. **~rle a uno** beat s.o. **~rse la vida** earn a living. **salir ~ndo** come out better off

ganch|illo m crochet. **hacer ~illo** crochet. **~o** m hook; (LAm, colgador) hanger. **tener ~o** be very attractive

ganga f bargain

ganso m goose

garabat|ear vt/i scribble. **~o** m scribble

garaje m garage

garant|e m & f guarantor. **~ía** f guarantee. **~izar** 🔟 vt guarantee

garapiña f (Mex) pineapple squash. **~do** adj. **almendras** fpl **~das** sugared almonds

garbanzo m chick-pea

garbo m poise; (de escrito) style. **~so** adj elegant

garganta f throat; (valle) gorge

gárgaras fpl. **hacer** ~ gargle

garita t hut; (de centinela) sentry box

garra f (de animal) claw; (de ave) talon

garrafa f carafe

garrafal adj huge

garrapata f tick

garrapat|ear vi scribble. **~o** m scribble

garrote m club, cudgel; (tormento) garrotte

gar|úa f (LAm) drizzle. **~uar** vi 🌂 (LAm) drizzle

garza f heron

gas m gas. **con** ~ fizzy. **sin** ~ still

gasa t gauze

gaseosa f fizzy drink

gas|óleo m diesel. **~olina** f petrol (Brit), gasoline (Amer), gas (Amer). **~olinera** f petrol station (Brit), gas station (Amer)

gast|ado adj spent; (vestido etc) worn out. **~ador** m spendthrift. **~ar** vt spend; (consumir) use; (malgastar) waste; (desgastar) wear out; wear (vestido etc); crack (broma). **~arse** vpr wear out. **~o** m expense; (acción de gastar) spending

gastronomía f gastronomy

gat|a f cat. **a ~as** on all fours. **~ear** vi crawl

gatillo m trigger

gat|ito m kitten. **~o** m cat. **dar ~o**

🔲 see A-Z of Spanish life and culture

por liebre take s.o. in

🔲 **gaucho** m Gaucho

gaveta f drawer

gaviota f seagull

🔲 **gazpacho** m gazpacho

gelatina f gelatine; (jalea) jelly

gema f gem

gemelo m twin. ~s mpl (anteojos) binoculars; (de camisa) cuff-links

gemido m groan

Géminis m Gemini

gemir 5 vi moan; (animal) whine, howl

gen m, **gene** m gene

geneal|ogía f genealogy. ~ógico adj genealogical. árbol m ~ógico family tree

generaci|ón f generation. ~onal adj generation

general adj general. **en ~** in general. **por lo ~** generally. ● m general. ~izar 10 vt/i generalize. ~mente adv generally

generar vt generate

género m type, sort; (en biología) genus; (Gram) gender; (en literatura etc) genre; (producto) product; (tela) material. ~s de punto knitwear. ~ humano mankind

generos|idad f generosity. ~o adj generous

genétic|a f genetics. ~o adj genetic

geni|al adj brilliant; (divertido) funny. ~o m temper; (carácter) nature; (talento, persona) genius

genital adj genital. ~es mpl genitals

genoma m genome

gente f people; (nación) nation; (fam, familia) family, folks; (Mex, persona) person. ● adj (LAm) respectable; (amable) kind

gentil adj charming. ~eza f

kindness. **tener la ~eza de** be kind enough to

gentío m crowd

genuflexión f genuflection

genuino adj genuine

ge|ografía f geography. ~ográfico adj geographical.

ge|ología f geology. ~ólogo m geologist

geom|etría f geometry. ~étrico adj geometrical

geranio m geranium

geren|cia f management. ~ciar vt (LAm) manage. ~te m & f manager

germen m germ

germinar vi germinate

gestación f gestation

gesticula|ción f gesticulation. ~r vi gesticulate

gesti|ón f step; (administración) management. ~onar vt take steps to arrange; (dirigir) manage

gesto m expression; (ademán) gesture; (mueca) grimace

gibraltareño adj & m Gibraltarian

gigante adj gigantic. ● m giant. ~sco adj gigantic

gimn|asia f gymnastics. ~asio m gymnasium, gym 🔲. ~asta m & f gymnast. ~ástic adj gymnastic

gimotear vi whine

ginebra f gin

ginec|ólogo m gynaecologist

gira f tour. ~r vt spin; draw (cheque); transfer (dinero). ● vi rotate, go round; (en camino) turn

girasol m sunflower

gir|atorio adj revolving. ~o m turn; (Com) draft; (locución) expression. ~o postal money order

🔲 **gitano** adj & m gypsy

glacia|l adj icy. ~r m glacier

glándula f gland

🔲 see A-Z of Spanish life and culture

glasear vt glaze; (Culin) ice

glob|al adj global; (fig) overall. ~o m globe; (aerostato, juguete) balloon

glóbulo m globule

gloria f glory; (placer) delight. ~rse vpr boast (**de** about)

glorieta f square; (Auto) roundabout (Brit), (traffic) circle (Amer)

glorificar 🔟 vt glorify

glorioso adj glorious

glotón adj gluttonous. •m glutton

gnomo /'nomo/ m gnome

gob|ernación f government. **Ministerio** m **de la G~ernación** Home Office (Brit), Department of the Interior (Amer). ~**ernador** adj governing. •m governor. ~**ernante** adj governing. •m & f leader. ~**ernar** 🔟 vt govern. ~**ierno** m government

goce m enjoyment

gol m goal

golf m golf

golfo m gulf; (niño) urchin; (holgazán) layabout

golondrina f swallow

golos|ina f titbit; (dulce) sweet. ~o adj fond of sweets

golpe m blow; (puñetazo) punch; (choque) bump; (de emoción) shock; (arg, atraco) job 🔟; (en golf, en tenis, de remo) stroke. ~ **de estado** coup d'etat. ~ **de fortuna** stroke of luck. ~ **de vista** glance. ~ **militar** military coup. **de** ~ suddenly. **de un** ~ in one go. ~**ar** vt hit; (dar varios golpes) beat; (con mucho ruido) bang; (con el puño) punch. •vi knock

goma f rubber; (para pegar) glue; (banda) rubber band; (de borrar) eraser. ~ **de mascar** chewing gum. ~ **espuma** foam rubber

googlear ® vt/i 🔟 to google

gord|a f (Mex) small thick tortilla. ~o adj (persona) (con ser) fat; (con

estar) have put on weight; (carne) fatty; (grueso) thick; (grande) large, big. •m first prize. ~**ura** f fatness; (grasa) fat

gorila f gorilla

gorje|ar vi chirp. ~o m chirping

gorra f cap. ~ **de baño** (LAm) bathing cap

gorrión m sparrow

gorro m cap; (de niño) bonnet. ~ **de baño** bathing cap

got|a f drop; (Med) gout. **ni** ~**a** nothing. ~**ear** vi drip. ~**era** f leak

gozar 🔟 vt enjoy. •vi. ~ **de** enjoy

gozne m hinge

gozo m pleasure; (alegría) joy. ~**so** adj delighted

graba|ción f recording. ~**do** m engraving, print; (en libro) illustration. ~**dora** f tape-recorder. ~**r** vt engrave; record (discos etc)

graci|a f grace; (favor) favour; (humor) wit. ~**as** fpl thanks. **¡~as!** thank you!, thanks! **dar las ~as** thank. **hacer** ~**a** amuse; (gustar) please. **¡muchas ~as!** thank you very much! **tener** ~**a** be funny. ~**oso** adj funny. •m fool, comic character

grad|a f step. ~**as** fpl stand(s). ~**ación** f gradation. ~**o** m degree; (en enseñanza) year (Brit), grade (Amer). **de buen** ~**o** willingly

gradua|ción f graduation; (de alcohol) proof. ~**do** m graduate. ~**l** adj gradual. ~**r** 🔟 vt graduate; (regular) adjust. ~**rse** vpr graduate

gráfic|a f graph. ~**o** adj graphic. •m graph

gram|ática f grammar. ~**atical** adj grammatical

gramo m gram, gramme (Brit)

gran adj véase GRANDE

grana f (color) deep red

granada f pomegranate; (Mil) grenade

granate m (color) maroon

Gran Bretaña f Great Britain

grande adj (delante de nombre en singular **gran**) big, large; (alto) tall; (fig) great; (LAm, de edad) grown up. **~za** f greatness

grandioso adj magnificent

granel m. **a ~** in bulk; (suelto) loose; (fig) in abundance

granero m barn

g

granito m granite; (grano) small grain

graniz|ado m iced drink. **~ar** 10 vi hail. **~o** m hail

granj|a f farm. **~ero** m farmer

grano m grain; (semilla) seed; (de café) bean; (Med) spot. **~s** mpl cereals

granuja m & f rogue

grapa f staple. **~r** vt staple

gras|a f grease; (Culin) fat. **~iento** adj greasy

gratifica|ción f (de sueldo) bonus (recompensa) reward. **~r** 7 vt reward

grat|is adv free. **~itud** f gratitude. **~o** adj pleasant **~uito** adj free; (fig) uncalled for

grava|men m tax; (carga) burden; (sobre inmueble) encumbrance. **~r** vt tax; (cargar) burden

grave adj serious; (voz) deep; (sonido) low; (acento) grave. **~dad** f gravity

gravilla f gravel

gravitar vi gravitate; (apoyarse) rest (**sobre** on); (peligro) hang (**sobre** over)

gravoso adj costly

graznar vi (cuervo) caw; (pato) quack; honk (ganso)

Grecia f Greece

gremio m union

greña f mop of hair

gresca f rumpus; (riña) quarrel

griego adj & m Greek

grieta f crack

grifo m tap, faucet (Amer)

grilletes mpl shackles

grillo m cricket. **~s** mpl shackles

gringo m (LAm) foreigner; (norteamericano) Yankee !

gripe f flu

gris adj grey. • m grey; (fam, policía) policeman

grit|ar vi shout. **~ería** f, **~erío** m uproar. **~o** m shout; (de dolor, sorpresa) cry; (chillido) scream. **dar ~s** shout

grosella f redcurrant. **~ negra** blackcurrant

groser|ía f rudeness; (ordinariez) coarseness; (comentario etc) coarse remark; (palabra) swearword. **~o** adj coarse; (descortés) rude

grosor m thickness

grotesco adj grotesque

grúa f crane

grueso adj thick; (persona) fat, stout. • m thickness; (fig) main body

grumo m lump

gruñi|do m grunt; (de perro) growl. **~r** 22 vi grunt; (perro) growl

grupa f hindquarters

grupo m group

gruta f grotto

guacamole m guacamole

guadaña f scythe

guaje m (Mex) gourd

guajolote m (Mex) turkey

guante m glove

guapo adj good-looking; (chica) pretty; (elegante) smart

guarda m & f guard; (de parque etc) keeper. **~barros** m invar mudguard. **~bosque** m gamekeeper. **~costas** m invar coastguard vessel. **~espaldas** m invar bodyguard. **~meta** m goalkeeper. **~r** vt keep; (proteger) protect; (en un lugar) put away; (reservar) save, keep. **~rse** vpr. **~rse de** (+ infinitivo) avoid (+ gerundio). **~rropa** m wardrobe; (en local público) cloakroom. **~vallas** m invar (LAm) goalkeeper

🔲**guardería** f nursery

guardia f guard; (policía) policewoman; (de médico) shift. 🔲**G~ Civil** Civil Guard. **~ municipal** police. **estar de ~** be on duty. **estar en ~** be on one's guard. **montar la ~** mount guard. ● m policeman. **~ jurado** m & f security guard. **~ de tráfico** m traffic policeman. ● f traffic policewoman

guardián m guardian; (de parque etc) keeper; (de edificio) security guard

guar|ecer 🔢 vt (albergar) give shelter to. **~ecerse** vpr take shelter. **~ida** f den, lair; (de personas) hideout

guarn|ecer 🔢 vt (adornar) adorn; (Culin) garnish. **~ición** f adornment; (de caballo) harness; (Culin) garnish; (Mil) garrison; (de piedra preciosa) setting

guas|a f joke. **~ón** adj humorous. ● m joker

Guatemala f Guatemala

guatemalteco adj & m Guatemalan

guateque m party, bash

guayab|a f guava; (dulce) guava jelly. **~era** f lightweight jacket

gubernatura f (Mex) government

güero adj (Mex) fair

guerr|a f war; (método) warfare. **dar ~a** annoy. **~ero** adj warlike; (belicoso) fighting. ● m warrior. **~illa** f band of guerrillas. **~illero** m guerrilla

guía m & f guide. ● f guidebook; (de teléfonos) directory

guiar 🔢 vt guide; (llevar) lead; (Auto) drive. **~se** vpr be guided (**por** by)

guijarro m pebble

guillotina f guillotine

guind|a f morello cherry. **~illa** f chilli

guiñapo m rag; (fig, persona) wreck

guiñ|ar vt/i wink. **~o** m wink. **hacer ~os** wink

gui|ón m hyphen, dash; (de película etc) script. **~onista** m & f scriptwriter

guirnalda f garland

guisado m stew

guisante m pea. **~ de olor** sweet pea

guis|ar vt/i cook. **~o** m stew

guitarr|a f guitar. **~ista** m & f guitarist

gula f gluttony

gusano m worm; (larva de mosca) maggot

---

gustar

● verbo intransitivo

❗ Cuando el verbo **gustar** va precedido del complemento indirecto **le** (o **les, nos** etc), el sujeto en español pasa a ser el objeto en inglés. **me gusta mucho la música** *I like music very much*. **le gustan los helados** *he likes ice cream*. **a Juan no le gusta** *Juan doesn't like it* (or *her etc*)

····➤ **gustar** + infinitivo. **les gusta ver televisión** they like watching television

····➤ **gustar que** + subjuntivo. **me ~ía que vinieras** I'd like you to come. **no le gusta que lo corrijan** he doesn't like being corrected. **¿te ~ía que te lo comprara?** would you like me to buy it for you?

····➤ **gustar de algo** to like sth. **gustan de las fiestas** they

....

🔲 *see* A-Z of Spanish life and culture

like parties

····▸ (*tener acogida*) to go down well. **ese tipo de cosas que siempre gusta** those sort of things always go down well. **el libro no gustó** the book didn't go down well

····▸ (*en frases de cortesía*) to wish. **como guste** as you wish. **cuando gustes** whenever you wish

● verbo transitivo

····▸ (*LAm, querer*) **¿gusta un café?**

would you like a coffee? **¿gustan pasar?** would you like to come in? **gustarse** verbo pronominal to like each other

gusto m taste; (*placer*) pleasure. **a ∼** comfortable. **a mi ∼** to my liking. **buen ∼** good taste. **con mucho ∼** with pleasure. **dar ∼** please. **mucho ∼** pleased to meet you. **∼so** adj tasty; (*de buen grado*) willingly

gutural adj guttural

Hh

ha vb véase **HABER**

haba f broad bean

Habana f **La ∼** Havana

habano m (*puro*) Havana

haber verbo auxiliar **30** have. ●v impersonal (*presente* s & pl **hay**, *imperfecto* s & pl **había**, *pretérito* s & pl **hubo**). **hay una carta para ti** there's a letter for you. **hay 5 bancos en la plaza** there are 5 banks in the square. **hay que hacerlo** it must be done, you have to do it. **he aquí** here is, here are. **no hay de qué** don't mention it, not at all. **¿qué hay?** (*¿qué pasa?*) what's the matter?; (*¿qué tal?*) how are you?

habichuela f bean

hábil adj skilful; (*listo*) clever; (*día*) working; (*Jurid*) competent

habili|dad f skill; (*astucia*) cleverness; (*Jurid*) competence. **∼tar** vt qualify

habita|ción f room; (*dormitorio*) bedroom; (*en biología*) habitat. **∼ción de matrimonio, ∼ción doble** double room. **∼ción individual, ∼ción sencilla** single room. **∼do** adj inhabited. **∼nte** m inhabitant. **∼r** vt live in. ●vi live

hábito m habit

habitua|l adj usual, habitual; (*cliente*) regular. **∼r** **21** vt accustom. **∼rse** vpr. **∼rse a** get used to

habla f speech; (*idioma*) language; (*dialecto*) dialect. **al ∼** (*al teléfono*) speaking. **ponerse al ∼ con** get in touch with. **∼dor** adj talkative. ●m & f speaker. **∼duría** f rumour. **∼durías** fpl gossip. **∼nte** adj speaking. ●m & f speaker. **∼r** vt speak. ●vi speak, talk (**con** to); (*Mex, por teléfono*) call. **¡ni ∼r!** out of the question! **se ∼ español** Spanish spoken

hacend|ado m landowner; (*LAm*) farmer. **∼oso** adj hard-working

hacer **31**

● verbo transitivo

····▸ to do. **¿qué haces?** what are you doing? **∼ los deberes** to do one's homework. **no sé qué ∼** I don't know what to do. **hazme un favor** can you do me a favour?

····▸ (*fabricar, preparar, producir*) to make. **me hizo un vestido** she made me a dress. **∼ un café** to make a (cup of) coffee. **no hagas tanto ruido** don't make so much noise

••••▸ (construir) to build (casa, puente)

••••▸ **hacer que uno haga algo** to make s.o. do sth. **haz que se vaya** make him leave. **hizo que se equivocara** he made her go wrong

••••▸ **hacer hacer algo** to have sth done. **hizo arreglar el techo** he had the roof repaired

▶ Cuando el verbo **hacer** se emplea en expresiones como **hacer una pregunta, hacer trampa** etc., ver bajo el respectivo nombre

• verbo intransitivo

••••▸ (actuar, obrar) to do. **hiciste bien en llamar** you did the right thing to call **¿cómo haces para parecer tan joven?** what do you do to look so young?

••••▸ (fingir, simular) **hacer como que** to pretend. **hizo como que no me conocía** he pretended not to know me. **haz como que estás dormido** pretend you're asleep

••••▸ **hacer de** (en teatro) to play the part of; (ejercer la función de) to act as

••••▸ (LAm, sentar) **tanta sal hace mal** so much salt is not good for you. **dormir le hizo bien** the sleep did him good. **el pepino me hace mal** cucumber doesn't agree with me verbo impersonal

••••▸ (hablando del tiempo atmosférico) to be. **hace sol** it's sunny. **hace 3 grados** it's 3 degrees

••••▸ (con expresiones temporales) **hace una hora que espero** I've been waiting for an hour. **llegó hace 3 días** he arrived 3 days ago. **hace mucho tiempo** a long time ago. **hasta hace poco** until recently

• **hacerse** verbo pronominal

••••▸ (para sí) to make o.s. (falda,

café)

••••▸ (hacer que otro haga) **se hizo la permanente** she had her hair permed. **me hice una piscina** I had a pool built

••••▸ (convertirse en) to become. **se hicieron amigos** they became friends

••••▸ (acostumbrarse) **~se a algo** to get used to sth

••••▸ (fingirse) **~se el enfermo** to pretend to be ill

••••▸ (moverse) to move. **hazte para atrás** move back

••••▸ **hacerse de** (LAm) to make (amigo, dinero)

hacha f axe; (antorcha) torch

hacia prep towards; (cerca de) near; (con tiempo) at about. **~ abajo** downwards. **~ arriba** upwards. **~ atrás** backwards. **~ las dos** (at) about two o'clock

hacienda † country estate; (en LAm) ranch; **la ~ pública** the Treasury. **Ministerio m de H~** Ministry of Finance; (en Gran Bretaña) Exchequer; (en Estados Unidos) Treasury

hada f fairy. **el ~ madrina** the fairy godmother

hago vb véase HACER

Haití m Haiti

halag|ar 12 vt flatter. **~üeño** adj flattering; (esperanzador) promising

halcón m falcon

halla|r vt find; (descubrir) discover. **~rse** vpr be. **~zgo** m discovery

hamaca f hammock; (asiento) deck-chair

hambr|e f hunger; (de muchos) famine. **tener ~e** be hungry. **~iento** adj starving

hamburguesa f hamburger

harag|án adj lazy, idle. •m layabout. **~anear** vi laze around

harap|iento adj in rags. **~o** m rag

harina f flour

hart|ar vt (fastidiar) annoy. **me estás**

~**ando** you're annoying me. ~**arse** vpr (llenarse) gorge o.s. (**de** on); (cansarse) get fed up (**de** with). ~**o** adj full; (cansado) tired; (fastidiado) fed up (**de** with). •adv (LAm) (muy) very; (mucho) a lot

hasta prep as far as; (en el tiempo) until, till; (Mex) not until. ~ even. **¡~ la vista!** goodbye!, see you! ① **¡~ luego!** see you later! **¡~ mañana!** see you tomorrow! **¡~ pronto!** see you soon!

hast|iar ⑳ vt (cansar) weary, tire; (aburrir) bore. ~**iarse** vpr get fed up (**de** with). ~**ío** m weariness; (aburrimiento) boredom

haya f beech (tree). •vb véase **HABER**

hazaña f exploit

hazmerreír m laughing stock

he vb véase **HABER**

hebilla f buckle

hebra f thread; (fibra) fibre

hebreo adj & m Hebrew

hechi|cería f witchcraft. ~**cero** m wizard. ~**zar** ⑩ vt cast a spell on; (fig) captivate. ~**zo** m spell; (fig) charm

hech|o pp de **hacer**. •adj (manufacturado) made; (terminado) done; (vestidos etc) ready-made; (Culin) done. •m fact; (acto) deed; (cuestión) matter; (suceso) event. **de ~o** in fact. ~**ura** f making; (forma) form; (del cuerpo) build; (calidad de fabricación) workmanship

hed|er ① vi stink. ~**iondez** f stench. ~**iondo** adj stinking, smelly. ~**or** m stench

hela|da f frost. ~**dera** f (LAm) fridge, refrigerator. ~**dería** f ice-cream shop. ~**do** adj freezing; (congelado) frozen; (LAm, bebida) chilled. •m ice-cream. ~**r** ① vt/i freeze. **anoche heló** there was a frost last night. ~**rse** vpr freeze

helecho m fern

hélice f propeller

helicóptero m helicopter

hembra f female; (mujer) woman

hemorr|agia f haemorrhage. ~**oides** fpl haemorrhoids

hendidura f crack, split; (en geología) fissure

heno m hay

heráldica f heraldry

hered|ar vt/i inherit. ~**era** f heiress. ~**ero** m heir. ~**itario** adj hereditary

herej|e m heretic. ~**ía** f heresy

herencia f inheritance; (fig) heritage

heri|da f injury; (con arma) wound. ~**do** adj injured; (con arma) wounded; (fig) hurt. •m injured person. ~**r** ④ vt injure; (con arma) wound; (fig) hurt. ~**rse** vpr hurt o.s.

herman|a f sister. ~**a política** sister-in-law. ~**astra** f stepsister. ~**astro** m stepbrother. ~**o** m brother. ~**o político** brother-in-law. ~**os** mpl brothers; (chicos y chicas) brothers and sisters. ~**os gemelos** twins

hermético adj hermetic; (fig) watertight

hermos|o adj beautiful; (espléndido) splendid. ~**ura** f beauty

héroe m hero

hero|ico adj heroic. ~**ína** f heroine; (droga) heroin. ~**ísmo** m heroism

herr|adura f horseshoe. ~**amienta** f tool. ~**ero** m blacksmith

herv|idero m (fig) hotbed; (multitud) throng. ~**ir** ④ vt/i boil. ~**or** m (fig) ardour. **romper el ~** come to the boil

hiberna|ción f hibernation. ~**r** vi hibernate

híbrido adj & m hybrid

hice vb véase **HACER**

hidalgo m nobleman

hidrata|nte adj moisturizing. ~**r** vt hydrate; (crema etc) moisturize

hidráulico adj hydraulic

hidr|oavión m seaplane.
~**oeléctrico** adj hydroelectric.
~**ofobia** f rabies. ~**ófobo** adj
rabid. ~**ógeno** m hydrogen

hiedra f ivy

hielo m ice

hiena f hyena

hierba f grass; (Culin, Med) herb
mala ~ weed. ~**buena** f mint.

hierro m iron

hígado m liver

higi|ene f hygiene. ~**énico** adj
hygienic

hig|o m fig. ~**uera** f fig tree

hij|a f daughter. ~**astra** f
stepdaughter. ~**astro** m stepson.
~**o** m son. ~**os** mpl sons; (chicos y
chicas) children

hilar vt spin. ~ **delgado** split hairs

hilera f row; (Mil) file

hilo m thread; (Elec) wire; (de líquido)
trickle; (lino) linen

hilv|án m tacking. ~**anar** vt tack;
(fig) put together

himno m hymn. ~ **nacional**
anthem

hincapié m. **hacer** ~ **en** stress,
insist on

hincar 🔟 vt drive (estaca) (**en** into).
~**se** vpr. ~**se de rodillas** kneel
down

hincha f 🔟 grudge. ●m & f (fam,
aficionado) fan

hincha|do adj inflated; (Med)
swollen. ~**r** vt inflate, blow up.
~**rse** vpr swell up; (fig, fam, comer
mucho) gorge o.s. ~**zón** f swelling

hinojo m fennel

hiper|mercado m hypermarket.
~**sensible** adj hypersensitive.
~**tensión** f high blood pressure

hípic|a f horse racing. ~**o** adj horse

hipn|osis f hypnosis. ~**otismo** m
hypnotism. ~**otizar** 🔟 vt
hypnotize

hipo m hiccup. **tener** ~ have
hiccups

hipo|alérgeno adj hypoallergenic.
~**condríaco** adj & m
hypochondriac

hip|ocresía f hypocrisy. ~**ócrita**
adj hypocritical. ●m & f hypocrite

hipódromo m racecourse

hipopótamo m hippopotamus

hipoteca f mortgage. ~**r** 🔟 vt
mortgage

hip|ótesis f invar hypothesis.
~**otético** adj hypothetical

hiriente adj offensive, wounding

hirsuto adj (barba) bristly; (pelo)
wiry

hispánico adj Hispanic

Hispanoamérica f Spanish
America

hispano|americano adj Spanish
American. ~**hablante** adj
Spanish-speaking

hist|eria f hysteria. ~**érico** adj
hysterical

hist|oria f history; (relato) story;
(excusa) tale, excuse. **pasar a la**
~**oria** go down in history.
~**oriador** m historian. ~**órico** adj
historical. ~**orieta** f tale; (con
dibujos) strip cartoon

hito m milestone

hizo vb véase HACER

hocico m snout

hockey /'(x)oki/ m hockey. ~
sobre hielo ice hockey

hogar m home; (chimenea) hearth.
~**eño** adj domestic; (persona) home-
loving

hoguera f bonfire

hoja f leaf; (de papel, metal etc) sheet;
(de cuchillo, espada etc) blade. ~ **de
afeitar** razor blade. ~**lata** f tin

hojaldre m puff pastry

hojear vt leaf through

hola int hello!

Holanda f Holland

h

holand|és adj Dutch. ●m Dutchman; (lengua) Dutch. **~esa** f Dutchwoman. **los ~eses** the Dutch

holg|ado adj loose; (fig) comfortable. **~ar 2 & 12** vi. **huelga decir que** needless to say. **~azán** adj lazy. ●m idler. **~ura** f looseness; (fig) comfort

hollín m soot

hombre m man; (especie humana) man(kind). ●int Good Heavens!; (de duda) well. **~ de negocios** businessman. **~ rana** frogman

hombr|era f shoulder pad. **~o** m shoulder

homenaje m homage, tribute. **rendir ~ a** pay tribute to

home|ópata m homoeopath. **~opatía** f homoeopathy. **~opático** adj homoeopathic

homicid|a adj murderous. ●m & f murderer. **~io** m murder

homosexual adj & m & f homosexual. **~idad** f homosexuality

hond|o adj deep. **~onada** f hollow

Honduras f Honduras

hondureño adj & m Honduran

honest|idad f honesty. **~o** adj honest

hongo m fungus; (LAm, Culin) mushroom; (venenoso) toadstool

hon|or m honour. **~orable** adj honourable. **~orario** adj honorary. **~orarios** mpl fees. **~ra** f honour; (buena fama) good name. **~radez** f honesty. **~rado** adj honest. **~rar** vt honour

hora f hour; (momento puntual) time; (cita) appointment. **~ pico, ~ punta** rush hour. **~s** fpl **de trabajo** working hours. **~s** fpl **extraordinarias** overtime. **~s** fpl **libres** free time. **a estas ~s** now. **¿a qué ~?** (at) what time? **a última ~** at the last moment. **de última ~** last-minute. **en buena ~** at the right time. **media ~**

half an hour. **pedir ~** to make an appointment. **¿qué ~ es?** what time is it?

horario adj hourly. ●m timetable. **~ de trabajo** working hours

horca f gallows

horcajadas fpl. **a ~** astride

horchata f tiger-nut milk

horizont|al adj & f horizontal. **~e** m horizon

horma f mould; (para fabricar calzado) last; (para conservar su forma) shoe-tree. **de ~ ancha** broad-fitting

hormiga f ant

hormigón m concrete

hormigue|ar vi tingle; (bullir) swarm. **me ~a la mano** I've got pins and needles in my hand. **~o** m tingling; (fig) anxiety

hormiguero m anthill; (de gente) swarm

hormona f hormone

horn|ada f batch. **~illa** f (LAm) burner. **~illo** m burner; (cocina portátil) portable electric cooker. **~o** m oven; (para cerámica etc) kiln; (Tec) furnace

horóscopo m horoscope

horquilla f pitchfork; (para el pelo) hairpin

horr|endo adj awful. **~ible** adj horrible. **~ipilante** adj terrifying. **~or** m horror; (atrocidad) atrocity. **¡qué ~or!** how awful!. **~orizar 10** vt horrify. **~orizarse** vpr be horrified. **~oroso** adj horrifying

hort|aliza f vegetable. **~elano** m market gardener

hosco adj surly

hospeda|je m accommodation. **~r** vt put up. **~rse** vpr stay

hospital m hospital. **~ario** adj hospitable. **~idad** f hospitality

hostal m boarding-house

hostería f inn

hostia f (Relig) host

hostigar 12 vt whip; (fig, molestar) pester

hostil adj hostile. **~idad** f hostility

hotel m hotel. **~ero** adj hotel. •m hotelier

hoy adv today. **~ (en) día** nowadays. **~ por ~** at the present time. **de ~ en adelante** from now on

hoy|o m hole. **~uelo** m dimple

hoz f sickle

hube vb véase **HABER**

hucha f money box

hueco adj hollow; (palabras) empty; (voz) resonant; (persona) superficial. •m hollow; (espacio) space; (vacío) gap

huelg|a f strike. **~a de brazos caídos** sit-down strike. **~a de hambre** hunger strike. **declararse en ~a** come out on strike. **~uista** m & f striker

huella f footprint; (de animal, vehículo etc) track. **~ digital** fingerprint

huelo vb véase **OLER**

huérfano adj orphaned. •m orphan. **~ de** without

huert|a f market garden (Brit), truck farm (Amer); (terreno de regadío) irrigated plain. **~o** m vegetable garden; (de árboles frutales) orchard

hueso m bone; (de fruta) stone

huésped m guest; (que paga) lodger

huesudo adj bony

huev|a f roe. **~o** m egg. **~o duro** hard-boiled egg. **~o escalfado** poached egg. **~o estrellado, ~o frito** fried egg. **~o pasado por agua** boiled egg. **~os revueltos** scrambled eggs. **~o tibio** (Mex) boiled egg

hui|da f flight, escape. **~dizo** adj (tímido) shy; (esquivo) elusive

▣ **huipil** m (Mex) traditional embroidered smock

huir vi 17 flee, run away; (evitar). **~**

de avoid. **me huye** he avoids me

huitlacoche m (Mex) edible black fungus

hule m oilcloth; (Mex, goma) rubber

human|idad f mankind; (fig) humanity. **~itario** adj humanitarian. **~o** adj human; (benévolo) humane

humareda f cloud of smoke

humed|ad f dampness; (en meteorología) humidity; (gotitas de agua) moisture. **~ecer** 11 vt moisten. **~ecerse** vpr become moist

húmedo adj damp; (clima) humid; (labios) moist; (mojado) wet

humi|ldad f humility. **~lde** adj humble. **~llación** f humiliation. **~llar** vt humiliate. **~llarse** vpr lower o.s.

humo m smoke; (vapor) steam; (gas nocivo) fumes. **~s** mpl airs

humor m mood, temper; (gracia) humour, **estar de mal ~** be in a bad mood. **~ista** m & f humorist. **~ístico** adj humorous

hundi|miento m sinking. **~r** vt sink; destroy (persona). **~rse** vpr sink; (edificio) collapse

húngaro adj & m Hungarian

Hungría f Hungary

huracán m hurricane

huraño adj unsociable

hurgar 12 vi rummage (**en** through). **~se la nariz** pick one's nose

hurra int hurray!

hurtadillas fpl. **a ~** stealthily

hurt|ar vt steal. **~o** m theft; (cosa robada) stolen object

husmear vt sniff out; (fig) pry into

huyo vb véase **HUIR**

▣ see A-Z of Spanish life and culture

Ii

iba véase **IR**

ibérico adj Iberian

iberoamericano adj & m Latin American

iceberg /iθ'ber/ m (pl **~s**) iceberg

ictericia f jaundice

ida f outward journey; (partida) departure. **de ~ y vuelta** (billete) return (Brit), round-trip (Amer); (viaje) round

idea f idea; (opinión) opinion. **cambiar de ~** change one's mind. **no tener la más remota ~, no tener la menor ~** not have the slightest idea, not have a clue 🔢

ideal adj & m ideal. **~ista** m & f idealist. **~izar** 🔟 vt idealize

idear vt think up, conceive; (inventar) invent

ídem pron & adv the same

idéntico adj identical

identi|dad f identity. **~ficación** f identification. **~ficar** 🔢 vt identify. **~ficarse** vpr identify o.s. **~ficarse con** identify with

ideol|ogía f ideology. **~ógico** adj ideological

idílico adj idyllic

idilio m idyll

idiom|a m language. **~ático** adj idiomatic

idiosincrasia f idiosyncrasy

idiot|a adj idiotic. **•**m & f idiot. **~ez** f stupidity

idolatrar vt worship; (fig) idolize

ídolo m idol

idóneo adj suitable (**para** for)

iglesia f church

iglú m igloo

ignora|ncia f ignorance. **~nte** adj ignorant. **•**m ignoramus. **~r** vt not know, be unaware of; (no hacer caso de) ignore

igual adj equal; (mismo) the same; (similar) like; (llano) even; (liso) smooth. **•**adv the same. **•**m equal. **~ que** (the same) as. **al ~ que** the same as. **da ~, es ~** it doesn't matter. **sin ~** unequalled

igual|ar vt make equal; equal (éxito, récord); (allanar) level. **~arse** vpr be equal. **~dad** f equality. **~mente** adv equally; (también) also, likewise; (respuesta de cortesía) the same to you

ilegal adj illegal

ilegible adj illegible

ilegítimo adj illegitimate

ileso adj unhurt

ilícito adj illicit

ilimitado adj unlimited

ilógico adj illogical

ilumina|ción f illumination; (alumbrado) lighting. **~r** vt light (up). **~rse** vpr light up

ilusi|ón f illusion; (sueño) dream; (alegría) joy. **hacerse ~ones** build up one's hopes. **me hace ~ón** I'm thrilled; I'm looking forward to (algo en el futuro). **~onado** adj excited. **~onar** vt give false hope. **~onarse** vpr have false hopes

ilusionis|mo m conjuring. **~ta** m & f conjurer

iluso adj naive. **•**m dreamer. **~rio** adj illusory

ilustra|ción f learning; (dibujo) illustration. **~do** adj learned; (con dibujos) illustrated. **~r** vt explain; (instruir) instruct; (añadir dibujos etc) illustrate. **~rse** vpr acquire knowledge. **~tivo** adj illustrative

ilustre adj illustrious

imagen f image; (TV etc) picture

imagina|ble adj imaginable. **~ción** f imagination. **~r** vt imagine. **~rse** vpr imagine. **~rio** m imaginary. **~tivo** adj imaginative

imán m magnet

imbécil adj stupid. ● m & f idiot

imborrable adj indelible; (recuerdo etc) unforgettable

imita|ción f imitation. **~r** vt imitate

impacien|cia f impatience. **~tarse** vpr lose one's patience. **~te** adj impatient

impacto m impact; (huella) mark. **~ de bala** bullet hole

impar adj odd

imparcial adj impartial. **~idad** f impartiality

impartir vt impart, give

impasible adj impassive

impávido adj fearless; (impasible) impassive

impecable adj impeccable

impedi|do adj disabled. **~mento** m impediment. **~r** [5] vt prevent; (obstruir) hinder

impenetrable adj impenetrable

impensa|ble adj unthinkable. **~do** adj unexpected

impera|r vi prevail. **~tivo** adj imperative; (necesidad) urgent

imperceptible adj imperceptible

imperdible m safety pin

imperdonable adj unforgivable

imperfec|ción f imperfection. **~to** adj imperfect

imperi|al adj imperial. **~alismo** m imperialism. **~o** m empire; (poder) rule. **~oso** adj imperious

impermeable adj waterproof. ● m raincoat

impersonal adj impersonal

impertinen|cia f impertinence. **~te** adj impertinent

imperturbable adj imperturbable

ímpetu m impetus; (impulso) impulse; (violencia) force

impetuos|idad f impetuosity. **~o** adj impetuous

implacable adj implacable

implantar vt introduce

implementación f implementation

implica|ción f implication. **~r** [7] vt implicate; (significar) imply

implícito adj implicit

implorar vt implore

impon|ente adj imposing; [1] terrific. **~er** [34] vt impose; (requerir) demand; deposit (dinero). **~erse** vpr (hacerse obedecer) assert o.s., (hacerse respetar) command respect; (prevalecer) prevail. **~ible** adj taxable

importa|ción f importation; (artículo) import. **~ciones** fpl imports. **~dor** adj importing. ● m importer

importa|ncia f importance. **~nte** adj important; (en cantidad) considerable. **~r** vt import; (ascender a) amount to. ● vi be important, matter. **¿le ~ría...?** would you mind...? **no ~** it doesn't matter

importe m price; (total) amount

importun|ar vt bother. **~o** adj troublesome; (inoportuno) inopportune

imposib|ilidad f impossibility. **~le** adj impossible. **hacer lo ~le para** do all one can to

imposición f imposition; (impuesto) tax

impostor m impostor

impoten|cia f impotence. **~te** adj impotent

impracticable adj impracticable;

(intransitable) unpassable

imprecis|ión f vagueness; (error) inaccuracy. ~**o** adj imprecise

impregnar vt impregnate; (empapar) soak

imprenta f printing; (taller) printing house, printer's

imprescindible adj indispensable, essential

impresi|ón f impression; (acción de imprimir) printing; (tirada) edition; (huella) imprint. ~**onable** adj impressionable. ~**onante** adj impressive; (espantoso) frightening. ~**onar** vt impress; (negativamente) shock; (conmover) move; (Foto) expose. ~**onarse** vpr be impressed; (negativamente) be shocked; (conmover) be moved

impresionis|mo m impressionism. ~**ta** adj & m & f impressionist

impreso adj printed. •m form. ~**s** mpl printed matter. ~**ra** f printer

imprevis|ible adj unforeseeable. ~**to** adj unforeseen

imprimir (pp **impreso**) vt print (libro etc)

improbab|ilidad f improbability. ~**le** adj unlikely, improbable

improcedente adj inadmissible; (conducta) improper; (despido) unfair

improductivo adj unproductive

improperio m insult. ~**s** mpl abuse

impropio adj improper

improvis|ación f improvisation. ~**ado** adj improvised. ~**ar** vt improvise. ~**o** adj. **de** ~**o** unexpectedly

impruden|cia f imprudence. ~**te** adj imprudent

imp|udicia f indecency; (desvergüenza) shamelessness. ~**údico** adj indecent; (desvergonzado) shameless. ~**udor** m indecency;

(desvergüenza) shamelessness

impuesto adj imposed. •m tax. ~ **a la renta** income tax. ~ **sobre el valor agregado** (LAm), ~ **sobre el valor añadido** VAT, value added tax

impuls|ar vt propel; drive (persona); boost (producción etc). ~**ividad** f impulsiveness. ~**ivo** adj impulsive. ~**o** m impulse

impun|e adj unpunished. ~**idad** f impunity

impur|eza f impurity. ~**o** adj impure

imputa|ción f charge. ~**r** vt attribute; (acusar) charge

inaccesible adj inaccessible

inaceptable adj unacceptable

inactiv|idad f inactivity. ~**o** adj inactive

inadaptado adj maladjusted

inadecuado adj inadequate; (inapropiado) unsuitable

inadmisible adj inadmissible; (inaceptable) unacceptable

inadvertido adj distracted. **pasar** ~ go unnoticed

inagotable adj inexhaustible

inaguantable adj unbearable

inaltera|ble adj impassive; (color) fast; (convicción) unalterable. ~**do** adj unchanged

inapreciable adj invaluable; (imperceptible) imperceptible

inapropiado adj inappropriate

inasequible adj out of reach

inaudito adj unprecedented

inaugura|ción f inauguration. ~**l** adj inaugural. ~**r** vt inaugurate

🖪 **inca** adj & m & f Inca. ~**ico** adj Inca

incalculable adj incalculable

incandescente adj incandescent

incansable adj tireless

incapa|cidad f incapacity; (física) disability. ~**citado** adj disabled.

🖪 *see* A-Z of Spanish life and culture

~**citar** vt incapacitate. ~**z** adj incapable

incauto adj unwary; (fácil de engañar) gullible

incendi|ar vt set fire to. ~**arse** vpr catch fire. ~**ario** adj incendiary. • m arsonist. ~**o** m fire

incentivo m incentive

incertidumbre f uncertainty

incesante adj incessant

incest|o m incest. ~**uoso** adj incestuous

inciden|cia f incidence; (efecto) impact; (incidente) incident. ~**tal** adj incidental. ~**te** m incident

incidir vi fall (**en** into); (influir) influence

incienso m incense

incierto adj uncertain

incinera|dor m incinerator. ~**r** vt incinerate; cremate (cadáver)

incipiente adj incipient

incisi|ón f incision. ~**vo** adj incisive. • m incisor

incitar vt incite

inclemen|cia f harshness. ~**te** adj harsh

inclina|ción f slope; (de la cabeza) nod; (fig) inclination. ~**r** vt tilt; (inducir) incline. ~**rse** vpr lean; (en saludo) bow; (tender) be inclined (**a** to)

inclu|ido adj included; (precio) inclusive. ~**ir** 17 vt include; (en cartas) enclose. ~**sión** f inclusion. ~**sive** adv inclusive. **hasta el lunes** ~**sive** up to and including Monday. ~**so** adv even

incógnito adj unknown. **de** ~ incognito

incoheren|cia f incoherence. ~**te** adj incoherent

incoloro adj colourless

incomestible adj, **incomible** adj uneatable, inedible

incomodar vt inconvenience; (causar vergüenza) make feel uncomfortable. ~**se** vpr feel uncomfortable; (enojarse) get angry

incómodo adj uncomfortable; (inconveniente) inconvenient

incomparable adj incomparable

incompatib|ilidad f incompatibility. ~**le** adj incompatible

incompeten|cia f incompetence. ~**te** adj & m & f incompetent

incompleto adj incomplete

incompren|dido adj misunderstood. ~**sible** adj incomprehensible. ~**sión** f incomprehension

incomunicado adj cut off; (preso) in solitary confinement

inconcebible adj inconceivable

inconcluso adj unfinished

incondicional adj unconditional

inconfundible adj unmistakable

incongruente adj incoherent; (contradictorio) inconsistent

inconmensurable adj immeasurable

inconscien|cia f unconsciousness; (irreflexión) recklessness. ~**te** adj unconscious; (irreflexivo) reckless

inconsecuente adj inconsistent

inconsistente adj flimsy

inconsolable adj unconsolable

inconstan|cia f lack of perseverance. ~**te** adj changeable; (persona) lacking in perseverance; (voluble) fickle

incontable adj countless

incontenible adj irrepressible

incontinen|cia f incontinence. ~**te** adj incontinent

inconvenien|cia f inconvenience. ~**te** adj inconvenient; (inapropiado) inappropriate; (incorrecto) improper. • m problem; (desventaja) drawback

incorpora|ción f incorporation. ~**r** vt incorporate; (Culin) add.

~**rse** vpr sit up; join (sociedad, regimiento etc)

incorrecto adj incorrect; (descortés) discourteous

incorregible adj incorrigible

incorruptible adj incorruptible

incrédulo adj sceptical; (mirada, gesto) incredulous

increíble adj incredible

increment|ar vt increase. ~**o** m increase

incriminar vt incriminate

incrustar vt encrust

incuba|ción f incubation. ~**dora** f incubator. ~**r** vt incubate; (fig) hatch

incuestionable adj unquestionable

inculcar 7 vt inculcate

inculpar vt accuse

inculto adj uneducated

incumplimiento m non-fulfilment; (de un contrato) breach

incurable adj incurable

incurrir vi. ~ **en** incur (gasto); fall into (error); commit (crimen)

incursión f raid

indagar 12 vt investigate

indebido adj unjust; (uso) improper

indecen|cia f indecency. ~**te** adj indecent

indecible adj indescribable

indecis|ión f indecision. ~**o** adj (con ser) indecisive; (con estar) undecided

indefenso adj defenceless

indefini|ble adj indefinable. ~**do** adj indefinite; (impreciso) undefined

indemnizar 10 vt compensate

independ|encia f independence. ~**iente** adj independent. ~**izarse** 10 vpr become independent

indes|cifrable adj indecipherable.

~**criptible** adj indescribable

indeseable adj undesirable

indestructible adj indestructible

indetermina|ble adj indeterminable. ~**do** adj indeterminate; (tiempo) indefinite

India f. **la** ~ India

indica|ción f indication; (señal) signal. ~**ciones** fpl directions. ~**dor** m indicator; (Tec) gauge. ~**r** 7 vt show, indicate; (apuntar) point at; (hacer saber) point out; (aconsejar) advise. ~**tivo** adj indicative. • m indicative; (al teléfono) dialling code

índice m index; (dedo) index finger; (catálogo) catalogue; (indicación) indication; (aguja) pointer

indicio m indication, sign; (vestigio) trace

indiferen|cia f indifference. ~**te** adj indifferent. **me es** ~**te** it's all the same to me

indígena adj indigenous. • m & f native

indigen|cia f poverty. ~**te** adj needy

indigest|ión f indigestion. ~**o** adj indigestible

indign|ación f indignation. ~**ado** adj indignant. ~**ar** vt make indignant. ~**arse** vpr become indignant. ~**o** adj unworthy; (despreciable) contemptible

indio adj & m Indian

indirect|a f hint. ~**o** adj indirect

indisciplinado adj undisciplined

indiscre|ción f indiscretion. ~**to** adj indiscreet

indiscutible adj unquestionable

indisoluble adj indissoluble

indispensable adj indispensable

indisp|oner 34 vt (enemistar) set against. ~**onerse** vpr fall out; (ponerse enfermo) fall ill. ~**osición** f indisposition. ~**uesto** adj indisposed

individu|al adj individual; (cama)

single. ●m (en tenis etc) singles.
~**alidad** f individuality. ~**alista**
m & f individualist. ~**alizar** 🔟 vt
individualize. ~**o** m individual

indocumentado m *person without
identity papers*; (inmigrante) illegal
immigrant

índole f nature; (clase) type

indolen|cia f indolence. ~**te** adj
indolent

indoloro adj painless

indomable adj untameable

inducir 🔟 vt induce. ~ **a error** be
misleading

indudable adj undoubted

indulgen|cia f indulgence. ~**te**
adj indulgent

indult|ar vt pardon. ~**o** m pardon

industria f industry. ~**l** adj
industrial. ●m & f industrialist.
~**lización** f industrialization.
~**lizar** 🔟 vt industrialize

inédito adj unpublished; (fig)
unknown

inefable adj indescribable

ineficaz adj ineffective; (sistema etc)
inefficient

ineficiente adj inefficient

ineludible adj inescapable,
unavoidable

inept|itud f ineptitude. ~**o** adj
inept

inequívoco adj unequivocal

inercia f inertia

inerte adj inert; (sin vida) lifeless

inesperado adj unexpected

inestable adj unstable

inestimable adj inestimable

inevitable adj inevitable

inexistente adj non-existent

inexorable adj inexorable

inexper|iencia f inexperience.
~**to** adj inexperienced

inexplicable adj inexplicable

infalible adj infallible

infam|ar vt defame. ~**atorio** adj
defamatory. ~**e** adj infamous; (fig,
fam, muy malo) awful. ~**ia** f infamy

infancia f infancy

infant|a f infanta, princess. ~**e** m
infante, prince. ~**ería** f infantry.
~**il** adj children's; (población) child;
(actitud etc) childish, infantile

infarto m heart attack

infec|ción f infection. ~**cioso** adj
infectious. ~**tar** vt infect. ~**tarse**
vpr become infected. ~**to** adj
infected; 🔟 disgusting

infeli|cidad f unhappiness. ~**z** adj
unhappy

inferior adj inferior. ●m & f
inferior. ~**idad** f inferiority

infernal adj infernal, hellish

infestar vt infest; (fig) inundate

infi|delidad f unfaithfulness. ~**el**
adj unfaithful

infierno m hell

infiltra|ción f infiltration. ~**rse**
vpr infiltrate

ínfimo adj lowest; (calidad) very
poor

infini|dad f infinity. ~**tivo** m
infinitive. ~**to** adj infinite. ●m. **el
~to** the infinite; (en matemáticas)
infinity. ~**dad de** countless

inflación f inflation

inflama|ble adj (in)flammable.
~**ción** f inflammation. ~**r** vt set
on fire; (fig, Med) inflame. ~**rse** vpr
catch fire; (Med) become inflamed

inflar vt inflate; blow up (globo);
(fig, exagerar) exaggerate

inflexi|ble adj inflexible. ~**ón** f
inflexion

influ|encia f influence (**en** on).
~**ir** 🔟 vt influence. ●vi. ~ **en**
influence. ~**jo** m influence.
~**yente** adj influential

informa|ción f information;
(noticias) news; (en aeropuerto etc)
information desk; (de teléfonos)

directory enquiries. **~dor** m
informant

informal adj informal; (persona)
unreliable

inform|ante m & f informant. **~ar**
vt/i inform. **~arse** vpr find out.
~ática f information technology,
computing. **~ativo** adj
informative; (programa) news.
~atizar 🔟 vt computerize

informe adj shapeless. •m report.
~s fpl references, information

infracción f infringement. **~ de
tráfico** traffic offence

infraestructura f infrastructure

infranqueable adj impassable;
(fig) insuperable

infrarrojo adj infrared

infringir 🔢 vt infringe

infructuoso adj fruitless

ínfulas fpl. **darse ~** give o.s. airs.
tener ~ de fancy o.s. as

infundado adj unfounded

infu|ndir vt instil. **~sión** f
infusion

ingeni|ar vt invent. **~árselas
para** find a way to

ingenier|ía f engineering. **~o** m
engineer

ingenio m ingenuity; (agudeza) wit;
(LAm, de azúcar) refinery. **~so** adj
ingenious

ingenu|idad f naivety. **~o** adj
naive

Inglaterra f England

ingl|és adj English. •m Englishman;
(lengua) English. **~esa** f
Englishwoman. **los ~eses** the
English

ingrat|itud f ingratitude. **~o** adj
ungrateful; (desagradable) thankless

ingrediente m ingredient

ingres|ar vt deposit. •vi. **~ar en**
come in, enter; join (sociedad). **~o**
m entrance; (de dinero) deposit; (en
sociedad, hospital) admission. **~os** mpl
income

inh|ábil adj unskilful; (no apto)
unfit. **~abilidad** f unskilfulness;
(para cargo) ineligibility

inhabitable adj uninhabitable

inhala|dor m inhaler. **~r** vt inhale

inherente adj inherent

inhibi|ción f inhibition. **~r** vt
inhibit

inhóspito adj inhospitable

inhumano adj inhuman

inici|ación f beginning. **~al** adj & f
initial. **~ar** vt initiate; (comenzar)
begin, start. **~ativa** f initiative.
~o m beginning

inigualado adj unequalled

ininterrumpido adj
uninterrupted

injert|ar vt graft. **~to** m graft

injuri|a f insult. **~ar** vt insult.
~oso adj insulting

injust|icia f injustice. **~o** adj
unjust, unfair

inmaculado adj immaculate

inmaduro adj unripe; (persona)
immature

inmediaciones fpl. **las ~** the
vicinity, the surrounding area

inmediat|amente adv
immediately. **~o** adj immediate;
(contiguo) next. **de ~o** immediately

inmejorable adj excellent

inmemorable adj immemorial

inmens|idad f immensity. **~o** adj
immense

inmersión f immersion

inmigra|ción f immigration.
~nte adj & m & f immigrant. **~r** vt
immigrate

inminen|cia f imminence. **~te** adj
imminent

inmiscuirse 🔢 vpr interfere

inmobiliario adj property

inmolar vt sacrifice

inmoral adj immoral. **~idad** f
immorality

inmortal adj immortal. **~izar** 🔟 vt immortalize

inmóvil adj immobile

inmovilizador m immobilizer

inmueble adj. **bienes ~s** property

inmund|icia f filth. **~o** adj filthy

inmun|e adj immune. **~idad** f immunity. **~ización** f immunization. **~izar** 🔟 vt immunize

inmuta|ble adj unchangeable. **~rse** vpr be perturbed. **sin ~rse** unperturbed

innato adj innate

innecesario adj unnecessary

innegable adj undeniable

innova|ción f innovation. **~r** vi innovate. ●vt make innovations in

innumerable adj innumerable

inocen|cia f innocence. **~tada** f practical joke. **~te** adj innocent. **~tón** adj naïve

inocuo adj innocuous

inodoro adj odourless. ●m toilet

inofensivo adj inoffensive

inolvidable adj unforgettable

inoperable adj inoperable

inoportuno adj untimely; (comentario) ill-timed

inoxidable adj stainless

inquiet|ar vt worry. **~arse** vpr get worried. **~o** adj worried; (agitado) restless. **~ud** f anxiety

inquilino m tenant

inquirir 🔟 vt enquire into, investigate

insaciable adj insatiable

insalubre adj unhealthy

insatisfecho adj unsatisfied; (descontento) dissatisfied

inscri|bir (pp **inscrito**) vt (en registro) register; (en curso) enrol; (grabar) inscribe. **~birse** vpr register. **~pción** f inscription; (registro) registration

insect|icida m insecticide. **~o** m insect

insegur|idad f insecurity. **~o** adj insecure; (ciudad) unsafe, dangerous

insemina|ción f insemination. **~r** vt inseminate

insensato adj foolish

insensible adj insensitive

inseparable adj inseparable

insertar vt insert

insidi|a f malice. **~oso** adj insidious

insigne adj famous

insignia f badge; (bandera) flag

insignificante adj insignificant

insinua|ción f insinuation. **~ante** adj insinuating. **~ar** 🗗 vt imply; insinuate (algo ofensivo). **~arse** vpr. **~ársele a** make a pass at

insípido adj insipid

insist|encia f insistence. **~ente** adj insistent. **~ir** vi insist; (hacer hincapié) stress

insolación f sunstroke

insolen|cia f rudeness, insolence. **~te** adj rude, insolent

insólito adj unusual

insolven|cia f insolvency. **~te** adj & m & f insolvent

insomn|e adj sleepless. ●m & f insomniac. **~io** m insomnia

insondable adj unfathomable

insoportable adj unbearable

insospechado adj unexpected

insostenible adj untenable

inspec|ción f inspection. **~cionar** vt inspect. **~tor** m inspector

inspira|ción f inspiration. **~r** vt inspire. **~rse** vpr be inspired

instala|ción f installation. **~r** vt install. **~rse** vpr settle

instancia f request. **en última ~** as a last resort

instant|ánea f snapshot. **∼áneo** adj instantaneous; (café etc) instant. **∼e** m instant. **a cada ∼e** constantly. **al ∼e** immediately

instaura|ción f establishment. **∼r** vt establish

instiga|ción f instigation. **∼dor** m instigator. **∼r** 🔢 vt instigate; (incitar) incite

instint|ivo adj instinctive. **∼o** m instinct

institu|ción f institution. **∼cional** adj institutional. **∼ir** 🔢 vt establish. 🔲**∼to** m institute; (en enseñanza) (secondary) school. **∼triz** f governess

instru|cción f education; (Mil) training. **∼cciones** fpl instruction. **∼ctivo** adj instructive; (película etc) educational. **∼ctor** m instructor. **∼ir** 🔢 vt instruct, teach; (Mil) train

instrument|ación f instrumentation. **∼al** adj instrumental. **∼o** m instrument; (herramienta) tool

insubordina|ción f insubordination. **∼r** vt stir up. **∼rse** vpr rebel

insuficien|cia f insufficiency; (inadecuación) inadequacy. **∼te** adj insufficient

insufrible adj insufferable

insular adj insular

insulina f insulin

insulso adj tasteless; (fig) insipid

insult|ar vt insult. **∼o** m insult

insuperable adj insuperable; (inmejorable) unbeatable

insurgente adj insurgent

insurrec|ción f insurrection. **∼to** adj insurgent

intachable adj irreproachable

intacto adj intact

intangible adj intangible

integra|ción f integration. **∼l** adj

🔲 *see* A-Z of Spanish life and culture

integral; (completo) complete; (incorporado) built-in; (pan) wholemeal (Brit), wholewheat (Amer). **∼r** vt make up

integridad f integrity; (entereza) wholeness

íntegro adj complete; (fig) upright

intelect|o m intellect. **∼ual** adj & m & f intellectual

inteligen|cia f intelligence. **∼te** adj intelligent

inteligible adj intelligible

intemperie f. **a la ∼** in the open

intempestivo adj untimely

intenci|ón f intention. **con doble ∼ón** implying sth else. **∼onado** adj deliberate. **bien ∼onado** well-meaning. **mal ∼onado** malicious. **∼onal** adj intentional

intens|idad f intensity. **∼ificar** 🔢 vt intensify. **∼ivo** adj intensive. **∼o** adj intense

intent|ar vt try. **∼o** m attempt; (Mex, propósito) intention

inter|calar vt insert. **∼cambio** m exchange. **∼ceder** vt intercede

interceptar vt intercept

interdicto m ban

inter|és m interest; (egoísmo) self-interest. **∼esado** adj interested; (parcial) biassed; (egoísta) selfish. **∼esante** adj interesting. **∼esar** vt interest; (afectar) concern. ●vi be of interest. **∼esarse** vpr take an interest (**por** in)

interfaz m & f interface

interfer|encia f interference. **∼ir** 🔢 vi interfere

interfono m intercom

interino adj temporary; (persona) acting. ●m stand-in

interior adj interior; (comercio etc) domestic. ●m inside. **Ministerio del I∼** Interior Ministry

interjección f interjection

inter|locutor m speaker. **∼mediario** adj & m intermediary.

~**medio** adj intermediate. •m interval

interminable adj interminable

intermitente adj intermittent. •m indicator

internacional adj international

intern|ado m (Escol) boarding-school. ~**ar** vt (en manicomio) commit; (en hospital) admit. ~**arse** vpr penetrate

internauta m & f netsurfer

Internet m Internet

interno adj internal; (en enseñanza) boarding. •m boarder

interponer 34 vt interpose. ~**se** vpr intervene

int|erpretación f interpretation. ~**erpretar** vt interpret; (Mús etc) play. ~**érprete** m interpreter; (Mus) performer

interroga|ción f interrogation; (signo) question mark. ~**r** 12 vt question. ~**tivo** adj interrogative

interru|mpir vt interrupt; cut off (suministro); cut short (viaje etc.); block (tráfico). ~**pción** f interruption. ~**ptor** m switch

inter|sección f intersection. ~**urbano** adj inter-city; (llamada) long-distance

intervalo m interval; (espacio) space. **a** ~**s** at intervals

interven|ir 53 vt control; (Med) operate on. •vi intervene; (participar) take part. ~**tor** m inspector; (Com) auditor

intestino m intestine

intim|ar vi become friendly. ~**idad** f intimacy

intimidar vt intimidate

íntimo adj intimate; (amigo) close. •m close friend

intolera|ble adj intolerable. ~**nte** adj intolerant

intoxicar 7 vt poison

intranquilo adj worried

intransigente adj intransigent

intransitable adj impassable

intransitivo adj intransitive

intratable adj impossible

intrépido adj intrepid

intriga f intrigue. ~**nte** adj intriguing. ~**r** 12 vt intrigue

intrincado adj intricate

intrínseco adj intrinsic

introduc|ción f introduction. ~**ir** 47 vt introduce; (meter) insert. ~**irse** vpr get into

intromisión f interference

introvertido adj introverted. •m introvert

intruso m intruder

intui|ción f intuition. ~**r** 17 vt sense. ~**tivo** adj intuitive

inunda|ción f flooding. ~**r** vt flood

inusitado adj unusual

in|útil adj useless; (vano) futile. ~**utilidad** f uselessness

invadir vt invade

inv|alidez f invalidity; (Med) disability. ~**álido** adj & m invalid

invariable adj invariable

invas|ión f invasion. ~**or** adj invading. •m invader

invencible adj invincible

inven|ción f invention. ~**tar** vt invent

inventario m inventory

invent|iva f inventiveness. ~**ivo** adj inventive. ~**or** m inventor

invernadero m greenhouse

invernal adj winter

inverosímil adj implausible

inver|sión f inversion; (Com) investment. ~**sionista** m & f investor

inverso adj inverse; (contrario) opposite. **a la inversa** the other way round. **a la inversa de** contrary to

inversor | irreconocible

138

inversor m investor

invertir 4 vt reverse; (Com) invest; put in (tiempo)

investidura f investiture

investiga|ción f investigation; (Univ) research. ~**dor** m investigator; (Univ) researcher. ~**r** 12 vt investigate; (Univ) research

investir 5 vt invest

invicto adj unbeaten

invierno m winter

inviolable adj inviolate

invisible adj invisible

invita|ción f invitation. ~**do** m guest. ~**r** vt invite. **te invito a una copa** I'll buy you a drink

invocar 7 vt invoke

involuntario adj involuntary

invulnerable adj invulnerable

inyec|ción f injection. ~**tar** vt inject

---

ir 49

● verbo intransitivo

••••▶ to go. **fui a verla** I went to see her. **ir a pie** to go on foot. **ir en coche** to go by car. **vamos a casa** let's go home. **fue (a) por el pan** he went to get some bread

! Cuando la acción del verbo **ir** significa trasladarse hacia o con el interlocutor la traducción es *to come*, p.ej: **¡ya voy!** *I'm coming!* **yo voy contigo** *I'll come with you*

••••▶ *(estar)* to be. **iba con su novio** she was with her boyfriend. **¿cómo te va?** how are you?

••••▶ *(sentar)* to suit. **ese color no le va** that colour doesn't suit her. **no me va ni me viene** I don't mind at all

••••▶ *(Méx, apoyar)* **irle a** to support. **le va al equipo local** he supports the local team

••••▶ *(en exclamaciones)* **¡vamos!**

come on! **¡vaya!** what a surprise!; *(contrariedad)* oh, dear! **¡vaya noche!** what a night! **¡qué va!** nonsense!

▶ Cuando el verbo intransitivo se emplea con expresiones como **ir de paseo, ir de compras, ir tirando** etc., ver bajo el respectivo nombre, verbo etc.

● verbo auxiliar

••••▶ **ir a** + infinitivo *(para expresar futuro, propósito)* to be going to + infinitive; *(al prevenir)* **no te vayas a caer** be careful you don't fall. **no vaya a ser que llueva** in case it rains; *(en sugerencias)* **vamos a dormir** let's go to sleep. **vamos a ver** let's see

••••▶ **ir** + gerundio. **ve arreglándote** start getting ready. **el tiempo va mejorando** the weather is gradually getting better.

● **irse** verbo pronominal

••••▶ to go. **se ha ido a casa** he's gone home

••••▶ *(marcharse)* to leave. **se fue sin despedirse** he left without saying goodbye. **se fue de casa** she left home

ira f anger. ~**cundo** adj irascible

Irak m Iraq

Irán m Iran

iraní adj & m & f Iranian

iraquí adj & m & f Iraqi

iris m (del ojo) iris

Irlanda f Ireland

irland|és adj Irish. ● m Irishman; (lengua) Irish. ~**esa** f Irishwoman. **los ~eses** the Irish

ir|onía f irony. ~**ónico** adj ironic

irracional adj irrational

irradiar vt radiate

irreal adj unreal. ~**idad** f unreality

irrealizable adj unattainable

irreconciliable adj irreconcilable

irreconocible adj unrecognizable

irrecuperable adj irretrievable

irreflexión f impetuosity

irregular adj irregular. **~idad** f irregularity

irreparable adj irreparable

irreprimible adj irrepressible

irreprochable adj irreproachable

irresistible adj irresistible

irrespetuoso adj disrespectful

irresponsable adj irresponsible

irriga|ción f irrigation. **~r** 12 vt irrigate

irrisorio adj derisory

irrita|ble adj irritable. **~ción** f irritation. **~r** vt irritate. **~rse** vpr get annoyed

irrumpir vi burst (**en** in)

isla f island. **las I~s Británicas** the British Isles

islámico adj Islamic

islandés adj Icelandic. ●m Icelander; (lengua) Icelandic

Islandia f Iceland

isleño adj island. ●m islander

Israel m Israel

israelí adj & m Israeli

Italia f Italy

italiano adj & m Italian

itinerario adj itinerary

IVA abrev (**impuesto sobre el valor agregado** (LAm), **impuesto sobre el valor añadido**) VAT

izar 10 vt hoist

izquierd|a f. **la ~a** the left hand; (Pol) left. **a la ~a** on the left; (con movimiento) to the left. **de ~a** left-wing. **~ista** m & f leftist. **~o** adj left

Jj

ja int ha!

jabalí m (pl **~es**) wild boar

jabalina f javelin

jab|ón m soap. **~onar** vt soap. **~onoso** adj soapy

jaca f pony

jacinto m hyacinth

jactarse vpr boast

jadea|nte adj panting. **~r** vi pant

jaguar m jaguar

jaiba f (LAm) crab

jalar vt (LAm) pull

jalea f jelly

jaleo m row, uproar. **armar un ~** kick up a fuss

jalón m (LAm, tirón) pull; (Mex fam, trago) drink; (Mex, tramo) stretch

jamás adv never. **nunca ~** never ever

jamelgo m nag

jamón m ham. **~ de York** boiled ham. **~ serrano** cured ham

Japón m. **el ~** Japan

japonés adj & m Japanese

jaque m check. **~ mate** checkmate

jaqueca f migraine

jarabe m syrup

jardín m garden. **~ de la infancia**, (Mex) **~ de niños** kindergarten, nursery school

jardiner|ía f gardening. **~o** m gardener

jarr|a f jug. **en ~as** with hands on hips. **~o** m jug. **caer como un ~o de agua fría** come as a shock. **~ón** m vase

jaula f cage

jauría f pack of hounds

jazmín m jasmine

jef|a f boss. ~**atura** f leadership; (sede) headquarters. ~**e** m boss; (Pol etc) leader. ~**e de camareros** head waiter. ~**e de estación** station-master. ~**e de ventas** sales manager

jengibre m ginger

jer|arquía f hierarchy. ~**árquico** adj hierarchical

■**jerez** m sherry. **al** ~ with sherry

jerga f coarse cloth; (argot) jargon

jerigonza f jargon; (galimatías) gibberish

jeringa f syringe; (LAm, fam, molestia) nuisance. ~**r** 12 vt (fig, fam, molestar) annoy

jeroglífico m hieroglyph(ic)

jersey m (pl ~s) jersey

Jesucristo m Jesus Christ. **antes de** ~ BC, before Christ

jesuita adj & m Jesuit

Jesús m Jesus. ●int good heavens!; (al estornudar) bless you!

jícara f (Mex) gourd

jilguero m goldfinch

jinete m & f rider

jipijapa m panama hat

jirafa f giraffe

jirón m shred, tatter

jitomate m (Mex) tomato

jorna|da f working day; (viaje) journey; (etapa) stage. ~**l** m day's wage. ~**lero** m day labourer

joroba f hump. ~**do** adj hunchbacked. ●m hunchback. ~**r** vt 🔟 annoy

jota f letter J; (danza) jota, popular dance. **ni** ~ nothing

joven (pl **jóvenes**) adj young. ●m young man. ●f young woman

■ *see* A-Z of Spanish life and culture

jovial adj jovial

joy|a f jewel. ~**as** fpl jewellery. ~**ería** f jeweller's (shop). ~**ero** m jeweller; (estuche) jewellery box

juanete m bunion

jubil|ación f retirement. ~**ado** adj retired. ~**ar** vt pension off. ~**arse** vpr retire. ~**eo** m jubilee

júbilo m joy

judaísmo m Judaism

judía f Jewish woman; (alubia) bean. ~ **blanca** haricot bean. ~ **escarlata** runner bean. ~ **verde** French bean

judicial adj judicial

judío adj Jewish. ●m Jewish man

judo m judo

juego m play; (de mesa, niños) game; (de azar) gambling; (conjunto) set. **estar en** ~ be at stake. **estar fuera de** ~ be offside. **hacer** ~ match. ~**s** mpl **malabares** juggling. **J~s** mpl **Olímpicos** Olympic Games. ●vb *véase* JUGAR

juerga f spree

jueves m invar Thursday

juez m judge. ~ **de instrucción** examining magistrate. ~ **de línea** linesman

juga|dor m player; (habitual, por dinero) gambler. ~**r** 🔳 vt play. ●vi play; (apostar fuerte) gamble. ~**rse** vpr risk. ~**r al fútbol**, (LAm) ~**r fútbol** play football

juglar m minstrel

jugo m juice; (de carne) gravy; (fig) substance. ~**so** adj juicy; (fig) substantial

juguet|e m toy. ~**ear** vi play. ~**ón** adj playful

juicio m judgement; (opinión) opinion; (razón) reason. **a mi** ~ in my opinion. ~**so** adj wise

juliana f vegetable soup

julio m July

junco m rush, reed

jungla f jungle

junio m June

junt|a f meeting; (consejo) board, committee; (Pol) junta; (Tec) joint. **~ar** vt join; (reunir) collect. **~arse** vpr join; (gente) meet. **~o** adj joined; (en plural) together. **~o a** next to. **~ura** f joint

jura|do adj sworn. ● m jury; (miembro de jurado) juror. **~mento** m oath. **prestar ~mento** take an oath. **~r** vt/i swear. **~r en falso** commit perjury. **jurárselas a uno** have it in for s.o.

jurel m (type of) mackerel

jurídico adj legal

juris|dicción f jurisdiction. **~prudencia** f jurisprudence

justamente adj exactly; (con justicia) fairly

justicia f justice

justifica|ción f justification. **~r** 🄷 vt justify

justo adj fair, just; (exacto) exact; (ropa) tight. ● adv just. **~ a tiempo** just in time

juven|il adj youthful. **~tud** f youth; (gente joven) young people

juzga|do m (tribunal) court. **~r** 🄓 vt judge. **a ~r por** judging by

Kk

kilo m, **kilogramo** m kilo, kilogram

kil|ometraje m distance in kilometres, mileage. **~ométrico** adj 🄷 endless. **~ómetro** m

kilometre. **~ómetro cuadrado** square kilometre

kilovatio m kilowatt

kiosco m kiosk

Ll

la artículo definido femenino (pl **las**)

••••► the. **la flor azul** the blue flower. **la casa de al lado** the house next door. **cerca de la iglesia** near the church No se traduce en los siguientes casos:

••••► (con nombre abstracto, genérico) **la paciencia es una virtud** patience is a virtue. **odio la leche** I hate milk. **la madera es muy versátil** wood is very versatile

••••► (con algunas instituciones) **termino la universidad mañana**

I finish university tomorrow. **no va nunca a la iglesia** he never goes to church. **está en la cárcel** he's in jail

••••► (con nombres propios) **la Sra. Díaz** Mrs Díaz. **la doctora Lara** doctor Lara

••••► (con partes del cuerpo, artículos personales) se traduce por un posesivo. **apretó la mano** he clenched his fist. **tienes la camisa desabrochada** your shirt is undone

••••► **la + de. es la de Ana** it's

Ana's. **la del sombrero** the one with the hat

····▶ **la que me atendió** (*persona*) the one who served me. (*cosa*) **la que se rompió** the one that broke

····▶ **la + que** + subjuntivo (*quienquiera*) whoever. **la que gane pasará a la final** whoever wins will go to the final. (*cualquiera*) whichever. **compra la que sea más barata** buy whichever is cheaper

laberinto m labyrinth, maze

labia f gift of the gab

labio m lip

labor f work. **~es de aguja** needlework. **~es de ganchillo** crochet. **~es de punto** knitting. **~es domésticas** housework. **~able** adj working. **~ar** vi work

laboratorio m laboratory

laborioso adj laborious

laborista adj Labour. • m & f member of the Labour Party

labra|do adj worked; (*madera*) carved; (*metal*) wrought; (*tierra*) ploughed. **~dor** m farmer; (*obrero*) farm labourer. **~nza** f farming. **~r** vt work; carve (*madera*); cut (*piedra*); till (*la tierra*). **~rse** vpr. **~rse un porvenir** carve out a future for o.s.

labriego m peasant

laca f lacquer

lacayo m lackey

lacio adj straight; (*flojo*) limp

lacón m shoulder of pork

lacónico adj laconic

lacr|ar vt seal. **~e** m sealing wax

lactante adj (*niño*) still on milk

lácteo adj milky. **productos** mpl **~s** dairy products

ladear vt tilt. **~se** vpr lean

ladera f slope

ladino adj astute

lado m side. **al ~** near. **al ~ de** next to, beside. **de ~** sideways. **en todos ~s** everywhere. **los de al ~** the next door neighbours. **por otro ~** on the other hand. **por todos ~s** everywhere. **por un ~** on the one hand

ladr|ar vi bark. **~ido** m bark

ladrillo m brick

ladrón m thief, robber; (*de casas*) burglar

lagart|ija f (small) lizard. **~o** m lizard

lago m lake

lágrima f tear

lagrimoso adj tearful

laguna f small lake; (*fig, omisión*) gap

laico adj lay

lament|able adj deplorable; (*que da pena*) pitiful; (*pérdida*) sad. **~ar** vt be sorry about. **~arse** vpr lament; (*quejarse*) complain. **~o** m moan

lamer vt lick

lámina f sheet; (*ilustración*) plate; (*estampa*) picture card

lamina|do adj laminated. **~r** vt laminate

lámpara f lamp. **~ de pie** standard lamp

lamparón m stain

lampiño adj beardless; (*cuerpo*) hairless

lana f wool. **de ~** wool(len)

lanceta f lancet

lancha f boat. **~ motora** motor boat. **~ salvavidas** lifeboat

langost|a f (*de mar*) lobster; (*insecto*) locust. **~ino** m king prawn

languide|cer 11 vi languish. **~z** f languor

lánguido adj languid; (*decaído*) listless

lanilla f nap; (*tela fina*) flannel

lanudo adj woolly; (*perro*) shaggy

lanza f lance, spear

lanza|llamas m invar flame-thrower. **∼miento** m throw; (acción de lanzar) throwing; (de proyectil, de producto) launch. **∼miento de peso**, (LAm) **∼miento de bala** shot put. **∼r** 🔟 vt throw; (de un avión) drop; launch (proyectil, producto). **∼rse** vpr throw o.s.

lapicero m (propelling) pencil

lápida f tombstone; (placa conmemorativa) memorial tablet

lapidar vt stone

lápiz m pencil. **∼ de labios** lipstick. **a ∼** in pencil

lapso m lapse

laptop m laptop

larg|a f. **a la ∼a** in the long run. **dar ∼as** put off. **∼ar** 🔢 vt (Naut) let out; (fam, dar) give; 🇹 deal (bofetada etc). **∼arse** vpr 🇹 beat it 🇹. **∼o** adj long. **¡∼o!** go away! **a lo ∼o** lengthwise. **a lo ∼o de** along. **tener 100 metros de ∼o** be 100 metres long

laring|e f larynx. **∼itis** f laryngitis

larva f larva

las artículo definido fpl the. véase tb LA. • pron them. **∼ de** those, the ones. **∼ de Vd** your ones, yours. **∼ que** whoever, the ones

láser m laser

lástima f pity; (queja) complaint. **da ∼ verlo así** it's sad to see him like that. **ella me da ∼** I feel sorry for her. **¡qué ∼!** what a pity!

lastim|ado adj hurt. **∼ar** vt hurt. **∼arse** vpr hurt o.s. **∼ero** adj doleful. **∼oso** adj pitiful

lastre m ballast; (fig) burden

lata f tinplate; (envase) tin (esp Brit), can; (fam, molestia) nuisance. **dar la ∼** be a nuisance. **¡qué ∼!** what a nuisance!

latente adj latent

lateral adj side, lateral

latido m beating; (cada golpe) beat

latifundio m large estate

latigazo m (golpe) lash; (chasquido) crack

látigo m whip

latín m Latin. **saber ∼** 🇹 know what's what 🇹

latino adj Latin. **L∼américa** f Latin America. **∼americano** adj & m Latin American

latir vi beat; (herida) throb

latitud f latitude

latón m brass

latoso adj annoying; (pesado) boring

laúd m lute

laureado adj honoured; (premiado) prize-winning

laurel m laurel; (Culin) bay

lava f lava

lava|ble adj washable. **∼bo** m wash-basin; (retrete) toilet. **∼dero** m sink. **∼do** m washing. **∼do de cerebro** brainwashing. **∼do en seco** dry-cleaning. **∼dora** f washing machine. **∼ndería** f laundry, **∼ndería automática** launderette, laundromat (esp Amer). **∼platos** m & f invar dishwasher. • m (Mex, fregadero) sink. **∼r** vt wash. **∼r en seco** dry-clean. **∼rse** vpr have a wash. **∼rse las manos** (incl fig) wash one's hands. **∼tiva** f enema. **∼vajillas** m invar dishwasher; (detergente) washing-up liquid (Brit), dishwashing liquid (Amer)

laxante adj & m laxative

lazada f bow

lazarillo m guide for a blind person

lazo m knot; (lazada) bow; (fig, vínculo) tie; (con nudo corredizo) lasso; (Mex, cuerda) rope

le pron (acusativo, él) him; (acusativo, Vd) you; (dativo, él) (to) him; (dativo, ella) (to) her; (dativo, cosa) (to) it; (dativo, Vd) (to) you

leal adj loyal; (fiel) faithful. ~**tad** f loyalty; (fidelidad) faithfulness

lección f lesson

leche f milk; (golpe) bash. ~ **condensada** condensed milk. ~ **desnatada** skimmed milk. ~ **en polvo** powdered milk. ~ **sin desnatar** whole milk. **tener mala** ~ be spiteful. ~**ra** f (vasija) milk jug. ~**ría** f dairy. ~**ro** adj milk, dairy. •m milkman

lecho m (en literatura) bed. ~ **de río** river bed

lechoso adj milky

lechuga f lettuce

lechuza f owl

lect|or m reader; (Univ) language assistant. ~**ura** f reading

leer 18 vt/i read

legación f legation

legado m legacy; (enviado) legate

legajo m bundle, file

legal adj legal. ~**idad** f legality. ~**izar** 10 vt legalize; (certificar) authenticate. ~**mente** adv legally

legar 12 vt bequeath

legible adj legible

legi|ón f legion. ~**onario** m legionary. ~**onella** f legionnaire's disease

legisla|ción f legislation. ~**dor** m legislator. ~**r** vi legislate. ~**tura** f term (of office); (año parlamentario) session; (LAm, cuerpo) legislature

leg|itimidad f legitimacy. ~**ítimo** adj legitimate; (verdadero) real

lego adj lay; (ignorante) ignorant. •m layman

legua f league

legumbre f vegetable

lejan|ía f distance. ~**o** adj distant

lejía f bleach

lejos adv far. ~ **de** far from. **a lo** ~ in the distance. **desde** ~ from

a distance, from afar

lema m motto

lencería f linen; (de mujer) lingerie

🔲**lengua** f tongue; (idioma) language. **irse de la** ~ talk too much. **morderse la** ~ hold one's tongue

lenguado m sole

lenguaje m language

lengüeta f (de zapato) tongue. ~**da** f, ~**zo** m lick

lente f lens. ~**s** mpl glasses. ~**s de contacto** contact lenses

lentej|a f lentil. ~**uela** f sequin

lentilla f contact lens

lent|itud f slowness. ~**o** adj slow

leñ|a f firewood. ~**ador** m woodcutter. ~**o** m log

Leo m Leo

le|ón m lion. ~**ona** f lioness

leopardo m leopard

leotardo m thick tights

lepr|a f leprosy. ~**oso** m leper

lerdo adj dim; (torpe) clumsy

les pron (acusativo) them; (acusativo, Vds) you; (dativo) (to) them; (dativo, Vds) (to) you

lesbiana f lesbian

lesi|ón f wound. ~**onado** adj injured. ~**onar** vt injure; (dañar) damage

letal adj lethal

let|árgico adj lethargic. ~**argo** m lethargy

letr|a f letter; (escritura) handwriting; (de una canción) words, lyrics. ~**a de cambio** bill of exchange. ~**a de imprenta** print. ~**ado** adj learned. ~**ero** m notice; (cartel) poster

letrina f latrine

leucemia f leukaemia

levadura f yeast. ~ **en polvo** baking powder

levanta|miento m lifting;

🔲 *see* A-Z of Spanish life and culture

(sublevación) uprising. **~r** vt raise, lift; (construir) build; (recoger) pick up. **~rse** vpr get up; (ponerse de pie) stand up; (erguirse, sublevarse) rise up

levante m east; (viento) east wind

levar vt. **~ anclas** weigh anchor

leve adj light; (sospecha etc) slight; (enfermedad) mild; (de poca importancia) trivial. **~dad** f lightness; (fig) slightness

léxico m vocabulary

lexicografía f lexicography

ley f law; (parlamentaria) act

leyenda f legend

liar 🗓 vt tie; (envolver) wrap up; roll (cigarrillo); (fig, confundir) confuse; (fig, enredar) involve. **~se** vpr get involved

libanés adj & m Lebanese

libelo m (escrito) libellous article; (Jurid) petition

libélula f dragonfly

libera|ción f liberation. **~dor** adj liberating. •m liberator

liberal adj & m & f liberal. **~idad** f liberality

liber|ar vt free. **~tad** f freedom. **~tad de cultos** freedom of worship. **~tad de imprenta** freedom of the press. **~tad provisional** bail. **en ~tad** free. **~tador** m liberator. **~tar** vt free

libertino m libertine

libido f libido

libio adj & m Libyan

libra f pound. **~ esterlina** pound sterling

Libra m Libra

libra|dor m (Com) drawer. **~r** vt free; (de un peligro) save. **~rse** vpr free o.s. **~rse de** get rid of

libre adj free. **estilo ~** (en natación) freestyle. **~ de impuestos** tax-free

librea f livery

libr|ería f bookshop (Brit),

bookstore (Amer); (mueble) bookcase. **~ero** m bookseller; (Mex, mueble) bookcase. **~eta** f notebook. **~o** m book. **~o de bolsillo** paperback. **~o de ejercicios** exercise book. **~o de reclamaciones** complaints book

licencia f permission; (documento) licence. **~do** m graduate; (Mex, abogado) lawyer. **~ para manejar** (Mex) driving licence. **~r** vt (Mil) discharge; (echar) dismiss. **~tura** f degree

licencioso adj licentious

licitar vt bid for

lícito adj legal; (permisible) permissible

licor m liquor; (dulce) liqueur

licua|dora f blender. **~r** 🗓 liquefy; (Culin) blend

lid f fight. **en buena ~** by fair means. **~es** fpl matters

líder m leader

liderato m, **liderazgo** m leadership

lidia f bullfighting; (lucha) fight. **~r** vt/i fight

liebre f hare

lienzo m linen; (del pintor) canvas; (muro, pared) wall

liga f garter; (alianza) league; (LAm, gomita) rubber band. **~dura** f bond; (Mus) slur; (Med) ligature. **~mento** m ligament. **~r** 🗓 vt bind; (atar) tie; (Mus) slur. •vi mix. **~r con** (fig) pick up. **~rse** vpr (fig) commit o.s.

liger|eza f lightness; (agilidad) agility; (rapidez) swiftness; (de carácter) fickleness. **~o** adj light; (rápido) quick; (ágil) agile; (superficial) superficial; (de poca importancia) slight. •adv quickly. **a la ~a** lightly, superficially

liguero m suspender belt

lija f dogfish; (papel de lija) sandpaper. **~r** vt sand

lila f lilac. •m (color) lilac

lima f file; (fruta) lime. **~duras** fpl

filings. **~r** vt file (down)

limita|ción f limitation. **~do** adj limited. **~r** vt limit. **~r con** border on. **~tivo** adj limiting

límite m limit. **~ de velocidad** speed limit

limítrofe adj bordering

lim|ón m lemon; (Mex) lime. **~onada** f lemonade

limosn|a f alms. **pedir ~a** beg. **~ear** vi beg

limpia|botas m invar bootblack. **~parabrisas** m invar windscreen wiper (Brit), windshield wiper (Amer). **~pipas** m invar pipe-cleaner. **~r** vt clean; (enjugar) wipe. **~vidrios** m invar (LAm) window cleaner

limpi|eza f cleanliness; (acción de limpiar) cleaning. **~eza en seco** dry-cleaning. **~o** adj clean; (cielo) clear; (fig, honrado) honest; (neto) net. **pasar a ~o**, (LAm) **pasar en ~o** make a fair copy. ● adv fairly. **jugar ~o** play fair

linaje m lineage; (fig, clase) kind

lince m lynx

linchar vt lynch

lind|ar vi border (**con** on). **~e** f boundary. **~ero** m border

lindo adj pretty, lovely. **de lo ~** 🅵 a lot

línea f line. **en ~s generales** broadly speaking. **guardar la ~** watch one's figure

lingote m ingot

lingü|ista m & f linguist. **~ística** f linguistics. **~ístico** adj linguistic

lino m flax; (tela) linen

linterna f lantern; (de bolsillo) torch, flashlight (Amer)

lío m bundle; (jaleo) fuss; (embrollo) muddle; (amorío) affair

liquida|ción f liquidation; (venta especial) sale. **~r** vt liquify; (Com) liquidate; settle (cuenta)

líquido adj liquid; (Com) net. ● m liquid; (Com) cash

lira f lyre; (moneda italiana) lira

líric|a f lyric poetry. **~o** adj lyric(al)

lirio m iris

lirón m dormouse; (fig) sleepyhead. **dormir como un ~** sleep like a log

lisiado adj crippled

liso adj smooth; (pelo) straight; (tierra) flat; (sencillo) plain

lisonj|a f flattery. **~eador** adj flattering. ● m flatterer. **~ear** vt flatter. **~ero** adj flattering

lista f stripe; (enumeración) list. **~ de correos** poste restante. **a ~s** striped. **pasar ~** take the register. **~do** adj striped

listo adj clever; (preparado) ready

listón m strip; (en saltos) bar; (Mex, cinta) ribbon

litera f (en barco, tren) berth; (en habitación) bunk bed

literal adj literal

litera|rio adj literary. **~tura** f literature

litig|ar 12 vi dispute; (Jurid) litigate. **~io** m dispute; (Jurid) litigation

litografía f (arte) lithography; (cuadro) lithograph

litoral adj coastal. ● m coast

litro m litre

lituano adj & m Lithuanian

liturgia f liturgy

liviano adj fickle; (LAm, de poco peso) light

lívido adj livid

llaga f wound; (úlcera) ulcer

llama f flame; (animal) llama

llamada f call

llama|do adj called. ● m (LAm) call. **~miento** m call. **~r** vt call; (por teléfono) phone. ● vi call; (golpear en la puerta) knock; (tocar el timbre) ring. **~r por teléfono** phone, telephone. **~rse** vpr be called.

¿cómo te ~s? what's your name?

llamarada f sudden blaze; (fig, de pasión etc) outburst

llamativo adj flashy; (color) loud; (persona) striking

llamear vi blaze

llano adj flat, level; (persona) natural; (sencillo) plain. •m plain

llanta f (Auto) (wheel) rim; (LAm, neumático) tyre

llanto m crying

llanura f plain

llave f key; (para tuercas) spanner; (LAm, del baño etc) tap (Brit), faucet (Amer); (Elec) switch. **~ inglesa** monkey wrench. **cerrar con ~** lock. **echar la ~** lock up. **~ro** m key-ring

llega|da f arrival. **~r** vi arrive, come; (alcanzar) reach; (bastar) be enough. **~r a** (conseguir) manage to. **~r a saber** find out. **~r a ser** become. **~r hasta** go as far as

llen|ar vt fill (up); (rellenar) fill in; (cubrir) cover (**de** with). **~o** adj full. •m (en el teatro etc) full house. **de ~** entirely

lleva|dero adj tolerable. **~r** vt carry; (inducir, conducir) lead; (acompañar) take; wear (ropa). **¿cuánto tiempo ~s aquí?** how long have you been here? **llevo 3 años estudiando inglés** I've been studying English for 3 years. **~rse** vpr take away; win (premio etc); (comprar) take. **~rse bien** get on well together

llor|ar vi cry; (ojos) water. **~iquear** vi whine. **~iqueo** m whining. **~o** m crying. **~ón** adj whining. •m cry-baby. **~oso** adj tearful

llov|er 2 vi rain. **~izna** f drizzle. **~iznar** vi drizzle

llueve vb véase LLOVER

lluvi|a f rain; (fig) shower. **~oso** adj rainy; (clima) wet

lo artículo definido neutro. **~ importante** what is important, the important thing. •pron (él)

him; (cosa) it. **~ que** what, that which

loa f praise. **~ble** adj praiseworthy. **~r** vt praise

lobo m wolf

lóbrego adj gloomy

lóbulo m lobe

local adj local. •m premises. **~idad** f locality; (de un espectáculo) seat; (entrada) ticket. **~izador** m pager; (de reserva) booking reference. **~izar** 10 vt find, locate

loción f lotion

loco adj mad, crazy. •m lunatic. **~ de alegría** mad with joy. **estar ~ por** be crazy about. **volverse ~** go mad

locomo|ción f locomotion. **~tora** f locomotive

locuaz adj talkative

locución f expression

locura f madness; (acto) crazy thing. **con ~** madly

locutor m broadcaster

lod|azal m quagmire. **~o** m mud

lógic|a f logic. **~o** adj logical

logr|ar vt get; win (premio). **~ hacer** manage to do. **~o** m achievement; (de premio) winning; (éxito) success

loma f small hill

lombriz f worm

lomo m back; (de libro) spine. **~ de cerdo** loin of pork

lona f canvas

loncha f slice; (de tocino) rasher

londinense adj from London. •m & f Londoner

Londres m London

loneta f thin canvas

longaniza f sausage

longev|idad f longevity. **~o** adj long-lived

longitud f length; (en geografía) longitude

lonja f slice; (de tocino) rasher; (Com) market

loro m parrot

los artículo definido mpl the. véase tb EL. • pron them. ~ **de Antonio** Antonio's. ~ **que** whoever, the ones

losa f (baldosa) flagstone. ~ **sepulcral** tombstone

lote m share; (de productos) batch; (terreno) plot (Brit), lot (Amer)

■lotería f lottery

loto m lotus

loza f crockery; (fina) china

lozano adj fresh; (vegetación) lush; (persona) healthy-looking

lubina f sea bass

lubrica|nte adj lubricating. • m lubricant. ~**r** 7 vt lubricate

lucero m bright star. ~ **del alba** morning star

lucha f fight; (fig) struggle. ~**dor** m fighter. ~**r** vi fight; (fig) struggle

lucid|ez f lucidity. ~**o** adj splendid

lúcido adj lucid

luciérnaga f glow-worm

lucimiento m brilliance

lucio m pike

lucir 11 vt (fig) show off. • vi shine; (joya) sparkle; (LAm, mostrarse) look. ~**se** vpr (fig) shine, excel; (presumir) show off

lucr|ativo adj lucrative. ~**o** m gain

luego adv then; (más tarde) later

....

■ see A-Z of Spanish life and culture

(on); (Mex, pronto) soon. • conj therefore. ~ **que** as soon as. **desde** ~ of course

lugar m place; (espacio libre) room. ~ **común** cliché. **dar** ~ **a** give rise to. **en** ~ **de** instead of. **en primer** ~ first. **hacer** ~ make room. **tener** ~ take place. ~**eño** adj local, village

lugarteniente m deputy

lúgubre adj gloomy

lujo m luxury. ~**so** adj luxurious. **de** ~ luxury

lumbago m lumbago

lumbre f fire; (luz) light

luminoso adj luminous; (fig) bright; (letrero) illuminated

luna f moon; (espejo) mirror. ~ **de miel** honeymoon. **claro de** ~ moonlight. **estar en la** ~ be miles away. ~**r** adj lunar. • m mole; (en tela) spot

lunes m invar Monday

lupa f magnifying glass

lustr|abotas m invar (LAm) bootblack. ~**ar** vt shine, polish. ~**e** m shine; (fig, esplendor) splendour. **dar** ~**e a**, **sacar** ~**e a** polish. ~**oso** adj shining

luto m mourning. **estar de** ~ be in mourning

luz f light; (electricidad) electricity. **luces altas** (LAm) headlights on full beam. **luces antiniebla** fog light. **luces bajas** (LAm), **luces cortas** dipped headlights. **luces largas** headlights on full beam. **a la** ~ **de** in the light of. **a todas luces** obviously. **dar a** ~ give birth. **hacer la** ~ **sobre** shed light on. **sacar a la** ~ bring to light

Mm

macabro adj macabre

macaco m macaque (monkey)

macanudo adj 🆃 great 🆃

macarrones mpl macaroni

macerar vt macerate (fruta); marinade (carne etc)

maceta f mallet; (tiesto) flowerpot

machacar 🔽 vt crush. •vi go on (**sobre** about)

machamartillo. a ~ adj ardent; (como adv) firmly

machet|azo m blow with a machete; (herida) wound from a machete. **~e** m machete

mach|ista m male chauvinist. **~o** adj male; (varonil) macho

machu|car 🔽 vt bruise; (aplastar) crush. **~cón** m (LAm) bruise

macizo adj solid. •m mass; (de plantas) bed

madeja f skein

madera m (vino) Madeira. •f wood, (naturaleza) nature. **~ble** adj yielding timber. **~men** m woodwork

madero m log; (de construcción) timber

madona f Madonna

madr|astra f stepmother. **~e** f mother. **~eperla** f mother-of-pearl. **~eselva** f honeysuckle

madrigal m madrigal

madriguera f den; (de conejo) burrow

madrileño adj of Madrid. •m person from Madrid

madrina f godmother; (en una boda) matron of honour

madrug|ada f dawn. **de ~ada** at dawn. **~ador** adj who gets up early. •m early riser. **~ar** 🔢 vi get up early

madur|ación f maturing; (de fruta) ripening. **~ar** vt/i mature; (fruta) ripen. **~ez** f maturity; (de fruta) ripeness. **~o** adj mature; (fruta) ripe

maestr|ía f skill; (Univ) master's degree. **~o** m master; (de escuela) schoolteacher

mafia f mafia

magdalena f fairy cake (Brit), cup cake (Amer)

magia f magic

mágico adj magic; (maravilloso) magical

magist|erio m teaching (profession); (conjunto de maestros) teachers. **~rado** m magistrate; (juez) judge. **~ral** adj teaching; (bien hecho) masterly. **~ratura** f magistracy

magn|animidad f magnanimity. **~ánimo** adj magnanimous. **~ate** m magnate, tycoon

magnavoz m (Mex) megaphone

magnético adj magnetic

magneti|smo m magnetism. **~zar** 🔟 vt magnetize

magn|ificar vt extol; (LAm) magnify (objeto). **~ificencia** f magnificence. **~ífico** adj magnificent. **~itud** f magnitude

magnolia f magnolia

mago m magician; (en cuentos) wizard

magro adj lean; (tierra) poor

magulla|dura f bruise. **~r** vt bruise. **~rse** vpr bruise

mahometano adj Islamic

m

maíz m maize, corn (Amer)

majada f sheepfold; (estiércol) manure; (LAm) flock of sheep

majader|ía f silly thing. ~**o** m idiot. •adj stupid

majest|ad f majesty. ~**uoso** adj majestic

majo adj nice

mal adv badly; (poco) poorly; (difícilmente) hardly; (equivocadamente) wrongly; (desagradablemente) bad. •adj. **estar** ~ be ill; (animicamente) be in a bad way; (incorrecto) be wrong. **estar** ~ **de** (escaso de) be short of. véase tb **MALO**. •m evil; (daño) harm; (enfermedad) illness. ~ **que bien** somehow (or other). **de** ~ **en peor** from bad to worse. **hacer** ~ **en** be wrong to. **¡menos** ~**!** thank goodness!

malabaris|mo m juggling. ~**ta** m & f juggler

mala|consejado adj ill-advised. ~**costumbrado** adj spoilt. ~**crianza** (LAm) rudeness. ~**gradecido** adj ungrateful

malagüeño adj of Málaga. •m person from Málaga

malaria f malaria

Malasia f Malaysia

malavenido adj incompatible

malaventura adj unfortunate

malayo adj Malay(an)

malbaratar vt sell off cheap; (malgastar) squander

malcarado adj nasty looking

malcriado adj (niño) spoilt

maldad f evil; (acción) wicked thing

maldecir 46 (pero imperativo **maldice**, futuro y condicional regulares, pp **maldecido** o **maldito**) vt curse. •vi curse; speak ill (**de** of)

maldi|ciente adj backbiting; (que blasfema) foul-mouthed. ~**ción** f curse. ~**to** adj damned. **¡~to sea!** damn (it)!

maleab|ilidad f malleability. ~**le** adj malleable

malea|nte m criminal. ~**r** vt damage; (pervertir) corrupt. ~**rse** vpr be spoilt; (pervertirse) be corrupted

malecón m breakwater; (embarcadero) jetty; (Rail) embankment; (LAm, paseo marítimo) seafront

maledicencia f slander

mal|eficio m curse. ~**éfico** adj evil

malestar m discomfort; (fig) uneasiness

malet|a f (suit)case. **hacer la** ~**a** pack (one's case). ~**ero** m porter; (Auto) boot, trunk (Amer). ~**ín** m small case; (para documentos) briefcase

mal|evolencia f malevolence. ~**évolo** adj malevolent

maleza f weeds; (matorral) undergrowth

mal|gastar vt waste. ~**hablado** adj foul-mouthed. ~**hechor** m criminal. ~**humorado** adj bad-tempered

malici|a f malice; (picardía) mischief. ~**arse** vpr suspect. ~**oso** adj malicious; (pícaro) mischievous

maligno adj malignant; (persona) evil

malintencionado adj malicious

malla f mesh; (de armadura) mail; (de gimnasia) leotard

Mallorca f Majorca

mallorquín adj & m Majorcan

malmirado adj (con estar) frowned upon

malo adj (delante de nombre masculino en singular **mal**) bad; (enfermo) ill. ~ **de** difficult to. **estar de malas** (malhumorado) be in a bad mood; (LAm, con mala suerte) be out of luck. **lo** ~ **es que** the trouble is that. **por las malas** by force

malogr|ar vt waste; (estropear) spoil. ~**arse** vpr fall through

maloliente adj smelly

malpensado adj nasty, malicious

malsano adj unhealthy

malsonante adj ill-sounding; (grosero) offensive

malt|a f malt. **~eada** f (LAm) milk shake. **~ear** vt malt

maltr|atar vt ill-treat; (pegar) batter; mistreat (juguete etc). **~echo** adj battered

malucho adj 🗈 under the weather

malva f mallow. **(color de) ~** adj invar mauve

malvado adj wicked

malvavisco m marshmallow

malversa|ción f embezzlement. **~dor** adj embezzling. •m embezzler. **~r** vt embezzle

Malvinas fpl. **las (islas) ~** the Falklands, the Falkland Islands

mama f mammary gland; (de mujer) breast

mamá f mum; (usado por niños) mummy

mama|da f sucking. **~r** vt suck; (fig) grow up with. •vi (bebé) feed; (animal) suckle. **dar de ~** breastfeed

mamario adj mammary

mamarracho m clown; (cosa ridícula) (ridiculous) sight; (cosa mal hecha) botch; (cosa fea) mess. **ir hecho un ~** look a sight

mameluco m (LAm) overalls; (de niño) rompers

mamífero adj mammalian. •m mammal

mamila f (Mex) feeding bottle

mamotreto m (libro) hefty volume; (armatoste) huge thing

mampara f screen

mampostería f masonry

mamut m mammoth

manada f herd; (de lobos) pack; (de leones) pride. **en ~** in crowds

mana|ntial m spring; (fig) source. **~r** vi flow; (fig) abound. •vt drip with

manaza f big hand

mancha f stain; (en la piel) blotch. **~do** adj stained; (sucio) dirty; (animal) spotted. **~r** vt stain; (ensuciar) dirty. **~rse** vpr get stained; (ensuciarse) get dirty

manchego adj de la Mancha. •m person from la Mancha

manchón m large stain

mancilla f blemish. **~r** vt stain

manco adj (de una mano) one-handed; (de las dos manos) handless; (de un brazo) one-armed; (de los dos brazos) armless

mancomun|adamente adv jointly. **~ar** vt unite; (Jurid) make jointly liable. **~arse** vpr unite. **~idad** f union

manda f (Mex) religious offering

manda|dero m messenger. **~do** m (LAm) shopping; (diligencia) errand. **hacer los ~dos** (LAm) do the shopping. **~miento** m order; (Relig) commandment. **~r** vt order; (enviar) send; (gobernar) rule. •vi be in command. **¿mandé?** (Mex) pardon?

mandarin|a f (naranja) mandarin (orange). **~o** m mandarin tree

mandat|ario m attorney; (Pol) head of state. **~o** m mandate; (Pol) term of office

mandíbula f jaw

mando m command. **~ a distancia** remote control. **al ~ de** in charge of. **altos ~s** mpl high-ranking officers

mandolina f mandolin

mandón adj bossy

manducar 🗇 vt 🗈 stuff oneself with

manecilla f hand

manej|able adj manageable. **~ar** vt use; handle (asunto etc); (fig) manage; (LAm, conducir) drive. **~arse** vpr get by. **~o** m handling. **~os** mpl scheming

manera f way. **~s** fpl manners. **de**

alguna ~ somehow. **de** ~ **que** so (that). **de ninguna** ~ by no means. **de otra** ~ otherwise. **de todas** ~s anyway

manga f sleeve; (tubo de goma) hose; (red) net; (para colar) filter; (LAm, de langostas) swarm

mango m handle; (fruta) mango. ~**near** vt boss about. •vi (entrometerse) interfere

manguera f hose(pipe)

manguito m muff

maní m (pl ~**es**) (LAm) peanut

manía f mania; (antipatía) dislike. **tener la** ~ **de** have an obsession with

maniaco adj, **maníaco** adj maniac(al). •m maniac

maniatar vt tie s.o.'s hands

maniático adj maniac(al); (obsesivo) obsessive; (loco) crazy; (delicado) finicky

manicomio m lunatic asylum

manicura f manicure; (mujer) manicurist

manido adj stale

manifesta|ción f manifestation, sign; (Pol) demonstration. ~**nte** m demonstrator. ~**r 1** vt show; (Pol) state. ~**rse** vpr show; (Pol) demonstrate

manifiesto adj clear; (error) obvious; (verdad) manifest. •m manifesto

manilargo adj light-fingered

manilla f (de cajón etc) handle; (de reloj) hand. ~**r** m handlebar(s)

maniobra f manoeuvre. ~**r** vt operate; (Rail) shunt. •vt/i manoeuvre. ~**s** fpl (Mil) manoeuvres

manipula|ción f manipulation. ~**r** vt manipulate

maniquí m dummy. •m & f model

mani|rroto adj & m spendthrift. ~**ta** f, (LAm) ~**to** m little hand

manivela f crank

manjar m delicacy

mano f hand; (de animales) front foot; (de perros, gatos) front paw. ~ **de obra** work force. **¡~s arriba!** hands up! **a** ~ by hand; (próximo) handy. **a** ~ **derecha** on the right. **de segunda** ~ second hand. **echar una** ~ lend a hand. **tener buena** ~ **para** be good at. •m (LAm, fam) mate (Brit), buddy (Amer)

manojo m bunch

manose|ar vt handle. ~**o** m handling

manotada f, **manotazo** m slap

manote|ar vi gesticulate. ~**o** m gesticulation

mansalva: **a** ~ adv without risk

mansarda f attic

mansión f mansion. ~ **señorial** stately home

manso adj gentle; (animal) tame

manta f blanket

mantec|a f fat. ~**oso** adj greasy

mantel m tablecloth; (del altar) altar cloth. ~**ería** f table linen

manten|er 40 vt support; (conservar) keep; (sostener) maintain. ~**erse** vpr support o.s.; (permanecer) remain. ~**se de/con** live off. ~**imiento** m maintenance

mantequ|era f butter churn. ~**illa** f butter

mant|illa f mantilla. ~**o** m cloak. ~**ón** m shawl

manual adj & m manual

manubrio m crank; (LAm, de bicicleta) handlebars

manufactura f manufacture. ~**r** vt manufacture, make

manuscrito adj handwritten. •m manuscript

manutención f maintenance

manzana f apple; (de edificios) block. ~**r** m (apple) orchard. ~ **de Adán** (LAm) Adam's apple

manzan|illa f camomile tea. •m

manzanilla, pale dry sherry. **~o** m apple tree

maña f skill. **~s** fpl cunning

mañan|a f morning. **~a por la ~a** tomorrow morning. **pasado ~a** the day after tomorrow. **en la ~a** (LAm), **por la ~a** in the morning. ● m future. ● adv tomorrow. **~ero** adj who gets up early. ● m early riser

mañoso adj clever; (astuto) crafty; (LAm, caprichoso) difficult

mapa m map

mapache m racoon

maqueta f scale model

maquiladora f (Mex) cross-border assembly plant

maquilla|je m make-up. **~r** vt make up. **~rse** vpr make up

máquina f machine; (Rail) engine. **~ de afeitar** shaver. **~ de escribir** typewriter. **~ fotográfica** camera

maquin|ación f machination. **~al** adj mechanical. **~aria** f machinery. **~ista** m & f operator; (Rail) engine driver

mar m & f sea. **alta ~** high seas. **la ~ de** 🔲 lots of

maraña f thicket; (enredo) tangle; (embrollo) muddle

maratón m & f marathon

maravill|a f wonder. **a las mil ~as, de ~as** marvellously. **contar/decir ~as de** speak wonderfully of. **hacer ~as** work wonders. **~ar** vt astonish. **~arse** vpr be astonished (**de** at). **~oso** adj marvellous, wonderful

marca f mark; (de coches etc) make; (de alimentos, cosméticos) brand; (Deportes) record. **de ~** brand name; (fig) excellent. **de ~ mayor** 🔲 absolute. **~do** adj marked. **~dor** m marker; (Deportes) scoreboard. **~r** 🔳 vt mark; (señalar) show; score (un gol); dial (número de teléfono). ● vi score

marcha f (incl Mus) march; (Auto) gear; (desarrollo) course; (partida) departure. **a toda ~** at full speed. **dar/hacer ~ atrás** put into reverse. **poner en ~** start; (fig) set in motion

marchante m (f **marchanta**) art dealer; (Mex, en mercado) stall holder

marchar vi go; (funcionar) work, go; (Mil) march. **~se** vpr leave

marchit|ar vt wither. **~arse** vpr wither. **~o** adj withered

marcial adj martial

marciano adj & m Martian

marco m frame; (moneda alemana) mark; (deportes) goal-posts

marea f tide. **~do** adj sick; (en el mar) seasick; (aturdido) dizzy; (borracho) drunk. **~r** vt make feel sick; (aturdir) make feel dizzy; (confundir) confuse. **~rse** vpr feel sick; (en un barco) get seasick; (estar aturdido) feel dizzy; (irse la cabeza) feel faint; (emborracharse) get slightly drunk; (confundirse) get confused

marejada f swell; (fig) wave

mareo m sickness; (en el mar) seasickness; (aturdimiento) dizziness; (confusión) muddle

marfil m ivory

margarina f margarine

margarita f daisy; (cóctel) margarita

marg|en m margin; (de un camino) side. ● f (de un río) bank. **~inado** adj excluded. ● m outcast. **al ~en** (fig) outside. **~inal** adj marginal. **~inar** vt (excluir) exclude; (fijar márgenes) set margins

🔳**mariachi** m (Mex) (música popular de Jalisco) Mariachi music; (conjunto) Mariachi band; (músico) Mariachi musician

maric|a m 🔲 sissy 🔲. **~ón** m 🔲 homosexual, queer 🔲; (LAm, cobarde) wimp

....

🔳 *see A-Z of Spanish life and culture*

marido m husband

mariguana f, marihuana f marijuana

marimacho f mannish woman

marimba f (type of) drum (LAm, especie de xilofón) marimba

marin|a f navy; (barcos) fleet; (cuadro) seascape. **~a de guerra** navy. **~a mercante** merchant navy. **~ería** f seamanship; (marineros) sailors. **~ero** adj marine; (barco) seaworthy. ● m sailor. **a la ~era** in tomato and garlic sauce. **~o** adj marine

marioneta f puppet. **~s** fpl puppet show

maripos|a f butterfly. **~a nocturna** moth. **~ear** vi be fickle; (galantear) flirt. **~ón** m flirt

mariquita f ladybird (Brit), ladybug (Amer). ● m 🇮 sissy 🇮

mariscador m shell-fisher

mariscal m marshal

maris|car vt fish for shellfish. **~co** m seafood, shellfish. **~quero** m (pescador de mariscos) seafood fisherman; (vendedor de mariscos) seafood seller

marital adj marital; (vida) married

marítimo adj maritime; (ciudad etc) coastal, seaside

marmita f cooking pot

mármol m marble

marmota f marmot

maroma f rope; (Mex, voltereta) somersault

marqu|és m marquess. **~esa** f marchioness. **~esina** f glass canopy; (en estadio) roof

marran|a f sow. **~ada** f filthy thing; (cochinada) dirty trick. **~o** adj filthy. ● m hog

marrón adj & m brown

marroqu|í adj, m & f Moroccan. ● m (leather) morocco. **~inería** f leather goods

Marruecos m Morocco

marsopa f porpoise

marsupial adj & m marsupial

marta f marten

martajar vt (Mex) crush (maíz)

Marte m Mars

martes m invar Tuesday. **~ de carnaval** Shrove Tuesday

martill|ar vt hammer. **~azo** m blow with a hammer. **~ear** vt hammer. **~eo** m hammering. **~o** m hammer

martín m **pescador** kingfisher

martinete m (del piano) hammer; (ave) heron

martingala f (ardid) trick

mártir m & f martyr

martir|io m martyrdom; (fig) torment. **~izar** 🔟 vt martyr; (fig) torment, torture

marxis|mo m Marxism. **~ta** adj & m & f Marxist

marzo m March

más adv & adj (comparativo) more; (superlativo) most. **~ caro** dearer. **~ doloroso** more painful. **el ~ caro** the dearest; (de dos) the dearer. **el ~ curioso** the most curious; (de dos) the more curious. ● prep plus. ● m plus (sign). **~ bien** rather. **~ de** (cantidad indeterminada) more than. **~ o menos** more or less. **~ que** more than. **~ y ~** more and more. **a lo ~** at (the) most. **dos ~ dos** two plus two. **de ~** too many. **es ~** moreover. **nadie ~** nobody else. **no ~** no more

masa f mass; (Culin) dough. **en ~** en masse

masacre f massacre

masaj|e m massage. **~ear** vt massage. **~ista** m masseur. ● f masseuse

mascada f (Mex) scarf

mascar 🔟 vt chew

máscara f mask

mascar|ada f masquerade. **~illa** f

mask. **~ón** m (Naut) figurehead

mascota f mascot

masculin|idad f masculinity. **~o** adj masculine; (sexo) male. ●m masculine

mascullar 🖪 vt mumble

masilla f putty

masivo adj massive, large-scale

mas|ón m Freemason. **~onería** f Freemasonry. **~ónico** adj Masonic

masoquis|mo m masochism. **~ta** adj masochistic. ●m & f masochist

mastica|ción f chewing. **~r** 🖪 vt chew

mástil m (Naut) mast; (de bandera) flagpole; (de guitarra, violín) neck

mastín m mastiff

mastodonte m mastodon; (fig) giant

masturba|ción f masturbation. **~rse** vpr masturbate

mata f (arbusto) bush; (LAm, planta) plant

matad|ero m slaughterhouse. **~or** adj killing. ●m (torero) matador

matamoscas m invar fly swatter

mata|nza f killing. **~r** vt kill (personas); slaughter (reses). **~rife** m butcher. **~rse** vpr kill o.s. (en un accidente) be killed; (Mex, para un examen) cram. **~rse trabajando** work like mad

mata|polillas m invar moth killer. **~rratas** m invar rat poison

matasanos m invar quack

matasellos m invar postmark

mate adj matt. ●m (ajedrez) (check)mate (LAm, bebida) maté

matemátic|as fpl mathematics, maths (Brit), math (Amer). **~o** adj mathematical. ●m mathematician

materia f matter; (material) material; (LAm, asignatura) subject. **~ prima** raw material. **en ~ de** on the question of

material adj & m material. **~idad** f

material nature. **~ismo** m materialism. **~ista** adj materialistic. ●m & f materialist; (Mex, constructor) building contractor. **~izar** 🔟 vt materialize. **~izarse** vpr materialize. **~mente** adv materially; (absolutamente) absolutely

matern|al adj maternal; (amor) motherly. **~idad** f motherhood; (hospital) maternity hospital; (sala) maternity ward. **~o** adj motherly; (lengua) mother

matin|al adj morning. **~ée** m matinée

matiz m shade; (fig) nuance. **~ación** f combination of colours. **~ar** 🔟 vt blend (colores); (introducir variedad) vary; (teñir) tinge (**de** with)

mat|ón m bully; (de barrio) thug. **~onismo** m bullying, (de barrio) thuggery

matorral m scrub; (conjunto de matas) thicket

matraca f rattle. **dar ~** pester

matraz m flask

matriarca f matriarch. **~do** m matriarchy. **~l** adj matriarchal

matr|ícula f (lista) register, list; (inscripción) registration; (Auto) registration number; (placa) licence plate. **~icular** vt register. **~icularse** vpr enrol, register

matrimoni|al adj matrimonial. **~o** m marriage; (pareja) married couple

matriz f matrix; (molde) mould; (útero) womb, uterus

matrona f matron; (partera) midwife

matutino adj morning

maull|ar vi miaow. **~ido** m miaow

mausoleo m mausoleum

maxilar adj maxillary. ●m jaw(bone)

máxim|a f maxim. **~e** adv

m

especially. **~o** adj maximum;
(punto) highest. ●m maximum

maya f daisy. ●adj Mayan. ●m & f
(persona) Maya

mayo m May

mayonesa f mayonnaise

mayor adj (más grande, comparativo)
bigger; (más grande, superlativo)
biggest; (de edad, comparativo) older;
(de edad, superlativo) oldest; (adulto)
grown-up; (principal) main, major;
(Mus) major. ●m & f (adulto) adult.
al por ~ wholesale. **~al** m
foreman. **~azgo** m entailed estate

mayordomo m butler

mayor|ía f majority. **~ista** m & f
wholesaler. **~itario** adj majority;
(socio) principal. **~mente** adv
especially

mayúscul|a f capital (letter). **~o**
adj capital; (fig, grande) big

mazacote m hard mass

mazapán m marzipan

mazmorra f dungeon

mazo m mallet; (manojo) bunch;
(LAm, de naipes) pack (Brit), deck
(Amer)

mazorca f cob. **~ de maíz**
corncob

me pron (acusativo) me; (dativo) (to)
me; (reflexivo) (to) myself

mecánic|a f mechanics. **~o** adj
mechanical. ●m mechanic

mecani|smo m mechanism.
~zación f mechanization. **~zar**
🔟 vt mechanize

mecanograf|ía f typing. **~iado**
adj typed, typewritten. **~iar** 🔟 vt
type

mecanógrafo m typist

mecate m (Mex) string; (más grueso)
rope

mecedora f rocking chair

mecenas m & f invar patron

mecer 🔟 vt rock; swing (columpio).

....
🔳 *see* A-Z of Spanish life and culture

~se vpr rock; (en un columpio) swing

mecha f (de vela) wick; (de explosivo)
fuse. **~s** fpl highlights

mechar vt stuff, lard

mechero m (cigarette) lighter

mechón m (de pelo) lock

medall|a f medal. **~ón** m
medallion; (relicario) locket

media f stocking; (promedio)
average. **a ~s** half each

mediación f mediation

mediado adj half full; (a mitad de)
halfway through. **~s** mpl. **a ~s de
marzo** in mid-March

mediador m mediator

medialuna f (pl **mediaslunas**)
croissant

median|amente adv fairly. **~a** f
(Auto) central reservation (Brit),
median strip (Amer). **~era** f party
wall. **~ero** adj (muro) party. **~o** adj
medium; (mediocre) average,
mediocre

medianoche f (pl **mediasnoches**)
midnight; (Culin) type of roll

mediante prep through, by
means of

mediar vi mediate; (llegar a la mitad)
be halfway through; (interceder)
intercede (**por** for)

medic|ación f medication.
~amento m medicine. **~ina** f
medicine. **~inal** adj medicinal

medición f measurement

médico adj medical. ●m doctor.
🔳**~ de cabecera** GP, general
practitioner

medid|a f measurement; (unidad)
measure; (disposición) measure,
step; (prudencia) moderation. **a la
~a** made to measure. **a ~a que**
as. **en cierta ~a** to a certain
extent. **~or** m (LAm) meter

medieval adj medieval. **~ista** m &
f medievalist

medio adj half (a); (mediano)
average. **dos horas y media** two

and a half hours. ~ **litro** half a litre. **las dos y media** half past two. • m middle; (Math) half; (manera) means; (en deportes) half(-back). **en** ~ in the middle (**de** of). **por** ~ **de** through. ~ **ambiente** m environment

medioambiental adj environmental

mediocr|e adj mediocre. ~**idad** f mediocrity

mediodía m midday, noon; (sur) south

medioevo m Middle Ages

Medio Oriente m Middle East

medir 5 vt measure; weigh up (palabras etc). • vi measure, be. **¿cuánto mide de alto?** how tall is it? ~**se** vpr (moderarse) measure o.s.; (Mex, probarse) try on

medita|bundo adj thoughtful. ~**ción** f meditation. ~**r** vt think about. • vi meditate

mediterráneo adj Mediterranean

Mediterráneo m Mediterranean

médium m & f medium

médula f marrow

medusa f jellyfish

megáfono m megaphone

megalómano m megalomaniac

mejicano adj & m Mexican

Méjico m Mexico

mejilla f cheek

mejillón m mussel

mejor adj & adv (comparativo) better; (superlativo) best. ~ **dicho** rather. **a lo** ~ perhaps. **tanto** ~ so much the better. ~**a** f improvement. ~**able** adj improvable. ~**amiento** m improvement

mejorana f marjoram

mejorar vt improve, better. • vi get better. ~**se** vpr get better

mejunje m mixture

melanc|olía f melancholy. ~**ólico** adj melancholic

melaza f molasses

melen|a f long hair; (de león) mane. ~**udo** adj long-haired

melindr|es mpl affectation. **hacer** ~**es con la comida** be picky about food. ~**oso** adj affected

mellizo adj & m twin

melocot|ón m peach. ~**onero** m peach tree

mel|odía f melody. ~**ódico** adj melodic. ~**odioso** adj melodious

melodram|a m melodrama. ~**ático** adj melodramatic

melómano m music lover

melón m melon

meloso adj sickly-sweet; (canción) slushy

membran|a f membrane. ~**oso** adj membranous

membrete m letterhead

membrill|ero m quince tree. ~**o** m quince

memo adj stupid. • m idiot

memorable adj memorable

memorando m, **memorándum** m notebook; (nota) memorandum, memo

memori|a f memory; (informe) report; (tesis) thesis. ~**as** fpl (autobiografía) memoirs. **de** ~**a** by heart; (citar) from memory. ~**al** m memorial. ~**ón** m good memory. ~**zación** f memorizing. ~**zar** 10 vt memorize

menaje m household goods. ~ **de cocina** kitchenware

menci|ón f mention. ~**onado** adj aforementioned. ~**onar** vt mention

mendi|cidad f begging. ~**gar** 12 vt beg for. • vi beg. ~**go** m beggar

mendrugo m piece of stale bread

mene|ar vt wag (rabo); shake (cabeza); wiggle (caderas). ~**arse** vpr move; (con inquietud) fidget; (balancearse) swing. ~**o** m movement; (sacudida) shake

menester m occupation. **ser ∼** be necessary. **∼oso** adj needy

menestra f vegetable stew

mengano m so-and-so

mengua f decrease; (falta) lack. **∼do** adj diminished. **∼nte** adj (luna) waning; (marea) ebb. **∼r** vt/i decrease, diminish

meningitis f meningitis

menjurje m mixture

menopausia f menopause

menor adj (más pequeño, comparativo) smaller; (más pequeño, superlativo) smallest; (más joven, comparativo) younger; (más joven, superlativo) youngest; (Mus) minor. ● m & f (menor de edad) minor. **al por ∼** retail

menos adj (comparativo) less; (comparativo, con plural) fewer; (superlativo) least; (superlativo, con plural) fewest. ● adv (comparativo) less; (superlativo) least. ● prep except. **al ∼** at least. **a ∼ que** unless. **las dos ∼ diez** ten to two. **ni mucho ∼** far from it. **por lo ∼** at least. **∼cabar** vt lessen; (fig, estropear) damage. **∼cabo** m lessening. **∼preciable** adj contemptible. **∼preciar** vt despise. **∼precio** m contempt

mensaje m message. **∼ro** m messenger

menso adj (LAm, fam) stupid

menstru|ación f menstruation. **∼al** adj menstrual. **∼ar** vi menstruate

mensual adj monthly. **∼idad** f monthly pay; (cuota) monthly payment

mensurable adj measurable

menta f mint

mental adj mental. **∼idad** f mentality. **∼mente** adv mentally

mentar vt mention, name

mente f mind

mentecato adj stupid. ● m idiot

mentir vi lie. **∼a** f lie. **∼ijillas** fpl. **de ∼ijillas** for a joke. **∼oso** adj lying. ● m liar

mentís m invar denial

mentor m mentor

menú m menu

menud|ear vi happen frequently; (Mex, Com) sell retail. **∼encia** f trifle. **∼encias** fpl (LAm) giblets. **∼eo** m (Mex) retail trade. **∼illos** mpl giblets. **∼o** adj small; (lluvia) fine. **a ∼o** often. **∼os** mpl giblets

meñique adj (dedo) little. ● m little finger

meollo m (médula) marrow; (de tema etc) heart

merca|chifle m hawker; (fig) profiteer. **∼der** m merchant. **∼dería** f (LAm) merchandise. **∼do** m market. **M∼do Común** Common Market. **∼do negro** black market

mercan|cía(s) f(pl) goods, merchandise. **∼te** adj merchant. ● m merchant ship. **∼til** adj mercantile, commercial. **∼tilismo** m mercantilism

merced f favour. **su/vuestra ∼** your honour

mercenario adj & m mercenary

mercer|ía f haberdashery (Brit), notions (Amer).

mercurial adj mercurial

mercurio m mercury

merec|edor adj worthy (**de** of). **∼er** vt deserve. **∼erse** vpr deserve. **∼idamente** adv deservedly. **∼ido** adj well deserved. **∼imiento** m (mérito) merit

merend|ar vt have as an afternoon snack. ● vi have an afternoon snack. **∼ero** m snack bar; (lugar) picnic area

merengue m meringue

meridi|ano adj midday; (fig) dazzling. ● m meridian. **∼onal** adj southern. ●m southerner

merienda f afternoon snack

merino adj merino

mérito m merit; (valor) worth

meritorio adj praiseworthy. ●m unpaid trainee

merluza f hake

merma f decrease. ∼**r** vt/i decrease, reduce

mermelada f jam

mero adj mere; (Mex, verdadero) real. ●adv (Mex, precisamente) exactly; (Mex, casi) nearly. ●m grouper

merode|ador m prowler. ∼**ar** vi prowl

mes m month

mesa f table; (para escribir o estudiar) desk. **poner la** ∼ lay the table

mesarse vpr tear at one's hair

meser|a f (LAm) waitress. ∼**o** m (LAm) waiter

meseta f plateau; (descansillo) landing

Mesías m Messiah

mesilla f, **mesita** f small table. ∼ **de noche** bedside table

mesón m inn

mesoner|a f landlady. ∼**o** m landlord

mestiz|aje m crossbreeding. ∼**o** adj (persona) half-caste; (animal) cross-bred. ●m (persona) half-caste; (animal) cross-breed

mesura f moderation. ∼**do** adj moderate

meta f goal; (de una carrera) finish

metabolismo m metabolism

metafísic|a f metaphysics. ∼**o** adj metaphysical

met|áfora f metaphor. ∼**afórico** adj metaphorical

met|al m metal; (de la voz) timbre. ∼**ales** mpl (instrumentos de latón) brass. ∼**álico** adj (objeto) metal; (sonido) metallic

metal|urgia f metallurgy. ∼**úrgico** adj metallurgical

metamorfosis f invar metamorphosis

metedura de pata f blunder

mete|órico adj meteoric. ∼**orito** m meteorite. ∼**oro** m meteor. ∼**orología** f meteorology. ∼**orológico** adj meteorological. ∼**orólogo** m meteorologist

meter vt put; score (un gol); (enredar) involve; (causar) make. ∼**se** vpr get involved (**en** in); (entrometerse) meddle. ∼**se con uno** pick a quarrel with s.o.

meticulos|idad f meticulousness. ∼**o** adj meticulous

metida de pata f (LAm) blunder

metido m reprimand. ●adj. ∼ **en años** getting on. **estar** ∼ **en algo** be involved in sth. **estar muy** ∼ **con uno** be well in with s.o.

metódico adj methodical

metodis|mo m Methodism. ∼**ta** adj & m & f Methodist

método m method

metodología f methodology

metraje m length. **de largo** ∼ (película) feature

metrall|a f shrapnel. ∼**eta** f submachine gun

métric|a f metrics. ∼**o** adj metric; (verso) metrical

metro m metre; (tren) underground (Brit), subway (Amer). ∼ **cuadrado** square metre

metrónomo m metronome

metr|ópoli f metropolis. ∼**opolitano** adj metropolitan. ●m metropolitan; (tren) underground (Brit), subway (Amer)

mexicano adj & m Mexican

México m Mexico. ∼ **D. F.** Mexico City

mezcal m (Mex) mescal

mezc|la f (acción) mixing; (substancia) mixture; (argamasa) mortar.

~**lador** m mixer. ~**lar** vt mix; shuffle (los naipes). ~**larse** vpr mix; (intervenir) interfere. ~**olanza** f mixture

mezquin|dad f meanness. ~**o** adj mean; (escaso) meagre. •m mean person

mezquita f mosque

mi adj my. •m (Mus) E; (solfa) mi

mí pron me

miau m miaow

mica f (silicato) mica

mico m (long-tailed) monkey

micro|bio m microbe. ~**biología** f microbiology. ~**cosmos** m invar microcosm. ~**film(e)** m microfilm

micrófono m microphone

microonda f microwave. ~**s** m invar microwave oven

microordenador m microcomputer

micros|cópico adj microscopic. ~**copio** m microscope. ~**urco** m long-playing record

miedo m fear (**a** for). **dar** ~ frighten. **morirse de** ~ be scared to death. **tener** ~ be frightened. ~**so** adj fearful

miel f honey

miembro m limb; (persona) member

mientras conj while. •adv meanwhile. ~ **que** whereas. ~ **tanto** in the meantime

miércoles m invar Wednesday. ~ **de ceniza** Ash Wednesday

mierda f (▣) shit

mies f ripe, grain

miga f crumb; (fig, meollo) essence. ~**jas** fpl crumbs; (sobras) scraps. ~**r** ⑫ vt crumble

migra|ción f migration. ~**torio** adj migratory

mijo m millet

mil adj & m a/one thousand. ~**es de** thousands of. ~ **novecientos noventa y nueve** nineteen

ninety-nine. ~ **euros** a thousand euros

milagro m miracle. ~**so** adj miraculous

milen|ario adj millenial. ~**io** m millennium

milésimo adj & m thousandth

mili f 🆃 military service. ~**cia** f soldiering; (gente armada) militia

mili|gramo m milligram. ~**litro** m millilitre

milímetro m millimetre

militante adj & m & f activist

militar adj military. •m soldier. ~**ismo** m militarism. ~**ista** adj militaristic. •m & f militarist. ~**izar** ⑩ vt militarize

milla f mile

millar m thousand. **a** ~**es** by the thousand

mill|ón m million. **un** ~**ón de libros** a million books. ~**onada** f fortune. ~**onario** m millionaire. ~**onésimo** adj & m millionth

milonga f popular dance and music from the River Plate region

milpa f (Mex) maize field, cornfield (Amer)

milpies m invar woodlouse

mimar vt spoil

mimbre m & f wicker. ~**arse** vpr sway. ~**ra** f osier. ~**ral** m osier-bed

mimetismo m mimicry

mímic|a f mime. ~**o** adj mimic

mimo m mime; (a un niño) spoiling; (caricia) cuddle

mimosa f mimosa

mina f mine. ~**r** vt mine; (fig) undermine

minarete m minaret

mineral m mineral; (mena) ore. ~**ogía** f mineralogy. ~**ogista** m & f mineralogist

miner|ía f mining. ~**o** adj mining. •m miner

miniatura f miniature

minifundio m smallholding

minimizar 🔟 vt minimize

mínim|o adj & m minimum. **como ~** at least. **~um** m minimum

minino m 🔢 cat, puss 🔢

minist|erial adj ministerial; (reunión) cabinet. **~erio** m ministry. **~ro** m minister

minor|ía f minority. **~idad** f minority. **~ista** m & f retailer

minuci|a f trifle. **~osidad** f thoroughness. **~oso** adj thorough; (detallado) detailed

minúscul|a f lower case letter. **~o** adj tiny

minuta f draft copy; (de abogado) bill

minut|ero m minute hand. **~o** m minute

mío adj & pron mine. **un amigo ~** a friend of mine

miop|e adj short-sighted. ●m & f short-sighted person. **~ía** f short-sightedness

mira f sight; (fig intención) aim. **a la ~** on the lookout. **con ~s a** with a view to. **~da** f look. **echar una ~da a** a glance at. **~do** adj careful with money; (comedido) considerate. **bien ~do** highly regarded. **no estar bien ~do** be frowned upon. **~dor** m viewpoint. **~miento** m consideration. **~r** vt look at; (observar) watch; (considerar) consider. **~r fijamente a** stare at. ●vi look (edificio etc). **~ hacia** face. **~rse** vpr (personas) look at each other

mirilla f peephole

miriñaque m crinoline

mirlo m blackbird

mirón adj nosey. ●m nosey-parker; (espectador) onlooker

mirto m myrtle

misa f mass. **~l** m missal

misántropo m misanthropist

miscelánea f miscellany; (Mex, tienda) corner shop (Brit), small general store (Amer)

miser|able adj very poor; (lastimoso) miserable; (tacaño) mean. **~ia** f extreme poverty; (suciedad) squalor

misericordi|a f pity; (piedad) mercy. **~oso** adj merciful

mísero adj miserable; (tacaño) mean; (malvado) wicked

misil m missile

misi|ón f mission. **~onero** m missionary

misiva f missive

mism|ísimo adj very same. **~o** adj same; (después de pronombre personal) myself, yourself, himself, herself, itself, ourselves, yourselves, themselves; (enfático) very. ●adv. **ahora ~** right now. **aquí ~** right here. **lo ~** the same

misterio m mystery. **~so** adj mysterious

mística f mysticism. **~o** adj mystical. ●m mystic

mistifica|ción f mystification. **~r** 🔢 vt mystify

mitad f half; (centro) middle. **cortar algo por la ~** cut sth in half

mitigar 🔢 vt mitigate; quench (sed); relieve (dolor etc)

mitin m, mitín m meeting

mito m myth. **~logía** f mythology. **~lógico** adj mythological

mitón m mitten

mitote m (Mex) Aztec dance

mixt|o adj mixed. **educación mixta** coeducation

mobbing m harassment

mobiliario m furniture

moce|dad f youth. **~río** m young people. **~tón** m strapping lad. **~tona** f strapping girl

mochales adj invar. **estar ~** be round the bend

mochila f rucksack

mocho adj blunt. ●m butt end

mochuelo m little owl

moción f motion

moco m mucus. **limpiarse los** ∼**s** blow one's nose

moda f fashion. **estar de** ∼ be in fashion. ∼**l** adj modal. ∼**les** mpl manners. ∼**lidad** f kind

model|ado m modelling. ∼**ador** m modeller. ∼**ar** vt model; (fig, configurar) form. ∼**o** m & f model

módem m modem

modera|ción f moderation. ∼**do** adj moderate. ∼**r** vt moderate; reduce (velocidad). ∼**rse** vpr control oneself

modern|idad f modernity. ∼**ismo** m modernism. ∼**ista** m & f modernist. ∼**izar** 10 vt modernize. ∼**o** adj modern; (a la moda) fashionable

modest|ia f modesty. ∼**o** adj modest

módico adj moderate

modifica|ción f modification. ∼**r** 7 vt modify

modismo m idiom

modist|a f dressmaker. ∼**o** m designer

modo m manner, way; (Gram) mood; (Mus) mode. ∼ **de ser** character. **de** ∼ **que** so that. **de ningún** ∼ certainly not. **de todos** ∼**s** anyhow. **ni** ∼ (LAm) no way

modorra f drowsiness

modula|ción f modulation. ∼**dor** m modulator. ∼**r** vt modulate

módulo m module

mofa f mockery. ∼**rse** vpr. ∼**rse de** make fun of

mofeta f skunk

moflet|e m chubby cheek. ∼**udo** adj with chubby cheeks

mohín m grimace. **hacer un** ∼ pull a face

moho m mould; (óxido) rust. ∼**so** adj mouldy; (metales) rusty

moisés m Moses basket

mojado adj wet

mojar vt wet; (empapar) soak; (humedecer) moisten, dampen

mojigat|ería f prudishness. ∼**o** m prude. ●adj prudish

mojón m boundary post; (señal) signpost

molar m molar

mold|e m mould; (aguja) knitting needle. ∼**ear** vt mould, shape; (fig) form. ∼**ura** f moulding

mole f mass, bulk. ●m (Mex, salsa) chili sauce with chocolate and sesame

mol|écula f molecule. ∼**ecular** adj molecular

mole|dor adj grinding. ●m grinder. ∼**r** 2 grind

molest|ar vt annoy; (incomodar) bother. **¿le** ∼**a que fume?** do you mind if I smoke? ●vi be a nuisance. **no** ∼**ar** do not disturb. ∼**arse** vpr bother; (ofenderse) take offence. ∼**ia** f bother, nuisance; (inconveniente) inconvenience; (incomodidad) discomfort. ∼**o** adj annoying; (inconveniente) inconvenient; (ofendido) offended

molicie f softness; (excesiva comodidad) easy life

molido adj ground; (fig, muy cansado) worn out

molienda f grinding

molin|ero m miller. ∼**ete** m toy windmill. ∼**illo** m mill; (juguete) toy windmill. ∼**o** m mill. ∼ **de agua** watermill. ∼**o de viento** windmill

molleja f gizzard

mollera f (de la cabeza) crown; (fig, sesera) brains

molusco m mollusc

moment|áneamente adv momentarily. ∼**áneo** adj (breve) momentary; (pasajero) temporary.

~o m moment; (ocasión) time. **al ~o** at once. **de ~o** for the moment

momi|a f mummy. ~**ficar** 7 vt mummify. ~**ficarse** vpr become mummified

monacal adj monastic

monada f beautiful thing; (niño bonito) cute kid; (acción tonta) silliness

monaguillo m altar boy

mon|arca m & f monarch. ~**arquía** f monarchy. ~**árquico** adj monarchical

monasterio m monastery

mond|a f peeling; (piel) peel. ~**adientes** m invar toothpick. ~**adura** f peeling; (piel) peel. ~**ar** vt peel (fruta etc). ~**o** adj (sin pelo) bald

mondongo m innards

moned|a f coin; (de un país) currency. ~**ero** m purse (Brit), change purse (Amer)

monetario adj monetary

mongolismo m Down's syndrome

monigote m weak character; (muñeco) rag doll; (dibujo) doodle

monitor m monitor

monj|a f nun. ~**e** m monk. ~**il** adj nun's; (como de monja) like a nun

mono m monkey; (sobretodo) overalls. •adj pretty

monocromo adj & m monochrome

monóculo m monocle

mon|ogamia f monogamy. ~**ógamo** adj monogamous

monogra|fía f monograph. ~**ma** m monogram

mon|ologar 12 vi soliloquize. ~**ólogo** m monologue

monoplano m monoplane

monopoli|o m monopoly. ~**zar** 10 vt monopolize

monos|ilábico adj monosyllabic. ~**ílabo** m monosyllable

monoteís|mo m monotheism. ~**ta** adj monotheistic. •m & f monotheist

mon|otonía f monotony. ~**ótono** adj monotonous

monseñor m monsignor

monstru|o m monster. ~**sidad** f monstrosity; (atrocidad) atrocity. ~**so** adj monstrous

monta f mounting; (valor) total value

montacargas m invar service lift (Brit), service elevator (Amer)

monta|dor m fitter. ~**je** m assembly; (Cine) montage; (teatro) staging, production

montañ|a f mountain. ~**a rusa** roller coaster. ~**ero** adj mountaineer. ~**és** adj mountain. •m highlander. ~**ismo** m mountaineering. ~**oso** adj mountainous

montaplatos m invar dumb waiter

montar vt ride; (subirse a) get on; (ensamblar) assemble; cock (arma); set up (una casa, un negocio). •vi ride; (subirse) mount. ~ **a caballo** ride a horse

monte m (montaña) mountain; (terreno inculto) scrub; (bosque) woodland. ~ **de piedad** pawnshop

montepío m charitable fund for dependents

montés adj wild

montevideano adj & m Montevidean

montículo m hillock

montón m heap, pile. **a montones** in abundance. **un ~ de** loads of

montura f mount; (silla) saddle

monument|al adj monumental; (fig, muy grande) enormous. ~**o** m monument

monzón m & f monsoon

moñ|a f ribbon. ~**o** m bun; (LAm, lazo) bow

moque|o m runny nose. ~**ro** m 🔲 handkerchief

moqueta f fitted carpet

moquillo m distemper

mora f mulberry; (de zarzamora) blackberry; (Jurid) default

morada f dwelling

morado adj purple

morador m inhabitant

moral m mulberry tree. ●f morals. ●adj moral. ~**eja** f moral. ~**idad** f morality. ~**ista** m & f moralist. ~**izador** adj moralizing. ●m moralist. ~**izar** 🔟 vt moralize

morar vi live

moratoria f moratorium

mórbido adj soft; (malsano) morbid

morbo m illness. ~**sidad** f morbidity. ~**so** adj unhealthy

morcilla f black pudding

morda|cidad f sharpness. ~**z** adj scathing

mordaza f gag

morde|dura f bite. ~**r** 🔢 vt bite; (Mex, exigir soborno a) extract a bribe from. ●vi bite. ~**rse** vpr bite o.s. ~**rse las uñas** bite one's nails

mordi|da f (Mex) bribe. ~**sco** m bite. ~**squear** vt nibble (at)

moreno adj (con ser) dark; (de pelo obscuro) dark-haired; (de raza negra) dark-skinned; (con estar) brown, tanned

morera f white mulberry tree

moretón m bruise

morfema m morpheme

morfin|a f morphine. ~**ómano** m morphine addict

morfol|ogía f morphology. ~**ógico** adj morphological

moribundo adj dying

morir 🔢 (pp **muerto**) vi die; (fig, extinguirse) die away; (fig, terminar) end. ~ **ahogado** drown. ~**se** vpr die. ~**se de hambre** starve to death; (fig) be starving. **se muere por una flauta** she's dying to have a flute

morisco adj Moorish. ●m Moor

morm|ón m Mormon. ~**ónico** adj Mormon. ~**onismo** m Mormonism

moro adj Moorish. ●m Moor

morral m (mochila) rucksack; (de cazador) gamebag; (para caballos) nosebag

morrillo m nape of the neck

morriña f homesickness

morro m snout

morrocotudo adj (🔲, tremendo) terrible; (estupendo) terrific 🔲

morsa f walrus

mortaja f shroud

mortal adj & m & f mortal. ~**idad** f mortality. ~**mente** adv mortally

mortandad f loss of life; (Mil) carnage

mortecino adj failing; (color) pale

mortero m mortar

mortífero adj deadly

mortifica|ción f mortification. ~**r** 🔢 vt (atormentar) torment. ~**rse** vpr distress o.s.

mortuorio adj death

mosaico m mosaic; (Mex, baldosa) floor tile

mosca f fly. ~**rda** f blowfly. ~**rdón** m botfly; (de cuerpo azul) bluebottle

moscatel adj muscatel

moscón m botfly; (mosca de cuerpo azul) bluebottle

moscovita adj & m & f Muscovite

mosque|arse vpr get cross. ~**o** m resentment

mosquete m musket. ~**ro** m musketeer

mosquit|ero m mosquito net. ~**o** m mosquito

mostacho m moustache

mostaza f mustard

mosto m must, grape juice

mostrador m counter

mostrar ② vt show. **~se** vpr (show oneself to) be. **se mostró muy amable** he was very kind

mota f spot, speck

mote m nickname

motea|do adj speckled. **~r** vt speckle

motejar vt call

motel m motel

motete m motet

motín m riot; (de tropas, tripulación) mutiny

motiv|ación f motivation. **~ar** vt motivate. **~o** m reason. **con ~o de** because of

motocicl|eta f motor cycle, motor bike Ⅲ. **~ista** m & f motorcyclist

motoneta f (LAm) (motor) scooter

motor adj motor. ●m motor, engine. **~ de arranque** starter motor. **~a** f motor boat. **~ismo** m motorcycling. **~ista** m & f motorist; (de una moto) motorcyclist. **~izar** Ⅲ vt motorize

motriz adj motor

move|dizo adj movable; (poco firme) unstable; (persona) fickle. **~r** ② vt move; shake (la cabeza); (provocar) cause. **~rse** vpr move; (darse prisa) hurry up

movi|ble adj movable. **~do** adj moved; (Foto) blurred

móvil adj mobile; (Esp, teléfono) mobile phone, cellphone. ●m motive

movili|dad f mobility. **~zación** f mobilization. **~zar** Ⅲ vt mobilize

movimiento m movement, motion; (agitación) bustle

moza f young girl. **~lbete** m lad

mozárabe adj Mozarabic. ●m & f Mozarab

moz|o m young boy. **~uela** f young girl. **~uelo** m young boy/lad

mucam|a f (LAm) servant. **~o** m (LAm) servant

muchach|a f girl; (sirvienta) servant, maid. **~o** m boy, lad

muchedumbre f crowd

mucho adj a lot of; (en negativas, preguntas) much, a lot of. **~s** a lot of; (en negativas, preguntas) many, a lot of. ●pron a lot; (personas) many (people). **como ~** at the most. **ni ~ menos** by no means. **por ~ que** however much. ●adv a lot, very much; (tiempo) long, a long time

mucos|idad f mucus. **~o** adj mucous

muda f change of clothing; (de animales) shedding. **~ble** adj changeable; (personas) fickle. **~nza** f move, removal (Brit). **~r** vt change; shed (piel). **~rse** vpr (de ropa) change one's clothes; (de casa) move (house)

mudéjar adj & m & f Mudejar

mud|ez f dumbness. **~o** adj dumb; (callado) silent

mueble adj movable. ●m piece of furniture. **~s** mpl furniture

mueca f grimace, face. **hacer una ~** pull a face

muela f back tooth, molar; (piedra de afilar) grindstone; (piedra de molino) millstone. **~ del juicio** wisdom tooth

muelle adj soft. ●m spring; (Naut) wharf; (malecón) jetty

muérdago m mistletoe

muero vb véase MORIR

muert|e f death; (homicidio) murder. **~o** adj dead. ●m dead person

muesca f nick; (ranura) slot

muestra f sample; (prueba) proof; (modelo) model; (señal) sign. **~rio** m collection of samples

muestro vb véase MOSTRAR

muevo vb véase MOVER

mugi|do m moo. **~r** 14 vi moo

mugr|e m dirt. **~iento** adj dirty, filthy

mugrón m sucker

mujer f woman; (esposa) wife. • int my dear! **~iego** adj fond of the women. • m womanizer. **~zuela** f prostitute

mula f mule. **~da** f drove of mules

mulato adj of mixed race (black and white). • m person of mixed race

mulero m muleteer

muleta f crutch; (toreo) stick with a red flag

mulli|do adj soft. **~r** 22 vt soften

mulo m mule

multa f fine. **~r** vt fine

multi|color adj multicoloured. **~copista** m duplicator. **~cultural** adj multicultural. **~forme** adj multiform. **~lateral** adj multilateral. **~lingüe** adj multilingual. **~millonario** m multimillionaire

múltiple adj multiple

multiplic|ación f multiplication. **~ar** 7 vt multiply. **~arse** vpr multiply. **~idad** f multiplicity

múltiplo m multiple

multitud f multitude, crowd. **~inario** adj mass; (concierto) with mass audience

mund|ano adj wordly; (de la sociedad elegante) society. **~ial** adj world-wide. **la segunda guerra ~ial** the Second World War. **~illo** m world, circles. **~o** m world. **todo el ~o** everybody

munición f ammunition; (provisiones) supplies

municip|al adj municipal. **~alidad** f municipality. 🎴**~io** m municipality; (ayuntamiento) town council

muñe|ca f (en anatomía) wrist; (juguete) doll; (maniquí) dummy.

🎴 see A-Z of Spanish life and culture

~co m doll. **~quera** f wristband

muñón m stump

mura|l adj mural, wall. • m mural. **~lla** f (city) wall. **~r** vt wall

murciélago m bat

murga f street band

murmullo m (incl fig) murmur

murmura|ción f gossip. **~dor** adj gossiping. • m gossip. **~r** vi murmur; (criticar) gossip

muro m wall

murria f depression

mus m card game

musa f muse

musaraña f shrew

muscula|r adj muscular. **~tura** f muscles

músculo m muscle

musculoso adj muscular

muselina f muslin

museo m museum. **~ de arte** art gallery

musgo m moss. **~so** adj mossy

música f music

musical adj & m musical

músico adj musical. • m musician

music|ología f musicology. **~ólogo** m musicologist

muslo m thigh

mustio adj (plantas) withered; (cosas) faded; (personas) gloomy; (Mex, hipócrita) two-faced

musulmán adj & m Muslim

muta|bilidad f mutability. **~ción** f mutation

mutila|ción f mutilation. **~do** adj crippled. • m cripple. **~r** vt mutilate; maim (persona)

mutis m (en el teatro) exit. **~mo** m silence

mutu|alidad f mutuality; (asociación) friendly society. **~amente** adv mutually. **~o** adj mutual

muy adv very; (demasiado) too

Nn

nabo m turnip

nácar m mother-of-pearl

nac|er 🔟 vi be born; (pollito) hatch out; (planta) sprout. ~**ido** adj born. **recien** ~**ido** newborn. ~**iente** adj (sol) rising. ~**imiento** m birth; (de rio) source; (belén) crib. **lugar** m **de** ~**imiento** place of birth

naci|ón f nation. ~**onal** adj national. ~**onalidad** f nationality. ~**onalismo** m nationalism. ~**onalista** m & f nationalist. ~**onalizar** 🔟 vt nationalize. ~**onalizarse** vpr become naturalized

nada pron nothing, not anything. ● adv not at all. **¡~ de eso!** nothing of the sort! **antes que** ~ first of all. **¡de ~!** (después de 'gracias') don't mention it! **para** ~ (not) at all. **por ~ del mundo** not for anything in the world

nada|dor m swimmer. ~**r** vi swim. ~**r de espalda(s)** do (the) backstroke

nadería f trifle

nadie pron no one, nobody

nado m (Mex) swimming. ● adv **a** ~ swimming

naipe m (playing) card. **juegos** mpl **de** ~**s** card games

nalga f buttock. ~**s** fpl bottom. ~**da** f (Mex) smack on the bottom

nana f lullaby

naranj|a f orange. ~**ada** f orangeade. ~**al** m orange grove. ~**ero** m orange tree

narcótico adj & m narcotic

nariz f nose. **¡narices!** rubbish!

narra|ción f narration. ~**dor** m

narrator. ~**r** vt tell. ~**tivo** adj narrative

nasal adj nasal

nata f cream

natación f swimming

natal adj native; (pueblo etc) home. ~**idad** f birth rate

natillas fpl custard

nativo adj & m native

nato adj born

natural adj natural. ● m native. ~**eza** f nature. ~**eza muerta** still life. ~**idad** f naturalness. ~**ista** m & f naturalist. ~**izar** 🔟 vt naturalize. ~**izarse** vpr become naturalized. ~**mente** adv naturally. ● int of course!

naufrag|ar 🔢 vi (barco) sink; (persona) be shipwrecked; (fig) fail. ~**io** m shipwreck

náufrago adj shipwrecked. ● m shipwrecked person

náuseas fpl nausea. **dar** ~**s a uno** make s.o. feel sick. **sentir** ~**s** feel sick

náutico adj nautical

navaja f penknife; (de afeitar) razor. ~**zo** m slash

naval adj naval

nave f ship; (de iglesia) nave. ~ **espacial** spaceship. **quemar las** ~**s** burn one's boats

navega|ble adj navigable; (barco) seaworthy. ~**ción** f navigation; (tráfico) shipping. ~**dor** m (Informática) browser. ~**nte** m & f navigator. ~**r** 🔢 vi sail; (Informática) browse

Navid|ad f Christmas. ~**eño** adj Christmas. **en** ~**ades** at

n

Christmas. **¡feliz ~ad!** Happy Christmas! **por ~ad** at Christmas

nazi adj & m & f Nazi. **~smo** m Nazism

neblina f mist

nebuloso adj misty; (fig) vague

necedad f foolishness. **decir ~es** talk nonsense. **hacer una ~** do sth stupid

necesari|amente adv necessarily. **~o** adj necessary

necesi|dad f need; (cosa esencial) necessity; (pobreza) poverty. **~dades** fpl hardships. **no hay ~dad** there's no need. **por ~dad** (out) of necessity. **~tado** adj in need (**de** of). **~tar** vt need. • vi. **~tar de** need

necio adj silly. • m idiot

néctar m nectar

nectarina f nectarine

nefasto adj unfortunate; (consecuencia) disastrous; (influencia) harmful

nega|ción f denial; (Gram) negative. **~do** adj useless. **~r 1** & **12** vt deny; (rehusar) refuse. **~rse** vpr refuse (**a** to). **~tiva** f (acción) denial; (acción de rehusar) refusal. **~tivo** adj & m negative

negligen|cia f negligence. **~te** adj negligent

negoci|able adj negotiable. **~ación** f negotiation. **~ante** m & f dealer. **~ar** vt/i negotiate. **~ar en** trade in. **~o** m business; (Com, trato) deal. **~os** mpl business. **hombre de ~os** businessman

negr|a f black woman; (Mus) crotchet. **~o** adj black; (ojos) dark. • m (color) black; (persona) black man. **~ura** f blackness. **~uzco** adj blackish

nen|a f little girl. **~o** m little boy

nenúfar m water lily

neocelandés adj from New Zealand. • m New Zealander

neón m neon

nepotismo m nepotism

nervio m nerve; (tendón) sinew; (en botánica) vein. **~sidad** f, **~sismo** m nervousness; (impaciencia) impatience. **~so** adj nervous; (de temperamento) highly-strung. **ponerse ~so** get nervous

neto adj clear; (verdad) simple; (Com) net

neumático adj pneumatic. • m tyre

neumonía f pneumonia

neur|algia f neuralgia. **~ología** f neurology. **~ólogo** m neurologist. **~osis** f neurosis. **~ótico** adj neurotic

neutr|al adj neutral. **~alidad** f neutrality. **~alizar 10** vt neutralize. **~o** adj neutral; (Gram) neuter

neva|da f snowfall. **~r 1** vi snow. **~sca** f blizzard

nevera f refrigerator, fridge (Brit)

nevisca f light snowfall

nexo m link

ni conj. **~... ~** neither... nor. **~ aunque** not even if. **~ siquiera** not even. **sin...~ ...** without ... or...

Nicaragua f Nicaragua

nicaragüense adj & m & f Nicaraguan

nicho m niche

nicotina f nicotine

nido m nest; (de ladrones) den

niebla f fog. **hay ~** it's foggy. **un día de ~** a foggy day

niet|a f granddaughter. **~o** m grandson. **~os** mpl grandchildren

nieve f snow; (Mex, helado) sorbet

niki m polo shirt

nimi|edad f triviality. **~o** adj insignificant

ninfa f nymph

ningún véase NINGUNO

ninguno adj (delante de nombre

masculino en singular **ningún**) no; (con otro negativo) any. **de ninguna manera, de ningún modo** by no means. **en ninguna parte** nowhere. **sin ningún amigo** without any friends. ●pron (de dos) neither; (de más de dos) none; (nadie) no-one, nobody

niñ|a f (little) girl. **~era** f nanny. **~ería** f childish thing. **~ez** f childhood. **~o** adj childish. ●m (little) boy **de ~o** as a child. **desde ~o** from childhood

níquel m nickel

níspero m medlar

nitidez f clarity; (de foto, imagen) sharpness

nítido adj clear; (foto, imagen) sharp

nitrógeno m nitrogen

nivel m level; (fig) standard. **~ de vida** standard of living. **~ar** vt level. **~arse** vpr become level

no adv not; (como respuesta) no. **¿~?** isn't it? **¡a que ~!** I bet you don't! **¡cómo ~!** of course! **Felipe ~ tiene hijos** Felipe has no children. **¡que ~!** certainly not!

nob|iliario adj noble. **~le** adj & m & f noble. **~leza** f nobility

noche f night. ▣**~ vieja** New Year's Eve. **de ~** at night. **hacerse de ~** get dark. **hacer ~** spend the night. **media ~** midnight. **en la ~** (LAm), **por la ~** at night

Nochebuena f Christmas Eve

noción f notion. **nociones** fpl rudiments

nocivo adj harmful

nocturno adj nocturnal; (clase) evening; (tren etc) night. ●m nocturne

nodriza f wet nurse

nogal m walnut tree; (madera) walnut

nómada adj nomadic. ●m & f nomad

nombr|ado adj famous; (susodicho) aforementioned. **~amiento** m appointment. **~ar** vt appoint; (citar) mention. **~e** m name; (Gram) noun; (fama) renown. **~e de pila** Christian name. **en ~e de** in the name of. **no tener ~e** be unspeakable. **poner de ~e** call

nomeolvides m invar forget-me-not

nómina f payroll

nomina|l adj nominal. **~tivo** adj & m nominative. **~tivo a** (cheque etc) made out to

non adj odd. ●m odd number. **pares y ~es** odds and evens

nono adj ninth

nordeste adj (región) north-eastern; (viento) north-easterly. ●m northeast

nórdico adj Nordic. ●m Northern European

noria f water-wheel; (en una feria) big wheel (Brit), Ferris wheel (Amer)

norma f rule

normal adj normal. ●f teachers' training college. **~idad** f normality (Brit), normalcy (Amer). **~izar** ⑩ vt normalize. **~mente** adv normally, usually

noroeste adj (región) north-western; (viento) north-westerly. ●m northwest

norte adj (región) northern; (viento, lado) north. ●m north; (fig, meta) aim

Norteamérica f (North) America

norteamericano adj & m (North) American

norteño adj northern. ●m northerner

Noruega f Norway

noruego adj & m Norwegian

nos pron (acusativo) us; (dativo) (to) us; (reflexivo) (to) ourselves;

n

....
▣ see A-Z of Spanish life and culture

(recíproco) (to) each other

nosotros pron we; (con prep) us

nost|algia f nostalgia; (de casa, de patria) homesickness. **~álgico** adj nostalgic

nota f note; (de examen etc) mark. **de ~** famous. **de mala ~** notorious. **digno de ~** notable. **~ble** adj notable. **~ción** f notation. **~r** vt notice. **es de ~r** it should be noted. **hacerse ~r** stand out

notario m notary

notici|a f (piece of) news. **~as** fpl news. **atrasado de ~as** behind with the news. **tener ~as de** hear from. **~ario**, (LAm) **~ero** m news

notifica|ción f notification. **~r** 7 vt notify

notori|edad f notoriety. **~o** adj well-known; (evidente) obvious; (notable) marked

novato adj inexperienced. ● m novice

novecientos adj & m nine hundred

noved|ad f newness; (cosa nueva) innovation; (cambio) change; (moda) latest fashion. **llegar sin ~ad** arrive safely. **~oso** adj novel

novel|a f novel. **~ista** m & f novelist

noveno adj ninth

noventa adj & m ninety; (nonagésimo) ninetieth

novia f girlfriend; (prometida) fiancée; (en boda) bride. **~r** vi (LAm) go out together. **~zgo** m engagement

novicio m novice

noviembre m November

novill|a f heifer. **~o** m bullock. **hacer ~os** play truant

novio m boyfriend; (prometido) fiancé; (en boda) bridegroom. **los ~s** the bride and groom

nub|arrón m large dark cloud. **~e** f cloud; (de insectos etc) swarm.

~lado adj cloudy, overcast. ● m cloud. **~lar** vt cloud. **~larse** vpr become cloudy; (vista) cloud over. **~oso** adj cloudy

nuca f back of the neck

nuclear adj nuclear

núcleo m nucleus

nudillo m knuckle

nudis|mo m nudism. **~ta** m & f nudist

nudo m knot; (de asunto etc) crux. **tener un ~ en la garganta** have a lump in one's throat. **~so** adj knotty

nuera f daughter-in-law

nuestro adj our. ● pron ours. **~ amigo** our friend. **un coche ~** a car of ours

nueva f (piece of) news. **~s** fpl news. **~mente** adv again

Nueva Zelanda f, (LAm) **Nueva Zelandia** f New Zealand

nueve adj & m nine

nuevo adj new. **de ~** again. **estar ~** be as good as new

nuez f walnut. **~ de Adán** Adam's apple. **~ moscada** nutmeg

nul|idad f nullity; (fam, persona) dead loss 🆧. **~o** adj useless; (Jurid) null and void

num|eración f numbering. **~eral** adj & m numeral. **~erar** vt number. **~érico** adj numerical

número m number; (arábigo, romano) numeral; (de zapatos etc) size; (billete de lotería) lottery ticket; (de publicación) issue. **sin ~** countless

numeroso adj numerous

nunca adv never. **~ (ja)más** never again. **casi ~** hardly ever. **como ~** like never before. **más que ~** more than ever

nupcial adj nuptial. **banquete ~** wedding breakfast

nutria f otter
nutri|ción f nutrition. ~**do** adj nourished, fed; (fig) large; (aplausos) loud; (fuego) heavy. ~**r** vt nourish, feed; (fig) feed. ~**tivo** adj nutritious. **valor** m ~**tivo** nutritional value
nylon m nylon

Ññ

ñapa f (LAm) extra goods given free
ñato adj (LAm) snub-nosed
ñoñ|ería f, ~**ez** f insipidity. ~**o** adj insipid; (tímido) bashful; (quisquilloso) prudish

Oo

o conj or. ~ **bien** rather. ~... ~ either ... or
oasis m invar oasis
obed|ecer 11 vt/i obey. ~**iencia** f obedience. ~**iente** adj obedient
obes|idad f obesity. ~**o** adj obese
obispo m bishop
obje|ción f objection. ~**tar** vt/i object
objetivo adj objective. ● m objective; (foto etc) lens
objeto m object. ~**r** m objector. ~ **de conciencia** conscientious objector
oblicuo adj oblique
obliga|ción f obligation; (Com) bond. ~**do** adj obliged; (forzoso) obligatory; ~**r** 12 vt force, oblige. ~**rse** vpr. ~**rse a** undertake to. ~**torio** adj obligatory
oboe m oboe. ● m & f (músico) oboist
obra f work; (acción) deed; (de teatro) play; (construcción) building work. ~ **maestra** masterpiece. **en** ~**s**

under construction. **por** ~ **de** thanks to. ~**r** vt do
obrero adj labour; (clase) working. ● m workman; (de fábrica, construcción) worker
obscen|idad f obscenity. ~**o** adj obscene
obscu... véase **oscu...**
obsequi|ar vt lavish attention on. ~**ar con** give, present with. ~**o** m gift, present; (agasajo) attention. ~**oso** adj obliging
observa|ción f observation. **hacer una** ~**ción** make a remark. ~**dor** m observer. ~**ncia** f observance. ~**r** vt observe; (notar) notice. ~**torio** m observatory
obses|ión f obsession. ~**ionar** vt obsess. ~**ivo** adj obsessive. ~**o** adj obsessed
obst|aculizar 10 vt hinder; hold up (tráfico). ~**áculo** m obstacle
obstante: **no** ~ adv however, nevertheless; (como prep) in spite of

n
o

obstar vi. **eso no obsta para que vaya** that should not prevent him from going

obstina|do adj obstinate. **~rse** vpr. **~rse en** (+ infinitivo) insist on (+ gerundio)

obstru|cción f obstruction. **~ir** 🔟 vt obstruct

obtener 🔟 vt get, obtain

obtura|dor m (Foto) shutter. **~r** vt plug; fill (muela etc)

obvio adj obvious

oca f goose

ocasi|ón f occasion; (oportunidad) opportunity. **aprovechar la ~ón** take the opportunity. **con ~ón de** on the occasion of. **de ~ón** bargain; (usado) second-hand. **en ~ones** sometimes. **perder una ~ón** miss a chance. **~onal** adj chance. **~onar** vt cause

ocaso m sunset; (fig) decline

occident|al adj western. •m & f westerner. **~e** m west

océano m ocean

ochenta adj & m eighty

ocho adj & m eight. **~cientos** adj & m eight hundred

ocio m idleness; (tiempo libre) leisure time. **~sidad** f idleness. **~so** adj idle; (inútil) pointless

oct|agonal adj octagonal. **~ágono** m octagon

octano m octane

octav|a f octave. **~o** adj & m eighth

octogenario adj & m octogenarian

octubre m October

ocular adj eye

oculista m & f ophthalmologist, ophthalmic optician

ocult|ar vt hide. **~arse** vpr hide. **~o** adj hidden; (secreto) secret

ocupa|ción f occupation. **~do** adj occupied; (persona) busy. **estar ~do** (asiento) be taken; (línea telefónica) be engaged (Brit), be busy

(Amer). **~nte** m & f occupant. **~r** vt occupy, take up (espacio). **~rse** vpr look after

ocurr|encia f occurrence, event; (idea) idea; (que tiene gracia) witty remark. **~ir** vi happen. **¿qué ~e?** what's the matter? **~irse** vpr occur. **se me ~e que** it occurs to me that

oda f ode

odi|ar vt hate. **~o** m hatred. **~oso** adj hateful; (persona) horrible

oeste adj (región) western; (viento, lado) west. •m west

ofen|der vt offend; (insultar) insult. **~derse** vpr take offence. **~sa** f offence. **~siva** f offensive. **~sivo** adj offensive

oferta f offer; (en subasta) bid. **~s de empleo** situations vacant. **en ~** on (special) offer

oficial adj official. •m skilled worker; (Mil) officer

oficin|a f office. **~a de colocación** employment office. **~a de turismo** tourist office. **horas** fpl **de ~a** business hours. **~ista** m & f office worker

oficio m trade. **~so** adj (no oficial) unofficial

ofrec|er 🔟 vt offer; give (fiesta, banquete etc); (prometer) promise. **~erse** vpr (persona) volunteer. **~imiento** m offer

ofrenda f offering. **~r** vt offer

ofuscar 🔟 vt blind; (confundir) confuse. **~se** vpr get worked up

oí|ble adj audible. **~do** m ear; (sentido) hearing. **al ~do** in one's ear. **de ~das** by hearsay. **conocer de ~das** have heard of. **de ~do** by ear. **duro de ~do** hard of hearing

oigo vb véase **OÍR**

oír 🔟 vt hear. **¡oiga!** listen!; (al teléfono) hello!

ojal m buttonhole

ojalá int I hope so! •conj if only

ojea|da f glance. **dar una ~da a**, **echar una ~da a** have a quick glance at. **~r** vt have a look at

ojeras fpl rings under one's eyes

ojeriza f ill will. **tener ~ a** have a grudge against

ojo m eye; (de cerradura) keyhole; (de un puente) span. **¡~!** careful!

ola f wave

olé int bravo!

olea|da f wave. **~je** m swell

óleo m oil; (cuadro) oil painting

oleoducto m oil pipeline

oler ② (las formas que empiecen por **ue** se escriben **hue**) vt smell. ●vi smell (**a** of). **me huele mal** (fig) it sounds fishy to me

olfat|ear vt sniff; scent (rastro). **~o** m (sense of) smell; (fig) intuition

olimpiada f, **olimpíada** f Olympic games, Olympics

olímpico adj Olympic; (fig, fam) total

oliv|a f olive. **~ar** m olive grove. **~o** m olive tree

olla f pot, casserole. **~ a/de presión**, **~ exprés** pressure cooker

olmo m elm (tree)

olor m smell. **~oso** adj sweet-smelling

olvid|adizo adj forgetful. **~ar** vt forget. **~arse** vpr forget. **~arse de** forget. **se me ~ó** I forgot. **~o** m oblivion; (acto) omission

ombligo m navel

omi|sión f omission. **~tir** vt omit

ómnibus adj omnibus

omnipotente adj omnipotent

omóplato m shoulder blade

once adj & m eleven

ond|a f wave. **~a corta** short wave. **~a larga** long wave. **longitud f de ~a** wavelength. **~ear** vi wave; (agua) ripple.

~ulación f undulation; (del pelo) wave. **~ular** vi wave

onomásti|co adj (índice) of names. ●m (LAm) saint's day

ONU abrev (**Organización de las Naciones Unidas**) UN

OPA f take-over bid

opac|ar ⑦ (LAm) make opaque; (deslucir) mar; (anular) overshadow. **~o** adj opaque; (fig) dull

opci|ón f option. **~onal** adj optional

open-jaw m open jaws ticket

ópera f opera

opera|ción f operation; (Com) transaction; **~ retorno** (Esp) return to work (after the holidays). **~dor** m operator; (TV) cameraman; (Mex, obrero) machinist. **~r** vt operate on; work (milagro etc); (Mex) operate (máquina). ●vi operate; (Com) deal. **~rio** m machinist. **~rse** vpr take place; (Med) have an operation. **~torio** adj operative

opereta f operetta

opin|ar vi express one's opinion. ●vt think. **~ que** think that. **¿qué opinas?** what do you think? **~ión** f opinion. **la ~ión pública** public opinion

opio m opium

opone|nte adj opposing. ●m & f opponent. **~r** vt oppose; offer (resistencia); raise (objeción). **~rse** vpr be opposed; (dos personas) oppose each other

oporto m port (wine)

oportun|idad f opportunity; (cualidad de oportuno) timeliness; (LAm, ocasión) occasion. **~ista** m & f opportunist. **~o** adj opportune; (apropiado) suitable

oposi|ción f opposition. **~ciones** fpl public examination. **~tor** m candidate; (Pol) opponent

opres|ión f oppression; (ahogo)

····················

 see A-Z of Spanish life and culture

difficulty in breathing. ~**ivo** adj oppressive. ~**or** m oppressor

oprimir vt squeeze; press (botón etc); (ropa) be too tight for; (fig) oppress

optar vi choose. ~ **por** opt for

óptic|a f optics; (tienda) optician's (shop). ~**o** adj optic(al). ●m optician

optimis|mo m optimism. ~**ta** adj optimistic. ●m & f optimist

óptimo adj ideal; (condiciones) perfect

opuesto adj opposite; (opiniones) conflicting

opulen|cia f opulence. ~**to** adj opulent

oración f prayer; (Gram) sentence

ora|dor m speaker. ~**l** adj oral

órale int (Mex) come on!; (de acuerdo) OK!

orar vi pray (**por** for)

órbita f orbit

orden f order. ~ **del día** agenda. **órdenes** fpl **sagradas** Holy Orders. **a sus órdenes** (esp Mex) can I help you? ~ **de arresto** arrest warrant. **en** ~ in order. **por** ~ in turn. ~**ado** adj tidy

ordenador m computer

ordena|nza f ordinance. ●m (Mil) orderly. ~**r** vt put in order; (mandar) order; (Relig) ordain; (LAm, en restaurante) order

ordeñar vt milk

ordinario adj ordinary; (grosero) common; (de mala calidad) poor-quality

orear vt air

orégano m oregano

oreja f ear

orfanato m orphanage

orfebre m goldsmith, silversmith

orfeón m choral society

orgánico adj organic

organillo m barrel-organ

organismo m organism

organista m & f organist

organiza|ción f organization. ~**dor** m organizer. ~**r** 🔟 vt organize. ~**rse** vpr get organized

órgano m organ

orgasmo m orgasm

orgía f orgy

orgullo m pride. ~**so** adj proud

orientación f orientation; (guía) guidance; (Archit) aspect

oriental adj & m & f oriental

orientar vt position; advise (persona). ~**se** vpr point; (persona) find one's bearings

oriente m east

orificio m hole

orig|en m origin. **dar** ~**en a** give rise to. ~**inal** adj original; (excéntrico) odd. ~**inalidad** f originality. ~**inar** vt give rise to. ~**inario** adj original; (nativo) native. **ser** ~**inario de** come from. ~**inarse** vpr originate; (incendio) start

orilla f (del mar) shore; (de río) bank; (borde) edge. **a** ~**s del mar** by the sea

orina f urine. ~**l** m chamber-pot. ~**r** vi urinate

oriundo adj native. **ser** ~ **de** (persona) come from; (especie etc) native to

ornamental adj ornamental

ornitología f ornithology

oro m gold. ~**s** mpl Spanish card suit. ~ **de ley** 9 carat gold. **hacerse de** ~ make a fortune. **prometer el** ~ **y el moro** promise the moon

orquesta f orchestra. ~**l** adj orchestral. ~**r** vt orchestrate

orquídea f orchid

ortiga f nettle

ortodoxo adj orthodox

ortografía f spelling

ortopédico adj orthopaedic

oruga f caterpillar

orzuelo m sty

os pron (acusativo) you; (dativo) (to) you; (reflexivo) (to) yourselves; (recíproco) (to) each other

osad|ía f boldness. ~o adj bold

oscila|ción f swinging; (de precios) fluctuation; (Tec) oscillation. ~r vi swing; (precio) fluctuate; (Tec) oscillate

oscur|ecer 11 vi get dark. ●vt darken; (fig) obscure. ~ecerse vpr grow dark; (nublarse) cloud over. ~idad f darkness, (fig) obscurity. ~o adj dark; (fig) obscure. a ~as in the dark

óseo adj bone

oso m bear. **~ de felpa**, **~ de peluche** teddy bear

ostensible adj obvious

ostent|ación f ostentation. ~ar vt show off; (mostrar) show. ~oso adj ostentatious

osteópata m & f osteopath

ostión m (esp Mex) oyster

ostra f oyster

ostracismo m ostracism

Otan abrev (**Organización del Tratado del Atlántico Norte**) NATO, North Atlantic Treaty Organization

otitis f inflammation of the ear

otoño m autumn (Brit), fall (Amer)

otorga|miento m granting. ~r 12 vt give; grant (préstamo); (Jurid) draw up (testamento)

otorrinolaringólogo m ear, nose and throat specialist

otro, otra

●adjetivo

····▸ another; (con artículo, posesivo) other. **come ~ pedazo** have another piece. **el ~ día** the other day. **mi ~ coche** my other car. **otra cosa** something else. **otra persona** somebody else. **otra vez** again

····▸ (en plural) other; (con numeral) another. **en otras ocasiones** on other occasions. **~s 3 vasos** another 3 glasses

····▸ (siguiente) next. **al ~ día** the next day. **me bajo en la otra estación** I get off at the next station

●pronombre

····▸ (cosa) another one. **lo cambié por ~** I changed it for another one

····▸ (persona) someone else. **invitó a ~** she invited someone else

····▸ (en plural) (some) others. **tengo ~s en casa** I have (some) others at home. **~s piensan lo contrario** others think the opposite

····▸ (con artículo) **el ~** the other one. **los ~s** the others. **uno detrás del ~** one after the other. **los ~s no vinieron** the others didn't come. **esta semana no, la otra** not this week, next week. **de un día para el ~** from one day to the next

▶ Para usos complementarios ver **uno, tanto**

ovación f ovation

oval adj, **ovalado** adj oval

óvalo m oval

ovario m ovary

oveja f sheep; (hembra) ewe

overol m (LAm) overalls

ovillo m ball. **hacerse un ~** curl up

OVNI abrev (**objeto volante no**

identificado) UFO
ovulación f ovulation
oxida|ción f rusting. ~**r** vi rust.
~**rse** vpr go rusty
óxido m rust; (en química) oxide

oxígeno m oxygen
oye vb véase **oír**
oyente adj listening. ●m & f
listener; (Univ) occasional student
ozono m ozone

Pp

pabellón m pavilion; (en jardín)
summerhouse; (en hospital) block;
(de instrumento) bell; (bandera) flag
pacer 11 vi graze
pachucho adj (fruta) overripe;
(persona) poorly
pacien|cia f patience. **perder la**
~**cia** lose patience. ~**te** adj & m & f
patient
pacificar 7 vt pacify. ~**se** vpr calm
down
pacífico adj peaceful. **el (Océano)**
P~ the Pacific (Ocean)
pacifis|mo m pacifism. ~**ta** adj & m
& f pacifist
pact|ar vi agree, make a pact. ~**o**
m pact, agreement
padec|er 11 vt/i suffer (**de** from);
(soportar) bear. ~**er del corazón**
have heart trouble. ~**imiento** m
suffering
padrastro m stepfather
padre adj 1 terrible; (Mex, estupendo)
great. ●m father. ~**s** mpl parents
padrino m godfather; (en boda)
man who gives away the bride
padrón m register. ~ **electoral**
(LAm) electoral roll
paella f paella
paga f payment; (sueldo) pay.
~**dero** adj payable
pagano adj & m pagan

··
⛿ see A-Z of Spanish life and culture

pagar 12 vt pay; pay for (compras).
●vi pay. ~**é** m IOU
página f page
pago m payment
país m country; (ciudadanos) nation.
~ **natal** native land. **⛿el P**~
Vasco the Basque Country. **los**
P~**es Bajos** the Low Countries
paisaje m landscape, scenery
paisano m compatriot
paja f straw; (en texto) padding
pájaro m bird. ~ **carpintero**
woodpecker
paje m page
pala f shovel; (para cavar) spade; (para
basura) dustpan; (de pimpón) bat
palabr|a f word; (habla) speech.
pedir la ~**a** ask to speak. **tomar**
la ~**a** take the floor. ~**ota** f
swear-word. **decir** ~**otas** swear
palacio m palace
paladar m palate
palanca f lever; (fig) influence. ~
de cambio (de velocidades) gear
lever (Brit), gear shift (Amer)
palangana f washbasin (Brit),
washbowl (Amer)
palco m (en el teatro) box
palestino adj & m Palestinian
paleta f (de pintor) palette; (de
albañil) trowel
paleto m yokel
paliativo adj & m palliative

palide|cer ⚀ vi turn pale. **~z** f paleness

pálido adj pale. **ponerse ~** turn pale

palillo m (de dientes) toothpick; (para comer) chopstick

paliza f beating

palma f (de la mano) palm; (árbol) palm (tree); (de dátiles) date palm. **dar ~s** clap. **~da** f pat; (LAm) slap. **~das** fpl applause

palmera f palm tree

palmo m span; (fig) few inches. **~ a ~** inch by inch

palmote|ar vi clap. **~o** m clapping, applause

palo m stick; (de valla) post; (de golf) club; (golpe) blow; (de naipes) suit; (mástil) mast

paloma f pigeon; (blanca, símbolo) dove

palomitas fpl popcorn

palpar vt feel

palpita|ción f palpitation. **~nte** adj throbbing. **~r** vi beat, (latir con fuerza) pound; (vena, sien) throb

palta f (LAm) avocado (pear)

paludismo m malaria

pamela f (woman's) broad-brimmed dress hat

pamp|a f pampas. **~ero** adj of the pampas

pan m bread; (barra) loaf. **~ integral** wholewheat bread, wholemeal bread (Brit). **~ tostado** toast. **~ rallado** breadcrumbs. **ganarse el ~** earn one's living

pana f corduroy

panader|ía f bakery; (tienda) baker's (shop). **~o** m baker

panal m honeycomb

panameño adj & m Panamanian

pancarta f banner, placard

panda m panda

pander|eta f (small) tambourine

~o m tambourine

pandilla f gang

panecillo m (bread) roll

panel m panel

panfleto m pamphlet

pánico m panic. **tener ~** be terrified (**a** of)

panor|ama m panorama. **~ámico** adj panoramic

panque m (Mex) sponge cake

pantaletas fpl (Mex) panties, knickers (Brit)

pantalla f screen; (de lámpara) (lamp)shade

pantalón m, **pantalones** mpl trousers. **~ a la cadera** bumsters

pantano m marsh; (embalse) reservoir. **~so** adj marshy

pantera f panther

panti m, (Mex) **pantimedias** fpl tights (Brit), pantyhose (Amer)

pantomima f pantomime

pantorrilla f calf

pantufla f slipper

panz|a f belly. **~udo** adj pot bellied

pañal m nappy (Brit), diaper (Amer)

paño m material; (de lana) woollen cloth; (trapo) cloth. **~ de cocina** dishcloth; (para secar) tea towel. **~ higiénico** sanitary towel. **en ~s menores** in one's underclothes

pañuelo m handkerchief; (de cabeza) scarf

papa m pope. ● f (LAm) potato. **~s fritas** (LAm) chips (Brit), French fries (Amer); (de paquete) crisps (Brit), chips (Amer)

papá m dad(dy). **~s** mpl parents. **P~ Noel** Father Christmas

papada f (de persona) double chin

papagayo m parrot

papalote m (Mex) kite

papanatas m invar simpleton

paparrucha f (tontería) silly thing

papaya f papaya, pawpaw

papel m paper; (en el teatro etc) role. **~ carbón** carbon paper. **~ de calcar** tracing paper. **~ de envolver** wrapping paper. **~ de plata** silver paper. **~ higiénico** toilet paper. **~ pintado** wallpaper. **~ secante** blotting paper. **~eo** m paperwork. **~era** f waste-paper basket. **~ería** f stationer's (shop). **~eta** f (para votar) (ballot) paper

paperas fpl mumps

paquete m packet; (bulto) parcel; (LAm, de papas fritas) bag; (Mex, problema) headache. **~ postal** parcel

Paquistán m Pakistan

paquistaní adj & m Pakistani

par adj (número) even. •m couple; (dos cosas iguales) pair. **a ~es** two by two. **de ~ en ~** wide open. **~es y nones** odds and evens. **sin ~** without equal. •f par. **a la ~** (Com) at par. **a la ~ que** at the same time

para preposición

····▸ for. **es ~ ti** it's for you. **~ siempre** for ever. **¿~ qué?** what for? **~ mi cumpleaños** for my birthday

····▸ (con infinitivo) to. **es muy tarde ~ llamar** it's too late to call. **salió ~ divertirse** he went out to have fun. **lo hago ~ ahorrar** I do it (in order) to save money

····▸ (dirección) **iba ~ la oficina** he was going to the office. **empújalo ~ atrás** push it back. **¿vas ~ casa?** are you going home?

····▸ (tiempo) by. **debe estar listo ~ el 5** it must be ready by the 5th. **~ entonces** by then

····▸ (LAm, hora) to. **son 5 ~ la** una it's 5 to one

····▸ **~ que** so (that). **grité ~ que me oyera** I shouted so (that) he could hear me.

Note that **para que** is always followed by a verb in the subjunctive

parabienes mpl congratulations

parábola f (narración) parable

parabólica f satellite dish

para|brisas m invar windscreen (Brit), windshield (Amer). **~caídas** m invar parachute. **~caidista** m & f parachutist; (Mil) paratrooper. **~choques** m invar bumper (Brit), fender (Amer) (Rail) buffer

parad|a f (acción) stop; (lugar) bus stop; (de taxis) rank; (Mil) parade. **~ero** m whereabouts; (LAm, lugar) bus stop. **~o** adj stationary; (desempleado) unemployed. **estar ~** (LAm, de pie) be standing

paradoja f paradox

🄲 **parador** m state-owned hotel

parafina f paraffin

paraguas m invar umbrella

Paraguay m Paraguay

paraguayo adj & m Paraguayan

paraíso m paradise; (en el teatro) gallery

parallel|a f parallel (line). **~as** fpl parallel bars. **~o** adj & m parallel

par|álisis f invar paralysis. **~alítico** adj paralytic. **~alizar** 🔟 vt paralyse

parámetro m parameter

paramilitar adj paramilitary

páramo m bleak upland

parangón m comparison.

paraninfo m main hall

paranoi|a f paranoia. **~co** adj paranoiac

parar vt/i stop. **sin ~** continuously. **~se** vpr stop; (LAm, ponerse de pie) stand

p

pararrayos m invar lightning conductor

parásito adj parasitic. •m parasite

parcela f plot. ~r vt divide into plots

parche m patch

parcial adj partial. **a tiempo ~** part-time. ~**idad** f prejudice

parco adj laconic; (sobrio) sparing, frugal

parear vt put into pairs

parec|er m opinion. **al ~er** apparently. **a mi ~er** in my opinion. •vi 🔢 seem; (asemejarse) look like; (tener aspecto de) look. **me ~e** I think. ~**e fácil** it looks easy. **¿qué te ~e?** what do you think? **según ~e** apparently. ~**erse** vpr resemble, look like. ~**ido** adj similar. **bien ~ido** good-looking. •m similarity

pared f wall. ~ **por medio** next door. ~**ón** m (de fusilamiento) wall. **llevar al ~ón** shoot

parej|a f pair; (hombre y mujer) couple, (compañero) partner. ~**o** adj the same; (LAm, sin desniveles) even; (LAm, liso) smooth; (Mex, equitativo) equal. •adv (LAm) evenly

parente|la f relations. ~**sco** m relationship

paréntesis m invar parenthesis, bracket (Brit); (intervalo) break. **entre ~** in brackets (Brit), in parenthesis; (fig) by the way

paria m & f outcast

paridad f equality; (Com) parity

pariente m & f relation, relative

parir vt give birth to. •vi give birth

parisiense adj, m & f, **parisino** adj & m Parisian

parking /'parkin/ m car park (Brit), parking lot (Amer)

parlament|ar vi talk. ~**ario** adj parliamentary. •m member of parliament (Brit), congressman

(Amer). 🔢~**o** m parliament

parlanchín adj talkative. •m chatterbox

parlante m (LAm) loudspeaker

🔢**paro** m stoppage; (desempleo) unemployment; (subsidio) unemployment benefit; (LAm, huelga) strike. ~ **cardíaco** cardiac arrest

parodia f parody

parpadear vi blink; (luz) flicker

párpado m eyelid

parque m park. ~ **de atracciones** funfair. ~ **eólico** wind farm. ~ **infantil** playground. ~ **zoológico** zoo, zoological gardens

parquímetro m parking meter

parra f grapevine

párrafo m paragraph

parrilla f grill; (LAm, Auto) luggage rack. **a la ~** grilled. ~**da** f grill

párroco m parish priest

parroquia f parish; (iglesia) parish church. ~**no** m parishioner

parte m (informe) report. **dar ~** report. **de mi ~** for me •f part; (porción) share; (Jurid) party; (Mex, repuesto) spare (part). **de ~ de** from. **¿de ~ de quién?** (al teléfono) who's speaking? **en cualquier ~** anywhere. **en gran ~** largely. **en ~** partly. **en todas ~s** everywhere. **la mayor ~** the majority. **la ~ superior** the top. **ninguna ~** nowhere. **por otra ~** on the other hand. **por todas ~s** everywhere

partera f midwife

partición f division; (Pol) partition

participa|ción f participation; (noticia) announcement; (de lotería) share. ~**nte** adj participating. •m & f participant. ~**r** vt announce. •vi take part

participio m participle

particular adj particular; (clase)

....

🔢 *see* A-Z of Spanish life and culture

p

private. **nada de** ∼ nothing
special. •m private individual.

partida f departure; (en registro)
entry; (documento) certificate; (de
mercancías) consignment; (juego)
game; (de gente) group

partidario adj & m partisan. ∼ **de**
in favour of

parti|do m (Pol) party; (encuentro)
match, game; (LAm, de ajedrez) game.
∼**r** vt cut; (romper) break; crack
(nueces). •vi leave. **a** ∼**r de** from.
∼ **de** start from. ∼**rse** vpr
(romperse) break; (dividirse) split

partitura f (Mus) score

parto m labour. **estar de** ∼ be in
labour

parvulario m kindergarten,
nursery school (Brit)

pasa f raisin. ∼ **de Corinto**
currant

pasa|da f passing; (de puntos) row.
de ∼**da** in passing. ∼**dero** adj
passable. ∼**dizo** m passage. ∼**do**
adj past; (día, mes etc) last; (anticuado)
old-fashioned; (comida) bad, off.
∼**do mañana** the day after
tomorrow. ∼**dos tres días** after
three days. ∼**dor** m bolt; (de pelo)
hair-slide

pasaje m passage; (pasajeros)
passengers; (LAm, de avión etc)
ticket. ∼**ro** adj passing. •m
passenger

pasamano(s) m handrail; (barandilla
de escalera) banister(s)

pasamontañas m invar balaclava

pasaporte m passport

pasar vt pass; (atravesar) go through;
(filtrar) strain; spend (tiempo);
(película) show; (tolerar) tolerate; give
(mensaje, enfermedad). •vi
(suceder) happen; (ir) go; (venir)
come; (tiempo) go by. ∼ **de** have no
interest in. ∼**lo bien** have a good
time. ∼ **frío** be cold. ∼ **la
aspiradora** vacuum. ∼ **por alto**
leave out. **lo que pasa es que**
the fact is that. **pase lo que pase**
whatever happens. **¡pase Vd!**

come in!, go in! **¡que lo pases
bien!** have a good time! **¿qué
pasa?** what's the matter?, what's
happening? ∼**se** vpr pass; (dolor) go
away; (flores) wither; (comida) go
bad; spend (tiempo); (excederse) go
too far

pasarela f footbridge; (Naut)
gangway

pasatiempo m hobby, pastime

Pascua f (fiesta de los hebreos)
Passover; (de Resurrección) Easter;
(Navidad) Christmas. ∼**s** fpl
Christmas

pase m pass

pase|ante m & f passer-by. ∼**ar** vt
walk (perro); (exhibir) show off. •vi
walk. **ir a** ∼**ar, salir a** ∼**ar** walk.
∼**arse** vpr walk. ∼**o** m walk; (en
coche etc) ride; (calle) avenue. ∼**o
marítimo** promenade. **dar un**
∼**o, ir de** ∼ go for a walk. **¡vete
a** ∼**o!** 🄸 get lost! 🄸

pasillo m corridor; (de cine, avión)
aisle

pasión f passion

pasivo adj passive

pasm|ar vt astonish. ∼**arse** vpr be
astonished

paso m step; (acción de pasar) passing;
(camino) way; (entre montañas) pass;
(estrecho) strait(s). ∼ **a nivel** level
crossing (Brit), grade crossing
(Amer). ∼ **de cebra** zebra
crossing. ∼ **de peatones**
pedestrian crossing. ∼ **elevado**
flyover (Brit), overpass (Amer). **a
cada** ∼ at every turn. **a dos** ∼**s**
very near. **de** ∼ in passing. **de** ∼
por just passing through. **oír** ∼**s**
hear footsteps. **prohibido el** ∼
no entry

pasota m & f drop-out

pasta f paste; (masa) dough; (sl,
dinero) dough ⊠. ∼**s** fpl pasta;
(pasteles) pastries. ∼ **de dientes**,
∼ **dentífrica** toothpaste

pastel m cake; (empanada) pie; (lápiz)
pastel. ∼**ería** f cake shop

pasteurizado adj pasteurized

pastilla f pastille; (de jabón) bar; (de chocolate) piece

pasto m pasture; (hierba) grass; (LAm, césped) lawn. **~r** m shepherd; (Relig) minister. **~ra** f shepherdess

pata f leg; (pie de perro, gato) paw; (de ave) foot. **~s arriba** upside down. **a cuatro ~s** on all fours. **meter la ~** put one's foot in it. **tener mala ~** have bad luck. **~da** f kick. **~lear** vi stamp one's feet; (niño) kick

patata f potato. **~s fritas** chips (Brit), French fries (Amer); (de bolsa) (potato) crisps (Brit), (potato) chips (Amer)

patente adj obvious. •f licence

patern|al adj paternal; (cariño etc) fatherly. **~idad** f paternity. **~o** adj paternal; (cariño etc) fatherly

patético adj moving

patillas fpl sideburns

patín m skate; (con ruedas) roller skate. **patines en línea** Rollerblades (P)

patina|dor m skater **~je** m skating. **~r** vi skate, (resbalar) slide; (coche) skid

patio m patio. **~ de butacas** stalls (Brit), orchestra (Amer)

pato m duck

patológico adj pathological

patoso adj clumsy

patraña f hoax

patria f homeland

patriarca m patriarch

patrimonio m patrimony; (fig) heritage

patri|ota adj patriotic. •m & f patriot. **~otismo** m patriotism

patrocin|ar vt sponsor. **~io** m sponsorship

patrón m (jefe) boss; (de pensión etc) landlord; (en costura) pattern

patrulla f patrol; (fig, cuadrilla) group. **~r** vt/i patrol

pausa f pause. **~do** adj slow

pauta f guideline

paviment|ar vt pave. **~o** m pavement

pavo m turkey. **~ real** peacock

pavor m terror

payas|ada f buffoonery. **~o** m clown

paz f peace

peaje m toll

peatón m pedestrian

peca f freckle

peca|do m sin; (defecto) fault. **~dor** m sinner. **~minoso** adj sinful. **~r** **7** vi sin

pech|o m chest; (de mujer) breast; (fig, corazón) heart. **dar el ~o a un niño** breast-feed a child. **tomar a ~o** take to heart. **~uga** f breast

pecoso adj freckled

peculiar adj peculiar, particular. **~idad** f peculiarity

pedal m pedal. **~ear** vi pedal

pedante adj pedantic

pedazo m piece, bit. **a ~s in pieces. hacer(se) ~s** smash

pediatra m & f paediatrician

pedicuro m chiropodist

pedi|do m order; (LAm, solicitud) request. **~r** **5** vt ask for; (Com, en restaurante) order. •vi ask. **~r prestado** borrow

pega|dizo adj catchy. **~joso** adj sticky

pega|mento m glue. **~r** **12** vt stick (on); (coser) sew on; give (enfermedad etc); (juntar) join; (golpear) hit; (dar) give. **~r fuego a** set fire to •vi stick. **~rse** vpr stick; (pelearse) hit each other. **~tina** f sticker

pein|ado m hairstyle. **~ar** vt comb. **~arse** vpr comb one's hair. **~e** m comb. **~eta** f ornamental comb

p.ej. abrev (**por ejemplo**) e.g.

pelado adj (fruta) peeled; (cabeza) bald; (terreno) bare

p

pela|je m (de animal) fur; (fig, aspecto) appearance. **∼mbre** m (de animal) fur; (de persona) thick hair

pelar vt peel; shell (habas); skin (tomates); pluck (ave)

peldaño m step; (de escalera de mano) rung

pelea f fight; (discusión) quarrel. **∼r** vi fight; (discutir) quarrel. **∼rse** vpr fight; (discutir) quarrel

peletería f fur shop

peliagudo adj difficult, tricky

pelícano m pelican

película f film (esp Brit), movie (esp Amer). **∼ de dibujos animados** cartoon (film)

peligro m danger; (riesgo) hazard, risk. **poner en ∼** endanger. **∼so** adj dangerous

pelirrojo adj red-haired

pellejo m skin

pellizc|ar 7 vt pinch. **∼o** m pinch

pelma m & f, **pelmazo** m bore, nuisance

pelo m hair. **no tener ∼s en la lengua** be outspoken. **tomar el ∼ a uno** pull s.o.'s leg

pelota f ball. **∼ vasca** pelota. **hacer la ∼ a uno** suck up to s.o.

pelotera f squabble

peluca f wig

peludo adj hairy

peluquer|ía f hairdresser's. **∼o** m hairdresser

pelusa f down

pena f sadness; (lástima) pity; (LAm, vergüenza) embarrassment; (Jurid) sentence. **∼ de muerte** death penalty. **a duras ∼s** with difficulty. **da ∼ que** it's a pity that. **me da ∼** it makes me sad. **merecer la ∼** be worthwhile. **pasar ∼s** suffer hardship. **¡qué ∼!** what a pity! **valer la ∼** be worthwhile

penal adj penal; (derecho) criminal. ● m prison; (LAm, penalty) penalty.

∼idad f suffering; (Jurid) penalty. **∼ty** m penalty

pendiente adj hanging; (cuenta) outstanding; (asunto etc) pending. ● m earring. ● f slope

péndulo m pendulum

pene m penis

penetra|nte adj penetrating; (sonido) piercing; (viento) bitter. **∼r** vt penetrate; (fig) pierce. ● vi. **∼r en** penetrate; (entrar) go into

penicilina f penicillin

pen|ínsula f peninsula. **∼insular** adj peninsular

penique m penny

penitencia f penitence; (castigo) penance

penoso adj painful; (difícil) difficult; (LAm, tímido) shy; (LAm, embarazoso) embarrassing

pensa|do adj. **bien ∼do** all things considered. **menos ∼do** least expected. **∼dor** m thinker. **∼miento** m thought. **∼r** 1 vt think; (considerar) consider. **cuando menos se piensa** when least expected. **¡ni ∼rlo!** no way! **pienso que sí** I think so. ● vi think. **∼r en** think about. **∼tivo** adj thoughtful

pensi|ón f pension; (casa de huéspedes) guest-house. **∼ón completa** full board. **∼onista** m & f pensioner; (huésped) lodger

penúltimo adj & m penultimate, last but one

penumbra f half-light

penuria f shortage. **pasar ∼s** suffer hardship

peñ|a f rock; (de amigos) group; (LAm, club) folk club. **∼ón** m rock. **el P∼ón de Gibraltar** The Rock (of Gibraltar)

peón m labourer; (en ajedrez) pawn; (en damas) piece

peonza f (spinning) top

peor adj (comparativo) worse; (superlativo) worst. ● adv worse. **de**

mal en ~ from bad to worse. **lo** ~ the worst thing. **tanto** ~ so much the worse

pepin|illo m gherkin. ~**o** m cucumber. **(no) me importa un** ~**o** I couldn't care less

pepita f pip; (de oro) nugget

pequeñ|ez f smallness; (minucia) trifle. ~**o** adj small, little; (de edad) young; (menor) younger. • m little one. **es el** ~**o** he's the youngest

pera f (fruta) pear. ~**l** m pear (tree)

percance m mishap

percatarse vpr. ~ **de** notice

perc|epción f perception. ~**ibir** vt perceive; earn (dinero)

percha f hanger; (de aves) perch

percusión f percussion

perde|dor adj losing. • m loser. ~**r** 🚺 vt lose; (malgastar) waste; miss (tren etc). • vi lose. ~**rse** vpr get lost; (desaparecer) disappear; (desperdiciarse) be wasted; (estropearse) be spoilt. **echar(se) a** ~**r** spoil

pérdida f loss; (de líquido) leak; (de tiempo) waste

perdido adj lost

perdiz f partridge

perd|ón m pardon, forgiveness. **pedir** ~**ón** apologize. • int sorry! ~**onar** vt excuse, forgive; (Jurid) pardon. **¡**~**one (Vd)!** sorry!

perdura|ble adj lasting. ~**r** vi last

perece|dero adj perishable. ~**r** 🚺 vi perish

peregrin|ación f pilgrimage. ~**o** adj strange. • m pilgrim

perejil m parsley

perengano m so-and-so

perenne adj everlasting; (planta) perennial

perez|a f laziness. ~**oso** adj lazy

perfec|ción f perfection. **a la** ~**ción** perfectly, to perfection. ~**cionar** vt perfect; (mejorar) improve. ~**cionista** m & f

perfectionist. ~**to** adj perfect; (completo) complete

perfil m profile; (contorno) outline. ~**ado** adj well-shaped

perfora|ción f perforation. ~**dora** f punch. ~**r** vt pierce, perforate; punch (papel, tarjeta etc)

perfum|ar vt perfume. ~**arse** vpr put perfume on. ~**e** m perfume, scent. ~**ería** f perfumery

pericia f skill

perif|eria f (de ciudad) outskirts. ~**érico** adj (barrio) outlying. • m (Mex, carretera) ring road

perilla f (barba) goatee

perímetro m perimeter

periódico adj periodic(al). • m newspaper

periodis|mo m journalism. ~**ta** m & f journalist

período m, **periodo** m period

periquito m budgerigar

periscopio m periscope

perito adj & m expert

perju|dicar 🚼 vt damage; (desfavorecer) not suit. ~**dicial** adj damaging. ~**icio** m damage. **en** ~**icio de** to the detriment of

perla f pearl. **de** ~**s** adv very well

permane|cer 🚻 vi remain. ~**ncia** f permanence; (estancia) stay. ~**nte** adj permanent. • f perm. • m (Mex) perm

permi|sivo adj permissive. ~**so** m permission; (documento) licence; (Mil etc) leave. ~**so de conducir** driving licence (Brit), driver's license (Amer). **con** ~**so** excuse me. ~**tir** vt allow, permit. **¿me** ~**te?** may I? ~**tirse** vpr allow s.o.

pernicioso adj pernicious; (persona) wicked

perno m bolt

pero conj but. • m fault; (objeción) objection

perogrullada f platitude

p

perpendicular | petrificar

perpendicular adj & f perpendicular

perpetrar vt perpetrate

perpetu|ar 21 vt perpetuate. ~o adj perpetual

perplejo adj perplexed

perr|a f (animal) bitch; (moneda) coin, penny (Brit); cent (Amer); (rabieta) tantrum. **estar sin una ~a** be broke. ~era f dog pound; (vehículo) dog catcher's van. ~o adj awful. ●m dog. ~o galgo greyhound. de ~os awful

persa adj & m & f Persian

perse|cución f pursuit; (política etc) persecution. ~guir 5 & 13 vt pursue; (por ideología etc) persecute

persevera|nte adj persevering. ~r vi persevere

persiana f blind; (LAm, contraventana) shutter

persignarse vpr cross o.s.

persist|ente adj persistent. ~ir vi persist

person|a f person. ~as fpl people. ~aje m (persona importante) important figure; (de obra literaria) character. ~al adj personal. ●m staff. ~alidad f personality. ~arse vpr appear in person. ~ificar 7 vt personify

perspectiva f perspective

perspica|cia f shrewdness; (de vista) keen eyesight. ~z adj shrewd; (vista) keen

persua|dir vt persuade. ~sión f persuasion. ~sivo adj persuasive

pertenecer 11 vi belong

pértiga f pole. **salto m con ~** pole vault

pertinente adj relevant

perturba|ción f disturbance. ~ción del orden público breach of the peace. ~r vt disturb; disrupt (orden)

Perú m. **el ~** Peru

peruano adj & m Peruvian

perver|so adj evil. ●m evil person. ~tir 4 vt pervert

pesa f weight. ~dez f weight; (de cabeza etc) heaviness; (lentitud) sluggishness; (cualidad de fastidioso) tediousness; (cosa fastidiosa) bore, nuisance

pesadilla f nightmare

pesado adj heavy; (sueño) deep; (viaje) tiring; (duro) hard; (aburrido) boring, tedious

pésame m sympathy, condolences

pesar vt weigh. ●vi be heavy. ●m sorrow; (remordimiento) regret. **a ~ de (que)** in spite of. **pese a (que)** in spite of

pesca f fishing; (peces) fish; (pescado) catch. **ir de ~** go fishing. ~da f hake. ~dería f fish shop. ~dilla f whiting. ~do m fish. ~dor adj fishing. ●m fisherman. ~r 7 vt catch. ●vi fish

pescuezo m neck

pesebre m manger

pesero m (Mex) minibus

peseta f peseta

pesimista adj pessimistic. ●m & f pessimist

pésimo adj very bad, awful

peso m weight; (moneda) peso. ~ bruto gross weight. ~ neto net weight. **al ~** by weight. **de ~** influential

pesquero adj fishing

pestaña f eyelash. ~ear vi blink

pest|e f plague; (hedor) stench. ~icida m pesticide

pestillo m bolt; (de cerradura) latch

petaca f cigarette case; (Mex, maleta) suitcase

pétalo m petal

petardo m firecracker

petición f request; (escrito) petition

petirrojo m robin

petrificar 7 vt petrify

petr|óleo m oil. **~olero** adj oil. •m oil tanker

petulante adj smug

peyorativo adj pejorative

pez f fish; (substancia negruzca) pitch. **~ espada** swordfish

pezón m nipple

pezuña f hoof

piadoso adj compassionate; (devoto) devout

pian|ista m & f pianist. **~o** m piano. **~o de cola** grand piano

piar 20 vi chirp

picad|a f. **caer en ~a** (LAm) nosedive. **~o** adj perforated; (carne) minced (Brit), ground (Amer); (ofendido) offended; (mar) choppy; (diente) bad. •m. **caer en ~o** nosedive. **~ura** f bite, sting; (de polilla) moth hole

picaflor m (LAm) hummingbird

picante adj hot; (chiste etc) risqué

picaporte m door-handle; (aldaba) knocker

picar 7 vt (ave) peck; (insecto, pez) bite; (abeja, avispa) sting; (comer poco) pick at; mince (Brit), grind (Amer) (carne); chop (up) (cebolla etc); (Mex, pinchar) prick. •vi itch; (ave) peck; (insecto, pez) bite; (sol) scorch; (comida) be hot

picardía f craftiness; (travesura) naughty thing

pícaro adj crafty; (niño) mischievous. •m rogue

picazón f itch

pichón m pigeon; (Mex, novato) beginner

pico m beak; (punta) corner; (herramienta) pickaxe; (cima) peak. **y ~** (con tiempo) a little after; (con cantidad) a little more than. **~tear** vt peck; (fam, comer) pick at

picudo adj pointed

pido vb véase PEDIR

pie m foot; (Bot, de vaso) stem. **~ cuadrado** square foot. **a cuatro**

~s on all fours. **al ~ de la letra** literally. **a ~** on foot. **a ~(s) juntillas** (fig) firmly. **buscarle tres ~s al gato** split hairs. **de ~** standing (up). **de ~s a cabeza** from head to toe. **en ~** standing (up). **ponerse de ~** stand up

piedad f pity; (Relig) piety

piedra f stone; (de mechero) flint

piel f skin; (cuero) leather

pienso vb véase PENSAR

pierdo vb véase PERDER

pierna f leg

pieza f piece; (parte) part; (obra teatral) play; (moneda) coin; (habitación) room. **~ de recambio** spare part

pijama m pyjamas

pila f (montón) pile; (recipiente) basin; (eléctrica) battery. **~ bautismal** font **~r** m pillar

píldora f pill

pilla|je m pillage. **~r** vt catch

pillo adj wicked •m rogue

pilot|ar vt pilot. **~o** m pilot

pim|entero m (vasija) pepperpot. **~entón** m paprika; (LAm, fruto) pepper. **~ienta** f pepper. **grano m de ~ienta** peppercorn. **~iento** m pepper

pináculo m pinnacle

pinar m pine forest

pincel m paintbrush. **~ada** f brush-stroke. **la última ~ada** (fig) the finishing touch

pinch|ar vt pierce, prick; puncture (neumático); (fig, incitar) push; (Med, fam) give an injection to. **~azo** m prick; (en neumático) puncture. **~itos** mpl kebab(s); (tapas) savoury snacks. **~o** m point

ping-pong m table tennis, pingpong

pingüino m penguin

pino m pine (tree)

pint|a f spot; (fig, aspecto)

appearance. **tener ~a de** look like. **~ada** f graffiti. **~ar** vt paint. **no ~a nada** (fig) it doesn't count. **~arse** vpr put on make-up. **~or** m painter. **~oresco** adj picturesque. **~ura** f painting; (material) paint

pinza f (clothes-)peg (Brit), clothespin (Amer); (de cangrejo etc) claw. **~s** fpl tweezers

piñ|a f pine cone; (fruta) pineapple. **~ón** m (semilla) pine nut

pío adj pious. ● m chirp. **no decir ni ~** not say a word

piojo m louse

pionero m pioneer

pipa f pipe; (semilla) seed; (de girasol) sunflower seed

pique m resentment; (rivalidad) rivalry. **irse a ~** sink

piquete m picket; (Mex, herida) prick; (Mex, de insecto) sting

piragua f canoe

pirámide f pyramid

pirata adj invar pirate. ● m & f pirate

Pirineos mpl. **los ~**the Pyrenees

piropo m flattering comment

pirueta f pirouette

pirulí m lollipop

pisa|da f footstep; (huella) footprint. **~papeles** m invar paperweight. **~r** vt tread on. ● vi tread

piscina f swimming pool

Piscis m Pisces

piso m floor; (vivienda) flat (Brit), apartment (Amer); (de autobús) deck

pisotear vt trample (on)

pista f track; (fig, indicio) clue. **~ de aterrizaje** runway. **~ de baile** dance floor. **~ de carreras** racing track. **~ de hielo** ice-rink. **~ de tenis** tennis court

pistol|a f pistol. **~era** f holster. **~ero** m gunman

pistón m piston

pit|ar, (LAm) **~ear** vt whistle at;

(conductor) hoot at; award (falta). ● vi blow a whistle; (Auto) sound one's horn. **~ido** m whistle

pitill|era f cigarette case. **~o** m cigarette

pito m whistle; (Auto) horn

pitón m python

pitorre|arse vpr. **~arse de** make fun of. **~o** m teasing

pitorro m spout

piyama m (LAm) pyjamas

pizarr|a f slate; (en aula) blackboard. **~ón** m (LAm) blackboard

pizca f 🔢 tiny piece; (de sal) pinch. **ni ~** not at all

placa f plate; (con inscripción) plaque; (distintivo) badge. **~ de matrícula** number plate

place|ntero adj pleasant. **~r** 🔢 vi. **haz lo que te plazca** do as you please. **me ~ hacerlo** I'm pleased to do it. ● m pleasure

plácido adj placid

plaga f (also fig) plague. **~do** adj. **~do de** filled with

plagio m plagiarism

plan m plan. **en ~ de** as

plana f page. **en primera ~** on the front page

plancha f iron; (lámina) sheet. **a la ~** grilled. **tirarse una ~** put one's foot in it. **~do** m ironing. **~r** vt iron. ● vi do the ironing

planeador m glider

planear vt plan. ● vi glide

planeta m planet

planicie f plain

planifica|ción f planning. **~r** 🔢 vt plan

planilla f (LAm) payroll; (personal) staff

plano adj flat. ● m plane; (de edificio) plan; (de ciudad) street plan. **primer ~** foreground; (Foto) close-up

planta f (del pie) sole; (en botánica, fábrica) plant; (piso) floor. **~ baja** ground floor (Brit), first floor (Amer)

planta|ción f plantation. **~r** vt plant; deal (golpe). **~r en la calle** throw out. **~rse** vpr stand; (fig) stand firm

plantear vt (exponer) expound; (causar) create; raise (cuestión)

plantilla f insole; (nómina) payroll; (personal) personnel

plaqué m plating. **de ~** plated

plástico adj & m plastic

plata f silver; (fig, fam, dinero) money. **~ de ley** hallmarked silver

plataforma f platform

plátano m plane (tree); (fruta) banana. **platanero** m banana tree

platea f stalls (Brit), orchestra (Amer)

plateado adj silver-plated; (color de plata) silver

pl|ática f talk. **~aticar** 7 vi (Mex) talk. ● vt (Mex) tell

platija f plaice

platillo m saucer; (Mus) cymbal. **~ volador** (LAm), **~ volante** flying saucer

platino m platinum. **~s** mpl (Auto) points

plato m plate; (comida) dish; (parte de una comida) course

platónico adj platonic

playa f beach; (fig) seaside

plaza f square; (mercado) market (place); (sitio) place; (empleo) job. **~ de toros** bullring

plazco vb véase PLACER

plazo m period; (pago) instalment; (fecha) date. **comprar a ~s** buy on hire purchase (Brit), buy on the installment plan (Amer)

plazuela f little square

pleamar f high tide

pleb|e f common people. **~eyo** adj & m plebeian. **~iscito** m plebiscite

plega|ble adj pliable; (silla) folding. **~r** 1 & 12 vt fold. **~rse** vpr bend; (fig) yield

pleito m (court) case; (fig) dispute

plenilunio m full moon

plen|itud f fullness; (fig) height. **~o** adj full. **en ~o día** in broad daylight. **en ~o verano** at the height of the summer

plieg|o m sheet. **~ue** m fold; (en ropa) pleat

plisar vt pleat

plom|ero m (LAm) plumber. **~o** m lead; (Elec) fuse. **con ~o** leaded. **sin ~o** unleaded

pluma f feather; (para escribir) pen. **~ atómica** (Mex) ballpoint pen. **~ estilográfica** fountain pen. **~je** m plumage

plum|ero m feather duster; (para plumas, lápices etc) pencil-case. **~ón** m down; (edredón) down-filled quilt

plural adj & m plural. **en ~** in the plural

pluri|empleo m having more than one job. **~partidismo** m multi-party system. **~étnico** adj multiethnic

plus m bonus

pluscuamperfecto m pluperfect

plusvalía f capital gain

pluvial adj rain

pobla|ción f population; (ciudad) city, town; (pueblo) village. **~do** adj populated. ● m village. **~r** 2 vt populate; (habitar) inhabit. **~rse** vpr get crowded

pobre adj poor. ● m & f poor person; (fig) poor thing. **¡~cito!** poor (little) thing! **¡~ de mí!** poor (old) me! **~za** f poverty

pocilga f pigsty

poción f potion

poco

● adjetivo/pronombre

····▶ poco, poca little, not much. **tiene poca paciencia** he has little patience. **¿cuánta leche queda? - poca** how much milk is there left? - not much

····▶ pocos, pocas few. **muy ~s días** very few days. **unos ~s dólares** a few dollars. **compré unos ~s** I bought a few. **aceptaron a muy ~s** very few (people) were accepted

····▶ a ~ de llegar soon after he arrived. **¡a ~ !** (Mex) really? **dentro de ~** soon. **~ a ~,** (LAm) **de a ~** gradually, little by little. **hace ~** recently, not long ago. **por ~** nearly. **un ~** (cantidad) a little; (tiempo) a while. **un ~ de** a (little) bit of, a little, some

● adverbio

····▶ (con verbo) not much. **lee muy ~** he doesn't read very much

····▶ (con adjetivo) **un lugar ~ conocido** a little known place. **es ~ inteligente** he's not very intelligent

! Cuando **poco** modifica a un adjetivo, muchas veces el inglés prefiere el uso del prefijo *un-,* p. ej. **poco amistoso** *unfriendly.* **poco agradecido** *ungrateful*

podar vt prune

poder 33 verbo auxiliar be able to. **no voy a ~ terminar** I won't be able to finish. **no pudo venir** he couldn't come. **¿puedo hacer algo?** can I do anything? **¿puedo pasar?** may I come in? **no ~ con** not be able to cope with; (no aguantar) not be able to stand. **no ~ más** be exhausted; (estar harto de algo) not be able to manage any more. **no ~ menos que** have no alternative but. **puede que** it is possible that. **puede ser** it is possible. **¿se puede ...?** may I...? ● m power. **en el ~** in power. **~es**

públicos authorities. **~oso** adj powerful

podrido adj rotten

po|ema m poem. **~esía** f poetry; (poema) poem. **~eta** m & f poet. **~ético** adj poetic

polaco adj Polish. ● m Pole; (lengua) Polish

polar adj polar. **estrella ~** polestar

polea f pulley

pol|émica f controversy. **~emizar** 10 vi argue

polen m pollen

policía f police (force); (persona) policewoman. ● m policeman. **~co** adj police; (novela etc) detective

policromo adj, **polícromo** adj polychrome

polideportivo m sports centre

polietileno m polythene

poligamia f polygamy

polígono m polygon

polilla f moth

polio(mielitis) f polio(myelitis)

polític|a f politics; (postura) policy; (mujer) politician. **~ interior** domestic policy. **~o** adj political. **familia ~a** in-laws. ● m politician

póliza f (de seguros) policy

poll|o m chicken; (gallo joven) chick. **~uelo** m chick

polo m pole; (helado) ice lolly (Brit), Popsicle (P) (Amer); (juego) polo. **P~ norte** North Pole

Polonia f Poland

poltrona f armchair

polución f pollution

polv|areda f dust cloud; (fig, escándalo) uproar. **~era** f compact. **~o** m powder; (suciedad) dust. **~os** mpl powder. **en ~o** powdered. **estar hecho ~o** be exhausted. **quitar el ~o** dust

pólvora f gunpowder; (fuegos

artificiales) fireworks

polvoriento adj dusty

pomada f ointment

pomelo m grapefruit

pómez adj. **piedra** f ~ pumice stone

pomp|a f bubble; (esplendor) pomp. ~**as fúnebres** funeral. ~**oso** adj pompous; (espléndido) splendid

pómulo m cheekbone

ponchar vt (Mex) puncture

ponche m punch

poncho m poncho

ponderar vt (alabar) speak highly of

poner 34 vt put; put on (ropa, obra de teatro, TV etc); lay (la mesa, un huevo); set (examen, deberes); (contribuir) contribute, give (nombre); make (nervioso); pay (atención); show (película, interés); open (una tienda); equip (una casa). ~ **con** (al teléfono) put through to. ~ **por escrito** put into writing. ~ **una multa** fine. **pongamos** let's suppose. ● vi lay. ~**se** vpr put o.s.; (volverse) get; put on (ropa); (sol) set. ~**se a** start to. ~**se a mal con uno** fall out with s.o.

pongo vb véase PONER

poniente m west; (viento) west wind

pont|ificar 7 vi pontificate. ~**ífice** m pontiff

popa f stern

popote m (Mex) (drinking) straw

popul|acho m masses. ~**ar** adj popular; (costumbre) traditional; (lenguaje) colloquial. ~**aridad** f popularity. ~**arizar** 10 vt popularize.

póquer m poker

poquito m. **un** ~ a little bit. ● adv a little

por preposición

····➤ for. **es** ~ **tu bien** it's for your own good. **lo compró por 5 dólares** he bought it for 5 dollars. **si no fuera por ti** if it weren't for you. **vino por una semana** he came for a week

▶ Para expresiones como **por la mañana, por la noche** etc., ver bajo el respectivo nombre

····➤ (causa) because of. **se retrasó** ~ **la lluvia** he was late because of the rain. **no hay trenes** ~ **la huelga** there aren't any trains because of the strike

····➤ (medio, agente) by. **lo envié** ~ **correo** I sent it by post. **fue destruida** ~ **las bombas** it was destroyed by the bombs

····➤ (a través de) through. **entró** ~ **la ventana** he got in through the window. **me enteré** ~ **un amigo** I found out through a friend. ~ **todo el país** throughout the country

····➤ (a lo largo de) along. **caminar** ~ **la playa** to walk along the beach. **cortar** ~ **la línea de puntos** cut along the dotted line

····➤ (proporción) per. **cobra 30 dólares** ~ **hora** he charges 30 dollars per hour. **uno** ~ **persona** one per person. **10** ~ **ciento** 10 per cent

····➤ (Mat) times. **dos** ~ **dos (son) cuatro** two times two is four

····➤ (modo) in. ~ **escrito** in writing. **pagar** ~ **adelantado** to pay in advance

▶ Para expresiones como **por dentro, por fuera** etc., ver bajo el respectivo adverbio

····➤ (en locuciones) ~ **más que** no matter how much. **¿**~ **qué?** why? ~ **si** in case. ~ **supuesto** of course

porcelana f china

porcentaje m percentage

p

porcino adj pig

porción f portion; (de chocolate) piece

pordiosero m beggar

porfia|do adj stubborn. **~r** 20 vi insist

pormenor m detail

pornogr|afía f pornography. **~áfico** adj pornographic

poro m pore; (Mex, puerro) leek. **~so** adj porous

porque conj because; (para que) so that

porqué m reason

porquería f filth; (basura) rubbish; (grosería) dirty trick

porra f club

porrón m wine jug (with a long spout)

portaaviones m invar aircraft carrier

portada f (de libro) title page; (de revista) cover

portadocumentos m invar (LAm) briefcase

portador m bearer

portaequipaje(s) m invar boot (Brit), trunk (Amer); (encima del coche) roof-rack

portal m hall; (puerta principal) main entrance. **~es** mpl arcade

porta|ligas m invar suspender belt. **~monedas** m invar purse

portarse vpr behave

portátil adj portable. •m portable computer, laptop

portavoz m spokesman. •f spokeswoman

portazo m bang. **dar un ~** slam the door

porte m transport; (precio) carriage; (LAm, tamaño) size. **~ador** m carrier

portento m marvel

porteño adj from Buenos Aires

porter|ía f porter's lodge; (en deportes) goal. **⧉~o** m caretaker, porter; (en deportes) goalkeeper. **~o automático** entryphone

pórtico m portico

portorriqueño adj & m Puerto Rican

Portugal m Portugal

portugués adj & m Portuguese

porvenir m future

posada f inn. **dar ~** give shelter

posar vt put. •vi pose. **~se** vpr (pájaro) perch; (avión) land

posdata f postscript

pose|edor m owner; (de récord, billete, etc) holder. **~er** 18 vt own; hold (récord); have (conocimientos). **~sión** f possession. **~sionarse** vpr. **~sionarse de** take possession of. **~sivo** adj possessive

posgraduado adj & m postgraduate

posguerra f post-war years

posib|ilidad f possibility. **~le** adj possible. **de ser ~le** if possible. **en lo ~le** as far as possible. **si es ~le** if possible

posición f position; (en sociedad) social standing

positivo adj positive

poso m sediment

posponer 34 vt put after; (diferir) postpone

posta f. **a ~** on purpose

postal adj postal. •f postcard

poste m pole; (de valla) post

póster m (pl **~s**) poster

postergar 12 vt pass over; (diferir) postpone

posteri|dad f posterity. **~or** adj back; (años) later; (capítulos) subsequent. **~ormente** adv later

postigo m door; (contraventana) shutter

⧉ *see* A-Z of Spanish life and culture

postizo adj false, artificial. ●m hairpiece

postrarse vpr prostrate o.s.

postre m dessert, pudding (Brit)

postular vt postulate; (LAm) nominate (candidato)

póstumo adj posthumous

postura f position, stance

potable adj drinkable; (agua) drinking

potaje m vegetable stew

potasio m potassium

pote m pot

poten|cia f power. ~**cial** adj & m potential. ~**te** adj powerful

potro m colt; (en gimnasia) horse

pozo m well; (hoyo seco) pit; (de mina) shaft; (fondo común) pool

práctica f practice. **en la** ~ in practice

practica|nte m & f nurse. ~**r** 7 vt practise; play (deportes); (ejecutar) carry out

práctico adj practical; (conveniente, útil) handy. ●m practitioner

prad|era f meadow; (terreno grande) prairie. ~**o** m meadow

pragmático adj pragmatic

preámbulo m preamble

precario adj precarious; (medios) scarce

precaución f precaution; (cautela) caution. **con** ~ cautiously

precaverse vpr take precautions

precede|ncia f precedence; (prioridad) priority. ~**nte** adj preceding. ●m precedent. ~**r** vt/i precede

precepto m precept. ~**r** m tutor

precia|do adj valued; (don) valuable. ~**rse** vpr. ~**rse de** pride o.s. on

precio m price. ~ **de venta al público** retail price. **al** ~ **de** at the cost of. **no tener** ~ be

priceless. **¿qué** ~ **tiene?** how much is it?

precios|idad f (cosa preciosa) beautiful thing. **¡es una** ~**idad!** it's beautiful! ~**o** adj precious; (bonito) beautiful

precipicio m precipice

precipita|ción f precipitation; (prisa) rush. ~**damente** adv hastily. ~**do** adj hasty. ~**r** vt (apresurar) hasten; (arrojar) hurl. ~**rse** vpr throw o.s.; (correr) rush; (actuar sin reflexionar) act rashly

precis|amente adj exactly. ~**ar** vt require; (determinar) determine. ~**ión** f precision. ~**o** adj precise; (necesario) necessary. **si es** ~**o** if necessary

preconcebido adj preconceived

precoz adj early; (niño) precocious

precursor m forerunner

predecesor m predecessor

predecir 46, (pero imperativo **predice**, futuro y condicional regulares) vt foretell

predestinado adj predestined

prédica f sermon

predicar 7 vt/i preach

predicción f prediction; (del tiempo) forecast

predilec|ción f predilection. ~**to** adj favourite

predisponer 34 vt predispose

predomin|ante adj predominant. ~**ar** vi predominate. ~**io** m predominance

preeminente adj pre-eminent

prefabricado adj prefabricated

prefacio m preface

prefer|encia f preference; (Auto) right of way. **de** ~**encia** preferably. ~**ente** adj preferential. ~**ible** adj preferable. ~**ido** adj favourite. ~**ir** 4 vt prefer

prefijo m prefix; (telefónico) dialling code

pregonar vt announce

p

pregunta | prestar

pregunta f question. **hacer una ~** ask a question. **~r** vt/i ask (**por** about). **~rse** vpr wonder

prehistórico adj prehistoric

preju|icio m prejudice. **~zgar** 12 vt prejudge

preliminar adj & m preliminary

preludio m prelude

premarital adj, **prematrimonial** adj premarital

prematuro adj premature

premedita|ción f premeditation. **~r** vt premeditate

premi|ar vt give a prize to; (recompensar) reward. **~o** m prize; (recompensa) reward. **~o gordo** jackpot

premonición f premonition

prenatal adj antenatal

prenda f garment; (garantía) surety; (en juegos) forfeit. **en ~ de** as a token of. **~r** vt captivate. **~rse** vpr fall in love (**de** with)

prende|dor m brooch. **~r** vt capture; (sujetar) fasten; light (cigarrillo); (LAm) turn on (gas, radio, etc). ●vi catch; (arraigar) take root. **~rse** vpr (encenderse) catch fire

prensa f press. **~r** vt press

preñado adj pregnant; (fig) full

preocupa|ción f worry. **~do** adj worried. **~r** vt worry. **~rse** vpr worry. **~rse de** look after

prepara|ción f preparation. **~do** adj prepared. ●m preparation. **~r** vt prepare. **~rse** vpr get ready. **~tivos** mpl preparations. **~torio** adj preparatory

preposición f preposition

prepotente adj arrogant; (actitud) high-handed

prerrogativa f prerogative

presa f (cosa) prey; (embalse) dam

presagi|ar vt presage. **~o** m omen

presb|iteriano adj & m

Presbyterian. **~ítero** m priest

prescindir vi. **~ de** do without; (deshacerse de) dispense with

prescri|bir (pp **prescrito**) vt prescribe. **~pción** f prescription

presencia f presence; (aspecto) appearance. **en ~ de** in the presence of. **~r** vt be present at; (ver) witness

presenta|ble adj presentable. **~ción** f presentation; (de una persona a otra) introduction. **~dor** m presenter. **~r** vt (ofrecer) offer; (entregar) hand in; (hacer conocer) introduce; show (película). **~rse** vpr present o.s.; (hacerse conocer) introduce o.s.; (aparecer) turn up

presente adj present; (actual) this. ●m present. **los ~s** those present. **tener ~** remember

presenti|miento m premonition. **~r** 4 vt have a feeling (**que** that)

preserva|r vt preserve. **~tivo** m condom

presiden|cia f presidency; (de asamblea) chairmanship. **~cial** adj presidential. **~ta** f (woman) president. **~te** m president; (de asamblea) chairman. ▣**~te del gobierno** prime minister

presidi|ario m convict. **~o** m prison

presidir vt be president of; preside over (tribunal); chair (reunión, comité)

presi|ón f pressure. **a ~ón** under pressure. **hacer ~ón** press. **~onar** vt press; (fig) put pressure on

preso adj. **estar ~** be in prison. **llevarse ~ a uno** take s.o. away under arrest. ●m prisoner

presta|do adj (de uno) lent; (a uno) borrowed. **pedir ~do** borrow. **~mista** m & f moneylender

préstamo m loan; (acción de pedir prestado) borrowing; (acción de prestar) lending

prestar vt lend; give (ayuda etc); pay

▣ see A-Z of Spanish life and culture

p

(atención). ~**se** vpr. ~**se a** be open to; (ser apto) be suitable (**para** for)

prestidigita|ción f conjuring. ~**dor** m conjurer

prestigio m prestige. ~**so** adj prestigious

presu|mido adj conceited. ~**mir** vi show off; boast (**de** about). ~**nción** f conceit; (suposición) presumption. ~**nto** adj alleged. ~**ntuoso** adj conceited

presup|oner 34 vt presuppose. ~**uesto** m budget; (precio estimado) estimate

preten|cioso adj pretentious. ~**der** vt try to; (afirmar) claim; (solicitar) apply for; (cortejar) court. ~**diente** m pretender; (a una mujer) suitor. ~**sión** f pretension; (aspiración) aspiration

pretérito m preterite, past

pretexto m pretext. **con el ~ de** on the pretext of

prevalecer 11 vi prevail (**sobre** over)

preven|ción f prevention; (prejuicio) prejudice. ~**ido** adj ready; (precavido) cautious. ~**ir** 53 vt prevent; (advertir) warn. ~**tiva** f (Mex) amber light. ~**tivo** adj preventive

prever 43 vt foresee; (planear) plan

previo adj previous

previs|ible adj predictable. ~**ión** f forecast; (prudencia) precaution

prima f (pariente) cousin; (cantidad) bonus

primario adj primary

primavera f spring. ~**l** adj spring

primer adj véase PRIMERO. ~**a** f (Auto) first (gear); (en tren etc) first class. ~**o** adj (delante de nombre masculino en singular **primer**) first; (mejor) best; (principal) leading. **la ~a fila** the front row. **lo ~o es** the most important thing is. ~**a enseñanza** primary education. **a ~os de** at the beginning of. **de**

~**a** first-class. ●n (the) first. ●adv first

primitivo adj primitive

primo m cousin; 🅵 fool. **hacer el ~** be taken for a ride

primogénito adj & m first-born, eldest

primor m delicacy; (cosa) beautiful thing

primordial adj fundamental; (interés) paramount

princesa f princess

principal adj main. **lo ~ es que** the main thing is that

príncipe m prince

principi|ante m & f beginner. ~**o** m beginning; (moral, idea) principle; (origen) origin. **al ~o** at first. **a ~o(s) de** at the beginning of. **desde el ~o** from the start. **en ~o** in principle. ~**os** mpl (nociones) rudiments

prión m prion

prioridad f priority

prisa f hurry, haste. **darse ~** hurry (up). **de ~** quickly. **tener ~** be in a hurry

prisi|ón f prison; (encarcelamiento) imprisonment. ~**onero** m prisoner

prismáticos mpl binoculars

priva|ción f deprivation. ~**da** f (Mex) private road. ~**do** adj (particular) private. ~**r** vt deprive (**de** of). ~**tivo** adj exclusive (**de** to)

privilegi|ado adj privileged; (muy bueno) exceptional. ~**o** m privilege

pro prep. **en ~ de** for, in favour of. ●m advantage. **los ~s y los contras** the pros and cons

proa f bow

probab|ilidad f probability. ~**le** adj probable, likely. ~**lemente** adv probably

proba|dor m fitting-room. ~**r** 2 vt try; try on (ropa); (demostrar) prove.

•vi try. **~rse** vpr try on

probeta f test-tube

problema m problem. **hacerse ~as** (LAm) worry

procaz adj indecent

proced|encia f origin. **~ente** adj (razonable) reasonable. **~ente de** (coming) from. **~er** m conduct. •vi proceed. **~er contra** start legal proceedings against. **~er de** come from. **~imiento** m procedure; (sistema) process; (Jurid) proceedings

proces|ador m. **~ador de textos** word processor. **~al** adj procedural. **costas ~ales** legal costs. **~amiento** m processing; (Jurid) prosecution. **~amiento de textos** word-processing.. **~ar** vt process; (Jurid) prosecute

procesión f procession

proceso m process; (Jurid) trial; (transcurso) course

proclamar vt proclaim

procrea|ción f procreation. **~r** vt procreate

procura|dor m attorney, solicitor; (asistente) clerk (Brit), paralegal (Amer). **~r** vt try; (obtener) obtain

prodigar vt lavish

prodigio m prodigy; (maravilla) wonder; (milagro) miracle. **~so** adj prodigious

pródigo adj prodigal

produc|ción f production. **~ir** vt produce; (causar) cause. **~irse** vpr (suceder) happen. **~tivo** adj productive. **~to** m product. **~tos agrícolas** farm produce. **~tos alimenticios** foodstuffs. **~tos de belleza** cosmetics. **~tos de consumo** consumer goods. **~tor** m producer.

proeza f exploit

profan|ación f desecration. **~ar** vt desecrate. **~o** adj profane

profecía f prophecy

proferir vt utter; hurl (insultos etc)

profes|ión f profession. **~ional** adj professional. **~or** m teacher; (en universidad) lecturer. **~orado** m teaching profession; (conjunto de profesores) staff

prof|eta m prophet. **~etizar** vt/i prophesize

prófugo adj & m fugitive

profund|idad f depth. **~o** adj deep; (fig) profound. **poco ~o** shallow

progenitor m ancestor

programa m programme; (de estudios) syllabus. **~ concurso** quiz show. **~ de entrevistas** chat show. **~ción** f programming; (TV etc) programmes; (en periódico) TV guide. **~r** vt programme. **~dor** m computer programmer

progres|ar vi (make) progress. **~ión** f progression. **~ista** adj progressive. **~ivo** adj progressive. **~o** m progress. **hacer ~os** make progress

prohibi|ción f prohibition. **~do** adj forbidden. **prohibido fumar** no smoking. **~r** vt forbid. **~tivo** adj prohibitive

prójimo m fellow man

prole f offspring

proletari|ado m proletariat. **~o** adj & m proletarian

prol|iferación f proliferation. **~iferar** vi proliferate. **~ífico** adj prolific

prolijo adj long-winded

prólogo m prologue

prolongar vt prolong; (alargar) lengthen. **~se** vpr go on

promedio m average. **como ~** on average

prome|sa f promise. **~ter** vt promise. •vi show promise. **~terse** vpr (novios) get engaged. **~tida** f fiancée. **~tido** adj promised; (novios) engaged. •m fiancé

prominente f prominence
promiscu|idad f promiscuity. ∼o adj promiscuous
promo|ción f promotion. ∼tor m promoter. ∼ver **2** vt promote; (causar) cause
promulgar **12** vt promulgate
pronombre m pronoun
pron|osticar **7** vt predict; forecast (tiempo). ∼óstico m prediction; (del tiempo) forecast; (Med) prognosis
pront|itud f promptness. ∼o adj quick. ● adv quickly; (dentro de poco) soon; (temprano) early. **de** ∼o suddenly. **por lo** ∼o for the time being. **tan** ∼o **como** as soon as
pronuncia|ción f pronunciation. ∼miento m revolt. ∼r vt pronounce; deliver (discurso). ∼rse vpr declare o.s.; (sublevarse) rise up
propagación f propagation
propaganda f propaganda; (anuncios) advertising
propagar **12** vt/i propagate. ∼se vpr spread
propasarse vpi go too far
propens|ión f inclination. ∼o adj inclined
propici|ar vt favour; (provocar) bring about. ∼o adj favourable
propie|dad f property. ∼tario m owner
propina f tip
propio adj own; (característico) typical; (natural) natural; (apropiado) proper. **el** ∼ **médico** the doctor himself
proponer **34** vt propose; put forward (persona). ∼se vpr. ∼se **hacer** intend to do
proporci|ón f proportion. ∼onado adj proportioned. ∼onal adj proportional. ∼onar vt provide
proposición f proposition
propósito m intention. **a** ∼

(adrede) on purpose; (de paso) by the way. **a** ∼ **de** with regard to
propuesta f proposal
propuls|ar vt propel; (fig) promote. ∼ión f propulsion. ∼ión a **chorro** jet propulsion
prórroga f extension
prorrogar **12** vt extend
prosa f prose. ∼ico adj prosaic
proscri|bir (pp **proscrito**) vt exile; (prohibir) ban. ∼to adj banned. ● m exile; (bandido) outlaw
proseguir **5** & **13** vt/i continue
prospecto m prospectus; (de fármaco) directions for use
prosper|ar vi prosper; (persona) do well. ∼idad f prosperity
próspero adj prosperous. **¡P∼ Año Nuevo!** Happy New Year!
prostit|ución f prostitution. ∼uta f prostitute
protagonista m & f protagonist
prote|cción f protection. ∼ctor adj protective. ● m protector; (benefactor) patron. ∼ger **14** vt protect. ∼gida f protégée. ∼gido adj protected. ● m protegé
proteína f protein
protesta f protest; (manifestación) demonstration; (Mex, promesa) promise; (Mex, juramento) oath
protestante adj & m & f Protestant
protestar vt/i protest
protocolo m protocol
provecho m benefit. **¡buen** ∼! enjoy your meal! **de** ∼ useful. **en** ∼ **de** to the benefit of. **sacar** ∼ **de** benefit from
proveer **18** (pp **proveído** y **provisto**) vt supply, provide
provenir **53** vi come (**de** from)
proverbi|al adj proverbial. ∼o m proverb
🔲**provincia** f province. ∼l adj, ∼no adj provincial

🔲 see A-Z of Spanish life and culture

provisional adj provisional

provisto adj provided (**de** with)

provoca|ción f provocation. **~r** 🛚 vt provoke; (causar) cause. **~tivo** adj provocative

proximidad f proximity

próximo adj next; (cerca) near

proyec|ción f projection. **~tar** vt hurl; cast (luz); show (película). **~til** m missile. **~to** m plan. **~to de ley** bill. **en ~to** planned. **~tor** m projector

pruden|cia f prudence; (cuidado) caution. **~te** adj prudent, sensible

prueba f proof; (examen) test; (de ropa) fitting. **a ~** on trial. **a ~ de** proof against. **a ~ de agua** waterproof. **poner a ~** test

pruebo vb véase PROBAR

psicoan|álisis f psychoanalysis. **~alista** m & f psychoanalyst. **~alizar** 🔟 vt psychoanalyse

psic|ología f psychology. **~ológico** adj psychological. **~ólogo** m psychologist. **~ópata** m & f psychopath. **~osis** f invar psychosis

psiqu|e f psyche. **~iatra** m & f psychiatrist. **~iátrico** adj psychiatric

psíquico adj psychic

ptas, pts abrev (**pesetas**) pesetas

púa f sharp point; (espina) thorn; (de erizo) quill; (de peine) tooth; (Mus) plectrum

pubertad f puberty

publica|ción f publication. **~r** 🛚 vt publish

publici|dad f publicity; (Com) advertising. **~tario** adj advertising

público adj public. ● m public; (de espectáculo etc) audience

puchero m cooking pot; (guisado) stew. **hacer ~s** (fig, fam) pout

pude vb véase PODER

pudor m modesty. **~oso** adj modest

pudrir (pp **podrido**) vt rot; (fig, molestar) annoy. **~se** vpr rot

puebl|ecito m small village. **~erino** m country bumpkin. **~o** m town; (aldea) village; (nación) nation, people

puedo vb véase PODER

🅿 **puente** m bridge; (fig, fam) long weekend. **~ colgante** suspension bridge. **~ levadizo** drawbridge. **hacer ~** 🅿 have a long weekend

puerco adj filthy; (grosero) coarse. ● m pig. **~ espín** porcupine

puerro m leek

puerta f door; (en deportes) goal; (de ciudad, en jardín) gate. **~ principal** main entrance. **a ~ cerrada** behind closed doors

puerto m port; (fig, refugio) refuge; (entre montañas) pass. **~ franco** free port

puertorriqueño adj & m Puerto Rican

pues adv (entonces) then; (bueno) well. ● conj since

puest|a f setting; (en juegos) bet. **~a de sol** sunset. **~a en escena** staging. **~a en marcha** starting. **~o** adj put; (vestido) dressed. ● m place; (empleo) position, job; (en mercado etc) stall. ● conj. **~o que** since

pugna f struggle. **~r** vi. **~r por** strive to

puja f struggle (**por** to); (en subasta) bid. **~r** vt struggle; (en subasta) bid

pulcro adj neat

pulga f flea. **tener malas ~s** be bad-tempered

pulga|da f inch. **~r** m thumb; (del pie) big toe

puli|do adj polished; (modales) refined. **~r** vt polish; (suavizar) smooth

pulla f gibe

pulm|ón m lung. **~onar** adj

🅿 see A-Z of Spanish life and culture

pulmonary. **~onía** f pneumonia

pulpa f pulp

pulpería f (LAm) grocer's shop (Brit), grocery store (Amer)

púlpito m pulpit

pulpo m octopus

pulque m (Mex) pulque, alcoholic Mexican drink. **~ría** f bar

pulsa|ción f pulsation. **~dor** m button. **~r** vt press; (Mus) pluck

pulsera f bracelet

pulso m pulse; (firmeza) steady hand. **echar un ~** arm wrestle. **tomar el ~ a uno** take s.o.'s pulse

pulular vi teem with

puma m puma

puna f puna, high plateau

punitivo adj punitive

punta f point; (extremo) tip. **estar de ~** be in a bad mood. **ponerse de ~ con uno** fall out with s.o. **sacar ~ a** sharpen

puntada f stitch

puntaje m (LAm) score

puntal m prop, support

puntapié m kick

puntear vt mark; (Mus) pluck; (LAm, en deportes) lead

puntería f aim; (destreza) markmanship

puntiagudo adj pointed; (afilado) sharp

puntilla f (encaje) lace. **en ~s** (LAm), **de ~s** on tiptoe

punto m point; (señal, trazo) dot; (de examen) mark; (lugar) spot, place; (de taxis) stand; (momento) moment; (punto final) full stop (Brit), period (Amer); (puntada) stitch. **~ de vista** point of view. **~ com** dot-com. **~ final** full stop (Brit), period (Amer). **~ muerto** (Auto) neutral (gear). **~ y aparte** full stop, new paragraph (Brit), period, new paragraph (Amer). **~ y coma**

semicolon. **a ~** on time; (listo) ready. **a ~ de** on the point of. **de ~** knitted. **dos ~s** colon. **en ~** exactly. **hacer ~** knit. **hasta cierto ~** to a certain extent

puntuación f punctuation; (en deportes, acción) scoring; (en deportes, número de puntos) score

puntual adj punctual; (exacto) accurate. **~idad** f punctuality; (exactitud) accuracy

puntuar 21 vt punctuate; mark (Brit), grade (Amer) (examen). ●vi score (points)

punza|da f sharp pain; (fig) pang. **~nte** adj sharp. **~r** 10 vt prick

puñado m handful. **a ~s** by the handful

puñal m dagger. **~ada** f stab

puñ|etazo m punch. **~o** m fist; (de ropa) cuff; (mango) handle. **de su ~o (y letra)** in his own handwriting

pupa f (fam, en los labios) cold sore

pupila f pupil

pupitre m desk

puré m purée; (sopa) thick soup. **~ do papas** (LAm), **~ de patatas** mashed potatoes

pureza f purity

purga f purge. **~torio** m purgatory

puri|ficación f purification. **~ficar** 7 vt purify. **~sta** m & f purist. **~tano** adj puritanical. ●m puritan

puro adj pure; (cielo) clear. **de pura casualidad** by sheer chance. **de ~ tonto** out of sheer stupidity. ●m cigar

púrpura f purple

pus m pus

puse vb véase PONER

pusilánime adj fainthearted

puta f (vulg) whore

p

Qq

que pron rel (personas, sujeto) who; (personas, complemento) whom; (cosas) which, that. ● conj that. **¡~ tengan Vds buen viaje!** have a good journey! **¡~ venga!** let him come! **~ venga o no venga** whether he comes or not. **creo ~ tiene razón** I think (that) he is right. **más ~** more than. **lo ~** what. **yo ~ tú** if I were you

qué adj (con sustantivo) what; (con a o adv) how. ● pron what. **¡~ bonito!** how nice!. **¿en ~ piensas?** what are you thinking about?

quebra|da f gorge; (paso) pass. **~dizo** adj fragile. **~do** adj broken; (Com) bankrupt. ● m (Math) fraction. **~ntar** vt break; disturb (paz). **~nto** m (pérdida) loss; (daño) damage. **~r 1** vt break. ● vi break; (Com) go bankrupt. **~rse** vpr break

quechua adj Quechua. ● m & f Quechuan. ● m (lengua) Quechua

quedar vi stay, remain; (estar) be; (haber todavía) be left. **~ bien** come off well. **~se** vpr stay. **~ en** agree to. **~ en nada** come to nothing. **~ por** (+ infinitivo) remain to be (+ pp)

quehacer m work. **~es domésticos** household chores

quej|a f complaint; (de dolor) moan. **~arse** vpr complain (**de** about); (gemir) moan. **~ido** m moan

quema|do adj burnt; (LAm, bronceado) tanned; (fig) annoyed. **~dor** m burner. **~dura** f burn. **~r** vt/i burn. **~rse** vpr burn o.s.; (consumirse) burn up; (con el sol) get sunburnt. **~rropa** adv. **a ~rropa** point-blank

quena f Indian flute

quepo vb véase CABER

querella f (riña) quarrel, dispute; (Jurid) criminal action

quer|er 35 vt want; (amar) love; (necesitar) need. **~er decir** mean. ● m love; (amante) lover. **como quiera que** however. **cuando quiera que** whenever. **donde quiera** wherever. **¿quieres darme ese libro?** would you pass me that book? **¿quieres un helado?** would you like an ice-cream? **quisiera ir a la playa** I'd like to go to the beach. **sin ~er** without meaning to. **~ido** adj dear; (amado) loved

querosén m, **queroseno** m kerosene

querubín m cherub

ques|adilla f (Mex) tortilla filled with cheese. **~o** m cheese

quetzal m (unidad monetaria ecuatoriana) quetzal

quicio m frame. **sacar de ~ a uno** infuriate s.o.

quiebra f (Com) bankruptcy

quien pron rel (sujeto) who; (complemento) whom

quién pron interrogativo (sujeto) who; (tras preposición) **¿con ~?** who with?, to whom?. **¿de ~ son estos libros?** whose are these books?

quienquiera pron whoever

quiero vb véase QUERER

quiet|o adj still; (inmóvil) motionless; (carácter etc) calm. **~ud** f stillness

quijada f jaw

quilate m carat

quilla f keel

quimera f (fig) illusion

químic|a f chemistry. ~o adj chemical. •m chemist

quince adj & m fifteen. ~ **días** a fortnight. ~**na** f fortnight. ~**nal** adj fortnightly

quincuagésimo adj fiftieth

quiniela f pools coupon. ~s fpl (football) pools

quinientos adj & m five hundred

quinquenio m (period of) five years

quinta f (casa) villa

quintal m a hundred kilograms

quinteto m quintet

quinto adj & m fifth

quiosco m kiosk; (en jardín)
summerhouse; (en parque etc) bandstand

quirúrgico adj surgical

quise vb véase QUERER

quisquill|a f trifle; (camarón) shrimp. ~**oso** adj irritable; (exigente) fussy

quita|esmalte m nail polish remover. ~**manchas** m invar stain remover. ~**nieves** m invar snow plough. ~**r** vt remove, take away; take off (ropa); (robar) steal. ~**ndo** (fam, a excepción de) apart from. ~**rse** vpr get rid of (dolor); take off (ropa). ~**rse de** (no hacerlo más) stop. ~**rse de en medio** get out of the way. ~**sol** m sunshade

quizá(s) adv perhaps

quórum m quorum

Rr

rábano m radish. ~ **picante** horseradish. **me importa un** ~ I couldn't care less

rabi|a f rabies; (fig) rage. ~**ar** vi (de dolor) be in great pain; (estar enfadado) be furious. **dar** ~**a** infuriate. ~**eta** f tantrum

rabino m rabbi

rabioso adj rabid; (furioso) furious

rabo m tail

racha f gust of wind; (fig) spate. **pasar por una mala** ~ go through a bad patch

racial adj racial

racimo m bunch

ración f share, ration; (de comida) portion

racional adj rational. ~**lizar** vt rationalize. ~**r** vt (limitar) ration; (repartir) ration out

racis|mo m racism. ~**ta** adj racist

radar m radar

radiación f radiation

radiactiv|idad f radioactivity. ~**o** adj radioactive

radiador m radiator

radiante adj radiant; (brillante) brilliant

radical adj & m & f radical

radicar vi lie (**en** in). ~**se** vpr settle

radio m radius; (de rueda) spoke; (LAm) radio. •f radio. ~**actividad** f radioactivity. ~**activo** adj radioactive. ~**difusión** f broadcasting. ~**emisora** f radio station. ~**escucha** m & f listener. ~**grafía** f radiography

radi|ólogo m radiologist. ~**oterapia** f radiotherapy

⚑ see A-Z of Spanish life and culture

radioyente m & f listener

raer 🟨 vt scrape; (quitar) scrape off

ráfaga f (de viento) gust; (de ametralladora) burst

rafia f raffia

raído adj threadbare

raíz f root. **a ∼ de** as a result of. **echar raíces** (fig) settle

raja f split; (Culin) slice. **∼r** vt split. **∼rse** vpr split; (fig) back out

rajatabla: **a ∼** rigorously

ralea f sort

ralla|dor m grater. **∼r** vt grate

ralo adj (pelo) thin

rama f branch. **∼je** m branches. **∼l** m branch

rambla f watercourse; (avenida) avenue

ramera f prostitute

ramifica|ción f ramification. **∼rse** 🟨 vpr branch out

ram|illete m bunch. **∼o** m branch; (de flores) bunch, bouquet

rampa f ramp, slope

rana f frog

ranch|era f (Mex) folk song. **∼ero** m cook; (Mex, hacendado) rancher. **∼o** m (LAm, choza) hut; (LAm, casucha) shanty; (Mex, hacienda) ranch

rancio adj rancid; (vino) old; (fig) ancient

rango m rank

ranúnculo m buttercup

ranura f groove; (para moneda) slot

rapar vt shave; crop (pelo)

rapaz adj rapacious; (ave) of prey

rape m monkfish

rapidez f speed

rápido adj fast, quick. ●adv quickly. ●m (tren) express. **∼s** mpl rapids

rapiña f robbery. **ave f de ∼** bird of prey

rapsodia f rhapsody

rapt|ar vt kidnap. **∼o** m kidnapping; (de ira etc) fit

raqueta f racquet

rar|eza f rarity; (cosa rara) oddity. **∼o** adj rare; (extraño) odd. **es ∼o que** it is strange that. **¡qué ∼o!** how strange!

ras. **a ∼ de** level with

rasca|cielos m invar skyscraper. **∼r** 🟨 vt scratch; (raspar) scrape

rasgar 🟨 vt tear

rasgo m characteristic; (gesto) gesture; (de pincel) stroke. **∼s** mpl (facciones) features

rasguear vt strum

rasguñ|ar vt scratch. **∼o** m scratch

raso adj (cucharada etc) level; (vuelo etc) low. **al ∼** in the open air. ●m satin

raspa|dura f scratch; (acción) scratching. **∼r** vt scratch; (rozar) scrape

rastr|a: **a ∼as** dragging. **∼ear** vt track. **∼ero** adj creeping. **∼illar** vt rake. **∼illo** m rake. **∼o** m track; (señal) sign. **ni ∼o** not a trace

rata f rat

ratero m petty thief

ratifica|ción f ratification. **∼r** 🟨 vt ratify

rato m moment, short time. **∼s libres** spare time. **a ∼s** at times. **a cada ∼** (LAm) always. **hace un ∼** a moment ago. **pasar un mal ∼** have a rough time

rat|ón m mouse. **∼onera** f mousetrap; (madriguera) mouse hole

raudal m torrent. **a ∼les** in abundance

raya f line; (lista) stripe; (de pelo) parting. **a ∼s** striped. **pasarse de la ∼** go too far. **∼r** vt scratch. **∼r en** border on

rayo m ray; (descarga eléctrica) lightning. **∼ de luna** moonbeam. **∼ láser** laser beam. **∼s X** X-rays

raza f race; (de animal) breed. **de ∼**

r

(caballo) thoroughbred; (perro) pedigree

raz|ón f reason. **a ~ón de** at the rate of. **tener ~ón** be right. **~onable** adj reasonable. **~onar** vt reason out. • vi reason

RDSI abrev (**Red Digital de Servicios Integrados**) ISDN

re m D; (solfa) re

reac|ción f reaction; (LAm, Pol) right wing. **~ción en cadena** chain reaction. **~cionario** adj & m reactionary. **~tor** m reactor; (avión) jet

real adj real; (de rey etc) royal; (hecho) true. • m real, old Spanish coin

realidad f reality; (verdad) truth. **en ~** in fact. **hacerse ~** come true

realis|mo m realism. **~ta** adj realistic. • m & f realist

realiza|ción f fulfilment. **~r** vt carry out; make (viaje); fulfil (ilusión); (vender) sell. **~rse** vpr (sueño, predicción etc) come true; (persona) fulfil o.s.

realzar vt (fig) enhance

reanimar vt revive. **~se** vpr revive

reanudar vt resume; renew (amistad)

reavivar vt revive

rebaja f reduction. **en ~s** in the sale. **~do** adj (precio) reduced. **~r** vt lower; lose (peso)

rebanada f slice

rebaño m herd; (de ovejas) flock

rebasar vt exceed; (dejar atrás) leave behind; (Mex, Auto) overtake

rebatir vt refute

rebel|arse vpr rebel. **~de** adj rebellious; (grupo) rebel. • m rebel. **~día** f rebelliousness. **~ión** f rebellion

rebosa|nte adj brimming (**de** with). **~r** vi overflow; (abundar) abound

rebot|ar vt bounce; (rechazar) repel.

• vi bounce; (bala) ricochet. **~e** m bounce, rebound. **de ~e** on the rebound

reboz|ar vt wrap up; (Culin) coat in batter. **~o** m (LAm) shawl

rebusca|do adj affected; (complicado) over-elaborate. **~r** vt search through

rebuznar vi bray

recado m errand; (mensaje) message

reca|er vi fall back; (Med) relapse; (fig) fall. **~ída** f relapse

recalcar vt stress

recalcitrante adj recalcitrant

recalentar vt reheat; (demasiado) overheat

recámara f small room; (de arma de fuego) chamber; (Mex, dormitorio) bedroom

recambio m (Mec) spare (part); (de pluma etc) refill. **de ~** spare

recapitular vt sum up

recarg|ar vt overload; (aumentar) increase; recharge (batería). **~o** m increase

recat|ado adj modest. **~o** m prudence; (modestia) modesty. **sin ~o** openly

recauda|ción f (cantidad) takings. **~dor** m tax collector. **~r** vt collect

recel|ar vt suspect. • vi be suspicious (**de** of). **~o** m distrust; (temor) fear. **~oso** adj suspicious

recepci|ón f reception. **~onista** m & f receptionist

receptáculo m receptacle

receptor m receiver

recesión f recession

receta f recipe; (Med) prescription

rechaz|ar vt reject; defeat (moción); repel (ataque); (no aceptar) turn down. **~o** m rejection

rechifla f booing

rechinar vi squeak. **le rechinan los dientes** he grinds his teeth

rechoncho adj stout

recib|imiento m (acogida) welcome. **∼ir** vt receive; (acoger) welcome ●vi entertain. **∼irse** vpr graduate. ●**o** m receipt. **acusar ∼o** acknowledge receipt

reci|én adv recently; (LAm, hace poco) just. **∼én casado** newly married. **∼én nacido** newborn. **∼ente** adj recent; (Culin) fresh

recinto m enclosure; (local) premises

recio adj strong; (voz) loud. ●adv hard; (en voz alta) loudly

recipiente m receptacle. ●m & f recipient

recíproco adj reciprocal; (sentimiento) mutual

recita|l m recital; (de poesías) reading. **∼r** vt recite

reclama|ción f claim; (queja) complaint. **∼r** vt claim. ●vi appeal

réclame m (LAm) advertisement

reclamo m (LAm) complaint

reclinar vi lean. **∼se** vpr lean

reclus|ión f imprisonment. **∼o** m prisoner

recluta m & f recruit. **∼miento** m recruitment. **∼r** vt recruit

recobrar vt recover. **∼se** vpr recover

recodo m bend

recog|er 14 vt collect; pick up (cosa caída); (cosechar) harvest. **∼erse** vpr withdraw; (ir a casa) go home; (acostarse) go to bed. **∼ida** f collection; (cosecha) harvest

recomenda|ción f recommendation. **∼r** 1 vt recommend; (encomendar) entrust

recomenzar 1 & 10 vt/i start again

recompensa f reward. **∼r** vt reward

reconcilia|ción f reconciliation. **∼r** vt reconcile. **∼rse** vpr be reconciled

Ⓒ *see* A-Z of Spanish life and culture

reconoc|er 11 vt recognize; (admitir) acknowledge; (examinar) examine. **∼imiento** m recognition; (admisión) acknowledgement; (agradecimiento) gratitude; (examen) examination

reconozco vb *véase* RECONOCER

Ⓒreconquista f reconquest. **∼r** vt reconquer; (fig) win back

reconsiderar vt reconsider

reconstruir 17 vt reconstruct

récord /'rekor/ m (pl **∼s**) record

recordar 2 vt remember; (hacer acordar) remind. ●vi remember. **que yo recuerde** as far as I remember. **si mal no recuerdo** if I remember rightly

recorr|er vt tour (país); go round (zona, museo); cover (distancia). **∼ mundo** travel all around the world. **∼ido** m journey; (trayecto) route

recort|ar vt cut (out). **∼e** m cutting (out); (de periódico etc) cutting

recostar 2 vt lean. **∼se** vpr lie down

recoveco m bend; (rincón) nook

recre|ación f recreation. **∼ar** vt recreate; (divertir) entertain. **∼arse** vpr amuse o.s. **∼ativo** adj recreational. **∼o** m recreation; (en escuela) break

recrudecer 11 vi intensify

recta f straight line. **∼ final** home stretch

rect|angular adj rectangular. **∼ángulo** adj rectangular; (triángulo) right-angled. ●m rectangle

rectifica|ción f rectification. **∼r** 7 vt rectify

rect|itud f straightness; (fig) honesty. **∼o** adj straight; (fig, justo) fair; (fig, honrado) honest. **todo ∼o** straight on. ●m rectum

rector adj governing. ●m rector

recubrir (pp **recubierto**) vt cover (**con**, **de** with)

recuerdo m memory; (regalo)

souvenir. **~s** mpl (saludos) regards.
● vb véase **RECORDAR**

recupera|ción f recovery. **~r** vt
recover. **~r el tiempo perdido**
make up for lost time. **~rse** vpr
recover

recur|rir vi. **~rir a** resort to (cosa);
turn to (persona). **~so** m resort;
(medio) resource; (Jurid) appeal.
~sos mpl resources

red f network; (malla) net; (para
equipaje) luggage rack; (Com) chain;
(Elec, gas) mains. **la R~** the Net

redac|ción f writing; (lenguaje)
wording; (conjunto de redactores)
editorial staff; (oficina) editorial
office; (Escol, Univ) essay. **~tar** vt
write. **~tor** m writer; (de periódico)
editor

redada f catch; (de policía) raid

redecilla f small net; (para el pelo)
hairnet

redentor adj redeeming

redimir vt redeem

redoblar vt redouble; step up
(vigilancia)

redomado adj utter

redond|a f (de imprenta) roman
(type); (Mus) semibreve (Brit),
whole note (Amer). **a la ~a**
around. **~ear** vt round off. **~el** m
circle; (de plaza de toros) arena. **~o**
adj round; (completo) complete; (Mex,
boleto) return, round-trip (Amer).
en ~o round; (categóricamente)
flatly

reduc|ción f reduction. **~ido** adj
reduced; (limitado) limited; (pequeño)
small; (precio) low. **~ir** 47 vt
reduce. **~irse** vpr be reduced; (fig)
amount

reduje vb véase **REDUCIR**

redundan|cia f redundancy. **~te**
adj redundant

reduzco vb véase **REDUCIR**

reembols|ar vt reimburse. **~o** m
repayment. **contra ~o** cash on
delivery

reemplaz|ar 10 vt replace. **~o** m
replacement

refacci|ón f (LAm) refurbishment;
(Mex, Mec) spare part. **~onar** vt
(LAm) refurbish. **~onaria** f (Mex)
repair shop

referencia f reference; (información)
report. **con ~ a** with reference
to. **hacer ~ a** refer to

referéndum m (pl **~s**)
referendum

referir 4 vt tell; (remitir) refer. **~se**
vpr refer. **por lo que se refiere a**
as regards

refiero vb véase **REFERIR**

refilón: de ~ obliquely

refin|amiento m refinement. **~ar**
vt refine. **~ería** f refinery

reflector m reflector; (proyector)
searchlight

reflej|ar vt reflect. **~o** adj reflex.
● m reflection; (Med) reflex; (en el
pelo) highlights

reflexi|ón f reflection. **sin ~ón**
without thinking. **~onar** vi
reflect. **~vo** adj (persona)
thoughtful; (Gram) reflexive

reforma f reform. **~s** fpl
(reparaciones) repairs. **~r** vt reform
~rse vpr reform

reforzar 2 & 10 vt reinforce

refrac|ción f refraction. **~tario** adj
heat-resistant

refrán m saying

refregar 1 & 12 vt scrub

refresc|ar 7 vt refresh; (enfriar)
cool. ● vi get cooler. **~arse** vpr
refresh o.s. **~o** m cold drink. **~os**
mpl refreshments

refrigera|ción f refrigeration;
(aire acondicionado) air-conditioning;
(de motor) cooling. **~r** vt
refrigerate; air-condition (lugar);
cool (motor). **~dor** m refrigerator

refuerzo m reinforcement

refugi|ado m refugee. **~arse** vpr
take refuge. **~o** m refuge, shelter

r

refunfuñar vi grumble

refutar vt refute

regadera f watering-can; (Mex, ducha) shower

regala|do adj as a present; free; (cómodo) comfortable. ~**r** vt give

regalo m present, gift

regañ|adientes: **a** ~**adientes** reluctantly. ~**ar** vt scold. ●vi moan; (dos personas) quarrel. ~**o** m (represión) scolding

regar 1 & 12 vt water

regata f boat race; (serie) regatta

regate|ar vt haggle over; (economizar) economize on. ●vi haggle; (en deportes) dribble. ~**o** m haggling; (en deportes) dribbling

regazo m lap

regenerar vt regenerate

régimen m (pl **regímenes**) regime; (Med) diet; (de lluvias) pattern

regimiento m regiment

regi|ón f region. ~**onal** adj regional

regir 5 & 14 vt govern. ●vi apply, be in force

registr|ado adj registered. ~**ar** vt register; (Mex) check in (equipaje); (grabar) record; (examinar) search. ~**arse** vpr register; (darse) be reported. ~**o** m (acción de registrar) registration; (libro) register; (cosa anotada) entry; (inspección) search. ~**o civil** (oficina) registry office

regla f ruler; (norma) rule; (menstruación) period. **en** ~ in order. **por** ~ **general** as a rule. ~**mentación** f regulation. ~**mentar** vt regulate. ~**mentario** adj regulation; (horario) set. ~**mento** m regulations

regocij|arse vpr be delighted. ~**o** m delight

regode|arse vpr (+ gerundio) delight in (+ gerund). ~**o** m delight

regordete adj chubby

regres|ar vi return; (LAm) send

back (persona). ~**arse** vpr (LAm) return. ~**ivo** adj backward. ~**o** m return

regula|ble adj adjustable. ~**dor** m control. ~**r** adj regular; (mediano) average; (no bueno) so-so. ●vt regulate; adjust (volumen etc). ~**ridad** f regularity. **con** ~**ridad** regularly

rehabilita|ción f rehabilitation; (en empleo etc) reinstatement. ~**r** vt rehabilitate; (en cargo) reinstate

rehacer 31 vt redo; (repetir) repeat; rebuild (vida). ~**se** vpr recover

rehén m hostage

rehogar 12 vt sauté

rehuir 17 vt avoid

rehusar vt/i refuse

reimpr|esión f reprinting. ~**imir** (pp **reimpreso**) vt reprint

reina f queen. ~**do** m reign. ~**nte** adj ruling; (fig) prevailing. ~**r** vi reign; (fig) prevail

reincidir vi (Jurid) reoffend

reino m kingdom. **R~ Unido** United Kingdom

reintegr|ar vt reinstate (persona); refund (cantidad). ~**arse** vpr return. ~**o** m refund

reír 51 vi laugh. ~**se** vpr laugh. ~**se de** laugh at. **echarse a** ~ burst out laughing

reivindica|ción f claim. ~**r** 7 vt claim; (rehabilitar) restore

rej|a f grille; (verja) railing. **entre** ~**as** behind bars. ~**illa** f grille, grating; (red) luggage rack

rejuvenecer 11 vt/i rejuvenate. ~**se** vpr be rejuvenated

relaci|ón f connection; (trato) relation(ship); (relato) account; (lista) list. **con** ~**ón a, en** ~**ón a** in relation to. ~**onado** adj related. **bien** ~**onado** well-connected. ~**onar** vt relate (**con** to). ~**onarse** vpr be connected; (tratar) mix (**con** with)

relaja|ción f relaxation;

(aflojamiento) slackening. ~**do** adj
relaxed. ~**r** vt relax; (aflojar)
slacken. ~**rse** vpr relax

relamerse vpr lick one's lips

relámpago m (flash of) lightning

relatar vt tell, relate

relativ|idad f relativity. ~**o** adj
relative

relato m tale; (relación) account

relegar 12 vt relegate. ~ **al olvido**
consign to oblivion

relev|ante adj outstanding. ~**ar** vt
relieve; (substituir) replace. ~**o** m
relief. **carrera** f **de** ~**os** relay race

relieve m relief; (fig) importance.
de ~ important. **poner de** ~
emphasize

religi|ón f religion. ~**osa** f nun.
~**oso** adj religious. ● m monk

relinch|ar vi neigh. ~**o** m neigh

reliquia f relic

rellano m landing

rellen|ar vt refill; (Culin) stuff; fill
in (formulario). ~**o** adj full up; (Culin)
stuffed. ● m filling; (Culin) stuffing

reloj m clock, (de bolsillo o pulsera)
watch. ~ **de caja** grandfather
clock. ~ **de pulsera** wrist-watch.
~ **de sol** sundial. ~
despertador alarm clock. ~**ería** f
watchmaker's (shop). ~**ero** m
watchmaker

reluci|ente adj shining. ~**r** 11 vi
shine; (destellar) sparkle

relumbrar vi shine

remach|ar vt rivet. ~**e** m rivet

remangar 12 vt roll up

remar vi row

remat|ado adj (total) complete.
~**ar** vt finish off; (agotar) use up;
(Com) sell off cheap; (LAm, subasta)
auction; (en tenis) smash. ~**e** m
end; (fig) finishing touch; (LAm,
subastar) auction; (en tenis) smash.
de ~**e** completely

remedar vt imitate

remedi|ar vt remedy; repair (daño);
(fig, resolver) solve. **no lo pude** ~**ar**
I couldn't help it. ~**o** m remedy;
(fig) solution; (LAm, medicamento)
medicine. **como último** ~**o** as a
last resort. **no hay más** ~**o**
there's no other way. **no tener
más** ~**o** have no choice

remedo m poor imitation

rem|endar 1 vt repair. ~**iendo** m
patch

remilg|ado adj fussy; (afectado)
affected. ~**o** m fussiness;
(afectación) affectation. ~**oso** adj
(Mex) fussy

reminiscencia f reminiscence

remisión f remission; (envío)
sending; (referencia) reference

remit|e m sender's name and
address. ~**ente** m sender. ~**ir** vt
send; (referir) refer ● vi diminish

remo m oar

remoj|ar vt soak; (fig, fam)
celebrate. ~**o** m soaking. **poner a**
~**o** soak

remolacha f beetroot. ~
azucarera sugar beet

remolcar 7 vt tow

remolino m swirl; (de aire etc) whirl

remolque m towing; (cabo) tow-
rope; (vehículo) trailer. **a** ~ on tow.
dar ~ **a** tow

remontar vt overcome. ~ **el
vuelo** soar up; (avión) gain height.
~**se** vpr soar up; (en el tiempo) go
back to

remord|er 2 vi. **eso le remuerde**
he feels guilty for it. **me
remuerde la conciencia** I have a
guilty conscience. ~**imiento** m
remorse. **tener** ~**imientos** feel
remorse

remoto adj remote; (época) distant

remover 2 vt stir (líquido); turn
over (tierra); (quitar) remove; (fig,
activar) revive

remunera|ción f remuneration.
~**r** vt remunerate

renac|er 11 vi be reborn; (fig)

r

revive. ~imiento m rebirth.
R~imiento Renaissance

renacuajo m tadpole; (fig) tiddler

rencilla f quarrel

rencor m bitterness. guardar ~ a
have a grudge against. ~oso adj
resentful

rendi|ción f surrender. ~do adj
submissive; (agotado) exhausted

rendija f crack

rendi|miento m performance;
(Com) yield. ~r 5 vt yield; (agotar)
exhaust; pay (homenaje); present
(informe). •vi pay; (producir) produce.
~rse vpr surrender

renegar 1 & 12 vt deny. •vi
grumble. ~ de renounce (fe etc);
disown (personas)

renglón m line; (Com) item. a ~
seguido straight away

reno m reindeer

renombr|ado adj renowned. ~e m
renown

renova|ción f renewal; (de edificio)
renovation; (de mobiliario) complete
change. ~r vt renew; renovate
(edificio); change (mobiliario)

rent|a f income; (Mex, alquiler) rent.
~a vitalicia (life) annuity.
~able adj profitable. ~ar vt yield;
(Mex, alquilar) rent, hire. ~ista m & f
person of independent means

renuncia f renunciation; (dimisión)
resignation. ~r vi. ~r a renounce,
give up; (dimitir) resign

reñi|do adj hard-fought. estar
~do con be incompatible with
(cosa); be on bad terms with
(persona). ~r 5 & 22 vt scold. •vi
quarrel

reo m & f (Jurid) accused; (condenado)
convicted offender; (pez) sea trout

reojo: mirar de ~ look out of the
corner of one's eye at

reorganizar 10 vt reorganize

repar|ación f repair; (acción)
repairing (fig, compensación)
reparation. ~ar vt repair; (fig)

make amends for; (notar) notice.
•vi. ~ar en notice; (hacer caso de)
pay attention to. ~o m fault;
(objeción) objection. poner ~os
raise objections

repart|ición f distribution. ~idor
m delivery man. ~imiento m
distribution. ~ir vt distribute,
share out; deliver (cartas, leche etc);
hand out (folleto, premio). ~o m
distribution; (de cartas, leche etc)
delivery; (actores) cast

repas|ar vt go over; check (cuenta);
revise (texto); (leer a la ligera) glance
through; (coser) mend. •vi revise.
~o m revision; (de ropa) mending.
dar un ~o look through

repatria|ción f repatriation. ~r vt
repatriate

repele|nte adj repulsive. •m insect
repellent. ~r vt repel

repent|e. de ~ suddenly. ~ino adj
sudden

repercu|sión f repercussion. ~tir
vi reverberate; (fig) have
repercussions (en on)

repertorio m repertoire

repeti|ción f repetition; (de
programa) repeat. ~damente adv
repeatedly. ~r 5 vt repeat; have a
second helping of (plato); (imitar)
copy. •vi have a second helping of

repi|car 7 vt ring (campanas). ~que
m peal

repisa f shelf. ~ de chimenea
mantelpiece

repito vb véase REPETIR

replegarse 1 & 12 vpr withdraw

repleto adj full up. ~ de gente
packed with people

réplica adj reply; (copia) replica

replicar 7 vi reply

repollo m cabbage

reponer 34 vt replace; revive (obra
de teatro); (contestar) reply. ~se vpr
recover

report|aje m report; (LAm, entrevista)
interview. ~ar vt yield; (LAm,

denunciar) report. ~**e** m (Mex, informe) report; (Mex, queja) complaint. ~**ero** m reporter

repos|ado adj quiet; (sin prisa) unhurried. ~**ar** vi rest; (líquido) settle. ~**o** m rest

repost|ar vt replenish. ●vi (avión) refuel; (Auto) fill up. ~**ería** f pastrymaking

reprender vt reprimand

represalia f reprisal. **tomar ~s** retaliate

representa|ción f representation; (en el teatro) performance. **en ~ción de** representing. ~**nte** m representative. ~**r** vt represent; perform (obra de teatro); play (papel); (aparentar) look. ~**rse** vpr imagine. ~**tivo** adj representative

represi|ón f repression. ~**vo** adj repressive

reprimenda f reprimand

reprimir vt supress. ~**se** vpr control o.s.

reprobar 2 vt condemn; (LAm, Univ, etc) fail

reproch|ar vt reproach. ~**e** m reproach

reproduc|ción f reproduction. ~**ir** 47 vt reproduce. ~**tor** adj reproductive; (animal) breeding

reptil m reptile

rep|ública f republic. ~**ublicano** adj & m republican

repudiar vt condemn; (Jurid) repudiate

repuesto m (Mec) spare (part). **de ~** spare

repugna|ncia f disgust. ~**nte** adj repugnant; (olor) disgusting. ~**r** vt disgust

repuls|a f rebuff. ~**ión** f repulsion. ~**ivo** adj repulsive

reputa|ción f reputation. ~**do** adj reputable. ~**r** vt consider

requeri|miento m request; (necesidad) requirement. ~**r** 4 vt

require; summons (persona)

requesón m curd cheese

requete... prefijo (fam) extremely

requis|a f requisition; (confiscación) seizure; (inspección) inspection; (Mil) requisition. ~**ar** vt requisition; (confiscar) seize; (inspeccionar) inspect. ~**ito** m requirement

res f animal. ~ **lanar** sheep. ~ **vacuna** (vaca) cow; (toro) bull; (buey) ox. **carne de ~** (Mex) beef

resabido adj well known; (persona) pedantic

resaca f undercurrent; (después de beber) hangover

resaltar vi stand out. **hacer ~** emphasize

resarcir 9 vt repay; (compensar) compensate. ~**se** vpr make up for

resbal|adilla f (Mex) slide. ~**adizo** adj slippery. ~**ar** vi slip; (Auto) skid; (líquido) trickle. ~**arse** vpr slip; (Auto) skid; (líquido) trickle. ~**ón** m slip; (de vehículo) skid. ~**oso** adj (LAm) slippery

rescat|ar vt rescue; (fig) recover. ~**e** m ransom; (recuperación) recovery; (salvamento) rescue

rescoldo m embers

resecar 7 vt dry up. ~**se** vpr dry up

resenti|do adj resentful. ~**miento** m resentment. ~**rse** vpr feel the effects; (debilitarse) be weakened; (ofenderse) take offence (**de** at)

reseña f summary; (de persona) description; (en periódico) report, review. ~**r** vt describe; (en periódico) report on, review

reserva f reservation; (provisión) reserve(s). **de ~** in reserve. ~**ción** f (LAm) reservation. ~**do** adj reserved. ~**r** vt reserve; (guardar) keep, save. ~**rse** vpr save o.s.

resfria|do m cold. ~**rse** vpr catch a cold

resguard|ar vt protect. ~**arse** vpr protect o.s.; (fig) take care. ~**o** m

r

protection; (garantía) guarantee; (recibo) receipt

resid|encia f residence; (Univ) hall of residence (Brit), dormitory (Amer); (de ancianos etc) home. ~encial adj residential. ~ente adj & m & f resident. ~ir vi reside; (fig) lie (en in)

residu|al adj residual. ~o m residue. ~os mpl waste

resigna|ción f resignation. ~rse vpr resign o.s. (a to)

resist|encia f resistence. ~ente adj resistent. ~ir vt resist; (soportar) bear. • vi resist. **ya no resisto más** I can't take it any more

resol|ución f resolution; (solución) solution; (decisión) decision. ~ver 2 (pp **resuelto**) resolve; solve (problema etc). ~verse vpr resolve itself; (resultar bien) work out; (decidir) decide

resona|ncia f resonance. **tener ~ncia** cause a stir. ~nte adj resonant; (fig) resounding. ~r 2 vi resound

resorte m spring; (Mex, elástico) elastic. **tocar (todos los) ~s** (fig) pull strings

respald|ar vt back; (escribir) endorse. ~arse vpr lean back. ~o m backing; (de asiento) back

respect|ar vi. **en lo que ~a a** with regard to. **en lo que a mí ~a** as far as I'm concerned. ~ivo adj respective. ~o m respect. **al ~o** on this matter. **(con) ~o a** with regard to

respet|able adj respectable. • m audience. ~ar vt respect. ~o m respect. **faltar al ~o a** be disrespectful to. ~uoso adj respectful

respir|ación f breathing; (ventilación) ventilation. ~ar vi breathe; (fig) breathe a sigh of relief. ~o m breathing; (fig) rest

respland|ecer 11 vi shine. ~eciente adj shining. ~or m brilliance; (de llamas) glow

responder vi answer; (replicar) answer back; (reaccionar) respond. ~ de be responsible for. ~ por uno vouch for s.o.

responsab|ilidad f responsibility. ~le adj responsible

respuesta f reply, answer

resquebrajar vt crack. ~se vpr crack

resquemor m (fig) uneasiness

resquicio m crack; (fig) possibility

resta f subtraction

restablecer 11 vt restore. ~se vpr recover

rest|ante adj remaining. **lo ~nte** the rest. ~ar vt take away; (substraer) subtract. • vi be left

restaura|ción f restoration. ~nte m restaurant. ~r vt restore

restitu|ción f restitution. ~ir 17 vt return; (restaurar) restore

resto m rest, remainder; (en matemática) remainder. ~s mpl remains; (de comida) leftovers

restorán m restaurant

restregar 1 & 12 vt rub

restri|cción f restriction. ~ngir 14 vt restrict, limit

resucitar vt resuscitate; (fig) revive. • vi return to life

resuello m breath; (respiración) heavy breathing

resuelto adj resolute

resulta|do m result (en in). ~r vi result; (salir) turn out; (dar resultado) work; (ser) be; (costar) come to

resum|en m summary. **en ~en** in short. ~ir vt summarize; (recapitular) sum up

resur|gir 14 vi reemerge; (fig) revive. ~gimiento m resurgence. ~rección f resurrection

retaguardia f (Mil) rearguard

retahíla f string

retar vt challenge

retardar vt slow down; (demorar) delay

retazo m remnant; (fig) piece, bit

reten|ción f retention. **~er** 40 vt keep; (en la memoria) retain; (no dar) withhold

reticencia f insinuation; (reserva) reluctance

retina f retina

retir|ada f withdrawal. **~ado** adj remote; (vida) secluded; (jubilado) retired. **~ar** vt move away; (quitar) remove; withdraw (dinero); (jubilar) pension off. **~arse** vpr draw back; (Mil) withdraw; (jubilarse) retire; (acostarse) go to bed. **~o** m retirement; (pensión) pension; (lugar apartado) retreat; (LAm, de apoyo, fondos) withdrawal

reto m challenge

retocar 7 vt retouch

retoño m shoot; (fig) kid

retoque m (acción) retouching; (efecto) finishing touch

retorc|er 2 & 9 vt twist; wring (ropa). **~erse** vpr get twisted up; (de dolor) writhe. **~ijón** m (LAm) stomach cramp

retóric|a f rhetoric; (grandilocuencia) grandiloquence. **~o** m rhetorical

retorn|ar vt/i return. **~o** m return

retortijón m twist; (de tripas) stomach cramp

retractarse vpr retract. **~ de lo dicho** withdraw what one said

retransmitir vt repeat; (radio, TV) broadcast. **~ en directo** broadcast live

retras|ado adj (con ser) mentally handicapped; (con estar) behind; (reloj) slow; (poco desarrollado) backward; (anticuado) old-fashioned. **~ar** vt delay; put back (reloj); (retardar) slow down; (posponer) postpone. ● vi (reloj) be slow. **~arse** vpr be late; (reloj) be slow. **~o** m delay; (poco desarrollo) backwardness; (de reloj) slowness. **traer ~o** be late. **~os** mpl arrears

retrato m portrait; (fig, descripción) description. **ser el vivo ~ de** be the living image of

retrete m toilet

retribu|ción f payment; (recompensa) reward. **~ir** 17 vt pay; (recompensar) reward; (LAm) return (favor)

retroce|der vi move back; (fig) back down. **~so** m backward movement; (de arma de fuego) recoil; (Med) relapse

retrógrado adj & m (Pol) reactionary

retrospectivo adj retrospective

retrovisor m rear-view mirror

retumbar vt echo; (trueno etc) boom

reum|a m, **reúma** m rheumatism. **~ático** adj rheumatic. **~atismo** m rheumatism

reuni|ón f meeting; (entre amigos) reunion. **~r** 23 vt join together; (recoger) gather (together); raise (fondos). **~rse** vpr meet; (amigos etc) get together

revalidar vt confirm; (Mex, estudios) validate

revalorizar 10 vt, (LAm) **revaluar** 21 vt revalue; increase (pensiones). **~se** vpr appreciate

revancha f revenge; (en deportes) return match. **tomar la ~** get one's own back

revela|ción f revelation. **~do** m developing. **~dor** adj revealing. **~r** vt reveal; (Foto) develop

revent|ar 1 vi burst; (tener ganas) be dying to. **~arse** vpr burst. **~ón** m burst; (Auto) blow out; (Mex, fiesta) party

reveren|cia f reverence; (de hombre, niño) bow; (de mujer) curtsy. **~ciar** vt revere. **~do** adj (Relig) reverend. **~te** adj reverent

revers|ible adj reversible. **~o** m reverse; (de papel) back

revertir 4 vi revert (**a** to)

revés m wrong side; (de prenda)

r

inside; (contratiempo) setback; (en deportes) backhand. **al ~** the other way round; (con lo de arriba abajo) upside down; (con lo de dentro fuera) inside out

revesti|miento m coating. **~r** 5 vt cover

revis|ar vt check; overhaul (mecanismo); service (coche etc); (LAm, equipaje) search. **~ión** f check(ing)); (Med) checkup; (de coche etc) service; (LAm, de equipaje) inspection. **~or** m inspector

revista f magazine; (inspección) inspection; (artículo) review; (espectáculo) revue. **pasar ~ a** inspect

revivir vi revive

revolcar 2 & 7 vt knock over. **~se** vpr roll around

revolotear vi flutter

revoltijo m, **revoltillo** m mess

revoltoso adj rebellious; (niño) naughty

revoluci|ón f revolution. **~onar** vt revolutionize. **~onario** adj & m revolutionary

revolver 2 (pp **revuelto**) vt mix; stir (líquido); (desordenar) mess up

revólver m revolver

revuelo m fluttering; (fig) stir

revuelt|a f revolt; (conmoción) disturbance. **~o** adj mixed up; (líquido) cloudy; (mar) rough; (tiempo) unsettled; (huevos) scrambled

rey m king. **los ~es** the king and queen. **los R~es Magos** the Three Wise Men

reyerta f brawl

rezagarse 12 vpr fall behind

rez|ar 10 vt say. ● vi pray; (decir) say. **~o** m praying; (oración) prayer

rezongar 12 vi grumble

ría f estuary

riachuelo m stream

riada f flood

ribera f bank

ribete m border; (fig) embellishment

rico adj rich; (Culin, fam) good, nice. ● m rich person

rid|ículo adj ridiculous. **~iculizar** 10 vt ridicule

riego m watering; (irrigación) irrigation

riel m rail

rienda f rein

riesgo m risk. **correr (el) ~ de** run the risk of

rifa f raffle. **~r** vt raffle

rifle m rifle

rigidez f rigidity; (fig) inflexibility

rígido adj rigid; (fig) inflexible

rig|or m strictness; (exactitud) exactness; (de clima) severity. **de ~or** compulsory. **en ~or** strictly speaking. **~uroso** adj rigorous

rima f rhyme. **~r** vt/i rhyme

rimbombante adj resounding; (lenguaje) pompous; (fig, ostentoso) showy

rímel m mascara

rin m (Mex) rim

rincón m corner

rinoceronte m rhinoceros

riña f quarrel; (pelea) fight

riñón m kidney

río m river; (fig) stream. **~ abajo** downstream. **~ arriba** upstream. ● vb véase **REÍR**

riqueza f wealth; (fig) richness. **~s** fpl riches

ris|a f laugh. **desternillarse de ~a** split one's sides laughing. **la ~a** laughter. **~otada** f guffaw. **~ueño** adj smiling; (fig) cheerful

rítmico adj rhythmic(al)

ritmo m rhythm; (fig) rate

rit|o m rite; (fig) ritual. **~ual** adj & m ritual

rival adj, m & f rival. **~idad** f

rivalry. **~izar** 10 vi rival

riz|ado adj curly. **~ar** 10 vt curl; ripple (agua). **~o** m curl; (en agua) ripple

róbalo m bass

robar vt steal (cosa); rob (banco); (raptar) kidnap

roble m oak (tree)

robo m theft; (de banco, museo) robbery; (en vivienda) burglary

robusto adj robust

roca f rock

roce m rubbing; (señal) mark; (fig, entre personas) regular contact; (Pol) friction. **tener un ~ con uno** have a brush with s.o.

rociar 20 vt spray

rocín m nag

rocío m dew

rodaballo m turbot

rodaja f slice. **en ~s** sliced

roda|je m (de película) shooting; (de coche) running in. **~r** 2 vt shoot (película); run in (coche). ●vi roll; (coche) run; (hacer una película) shoot

rode|ar vt surround, (LAm) round up (ganado). **~arse** vpr surround o.s. (**de** with). **~o** m detour; (de ganado) round up. **andar con ~os** beat about the bush. **sin ~os** plainly

rodill|a f knee. **ponerse de ~as** kneel down. **~era** f knee-pad

rodillo m roller; (Culin) rolling-pin

roe|dor m rodent. **~r** 37 vt gnaw

rogar 2 & 12 vt/i beg; (Relig) pray; **se ruega a los Sres. pasajeros...** passengers are requested.... **se ruega no fumar** please do not smoke

roj|izo adj reddish. **~o** adj & m red. **ponerse ~o** blush

roll|izo adj plump; (bebé) chubby. **~o** m roll; (de cuerda) coil; (Culin, rodillo) rolling-pin; (fig, fam, pesadez) bore

romance adj Romance. ●m (idilio)

romance; (poema) ballad

roman|o adj & m Roman. **a la ~a** (Culin) (deep-)fried in batter

rom|anticismo m romanticism. **~ántico** adj romantic

romería f pilgrimage; (LAm, multitud) mass

romero m rosemary

romo adj blunt; (nariz) snub

rompe|cabezas m invar puzzle; (de piezas) jigsaw (puzzle). **~olas** m invar breakwater

romp|er (pp **roto**) vt break; tear (hoja, camisa etc); break off (relaciones etc). ●vi break; (novios) break up. **~er a** burst out. **~erse** vpr break

ron m rum

ronc|ar 7 vi snore. **~o** adj hoarse

roncha f lump; (por alergia) rash

ronda f round; (patrulla) patrol; (serenata) serenade. **~r** vt patrol. ●vi be on patrol; (merodear) hang around

ronqu|era f hoarseness. **~ido** m snore

ronronear vi purr

roñ|a f (suciedad) grime. **~oso** adj dirty; (oxidado) rusty; (tacaño) mean

rop|a f clothes, clothing. **~a blanca** linen, underwear. **~a de cama** bedclothes. **~a interior** underwear. **~aje** m robes; (excesivo) heavy clothing. **~ero** m wardrobe

ros|a adj invar pink. ●f rose. ●m pink. **~áceo** adj pinkish. **~ado** adj pink; (mejillas) rosy. ●m (vino) rosé. **~al** m rose-bush

rosario m rosary; (fig) series

ros|ca f (de tornillo) thread; (de pan) roll; (bollo) type of doughnut. **~co** m roll. **~quilla** f type of doughnut

rostro m face

rota|ción f rotation. **~r** vt/i rotate. **~rse** vpr take turns. **~tivo** adj rotary

roto adj broken

rótula f kneecap

rotulador m felt-tip pen

rótulo m sign; (etiqueta) label; (logotipo) logo

rotundo adj categorical

rotura f tear; (grieta) crack

rozadura f scratch

rozagante adj (LAm) healthy

rozar vt rub against; (ligeramente) brush against; (raspar) graze. **~se** vpr rub; (con otras personas) mix

Rte. abrev (**Remite(nte)**) sender

rubéola f German measles

rubí m ruby

rubicundo adj ruddy

rubio adj (pelo) fair; (persona) fair-haired; (tabaco) Virginia

rubor m blush; (Mex, cosmético) blusher. **~izarse** 10 vpr blush

rúbrica f (de firma) flourish; (firma) signature; (título) heading

rudeza f roughness

rudiment|ario adj rudimentary. **~os** mpl rudiments

rueca f distaff

rueda f wheel; (de mueble) castor; (de personas) ring; (Culin) slice. **~ de prensa** press conference

ruedo m edge; (redondel) bullring

ruego m request; (súplica) entreaty. • vb véase ROGAR

rufián m pimp; (granuja) rogue

rugby m rugby

rugi|do m roar. **~r** 14 vi roar

ruibarbo m rhubarb

ruido m noise. **~so** adj noisy; (fig) sensational

ruin adj despicable; (tacaño) mean

ruin|a f ruin; (colapso) collapse. **~oso** adj ruinous

ruiseñor m nightingale

ruleta f roulette

rulo m curler

rumano adj & m Romanian

rumbo m direction; (fig) course; (fig, esplendidez) lavishness. **con ~ a** in the direction of. **~so** adj lavish

rumia|nte adj & m ruminant. **~r** vt chew; (fig) brood over. • vi ruminate

rumor m rumour; (ruido) murmur. **~earse** vpr **se ~ea que** rumour has it that. **~oso** adj murmuring

runrún m (de voces) murmur; (de motor) whirr

ruptura f breakup; (de relaciones etc) breaking off; (de contrato) breach

rural adj rural

ruso adj & m Russian

rústico adj rural; (de carácter) coarse. **en rústica** paperback

ruta f route; (fig) course

rutina f routine. **~rio** adj routine; (trabajo) monotonous

Ss

S.A. abrev (**Sociedad Anónima**) Ltd, plc, Inc (Amer)

sábado m Saturday

sábana f sheet

sabañón m chilblain

sabático adj sabbatical

sab|elotodo m & f invar know-all 1. **~er** 38 vt know; (ser capaz de) be able to, know how to; (enterarse de) find out. • vi know. **~er a** taste of. **hacer ~er** let know. **¡qué sé yo!**

how should I know? **que yo sepa** as far as I know. **¿~es nadar?** can you swim? **un no sé qué** a certain sth. **¡yo qué sé!** how should I know? **¡vete a ~er!** who knows? **~er** m knowledge. **~ido** adj well-known. **~iduría** f wisdom; (conocimientos) knowledge

sabi|endas. a ~ knowingly; (a propósito) on purpose. **~hondo** m know-all. **~o** adj learned; (prudente) wise

sabor m taste, flavour; (fig) flavour. **~ear** vt taste; (fig) savour

sabot|aje m sabotage. **~eador** m saboteur. **~ear** vt sabotage

sabroso adj tasty; (chisme) juicy; (LAm, agradable) pleasant

sabueso m (perro) bloodhound; (fig, detective) detective

saca|corchos m invar corkscrew. **~puntas** m invar pencil-sharpener

sacar ⑦ vt take out; put out (parte del cuerpo); (quitar) remove; take (foto); win (premio); get (billete, entrada); withdraw (dinero); reach (solución); draw (conclusión); make (copia). **~ adelante** bring up (niño); carry on (negocio)

sacarina f saccharin

sacerdo|cio m priesthood. **~te** m priest

saciar vt satisfy; quench (sed)

saco m sack; (LAm, chaqueta) jacket. **~ de dormir** sleeping-bag

sacramento m sacrament

sacrific|ar ⑦ vt sacrifice; slaughter (res); put to sleep (perro, gato). **~arse** vpr sacrifice o.s. **~io** m sacrifice; (de res) slaughter

sacr|ilegio m sacrilege. **~ílego** adj sacrilegious

sacudi|da f shake; (movimiento brusco) jolt, jerk; (fig) shock. **~da eléctrica** electric shock. **~r** vt shake; (golpear) beat. **~rse** vpr shake off; (fig) get rid of

sádico adj sadistic. ●m sadist

sadismo m sadism

safari m safari

sagaz adj shrewd

Sagitario m Sagittarius

sagrado adj (lugar) holy, sacred; (altar, escrituras) holy; (fig) sacred

sal f salt. ●vb véase SALIR

sala f room; (en casa) living room; (en hospital) ward; (para reuniones etc) hall; (en teatro) house; (Jurid) courtroom. **~ de embarque** departure lounge. **~ de espera** waiting room. **~ de estar** living room. **~ de fiestas** nightclub

salado adj salty; (agua del mar) salt; (no dulce) savoury; (fig) witty

salario m wage

salchich|a f (pork) sausage. **~ón** m salami

sald|ar vt settle (cuenta); (vender) sell off. **~o** m balance. **~os** mpl sales. **venta de ~os** clearance sale

salero m salt-cellar

salgo vb véase SALIR

sali|da f departure; (puerta) exit, way out (de gas, de líquido) leak; (de astro) rising; (Com, venta) sale; (chiste) witty remark; (fig) way out. **~da de emergencia** emergency exit. **~ente** adj (Archit) projecting; (pómulo etc) prominent. **~r** ⓹ vi leave; (ir afuera) go out; (Informática) exit; (revista etc) be published; (resultar) turn out; (astro) rise; (aparecer) appear. **~r adelante** get by. **~rse** vpr leave; (recipiente, líquido etc) leak. **~rse con la suya** get one's own way

saliva f saliva

salmo m psalm

salm|ón m salmon. **~onete** m red mullet

salón m living-room, lounge. **~ de actos** assembly hall. **~ de clases** classroom. **~ de fiestas** dancehall

salpica|dera f (Mex) mudguard. **~dero** m (Auto) dashboard. **~dura** f splash; (acción) splashing. **~r** ⑦ vt

S

splash; (fig) sprinkle

sals|a f sauce; (para carne asada) gravy; (Mus) salsa. **~a verde** parsley sauce. **~era** f sauce-boat

salt|amontes m invar grasshopper. **~ar** vt jump (over); (fig) miss out. ●vi jump; (romperse) break; (líquido) spurt out; (desprenderse) come off; (pelota) bounce; (estallar) explode. **~eador** m highwayman. **~ear** vt (Culin) sauté

salt|o m jump; (al agua) dive. **~o de agua** waterfall. **~o mortal** somersault. **de un ~o** with one jump. **~ón** adj (ojos) bulging

salud f health. ●int cheers!; (LAm, al estornudar) bless you! **~able** adj healthy

salud|ar vt greet, say hello to; (Mil) salute. **lo ~a atentamente** (en cartas) yours faithfully. **~ar con la mano** wave. **~o** m greeting; (Mil) salute. **~os** mpl best wishes

salva f salvo. **una ~ de aplausos** a burst of applause

salvación f salvation

salvado m bran

salvaguardia f safeguard

salvaje adj (planta, animal) wild; (primitivo) savage. ●m & f savage

salva|mento m rescue. **~r** vt save, rescue; (atravesar) cross (recorrer); travel (fig) overcome. **~rse** vpr save o.s. **~vidas** m & f invar lifeguard. ●m lifebelt. **chaleco m ~vidas** life-jacket

salvo adj safe. ●adv & prep except (for). **a ~** out of danger. **poner a ~** put in a safe place. **~ que** unless. **~conducto** m safe-conduct.

San adj Saint, St. **~ Miguel** St Michael

sana|r vt cure. ●vi recover; heal (herida). **~torio** m sanatorium

sanci|ón f sanction. **~onar** vt sanction

sandalia f sandal

sandía f watermelon

sándwich /'sangwitʃ/ m (pl **~s,** **~es**) sandwich

sangr|ante adj bleeding; (fig) flagrant. **~ar** vt/i bleed. **~e** f blood. **a ~e fría** in cold blood

sangría f (bebida) sangria

sangriento adj bloody

sangu|ijuela f leech. **~íneo** adj blood

san|idad f health. **~itario** adj sanitary. ●m (Mex) toilet. **~o** adj healthy; (mente) sound. **~o y salvo** safe and sound. **cortar por lo ~o** settle things once and for all

santiamén m. **en un ~** in an instant

sant|idad f sanctity. **~ificar** 🔟 vt sanctify. **~iguarse** 🔟 vpr cross o.s. **~o** adj holy; (delante de nombre) Saint, St. ●m saint; (día) saint's day, name day. **~uario** m sanctuary. **~urrón** adj sanctimonious

saña f viciousness. **con ~** viciously

sapo m toad

saque m (en tenis) service; (inicial en fútbol) kick-off. **~ de banda** throw-in; (en rugby) line-out. **~ de esquina** corner (kick)

saque|ar vt loot. **~o** m looting

sarampión m measles

sarape m (Mex) colourful blanket

sarc|asmo m sarcasm. **~ástico** adj sarcastic

sardina f sardine

sargento m sergeant

sarpullido m rash

sartén f or m frying-pan (Brit), fry-pan (Amer)

sastre m tailor. **~ría** f tailoring; (tienda) tailor's (shop)

Sat|anás m Satan. **~ánico** adj satanic

satélite m satellite

satinado adj shiny

sátira f satire

satírico adj satirical. ●m satirist

satisf|acción f satisfaction. ~acer **51** vt satisfy; (pagar) pay; (gustar) please; meet (gastos, requisitos). ~acerse vpr satisfy o.s.; (vengarse) take revenge. ~actorio adj satisfactory. ~echo adj satisfied. ~echo de sí mismo smug

satura|ción f saturation. ~r vt saturate

Saturno m Saturn

sauce m willow. ~ llorón weeping willow

sauna f, (LAm) **sauna** m sauna

saxofón m, **saxófono** m saxophone

sazona|do adj ripe; (Culin) seasoned. ~r vt ripen; (Culin) season

se pronombre

●(en lugar de le, les) **se lo di** (a él) I gave it to him; (a ella) I gave it to her; (a usted, ustedes) I gave it to you; (a ellos, ellas) I gave it to them. **se lo compré** I bought it for him (or her etc). **se lo quité** I took it away from him (or her etc). **se lo dije** I told him (or her etc)

····▸ (reflexivo) **se secó** (él) he dried himself; (ella) she dried herself; (usted) you dried yourself. (sujeto no humano) it dried itself. **se secaron** (ellos, ellas) they dried themselves. (ustedes) you dried yourselves. (con partes del cuerpo) **se lavó la cara** (él) he washed his face; (con efectos personales) **se limpian los zapatos** they clean their shoes

····▸ (recíproco) each other, one another. **se ayudan mucho** they help each other a lot. **no se hablan** they don't speak to each other

····▸ (cuando otro hace la acción) **va a operarse** she's going to have an operation. **se cortó el pelo**

he had his hair cut

····▸ (enfático) **se bebió el café** he drank his coffee. **se subió al tren** he got on the train

▶ **se** also forms part of certain pronominal verbs such as **equivocarse, arrepentirse, caerse** etc., which are treated under the respective entries

····▸ (voz pasiva) **se construyeron muchas casas** many houses were built. **se vendió rápidamente** it was sold very quickly

····▸ (impersonal) **antes se escuchaba más radio** people used to listen to the radio more in the past. **no se puede entrar aquí** you can't get in. **se está bien aquí** it's very nice here

····▸ (en instrucciones) **sírvase frío** serve cold

sé vb véase SABER y SER

sea vb véase SER

seca|dor m drier; (de pelo) hairdrier. ~nte adj drying. ●m blotting-paper. ~r **7** vt dry. ~rse vpr dry; (río etc) dry up; (persona) dry o.s.

sección f section

seco adj dry; (frutos, flores) dried; (flaco) thin; (respuesta) curt. **a secas** just. **en ~** (bruscamente) suddenly. **lavar en ~** dry-clean

secretar|ía f secretariat; (Mex, ministerio) ministry. ~io m secretary; (Mex, Pol) minister

secreto adj & m secret

secta f sect. ~rio adj sectarian

sector m sector

secuela f consequence

secuencia f sequence

secuestr|ar vt confiscate; kidnap (persona); hijack (avión). ~o m seizure; (de persona) kidnapping; (de avión) hijack(ing)

secundar vt second, help. ~io adj secondary

sed f thirst. •vb véase SER. **tener ~** be thirsty. **tener ~ de** (fig) be hungry for

seda f silk. **~ dental** dental floss

sedante adj & m sedative

sede f seat; (Relig) see; (de organismo) headquarters; (de congreso, juegos etc) venue

sedentario adj sedentary

sedici|ón f sedition. **~oso** adj seditious

sediento adj thirsty

seduc|ción f seduction. **~ir** 47 vt seduce; (atraer) attract. **~tor** adj seductive. •m seducer

seglar adj secular. •m layman

segrega|ción f segregation. **~r** 12 vt segregate

segui|da f. **en ~da** immediately. **~do** adj continuous; (en plural) consecutive. **~da de** followed by. •adv straight; (LAm, a menudo) often. **todo ~do** straight ahead. **~dor** m follower; (en deportes) supporter. **~r** 5 & 13 vt follow. •vi (continuar) continue; (por un camino) go on. **~r adelante** carry on

según prep according to. •adv it depends; (a medida que)

segund|a f (Auto) second gear; (en tren, avión etc) second class. **~o** adj & m second

segur|amente adv certainly; (muy probablemente) surely. **~idad** f security; (ausencia de peligro) safety; (certeza) certainty; (aplomo) confidence. **~idad en sí mismo** self-confidence. **~idad social** social security. **~o** adj safe; (cierto) certain, sure; (estable) secure; (de fiar) reliable. •adv for certain. •m insurance; (dispositivo de seguridad) safety device. **~o de sí mismo** self-confident. **~o contra terceros** third-party insurance

seis adj & m six. **~cientos** adj & m six hundred

....
🔲 see A-Z of Spanish life and culture

seísmo m earthquake

selec|ción f selection. **~cionar** vt select, choose. **~tivo** adj selective. **~to** adj selected; (fig) choice

sell|ar vt stamp; (cerrar) seal. **~o** m stamp; (precinto) seal; (fig, distintivo) hallmark; (LAm, en moneda) reverse

selva f forest; (jungla) jungle

semáforo m (Auto) traffic lights; (Rail) signal; (Naut) semaphore

semana f week. **🔲S~ Santa** Holy Week. **~l** adj weekly. **~rio** adj & m weekly

semántic|a f semantics. **~o** adj semantic

semblante m face; (fig) look

sembrar 1 vt sow; (fig) scatter

semeja|nte adj similar; (tal) such. •m fellow man. **🔲~nza** f similarity. **a ~nza de** like. **~r** vi. **~r a** resemble

semen m semen. **~tal** adj stud. •m stud animal

semestr|al adj half-yearly. **~e** m six months

semi|circular adj semicircular. **~círculo** m semicircle. **~final** f semifinal

semill|a f seed. **~ero** m seedbed; (fig) hotbed

seminario m (Univ) seminar; (Relig) seminary

sémola f semolina

🔲senado m senate. **~r** m senator

sencill|ez f simplicity. **~o** adj simple; (para viajar) single ticket; (disco) single; (LAm, dinero suelto) change

senda f, **sendero** m path

sendos adj pl each

seno m bosom. **~ materno** womb

sensaci|ón f sensation; (percepción, impresión) feeling. **~onal** adj sensational

sensat|ez f good sense. **~o** adj sensible

sensi|bilidad f sensibility. **~ble**
adj sensitive; (notable) notable;
(lamentable) lamentable. **~tivo** adj
(órgano) sense

sensual adj sensual. **~idad** f
sensuality

senta|do adj sitting (down); **dar
algo por ~do** take something
for granted. **~dor** adj (LAm)
flattering. **~r 1** vt sit; (establecer)
establish. ● vi suit; (de medidas) fit;
(comida) agree with. **~rse** vpr sit
(down)

sentencia f (Jurid) sentence. **~r** vt
sentence (**a** to)

sentido adj heartfelt; (sensible)
sensitive. ● m sense; (dirección)
direction; (conocimiento)
consciousness. **~ común** common
sense. **~ del humor** sense of
humour. **~ único** one-way. **doble
~** double meaning. **no tener ~**
not make sense. **perder el ~**
faint. **sin ~** senseless

sentim|ental adj sentimental.
~iento m feeling; (sentido) sense;
(pesar) regret

sentir 4 vt feel; (oír) hear; (lamentar)
be sorry for. **lo siento mucho**
I'm really sorry. ● m (opinión)
opinion **~se** vpr feel, (Mex,
ofenderse) be offended

seña f sign. **~s** fpl (dirección)
address; (descripción) description.
dar ~s de show signs of

señal f signal; (letrero, aviso) sign;
(telefónica) tone; (Com) deposit. **dar
~es de** show signs of. **en ~ de**
as a token of. **~ado** adj (hora, día)
appointed. **~ar** vt signal; (poner
señales en) mark; (apuntar) point out;
(manecilla, aguja) point to; (determinar)
fix. **~arse** vpr stand out

señor m man, gentleman; (delante de
nombre propio) Mr; (tratamiento directo)
sir. **~a** f lady, woman; (delante de
nombre propio) Mrs; (esposa) wife;
(tratamiento directo) madam. **el ~** Mr.
muy ~ mío Dear Sir. **¡no ~!**
certainly not!. **~ial** adj (casa)
stately. **~ita** f young lady; (delante

de nombre propio) Miss; (tratamiento
directo) miss. **~ito** m young
gentleman

señuelo m lure

sepa vb véase **SABER**

separa|ción f separation. **~do** adj
separate. **por ~do** separately. **~r**
vt separate; (de empleo) dismiss.
~rse vpr separate; (amigos) part.
~tista adj & m & f separatist

septentrional adj north(ern)

septiembre m September

séptimo adj seventh

sepulcro m sepulchre

sepult|ar vt bury. **~ura** f burial;
(tumba) grave. **~urero** m
gravedigger

sequ|edad f dryness. **~ía** f
drought

séquito m entourage; (fig) train

---

ser 39

● verbo intransitivo

····► to be. **es bajo** he's short. **es
abogado** he's a lawyer. **ábreme,
soy yo** open up, it's me. **¿cómo
es?** (como persona) what's he
like?; (físicamente) what does he
look like? **era invierno** it was
winter

····► **ser de** (indicando composición)
to be made of. **es de hierro** it's
made of iron. (provenir de) to be
from. **es de México** he's from
Mexico. (pertenecer a) to belong
to. **el coche es de Juan** the car
belongs to Juan, it's Juan's car

····► (sumar) **¿cuánto es todo?**
how much is that altogether?
son 40 dólares that's 40 dollars.
somos 10 there are 10 of us

····► (con la hora) **son las 3** it's 3
o'clock. **~ía la una** it must have
been one o'clock

····► (tener lugar) to be held. **~á
en la iglesia** it will be held in
the church

····► (ocurrir) to happen **¿dónde**

fue el accidente? where did the accident happen? **me contó cómo fue** he told me how it happened

····▶ (*en locuciones*) **a no ∼ que** unless. **como sea** no matter what. **cuando sea** whenever. **donde sea** wherever. **¡eso es!** that's it! **es que** the thing is. **lo que sea** anything. **no sea que, no vaya a ∼ que** in case. **o sea** in other words. **sea ... sea ...** either ... or ... **sea como sea** at all costs

●nombre masculino being; (*persona*) person. **el ∼ humano** the human being. **un ∼ amargado** a bitter person. **los ∼es queridos** the loved ones

seren|ar vt calm down. **∼arse** vpr calm down. **∼ata** f serenade. **∼idad** f serenity. **∼o** adj serene; (*cielo*) clear; (*mar*) calm

seri|al m serial. **∼e** f series. **fuera de ∼e** (*fig*) out of this world. **producción** f **en ∼e** mass production

seri|edad f seriousness. **∼o** adj serious; (*confiable*) reliable; **en ∼o** seriously. **poco ∼o** frivolous

sermón m sermon; (*fig*) lecture

serp|enteante adj winding. **∼entear** vi wind. **∼iente** f snake. **∼iente de cascabel** rattlesnake

serr|ar 🔳 vt saw. **∼ín** m sawdust. **∼uchar** vt (LAm) saw. **∼ucho** m (hand)saw

servi|cial adj helpful. **∼cio** m service; (*conjunto*) set; (*aseo*) toilet; **∼cio a domicilio** delivery service. **∼dor** m servant. **su (seguro) ∼dor** (*en cartas*) yours faithfully. **∼dumbre** f servitude; (*criados*) servants, staff. **∼l** adj servile

servidor m server; (*criado*) servant

servilleta f napkin, serviette

servir 🔳 vt serve; (*en restaurante*) wait on. ●vi serve; (*ser útil*) be of use. **∼se** vpr help o.s.. **∼se de** use.

no ∼ de nada be useless. **para ∼le** at your service. **sírvase sentarse** please sit down

sesent|a adj & m sixty. **∼ón** adj & m sixty-year-old

seseo m pronunciation of the Spanish c as an s

sesión f session; (*en el cine, teatro*) performance

seso m brain

seta f mushroom

sete|cientos adj & m seven hundred. **∼nta** adj & m seventy. **∼ntón** adj & m seventy-year-old

setiembre m September

seto m fence; (*de plantas*) hedge. **∼ vivo** hedge

seudónimo m pseudonym

sever|idad f severity; (*de profesor etc*) strictness. **∼o** adj severe; (*profesor etc*) strict

sevillan|as fpl popular dance from Seville. **∼o** m person from Seville

sexo m sex

sext|eto m sextet. **∼o** adj sixth

sexual adj sexual. **∼idad** f sexuality

si m (Mus) B; (*solfa*) te. ●conj if; (*dubitativo*) whether; **∼ no** otherwise. **por ∼ (acaso)** in case

sí¹ pron reflexivo (*él*) himself; (*ella*) herself; (*de cosa*) itself; (*uno*) oneself; (*Vd*) yourself; (*ellos, ellas*) themselves; (*Vds*) yourselves; (*recíproco*) each other

sí² adv yes. ●m consent

sida m Aids

sidra f cider

siembra f sowing; (*época*) sowing time

siempre adv always; (LAm, *todavía*) still; (Mex, *por fin*) after all. **∼ que** if; (*cada vez*) whenever. **como ∼** as usual. **de ∼** (*acostumbrado*) usual. **lo de ∼** the usual thing. **para ∼** for ever

sien f temple

siento vb véase SENTAR y SENTIR

sierra f saw; (cordillera) mountain range

◼**siesta** f nap, siesta

siete adj & m seven

sífilis f syphilis

sifón m U-bend; (de soda) syphon

sigilo m stealth; (fig) secrecy

sigla f abbreviation

siglo m century; (época) age. **hace ~s que no escribe** he hasn't written for ages

significa|ción f significance. ~**do** adj (conocido) well-known. ●m meaning; (importancia) significance. ~**r** 7 vt mean; (expresar) express. ~**tivo** adj meaningful; (importante) significant

signo m sign. ~ **de admiración** exclamation mark. ~ **de interrogación** question mark

sigo vb véase SEGUIR

siguiente adj following, next. **lo ~** the following

sílaba f syllable

silb|ar vt/i whistle. ~**ato** m, ~**ido** m whistle

silenci|ador m silencer. ~**ar** vt hush up. ~**o** m silence. ~**oso** adj silent

sill|a f chair; (de montar) saddle (Relig) see ~**a de ruedas** wheelchair. ~**ín** m saddle. ~**ón** m armchair

silueta f silhouette; (dibujo) outline

silvestre adj wild

simb|ólico adj symbolic(al). ~**olismo** m symbolism. ~**olizar** 10 vt symbolize

símbolo m symbol

sim|etría f symmetry. ~**étrico** adj symmetric(al)

similar adj similar (**a** to)

simp|atía f friendliness; (cariño) affection. ~**ático** adj nice, likeable; (ambiente) pleasant.

~**atizante** m & f sympathizer. ~**atizar** 10 vi get on (well together)

simpl|e adj simple; (mero) mere. ~**eza** f simplicity; (tontería) stupid thing; (insignificancia) trifle. ~**icidad** f simplicity. ~**ificar** 7 vt simplify. ~**ista** adj simplistic. ~**ón** m simpleton

simula|ción f simulation. ~**r** vt simulate; (fingir) feign

simultáneo adj simultaneous

sin prep without. ~ **saber** without knowing. ~ **querer** accidentally

sinagoga f synagogue

sincer|idad f sincerity. ~**o** adj sincere

sincronizar 10 vt synchronize

sindica|l adj (trade-)union. ~**lista** m & f trade-unionist. ~**to** m trade union

síndrome m syndrome

sinfín m endless number (**de** of)

sinfonía f symphony

singular adj singular; (excepcional) exceptional. ~**izarse** vpr stand out

siniestro adj sinister. ●m disaster; (accidente) accident

sinnúmero m endless number (**de** of)

sino m fate. ●conj but

sinónimo adj synonymous. ●m synonym (**de** for)

sintaxis f syntax

síntesis f invar synthesis; (resumen) summary

sint|ético adj synthetic. ~**etizar** 10 vt synthesize; (resumir) summarize

síntoma f symptom

sintomático adj symptomatic

sinton|ía f tuning; (Mus) signature tune. ~**izar** 10 vt (con la radio) tune (in) to

◼ *see* A-Z of Spanish life and culture

sinvergüenza m & f crook

siquiera conj even if. ●adv at least. **ni** ~ not even

sirena f siren; (en cuentos) mermaid

sirio adj & m Syrian

sirvient|a f maid. ~e m servant

sirvo vb véase SERVIR

sísmico adj seismic

sismo m earthquake

sistem|a m system. **por** ~**a** as a rule. ~**ático** adj systematic

sitiar vt besiege; (fig) surround

sitio m place; (espacio) space; (Mil) siege; (Mex, parada de taxi) taxi rank. **en cualquier** ~ anywhere. ~ **web** website

situa|ción f situation; (estado, condición) position. ~**r** 21 vt place, put; locate (edificio). ~**rse** vpr be successful, establish o.s.

slip /es'lip/ m (pl ~**s**) underpants, briefs

smoking /es'mokin/ m (pl ~**s**) dinner jacket (Brit), tuxedo (Amer)

sobaco m armpit

sobar vt handle; knead (masa)

soberan|ía f sovereignty. ~**o** adj sovereign; (fig) supreme. ●m sovereign

soberbi|a f pride; (altanería) arrogance. ~**o** adj proud; (altivo) arrogant

soborn|ar vt bribe. ~**o** m bribe

sobra f surplus. **de** ~ more than enough. ~**s** fpl leftovers. ~**do** adj more than enough. ~**nte** adj surplus. ~**r** vi be left over; (estorbar) be in the way

sobre prep on; (encima de) on top of; (más o menos) about; (por encima de) above; (sin tocar) over. ~ **todo** above all, especially. ●m envelope. ~**cargar** 12 vt overload. ~**coger** 14 vt startle; (conmover) move. ~**cubierta** f dustcover. ~**dosis** f invar overdose. ~**entender** 1 vt understand, infer. ~**girar** vt (LAm)

overdraw. ~**giro** m (LAm) overdraft. ~**humano** adj superhuman. ~**llevar** vt bear. ~**mesa** f. **de** ~**mesa** after-dinner. ~**natural** adj supernatural. ~**nombre** m nickname. ~**pasar** vt exceed. ~**peso** m (LAm) excess baggage. ~**poner** 34 vt superimpose. ~**ponerse** vpr overcome. ~**saliente** adj (fig) outstanding. ●m excellent mark. ~**salir** 52 vi stick out; (fig) stand out. ~**saltar** vt startle. ~**salto** m fright. ~**sueldo** m bonus. ~**todo** m overcoat. ~**venir** 53 vi happen. ~**viviente** adj surviving. ●m & f survivor. ~**vivir** vi survive. ~**volar** vt fly over

sobriedad f moderation; (de estilo) simplicity

sobrin|a f niece. ~**o** m nephew. ~**os** (varones) nephews; (varones y mujeres) nieces and nephews

sobrio adj moderate, sober

socavar vt undermine

soci|able adj sociable. ~**al** adj social. ~**aldemócrata** m & f social democrat. ~**alismo** m socialism. ~**alista** adj & m & f socialist. ~**edad** f society; (Com) company. ~**edad anónima** limited company. ~**o** m member; (Com) partner. ~**ología** f sociology. ~**ólogo** m sociologist

socorr|er vt help. ~**o** m help

soda f (bebida) soda (water)

sodio m sodium

sofá m sofa, settee

sofistica|ción f sophistication. ~**do** adj sophisticated

sofo|cante adj suffocating; (fig) stifling. ~**car** 7 vt smother (fuego); (fig) stifle. ~**carse** vpr get upset

soga f rope

soja f soya (bean)

sojuzgar 12 vt subdue

sol m sun; (luz) sunlight; (Mus) G; (solfa) soh. **al** ~ in the sun. **día** m

de ~ sunny day. **hace** ~, **hay** ~ it is sunny. **tomar el** ~ sunbathe

solamente adv only

solapa f lapel; (de bolsillo etc) flap. ~**do** adj sly

solar adj solar. • m plot

solariego adj (casa) ancestral

soldado m soldier. ~ **raso** private

solda|dor m welder; (utensilio) soldering iron. ~**r** ② vt weld, solder

soleado adj sunny

soledad f solitude; (aislamiento) loneliness

solemn|e adj solemn. ~**idad** f solemnity

soler ② vi be in the habit of. **suele despertarse a las 6** he usually wakes up at 6 o'clock

soli|citante m applicant. ~ **de asilo** asylum seeker. ~**icitar** vt request, ask for; apply for (empleo). ~**ícito** adj solicitous. ~**icitud** f request; (para un puesto) application; (formulario) application form; (preocupación) concern

solidaridad f solidarity

solid|ez f solidity; (de argumento etc) soundness. ~**ificarse** ⑦ vpr solidify

sólido adj solid; (argumento etc) sound. • m solid

soliloquio m soliloquy

solista m & f soloist

solitario adj solitary; (aislado) lonely. • m loner; (juego, diamante) solitaire

solloz|ar ⑩ vi sob. ~**o** m sob

solo adj (sin compañía) alone; (aislado) lonely; (sin ayuda) by oneself; (único) only; (Mus) solo; (café) black. • m solo; (juego) solitaire. **a solas** alone

sólo adv only. ~ **que** except that. **no** ~**... sino también** not only... but also.... **tan** ~ only

solomillo m sirloin

soltar ② vt let go of; (dejar ir) release; (dejar caer) drop; (dejar salir, decir) let out; give (golpe etc). ~**se** vpr come undone; (librarse) break loose

solter|a f single woman. ~**o** adj single. • m bachelor

soltura f looseness; (fig) ease, fluency

solu|ble adj soluble. ~**ción** f solution. ~**cionar** vt solve; settle (huelga, asunto)

solvente adj & m solvent

sombr|a f shadow; (lugar sin sol) shade. **a la** ~**a** in the shade. ~**eado** adj shady

sombrero m hat. ~ **hongo** bowler hat

sombrío adj sombre

somero adj superficial

someter vt subdue; subject (persona); (presentar) submit. ~**se** vpr give in

somn|oliento adj sleepy. ~**ífero** m sleeping-pill

somos vb véase SER

son m sound. • vb véase SER

sonámbulo m sleepwalker. **ser** ~ walk in one's sleep

sonar ② vt blow; ring (timbre). • vi sound; (timbre, teléfono etc) ring; (despertador) go off; (Mus) play; (fig, ser conocido) be familiar. ~ **a** sound like. ~**se** vpr blow one's nose

sonde|ar vt sound out; explore (espacio); (Naut) sound. ~**o** m poll; (Naut) sounding

soneto m sonnet

sonido m sound

sonoro adj sonorous; (ruidoso) loud

sonr|eír ⑤ vi smile. ~**eírse** vpr smile. ~**isa** f smile

sonroj|arse vpr blush. ~**o** m blush

sonrosado adj rosy, pink

sonsacar ⑦ vt wheedle out

soñ|ado adj dream. ~**ador** m

dreamer. ~**ar 2** vi dream (**con** of). **¡ni ~arlo!** not likely!

sopa f soup

sopesar vt (fig) weigh up

sopl|ar vt blow; blow out (vela); blow off (polvo); (inflar) blow up. • vi blow. ~**ete** m blowlamp. ~**o** m puff

soport|al m porch. ~**ales** mpl arcade. ~**ar** vt support; (fig) bear, put up with. ~**e** m support

soprano f soprano

sor f sister

sorb|er vt sip; (con ruido) slurp; (absorber) absorb. ~**er por la nariz** sniff. ~**ete** m sorbet, water-ice. ~**o** m (pequeña cantidad) sip; (trago grande) gulp

sordera f deafness

sórdido adj squalid; (asunto) sordid

sordo adj deaf; (ruido etc) dull. • m deaf person. **hacerse el ~** turn a deaf ear. ~**mudo** adj deaf and dumb

soroche m (LAm) mountain sickness

sorpre|ndente adj surprising. ~**nder** vt surprise. ~**nderse** vpr be surprised. ~**sa** f surprise

sorte|ar vt draw lots for; (fig) avoid. ~**o** m draw. **por ~o** by drawing lots

sortija f ring; (de pelo) ringlet

sortilegio m sorcery; (embrujo) spell

sos|egar 1 & 12 vt calm. ~**iego** m calmness

soslayo: de ~ sideways

soso adj tasteless; (fig) dull

sospech|a f suspicion. ~**ar** vt suspect. • vi. ~ **de** suspect. ~**oso** adj suspicious. • m suspect

sost|én m support; (prenda femenina) bra 1, brassière. ~**ener 40** vt support; bear (peso); (sujetar) hold; (sustentar) maintain; (alimentar) sustain. ~**enerse** vpr support o.s.;

(continuar) remain. ~**enido** adj sustained; (Mus) sharp. • m (Mus) sharp

sota f (de naipes) jack

sótano m basement

soviético adj (Historia) Soviet

soy vb véase SER

Sr. abrev (**Señor**) Mr. ~**a.** abrev (**Señora**) Mrs. ~**ta.** abrev (**Señorita**) Miss

su adj (de él) his; (de ella) her; (de animal, objeto) its; (de uno) one's; (de Vd) your; (de ellos, de ellas) their; (de Vds) your

suav|e adj smooth; (fig) gentle; (color, sonido) soft; (tabaco, sedante) mild. ~**idad** f smoothness, softness. ~**izante** m conditioner; (para ropa) softener. ~**izar 10** vt smooth, soften

subalimentado adj underfed

subarrendar 1 vt sublet

subasta f auction. ~**r** vt auction

sub|campeón m runner-up. ~**consciencia** f subconscious. ~**consciente** adj & m subconscious. ~**continente** m subcontinent. ~**desarrollado** adj under-developed. ~**director** m assistant manager

súbdito m subject

sub|dividir vt subdivide. ~**estimar** vt underestimate

subi|da f rise; (a montaña) ascent; (pendiente) slope. ~**do** adj (color) intense. ~**r** vt go up; climb (mountain); (llevar) take up; (aumentar) raise; turn up (radio, calefacción). • vi go up. ~**r a** get into (coche); get on (autobús, avión, barco, tren); (aumentar) rise. ~**r a pie** walk up. ~**rse** vpr climb up. ~**rse a** get on (tren etc)

súbito adj sudden. **de ~** suddenly

subjetivo adj subjective

subjuntivo adj & m subjunctive

subleva|ción f uprising. ~**rse** vpr rebel

sublim|ar vt sublimate. **~e** adj sublime

submarino adj underwater. ●m submarine

subordinado adj & m subordinate

subrayar vt underline

subsanar vt rectify; overcome (dificultad); make up for (carencia)

subscri|blr vt (pp **subscrito**) sign. **~birse** vpr subscribe (**a** to). **~pción** f subscription

subsidi|ario adj subsidiary. **~o** m subsidy. **~o de desempleo, ~ de paro** unemployment benefit

subsiguiente adj subsequent

subsist|encia f subsistence. **~ir** vi subsist; (perdurar) survive

substraer 🔟 vt take away

subterráneo adj underground

subtítulo m subtitle

suburb|ano adj suburban. **~io** m suburb; (barrio pobre) depressed area

subvenci|ón f subsidy. **~onar** vt subsidize

subver|sión f subversion. **~sivo** adj subversive. **~tir** 🔟 vt subvert

succi|ón f suction. **~onar** vt suck

suce|der vi happen; (seguir) **~ a** follow. ●vt (substituir) succeed. **lo que ~de es que** the trouble is that. **¿qué ~de?** what's the matter? **~sión** f succession. **~sivo** adj successive; (consecutivo) consecutive. **en lo ~sivo** in future. **~so** m event; (incidente) incident. **~sor** m successor

suciedad f dirt; (estado) dirtiness

sucinto adj concise; (prenda) scanty

sucio adj dirty; (conciencia) guilty. **en ~** in rough

sucre m (unidad monetaria del Ecuador) sucre

suculento adj succulent

sucumbir vi succumb (**a** to)

sucursal f branch (office)

Sudáfrica f South Africa

sudafricano adj & m South African

Sudamérica f South America

sudamericano adj & m South American

sudar vi sweat

sud|este m south-east. **~oeste** m south-west

sudor m sweat

Suecia f Sweden

sueco adj Swedish. ●m (persona) Swede; (lengua) Swedish. **hacerse el ~** pretend not to hear

suegr|a f mother-in-law. **~o** m father-in-law. **mis ~os** my in-laws

suela f sole

sueldo m salary

suelo m ground; (dentro de edificio) floor; (territorio) soil; (en la calle etc) road surface. ●vb véase **SOLER**

suelto adj loose; (cordones) undone; (sin pareja) odd; (lenguaje) fluent. **con el pelo ~** with one's hair down. ●m change

sueño m sleep; (lo soñado, ilusión) dream. **tener ~** be sleepy

suerte f luck; (destino) fate; (azar) chance. **de otra ~** otherwise. **de ~ que** so. **echar ~s** draw lots. **por ~** fortunately. **tener ~** be lucky

suéter m sweater, jersey

suficien|cia f (aptitud) aptitude; (presunción) smugness. **~te** adj enough, sufficient; (presumido) smug. **~temente** adv sufficiently

sufijo m suffix

sufragio m (voto) vote

sufri|miento m suffering. **~r** vt suffer; undergo (cambio); have (accident). ●vi suffer

suge|rencia f suggestion. **~rir** 🔟 vt suggest. **~stión** f (en psicología) suggestion. **es pura ~stión** it's all in one's mind. **~stionable** adj impressionable. **~stionar** vt influence. **~stivo** adj (estimulante) stimulating; (atractivo) sexy

suicid|a adj suicidal. ●m & f suicide victim; (fig) maniac. **~arse** vpr commit suicide. **~io** m suicide

Suiza f Switzerland

suizo adj & m Swiss

suje|ción f subjection. **con ~ción a** in accordance with. **~tador** m bra 🔟, brassière. **~tapapeles** m invar paper-clip. **~tar** vt fasten; (agarrar) hold. **~tarse** vpr. **~se a** hold on to; (someterse) abide by. **~to** adj fastened; (susceptible) subject (**a** to). ●m individual; (Gram) subject.

suma f sum; (Math) addition; (combinación) combination. **en ~** in short. **~mente** adv extremely. **~r** vt add (up); (totalizar) add up to. ●vi add up. **~rse** vpr. **~rse a** join in

sumario adj brief; (Jurid) summary. ●m table of contents; (Jurid) pre-trial proceedings

sumergi|ble adj submersible. **~r** 🔟 vt submerge

suministr|ar vt supply. **~o** m supply; (acción) supplying

sumir vt sink; (fig) plunge

sumis|ión f submission. **~o** adj submissive

sumo adj great; (supremo) supreme. **a lo ~** at the most

suntuoso adj sumptuous

supe vb véase **SABER**

superar vt surpass; (vencer) overcome; beat (marca); (dejar atrás) get over. **~se** vpr better o.s.

superchería f swindle

superfici|al adj superficial. **~e** f surface; (extensión) area. **de ~e** surface

superfluo adj superfluous

superior adj superior; (más alto) higher; (mejor) better; (piso) upper. ●m superior. **~idad** f superiority

superlativo adj & m superlative

supermercado m supermarket

superstici|ón f superstition. **~oso** adj superstitious

supervis|ar vt supervise. **~ión** f supervision. **~or** m supervisor

superviv|encia f survival. **~iente** adj surviving. ●m & f survivor

suplantar vt supplant

suplement|ario adj supplementary. **~o** m supplement

suplente adj & m & f substitute

súplica f entreaty; (Jurid) request

suplicar 🔟 vt beg

suplicio m torture

suplir vt make up for; (reemplazar) replace

supo|ner 🔟 vt suppose; (significar) mean; involve (gasto, trabajo). **~sición** f supposition

suprem|acía f supremacy. **~o** adj supreme

supr|esión f suppression; (de impuesto) abolition; (de restricción) lifting. **~imir** vt suppress; abolish (impuesto); lift (restricción); delete (párrafo)

supuesto adj supposed; (falso) false; (denominado) so-called. ●m assumption. **¡por ~!** of course!

sur m south; (viento) south wind

surc|ar 🔟 vt plough; cut through (agua). **~o** m furrow; (de rueda) rut

surfear vi (Informática) surf

surgir 🔟 vi spring up; (elevarse) loom up; (aparecer) appear; (dificultad, oportunidad) arise

surrealis|mo m surrealism. **~ta** adj & m & f surrealist

surti|do adj well-stocked; (variado) assorted. ●m assortment, selection. **~dor** m (de gasolina) petrol pump (Brit), gas pump (Amer). **~r** vt supply; have (efecto). **~rse** vpr provide o.s. (**de** with)

susceptib|ilidad f sensitivity. **~le** adj susceptible; (sensible) sensitive

suscitar vt provoke; arouse (curiosidad, interés)

suscr... véase SUBSCR...

susodicho adj aforementioned

suspen|der vt suspend; stop (tratamiento); call off (viaje); (en examen) fail; (colgar) hang (**de** from). **~se** m suspense. **novela de ~se** thriller. **~sión** f suspension. **~so** m fail; (LAm, en libro, película) suspense. **en ~so** suspended

suspir|ar vi sigh. **~o** m sigh

sust... véase SUBST...

sustanci|a f substance. **~al** adj substantial. **~oso** adj substantial

sustantivo m noun

sustent|ación f support. **~ar** vt

support; (alimentar) sustain; (mantener) maintain. **~o** m support; (alimento) sustenance

sustitu|ción f substitution; (permanente) replacement. **~ir** 🔟 vt substitute, replace. **~to** m substitute; (permanente) replacement

susto m fright

susurr|ar vi (persona) whisper; (agua) murmur; (hojas) rustle

sutil adj fine; (fig) subtle. **~eza** f subtlety

suyo adj & pron (de él) his; (de ella) hers; (de animal) its; (de Vd) yours; (de ellos, de ellas) theirs; (de Vds) yours. **un amigo ~** a friend of his, a friend of theirs, etc

Tt

tabac|alera f (state) tobacco monopoly. **~o** m tobacco; (cigarrillos) cigarettes

tabern|a f bar. **~ero** m barman; (dueño) landlord

tabique m partition wall; (Mex, ladrillo) brick

tabl|a f plank; (del suelo) floorboard; (de vestido) pleat; (índice) index; (gráfico, en matemática etc) table. **hacer ~as** (en ajedrez) draw. **~a de surf** surfboard. **~ado** m platform; (en el teatro) stage. **~ao** m place where flamenco shows are held. **~ero** m board. **~ero de mandos** dashboard

tableta f tablet; (de chocolate) bar

tabl|illa f splint; (Mex, de chocolate) bar. **~ón** m plank. **~ón de anuncios** notice board (esp Brit), bulletin board (Amer)

tabú m (pl **~es**, **~s**) taboo

tabular vt tabulate

taburete m stool

tacaño adj mean

tacha f stain, blemish. **sin ~** unblemished; (conducta) irreproachable. **~r** vt (con raya) cross out; (Jurid) impeach. **~ de** accuse of

tácito adj tacit

taciturno adj taciturn; (triste) glum

taco m plug; (LAm, tacón) heel; (de billar) cue; (de billetes) book; (fig, fam, lío) mess; (palabrota) swearword; (Mex, Culin) taco, filled tortilla

tacón m heel

táctic|a f tactics. **~o** adj tactical

táctil adj tactile

tacto m touch; (fig) tact

tahúr m card-sharp

tailandés adj & m Thai

s
t

Tailandia f Thailand

taimado adj sly

taj|ada f slice. **sacar ~ada** profit. **~ante** adj categorical; (tono) sharp. **~ear** vt (LAm) slash. **~o** m cut; (en mina) face

tal adj such. **de ~ manera** in such a way. **un ~** someone called. ●pron. **como ~** as such. **y ~** and things like that. ●adv. **con ~ de que** as long as. **~ como** the way. **~ para cual** 🅣 two of a kind. **~ vez** maybe. **¿qué ~?** how are you? **¿qué ~ es ella?** what's she like?

taladr|ar vt drill. **~o** m drill

talante m mood. **de buen ~** (estar) in a good mood; (ayudar) willingly

talar vt fell

talco m talcum powder

talega f, **talego** m sack

talento m talent; (fig) talented person

talismán m talisman

talla f carving; (de diamante etc) cutting; (estatura) height; (tamaño) size. **~do** m carving; (de diamante etc) cutting. **~dor** m carver; (cortador) cutter; (LAm, de naipes) dealer. **~r** vt carve; sculpt (escultura); cut (diamante); (Mex, restregar) scrub. **~rse** vpr (Mex) rub o.s.

tallarín m noodle

talle m waist; (figura) figure

taller m workshop; (de pintor etc) studio; (Auto) garage

tallo m stem, stalk

tal|ón m heel; (recibo) counterfoil; (cheque) cheque. **~onario** m receipt book; (de cheques) cheque book

tamal m (LAm) tamale

tamaño adj such a. ●m size. **de ~ natural** life-size

tambalearse vpr (persona) stagger; (cosa) wobble

también adv also, too

tambor m drum. **~ del freno** brake drum. **~ilear** vi drum

tamiz m sieve. **~ar** 🔟 vt sieve

tampoco adv neither, nor, not either. **yo ~ fui** I didn't go either

tampón m tampon; (para entintar) ink-pad

tan adv so. **~... como** as... as. **¿qué ~...?** (LAm) how...?

tanda f group; (de obreros) shift

tang|ente adj & f tangent. **~ible** adj tangible

tango m tango

tanque m tank

tante|ar vt estimate; sound up (persona); (ensayar) test; (fig) weigh up; (LAm, palpar) feel. ●vi (LAm) feel one's way. **~o** m estimate; (prueba) test; (en deportes) score

tanto adj (en singular) so much; (en plural) so many; (comparación en singular) as much; (comparación en plural) as many. ●pron so much; (en plural) so many. ●adv so; (con verbo) so much. **hace ~ tiempo** it's been so long. **~... como** both...and. **¿qué ~...?** (LAm) how much...? **~ como** as well as; (cantidad) as much as. **~ más... cuanto que** all the more ... because. **~ si... como si** whether ... or. **a ~s de** sometime in. **en ~, entre ~** meanwhile. **en ~ que** while. **entre ~** meanwhile. **hasta ~ que** until. **no es para ~** it's not as bad as all that. **otro ~ the** same; (el doble) as much again. **por (lo) ~** therefore. ●m certain amount; (punto) point; (gol) goal. **estar al ~ de** be up to date with

tañer 🔢 vi peal

tapa f lid; (de botella) top; (de libro) cover. 🅖**~s** fpl savoury snacks. **~dera** f cover, lid; (fig) cover. **~r** vt cover; (abrigar) wrap up; (obturar) plug. **~rrabo(s)** m invar loincloth

tapete m (de mesa) table cover; (Mex, alfombra) rug

tapia f wall. ~**r** vt enclose

tapi|cería f tapestry; (de muebles) upholstery. ~**z** m tapestry. ~**zar** 🔟 vt upholster (muebles)

tapón m stopper; (Tec) plug

taqui|igrafía f shorthand. ~**ígrafo** m shorthand writer

taquill|a f ticket office; (fig, dinero) takings. ~**ero** adj box-office

tara f (peso) tare; (defecto) defect

tarántula f tarantula

tararear vt/i hum

tarda|nza f delay. ~**r** vt take. ●vi (retrasarse) be late; (emplear mucho tiempo) take a long time. **a más ~r** at the latest. **sin ~r** without delay

tard|e adv late. ●f (antes del atardecer) afternoon; (después del atardecer) evening. **en la ~e** (LAm), **por la ~e** in the afternoon. ~**ío** adj late

tarea f task, job

tarifa f rate; (en transporte) fare; (lista de precios) tariff

tarima f dais

tarjeta f card. ~ **de crédito** credit card. ~ **de fidelidad** loyalty card. ~ **postal** postcard. ~ **telefónica** telephone card

tarro m jar; (Mex, taza) mug

tarta f cake; (con base de masa) tart. ~ **helada** ice-cream gateau

tartamud|ear vi stammer. ~**o** adj. **es ~o** he stammers

tasa f valuation; (impuesto) tax; (índice) rate. ~**r** vt value; (limitar) ration

tasca f bar

tatarabuel|a f great-great-grandmother. ~**o** m great-great-grandfather. ~**os** mpl great-great-grandparents

tatua|je m (acción) tattooing; (dibujo) tattoo. ~**r** 🔢 vt tattoo

taurino adj bullfighting

Tauro m Taurus

tauromaquia f bullfighting

taxi m taxi. ~**ista** m & f taxi-driver

taz|a f cup. ~**ón** m bowl

te pron (acusativo) you; (dativo) (to) you; (reflexivo) (to) yourself

té m tea; (LAm, reunión) tea party

teatr|al adj theatre; (exagerado) theatrical. ~**o** m theatre; (literatura) drama

tebeo m comic

tech|ado m roof. ~**ar** vt roof. ~**o** m (interior) ceiling; (LAm, tejado) roof. ~**umbre** f roof

tecl|a f key. ~**ado** m keyboard. ~**ear** vt key in

técnica f technique

tecnicismo m technical nature; (palabra) technical term

técnico adj technical. ●m technician; (en deportes) trainer

tecnol|ogía f technology. ~**ógico** adj technological

tecolote m (Mex) owl

teja f tile. ~**s de pizarra** slates. ~**do** m roof. **a toca ~** cash

teje|do|r m weaver. ~**r** vt weave; (hacer punto) knit

teje|maneje m 🔟 intrigue. ~**s** mpl scheming

tejido m material; (Anat, fig) tissue. ~**s** mpl textiles

tejón m badger

tela f material, fabric; (de araña) web; (en líquido) skin

telar m loom. ~**es** mpl textile mill

telaraña f spider's web, cobweb

tele f 🔟 TV, telly

tele|banca f telephone banking. ~**comunicación** f telecommunication. ~**diario** m television news. ~**dirigido** adj remote-controlled; (misil) guided. ~**férico** m cable-car

tel|efonear vt/i telephone.

t

~**efónico** adj telephone. ~**efonista** m & f telephonist.

teléfono m telephone. ~ **celular** (LAm) mobile phone, cellular phone. ~ **móvil** (Esp) mobile phone, cellular phone. ~ **satélite** satphone

tel|egrafía f telegraphy. ~**égrafo** m telegraph. ~**egrama** m telegram

telenovela f television soap opera

teleobjetivo m telephoto lens

telep|atía f telepathy. ~**ático** adj telepathic

telesc|ópico adj telescopic. ~**opio** m telescope

telesilla m & f chair-lift

telespectador m viewer

telesquí m ski-lift

televi|dente m & f viewer. ~**sar** vt televise. ~**sión** f television. ~**sor** m television (set)

télex m invar telex

telón m curtain

tema m subject; (Mus) theme

tembl|ar ■ vi shake; (de miedo) tremble; (de frío) shiver. ~**or** m shaking; (de miedo) trembling; (de frío) shivering. ~**or de tierra** earth tremor. ~**oroso** adj trembling

tem|er vt be afraid (of). • vi be afraid. ~**erse** vpr be afraid. ~**erario** adj reckless. ~**eroso** adj frightened. ~**ible** adj fearsome. ~**or** m fear

témpano m floe

temperamento m temperament

temperatura f temperature

tempest|ad f storm. ~**uoso** adj stormy

templ|ado adj (tibio) warm; (clima, tiempo) mild; (valiente) courageous. ~**anza** f mildness. ~**ar** vt temper; (calentar) warm up. ~**e** m tempering; (coraje) courage; (humor) mood

templo m temple

tempora|da f season. ~**l** adj temporary. • m storm

tempran|ero adj (frutos) early. **ser** ~**ero** be an early riser. ~**o** adj & adv early

tenacidad f tenacity

tenacillas fpl tongs

tenaz adj tenacious

tenaza f, **tenazas** fpl pliers; (de chimenea, Culin) tongs; (de cangrejo) pincer

tende|ncia f tendency. ~**nte** adj. ~**nte a** aimed at. ~**r** ■ vt spread (out); hang out (ropa a secar); (colocar) lay. • vi tend (**a** to). ~**rse** vpr lie down

tender|ete m stall. ~**o** m shopkeeper

tendido adj spread out; (ropa) hung out; (persona) lying down. • m (en plaza de toros) front rows

tendón m tendon

tenebroso adj gloomy; (asunto) sinister

tenedor m fork; (poseedor) holder

---

tener ⁴⁰

• verbo transitivo

❗ El presente del verbo **tener** admite dos traducciones: *to have* y *to have got*, este último de uso más extendido en el inglés británico

····▶ to have. **¿tienen hijos?** do you have any children?, have you got any children? **no tenemos coche** we don't have a car, we haven't got a car. **tiene gripe** he has (the) flu, he's got (the) flu

····▶ to be. (dimensiones, edad) **tiene 1 metro de largo** it's 1 meter long. **tengo 20 años** I'm 20 (years old)

····▶ (sentir) **tener** + nombre to be + adjective. ~ **celos** to be jealous.

~ **frío** to be cold

····▸ *(sujetar, sostener)* to hold. **tenme la escalera** hold the ladder for me

····▸ *(indicando estado)* **tiene las manos sucias** his hands are dirty. **me tiene preocupada** I'm worried about him. **me tuvo esperando** he kept me waiting

····▸ *(llevar puesto)* to be wearing, to have on. **¡qué zapatos más elegantes tienes!** those are very smart shoes you're wearing! **tienes el suéter al revés** you have your sweater on inside out

····▸ *(considerar)* ~ **a uno por algo** to think s.o. is sth. **lo tenía por tímido** I thought he was shy

●verbo auxiliar

····▸ ~ **que hacer algo** to have to do sth. **tengo que irme** I have to go

····▸ **tener** + participio pasado. **tengo pensado comprarlo** I'm thinking of buying it. **tenía entendido otra cosa** I understood something else

····▸ *(LAm, con expresiones temporales)* **tienen 2 años de estar aquí** they've been here for 2 months. **tiene mucho tiempo sin verlo** she hasn't seen him for a long time

····▸ *(en locuciones)* **aquí tiene** here you are. **¿qué tienes?** what's the matter with you? **¿y eso qué tiene?** (LAm) and what's wrong with that?

●**tenerse** verbo pronominal

····▸ *(sostenerse)* **no podía** ~**se en pie** *(de cansancio)* he was dead on his feet; *(de borracho)* he could hardly stand

····▸ *(considerarse)* to consider o.s. **se tiene por afortunado** he considers himself lucky

tengo vb véase TENER

teniente m lieutenant

tenis m tennis. ~ **de mesa** table tennis. ~**ta** m & f tennis player

tenor m sense; (Mus) tenor. **a** ~ **de** according to

tens|ión f tension; (arterial) blood pressure; (Elec) voltage; (estrés) strain. ~**o** adj tense

tentación f temptation

tentáculo m tentacle

tenta|dor adj tempting. ~**r 1** vt tempt; (palpar) feel

tentativa f attempt

tenue adj thin; (luz, voz) faint; (color) subdued

teñi|r 5 & **22** vt dye; (fig) tinge (**de** with). ~**rse** vpr dye one's hair

teología f theology

te|oría f theory. ~**órico** adj theoretical

tequila f tequila

terap|euta m & f therapist. ~**éutico** adj therapeutic. ~**ia** f therapy

terc|er adj véase TERCERO. ~**era** f (Auto) third (gear). ~**ero** adj (delante de nombre masculino en singular **tercer**) third. ●m third party. ~**io** m third

terciopelo m velvet

terco adj obstinate

tergiversar vt distort

termal adj thermal

térmico adj thermal

termina|ción f ending; (conclusión) conclusion. ~**l** adj & m terminal. ~**nte** adj categorical. ~**r** vt finish, end. ~**r por** end up. ~**rse** vpr come to an end

término m end; (palabra) term; (plazo) period. ~ **medio** average. **dar** ~ **a** finish off. **en primer** ~ first of all. **en último** ~ as a last resort. **estar en buenos** ~**s con** be on good terms with. **llevar a** ~ carry out

terminología f terminology

termita f termite

termo m Thermos ® flask, flask

termómetro m thermometer

termo|nuclear adj thermonuclear. **~stato** m thermostat

terner|a f (carne) veal. **~o** m calf

ternura f tenderness

terquedad f stubbornness

terrado m flat roof

terraplén m embankment

terrateniente m & f landowner

🄲**terraza** f terrace; (balcón) balcony; (terrado) flat roof

terremoto m earthquake

terre|no adj earthly. ●m land; (solar) plot (fig) field. **~stre** adj land; (Mil) ground

terrible adj terrible. **~mente** adv awfully

territori|al adj territorial. **~o** m territory

terrón m (de tierra) clod; (Culin) lump

terror m terror. **~ífico** adj terrifying. **~ismo** m terrorism. **~ista** m & f terrorist

terso adj smooth

tertulia f gathering

tesina f dissertation

tesón m tenacity

tesor|ería f treasury. **~ero** m treasurer. **~o** m treasure; (tesorería) treasury; (libro) thesaurus

testaferro m figurehead

testa|mento m will. **T~mento** (Relig) Testament. **~r** vi make a will

testarudo adj stubborn

testículo m testicle

testi|ficar 🄷 vt/i testify. **~go** m witness. **~go ocular**, **~go presencial** eyewitness. **ser ~go de** witness. **~monio** m testimony

teta f tit (fam o vulg); (de biberón) teat

tétanos m tetanus

tetera f (para el té) teapot

....

🄲 *see* A-Z of Spanish life and culture

tetilla f nipple; (de biberón) teat

tétrico adj gloomy

textil adj & m textile

text|o m text. **~ual** adj textual; (traducción) literal; (palabras) exact

textura f texture

tez f complexion

ti pron you

tía f aunt; 🄸 woman

tiara f tiara

tibio adj lukewarm

tiburón m shark

tiempo m time; (atmosférico) weather; (Mus) tempo; (Gram) tense; (en partido) half. **a su ~** in due course. **a ~** in time. **¿cuánto ~?** how long? **hace buen ~** the weather is fine. **hace ~** some time ago. **mucho ~** a long time. **perder el ~** waste time

🄲**tienda** f shop (esp Brit), store (esp Amer); (de campaña) tent. **~ de comestibles**, **~ de ultramarinos** grocer's (shop) (Brit), grocery store (Amer)

tiene vb véase TENER

tienta: andar a ~s feel one's way

tierno adj tender; (joven) young

tierra f land; (planeta, Elec) earth; (suelo) ground; (en geología) soil, earth; (LAm, polvo) dust. **por ~** overland, by land

tieso adj stiff; (engreído) conceited

tiesto m flowerpot

tifón m typhoon

tifus m typhus; (fiebre tifoidea) typhoid (fever)

tigre m tiger. **~sa** f tigress

tijera f, **tijeras** fpl scissors; (de jardín) shears

tijeretear vt snip

tila f (infusión) lime tea

tild|ar vt. **~ar de** (fig) brand as. **~e** f tilde

tilo m lime(-tree)

timar vt swindle

timbal m kettledrum; (Culin) timbale, meat pie. ~es mpl (Mus) timpani

timbr|ar vt stamp. ~e m (sello) fiscal stamp; (Mex) postage stamp; (Elec) bell; (sonido) timbre

timidez f shyness

tímido adj shy

timo m swindle

timón m rudder; (rueda) wheel; (fig) helm

tímpano m eardrum

tina f tub. ~co m (Mex) water tank. ~ja f large earthenware jar

tinglado m mess; (asunto) racket

tinieblas fpl darkness; (fig) confusion

tino f good sense; (tacto) tact

tint|a f ink. **de buena ~a** on good authority. ~e m dyeing; (color) dye; (fig) tinge. ~ero m ink-well

tintinear vi tinkle; (vasos) chink, clink

tinto adj (vino) red

tintorería f dry cleaner's

tintura f dyeing; (color) dye

tío m uncle; 🄵 man. ~s mpl uncle and aunt

tiovivo m merry-go-round

típico adj typical

tipo m type; (fam, persona) person; (figura de mujer) figure; (figura de hombre) build; (Com) rate

tip|ografía f typography. ~ográfico adj typographic(al)

tira f strip. **la ~ de** lots of

tirabuzón m corkscrew; (de pelo) ringlet

tirad|a f distance; (serie) series; (de periódico etc) print-run. **de una ~a** in one go. ~o adj (barato) very cheap; (fam, fácil) very easy. ~or m (asa) handle

tiran|ía f tyranny. ~izar 🔟 vt

tyrannize. ~o adj tyrannical. ●m tyrant

tirante adj tight; (fig) tense; (relaciones) strained. ●m strap. ~s mpl braces (esp Brit), suspenders (Amer)

tirar vt throw; (desechar) throw away; (derribar) knock over; drop (bomba); fire (cohete); (imprimir) print. ●vi (disparar) shoot. ~ a tend to (be); (parecerse a) resemble. ~ **abajo** knock down. ~ **de** pull. **a todo ~** at the most. **ir tirando** get by. ~se vpr throw o.s.; (tumbarse) lie down

tirita f (sticking) plaster

tiritar vi shiver (**de** with)

tiro m throw; (disparo) shot. ~ **libre** free kick. **a ~** within range. **errar el ~** miss. **pegarse un ~** shoot o.s.

tiroides m thyroid (gland)

tirón m tug. **de un ~** in one go

tirote|ar vt shoot at. ~o m shooting

tisana f herb tea

tisú m (pl ~s, ~es) tissue

títere m puppet. ~s mpl puppet show

titilar vi (estrella) twinkle

titiritero m puppeteer; (acróbata) acrobat

titube|ante adj faltering; (fig) hesitant. ~ar vi falter. ~o m hesitation

titula|do adj (libro) entitled; (persona) qualified. ~r m headline; (persona) holder. ●vt call. ~rse vpr be called; (persona) graduate

título m title; (académico) qualification; (Univ) degree. **a ~ de** as, by way of

tiza f chalk

tiz|nar vt dirty. ~ne m soot

toall|a f towel. ~ero m towel-rail

tobillo m ankle

tobogán m slide; (para la nieve) toboggan

tocadiscos m invar record-player

toca|do adj touched ⚠. ● m headdress. **~dor** m dressing-table. **~nte** adj. **en lo ~nte a** with regard to. **~r** 7 vt touch; (palpar) feel; (Mus) play; ring (timbre); (mencionar) touch on; (barco) stop at. ● vi ring; (corresponder a uno). **te ~ a ti** it's your turn. **en lo que ~ a** as for. **~rse** vpr touch; (personas); touch each other

tocayo m namesake

tocino m bacon

tocólogo m obstetrician

todavía adv still; (con negativos) yet. **~ no** not yet

todo , **toda**
● adjetivo
····▸ (la totalidad) all. **~ el vino** all the wine. **~s los edificios** all the buildings. **~ ese dinero** all that money. **~ el mundo** everyone. (como adv) **está toda sucia** it's all dirty

····▸ (entero) whole. **~ el día** the whole day, all day. **toda su familia** his whole family. **~ el tiempo** the whole time, all the time

····▸ (cada, cualquiera) every. **~ tipo de coche** every type of car. **~s los días** every day

····▸ (enfático) **a toda velocidad** at top speed. **es ~ un caballero** he's a real gentleman

····▸ (en locuciones) **ante ~** above all. **a ~ esto** meanwhile. **con ~** even so. **del ~** totally. **~ lo contrario** quite the opposite

▶ Para expresiones como **todo recto, todo seguido** etc., ver bajo el respectivo adjetivo

● pronombre
····▸ all; (todas las cosas) everything. **eso es ~** that's all.

lo perdieron ~ they lost everything. **quiere comprar ~** he wants to buy everything
····▸ **todos, todas** all; (todo el mundo) everyone. **los compró ~s** he bought them all, he bought all of them. **~s queríamos ir** we all wanted to go. **vinieron ~s** everyone came
● nombre masculino **el/un ~** the/a whole

toldo m awning

tolera|ncia f tolerance. **~nte** adj tolerant. **~r** vt tolerate

toma f taking; (de universidad etc) occupation; (Med) dose; (de agua) intake; (Elec) socket; (LAm, acequia) irrigation channel. ● int well!, fancy that! **~ de corriente** power point. **~dura** f. **~dura de pelo** hoax. **~r** vt take; catch (autobús, tren); occupy (universidad etc); (beber) drink, have; (comer) eat, have. ● vi take; (esp LAm, beber) drink; (LAm, dirigirse) go. **~r a bien** take well. **~r a mal** take badly. **~r en serio** take seriously. **~rla con uno** pick on s.o. **~r por** take for. **~ y daca** give and take. **¿qué va a ~r?** what would you like? **~rse** vpr take; (beber) drink, have; (comer) eat, have

tomate m tomato

tomillo m thyme

tomo m volume

ton: **sin ~ ni son** without rhyme or reason

tonad|a f tune; (canción) popular song; (LAm, acento) accent. **~illa** f tune

tonel m barrel. **~ada** f ton. **~aje** m tonnage

tónic|a f trend; (bebida) tonic water. **~o** adj tonic; (sílaba) stressed. ● m tonic

tonificar 7 vt invigorate

tono m tone; (Mus, modo) key; (color) shade

tont|ería f silliness; (cosa) silly

thing; (dicho) silly remark. **dejarse de ~erías** stop fooling around. **~o** adj silly. ●m fool, idiot; (payaso) clown. **hacer el ~o** act the fool. **hacerse el ~o** act dumb

topacio m topaz

topar vi. **~ con** run into

tope adj maximum. ●m end; (de tren) buffer; (Mex, Auto) speed bump. **hasta los ~s** crammed full. **ir a ~** go flat out

tópico adj trite. **de uso ~** (Med) for external use only. ●m cliché

topo m mole

topogr|afía f topography. **~áfico** adj topographical

toque m touch; (sonido) sound; (de campana) peal; (de reloj) stroke. **~ de queda** curfew. **dar los últimos ~s** put the finishing touches. **~tear** vt fiddle with

toquilla f shawl

tórax m invar thorax

torcer 2 & 9 vt twist; (doblar) bend; wring out (ropa). ●vi turn. **~se** vpr twist

tordo adj dapple grey. ●m thrush

tore|ar vt fight; (evitar) dodge. ●vi fight (bulls). **~o** m bullfighting. **~ro** m bullfighter

torment|a f storm. **~o** m torture. **~oso** adj stormy

tornado m tornado

tornasolado adj irridescent

torneo m tournament

tornillo m screw

torniquete m (Med) tourniquet; (entrada) turnstile

torno m lathe; (de alfarero) wheel. **en ~ a** around

⚅**toro** m bull. **~s** mpl bullfighting. **ir a los ~s** go to a bullfight

toronja f (LAm) grapefruit

torpe adj clumsy; (estúpido) stupid

torpedo m torpedo

torpeza f clumsiness; (de inteligencia)

slowness. **una ~** a blunder

torre f tower; (en ajedrez) castle, rook; (Elec) pylon; (edificio) tower block (Brit), apartment block (Amer)

torren|cial adj torrential. **~te** m torrent; (circulatorio) bloodstream; (fig) flood

tórrido adj torrid

torsión f twisting

torso m torso

torta f tart; (LAm, de verduras) pie; (golpe) slap, punch; (Mex, bocadillo) filled roll. **no entender ni ~** not understand a thing. **~zo** m slap, punch. **pegarse un ~zo** have a bad accident

tortícolis f stiff neck

tortilla f omelette; (Mex, de maíz) tortilla. **~ española** potato omelette. **~ francesa** plain omelette

tórtola f turtle-dove

tortuoso adj winding; (fig) devious

tortura f torture. **~r** vt torture

tos f cough. **~ ferina** whooping cough

tosco adj crude; (persona) coarse

toser vi cough

tost|ada f piece of toast. **~adas** fpl toast; (Mex, de tortilla) fried tortillas. **~ado** adj (pan) toasted; (café) roasted; (persona, color) tanned. **~ar** vt toast (pan); roast (café); tan (piel)

total adj total. ●adv after all. **~ que** so, to cut a long story short. ●m total; (totalidad) whole. **~idad** f whole. **~itario** adj totalitarian. **~izar** 10 vt total

tóxico adj toxic

toxi|cómano m drug addict. **~na** f toxin

tozudo adj stubborn

traba f catch; (fig, obstáculo) obstacle. **poner ~s a** hinder

trabaj|ador adj hard-working. ●m

··

⚅ *see* A-Z of Spanish life and culture

worker. **~ar** vt work; knead (masa).
• vi work (**de** as); (actor) act. **¿en
qué ~as?** what do you do? **~o** m
work. **costar ~o** be difficult.
~oso adj hard

trabalenguas m invar
tonguetwister

traba|r vt (sujetar) fasten; (unir) join;
(entablar) strike up. **~rse** vpr get
stuck. **trabársele la lengua** get
tongue-tied

trácala m (Mex) cheat. • f (Mex)
trick

tracción f traction

tractor m tractor

tradici|ón f tradition. **~onal** adj
traditional

traduc|ción f translation. **~ir** 47 vt
translate (**a** into). **~tor** m
translator

traer 41 vt bring; (llevar) carry;
(causar) cause. **traérselas** be
difficult

trafica|nte m & f dealer. **~r** 7 vi
deal

tráfico m traffic; (Com) trade

traga|luz m skylight. **~perras** f
invar slot-machine. **~r** 12 vt
swallow; (comer mucho) devour;
(soportar) put up with. **no lo trago**
I can't stand him. **~rse** vpr
swallow; (fig) swallow up

tragedia f tragedy

trágico adj tragic. • m tragedian

trag|o m swallow, gulp; (pequeña
porción) sip; (fig, disgusto) blow; (LAm,
bebida alcohólica) drink. **echar(se)
un ~o** have a drink. **~ón** adj
greedy. • m glutton

trai|ción f treachery; (Pol) treason.
~cionar vt betray. **~cionero** adj
treacherous. **~dor** adj
treacherous. • m traitor

traigo vb véase TRAER

traje m dress; (de hombre) suit. **~ de
baño** swimming-costume. **~ de
etiqueta**, **~ de noche** evening
dress. • vb véase TRAER.

traj|ín m coming and going; (ajetreo)
hustle and bustle. **~inar** vi bustle
about

trama f weft; (fig, argumento) plot.
~r vt weave; (fig) plot

tramitar vt negotiate

trámite m step. **~s** mpl procedure

tramo m (parte) section; (de escalera)
flight

tramp|a f trap; (fig) trick. **hacer
~a** cheat. **~illa** f trapdoor

trampolín m trampoline; (de
piscina) springboard; (rígido) diving
board

tramposo adj cheating. • m cheat

tranca f bar. **~r** vt bar

trance m moment; (hipnótico etc)
trance

tranco m stride

tranquil|idad f peace; (de espíritu)
peace of mind. **con ~** calmly.
~izar 10 vt calm down; (reconfortar)
reassure. **~o** adj calm; (lugar) quiet;
(conciencia) clear. **estáte ~o** don't
worry

transa|cción f transaction;
(acuerdo) settlement. **~r** vi (LAm)
compromise

transatlántico adj transatlantic.
• m (ocean) liner

transbord|ador m ferry. **~ar** vt
transfer. **~o** m transfer. **hacer ~o**
change (**en** at)

transcri|bir (pp transcrito) vt
transcribe. **~pción** f transcription

transcur|rir vi pass. **~so** m course

transeúnte m & f passer-by

transfer|encia f transfer. **~ir** 4
vt transfer

transforma|ción f
transformation. **~dor** m
transformer. **~r** vt transform

transfusión f transfusion

transgre|dir vt transgress. **~sión**
f transgression

transición f transition

transigir 🖽 vi give in, compromise

transistor m transistor

transita|ble adj passable. **~r** vi go

transitivo adj transitive

tránsito m transit; (tráfico) traffic

transitorio adj transitory

transmi|sión f transmission; (radio, TV) broadcast **~sor** m transmitter. **~sora** f broadcasting station. **~tir** vt transmit; (radio, TV) broadcast; (fig) pass on

transparen|cia f transparency. **~tar** vt show. **~te** adj transparent

transpira|ción f perspiration. **~r** vi transpire; (sudar) sweat

transport|ar vt transport. **~e** m transport. **empresa** f **de ~es** removals company

transversal adj transverse. **una calle ~ a la Gran Vía** a street which crosses the Gran Vía

tranvía m tram

trapear vt (LAm) mop

trapecio m trapeze; (Math) trapezium

trapo m cloth. **~s** mpl rags; (🏛, ropa) clothes **a todo ~** out of control

tráquea f windpipe, trachea

traquete|ar vt bang, rattle; (persona) rush around. **~o** m banging, rattle

tras prep after; (detrás) behind

trascende|ncia f significance; (alcance) implication. **~ntal** adj transcendental; (importante) important. **~r** 🗊 vi (saberse) become known; (extenderse) spread

trasero adj back, rear. ● m (de persona) bottom

trasfondo m background

traslad|ar vt move; transfer (empleado etc); (aplazar) postpone. **~o** m transfer; (copia) copy. (mudanza) removal. **dar ~o** notify

trasl|úcido adj translucent.

~ucirse 🖽 vpr be translucent; (dejarse ver) show through; (fig, revelarse) be revealed. **~uz** m. **al ~uz** against the light

trasmano: a ~ out of the way

trasnochar vt (acostarse tarde) go to bed late; (no acostarse) stay up all night; (no dormir) be unable to sleep

traspas|ar vt go through; (transferir) transfer; go beyond (limite). **se ~a** for sale. **~o** m transfer

traspié m trip; (fig) slip. **dar un ~** stumble; (fig) slip up

trasplant|ar vt transplant. **~e** m transplant

trastada f prank; (jugada) dirty trick

traste m fret. **dar al ~ con** ruin. **ir al ~** fall through. **~s** mpl (Mex) junk

trastero m storeroom

trasto m piece of junk. ● **~s** mpl junk

trastorn|ado adj mad. **~ar** vt upset; (volver loco) drive mad; (fig, fam, gustar mucho) delight. **~arse** vpr get upset; (volverse loco) go mad. **~o** m (incl Med) upset; (Pol) disturbance; (fig) confusion

trat|able adj friendly; (Med) treatable. **~ado** m treatise; (acuerdo) treaty. **~amiento** m treatment; (título) title. **~ante** m & f dealer. **~ar** vt (incl Med) treat; deal with (asunto etc); (manejar) handle; (de tú, de Vd) address (**de** as). ● vi deal (with). **~ar con** have to do with; (Com) deal in. **~ar de** be about; (intentar) try. **¿de qué se ~a?** what's it about? **~o** m treatment; (acuerdo) agreement; (título) title; (relación) relationship. **¡~o hecho!** agreed! **~os** mpl dealings

traum|a m trauma. **~ático** adj traumatic

través: **a ~ de** through; (de lado a lado) crossways

travesaño m crossbeam; (de portería) crossbar

travesía f crossing; (calle) sidestreet

trav|esura f prank. **~ieso** adj (niño) mischievous, naughty

trayecto m (tramo) stretch; (ruta) route; (viaje) journey. **~ria** f trajectory; (fig) course

traz|a f (aspecto) appearance. **~as** fpl signs. **~ado** m plan. **~ar** 10 vt draw; (bosquejar) sketch. **~o** m stroke; (línea) line

trébol m clover. **~es** mpl (en naipes) clubs

trece adj & m thirteen

trecho m stretch; (distancia) distance; (tiempo) while. **a ~s** here and there. **de ~ en ~** at intervals

tregua f truce; (fig) respite

treinta adj & m thirty

tremendo adj terrible; (extraordinario) terrific

tren m train. **~ de aterrizaje** landing gear. **~ de vida** lifestyle

tren|cilla f braid. **~za** f braid; (de pelo) plait. **~zar** 10 vt plait

trepa|dor adj climbing. **~dora** f climber. **~r** vt/i climb. **~rse** vpr. **~rse a** climb (árbol); climb onto (silla etc)

tres adj & m three. **~cientos** adj & m three hundred. **~illo** m threepiece suite; (Mus) triplet

treta f trick

tri|angular adj triangular. **~ángulo** m triangle

trib|al adj tribal. **~u** f tribe

tribuna f platform; (de espectadores) stand. **~l** m court; (de examen etc) board; (fig) tribunal

tribut|ar vt pay. **~o** m tribute; (impuesto) tax

triciclo m tricycle

tricolor adj three-coloured

tricotar vt/i knit

tridimensional adj three-dimensional

trig|al m wheat field. **~o** m wheat

trigésimo adj thirtieth

trigueño adj olive-skinned; (pelo) dark blonde

trilla|do adj (fig, manoseado) trite; (fig, conocido) well-known. **~r** vt thresh

trilogía f trilogy

trimestr|al adj quarterly. **~e** m quarter; (en enseñanza) term

trin|ar vi warble. **estar que trina** be furious

trinchar vt carve

trinchera f ditch; (Mil) trench; (abrigo) trench coat

trineo m sledge

trinidad f trinity

trino m warble

trío m trio

tripa f intestine; (fig, vientre) tummy, belly. **~s** fpl (de máquina etc) parts, workings. **revolver las ~s** turn one's stomach

tripl|e adj triple. •m. **el ~e (de)** three times as much (as). **~icado** adj. **por ~icado** in triplicate. **~icar** 7 vt treble

tripula|ción f crew. **~nte** m & f member of the crew. **~r** vt man

tris m. **estar en un ~** be on the point of

triste adj sad; (paisaje, tiempo etc) gloomy; (fig, insignificante) miserable. **~za** f sadness

triturar vt crush

triunf|al adj triumphal. **~ante** adj triumphant. **~ar** vi triumph (**de**, **sobre** over). **~o** m triumph

trivial adj trivial. **~idad** f triviality

trizas. hacer algo ~ smash sth to pieces. **hacerse ~** smash

trocear vt cut up, chop

trocha f narrow path; (LAm, rail) gauge

trofeo m trophy

tromba f whirlwind; (marina) waterspout. **~ de agua** heavy downpour

trombón m trombone

trombosis f invar thrombosis

trompa f horn; (de orquesta) French horn; (de elefante) trunk; (hocico) snout; (en anatomía) tube. **coger una ~** 🔢 get drunk. **~zo** m bump

trompet|a f trumpet; (músico) trumpet player; (Mil) trumpeter. **~illa** f ear-trumpet

trompo m (juguete) (spinning) top

tronar vt (Mex) shoot. ● vi thunder

tronchar vt bring down; (fig) cut short. **~se de risa** laugh a lot

tronco m trunk. **dormir como un ~** sleep like a log

trono m throne

trop|a f troops. **~el** m mob

tropez|ar 🔢 & 🔟 vi trip; (fig) slip up. **~ar con** run into. **~ón** m stumble; (fig) slip

tropical adj tropical

trópico adj tropical. ● m tropic

tropiezo m slip; (desgracia) hitch

trot|ar vi trot. **~e** m trot; (fig) toing and froing. **al ~e** at a trot; (de prisa) in a rush. **de mucho ~e** hard-wearing

trozo m piece, bit. **a ~s** in bits

trucha f trout

truco m trick. **coger el ~** get the knack

trueno m thunder; (estampido) bang

trueque m exchange; (Com) barter

trufa f truffle

truhán m rogue

truncar 🔢 vt truncate; (fig) cut short

tu adj your

tú pron you

tuba f tuba

tubérculo m tuber

tuberculosis f tuberculosis

tub|ería f pipes; (oleoducto etc) pipeline. **~o** m tube. **~o de ensayo** test tube. **~o de escape** (Auto) exhaust (pipe). **~ular** adj tubular

tuerca f nut

tuerto adj one-eyed, blind in one eye. ● m one-eyed person

tuétano m marrow; (fig) heart. **hasta los ~s** completely

tufo m stench

tugurio m hovel

tul m tulle

tulipán m tulip

tulli|do adj paralysed. **~r** 🔢 vt cripple

tumba f grave, tomb

tumb|ar vt knock over, knock down (estructura); (fig, fam, en examen) fail. **~arse** vpr lie down. **~o** m jolt. **dar un ~o** tumble. **~ona** f sun lounger

tumor m tumour

tumulto m turmoil; (Pol) riot

tuna f prickly pear; (de estudiantes) student band

tunante m & f rogue

túnel m tunnel

túnica f tunic

tupé m toupee; (fig) nerve

tupido adj thick

turba f peat; (muchedumbre) mob

turbado adj upset

turbante m turban

turbar vt upset; (molestar) disturb. **~se** vpr be upset

turbina f turbine

turbi|o adj cloudy; (vista) blurred; (asunto etc) shady. **~ón** m squall

turbulen|cia f turbulence; (disturbio) disturbance. **~te** adj turbulent

turco adj Turkish. ● m Turk; (lengua) Turkish

🔲 **tur|ismo** m tourism; (coche) car. **hacer ~** travel around. **~ cultural** heritage tourism. **~ patrimonial** (LAm) heritage tourism. **~ista** m & f tourist. **~ístico** adj tourist

turn|arse vpr take turns (**para** to). **~o** m turn; (de trabajo) shift. **de ~** on duty

turquesa f turquoise

Turquía f Turkey

turrón m nougat

tutear vt address as tú. **~se** vpr be on familiar terms

tutela f (Jurid) guardianship; (fig) protection

tutor m guardian; (en enseñanza) form master

tuve vb véase TENER

tuyo adj & pron yours. **un amigo ~** a friend of yours

Uu

u conj or

ubic|ar vt (LAm) place; (localizar) find. **~arse** vpr be situated; (orientarse) find one's way around

ubre f udder

Ud. abrev (**Usted**) you

UE abrev (**Unión Europea**) EU

uf int phew!; (de repugnancia) ugh!

ufan|arse vpr be proud (**con, de** of); (jactarse) boast (**con, de** about). **~o** adj proud

úlcera f ulcer

últimamente adv (recientemente) recently; (finalmente) finally

ultim|ar vt complete; (LAm, matar) kill. **~átum** m ultimatum

último adj last; (más reciente) latest; (más lejano) furthest; (más alto) top; (más bajo) bottom; (definitivo) final. ● m last one. **estar en las últimas** be on one's last legs; (sin dinero) be down to one's last penny. **por ~** finally. **vestido a la última** dressed in the latest fashion

ultra adj ultra, extreme

....
🔲 *see* A-Z of Spanish life and culture

ultraj|ante adj offensive. **~e** m insult, outrage

ultramar m. **de ~** overseas; (productos) foreign. **~inos** mpl groceries. **tienda de ~s** grocer's (shop) (Brit), grocery store (Amer)

ultranza. a ~ (con decisión) decisively; (extremo) out-and-out

ultravioleta adj invar ultraviolet

umbilical adj umbilical

umbral m threshold

---

un , **una** artículo indefinido

❗ The masculine article **un** is also used before feminine nouns which begin with stressed **a** or **ha**, e.g. **un alma piadosa, un hada madrina**

····▸ (en sing) a; (antes de sonido vocálico) an. **un perro** a dog. **una hora** an hour

····▸ **unos, unas** (cantidad incierta) some. **compré ~os libros** I bought some books. (cantidad cierta) **tiene ~os ojos preciosos** she has beautiful eyes. **tiene ~os hijos muy buenos** her children are very good. (en aproximaciones) about. **en ∼as 3 horas** in about 3 hours

▶ For further information see **uno**

un|ánime adj unanimous. **∼animidad** f unanimity

undécimo adj eleventh

ungüento m ointment

únic|amente adv only. **∼o** adj only; (fig, incomparable) unique

unicornio m unicorn

unid|ad f unit; (cualidad) unity. **∼ad de disco** disk drive. **∼o** adj united

unifica|ción f unification. **∼r 7** vt unite, unify

uniform|ar vt standardize. **∼e** adj & m uniform. **∼idad** f uniformity

unilateral adj unilateral

uni|ón f union; (cualidad) unity; (Tec) joint. **∼r** vt join; mix (líquidos). **∼rse** vpr join together; (caminos) converge; (compañías) merge

unísono m unison. **al ∼** in unison

univers|al adj universal. **∼idad** f university. **∼itario** adj university. **∼o** m universe

uno , una

● adjetivo

Note that **uno** becomes **un** before masculine nouns

one. **una peseta** one peseta. **un dólar** one dollar. **ni una persona** not one person, not a single person. **treinta y un años** thirty one years

● pronombre

····▸ one. **∼ es mío** one (of them) is mine. **es la una** it's one o'clock. **se ayudan el ∼ al otro** they help one another, they help each other. **lo que sienten el ∼ por el otro** what they feel for each other

····▸ (fam, alguien) someone. **le**

preguntè a ∼ l asked someone

····▸ **unos, unas** some. **no tenía vasos así es que le prestè ∼s** she didn't have any glasses so l lent her some. **a ∼s les gusta, a otros no** some like it, others don't. **los ∼s a los otros** one another, each other

····▸ (impersonal) you. **∼ no sabe qué decir** you don't know what to say

untar vt grease; (cubrir) spread; (fig, fam, sobornar) bribe

uña f nail; (de animal) claw; (casco) hoof

uranio m uranium

Urano m Uranus

urban|idad f politeness. **∼ismo** m town planning. **∼ización** f development. **∼izar 10** vt develop. **∼o** adj urban

urbe f big city

urdir vt (fig) plot

urg|encia f urgency; (emergencia) emergency. **∼encias** A & E, (Amer) emergency room. **∼ente** adj urgent; (carta) express. **∼ir 14** vi be urgent.

urinario m urinal

urna f urn; (Pol) ballot box

urraca f magpie

URSS abrev (Historia) USSR

Uruguay m. **el ∼** Uruguay

uruguayo adj & m Uruguayan

us|ado adj (con estar) used; (ropa etc) worn; (con ser) secondhand. **∼ar** vt use; (llevar) wear. **∼arse** vpr (LAm) be in fashion. **∼o** m use; (costumbre) custom. **al ∼o de** in the style of

usted pron you. **∼es** you

usual adj usual

usuario adj user

usur|a f usury. **∼ero** m usurer

....

 see A-Z of Spanish life and culture

u

usurpar vt usurp

utensilio m utensil; (herramienta) tool

útero m womb, uterus

útil adj useful. **~es** mpl implements; (equipo) equipment

utili|dad f usefulness. **~dades** fpl (LAm) profits. **~zación** f use, utilization. **~zar** [10] vt use, utilize

utopía f Utopia

uva f grape. **~ pasa** raisin. **mala ~** bad mood

Vv

vaca f cow. **carne de ~** beef

vacaciones fpl holiday(s), vacation(s) (Amer). **de ~** on holiday, on vacation (Amer)

vacante adj vacant. •f vacancy

vaciar [20] vt empty; (ahuecar) hollow out; (en molde) cast

vacila|ción f hesitation. **~nte** adj unsteady; (fig) hesitant. **~r** vi hesitate ([I], bromear) tease; (LAm, divertirse) have fun

vacío adj empty; (frívolo) frivolous. •m empty space; (estado) emptiness; (en física) vacuum; (fig) void

vacuna f vaccine. **~ción** f vaccination. **~r** vt vaccinate

vacuno adj bovine

vad|ear vt ford. **~o** m ford

vaga|bundear vi wander. **~bundo** adj vagrant; (perro) stray. **niño ~** street urchin. •m tramp, vagrant. **~ncia** f vagrancy; (fig) laziness. **~r** [12] vi wander (about)

vagina f vagina

vago adj vague; (holgazán) lazy. •m layabout

vagón m coach, carriage; (de mercancías) wagon. **~ón restaurante** dining-car. **~oneta** f small freight wagon; (Mex, para pasajeros) van

vaho m breath; (vapor) steam. **~s** mpl inhalation

vain|a f sheath; (de semillas) pod. **~illa** f vanilla

vaivén m swinging; (de tren etc) rocking. **~enes** mpl (fig, de suerte) swings

vajilla f dishes, crockery

vale m voucher; (pagaré) IOU. **~dero** adj valid

valenciano adj from Valencia

valentía f bravery, courage

valer [42] vt be worth; (costar) cost; (fig, significar) mean. •vi be worth; (costar) cost; (servir) be of use; (ser valedero) be valid; (estar permitido) be allowed. **~ la pena** be worthwhile, be worth it. **¿cuánto vale?** how much is it? **no ~ para nada** be useless. **eso no me vale** (Mex, fam) I don't give a damn about that. **¡vale!** all right!, OK! [I]

valeroso adj courageous

valgo vb véase **VALER**

valía f worth

validez f validity. **dar ~ a** validate

válido adj valid

valiente adj brave; (en sentido irónico) fine. •m brave person

valija f suitcase. **~ diplomática** diplomatic bag

valioso adj valuable

valla f fence; (en atletismo) hurdle

valle m valley

val|or m value, worth; (coraje) courage. **objetos** mpl **de ~or** valuables. **sin ~or** worthless. **~ores** mpl securities. **~oración** f valuation. **~orar** vt value

vals m invar waltz

válvula f valve

vampiro m vampire

vanagloriarse vpr boast

vandalismo m vandalism

vándalo m & f vandal

vanguardia f vanguard. **de ~** (en arte, música etc) avant-garde

van|idad f vanity. **~idoso** adj vain. **~o** adj vain; (inútil) futile; (palabras) empty. **en ~o** in vain

vapor m steam, vapour; (Naut) steamer. **al ~** (Culin) steamed. **~izador** m vaporizer. **~izar** ⑩ vaporize

vaquer|o m cowherd, cowboy. **~os** mpl jeans

vara f stick; (de autoridad) staff (medida) yard

varar vi run aground

varia|ble adj & f variable. **~ción** f variation. **~do** adj varied. **~nte** f variant; (Auto) by-pass. **~ntes** fpl hors d'oeuvres. **~r** ⑳ vt change; (dar variedad a) vary. ● vi vary; (cambiar) change

varicela f chickenpox

variedad f variety

varilla f stick; (de metal) rod

varios adj several

varita f wand

variz f (pl **varices**, (LAm) **várices**) varicose vein

var|ón adj male. ● m man; (niño) boy. **~onil** adj manly

vasco adj & m Basque

vaselina f Vaseline (P), petroleum jelly

vasija f vessel, pot

vaso m glass; (en anatomía) vessel

vástago m shoot; (descendiente) descendant

vasto adj vast

vaticin|ar vt forecast. **~io** m prediction, forecast

vatio m watt

vaya vb véase IR

Vd. abrev (**Usted**) you

vecin|al adj local. **~dad** f neighbourhood; (vecinos) residents; (Mex, edificio) tenement house. **~dario** m neighbourhood; (vecinos) residents. **~o** adj neighbouring. ● m neighbour; (de barrio, edificio) resident

ve|da f close season. **~do** m reserve. **~do de caza** game reserve. **~r** vt prohibit

vega f fertile plain

vegeta|ción f vegetation. **~l** adj & m plant, vegetable. **~r** vi grow; (persona) vegetate. **~riano** adj & m vegetarian

vehemente adj vehement

vehículo m vehicle

veinte adj & m twenty

veinti|cinco adj & m twenty-five. **~cuatro** adj & m twenty-four. **~dós** adj & m twenty-two. **~nueve** adj & m twenty-nine. **~ocho** adj & m twenty-eight. **~séis** adj & m twenty-six. **~siete** adj & m twenty-seven. **~trés** adj & m twenty-three. **~uno** adj & m (delante de nombre masculino **veintiún**) twenty-one

vejación f humiliation

vejar vt ill-treat

veje|storio m old crock; (LAm, cosa) old relic. **~z** f old age

vejiga f bladder

vela f (Naut) sail; (de cera) candle; (vigilia) vigil. **pasar la noche en ~** have a sleepless night

velada f evening

vela|do adj veiled; (Foto) exposed. **~r** vt watch over; hold a wake

V

over (difunto); (encubrir) veil; (Foto) expose. •vi stay awake. **~r por** look after. **~rse** vpr (Foto) get exposed

velero m sailing-ship

veleta f weather vane

vell|o m hair; (pelusa) down. **~ón** m fleece

velo m veil

veloc|idad f speed; (Auto, Mec) gear. **a toda ~idad** at full speed. **~ímetro** m speedometer. **~ista** m & f sprinter

velódromo m cycle-track

veloz adj fast, quick

vena f vein; (en madera) grain. **estar de/en ~** be in the mood

venado m deer; (Culin) venison

vencedor adj winning. •m winner

venc|er 🖥 vt defeat; (superar) overcome. •vi win; (pasaporte) expire. **~erse** vpr collapse; (LAm, pasaporte) expire. **~ido** adj beaten; (pasaporte) expired; (Com, atrasado) in arrears. **darse por ~ido** give up. **~imiento** m due date; (de pasaporte) expiry date

venda f bandage. **~je** m dressing. **~r** vt bandage

vendaval m gale

vende|dor adj selling. •m seller; (en tienda) salesperson. **~dor ambulante** pedlar. **~r** vt sell. **se ~** for sale. **~rse** vpr (persona) sell out

vendimia f grape harvest

veneciano adj Venetian

veneno m poison; (malevolencia) venom. **~so** adj poisonous

venera|ble adj venerable. **~ción** f reverence. **~r** vt revere

venéreo adj venereal

venezolano adj & m Venezuelan

Venezuela f Venezuela

venga|nza f revenge. **~r** 🖩 vt avenge. **~rse** vpr take revenge

(**de, por**) for) (**en** on). **~tivo** adj vindictive

vengo vb véase **VENIR**

venia f (permiso) permission. **~l** adj venial

veni|da f arrival; (vuelta) return. **~dero** adj coming. **~r** 🖩 vi come. **~r bien** suit. **la semana que viene** next week. **¡venga!** come on!

venta f sale; (posada) inn. **en ~** for sale

ventaj|a f advantage. **~oso** adj advantageous

ventan|a f (inc informática) window; (de la nariz) nostril. **~illa** f window

ventarrón m 🖪 strong wind

ventila|ción f ventilation. **~dor** m fan. **~r** vt air

vent|isca f blizzard. **~olera** f gust of wind. **~osa** f sucker. **~osidad** f wind, flatulence. **~oso** adj windy

ventrílocuo m ventriloquist

ventur|a f happiness; (suerte) luck. **a la ~a** with no fixed plan. **echar la buena ~a a uno** tell s.o.'s fortune. **por ~a** fortunately; (acaso) perhaps. **~oso** adj happy, lucky

Venus m Venus

ver 🖪 vt see; watch (televisión). •vi see. **a mi modo de ~** in my view. **a ~** let's see. **dejarse ~** show. **no lo puedo ~** I can't stand him. **no tener nada que ~ con** have nothing to do with. **vamos a ~** let's see. **ya lo veo** that's obvious. **ya ~emos** we'll see. **~se** vpr see o.s.; (encontrarse) find o.s.; (dos personas) meet; (LAm, parecer) look

veran|eante m & f holidaymaker, vacationer (Amer). **~ear** vi spend one's summer holiday. **~eo** m. **ir de ~eo** spend one's summer holiday. **lugar** m **de ~eo** summer resort. **~iego** adj summer. **~o** m summer

V

vera|s: de ~ really; (verdadero) real. **~z** adj truthful

verbal adj verbal

verbena f (fiesta) fair; (baile) dance

verbo m verb. **~so** adj verbose

verdad f truth. **¿~?** isn't it?, aren't they?, won't it? etc. **a decir ~** to tell the truth. **de ~** really. **~eramente** adv really. **~ero** adj true; (fig) real

verd|e adj green; (fruta) unripe; (chiste) dirty. • m green; (hierba) grass. **~or** m greenness

verdugo m executioner; (fig) tyrant

verdu|lería f greengrocer's (shop). **~lero** m greengrocer

vereda f path; (LAm, acera) pavement (Brit), sidewalk (Amer)

veredicto m verdict

verg|onzoso adj shameful; (timido) shy. **~üenza** f shame; (bochorno) embarrassment. **¡es una ~üenza!** it's a disgrace! **me da ~üenza** I'm ashamed/embarrassed. **tener ~üenza** be ashamed/embarrassed

verídico adj true

verifica|ción f verification. **~r** 7 vt check. **~rse** vpr take place; (resultar verdad) come true

verja f (cerca) railings; (puerta) iron gate

vermú m, **vermut** m vermouth

verosímil adj likely; (relato) credible

verruga f wart

versa|do adj versed. **~r** vi. **~ sobre** deal with

versátil adj versatile; (fig) fickle

versión f version; (traducción) translation

verso m verse; (poema) poem

vértebra f vertebra

verte|dero m dump; (desagüe) drain. **~r** 1 vt pour; (derramar) spill • vi flow

vertical adj & f vertical

vértice f vertex

vertiente f slope

vertiginoso adj dizzy

vértigo m (Med) vertigo. **dar ~** make dizzy

vesícula f vesicle. **~ biliar** gall bladder

vespertino adj evening

vestíbulo m hall; (de hotel, teatro) foyer

vestido m dress

vestigio m trace. **~s** mpl remains

vest|imenta f clothes. **~ir** 5 vt (llevar) wear; dress (niño etc). • vi dress. **~ir de** wear. **~irse** vpr get dressed. **~irse de** wear; (disfrazarse) dress up as. **~uario** m wardrobe; (en gimnasio etc) changing room (Brit), locker room (Amer)

vetar vt veto

veterano adj veteran

veterinari|a f veterinary science. **~o** adj veterinary. • m vet 🄸, veterinary surgeon (Brit), veterinarian (Amer)

veto m veto

vez f time; (turno) turn. **a la ~** at the same time. **alguna ~** sometimes; (en preguntas) ever. **algunas veces** sometimes. **a su ~** in turn. **a veces** sometimes. **cada ~** each time. **~ más** more and more. **de una ~** in one go. **de una ~ para siempre** once and for all. **de ~ en cuando** from time to time. **dos veces** twice. **en ~ de** instead of. **érase una ~, había una ~** once upon a time there was. **otra ~** again. **pocas veces, rara ~** seldom. **una ~ (que)** once

vía f road; (Rail) line; (en anatomía) tract; (fig) way. **~ férrea** railway (Brit), railroad (Amer). **~ rápida** fast lane. **estar en ~s de** be in the process of. • prep vía. **~ aérea** by air. **~ de comunicación** means of communication.

V

viab|ilidad f viability. ~**le** adj
viable

viaducto m viaduct

viaj|ante m & f commercial
traveller. ~**ar** vi travel. ~**e** m
journey; (corto) trip. ~**e de
novios** honeymoon. **¡buen ~e!**
have a good journey!. **estar de
~e** be away. **salir de ~e** go on a
trip. ~**ero** m traveller; (pasajero)
passenger

víbora f viper

vibra|ción f vibration. ~**nte** adj
vibrant. ~**r** vt/i vibrate

vicario m vicar

viceversa adv vice versa

vici|ado adj (texto) corrupt; (aire)
stale. ~**ar** vt corrupt; (estropear)
spoil. ~**o** m vice; (mala costumbre)
bad habit. ~**oso** adj dissolute;
(círculo) vicious

víctima f victim; (de un accidente)
casualty

victori|a f victory. ~**oso** adj
victorious

vid f vine

vida f life; (duración) lifetime. **¡~
mía!** my darling! **de por ~** for
life. **en mi ~** never (in my life).
estar con ~ be still alive

vídeo m, (LAm) **video** m video;
(cinta) videotape; (aparato) video
recorder

videojuego m video game

vidri|era f stained glass window;
(puerta) glass door; (LAm, escaparate)
shop window. ~**ería** f glass works.
~**ero** m glazier. ~**o** m glass; (LAm,
en ventana) window pane. **limpiar
los ~os** clean the windows.
~**oso** adj glassy

vieira f scallop

viejo adj old. ● m old person

viene vb véase VENIR

viento m wind. **hacer ~** be windy

vientre m stomach; (cavidad)
abdomen; (matriz) womb; (intestino)
bowels; (de vasija etc) belly

viernes m invar Friday. **V~ Santo**
Good Friday

viga f beam; (de metal) girder

vigen|cia f validity. ~**te** adj valid;
(ley) in force. **entrar en ~cia**
come into force

vigésimo adj twentieth

vigía f watch-tower. ● m & f (persona)
lookout

vigil|ancia f vigilance. ~**ante** adj
vigilant. ● m & f security guard;
(nocturno) watchman. ~**ar** vt keep
an eye on. ● vi be vigilant; (vigía)
keep watch. ~**ia** f vigil; (Relig)
fasting

vigor m vigour; (vigencia) force.
entrar en ~ come into force.
~**oso** adj vigorous

vil adj vile. ~**eza** f vileness; (acción)
vile deed

villa f (casa) villa; (Historia) town. **la
V~** Madrid

villancico m (Christmas) carol

villano adj villanous; (Historia)
peasant

vilo: **en ~** in the air

vinagre m vinegar. ~**ra** f vinegar
bottle. ~**ras** fpl cruet. ~**ta** f
vinaigrette

vincular vt bind

vínculo m tie, bond

vindicar ⁊ vt (rehabilitar) vindicate

vine vb véase VENIR

vinicult|or m wine-grower. ~**ura** f
wine growing

vino m wine. ~ **de la casa** house
wine. ~ **de mesa** table wine. ~
tinto red wine

viñ|a f vineyard. ~**atero** m (LAm)
wine-grower. ~**edo** m vineyard

viola f viola

viola|ción f violation; (de una mujer)
rape. ~**r** vt violate; break (ley);
rape (mujer)

violen|cia f violence; (fuerza) force.

~**tarse** vpr get embarrassed. ~**to** adj violent; (fig) awkward

violeta adj invar & f violet

viol|ín m violin. ●m & f (músico) violinist. ~**inista** m & f violinist. ~**ón** m double bass. ~**onc(h)elista** m & f cellist. ~**onc(h)elo** m cello

vira|je m turn. ~**r** vt turn. ●vi turn; (fig) change direction. ~**r bruscamente** swerve

virg|en adj. **ser** ~**en** be a virgin. ●f virgin. ~**inal** adj virginal. ~**inidad** f virginity

Virgo m Virgo

viril adj virile. ~**idad** f virility

virtu|al adj virtual. ~**d** f virtue; (capacidad) power. **en** ~ **de** by virtue of. ~**oso** adj virtuous. ●m virtuoso

viruela f smallpox

virulento adj virulent

virus m invar virus

visa f (LAm) visa. ~**do** m visa. ~**r** vt endorse

vísceras fpl entrails

viscoso adj viscous

visera f visor; (de gorra) peak

visib|ilidad f visibility. ~**le** adj visible

visillo m (cortina) net curtain

visi|ón f vision; (vista) sight. ~**onario** adj & m visionary

visita f visit; (visitante) visitor; (invitado) guest; (Internet) hit. ~**nte** m & f visitor. ~**r** vt visit

vislumbrar vt glimpse

viso m sheen; (aspecto) appearance

visón m mink

visor m viewfinder

víspera f day before, eve

vista f sight, vision; (aspecto, mirada) look; (panorama) view. **apartar la** ~ look away. **a primera** ~, **a simple** ~ at first sight. **con** ~**s a**

with a view to. **en** ~ **de** in view of. **estar a la** ~ be obvious. **hacer la** ~ **gorda** turn a blind eye. **perder la** ~ lose one's sight. **tener a la** ~ have in front of one. **volver la** ~ **atrás** look back. ~**zo** m glance. **dar/echar un** ~**zo a** glance at

visto adj seen; (poco original) common (considerado) considered. ~ **que** since. **bien** ~ acceptable. **está** ~ **que** it's obvious that. **mal** ~ unacceptable. **por lo** ~ apparently. ●vb véase **VESTIR.** ~ **bueno** m approval. ~**so** adj colourful, bright

visual adj visual. **campo** ~ field of vision

vital adj vital. ~**icio** adj life; (cargo) held for life. ~**idad** f vitality

vitamina f vitamin

viticult|or m wine-grower. ~**ura** f wine growing

vitorear vt cheer

vítreo adj vitreous

vitrina f showcase; (en casa) glass cabinet; (LAm, escaparate) shop window

viud|a f widow. ~**ez** f widowhood. ~**o** adj widowed. ●m widower

viva m cheer. ~**cidad** f liveliness. ~**mente** adv vividly. ~**z** adj lively

víveres mpl supplies

vivero m nursery; (de peces) hatchery; (de moluscos) bed

viveza f vividness; (de inteligencia) sharpness; (de carácter) liveliness

vívido adj vivid

vividor m pleasure seeker

vivienda f housing; (casa) house; (piso) flat (Brit), apartment (esp Amer). **sin** ~ homeless

viviente adj living

vivificar 7 vt (animar) enliven

vivir vt live through. ●vi live; (estar vivo) be alive. **¡viva!** hurray! **¡viva**

V

el rey! long live the king! •m life. ~ **de** live on. **de mal** ~ dissolute

vivisección f vivisection

vivo adj alive; (viviente) living; (color) bright; (listo) clever; (fig) lively. •m sharp operator

vocab|lo m word. ~**ulario** m vocabulary

vocación f vocation

vocal adj vocal. •f vowel. •m & f member. ~**ista** m & f vocalist

voce|ar vt call (mercancías); (fig) proclaim; (Mex) page (persona). •vi shout. ~**río** m shouting. ~**ro** (LAm) spokesperson

vociferar vi shout

vola|dor adj flying. •m rocket. ~**ndas. en** ~**ndas** in the air. ~**nte** adj flying. •m (Auto) steering-wheel; (nota) note; (rehilete) shuttlecock. ~**r 2** vt blow up. •vi fly; (fam, desaparecer) disappear

volátil adj volatile

volcán m volcano. ~**ico** adj volcanic

volcar 2 & 7 vt knock over; (vaciar) empty out; turn over (molde). •vi overturn. ~**se** vpr fall over; (vehículo) overturn; (fig) do one's utmost. ~**se en** throw o.s. into

vóleibol m, (Mex) **volibol** m volleyball

voltaje m voltage

volte|ar vt turn over; (en el aire) toss; ring (campanas); (LAm) turn over (colchón etc); (LAm) turn around; (carro) overturn. ~**arse** vpr (LAm) turn around; (carro) overturn. ~**reta** f somersault

voltio m volt

voluble adj (fig) fickle

volum|en m volume. ~**inoso** adj voluminous

voluntad f will; (fuerza de voluntad) willpower; (deseo) wish; (intención) intention. **buena** ~ goodwill. **mala** ~ ill will

voluntario adj voluntary. •m volunteer

voluptuoso adj voluptuous

volver 2 (pp **vuelto**) vt turn; (de arriba a abajo) turn over; (devolver) restore. •vi return; (fig) revert. ~ **a hacer algo** do sth again. ~ **en sí** come round. ~**se** vpr turn round; (hacerse) become

vomit|ar vt bring up. •vi be sick, vomit. ~**ivo** adj disgusting

vómito m vomit; (acción) vomiting

voraz adj voracious

vos pron (LAm) you. ~**otros** pron you; (reflexivo) yourselves

vot|ación f voting; (voto) vote. ~**ante** m & f voter. ~**ar** vt vote for. •vi vote (**por** for). ~**o** m vote; (Relig) vow

voy vb véase **IR**

voz f voice; (rumor) rumour; (palabra) word. ~ **pública** public opinion. **a media** ~ softly. **a una** ~ unanimously. **dar voces** shout. **en** ~ **alta** loudly

vuelco m upset. **el corazón me dio un** ~ my heart missed a beat

vuelo m flight; (acción) flying; (de ropa) flare. **al** ~ in flight; (fig) in passing

vuelta f turn; (curva) bend; (paseo) walk; (revolución) revolution; (regreso) return; (dinero) change. **a la** ~ on one's return. **a la** ~ **de la esquina** round the corner. **dar la** ~ **al mundo** go round the world. **dar una** ~ go for a walk. **estar de** ~ be back

vuelvo vb véase **VOLVER**

vuestro adj your. •pron yours. **un amigo** ~ a friend of yours

vulg|ar adj vulgar; (persona) common. ~**aridad** f vulgarity. ~**arizar 10** vt popularize. ~**o** m common people

vulnerable adj vulnerable

Ww

wáter /'(g)water/ m toilet
Web m /'(g)web/. **el ~** the Web
whisky /'(g)wiski/ m whisky

Xx

xenofobia f xenophobia
xilófono m xylophone

Yy

y conj and
ya adv already; (ahora) now; (con negativos) any more; (para afirmar) yes, sure; (en seguida) immediately; (pronto) soon. **~ mismo** (LAm) right away. ●int of course! **~ no** no longer. **~ que** since. **¡~, ~!** oh sure!
yacaré m (LAm) alligator
yac|er 🔢 vi lie. **~imiento** m deposit; (de petróleo) oilfield
yanqui m & f American, Yank(ee)
yate m yacht
yegua f mare
yelmo m helmet
yema f (en botánica) bud; (de huevo) yolk; (golosina) sweet. **~ del dedo** fingertip
yerba f (LAm) grass; (Med) herb
yergo vb véase ERGUIR

yermo adj uninhabited; (no cultivable) barren. ●m wasteland
yerno m son-in-law
yerro m mistake. ●vb véase ERRAR
yeso m plaster; (mineral) gypsum
yo pron I. **~ mismo** myself. **¿quién, ~?** who, me? **soy ~** it's me
yodo m iodine
yoga m yoga
yogur m yog(h)urt
yuca f yucca
yugo m yoke
Yugoslavia f Yugoslavia
yugoslavo adj & m Yugoslav
yunque m anvil
yunta f yoke

Zz

zafarrancho m (confusión) mess; (riña) quarrel

zafarse vpr escape; get out of (obligación etc); (Mex, dislocarse) dislocate

zafiro m sapphire

zaga f rear; (en deportes) defence. **a la ~** behind

zaguán m hall

zaherir 4 vt hurt

zahorí m dowser

zaino adj (caballo) chestnut; (vaca) black

zalamer|ía f flattery. **~o** adj flattering. ● m flatterer

zamarra f (piel) sheepskin; (prenda) sheepskin jacket

zamarrear vt shake

zamba f South American dance

zambulli|da f dive; (baño) dip. **~rse** vpr dive

zamparse vpr gobble up

zanahoria f carrot

zancad|a f stride. **~illa** f trip. **hacer una ~illa a uno** trip s.o. up

zanc|o m stilt. **~udo** adj long-legged; (ave) wading. ● m (LAm) mosquito

zanganear vi idle

zángano m drone. ● m & f (persona) idler

zangolotear vt shake. ● vi rattle; (persona) fidget

zanja f ditch; (para tuberías etc) trench. **~r** vt (fig) settle

zapat|ear vi tap with one's feet.

....

~ería f shoe shop; (arte) shoemaking. **~ero** m shoemaker; (el que remienda zapatos) cobbler. **~illa** f slipper; (de deportes) trainer. **~illa de ballet** ballet shoe. **~o** m shoe

zarand|a f sieve. **~ear** vt (sacudir) shake

zarcillo m earring

zarpa f paw

zarpar vi set sail, weigh anchor

zarza f bramble. **~mora** f blackberry

zarzuela f Spanish operetta

zigzag m zigzag. **~uear** vi zigzag

zinc m zinc

zócalo m skirting-board; (pedestal) plinth; (Mex, plaza) main square

zodiaco m, **zodíaco** m zodiac

zona f zone; (área) area

zoo m zoo. **~logía** f zoology. **~lógico** adj zoological

zoólogo m zoologist

zopenco adj stupid. ● m idiot

zoquete m blockhead

zorr|a f vixen **~illo** m (LAm) skunk. **~o** m fox

zorzal m thrush

zozobra f (fig) anxiety. **~r** vi founder

zueco m clog

zumb|ar vt 1 give (golpe etc). ● vi buzz. **~ido** m buzzing

zumo m juice

zurci|do m darning. **~r** 9 vt darn

zurdo adj left-handed; (mano) left

zurrar vt (fig, fam, dar golpes) beat (up)

zutano m so-and-so

Z 🔳 *see* A-Z of Spanish life and culture

Test yourself with word games

This section contains a number of word games which will help you to use your dictionary more effectively and to build up your knowledge of Spanish vocabulary and usage in a fun and entertaining way. You will find answers to all puzzles and games at the end of the section.

1 X files

A freak power cut in the office has caused all the computers to go down. When they are re-booted, all the words on the screen have become mysteriously jumbled. Use the English to Spanish side of the dictionary to help you decipher these Spanish names of everyday office and computer equipment.

ZIPLÁ

ÓCNAJ

AERODONRD

PRACATE

ODCSI

MOAG

GLOBAFÍRO

TAPALLAN

2 Odd meaning Out

Watch out: one word can have different meanings. In the following exercise, only two of the suggested translations are correct. Use the dictionary to spot the odd one out, then find the correct Spanish translation for it.

vela — sail, veil, candle

boot, jar, boat — bote

talón — cheque, heel, talon

smooth, suave, soft — suave

muelle — wharf, mussel, jetty

buffet, writing desk, lawyer's office — bufete

3 Mystery Word

The following crossword is composed entirely of musical instruments.
Put the Spanish translation of the pictures of instruments in the right
boxes to form the name of a Spanish composer in the vertical column.

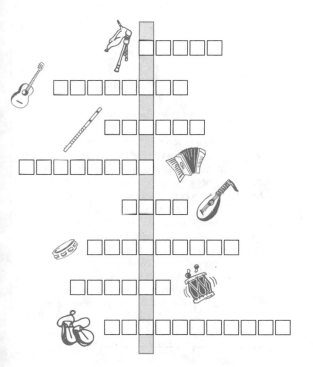

The composer is _ .

4 Doña Paquita's shooting stars

Doña Paquita is very good at predicting the future, but she is not very good at using the subjunctive. Help her to replace the verbs between brackets with the correct part of the present subjunctive.

ARIES: Estás en el apogeo de tu vida, tanto en tu carrera profesional como en el ámbito personal. Pero tienes que evitar que todo (echarse) a perder. Con la influencia maléfica de Saturno situada actualmente en tu astro, siempre es posible que (suceder) algo negativo. Además, los aries son impacientes por naturaleza y quieren que las cosas (hacerse) lo antes posible. Por lo tanto te aconsejo que no (precipitarse) a la hora de tomar decisiones importantes. Aunque tu situación económica te (parecer) segura, no (contar) con el apoyo de los demás. Sin embargo, con el aspecto favorable de Venus es muy posible que dentro de poco (conocer) a tu pareja ideal. ¡No (dejar) de reconocerlo! ¡Suerte!

5 Write it right

A mother and daughter are getting a little bit annoyed with each other.
In the fraught atmosphere, many of the Spanish accents and some
punctuation marks have been left out of the dialogue. You have a box
full of characters to be substituted or added in the right place in the
text. They must all be used up.

— ¡Raquel! ¿Donde estás?

— Aquí, mama. ¿Que pasa? Por que me gritas así?

— Porque tu no me haces caso. Mira, ¿cuando vas a ordenar tu
habitación?

— Cuando tenga tiempo. Quizá manana. No me des la lata ahora!

— Eso me dices todos los días, pero jamas lo haces. No me ayudas
nada en la casa y encima me contestas mal. Eres una sinverguenza
y pienso decirselo a tu padre cuando vuelva.

— Perdon, mama. Lo siento. Me pasé, lo se.

6 Crowded suitcase

You are at the airport on your way to visit your Welsh cousins in Patagonia when you are told that your suitcase is overweight. Luckily, you had packed a number of things you did not need because you had forgotten that it was wintertime in the southern hemisphere. Decide which 5 items to jettison from your luggage.

gafas de sol   calcetines de lana   **alpargatas**   *camisón*

esterilla   cepillo de dientes   camiseta

crema bronceadora   camisa de manga corta   *cinturón*

bañador   abrigo   **unas revistas**

pantalón corto   bufanda

7 Crossword

Across

1. we inhabit
7. dative of 'them'
9. scarcely
10. the letter 'n' as spoken (or written)
11. evade – present subjunctive
    (1st or 3rd person singular)
13. reindeer, in reverse
14. swim! – polite imperative (singular)
15. nor
16. clear
18. religious sister
20. go! – familiar imperative (plural)
21. I heard
22. woman's name
23. do! – familiar imperative (singular)
24. sarcasm

Down

2. mountaineers
3. to be unaware of
4. absence
5. wave (figurative sense)
6. paths
8. present subjunctive of 'ser'
    (1st or 3rd person singular)
12. you (singular) will be worth
13. half of the number eleven
17. they were hearing
19. ounce
21. plural of 'te'

8 Liar, liar

Miguel is telling his parents what he did on his day off while his younger brother Félix was meant to be at school, but he makes a blunder. Once the truth is out, as a punishment they both have to write out the story with the correct plural endings and pronouns. Use the verb tables at the back of the dictionary to help you make the necessary alterations to the text.

Iba andando a la playa cuando de repente me encontré con Paco. Me acompañó hasta la tienda de la esquina donde dijo:

—Mira, ¿quieres que te preste mi bicicleta para que llegues más rápido?

Estaba muy cansado y no quería seguir caminando así que acepté con mucho gusto y me fui contentísimo por el camino. Me costó un poco controlar la bici porque era tan grande y casi me caigo un par de veces. La gente me miraba como si estuviera loco y varias personas me gritaban "¡Bravo!"

Cuando estaba ya en la playa se me salieron los pies de los pedales y perdí el control. Bajaba a toda velocidad hacia el agua, de repente frené y—¡plaf!— me caí al agua.

Más tarde, me dio vergüenza devolverle la bicicleta a Paco y naturalmente se echó a reír:

—Pero, ¿qué pasó?—me dijo—¿te diste un buen baño? Le contesté:

—Fue culpa de él—y dije dándome la vuelta hacia atrás—¡Nunca más voy a montar en un tándem contigo, Félix!

9 Hidden words—false friends

Hidden in the grid are nine Spanish words. First look at the list of false friends below—look up the translation of the Spanish words listed, then using your own knowledge and the dictionary, find the translations of the English to search for in the grid.

O	S	É	T	R	O	C	S	E	D
H	I	G	A	E	C	Í	J	A	O
A	D	O	R	A	R	H	D	E	L
F	O	B	I	N	S	A	H	O	M
N	F	T	É	P	N	L	E	P	A
Ú	R	E	L	A	V	E	Ú	O	S
T	E	R	P	T	O	T	I	T	É
A	C	M	D	Z	A	A	S	I	T
M	E	A	C	R	X	P	O	N	U
S	R	O	J	O	N	Í	A	E	L

English   Spanish

pie	pie	....
dote	dote	....
red	red	....
tuna	atún	....
lid	lid	....
fin	fin	....
rude	rudo	....
mole	mole	....
tea	tea	....

10 Word Families

It's good to build up word families to increase your vocabulary, but it's important to know the part of speech of each word and how it can fit into a sentence. Pick the right word from each family to go in the space. Everything you need to know for this exercise is in the dictionary.

le falta	preparado
	preparación
	preparó
tuvieron que	esconder
	escondrijo
	esconderse
una mujer ... en años	entrada
	entró
	entrante
no se hace así en la ...	actualmente
	actualidad
	actualización
y por ... agregarle el agua	ultimar
	últimamente
	último
la industria ... de esa región	floreciente
	florista
	florida
su timidez me	desconcierto
	desconcertante
	deconcierta

11 My life's a mess

Pilar Jiménez has a busy schedule but she is a creature of habit and likes to stick to her daily routine. The order of her normal workday has been muddled up in the sentences below. Link up the matching halves of each sentence in the two columns and then try to put the complete sentences in sequence. Be careful, some can link up with more than one of the other column, so you'll have to do them all before you can be sure which go together best.

sólo lee el periódico	para comer
llega a casa	lee la correspondencia
nunca toma café durante	antes de las nueve y media
normalmente saca al perro	muy cansada
le gusta	durante el viaje de vuelta
primero	antes de acostarse
suele salir a mediodía	una reunión
prefiere ducharse antes	por la mañana
siempre entra al trabajo	dar una vuelta antes de volver a la oficina
insiste en tener las reuniones	de cenar

12 Recipe of the Week

The printers have left out some important words from this recipe.
Can you supply the missing words from the jumble below?

COCINA: Receta de la semana

Limpiar y lavar los .... y cortarlos en rodajas finas.
Calentar el ...... en una sartén de hierro y freír la ..... picada,
los puerros y dos dientes de .... . Agregar el vaso de .... y
dejar cocer a .... lento durante 10 minutos. Sazonar con ....,
.... y ...... picado.

En otra sartén aparte, saltear los trocitos de ..... en el resto
del aceite de oliva hasta que empiecen a dorarse. Regar
con dos cucharadas de ..... y dejar cocer unos minutos más.
Incorporar las .... y la ......

Distribuir los puerros uniformemente en platos calientes y
colocar el pollo salteado encima. Salar al gusto. Servir
acompañado de una guarnición de ...... al vapor.

puerros	aceite de oliva	**fuego**
cebolla	ajo	vino blanco	**sal**
pimienta	**pollo**	**perejil**	jerez
aceitunas	**nata**	patatas	

13 Link-up

The Spanish nouns on the left-hand side are all made up of two
separate words but they have been split apart. Try to link up the two
halves of each compound, then do the same for the English
compounds in the right-hand columns. Now you can match up the
Spanish compounds with their English translations.

espanta	corchos	pencil	sport
sujeta	pipas	birth	cleaner
porta	césped	paper	screw
agua	aviones	flame	day
saca	años	spoil	crow
lanza	puntas	lawn	sharpener
limpia	fiestas	aircraft	thrower
corta	papeles	pipe	clip
cumple	llamas	scare	carrier
saca	pájaros	cork	mower

Answers

1

lápiz	disco
cajón	goma
ordenador	bolígrafo
carpeta	pantalla

2

veil – velo	suave – zalamero
boot – bota	mussel – mejillón
talon – garra	buffet – bufé

3

gaita	laúd
guitarra	pandereta
flauta	tambor
acordeón	castañuelas

The composer's name is Granados (1867–1916)

4

se eche	parezca
suceda	cuentes
se hagan	conozcas
te precipites	dejes

5

— ¡Raquel! ¿Dónde estás?
—Aquí, mamá. ¿Qué pasa? ¿Por qué me gritas así?
—Porque tú no me haces caso. Mira, ¿cuándo vas a ordenar tu habitación?
—Cuando tenga tiempo. Quizá mañana. ¡No me des la lata ahora!
—Eso me dices todos los días, pero jamás lo haces. No me ayudas nada en la casa y encima me contestas mal. Eres una sinvergüenza y pienso decírselo a tu padre cuando vuelva.
—Perdón, mamá. Lo siento. Me pasé, lo sé.

6

alpargatas
esterilla
crema bronceadora
camisa de manga corta
pantalón corto

7

Across	Down
1 habitamos	2 alpinistas
7 les	3 ignorar
9 apenas	4 ausencia
10 ene	5 oleada
11 evada	6 senderos
13 oner (= reno)	8 sea
14 nade	12 valdrás
15 n	13 on (from ('once')
16 claro	17 oían
18 sor	19 onza
20 id	21 os
21 oí	
22 Marisa	
23 haz	
24 sarcasmo	

8

There are two boys going to the beach, the narrator and Félix. The bike is a tandem.

Íbamos   nos encontramos   Nos acompaño   nos dijo

—Mirad, ¿queréis que os preste...?

Estábamos muy cansados y no queríamos   aceptamos

y nos fuimos contentísimos   Nos costó

casi nos caemos   nos miraba

como si estuviéramos locos   nos gritaban

estábamos   se nos salieron   perdimos el control

Bajábamos   frenamos   Nos dio vergüenza

¿os disteis un buen baño?

Note that the second person plural verb endings given here are all the 'vosotros' form used in Spain. In Latin America this would be replaced by the 'ustedes' form, as follows:

—Miren, ¿quieren que les preste ...?

¿se dieron un buen baño?

9

foot	empanada	
dowry	adorar	
	(= dote on)	
net	rojo	
torch	té	
fight	tapa	
end	aleta	
rough	descortés	
prickly pear	atún	
mass, bulk	topo	

10

preparación
esconderse
entrada
actualidad
último
floreciente
desconcierta

11

siempre entra al trabajo antes de las nueve y media
primero lee la correspondencia
insiste en tener las reuniones por la mañana
nunca toma café durante una reunión
suele salir a mediodía para comer
le gusta dar una vuelta antes de volver a la oficina
sólo lee el periódico durante el viaje de vuelta
llega a casa muy cansada
prefiere ducharse antes de cenar
normalmente saca al perro antes de acostarse

12

Limpiar y lavar los PUERROS y cortarlos en rodajas finas.
Calentar el ACEITE DE OLIVA en una sartén de hierro y freír la CEBOLLA picada, los puerros y dos dientes de AJO. Agregar el vaso de VINO BLANCO y dejar cocer a FUEGO lento durante 10 minutos. Sazonar con SAL, PIMIENTA y PEREJIL picado.

En otra sartén aparte, saltear los trocitos de POLLO en el resto del aceite de oliva hasta que empiecen a dorarse. Regar con dos cucharadas de JEREZ y dejar cocer unos minutos más. Incorporar las ACEITUNAS y la NATA.

Distribuir los puerros uniformemente en platos calientes y colocar el pollo salteado encima. Salar al gusto. Servir acompañado de una guarnición de PATATAS al vapor.

13

espantapájaros	=	scarecrow
sujetapapeles	=	paper clip
portaaviones	=	aircraft carrier
aguafiestas	=	spoilsport
sacacorchos	=	corkscrew
lanzallamas	=	flame thrower
cumpleaños	=	birthday
limpiapipas	=	pipe cleaner
cortacésped	=	lawn-mower
sacapuntas	=	pencil sharpener

Calendar of traditions, festivals, and holidays in Spanish-speaking countries

January
1 8 15 22 29
2 9 16 23 30
3 10 17 24 31
4 11 18 25
5 12 19 26
6 13 **20** 27
7 14 21 28

February
1 8 15 22
2 9 16 23
3 10 17 24
4 11 18 25
5 12 19 **26**
6 13 20 27
7 14 **21** 28

March
1 8 15 22 29
2 9 16 23 30
3 10 17 24 31
4 11 18 25
5 12 19 26
6 13 20 27
7 14 21 28

April
1 8 15 22 29
2 9 16 **23** 30
3 10 17 24 31
4 11 18 25
5 12 19 26
6 13 20 27
7 **14** 21 28

May
1 8 15 22 29
2 9 16 23 30
3 10 17 24 31
4 11 18 **25**
5 12 19 26
6 13 20 27
7 14 21 28

June
1 8 15 22 29
2 9 16 23 30
3 10 17 **24**
4 11 18 25
5 12 19 26
6 13 **20** 27
7 14 21 28

July
1 8 15 22 29
2 **9** 16 23 30
3 10 17 24 31
4 11 18 **25**
5 12 19 26
6 13 20 27
7 14 21 **28**

August
1 8 15 22 29
2 9 16 23 30
3 **10** **17** 24 31
4 11 18 **25**
5 12 19 26
6 13 20 27
7 14 21 28

September
1 8 **15** 22 29
2 9 16 23 30
3 10 17 24
4 **11** **18** 25
5 12 19 26
6 **13** 20 27
7 14 21 28

October
1 8 15 22 29
2 9 16 23 30
3 10 17 24 **31**
4 11 18 25
5 **12** 19 26
6 13 20 27
7 14 21 28

November
1 8 15 22 29
2 9 16 23 30
3 **10** 17 24
4 11 18 25
5 12 19 26
6 13 **20** 27
7 14 21 28

December
1 8 15 22 29
2 9 16 23 30
3 10 17 24 **31**
4 11 18 **25**
5 12 19 26
6 13 20 27
7 14 21 **28**

1 January
Año Nuevo (New Year's Day). A public holiday in all Spanish-speaking countries.

5 January (Mexico)
Día de la Constitución (Constitution Day). A public holiday.

6 January
Día de Reyes (Epiphany/Twelfth Night). In many Spanish-speaking countries, this is when presents are given, rather than on Christmas Day.

20 January
San Sebastián (Saint Sebastian's Day). Celebrated in Spain with parades, sporting events, and bullfights, it is also a day of celebration and dancing for the people of the Basque city that bears the name of the saint.

2 February
La Candelaria (Candlemas). An occasion for celebrations and parades in many Spanish-speaking countries.

3 February
Fiesta de San Blas (patron saint of Paraguay). A public holiday.

21 February (Mexico)
Anniversary of the birth of Benito Juárez, a famous nineteenth-century statesman, who was twice president. A public holiday.

26 February
Aberri Eguna – Basque national day and a public holiday in the Basque country of Spain.

12–19 March
Las Fallas are one of the best known *fiestas* in Spain. They are held in Valencia in eastern Spain. The high point of the celebration is on the last night, when the *cabezudos* (carnival figures with large heads), which have been carefully prepared by the *falleros*, are paraded through the streets and then burned, all this to the accompaniment of an enormous fireworks display.

14 April (Paraguay)
Día de la Independencia. A public holiday.

23 April
San Jordi The feast day of Catalonia's patron saint. According to custom, women give men books and men give women roses on this Catalan version of St Valentine's Day.

1 May
Día del Trabajo (Labor Day). A public holiday in all Spanish-speaking countries.

5 May (Mexico)
The anniversary of the victory of the state of Puebla against the French invasion of 1862. A public holiday.

25 May (Argentina)
The anniversary of the May revolution of 1810.

20 June (Argentina)
Día de la Bandera (Argentinian National Day). A public holiday.

(Colombia)
Día de la Independencia.
A public holiday.

24 June

San Juan (Feast of St John).
Traditionally fires are lit on the night of San Juan in order to keep away the cold of winter. In some places, people jump over the fires and in others the faithful will try to walk through them barefoot. The custom is slowly dying out, but continues in many parts of the Spanish-speaking world.

5 July (Venezuela)

Día de la Independencia.
A public holiday.

6–14 July

Sanfermines. The festival of *el encierro* (the 'running of the bulls'), takes place in Pamplona in northern Spain. The animals are released into the barricaded streets and people run in front of them, in honor of the town's patron saint, San Fermín, who was put to death by being dragged by bulls.

9 July (Argentina)

Día de la Independencia.
A public holiday.

25 July

Fiesta de Santiago (Feast of St James). The famous *Camino de Santiago*, the pilgrimage of thousands of people from all over Spain and many other parts of Europe to the holy city of Santiago de Compostela, takes place in the week leading up to St James' Day, 25 July. The city also has its *fiestas* around this time. The streets are full of musicians and

performers for two weeks of celebrations culminating in the *Festival del Apóstol*.

28 July (Peru)

Día de la Independencia.
A public holiday.

6 August (Bolivia)

Día de la Independencia.
A public holiday.

10 August (Ecuador)

Primer Grito de Independencia.
A public holiday commemorating the first cry of independence in 1809.

17 August (Argentina)

A public holiday to celebrate the anniversary of the death of the San Martín who liberated Argentina from Spanish rule in 1816.

25 August (Uruguay)

Día de la Independencia.
A public holiday.

11 September

Día Nacional de Cataluña.
Catalonian National Day and a public holiday in Catalonia.

13 September (Mexico)

Commemoration of the *Niños Héroes* (child heroes) who fell while defending the castle of Chapultepec against European invaders in 1847.

15 September (Mexico)

Conmemoración de la Proclamación de la Independencia.
Throughout the country, at 11 o'clock at night, there is a communal shout, *El Grito*, in memory of Padre Hidalgo's

cry of independence from the Spanish in the town of Dolores.

18 September (Chile)

Día de la Independencia.
A public holiday.

12 October

Día de la Hispanidad.
A public holiday, this is also
Columbus Day, which is celebrated in all Spanish-speaking countries, as well as the US, in commemoration of the discovery of the Americas by Christopher Columbus in 1492.
In Spanish-speaking countries of the Americas, it is also called the **Día de la Raza** (literally, Day of the Race) in celebration of the *mestizaje*, the mingling of races, which gave birth to the populations of today.

31 October

Todos los Santos (All Saints). People all over the Spanish-speaking world flock to the cemeteries on this and the following day *el día de los Difuntos/ Muertos* to put flowers on the graves of relatives and friends and to remember the dead. In Mexico this is an important festival in which Catholic traditions are mixed with those of pre-Hispanic religions.

10 November (Argentina)

Fiesta de la Tradición. This festival takes place throughout the country but is especially important in the town of San Antonio de Areco, near Buenos Aires. The capital also holds a festival in November, the **Semana de Buenos Aires**, in honor of its patron saint San Martín de Tours.

20 November (Mexico)

Día de la Revolución de 1910.
A public holiday to celebrate the revolution of 1910.

2 December (Mexico)

Virgen de Guadalupe. Celebrations are held in honor of the patron saint of the country, with music and dancers, in particular the *concheros*, who dance, wearing bells around their ankles, to the sound of stringed instruments and conches.

25 December

Navidad (Christmas Day). A time of great religious celebration in all Spanish-speaking countries. In many places, reenactments of the nativity are held, with a variety of traditions, parades, and costumes.

28 December

Día de los Inocentes. This is the equivalent to April Fool's Day. In most Spanish-speaking countries it is a day for playing tricks on people. And if you trick someone into lending you money for that day, you keep it and tell them *que te lo paguen los Santos Inocentes* (let the Holy Innocents pay you back).

31 December

La noche de Fin de Año.
This is often the occasion for parties, and at midnight the New Year is welcomed with much noise and merrymaking. In Spain and in many other Spanish-speaking countries, the families gather together twelve seconds before midnight *para tomar las uvas* (to see the New Year in by eating one grape on each chime of the clock) for good luck.

Movable feasts and holidays

Martes de Carnaval (Shrove Tuesday). The last Tuesday before the beginning of *Cuaresma* (Lent). *Carnaval* is celebrated in many Spanish-speaking countries just before this date. In many places, there are masked balls and parades. The biggest in Spain are those of Cádiz, on the south coast, and Madrid, where a strange ceremony called *el entierro de la sardina* (literally the *burial of the sardine*) takes place. In Mexico, the best-known are in Veracruz and Mazatlán.

Pascua (Easter) – **Semana Santa** (Holy Week). The week leading up to Easter Sunday is the most important time of religious celebration throughout the Spanish-speaking world. In many places, there are processions in which statues of Christ or the Virgin Mary, often covered in jewels and flowers, are carried to the church.

Seville's famous **Feria de abril** (April festival) takes place in the week following Easter. The site of the *feria* is decked out with hundreds of *casetas* or small marquees, hired by companies or private individuals, in which people entertain, eat *tapas*, drink *manzanilla* (a pale dry sherry), play music, and dance *sevillanas*, the popular dances of Andalucía. Many people dress up in colourful traditional costumes, some of them on horseback or in horse-drawn carriages.

Corpus Christi – 9 weeks after Easter is celebrated in most Spanish-speaking countries with religious parades.

A–Z of spanish life and culture

ABC
One of the Spanish national daily newspapers. *ABC* holds conservative political views and is a firm supporter of the monarchy. It is considered to be one of the high-quality newspapers in Spain.

aberzale or abertzale
This term is used to refer to the political and social ideology of Basque nationalism, and to its followers. It embraces different degrees of radicalism in the movement's objectives and in its support of violence as a means to achieve independence.

alcalde/alcaldesa
President of the AYUNTAMIENTO (local council), who is in charge of running the administration of the MUNICIPIO. The *alcalde* is elected by proportional representation from the candidates put forward by the political parties. The approximate equivalent position in Britain would be that of mayor.

ambulatorio (de la seguridad social)
Medical centre, part of the social security system, where people can go to see a MÉDICO DE CABECERA (general practitioner). It is a day centre and does not take in-patients. It has the same function as the CENTRO DE SALUD, but is generally bigger.

Antena 3
One of the main national Spanish commercial TV channels, broadcasting films and entertainment programmes.

As
Daily newspaper dealing exclusively with sports information and reports, mainly football. It is published in Madrid and distributed over the whole of Spain.

autonomía
One of the autonomous regions of which Spain is made up. There are 19 *autonomías* in Spain: Andalucía, Aragón, Baleares, Canarias, Cantabria, Castilla-La Mancha, Castilla y León, Cataluña, Ceuta, Comunidad Valenciana, Extremadura, Galicia, La Rioja, Madrid, Melilla, Navarra, País Vasco (or Euskadi), Principado de Asturias, and Región de Murcia. Each *autonomía* has its own administrative, legislative, and judicial powers and its own assemblies or parliaments.

AVE
High-speed train that completes the Madrid-Seville route in two and a half hours. It was introduced to coincide with the international exhibition, Expo-92, that took place in Seville in 1992. It is the only high-speed train in use at the moment in Spain, although there are plans to use them on other routes.

ayuntamiento

Governing body (similar to a council) that is in charge of the administration of a MUNICIPIO. It comprises the ALCALDE and the CONCEJALES, each of them with responsibility for a particular area of government. The building where the ALCALDE and CONCEJALES work is also called the *ayuntamiento*.

Aztecas

A Náhuatl-speaking people who in the fourteenth century established a brilliant and tyrannical civilization in central and southern Mexico. Its capital was Tenochtitlán, built on reclaimed marshland, and which became Mexico City. The Aztec empire collapsed in 1521 after defeat by the Spaniards led by Hermán Cortés.

bable

Bable is spoken in Asturias. It is very similar to Castilian.

bacalao or bakalao

Name given in Spain to modern music that has a very strong repetitive rhythm, such as house music.

Bachillerato

Educational level that comes after the ESO and before the COU, for pupils between 16 and 18. It comprises two years of non-compulsory education. This level is normally taken by pupils who want to go on to university and it has an academic focus. Pupils can choose one from among several *modalidades* (groups of subjects) to study. These *modalidades* are made up of a small number of core subjects (such as Spanish language and the language of the AUTONOMÍA) common to all of them, plus a combination of subjects that are geared more to sciences or arts, etc., according to the pupils' interests and to what they want to study at university. In addition to these, they can choose a number of optional subjects. The qualification that is awarded after completing these two years is called *Título de Bachiller*.

balseros

The name given to illegal immigrants who try to enter a country in small boats or on rafts. It applies particularly to Cubans who try to enter the US by sailing to Florida and to immigrants attempting to enter Spain by crossing the Straits of Gibraltar.

bar

*In Spain a bar se*lls all types of drinks, hot and cold, alcoholic and non-alcoholic. *Bares* also sell snack food such as TAPAS or RACIONES, or *bocadillos* (sandwiches made with a baguette-type loaf), and pastries to have with coffee. They can also offer full meals at lunchtime. *Bares* open all day, from early in the morning, for people to have breakfast, till late in the evening (sometimes just before midnight). There is sometimes little distinction between a BAR and a CAFETERÍA.

barrio

Area of a city or town. Many of them have a very strong identity and they often have their own residents' association that organizes events.

BNG

Political party of Galicia with a nationalist ideology.

BOE – Boletín Oficial del Estado

Name of the official news bulletin published by the government. It publishes all general regulations and laws that have been passed by Parliament. A new law comes into effect 21 days after it has appeared in the BOE.

bonhotel or bonotel

Voucher with which the holder can book nights in a hotel at a special rate. They are sold by travel agents and some department stores and banks.

bonobús

Special ticket that allows the purchaser to travel by bus a certain number of times (normally 10), at a cheaper rate than if individual tickets are purchased. On boarding the bus, the holder has to enter the ticket in a machine that punches out a small square in the ticket. *Bonobuses* can be bought in the ESTANCOS, at newspaper kiosks, and at special ticket stands.

bonoloto

National lottery that runs four times a week. The player has to bet on six numbers which he or she marks in a square consisting of forty-nine numbers. The winner is the person whose numbers coincide with the numbers that are drawn. The prizes are normally substantial.

bonometro

Special ticket that allows the purchaser to travel by bus or underground a certain number of times (normally 10), at a cheaper rate than if individual tickets are purchased. The ticket has to be put through a machine that registers the number of trips remaining and then prints the date and code of each journey. They can be bought in the ESTANCOS, at newspaper kiosks, and at special ticket stands.

BUP

The old educational level that used to exist in place of the current BACHILLERATO before the 1990 educational reform. The *BUP* used to last three years, whereas now the *Bachillerato* is only two, since the *reforma* (education reform) increased by one year the length of compulsory education. Like the current BACHILLERATO, it was taken by pupils who wanted to go on to university education.

cabalgata de Reyes

Parade that takes place in the streets of villages, towns, and cities on 5 January, the night before the DÍA DE REYES, the day on which Christmas presents are exchanged in Spain. The parade includes the *Reyes Magos* (the Three Wise Men) coming into the village, town, or city, with cartloads of presents to give to the people. It is an event aimed mainly at children, since they believe that it is the *Reyes Magos* who give out the presents.

Cadena SER

Commercial radio station offering a high level of information and political debate. Its political views are considered left of centre.

cafetería

Establishment with tables where you can sit down and have a coffee or other hot drink, and pastries or cakes. It also serves many other types of drink, such as soft drinks and beer. Often there is a supplementary charge for sitting at a table. *Cafeterías* are often combined with BARES and there is often little distinction between them in terms of what you can have.

Cámara de los diputados

The lower of the two chambers that form the Spanish CORTES or Parliament. Its members, the *diputados*, are elected by proportional representation during the general elections and they meet to debate issues of current national and international politics and to vote on proposed legislation. The place where the *diputados* meet is also called *la Cámara de los diputados* or EL CONGRESO.

Camino de Santiago

A pilgrimage route since the Middle Ages across north-western Spain to Santiago de Compostela in Galicia. The city was founded at a place where a shepherd is said to have discovered the tomb of St James the Apostle, and its cathedral reputedly houses the saint's relics.

campamentos

Summer camps where groups of children go to spend their summer holidays. Every day there are different activities for the children, ranging from ceramics to survival games. Some *campamentos* are organized by large companies (such as CORREOS or banks), some by the councils.

Canal + (Canal plus)

Privately owned television channel specializing in showing films that have been recently released. It is paid for by subscription and the subscriber must have a decoder to be able to receive the channel. Films are shown on this channel before going to the national television channels.

Canal 9

Television channel of Cataluña, Valencia, and Baleares. It broadcasts in CATALÁN.

Canal Sur

Television channel of Andalucía.

CAP – Curso de adaptación pedagógica

Course taken by graduates who have a degree in a subject other than education, and who want to teach in COLEGIOS or INSTITUTOS.

carnaval

Popular festival that takes place before Lent. Schools give three or more days' holiday, depending on the AUTONOMÍA. During *carnaval* there are street parades and festivals in most towns and cities, at which people dress up in fancy dress. The *carnavales* in Cádiz and the Canary Islands are particularly spectacular.

carnet de conducir

The card given to people who have passed their driving test. It must always be carried with you when you are driving.

carnet de identidad

Identity card that is compulsory for all Spanish residents over 14 years of age. It is also called *DNI*, short for *Documento Nacional de Identidad* (National Identity Document). This card, which states the name of the person, their date of birth, their address, and the name of their parents, must be carried at all times. It also has a picture of the person and a code which refers to the person's fingerprints. Each person is given an identity card number, consisting of a series of figures followed by a letter. The identity card number is the same as the **NIF**, and people are required to give it as proof of identity and as part of their personal details when filling in official forms, applying for a loan, etc.

castellano

The language that is spoken all over Spain and, with regional differences, in most of Latin America. It is also referred to as 'español'. A foreigner learning Spanish is learning *castellano*. *Castellano* is the official language of the whole of Spain and is a compulsory subject in schools in all **AUTONOMÍAS**. Like **CATALÁN** and **GALLEGO**, it is a member of the group of Romance languages that derived from Latin.

catalán

The main language spoken in Cataluña, and, with some regional differences, in Valencia and Baleares. In all these areas it is the official language, together with **CASTELLANO** (Castilian), and is an official requirement for many official and academic positions as well as a compulsory subject in school. *Catalán* is spoken by around 11 million people. A large number of books are published in *catalán*, either originally

written in this language or translated into it. *Catalán*, like **CASTELLANO** and **GALLEGO**, is part of the group of Romance languages that are derived from Latin. The Catalan name for this language is *Catalá*.

cava

Spanish sparkling wine, made by the same method as Champagne. *Cava* is made in the area of Cataluña and produced to a very high standard. There are three types, depending on dryness: *Brut*, *Sec*, and *Semi-Sec*, *Brut* being the driest.

CC – Coalición Canaria

Political party of the Canary Islands with a nationalist ideology.

CCOO – Comisiones Obreros

One of the main trade unions in Spain. It is a unitary national organization, drawing its members from all occupations. It has historical links with the Spanish Communist Party. Nowadays, it is still considered to be associated with the current political parties of the left.

CEIP – Colegio de Educación Infantil y Primaria

Official name given to the **COLEGIOS ESTATALES** (state infant and primary schools).

centro de salud

Medical centre, part of the social security system, where people can go to see a **MÉDICO DE CABECERA** (general practitioner). It is a day centre and does not take in-patients. It has the same function as the

AMBULATORIO, but is generally smaller.

charcutería

Name used to refer to a shop or supermarket counter selling pork products, such as *chorizo* (spicy cured sausage), cured and cooked ham, sausages, etc.

Chicano

Chicanos are Mexican Americans, descendants of Mexican immigrants living in the US. For long looked down on by Americans of European descent, Chicanos have found a new pride in their origins and culture. There are numerous Chicano radio stations and many universities and colleges now offer courses in Chicano studies.

CiU

Political party in Cataluña. It has a nationalist ideology and is represented in the central parliament as well as in the GENERALITAT, the parliament of Cataluña. Its influence in central government has been considerable, as often the main political party in power (whether PSOE or PP) has been forced to form a pact with it in order to be able to outvote the opposition.

colegio concertado

School that is privately owned but receives a grant from central government. Parents have to pay a monthly fee for tuition, but not as much as in a COLEGIO PRIVADO. It normally covers all stages of education: EDUCACIÓN PRIMARIA, ESO, BACHILLER, and COU. Some might also offer classes for children aged 3-6, which is called EDUCACIÓN INFANTIL and is not compulsory.

These schools have a reputation for a high standard of education, and often are, or were in the past, religious schools.

colegio estatal

Its official name is CEIP, Colegio de Educación Infantil y Primaria (School of Infant and Primary Education). It is part of the free state school system, meaning that parents do not have to pay for their children's education. It offers EDUCACIÓN PRIMARIA for children aged from 6 to 12. Some might also offer classes for children aged 3-6, which is called EDUCACIÓN INFANTIL and is not compulsory. After finishing the EDUCACIÓN PRIMARIA in a CEIP, children go to an INSTITUTO for their secondary education.

colegio privado

School that is privately owned and receives no money at all from central government. The costs of tuition are covered by the parents in the form of monthly fees, which are normally quite high. It usually covers all stages of education: EDUCACIÓN PRIMARIA, ESO, BACHILLER, and COU. Some might also offer classes for children aged 3–6, which is called EDUCACIÓN INFANTIL and is not compulsory.

Comunidad Autónoma

In 1978 Spain was divided into *comunidades autónomas* or *autonomías*, which have far greater powers than the old *regiones*. The *comunidades autónomas* are: Andalusia, Aragon, Asturias, Balearic Islands, the Basque Country, Canary Islands, Cantabria, Castilla y León, Castilla-La Mancha, Catalonia, Extremadura, Galicia, Madrid, Murcia, Navarre, La Rioja, Valencia and the

North African enclaves of Ceuta and Melilla.

comunidad de vecinos

Name given to the group of people who live in a block of flats. They have regular meetings to discuss and decide things concerning the maintenance of the building, lifts, central heating system, etc. Each of the tenants must also pay a sum of money every month into a fund that goes to pay for any repairs that are needed, as well as to cover the services of a PORTERO, if the building has one. This is called *pagar la comunidad* (to pay the community charge). Each *comunidad* must elect a president, who calls the meetings, and employs the services of an administrator, who is in charge of getting quotes, paying the salary of the PORTERO, etc.

concejal

Person in charge of an area of local government (such as town planning, traffic, or the environment) in a MUNICIPIO. They are appointed by the ALCALDE.

el Congreso

See CÁMARA DE LOS DIPUTADOS.

consejo escolar

Administrative body in a school comprising the school management team, representatives of teachers, parents, and students (although students cannot vote), and one representative of the council and one of the non-teaching staff. They meet to discuss and decide issues regarding the running of the school.

Conquistadores

The collective term for the succession of explorers, soldiers, and adventurers who, from the sixteenth century onward led the settlement and exploitation of Spain's Latin American colonies.

Correos

Name given to the state-run postal system in Spain. In Spain, stamps can be bought in ESTANCOS, although if you want to send a parcel or letter by registered or express post you need to go to an *estafeta de correos* (post office). Postboxes in Spain are yellow.

corrida

The Spanish word for a bullfight. *Toreo* (bullfighting) has ancient origins, with Phoenician and Roman roots, and is a very popular spectacle in Spain. *Corridas* are regularly broadcast on television when the season starts. During the *corrida* three *matadores* (bullfighters) fight a total of six bulls, two each.

las Cortes

The name by which the national parliament is known in Spain. The name derives from a body that existed in the old kingdoms of Castilla, Aragón, Valencia, Navarra, and Cataluña, formed by people who were authorized to take part in government business, either in a personal capacity or as representatives of a particular social or economic group. Today it is used to refer to the two bodies that form the Spanish parliament: the CÁMARA DE LOS DIPUTADOS and the SENADO.

COU – Curso de orientación universitaria

One-year course taken by students who wish to go to university. The course prepares students for the university entrance exam, SELECTIVIDAD. Students normally carry on studying the subjects they have chosen for the BACHILLERATO. However, the *COU* will be phased out as part of the changes introduced by the REFORMA.

créditos

Number of points or credits awarded for each subject studied at university. To get their degree, students must accumulate a certain number of these points.

Defensor del pueblo

Ombudsman who, in Spain, is nominated by the PARLAMENTO to preside over the institution in charge of defending the fundamental rights of Spanish citizens against the administration. Citizens can write to the *Defensor del pueblo* if they feel that their constitutional rights have not been respected. The *Defensor del pueblo* decides whether they are right or not, and, if they are, writes to the administration advising what steps should be taken to compensate them. He also reports to Parliament at least once a year or on request.

despacho de lotería y apuestas del estado

Often just called *despachos de lotería*, this is a shop licensed to sell tickets for a lottery, such as the BONOLOTO or the LOTERÍA DE NAVIDAD. Some people always like to buy their ticket from the same shop as they think this might bring them good luck. Also, the *despacho* that sells the GORDO DE NAVIDAD at Christmas time normally gets a lot of people buying from it the following year.

Día de la raza

In Latin America, the anniversary of Columbus's discovery of America, October 12. In Spain it is known as *Día de la Hispanidad*. It is a celebration of the cultural ties shared by Spanish-speaking countries.

Día de Reyes

Name given in Spain to the Epiphany, 6 January. It is the day when Christmas presents are given and exchanged. Young children in Spain believe that the *Reyes Magos* (Three Wise Men) come to every house and leave presents for everybody. The night before, people leave a pair of shoes belonging to each member of the family close to a window or balcony door, which is how the *Reyes Magos* get into the house or flat. The *Reyes Magos* leave next to each pair of shoes the presents that correspond to that person. People also put out some Christmas sweets and spirits for the *Reyes Magos*, and some water for the camels. The tradition is based on the *Reyes Magos* (Three Wise Men) who came to offer presents to baby Jesus in Bethlehem.

Dicen

Daily newspaper dealing exclusively with sports information and reports, mainly football. It is published in Barcelona and distributed over the whole of Spain.

documento de identidad

An identity card that all residents over a certain age in Spain and Latin America must carry at all times. Holders must quote their identity card number on most official forms. The card is also known as *carné de identidad*, and in Spain as the *DNI*

(*Documento Nacional de Identidad*).

droguería
Shop selling household and cleaning products and utensils, as well as DIY products such as paint, plaster, etc.

duro
Informal name given to a five-peseta coin. 'Duro' is often used in conversation when talking about a relatively low amount of money. For instance, people very often say 'veinte duros' (= 'twenty duros') meaning 100 pesetas, or 'diez duros' (= 'ten duros') meaning 50 pesetas.

educación infantil
Period of pre-school education that is not part of the compulsory educational system but has a certain academic orientation and aims to prepare children for formal education. It provides care and education for children from 0 to 6 years of age (at 6 children will start formal education). Parents wishing their children to receive *educación infantil* can take them to those GUARDERÍAS that cater for children up to 6 years of age or to COLEGIOS (which only offer *educación infantil* to children from 3 to 6 years of age). Since pre-school education is not compulsory, parents must pay for it. Depending on whether the GUARDERÍAS are fully private or run by the council, they can be more or less expensive.

educación primaria, enseñanza primaria
See PRIMARIA

educación secundaria, enseñanza secundaria
See ESO

EGB – Enseñanza General Básica
The old level of compulsory education that used to exist before the REFORMA. It was for pupils between 6 and 14 years of age. Students who wished to carry on studying could go on to study FORMACIÓN PROFESIONAL, which had a vocational focus, or BUP, which had a more academic approach.

EH – Euskal Herritarrok
EH is the political platform on which the Basque political party, **HB**, runs for elections. It was formed by **HB** in 1998.

elecciones
There are three types of election in Spain: *generales*, *autonómicas*, and *municipales*. The *elecciones generales* (general elections) elect members to the central PARLAMENTO of Spain. The *elecciones autonómicas* (elections in the autonomous regions) elect members to the parliaments of the AUTONOMÍAS, Cataluña, Euskadi, Andalucía, etc. The *elecciones municipales* (local elections) elect the ALCALDE and the party that will be in charge of the local government. The elections normally take place at different times, and they are held at least every four years. All elections follow a system of proportional representation.

Ertzaintza
Regional police of the Basque country. They come under the authority of the parliament of the PAÍS VASCO. Their members are called *ertzainas*.

ESO – Enseñanza Secundaria Obligatoria

The name given to Spanish secondary education, coming after the ENSEÑANZA PRIMARIA, for pupils from 12 to 16 years of age. The *ESO* is compulsory, and comprises two cycles of two academic years each. At the end of the *ESO* the student will get a qualification called *Graduado en Educación Secundaria*. Students wishing to carry on studying can then study either FORMACIÓN PROFESIONAL, which has a vocational focus, or BACHILLERATO, which has a more traditional academic approach.

estanco

In Spain, many bars and restaurants sell cigarettes, either over the bar, or, more commonly nowadays, in cigarette machines. However, the main shop that sells cigarettes, cigars, pipe tobacco, etc. is an *estanco*. *Estancos* also sell stamps and some writing materials such as envelopes, pens, ink, etc. However, if you want to send a parcel or letter by registered or express post you need to go to an *estafeta de correos* (post office). In the *estancos* you can also buy the special 10-journey bus and metro tickets: BONOBÚS and BONOMETRO.

ETA – Euskadi Ta Askatasuna

Terrorist organization of a nationalist character, whose aim is to achieve political independence for the Basque Country (EUSKADI) from the Spanish central government.

ETB

Television channel of the Basque Country. It broadcasts only in the PAÍS VASCO and in the language of that region, EUSKERA.

Euskadi

Name in Basque (EUSKERA) for the Basque Country. See PAÍS VASCO.

euskera (Basque)

Language spoken in the Basque Country (EUSKADI) and parts of Navarra. Together with Castilian, it is the official language of this AUTONOMÍA and is a compulsory subject in schools. It is spoken by around 750,000 people and is an official requirement for many official and administrative positions in the Basque Country. A considerable number of books are published in *euskera*, either originally written in this language or translated into it. It is also spoken in the French Basque country, though there it is not an official language. *Euskera* is a language unrelated to the Romance languages derived from Latin which are spoken in Spain: GALLEGO, CASTELLANO, and CATALÁN. Its origins are, in fact, unknown. It has been linked to Caucasian, Asian, and North African languages, but there is no strong evidence relating it to any of them. Many think it is a language that preceded Indo-European languages. Current official *euskera* is a language that was 'created' by fusing the different dialects that already existed and it is called *euskera batua*.

facultad

Each of the branches of study that are offered in a university, such as medicine, architecture, social studies, etc. Each university offers a wide range of *facultades*. The buildings and departments where the study of a particular branch takes place are also called the *facultad* of that particular area of study. For instance, *Facultad de Medicina* (Faculty of Medicine) is where you go to study medicine.

fallas

Popular festival that takes place in Valencia on 19 March and the preceding days. Huge figures of papier maché are constructed during this time, often representing popular public figures, or making reference to social or political events. They are displayed and then burnt on the 19th in the streets. There are numerous street parties and other types of events during the period of the *fallas*.

farmacia

Shop licensed to sell drugs and medicines. The pharmacists must be graduates in pharmacy, as they are supposed to offer medical advice for simple ailments such as colds and headaches. Pharmacies can also sell cosmetics and hygiene products and are identified by a street sign with a green cross. Some are also *farmacias de guardia*, which means that they open outside the normal hours as part of a local rota, in order to sell medicines in cases of emergency. There is a notice outside each pharmacy indicating the *farmacia de guardia* for each day/week of the month and its address. The same information also appears in local newspapers.

fiesta

Every town and village in Spain has its *fiesta*. This is a period, lasting from a few days to a couple of weeks, that precedes the day of the saint of the locality, which can also be a holiday. During the *fiesta*, the town or village is decorated and various cultural and social events take place, such as communal dances, concerts, games, etc. Some of these events are very traditional, going back hundreds of years, and they can be something like a parade or the re-enacting of a historical event or battle. Some *fiestas* are very big and famous, even outside Spain, such as the FALLAS in Valencia or SAN FERMINES in Navarra.

flamenco

Style of songs and dance typical of the south of Spain, of GITANO origins. It is characterized by the passionate and powerful expression of feelings, often tragic.

Formación Profesional (FP)

After finishing the compulsory years of education (ESO), pupils can go on to the BACHILLERATO, which has a more traditional academic approach, or to the *Formación Profesional*, which has a vocational focus. *FP* comprises two cycles, one for students from 16 to 18 years of age and another which runs parallel to university education, for students of 18 years and upwards. For each of these stages pupils are given a qualification, either *técnico* or *asistente*, which qualifies them for a specific occupation or to continue to a more specialized course. It is possible to access the BACHILLERATO or university education from the *Formación Profesional*.

gallego (galego)

Language spoken in Galicia. It is very similar to Portuguese, from which it derived in the 14th century. Together with Castilian, it is the official language of this AUTONOMÍA, where it is an official requirement for many official and academic positions, as well as a compulsory subject in school. It is spoken by around three million people in Galicia, but there is also a substantial number of speakers of *gallego* living outside Galicia, both in Spain and abroad, since in the past it was an area that produced a large number of emigrants. A considerable number of books are published in *gallego*, either originally written in this language or translated into it. *Gallego*, like CASTELLANO and CATALÁN, is part of the group of Romance languages that derived from Latin. The Galician name for the language is *galego*.

gaucho

A peasant of the pampas of Argentina, Uruguay and Brazil. Modern gauchos work as foremen on farms and ranches and take part in rodeos. Traditionally, a gaucho's outfit was characterized by its baggy trousers, leather chaps, and *chiripá*, a waist-high garment. They also used *boleadoras* for catching cattle.

gazpacho

Traditional cold summer soup made with water, tomatoes, cucumber, green pepper, onion, garlic, and dry bread. It originated in the region of Andalucía but is very popular all over Spain.

Generalitat

Name given in Cataluña and Valencia to their parliaments.

gitano

Member of the Spanish gypsy community, which has its roots in a Hindu ethnic group that spread around the north of Africa and Europe. The gypsies often live in camps and retain their nomadic habits, deriving a living from trading and selling things in markets. They also keep a lot of their customs and do not usually integrate into the mainstream of Spanish society. Flamenco dance and songs have gypsy origins and many of the best performers come from the *gitano* community.

El Gordo de Navidad

This name means 'the fat one of Christmas' and it is the name given to the biggest prize in the LOTERÍA DE NAVIDAD (Christmas Lottery), which takes place shortly before 24 December.

Goyas

Prizes awarded by the AACC, *Academia de las Artes y las Ciencias Cinematográficas de España* (Academy of the Cinematographic Arts and Sciences of Spain) for achievement in the Spanish film industry. They are the Spanish equivalent of the Oscars and there are different categories such as best film, best main actor and actress, etc. The winners receive a replica bust of the painter *Goya*, hence the name of the prize.

guardería

Centre that looks after small children who are under the compulsory school age (6 years old). It is similar to a nursery in the UK. The *guarderías* normally look after children from a few months old up to 4 years, or sometimes up to 6. Some *guarderías* are private, while some are run and subsidized by the council, or in some cases by the government, and are part of a COLEGIO, but parents must always pay a certain amount for their children to attend.

guardia civil

Military body in Spain which is in charge of security in rural areas and on the coast, and of the protection of the Spanish public bodies (*organismos públicos*). It has a military organization and a strong army ethos, even though it carries out police work. Its members are also called *guardias civiles* and they used to have a very characteristic three-pointed hat, called *tricornio*, as part of their uniform, but this is no longer used.

HB – Herri Batasuna

Coalition of nationalist political parties of Marxist-Leninist ideology formed in 1978. It is described as the 'political arm' of ETA and, like ETA, it aims to achieve political independence for the PAÍS VASCO (the Basque Country) from the Spanish central government. Its political platform is EH.

huipil

A traditional garment worn by Indian and mestizo women in Mexico and Central America. *Huipiles* are generally made of richly embroidered cotton. They are very wide and low-cut, and are either waist- or thigh-length.

Iberia

Spanish national commercial airline company.

ikastola

School where the teaching is done in EUSKERA (Basque).

Incas

Founded in the twelfth century, the Andean empire of the Quechua-speaking Incas grew and extended from southern Colombia to Argentina and central Chile. Its capital was Cuzco. The Incas built an extensive road network and impressive buildings, including Machu Picchu. The empire collapsed in 1533 after defeat by the Spaniards led by Francisco Pizarro.

instituto

Centre of secondary education providing ESO (compulsory secondary education for children 12 to 16), the two years of BACHILLERATO (non-compulsory secondary education for children 16 to 18), and the one year pre university course, COU. These establishments are part of the state school system and therefore free of charge.

jerez

Sherry is produced in an area around Jerez de la Frontera near Cádiz. Sherries are drunk worldwide as an aperitif, and in Spain as an accompaniment to *tapas*. The main types are the pale *fino* and *manzanilla* and the darker *oloroso* and *amontillado*. It is from *Jerez* that sherry takes its English name.

La 2

Spanish commercial television channel, broadcasting documentaries and educational and news programmes. It is considered to be the channel that maintains the highest quality in Spanish television.

lehendakari

President of the parliament of EUSKADI. Each party running for the ELECCIONES AUTONÓMICAS in the PAÍS VASCO nominates a person, who can also, but does not have to, be the leader of the party, to become the president in the event of the party winning the elections. Apart from presiding over Parliament and running the administration of the AUTONOMÍA of the PAÍS VASCO, the *lehendakari* has an important role in liaising with the president of the Spanish central government.

lenguas cooficiales

The regional languages of Spain, *catalán*, *euskera* and *gallego*, which now have equal status with Castilian in the regions where they are spoken. Banned under Franco, they continued to be spoken privately. They are now widely used in public life, education, the media, cinema and literature.

lotería de Navidad and lotería del Niño

Name given to the special national lottery draws that take place at Christmas time. There are two main draws: *Lotería de Navidad* (that takes place a couple of days before the 24th), and *Lotería del Niño* (that takes place on 5 January, before the DÍA DE REYES). The prizes may not be as big as the LOTERÍA PRIMITIVA or the BONOLOTO, but it is a big social event. It is traditional to buy tickets and give them as presents to friends and relatives, or for a group of friends or colleagues at work to buy

a number together. This means that the prize is normally shared between people who are related or know each other. The draw, with children singing the numbers as they come out of the drum, is shown on television and later the winners are shown and interviewed on the national news.

lotería primitiva

This is the national lottery, which takes place three times a week. People playing have to bet on six numbers which they mark in a square consisting of 49 numbers. The winner is the person whose numbers coincide with the numbers that come out in the draw. The prizes are normally substantial.

Marca

Daily newspaper dealing exclusively with sports information and reports, mainly football. It is published in Madrid and distributed all over Spain. It is the highest-circulation newspaper in Spain, well ahead any of the daily non-sports newspapers, such as **ABC** or EL PAÍS.

mariachi

The word can mean the traditional Mexican musical ensemble, the musicians and the lively mestizo music they play. *Mariachis* wearing costumes based on those worn by *charros* can be seen in the Plaza Garibaldi, in Mexico City, where they are hired for parties, or to sing *mañanitas* or *serenades*.

médico de cabecera

Doctor who is a general practitioner. People go to see the *médico de cabecera* for common illnesses that are not of a serious nature, or to get referred to a specialist.

mercado

Even though every day there are
more and more supermarkets in
Spain, people still like, or even prefer,
to buy in *mercados* (markets). The
markets normally comprise a group
of stalls set up in a covered square or
in a building. They are open every
day except Sunday.

Mossos d'Esquadra

The police force of Cataluña. It
comes under the authority of the
GENERALITAT, the parliament of
Cataluña.

El Mundo

A Spanish daily national newspaper.
It is considered to be close to the
Conservative party, the **PP**.

municipio

Each of the administrative areas into
which a PROVINCIA is divided. A
municipio can be a town, a city, or a
village. Each *municipio* has an
ALCALDE and several CONCEJALES,
who deal with the administration and
government of the area. This
governing body comprising the
ALCALDE and the CONCEJALES is also
called *municipio*.

NIF – Número de identificación fiscal

Tax identification code that all
residents must have in Spain. People
must give it as part of the personal
details provided when applying for a
loan, opening a bank account, etc.
It is the same number as a person's
identity number (and passport
number), with the addition of a
letter. It is used to keep tax control
over people's financial transactions.

Nochevieja

In Spain and other Spanish-speaking
countries, where it is known as Año
Nuevo, it is customary to see in the
New Year by eating twelve grapes for
good luck, one on each chime of the
clock at midnight.

ONG – Organización no Gubernamental

The ONGs (non-governmental
organizations) are not set up by a
government or any agreement
between governments. They are non-
profit-making and are partly financed
by governments and administrative
bodies, although mainly by the
general public. They are normally
concerned with social issues, such as
homelessness or drug addiction. A lot
of them work in Spain although
many also work abroad in the
developing world. There are currently
around 70 *ONGs* in Spain.

oposición

This is a competitive exam for people
wanting to get a job in the
administration, or as a teacher in a
secondary school (INSTITUTO), or to
become a judge. The candidates are
examined by a tribunal. When the
candidate is applying for the position
of a teacher in an INSTITUTO or to
become a judge, passing the exam
often means studying for several
years and sitting more than once for
the exam, as the exams are very hard
and there are thousands of applicants
for very few positions.

PA – Partido Andaluz

Nationalist political party of
Andalucía. It is one of the main
political parties of this autonomous
region and has representatives both

in the central parliament and in the parliament of Andalucía.

paga extra, paga extraordinaria

Name for a bonus payment that most people receive at work twice a year, at Christmas and in July before the summer holidays, on top of their monthly salary.

El País

A Spanish national newspaper which is published daily. Its political views are to the left of centre and it gives considerable coverage to social issues and the arts. It also publishes a number of supplements on different subjects such as the economy and culture. It was founded in 1976, just as Spain was starting the democratic process of transition following General Franco's dictatorship, and its importance and influence on Spanish society at that critical time was considerable. It is considered to represent a very high standard of journalism.

País Vasco

Name used in Spain to refer to the AUTONOMÍA formed by the provinces of Álava, Guipúzcoa, and Vizcaya, in the north of Spain. Some people consider that, for historical and cultural reasons, it extends on both sides of the Pyrenees where Basque or EUSKERA is spoken. Therefore, people also talk of the *País Vasco–Francés* and *País Vasco–Español*. The *País Vasco–Francés* (French Basque region) does not have autonomous status, and Basque is not recognized as an official language there, whereas the *País Vasco–Español* is an autonomous region within the

Spanish State, with its own parliament, and its own administrative, legislative, and judicial powers. The name given to the *País Vasco* in EUSKERA (the Basque language) is EUSKADI.

parador

Hotel that is situated in a big historic house, typical of the region or area where it is located, or sometimes in an old palace, which has been renovated, thus preserving the character of the building. Normally of very high quality, they were created as a way of giving buildings of historical or architectural importance a new lease of life. They used to be controlled by the Ministry of Tourism but are now independent.

Parlamento

The Spanish parliament, also known as *las Cortes*. It is formed by two bodies: a Lower Chamber or CÁMARA DE LOS DIPUTADOS and an Upper Chamber or SENADO.

paro

Name given in Spain to unemployment and to the unemployment benefit received by people out of work. The payment is not the same fixed amount for everybody, but varies according to the National Insurance contributions that have been made during the period of employment. The period during which unemployment pay can be claimed depends on the period of time a person has been working, and it can range from three months to a maximum of two years.

Unemployment pay also decreases over the period of unemployment. For instance, someone who has worked for six months will receive three months' unemployment pay, and a maximum of 70% of their salary, which might go down in the following months. To receive unemployment benefit is called *cobrar el paro*.

payo
Name given by members of the gypsy community to all non-gypsies.

PNV – Partido Nacionalista Vasco
Main political party in the PAÍS VASCO. It has a nationalist ideology and is represented in the central parliament as well as in the parliament of the PAÍS VASCO. Its influence in central government has been considerable, as often the main political party in power (whether PSOE or PP) has been forced to enter into a pact with it in order to be able to outvote the opposition.

portero
The name given in Spain to the caretaker of a block of flats who looks after the building, keeps it clean, and also keeps an eye on who comes and goes. *Porteros* are also in charge of collecting the rubbish and delivering the mail to each mailbox. Their salary comes from the money paid by the COMUNIDAD DE VECINOS and they are often given a flat in the building to live in, as part of their payment. However, a lot of buildings now do not have *porteros* and their inhabitants either share the cleaning by rota or employ someone to do it. Where there is no *portero*, access is regulated by an entryphone, which in Spain is called *portero automático* (automatic caretaker).

PP – Partido Popular
One of the two main political parties in Spain with representation in the central government and in the government of the AUTONOMÍAS. Its ideology is right of centre.

Premio Cervantes
Prize awarded in Spain for literary achievement. It is considered to be the most prestigious prize among Spanish intellectuals and writers. The prize is not awarded for a particular piece of writing, but for a writer's work as a whole.

Presidente del gobierno
President of the Spanish central parliament, the equivalent of the Prime Minister in the UK. Each party running for the ELECCIONES *generales* in Spain nominates a person, usually, but not necessarily, the leader of the party, to become the president in the event of that party winning the elections. Apart from presiding over the parliament and running the administration of the state, the *Presidente* has an important role in liaising and meeting with the prime ministers of other countries and with the presidents of the different AUTONOMÍAS of Spain.

Primaria
The name given in Spain to the first of the two compulsory levels of education. The *Primaria* is for pupils between 6 and 12 years of age and leads on to the ESO. It is compulsory and is taught in COLEGIOS.

provincia

Each of the different administrative areas into which Spain is divided. The current division was established in 1833. Each *provincia* includes a main city or town, sometimes more, depending on their social and economic power. Most AUTONOMÍAS comprise at least two or more *provincias*, except Madrid and Murcia, which consist of just one *provincia*. The city of Madrid is the capital of the province and of the AUTONOMÍA of Madrid, as well as being the capital of Spain.

PSOE – Partido Socialista Obrero Español

One of the two main political parties in Spain with representation in the central government and in the governments of the AUTONOMÍAS. Its ideology is left of centre.

pub

Name used in Spain to refer to an establishment where drinks are served and sometimes also snacks. Although the name comes from English, Spanish *pubs* look very different from English pubs. They are usually decorated in a very stylish modern fashion, and are sometimes theme-based. Often concentrated in a particular area of a town or city, they are aimed at young people going out in the evening and are open till the early hours of the morning. They always have music, which can be very loud.

puente

Holidays in Spain are fixed on specific dates in the calendar. This means that each year the day of the week on which they fall will vary. If one year a holiday falls on a Tuesday or a Thursday, some companies and most schools will also give a holiday on the day between the holiday and the weekend (i.e. the Monday or the Friday). This is called a *puente* (bridge), while to give this holiday is called *dar puente* and to take this holiday is *hacer puente*.

quiniela

Name given to football and horse racing pools in Spain. The paper on which the bet is written is also called the *quiniela*. The punters must state what they think will be the result of a match or a race. In the case of football pools, for each match, they must write 1, 2, or X: '1' if they think the home team is going to win, '2' if they think the away team is going to win, and 'X' if they think it is going to be a draw. The total number of matches is 14, and people who get either 13 or 14 correct results share the prize money.

ración

This is a small portion of food that you have in a bar with a drink. *Raciones* are bigger than TAPAS and normally shared between two or three people. It is common for a group of friends in Spain to meet and go out to a bar, or from one bar to another, having a drink and a selection of TAPAS and *raciones*, either as an aperitif before lunch or in the evening instead of having dinner.

RAE – Real Academia Española

Official body created in the 18th century with the aim of preserving the purity of the Spanish language. It is made up of *académicos,* who are normally well-known writers or academic experts on the Spanish language, both from Spain and abroad. The *RAE* has published different editions of a Dictionary of Spanish and a Spanish Grammar, incorporating changes that have taken place in the language. These books are regarded as an authority on what is acceptable and correct Spanish. However, the *RAE* is often criticized as being conservative and slow in accepting the changes that take place in the language. There are also *RAEs* in most Latin American countries.

rastro

Name given to an open-air flea market that normally takes place once a week and where all types of new and old items are sold, including a lot of handicrafts. The name *El rastro* is used to refer to a very big market of this type that takes place in an old and very traditional part of Madrid at the weekend, but smaller *rastros* take place all over Madrid and other towns and they are often called *rastrillos*.

Reconquista

The period in Spain's history during which the Christian kingdoms slowly recovered the territories occupied by the Moslem Moors of North Africa. The Moorish invasion began in 711 AD and was halted in 718. The expulsion of the last Moorish ruler of Granada in 1492 completed the *Reconquista*.

la reforma (educativa)

Name used to refer to the change in the educational system that was introduced gradually from 1990 onwards. The main changes were the extension of compulsory education by one year (up to 16 years of age), with the introduction of the ESO that replaced EGB.

RENFE – Red Nacional de los Ferrocarriles Españoles

State-run railway system. Trains in Spain are often cheaper than in the UK, and it is a generally efficient system. The most common trains are *Intercity* and *TALGO*. Tickets can be booked over the phone, and then collected, or if you pay a supplement they are delivered to your address.

San Fermines

Popular festival that takes place in Pamplona on 7 July and the preceding days. During these days, a series of *encierros* take place, events in which people must run in front of a herd of bulls in narrow streets, leading them to the bullring where there is later a CORRIDA (bullfight). *San Fermines* is a very popular festival, well-known also abroad, and a lot of foreigners like to try their skill at running in front of the bulls.

santo

Day that has been assigned by the church to a particular saint. In Spain people celebrate their name days as well as birthdays, although this varies according to the region. Some saints' days are very important celebrations in certain areas, such as San Juan in Valencia (known locally as San Joan) and San Fermín in Pamplona (see **SAN FERMINES**).

Selectividad

Examination that takes place after COU, when students are normally 17 or 18. Students sit exams in the core subjects, such as history and Spanish language, which are common to all students, and in the subject they have chosen as their specialism (for example literature or chemistry). An average is taken of the results of the exams and this is worked out against the average of the year's results in **BACHILLERATO**. The final result is a figure out of 10, and this figure is taken as a qualification for entering university. So, for instance, different **FACULTADES** will only accept students who have obtained a grade in *Selectividad* above a certain figure.

Semana Santa

The most famous Holy Week celebrations in the Spanish-speaking world are held in Sevilla between Palm Sunday and Easter Sunday. Lay brotherhoods, *cofradías*, process through the city in huge parades. During the processions they sing *saetas*, flamenco verses mourning Christ's passion.

Senado

The upper of the two chambers in **LAS CORTES**. Its members, the *senadores*, are elected during the general elections. The Senate's function is to discuss and either approve or suggest amendments to legislation passed by the **CÁMARA DE LOS DIPUTADOS**. The place where the *senadores* meet is also called the *Senado*.

senyera

Name given in Cataluña and Valencia to the flag of these autonomous regions.

siesta

Nap that some people in Spain take after lunch and especially at the weekends and in the heat of the summer. Nowadays it is not such a common practice, owing to the change in lifestyle and in working hours (in the past most jobs used to have a long break at lunch).

Sport

Daily newspaper dealing exclusively with sports information and reports, mainly football. It is published in Barcelona and distributed all over Spain.

tapas

Small snack eaten with a drink. *Tapas* is a popular form of food all over Spain. It is common for a group of friends in Spain to meet and go out to a bar, or from one bar to another, having a drink and a selection of *tapas*, either as an aperitif before lunch or in the evening instead of having dinner. This is called *ir de tapas*. You can also have **RACIONES**, which are bigger portions, on such outings.

Tele 5

One of the main national Spanish commercial TV channels, broadcasting films and entertainment programmes.

Telefónica (de España S.A.)

This is the largest telephone company

in Spain. It used to be a state company but it was privatized in 1999. There are a number of other privately owned telephone companies now operating in Spain.

terraza

Area outside a bar, café, or restaurant where people can sit and have a drink or eat in the open air. Some *terrazas* are very trendy and popular among young people going out in the evening. These can be very large, open until late into the night, and they can even have music.

tiendas

Shops in Spain are open from nine or ten in the morning until one or two in the afternoon. They close for lunch and then are open again from five o'clock until eight or nine in the evening. Shops close on Sundays, except around Christmas time. Big stores are only allowed to open a certain number of Sundays during the year, in order to protect small shops. There are a lot more small independent shops in Spain than in the UK.

(la fiesta de) los toros

Bullfighting is popular in Spain and some Latin American countries. The season runs from March to October in Spain, from November to March in Latin America. The bullfighters who take place in a *corrida* gather in *cuadrillas*. The principal bullfighter or *matador* is assisted by *peones*.

turismo rural

Name used to refer to a form of tourism that rents out renovated houses in the country and in old Spanish villages to people on holiday. Houses are given a grant to be renovated on the condition that they are rented out for this purpose. The aim of the initiative was to promote tourism in rural areas, thereby providing an income to farmers and helping to preserve village architecture.

TV1

One of the main national Spanish commercial TV channels, broadcasting films and entertainment programmes.

TV-3

Television channel of Cataluña, Valencia, and Baleares. It broadcasts in CATALÁN.

TVAC

Television channel of the Canary Islands.

TVG

Television channel of Galicia. It broadcasts in GALLEGO.

UGT – Union General de Trabajadores

One of the main trade unions in Spain, traditionally linked to the Socialist party and movement. It is a unitary national organization, drawing its members from all occupations.

UNED – Universidad Nacional de Educación a Distancia

Spanish national university for distance learning. Students receive the booklist and the syllabus of the subject and submit their assignments by post. They also have regular meetings, individually or in small groups, with a tutor, and on occasions they also attend lectures.

universidad

Educational body in charge of higher education. It is made up of various FACULTADES and university schools, each offering a different branch of study. There are private universities and universities that form part of the state system of education. Students have to pay fees in both, but these are much higher in private universities. Since students are not given grants unless the income of their family falls below a certain level, they normally live at home with their parents while at university, usually attending the university that is nearest to their home. Language is also a deciding factor, since a student wishing to go to a university in Cataluña, for instance, would need to attend classes in CATALÁN. Students can choose different subjects within their degree, following a system of points called CRÉDITOS.

vacaciones de verano

In Spain a lot of companies allow their employees to take their summer holidays only during the months of July, August, and September. Some companies close during the month of

August. This means that most people tend to have their summer holidays at the same time of the year. However, during the rest of the year people can have PUENTES, which are small holidays given around a bank holiday.

La Vanguardia

Daily newspaper published in Barcelona and distributed all over Spain. It is the newspaper with the largest number of subscribers and has a series of supplements on different subjects. It is a prestigious newspaper with a strong influence in Catalan society and is also published on the Internet.

Xunta

The parliament of Galicia.

zarzuela

A musical drama consisting of alternating passages of dialogue, songs, choruses, and dancing that originated in Spain in the seventeenth century. Also popular in Latin America, its name derives from the Palacio de la Zarzuela, the Madrid palace where the Royal family now lives.

Letter-writing

Holiday postcard

■ Beginning (quite informal): this formula is used among young people, very close friends, and, generally speaking, when addressee and sender address each other using the familiar form tú. *Querido Juan* can also be used, or *Querida Ana* if the addressee is a woman. If addressed to two or more people, males and females or only males, the masculine plural *Queridos* is always used: *Queridos Juan y Ana, Queridos amigos, Queridos Juan y Pedro. Queridas* is used if the card or letter is addressed to more than one female: *Queridas chicas, Queridas Ana y Conchita*

■ Address: Note that the title (*Sr., Sra., Srta.*) is always followed by a full stop and stands next to the name.

The house number (sometimes also N° ...) comes after the street name. In addresses of apartments in Spain, this is often followed by a floor number and sometimes the apartment's position on the landing: *c/ Hermosilla 98, 6° Dcha.*

The post code or zip code comes before the place

Hola Juan

¿Qué tal? Hemos llegado a esta maravilla de ciudad hace dos días y estamos disfrutando muchísimo de todo lo que vemos, ¡a pesar del tiempo! Ya sabes tú como es el clima por aquí.

Hemos visitado los baños romanos (por supuesto), la catedral y sus alrededores. Hicimos un paseo por el río en barca y hemos recorrido la ciudad a pie. Es la mejor forma de apreciar la increíble arquitectura de este lugar.

¡Ah! También tomamos un té inglés como es debido, con sándwichs de pepino incluidos, en la elegante "Pump Room". Mañana regresamos a Londres y luego de vuelta a la dura realidad.

Esperamos que todo te haya ido bien con el cambio de trabajo. Ya nos contarás.

Hasta pronto.

Ana y Eduardo

Bath, 8 de octubre 2007 **1**

Sr. Juan Elizalde

Pº Pintor Rosales 101

28008 Madrid

Spain

■ Endings (informal): *Un fuerte abrazo, Muchos saludos, Muchos besos y abrazos.* Also in Latin America: *Cariños* (NB not between men), *Hasta pronto* (See you soon).

1 Not only on postcards, but on most personal letters, Spanish speakers do not put the address at the top, but just the name of the place and the date. The sender's address is recorded on the back of the envelope.

Christmas and New Year wishes

On a card:

Feliz Navidad **1** y Próspero Año Nuevo **2**

Feliz Navidad **1** y los mejores deseos para el Año Nuevo **3**

1 Or: Felices Pascuas, Felices Navidades.

2 Or: Próspero Año 2007.

3 Or: para el Año 2007.

In a letter:

■ Beginning: the name on the first line is usually followed by a colon.

4 This is a letter to friends who are addressed as *vosotros*, the plural of the familiar form *tú*. However, Latin American Spanish uses the formal plural *ustedes* instead of this form, so should replace the words marked * in the letter as follows: *vosotros* by *ustedes*, *vuestro* and *vuestra* by *su* or *de ustedes*, *os* by *les* or *los*. The verbs, marked **, should be replaced by the formal plural form, e.g. *estéis* by *estén*.

5 Or (if the children are older): *para vosotros y los chicos* (or *y las chicas* if there are only females), *para vosotros y para toda la familia*.

6 Or: *todos muy bien*.

Barcelona, 18 de diciembre de 2001

Queridos Juan y Elsa:

4 Antes que nada, os* deseamos a vosotros* y a los niños **5** unas muy felices Navidades y os* enviamos nuestros mejores deseos para el año 2000. Esperamos que estéis** todos estupendamente **6**. No sabéis** cómo nos alegramos con el anuncio de vuestro* viaje para enero. Ya tenemos pensado todo lo que podemos hacer durante vuestra* estancia aquí. Os* esperamos.

Conchita hizo los exámenes del último año de su carrera y sacó muy buenas notas. Ahora tiene que hacer su trabajo de práctica. Elena está bien y muy contenta en el colegio. Tiene muchísimos amigos y es muy buena chica. Luis y yo estamos bien también y sumamente felices con la reciente noticia del próximo ascenso de Luis. En definitiva, 1999 ha sido un buen año y no nos podemos quejar. Confiamos en que el próximo será aún mejor.

Decidnos** con antelación la fecha de vuestro* viaje para que podamos ir a esperaros* al aeropuerto.

Recibid** todo nuestro cariño y un fuerte abrazo.

Luis y Ana.

Invitation (informal)

> Hamm, den 22.4.2007
>
> Madrid, 22 de abril del 2007
>
> Querido James:
>
> Te escribo para preguntarte si te apetecería **1** pasar las
> vacaciones de verano con nosostros. A Tito y a Pilar les haría
> mucha ilusión (y también a Juan y a mí, por supuesto).
> Pensamos ir al noreste del país a finales de julio o a principios
> de agosto. Es una región realmente hermosa y nos encantaría
> que tú también vinieras. Es muy probable que llevemos tiendas
> de campaña ¡espero que no te importe dormir en el suelo!
>
> Te agradecería que me avisaras lo más pronto posible si puedes
> venir.
>
> Un cariñoso saludo,
>
> Ana de Salas

1 Or (in Latin America and also in Spain): *si te gustaría*

Invitation (formal)

Invitations to parties are usually by word of mouth, while for weddings announcements
are usually sent out.

> Carmen S.de Pérez y Ramón Pérez Arrate, Lucía N.de Salas y Mario
> Salas Moro Participan a Ud. de la boda de sus hijos
>
> Consuelo y Hernán
>
> Y le invitan a la ceremonia religiosa que se efectuará en la Capilla del
> Sagrado Corazón, de Mirasierra, Madrid, el sábado 25 de julio del 2007
> a las 7 p.m.
>
> Y luego a una recepción en la Sala de Banquetes del Restaurante Galán
> en C/Los Santos 10 de Majadahonda, Madrid.
>
> S.R.C.2

■ In Latin America invitations to the
reception are sent to relatives and close
friends in a separate smaller card
enclosed with the announcement.

■ In Spanish-speaking countries, the
answer is not usually given in writing.
2 In Latin America: R.S.V.P.

Accepting an invitation

Winchester, 2 de mayo del 2007

Estimada Sra. de Salas:

Muchísimas gracias por su amable carta y su invitación **1**.

No tengo nada planeado para las vacaciones de verano, así es que me encantaría acompañarles **2** *al norte. Desgraciadamente, no podré quedarme más de cinco o seis días debido a que mi madre no se encuentra muy bien y no me gustaría estar mucho tiempo fuera de casa.*

Por favor dígame lo que tengo que llevar. ¿Hace mucho calor en la región adonde vamos? ¿Hay mar o río donde se pueda nadar? En cuanto a hacer camping, no tengo ningún problema. Nosotros siempre llevamos nuestras tiendas de campaña a todas partes.

Esperando verles **3** *pronto otra vez,*

Un afectuoso saludo,

James

1 Since this is a letter from a younger person writing to the mother of a friend, he uses the formal *usted* form and the possessive *su*, and writes to her as *Sra. de Salas* and *Estimada*, which is normally used to begin a letter when the relationship is not too close. *Querida ...* could also be used (*Estimado Sr. ...* or *Querido Sr. ...* if the addressee is a man). On the other hand it was quite natural for *Sra. de Salas* to use the informal *tú* form to him.

2 In Latin America: *acompañarlos*.

3 In Latin America: *verlos*.

■ Ending: This is normally used when the relationship is not too close, generally when the person is known to you but the usted form would be used. *Un saludo muy afectuoso* is also possible.

Enquiry to a tourist office

- This is a standard formula for starting a business letter addressed to a firm or organization, and not to a particular person. Alternatively, *Estimados señores* and, also in Latin America, *De nuestra mayor consideración*, could be used.

  - A simple business-style letter. The sender's address is on the top left-hand corner, the date is on the right, and the recipient's address is on the left, beneath the sender's address.

Sally McGregor
16 Victoria Road
Brixton
London SW2 5HU

4 de mayo del 2007

Oficina de Información y Turismo
Princesa 5
Oviedo

Muy señores míos:

Les agradecería me remitieran a la mayor brevedad una lista de hoteles y pensiones, de precio medio, en Oviedo y los pueblos de la provincia.

También me interesaría obtener información acerca de excursiones en autocar **1** a los lugares de interés de la zona durante la segunda mitad de agosto.

Agradeciendo de antemano su atención, les saluda atentamente,

Sally McGregor

- *Les* (*Los* in Latin America) *saluda atentamente* is the standard ending for a formal or business letter. Other possibilities are: *Me despido de ustedes atentamente* or *Reciban un atento saludo de …*

1 In Latin America: *autobús*.

Booking a hotel room

Luis Granados
C/Felipe V 32
Segovia

23 de abril del 2007

Sr. Director
Hotel Los Palomos
C/Piedrabuena 40
Cádiz

Apreciado señor: **1**

Su hotel aparece en un folleto turístico sobre la zona para el año 2007 y me ha causado muy buena impresión. Por ello le escribo para reservar una habitación doble con baño y una habitación individual **2** para nuestro hijo, desde el 2 hasta 11 de agosto (nueve noches). Preferiblemente ambas habitaciones con vista al mar.

Si tiene disponibilidad para esas fechas, le rogaría que me comunicara el precio y si se requiere depósito.

Sin otro particular le saluda **3** atentamente,

Luis Granados

1 Also: *Estimado Sr.*
2 Or: *una habitación doble y una individual para nuestro hijo, ambas con baño.*
3 In Latin America: *lo saluda …*

Booking a campsite

Urbanización El Molino
Chalet 88
Villanueva de la Cañada
Madrid

25 de abril del 2007

Camping Loredo
Sr. Roberto Loredo
Nájera
La Rioja

Muy señor mío:

Un amigo que suele acampar en la zona me ha recomendado su camping **1**, por lo que quisiera reservar una plaza para una tienda **2**, preferiblemente en un lugar abrigado **3**. Dos amigos y yo queremos pasar una semana allí, desde el 18 al 25 de julio inclusive.

Le agradecería que me confirmara la reserva lo antes posible y que me dijera si se requiere depósito. También le estaría muy agradecido si me enviara indicaciones para llegar al camping desde la carretera.

A la espera de su confirmación, le saluda **4** atentamente,

Pedro Salguedo

1 Or: *Su camping aparece anunciado en la revista Guía del Buen Campista.*
2 Other possibility: *para una caravana.*
3 Alternatively: *en un lugar sombreado/ cerca de la playa.*
4 In Latin America: *lo saluda* ...

Cancelling a reservation

Sra. Rosario de Barros
Av. Colonial
San Isidro
Lima

20 de julio de 2007

Estimada señora (de Barros):

Debido a circunstancias ajenas a nuestra voluntad **1**, nos
hemos visto obligados a cambiar nuestros planes para las
vacaciones, por lo que le rogaría cancelara la reserva **2**
hecha a mi nombre para la semana del 7 al 14 de agosto.

Lamento muchísimo tener que hacer esta cancelación
(tan a último momento) y espero que esto no le cause
muchos inconvenientes.

La saluda atentamente,

Paul Roberts
2633 Higland Avenue
Urbandale, IA 51019
EEUU

In Latin America if the full address is
given, it is usually written in the bottom
left-hand corner, beneath the
signature.

1 Or: *Debido al repentino fallecimiento
de mi marido/a la hospitalización de mi
hijo/a la enfermedad de mi marido* etc.

2 Also in Latin America: *reservación*.

Sending an e-mail

The illustration shows a typical interface for sending e-mail.

File menu	Edit menu	View menu	Mail menu	Insert menu	Format menu	Help menu

Archivo Edicion Ver Correo Insertar Formato Ayuda

To: someone@somewhere.co.uk
cc: click here to enter carbon copy recipients
Subject: click here to enter the subject

> Querida Cristina:
>
> Solo un par de líneas para confirmar el recibo de tu e-mail de prueba. Me alegro que desde ahora nos podamos comunicar por Internet. Quedo a la espera del documento adjunto que me prometiste.
>
> Un fuerte abrazo,
>
> Carmen

Texting

The basic principles governing Spanish SMS abbreviations are similar to English ones. Certain words or syllables can be represented by letters or numbers that sound the same but take up less space. Also, points, accents and other diacritics are generally omitted altogether. For example, the syllable -ca can be replaced by the letter k and the conjunction 'que' by 'ke'. Another way of shortening words is simply to omit certain letters, especially vowels. For example, 'bastante' becomes 'bstnt' and 'gente' becomes 'gnt'.

As in English, 'emoticons' are very popular, and some of the more established ones are included in the table below.

Glossary of Spanish SMS abbreviations

Abbreviation	Full word	Abbreviation	Full word	Abbreviation	Full word
a2	adiós	kro	caro	txt	texto
aa	años	lgr	lugar	t2	todos
archvo	archivo	lu	lunes	vi	viernes
artclo	artículo	mar	martes	xa	para
bstnt	bastante	mñna/mñn	mañana	x	por
b	beso	mktg	marketing	xfa	por favor
cia	compañia	+	más	xq	porque
compljo	complejo	+tikr	masticar	xtrangro	extranjero
complikdo	complicado	mjr	mejor		
comnikr	comunicar	msj/sms	mensaje/	Emoticons*	
d	de		mens.móvil	:-)	Cara feliz
dcir	decir	msjr	mensajero	:-|	Ceñudo
dd	días	mm	meses	:-e	Desilusión
dir	dirección	mi	miércoles	:-(	Cara triste
do	domingo	'	minuto	%-)	Confundido
exclnt	excelente	's	minutos	:~(o :'-(	Llorando
fsta	fiesta	nd	nada	;-)	Guiñando el ojo
fvor	favor	-	negativo, no	l-o	Aburrido,
garntzr	garantizar	0/ning	ninguno		durmiendo
gf	jefe	nka	nunca	:-\	Escéptico
gral	general	pers	personas	:-D	Sonrisa grande,
grduar	graduar	prblm	problema		cara sonriente
gralmnt	generalmente	prpar2	preparados	:-<>	Asombrado
gnt	gente	q	que	:-@	Enfadado
hab	habitación	qn	quien	:-p	Sacando la
hcer	hacer	qndo	cuando		lengua
hno	hermano	s	ese	:-O	Gritando
hr	hora	sa	sábado	O:-)	Ángel
hl	hola	salu2	saludos	:-* o :-x	Un beso
infrmal	informal	"	segundos	:-o	Shock
info	información	stndar	estándar	@}-,-'—	Una rosa
jf	jefe	st	este		
ju	jueves	s3	estrés	* NB: the '-' which depicts the
klidad	calidad	tb	también	nose is often omitted or replaced
kntidad	cantidad	thanx	gracias	by an 'o' e.g., :) or :o)
kpaz	capaz	tx	taxi	

The spanish words you must know

A
a
abajo (de)
abierto
abogado, el
abrigo, el
abril
abrir
abuelo, el
aburrido
acabar (de)
accidente, el
aceite, el
aceituna, la
acento, el
aceptar
acordarse
acostarse
actividad, la
activo
adentro
adiós
¿adónde?
adulto
aeropuerto, el
aficionado, el
afuera
agosto
agua (f), el
ahí
ahora (mismo)
aire, el
ajo, el
alcanzar
alcohólico
alegre
alegría, la
alemán
alfombra, la
algo
alguno
allá

allí
almuerzo, el
alojarse
alquilar
alrededor (de)
alto
alumno, el
amarillo
ambiente, el
amigo, el
ancho
anciano
andar
año, el
anoche
antes (de)
antiguo
anuncio, el
apagar
aparcamiento, el
aparecer
apartamento, el
apellido, el
aprender (a)
aprobar
apropiado
aquel
aquello
aquí
árbol, el
armario, el
arreglar
arriba (de)
arroz, el
asado
ascensor, el
asiento, el
asistir
atención, la
atún, el
autobús, el
autocar, el

autopista, la
avenida, la
avión, el
ayer
ayuda, la
azúcar, el
azul

B
baile, el
bajo
banco, el
bañador, el
bañarse
baño, el
barato
barco, el
barrio, el
bastante
basura, la
bebé, el
beber
bebida, la
biblioteca, la
bien
blanco
bloque, el
blusa, la
boca, la
bocadillo, el
boda, la
bolsa, la
bolso, el
bomberos, los
bonito
bosque, el
botella, la
brazo, el
británico
buenas noches
buenas tardes
bueno

buenos días
buscar

C
caballero(s)
caballo, el
cabeza, la
cada
caer(se)
café, el
caja, la
cajero automático,
   el
calamares, los
calefacción, la
caliente
calle, la
calor, el
cama, la
cambiar
caminar
camisa, la
camiseta, la
campeón, el
campo, el
canción, la
cansado
cantar
cantidad, la
capaz
capital, la
cara, la
caravana, la
carne, la
caro
carrera, la
carretera, la
carta, la
cartón, el
casa, la
casado
casi
castañuelas, las

castellano
castigo, el
castillo, el
catalán
catedral, la
causa, la
cebolla, la
cena, la
centímetro, el
céntimo, el
centro, el
cepillo, el
cerca (de)
cerrado
cerrar
cerveza, la
champiñones, los
champú, el
cheque, el
chico, el
chimenea, la
chuleta, la
cielo, el
cierto
cigarrillo, el
cine, el
cinturón, el
ciudad, la
claro
clase, la
coche, el
cocina, la
coger
col, la
colegio, el
coliflor, la
color, el
comedor, el
comenzar
comer
comida, la
como
¿cómo?
cómodo
compañero, el
compañía, la
completo
comprar

compras, las
conductor, el
conejo, el
confitería, la
congelador, el
conocer
conseguir
consejo, el
contaminación, la
contar
contento
contestar
continuar
contra
controlar
conversación, la
copa, la
corbata, la
corregir
correo, el
correo electrónico, el
correr
corrida de toros, la
corto
cosa, la
costa, la
costar
crema, la
cristal, el
cruce, el
cuaderno, el
¿cuál(es)?
cualidad, la
cualquier(a)
cuando
¿cuándo?
¿cuánto(s)?
cuarto, el
cuchara, la
cuenta, la
cuero, el
cuerpo, el
cuidado, el
cuidar
cumplir

D
dar
de
de nada
de nuevo
debajo (de)
deber vb, el
decidir
décimo
decir
dedo, el
defecto, el
dejar
dejar de
delante (de)
delgado
delicioso
demasiado
dentro (de)
dependiente, el
deporte, el
deprisa
derecha, la
derecho
desaparecer
desastre, el
desayuno, el
descansar
descripción, la
desde
despacho, el
despacio
despertarse
después (de)
destino, el
detalle, el
detrás (de)
día, el
diálogo, el
dibujo, el
diciembre
diente, el
diferencia, la
diferente (de)
difícil
¡diga!
dinero, el
dirección, la

director, el
discoteca, la
disculpa, la
distinto (de)
divertido
divorciado
doble
docena, una
doler
dolor, el
domingo, el
donde
¿dónde?
dormir(se)
droga, la
ducha, la
dueño, el
dulce
durante
durar
duro

E
económico
edad, la
edificio, el
ejemplo, el
ejercicio, el
ejército, el
empezar
empleado, el
empujar
en
en seguida
encender
encima (de)
encontrar(se)
enero
enfadado
enfermedad, la
enfermo
enfrente (de)
ensalada, la
enseñar
entender
entonces
entrada, la
entrar

entre
enviar
época, *la*
equipaje, *el*
equipo, *el*
equivocarse
esa
escalera, *la*
escocés
Escocia
escoger
escribir
escuchar
escuela, *la*
ese
eso
espalda, *la*
España
español
especial
espectáculo, *el*
espejo, *el*
esperar
esposo, *el*
esquí, *el*
esquina, *la*
esta
estación, *la*
estado civil, *el*
estanco, *el*
estar
este
Este, *el*
esto
estómago, *el*
estrecho
estrella, *la*
estricto
estropear
estudiante, *el*
estudios, *los*
euro, *el*
Europa
europeo
evitar
examen, *el*
excelente
éxito, *el*

experiencia, *la*
explicar
extranjero, *el*

F

fábrica, *la*
fácil
falda, *la*
falso
faltar
familia, *la*
famoso
farmacia, *la*
febrero
fecha, *la*
feliz
feo
fiebre, *la*
fiesta, *la*
fin, *el*
final, *el*
firmar
flan, *el*
flojo
flor, *la*
formal
foto(grafía), *la*
fracasar
frase, *la*
freír
fresa, *la*
fresco
frigorífico, *el*
frío, *el*
fruta, *la*
fuera (de)
fuerte
fumador
fumar
función, *la*
funcionar
fútbol, *el*

G

gafas, *las*
galería (de arte), *la*
galés
gallego

gambas, *las*
ganar
garaje, *el*
gasolinera, *la*
gastar
gato, *el*
generoso
gente, *la*
gimnasia, *la*
gol, *el*
goma, *la*
gracias
grande
granja, *la*
gris
gritar
grueso
grupo, *el*
guantes, *los*
guapo
guardar
guía, *el*, *la*
guitarra, *la*
gustar

H

habitación, *la*
hablar
hacer
hacerse
hacia
hambre, *el*
hamburguesa, *la*
hasta
hay
helado, *el*
herida, *la*
hermano, *el*
hierba, *la*
hierro, *el*
hijo, *el*
historia, *la*
histórico
hola
hombre, *el*
hora, *la*
horario, *el*
hospital, *el*

hotel, *el*
hoy
huevo, *el*
humo, *el*

I

idioma, *el*
iglesia, *la*
igual
impermeable, *el*
importante
imposible
incluir
inconveniente, *el*
indicar
industria, *la*
informática, *la*
ingeniero, *el*
inglés, *(el)*
inteligente
intercambio, *el*
interesante
interesar(se)
interior, *el*
Internet, *(la)*
inútil
invierno, *el*
invitar
ir (a/en)
irlandés
izquierda, *la*

J

jabón, *el*
jamás
jamón, *el*
jardín, *el*
jardinero, *el*
jefe, *el*
joven
judías verdes, *las*
juego, *el*
jueves, *el*
jugador, *el*
jugar
juguete, *el*
julio
junio

K

kilo, el
kilómetro, el

L

lado, el
lago, el
lámpara, la
lana, la
lápiz, el
largo
lata, la
lavabo, el
lavadora, la
lavar
leche, la
lechuga, la
leer
lejos (de)
lengua, la
lentillas, las
lento
letra, la
levantarse
libre
librería, la,
libro, el
limpio
línea, la
lista, la
litro, el
llamar
llamarse
llave, la
llegada, la
llegar (a/de)
lleno
llevar
llorar
llover
lluvia, la
lotería, la
luego
lugar, el
lunes, el
luz, la

M

madera, la
madre, la
mal
maleta, la
malo
mañana, la
mandar
mano, la
manta, la
mantequilla, la
manzana, la
mapa, el
máquina, la
máquina de fotos,
la
mar, el
marca, la
marcar
marido, el
mariscos, los
marrón
martes, el
marzo
más
matemáticas, las
matrimonio, el
mayor
mayoría, la
medalla, la
medias, las
medicina, la
médico, el
medida, la
medio
medio ambiente,
el
mediodía
mejor
mejorar(se)
melocotón, el
melón, el
menor
menos
mensaje, el
mentira, la
menú, el
mercado, el

merienda, la
mermelada, la
mes, el
mesa, la
metro, el
miedo
miembro, el
mientras (que)
miércoles, el
minuto, el
mirar
mismo
mitad, la
mochila, la
moderno
moneda, la
montaña, la
moreno
morir
moto, la
mucho
mucho gusto
mudarse (de casa)
muebles, los
muerto
mujer, la
mundo, el
museo, el
música, la
muy

N

nacer
nacimiento, el
nada
nada más
nadar
nadie
naranja
naranja, la
nariz, la
nata, la
necesario
necesitar
negro
nevera, la
niebla, la
nieto, el

nieve, la
ninguno
niño, el
no
noche, la
nombre, el
normal
Norte, el
nota, la
noticias, las
novela, la
noviembre
novio, el
nube, la
nuevo
número, el
nunca

O

obrero, el
obtener
ocupado
ocurrir
Oeste, el
oferta, la
oficina, la
¡oiga!
oír
ojo, el
olor, el
olvidar
opinión, la
ordenador, el
oreja, la
organizar
oro, el
oscuro
otoño, el
otro

P

padre, el
pagar
página, la
país, el
pájaro, el
palabra, la
palacio, el

pan, *el*
panadería, *la*
pantalón, *el*
papel, *el*
paquete, *el*
para
parada, *la*
parado
paraguas, *el*
parar
parecer
parecerse (a)
pared, *la*
pareja, *la*
parientes, *los*
parque, *el*
parte, *la*
participar
partido, *el*
pasado, *el*
pasajero, *el*
pasaporte, *el*
pasar
pasatiempo, *el*
paseo, *el*
paso, *el*
pastelería, *la*
pastilla, *la*
patata, *la*
patio, *el*
peatón, *el*
pedazo, *el*
pedir
peine, *el*
película, *la*
peligroso
pelo, *el*
pelota, *la*
peluquería, *la*
pensar
pensión, *la*
pequeño
pera, *la*
perder
perdón
periódico, *el*
permitir
pero

perro, *el*
persona, *la*
pertenecer
pesar
pescadería, *la*
pescado, *el*
peso, *el*
pez, *el*
picante
pie, *el*
piel, *la*
pierna, *la*
pimienta, *la*
pimiento, *el*
piña, *la*
piscina, *la*
piso, *el*
plano, *el*
plástico, *el*
plata, *la*
plátano, *el*
plato, *el*
playa, *la*
plaza, *la*
pobre
poco, (un)
poder
policía, el, la
poner
ponerse
por
porque
¿por qué?
posibilidad, *la*
postre, *el*
practicar
precio, *el*
preferir
pregunta, (*la*)
premio, *el*
preocupar(se)
preparar
presente
prestar
primavera, *la*
primero
primo, *el*
principio, al

probar
problema, *el*
profesor, *el*
programa, *el*
prohibido
prohibir
pronto
propina, *la*
próximo
prueba, *la*
publicidad, *la*
público, (*el*)
pueblo, *el*
puente, *el*
puerta, *la*
puerto, *el*
pues

Q
que
¿qué?
quedar
queja, *la*
quemadura, *la*
querer
querido
queso, *el*
¿quién?
quitarse
quizá(s)

R
ración, *la*
radio, *la*
rápido
raro
rato, *el*
ratón, *el*
razón, *la*
recepción, *la*
recibo, *el*
recordar
recto
recuerdo, *el*
redondo
regalo, *el*
región, *la*
regla,

reír(se)
religión, *la*
reloj, *el*
reserva, *la*
reservar
resfriado, *el*
respeto, *el*
responder
responsable
respuesta, *la*
restaurante, *el*
retraso, *el*
revista, *la*
rico
río, *el*
rojo
romper(se)
ropa, *la*
rosa
roto
rubio
rueda, *la*
ruido, *el*

S
sábado, *el*
saber
sabor, *el*
sacar
sal, *la*
sala, *la*
salado
salchicha, *la*
salida, *la*
salir (a/de)
salón, *el*
salsa, *la*
salud, *la*
saludos
sardina, *la*
septiembre
sección, *la*
sed, *la*
seguir
segundo (*el*)
sello, *el*
semáforo, *el*
semana, *la*

señal, *la*
sencillo
señor
señora
señorita
sentarse
sentido, *el*
sentir (se)
séptimo
ser
serio
servicio, *el*
servicios, los
servir
sexo, *el*
si
sí
siempre
sierra, *la*
siguiente
silencio, *el*
silla, *la*
sillón, *el*
simpático
sin
sino
sitio, *el*
sobre
socio, *el*
sofá, *el*
sol, *el*
solamente
soldado, *el*
solo
sólo
soltero
sombrero, *el*
sonar
sonido, *el*
sopa, *la*
sorpresa, *la*
subir
sucio

suelo, *el*
sueño, *el*
suerte, *la*
sugerir
supermercado, *el*
Sur, *el*

T

tabaco, *el*
taller, *el*
tamaño, *el*
también
tampoco
tan
tanto
tapas, *las*
taquilla, *la*
tarde, (*la*)
tarjeta, *la*
tarta, *la*
taza, *la*
té, *el*
techo, *el*
técnico, (*el*)
tejado, *el*
tela, *la*
teléfono (móvil), *el*
televisión, *la*
temperatura, *la*
temprano
tenedor, *el*
tener
tercero
terminar
terraza, *la*
tiempo, *el*
tienda, *la*
tierra, *la*
tijeras, *las*
tío, *el*
típico
tipo, *el*
tirar

toalla, *la*
tocar
todavía
todo
tomar
tomate, *el*
tonto
torcer
torero, *el*
toro, *el*
tortilla, *la*
tostada, *la*
trabajador, (*el*)
trabajar
trabajo, *el*
traer
tráfico, *el*
traje, *el*
tranquilo
transporte, *el*
tratar de
tren, *el*
triste
trozo, *el*
tu
tú
turista, *el*

U

último
único
universidad, *la*
uno
urgencias, *las*
usar
usted(es)
útil

V

vacaciones, *las*
vacío
valle, *el*
vaqueros, los

vaso, *el*
vecino, *el*
vender
venir
ventaja, *la*
ventana, *la*
ver
verano, *el*
verdad, *la*
verde
vestido, *el*
vestirse
vez, *la*
viaje, *el*
viajero, *el*
vida, *la*
vidrio, *el*
viejo
viento, *el*
viernes, *el*
vino, *el*
visita, *la*
visitar
vista, *la*
vivir
vivo
volver (a/de)
vosotros
voz, *la*
vuelo, *el*

Y

y/e
ya

Z

zanahoria, *la*
zapatos, *los*
zona, *la*
zumo, *el*

Aa

a /ə/, stressed form /eɪ/

before vowel sound or silent 'h' **an**

indefinite article

····▶ un (m), una (f). **a problem** un problema. **an apple** una manzana. **have you got a pencil?** ¿tienes un lápiz?

! Feminine singular nouns beginning with stressed a or ha take the article un instead of una, e.g. un águila, un hada

····▶ (when talking about prices and quantities) por. **30 miles an hour** 30 millas por hora. **twice a week** dos veces por semana, dos veces a la semana

! There are many cases in which **a** is not translated, such as when talking about people's professions, in exclamations, etc: **she's a lawyer** es abogada. **what a beautiful day!** ¡qué día más precioso!. **have you got a car?** ¿tienes coche? **half a cup** media taza

A & E /eɪənd'iː/ n urgencias fpl

aback /ə'bæk/ adv. **be taken ~** quedar desconcertado

abandon /ə'bændən/ vt abandonar. ●n abandono m, desenfado m. ~**ed** adj abandonado

abashed /ə'bæʃt/ adj confuso

abate /ə'beɪt/ vi disminuir; (storm etc) calmarse

abattoir /'æbətwɑː(r)/ n matadero m

abbess /'æbɪs/ n abadesa f

abbey /'æbɪ/ n abadía f

abbot /'æbət/ n abad m

abbreviat|e /ə'briːvɪeɪt/ vt abreviar. ~**ion** /-'eɪʃn/ n abreviatura f; (act) abreviación f

abdicat|e /'æbdɪkeɪt/ vt/i abdicar. ~**ion** /-'eɪʃn/ n abdicación f

abdom|en /'æbdəmən/ n abdomen m. ~**inal** /-'dɒmɪnl/ adj abdominal

abduct /æb'dʌkt/ vt secuestrar. ~**ion** /-ʃn/ n secuestro m

abhor /əb'hɔː(r)/ vt (pt **abhorred**) aborrecer. ~**rence** /-'hɒrəns/ n aborrecimiento m. ~**rent** /-'hɒrənt/ adj aborrecible

abide /ə'baɪd/ vt (pt **abided**) soportar. ●vi (old use, pt **abode**) morar. ■ ~ **by** atenerse a; cumplir (promise)

ability /ə'bɪlətɪ/ n capacidad f; (cleverness) habilidad f

abject /'æbdʒekt/ adj (wretched) miserable

ablaze /ə'bleɪz/ adj en llamas

able /'eɪbl/ adj (**-er, -est**) capaz. **be ~** poder; (know how to) saber. ~**-bodied** /-'bɒdɪd/ adj sano, no discapacitado

ably /'eɪblɪ/ adv hábilmente

abnormal /æb'nɔːml/ adj anormal. ~**ity** /-'mælətɪ/ n anormalidad f

aboard /ə'bɔːd/ adv a bordo. ●prep a bordo de

abode /ə'bəʊd/ see ABIDE. ●n (old use) domicilio m

aboli|sh /ə'bɒlɪʃ/ vt abolir. ~**tion** /æbə'lɪʃn/ n abolición f

abominable /ə'bɒmɪnəbl/ adj abominable

aborigin|al /æbə'rɪdʒənl/ adj & n aborigen (m & f), indígena (m & f). ~**es** /-iːz/ npl aborígenes mpl

abort /ə'bɔːt/ vt hacer abortar. ~**ion** /-ʃn/ n aborto m provocado;

a

(fig) aborto m. **have an ~ion** hacerse un aborto. **~ive** adj fracasado

abound /ə'baʊnd/ vi abundar (**in** en)

about /ə'baʊt/ adv (approximately) alrededor de; (here and there) por todas partes; (in existence) por aquí. **~ here** por aquí. **be ~ to** estar a punto de. ● prep sobre; (around) alrededor de; (somewhere in) en. **talk ~** hablar de. **~-face**, **~-turn** n (fig) cambio m rotundo

above /ə'bʌv/ ● prep encima de; (more than) más de. **~ all** sobre todo. **~ board** adj legítimo. ● adv abiertamente. **~-mentioned** adj susodicho

abrasi|on /ə'breɪʒn/ n abrasión f. **~ve** /-sɪv/ adj abrasivo

abreast /ə'brest/ adv. **march four ~** marchar en columna de cuatro en fondo. **keep ~ of** mantenerse al corriente de

abroad /ə'brɔːd/ adv (be) en el extranjero; (go) al extranjero; (far and wide) por todas partes

abrupt /ə'brʌpt/ adj brusco. **~ly** (suddenly) repentinamente; (curtly) bruscamente

abscess /'æbsɪs/ n absceso m

abscond /əb'skɒnd/ vi fugarse

absen|ce /'æbsəns/ n ausencia f; (lack) falta f. **~t** /'æbsənt/ adj ausente. **~t-minded** /-'maɪndɪd/ adj distraído. **~t-mindedness** n distracción f, despiste m. **~tee** /-'tiː/ n ausente m & f. **~teeism** n absentismo m, ausentismo m (LAm)

absolute /'æbsəluːt/ adj absoluto. **~ly** adv absolutamente

absolve /əb'zɒlv/ vt (from sin) absolver; (from obligation) liberar

absor|b /əb'zɔːb/ vt absorber. **~bent** /-bent/ adj absorbente. **~bent cotton** (Amer) algodón m hidrófilo. **~ption** /əb'zɔːpʃən/ n absorción f

abstain /əb'steɪn/ vi abstenerse (**from** de)

abstemious /əb'stiːmɪəs/ adj abstemio

abstention /əb'stenʃn/ n abstención f

abstract /'æbstrækt/ adj abstracto. ● n (summary) resumen m; (painting) cuadro m abstracto. ● /əb'strækt/ vt extraer; (summarize) resumir. **~ion** /-ʃn/ n abstracción f

absurd /əb'sɜːd/ adj absurdo. **~ity** n absurdo m, disparate m

abundan|ce /ə'bʌndns/ n abundancia f. **~t** adj abundante

abus|e /ə'bjuːz/ vt (misuse) abusar de; (ill-treat) maltratar; (insult) insultar. ● /ə'bjuːs/ n abuso m; (insults) insultos mpl. **~ive** /ə'bjuːsɪv/ adj injurioso

abysmal /ə'bɪzməl/ adj 🄴 pésimo

abyss /ə'bɪs/ n abismo m

academic /ækə'demɪk/ adj académico; (pej) teórico. ● n universitario m, catedrático m

academy /ə'kædəmɪ/ n academia f.

accelerat|e /ək'seləreɪt/ vt acelerar. ● vi acelerar; (Auto) apretar el acelerador. **~ion** /-'reɪʃn/ n aceleración f. **~or** n acelerador m

accent /'æksənt/ n acento m

accept /ək'sept/ vt aceptar. **~able** adj aceptable. **~ance** n aceptación f; (approval) aprobación f

access /'ækses/ n acceso m. **~ible** /ək'sesəbl/ adj accesible; (person) tratable

accession /æk'seʃn/ n (to power, throne etc) ascenso m; (thing added) adquisición f

accessory /ək'sesərɪ/ adj accesorio. ● n accesorio m, complemento m; (Jurid) cómplice m & f

accident /'æksɪdənt/ n accidente m; (chance) casualidad f. **by ~** sin querer; (by chance) por casualidad. **~al** /-'dentl/ adj accidental, fortuito. **~ally** /-'dentəlɪ/ adv sin querer; (by chance) por casualidad. **~-prone** adj propenso a los accidentes

acclaim /əˈkleɪm/ vt aclamar. •n aclamación f

accolade /ˈækəleɪd/ n (praise) encomio m

accommodat|e /əˈkɒmədeɪt/ vt (give hospitality to) alojar; (adapt) acomodar; (oblige) complacer. ~ing adj complaciente. ~ion /-ˈdeɪʃn/ n, ~ions npl (Amer) alojamiento m

accompan|iment /əˈkʌmpənɪmənt/ n acompañamiento m. ~ist n acompañante m & f. ~y /əˈkʌmpənɪ/ vt acompañar

accomplice /əˈkʌmplɪs/ n cómplice m & f

accomplish /əˈkʌmplɪʃ/ vt (complete) acabar; (achieve) realizar; (carry out) llevar a cabo. ~ed adj consumado. ~ment n realización f; (ability) talento m; (thing achieved) triunfo m, logro m

accord /əˈkɔːd/ vi concordar. •vt conceder. •n acuerdo m; (harmony) armonía f. **of one's own ~** espontáneamente. ~ance n. **in ~ance with** de acuerdo con. ~ing adv. ~ing to según. ~ingly adv en conformidad; (therefore) por consiguiente

accordion /əˈkɔːdɪən/ n acordeón m

accost /əˈkɒst/ vt abordar

account /əˈkaʊnt/ n cuenta f; (description) relato m. ~s npl (in business) contabilidad f. **on no ~** de ninguna manera. **on this ~** por eso. **take into ~** tener en cuenta. •vt considerar. ∎ **~ for** vt dar cuenta de, explicar

accountan|cy /əˈkaʊntənsɪ/ n contabilidad f. ~t n contable m & f, contador m (LAm)

accumulat|e /əˈkjuːmjʊleɪt/ vt acumular. •vi acumularse. ~ion /-ˈleɪʃn/ n acumulación f

accura|cy /ˈækjərəsɪ/ n exactitud f, precisión f. ~te /-ət/ adj exacto, preciso

accus|ation /ækjuːˈzeɪʃn/ n acusación f. ~e /əˈkjuːz/ vt acusar

accustom /əˈkʌstəm/ vt acostumbrar. ~ed adj. **be ~ed (to)** estar acostumbrado (a). **get ~ed (to)** acostumbrarse (a)

ace /eɪs/ n as m

ache /eɪk/ n dolor m. •vi doler. **my leg ~s** me duele la pierna

achieve /əˈtʃiːv/ vt realizar; lograr (success). ~ment n realización f; (feat) proeza f; (thing achieved) logro m

acid /ˈæsɪd/ adj & n ácido (m). ~ic /əˈsɪdɪk/ adj ácido. ~ **rain** n lluvia f ácida

acknowledge /əkˈnɒlɪdʒ/ vt reconocer. ~ **receipt of** acusar recibo de. ~ment n reconocimiento m; (Com) acuse m de recibo

acne /ˈæknɪ/ n acné m

acorn /ˈeɪkɔːn/ n bellota f

acoustic /əˈkuːstɪk/ adj acústico. ~s npl acústica f

acquaint /əˈkweɪnt/ vt. ~ **s.o. with** poner a uno al corriente de. **be ~ed with** conocer (person); saber (fact). ~ance n conocimiento m; (person) conocido m

acquiesce /ækwɪˈes/ vi consentir (in en). ~nce n aquiescencia f, consentimiento m

acqui|re /əˈkwaɪə(r)/ vt adquirir; aprender (language). ~**re a taste for** tomar gusto a. ~**sition** /ækwɪˈzɪʃn/ n adquisición f. ~**sitive** /əˈkwɪzətɪv/ adj codicioso

acquit /əˈkwɪt/ vt (pt **acquitted**) absolver. ~**tal** n absolución f

acre /ˈeɪkə(r)/ n acre m

acrid /ˈækrɪd/ adj acre

acrimonious /ækrɪˈməʊnɪəs/ adj cáustico, mordaz

acrobat /ˈækrəbæt/ n acróbata m & f. ~**ic** /-ˈbætɪk/ adj acrobático. ~**ics** npl acrobacia f

acronym /ˈækrənɪm/ n acrónimo m, siglas fpl

across /əˈkrɒs/ adv & prep (side to side) de un lado al otro; (on other side) al otro lado de; (crosswise) a través. **it is 20 metres ~** tiene 20 metros de ancho. **go** or **walk ~** atravesar, cruzar

act /ækt/ n acto m; (action) acción f; (in variety show) número m; (decree) decreto m. •vt hacer (part, role). •vi actuar; (pretend) fingir. **~ as** actuar de; (object) servir de. **~ for** representar. **~ing** adj interino. •n (of play) representación f; (by actor) interpretación f; (profession) profesión f de actor

action /ˈækʃn/ n acción f; (Jurid) demanda f; (plot) argumento m. **out of ~** (on sign) no funciona. **put out of ~** inutilizar. **take ~** tomar medidas. **~ replay** n repetición f de la jugada

activate /ˈæktɪveɪt/ vt activar

activ|e /ˈæktɪv/ adj activo; (energetic) lleno de energía; (volcano) en actividad. **~ist** n activista m & f. **~ity** /-ˈtɪvəti/ n actividad f

act|or /ˈæktə(r)/ n actor m. **~ress** /-trɪs/ n actriz f

actual /ˈæktʃʊəl/ adj verdadero. **~ly** adv en realidad, efectivamente; (even) incluso

acute /əˈkjuːt/ adj agudo. **~ly** adv agudamente

ad /æd/ n 🇬🇧 anuncio m, aviso m (LAm)

AD /erˈdiː/ abbr (= **Anno Domini**) d. de J.C.

Adam's apple /ædəmzˈæpl/ n nuez f (de Adán)

adapt /əˈdæpt/ vt adaptar. •vi adaptarse. **~ability** /-əˈbɪləti/ n adaptabilidad f. **~able** /-əbl/ adj adaptable. **~ation** /ædæpˈteɪʃn/ n adaptación f; (of book etc) versión f. **~or** /əˈdæptə(r)/ n (Elec, with several sockets) enchufe m múltiple; (Elec, for different sockets) adaptador m

add /æd/ vt añadir. •vi sumar. ∎ **~**

up vt sumar; (fig) tener sentido. **~ up to** equivaler a

adder /ˈædə(r)/ n víbora f

addict /ˈædɪkt/ n adicto m; (fig) entusiasta m & f. **~ed** /əˈdɪktɪd/ adj. **~ed to** adicto a; (fig) fanático de. **~ion** /əˈdɪkʃn/ n (Med) dependencia f; (fig) afición f. **~ive** /əˈdɪktɪv/ adj que crea adicción; (fig) que crea hábito

addition /əˈdɪʃn/ n suma f. **in ~** además. **~al** adj suplementario

address /əˈdres/ n dirección f; (on form) domicilio m; (speech) discurso m. •vt poner la dirección en; (speak to) dirigirse a. **~ book** libreta f de direcciones. **~ee** /ædreˈsiː/ n destinatario m

adept /ˈædept/ adj & n experto (m)

adequa|cy /ˈædɪkwəsi/ n suficiencia f. **~te** /-ət/ adj suficiente, adecuado. **~tely** adv suficientemente, adecuadamente

adhere /ədˈhɪə(r)/ vi adherirse (**to** a); observar (rule). **~nce** /-rəns/ n adhesión f; (to rules) observancia f

adhesi|on /ədˈhiːʒn/ n adherencia f. **~ve** /-sɪv/ adj & n adhesivo (m)

adjacent /əˈdʒeɪsnt/ adj contiguo

adjective /ˈædʒɪktɪv/ n adjetivo m

adjourn /əˈdʒɜːn/ vt aplazar; suspender (meeting etc). •vi suspenderse

adjust /əˈdʒʌst/ vt ajustar (machine); (arrange) arreglar. •vi. **~ (to)** adaptarse (a). **~able** adj ajustable. **~ment** n adaptación f; (Tec) ajuste m

administer /ədˈmɪnɪstə(r)/ vt administrar

administrat|ion /ədmɪnɪˈstreɪʃn/ n administración f. **~ive** /ədˈmɪnɪstrətɪv/ adj administrativo. **~or** /ədˈmɪnɪstreɪtə(r)/ n administrador m

admirable /ˈædmərəbl/ adj admirable

admiral /ˈædmərəl/ n almirante m

admir|ation /ædməˈreɪʃn/ n

admiración f. **~e** /ədˈmaɪə(r)/ vt admirar. **~er** /ədˈmaɪərə(r)/ n admirador m

admission /ədˈmɪʃn/ n admisión f; (entry) entrada f

admit /ədˈmɪt/ vt (pt **admitted**) dejar entrar; (acknowledge) admitir, reconocer. **~ to** confesar. **be ~ted** (to hospital etc) ingresar. **~tance** n entrada f. **~tedly** adv es verdad que

admonish /ədˈmɒnɪʃ/ vt reprender; (advise) aconsejar

ado /əˈduː/ n alboroto m; (trouble) dificultad f. **without more or further ~** en seguida, sin más

adolescen|ce /ædəˈlesns/ n adolescencia f. **~t** adj & n adolescente (m & f)

adopt /əˈdɒpt/ vt adoptar. **~ed** adj (child) adoptivo. **~ion** /-ʃn/ n adopción f

ador|able /əˈdɔːrəbl/ adj adorable. **~ation** /ædəˈreɪʃn/ n adoración f. **~e** /əˈdɔː(r)/ vt adorar

adorn /əˈdɔːn/ vt adornar. **~ment** n adorno m

adrift /əˈdrɪft/ adj & adv a la deriva

adult /ˈædʌlt/ adj & n adulto (m)

adulter|er /əˈdʌltərə(r)/ n adúltero m. **~ess** /-ɪs/ n adúltera f. **~y** n adulterio m

advance /ədˈvɑːns/ vt adelantar. ●vi adelantarse. ●n adelanto m. **in ~** con anticipación, por adelantado. **~d** adj avanzado; (studies) superior

advantage /ədˈvɑːntɪdʒ/ n ventaja f. **take ~ of** aprovecharse de; abusar de (person). **~ous** /ædvənˈteɪdʒəs/ adj ventajoso

advent /ˈædvənt/ n venida f. **A~** n adviento m

adventur|e /ədˈventʃə(r)/ n aventura f. **~er** n aventurero m. **~ous** adj (person) aventurero; (thing) arriesgado; (fig, bold) audaz

adverb /ˈædvɜːb/ n adverbio m

adversary /ˈædvəsəri/ n adversario m

advers|e /ˈædvɜːs/ adj adverso, contrario, desfavorable. **~ity** /ədˈvɜːsəti/ n infortunio m

advert /ˈædvɜːt/ n **▣** anuncio m, aviso m (LAm). **~ise** /ˈædvətaɪz/ vt anunciar. ●vi hacer publicidad. (seek, sell) poner un anuncio. **~isement** /ədˈvɜːtɪsmənt/ n anuncio m, aviso m (LAm). **~iser** /ˈædvətaɪzə(r)/ n anunciante m & f

advice /ədˈvaɪs/ n consejo m; (report) informe m

advis|able /ədˈvaɪzəbl/ adj aconsejable. **~e** /ədˈvaɪz/ vt aconsejar; (inform) avisar. **~e against** aconsejar en contra de. **~er** n consejero m; (consultant) asesor m. **~ory** adj consultivo

advocate /ˈædvəkət/ n defensor m; (Jurid) abogado m. ●/ˈædvəkeɪt/ vt recomendar

aerial /ˈeəriəl/ adj aéreo. ●n antena f

aerobics /eəˈrəʊbɪks/ npl aeróbica f

aerodrome /ˈeərədrəʊm/ n aeródromo m

aerodynamic /ˌeərəʊdaɪˈnæmɪk/ adj aerodinámico

aeroplane /ˈeərəpleɪn/ n avión m

aerosol /ˈeərəsɒl/ n aerosol m

aesthetic /iːsˈθetɪk/ adj estético

afar /əˈfɑː(r)/ adv lejos

affable /ˈæfəbl/ adj afable

affair /əˈfeə(r)/ n asunto m. **(love) ~** aventura f, amorío m. **~s** npl (business) negocios mpl

affect /əˈfekt/ vt afectar; (pretend) fingir. **~ation** /æfekˈteɪʃn/ n afectación f. **~ed** adj afectado, amanerado

affection /əˈfekʃn/ n cariño m. **~ate** /-ət/ adj cariñoso

affiliate /əˈfɪlieɪt/ vt afiliar

affirm /əˈfɜːm/ vt afirmar. **~ative** /-ətɪv/ adj afirmativo. ●n respuesta f afirmativa

afflict /əˈflɪkt/ vt afligir. **~ion** /-ʃn/ n aflicción f, pena f

a

affluen|ce /'æfluəns/ n riqueza f. **~t** adj rico.

afford /ə'fɔːd/ vt permitirse; (provide) dar. **he can't ~ a car** no le alcanza el dinero para comprar un coche

affront /ə'frʌnt/ n afrenta f, ofensa f. ●vt afrentar, ofender

afield /ə'fiːld/ adv. **far ~** muy lejos

afloat /ə'fləʊt/ adv a flote

afraid /ə'freɪd/ adj. **be ~** tener miedo (**of** a); (be sorry) sentir, lamentar

afresh /ə'freʃ/ adv de nuevo

Africa /'æfrɪkə/ n África f. **~n** adj & n africano (m). **~n-American** adj & n norteamericano (m) de origen africano

after /'ɑːftə(r)/ adv después; (behind) detrás. ●prep después de; (behind) detrás de. **it's twenty ~ four** (Amer) son las cuatro y veinte. **be ~** (seek) andar en busca de. ●conj después de que. ●adj posterior. **~-effect** n consecuencia f, efecto m secundario. **~math** /'ɑːftəmæθ/ n secuelas fpl. **~noon** /-'nuːn/ n tarde f. **~shave** n loción f para después de afeitarse. **~thought** n ocurrencia f tardía. **~wards** /-wədz/ adv después

again /ə'gen/ adv otra vez; (besides) además. **do ~** volver a hacer, hacer otra vez. **~ and ~** una y otra vez

against /ə'genst/ prep contra; (in opposition to) en contra de, contra

age /eɪdʒ/ n edad f. **at four years of ~** a los cuatro años. **under ~** menor de edad. **~s** npl ▣ siglos mpl. ●vt/i (pres p **ageing**) envejecer. **~d** /'eɪdʒd/ adj de ... años. **~d 10** de 10 años. **~d** /'eɪdʒɪd/ adj viejo, anciano

agency /'eɪdʒənsɪ/ n agencia f; (department) organismo m

agenda /ə'dʒendə/ n orden m del día

agent /'eɪdʒənt/ n agente m & f; (representative) representante m & f

aggravat|e /'ægrəveɪt/ vt agravar; (fam, irritate) irritar. **~ion** /-'veɪʃn/ n agravación f; (fam, irritation) irritación f

aggress|ion /ə'greʃn/ n agresión f. **~ive** adj agresivo. **~iveness** n agresividad f. **~or** n agresor m

aggrieved /ə'griːvd/ adj apenado, ofendido

aghast /ə'gɑːst/ adj horrorizado

agil|e /'ædʒaɪl/ adj ágil. **~ity** /ə'dʒɪlətɪ/ n agilidad f

aging /'eɪdʒɪŋ/ adj envejecido. ●n envejecimiento m

agitat|e /'ædʒɪteɪt/ vt agitar. **~ed** adj nervioso. **~ion** /-'teɪʃn/ n agitación f, excitación f. **~or** n agitador m

ago /ə'gəʊ/ adv. **a long time ~** hace mucho tiempo. **3 days ~** hace 3 días

agon|ize /'ægənaɪz/ vi atormentarse. **~izing** adj (pain) atroz; (experience) angustioso. **~y** n dolor m (agudo); (mental) angustia f

agree /ə'griː/ vt acordar. ●vi estar de acuerdo; (of figures) concordar; (get on) entenderse. ■ **~ on** vt acordar (date, details). **~ with** vt (of food etc) sentarle bien a. **~able** /ə'griːəbl/ adj agradable. **~able** (willing) estar de acuerdo. **~d** adj (time, place) convenido. **~ment** /-mənt/ n acuerdo m. **in ~ment** de acuerdo

agricultur|al /ægrɪ'kʌltʃərəl/ adj agrícola. **~e** /'ægrɪkʌltʃə(r)/ n agricultura f

aground /ə'graʊnd/ adv. **run ~** (of ship) varar, encallar

ahead /ə'hed/ adv delante; (in time) antes de. **be ~** ir delante

aid /eɪd/ vt ayudar. ●n ayuda f. **in ~ of** a beneficio de

AIDS /eɪdz/ n sida m

ailment /'eɪlmənt/ n enfermedad f

aim /eɪm/ vt apuntar; (fig) dirigir. ●vi apuntar; (fig) pretender. ●n puntería f; (fig) objetivo m. **~less**

adj, **~lessly** adv sin objeto, sin rumbo

air /eə(r)/ n aire m. **be on the ~** (Radio, TV) estar en el aire. **put on ~s** darse aires. • vt airear. **~ bag** n (Auto) bolsa f de aire. **~ base** n base f aérea. **~borne** adj en el aire; (Mil) aerotransportado. **~-conditioned** adj climatizado, con aire acondicionado. **~ conditioning** n aire m acondicionado. **~craft** n (pl invar) avión m. **~craft carrier** n portaaviones m. **~field** n aeródromo m. **A~ Force** n fuerzas fpl aéreas. **~ freshener** n ambientador m. **~gun** n escopeta f de aire comprimido. **~ hostess** n azafata f, aeromoza f (LAm). **~line** n línea f aérea. **~ mail** n correo m aéreo. **~plane** n (Amer) avión m. **~port** n aeropuerto m. **~sick** adj mareado (en un avión). **~tight** adj hermético. **~ traffic controller** n controlador m aéreo. **~y** adj (**-ier**, **-iest**) aireado; (manner) desenfadado

aisle /aɪl/ n nave f lateral; (gangway) pasillo m

ajar /ə'dʒɑ:(r)/ adj entreabierto

alarm /ə'lɑ:m/ n alarma f. • vt asustar. **~ clock** n despertador m. **~ist** n alarmista m & f

Albania /æl'beɪnɪə/ n Albania f. **~n** adj & n albanés (m)

albatross /'ælbətrɒs/ n albatros m

album /'ælbəm/ n álbum m

alcohol /'ælkəhɒl/ n alcohol m. **~ic** /-'hɒlɪk/ adj & n alcohólico (m)

alcove /'ælkəʊv/ n nicho m

ale /eɪl/ n cerveza f

alert /ə'lɜ:t/ adj vivo; (watchful) vigilante. • n alerta f. **on the ~** alerta. • vt avisar

algebra /'ældʒɪbrə/ n álgebra f

Algeria /æl'dʒɪərɪə/ n Argelia f. **~n** adj & n argelino (m)

alias /'eɪlɪəs/ n (pl **-ases**) alias m. • adv alias

alibi /'ælɪbaɪ/ n (pl **-is**) coartada f

alien /'eɪlɪən/ n extranjero m. • adj ajeno. **~ate** /-eɪt/ vt enajenar. **~ation** /-'neɪʃn/ n enajenación f

alienat|e /'eɪlɪəneɪt/ vt enajenar. **~ion** /-'neɪʃn/ n enajenación f

alight /ə'laɪt/ adj ardiendo; (light) encendido

align /ə'laɪn/ vt alinear. **~ment** n alineación f

alike /ə'laɪk/ adj parecido, semejante. **look** or **be ~** parecerse. • adv de la misma manera

alive /ə'laɪv/ adj vivo. **~ with** lleno de

alkali /'ælkəlaɪ/ n (pl **-is**) álcali m. **~ne** adj alcalino

all /ɔ:l/

• adjective todo, -da; (pl) todos, -das. **~ day** todo el día. **~ the windows** todas las ventanas. **~ four of us went** fuimos los cuatro

• pronoun

·····▶ (everything) todo. **that's ~** eso es todo. **I did ~ I could to persuade her** hice todo lo que pude para convencerla

·····▶ (after pronoun) todo, -da; (pl) todos, -das. **he helped us ~** nos ayudó a todos

·····▶ **all of** todo, -da, (pl) todos, -das. **~ of the paintings** todos los cuadros. **~ of the milk** toda la leche

·····▶ (in phrases) **all in all** en general. **not at all** (in no way) de ninguna manera; (after thanks) de nada, no hay de qué. **it's not at ~ bad** no está nada mal. **I don't like it at ~** no me gusta nada

• adverb

·····▶ (completely) completamente. **she was ~ alone** estaba completamente sola. **I got ~ dirty** me ensucié todo/toda. **I** don't know him ~ that well no lo conozco tan bien

····▶ (in scores) **the score was one ~** iban empatados uno a uno

····▶ (in phrases) **to be all for sth** estar completamente a favor de algo. **to be all in** ⊤ estar rendido

all-around /ɔːlə'raʊnd/ adj (Amer) completo

allay /ə'leɪ/ vt aliviar (pain); aquietar (fears etc)

all-clear /ɔːl'klɪə(r)/ n fin m de (la) alarma; (permission) visto m bueno

alleg|ation /ælɪ'geɪʃn/ n alegato m. **~e** /ə'ledʒ/ vt alegar. **~ed** adj presunto. **~edly** /-ɪdlɪ/ adv según se dice, supuestamente

allegiance /ə'liːdʒəns/ n lealtad f

allegory /'ælɪgərɪ/ n alegoría f

allerg|ic /ə'lɜːdʒɪk/ adj alérgico (**to** a). **~y** /'ælədʒɪ/ n alergia f

alleviate /ə'liːvɪeɪt/ vt aliviar

alley /'ælɪ/ (pl **-eys**) n callejuela f

alliance /ə'laɪəns/ n alianza f

alligator /'ælɪgeɪtə(r)/ n caimán m

allocat|e /'æləkeɪt/ vt asignar; (share out) repartir. **~ion** /-'keɪʃn/ n asignación f; (distribution) reparto m

allot /ə'lɒt/ vt (pt **allotted**) asignar. **~ment** n asignación f; (land) parcela f

allow /ə'laʊ/ vt permitir; (grant) conceder; (reckon on) prever; (agree) admitir. ∎ **~ for** vt tener en cuenta. **~ance** /ə'laʊəns/ n concesión f; (pension) pensión f; (Com) rebaja f. **make ~ances for** ser indulgente con (person); (take into account) tener en cuenta

alloy /'ælɔɪ/ n aleación f

all: ~ right adj & adv bien. ● int ¡vale!, ¡okey! (esp LAm), ¡órale! (Mex). **~-round** adj completo

allusion /ə'luːʒn/ n alusión f

ally /'ælaɪ/ n aliado m. ● /ə'laɪ/ vt. **~ o.s.** aliarse (**with** con)

almighty /ɔːl'maɪtɪ/ adj todopoderoso

almond /'ɑːmənd/ n almendra f

almost /'ɔːlməʊst/ adv casi

alone /ə'ləʊn/ adj solo. ● adv sólo, solamente

along /ə'lɒŋ/ prep por, a lo largo de. ● adv. **~ with** junto con. **all ~** todo el tiempo. **come ~** venga. **~side** /-'saɪd/ adv (Naut) al costado. ● prep al lado de

aloof /ə'luːf/ adv apartado. ● adj reservado

aloud /ə'laʊd/ adv en voz alta

alphabet /'ælfəbet/ n alfabeto m. **~ical** /-'betɪkl/ adj alfabético

Alps /ælps/ npl. **the ~** los Alpes

already /ɔːl'redɪ/ adv ya

Alsatian /æl'seɪʃn/ n pastor m alemán

also /'ɔːlsəʊ/ adv también; (moreover) además

altar /'ɔːltə(r)/ n altar m

alter /'ɔːltə(r)/ vt cambiar. ● vi cambiarse. **~ation** /-'reɪʃn/ n modificación f; (to garment) arreglo m

alternate /ɔːl'tɜːnət/ adj alterno; (Amer) see **ALTERNATIVE.** ● /'ɔːltənət/ vt/i alternar. **~ly** /ɔːl'tɜːnətlɪ/ adv alternativamente

alternative /ɔːl'tɜːnətɪv/ adj alternativo. ● n alternativa f. **~ly** adv en cambio, por otra parte

although /ɔːl'ðəʊ/ conj aunque

altitude /'æltɪtjuːd/ n altitud f

altogether /ɔːltə'geðə(r)/ adv completamente; (on the whole) en total

aluminium /æljʊ'mɪnɪəm/, **aluminum** /ə'luːmɪnəm/ (Amer) n aluminio m

always /'ɔːlweɪz/ adv siempre

am /æm/ see **BE**

a.m. abbr (= ante meridiem) de la mañana

amalgamate /ə'mælgəmeɪt/ vt amalgamar. •vi amalgamarse

amass /ə'mæs/ vt acumular

amateur /'æmətə(r)/ adj & n amateur (m & f). ~**ish** adj (pej) torpe, chapucero

amaz|e /ə'meɪz/ vt asombrar. ~**ed** adj asombrado, estupefacto. **be** ~**ed at** quedarse asombrado de, asombrarse de. ~**ement** n asombro m. ~**ing** adj increíble

ambassador /æm'bæsədə(r)/ n embajador m

ambigu|ity /æmbɪ'gjuːətɪ/ n ambigüedad f. ~**ous** /æm'bɪgjʊəs/ adj ambiguo

ambiti|on /æm'bɪʃn/ n ambición f. ~**ous** /-ʃəs/ adj ambicioso

ambivalent /æm'bɪvələnt/ adj ambivalente

amble /'æmbl/ vi andar despacio, andar sin prisa

ambulance /'æmbjʊləns/ n ambulancia f

ambush /'æmbʊʃ/ n emboscada f. •vt tender una emboscada a

amen /ɑː'men/ int amén

amend /ə'mend/ vt enmendar. ~**ment** n enmienda f. ~**s** npl. **make** ~**s** reparar

amenities /ə'miːnətɪz/ npl servicios mpl; (of hotel, club) instalaciones fpl

America /ə'merɪkə/ n (continent) América; (North America) Estados mpl Unidos, Norteamérica f. ~**n** adj & n americano (m); (North American) estadounidense (m & f), norteamericano (m). ~**nism** n americanismo m

amiable /'eɪmɪəbl/ adj simpático

amicable /'æmɪkəbl/ adj amistoso

amid(st) /ə'mɪd(st)/ prep entre, en medio de

ammonia /ə'məʊnɪə/ n amoníaco m, amoniaco m

ammunition /æmjʊ'nɪʃn/ n municiones fpl

amnesty /'æmnəstɪ/ n amnistía f

amok /ə'mɒk/ adv. **run** ~ volverse loco

among(st) /ə'mʌŋ(st)/ prep entre

amount /ə'maʊnt/ n cantidad f; (total) total m, suma f. ■ ~ **to** vt sumar; (fig) equivaler a, significar

amp(ere) /'æmp(eə(r))/ n amperio m

amphibi|an /æm'fɪbɪən/ n anfibio m. ~**ous** /-əs/ adj anfibio

amphitheatre /'æmfɪθɪətə(r)/ n anfiteatro m

ampl|e /'æmpl/ adj (**-er**, **-est**) amplio; (enough) suficiente; (plentiful) abundante. ~**y** adv ampliamente, bastante

amplif|ier /'æmplɪfaɪə(r)/ n amplificador m. ~**y** /'æmplɪfaɪ/ vt amplificar

amputat|e /'æmpjʊteɪt/ vt amputar. ~**ion** /-'teɪʃn/ n amputación f

amus|e /ə'mjuːz/ vt divertir. ~**ed** adj (expression) divertido. **keep s.o.** ~**ed** entretener a uno. ~**ement** n diversión f. ~**ing** adj divertido

an /ən, æn/ see A

anaemi|a /ə'niːmɪə/ n anemia f. ~**c** adj anémico

anaesthe|tic /ænɪs'θetɪk/ n anestésico m. ~**tist** /ə'niːsθɪtɪst/ n anestesista m & f

anagram /'ænəgræm/ n anagrama m

analogy /ə'nælədʒɪ/ n analogía f

analy|se /'ænəlaɪz/ vt analizar. ~**sis** /ə'næləsɪs/ n (pl **-ses** /-siːz/) análisis m. ~**st** /'ænəlɪst/ n analista m & f. ~**tic(al)** /ænə'lɪtɪk(əl)/ adj analítico

anarch|ist /'ænəkɪst/ n anarquista m & f. ~**y** n anarquía f

anatom|ical /ænə'tɒmɪkl/ adj anatómico. ~**y** /ə'nætəmɪ/ n anatomía f

ancest|or /'ænsestə(r)/ n

antepasado m. ∼ral /-'sestrəl/ adj ancestral. ∼ry /'ænsestrɪ/ n ascendencia f

anchor /'æŋkə(r)/ n ancla f. •vt anclar; (fig) sujetar. •vi anclar. ∼**man** n (on TV) presentador m. ∼**woman** n (on TV) presentadora f.

ancient /'eɪnʃənt/ adj antiguo, viejo

ancillary /æn'sɪlərɪ/ adj auxiliar

and /ənd, ænd/ conj y; (before i- and hi-) e. **bread** ∼ **butter** pan m con mantequilla. **go** ∼ **see him** ve a verlo. **more** ∼ **more** cada vez más. **try** ∼ **come** trata de venir

anecdot|al /ænɪk'dəʊtl/ adj anecdótico. ∼**e** /'ænɪkdəʊt/ n anécdota f

anew /ə'njuː/ adv de nuevo

angel /'eɪndʒl/ n ángel m. ∼**ic** /æn'dʒelɪk/ adj angélico

anger /'æŋgə(r)/ n ira f. •vt enfadar, (esp LAm) enojar

angle /'æŋgl/ n ángulo m; (fig) punto m de vista. ∼**r** /'æŋglə(r)/ n pescador m

Anglican /'æŋglɪkən/ adj & n anglicano (m)

angr|ily /'æŋgrɪlɪ/ adv con enfado, (esp LAm) con enojo. ∼**y** /'æŋgrɪ/ adj (-ier, -iest) enfadado, (esp LAm) enojado. **get** ∼**y** enfadarse, enojarse (esp LAm)

anguish /'æŋgwɪʃ/ n angustia f

animal /'ænɪməl/ adj & n animal (m)

animat|e /'ænɪmeɪt/ vt animar. ∼**ion** /-'meɪʃn/ n animación f

animosity /ænɪ'mɒsətɪ/ n animosidad f

ankle /'æŋkl/ n tobillo m. ∼ **boot** botín m. ∼ **sock** calcetín m corto

annexe /'æneks/ n anexo m

annihilat|e /ə'naɪəleɪt/ vt aniquilar. ∼**ion** /-'leɪʃn/ n aniquilación f

anniversary /ænɪ'vɜːsərɪ/ n aniversario m

announce /ə'naʊns/ vt anunciar, comunicar. ∼**ment** n anuncio m;

(official) comunicado m. ∼**r** n (Radio, TV) locutor m

annoy /ə'nɔɪ/ vt molestar. ∼**ance** n molestia m. ∼**ed** adj enfadado, enojado (LAm). ∼**ing** adj molesto

annual /'ænjʊəl/ adj anual. •n anuario m. ∼**ly** adv cada año

annul /ə'nʌl/ vt (pt **annulled**) anular. ∼**ment** n anulación f

anonymous /ə'nɒnɪməs/ adj anónimo

anorak /'ænəræk/ n anorac m

another /ə'nʌðə(r)/ adj & pron otro. ∼ **10 minutes** 10 minutos más. **in** ∼ **way** de otra manera. **one** ∼ el uno al otro; (pl) unos a otros

answer /'ɑːnsə(r)/ n respuesta f; (solution) solución f. •vt contestar; escuchar, oír (prayer). ∼ **the door** abrir la puerta. •vi contestar. ∎ ∼ **back** vi contestar. ∎ ∼ **for** vt ser responsable de. ∼**able** adj responsable. ∼**ing machine** n contestador m automático

ant /ænt/ n hormiga f

antagoni|sm /æn'tægənɪzəm/ n antagonismo m. ∼**stic** /-'nɪstɪk/ adj antagónico, opuesto. ∼**ze** /æn'tægənaɪz/ vt provocar la enemistad de

Antarctic /æn'tɑːktɪk/ adj antártico. •n **the** ∼ la región antártica

antelope /'æntɪləʊp/ n antílope m

antenatal /'æntɪneɪtl/ adj prenatal

antenna /æn'tenə/ (pl **-nae** /-niː/) (of insect etc) n antena f; (pl **-nas**) (of radio, TV) antena f

anthem /'ænθəm/ n himno m

anthology /æn'θɒlədʒɪ/ n antología f

anthrax /'ænθræks/ n ántrax m

anthropolog|ist /ænθrə'pɒlədʒɪst/ n antropólogo m. ∼**y** n antropología f

anti-... /ænti/ pref anti... ∼**aircraft** /-'eəkrɑːft/ adj antiaéreo

antibiotic /æntɪbar'ɒtɪk/ adj & n antibiótico (m)

anticipat|e /æn'tɪsɪpeɪt/ vt anticiparse a; (foresee) prever; (forestall) prevenir. **~ion** /-'peɪʃn/ n (foresight) previsión f; (expectation) expectativa f

anti /~'klaɪmæks/ n decepción f. **~clockwise** /-'klɒkwaɪz/ adv & adj en sentido contrario al de las agujas del reloj

antidote /'æntɪdəʊt/ m antídoto m

antifreeze /'æntɪfriːz/ n anticongelante m

antiperspirant /æntɪ'pɜːspɪrənt/ n antitranspirante m

antiquated /'æntɪkweɪtɪd/ adj anticuado

antique /æn'tiːk/ adj antiguo. ● n antigüedad f. **~ dealer** anticuario m. **~ shop** tienda f de antigüedades

antiquity /æn'tɪkwətɪ/ n antigüedad f

anti /~'septɪk/ /-'septɪk/ adj & n antiséptico (m). **~social** /-'səʊʃl/ adj antisocial

antlers /'æntləz/ npl cornamenta f

anus /'eɪnəs/ n ano m

anvil /'ænvɪl/ n yunque m

anxi|ety /æŋ'zaɪətɪ/ n ansiedad f; (worry) inquietud f; (eagerness) anhelo m. **~ous** /'æŋkʃəs/ adj inquieto; (eager) deseoso. **~ously** adv con inquietud; (eagerly) con impaciencia

any /'enɪ/ adj algún; (negative) ningún m; (whatever) cualquier; (every) todo. **at ~ moment** en cualquier momento. **have you ~ wine?** ¿tienes vino? ● pron alguno; (negative) ninguno. **have we ~?** ¿tenemos algunos? **not ~** ninguno. ● adv (a little) un poco, algo. **is it ~ better?** ¿está algo mejor?

anybody /'enɪbɒdɪ/ pron alguien; (after negative) nadie. **~ can do it** cualquiera puede hacerlo

anyhow /'enɪhaʊ/ adv de todas formas; (in spite of all) a pesar de

todo; (badly) de cualquier manera

anyone /'enɪwʌn/ pron see ANYBODY

anything /'enɪθɪŋ/ pron algo; (whatever) cualquier cosa; (after negative) nada. **~ but** todo menos

anyway /'enɪweɪ/ adv de todas formas

anywhere /'enɪweə(r)/ adv en cualquier parte; (after negative) en ningún sitio. **~ else** en cualquier otro lugar. **~ you go** dondequiera que vayas

apart /ə'pɑːt/ adv aparte; (separated) separado. **~ from** aparte de. **come ~** romperse. **take ~** desmontar

apartheid /ə'pɑːtheɪt/ n apartheid m

apartment /ə'pɑːtmənt/ n (Amer) apartamento m, piso m. **~ building** (Amer) edificio m de apartamentos, casa f de pisos

apath|etic /æpə'θetɪk/ adj apático. **~y** /'æpəθɪ/ n apatía f

ape /eɪp/ n mono m. ● vt imitar

aperitif /ə'perətɪf/ n aperitivo m

aperture /'æpətʃʊə(r)/ n abertura f

apex /'eɪpeks/ n ápice m

aphrodisiac /æfrə'dɪzɪæk/ adj & n afrodisíaco (m), afrodisiaco (m)

apolog|etic /əpɒlə'dʒetɪk/ adj lleno de disculpas. **be ~etic** disculparse. **~ize** /ə'pɒlədʒaɪz/ vi disculparse (**for** de). **~y** /ə'pɒlədʒɪ/ n disculpa f

apostle /ə'pɒsl/ n apóstol m

apostrophe /ə'pɒstrəfɪ/ n apóstrofo m

appal /ə'pɔːl/ vt (pt **appalled**) horrorizar. **~ling** adj espantoso

apparatus /æpə'reɪtəs/ n aparato m

apparel /ə'pærəl/ n (Amer) ropa f

apparent /ə'pærənt/ adj aparente; (clear) evidente. **~ly** adv por lo visto

apparition /æpə'rɪʃn/ n aparición f

appeal /ə'piːl/ vi apelar; (attract)

atraer. • n llamamiento m; (attraction) atractivo m; (Jurid) apelación f. **~ing** adj atrayente

appear /ə'pɪə(r)/ vi aparecer; (seem) parecer; (in court) comparecer. **~ance** n aparición f; (aspect) aspecto m; (in court) comparecencia f

appease /ə'piːz/ vt aplacar; (pacify) apaciguar

append /ə'pend/ vt adjuntar

appendicitis /əpendɪ'saɪtɪs/ n apendicitis f

appendix /ə'pendɪks/ n (pl **-ices** /-ɪsiːz/) (of book) apéndice m. (pl **-ixes**) (organ) apéndice m

appetite /'æpɪtaɪt/ n apetito m

applau|d /ə'plɔːd/ vt/i aplaudir. **~se** /ə'plɔːz/ n aplausos mpl. **round of ~se** n aplauso m

apple /'æpl/ n manzana f. **~ tree** n manzano m

appliance /ə'plaɪəns/ n aparato m. **electrical ~** electrodoméstico m

applic|able /'æplɪkəbl/ adj aplicable; (relevant) pertinente. **~ant** /'æplɪkənt/ n candidato m, solicitante m & f. **~ation** /æplɪ'keɪʃn/ n aplicación f; (request) solicitud f. **~ation form** formulario m (de solicitud)

appl|ied /ə'plaɪd/ adj aplicado. **~y** /ə'plaɪ/ vt aplicar. • vi aplicarse; (ask) presentar una solicitud. **~y for** solicitar (job etc)

appoint /ə'pɔɪnt/ vt nombrar; (fix) señalar. **~ment** n cita f

apprais|al /ə'preɪzl/ n evaluación f. **~e** /ə'preɪz/ vt evaluar

appreciable /ə'priːʃəbl/ adj (considerable) considerable

appreciat|e /ə'priːʃɪeɪt/ vt (value) apreciar; (understand) comprender; (be grateful for) agradecer. **~ion** /-'eɪʃn/ n aprecio m; (gratitude) agradecimiento m. **~ive** /ə'priːʃɪətɪv/ adj agradecido

apprehen|sion /æprɪ'henʃn/ n (fear) recelo m. **~sive** adj aprensivo

apprentice /ə'prentɪs/ n aprendiz m. • vt. **be ~d to s.o.** estar de aprendiz con uno. **~ship** n aprendizaje m

approach /ə'prəʊtʃ/ vt acercarse a. • vi acercarse. • n acercamiento m; (to problem) enfoque m; (access) acceso m

appropriate /ə'prəʊprɪət/ adj apropiado. • /ə'prəʊprɪeɪt/ vt apropiarse de. **~ly** /-ətlɪ/ adv apropiadamente

approv|al /ə'pruːvl/ n aprobación f. **on ~al** a prueba. **~e** /ə'pruːv/ vt/i aprobar. **~ingly** adv con aprobación

approximat|e /ə'prɒksɪmət/ adj aproximado. • /ə'prɒksɪmeɪt/ vt aproximarse a. **~ely** /-ətlɪ/ adv aproximadamente. **~ion** /-'meɪʃn/ n aproximación f

apricot /'eɪprɪkɒt/ n albaricoque m, chabacano m (Mex)

April /'eɪprəl/ n abril m. **~ fool!** ¡inocentón!

apron /'eɪprən/ n delantal m

apt /æpt/ adj apropiado. **be ~ to** tener tendencia a. **~itude** /'æptɪtjuːd/ n aptitud f. **~ly** adv acertadamente

aquarium /ə'kweərɪəm/ n (pl **-ums**) acuario m

Aquarius /ə'kweərɪəs/ n Acuario m

aquatic /ə'kwætɪk/ adj acuático

aqueduct /'ækwɪdʌkt/ n acueducto m

Arab /'ærəb/ adj & n árabe (m & f). **~ian** /ə'reɪbɪən/ adj árabe. **~ic** /'ærəbɪk/ adj & n árabe (m). **~ic numerals** números mpl arábigos

arable /'ærəbl/ adj cultivable

arbitrary /'ɑːbɪtrərɪ/ adj arbitrario

arbitrat|e /'ɑːbɪtreɪt/ vi arbitrar. **~ion** /-'treɪʃn/ n arbitraje m. **~or** n árbitro m

arc /ɑːk/ n arco m

arcade /ɑː'keɪd/ n arcada f; (around

square) soportales mpl; (shops) galería f

arch /ɑːtʃ/ n arco m. • vt arquear. • vi arquearse

archaeolog|ical /ɑːkɪəˈlɒdʒɪkl/ adj arqueológico. **~ist** /ɑːkɪˈɒlədʒɪst/ n arqueólogo m. **~y** /ɑːkɪˈɒlədʒɪ/ n arqueología f

archaic /ɑːˈkeɪɪk/ adj arcaico

archbishop /ɑːtʃˈbɪʃəp/ n arzobispo m

archer /ˈɑːtʃə(r)/ n arquero m. **~y** n tiro m con arco

architect /ˈɑːkɪtekt/ n arquitecto m. **~ure** /-tʃə(r)/ n arquitectura f. **~ural** /-ˈtektʃərəl/ adj arquitectónico

archives /ˈɑːkaɪvz/ npl archivo m

archway /ˈɑːtʃweɪ/ n arco m

Arctic /ˈɑːktɪk/ adj ártico. • n. **the ~** el Ártico

ard|ent /ˈɑːdənt/ adj fervoroso; (supporter, lover) apasionado. **~our** /ˈɑːdə(r)/ n fervor m; (love) pasión f

arduous /ˈɑːdjʊəs/ adj arduo

are /ɑː(r)/ see BE

area /ˈeərɪə/ n (Math) superficie f; (of country) zona f; (of city) barrio m

arena /əˈriːnə/ n arena f; (scene of activity) ruedo m

aren't /ɑːnt/ = are not

Argentin|a /ɑːdʒənˈtiːnə/ n Argentina f. **~ian** /-ˈtɪnɪən/ adj & n argentino (m)

argu|able /ˈɑːgjʊəbl/ adj discutible. **~e** /ˈɑːgjuː/ vi discutir; (reason) razonar. **~ment** /ˈɑːgjʊmənt/ n disputa f; (reasoning) argumento m. **~mentative** /ɑːgjʊˈmentətɪv/ adj discutidor

arid /ˈærɪd/ adj árido

Aries /ˈeəriːz/ n Aries m

arise /əˈraɪz/ vi (pt **arose**, pp **arisen**) surgir (**from** de)

aristocra|cy /ærɪˈstɒkrəsɪ/ n aristocracia f. **~t** /ˈærɪstəkræt/ n

aristócrata m & f. **~tic** /-ˈkrætɪk/ adj aristocrático

arithmetic /əˈrɪθmətɪk/ n aritmética f

ark /ɑːk/ n (Relig) arca f

arm /ɑːm/ n brazo m; (of garment) manga f. **~s** npl armas fpl. • vt armar

armament /ˈɑːməmənt/ n armamento m

arm: ~band n brazalete m. **~chair** n sillón m

armed /ɑːmd/ adj armado. **~ robbery** n robo m a mano armada

armful /ˈɑːmfʊl/ n brazada f

armour /ˈɑːmə(r)/ n armadura f. **~ed** /ˈɑːməd/ adj blindado. **~y** /ˈɑːmərɪ/ n arsenal m

armpit /ˈɑːmpɪt/ n sobaco m, axila f

army /ˈɑːmɪ/ n ejército m

aroma /əˈrəʊmə/ n aroma m

arose /əˈrəʊz/ see ARISE

around /əˈraʊnd/ adv alrededor; (near) cerca. **all ~** por todas partes. • prep alrededor de; (with time) a eso de

arouse /əˈraʊz/ vt despertar

arrange /əˈreɪndʒ/ vt arreglar; (fix) fijar. **~ment** n arreglo m; (agreement) acuerdo m. **~ments** npl (plans) preparativos mpl

arrears /əˈrɪəz/ npl atrasos mpl. **in ~** atrasado en el pago (**with** de)

arrest /əˈrest/ vt detener. • n detención f. **under ~** detenido

arriv|al /əˈraɪvl/ n llegada f. **new ~al** recién llegado m. **~e** /əˈraɪv/ vi llegar

arrogan|ce /ˈærəgəns/ n arrogancia f. **~t** adj arrogante. **~tly** adv con arrogancia

arrow /ˈærəʊ/ n flecha f

arse /ɑːs/ n (vulgar) culo m

arsenal /ˈɑːsənl/ n arsenal m

arsenic /ˈɑːsnɪk/ n arsénico m

arson /ˈɑːsn/ n incendio m

a

provocado. **~ist** n incendiario m

art¹ /ɑːt/ n arte m. **A~s** npl (Univ) Filosofía y Letras fpl. **fine ~s** bellas artes fpl

art² /ɑːt/ (old use, with **thou**) see ARE

artery /'ɑːtərɪ/ n arteria f

art gallery n museo m de arte, pinacoteca f; (commercial) galería f de arte

arthritis /ɑː'θraɪtɪs/ n artritis f

article /'ɑːtɪkl/ n artículo m. **~ of clothing** prenda f de vestir

articulat|e /ɑː'tɪkjʊlət/ adj (utterance) articulado; (person) que sabe expresarse. ● /ɑː'tɪkjʊleɪt/ vt/i articular. **~ed lorry** n camión m articulado. **~ion** /-'leɪʃn/ n articulación f

artificial /ɑːtɪ'fɪʃl/ adj artificial. **~ respiration** respiración f artificial

artillery /ɑː'tɪlərɪ/ n artillería f

artist /'ɑːtɪst/ n artista m & f. **~tic** /ɑː'tɪstɪk/ adj artístico. **~ry** /'ɑːtɪstrɪ/ n arte m, habilidad f

as /æz, əz/ adv & conj como; (since) ya que; (while) mientras. **~ big** ~ tan grande como. **~ far** ~ (distance) hasta; (qualitative) en cuanto a. **~ far** ~ **I know** que yo sepa. **~ if** como si. **~ long** ~ mientras. **~ much** ~ tanto como. **~ soon** ~ tan pronto como. **~ well** también

asbestos /æz'bestɒs/ n amianto m, asbesto m

ascen|d /ə'send/ vt/i subir. **A~sion** /ə'senʃn/ n. **the A~sion** la Ascensión f. **~t** /ə'sent/ n subida f

ascertain /æsə'teɪn/ vt averiguar

ash /æʃ/ n ceniza f. ●n. ~ **(tree)** fresno m

ashamed /ə'ʃeɪmd/ adj avergonzado (**of** de). **be** ~ **of s.o.** avergonzarse de uno

ashore /ə'ʃɔː(r)/ adv a tierra. **go** ~ desembarcar

ash: ~tray n cenicero m. **A~ Wednesday** n Miércoles m de Ceniza

Asia /'eɪʃə/ n Asia f. **~n** adj & n asiático (m). **~tic** /-ɪ'ætɪk/ adj asiático

aside /ə'saɪd/ adv a un lado. ●n (in theatre) aparte m

ask /ɑːsk/ vt pedir; hacer (question); (invite) invitar. **~ about** enterarse de. ~ **s.o. to do something** pedirle a uno que haga algo. ■ ~ **after** vt preguntar por. ■ ~ **for** vt. ~ **for help** pedir ayuda. ~ **for trouble** buscarse problemas. ■ ~ **in** vt. ~ **s.o. in** invitar a uno a pasar

askew /ə'skjuː/ adv & adj torcido

asleep /ə'sliːp/ adv & adj dormido. **fall** ~ dormirse

asparagus /ə'spærəgəs/ n espárrago m

aspect /'æspekt/ n aspecto m

asphalt /'æsfælt/ n asfalto m. ●vt asfaltar

aspir|ation /æspə'reɪʃn/ n aspiración f. **~e** /ə'spaɪə(r)/ vi aspirar

aspirin /'æsprɪn/ n aspirina f

ass /æs/ n asno m; (fig, fam) imbécil m; (Amer vulgar) culo m

assassin /ə'sæsɪn/ n asesino m. **~ate** /-eɪt/ vt asesinar. **~ation** /-'eɪʃn/ n asesinato m

assault /ə'sɔːlt/ n (Mil) ataque m; (Jurid) atentado m. ●vt asaltar

assembl|e /ə'sembl/ vt reunir; (Mec) montar. ●vi reunirse. **~y** n reunión f; (Pol etc) asamblea f. **~y line** n línea f de montaje

assent /ə'sent/ n asentimiento m. ●vi asentir

assert /ə'sɜːt/ vt afirmar; hacer valer (one's rights). **~ion** /-ʃn/ n afirmación f. **~ive** adj positivo, firme

assess /ə'ses/ vt evaluar; (determine) determinar; fijar (tax etc). **~ment** n evaluación f

asset /'æset/ n (advantage) ventaja f. **~s** npl (Com) bienes mpl

assign /əˈsaɪn/ vt asignar; (appoint) nombrar. **~ment** n asignación f; (mission) misión f; (task) función f; (for school) trabajo m

assimilate /əˈsɪmɪleɪt/ vt asimilar. • vi asimilarse

assist /əˈsɪst/ vt/i ayudar. **~ance** n ayuda f. **~ant** n ayudante m & f; (shop) dependienta f, dependiente m. • adj auxiliar, adjunto

associat|e /əˈsəʊʃɪeɪt/ vt asociar. • vi asociarse. /əˈsəʊʃɪət/ adj asociado. • n colega m & f; (Com) socio m. **~ion** /-ˈeɪʃn/ n asociación f.

assort|ed /əˈsɔːtɪd/ adj surtido. **~ment** n surtido m

assum|e /əˈsjuːm/ vt suponer; tomar (power, attitude); asumir (role, burden). **~ption** /əˈsʌmpʃn/ n suposición f

assur|ance /əˈʃʊərəns/ n seguridad f; (insurance) seguro m. **~e** /əˈʃʊə(r)/ vt asegurar. **~ed** adj seguro

asterisk /ˈæstərɪsk/ n asterisco m

asthma /ˈæsmə/ n asma f. **~tic** /-ˈmætɪk/ adj & n asmático (m)

astonish /əˈstɒnɪʃ/ vt asombrar. **~ed** adj asombrado. **~ing** adj asombroso. **~ment** n asombro m

astound /əˈstaʊnd/ vt asombrar. **~ed** adj atónito. **~ing** adj increíble

astray /əˈstreɪ/ adv. **go ~** extraviarse. **lead ~** llevar por mal camino

astrology /əˈstrɒlədʒɪ/ n astrología f

astronaut /ˈæstrənɔːt/ n astronauta m & f

astronom|er /əˈstrɒnəmə(r)/ n astrónomo m. **~ical** /æstrəˈnɒmɪkl/ adj astronómico. **~y** /əˈstrɒnəmɪ/ n astronomía f

astute /əˈstjuːt/ adj astuto

asylum /əˈsaɪləm/ n asilo m. **lunatic ~** manicomio m. **~ seeker** n solicitante m & f de asilo

at /æt/ preposition

····▸ (location) en. **she's at the office** está en la oficina. **at home** en casa. **call me at the office** llámame a la oficina

▷ For translations of phrases such as **at the top**, **at the front of**, **at the back of** see entries **top**, **front** etc

····▸ (at the house of) en casa de. **I'll be at Rachel's** estaré en casa de Rachel

····▸ (Comput: @) arroba f

····▸ (talking about time) **at 7 o'clock** a las siete. **at night** por la noche, de noche, en la noche (LAm). **at Christmas** en Navidad

····▸ (talking about age) a. **at six (years of age)** a los seis años

····▸ (with measurements, numbers etc) a. **at 60 miles an hour** a 60 millas por hora. **at a depth of** a una profundidad de. **three at a time** de tres en tres

▷ For translations of phrasal verbs with **at**, such as **look at**, see entries for those verbs

ate /et/ see EAT

atheis|m /ˈeɪθɪɪzəm/ n ateísmo m. **~t** n ateo m

athlet|e /ˈæθliːt/ n atleta m & f. **~ic** /-ˈletɪk/ adj atlético. **~ics** npl atletismo m; (Amer, Sport) deportes mpl

Atlantic /ətˈlæntɪk/ adj atlántico. • n. **the ~ (Ocean)** el (Océano) Atlántico

atlas /ˈætləs/ n atlas m

ATM abbr (= **automated teller machine**) cajero m automático

atmospher|e /ˈætməsfɪə(r)/ n atmósfera f; (fig) ambiente m. **~ic** /-ˈferɪk/ adj atmosférico

atom /ˈætəm/ n átomo m. **~ic** /əˈtɒmɪk/ adj atómico

atroci|ous /əˈtrəʊʃəs/ adj atroz. **~ty** /əˈtrɒsətɪ/ n atrocidad f

a

a

attach /əˈtætʃ/ vt sujetar; adjuntar (document etc). **be ~ed to** (be fond of) tener cariño a. **~ment** n (affection) cariño m; (tool) accesorio m

attack /əˈtæk/ n ataque m. •vt/i atacar. **~er** n agresor m

attain /əˈteɪn/ vt conseguir. **~able** adj alcanzable

attempt /əˈtempt/ vt intentar. •n tentativa f; (attack) atentado m

attend /əˈtend/ vt asistir a; (escort) acompañar. •vi prestar atención. ■ **~ to** vt (look after) ocuparse de. **~ance** n asistencia f; (people present) concurrencia f.

atten|tion /əˈtenʃn/ n atención f. **~tion!** (Mil) ¡firmes! **pay ~tion** prestar atención. **~tive** adj atento

attic /ˈætɪk/ n desván m

attire /əˈtaɪə(r)/ n atavío m. •vt ataviar

attitude /ˈætɪtjuːd/ n postura f

attorney /əˈtɜːnɪ/ n (pl **-eys**) (Amer) abogado m

attract /əˈtrækt/ vt atraer. **~ion** /-ʃn/ n atracción f; (charm) atractivo m. **~ive** adj atractivo; (interesting) atrayente

attribute /əˈtrɪbjuːt/ vt atribuir. •/ˈætrɪbjuːt/ n atributo m

aubergine /ˈəʊbəʒiːn/ n berenjena f

auction /ˈɔːkʃn/ n subasta f. •vt subastar. **~eer** n /-əˈnɪə(r)/ n subastador m

audaci|ous /ɔːˈdeɪʃəs/ adj audaz. **~ty** /ɔːˈdæsətɪ/ n audacia f

audible /ˈɔːdəbl/ adj audible

audience /ˈɔːdɪəns/ n (at play, film) público m; (TV) audiencia f; (interview) audiencia f

audiovisual /ɔːdɪəʊˈvɪʒʊəl/ adj audiovisual

audit /ˈɔːdɪt/ n revisión f de cuentas. •vt revisar

audition /ɔːˈdɪʃn/ n audición f. •vt hacerle una audición a. •vi dar una audición (**for** para)

auditor /ˈɔːdɪtə(r)/ n interventor m de cuentas

auditorium /ɔːdɪˈtɔːrɪəm/ (pl **-riums** or **-ria** /-rɪə/) n sala f, auditorio m

augment /ɔːgˈment/ vt aumentar

augur /ˈɔːgə(r)/ vt augurar. **it ~s well** es de buen agüero

August /ˈɔːgəst/ n agosto m

aunt /ɑːnt/ n tía f

au pair /əʊˈpeə(r)/ n chica f au pair

aura /ˈɔːrə/ n aura f, halo m

auster|e /ɔːˈstɪə(r)/ adj austero. **~ity** /ɔːˈsterətɪ/ n austeridad f

Australia /ɒˈstreɪlɪə/ n Australia f. **~n** adj & n australiano (m)

Austria /ˈɒstrɪə/ n Austria f. **~n** adj & n austríaco (m)

authentic /ɔːˈθentɪk/ adj auténtico. **~ate** /-keɪt/ vt autenticar. **~ity** /-ənˈtɪsətɪ/ n autenticidad f

author /ˈɔːθə(r)/ n autor m. **~ess** /-ɪs/ n autora f

authoritative /ɔːˈθɒrɪtətɪv/ adj autorizado; (manner) autoritario

authority /ɔːˈθɒrətɪ/ n autoridad f; (permission) autorización f

authoriz|ation /ɔːθəraɪˈzeɪʃn/ n autorización f. **~e** /ˈɔːθəraɪz/ vt autorizar

autobiography /ɔːtəʊbaɪˈɒɡrəfɪ/ n autobiografía f

autograph /ˈɔːtəɡrɑːf/ n autógrafo m. •vt firmar, autografiar

automat|e /ˈɔːtəmeɪt/ vt automatizar. **~ic** /-ˈmætɪk/ adj automático. **~ion** /-ˈmeɪʃn/ n automatización f. **~on** /ɔːˈtɒmətən/ n (pl **-tons** or **-ta** /-tə/) autómata m

automobile /ˈɔːtəməbiːl/ n (Amer) coche m, carro m (LAm), automóvil m

autonom|ous /ɔːˈtɒnəməs/ adj autónomo. **~y** n autonomía f

autopsy /ˈɔːtɒpsɪ/ n autopsia f

autumn /'ɔːtəm/ n otoño m. ~**al** /ɔː'tʌmnəl/ adj otoñal

auxiliary /ɔːg'zɪlɪərɪ/ adj & n auxiliar (m & f)

avail /ə'veɪl/ n. **to no ~** inútil

availab|ility /əveɪlə'bɪlətɪ/ n disponibilidad f. ~**le** /ə'veɪləbl/ adj disponible

avalanche /'ævəlɑːnʃ/ n avalancha f

avaric|e /'ævərɪs/ n avaricia f. ~**ious** /-'rɪʃəs/ adj avaro

avenue /'ævənjuː/ n avenida f; (fig) vía f

average /'ævərɪdʒ/ n promedio m. **on ~** por término medio. ●adj medio

avers|e /ə'vɜːs/ adj. **be ~e to** ser reacio a. ~**ion** /-ʃn/ n repugnancia f

avert /ə'vɜːt/ vt (turn away) apartar; (ward off) desviar

aviation /eɪvɪ'eɪʃn/ n aviación f

avid /'ævɪd/ adj ávido

avocado /ævə'kɑːdəʊ/ n (pl -**os**) aguacate m

avoid /ə'vɔɪd/ vt evitar. ~**able** adj evitable. ~**ance** n el evitar

await /ə'weɪt/ vt esperar

awake /ə'weɪk/ vt/i (pt **awoke**, pp **awoken**) despertar. ●adj despierto. **wide ~** completamente

despierto; (fig) despabilado. ~**n** /ə'weɪkən/ vt/i despertar. ~**ning** n el despertar

award /ə'wɔːd/ vt otorgar; (Jurid) adjudicar. ●n premio m; (Jurid) adjudicación f; (scholarship) beca f

aware /ə'weə(r)/ adj. **be ~ of sth** ser consciente de algo, darse cuenta de algo. ~**ness** n conciencia f

awash /ə'wɒʃ/ adj inundado

away /ə'weɪ/ adv (absent) fuera. **far ~** muy lejos. ●adj ~ **match** partido m fuera de casa

awe /ɔː/ n temor m. ~-**inspiring** adj impresionante. ~**some** /-səm/ adj imponente

awful /'ɔːfʊl/ adj terrible, malísimo. **feel ~** sentirse muy mal

awkward /'ɔːkwəd/ adj difícil; (inconvenient) inoportuno; (clumsy) desmañado; (embarrassed) incómodo. ~**ness** n dificultad f; (discomfort) molestia f; (clumsiness) torpeza f

awning /'ɔːnɪŋ/ n toldo m

awoke /ə'wəʊk/, **awoken** /ə'wəʊkən/ see **AWAKE**

axe /æks/ n hacha f. ●vt (pres p **axing**) cortar con hacha; (fig) recortar

axis /'æksɪs/ n (pl **axes** /-iːz/) eje m

axle /'æksl/ n eje m

Bb

BA /biː'eɪ/ abbr see **BACHELOR**

babble /'bæbl/ vi balbucir; (chatter) parlotear; (stream) murmullar.

baboon /bə'buːn/ n mandril m

baby /'beɪbɪ/ n niño m, bebé m. ~ **buggy**, ~ **carriage** n (Amer) cochecito m. ~**ish** adj /'beɪbɪʃ/

infantil. ~-**sit** vi cuidar a los niños, hacer de canguro. ~-**sitter** n baby sitter m & f, canguro m & f

bachelor /'bætʃələ(r)/ n soltero m. **B~ of Arts (BA)** licenciado m en filosofía y letras. **B~ of Science (BSc)** licenciado m en ciencias

back /bæk/ n espalda f; (of car)

parte f trasera; (of chair) respaldo m; (of cloth) revés m; (of house) parte f de atrás; (of animal, book) lomo m; (of hand, document) dorso m; (football) defensa m & f. **in the ~ of beyond** en el quinto infierno. • adj trasero. **the ~ door** la puerta trasera. • adv atrás; (returned) de vuelta. • vt apoyar; (betting) apostar a; dar marcha atrás a (car). • vi retroceder; (car) dar marcha atrás. ■~ **down** vi volverse atrás. ■~ **out** vi retirarse. ■~ **up** vt apoyar; (Comp) hacer una copia de seguridad de. ~**ache** n dolor m de espalda. ~**bone** n columna f vertebral; (fig) pilar m. ~**date** /-'deɪt/ vt antedatar. ~**er** n partidario m; (Com) financiador m. ~**fire** /-'faɪə(r)/ vi (Auto) petardear; (fig) fallar. **his plan ~fired on him** le salió el tiro por la culata. ~**ground** n fondo m; (environment) antecedentes mpl. ~**hand** n (Sport) revés m. ~**ing** n apoyo m. ~**lash** n reacción f. ~**log** n atrasos mpl. ~**side** /-'saɪd/ n 🆎 trasero m. ~**stage** /-'steɪdʒ/ adj de bastidores. • adv entre bastidores. ~**stroke** n (tennis etc) revés m; (swimming) estilo m espalda, estilo m dorso (Mex). ~-**up** n apoyo m; (Comp) copia f de seguridad. ~**ward** /-wəd/ adj (step etc) hacia atrás; (retarded) retrasado; (undeveloped) atrasado. • adv (Amer) see **BACKWARDS**. ~**wards** adv hacia atrás; (fall) de espaldas; (back to front) al revés. **go ~wards and forwards** ir de acá para allá. ~**water** n agua f estancada; (fig) lugar m apartado

bacon /'beɪkən/ n tocino m

bacteria /bæk'tɪərɪə/ npl bacterias fpl

bad /bæd/ adj (**worse, worst**) malo, (before masculine singular noun) mal; (serious) grave; (harmful) nocivo; (language) indecente. **feel ~** sentirse mal

bade /beɪd/ see **BID**

badge /bædʒ/ n distintivo m, chapa f

badger /'bædʒə(r)/ n tejón m. • vt acosar

bad: ~**ly** adv mal. **want ~ly** desear muchísimo. ~**ly injured** gravemente herido. ~**ly off** mal de dinero. ~-**mannered** /-'mænəd/ adj mal educado

badminton /'bædmɪntən/ n bádminton m

bad-tempered /bæd'tempəd/ adj (always) de mal carácter; (temporarily) de mal humor

baffle /'bæfl/ vt desconcertar. ~**d** adj perplejo

bag /bæg/ n bolsa f; (handbag) bolso m. • vt (pt **bagged**) ensacar; (take) coger (esp Spain), agarrar (LAm). ~**s** npl (luggage) equipaje m

baggage /'bægɪdʒ/ n equipaje m. ~ **room** n (Amer) consigna f

baggy /'bægɪ/ adj (clothes) holgado

bagpipes /'bægpaɪps/ npl gaita f

baguette /bæ'get/ n baguette f

bail[1] /beɪl/ n fianza f. • vt poner en libertad bajo fianza. ~ **s.o. out** pagar la fianza a uno

bail[2] vt. ~ **out** (Naut) achicar

bait /beɪt/ n cebo m

bak|e /beɪk/ vt cocer al horno. • vi cocerse. ~**er** n panadero m. ~**ery** n panadería f

balance /'bæləns/ n equilibrio m; (Com) balance m; (sum) saldo m; (scales) balanza f; (remainder) resto m. • vt equilibrar (load); mantener en equilibrio (object); nivelar (budget). • vi equilibrarse; (Com) cuadrar. ~**d** adj equilibrado

balcony /'bælkənɪ/ n balcón m

bald /bɔːld/ adj (-**er**, -**est**) calvo, pelón (Mex)

bale /beɪl/ n bala f, fardo m. • vi. ~ **out** lanzarse en paracaídas

Balearic /bælɪ'ærɪk/ adj. **the ~ Islands** las Islas fpl Baleares

ball /bɔːl/ n bola f; (tennis etc) pelota f; (football etc) balón m, pelota f (esp

LAm); (of yarn) ovillo m; (dance)
baile m

ballad /'bæləd/ n balada f

ballast /'bæləst/ n lastre m

ball bearing n cojinete m de bolas

ballerina /bælə'ri:nə/ f bailarina f

ballet /'bæleɪ/ n ballet m. ~
dancer n bailarín m de ballet,
bailarina f de ballet

balloon /bə'lu:n/ n globo m

ballot /'bælət/ n votación f. ~ **box**
n urna f. ~ **paper** n papeleta f.

ball: ~**point** n. ~**point (pen)**
bolígrafo m, pluma f atómica (Mex).
~**room** n salón m de baile

bamboo /bæm'bu:/ n bambú m

ban /bæn/ vt (pt **banned**) prohibir.
~ **s.o. from sth** prohibir algo a
uno. ● n prohibición f

banal /bə'nɑ:l/ adj banal ~**ity**
/bə'nælətɪ/ n banalidad f

banana /bə'nɑ:nə/ n plátano m

band /bænd/ n (strip) banda f. ● n
(Mus) orquesta f; (military, brass)
banda f. ■ ~ **together** vi juntarse

bandage /'bændɪdʒ/ n venda f. ● vt
vendar

Band-Aid /'bændeɪd/ n (Amer, ®)
tirita f, curita f (LAm)

B & B /'bi:ənbi:/ abbr (= **bed and
breakfast**) cama f y desayuno;
(place) pensión f

bandit /'bændɪt/ n bandido m

band: ~**stand** n quiosco m de
música. ~**wagon** n. **jump on
the** ~**wagon** (fig) subirse al carro

bandy /'bændɪ/ adj (**-ier, -iest**)
patizambo

bang /bæŋ/ n (noise) ruido m; (blow)
golpe m; (of gun) estampido m; (of
door) golpe m. ● vt (strike) golpear. ~
the door dar un portazo. ● adv
exactamente. ● int ¡pum! ~**s** npl
(Amer) flequillo m, cerquillo m
(LAm), fleco m (Mex)

banger /'bæŋə(r)/ n petardo m; (🔧,
Culin) salchicha f

bangle /'bæŋgl/ n brazalete m

banish /'bænɪʃ/ vt desterrar

banisters /'bænɪstəz/ npl
pasamanos m

banjo /'bændʒəʊ/ n (pl **-os**) banjo m

bank /bæŋk/ n (Com) banco m; (of
river) orilla f. ● vt depositar. ● vi (in
flying) ladearse. ■ ~ **on** vt contar
con. ■ ~ **with** vi tener una cuenta
con. ~ **card** n tarjeta f bancaria;
(Amer) tarjeta f de crédito (expedida
por un banco). ~ **holiday** n día m festivo, día m
feriado (LAm). ~**ing** n (Com) banca
f. ~**note** n billete m de banco

bankrupt /'bæŋkrʌpt/ adj & n
quebrado (m). **go** ~ quebrar. ● vt
hacer quebrar. ~**cy** /-rʌpsɪ/ n
bancarrota f, quiebra f

bank statement n estado m de
cuenta

banner /'bænə(r)/ n bandera f; (in
demonstration) pancarta f

banquet /'bæŋkwɪt/ n banquete m

banter /'bæntə(r)/ n chanza f

bap /bæp/ n panecillo m blando

baptism /'bæptɪzəm/ n bautismo m;
(act) bautizo m

Baptist /'bæptɪst/ n bautista m & f

baptize /bæp'taɪz/ vt bautizar

bar /bɑ:(r)/ n barra f; (on window)
reja f; (of chocolate) tableta f; (of
soap) pastilla f; (pub) bar m; (Mus)
compás m; (Jurid) abogacía f; (fig)
obstáculo m. ● vt (pt **barred**)
atrancar (door); (exclude) excluir;
(prohibit) prohibir. ● prep excepto

barbar|ian /bɑ:'beərɪən/ adj & n
bárbaro (m). ~**ic** /bɑ:'bærɪk/ adj
bárbaro

barbecue /'bɑ:bɪkju:/ n barbacoa f.
● vt asar a la parilla

barbed wire /bɑ:bd 'waɪə(r)/ n
alambre m de púas

barber /'bɑ:bə(r)/ n peluquero m,
barbero m

barbwire /'bɑ:b'waɪə(r)/ n (Amer)
see **BARBED WIRE**

b

bare /beə(r)/ adj (**-er, -est**) desnudo; (room) con pocos muebles; (mere) simple; (empty) vacío. •vt desnudar; (uncover) descubrir. ~ **one's teeth** mostrar los dientes. ~**back** adv a pelo. ~**faced** adj descarado. ~**foot** adj descalzo. ~**headed** /-'hedɪd/ adj descubierto. ~**ly** adv apenas.

bargain /'bɑːgɪn/ n (agreement) pacto m; (good buy) ganga f. •vi negociar; (haggle) regatear. ■ ~ **for** vt esperar, contar con

barge /bɑːdʒ/ n barcaza f. •vi. ~ **in** irrumpir

baritone /'bærɪtəʊn/ n barítono m

bark /bɑːk/ n (of dog) ladrido m; (of tree) corteza f. •vi ladrar

barley /'bɑːlɪ/ n cebada f

bar: ~**maid** n camarera f. ~**man** /-mən/ n camarero m, barman m

barmy /'bɑːmɪ/ adj 🅇 chiflado

barn /bɑːn/ n granero m

barometer /bə'rɒmɪtə(r)/ n barómetro m

baron /'bærən/ n barón m. ~**ess** /-ɪs/ n baronesa f

barracks /'bærəks/ npl cuartel m

barrage /'bærɑːʒ/ n (Mil) barrera f; (dam) presa f. **a** ~ **of questions** un aluvión de preguntas

barrel /'bærəl/ n barril m; (of gun) cañón m

barren /'bærən/ adj estéril

barrette /bə'ret/ n (Amer) pasador m

barricade /bærɪ'keɪd/ n barricada f. •vt cerrar con barricadas

barrier /'bærɪə(r)/ n barrera f

barrister /'bærɪstə(r)/ n abogado m

bartender /'bɑːtendə(r)/ n (Amer) (male) camarero m, barman m; (female) camarera f

barter /'bɑːtə(r)/ n trueque m. •vt trocar

base /beɪs/ n base f. •vt basar. ~**ball** n béisbol m, beisbol m (Mex)

basement /'beɪsmənt/ n sótano m

bash /bæʃ/ vt golpear. •n golpe m. **have a** ~ 🅇 probar

bashful /'bæʃfl/ adj tímido

basic /'beɪsɪk/ adj básico, fundamental. ~**ally** adv fundamentalmente

basin /'beɪsn/ n (for washing) palangana f; (for food) cuenco m; (of river) cuenca f

basis /'beɪsɪs/ n (pl **bases** /-siːz/) base f

bask /bɑːsk/ vi asolearse; (fig) gozar (**in** de)

basket /'bɑːskɪt/ n cesta f; (big) cesto m. ~**ball** n baloncesto m, básquetbol m (LAm)

bass¹ /beɪs/ adj bajo. •n (Mus) bajo m

bass² /bæs/ n (fish) lubina f

bassoon /bə'suːn/ n fagot m

bastard /'bɑːstəd/ n bastardo m. **you** ~! (vulgar) ¡cabrón! (vulgar)

bat /bæt/ n (for baseball, cricket) bate m; (for table tennis) raqueta f; (mammal) murciélago m. **off one's own** ~ por sí solo. •vt (pt **batted**) golpear. **without** ~**ting an eyelid** sin pestañear. •vi batear

batch /bætʃ/ n (of people) grupo m; (of papers) pila f; (of goods) remesa f; (of bread) hornada f; (Comp) lote m

bated /'beɪtɪd/ adj. **with** ~ **breath** con aliento entrecortado

bath /bɑːθ/ n (pl **-s** /bɑːðz/) baño m; (tub) bañera f, tina f (LAm). ~**s** npl (swimming pool) piscina f, alberca f (Mex). **have a** ~, **take a** ~ (Amer) bañarse. •vt bañar. •vi bañarse

bathe /beɪð/ vt bañar. •vi bañarse. •n baño m. ~**r** n bañista m & f

bathing /'beɪðɪŋ/ n baños mpl. ~ **costume**, ~ **suit** n traje m de baño

bathroom /'bɑːθrʊm/ n cuarto m de baño; (Amer, toilet) servicio m, baño m (LAm)

batsman /'bætsmən/ n (pl **-men**) bateador m

battalion /bə'tælɪən/ n batallón m

batter /'bætə(r)/ vt (beat) apalear; (cover with batter) rebozar. ●n batido m para rebozar; (Amer, for cake) masa f. ~**ed** /'bætəd/ adj (car etc) estropeado; (wife etc) maltratado

battery /'bætərɪ/ n (Mil, Auto) batería f; (of torch, radio) pila f

battle /'bætl/ n batalla f; (fig) lucha f. ●vi luchar. ~**field** n campo m de batalla. ~**ship** n acorazado m

bawl /bɔːl/ vt/i gritar

bay /beɪ/ n (on coast) bahía f. **keep at** ~ mantener a raya

bayonet /'beɪənet/ n bayoneta f

bay window /beɪ 'wɪndəʊ/ n ventana f saledizza

bazaar /bə'zɑː(r)/ n bazar m

BC abbr (= **before Christ**) a. de C., antes de Cristo

---

be /biː/

present **am, are, is**; past **was, were**; past participle **been**

● intransitive verb

! Spanish has two verbs meaning *be*, *ser* and *estar*. See those entries for further information about the differences between them.

‥‥▸ (position, changed condition or state) estar. **where is the library?** ¿dónde está la biblioteca? **she's tired** está cansada. **how are you?** ¿cómo estás?

‥‥▸ (identity, nature or permanent characteristics) ser.**she's tall** es alta. **he's Scottish** es escocés. **I'm a journalist** soy periodista. **he's very kind** es muy bondadoso

‥‥▸ (feel) **to be** + adjective tener + sustantivo. **to be cold/hot** tener frío/calor. **he's hungry/thirsty** tiene hambre/sed

‥‥▸ (age) **he's thirty** tiene treinta años

‥‥▸ (weather) **it's cold/hot** hace frío/calor. **it was 40 degrees** hacía 40 grados

● auxiliary verb

‥‥▸ (in tenses) estar. **I'm working** estoy trabajando. **they were singing** estaban cantando, cantaban

‥‥▸ (in tag questions) **it's a beautiful house, isn't it?** es una casa preciosa, ¿verdad? or ¿no? or ¿no es cierto?

‥‥▸ (in short answers) **are you disappointed? - yes, I am** ¿estás desilusionado? - sí (lo estoy). **I'm surprised, aren't you?** estoy sorprendido, ¿tú no?

‥‥▸ (in passive sentences) **it was built in 1834** fue construido en 1834, se construyó en 1834. **she was told that ...** le dijeron que..., se le dijo que ...

! Note that passive sentences in English are often translated using the pronoun *se* or using the third person plural.

---

beach /biːtʃ/ n playa f

beacon /'biːkən/ n faro m

bead /biːd/ n cuenta f; (of glass) abalorio m

beak /biːk/ n pico m

beaker /'biːkə(r)/ n taza f (alta y sin asa)

beam /biːm/ n (of wood) viga f; (of light) rayo m; (Naut) bao m. ●vt emitir. ●vi irradiar; (smile) sonreír

bean /biːn/ n alubia f, frijol m (LAm); (broad bean) haba f; (of coffee) grano m

bear /beə(r)/ vt (pt bore, pp borne) llevar; parir (niño); (endure) soportar. ~ **right** torcer a la derecha. ~ **in mind** tener en cuenta. ■~ **with** vt tener paciencia con. ●n oso m. ~**able** adj soportable

beard /bɪəd/ n barba f. ~**ed** adj barbudo

bearer /'beərə(r)/ n portador m; (of passport) titular m & f

b

bearing /'beərɪŋ/ n
comportamiento m; (relevance)
relación f; (Mec) cojinete m. **get
one's ~s** orientarse. **lose one's
~s** desorientarse

beast /biːst/ n bestia f; (person)
bruto m. **~ly** adj (-ier, -iest)
bestial; 🔢 horrible

beat /biːt/ vt (pt **beat**, pp **beaten**)
(hit) pegar; (Culin) batir; (defeat)
derrotar; (better) sobrepasar; batir
(record); (baffle) dejar perplejo. **~ it**
🔢 largarse. ●vi (heart) latir. ●n
latido m; (Mus) ritmo m; (of
policeman) ronda f. ■ **~ up** vt darle
una paliza a; (Culin) batir. **~ up on**
(Amer, fam) darle una paliza a. **~er**
n batidor m. **~ing** n paliza f

beautician /bjuː'tɪʃn/ n esteticista
m & f

beautiful /'bjuːtɪfl/ adj hermoso.
~ly adv maravillosamente

beauty /'bjuːtɪ/ n belleza f. ~
salon, ~ shop (Amer) salón m de
belleza. **~ spot** n (on face) lunar m;
(site) lugar m pintoresco

beaver /'biːvə(r)/ n castor m

became /bɪ'keɪm/ see BECOME

because /bɪ'kɒz/ conj porque. ●adv.
~ of por, a causa de

beckon /'bekən/ vt/i. ~ **(to)** hacer
señas (a)

become /bɪ'kʌm/ vi (pt **became**, pp
become) hacerse, llegar a ser,
volverse, convertirse en. **what
has ~ of her?** ¿qué es de ella?

bed /bed/ n cama f; (layer) estrato m;
(of sea, river) fondo m; (of flowers)
macizo m. **go to ~** acostarse. ●vi
(pt **bedded**). **~ and breakfast (B
& B)** cama y desayuno; (place)
pensión f. **~bug** n chinche f.
~clothes npl, **~ding** n ropa f de
cama, cobijas fpl (LAm)

bed: ~room n dormitorio m,
cuarto m, habitación f, recámara f
(Mex). **~sitter** /-'sɪtə(r)/ n
habitación f con cama y uso de
cocina y baño compartidos,
estudio m. **~spread** n colcha f.

~time n hora f de acostarse

bee /biː/ n abeja f; (Amer, social
gathering) círculo m

beech /biːtʃ/ n haya f

beef /biːf/ n carne f de vaca, carne f
de res (Mex). ●vi 🔢 quejarse.
~burger n hamburguesa f. **~y** adj
(-ier, -iest) musculoso

bee: ~hive n colmena f. **~line** n.
make a ~line for ir en línea
recta hacia

been /biːn/ see BE

beer /bɪə(r)/ n cerveza f

beet /biːt/ n (Amer) remolacha f,
betabel f (Mex)

beetle /'biːtl/ n escarabajo m

beetroot /'biːtruːt/ n invar
remolacha f, betabel f (Mex)

befall /bɪ'fɔːl/ vt (pt **befell**, pp
befallen) ocurrirle a. ●vi ocurrir

before /bɪ'fɔː(r)/ prep (time) antes
de; (place) delante de. **~ leaving**
antes de marcharse. ●adv (place)
delante; (time) antes. **a week ~**
una semana antes. **the week ~**
la semana anterior. ●conj (time) antes
de que. **~ he leaves** antes de que
se vaya. **~hand** adv de antemano

befriend /bɪ'frend/ vt hacerse
amigo de

beg /beg/ vt/i (pt **begged**) mendigar;
(entreat) suplicar; (ask) pedir. **~
s.o.'s pardon** pedir perdón a uno.
I ~ your pardon! ¡perdone Vd! **I
~ your pardon?** ¿cómo?

began /bɪ'gæn/ see BEGIN

beggar /'begə(r)/ n mendigo m

begin /bɪ'gɪn/ vt/i (pt **began**, pp
begun, pres p **beginning**)
comenzar, empezar. **~ner** n
principiante m & f. **~ning** n
principio m

begrudge /bɪ'grʌdʒ/ vt envidiar;
(give) dar de mala gana

begun /bɪ'gʌn/ see BEGIN

behalf /bɪ'hɑːf/ n. **on ~ of, in ~
of** (Amer) de parte de, en
nombre de

behav|e /bɪ'heɪv/ vi comportarse, portarse. **~e (o.s.)** portarse bien. **~iour** /bɪ'heɪvjə(r)/ n comportamiento m

behead /bɪ'hed/ vt decapitar

behind /bɪ'haɪnd/ prep detrás de, atrás de (LAm). ● adv detrás; (late) atrasado. ● n 🄸 trasero m

beige /beɪʒ/ adj & n beige (m)

being /'biːɪŋ/ n ser m. **come into ~** nacer

belated /bɪ'leɪtɪd/ adj tardío

belch /beltʃ/ vi eructar. ■**~ out** vt arrojar (smoke)

belfry /'belfrɪ/ n campanario m

Belgi|an /'beldʒən/ adj & n belga (m & f). **~um** /'beldʒəm/ n Bélgica f

belie|f /bɪ'liːf/ n (trust) ⸵e †; (opinion) creencia f. **~ve** /bɪ'liːv/ vt/i creer. **~ve in** creer en. **make ~ve** fingir

belittle /bɪ'lɪtl/ vt menospreciar (achievements); denigrar (person)

bell /bel/ n campana f; (on door, bicycle) timbre m

belligerent /bɪ'lɪdʒərənt/ adj beligerante

bellow /'beləʊ/ vt gritar. ● vi bramar. **~s** npl fuelle m

bell pepper n (Amer) pimiento m

belly /'belɪ/ n barriga f

belong /bɪ'lɒŋ/ vi pertenecer (**to** a); (club) ser socio (**to** de); (have as usual place) ir. **~ings** /bɪ'lɒŋɪŋz/ npl pertenencias fpl. **personal ~ings** efectos mpl personales

beloved /bɪ'lʌvɪd/ adj querido

below /bɪ'ləʊ/ prep debajo de, abajo de (LAm); (fig) inferior a. ● adv abajo

belt /belt/ n cinturón m; (area) zona f. ● vt (fig) rodear; 🄸 darle una paliza a. **~way** n (Amer) carretera f de circunvalación

bench /bentʃ/ n banco m

bend /bend/ n curva f. ● vt (pt & pp **bent**) doblar; torcer (arm, leg). ● vi doblarse; (road) torcerse. ■**~**
down vi inclinarse ■**~ over** vi agacharse

beneath /bɪ'niːθ/ prep debajo de; (fig) inferior a. ● adv abajo

beneficial /benɪ'fɪʃl/ adj provechoso

beneficiary /benɪ'fɪʃərɪ/ n beneficiario m

benefit /'benɪfɪt/ n provecho m, ventaja f; (allowance) prestación f; (for unemployed) subsidio m; (perk) beneficio m. ● vt (pt **benefited**, pres p **benefiting**) beneficiar. ● vi beneficiarse

benevolent /bə'nevələnt/ adj benévolo

benign /bɪ'naɪn/ adj benigno

bent /bent/ see BEND. ● n inclinación f. ● adj torcido; (🄸, corrupt) corrompido

bereave|d /bɪ'riːvd/ n. **the ~d** la familia del difunto. **~ment** n pérdida f; (mourning) luto m

beret /'bereɪ/ n boina f

berry /'berɪ/ n baya f

berserk /bə'sɜːk/ adj. **go ~** volverse loco

berth /bɜːθ/ n litera f; (anchorage) amarradero m. **give a wide ~ to** evitar. ● vt/i atracar

beside /bɪ'saɪd/ prep al lado de. **be ~ o.s.** estar fuera de sí

besides /bɪ'saɪdz/ prep además de; (except) excepto. ● adv además

besiege /bɪ'siːdʒ/ vt sitiar, asediar; (fig) acosar

best /best/ adj (el) mejor. **the ~ thing is to...** lo mejor es... ● adv mejor. **like ~** preferir. ● n lo mejor. **at ~** a lo más. **do one's ~** hacer todo lo posible. **make the ~ of** contentarse con. **~ man** n padrino m (de boda)

bestow /bɪ'stəʊ/ vt conceder

bestseller /best'selə(r)/ n éxito m de librería, bestseller m

bet /bet/ n apuesta f. ● vt/i (pt **bet** or **betted**) apostar

betray /bɪ'treɪ/ vt traicionar. ∼al n traición f

better /'betə(r)/ adj & adv mejor. ∼ **off** en mejores condiciones; (richer) más rico. **get** ∼ mejorar. **all the** ∼ tanto mejor. **I'd** ∼ **be off** me tengo que ir. **the** ∼ **part of** la mayor parte de. ●vt mejorar; (beat) sobrepasar. ∼ **o.s.** superarse. ●n superior m. **get the** ∼ **of** vencer a. **my** ∼s mis superiores mpl

between /bɪ'twiːn/ prep entre. ●adv en medio

beverage /'bevərɪdʒ/ n bebida f

beware /bɪ'weə(r)/ vi tener cuidado. ●int ¡cuidado!

bewilder /bɪ'wɪldə(r)/ vt desconcertar. ∼ment n aturdimiento m

bewitch /bɪ'wɪtʃ/ vt hechizar; (delight) cautivar

beyond /bɪ'jɒnd/ prep más allá de; (fig) fuera de. ∼ **doubt** sin lugar a duda. ●adv más allá

bias /'baɪəs/ n tendencia f; (prejudice) prejuicio m. ●vt (pt **biased**) influir en. ∼ed adj parcial

bib /bɪb/ n babero m

Bible /'baɪbl/ n Biblia f

biblical /'bɪblɪkl/ adj bíblico

bibliography /bɪblɪ'ɒɡrəfɪ/ n bibliografía f

biceps /'baɪseps/ n invar bíceps m

bicker /'bɪkə(r)/ vi altercar

bicycle /'baɪsɪkl/ n bicicleta f

bid /bɪd/ n (offer) oferta f; (attempt) tentativa f. ●vi hacer una oferta. ●vt (pt & pp **bid**, pres p **bidding**) ofrecer; (pt **bid**, pp **bidden**, pres p **bidding**) mandar; dar (welcome, good day etc). ∼**der** n postor m. ∼**ding** n (at auction) ofertas fpl; (order) mandato m

bide /baɪd/ vt. ∼ **one's time** esperar el momento oportuno

bifocals /baɪ'fəʊklz/ npl gafas fpl bifocales, anteojos mpl bifocales (LAm)

big /bɪɡ/ adj (**bigger, biggest**) grande, (before singular noun) gran. ●adv. **talk** ∼ fanfarronear

bigam|ist /'bɪɡəmɪst/ n bígamo m. ∼**ous** /'bɪɡəməs/ adj bígamo. ∼**y** n bigamia f

big-headed /-'hedɪd/ adj engreído

bigot /'bɪɡət/ n fanático m. ∼**ed** adj fanático

bike /baɪk/ n 🔢 bici f 🔢

bikini /bɪ'kiːnɪ/ n (pl **-is**) bikini m

bile /baɪl/ n bilis f

bilingual /baɪ'lɪŋɡwəl/ adj bilingüe

bill /bɪl/ n cuenta f; (invoice) factura f; (notice) cartel m; (Amer, banknote) billete m; (Pol) proyecto m de ley; (of bird) pico m

billet /'bɪlɪt/ n (Mil) alojamiento m. ●vt alojar

billfold /'bɪlfəʊld/ n (Amer) cartera f, billetera f

billiards /'bɪlɪədz/ n billar m

billion /'bɪlɪən/ n billón m; (Amer) mil millones mpl

bin /bɪn/ n recipiente m; (for rubbish) cubo m de basura, bote m de basura (Mex); (for waste paper) papelera f

bind /baɪnd/ vt (pt **bound**) atar; encuadernar (book); (Jurid) obligar. ●n 🔢 lata f. ∼**ing** n (of books) encuadernación f; (braid) ribete m

binge /bɪndʒ/ n 🔢, (of food) comilona f; (of drink) borrachera f. **go on a** ∼ ir de juerga

bingo /'bɪŋɡəʊ/ n bingo m

binoculars /bɪ'nɒkjʊləz/ npl gemelos mpl

biograph|er /baɪ'ɒɡrəfə(r)/ n biógrafo m. ∼**y** n biografía f

biolog|ical /baɪə'lɒdʒɪkl/ adj biológico. ∼**ist** /baɪ'ɒlədʒɪst/ n biólogo m. ∼**y** /baɪ'ɒlədʒɪ/ n biología f

bioterrorism /baɪəʊ'terərɪzm/ n bioterrorismo m

birch /bɜːtʃ/ n (tree) abedul m

bird /bɜːd/ n ave f; (small) pájaro m; (sl, girl) chica f

Biro /'baɪərəʊ/ n (pl **-os**) (℗) bolígrafo m

birth /bɜːθ/ n nacimiento m. **give ~** dar a luz. **~ certificate** n partida f de nacimiento. **~ control** n control m de la natalidad. **~day** n cumpleaños m. **~mark** n marca f de nacimiento. **~place** n lugar m de nacimiento. **~ rate** n natalidad f

biscuit /'bɪskɪt/ n galleta f

bisect /baɪ'sekt/ vt bisecar

bishop /'bɪʃəp/ n obispo m; (Chess) alfil m

bit /bɪt/ see BITE. ●n trozo m; (quantity) poco m; (of horse) bocado m; (Mec) broca f; (Comp) bit m

bitch /bɪtʃ/ n perra f; (fam, woman) bruja f 🗓

bit|e /baɪt/ vt/i (pt **bit**, pp **bitten**) morder; (insect) picar. **~e one's nails** morderse las uñas. ●n mordisco m; (mouthful) bocado m; (of insect etc) picadura f. **~ing** /'baɪtɪŋ/ adj mordaz

bitter /'bɪtə(r)/ adj amargo; (of weather) glacial. ●n cerveza f amarga. **~ly** adv amargamente. **it's ~ly cold** hace un frío glacial. **~ness** n amargor m; (resentment) amargura f

bizarre /bɪ'zɑː(r)/ adj extraño

black /blæk/ adj (**-er, -est**) negro. **~ and blue** amoratado. ●n negro m; (coffee) solo, negro (LAm). ●vt ennegrecer; limpiar (shoes). **~ out** vi desmayarse. **~ and white** blanco y negro m. **~-and-white** adj en blanco y negro. **~berry** /-bərɪ/ n zarzamora f. **~bird** n mirlo m. **~board** n pizarra f. **~currant** /-ˈkʌrənt/ n grosella f negra. **~en** vt ennegrecer. **~ eye** n ojo m morado. **~list** vt poner en la lista negra. **~mail** n chantaje m. ●vt chantajear. **~mailer** n chantajista m & f. **~out** n apagón m; (Med) desmayo m; (of news) censura f. **~smith** n herrero m

bladder /'blædə(r)/ n vejiga f

blade /bleɪd/ n (of knife, sword) hoja f. **~ of grass** brizna f de hierba

blame /bleɪm/ vt echar la culpa a. **be to ~** tener la culpa. ●n culpa f. **~less** adj inocente

bland /blænd/ adj (**-er, -est**) suave

blank /blæŋk/ adj (page, space) en blanco; (cassette) virgen; (cartridge) sin bala; (fig) vacío. ●n blanco m

blanket /'blæŋkɪt/ n manta f, cobija f (LAm), frazada (LAm); (fig) capa f. ●vt (pt **blanketed**) (fig) cubrir (**in, with** de)

blare /bleə(r)/ vi sonar muy fuerte. ●n estrépito m

blasphem|e /blæs'fiːm/ vt/i blasfemar. **~ous** /'blæsfəməs/ adj blasfemo. **~y** /'blæsfəmɪ/ n blasfemia f

blast /blɑːst/ n explosión f; (gust) ráfaga f; (sound) toque m. ●vt volar. **~ed** adj maldito. **~-off** n (of missile) despegue m

blatant /'bleɪtnt/ adj patente; (shameless) descarado

blaze /bleɪz/ n llamarada f; (of light) resplandor m; (fig) arranque m. ●vi arder en llamas; (fig) brillar

blazer /'bleɪzə(r)/ n chaqueta f

bleach /bliːtʃ/ n lejía f, cloro m (LAm), blanqueador m (LAm). ●vt blanquear; decolorar (hair).

bleak /bliːk/ adj (**-er, -est**) desolado; (fig) sombrío

bleat /bliːt/ n balido m. ●vi balar

bleed /bliːd/ vt/i (pt **bled** /bled/) sangrar

bleep /bliːp/ n pitido m

blemish /'blemɪʃ/ n mancha f

blend /blend/ n mezcla f. ●vt mezclar. ●vi combinarse. **~er** n licuadora f

bless /bles/ vt bendecir. **~ you!** (on sneezing) ¡Jesús!, ¡salud! (Mex). **~ed** /'blesɪd/ adj bendito. **~ing** n bendición f; (advantage) ventaja f

blew /blu:/ see BLOW

blight /blaɪt/ n añublo m, tizón m; (fig) plaga f. •vt añublar, atizonar; (fig) destrozar

blind /blaɪnd/ adj ciego. ~ **alley** callejón m sin salida. •n persiana f; (fig) pretexto m. •vt dejar ciego; (dazzle) deslumbrar. ~**fold** adj & adv con los ojos vendados. •n venda f. •vt vendar los ojos a. ~**ly** adv a ciegas. ~**ness** n ceguera f

blink /blɪŋk/ vi parpadear; (light) centellear. ~**ers** npl (on horse) anteojeras fpl

bliss /blɪs/ n felicidad f. ~**ful** adj feliz

blister /'blɪstə(r)/ n ampolla f

blizzard /'blɪzəd/ n ventisca f

bloated /'bləʊtɪd/ adj hinchado (**with** de)

blob /blɒb/ n (drip) gota f; (stain) mancha f

bloc /blɒk/ n (Pol) bloque m

block /blɒk/ n bloque m; (of wood) zoquete m; (of buildings) manzana f, cuadra f (LAm). **in ~ letters** en letra de imprenta. ~ **of flats** edificio m de apartamentos, casa f de pisos. •vt bloquear. ~**ade** /blɒˈkeɪd/ n bloqueo m. •vt bloquear. ~**age** /-ɪdʒ/ n obstrucción f. ~**head** n 🄳 zopenco m

bloke /bləʊk/ n 🄳 tipo m, tío m 🄳

blond /blɒnd/ adj & n rubio (m), güero (m) (Mex fam). ~**e** adj & n rubia (f), güera (f) (Mex fam)

blood /blʌd/ n sangre f. ~**bath** n masacre m. ~**-curdling** /-kɜːdlɪŋ/adj horripilante. ~**hound** n sabueso m. ~ **pressure** n tensión f arterial. **high ~ pressure** hipertensión f. ~**shed** n derramamiento m de sangre. ~**shot** adj sanguinolento; (eye) inyectado de sangre. ~**stream** n torrente m sanguíneo. ~**thirsty** adj sanguinario. ~**y** adj (**-ier, -iest**) sangriento; (stained) ensangrentado; 🗴 maldito

bloom /blu:m/ n flor f. •vi florecer

blossom /'blɒsəm/ n flor f. •vi florecer. ~ **(out) into** (fig) llegar a ser

blot /blɒt/ n borrón m. •vt (pt **blotted**) manchar; (dry) secar. ■ ~ **out** vt oscurecer

blotch /blɒtʃ/ n mancha f. ~**y** adj lleno de manchas

blotting-paper /'blɒtɪŋ/ n papel m secante

blouse /blaʊz/ n blusa f

blow /bləʊ/ vt (pt **blew**, pp **blown**) soplar; fundir (fuse); tocar (trumpet).•vi soplar; (fuse) fundirse; (sound) sonar. •n golpe m. ■ ~ **down** vt derribar. ■ ~ **out** vi apagar (candle). ■ ~ **over** vi pasar. ■ ~ **up** vt inflar; (explode) volar; (Photo) ampliar. vi (explode) estallar; (burst) reventar. ~**-dry** vt secar con secador. ~**lamp** n soplete m. ~**out** n (of tyre) reventón m. ~ **torch** n soplete m

blue /blu:/ adj (**-er, -est**) azul; (joke) verde. •n azul m. **out of the ~** totalmente inesperado. ~**s** npl. **have the ~s** tener tristeza. ~**bell** n campanilla f. ~**berry** n arándano m. ~**bottle** n moscarda f. ~**print** n plano m; (fig, plan) programa m

bluff /blʌf/ n (poker) farol m, bluff m (LAm), blof m (Mex). •vt engañar. •vi tirarse un farol, hacer un bluf (LAm), blofear (Mex)

blunder /'blʌndə(r)/ vi cometer un error. •n metedura f de pata

blunt /blʌnt/ adj desafilado; (person) directo, abrupto. •vt desafilar. ~**ly** adv francamente

blur /blɜ:(r)/ n impresión f indistinta. •vt (pt **blurred**) hacer borroso

blurb /blɜ:b/ n resumen m publicitario

blurt /blɜ:t/ vt. ~ **out** dejar escapar

blush /blʌʃ/ vi ruborizarse. •n rubor m

boar /bɔ:(r)/ n verraco m. **wild ~** jabalí m

board /bɔ:d/ n tabla f, tablero m; (for notices) tablón m de anuncios, tablero m de anuncios (LAm); (blackboard) pizarra f; (food) pensión f; (of company) junta f. **~ and lodging** casa y comida. **full ~** pensión f completa. **go by the ~** ser abandonado. ●vt alojar; **~ a ship** embarcarse. ●vi alojarse (**with** en casa de); (at school) ser interno. **~er** n huésped m & f; (school) interno m. **~ing card** n tarjeta f de embarque. **~ing house** n casa f de huéspedes, pensión f. **~ing pass** n see **~ING CARD. ~ing school** n internado m

boast /bəʊst/ vt enorgullecerse de. ●vi jactarse. ●n jactancia f. **~ful** adj jactancioso

boat /bəʊt/ n barco m; (small) bote m, barca f

bob /bɒb/ vi (pt **bobbed**) menearse, subir y bajar. ■ **~ up** vi presentarse súbitamente

bobbin /'bɒbɪn/ n carrete m; (in sewing machine) canilla f, bobina f

bobby pin /'bɒbɪ/ n (Amer) horquilla f, pasador m (Mex). **~ sox** /sɒks/ npl (Amer) calcetines mpl cortos

bobsleigh /'bɒbsleɪ/ n bob(sleigh) m

bode /bəʊd/ vi. **~ well/ill** ser de buen/mal agüero

bodice /'bɒdɪs/ n corpiño m

bodily /'bɒdɪlɪ/ adj físico, corporal. ●adv físicamente

body /'bɒdɪ/ n cuerpo m; (dead) cadáver m. **~guard** n guardaespaldas m. **~ part** n pedazo m de cuerpo. **~work** n carrocería f

bog /bɒg/ n ciénaga f. ■ **~ down** vt (pt **bogged**). **get ~ged down** empantanarse

boggle /'bɒgl/ vi sobresaltarse. **the mind ~s** uno se queda atónito

bogus /'bəʊgəs/ adj falso

boil /bɔɪl/ vt/i hervir. **be ~ing hot** estar ardiendo; (weather) hacer mucho calor. ●n furúnculo m. ■ **~ away** vi evaporarse. ■ **~ down to** vt reducirse a. ■ **~ over** vi rebosar. **~ed** adj hervido; (egg) pasado por agua. **~er** n caldera f. **~er suit** n mono m, overol m (LAm)

boisterous /'bɔɪstərəs/ adj ruidoso, bullicioso

bold /bəʊld/ adj (**-er, -est**) audaz. **~ly** adv con audacia, audazmente

Bolivia /bə'lɪvɪə/ n Bolivia f. **~n** adj & n boliviano (m)

bolster /'bəʊlstə(r)/ ■ **~ up** vt sostener

bolt /bəʊlt/ n (on door) cerrojo m; (for nut) perno m; (lightning) rayo m; (leap) fuga f. ●vt echar el cerrojo a (door); engullir (food). ●vi fugarse. ●adv. **~ upright** rígido

bomb /bɒm/ n bomba f. ●vt bombardear. **~ard** /bɒm'bɑ:d/ vt bombardear **~er** /'bɒmə(r)/ n (plane) bombardero m; (terrorist) terrorista m & f. **~ing** /'bɒmɪŋ/ n bombardeo m. **~shell** n bomba f

bond /bɒnd/ n (agreement) obligación f; (link) lazo m; (Com) bono m. ●vi (stick) adherirse. **~age** /-ɪdʒ/ n esclavitud f

bone /bəʊn/ n hueso m; (of fish) espina f. ●vt deshuesar; quitar las espinas a (fish). **~-dry** adj completamente seco. **~ idle** adj holgazán

bonfire /'bɒnfaɪə(r)/ n hoguera f, fogata f

bonnet /'bɒnɪt/ n gorra f; (Auto) capó m, capote m (Mex)

bonus /'bəʊnəs/ n (payment) bonificación f; (fig) ventaja f

bony /'bəʊnɪ/ adj (**-ier, -iest**) huesudo; (fish) lleno de espinas

boo /bu:/ int ¡bu! ●vt/i abuchear

boob /bu:b/ n (fam, mistake) metedura f de pata. ●vi 🄵 meter la pata

book /bʊk/ n libro m; (of cheques etc)

b

talonario m, chequera f; (notebook) libreta f; (exercise book) cuaderno m. **~s** (mpl) (Com) cuentas fpl. • vt (enter) registrar; (reserve) reservar. • vi reservar. **~case** n biblioteca f, librería f, librero m (Mex). **~ing** n reserva f, reservación f (LAm). **~ing office** n (in theatre) taquilla f, boletería f (LAm). **~keeping** n contabilidad f. **~let** /'bʊklɪt/ n folleto m. **~maker** n corredor m de apuestas. **~mark** n señal f. **~seller** n librero m. **~shop**, (Amer) **~store** n librería f. **~worm** n (fig) ratón m de biblioteca

boom /buːm/ vi retumbar; (fig) prosperar. • n estampido m; (Com) boom m

boost /buːst/ vt estimular; reforzar (morale). • n empuje m. **~er** n (Med) revacunación f. **~er cable** n (Amer) cable m de arranque

boot /buːt/ n bota f; (Auto) maletero m, cajuela f (Mex). ■ **~ up** vt (Comp) cargar

booth /buːð/ n cabina f; (at fair) puesto m

booze /buːz/ vi 🔲 beber mucho. • n 🔲 alcohol m

border /'bɔːdə(r)/ n borde m; (frontier) frontera f; (in garden) arriate m. ■ **~ on** vt lindar con. **~line** n línea f divisoria. **~line case** n caso m dudoso

bor|e /bɔː(r)/ see BEAR. • vt (annoy) aburrir; (Tec) taladrar. • vi taladrar. • n (person) pelmazo m; (thing) lata f. **~ed** adj aburrido. **be ~ed** estar aburrido. **get ~ed** aburrirse. **~edom** /'bɔːdəm/ n aburrimiento m. **~ing** adj aburrido, pesado

born /bɔːn/ adj nato. **be ~** nacer

borne /bɔːn/ see BEAR

borough /'bʌrə/ n municipio m

borrow /'bɒrəʊ/ vt pedir prestado

boss /bɒs/ n 🔲 jefe m. • vt. **~ (about)** 🔲 dar órdenes a. **~y** adj mandón

botan|ical /bə'tænɪkl/ adj botánico. **~ist** n /'bɒtənɪst/ n botánico m. **~y**

/'bɒtənɪ/ n botánica f

both /bəʊθ/ adj & pron ambos (mpl), los dos (mpl). • adv al mismo tiempo, a la vez. **~ Ann and Brian came** tanto Ann como Bob vinieron.

bother /'bɒðə(r)/ vt (inconvenience) molestar; (worry) preocupar. **~ it!** ¡caramba! • vi molestarse. **~ about** preocuparse de. **~ doing** tomarse la molestia de hacer. • n molestia f

bottle /'bɒtl/ n botella, mamila f (Mex); (for baby) biberón m. • vt embotellar. ■ **~ up** vt (fig) reprimir. **~neck** n (traffic jam) embotellamiento m. **~ opener** n abrebotellas m, destapador m (LAm)

bottom /'bɒtəm/ n fondo m; (of hill) pie m; (buttocks) trasero m. • adj de más abajo; (price) más bajo; (lip, edge) inferior. **~less** adj sin fondo

bough /baʊ/ n rama f

bought /bɔːt/ see BUY

boulder /'bəʊldə(r)/ n canto m

bounce /baʊns/ vt hacer rebotar. • vi rebotar; (person) saltar; 🔲 (cheque) ser rechazado. • n rebote m

bound /baʊnd/ see BIND. • vi saltar. • n (jump) salto m. **~s** npl (limits) límites mpl. **out of ~s** zona f prohibida. • adj. **be ~ for** dirigirse a. **~ to** obligado a; (certain) seguro de

boundary /'baʊndərɪ/ n límite m

bouquet /bʊ'keɪ/ n ramo m; (of wine) buqué m, aroma m

bout /baʊt/ n período m; (Med) ataque m; (Sport) encuentro m

bow[1] /bəʊ/ n (weapon, Mus) arco m; (knot) lazo m, moño m (LAm)

bow[2] /baʊ/ n reverencia f; (Naut) proa f; • vi inclinarse. • vt inclinar

bowels /'baʊəlz/ npl intestinos mpl; (fig) entrañas fpl

bowl /bəʊl/ n (container) cuenco m; (for washing) palangana f; (ball) bola f. • vt (cricket) arrojar. • vi (cricket) arrojar la pelota. ■~ **over** vt derribar

bowl: ~**er** n (cricket) lanzador m. ~**er (hat)** sombrero m de hongo, bombín m. ~**ing** n bolos mpl. ~**ing alley** n bolera f

bow tie /bəʊ ˈtaɪ/ n corbata f de lazo, pajarita f

box /bɒks/ n caja f; (for jewels etc) estuche m; (in theatre) palco m. ●vt boxear contra. ~ **s.o.'s ears** dar una manotada a uno. ●vi boxear. ~**er** n boxeador m. ~**ing** n boxeo m. **B~ing Day** n el 26 de diciembre. ~ **office** n taquilla f, boletería f (LAm). ~ **room** n trastero m

boy /bɔɪ/ n chico m, muchacho m; (young) niño m

boy: ~ **band** n grupo m pop de chicos. ~**friend** n novio m. ~**hood** n niñez f. ~**ish** adj de muchacho; (childish) infantil

boycott /ˈbɔɪkɒt/ vt boicotear. ●n boicoteo m

bra /brɑː/ n sostén m, sujetador m, brasier m (Mex)

brace /breɪs/ n abrazadera f. ●vt asegurar. ~ **o.s.** prepararse. ~**s** npl tirantes mpl; (Amer, dental) aparato(s) m(pl)

bracelet /ˈbreɪslɪt/ n pulsera f

bracken /ˈbrækən/ n helecho m

bracket /ˈbrækɪt/ n soporte m; (group) categoría f; (parenthesis) paréntesis m. **square ~s** corchetes mpl. ●vt poner entre paréntesis; (join together) agrupar

brag /bræg/ vi (pt **bragged**) jactarse (**about** de)

braid /breɪd/ n galón m; (Amer, in hair) trenza f

brain /breɪn/ n cerebro m. ●vt romper la cabeza a. ~**child** n invento m. ~ **drain** n 🅸 fuga f de cerebros. ~**storm** n ataque m de locura; (Amer, brainwave) idea f genial. ~**wash** vt lavar el cerebro. ~**wave** n idea f genial. ~**y** adj (**-ier, -iest**) inteligente

brake /breɪk/ n freno m. ●vt/i frenar. ~ **fluid** n líquido m de freno. ~ **lights** npl luces fpl de freno

bramble /ˈbræmbl/ n zarza f

bran /bræn/ n salvado m

branch /brɑːntʃ/ n rama f; (of road) bifurcación f; (Com) sucursal m; (fig) ramo m. ■~ **off** vi bifurcarse. ■~ **out** vi ramificarse

brand /brænd/ n marca f. ●vt marcar; (label) tildar de

brandish /ˈbrændɪʃ/ vt blandir

brand: ~ **name**: n marca f. ~**-new** /-ˈnjuː/ adj flamante

brandy /ˈbrændɪ/ n coñac m

brash /bræʃ/ adj descarado

brass /brɑːs/ n latón m. **get down to ~ tacks** (fig) ir al grano. ~ **band** n banda f de música

brassière /ˈbræsɪə(r)/ n see BRA

brat /bræt/ n (pej) mocoso m

bravado /brəˈvɑːdəʊ/ n bravata f

brave /breɪv/ adj (**-er, -est**) valiente. ●n (North American Indian) guerrero m indio. **the ~** npl los valientes. ●vt afrontar. ~**ry** /-ərɪ/ n valentía f, valor m

brawl /brɔːl/ n alboroto m. ●vi pelearse

brazen /ˈbreɪzn/ adj descarado

Brazil /brəˈzɪl/ n Brasil m. ~**ian** /-jən/ adj & n brasileño (m)

breach /briːtʃ/ n infracción f, violación f; (of contract) incumplimiento m; (gap) brecha f. ~ **of the peace** alteración f del orden público. ●vt abrir una brecha en

bread /bred/ n pan m. **a loaf of ~** un pan. ~**crumbs** npl migajas fpl; (Culin) pan m rallado, pan m molido (Mex)

breadth /bredθ/ n anchura f

breadwinner /ˈbredwɪnə(r)/ n sostén m de la familia

break /breɪk/ vt (pt **broke**, pp

broken) romper; infringir, violar (law); batir (record); comunicar (news); interrumpir (journey). •vi romperse; (news) divulgarse. •n ruptura f; (interval) intervalo m; (fam, chance) oportunidad f; (in weather) cambio m. ∎ **~ away** vi escapar. ∎ **~ down** vt derribar; analizar (figures). vi estropearse, descomponerse (LAm); (Auto) averiarse; (cry) deshacerse en lágrimas. ∎ **~ in** vi (intruder) entrar (para robar). ∎ **~ into** vt entrar en (para robar) (house etc); (start doing) ponerse a. ∎ **~ off** vi interrumpirse. ∎ **~ out** vi (war, disease) estallar; (run away) escaparse. ∎ **~ up** vi romperse; (band, lovers) separarse; (schools) terminar. **~able** adj frágil. **~age** /-ɪdʒ/ n rotura f. **~down** n (Tec) falla f; (Med) colapso m, crisis f nerviosa; (of figures) análisis f. **~er** n (wave) ola f grande

breakfast /'brekfəst/ n desayuno m. **have ~** desayunar

break: **~through** n adelanto m. **~water** n rompeolas m

breast /brest/ n pecho m; (of chicken etc) pechuga f. **~stroke** n braza f, (estilo m) pecho m (LAm)

breath /breθ/ n aliento m, respiración f. **be out of ~** estar sin aliento. **hold one's ~** aguantar la respiración. **under one's ~** a media voz

breath|e /briːð/ vt/i respirar. **~er** n descanso m, pausa f. **~ing** n respiración f

breathtaking /'breθteɪkɪŋ/ adj impresionante

bred /bred/ see BREED

breed /briːd/ vt (pt bred) criar; (fig) engendrar. •vi reproducirse. •n raza f

breez|e /briːz/ n brisa f. **~y** adj de mucho viento

brew /bruː/ vt hacer (beer); preparar (tea). •vi hacer cerveza; (tea) reposar; (fig) prepararse. •n infusión f. **~er** n cervecero m.

~ery n cervecería f, fábrica f de cerveza

bribe /braɪb/ n soborno m. •vt sobornar. **~ry** /'braɪbəri/ n soborno m

brick /brɪk/ n ladrillo m. **~layer** n albañil m

bridal /'braɪdl/ adj nupcial

bride /braɪd/ m novia f. **~groom** n novio m. **~smaid** /'braɪdzmeɪd/ n dama f de honor

bridge /brɪdʒ/ n puente m; (of nose) caballete m; (Cards) bridge m. •vt tender un puente sobre. **~ a gap** llenar un vacío

bridle /'braɪdl/ n brida f. **~ path** n camino m de herradura

brief /briːf/ adj (-er, -est) breve. •n (Jurid) escrito m. •vt dar instrucciones a. **~case** n maletín m, portafolio(s) m (LAm). **~ly** adv brevemente. **~s** npl (man's) calzoncillos mpl; (woman's) bragas fpl, calzones mpl (LAm), pantaletas fpl (Mex)

brigade /brɪ'geɪd/ n brigada f

bright /braɪt/ adj (-er, -est) brillante, claro; (clever) listo; (cheerful) alegre. **~en** vt aclarar; hacer más alegre (house etc). •vi (weather) aclararse; (face) illuminarse

brillian|ce /'brɪljəns/ n brillantez f, brillo m. **~t** adj brillante

brim /brɪm/ n borde m; (of hat) ala f. ∎ **~ over** vi (pt **brimmed**) desbordarse

brine /braɪn/ n salmuera f

bring /brɪŋ/ vt (pt **brought**) traer; (lead) llevar. ∎ **~ about** vt causar. ∎ **~ back** vt devolver. ∎ **~ down** vt derribar. ∎ **~ off** vt lograr. ∎ **~ on** vt causar. ∎ **~ out** vt sacar; lanzar (product); publicar (book). ∎ **~ round/to** vt hacer volver en sí. ∎ **~ up** vt (Med) vomitar; educar (children); plantear (question)

brink /brɪŋk/ n borde m

brisk /brɪsk/ adj (**-er, -est**) enérgico, vivo

bristle /'brɪsl/ n cerda f. ●vi erizarse

Brit|ain /'brɪtən/ n Gran Bretaña f. **~ish** /'brɪtɪʃ/ adj británico. ●npl **the ~ish** los británicos. **~on** /'brɪtən/ n británico m

Brittany /'brɪtəni/ n Bretaña f

brittle /'brɪtl/ adj frágil, quebradizo

broach /brəʊtʃ/ vt abordar

broad /brɔːd/ adj (**-er, -est**) ancho. **in ~ daylight** a plena luz del día. **~ bean** n haba f **~cast** n emisión f. ●vt (pt **broadcast**) emitir. ●vi hablar por la radio. **~caster** n locutor m. **~casting** n radiodifusión f. **~en** vt ensanchar. ●vi ensancharse. **~ly** adv en general. **~-minded** /-'maɪndɪd/ adj de miras amplias, tolerante

broccoli /'brɒkəlɪ/ n invar brécol m

brochure /'brəʊʃə(r)/ n folleto m

broil /brɔɪl/ vt (Amer) asar a la parrilla **~er** n (Amer) parrilla f

broke /brəʊk/ see **BREAK**. ●adj 🔢 sin blanca, en la ruina

broken /'brəʊkən/ see **BREAK**. ●adj roto

broker /'brəʊkə(r)/ n corredor m

brolly /'brɒlɪ/ n 🔢 paraguas m

bronchitis /brɒŋ'kaɪtɪs/ n bronquitis f

bronze /brɒnz/ n bronce m. ●adj de bronce

brooch /brəʊtʃ/ n broche m

brood /bruːd/ n cría f; (humorous) prole m. ●vi empollar; (fig) meditar

brook /brʊk/ n arroyo m. ●vt soportar

broom /bruːm/ n escoba f. **~stick** n palo m de escoba

broth /brɒθ/ n caldo m

brothel /'brɒθl/ n burdel m

brother /'brʌðə(r)/ n hermano m. **~hood** n fraternidad f. **~-in-law** (pl **~s-in-law**) n cuñado m. **~ly** adj fraternal

brought /brɔːt/ see **BRING**

brow /braʊ/ n frente f; (of hill) cima f. **~beat** vt (pt **-beaten**, pp **-beat**) intimidar

brown /braʊn/ adj (**-er, -est**) marrón, café (Mex); (hair) castaño; (skin) moreno; (tanned) bronceado. ●n marrón m, café m (Mex). ●vt poner moreno; (Culin) dorar. ~ **bread** n pan m integral. ~ **sugar** /braʊn 'ʃʊgə(r)/ n azúcar m moreno, azúcar f morena

browse /braʊz/ vi (in a shop) curiosear; (animal) pacer; (Comp) navegar. **~r** (Comp) browser m, navegador m

bruise /bruːz/ n magulladura f. ●vt magullar; machucar (fruit)

brunch /brʌntʃ/ n 🔢 desayuno m tardío

brunette /bruː'net/ n morena f

brunt /brʌnt/ n. **bear** or **take the ~ of sth** sufrir algo

brush /brʌʃ/ n cepillo m; (large) escoba; (for decorating) brocha f; (artist's) pincel; (skirmish) escaramuza f. ●vt cepillar. ■ ~ **against** vt rozar. ■ ~ **aside** vt rechazar. ■ ~ **off** vt (rebuff) desairar. ■ ~ **up (on)** vt refrescar

brusque /bruːsk/ adj brusco. **~ly** adv bruscamente

Brussels /'brʌslz/ n Bruselas f. ~ **sprout** n col f de Bruselas

brutal /'bruːtl/ adj brutal. **~ity** /-'tælətɪ/ n brutalidad f. **~ly** adv brutalmente

brute /bruːt/ n bestia f. ~ **force** fuerza f bruta

BSc abbr see **BACHELOR**

BSE abbr (**bovine spongiform encephalopathy**) EBE f

bubbl|e /'bʌbl/ n burbuja f. ●vi burbujear. ■ ~ **over** vi desbordarse. **~ly** adj burbujeante

buck /bʌk/ adj macho. ●n (deer) ciervo m; (Amer fam) dólar m. **pass the ~** pasar la pelota

bucket | bunker

340

bucket /ˈbʌkɪt/ n balde m, cubo m, cubeta f (Mex)

buckle /ˈbʌkl/ n hebilla f. •vt abrochar. •vi torcerse

bud /bʌd/ n brote m. •vi (pt **budded**) brotar.

Buddhis|m /ˈbʊdɪzəm/ n budismo m. ~**t** adj & n budista (m & f)

budding /ˈbʌdɪŋ/ adj (fig) en ciernes

buddy /ˈbʌdɪ/ n 🔲 amigo m, cuate m (Mex)

budge /bʌdʒ/ vt mover. •vi moverse

budgerigar /ˈbʌdʒərɪgɑː(r)/ n periquito m

budget /ˈbʌdʒɪt/ n presupuesto m

buffalo /ˈbʌfələʊ/ n (pl **-oes** or **-o**) búfalo m

buffer /ˈbʌfə(r)/ n parachoques m

buffet[1] /ˈbʊfeɪ/ n (meal) buffet m; (in train) bar m

buffet[2] /ˈbʌfɪt/ n golpe m

bug /bʌg/ n bicho m; 🔲 (germ) microbio m; (fam, device) micrófono m oculto. •vt (pt **bugged**) 🔲 ocultar un micrófono en; (bother) molestar

buggy /ˈbʌgɪ/ n. **baby** ~ sillita f de paseo (plegable); (Amer) cochecito m

bugle /ˈbjuːgl/ n corneta f

build /bɪld/ vt/i (pt **built**) construir. •n (of person) figura f, tipo m. ∎ ~ **up** vt/i fortalecer; (increase) aumentar. ~**er** n (contractor) contratista m & f; (labourer) albañil m. ~**ing** n edificio m; (construction) construcción f. ~**up** n aumento m; (of gas etc) acumulación f

built /bɪlt/ see BUILD. ~**-in** adj empotrado. ~**-up area** n zona f urbanizada

bulb /bʌlb/ n bulbo m; (Elec) bombilla f, foco m (Mex)

Bulgaria /bʌlˈgeərɪə/ n Bulgaria f. ~**n** adj & n búlgaro (m)

bulg|e /bʌldʒ/ n protuberancia f. •vi pandearse. ~**ing** adj abultado; (eyes) saltón

bulk /bʌlk/ n bulto m, volumen m. **in** ~ a granel; (loose) suelto. **the** ~ **of** la mayor parte de. ~**y** adj voluminoso

bull /bʊl/ n toro m. ~**dog** n buldog m. ~**dozer** /-dəʊzə(r)/ n bulldozer m

bullet /ˈbʊlɪt/ n bala f

bulletin /ˈbʊlətɪn/ n anuncio m; (journal) boletín m. ~ **board** n (Amer) tablón m de anuncios, tablero m de anuncios (LAm)

bulletproof /ˈbʊlɪtpruːf/ adj a prueba de balas

bullfight /ˈbʊlfaɪt/ n corrida f (de toros). ~**er** n torero m. ~**ing** n (deporte m de) los toros

bull: ~ring n plaza f de toros. ~**'s-eye** n diana f. ~**shit** n (vulgar) sandeces fpl 🔲, gillipolleces fpl 🔲

bully /ˈbʊlɪ/ n matón m. •vt intimidar. ~**ing** n intimidación f

bum /bʌm/ n (fam, backside) trasero m; (Amer fam, tramp) holgazán m

bumblebee /ˈbʌmblbiː/ n abejorro m

bump /bʌmp/ vt chocar contra. •vi dar sacudidas. •n (blow) golpe m; (jolt) sacudida f. ∎ ~ **into** vt chocar contra; (meet) encontrar.

bumper /ˈbʌmpə(r)/ n parachoques m. •adj récord. ~ **edition** n edición f especial

bun /bʌn/ n bollo m; (bread roll) panecillo m, bolillo m (Mex); (hair) moño m, chongo m (Mex)

bunch /bʌntʃ/ n (of people) grupo m; (of bananas, grapes) racimo m; (of flowers) ramo m

bundle /ˈbʌndl/ n bulto m; (of papers) legajo m. ∎ ~ **up** vt atar

bungalow /ˈbʌŋgələʊ/ n casa f de un solo piso

bungle /ˈbʌŋgl/ vt echar a perder

bunk /bʌŋk/ n litera f

bunker /ˈbʌŋkə(r)/ n carbonera f; (Golf, Mil) búnker m

bunny /'bʌnɪ/ n conejito m

buoy /bɔɪ/ n boya f. ■ ~ **up** vt hacer flotar; (fig) animar

buoyant /'bɔɪənt/ adj flotante; (fig) optimista

burden /'bɜːdn/ n carga f. ●vt cargar (**with** de)

bureau /'bjʊərəʊ/ n (pl **-eaux** /-əʊz/) agencia f; (desk) escritorio m; (Amer, chest of drawers) cómoda f

bureaucra|cy /bjʊə'rɒkrəsɪ/ n burocracia f. **~t** /'bjʊərəkræt/ n burócrata m & f. **~tic** /-'krætɪk/ adj burocrático

burger /'bɜːɡə(r)/ n 🔢 hamburguesa f

burgl|ar /'bɜːɡlə(r)/ n ladrón m. **~ar alarm** n alarma f antirrobo. **~ary** n robo m (en casa o edificio). **~e** /'bɜːɡl/ vt entrar a robar en. **we were ~ed** nos entraron a robar

burial /'berɪəl/ n entierro m

burly /'bɜːlɪ/ adj (**-ier, -iest**) corpulento

burn /bɜːn/ vt (pt **burned** or **burnt**) quemar. ●vi quemarse. ●n quemadura f. **~er** n quemador m. ■ ~ **down** vt incendiar. vi incendiarse

burnt /bɜːnt/ see BURN

burp /bɜːp/ n 🔢 eructo m. ●vi 🔢 eructar

burrow /'bʌrəʊ/ n madriguera f. ●vt excavar

burst /bɜːst/ vt (pt **burst**) reventar. ●vi reventarse. ~ **into tears** echarse a llorar. ~ **out laughing** echarse a reír. ●n (Mil) ráfaga f; (of activity) arrebato; (of applause) salva f

bury /'berɪ/ vt enterrar; (hide) ocultar

bus /bʌs/ n (pl **buses**) autobús m, camión m (Mex)

bush /bʊʃ/ n arbusto m; (land) monte m. **~y** adj espeso

business /'bɪznɪs/ n negocio m; (Com) negocios mpl; (profession) ocupación f; (fig) asunto m. **mind one's own ~** ocuparse de sus propios asuntos. **~like** adj práctico, serio. **~man** /-mən/ n hombre m de negocios. **~woman** n mujer f de negocios

busker /'bʌskə(r)/ n músico m ambulante

bus stop n parada f de autobús, paradero m de autobús (LAm)

bust /bʌst/ n busto m; (chest) pecho m. ●vt (pt **busted** or **bust**) 🔢 romper. ●vi romperse. ●adj roto. **go ~** 🔢 quebrar

bust-up /'bʌstʌp/ n 🔢 riña f

busy /'bɪzɪ/ adj (**-ier, -iest**) ocupado; (street) concurrido. **be ~** (Amer) (phone) estar comunicando, estar ocupado (LAm). ●vt. ~ **o.s. with** ocuparse de. **~body** n entrometido m

but /bʌt/ conj pero; (after negative) sino. ●prep menos. ~ **for** si no fuera por. **last ~ one** penúltimo

butcher /'bʊtʃə(r)/ n carnicero m. ●vt matar; (fig) hacer una carnicería con

butler /'bʌtlə(r)/ n mayordomo m

butt /bʌt/ n (of gun) culata f; (of cigarette) colilla f; (target) blanco m; (Amer fam, backside) trasero m. ●vi topar. ■ ~ **in** vi interrumpir

butter /'bʌtə(r)/ n mantequilla f. ●vt untar con mantequilla. **~cup** n ranúnculo m. **~fingers** n manazas m, torpe m. **~fly** n mariposa f; (swimming) estilo m mariposa

buttock /'bʌtək/ n nalga f

button /'bʌtn/ n botón m. ●vt abotonar. ●vi abotonarse. **~hole** n ojal m. ●vt (fig) detener

buy /baɪ/ vt/i (pt **bought**) comprar. ●n compra f. **~er** n comprador m

buzz /bʌz/ n zumbido m. ●vi zumbar. ■ ~ **off** vi 🔢 largarse. **~er** n timbre m

by /baɪ/ prep por; (near) cerca de; (before) antes de; (according to) según. **~ and large** en conjunto, en general. **~ car** en coche. **~ oneself** por sí solo

bye /baɪ/, **bye-bye** /ˈbaɪbaɪ/ int 🅃 ¡adiós!

by: **~-election** n elección f parcial. **~-law** n reglamento m

(local). **~pass** n carretera f de circunvalación. ●vt eludir; (road) circunvalar. **~-product** n subproducto m. **~stander** /-stændə(r)/ n espectador m

byte /baɪt/ n (Comp) byte m, octeto m

Cc

cab /kæb/ n taxi m; (of lorry, train) cabina f

cabaret /ˈkæbəreɪ/ n cabaret m

cabbage /ˈkæbɪdʒ/ n col f, repollo m

cabin /ˈkæbɪn/ n (house) cabaña f; (in ship) camarote m; (in plane) cabina f

cabinet /ˈkæbɪnɪt/ n (cupboard) armario m; (for display) vitrina f. **C~** (Pol) gabinete m

cable /ˈkeɪbl/ n cable m. **~ car** n teleférico m. **~ TV** n televisión f por cable, cablevisión f (LAm)

cackle /ˈkækl/ n (of hen) cacareo m; (laugh) risotada f. ●vi cacarear; (laugh) reírse a carcajadas

cactus /ˈkæktəs/ n (pl **-ti** /-taɪ/ or **-tuses**) cacto m

caddie, caddy /ˈkædɪ/ n (golf) portador m de palos

cadet /kəˈdet/ n cadete m

cadge /kædʒ/ vt/i gorronear

café /ˈkæfeɪ/ n cafetería f

cafeteria /kæfɪˈtɪərɪə/ n restaurante m autoservicio

caffeine /ˈkæfiːn/ n cafeína f

cage /keɪdʒ/ n jaula f. ●vt enjaular

cake /keɪk/ n pastel m, tarta f; (sponge) bizcocho m. **~ of soap** pastilla f de jabón

calamity /kəˈlæmətɪ/ n calamidad f

calcium /ˈkælsɪəm/ n calcio m

calculat|e /ˈkælkjʊleɪt/ vt/i calcular. **~ion** /-ˈleɪʃn/ n cálculo m. **~or** n calculadora f

calculus /ˈkælkjʊləs/ n (Math) cálculo m

calendar /ˈkælɪndə(r)/ n calendario m

calf /kɑːf/ n (pl **calves**) (animal) ternero m; (of leg) pantorrilla f

calibre /ˈkælɪbə(r)/ n calibre m

call /kɔːl/ vt/i llamar. ●n llamada f; (shout) grito m; (visit) visita f. **be on ~** estar de guardia. **long-distance ~** llamada f de larga distancia, conferencia f. ■ **~ back** vt hacer volver; (on phone) volver a llamar. vi volver; (on phone) volver a llamar. ■ **~ for** vt pedir; (fetch) ir a buscar. ■ **~ off** vt suspender. ■ **~ on** vt pasar a visitar. ■ **~ out** vi dar voces. ■ **~ together** vt convocar. ■ **~ up** vt (Mil) llamar al servicio militar; (phone) llamar. **~ box** n cabina f telefónica. **~ centre** n centro m de llamadas. **~er** n visita f; (phone) persona que llama m. **~ing** n vocación f

callous /ˈkæləs/ adj insensible, cruel

calm /kɑːm/ adj (**-er, -est**) tranquilo; (sea) en calma. ●n tranquilidad f, calma f. ●vt calmar. ●vi calmarse. **~ down** vi tranquilizarse. vt calmar. **~ly** adv con calma

calorie /ˈkælərɪ/ n caloría f

calves /kɑːvz/ npl see **CALF**

camcorder /'kæmkɔːdə(r)/ n
videocámara f, camcórder m

came /keɪm/, see **COME**

camel /'kæml/ n camello m

camera /'kæmərə/ n cámara f,
máquina f fotográfica ∼**man**
/-mæn/ n camarógrafo m, cámara m

camouflage /'kæməflɑːʒ/ n
camuflaje m. •vt camuflar

camp /kæmp/ n campamento m. •vi
acampar. **go** ∼**ing** hacer camping

campaign /kæm'peɪn/ n campaña f.
•vi hacer campaña

camp: ∼**bed** n catre m de tijera.
∼**er** n campista m & f; (vehicle)
cámper m. ∼**ground** n (Amer) see
∼**site**. ∼**ing** n camping m. ∼**site**
n camping m

campus /'kæmpəs/ n (pl **-puses**)
campus m, ciudad f universitaria

can¹ /kæn/ /kən/

negative **can't**, **cannot** (formal);
past **could**

auxiliary verb

····▸ (be able to) poder. **I** ∼**'t lift it**
no lo puedo levantar. **she says
she** ∼ **come** dice que puede
venir

····▸ (be allowed to) poder. ∼ **I
smoke?** ¿puedo fumar?

····▸ (know how to) saber. ∼ **you
swim?** ¿sabes nadar?

····▸ (with verbs of perception) not
translated. **I** ∼**'t see you** no te
veo. **I** ∼ **hear you better now**
ahora te oigo mejor

····▸ (in requests) ∼ **I have a glass
of water, please?** ¿me trae un
vaso de agua, por favor? ∼ **I
have a kilo of cheese, please?**
¿me da un kilo de queso, por
favor?

····▸ (in offers) ∼ **I help you?** ¿te
ayudo?; (in shop) ¿lo/la
atienden?

can² /kæn/ n lata f, bote m. •vt (pt

canned) enlatar. ∼**ned music**
música f grabada

Canad|a /'kænədə/ n (el) Canadá
m. ∼**ian** /kə'neɪdɪən/ adj & n
canadiense (m & f)

canal /kə'næl/ n canal m

Canaries /kə'neərɪz/ npl = **CANARY
ISLANDS**

canary /kə'neərɪ/ n canario m. **C**∼
Islands npl. **the C**∼ **Islands** las
Islas Canarias

cancel /'kænsl/ vt (pt **cancelled**)
cancelar; anular (command, cheque);
(delete) tachar. ∼**lation** /-'leɪʃn/ n
cancelación f

cancer /'kænsə(r)/ n cáncer m. **C**∼
(in astrology) Cáncer m. ∼**ous** adj
canceroso

candid /'kændɪd/ adj franco

candidate /'kændɪdeɪt/ n
candidato m

candle /'kændl/ n vela f. ∼**stick** n
candelero m

candour /'kændə(r)/ n franqueza f

candy /'kændɪ/ n (Amer) caramelo m,
dulce m (LAm). ∼**floss** /-flɒs/ n
algodón m de azúcar

cane /keɪn/ n caña f; (for baskets)
mimbre m; (stick) bastón m; (for
punishment) palmeta f. •vt castigar
con palmeta

canister /'kænɪstə(r)/ n bote m

cannabis /'kænəbɪs/ n cáñamo m
índico, hachís m, cannabis m

cannibal /'kænɪbl/ n caníbal m.
∼**ism** n canibalismo m

cannon /'kænən/ n invar cañón m. ∼
ball n bala f de cañón

cannot /'kænət/ see **CAN¹**

canoe /kə'nuː/ n canoa f, piragua f.
•vi ir en canoa

canon /'kænən/ n canon m; (person)
canónigo m. ∼**ize** vt canonizar

can opener n abrelatas m

canopy /'kænəpɪ/ n dosel m

can't /kɑːnt/ see **CAN¹**

cantankerous | career   344

cantankerous /kæn'tæŋkərəs/ adj mal humorado

canteen /kæn'ti:n/ n cantina f; (of cutlery) juego m de cubiertos

canter /'kæntə(r)/ n medio galope m. •vi ir a medio galope

canvas /'kænvəs/ n lona f; (artist's) lienzo m

canvass /'kænvəs/ vi hacer campaña, solicitar votos. **~ing** n solicitación f (de votos)

canyon /'kænjən/ n cañón m

cap /kæp/ n gorra f; (lid) tapa f; (of cartridge) cápsula f; (of pen) capuchón m. •vt (pt **capped**) tapar, poner cápsula a; (outdo) superar

capab|ility /keɪpə'bɪlətɪ/ n capacidad f. **~le** /'keɪpəbl/ adj capaz

capacity /kə'pæsətɪ/ n capacidad f; (function) calidad f

cape /keɪp/ n (cloak) capa f; (headland) cabo m

capital /'kæpɪtl/ adj capital. **~ letter** mayúscula f. •n (town) capital f; (money) capital m. **~ism** n capitalismo m. **~ist** adj & n capitalista (m & f.) **~ize** vt capitalizar; escribir con mayúsculas (word). •vi. **~ize on** aprovechar

capitulat|e /kə'pɪtʃuleɪt/ vi capitular. **~ion** /-'leɪʃn/ n capitulación f

Capricorn /'kæprɪkɔːn/ n Capricornio m

capsize /kæp'saɪz/ vt hacer volcar. •vi volcarse

capsule /'kæpsjuːl/ n cápsula f

captain /'kæptɪn/ n capitán m; (of plane) comandante m & f. •vt capitanear

caption /'kæpʃn/ n (heading) título m; (of cartoon etc) leyenda f

captivate /'kæptɪveɪt/ vt encantar

captiv|e /'kæptɪv/ adj & n cautivo (m). **~ity** /-'tɪvətɪ/ n cautiverio m, cautividad f

capture /'kæptʃə(r)/ vt capturar; atraer (attention); (Mil) tomar. •n apresamiento m; (Mil) toma f

car /kɑː(r)/ n coche m, carro m (LAm); (Amer, of train) vagón m

caramel /'kærəmel/ n azúcar m quemado; (sweet) caramelo m, dulce m (LAm)

caravan /'kærəvæn/ n caravana f

carbohydrate /kɑːbəʊ'haɪdreɪt/ n hidrato m de carbono

carbon /'kɑːbən/ n carbono m; (paper) carbón m. **~ copy** n copia f al carbón. **~ dioxide** /daɪ'ɒksaɪd/ n anhídrido m carbónico. **~ monoxide** /mə'nɒksaɪd/ n monóxido de carbono

carburettor /kɑːbjʊ'retə(r)/ n carburador m

carcass /'kɑːkəs/ n cuerpo m de animal muerto; (for meat) res f muerta

card /kɑːd/ n tarjeta f; (for games) carta f; (membership) carnet m; (records) ficha f. **~board** n cartón m

cardigan /'kɑːdɪgən/ n chaqueta f de punto, rebeca f

cardinal /'kɑːdɪnl/ adj cardinal. •n cardenal m

care /keə(r)/ n cuidado m; (worry) preocupación f; (protection) cargo m. **~ of** a cuidado de, en casa de. **take ~** tener cuidado. **take ~ of** cuidar de (person); ocuparse de (matter). •vi interesarse. **I don't ~** me da igual. ∎**~ about** vt preocuparse por. ∎**~ for** vt cuidar de; (like) querer

career /kə'rɪə(r)/ n carrera f. •vi correr a toda velocidad

care:: ~free adj despreocupado. **~ful** adj cuidadoso; (cautious) prudente. **be ~ful** tener cuidado. **~fully** adv con cuidado. **~less** adj negligente; (not worried) indiferente. **~lessly** adv descuidadamente. **~lessness** n descuido m **~r** n persona que cuida de un discapacitado

caress /kə'res/ n caricia f. ●vt acariciar

caretaker /'keəteikə(r)/ n vigilante m; (of flats etc) portero m

car ferry n transbordador m de coches

cargo /'kɑ:gəʊ/ n (pl **-oes**) carga f

Caribbean /kærɪ'biːən/ adj caribeño. **the ~ (Sea)** n el mar Caribe

caricature /'kærɪkətʃʊə(r)/ n caricatura f. ●vt caricaturizar

carnage /'kɑ:nɪdʒ/ n carnicería f, matanza f

carnation /kɑ:'neɪʃn/ n clavel m

carnival /'kɑ:nɪvl/ n carnaval m

carol /'kærəl/ n villancico m

carousel /kærə'sel/ n tiovivo m, carrusel m (LAm); (for baggage) cinta f transportadora

carp /kɑ:p/ n invar carpa f. ■ **~ at** vi quejarse de

car park n aparcamiento m, estacionamiento m

carpent|er /'kɑ:pɪntə(r)/ n carpintero m. **~ry** /-trɪ/ n carpintería f

carpet /'kɑ:pɪt/ n alfombra f. **~ sweeper** n cepillo m mecánico

carriage /'kærɪdʒ/ n coche m; (Mec) carro m; (transport) transporte m; (cost, bearing) porte m; (of train) vagón m. **~way** n calzada f, carretera f

carrier /'kærɪə(r)/ n transportista m & f; (company) empresa f de transportes; (Med) portador m. **~ bag** n bolsa f

carrot /'kærət/ n zanahoria f

carry /'kærɪ/ vt llevar; transportar (goods); (involve) llevar consigo, implicar. ●vi (sounds) llegar, oírse. ■ **~ off** vt llevarse. ■ **~ on** vi seguir, continuar. ■ **~ out** vt realizar; cumplir (promise, threat). **~ cot** n cuna f portátil

carsick /'kɑ:sɪk/ adj mareado (por viajar en coche)

cart /kɑ:t/ n carro m; (Amer, in supermarket, airport) carrito m. ●vt acarrear; (fam, carry) llevar

carton /'kɑ:tən/ n caja f de cartón

cartoon /kɑ:'tu:n/ n caricatura f, chiste m; (strip) historieta f; (film) dibujos mpl animados

cartridge /'kɑ:trɪdʒ/ n cartucho m

carve /kɑ:v/ vt tallar; trinchar (meat)

cascade /kæs'keɪd/ n cascada f. ●vi caer en cascadas

case /keɪs/ n caso m; (Jurid) proceso m; (crate) cajón m; (box) caja f; (suitcase) maleta f, petaca f (Mex). **in any ~** en todo caso. **in ~ he comes** por si viene. **in ~ of** en caso de

cash /kæʃ/ n dinero m efectivo. **pay (in) ~** pagar al contado. ●vt cobrar. **~ in (on)** aprovecharse de. **~ desk** n caja f. **~ dispenser** n cajero m automático

cashier /kæ'ʃɪə(r)/ n cajero m

cashpoint /'kæʃpɔɪnt/ n cajero m automático

casino /kə'si:nəʊ/ n (pl **-os**) casino m

cask /kɑ:sk/ n barril m

casket /'kɑ:skɪt/ n cajita f; (Amer) ataúd m, cajón m (LAm)

casserole /'kæsərəʊl/ n cacerola f; (stew) guiso m, guisado m (Mex)

cassette /kə'set/ n cassette m & f

cast /kɑ:st/ vt (pt cast) arrojar; fundir (metal); emitir (vote). ●n lanzamiento m; (in play) reparto m; (mould) molde m

castanets /kæstə'nets/ npl castañuelas fpl

castaway /'kɑ:stəweɪ/ n náufrago m

caster /'kɑ:stə(r)/ n ruedecita f. **~ sugar** n azúcar m extrafino

Castil|e /kæ'sti:l/ n Castilla f. **~ian** /kæ'stɪlɪən/ adj & n castellano (m)

cast: ~ iron n hierro m fundido.

∼-iron adj (fig) sólido

castle /'kɑ:sl/ n castillo m; (Chess) torre f

cast-offs /'kɑ:stɒfs/ npl desechos mpl

castrat|e /kæ'streɪt/ vt castrar. **∼ion** /-ʃn/ n castración f

casual /'kæʒʊəl/ adj casual; (meeting) fortuito; (work) ocasional; (attitude) despreocupado; (clothes) informal, de sport. **∼ly** adv de paso

casualt|y /'kæʒʊəltɪ/ n (injured) herido m; (dead) víctima f; (in hospital) urgencias fpl. **∼ies** npl (Mil) bajas fpl

cat /kæt/ n gato m

Catalan /'kætəlæn/ adj & n catalán (m)

catalogue /'kætəlɒg/ n catálogo m. • vt catalogar

Catalonia /kætə'ləʊnɪə/ n Cataluña f

catalyst /'kætəlɪst/ n catalizador m

catamaran /kætəmə'ræn/ n catamarán m

catapult /'kætəpʌlt/ n catapulta f; (child's) tirachinas f, resortera f (Mex)

catarrh /kə'tɑ:(r)/ n catarro m

catastroph|e /kə'tæstrəfɪ/ n catástrofe m. **∼ic** /kætə'strɒfɪk/ adj catastrófico

catch /kætʃ/ vt (pt **caught**) coger (esp Spain), agarrar; tomar (train, bus); (unawares) sorprender, pillar; (understand) entender; contagiarse de (disease). **∼ a cold** resfriarse. **∼ sight of** avistar. • vi (get stuck) engancharse; (fire) prenderse. • n (by goalkeeper) parada f; (of fish) pesca f; (on door) pestillo m; (on window) cerradura f. **■ ∼ on** vi 🄸 hacerse popular. **■ ∼ up** vi poner al día. **∼ up with** alcanzar; ponerse al corriente de (news etc). **∼ing** adj contagioso. **∼phrase** n eslogan m. **∼y** adj pegadizo

categor|ical /kætɪ'gɒrɪkl/ adj categórico. **∼y** /'kætɪgərɪ/ n categoría f

cater /'keɪtə(r)/ vi encargarse del servicio de comida. **∼ for** proveer a (needs). **∼er** n proveedor m

caterpillar /'kætəpɪlə(r)/ n oruga f, azotador m (Mex)

cathedral /kə'θi:drəl/ n catedral f

catholic /'kæθəlɪk/ adj universal. **C∼** adj & n católico (m). **C∼ism** /kə'θɒlɪsɪzəm/ n catolicismo m

cat: ∼nap n sueñecito m. **C∼seyes** npl (®) catafaros mpl

cattle /'kætl/ npl ganado m

catwalk n pasarela f

Caucasian /kɔ:'keɪʒən/ n. **a male ∼** (Amer) un hombre de raza blanca

caught /kɔ:t/ see CATCH

cauliflower /'kɒlɪflaʊə(r)/ n coliflor f

cause /kɔ:z/ n causa f, motivo m. • vt causar

cautio|n /'kɔ:ʃn/ n cautela f; (warning) advertencia f. • vt advertir; (Jurid) amonestar. **∼us** /-ʃəs/ adj cauteloso, prudente

cavalry /'kævəlrɪ/ n caballería f

cave /keɪv/ n cueva f. **■ ∼ in** vi hundirse. **∼man** n troglodita m

cavern /'kævən/ n caverna f

caviare /'kævɪɑ:(r)/ n caviar m

cavity /'kævətɪ/ n cavidad f; (in tooth) caries f

CCTV abbr (**closed circuit television**) CCTV m

CD abbr (= **compact disc**) CD m. **∼ player** (reproductor m de) compact-disc m. **∼-ROM** n CD-ROM m

cease /si:s/ vt/i cesar. **∼fire** n alto el fuego

cedar /'si:də(r)/ n cedro m

ceiling /'si:lɪŋ/ n techo m

celebrat|e /'selɪbreɪt/ vt celebrar. • vi divertirse. **∼ed** adj célebre.

~ion /-'breɪʃn/ n celebración f; (party) fiesta f

celebrity /sɪ'lebrətɪ/ n celebridad f

celery /'selərɪ/ n apio m

cell /sel/ n celda f; (in plants, electricity) célula f

cellar /'selə(r)/ n sótano m; (for wine) bodega f

cello /'tʃeləʊ/ n (pl **-os**) violonc(h)elo m, chelo m

Cellophane /'seləfeɪn/ n (®) celofán m (®)

cellphone /'selfəʊn/ n celular m (LAm), móvil m (Esp)

cellul|ar /'seljʊlə(r)/ adj celular. ~ **phone** n teléfono celular m (LAm), teléfono móvil m (Esp). ~**oid** n celuloide m

Celsius /'selsɪəs/ adj. **20 degrees ~** 20 grados centígrados or Celsio(s)

cement /sɪ'ment/ n cemento m. ●vt cementar

cemetery /'semətrɪ/ n cementerio m

cens|or /'sensə(r)/ n censor m. ●vt censurar. ~**ship** n censura f. ~**ure** /'senʃə(r)/ vt censurar

census /'sensəs/ n censo m

cent /sent/ n ($) centavo m; (€) céntimo m

centenary /sen'ti:nərɪ/ n centenario m

centi|grade /'sentɪɡreɪd/ adj centígrado. ~**litre** n centilitro m. ~**metre** n centímetro m. ~**pede** /-pi:d/ n ciempiés m

central /'sentrəl/ adj central; (of town) céntrico. ~ **heating** n calefacción f central. ~**ize** vt centralizar

centre /'sentə(r)/ n centro m. ●vt (pt **centred**) centrar. ●vi centrarse (**on** en)

century /'sentʃərɪ/ n siglo m

cereal /'sɪərɪəl/ n cereal m

ceremon|ial /serɪ'məʊnɪəl/ adj & n

ceremonial (m). ~**y** /'serɪmənɪ/ n ceremonia f

certain /'sɜːtn/ adj cierto. **for ~** seguro. **make ~ of** asegurarse de. ~**ly** adv desde luego

certificate /sə'tɪfɪkət/ n certificado m; (of birth, death etc) partida f

certify /'sɜːtɪfaɪ/ vt certificar

chafe /tʃeɪf/ vt rozar. ●vi rozarse

chaffinch /'tʃæfɪntʃ/ n pinzón m

chagrin /'ʃæɡrɪn/ n disgusto m

chain /tʃeɪn/ n cadena f. ●vt encadenar. ~ **reaction** n reacción f en cadena. ~**-smoker** n fumador m que siempre tiene un cigarrillo encendido. ~ **store** n tienda f de una cadena

chair /tʃeə(r)/ n silla f; (Univ) cátedra f. ●vt presidir. ~**lift** n telesquí m, telesilla m (LAm). ~**man** /-mən/ n presidente m

chalet /'ʃæleɪ/ n chalé m

chalk /tʃɔːk/ n (in geology) creta f; (stick) tiza f, gis m (Mex)

challeng|e /'tʃælɪndʒ/ n desafío m; (fig) reto m. ●vt desafiar; (question) poner en duda. ~**ing** adj estimulante

chamber /'tʃeɪmbə(r)/ n (old use) cámara f. ~**maid** n camarera f. ~**pot** n orinal m

champagne /ʃæm'peɪn/ n champaña m, champán m

champion /'tʃæmpɪən/ n campeón m. ●vt defender. ~**ship** n campeonato m

chance /tʃɑːns/ n casualidad f; (likelihood) posibilidad f; (opportunity) oportunidad f; (risk) riesgo m. **by ~** por casualidad. ●adj fortuito

chancellor /'tʃɑːnsələ(r)/ n canciller m; (Univ) rector m. **C~ of the Exchequer** Ministro m de Hacienda

chandelier /ʃændə'lɪə(r)/ n araña f (de luces)

chang|e /tʃeɪndʒ/ vt cambiar; (substitute) reemplazar. ~ **one's**

mind cambiar de idea. •vi cambiarse. •n cambio m; (coins) cambio m, sencillo m (LAm), feria f (Mex); (money returned) cambio m, vuelta f, vuelto m (LAm). ~**eable** adj cambiable; (weather) variable. ~**ing room** n (Sport) vestuario m, vestidor m (Mex); (in shop) probador m

channel /'tʃænl/ n canal m; (fig) medio m. •vt (pt **channelled**) acanalar; (fig) encauzar. **the (English) C~** el Canal de la Mancha. **C~ Islands** npl. **the C~ Islands** las islas Anglonormandas. **C~ Tunnel** n. **the C~ Tunnel** el Eurotúnel

chant /tʃɑːnt/ n canto m. •vt/i cantar

chao|s /'keɪɒs/ n caos m. ~**tic** /-'ɒtɪk/ adj caótico

chap /tʃæp/ n 🇬🇧 tipo m, tío m 🇬🇧. •vt (pt **chapped**) agrietar. •vi agrietarse

chapel /'tʃæpl/ n capilla f

chaperon /'ʃæpərəʊn/ n acompañante f

chapter /'tʃæptə(r)/ n capítulo m

char /tʃɑː(r)/ vt (pt **charred**) carbonizar

character /'kærəktə(r)/ n carácter m; (in book, play) personaje m. in ~ característico. ~**istic** /-'rɪstɪk/ adj típico. •n característica f. ~**ize** vt caracterizar

charade /ʃə'rɑːd/ n farsa f. ~**s** npl (game) charada f

charcoal /'tʃɑːkəʊl/ n carbón m vegetal; (for drawing) carboncillo m

charge /tʃɑːdʒ/ n precio m; (Elec, Mil) carga f; (Jurid) acusación f; (task, custody) encargo m, responsibility) responsabilidad f. in ~ of responsable de, encargado de. **the person in ~** la persona responsable. **take ~ of** encargarse de. •vt pedir; (Elec, Mil) cargar; (Jurid) acusar. •vi cargar; (animal) embestir (**at** contra)

charit|able /'tʃærɪtəbl/ adj

caritativo. ~**y** /'tʃærɪtɪ/ n caridad f; (society) institución f benéfica

charm /tʃɑːm/ n encanto m; (spell) hechizo m; (on bracelet) dije m, amuleto m. •vt encantar. ~**ing** adj encantador

chart /tʃɑːt/ n (for navigation) carta f de navegación; (table) tabla f

charter /'tʃɑːtə(r)/ n carta f. •vt alquilar (bus, train); fletar (plane, ship). ~ **flight** n vuelo m chárter

chase /tʃeɪs/ vt perseguir. •vi correr (**after** tras). •n persecución f. ■ ~ **away**, ~ **off** vt ahuyentar

chassis /'ʃæsɪ/ n chasis m

chastise /tʃæs'taɪz/ vt castigar

chastity /'tʃæstɪtɪ/ n castidad f

chat /tʃæt/ n charla f, conversación f (LAm), plática f (Mex). •vi (pt **chatted**) charlar, conversar (LAm), platicar (Mex)

chatter /'tʃætə(r)/ n charla f. •vi charlar. **his teeth are ~ing** le castañetean los dientes. ~**box** n parlanchín m

chauffeur /'ʃəʊfə(r)/ n chófer m

chauvinis|m /'ʃəʊvɪnɪzəm/ n patriotería f; (male) machismo m. ~**t** n patriotero m; (male) machista m

cheap /tʃiːp/ adj (**-er, -est**) barato; (poor quality) de baja calidad; (rate) económico. ~**(ly)** adv barato, a bajo precio

cheat /tʃiːt/ vt defraudar; (deceive) engañar. •vi (at cards) hacer trampas. •n trampa f; (person) tramposo m

check /tʃek/ vt comprobar; (examine) inspeccionar; (curb) frenar. •vi comprobar. •n comprobación f; (of tickets) control m; (curb) freno m; (Chess) jaque m; (pattern) cuadro m; (Amer, bill) cuenta f; (Amer, cheque) cheque m. ■ ~ **in** vi registrarse; (at airport) facturar el equipaje, chequear el equipaje (LAm), registrar el equipaje (Mex). ■ ~ **out** vi pagar la cuenta y marcharse. ■ ~ **up** vi confirmar.

■ ~ **up on** vt investigar. ~**book** n (Amer) see CHEQUEBOOK. ~**ered** /'tʃekəd/ adj (Amer) see CHEQUERED

checkers /'tʃekəz/ n (Amer) damas fpl

check: ~**mate** n jaque m mate. •vt dar mate a. ~**out** n caja f. ~**point** control m. ~**up** n chequeo m, revisión

cheek /tʃiːk/ n mejilla f; (fig) descaro m. ~**bone** n pómulo m. ~**y** adj descarado

cheep /tʃiːp/ vi piar

cheer /tʃɪə(r)/ n alegría f; (applause) viva m. ~**s!** ¡salud!.•vt alegrar; (applaud) aplaudir. •vi alegrarse; (applaud) aplaudir. ~ **up!** ¡anímate! ~**ful** adj alegre

cheerio /tʃɪərɪ'əʊ/ int 🇬🇧 ¡adiós!, ¡hasta luego!

cheerless /'tʃɪəlɪs/ adj triste

cheese /tʃiːz/ n queso m

cheetah /'tʃiːtə/ n guepardo m

chef /ʃef/ n jefe m de cocina

chemical /'kemɪkl/ adj químico. •n producto m químico

chemist /'kemɪst/ n farmacéutico m; (scientist) químico m. ~**ry** n química f. ~**'s (shop)** n farmacia f

cheque /tʃek/ n cheque m, talón m. ~**book** n chequera f, talonario m

cherish /'tʃerɪʃ/ vt cuidar; (love) querer; abrigar (hope)

cherry /'tʃerɪ/ n cereza f. ~ **tree** n cerezo m

chess /tʃes/ n ajedrez m. ~**board** n tablero m de ajedrez

chest /tʃest/ n pecho m; (box) cofre m, cajón m

chestnut /'tʃesnʌt/ n castaña f. •adj castaño. ~ **tree** n castaño m

chest of drawers n cómoda f

chew /tʃuː/ vt masticar. ~**ing gum** n chicle m

chic /ʃiːk/ adj elegante

chick /tʃɪk/ n polluelo m. ~**en** /'tʃɪkɪn/ n pollo m. •adj 🇬🇧 cobarde. ■ ~**en out** vi 🇬🇧 acobardarse. ~**enpox** /'tʃɪkɪnpɒks/ n varicela f. ~**pea** n garbanzo m

chicory /'tʃɪkərɪ/ n (in coffee) achicoria f; (in salad) escarola f

chief /tʃiːf/ n jefe m. •adj principal. ~**ly** adv principalmente

chilblain /'tʃɪlbleɪn/ n sabañón m

child /tʃaɪld/ n (pl **children** /'tʃɪldrən/) niño m; (offspring) hijo m. ~**birth** n parto m. ~**hood** n niñez f. ~**ish** adj infantil. ~**less** adj sin hijos. ~**like** adj ingenuo, de niño

Chile /'tʃɪlɪ/ n Chile m. ~**an** adj & n chileno (m)

chill /tʃɪl/ n frío m; (illness) resfriado m. •adj frío. •vt enfriar; refrigerar (food)

chilli /'tʃɪlɪ/ n (pl **-ies**) chile m

chilly /'tʃɪlɪ/ adj frío

chime /tʃaɪm/ n carillón m. •vt tocar (bells); dar (hours). •vi repicar

chimney /'tʃɪmnɪ/ n (pl **-eys**) chimenea f. ~ **sweep** n deshollinador m

chimpanzee /tʃɪmpæn'ziː/ n chimpancé m

chin /tʃɪn/ n barbilla f

china /'tʃaɪnə/ n porcelana f

Chin|a /'tʃaɪnə/ n China f. ~**ese** /-'niːz/ adj & n chino (m)

chink /tʃɪŋk/ n (crack) grieta f; (sound) tintín m. •vi tintinear

chip /tʃɪp/ n pedacito m; (splinter) astilla f; (Culin) patata f frita, papa f frita (LAm); (in gambling) ficha f; (Comp) chip m. **have a ~ on one's shoulder** guardar rencor. •vt (pt **chipped**) desportillar. ■ ~ in vi 🇬🇧 interrumpir; (with money) contribuir

chiropodist /kɪ'rɒpədɪst/ n callista m & f, pedicuro m

chirp /tʃɜːp/ n pío m. •vi piar. ~**y** adj alegre

chisel /'tʃɪzl/ n formón m. •vt (pt **chiselled**) cincelar

chivalr|ous /ˈʃɪvəlrəs/ adj caballeroso. **~y** /-rɪ/ n caballerosidad f

chlorine /ˈklɔːriːn/ n cloro m

chock /tʃɒk/ n cuña f. **~-a-block** adj, **~-full** adj atestado

chocolate /ˈtʃɒklət/ n chocolate m; (individual sweet) bombón m, chocolate m (LAm)

choice /tʃɔɪs/ n elección f; (preference) preferencia f. ●adj escogido

choir /ˈkwaɪə(r)/ n coro m

choke /tʃəʊk/ vt sofocar. ●vi sofocarse. ●n (Auto) choke m, estárter m, ahogador m (Mex)

cholera /ˈkɒlərə/ n cólera m

cholesterol /kəˈlestərɒl/ n colesterol m

choose /tʃuːz/ vt/i (pt **chose**, pp **chosen**) elegir, escoger. **~y** adj 🄸 exigente

chop /tʃɒp/ vt (pt **chopped**) cortar. ●n (Culin) chuleta f. ■**~ down** vt talar. ■**~ off** vt cortar. **~per** n hacha f; (butcher's) cuchilla f. **~py** adj picado

chord /kɔːd/ n (Mus) acorde m

chore /tʃɔː(r)/ n tarea f, faena f. **household ~s** npl quehaceres mpl domésticos

chorus /ˈkɔːrəs/ n coro m; (of song) estribillo m

chose /tʃəʊz/, **chosen** /ˈtʃəʊzn/ see CHOOSE

Christ /kraɪst/ n Cristo m

christen /ˈkrɪsn/ vt bautizar. **~ing** n bautizo m

Christian /ˈkrɪstjən/ adj & n cristiano (m). **~ity** /krɪstɪˈænɪtɪ/ cristianismo m. **~ name** n nombre m de pila

Christmas /ˈkrɪsməs/ n Navidad f. **Merry ~!** ¡Feliz Navidad!, ¡Felices Pascuas! **Father ~** Papá m Noel. ●adj de Navidad, navideño. **~ card** n tarjeta f de Navidad f. **~ day** n día m de Navidad. **~ Eve** n Nochebuena f. **~ tree** n árbol m de Navidad

chrom|e /krəʊm/ n cromo m. **~ium** /ˈkrəʊmɪəm/ n cromo m

chromosome /ˈkrəʊməsəʊm/ n cromosoma m

chronic /ˈkrɒnɪk/ adj crónico; (fam, bad) terrible

chronicle /ˈkrɒnɪkl/ n crónica f. ●vt historiar

chronological /krɒnəˈlɒdʒɪkl/ adj cronológico

chubby /ˈtʃʌbɪ/ adj (**-ier, -iest**) regordete; (person) gordinflón 🄸

chuck /tʃʌk/ vt 🄸 tirar. ■**~ out** vt tirar

chuckle /ˈtʃʌkl/ n risa f ahogada. ●vi reírse entre dientes

chug /tʃʌg/ vi (pt **chugged**) (of motor) traquetear

chum /tʃʌm/ n amigo m, compinche m, cuate m (Mex)

chunk /tʃʌŋk/ n trozo m grueso. **~y** adj macizo

church /tʃɜːtʃ/ n iglesia f. **~yard** n cementerio m

churn /tʃɜːn/ n (for milk) lechera f, cántara f; (for making butter) mantequera f. ●vt agitar. ■**~ out** vt producir en profusión

chute /ʃuːt/ n tobogán m

cider /ˈsaɪdə(r)/ n sidra f

cigar /sɪˈgɑː(r)/ n puro m

cigarette /sɪɡəˈret/ n cigarrillo m. **~ end** n colilla f. **~ holder** n boquilla f. **~ lighter** n mechero m, encendedor m

cinecamera /ˈsɪnɪkæmərə/ n tomavistas m, filmadora f (LAm)

cinema /ˈsɪnəmə/ n cine m

cipher /ˈsaɪfə(r)/ n (Math, fig) cero m; (code) clave f

circle /ˈsɜːkl/ n círculo m; (in theatre) anfiteatro m. ●vt girar alrededor de. ●vi dar vueltas

circuit /ˈsɜːkɪt/ n circuito m

circular /'sɜːkjʊlə(r)/ adj & n circular (f)

circulat|e /'sɜːkjʊleɪt/ vt hacer circular. •vi circular. ~**ion** /-'leɪʃn/ n circulación f; (number of copies) tirada f

circumcise /'sɜːkəmsaɪz/ vt circuncidar

circumference /sə'kʌmfərəns/ n circunferencia f

circumstance /'sɜːkəmstəns/ n circunstancia f. ~**s** (means) npl situación f económica

circus /'sɜːkəs/ n circo m

cistern /'sɪstən/ n cisterna f

cite /saɪt/ vt citar

citizen /'sɪtɪzn/ n ciudadano m; (inhabitant) habitante m & f

citrus /'sɪtrəs/ n. ~ **fruits** cítricos mpl

city /'sɪtɪ/ n ciudad f; **the C~** el centro m financiero de Londres

civic /'sɪvɪk/ adj cívico

civil /'sɪvl/ adj civil; (polite) cortés

civilian /sɪ'vɪlɪən/ adj & n civil (m & f)

civiliz|ation /sɪvɪlaɪ'zeɪʃn/ n civilización f. ~**ed** /'sɪvɪlaɪzd/ adj civilizado

civil: ~ servant n funcionario m (del Estado), burócrata m & f (Mex). ~ **service** n administración f pública. ~ **war** n guerra f civil

clad /klæd/ see CLOTHE

claim /kleɪm/ vt reclamar; (assert) pretender. •n reclamación f; (right) derecho m; (Jurid) demanda f

clairvoyant /kleə'vɔɪənt/ n clarividente m & f

clam /klæm/ n almeja f. •vi (pt clammed). ~ **up** 🄳 ponerse muy poco comunicativo

clamber /'klæmbə(r)/ vi trepar a gatas

clammy /'klæmɪ/ adj (-ier, -iest) húmedo

clamour /'klæmə(r)/ n clamor m.

•vi. ~ **for** pedir a gritos

clamp /klæmp/ n abrazadera f; (Auto) cepo m. •vt sujetar con abrazadera; poner cepo a (car). ■~ **down on** vt reprimir

clan /klæn/ n clan m

clang /klæŋ/ n sonido m metálico

clap /klæp/ vt (pt clapped) aplaudir; batir (hands). •vi aplaudir. •n palmada f; (of thunder) trueno m

clarif|ication /klærɪfɪ'keɪʃn/ n aclaración f. ~**y** /'klærɪfaɪ/ vt aclarar. •vi aclararse

clarinet /klærɪ'net/ n clarinete m

clarity /'klærətɪ/ n claridad f

clash /klæʃ/ n choque m; (noise) estruendo m; (contrast) contraste m; (fig) conflicto m. •vt golpear. •vi encontrarse; (colours) desentonar

clasp /klɑːsp/ n cierre m. •vt agarrar; apretar (hand)

class /klɑːs/ n clase f. **evening** ~ n clase nocturna. •vt clasificar

classic /'klæsɪk/ adj & n clásico (m). ~**al** adj clásico ~**s** npl estudios mpl clásicos

classif|ication /klæsɪfɪ'keɪʃn/ n clasificación f. ~**y** /'klæsɪfaɪ/ vt clasificar

class: ~room n aula f, clase f. ~**y** adj 🄳 elegante

clatter /'klætə(r)/ n ruido m; (of train) traqueteo m. •vi hacer ruido

clause /klɔːz/ n cláusula f; (Gram) oración f

claustrophobia /klɔːstrə'fəʊbɪə/ n claustrofobia f

claw /klɔː/ n garra f; (of cat) uña f; (of crab) pinza f. •vt arañar

clay /kleɪ/ n arcilla f

clean /kliːn/ adj (-er, -est) limpio; (stroke) bien definido. •adv completamente. •vt limpiar. •vi limpiar. ■~ **up** vt hacer la limpieza. ~**er** n persona f que hace la limpieza. ~**liness** /'klenlɪnɪs/ n limpieza f

cleanse /klenz/ vt limpiar. **~er** n producto m de limpieza; (for skin) crema f de limpieza. **~ing cream** n crema f de limpieza

clear /klɪə(r)/ adj (**-er, -est**) claro; (transparent) transparente; (without obstacles) libre; (profit) neto; (sky) despejado. **keep ~ of** evitar. • adv claramente. • vt despejar; liquidar (goods); (Jurid) absolver; (jump over) saltar por encima de; quitar, levantar (LAm) (table). ∎ **~ off** vi 🗙, **~ out** vi (🗓, go away) largarse. ∎ **~ up** vt (tidy) ordenar; aclarar (mystery). vi (weather) despejarse. **~ance** n (removal of obstructions) despeje m; (authorization) permiso m; (by security) acreditación f. **~ing** n claro m. **~ly** adv evidentemente. **~way** n carretera f en la que no se permite parar

cleavage /'kli:vɪdʒ/ n escote m

clef /klef/ n (Mus) clave f

clench /klentʃ/ vt apretar

clergy /'klɜːdʒɪ/ n clero m. **~man** /-mən/ n clérigo m

cleric /'klerɪk/ n clérigo m. **~al** adj clerical; (of clerks) de oficina

clerk /klɑːk/ n empleado m; (Amer, salesclerk) vendedor m

clever /'klevə(r)/ adj (**-er, -est**) inteligente; (skilful) hábil. **~ly** adv inteligentemente; (with skill) hábilmente. **~ness** n inteligencia f

cliché /'kli:ʃeɪ/ n lugar m común m, cliché m

click /klɪk/ n golpecito m. • vi chascar; 🗓 llevarse bien. **~ on sth** hacer clic en algo. • vt chasquear

client /'klaɪənt/ n cliente m

cliff /klɪf/ n acantilado m

climat|e /'klaɪmət/ n clima m. **~ic** /-'mætɪk/ adj climático

climax /'klaɪmæks/ n clímax m; (orgasm) orgasmo m

climb /klaɪm/ vt subir (stairs); trepar (tree); escalar (mountain). • vi subir.

• n subida f. ∎ **~ down** vi bajar; (fig) ceder. **~er** n (Sport) alpinista m & f, andinista m & f (LAm); (plant) trepadora f

clinch /klɪntʃ/ vt cerrar (deal)

cling /klɪŋ/ vi (pt **clung**) agarrarse; (stick) pegarse

clinic /'klɪnɪk/ n centro m médico; (private hospital) clínica f. **~al** adj clínico

clink /klɪŋk/ n tintineo m. • vt hacer tintinear. • vi tintinear

clip /klɪp/ n (fastener) clip m; (for paper) sujetapapeles m; (for hair) horquilla f. • vt (pt **clipped**) (cut) cortar; (join) sujetar. **~pers** /'klɪpəz/ npl (for hair) maquinilla f para cortar el pelo; (for nails) cortauñas m. **~ping** n recorte m

cloak /kləʊk/ n capa f. **~room** n guardarropa m; (toilet) lavabo m, baño m (LAm)

clock /klɒk/ n reloj m. **~wise** a/adv en el sentido de las agujas del reloj. **~work** n mecanismo m de relojería. **like ~work** con precisión

clog /klɒg/ n zueco m. • vt (pt **clogged**) atascar

cloister /'klɔɪstə(r)/ n claustro m

clone /kləʊn/ n clon m

close[1] /kləʊs/ adj (**-er, -est**) cercano; (together) apretado; (friend) íntimo; (weather) bochornoso; (link etc) estrecho; (game, battle) reñido. **have a ~ shave** (fig) escaparse de milagro. • adv cerca

close[2] /kləʊz/ vt cerrar. • vi cerrarse; (end) terminar. **~ down** vt/i cerrar. • n fin m. **~d** adj cerrado

closely /'kləʊslɪ/ adv estrechamente; (at a short distance) de cerca; (with attention) detenidamente; (precisely) rigurosamente

closet /'klɒzɪt/ n (Amer) armario m; (for clothes) armario m, closet m (LAm)

close-up /ˈkləʊsʌp/ n (Cinema etc) primer plano m

closure /ˈkləʊʒə(r)/ n cierre m

clot /klɒt/ n (Med) coágulo m; 🔢 tonto m. • vi (pt **clotted**) cuajarse; (blood) coagularse

cloth /klɒθ/ n tela f; (duster) trapo m; (tablecloth) mantel m

cloth|e /kləʊð/ vt (pt **clothed** or **clad**) vestir. ~**es** /kləʊðz/ npl ropa. ~**espin**, ~**espeg** (Amer) n pinza f (para tender la ropa). ~**ing** n ropa f

cloud /klaʊd/ n nube f. • ~ **over** vi nublarse. ~**y** adj (**-ier, -iest**) nublado; (liquid) turbio

clout /klaʊt/ n bofetada f. • vt abofetear

clove /kləʊv/ n clavo m. ~ **of garlic** n diente m de ajo

clover /ˈkləʊvə(r)/ n trébol m

clown /klaʊn/ n payaso m. • vi hacer el payaso

club /klʌb/ n club m; (weapon) porra f; (golf club) palo m de golf; (at cards) trébol m. • vt (pt **clubbed**) aporrear. ■ ~ **together** vi contribuir con dinero (**to** para)

cluck /klʌk/ vi cloquear

clue /kluː/ n pista f; (in crosswords) indicación f. **not to have a ~** no tener la menor idea

clump /klʌmp/ n grupo m. • vt agrupar

clums|iness /ˈklʌmzɪnɪs/ n torpeza f. ~**y** /ˈklʌmzɪ/ adj (**-ier, -iest**) torpe

clung /klʌŋ/ see CLING

cluster /ˈklʌstə(r)/ n grupo m. • vi agruparse

clutch /klʌtʃ/ vt agarrar. • n (Auto) embrague m

clutter /ˈklʌtə(r)/ n desorden m. • vt. ~ **(up)** abarrotar. ~**ed** /ˈklʌtəd/ adj abarrotado de cosas

coach /kəʊtʃ/ n autocar m, autobús m; (of train) vagón m; (horse-drawn) coche m; (Sport) entrenador m. • vt (Sport) entrenar

coal /kəʊl/ n carbón m

coalition /kəʊəˈlɪʃn/ n coalición f

coarse /kɔːs/ adj (**-er, -est**) grueso; (material) basto; (person, language) ordinario

coast /kəʊst/ n costa f. • vi (with cycle) deslizarse sin pedalear; (with car) ir en punto muerto. ~**al** adj costero. ~**guard** n guardacostas m. ~**line** n litoral m

coat /kəʊt/ n abrigo m; (jacket) chaqueta f; (of animal) pelo m; (of paint) mano f. • vt cubrir, revestir. ~**hanger** n percha f, gancho m (LAm). ~**ing** n capa f. ~ **of arms** n escudo m de armas

coax /kəʊks/ vt engatusar

cobbler /ˈkɒblə(r)/ n zapatero m (remendón)

cobblestone /ˈkɒbəlstəʊn/ n adoquín m

cobweb /ˈkɒbweb/ n telaraña f

cocaine /kəˈkeɪn/ n cocaína f

cock /kɒk/ n (cockerel) gallo m; (male bird) macho m. • vt amartillar (gun), aguzar (ears). ~**erel** /ˈkɒkərəl/ n gallo m. ~**-eyed** /-aɪd/ adj 🔢 torcido

cockney /ˈkɒknɪ/ adj & n (pl **-eys**) londinense (m & f) (del este de Londres)

cockpit /ˈkɒkpɪt/ n (in aircraft) cabina f del piloto

cockroach /ˈkɒkrəʊtʃ/ n cucaracha f

cocktail /ˈkɒkteɪl/ n cóctel m

cock-up /ˈkɒkʌp/ n 🔢 lío m

cocky /ˈkɒkɪ/ adj (**-ier, -iest**) engreído

cocoa /ˈkəʊkəʊ/ n cacao m; (drink) chocolate m, cocoa f (LAm)

coconut /ˈkəʊkənʌt/ n coco m

cocoon /kəˈkuːn/ n capullo m

cod /kɒd/ n invar bacalao m

code /kəʊd/ n código m; (secret) clave f; **in ~** en clave

C

coeducational /kəʊedʒʊˈkeɪʃənl/ adj mixto

coerc|e /kəʊˈɜːs/ vt coaccionar. **~ion** /-ʃn/ n coacción f

coffee /ˈkɒfɪ/ n café m. **~ bean** n grano m de café. **~ maker** n cafetera f. **~pot** n cafetera f

coffin /ˈkɒfɪn/ n ataúd m, cajón m (LAm)

cog /kɒg/ n diente m; (fig) pieza f

coherent /kəʊˈhɪərənt/ adj coherente

coil /kɔɪl/ vt enrollar. ●n rollo m; (one ring) vuelta f

coin /kɔɪn/ n moneda f. ●vt acuñar

coincide /kəʊɪnˈsaɪd/ vi coincidir. **~nce** /kəʊˈɪnsɪdəns/ n casualidad f. **~ntal** /kəʊɪnsɪˈdentl/ adj casual

coke /kəʊk/ n (coal) coque m. **C~** (®) Coca-Cola f (®)

colander /ˈkʌləndə(r)/ n colador m

cold /kəʊld/ adj (-er, -est) frío. **be ~** (person) tener frío. **it is ~** (weather) hace frío. ●n frío m; (Med) resfriado m. **have a ~** estar resfriado. **~-blooded** /-ˈblʌdɪd/ adj (animal) de sangre fría; (murder) a sangre fría. **~-shoulder** /-ˈʃəʊldə(r)/ vt tratar con frialdad. **~ sore** n herpes m labial. **~ storage** n conservación f en frigorífico

coleslaw /ˈkəʊlslɔː/ n ensalada f de col

collaborat|e /kəˈlæbəreɪt/ vi colaborar. **~ion** /-ˈreɪʃn/ n colaboración f. **~or** n colaborador m

collaps|e /kəˈlæps/ vi derrumbarse; (Med) sufrir un colapso. ●n derrumbamiento m; (Med) colapso m. **~ible** /-əbl/ adj plegable

collar /ˈkɒlə(r)/ n cuello m; (for animals) collar m. ●vt hurtar. **~bone** n clavícula f

colleague /ˈkɒliːg/ n colega m & f

collect /kəˈlekt/ vt reunir; (hobby) coleccionar, juntar (LAm); (pick up)

recoger; cobrar (rent). ●vi (people) reunirse; (things) acumularse. **~ion** /-ʃn/ n colección f; (in church) colecta f; (of post) recogida f. **~or** n coleccionista m & f

college /ˈkɒlɪdʒ/ n colegio m; (of art, music etc) escuela f; (Amer) universidad f

colli|de /kəˈlaɪd/ vi chocar. **~sion** /-ˈlɪʒn/ n choque m

colloquial /kəˈləʊkwɪəl/ adj coloquial

Colombia /kəˈlʌmbɪə/ n Colombia f. **~n** adj & n colombiano (m)

colon /ˈkəʊlən/ n (Gram) dos puntos mpl; (Med) colon m

colonel /ˈkɜːnl/ n coronel m

colon|ial /kəˈləʊnɪəl/ adj colonial. **~ize** /ˈkɒlənaɪz/ vt colonizar. **~y** /ˈkɒlənɪ/ n colonia f

colossal /kəˈlɒsl/ adj colosal

colour /ˈkʌlə(r)/ n color m. **off ~** (fig) indispuesto. ● adj de color(es), en color(es) ●vt colorear; (dye) teñir. **~-blind** adj daltónico. **~ed** /ˈkʌləd/ adj de color. **~ful** adj lleno de color; (fig) pintoresco. **~ing** n color; (food colouring) colorante m. **~less** adj incoloro

column /ˈkɒləm/ n columna f. **~ist** n columnista m & f

coma /ˈkəʊmə/ n coma m

comb /kəʊm/ n peine m. ●vt (search) registrar. **~ one's hair** peinarse

combat /ˈkɒmbæt/ n combate m. ●vt (pt **combated**) combatir

combination /kɒmbɪˈneɪʃn/ n combinación f

combine /kəmˈbaɪn/ vt combinar. ●vi combinarse. ● /ˈkɒmbaɪn/ n asociación f. **~ harvester** n cosechadora f

combustion /kəmˈbʌstʃən/ n combustión f

come /kʌm/ vi (pt **came**, pp **come**) venir; (occur) pasar. ■ **~ across** vt encontrarse con (person); encontrar (object). ■ **~ apart** vi deshacerse.

■ ~ **away** vi (leave) salir; (become detached) salirse. ■ ~ **back** vi volver. ■ ~ **by** vt obtener. ■ ~ **down** vi bajar. ■ ~ **in** vi entrar; (arrive) llegar. ■ ~ **into** vt entrar en; heredar (money). ■ ~ **off** vi desprenderse; (succeed) tener éxito. vt. ~ **off it!** 🔲 ¡no me vengas con eso! ■ ~ **on** vi (start to work) encenderse. ~ **on, hurry up!** ¡vamos, date prisa! ■ ~ **out** vi salir. ■ ~ **round** vi (after fainting) volver en sí; (be converted) cambiar de idea; (visit) venir. ■ ~ **to** vt llegar a (decision etc). ■ ~ **up** vi subir; (fig) surgir. ■ ~ **up with** vt proponer (idea). ~**back** n retorno m; (retort) réplica f

comedian /kə'miːdɪən/ n cómico m

comedy /'kɒmədɪ/ n comedia f

comet /'kɒmɪt/ n cometa m

comfort /'kʌmfət/ n comodidad f; (consolation) consuelo m. ●vt consolar. ~**able** adj cómodo. ~**er** n (for baby) chupete m, chupón m (LAm); (Amer; for bed) edredón m

comic /'kɒmɪk/ adj cómico. ●n cómico m; (periodical) revista f de historietas, tebeo m. ~**al** adj cómico. ~ **strip** n tira f cómica

coming /'kʌmɪŋ/ n llegada f. ~**s and goings** idas fpl y venidas. ●adj próximo, (week, month etc) que viene

comma /'kɒmə/ n coma f

command /kə'mɑːnd/ n orden f; (mastery) dominio m. ●vt ordenar; imponer (respect)

commandeer /kɒmən'dɪə(r)/ vt requisar

command: ~**er** n comandante m. ~**ing** adj imponente. ~**ment** n mandamiento m

commando /kə'mɑːndəʊ/ n (pl **-os**) comando m

commemorat|e /kə'meməreɪt/ vt conmemorar. ~**ion** /-'reɪʃn/ n conmemoración f. ~**ive** /-ətɪv/ adj conmemorativo

commence /kə'mens/ vt dar comienzo a. ●vi iniciarse

commend /kə'mend/ vt alabar. ~**able** adj loable. ~**ation** /kɒmen'deɪʃn/ n elogio m

comment /'kɒment/ n observación f. ●vi hacer observaciones (**on** sobre)

commentary /'kɒməntrɪ/ n comentario m; (Radio, TV) reportaje m

commentat|e /'kɒmənteɪt/ vi narrar. ~**or** n (Radio, TV) locutor m

commerc|e /'kɒmɜːs/ n comercio m. ~**ial** /kə'mɜːʃl/ adj comercial. ●n anuncio m; aviso m (LAm). ~**ialize** vt comercializar

commiserat|e /kə'mɪzəreɪt/ vi compadecerse (**with** de). ~**ion** /-'reɪʃn/ n conmiseración f

commission /kə'mɪʃn/ n comisión f. **out of** ~ fuera de servicio. ●vt encargar; (Mil) nombrar oficial

commissionaire /kəmɪʃə'neə(r)/ n portero m

commit /kə'mɪt/ vt (pt **committed**) cometer; (entrust) confiar. ~ **o.s.** comprometerse. ~**ment** n compromiso m

committee /kə'mɪtɪ/ n comité m

commodity /kə'mɒdətɪ/ n producto m, artículo m

common /'kɒmən/ adj (**-er, -est**) común; (usual) corriente; (vulgar) ordinario. ●n. **in** ~ en común. ~**er** n plebeyo m. ~ **law** n derecho m consuetudinario. ~**ly** adv comúnmente. **C~ Market** n Mercado m Común. ~**place** adj banal. ●n banalidad f. ~ **room** n sala f común, salón m común. **C~s** n. **the (House of) C~s** la Cámara de los Comunes. ~ **sense** n sentido m común. **C~wealth** n. **the C~wealth** la Mancomunidad f Británica

commotion /kə'məʊʃn/ n confusión f

commune /'kɒmjuːn/ n comuna f

communicat|e /kə'mjuːnɪkeɪt/ vt comunicar. ●vi comunicarse. ~**ion** /-'keɪʃn/ n comunicación f. ~**ive**

/-ətɪv/ adj comunicativo

communion /kəˈmjuːnɪən/ n comunión f

communis|m /ˈkɒmjʊnɪsəm/ n comunismo m. **~t** n comunista m & f

community /kəˈmjuːnəti/ n comunidad f. **~ centre** n centro m social

commute /kəˈmjuːt/ vi viajar diariamente (entre el lugar de residencia y el trabajo). ●vt (Jurid) conmutar. **~r** n viajero m diario

compact /kəmˈpækt/ adj compacto. ●/ˈkɒmpækt/ n (for powder) polvera f. **~ disc, ~ disk** /ˈkɒmpækt/ n disco m compacto, compact-disc m. **~ disc player** n (reproductor m de) compact-disc

companion /kəmˈpænɪən/ n compañero m. **~ship** n compañía f

company /ˈkʌmpəni/ n compañía f; (guests) visita f; (Com) sociedad f

compar|able /ˈkɒmpərəbl/ adj comparable. **~ative** /kəmˈpærətɪv/ adj comparativo; (fig) relativo. ●n (Gram) comparativo m. **~e** /kəmˈpeə(r)/ vt comparar. **~ison** /kəmˈpærɪsn/ n comparación f

compartment /kəmˈpɑːtmənt/ n compartim(i)ento m

compass /ˈkʌmpəs/ n brújula f. **~es** npl compás m

compassion /kəmˈpæʃn/ n compasión f. **~ate** /-ət/ adj compasivo

compatible /kəmˈpætəbl/ adj compatible

compel /kəmˈpel/ vt (pt **compelled**) obligar. **~ling** adj irresistible

compensat|e /ˈkɒmpənseɪt/ vt compensar; (for loss) indemnizar. ●vi. **~e for sth** compensar algo. **~ion** /-ˈseɪʃn/ n compensación f; (financial) indemnización f

compère /ˈkɒmpeə(r)/ n presentador m. ●vt presentar

compete /kəmˈpiːt/ vi competir

competen|ce /ˈkɒmpətəns/ n competencia f. **~t** adj competente

competit|ion /kɒmpəˈtɪʃn/ n (contest) concurso m; (Sport) competición f, competencia f (LAm); (Com) competencia f. **~ive** /kəmˈpetɪtɪv/ adj competidor; (price) competitivo. **~or** /kəmˈpetɪtə(r)/ n competidor m; (in contest) concursante m & f

compile /kəmˈpaɪl/ vt compilar

complacen|cy /kəmˈpleɪsənsi/ n autosuficiencia f. **~t** adj satisfecho de sí mismo

complain /kəmˈpleɪn/ vi. **~ (about)** quejarse (de). ●vt. **~ that** quejarse de que. **~t** n queja f; (Med) enfermedad f

complement /ˈkɒmplɪmənt/ n complemento m. ●vt complementar. **~ary** /-ˈmentrɪ/ adj complementario

complet|e /kəmˈpliːt/ adj completo; (finished) acabado; (downright) total. ●vt acabar; llenar (a form). **~ely** adv completamente. **~ion** /-ʃn/ n finalización f

complex /ˈkɒmpleks/ adj complejo. ●n complejo m

complexion /kəmˈplekʃn/ n tez f; (fig) aspecto m

complexity /kəmˈpleksəti/ n complejidad f

complicat|e /ˈkɒmplɪkeɪt/ vt complicar. **~ed** adj complicado. **~ion** /-ˈkeɪʃn/ n complicación f

compliment /ˈkɒmplɪmənt/ n cumplido m; (amorous) piropo m. ●vt felicitar. **~ary** /-ˈmentrɪ/ adj halagador; (given free) de regalo. **~s** npl saludos mpl

comply /kəmˈplaɪ/ vi. **~ with** conformarse con

component /kəmˈpəʊnənt/ adj & n componente (m)

compos|e /kəmˈpəʊz/ vt componer. **be ~ed of** estar compuesto de. **~er** n compositor m. **~ition** /kɒmpəˈzɪʃn/ n composición f

compost /ˈkɒmpɒst/ n abono m

composure /kəm'pəʊʒə(r)/ n
serenidad f

compound /'kɒmpaʊnd/ n
compuesto m; (enclosure) recinto m.
● adj compuesto; (fracture)
complicado

comprehen|d /kɒmprɪ'hend/ vt
comprender. ~**sion**
/kɒmprɪ'henʃn/ n comprensión f.
~**sive** /kɒmprɪ'hensɪv/ adj extenso;
(insurance) contra todo riesgo.
~**sive (school)** n instituto m de
enseñanza secundaria

compress /'kɒmpres/ n (Med)
compresa f. ● /kəm'pres/ vt
comprimir. ~**ion** /-'preʃn/ n
compresión f

comprise /kəm'praɪz/ vt
comprender

compromis|e /'kɒmprəmaɪz/ n
acuerdo m, compromiso m, arreglo
m. ● vt comprometer. ● vi llegar a
un acuerdo. ~**ing** adj (situation)
comprometido

compuls|ion /kəm'pʌlʃn/ n (force)
coacción f; (obsession) compulsión f.
~**ive** /kəm'pʌlsɪv/ adj compulsivo.
~**ory** /kəm'pʌlsərɪ/ adj obligatorio

comput|e /kəm'pju:t/ vb calcular.
comput|er n ordenador m,
computadora f (LAm). ~**erize** vt
computarizar, computerizar. ~**er
studies** n, ~**ing** n informática f,
computación f

comrade /'kɒmreɪd/ n camarada m
& f

con /kɒn/ vt (pt **conned**) 🔟 estafar.
● n (fraud) estafa f; (objection) see **PRO**

concave /'kɒŋkeɪv/ adj cóncavo

conceal /kən'si:l/ vt ocultar

concede /kən'si:d/ vt conceder

conceit /kən'si:t/ n vanidad f. ~**ed**
adj engreído

conceiv|able /kən'si:vəbl/ adj
concebible. ~**e** /kən'si:v/ vt/i
concebir

concentrat|e /'kɒnsəntreɪt/ vt
concentrar. ● vi concentrarse (**on**

en). ~**ion** /-'treɪʃn/ n
concentración f

concept /'kɒnsept/ n concepto m

conception /kən'sepʃn/ n
concepción f

concern /kən'sɜ:n/ n asunto m;
(worry) preocupación f; (Com)
empresa f. ● vt tener que ver con;
(deal with) tratar de. **as far as I'm
~ed** en cuanto a mí. **be ~ed
about** preocuparse por. ~**ing** prep
acerca de

concert /'kɒnsət/ n concierto m.
~**ed** /kən'sɜ:tɪd/ adj concertado

concertina /kɒnsə'ti:nə/ n
concertina f

concerto /kən'tʃɜ:təʊ/ n (pl **-os** or **-ti**
/-tɪ/) concierto m

concession /kən'seʃn/ n
concesión f

concise /kən'saɪs/ adj conciso

conclu|de /kən'klu:d/ vt/i concluir.
~**ding** adj final. ~**sion** /-ʃn/ n
conclusión f. ~**sive** /-sɪv/ adj
decisivo. ~**sively** adv
concluyentemente

concoct /kən'kɒkt/ vt confeccionar;
(fig) inventar. ~**ion** /-ʃn/ n mezcla
f; (drink) brebaje m

concrete /'kɒŋkri:t/ n hormigón m,
concreto m (LAm). ● adj concreto

concussion /kən'kʌʃn/ n
conmoción f cerebral

condemn /kən'dem/ vt condenar.
~**ation** /kɒndem'neɪʃn/ n
condena f

condens|ation /kɒnden'seɪʃn/ n
condensación f. ~**e** /kən'dens/ vt
condensar. ● vi condensarse

condescend /kɒndɪ'send/ vi
dignarse (**to** a). ~**ing** adj superior

condition /kən'dɪʃn/ n condición f.
on ~ that a condición de que. ● vt
condicionar. ~**al** adj condicional.
~**er** n (for hair) suavizante m,
enjuague m (LAm)

condo /'kɒndəʊ/ n (pl **-os**) (Amer fam)
see **CONDOMINIUM**

condolences /kən'dəʊlənsɪz/ npl
pésame m

condom /'kɒndɒm/ n condón m

condominium /kɒndə'mɪnɪəm/ n
(Amer) apartamento m, piso m (en
régimen de propiedad horizontal)

condone /kən'dəʊn/ vt condonar

conduct /kən'dʌkt/ vt llevar a cabo
(business, experiment); conducir
(electricity); dirigir (orchestra).
•/'kɒndʌkt/ n conducta f. ~or
/kən'dʌktə(r)/ n director m; (of bus)
cobrador m. ~ress /kən'dʌktrɪs/ n
cobradora f

cone /kəʊn/ n cono m; (for ice cream)
cucurucho m, barquillo m (Mex)

confectionery /kən'fekʃənrɪ/ n
productos mpl de confitería

confederation /kənfedə'reɪʃn/ n
confederación f

conference /'kɒnfərəns/ n
congreso m; **an international ~
on ...** un congreso internacional
sobre ...

confess /kən'fes/ vt confesar. •vi
confesarse. ~ion /-ʃn/ n
confesión f

confetti /kən'fetɪ/ n confeti m

confide /kən'faɪd/ vt/i confiar

confiden|ce /'kɒnfɪdəns/ n
confianza f; (self-confidence)
confianza f en sí mismo; (secret)
confidencia f. **~ce trick** n estafa f,
timo m. **~t** /'kɒnfɪdənt/ adj seguro
de sí mismo. **be ~t of** confiar en

confidential /kɒnfɪ'denʃl/ adj
confidencial. **~ity** /-denʃɪ'ælətɪ/ n
confidencialidad f

configur|ation /kənfɪgə'reɪʃn/ n
configuración f. **~e** /kən'fɪgə(r)/ vt
configurar

confine /kən'faɪn/ vt confinar;
(limit) limitar. **~ment** n
(imprisonment) prisión f

confirm /kən'fɜːm/ vt confirmar.
~ation /kɒnfə'meɪʃn/ n
confirmación f. **~ed** adj inveterado

confiscat|e /'kɒnfɪskeɪt/ vt

confiscar. ~ion /-'keɪʃn/ n
confiscación f

conflict /'kɒnflɪkt/ n conflicto m.
•/kən'flɪkt/ vi chocar. **~ing**
/kən'flɪktɪŋ/ adj contradictorio

conform /kən'fɔːm/ vi conformarse.
~ist n conformista m & f

confound /kən'faʊnd/ vt
confundir. **~ed** adj 🄸 maldito

confront /kən'frʌnt/ vt hacer
frente a; (face) enfrentarse con.
~ation /kɒnfrʌn'teɪʃn/ n
confrontación f

confus|e /kən'fjuːz/ vt confundir.
~ed adj confundido. **get ~ed**
confundirse. **~ing** adj confuso.
~ion /-ʒn/ n confusión f

congeal /kən'dʒiːl/ vi coagularse

congest|ed /kən'dʒestɪd/ adj
congestionado. **~ion** /-tʃən/ n
congestión f

congratulat|e /kən'grætjʊleɪt/ vt
felicitar. **~ions** /-'leɪʃnz/ npl
enhorabuena f, felicitaciones fpl
(LAm)

congregat|e /'kɒŋgrɪgeɪt/ vi
congregarse. **~ion** /-'geɪʃn/ n
asamblea f; (Relig) fieles mpl,
feligreses mpl

congress /'kɒŋgres/ n congreso m.
C~ (Amer) el Congreso. **~man**
/-mən/ n (Amer) miembro m del
Congreso. **~woman** n (Amer)
miembro f del Congreso

conifer /'kɒnɪfə(r)/ n conífera f

conjugat|e /'kɒndʒʊgeɪt/ vt
conjugar. **~ion** /-'geɪʃn/ n
conjugación f

conjunction /kən'dʒʌŋkʃn/ n
conjunción f

conjur|e /'kʌndʒə(r)/ vi hacer
juegos de manos. •vt. ■**~e up** vt
evocar. **~er, ~or** n
prestidigitador m

conk /kɒŋk/ vi. **~ out** 🄸 fallar;
(person) desmayarse

conker /'kɒŋkə(r)/ n 🄸 castaña f de
Indias

conman /'kɒnmæn/ n (pl -men) 🄸

estafador m, timador m

connect /kə'nekt/ vt conectar; (associate) relacionar. ● vi (be fitted) estar conectado (**to** a). ■ **~ with** vt (train) enlazar con. **~ed** adj unido; (related) relacionado. **be ~ed with** tener que ver con, estar emparentado con. **~ion** /-ʃn/ n conexión f; (Rail) enlace m; (fig) relación f. **in ~ion with** a propósito de, con respecto a

connive /kə'naɪv/ vi. **~e at** ser cómplice en

connoisseur /kɒnə'sɜː(r)/ n experto m

connotation /kɒnə'teɪʃn/ n connotación f

conquer /'kɒŋkə(r)/ vt conquistar; (fig) vencer. **~or** n conquistador m

conquest /'kɒŋkwest/ n conquista f

conscience /'kɒnʃəns/ n conciencia f

conscientious /kɒnʃɪ'enʃəs/ adj concienzudo

conscious /'kɒnʃəs/ adj consciente; (deliberate) intencional **~ly** adv a sabiendas. **~ness** n consciencia f, (Med) conocimiento m

conscript /'kɒnskrɪpt/ n recluta m & f, conscripto m (LAm). ● /kən'skrɪpt/ vt reclutar. **~ion** /kən'skrɪpʃn/ n reclutamiento m, conscripción f (LAm)

consecrate /'kɒnsɪkreɪt/ vt consagrar

consecutive /kən'sekjʊtɪv/ adj sucesivo

consensus /kən'sensəs/ n consenso m

consent /kən'sent/ vi consentir. ● n consentimiento m

consequen|ce /'kɒnsɪkwəns/ n consecuencia f. **~t** adj consiguiente. **~tly** adv por consiguiente

conservation /kɒnsə'veɪʃn/ n conservación f, preservación f. **~ist** n conservacionista m & f

conservative /kən'sɜːvətɪv/ adj

conservador; (modest) prudente, moderado. **C~** adj & n conservador (m)

conservatory /kən'sɜːvətrɪ/ n invernadero m

conserve /kən'sɜːv/ vt conservar

consider /kən'sɪdə(r)/ vt considerar; (take into account) tomar en cuenta. **~able** adj considerable. **~ably** adv considerablemente

considerat|e /kən'sɪdərət/ adj considerado. **~ion** /-'reɪʃn/ n consideración f. **take sth into ~ion** tomar algo en cuenta

considering /kən'sɪdərɪŋ/ prep teniendo en cuenta. ● conj. **~ (that)** teniendo en cuenta que

consign /kən'saɪn/ vt consignar; (send) enviar. **~ment** n envío m

consist /kən'sɪst/ vi. **~ of** consistir en. **~ency** n consistencia f; (fig) coherencia f. **~ent** adj coherente; (unchanging) constante. **~ent with** compatible con. **~ently** adv constantemente

consolation /kɒnsə'leɪʃn/ n consuelo m

console /kən'səʊl/ vt consolar. ● /'kɒnsəʊl/ n consola f

consolidate /kən'sɒlɪdeɪt/ vt consolidar

consonant /'kɒnsənənt/ n consonante f

conspicuous /kən'spɪkjʊəs/ adj (easily seen) visible; (showy) llamativo; (noteworthy) notable

conspir|acy /kən'spɪrəsɪ/ n conspiración f. **~ator** /kən'spɪrətə(r)/ n conspirador m. **~e** /kən'spaɪə(r)/ vi conspirar

constable /'kʌnstəbl/ n agente m & f de policía

constant /'kɒnstənt/ adj constante. **~ly** adv constantemente

constellation /kɒnstə'leɪʃn/ n constelación f

consternation /kɒnstə'neɪʃn/ n consternación f

constipat|ed /'kɒnstɪpeɪtɪd/ adj estreñido. **~ion** /-'peɪʃn/ n estreñimiento m

constituen|cy /kən'stɪtjʊənsɪ/ n distrito m electoral. **~t** n (Pol) elector m. ●adj constituyente, constitutivo

constitut|e /'kɒnstɪtjuːt/ vt constituir. **~ion** /-'tjuːʃn/ n constitución f. **~ional** /-'tjuːʃənl/ adj constitucional. ●n paseo m

constrict /kən'strɪkt/ vt apretar. **~ion** /-ʃn/ n constricción f

construct /kən'strʌkt/ vt construir. **~ion** /-ʃn/ n construcción f. **~ive** adj constructivo

consul /'kɒnsl/ n cónsul m & f. **~ate** /'kɒnsjʊlət/ n consulado m

consult /kən'sʌlt/ vt/i consultar. **~ancy** n asesoría. **~ant** n asesor m; (Med) especialista m & f; (Tec) consejero m técnico. **~ation** /kɒnsəl'teɪʃn/ n consulta f

consume /kən'sjuːm/ vt consumir. **~r** n consumidor m. ●adj de consumo

consummate /'kɒnsəmət/ adj consumado. ●/'kɒnsəmeɪt/ vt consumar

consumption /kən'sʌmpʃn/ n consumo m

contact /'kɒntækt/ n contacto m. ●vt ponerse en contacto con. **~ lens** n lentilla f, lente f de contacto (LAm)

contagious /kən'teɪdʒəs/ adj contagioso

contain /kən'teɪn/ vt contener. **~ o.s.** contenerse. **~er** n recipiente m; (Com) contenedor m

contaminat|e /kən'tæmɪneɪt/ vt contaminar. **~ion** /-'neɪʃn/ n contaminación f

contemplate /'kɒntəmpleɪt/ vt contemplar; (consider) considerar

contemporary /kən'tempərərɪ/ adj & n contemporáneo (m)

contempt /kən'tempt/ n desprecio m. **~ible** adj despreciable. **~uous** /-tjʊəs/ adj desdeñoso

contend /kən'tend/ vt competir. **~er** n aspirante m & f (**for a**)

content /kən'tent/ adj satisfecho. ●/'kɒntent/ n contenido m. **~ed** /kən'tentɪd/ adj satisfecho. **~ment** /kən'tentmənt/ n satisfacción f. **~s** /'kɒntents/ n contenido m; (of book) índice m de materias

contest /'kɒntest/ n (competition) concurso m; (Sport) competición f, competencia f (LAm). ●/kən'test/ vt disputar. **~ant** /kən'testənt/ n concursante m & f

context /'kɒntekst/ n contexto m

continent /'kɒntɪnənt/ n continente m. **the C~** Europa f. **~al** /-'nentl/ adj continental. **~al quilt** n edredón m

contingen|cy /kən'tɪndʒənsɪ/ n contingencia f. **~t** adj & n contingente (m)

continu|al /kən'tɪnjʊəl/ adj continuo. **~ally** adv continuamente. **~ation** /-'eɪʃn/ n continuación f. **~e** /kən'tɪnjuː/ vt/i continuar, seguir. **~ed** adj continuo. **~ity** /kɒntɪ'njuːətɪ/ n continuidad f. **~ous** /kən'tɪnjʊəs/ adj continuo. **~ously** adv continuamente

contort /kən'tɔːt/ vt retorcer. **~ion** /-ʃn/ n contorsión f. **~ionist** /-ʃənɪst/ n contorsionista m & f

contour /'kɒntʊə(r)/ n contorno m

contraband /'kɒntrəbænd/ n contrabando m

contracepti|on /kɒntrə'sepʃn/ n anticoncepción f. **~ve** /-tɪv/ adj & n anticonceptivo m

contract /'kɒntrækt/ n contrato m. ●/kən'trækt/ vt contraer. ●vi contraerse. **~ion** /kən'trækʃn/ n contracción f. **~or** /kən'træktə(r)/ n contratista m & f

contradict /kɒntrə'dɪkt/ vt contradecir. **~ion** /-ʃn/ n contradicción f. **~ory** adj contradictorio

contraption /kən'træpʃn/ n 🔲 artilugio m

contrary /'kɒntrərɪ/ adj contrario. **the ~** lo contrario. **on the ~** al contrario. • adv. **~ to** contrariamente a. • /kən'treərɪ/ adj (obstinate) terco

contrast /'kɒntrɑːst/ n contraste m. • /kən'trɑːst/ vt/i contrastar. **~ing** adj contrastante

contravene /kɒntrə'viːn/ vt contravenir

contribut|e /kən'trɪbjuːt/ vt contribuir con. • vi contribuir. **~e to** escribir para (newspaper). **~ion** /kɒntrɪ'bjuːʃn/ n contribución f. **~or** n contribuyente m & f; (to newspaper) colaborador m

contrite /'kɒntraɪt/ adj arrepentido, pesaroso

contriv|e /kən'traɪv/ vt idear. **~e to** conseguir. **~ed** adj artificioso

control /kən'trəʊl/ vt (pt **controlled**) controlar. • n control m. **~ler** n director m. **~s** npl (Mec) mandos mpl

controvers|ial /kɒntrə'vɜːʃl/ controvertido. **~y** /'kɒntrəvɜːsɪ/ n controversia f

conundrum /kə'nʌndrəm/ n adivinanza f

convalesce /kɒnvə'les/ vi convalecer. **~nce** n convalecencia f

convector /kən'vektə(r)/ n estufa f de convección

convene /kən'viːn/ vt convocar. • vi reunirse

convenien|ce /kən'viːnɪəns/ n conveniencia f, comodidad f. **all modern ~ces** todas las comodidades. **at your ~ce** según le convenga. **~ces** npl servicios mpl, baños mpl (LAm). **~t** adj conveniente; (place) bien situado; (time) oportuno. **be ~t** convenir. **~tly** adv convenientemente

convent /'kɒnvənt/ n convento m

convention /kən'venʃn/ n

convención f. **~al** adj convencional

converge /kən'vɜːdʒ/ vi converger

conversation /kɒnvə'seɪʃn/ n conversación f. **~al** adj familiar, coloquial.

converse /kən'vɜːs/ vi conversar. • /'kɒnvɜːs/ adj inverso. • n lo contrario. **~ly** adv a la inversa

conver|sion /kən'vɜːʃn/ n conversión f. **~t** /kən'vɜːt/ vt convertir. • /'kɒnvɜːt/ n converso m. **~tible** /kən'vɜːtɪbl/ adj convertible. • n (Auto) descapotable m, convertible m (LAm)

convex /'kɒnveks/ adj convexo

convey /kən'veɪ/ vt transportar (goods, people); comunicar (idea, feeling). **~or belt** n cinta f transportadora, banda f transportadora (LAm)

convict /kən'vɪkt/ vt condenar. • /'kɒnvɪkt/ n presidiario m. **~ion** /kən'vɪkʃn/ n condena f; (belief) creencia f

convinc|e /kən'vɪns/ vt convencer. **~ing** adj convincente

convoluted /'kɒnvəluːtɪd/ adj (argument) intrincado

convoy /'kɒnvɔɪ/ n convoy m

convuls|e /kən'vʌls/ vt convulsionar. **be ~ed with laughter** desternillarse de risa. **~ion** /-ʃn/ n convulsión f

coo /kuː/ vi arrullar

cook /kʊk/ vt hacer, preparar. • vi cocinar; (food) hacerse. • n cocinero m. ■ **~ up** vt 🔲 inventar. **~book** n libro m de cocina. **~er** n cocina f, estufa f (Mex). **~ery** n cocina f

cookie /'kʊkɪ/ n (Amer) galleta f

cool /kuːl/ adj (**-er**, **-est**) fresco; (calm) tranquilo; (unfriendly) frío. • n fresco m; 🗵 calma f. • vt enfriar. • vi enfriarse. ■ **~ down** vi (person) calmarse. **~ly** adv tranquilamente

coop /kuːp/ n gallinero m. ■ **~ up** vt encerrar

co-op /'kəʊɒp/ n cooperativa f

cooperat|e /kəʊ'ɒpəreɪt/ vi cooperar. **~ion** /-'reɪʃn/ n cooperación f. **~ive** /kəʊ'ɒpərətɪv/ adj cooperativo. ●n cooperativa f

co-opt /kəʊ'ɒpt/ vt cooptar

co-ordinat|e /kəʊ'ɔːdɪneɪt/ vt coordinar. ●/kəʊ'ɔːdɪnət/ n (Math) coordenada f. **~es** npl prendas fpl para combinar. **~ion** /kəʊ.ɔːdɪ'neɪʃn/ n coordinación f

cop /kɒp/ n 🄳 poli m & f 🄳, tira m & f (Mex, fam)

cope /kəʊp/ vi arreglárselas. **~ with** hacer frente a

copious /'kəʊpɪəs/ adj abundante

copper /'kɒpə(r)/ n cobre m; (coin) perra f; 🄳 poli m & f 🄳, tira m & f (Mex, fam). ●adj de cobre

copy /'kɒpɪ/ n copia f; (of book, newspaper) ejemplar m. ●vt copiar. **~right** n derechos mpl de reproducción

coral /'kɒrəl/ n coral m

cord /kɔːd/ n cuerda f; (fabric) pana f; (Amer, Elec) cordón m, cable m

cordial /'kɔːdɪəl/ adj cordial. ●n refresco m (concentrado)

cordon /'kɔːdn/ n cordón m. ■ **~ off** vt acordonar

core /kɔː(r)/ n (of apple) corazón m; (of Earth) centro m; (of problem) meollo m

cork /kɔːk/ n corcho m. **~screw** n sacacorchos m

corn /kɔːn/ n (wheat) trigo m; (Amer) maíz m; (hard skin) callo m

corned beef /kɔːnd 'biːf/ n carne f de vaca en lata

corner /'kɔːnə(r)/ n ángulo m; (inside) rincón m; (outside) esquina f; (football) córner m. ●vt arrinconar; (Com) acaparar

cornet /'kɔːnɪt/ n (Mus) corneta f; (for ice cream) cucurucho m, barquillo m (Mex)

corn: ~flakes npl copos mpl de maíz. **~flour** n maizena f (®)

Cornish /'kɔːnɪʃ/ adj de Cornualles

cornstarch /'kɔːnstɑːtʃ/ n (Amer) maizena f (®)

corny /'kɔːnɪ/ adj (fam, trite) gastado

coronation /kɒrə'neɪʃn/ n coronación f

coroner /'kɒrənə(r)/ n juez m de primera instancia

corporal /'kɔːpərəl/ n cabo m. ●adj corporal

corporate /'kɔːpərət/ adj corporativo

corporation /kɔːpə'reɪʃn/ n corporación f; (Amer) sociedad f anónima

corps /kɔː(r)/ n (pl **corps**/kɔːz/) cuerpo m

corpse /kɔːps/ n cadáver m

corpulent /'kɔːpjʊlənt/ adj corpulento

corral /kə'rɑːl/ n (Amer) corral m

correct /kə'rekt/ adj correcto; (time) exacto. ●vt corregir. **~ion** /-ʃn/ n corrección f

correspond /kɒrɪ'spɒnd/ vi corresponder; (write) escribirse. **~ence** n correspondencia f. **~ent** n corresponsal m & f

corridor /'kɒrɪdɔː(r)/ n pasillo m

corro|de /kə'rəʊd/ vt corroer. ●vi corroerse. **~sion** /-ʒn/ n corrosión f. **~sive** /-sɪv/ adj corrosivo

corrugated /'kɒrəgeɪtɪd/ adj ondulado. **~ iron** n chapa f de zinc

corrupt /kə'rʌpt/ adj corrompido. ●vt corromper. **~ion** /-ʃn/ n corrupción f

corset /'kɔːsɪt/ n corsé m

cosmetic /kɒz'metɪk/ adj & n cosmético (m)

cosmic /'kɒzmɪk/ adj cósmico

cosmopolitan /kɒzmə'pɒlɪtən/ adj & n cosmopolita (m & f)

cosmos /'kɒzmɒs/ n cosmos m

cosset /'kɒsɪt/ vt (pt **cosseted**) mimar

cost | court

cost /kɒst/ vt (pt **cost**) costar; (pt **costed**) calcular el coste de, calcular el costo de (LAm). • n coste m, costo m (LAm). **at all ∼s** cueste lo que cueste. **to one's ∼** a sus expensas. **∼s** npl (Jurid) costas fpl

Costa Rica /kɒstəˈriːkə/ n Costa f Rica. **∼n** adj & n costarricense (m & f), costarriqueño (m & f)

cost: **∼-effective** adj rentable. **∼ly** adj (-ier, -iest) costoso

costume /ˈkɒstjuːm/ n traje m; (for party, disguise) disfraz m

cosy /ˈkəʊzɪ/ adj (-ier, -iest) acogedor. • n cubreteras

cot /kɒt/ n cuna f

cottage /ˈkɒtɪdʒ/ n casita f. **∼ cheese** n requesón m. **∼ pie** n pastel m de carne cubierta con puré

cotton /ˈkɒtn/ n algodón m; (thread) hilo m; (Amer) see **WOOL**. ■**∼ on** vi 🔲 comprender. **∼ bud** n bastoncillo m, cotonete m (Mex). **∼ candy** n (Amer) algodón m de azúcar. **∼ swab** n (Amer) see **BUD**. **∼ wool** n algodón m hidrófilo

couch /kaʊtʃ/ n sofá m

cough /kɒf/ vi toser. • n tos f. ■**∼ up** vt 🔲 pagar. **∼ mixture** n jarabe m para la tos

could /kʊd/ pt of **CAN**[1]

couldn't /ˈkʊdnt/ = could not

council /ˈkaʊnsl/ n consejo m; (of town) ayuntamiento m. **∼ house** n vivienda f subvencionada. **∼lor** n concejal m

counsel /ˈkaʊnsl/ n consejo m; (pl invar) (Jurid) abogado m. • vt (pt **counselled**) aconsejar. **∼ling** n terapia f de apoyo. **∼lor** n consejero m

count /kaʊnt/ n recuento m; (nobleman) conde m. • vt/i contar. ■**∼ on** vt contar con. **∼down** n cuenta f atrás

counter /ˈkaʊntə(r)/ n (in shop) mostrador m; (in bank, post office) ventanilla f; (token) ficha f. • adv. **∼ to** en contra de. • adj opuesto. • vt oponerse a; parar (blow)

counter... /ˈkaʊntə(r)/ pref contra.... **∼act** /-ˈækt/ vt contrarrestar. **∼attack** n contraataque m. • vt/i contraatacar. **∼balance** n contrapeso m. • vt/i contrapesar. **∼clockwise** /-ˈklɒkwaɪz/ a/adv (Amer) en sentido contrario al de las agujas del reloj

counterfeit /ˈkaʊntəfɪt/ adj falsificado. • n falsificación f. • vt falsificar

counterfoil /ˈkaʊntəfɔɪl/ n matriz f, talón m (LAm)

counter-productive /kaʊntəprəˈdʌktɪv/ adj contraproducente

countess /ˈkaʊntɪs/ n condesa f

countless /ˈkaʊntlɪs/ adj innumerable

country /ˈkʌntrɪ/ n (native land) país m; (countryside) campo m; (Mus) (música f) country m. **∼-and-western** /-en'westən/ (música f) country m. **∼man** /-mən/ n (of one's own country) compatriota m. **∼side** n campo m; (landscape) paisaje m

county /ˈkaʊntɪ/ n condado m

coup /kuː/ n golpe m

couple /ˈkʌpl/ n (of things) par m; (of people) pareja f; (married) matrimonio m. **a ∼ of** un par de

coupon /ˈkuːpɒn/ n cupón m

courage /ˈkʌrɪdʒ/ n valor m. **∼ous** /kəˈreɪdʒəs/ adj valiente

courgette /kʊəˈʒet/ n calabacín m

courier /ˈkʊrɪə(r)/ n mensajero m; (for tourists) guía m & f

course /kɔːs/ n curso m; (behaviour) conducta f; (in navigation) rumbo m; (Culin) plato m; (for golf) campo m. **in due ∼** a su debido tiempo. **in the ∼ of** en el transcurso de, durante. **of ∼** claro, por supuesto. **of ∼ not** claro que no, por supuesto que no

court /kɔːt/ n corte f; (tennis) pista f;

cancha f (LAm); (Jurid) tribunal m.
• vt cortejar; buscar (danger)

courteous /'kɜːtɪəs/ adj cortés

courtesy /'kɜːtəsɪ/ n cortesía f

courtier /'kɔːtɪə(r)/ n (old use)
cortesano m

court:: ~ **martial** n (pl ~s
martial) consejo m de guerra.
-martial vt (pt ~-martialled)
juzgar en consejo de guerra.
~**ship** n cortejo m. ~**yard** n
patio m

cousin /'kʌzn/ n primo m. **first** ~
primo carnal. **second** ~ primo
segundo

cove /kəʊv/ n ensenada f, cala f

Coventry /'kɒvntrɪ/ n. **send s.o.
to** ~ hacer el vacío a uno

cover /'kʌvə(r)/ vt cubrir. • n
cubierta f; (shelter) abrigo m; (lid)
tapa f; (for furniture) funda f; (pretext)
pretexto m; (of magazine) portada f.
■ ~ **up** vt cubrir; (fig) ocultar.
~**age** n cobertura f. ~ **charge** n
precio m del cubierto. ~**ing** n
cubierta f. ~**ing letter** n carta f
adjunta

covet /'kʌvɪt/ vt codiciar

cow /kaʊ/ n vaca f

coward /'kaʊəd/ n cobarde m. ~**ice**
/'kaʊədɪs/ n cobardía f. ~**ly** adj
cobarde.

cowboy /'kaʊbɔɪ/ n vaquero m

cower /'kaʊə(r)/ vi encogerse,
acobardarse

coxswain /'kɒksn/ n timonel m

coy /kɔɪ/ adj (-er, -est) (shy) tímido;
(evasive) evasivo

crab /kræb/ n cangrejo m, jaiba f
(LAm)

crack /kræk/ n grieta f; (noise)
crujido m; (of whip) chasquido m;
(drug) crack m. • adj 🄻 de primera.
• vt agrietar; chasquear (whip,
fingers); cascar (nut); gastar (joke);
resolver (problem). • vi agrietarse.
get ~**ing** 🄻 darse prisa. ■ ~
down on vt 🄻 tomar medidas
enérgicas contra

cracker /'krækə(r)/ n (Culin) cracker
f, galleta f (salada); (Christmas cracker)
sorpresa f (que estalla al abrirla)

crackle /'krækl/ vi crepitar. • n
crepitación f, crujido m

crackpot /'krækpɒt/ n 🄻
chiflado m

cradle /'kreɪdl/ n cuna f. • vt acunar

craft /krɑːft/ n destreza f; (technique)
arte f; (cunning) astucia f. • n invar
(boat) barco m

craftsman /'krɑːftsmən/ n (pl
-men) artesano m. ~**ship** n
artesanía f

crafty /'krɑːftɪ/ adj (-ier, -iest)
astuto

cram /kræm/ vt (pt crammed)
rellenar. ~ **with** llenar de. • vi (for
exams) memorizar, empollar 🄍,
zambutir (Mex)

cramp /kræmp/ n calambre m

cramped /kræmpt/ adj apretado

crane /kreɪn/ n grúa f. • vt estirar
(neck)

crank /kræŋk/ n manivela f; (person)
excéntrico m. ~**y** adj excéntrico

cranny /'krænɪ/ n grieta f

crash /kræʃ/ n accidente m; (noise)
estruendo m; (collision) choque m;
(Com) quiebra f. • vt estrellar. • vi
quebrar con estrépito; (have
accident) tener un accidente; (car etc)
estrellarse, chocar; (fail) fracasar.
~ **course** n curso m intensivo. ~
helmet n casco m protector.
~-**land** vi hacer un aterrizaje
forzoso

crass /kræs/ adj craso, burdo

crate /kreɪt/ n cajón m. • vt embalar

crater /'kreɪtə(r)/ n cráter m

crav|e /kreɪv/ vt ansiar. ~**ing** n
ansia f

crawl /krɔːl/ vi (baby) gatear; (move
slowly) avanzar lentamente; (drag
o.s.) arrastrarse. ~ **to** humillarse
ante. ~ **with** hervir de. • n
(swimming) crol m. **at a** ~ a paso
lento

crayon /'kreɪən/ n lápiz m de color; (made of wax) lápiz m de cera, crayola f (®), crayón m (Mex)

craz|e /kreɪz/ n manía f. ~**y** /'kreɪzɪ/ adj (**-ier, -iest**) loco. **be ~y about** estar loco por

creak /kriːk/ n crujido m; (of hinge) chirrido m. •vi crujir; (hinge) chirriar

cream /kriːm/ n crema f; (fresh) nata f, crema f (LAm). •adj (colour) color crema. •vt (beat) batir. ~ **cheese** n queso m para untar, queso m crema (LAm). ~**y** adj cremoso

crease /kriːs/ n raya f, pliegue m (Mex); (crumple) arruga f. •vt plegar; (wrinkle) arrugar. •vi arrugarse

creat|e /kriː'eɪt/ vt crear. ~**ion** /-ʃn/ n creación f. ~**ive** adj creativo. ~**or** n creador m

creature /'kriːtʃə(r)/ n criatura f

crèche /kreʃ/ n guardería f (infantil)

credib|ility /kredə'bɪlətɪ/ n credibilidad f. ~**le** /'kredəbl/ adj creíble

credit /'kredɪt/ n crédito m; (honour) mérito m. **take the ~ for** atribuirse el mérito de. •vt (pt **credited**) acreditar; (believe) creer. ~ **s.o. with** atribuir a uno. ~ **card** n tarjeta f de crédito. ~**or** n acreedor m

creed /kriːd/ n credo m

creek /kriːk/ n ensenada f. **up the ~** 🅧 en apuros

creep /kriːp/ vi (pt **crept**) arrastrarse; (plant) trepar. •n 🅣 adulador m. ~**s** /kriːps/ npl. **give s.o. the ~s** poner los pelos de punta a uno. ~**er** n enredadera f

cremat|e /krɪ'meɪt/ vt incinerar. ~**ion** /-ʃn/ n cremación f. ~**orium** /kremə'tɔːrɪəm/ n (pl **-ia** /-ɪə/) crematorio m

crept /krept/ see CREEP

crescendo /krɪ'ʃendəʊ/ n (pl **-os**) crescendo m

crescent /'kresnt/ n media luna f; (street) calle f en forma de media luna

crest /krest/ n cresta f; (on coat of arms) emblema m

crevice /'krevɪs/ n grieta f

crew /kruː/ n tripulación f; (gang) pandilla f. ~ **cut** n corte m al rape

crib /krɪb/ n (Amer) cuna f; (Relig) belén m. •vt/i (pt **cribbed**) copiar

crick /krɪk/ n calambre m; (in neck) tortícolis f

cricket /'krɪkɪt/ n (Sport) críquet m; (insect) grillo m

crim|e /kraɪm/ n delito m; (murder) crimen m; (acts) delincuencia f. ~**inal** /'krɪmɪnl/ adj & n criminal (m & f)

crimson /'krɪmzn/ adj & n carmesí (m)

cringe /krɪndʒ/ vi encogerse; (fig) humillarse

crinkle /'krɪŋkl/ vt arrugar. •vi arrugarse. •n arruga f

cripple /'krɪpl/ n lisiado m. •vt lisiar; (fig) paralizar

crisis /'kraɪsɪs/ n (pl **crises** /-siːz/) crisis f

crisp /krɪsp/ adj (**-er, -est**) (Culin) crujiente; (air) vigorizador. ~**s** npl patatas fpl fritas, papas fpl fritas (LAm) (de bolsa)

crisscross /'krɪskrɒs/ adj entrecruzado. •vt entrecruzar. •vi entrecruzarse

criterion /kraɪ'tɪərɪən/ n (pl **-ia** /-ɪə/) criterio m

critic /'krɪtɪk/ n crítico m. ~**al** adj crítico. ~**ally** adv críticamente; (ill) gravemente

critici|sm /'krɪtɪsɪzəm/ n crítica f. ~**ze** /'krɪtɪsaɪz/ vt/i criticar

croak /krəʊk/ n (of person) gruñido m; (of frog) canto m. •vi gruñir; (frog) croar

Croat /'krəʊæt/ n croata m & f. ~**ia** /krəʊ'eɪʃə/ n Croacia f. ~**ian** adj croata

crochet /ˈkrəʊʃeɪ/ n crochet m, ganchillo m. •vt tejer a crochet or a ganchillo

crockery /ˈkrɒkərɪ/ n loza f

crocodile /ˈkrɒkədaɪl/ n cocodrilo m. ~ **tears** npl lágrimas fpl de cocodrilo

crocus /ˈkrəʊkəs/ n (pl **-es**) azafrán m de primavera

crook /krʊk/ n 🄸 sinvergüenza m & f. ~**ed** /ˈkrʊkɪd/ adj torcido, chueco (LAm); (winding) tortuoso; (dishonest) deshonesto

crop /krɒp/ n cosecha f; (haircut) corte m de pelo muy corto. •vt (pt **cropped**) cortar. ∎ ~ **up** vi surgir

croquet /ˈkrəʊkeɪ/ n croquet m

cross /krɒs/ n cruz f; (of animals) cruce m. •vt cruzar; (oppose) contrariar. ~ **s.o.'s mind** ocurrírsele a uno. •vi cruzar. ~ **o.s.** santiguarse. •adj enfadado, enojado (esp LAm). ∎ ~ **out** vt tachar. ~**bar** n travesaño m. ~**-examine** /-ɪgˈzæmɪn/ vt interrogar. ~**-eyed** adj bizco. ~**fire** n fuego m cruzado. ~**ing** n (by boat) travesía f; (on road) cruce m peatonal. ~**ly** adv con enfado, con enojo (esp LAm). ~**-purposes** /-ˈpɜːpəsɪz/ npl. **talk at** ~**-purposes** hablar sin entenderse. ~**-reference** /-ˈrefrəns/ n remisión f. ~**roads** n invar cruce m. ~**-section** /-ˈsekʃn/ n sección f transversal; (fig) muestra f representativa. ~**walk** n (Amer) paso m de peatones. ~**word** n ~**word (puzzle)** crucigrama m

crotch /krɒtʃ/ n entrepiernas fpl

crouch /kraʊtʃ/ vi agacharse

crow /krəʊ/ n cuervo m. **as the** ~ **flies** en línea recta. •vi cacarear. ~**bar** n palanca f

crowd /kraʊd/ n muchedumbre f. •vt amontonar; (fill) llenar. •vi amontonarse; (gather) reunirse. ~**ed** adj atestado

crown /kraʊn/ n corona f; (of hill) cumbre f; (of head) coronilla f. •vt coronar

crucial /ˈkruːʃl/ adj crucial

crucifix /ˈkruːsɪfɪks/ n crucifijo m. ~**ion** /-ˈfɪkʃn/ n crucifixión f

crucify /ˈkruːsɪfaɪ/ vt crucificar

crude /kruːd/ adj (**-er, -est**) (raw) crudo; (rough) tosco; (vulgar) ordinario

cruel /ˈkruːəl/ adj (**crueller, cruellest**) cruel. ~**ty** n crueldad f

cruet /ˈkruːɪt/ n vinagrera f

cruise /kruːz/ n crucero m. •vi hacer un crucero; (of car) circular lentamente. ~**r** n crucero m

crumb /krʌm/ n miga f

crumble /ˈkrʌmbl/ vt desmenuzar. •vi desmenuzarse; (collapse) derrumbarse

crummy /ˈkrʌmɪ/ adj (**-ier, -iest**) 🄳 miserable

crumpet /ˈkrʌmpɪt/ n bollo m blando

crumple /ˈkrʌmpl/ vt arrugar. •vi arrugarse

crunch /krʌntʃ/ vt hacer crujir; (bite) masticar. ~**y** adj crujiente

crusade /kruːˈseɪd/ n cruzada f. ~**r** n cruzado m

crush /krʌʃ/ vt aplastar; arrugar (clothes). •n (crowd) aglomeración f. **have a** ~ **on** 🄸 estar chiflado por

crust /krʌst/ n corteza f. ~**y** adj (bread) de corteza dura

crutch /krʌtʃ/ n muleta f; (between legs) entrepiernas fpl

crux /krʌks/ n (pl **cruxes**). **the** ~ **(of the matter)** el quid (de la cuestión)

cry /kraɪ/ n grito m. **be a far** ~ **from** (fig) distar mucho de. •vi llorar; (call out) gritar. ∎ ~ **off** vi echarse atrás, rajarse. ~**baby** n llorón m

crypt /krɪpt/ n cripta f

cryptic /ˈkrɪptɪk/ adj enigmático

crystal /'krɪstl/ n cristal m. ~**lize** vi cristalizarse

cub /kʌb/ n cachorro m. **C~ (Scout)** n lobato m

Cuba /'kju:bə/ n Cuba f. ~**n** adj & n cubano (m)

cubbyhole /'kʌbɪhəʊl/ n cuchitril m

cub|e /kju:b/ n cubo m. ~**ic** adj cúbico

cubicle /'kju:bɪkl/ n cubículo m; (changing room) probador m

cuckoo /'kʊku:/ n cuco m, cuclillo m

cucumber /'kju:kʌmbə(r)/ n pepino m

cuddl|e /'kʌdl/ vt abrazar. • vi abrazarse. • n abrazo m. ~**y** adj adorable

cue /kju:/ n (Mus) entrada f; (in theatre) pie m; (in snooker) taco m

cuff /kʌf/ n (Amer, of trousers) vuelta f, dobladillo m, (blow) bofetada f. **speak off the ~** hablar de improviso. • vt abofetear. ~**link** n gemelo m, mancuerna f (Mex)

cul de sac /'kʌldəsæk/ n callejón m sin salida

culinary /'kʌlɪnərɪ/ adj culinario

cull /kʌl/ vt sacrificar en forma selectiva (animals)

culminat|e /'kʌlmɪneɪt/ vi culminar. ~**ion** /-'neɪʃn/ n culminación f

culprit /'kʌlprɪt/ n culpable m & f

cult /kʌlt/ n culto m

cultivat|e /'kʌltɪveɪt/ vt cultivar. ~**ion** /-'veɪʃn/ n cultivo m

cultur|al /'kʌltʃərəl/ adj cultural. ~**e** /'kʌltʃə(r)/ n cultura f; (Bot etc) cultivo m. ~**ed** adj cultivado; (person) culto

cumbersome /'kʌmbəsəm/ adj incómodo; (heavy) pesado

cunning /'kʌnɪŋ/ adj astuto. • n astucia f

cup /kʌp/ n taza f; (trophy) copa f

cupboard /'kʌbəd/ n armario m

curator /kjʊə'reɪtə(r)/ n (of museum) conservador m

curb /kɜ:b/ n freno m; (Amer) bordillo m (de la acera), borde m de la banqueta (Mex). • vt refrenar

curdle /'kɜ:dl/ vt cuajar. • vi cuajarse; (go bad) cortarse

cure /kjʊə(r)/ vt curar. • n cura f

curfew /'kɜ:fju:/ n toque m de queda

curio|sity /kjʊərɪ'ɒsətɪ/ n curiosidad f. ~**us** /'kjʊərɪəs/ adj curioso

curl /kɜ:l/ vt rizar, enchinar (Mex). ~ **o.s. up** acurrucarse. • vi (hair) rizarse, enchinarse (Mex); (paper) ondularse. • n rizo m, chino m (Mex). ~**er** n rulo m, chino m (Mex). ~**y** adj (**-ier, -iest**) rizado, chino (Mex)

currant /'kʌrənt/ n pasa f de Corinto

currency /'kʌrənsɪ/ n moneda f

current /'kʌrənt/ adj & n corriente (f,l); (existing) actual. ~ **affairs** npl sucesos de actualidad. ~**ly** adv actualmente

curriculum /kə'rɪkjʊləm/ n (pl **-la**) programa m de estudios. ~ **vitae** n currículum m vitae

curry /'kʌrɪ/ n curry m. • vt preparar al curry

curse /kɜ:s/ n maldición f; (oath) palabrota f. • vt maldecir. • vi decir palabrotas

cursory /'kɜ:sərɪ/ adj superficial

curt /kɜ:t/ adj brusco

curtain /'kɜ:tn/ n cortina f; (in theatre) telón m

curtsey, curtsy /'kɜ:tsɪ/ n reverencia f. • vi hacer una reverencia

curve /kɜ:v/ n curva f. • vi estar curvado; (road) torcerse

cushion /'kʊʃn/ n cojín m, almohadón m

cushy /ˈkʊʃɪ/ adj (-ier, -iest) 🔲 fácil

custard /ˈkʌstəd/ n natillas fpl

custody /ˈkʌstədɪ/ n custodia f; **be in ~** Jurid estar detenido

custom /ˈkʌstəm/ n costumbre f; (Com) clientela f. **~ary** /-ərɪ/ adj acostumbrado. **~er** n cliente m. **~s** npl aduana f. **~s officer** n aduanero m

cut /kʌt/ vt/i (pt cut, pres p cutting) cortar; reducir (prices). ●n corte m; (reduction) reducción f. ■**~ across** vt cortar camino por. ■**~ back, ~ down** vt reducir. ■**~ in** vi interrumpir. ■**~ off** vt cortar; (phone) desconectar; (fig) aislar. ■**~ out** vt recortar; (omit) suprimir. ■**~ through** vt cortar camino por. ■**~ up** vt cortar en pedazos

cute /kjuːt/ adj (-er, -est) 🔲 mono, amoroso (LAm); (Amer, attractive) guapo, buen mozo (LAm)

cutlery /ˈkʌtlərɪ/ n cubiertos mpl

cutlet /ˈkʌtlɪt/ n chuleta f

cut: **~-price,** (Amer) **~-rate** adj a precio reducido. **~-throat** adj despiadado. **~ting** adj cortante; (remark) mordaz. ●n (from newspaper) recorte m; (of plant) esqueje m

CV n (= curriculum vitae) currículum m (vitae)

cyberspace /ˈsaɪbəspeɪs/ ciberespacio m

cycl|e /ˈsaɪkl/ n ciclo m; (bicycle) bicicleta f. ●vi ir en bicicleta. **~ing** n ciclismo m. **~ist** n ciclista m & f

cylind|er /ˈsɪlɪndə(r)/ n cilindro m. **~er head** (Auto) n culata f. **~rical** /-ˈlɪndrɪkl/ adj cilíndrico

cymbal /ˈsɪmbl/ n címbalo m

cynic /ˈsɪnɪk/ n cínico m. **~al** adj cínico. **~ism** /-sɪzəm/ n cinismo m

Czech /tʃek/ adj & n checo (m). **~oslovakia** /-əslə'vækɪə/ n (History) Checoslovaquia f. **~ Republic** n. **the ~ Republic** n la República Checa

Dd

dab /dæb/ vt (pt dabbed) tocar ligeramente. ●n toque m suave. **a ~ of** un poquito de

dad /dæd/ n 🔲 papá m. **~dy** n papi m. **~dy-long-legs** n invar (cranefly) típula f; (Amer, harvestman) segador m, falangio m

daffodil /ˈdæfədɪl/ n narciso m

daft /dɑːft/ adj (-er, -est) 🔲 tonto

dagger /ˈdægə(r)/ n daga f, puñal m

daily /ˈdeɪlɪ/ adj diario. ●adv diariamente, cada día

dainty /ˈdeɪntɪ/ adj (-ier, -iest) delicado

dairy /ˈdeərɪ/ n vaquería f; (shop) lechería f

daisy /ˈdeɪzɪ/ n margarita f

dam /dæm/ n presa f, represa f (LAm)

damag|e /ˈdæmɪdʒ/ n daño m; **~s** (npl, Jurid) daños mpl y perjuicios mpl. ●vt (fig) dañar, estropear. **~ing** adj perjudicial

dame /deɪm/ n (old use) dama f; (Amer, sl) chica f

damn /dæm/ vt condenar; (curse) maldecir. ●int 🔲 ¡caray! 🔲. ●adj maldito. ●n **I don't give a ~** (no) me importa un comino

damp /dæmp/ n humedad f. ●adj (-er, -est) húmedo. ●vt mojar. **~ness** n humedad f

danc|e /dɑːns/ vt/i bailar. ●n baile

m. ~**e hall** n salón m de baile. ~**er** n bailador m; (professional) bailarín m. ~**ing** n baile m

dandelion /'dændɪlaɪən/ n diente m de león

dandruff /'dændrʌf/ n caspa f

dandy /'dændɪ/ n petimetre m

Dane /deɪn/ n danés m

danger /'deɪndʒə(r)/ n peligro m; (risk) riesgo m. ~**ous** adj peligroso

dangle /'dæŋgl/ vt balancear. ●vi suspender, colgar

Danish /'deɪnɪʃ/ adj danés. ●m (language) danés m

dar|e /deə(r)/ vt desafiar. ●vi atreverse a. **I ~ say** probablemente. ~**edevil** n atrevido m. ~**ing** adj atrevido

dark /dɑːk/ adj (-er, -est) oscuro; (skin, hair) moreno. ●n oscuridad f; (nightfall) atardecer. **in the ~** a oscuras. ~**en** vt oscurecer. ●vi oscurecerse. ~**ness** n oscuridad f. ~**room** n cámara f oscura

darling /'dɑːlɪŋ/ adj querido. ●n cariño m

darn /dɑːn/ vt zurcir

dart /dɑːt/ n dardo m. ●vi lanzarse; (run) precipitarse. ~**board** n diana f. ~**s** npl los dardos mpl

dash /dæʃ/ vi precipitarse. ●vt tirar; (break) romper; defraudar (hopes). ●n (small amount) poquito m; (punctuation mark) guión m. ■ ~ **off** vi marcharse apresuradamente. ~ **out** vi salir corriendo. ~**board** n tablero m de mandos

data /'deɪtə/ npl datos mpl. ~**base** n base f de datos. ~ **processing** n proceso m de datos

date /deɪt/ n fecha f; (appointment) cita f; (fruit) dátil m. **to ~** hasta la fecha. ●vt fechar. ●vi datar; datar (remains); be old-fashioned) quedar anticuado. ~**d** adj pasado de moda

daub /dɔːb/ vt embadurnar

daughter /'dɔːtə(r)/ n hija f. ~**-in-law** n nuera f

dawdle /'dɔːdl/ vi andar despacio; (waste time) perder el tiempo

dawn /dɔːn/ n amanecer m. ●vi amanecer; (fig) nacer. **it ~ed on me that** caí en la cuenta de que

day /deɪ/ n día m; (whole day) jornada f; (period) época f. ~**break** n amanecer m. ~ **care center** n (Amer) guardería f infantil. ~**dream** n ensueño m. ●vi soñar despierto. ~**light** n luz f del día. ~**time** n día m

daze /deɪz/ vt aturdir. ●n aturdimiento m. **in a ~** aturdido. ~**d** adj aturdido

dazzle /'dæzl/ vt deslumbrar

dead /ded/ adj muerto; (numb) dormido. ●adv justo; (**fam**, completely) completamente. ~ **beat** rendido. ~ **slow** muy lento. **stop ~** parar en seco. ~**en** vt amortiguar (sound, blow); calmar (pain). ~ **end** n callejón m sin salida. ~**line** n fecha f tope, plazo m de entrega. ~**lock** n punto m muerto. ~**ly** adj (-ier, -iest) mortal

deaf /def/ adj (-er, -est) sordo. ~**en** vt ensordecer. ~**ness** n sordera f

deal /diːl/ n (agreement) acuerdo m; (treatment) trato m. **a good ~** bastante. **a great ~ (of)** muchísimo. ●vt (pt **dealt**) dar (a blow, cards). ●vi (cards) dar; repartir. ■ ~ **in** vt comerciar en. ■ ~ **out** vt repartir, distribuir. ■ ~ **with** vt tratar con (person); tratar de (subject); ocuparse de (problem). ~**er** n comerciante m. **drug ~er** traficante m & f de drogas

dean /diːn/ n deán m; (Univ) decano m

dear /dɪə(r)/ adj (-er, -est) querido; (expensive) caro. ●n querido m. ●adv caro. ●int. **oh ~!** ¡ay por Dios! ~ **me!** ¡Dios mío! ~**ly** adv (pay) caro; (very much) muchísimo

death /deθ/ n muerte f. ~ **sentence** n pena f de muerte. ~ **trap** n lugar m peligroso.

debat|able /dɪ'beɪtəbl/ adj discutible. ~**e** /dɪ'beɪt/ n debate m.

•vt debatir, discutir

debauchery /dɪˈbɔːtʃərɪ/ vt libertinaje m

debit /ˈdebɪt/ n débito m. •vt debitar, cargar. ~ **card** n tarjeta f de cobro automático

debris /ˈdebriː/ n escombros mpl

debt /det/ n deuda f. **be in** ~ tener deudas. ~**or** n deudor m

debut /ˈdebjuː/ debut m

decade /ˈdekeɪd/ n década f

decaden|ce /ˈdekədəns/ n decadencia f. ~**t** adj decadente

decay /dɪˈkeɪ/ vi descomponerse; (tooth) cariarse. •n descomposición f; (of tooth) caries f

deceased /dɪˈsiːst/ adj difunto

deceit /dɪˈsiːt/ n engaño m. ~**ful** adj falso. ~**fully** adv falsamente

deceive /dɪˈsiːv/ vt engañar

December /dɪˈsembə(r)/ n diciembre m

decen|cy /ˈdiːsənsɪ/ n decencia f. ~**t** adj decente; (fam, good) bueno; (fam, kind) amable. ~**tly** adv decentemente

decepti|on /dɪˈsepʃn/ n engaño m. ~**ve** /-tɪv/ adj engañoso

decibel /ˈdesɪbel/ n decibel(io) m

decide /dɪˈsaɪd/ vt/i decidir. ~**d** adj resuelto; (unquestionable) indudable

decimal /ˈdesɪml/ adj & n decimal (m). ~ **point** n coma f (decimal), punto m decimal

decipher /dɪˈsaɪfə(r)/ vt descifrar

decis|ion /dɪˈsɪʒn/ n decisión f. ~**ive** /dɪˈsaɪsɪv/ adj decisivo; (manner) decidido

deck /dek/ n (Naut) cubierta f; (Amer, of cards) baraja f; (of bus) piso m. •vt adornar. ~**chair** n tumbona f, silla f de playa

declar|ation /dekləˈreɪʃn/ n declaración f. ~**e** /dɪˈkleə(r)/ vt declarar

decline /dɪˈklaɪn/ vt rehusar; (Gram) declinar. •vi disminuir; (deteriorate) deteriorarse. •n decadencia f; (decrease) disminución f

decode /diːˈkəʊd/ vt descifrar

decompose /diːkəmˈpəʊz/ vi descomponerse

décor /ˈdeɪkɔː(r)/ n decoración f

decorat|e /ˈdekəreɪt/ vt adornar, decorar (LAm); empapelar y pintar (room). ~**ion** /-ˈreɪʃn/ n (act) decoración f; (ornament) adorno m. ~**ive** /-ətɪv/ adj decorativo. ~**or** n pintor m decorador

decoy /ˈdiːkɔɪ/ n señuelo m. •/dɪˈkɔɪ/ vt atraer con señuelo

decrease /dɪˈkriːs/ vt/i disminuir. •/ˈdiːkriːs/ n disminución f

decree /dɪˈkriː/ n decreto m. •vt decretar

decrepit /dɪˈkrepɪt/ adj decrépito

decriminalize /diːˈkrɪmɪnəlaɪz/ vt despenalizar

dedicat|e /ˈdedɪkeɪt/ vt dedicar. ~**ion** /-ˈkeɪʃn/ n dedicación f

deduce /dɪˈdjuːs/ vt deducir

deduct /dɪˈdʌkt/ vt deducir. ~**ion** /-ʃn/ n deducción f

deed /diːd/ n hecho m; (Jurid) escritura f

deem /diːm/ vt juzgar, considerar

deep /diːp/ adj (**-er**, **-est**) adv profundo. •adv profundamente. **be** ~ **in thought** estar absorto en sus pensamientos. ~**en** vt hacer más profundo. •vi hacerse más profundo. ~**freeze** n congelador m, freezer m (LAm). ~**ly** adv profundamente

deer /dɪə(r)/ n invar ciervo m

deface /dɪˈfeɪs/ vt desfigurar

default /dɪˈfɔːlt/ vi faltar. •n opción por defecto. **by** ~ en rebeldía

defeat /dɪˈfiːt/ vt vencer; (frustrate) frustrar. •n derrota f. ~**ism** n derrotismo m. ~**ist** adj & n derrotista (m & f)

defect /ˈdiːfekt/ n defecto m.

•/dɪˈfekt/ vi desertar. ~ **to** pasar a. ~**ion** /dɪˈfekʃn/ n (Pol) defección f. ~**ive** /dɪˈfektɪv/ adj defectuoso

defence /dɪˈfens/ n defensa f. ~**less** adj indefenso

defen|d /dɪˈfend/ vt defender. ~**dant** n (Jurid) acusado m. ~**sive** /-sɪv/ adj defensivo. • n defensiva f

defer /dɪˈfɜː(r)/ vt (pt **deferred**) aplazar. ~**ence** /ˈdefərəns/ n deferencia f. ~**ential** /defəˈrenʃl/ adj deferente

defian|ce /dɪˈfaɪəns/ n desafío m. **in ~ce of** a despecho de. ~**t** adj desafiante. ~**tly** adv con actitud desafiante

deficien|cy /dɪˈfɪʃənsɪ/ n falta f. ~**t** adj deficiente. **be ~t in** carecer de

deficit /ˈdefɪsɪt/ n déficit m

define /dɪˈfaɪn/ vt definir

definite /ˈdefɪnɪt/ adj (final) definitivo; (certain) seguro; (clear) claro; (firm) firme. ~**ly** adv seguramente; (definitively) definitivamente

definition /defɪˈnɪʃn/ n definición f

definitive /dɪˈfɪnɪtɪv/ adj definitivo

deflate /dɪˈfleɪt/ vt desinflar. • vi desinflarse

deflect /dɪˈflekt/ vt desviar

deform /dɪˈfɔːm/ vt deformar. ~**ed** adj deforme. ~**ity** n deformidad f

defrost /diːˈfrɒst/ vt descongelar. • vi descongelarse

deft /deft/ adj (**-er**, **-est**) hábil. ~**ly** adv hábilmente f

defuse /diːˈfjuːz/ vt desactivar (bomb); (fig) calmar

defy /dɪˈfaɪ/ vt desafiar

degenerate /dɪˈdʒenəreɪt/ vi degenerar. •/dɪˈdʒenərət/ adj & n degenerado (m)

degrad|ation /degrəˈdeɪʃn/ n degradación f. ~**e** /dɪˈgreɪd/ vt degradar

degree /dɪˈgriː/ n grado m; (Univ) licenciatura f; (rank) rango m. **to a**

certain ~ hasta cierto punto

deign /deɪn/ vi. ~ **to** dignarse

deity /ˈdiːɪtɪ/ n deidad f

deject|ed /dɪˈdʒektɪd/ adj desanimado. ~**ion** /-ʃn/ n abatimiento m

delay /dɪˈleɪ/ vt retrasar, demorar (LAm). • vi tardar, demorar (LAm). • n retraso m, demora f (LAm)

delegat|e /ˈdelɪgeɪt/ vt/i delegar. •/ˈdelɪgət/ n delegado m. ~**ion** /-ˈgeɪʃn/ n delegación f

delet|e /dɪˈliːt/ vt tachar. ~**ion** /-ʃn/ n supresión f

deliberat|e /dɪˈlɪbəreɪt/ vt/i deliberar. •/dɪˈlɪbərət/ adj intencionado; (steps etc) pausado. ~**ely** adv a propósito. ~**ion** /-ˈreɪʃn/ n deliberación f

delica|cy /ˈdelɪkəsɪ/ n delicadeza f; (food) manjar m. ~**te** /ˈdelɪkət/ adj delicado

delicatessen /delɪkəˈtesn/ n charcutería f, salchichonería f (Mex)

delicious /dɪˈlɪʃəs/ adj delicioso

delight /dɪˈlaɪt/ n placer m. • vt encantar. • vi deleitarse. ~**ed** adj encantado. ~**ful** adj delicioso

deliri|ous /dɪˈlɪrɪəs/ adj delirante. ~**um** /-əm/ n delirio m

deliver /dɪˈlɪvə(r)/ vt entregar; (distribute) repartir; (aim) lanzar; (Med) he ~**ed the baby** la asistió en el parto. ~**ance** n liberación f. ~**y** n entrega f; (of post) reparto m; (Med) parto m

delta /ˈdeltə/ n (of river) delta m

delude /dɪˈluːd/ vt engañar. ~ **o.s.** engañarse

deluge /ˈdeljuːdʒ/ n diluvio m

delusion /dɪˈluːʒn/ n ilusión f

deluxe /dɪˈlʌks/ adj de lujo

delve /delv/ vi hurgar. ~ **into** (investigate) ahondar en

demand /dɪˈmɑːnd/ vt exigir. • n petición f, pedido m (LAm); (claim) exigencia f; (Com) demanda f. **in ~** muy popular, muy solicitado. **on ~** a solicitud. **~ing** adj exigente. **~s** npl exigencias fpl

demented /dɪˈmentɪd/ adj demente

demo /ˈdeməʊ/ n (pl **-os**) ⊞ manifestación f

democra|cy /dɪˈmɒkrəsɪ/ n democracia f. **~t** /ˈdeməkræt/ n demócrata m & f. **D~t** adj & n (in US) demócrata (m & f). **~tic** /deməˈkrætɪk/ adj democrático

demoli|sh /dɪˈmɒlɪʃ/ vt derribar. **~tion** /deməˈlɪʃn/ n demolición f

demon /ˈdiːmən/ n demonio m

demonstrat|e /ˈdemənstreɪt/ vt demostrar. • vi manifestarse, hacer una manifestación. **~ion** /-ˈstreɪʃn/ n demostración f; (Pol) manifestación f. **~or** /ˈdemənstreɪtə(r)/n (Pol) manifestante m & f; (marketing) demostrador m

demoralize /dɪˈmɒrəlaɪz/ vt desmoralizar

demote /dɪˈməʊt/ vt bajar de categoría

demure /dɪˈmjʊə(r)/ adj recatado

den /den/ n (of animal) guarida f, madriguera f

denial /dɪˈnaɪəl/ n denegación f; (statement) desmentimiento m

denim /ˈdenɪm/ n tela f vaquera or de jeans, mezclilla (Mex) f. **~s** npl vaqueros mpl, jeans mpl, tejanos mpl, pantalones mpl de mezclilla (Mex)

Denmark /ˈdenmɑːk/ n Dinamarca f

denote /dɪˈnəʊt/ vt denotar

denounce /dɪˈnaʊns/ vt denunciar

dens|e /dens/ adj (**-er, -est**) espeso; (person) torpe. **~ely** adv densamente. **~ity** n densidad f

dent /dent/ n abolladura f. • vt abollar

dental /ˈdentl/ adj dental. **~ floss** /flɒs/ n hilo m or seda f dental. **~ surgeon** n dentista m & f

dentist /ˈdentɪst/ n dentista m & f. **~ry** n odontología f

dentures /ˈdentʃəz/ npl dentadura f postiza

deny /dɪˈnaɪ/ vt negar; desmentir (rumour); denegar (request)

deodorant /dɪˈəʊdərənt/ adj & n desodorante (m)

depart /dɪˈpɑːt/ vi partir, salir. **~ from** (deviate from) apartarse de

department /dɪˈpɑːtmənt/ n departamento m; (Pol) ministerio m, secretaría f (Mex). **~ store** n grandes almacenes mpl, tienda f de departamentos (Mex)

departure /dɪˈpɑːtʃə(r)/ n partida f; (of train etc) salida f

depend /dɪˈpend/ vi depender. **~ on** depender de. **~able** adj digno de confianza. **~ant** /dɪˈpendənt/ n familiar m & f dependiente. **~ence** n dependencia f. **~ent** adj dependiente. **be ~ent on** depender de

depict /dɪˈpɪkt/ vt representar; (in words) describir

deplete /dɪˈpliːt/ vt agotar

deplor|able /dɪˈplɔːrəbl/ adj deplorable. **~e** /dɪˈplɔː(r)/ vt deplorar

deploy /dɪˈplɔɪ/ vt desplegar

deport /dɪˈpɔːt/ vt deportar. **~ation** /-ˈteɪʃn/ n deportación f

depose /dɪˈpəʊz/ vt deponer

deposit /dɪˈpɒzɪt/ vt (pt **deposited**) depositar. • n depósito m

depot /ˈdepəʊ/ n depósito m; (Amer) estación f de autobuses

deprav|ed /dɪˈpreɪvd/ adj depravado. **~ity** /dɪˈprævətɪ/ n depravación f

depress /dɪˈpres/ vt deprimir; (press down) apretar. **~ed** adj deprimido. **~ing** adj deprimente. **~ion** /-ʃn/ n depresión f

depriv|ation /deprɪˈveɪʃn/ n privación f. **~e** /dɪˈpraɪv/ vt. **~e of** privar de. **~d** adj carenciado

depth /depθ/ n profundidad f. **be out of one's ~** perder pie; (fig) meterse en honduras. **in ~** a fondo

deput|ize /'depjʊtaɪz/ vi. **~ize for** sustituir a. **~y** /'depjʊtɪ/ n sustituto m. **~y chairman** n vicepresidente m

derail /dɪ'reɪl/ vt hacer descarrilar. **~ment** n descarrilamiento m

derelict /'derəlɪkt/ adj abandonado y en ruinas

deri|de /dɪ'raɪd/ vt mofarse de. **~sion** /dɪ'rɪʒn/ n mofa t. **~sive** /dɪ'raɪsɪv/ adj burlón. **~sory** /dɪ'raɪsərɪ/ adj (offer etc) irrisorio

deriv|ation /derɪ'veɪʃn/ n derivación f. **~ative** /dɪ'rɪvətɪv/ n derivado m. **~e** /dɪ'raɪv/ vt/i derivar

derogatory /dɪ'rɒgətrɪ/ adj despectivo

descen|d /dɪ'send/ vt/i descender, bajar. **~dant** n descendiente m & f. **~t** n descenso m, bajada f; (lineage) ascendencia f

descri|be /dɪs'kraɪb/ vt describir. **~ption** /-'krɪpʃn/ n descripción f. **~ptive** /-'krɪptɪv/ adj descriptivo

desecrate /'desɪkreɪt/ vt profanar

desert[1] /dɪ'zɜːt/ vt abandonar. ●vi (Mil) desertar. **~er** /dɪ'zɜːtə(r)/ n desertor m

desert[2] /'dezət/ adj & n desierto (m)

deserts /dɪ'zɜːts/ npl lo merecido. **get one's just ~** llevarse su merecido

deserv|e /dɪ'zɜːv/ vt merecer. **~ing** adj (cause) meritorio

design /dɪ'zaɪn/ n diseño m; (plan) plan m. **~s** (intentions) propósitos mpl. ●vt diseñar; (plan) planear

designate /'dezɪgneɪt/ vt designar

designer /dɪ'zaɪnə(r)/ n diseñador m; (fashion ~) diseñador m de modas. ●adj (clothes) de diseño exclusivo

desirable /dɪ'zaɪərəbl/ adj deseable

desire /dɪ'zaɪə(r)/ n deseo m. ●vt desear

desk /desk/ n escritorio m; (at school) pupitre m; (in hotel) recepción f; (Com) caja f. **~top publishing** n autoedición f, edición f electrónica

desolat|e /'desələt/ adj desolado; (uninhabited) deshabitado. **~ion** /-'leɪʃn/ n desolación f

despair /dɪ'speə(r)/ n desesperación f. **be in ~** estar desesperado. ●vi. **~ of** desesperarse de

despatch /dɪ'spætʃ/ vt, n see DISPATCH

desperat|e /'despərət/ adj desesperado. **~ely** adv desesperadamente. **~ion** /-'reɪʃn/ n desesperación f

despicable /dɪ'spɪkəbl/ adj despreciable

despise /dɪ'spaɪz/ vt despreciar

despite /dɪ'spaɪt/ prep a pesar de

despondent /dɪ'spɒndənt/ adj abatido

despot /'despɒt/ n déspota m

dessert /dɪ'zɜːt/ n postre m. **~spoon** n cuchara f de postre

destination /destɪ'neɪʃn/ n destino m

destiny /'destɪnɪ/ n destino m

destitute /'destɪtjuːt/ adj indigente

destroy /dɪ'strɔɪ/ vt destruir. **~er** n destructor m

destructi|on /dɪ'strʌkʃn/ n destrucción f. **~ve** /-ɪv/ adj destructivo

desultory /'desəltrɪ/ adj desganado

detach /dɪ'tætʃ/ vt separar. **~able** adj separable. **~ed** adj (aloof) distante; (house) no adosado. **~ment** n desprendimiento m; (Mil) destacamento m; (aloofness) indiferencia f

detail /'diːteɪl/ n detalle m. **explain sth in ~** explicar algo detalladamente. ●vt detallar; (Mil) destacar. ~ed adj detallado

detain /dɪˈteɪn/ vt detener; (delay) retener. ~ee /diːteɪˈniː/ n detenido m

detect /dɪˈtekt/ vt percibir; (discover) descubrir. ~ive n (private) detective m; (in police) agente m & f. ~or n detector m

detention /dɪˈtenʃn/ n detención f

deter /dɪˈtɜː(r)/ vt (pt **deterred**) disuadir; (prevent) impedir

detergent /dɪˈtɜːdʒənt/ adj & n detergente (m)

deteriorat|e /dɪˈtɪərɪəreɪt/ vi deteriorarse. ~ion /-ˈreɪʃn/ n deterioro m

determin|ation /dɪtɜːmɪˈneɪʃn/ n determinación f. ~e /dɪˈtɜːmɪn/ vt determinar; (decide) decidir. ~ed adj determinado; (resolute) decidido

deterrent /dɪˈterənt/ n elemento m de disuasión

detest /dɪˈtest/ vt aborrecer. ~able adj odioso

detonat|e /ˈdetəneɪt/ vt hacer detonar. • vi detonar. ~ion /-ˈneɪʃn/ n detonación f. ~or n detonador m

detour /ˈdiːtʊə(r)/ n rodeo m; (Amer, of transport) desvío m, desviación f. • vt (Amer) desviar

detract /dɪˈtrækt/ vi. ~ **from** disminuir

detriment /ˈdetrɪmənt/ n. **to the** ~ **of** en perjuicio de. ~al /-ˈmentl/ adj perjudicial

devalue /diːˈvæljuː/ vt desvalorizar

devastat|e /ˈdevəsteɪt/ vt devastar. ~ing adj devastador; (fig) arrollador. ~ion /-ˈsteɪʃn/ n devastación f

develop /dɪˈveləp/ vt desarrollar; contraer (illness); urbanizar (land). • vi desarrollarse; (appear) surgir. ~ing adj (country) en vías de desarrollo. ~ment n desarrollo m. **(new)** ~ment novedad f

deviant /ˈdiːvɪənt/ adj desviado

deviat|e /ˈdiːvɪeɪt/ vi desviarse. ~ion /-ˈeɪʃn/ n desviación f

device /dɪˈvaɪs/ n dispositivo m; (scheme) estratagema f

devil /ˈdevl/ n diablo m

devious /ˈdiːvɪəs/ adj taimado

devise /dɪˈvaɪz/ vt idear

devoid /dɪˈvɔɪd/ adj. **be** ~ **of** carecer de

devolution /diːvəˈluːʃn/ n descentralización f; (of power) delegación f

devot|e /dɪˈvəʊt/ vt dedicar. ~ed adj (couple) unido; (service) leal. ~ee /devəˈtiː/ n partidario m. ~ion /-ʃn/ n devoción f

devour /dɪˈvaʊə(r)/ vt devorar

devout /dɪˈvaʊt/ adj devoto

dew /djuː/ n rocío m

dexterity /dekˈsterəti/ n destreza f

diabet|es /daɪəˈbiːtiːz/ n diabetes f. ~ic /-ˈbetɪk/ adj & n diabético (m)

diabolical /daɪəˈbɒlɪkl/ adj diabólico

diagnos|e /ˈdaɪəgnəʊz/ vt diagnosticar. ~is /-ˈnəʊsɪs/ n (pl **-oses**/-siːz/) diagnóstico m

diagonal /daɪˈægənl/ adj & n diagonal (f)

diagram /ˈdaɪəgræm/ n diagrama m

dial /ˈdaɪəl/ n cuadrante m; (on clock, watch) esfera f; (on phone) disco m. • vt (pt **dialled**) marcar, discar (LAm)

dialect /ˈdaɪəlekt/ n dialecto m

dialling:: ~ code n prefijo m, código m de la zona (LAm). ~ **tone** n tono m de marcar, tono m de discado (LAm)

dialogue /ˈdaɪəlɒg/ n diálogo m

dial tone n (Amer) see **DIALLING TONE**

diameter /daɪˈæmɪtə(r)/ n diámetro m

diamond /ˈdaɪəmənd/ n diamante m; (shape) rombo m. ~s npl (Cards) diamantes mpl

diaper /ˈdaɪəpə(r)/ n (Amer) pañal m

diaphragm /ˈdaɪəfræm/ n
diafragma m

diarrhoea /daɪəˈrɪə/ n diarrea f

diary /ˈdaɪərɪ/ n diario m; (book)
agenda f

dice /daɪs/ n invar dado m. •vt (Culin)
cortar en cubitos

dictat|e /dɪkˈteɪt/ vt/i dictar. ~**ion**
/dɪkˈteɪʃn/ n dictado m. ~**or** n
dictador m. ~**orshlp** n dictadura f

dictionary /ˈdɪkʃənərɪ/ n
diccionario m

did /dɪd/ see DO

didn't /ˈdɪdnt/ = **did not**

die /daɪ/ vi (pres p **dying**) morir. **be
dying to** morirse por. ■ ~ **down**
vi irse apagando. ■ ~ **out** vi
extinguirse

diesel /ˈdiːzl/ n (fuel) gasóleo m. ~
engine n motor m diesel

diet /ˈdaɪət/ n alimentación f;
(restricted) régimen m. **be on a** ~
estar a régimen. •vi estar a
régimen

differ /ˈdɪfə(r)/ vi ser distinto;
(disagree) no estar de acuerdo.
~**ence** /ˈdɪfrəns/ n diferencia f;
(disagreement) desacuerdo m. ~**ent**
/ˈdɪfrənt/ adj distinto, diferente.
~**ently** adv de otra manera

difficult /ˈdɪfɪkəlt/ adj difícil ~**y** n
dificultad f

diffus|e & /dɪˈfjuːs/ adj difuso.
•/dɪˈfjuːz/ vt difundir. •vi
difundirse. ~**ion** /-ʒn/ n difusión f

dig /dɪg/ n (poke) empujón m; (poke
with elbow) codazo m; (remark)
indirecta f. ~**s** npl 🔲 alojamiento
m •vt (pt **dug**, pres p **digging**) cavar;
(thrust) empujar. •vi cavar. ■ ~ **out**
vt extraer. ■ ~ **up** vt desenterrar

digest /ˈdaɪdʒest/ n resumen m.
•/daɪˈdʒest/ vt digerir. ~**ion**
/-ˈdʒestʃn/ n digestión f. ~**ive**
/-ˈdʒestɪv/ adj digestivo

digger /ˈdɪgə(r)/ n (Mec)
excavadora f

digit /ˈdɪdʒɪt/ n dígito m; (finger)

dedo m. ~**al** /ˈdɪdʒɪtl/ adj digital

dignified /ˈdɪgnɪfaɪd/ adj solemne

dignitary /ˈdɪgnɪtərɪ/ n
dignatario m

dignity /ˈdɪgnətɪ/ n dignidad f

digress /daɪˈgres/ vi divagar. ~
from apartarse de. ~**ion** /-ʃn/ n
digresión f

dike /daɪk/ n dique m

dilapidated /dɪˈlæpɪdeɪtɪd/ adj
ruinoso

dilate /daɪˈleɪt/ vt dilatar. •vi
dilatarse

dilemma /daɪˈlemə/ n dilema m

diligent /ˈdɪlɪdʒənt/ adj diligente

dilute /daɪˈljuːt/ vt diluir

dim /dɪm/ adj (**dimmer, dimmest**)
(light) débil; (room) oscuro; (fam,
stupid) torpe. •vt (pt **dimmed**)
atenuar. ~ **one's headlights**
(Amer) poner las (luces) cortas or
de cruce, poner las (luces) bajas
(LAm). •vi (light) irse atenuando

dime /daɪm/ n (Amer) moneda de
diez centavos

dlmension /daɪˈmenʃn/ n
dimensión f

diminish /dɪˈmɪnɪʃ/ vt/i disminuir

dimple /ˈdɪmpl/ n hoyuelo m

din /dɪn/ n jaleo m

dine /daɪn/ vi cenar. ~**r** n comensal
m & f; (Amer, restaurant) cafetería f

dinghy /ˈdɪŋgɪ/ n bote m; (inflatable)
bote n neumático

dingy /ˈdɪndʒɪ/ adj (**-ier, -iest**)
miserable, sucio

dinner /ˈdɪnə(r)/ n cena f, comida f
(LAm). **have** ~ cenar, comer (LAm).
~ **party** n cena f, comida f (LAm)

dinosaur /ˈdaɪnəsɔː(r)/ n
dinosaurio m

dint /dɪnt/ n. **by** ~ **of** a fuerza de

dip /dɪp/ vt (pt **dipped**) meter; (in
liquid) mojar. ~ **one's headlights**
poner las (luces) cortas or de
cruce, poner las (luces) bajas

(LAm). ●vi bajar. ●n (slope) inclinación f; (in sea) baño m. ■~ **into** vt hojear (book)

diphthong /'dɪfθɒŋ/ n diptongo m

diploma /dɪ'pləʊmə/ n diploma m

diploma|cy /dɪ'pləʊməsɪ/ n diplomacia f. ~**t** /'dɪpləmæt/ n diplomático m. ~**tic** /-'mætɪk/ adj diplomático

dipstick /'dɪpstɪk/ n (Auto) varilla f del nivel de aceite

dire /daɪə(r)/ adj (-er, -est) terrible; (need, poverty) extremo

direct /dɪ'rekt/ adj directo. ●adv directamente. ●vt dirigir; (show the way) indicar. ~**ion** /-ʃn/ n dirección f. ~**ions** npl instrucciones fpl. ~**ly** adv directamente; (at once) en seguida. ●conj 🆒 en cuanto. ~**or** n director m; (of company) directivo m

directory /dɪ'rektərɪ/ n guía f; (Comp) directorio m

dirt /dɜːt/ n suciedad f. ~**y** adj (-ier, -iest) sucio. ●vt ensuciar

disab|ility /dɪsə'bɪlətɪ/ n invalidez f. ~**le** /dɪs'eɪbl/ vt incapacitar. ~**led** adj minusválido

disadvantage /dɪsəd'vɑːntɪdʒ/ n desventaja f. ~**d** adj desfavorecido

disagree /dɪsə'griː/ vi no estar de acuerdo (**with** con). ~ **with** (food, climate) sentarle mal a. ~**able** adj desagradable. ~**ment** n desacuerdo m; (quarrel) riña f

disappear /dɪsə'pɪə(r)/ vi desaparecer. ~**ance** n desaparición f

disappoint /dɪsə'pɔɪnt/ vt decepcionar. ~**ing** adj decepcionante. ~**ment** n decepción f

disapprov|al /dɪsə'pruːvl/ n desaprobación f. ~**e** /dɪsə'pruːv/ vi. ~**e of** desaprobar. ~**ing** adj de reproche

disarm /dɪs'ɑːm/ vt desarmar. ●vi desarmarse. ~**ament** n desarme m

disarray /dɪsə'reɪ/ n desorden m

disast|er /dɪ'zɑːstə(r)/ n desastre m. ~**rous** /-strəs/ adj catastrófico

disband /dɪs'bænd/ vt disolver. ●vi disolverse

disbelief /dɪsbɪ'liːf/ n incredulidad f

disc /dɪsk/ n disco m

discard /dɪs'kɑːd/ vt descartar; abandonar (beliefs etc)

discern /dɪ'sɜːn/ vt percibir. ~**ing** adj exigente; (ear, eye) educado

discharge /dɪs'tʃɑːdʒ/ vt descargar; cumplir (duty); (Mil) licenciar. ●/'dɪstʃɑːdʒ/ n descarga f; (Med) secreción f; (Mil) licenciamiento m

disciple /dɪ'saɪpl/ n discípulo m

disciplin|ary /dɪsə'plɪnərɪ/ adj disciplinario. ~**e** /'dɪsɪplɪn/ n disciplina f. ●vt disciplinar; (punish) sancionar

disc jockey /'dɪskdʒɒkɪ/ n pinchadiscos m & f

disclaim /dɪs'kleɪm/ vt desconocer. ~**er** n (Jurid) descargo m de responsabilidad

disclos|e /dɪs'kləʊz/ vt revelar. ~**ure** /-ʒə(r)/ n revelación f

disco /'dɪskəʊ/ n (pl -os) 🆒 discoteca f

discolour /dɪs'kʌlə(r)/ vt decolorar. ●vi decolorarse

discomfort /dɪs'kʌmfət/ n malestar m; (lack of comfort) incomodidad f

disconcert /dɪskən'sɜːt/ vt desconcertar

disconnect /dɪskə'nekt/ vt separar; (Elec) desconectar

disconsolate /dɪs'kɒnsələt/ adj desconsolado

discontent /dɪskən'tent/ n descontento m. ~**ed** adj descontento

discontinue /dɪskən'tɪnjuː/ vt interrumpir

discord /'dɪskɔːd/ n discordia f; (Mus) disonancia f. ~**ant**

/-'skɔːdənt/ adj discorde; (Mus) disonante

discotheque /'dɪskətek/ n discoteca f

discount /'dɪskaʊnt/ n descuento m. ●/dɪs'kaʊnt/ vt hacer caso omiso de; (Com) descontar

discourag|e /dɪs'kʌrɪdʒ/ vt desanimar; (dissuade) disuadir. ~ing adj desalentador

discourteous /dɪs'kɜːtɪəs/ adj descortés

discover /dɪs'kʌvə(r)/ vt descubrir. ~y n descubrimiento m

discredit /dɪs'kredɪt/ vt (pt **discredited**) desacreditar. ●n descrédito m

discreet /dɪs'kriːt/ adj discreto. ~ly adv discretamente

discrepancy /dɪ'skrepənsɪ/ n discrepancia f

discretion /dɪ'skreʃn/ n discreción f

discriminat|e /dɪs'krɪmɪneɪt/ vt discriminar. ~e **between** distinguir entre. ~ing adj perspicaz. ~ion /-'neɪʃn/ n discernimiento m; (bias) discriminación f

discus /'dɪskəs/ n disco m

discuss /dɪ'skʌs/ vt discutir. ~ion /-ʃn/ n discusión f

disdain /dɪs'deɪn/ n desdén m. ~ful adj desdeñoso

disease /dɪ'ziːz/ n enfermedad f

disembark /dɪsɪm'bɑːk/ vi desembarcar

disenchant|ed /dɪsɪn'tʃɑːntɪd/ adj desilusionado. ~ment n desencanto m

disentangle /dɪsɪn'tæŋgl/ vt desenredar

disfigure /dɪs'fɪgə(r)/ vt desfigurar

disgrace /dɪs'greɪs/ n vergüenza f. ●vt deshonrar. ~ful adj vergonzoso

disgruntled /dɪs'grʌntld/ adj descontento

disguise /dɪs'gaɪz/ vt disfrazar. ●n disfraz m. **in** ~ disfrazado

disgust /dɪs'gʌst/ n repugnancia f, asco m. ●vt dar asco a. ~ed adj indignado; (stronger) asqueado. ~ing adj repugnante, asqueroso

dish /dɪʃ/ n plato m. **wash** or **do the** ~es fregar los platos, lavar los trastes (Mex). ■ ~ **up** vt/i servir. ~**cloth** n bayeta f

disheartening /dɪs'hɑːtnɪŋ/ adj desalentador

dishonest /dɪs'ɒnɪst/ adj deshonesto. ~y n falta f de honradez

dishonour /dɪs'ɒnə(r)/ n deshonra f

dish: ~ **soap** n (Amer) lavavajillas m. ~ **towel** n paño m de cocina. ~**washer** n lavaplatos m, lavavajillas m. ~**washing liquid** n (Amer) see ~ SOAP

disillusion /dɪsɪ'luːʒn/ vt desilusionar. ~ment n desilusión f

disinfect /dɪsɪn'fekt/ vt desinfectar. ~ant n desinfectante m

disintegrate /dɪs'ɪntɪgreɪt/ vt desintegrar. ●vi desintegrarse

disinterested /dɪs'ɪntrəstɪd/ adj desinteresado

disjointed /dɪs'dʒɔɪntɪd/ adj inconexo

disk /dɪsk/ n disco m. ~ **drive** (Comp) unidad f de discos. ~**ette** /dɪs'ket/ n disquete m

dislike /dɪs'laɪk/ n aversión f. ●vt. **I** ~ **dogs** no me gustan los perros

dislocate /'dɪsləkeɪt/ vt dislocar(se) (limb)

dislodge /dɪs'lɒdʒ/ vt sacar

disloyal /dɪs'lɔɪəl/ adj desleal. ~ty n deslealtad f

dismal /'dɪzməl/ adj triste; (bad) fatal

dismantle /dɪs'mæntl/ vt desmontar

dismay /dɪs'meɪ/ n consternación f. ●vt consternar

dismiss /dɪs'mɪs/ vt despedir; (reject) rechazar. ~**al** n despido m; (of idea) rechazo m

dismount /dɪs'maʊnt/ vi desmontar

disobe|dience /dɪsə'biːdɪəns/ n desobediencia f. ~**dient** adj desobediente. ~**y** /dɪsə'beɪ/ vt/i desobedecer

disorder /dɪs'ɔːdə(r)/ n desorden m; (ailment) afección f. ~**ly** adj desordenado

disorganized /dɪs'ɔːgənaɪzd/ adj desorganizado

disorientate /dɪs'ɔːrɪənteɪt/ vt desorientar

disown /dɪs'əʊn/ vt repudiar

disparaging /dɪs'pærɪdʒɪŋ/ adj despreciativo

dispatch /dɪs'pætʃ/ vt despachar. ●n despacho m. ~ **rider** n mensajero m

dispel /dɪs'pel/ vt (pt **dispelled**) disipar

dispens|able /dɪs'pensəbl/ adj prescindible. ~**e** vt distribuir; (Med) preparar. ∎~ **with** vt prescindir de

dispers|al /dɪ'spɜːsl/ n dispersión f. ~**e** /dɪ'spɜːs/ vt dispersar. ●vi dispersarse

dispirited /dɪs'pɪrɪtɪd/ adj desanimado

display /dɪs'pleɪ/ vt exponer (goods); demostrar (feelings). ●n exposición f; (of feelings) demostración f

displeas|e /dɪs'pliːz/ vt desagradar. **be ~ed with** estar disgustado con. ~**ure** /-'pleʒə(r)/ n desagrado m

dispos|able /dɪs'pəʊzəbl/ adj desechable. ~**al** /dɪs'pəʊzl/ n (of waste) eliminación f. **at s.o.'s ~al** a la disposición de uno. ~**e of** /dɪs'pəʊz/ vt deshacerse de

disproportionate /dɪsprə'pɔːʃənət/ adj desproporcionado

disprove /dɪs'pruːv/ vt desmentir (claim); refutar (theory)

dispute /dɪs'pjuːt/ vt discutir. ●n disputa f. **in ~** disputado

disqualif|ication /dɪskwɒlɪfɪ'keɪʃn/ n descalificación f. ~**y** /dɪs'kwɒlɪfaɪ/ vt incapacitar; (Sport) descalificar

disregard /dɪsrɪ'gɑːd/ vt no hacer caso de. ●n indiferencia f (**for** a)

disreputable /dɪs'repjʊtəbl/ adj de mala fama

disrespect /dɪsrɪ'spekt/ n falta f de respeto

disrupt /dɪs'rʌpt/ vt interrumpir; trastornar (plans). ~**ion** /-ʃn/ n trastorno m. ~**ive** adj (influence) perjudicial, negativo

dissatis|faction /dɪsætɪs'fækʃn/ n descontento m. ~**fied** /dɪ'sætɪsfaɪd/ adj descontento

dissect /dɪ'sekt/ vt disecar

dissent /dɪ'sent/ vi disentir. ●n disentimiento m

dissertation /dɪsə'teɪʃn/ n (Univ) tesis f

dissident /'dɪsɪdənt/ adj & n disidente (m & f)

dissimilar /dɪ'sɪmɪlə(r)/ adj distinto

dissolute /'dɪsəluːt/ adj disoluto

dissolve /dɪ'zɒlv/ vt disolver. ●vi disolverse

dissuade /dɪ'sweɪd/ vt disuadir

distan|ce /'dɪstəns/ n distancia f. **from a ~ce** desde lejos. **in the ~ce** a lo lejos. ~**t** adj distante, lejano; (aloof) distante

distaste /dɪs'teɪst/ n desagrado m. ~**ful** adj desagradable

distil /dɪs'tɪl/ vt (pt **distilled**) destilar. ~**lery** /dɪs'tɪləri/ n destilería f

distinct /dɪs'tɪŋkt/ adj distinto; (clear) claro; (marked) marcado. ~**ion** /-ʃn/ n distinción f; (in exam)

sobresaliente m. ~**ive** adj
distintivo

distinguish /dɪsˈtɪŋgwɪʃ/ vt/i
distinguir. ~**ed** adj distinguido

distort /dɪsˈtɔːt/ vt torcer. ~**ion**
/-ʃn/ n deformación f

distract /dɪsˈtrækt/ vt distraer.
~**ed** adj distraído. ~**ion** /-ʃn/ n
distracción f; (confusion)
aturdimiento m

distraught /dɪsˈtrɔːt/ adj
consternado, angustiado

distress /dɪsˈtres/ n angustia f. • vt
afligir. ~**ed** adj afligido. ~**ing** adj
penoso

distribut|e /dɪˈstrɪbjuːt/ vt repartir,
distribuir. ~**ion** /-ˈbjuːʃn/ n
distribución f. ~**or** n distribuidor
m; (Auto) distribuidor m (del
encendido)

district /ˈdɪstrɪkt/ n zona f, región f;
(of town) barrio m

distrust /dɪsˈtrʌst/ n desconfianza
f. • vt desconfiar de

disturb /dɪsˈtɜːb/ vt molestar;
(perturb) inquietar; (move)
desordenar; (interrupt) interrumpir.
~**ance** n disturbio m; (tumult)
alboroto m. ~**ed** adj trastornado.
~**ing** adj inquietante

disused /dɪsˈjuːzd/ adj fuera de uso

ditch /dɪtʃ/ n zanja f; (for irrigation)
acequia f. • vt 🔲 abandonar

dither /ˈdɪðə(r)/ vi vacilar

ditto /ˈdɪtəʊ/ adv ídem

divan /dɪˈvæn/ n diván m

dive /daɪv/ vi tirarse (al agua),
zambullirse; (rush) meterse
(precipitadamente). • n (into water)
zambullida f; (Sport) salto m (de
trampolín); (of plane) descenso m
en picado, descenso m en picada
(LAm); (🔲, place) antro m. ~**r** n
saltador m; (underwater) buzo m

diverge /daɪˈvɜːdʒ/ vi divergir. ~**nt**
adj divergente

divers|e /daɪˈvɜːs/ adj diverso. ~**ify**
vt diversificar. ~**ity** n diversidad f

diver|sion /daɪˈvɜːʃn/ n desvío m;
desviación f; (distraction) diversión f.
~**t** /daɪˈvɜːt/ vt desviar; (entertain)
divertir

divide /dɪˈvaɪd/ vt dividir. • vi
dividirse. ~**d highway** n (Amer)
autovía f, carretera f de doble
pista

dividend /ˈdɪvɪdend/ n dividendo m

divine /dɪˈvaɪn/ adj divino

division /dɪˈvɪʒn/ n división f

divorce /dɪˈvɔːs/ n divorcio m. • vt
divorciarse de. **get** ~**d**
divorciarse. • vi divorciarse. ~**e**
/dɪvɔːˈsiː/ n divorciado m

divulge /daɪˈvʌldʒ/ vt divulgar

DIY abbr see **DO-IT-YOURSELF**

dizz|iness /ˈdɪzɪnɪs/ n vértigo m.
~**y** adj (**-ier, -iest**) mareado. **be** or
feel ~**y** marearse

DJ abbr see **DISC JOCKEY**

do /duː//də, də/

3rd person singular present **does**;
past **did**;
past participle **done**

• transitive verb

⋯▸ hacer. **he does what he
wants** hace lo que quiere. **to do
one's homework** hacer los
deberes. **to do the cooking**
preparar la comida, cocinar. **well
done!** ¡muy bien!

⋯▸ (clean) lavar (dishes). limpiar
(windows)

⋯▸ (as job) **what does he do?**
¿en qué trabaja?

⋯▸ (swindle) estafar. **I've been
done!** ¡me han estafado!

⋯▸ (achieve) **she's done it!** ¡lo ha
logrado!

• intransitive verb

⋯▸ hacer. **do as you're told!**
¡haz lo que se te dice!

⋯▸ (fare) **how are you doing?**
(with a task) ¿qué tal te va? **how
do you do?**, (as greeting) mucho
gusto, encantado

····▸ (perform) **she did well/badly** le fue bien/mal

····▸ (be suitable) **will this do?** ¿esto sirve?

····▸ (be enough) ser suficiente, bastar. **one box will do** con una caja basta, con una caja es suficiente

● auxiliary verb

····▸ (to form interrogative and negative) **do you speak Spanish?** ¿hablas español?. **I don't want to** no quiero. **don't shut the door** no cierres la puerta

····▸ (in tag questions) **you eat meat, don't you?** ¿comes carne, ¿verdad? or ¿no?. **he lives in London, doesn't he?** vive en Londres, ¿no? or ¿verdad? or ¿no es cierto?

····▸ (in short answers) **do you like it? - yes, I do** ¿te gusta? - sí. **who wrote it? - I did** ¿quién lo escribió? - yo

····▸ (emphasizing) **do come in!** ¡pase Ud!. **you do exaggerate!** ¡cómo exageras! ■ **do away with** vt abolir. ■ **do in** vt (sl, kill) eliminar. ■ **do up** vt abrochar (coat etc); arreglar (house). ■ **do with** (need) (with can, could) necesitar; (expressing connection) **it has nothing to do with that** no tiene nada que ver con eso. ■ **do without** vt prescindir de

docile /ˈdəʊsaɪl/ adj dócil

dock /dɒk/ n (Naut) dársena f; (wharf, quay) muelle m; (Jurid) banquillo m de los acusados. **~s** npl (port) puerto m. ● vt cortar (tail); atracar (ship). ● vi (ship) atracar. **~er** n estibador m. **~yard** n astillero m

doctor /ˈdɒktə(r)/ n médico m, doctor m

doctrine /ˈdɒktrɪn/ n doctrina f

document /ˈdɒkjʊmənt/ n documento m. **~ary** /-ˈmentrɪ/ adj & n documental (m)

dodge|e /dɒdʒ/ vt esquivar. ● vi esquivarse. ● n treta f. **~ems** /ˈdɒdʒəmz/ npl autos mpl de choque.

~y adj (-ier, -iest) (awkward) difícil

doe /dəʊ/ n (rabbit) coneja f; (hare) liebre f hembra; (deer) cierva f

does /dʌz/ see **DO**

doesn't /ˈdʌznt/ = **does not**

dog /dɒg/ n perro m. ● vt (pt **dogged**) perseguir

dogged /ˈdɒgɪd/ adj obstinado

doghouse /ˈdɒghaʊs/ n (Amer) casa f del perro. **in the ~** 𝕋 en desgracia

dogma /ˈdɒgmə/ n dogma m. **~tic** /-ˈmætɪk/ adj dogmático

do|ings npl actividades fpl. **~-it-yourself** /duːɪtjɔːˈself/ n bricolaje m

dole /dəʊl/ n subsidio m de paro, subsidio m de desempleo. **on the ~** 𝕋 parado, desempleado. ■ **~ out** vt distribuir

doleful /ˈdəʊlfl/ adj triste

doll /dɒl/ n muñeca f

dollar /ˈdɒlə(r)/ n dólar m

dollarization /dɒləraɪˈzeɪʃn/ n dolarización f

dollop /ˈdɒləp/ n 𝕋 porción f

dolphin /ˈdɒlfɪn/ n delfín m

domain /dəʊˈmeɪn/ n dominio m

dome /dəʊm/ n cúpula f

domestic /dəˈmestɪk/ adj doméstico; (trade, flights, etc) nacional. **~ated** /dəˈmestɪkeɪtɪd/ adj (animal) domesticado. **~ science** n economía f doméstica

domin|ance /ˈdɒmɪnəns/ n dominio m. **~ant** adj dominante. **~ate** /-eɪt/ vt/i dominar. **~ation** /-ˈneɪʃn/ n dominación f. **~eering** adj dominante

Dominican Republic /dəˈmɪnɪkən/ n República f Dominicana

dominion /dəˈmɪnjən/ n dominio m

domino /ˈdɒmɪnəʊ/ n (pl **-oes**) ficha f de dominó. **~es** npl (game) dominó m

donat|e /dəʊˈneɪt/ vt donar. **~ion**

/-ʃn/ n donativo m, donación f

done /dʌn/ see **DO**

donkey /'dɒŋkɪ/ n burro m, asno m. **~'s years** 🎏 siglos mpl

donor /'dəʊnə(r)/ n donante m & f

don't /dəʊnt/ = **do not**

doodle /'duːdl/ vi/t garrapatear

doom /duːm/ n destino m; (death) muerte f. ●vt. **be ~ed to** estar condenado a

door /dɔː(r)/ n puerta f. **~bell** n timbre m. **~knob** n pomo m (de la puerta). **~mat** n felpudo m. **~step** n peldaño m. **~way** n entrada f

dope /dəʊp/ n 🎏 droga f; (sl, idiot) imbécil m. ●vt 🎏 drogar

dormant /'dɔːmənt/ adj aletargado, (volcano) inactivo

dormice /'dɔːmaɪs/ see **DORMOUSE**

dormitory /'dɔːmɪtrɪ/ n dormitorio m

dormouse /'dɔːmaʊs/ n (pl **-mice**) lirón m

DOS /dɒs/ abbr (= **disc-operating system**) DOS m

dos|age /'dəʊsɪdʒ/ n dosis f. **~e** /dəʊs/ n dosis f

dot /dɒt/ n punto m. **on the ~** en punto. **~com** n punto m com. **~-com company** empresa f puntocom

dote /dəʊt/ vi. **~ on** adorar

dotty /'dɒtɪ/ adj (**-ier, -iest**) 🎏 chiflado

double /'dʌbl/ adj doble. ●adv el doble. ●n doble m; (person) doble m & f. **at the ~** corriendo. ●vt doblar; redoblar (efforts etc). ●vi doblarse. **~ bass** /beɪs/ n contrabajo m. **~ bed** n cama f de matrimonio, cama f de doa plazas (LAm). **~ chin** n papada f. **~ click** vt hacer doble clic en. **~-cross** /-'krɒs/ vt traicionar. **~-decker** /-'dekə(r)/ n autobús m de dos pisos. **~ Dutch** n 🎏 chino m. **~ glazing** /-'gleɪzɪŋ/ n doble ventana

f. **~s** npl (tennis) dobles mpl

doubly /'dʌblɪ/ adv doblemente

doubt /daʊt/ n duda f. ●vt dudar; (distrust) dudar de. **~ful** adj dudoso. **~less** adv sin duda

dough /dəʊ/ n masa f; (sl, money) pasta f 🔳, lana f (LAm fam). **~nut** n donut m, dona f (Mex)

dove /dʌv/ n paloma f

down /daʊn/ adv abajo. **~ with** abajo. **come ~** bajar. **go ~** bajar; (sun) ponerse. ●prep abajo. ●adj 🎏 deprimido. ●vt derribar; (fam, drink) beber. ●n (feathers) plumón m. **~ and out** adj en la miseria. **~cast** adj abatido. **~fall** n perdición f; (of king, dictator) caída f. **~-hearted** /-'hɑːtɪd/ adj abatido. **~hill** /-'hɪl/ adv cuesta abajo. **~load** /-'ləʊd/ vt (Comp) bajar. **~market** /-'mɑːkɪt/ adj (newspaper) popular; (store) barato. **~ payment** n depósito m. **~pour** n aguacero m. **~right** adj completo. ●adv completamente. **~s** npl colinas fpl. **~stairs** /-'steəz/ adv abajo. ●/-'steəz/ adj de abajo. **~stream** adv río abajo. **~-to-earth** /-tʊ'ɜːθ/ adj práctico. **~town** /-'taʊn/ n centro m (de la ciudad). ●adv. **go ~town** ir al centro. **~under** adv en las antípodas; (in Australia) en Australia. **~ward** /-wəd/ adj & adv, **~wards** adv hacia abajo

dowry /'daʊərɪ/ n dote f

doze /dəʊz/ vi dormitar

dozen /'dʌzn/ n docena f. **a ~ eggs** una docena de huevos. **~s of** 🎏 miles de, muchos

Dr /'dɒktə(r)/ abbr (**Doctor**)

drab /dræb/ adj monótono

draft /drɑːft/ n borrador m; (Com) letra f de cambio; (Amer, Mil) reclutamiento m; (Amer, of air) corriente f de aire. ●vt redactar el borrador de; (Amer, conscript) reclutar

drag /dræg/ vt (pt **dragged**) arrastrar. ●n 🎏 lata f

dragon /'drægən/ n dragón m. **~fly** n libélula f

drain /dreɪn/ vt vaciar (tank, glass); drenar (land); (fig) agotar. •vi escurrirse. •n (pipe) sumidero m, resumidero m (LAm); (plughole) desagüe m. **~board** (Amer), **~ing board** n escurridero m

drama /'drɑːmə/ n drama m; (art) arte m teatral. **~tic** /drə'mætɪk/ adj dramático. **~tist** /'dræmətɪst/ n dramaturgo m. **~tize** /'dræmətaɪz/ vt adaptar al teatro; (fig) dramatizar

drank /dræŋk/ see DRINK

drape /dreɪp/ vt cubrir; (hang) colgar. **~s** npl (Amer) cortinas fpl

drastic /'dræstɪk/ adj drástico

draught /drɑːft/ n corriente f de aire. **~ beer** n cerveza f de barril. **~s** npl (game) juego m de damas fpl. **~y** adj lleno de corrientes de aire

draw /drɔː/ vt (pt **drew**, pp **drawn**) tirar; (attract) atraer; dibujar (picture); trazar (line). **~ the line** trazar el límite. •vi (Art) dibujar; (Sport) empatar. **~ near** acercarse. •n (Sport) empate m; (in lottery) sorteo m. ■ **~ in** vi (days) acortarse. ■ **~ out** vt sacar (money). ■ **~ up** vi pararse. vt redactar (document); acercar (chair). **~back** n desventaja f. **~bridge** n puente m levadizo

drawer /drɔː(r)/ n cajón m, gaveta f (Mex). **~s** npl calzones mpl

drawing /'drɔːɪŋ/ n dibujo m. **~ pin** n tachuela f, chincheta f, chinche f. **~ room** n salón m

drawl /drɔːl/ n habla f lenta

drawn /drɔːn/ see DRAW

dread /dred/ n terror m. •vt temer. **~ful** adj terrible. **~fully** adv terriblemente

dream /driːm/ n sueño m. •vt/i (pt **dreamed** or **dreamt** /dremt/) soñar. ■ **~ up** vt idear. adj ideal. **~er** n soñador m

dreary /'drɪərɪ/ adj (-ier, -iest) triste; (boring) monótono

dredge /dredʒ/ n draga f. •vt dragar. **~r** n draga f

dregs /dregz/ npl posos mpl, heces fpl; (fig) hez f

drench /drentʃ/ vt empapar

dress /dres/ n vestido m; (clothing) ropa f. •vt vestir; (decorate) adornar; (Med) vendar. •vi vestirse. ■ **~ up** vi ponerse elegante. **~ up as** disfrazarse de. **~ circle** n primer palco m

dressing /'dresɪŋ/ n (sauce) aliño m; (bandage) vendaje m. **~-down** /-'daun/ n rapapolvo m, reprensión f. **~ gown** n bata f. **~ room** n vestidor m; (in theatre) camarín m. **~ table** n tocador m

dress: ~maker n modista m & f. **~making** n costura f. **~ rehearsal** n ensayo m general

drew /druː/ see DRAW

dribble /'drɪbl/ vi (baby) babear; (in football) driblar, driblear

drie|d /draɪd/ adj (food) seco; (milk) en polvo. **~r** /'draɪə(r)/ n secador m

drift /drɪft/ vi ir a la deriva; (snow) amontonarse. •n (movement) dirección f; (of snow) montón m

drill /drɪl/ n (tool) taladro m; (of dentist) torno m; (training) ejercicio m. •vt taladrar, perforar; (train) entrenar. •vi entrenarse

drink /drɪŋk/ vt/i (pt **drank**, pp **drunk**) beber, tomar (LAm). •n bebida f. **~able** adj bebible; (water) potable. **~er** n bebedor m. **~ing water** n agua f potable

drip /drɪp/ vi (pt **dripped**) gotear. •n gota f; (Med) goteo m intravenoso; (fam, person) soso m. **~-dry** /-'draɪ/ adj de lava y pon. **~ping** adj. **be ~ping wet** estar chorreando

drive /draɪv/ vt (pt **drove**, pp **driven**) conducir, manejar (LAm) (car etc). **~ s.o. mad** volver loco a uno. **~ s.o. to do sth** llevar a uno a hacer algo. •vi conducir, manejar (LAm). **~ at** querer decir. **~ in** (in car) entrar en coche. •n paseo m;

(road) calle f; (private road) camino m de entrada; (fig) empuje m. **~r** n conductor m, chofer m (LAm). **~r's license** n (Amer) see **DRIVING LICENSE**

drivel /'drɪvl/ n tonterías fpl

driving /'draɪvɪŋ/ n conducción f. **~ licence** n permiso m de conducir, licencia f de conducción (LAm), licencia f (de manejar) (Mex). **~ test** n examen m de conducir, examen m de manejar (LAm)

drizzle /'drɪzl/ n llovizna f. •vi lloviznar

drone /drəʊn/ n zumbido m. •vi zumbar

drool /druːl/ vi babear

droop /druːp/ vi inclinarse; (flowers) marchitarse

drop /drɒp/ n gota f; (fall) caída f; (decrease) descenso m. •vt (pt dropped) dejar caer; (lower) bajar. •vi caer. ∎ **~ in on** vt pasar por casa de. ∎ **~ off** vi (sleep) dormirse. ∎ **~ out** vi retirarse; (student) abandonar los estudios. **~out** n marginado m

drought /draʊt/ n sequía f

drove /drəʊv/ see **DRIVE**. •n manada f

drown /draʊn/ vt ahogar. •vi ahogarse

drowsy /'draʊzɪ/ adj soñoliento

drudgery /'drʌdʒərɪ/ n trabajo m pesado

drug /drʌg/ n droga f; (Med) medicamento m. •vt (pt drugged) drogar. **~ addict** n drogadicto m. **~gist** n (Amer) farmacéutico m. **~store** n (Amer) farmacia f (que vende otros artículos también)

drum /drʌm/ n tambor m; (for oil) bidón m. •vi (pt drummed) tocar el tambor. •vt. **~ sth into s.o.** hacerle aprender algo a uno a fuerza de repetírselo. **~mer** n tambor m; (in group) batería f. **~s** npl batería f. **~stick** n baqueta f; (Culin) muslo m

drunk /drʌŋk/ see **DRINK**. •adj borracho. **get ~** emborracharse. •n borracho m. **~ard** /-əd/ n borracho m. **~en** adj borracho

dry /draɪ/ adj (drier, driest) seco. •vt secar. •vi secarse. ∎ **~ up** vi (stream) secarse; (funds) agotarse. **~-clean** vt limpiar en seco. **~-cleaner's** tintorería f. **~er** n see **DRIER**

DTD abbrev **Document Type Definition** DTD m

dual /'djuːəl/ adj doble. **~ carriageway** n autovía f, carretera f de doble pista

dub /dʌb/ vt (pt dubbed) doblar (film)

dubious /'djuːbɪəs/ adj dudoso; (person) sospechoso

duchess /'dʌtʃɪs/ n duquesa f

duck /dʌk/ n pato m. •vt sumergir; bajar (head). •vi agacharse. **~ling** /'dʌklɪŋ/ n patito m

duct /dʌkt/ n conducto m

dud /dʌd/ adj inútil; (cheque) sin fondos

due /djuː/ adj debido; (expected) esperado. **~ to** debido a. •adv. **~ north** derecho hacia el norte. **~s** npl derechos mpl

duel /'djuːəl/ n duelo m

duet /djuː'et/ n dúo m

duffel, duffle /'dʌfl/: **~ bag** n bolsa f de lona. **~ coat** n trenca f

dug /dʌg/ see **DIG**

duke /djuːk/ n duque m

dull /dʌl/ adj (-er, -est) (weather) gris; (colour) apagado; (person, play, etc) pesado; (sound) sordo

dumb /dʌm/ adj (-er, -est) mudo; 🄸 estúpido. ∎ **~ down** vt reducir el valor intelectual de. **~found** /dʌm'faʊnd/ vt pasmar

dummy /'dʌmɪ/ n muñeco m; (of tailor) maniquí m; (for baby) chupete m. •adj falso. **~ run** prueba f

dump /dʌmp/ vt tirar, botar (LAm). •n vertedero m; (Mil) depósito m; 🄸 lugar m desagradable. **be down**

in the ~s estar deprimido

dumpling /'dʌmplɪŋ/ n bola f de masa hervida

Dumpster /'dʌmpstə(r)/ n (Amer, ®) contenedor m (para escombros)

dumpy /'dʌmpɪ/ adj (-ier, -iest) regordete

dunce /dʌns/ n burro m

dung /dʌŋ/ n (manure) estiércol m

dungarees /dʌŋgə'riːz/ npl mono m, peto m

dungeon /'dʌndʒən/ n calabozo m

dunk /dʌŋk/ vt remojar

dupe /djuːp/ vt engañar. ● n inocentón m

duplicat|e /'djuːplɪkət/ adj & n duplicado (m). ● /'djuːplɪkeɪt/ vt duplicar; (on machine) reproducir. ~ing machine, ~or n multicopista f

durable /'djʊərəbl/ adj durable

duration /djʊ'reɪʃn/ n duración f

duress /djʊ'res/ n. under ~ bajo coacción

during /'djʊərɪŋ/ prep durante

dusk /dʌsk/ n anochecer m

dust /dʌst/ n polvo m. ● vt quitar el polvo a; (sprinkle) espolvorear (**with** con). ~**bin** n cubo m de la basura, bote m de la basura (Mex).

~ **cloth** (Amer), ~**er** n trapo m. ~**jacket** n sobrecubierta f. ~**man** /-mən/ n basurero m. ~**pan** n recogedor m. ~**y** adj (-ier, -iest) polvoriento

Dutch /dʌtʃ/ adj holandés. ● n (language) holandés m. **the** ~ (people) los holandeses. ~**man** /-mən/ m holandés m. ~**woman** n holandesa f

duty /'djuːtɪ/ n deber m; (tax) derechos mpl de aduana. **on** ~ de servicio. ~**free** /-'friː/ adj libre de impuestos

duvet /'djuːveɪ/ n edredón m

dwarf /dwɔːf/ n (pl -s or **dwarves**) enano m

dwell /dwel/ vi (pt **dwelt** or **dwelled**) morar.■ ~ **on** vt detenerse en. ~**ing** n morada f

dwindle /'dwɪndl/ vi disminuir

dye /daɪ/ vt (pres p **dyeing**) teñir. ● n tinte m

dying /'daɪɪŋ/ see DIE

dynamic /daɪ'næmɪk/ adj dinámico. ~**s** npl dinámica f

dynamite /'daɪnəmaɪt/ n dinamita f. ● vt dinamitar

dynamo /'daɪnəməʊ/ n (pl **-os**) dinamo f, dínamo f, dinamo m (LAm), dínamo m (LAm)

dynasty /'dɪnəstɪ/ n dinastía f

Ee

E abbr (= **East**) E

each /iːtʃ/ adj cada. ● pron cada uno. ~ **one** cada uno. ~ **other** uno a otro, el uno al otro. **they love** ~ **other** se aman

eager /'iːgə(r)/ adj impaciente; (enthusiastic) ávido. ~**ness** n impaciencia f; (enthusiasm) entusiasmo m

eagle /'iːgl/ n águila f

ear /ɪə(r)/ n oído m; (outer) oreja f; (of corn) espiga f. ~**ache** n dolor m de oído. ~**drum** n tímpano m

earl /ɜːl/ n conde m

early /'ɜːlɪ/ adj (-ier, -iest) temprano; (before expected time) prematuro. ● adv temprano; (ahead of time) con anticipación

earn /ɜːn/ vt ganar; (deserve) merecer

earnest /ˈɜːnɪst/ adj serio. **in ~** en serio

earnings /ˈɜːnɪŋz/ npl ingresos mpl; (Com) ganancias fpl

ear: ~phone n audífono m. **~ring** n pendiente m, arete m (LAm). **~shot** n. **within ~shot** al alcance del oído

earth /ɜːθ/ n tierra f. **the E~** (planet) la Tierra. • vt (Elec) conectar a tierra. **~quake** n terremoto m

earwig /ˈɪəwɪɡ/ n tijereta f

ease /iːz/ n facilidad f; (comfort) tranquilidad f. **at ~** a gusto; (Mil) en posición de descanso. **ill at ~** molesto. **with ~** fácilmente. • vt calmar; aliviar (pain). • vi calmarse; (lessen) disminuir

easel /ˈiːzl/ n caballete m

easily /ˈiːzɪlɪ/ adv fácilmente

east /iːst/ n este m. • adj este, oriental; (wind) del este. • adv hacia el este.

Easter /ˈiːstə(r)/ n Semana f Santa; (Relig) Pascua f de Resurrección. **~ egg** n huevo m de Pascua

east: ~erly /-əlɪ/ adj (wind) del este **~ern** /-ən/ adj este, oriental. **~ward**/-wəd/, **~wards** adv hacia el este

easy /ˈiːzɪ/ adj (**-ier, -iest**) fácil. • adv. **go ~ on sth** 🔳 no pasarse con algo. **take it ~** tomarse las cosas con calma. • int ¡despacio! **~ chair** n sillón m. **~going** /-ˈɡəʊɪŋ/ adj acomodadizo

eat /iːt/ vt/i (pt **ate**, pp **eaten**) comer. **■ ~ into** vt corroer. **~er** n comedor m

eaves /iːvz/ npl alero m. **~drop** vi (pt **-dropped**). **~drop (on)** escuchar a escondidas

ebb /eb/ n reflujo m. • vi bajar; (fig) decaer

ebola /iːˈbəʊlə/ n Ébola m

ebony /ˈebənɪ/ n ébano m

EC /iːˈsiː/ abbr (= **European Community**) CE f (Comunidad f Europea)

eccentric /ɪkˈsentrɪk/ adj & n excéntrico (m). **~ity** /eksenˈtrɪsətɪ/ n excentricidad f

echo /ˈekəʊ/ n (pl **-oes**) eco m. • vi hacer eco

eclipse /ɪˈklɪps/ n eclipse m. • vt eclipsar

ecolog|ical /iːkəˈlɒdʒɪkl/ adj ecológico. **~y** n ecología f

e-commerce /iːˈkɒmɜːs/ n comercio m electrónico

econom|ic /iːkəˈnɒmɪk/ adj económico; **~ refugee** refugiado m económico. **~ical** adj económico. **~ics** n economía f. **~ist** /ɪˈkɒnəmɪst/ n economista m & f. **~ize** /ɪˈkɒnəmaɪz/ vi economizar. **~ize on sth** economizar algo. **~y** /ɪˈkɒnəmɪ/ n economía f

ecsta|sy /ˈekstəsɪ/ n éxtasis f. **~tic** /ɪkˈstætɪk/ adj extático

Ecuador /ˈekwədɔː(r)/ n Ecuador m. **~ean** /ekwəˈdɔːrɪən/ adj & n ecuatoriano (m)

edg|e /edʒ/ n borde m; (of knife) filo m; (of town) afueras fpl. **have the ~e on** 🔳 llevar la ventaja a. **on ~e** nervioso. • vt ribetear. • vi avanzar cautelosamente. **~eways** adv de lado. **~y** adj nervioso

edible /ˈedɪbl/ adj comestible

edit /ˈedɪt/ vt dirigir (newspaper); preparar una edición de (text); editar (film). **~ion** /ɪˈdɪʃn/ n edición f. **~or** n (of newspaper) director m; (of text) redactor m. **~orial** /edɪˈtɔːrɪəl/ adj editorial. • n artículo m de fondo

educat|e /ˈedʒʊkeɪt/ vt educar. **~ed** adj culto. **~ion** /-ˈkeɪʃn/ n educación f; (knowledge, culture) cultura f. **~ional** /-ˈkeɪʃənl/ adj instructivo

EC /iːˈsiː/ abbr (= **European Commission**) CE f (Comisión f Europea)

eel /iːl/ n anguila f

eerie /'ɪərɪ/ adj (-ier, -iest) misterioso

effect /ɪ'fekt/ n efecto m. **in ~** efectivamente. **take ~** entrar en vigor. **~ive** adj eficaz; (striking) impresionante; (real) efectivo. **~ively** adv eficazmente. **~iveness** n eficacia f

effeminate /ɪ'femɪnət/ adj afeminado

efficien|cy /ɪ'fɪʃənsɪ/ n eficiencia f; (Mec) rendimiento m. **~t** adj eficiente. **~tly** adv eficientemente

effort /'efət/ n esfuerzo m. **~less** adj fácil

e.g. /iː'dʒiː/ abbr (= **exempli gratia**) p.ej., por ejemplo

egg /eg/ n huevo m. ■ **~ on** vt 🔲 incitar. **~cup** n huevera f. **~plant** n (Amer) berenjena f. **~shell** n cáscara f de huevo

ego /'iːgəʊ/ n (pl **-os**) yo m. **~ism** n egoísmo m. **~ist** n egoísta m & f. **~centric** /iːgəʊ'sentrɪk/ adj egocéntrico. **~tism** n egotismo m. **~tist** n egotista m & f

eh /eɪ/ int 🔲 ¡eh!

eiderdown /'aɪdədaʊn/ n edredón m

eight /eɪt/ adj & n ocho (m). **~een** /eɪ'tiːn/ adj & n dieciocho (m). **~eenth** adj decimoctavo. ●n dieciochavo m. **~h** /eɪtθ/ adj & n octavo (m) **~ieth** /'eɪtɪəθ/ adj octogésimo. ●n ochentavo m. **~y** /'eɪtɪ/ adj & n ochenta (m)

either /'aɪðə(r)/ adj cualquiera de los dos; (negative) ninguno de los dos; (each) cada. ●pron uno u otro; (with negative) ni uno ni otro. ●adv (negative) tampoco. ●conj o. **~ Tuesday or Wednesday** o el martes o el miércoles; (with negative) ni el martes ni el miércoles

eject /ɪ'dʒekt/ vt expulsar

eke /iːk/ vt. **~ out** hacer alcanzar (resources). **~ out a living** ganarse la vida a duras penas

elaborate /ɪ'læbərət/ adj complicado. ●/ɪ'læbəreɪt/ vt elaborar. ●/ɪ'læbəreɪt/ vi explicarse

elapse /ɪ'læps/ vi transcurrir

elastic /ɪ'læstɪk/ adj & n elástico (m). **~ band** n goma f (elástica), liga f (Mex)

elat|ed /ɪ'leɪtɪd/ adj regocijado. **~ion** /-ʃn/ n regocijo m

elbow /'elbəʊ/ n codo m. ●vt dar un codazo a

elder /'eldə(r)/ adj mayor. ●n mayor m & f; (tree) saúco m. **~ly** /'eldəlɪ/ adj mayor, anciano

eldest /'eldɪst/ adj & n mayor (m & f)

elect /ɪ'lekt/ vt elegir. **~ to do** decidir hacer. ●adj electo. **~ion** /-ʃn/ n elección f. **~or** n elector m. **~oral** adj electoral. **~orate** /-ət/ n electorado m

electric /ɪ'lektrɪk/ adj eléctrico. **~al** adj eléctrico. **~ blanket** n manta f eléctrica. **~ian** /ɪlek'trɪʃn/ n electricista m & f. **~ity** /ɪlek'trɪsətɪ/ n electricidad f

electrify /ɪ'lektrɪfaɪ/ vt electrificar; (fig) electrizar

electrocute /ɪ'lektrəkjuːt/ vt electrocutar

electrode /ɪ'lektrəʊd/ n electrodo m

electron /ɪ'lektrɒn/ n electrón m

electronic /ɪlek'trɒnɪk/ adj electrónico. **~ mail** n correo m electrónico. **~s** n electrónica f

elegan|ce /'elɪgəns/ n elegancia f. **~t** adj elegante. **~tly** adv elegantemente

element /'elɪmənt/ n elemento m. **~ary** /-'mentrɪ/ adj elemental. **~ary school** n (Amer) escuela f primaria

elephant /'elɪfənt/ n elefante m

elevat|e /'elɪveɪt/ vt elevar. **~ion** /-'veɪʃn/ n elevación f. **~or** n (Amer) ascensor m

eleven /ɪ'levn/ adj & n once (m). **~th** adj undécimo. ●n onceavo m

elf /elf/ n (pl **elves**) duende m

eligible /'elɪdʒəbl/ adj elegible. **be ~ for** tener derecho a

eliminat|e /ɪ'lɪmɪneɪt/ vt eliminar. **~ion** /-'neɪʃn/ n eliminación f

élite /eɪ'liːt/ n elite f, élite f

ellip|se /ɪ'lɪps/ n elipse f. **~tical** adj elíptico

elm /elm/ n olmo m

elope /ɪ'ləʊp/ vi fugarse con el amante

eloquen|ce /'eləkwəns/ n elocuencia f. **~t** adj elocuente

El Salvador /el'sælvədɔː(r)/ n El Salvador

else /els/ adv. **somebody ~** otra persona. **everybody ~** todos los demás. **nobody ~** ningún otro, nadie más. **nothing ~** nada más. **or ~** o bien. **somewhere ~** en otra parte. **~where** adv en otra parte

elu|de /ɪ'luːd/ vt eludir. **~sive** /-sɪv/ adj esquivo

elves /elvz/ see ELF

emaciated /ɪ'meɪʃɪeɪtɪd/ adj consumido

email, e-mail /'iːmeɪl/ n correo m electrónico, correo-e m. •vt mandar por correo electrónico, emailear. **~ address** n casilla f electrónica, dirección f de correo electrónico

emancipat|e /ɪ'mænsɪpeɪt/ vt emancipar. **~ion** /-'peɪʃn/ n emancipación f

embankment /ɪm'bæŋkmənt/ n terraplén m; (of river) dique m

embargo /ɪm'bɑːɡəʊ/ n (pl -oes) embargo m

embark /ɪm'bɑːk/ vi embarcarse. **~ on** (fig) emprender. **~ation** /embɑː'keɪʃn/ n embarque m

embarrass /ɪm'bærəs/ vt avergonzar. **~ed** adj avergonzado. **~ing** adj embarazoso. **~ment** n vergüenza f

embassy /'embəsɪ/ n embajada f

embellish /ɪm'belɪʃ/ vt adornar.

~ment n adorno m

embers /'embəz/ npl ascuas fpl

embezzle /ɪm'bezl/ vt desfalcar. **~ment** n desfalco m

emblem /'embləm/ n emblema m

embrace /ɪm'breɪs/ vt abrazar; (fig) abarcar. •vi abrazarse. •n abrazo m

embroider /ɪm'brɔɪdə(r)/ vt bordar. **~y** n bordado m

embroil /ɪm'brɔɪl/ vt enredar

embryo /'embrɪəʊ/ n (pl -os) embrión m. **~nic** /-'ɒnɪk/ adj embrionario

emend /ɪ'mend/ vt enmendar

emerald /'emərəld/ n esmeralda f

emerge /ɪ'mɜːdʒ/ vi salir. **~nce** /-əns/ n aparición f

emergency /ɪ'mɜːdʒənsɪ/ n emergencia f; (Med) urgencia f. **in an ~** en caso de emergencia. **~ exit** n salida f de emergencia. **~ room** urgencias fpl

emigra|nt /'emɪɡrənt/ n emigrante m & f. **~te** /'emɪɡreɪt/ vi emigrar. **~tion** /-'ɡreɪʃn/ n emigración f

eminen|ce /'emɪnəns/ n eminencia f. **~t** adj eminente

emi|ssion /ɪ'mɪʃn/ n emisión f. **~t** vt (pt **emitted**) emitir

emoti|on /ɪ'məʊʃn/ n emoción f. **~onal** adj emocional; (person) emotivo; (moving) conmovedor. **~ve** /ɪ'məʊtɪv/ adj emotivo

empathy /'empəθɪ/ n empatía f

emperor /'empərə(r)/ n emperador m

empha|sis /'emfəsɪs/ n (pl **~ses** /-siːz/) énfasis m. **~size** /'emfəsaɪz/ vt enfatizar. **~tic** /ɪm'fætɪk/ adj (gesture) enfático; (assertion) categórico

empire /'empaɪə(r)/ n imperio m

empirical /ɪm'pɪrɪkl/ adj empírico

employ /ɪm'plɔɪ/ vt emplear. **~ee** /emplɔɪ'iː/ n empleado m. **~er** n patrón m. **~ment** n empleo m.

~**ment agency** n agencia f de trabajo

empower /ɪm'pavə(r)/ vt autorizar (**to do** a hacer)

empress /'emprɪs/ n emperatriz f

empty /'emptɪ/ adj vacío; (promise) vano. **on an ~y stomach** con el estómago vacío. •n ⊞ envase m (vacío). •vt vaciar. •vi vaciarse

emulate /'emjʊleɪt/ vt emular

emulsion /ɪ'mʌlʃn/ n emulsión f

enable /ɪ'neɪbl/ vt. **~ s.o. to do sth** permitir a uno hacer algo

enact /ɪ'nækt/ vt (Jurid) decretar; (in theatre) representar

enamel /ɪ'næml/ n esmalte m. •vt (pt **enamelled**) esmaltar

enchant /ɪn'tʃɑːnt/ vt encantar. ~**ing** adj encantador. ~**ment** n encanto m

encircle /ɪn'sɜːkl/ vt rodear

enclave /'enkleɪv/ n enclave m

enclos|e /ɪn'kləʊz/ vt cercar (land); (Com) adjuntar. ~**ed** adj (space) cerrado; (Com) adjunto. ~**ure** /ɪn'kləʊʒə(r)/ n cercamiento m

encode /ɪn'kəʊd/ vt codificar, cifrar

encore /'ɒŋkɔː(r)/ int ¡otra! •n bis m, repetición f

encounter /ɪn'kaʊntə(r)/ vt encontrar. •n encuentro m

encourag|e /ɪn'kʌrɪdʒ/ vt animar; (stimulate) fomentar. ~**ement** n ánimo m. ~**ing** adj alentador

encroach /ɪn'krəʊtʃ/ vi. **~ on** invadir (land); quitar (time)

encyclopaedi|a /ɪnsaɪklə'piːdɪə/ n enciclopedia f. ~**c** adj enciclopédico

end /end/ n fin m; (furthest point) extremo m. **in the ~** por fin. **make ~s meet** poder llegar a fin de mes. **put an ~ to** poner fin a. **no ~ of** muchísimos. **on ~** de pie; (consecutive) seguido. •vt/i terminar, acabar

endanger /ɪn'deɪndʒə(r)/ vt poner en peligro. ~**ed** adj (species) en peligro

endearing /ɪn'dɪərɪŋ/ adj simpático

endeavour /ɪn'devə(r)/ n esfuerzo m, intento m. •vi. **~ to** esforzarse por

ending /'endɪŋ/ n fin m

endless /'endlɪs/ adj interminable

endorse /ɪn'dɔːs/ vt endosar; (fig) aprobar. ~**ment** n endoso m; (fig) aprobación f; (Auto) nota f de inhabilitación

endur|ance /ɪn'djʊərəns/ n resistencia f. ~**e** /ɪn'djʊə(r)/ vt aguantar. ~**ing** adj perdurable

enemy /'enəmɪ/ adj & n enemigo (m)

energ|etic /enə'dʒetɪk/ adj enérgico. ~**y** /'enədʒɪ/ n energía f

enforce /ɪn'fɔːs/ vt hacer cumplir (law); hacer valer (claim). ~**d** adj forzado

engag|e /ɪn'geɪdʒ/ vt emplear (staff); captar (attention); (Mec) hacer engranar. •vi (Mec) engranar. ~**e in** dedicarse a. ~**ed** adj prometido, comprometido (LAm); (busy) ocupado. **be ~ed** (of phone) estar comunicando, estar ocupado (LAm). **get ~ed** prometerse, comprometerse (LAm). ~**ement** n compromiso m

engine /'endʒɪn/ n motor m; (of train) locomotora f. **~ driver** n maquinista m

engineer /endʒɪ'nɪə(r)/ n ingeniero m; (mechanic) mecánico m; (Amer, Rail) maquinista m. •vt (contrive) fraguar. ~**ing** n ingeniería f

England /'ɪŋɡlənd/ n Inglaterra f

English /'ɪŋɡlɪʃ/ adj inglés. •n (language) inglés m. •npl. **the ~** los ingleses. ~**man** /-mən/ n inglés m. ~**woman** n inglesa f

engrav|e /ɪn'greɪv/ vt grabar. ~**ing** n grabado m

engrossed /ɪn'ɡrəʊst/ adj absorto

engulf /ɪn'ɡʌlf/ vt envolver

enhance /ɪnˈhɑːns/ vt realzar; aumentar (value)

enigma /ɪˈnɪgmə/ n enigma m. **~tic** /enɪgˈmætɪk/ adj enigmático

enjoy /ɪnˈdʒɔɪ/ vt. **I ~ reading** me gusta la lectura. **~ o.s.** divertirse. **~able** adj agradable. **~ment** n placer m

enlarge /ɪnˈlɑːdʒ/ vt agrandar; (Photo) ampliar. • vi agrandarse. **~ upon** extenderse sobre. **~ment** n (Photo) ampliación f

enlighten /ɪnˈlaɪtn/ vt ilustrar. **~ment** n. **the E~ment** el siglo de la luces

enlist /ɪnˈlɪst/ vt alistar; conseguir (support). • vi alistarse

enliven /ɪnˈlaɪvn/ vt animar

enorm|ity /ɪˈnɔːmətɪ/ n enormidad f. **~ous** /ɪˈnɔːməs/ adj enorme. **~ously** adv enormemente

enough /ɪˈnʌf/ adj & adv bastante. • n bastante m, suficiente m. • int ¡basta!

enquir|e /ɪnˈkwaɪə(r)/ vt/i preguntar. **~e about** informarse de. **~y** n pregunta f; (investigation) investigación f

enrage /ɪnˈreɪdʒ/ vt enfurecer

enrol /ɪnˈrəʊl/ vt (pt enrolled) inscribir, matricular (student). • vi inscribirse, matricularse

ensue /ɪnˈsjuː/ vi seguir

ensure /ɪnˈʃʊə(r)/ vt asegurar

entail /ɪnˈteɪl/ vt suponer; acarrear (expense)

entangle /ɪnˈtæŋgl/ vt enredar. **~ment** n enredo m

enter /ˈentə(r)/ vt entrar en, entrar a (esp LAm); presentarse a (competition); inscribirse en (race); (write) escribir. • vi entrar

enterpris|e /ˈentəpraɪz/ n empresa f; (fig) iniciativa f. **~ing** adj emprendedor

entertain /entəˈteɪn/ vt entretener; recibir (guests); abrigar (ideas, hopes); (consider) considerar. **~ing** adj

entretenido. **~ment** n entretenimiento m; (show) espectáculo m

enthral /ɪnˈθrɔːl/ vt (pt enthralled) cautivar

enthuse /ɪnˈθjuːz/ vi. **~ over** entusiasmarse por

enthusias|m /ɪnˈθjuːzɪæzəm/ n entusiasmo m. **~t** n entusiasta m & f. **~tic** /-ˈæstɪk/ adj entusiasta. **~tically** adv con entusiasmo

entice /ɪnˈtaɪs/ vt atraer

entire /ɪnˈtaɪə(r)/ adj entero. **~ly** adv completamente. **~ty** /ɪnˈtaɪərətɪ/ n. **in its ~ty** en su totalidad

entitle /ɪnˈtaɪtl/ vt titular; (give a right) dar derecho a. **be ~d to** tener derecho a. **~ment** n derecho m

entity /ˈentətɪ/ n entidad f

entrails /ˈentreɪlz/ npl entrañas fpl

entrance /ˈentrəns/ n entrada f. • /ɪnˈtrɑːns/ vt encantar

entrant /ˈentrənt/ n participante m & f; (in exam) candidato m

entreat /ɪnˈtriːt/ vt suplicar. **~y** n súplica f

entrenched /ɪnˈtrentʃt/ adj (position) afianzado

entrust /ɪnˈtrʌst/ vt confiar

entry /ˈentrɪ/ n entrada f

entwine /ɪnˈtwaɪn/ vt entrelazar

enumerate /ɪˈnjuːməreɪt/ vt enumerar

envelop /ɪnˈveləp/ vt envolver

envelope /ˈenvələʊp/ n sobre m

enviable /ˈenvɪəbl/ adj envidiable

envious /ˈenvɪəs/ adj envidioso

environment /ɪnˈvaɪərənmənt/ n medio m ambiente. **~al** /-ˈmentl/ adj ambiental

envisage /ɪnˈvɪzɪdʒ/ vt prever; (imagine) imaginar

envision /ɪnˈvɪʒn/ vt (Amer) prever

envoy /ˈenvɔɪ/ n enviado m

e

envy /'envɪ/ n envidia f. • vt envidiar

enzyme /'enzaɪm/ n enzima f

ephemeral /ɪ'femərəl/ adj efímero

epic /'epɪk/ n épica f. • adj épico

epidemic /epɪ'demɪk/ n epidemia f. • adj epidémico

epilep|sy /'epɪlepsɪ/ n epilepsia f. ~**tic** /-'leptɪk/ adj & n epiléptico (m)

epilogue /'epɪlɒg/ n epílogo m

episode /'epɪsəʊd/ n episodio m

epitaph /'epɪtɑ:f/ n epitafio m

epitom|e /ɪ'pɪtəmɪ/ n personificación f, epítome m. ~**ize** vt ser la personificación de

epoch /'i:pɒk/ n época f

equal /'i:kwəl/ adj & n igual (m & f). ~ **to** (a task) a la altura de. • vt (pt **equalled**) ser igual a; (Math) ser. ~**ity** /ɪ'kwɒlətɪ/ n igualdad f. ~**ize** vt igualar. • vi (Sport) emapatar. ~**izer** n (Sport) gol m del empate. ~**ly** adv igualmente; (share) por igual

equation /ɪ'kweɪʒn/ n ecuación f

equator /ɪ'kweɪtə(r)/ n ecuador m. ~**ial** /ekwə'tɔ:rɪəl/ adj ecuatorial

equilibrium /i:kwɪ'lɪbrɪəm/ n equilibrio m

equinox /'i:kwɪnɒks/ n equinoccio m

equip /ɪ'kwɪp/ vt (pt **equipped**) equipar. ~ **sth with** proveer algo de. ~**ment** n equipo m

equivalen|ce /ɪ'kwɪvələns/ n equivalencia f. ~**t** adj & n equivalente (m). **be** ~**t to** equivaler

equivocal /ɪ'kwɪvəkl/ adj equívoco

era /'ɪərə/ n era f

eradicate /ɪ'rædɪkeɪt/ vt erradicar, extirpar

erase /ɪ'reɪz/ vt borrar. ~**r** n goma f (de borrar)

erect /ɪ'rekt/ adj erguido. • vt levantar. ~**ion** /-ʃn/ n construcción f; (physiology) erección f

ero|de /ɪ'rəʊd/ vt erosionar. ~**sion** /-ʒn/ n erosión f

erotic /ɪ'rɒtɪk/ adj erótico

err /ɜ:(r)/ vi errar; (sin) pecar

errand /'erənd/ n recado m, mandado m (LAm)

erratic /ɪ'rætɪk/ adj desigual; (person) voluble

erroneous /ɪ'rəʊnɪəs/ adj erróneo

error /'erə/ n error m

erudit|e /'eru:daɪt/ adj erudito. ~**ion** /-'dɪʃn/ n erudición f

erupt /ɪ'rʌpt/ vi entrar en erupción; (fig) estallar. ~**ion** /-ʃn/ n erupción f

escalat|e /'eskəleɪt/ vt intensificar. • vi intensificarse. ~**ion** /-'leɪʃn/ n intensificación f. ~**or** n escalera f mecánica

escapade /eskə'peɪd/ n aventura f

escap|e /ɪ'skeɪp/ vi escaparse. • vt evitar. • n fuga f; (of gas, water) escape m. **have a narrow** ~**e** escapar por un pelo. ~**ism** /-ɪzəm/ n escapismo m

escort /'eskɔ:t/ n acompañante m & f; (Mil) escolta f. • /ɪ'skɔ:t/ vt acompañar; (Mil) escoltar

Eskimo /'eskɪməʊ/ n (pl **-os** or invar) esquimal m & f

especial /ɪ'speʃl/ adj especial. ~**ly** adv especialmente

espionage /'espɪənɑ:ʒ/ n espionaje m

Esq. /ɪ'skwaɪə(r)/ abbr (= **Esquire**) (in address) **E. Ashton,** ~ Sr. Don E. Ashton

essay /'eseɪ/ n ensayo m; (at school) composición f

essence /'esns/ n esencia f. **in** ~ esencialmente

essential /ɪ'senʃl/ adj esencial. • n elemento m esencial. ~**ly** adv esencialmente

establish /ɪ'stæblɪʃ/ vt establecer. ~**ment** n establecimiento m. **the E**~**ment** los que mandan, el sistema

estate /ɪ'steɪt/ n finca f; (housing estate) complejo m habitacional, urbanización f, fraccionamiento m (Mex); (possessions) bienes mpl. ~ **agent** n agente m inmobiliario. ~ **car** n ranchera f, (coche m) familiar m, camioneta f (LAm)

esteem /ɪ'stiːm/ n estima f

estimat|e /'estɪmət/ n cálculo m; (Com) presupuesto m. • /'estɪmeɪt/ vt calcular. ~**ion** /-'meɪʃn/ n estimación f; (opinion) opinión f

estranged /ɪs'treɪndʒd/ adj alejado

estuary /'estʃʊərɪ/ n estuario m

etc /et'setrə/ abbr (= **et cetera**) etc., etcétera

etching /'etʃɪŋ/ n aguafuerte m

etern|al /ɪ'tɜːnl/ adj eterno. ~**ity** /-ətɪ/ n eternidad f

ether /'iːθə(r)/ n éter m

ethic /'eθɪk/ n ética f. ~**al** adj ético. ~**s** npl ética f

ethnic /'eθnɪk/ adj étnico

etiquette /'etɪket/ n etiqueta f

etymology /etɪ'mɒlədʒɪ/ n etimología f

EU /iː'juː/ abbr (**European Union**) UE (Unión Europea)

euphemism /'juːfəmɪzəm/ n eufemismo m

euphoria /juː'fɔːrɪə/ n euforia f

euro /'jʊərəʊ/ n euro m

Europe /'jʊərəp/ n Europa f. ~**an** /-'pɪən/ adj & n europeo (m). ~**an Union** n Unión f Europea

euthanasia /juːθə'neɪzɪə/ n eutanasia f

evacuat|e /ɪ'vækjʊeɪt/ vt evacuar; desocupar (building). ~**ion** /-'eɪʃn/ n evacuación f

evade /ɪ'veɪd/ vt evadir

evalua|te /ɪ'væljʊeɪt/ vt evaluar. ~**tion** /-'eɪʃn/ n evaluación f

evangelical /iːvæn'dʒelɪkl/ adj evangélico

evaporat|e /ɪ'væpəreɪt/ vi

evaporarse. ~**ion** /-'reɪʃn/ n evaporación f

evasi|on /ɪ'veɪʒn/ n evasión f. ~**ve** /ɪ'veɪsɪv/ adj evasivo

eve /iːv/ n víspera f

even /'iːvn/ adj (flat, smooth) plano; (colour) uniforme; (distribution) equitativo; (number) par. **get ~ with** desquitarse con. • vt nivelar. ■ ~ **up** vt equilibrar. • adv aun, hasta, incluso. ~ **if** aunque. ~ **so** aun así. **not** ~ ni siquiera

evening /'iːvnɪŋ/ n tarde f; (after dark) noche f. ~ **class** n clase f nocturna

event /ɪ'vent/ n acontecimiento m; (Sport) prueba f. **in the ~ of** en caso de. ~**ful** adj lleno de acontecimientos

eventual /ɪ'ventʃʊəl/ adj final, definitivo. ~**ity** /-'ælətɪ/ n eventualidad f. ~**ly** adv finalmente

ever /'evə(r)/ adv (negative) nunca, jamás; (at all times) siempre. **have you ~ been to Greece?** ¿has estado (alguna vez) en Grecia?, ~ **after** desde entonces. ~ **since** desde entonces. ~ **so** 🔲 muy. **for ~** para siempre. **hardly ~** casi nunca. ~**green** adj de hoja perenne. • n árbol m de hoja perenne. ~**lasting** adj eterno

every /'evrɪ/ adj cada, todo. ~ **child** todos los niños. ~ **one** cada uno. ~ **other day** un día sí y otro no. ~**body** pron todos, todo el mundo. ~**day** adj de todos los días. ~**one** pron todos, todo el mundo. ~**thing** pron todo. ~**where** adv (be) en todas partes, (go) a todos lados

evict /ɪ'vɪkt/ vt desahuciar. ~**ion** /-ʃn/ n desahucio m

eviden|ce /'evɪdəns/ n evidencia f; (proof) pruebas fpl; (Jurid) testimonio m; **give ~ce** prestar declaración. ~**ce of** señales de. **in ~ce** visible. ~**t** adj evidente. ~**tly** adv evidentemente

evil /'iːvl/ adj malvado. • n mal m

evo|cative /ɪ'vɒkətɪv/ adj evocador. **~ke** /ɪ'vəʊk/ vt evocar

evolution /iːvə'luːʃn/ n evolución f

evolve /ɪ'vɒlv/ vt desarrollar. •vi evolucionar

ewe /juː/ n oveja f

exact /ɪg'zækt/ adj exacto. •vt exigir (**from** a). **~ing** adj exigente. **~ly** adv exactamente

exaggerat|e /ɪg'zædʒəreɪt/ vt exagerar. **~ion** /-'reɪʃn/ n exageración f

exam /ɪg'zæm/ n examen m. **~ination** /ɪgzæmɪ'neɪʃn/ n examen m. **~ine** /ɪg'zæmɪn/ vt examinar; interrogar (witness). **~iner** n examinador m

example /ɪg'zɑːmpl/ n ejemplo m. **for** ~ por ejemplo. **make an** ~ **of s.o.** darle un castigo ejemplar a uno

exasperat|e /ɪg'zæspəreɪt/ vt exasperar. **~ing** adj exasperante. **~ion** /-'reɪʃn/ n exasperación f

excavat|e /'ekskəveɪt/ vt excavar. **~ion** /-'veɪʃn/ n excavación f

exceed /ɪk'siːd/ vt exceder. **~ingly** adv sumamente

excel /ɪk'sel/ vi (pt **excelled**) sobresalir. •vt. ~ **o.s.** lucirse. **~lence** /'eksələns/ n excelencia f. **~lent** adj excelente

except /ɪk'sept/ prep menos, excepto. ~ **for** si no fuera por. •vt exceptuar. **~ing** prep con excepción de

exception /ɪk'sepʃən/ n excepción f. **take** ~ **to** ofenderse por. **~al** adj excepcional. **~ally** adv excepcionalmente

excerpt /'eksɜːpt/ n extracto m

excess /ɪk'ses/ n exceso m. •/'ekses/ adj excedente. ~ **fare** suplemento m. ~ **luggage** exceso m de equipaje. **~ive** adj excesivo

exchange /ɪks'tʃeɪndʒ/ vt cambiar. •n intercambio m; (of money) cambio m. **(telephone)** ~ central f telefónica

excise /'eksaɪz/ n impuestos mpl interos. •/ek'saɪz/ vt quitar

excit|able /ɪk'saɪtəbl/ adj excitable. **~e** /ɪk'saɪt/ vt emocionar; (stimulate) excitar. **~ed** adj entusiasmado. **get ~ed** entusiasmarse. **~ement** n emoción f; (enthusiasm) entusiasmo m. **~ing** adj emocionante

excla|im /ɪk'skleɪm/ vi/t exclamar. **~mation** /ekskləˈmeɪʃn/ n exclamación f. **~mation mark** n signo m de admiración f

exclu|de /ɪk'skluːd/ vt excluir. **~sion** /-ʒən/ n exclusión f. **~sive** /ɪk'skluːsɪv/ adj exclusivo; (club) selecto. **~sive of** excluyendo. **~sively** adv exclusivamente

excruciating /ɪk'skruːʃieɪtɪŋ/ adj atroz, insoportable

excursion /ɪk'skɜːʃn/ n excursión f

excus|able /ɪk'skjuːzəbl/ adj perdonable. **~e** /ɪk'skjuːz/ vt perdonar. **~e from** dispensar de. **~e me!** ¡perdón! •/ɪk'skjuːs/ n excusa f

ex-directory /eksdɪ'rektərɪ/ adj que no figura en la guía telefónica, privado (Mex)

execut|e /'eksɪkjuːt/ vt ejecutar. **~ion** /eksɪ'kjuːʃn/ n ejecución f. **~ioner** n verdugo m

executive /ɪg'zekjʊtɪv/ adj & n ejecutivo (m)

exempt /ɪg'zempt/ adj exento (**from** de). •vt dispensar. **~ion** /-ʃn/ n exención f

exercise /'eksəsaɪz/ n ejercicio m. •vt ejercer. •vi hacer ejercicio. **~ book** n cuaderno m

exert /ɪg'zɜːt/ vt ejercer. ~ **o.s.** hacer un gran esfuerzo. **~ion** /-ʃn/ n esfuerzo m

exhale /eks'heɪl/ vt/i exhalar

exhaust /ɪg'zɔːst/ vt agotar. •n (Auto) tubo m de escape. **~ed** adj agotado. **~ion** /-stʃən/ n agotamiento m. **~ive** adj exhaustivo

exhibit /ɪgˈzɪbɪt/ vt exponer; (fig) mostrar. • n objeto m expuesto; (Jurid) documento m. ~ion /eksɪˈbrʃn/ n exposición. ~ionist n exhibicionista m & f. ~or /ɪgˈzɪbɪtə(r)/ n expositor m

exhilarat|ing /ɪgˈzɪlərertɪŋ/ adj excitante. ~ion /-ˈreɪʃn/ n regocijo m

exhort /ɪgˈzɔːt/ vt exhortar

exile /ˈeksaɪl/ n exilio m; (person) exiliado m. • vt desterrar

exist /ɪgˈzɪst/ vi existir. ~ence n existencia f. **in ~ence** existente

exit /ˈeksɪt/ n salida f

exorbitant /ɪgˈzɔːbɪtənt/ adj exorbitante

exorcis|e /ˈeksɔːsaɪz/ vt exorcizar. ~m /-sɪzəm/ n exorcismo m. ~t n exorcista m & f

exotic /ɪgˈzɒtɪk/ adj exótico

expand /ɪkˈspænd/ vt expandir; (develop) desarrollar. • vi expandirse

expanse /ɪkˈspæns/ n extensión f

expansion /ɪkˈspænʃn/ n expansión f

expatriate /eksˈpætrɪət/ adj & n expatriado (m)

expect /ɪkˈspekt/ vt esperar; (suppose) suponer; (demand) contar con. **I ~ so** supongo que sí. ~ancy n esperanza f. **life ~ancy** esperanza f de vida. ~ant adj expectante. ~ant mother n futura madre f

expectation /ekspekˈteɪʃn/ n expectativa f

expedient /ɪkˈspiːdɪənt/ adj conveniente. • n expediente m

expedition /ekspɪˈdɪʃn/ n expedición f

expel /ɪkˈspel/ vt (pt expelled) expulsar

expend /ɪkˈspend/ vt gastar. ~able adj prescindible. ~iture /-ɪtʃə(r)/ n gastos mpl

expens|e /ɪkˈspens/ n gasto m. **at

s.o.'s ~e a costa de uno. ~es npl (Com) gastos mpl. ~ive adj caro

experience /ɪkˈspɪərɪəns/ n experiencia. • vt experimentar. ~d adj con experiencia; (driver) experimentado

experiment /ɪkˈsperɪmənt/ n experimento m. • vi experimentar. ~al /-ˈmentl/ adj experimental

expert /ˈekspɜːt/ adj & n experto (m). ~ise /ekspɜːˈtiːz/ n pericia f. ~ly adv hábilmente

expir|e /ɪkˈspaɪə(r)/ vi (passport, ticket) caducar; (contract) vencer. ~y n vencimiento m, caducidad f

expla|in /ɪkˈspleɪn/ vt explicar. ~nation /ekspləˈneɪʃn/ n explicación f. ~natory /ɪksˈplænətərɪ/ adj explicativo

explicit /ɪkˈsplɪsɪt/ adj explícito

explode /ɪkˈspləʊd/ vt hacer explotar. • vi estallar

exploit /ˈeksplɔɪt/ n hazaña f. • /ɪkˈsplɔɪt/ vt explotar. ~ation /eksplɔɪˈteɪʃn/ n explotación f

explor|ation /ekspləˈreɪʃn/ n exploración f. ~atory /ɪkˈsplɔrətrɪ/ adj exploratorio. ~e /ɪkˈsplɔː(r)/ vt explorar. ~er n explorador m

explosi|on /ɪkˈspləʊʒn/ n explosión f. ~ve /-sɪv/ adj & n explosivo (m)

export /ɪkˈspɔːt/ vt exportar. • /ˈekspɔːt/ n exportación f; (item) artículo m de exportación. ~er /ɪksˈpɔːtə(r)/ exportador m

expos|e /ɪkˈspəʊz/ vt exponer; (reveal) descubrir. ~ure /-ʒə(r)/ n exposición f. **die of ~ure** morir de frío

express /ɪkˈspres/ vt expresar. • adj expreso; (letter) urgente. • adv (by express post) por correo urgente. • n (train) rápido m, expreso m. ~ion n expresión f. ~ive adj expresivo. ~ly adv expresamente. ~way n (Amer) autopista f

expulsion /ɪkˈspʌlʃn/ n expulsión f

exquisite /ˈekskwɪzɪt/ adj exquisito

exten|d /ɪkˈstend/ vt extender;

(prolong) prolongar; ampliar (house).
• vi extenderse. **~sion** /-ʃn/ n
extensión f; (of road, time)
prolongación f; (building) anejo m.
~sive /-sɪv/ adj extenso. **~sively**
adv extensamente. **~t** n extensión
f; (fig) alcance. **to a certain ~t**
hasta cierto punto

exterior /ɪkˈstɪərɪə(r)/ adj & n
exterior (m)

exterminat|e /ɪkˈstɜːmɪneɪt/ vt
exterminar. **~ion** /-ˈneɪʃn/ n
exterminio m

external /ɪkˈstɜːnl/ adj externo

extinct /ɪkˈstɪŋkt/ adj extinto. **~ion**
/-ʃn/ n extinción f

extinguish /ɪkˈstɪŋgwɪʃ/ vt
extinguir. **~er** n extintor m,
extinguidor m (LAm)

extol /ɪkˈstəʊl/ vt (pt **extolled**)
alabar

extort /ɪkˈstɔːt/ vt sacar por la
fuerza. **~ion** /-ʃn/ n exacción f.
~ionate /-ənət/ adj exorbitante

extra /ˈekstrə/ adj de más. • adv
extraordinariamente. • n
suplemento m; (Cinema) extra m & f

extract /ˈekstrækt/ n extracto m.
• /ɪkˈstrækt/ vt extraer. **~ion**
/ɪkˈstrækʃn/ n extracción f

extradit|e /ˈekstrədaɪt/ vt
extraditar. **~ion** /-ˈdɪʃn/ n
extradición f

extra: ~ordinary /ɪkˈstrɔːdnrɪ/
adj extraordinario. **~-sensory**
/ekstrəˈsensərɪ/ adj extrasensorial

extravagan|ce /ɪkˈstrævəgəns/ n
prodigalidad f; (of gestures, dress)
extravagancia f. **~t** adj pródigo;
(behaviour) extravagante. **~za** n
gran espectáculo m

extrem|e /ɪkˈstriːm/ adj & n
extremo (m). **~ely** adv
extremadamente. **~ist** n
extremista m & f

extricate /ˈekstrɪkeɪt/ vt
desenredar, librar

extrovert /ˈekstrəvɜːt/ n
extrovertido m

exude /ɪgˈzjuːd/ vt rezumar

exult /ɪgˈzʌlt/ vi exultar. **~ation**
/egzʌlˈteɪʃn/ n exultación f

eye /aɪ/ n ojo m. **keep an ~ on** no
perder de vista. **see ~ to ~ with
s.o.** estar de acuerdo con uno. • vt
(pt **eyed**, pres p **eyeing**) mirar.
~ball n globo m ocular. **~brow** n
ceja f. **~drops** npl colirio m. **~lash**
n pestaña f. **~lid** n párpado m.
~-opener n 🛈 revelación f.
~-shadow n sombra f de ojos.
~sight n vista f. **~sore** n (fig, fam)
monstruosidad f, adefesio m.
~witness n testigo m ocular

Ff

fable /ˈfeɪbl/ n fábula f

fabric /ˈfæbrɪk/ n tejido m, tela f

fabricate /ˈfæbrɪkeɪt/ vt inventar.
~ation /-ˈkeɪʃn/ n invención f

fabulous /ˈfæbjʊləs/ adj fabuloso

facade /fəˈsɑːd/ n fachada f

face /feɪs/ n cara f, rostro m; (of

watch) esfera f, carátula f (Mex);
(aspect) aspecto m. **~
down(wards)** boca abajo. **~
up(wards)** boca arriba. **in the ~
of** frente a. **lose ~** quedar mal.
pull ~s hacer muecas. • vt mirar
hacia; (house) dar a; (confront)
enfrentarse con. • vi volverse. ∎ **~
up to** vt enfrentarse con. **~**

flannel n paño m (para lavarse la cara). **~less** adj anónimo. **~ lift** n cirugía f estética en la cara

facetious /fəˈsiːʃəs/ adj burlón

facial /ˈfeɪʃl/ adj facial

facile /ˈfæsaɪl/ adj superficial, simplista

facilitate /fəˈsɪlɪteɪt/ vt facilitar

facility /fəˈsɪlɪtɪ/ n facilidad f

fact /fækt/ n hecho m. **as a matter of ~, in ~** en realidad, de hecho

faction /ˈfækʃn/ n facción f

factor /ˈfæktə(r)/ n factor m

factory /ˈfæktərɪ/ n fábrica f

factual /ˈfæktʃʊəl/ adj basado en hechos, factual

faculty /ˈfækəltɪ/ n facultad f

fad /fæd/ n manía f, capricho m

fade /feɪd/ vi (colour) desteñirse; (flowers) marchitarse; (light) apagarse; (memory, sound) desvanecerse

fag /fæg/ n (fam, chore) faena f; (sl, cigarette) cigarrillo m, pitillo m

Fahrenheit /ˈfærənhaɪt/ adj Fahrenheit

fail /feɪl/ vi fracasar; (brakes) fallar; (in an exam) suspender, ser reprobado (LAm). **he ~ed to arrive** no llegó. ● vt suspender, ser reprobado en (LAm) (exam); suspender, reprobar (LAm) (candidate). ● n. **without ~** sin falta. **~ing** n defecto m. ● prep. **~ing that, ...** si eso no resulta.... **~ure** /ˈfeɪljə(r)/ n fracaso m

faint /feɪnt/ adj (-er, -est) (weak) débil; (indistinct) indistinto. **feel ~** estar mareado. **the ~est idea** la más remota idea. ● vi desmayarse. ● n desmayo m. **~-hearted** /-ˈhɑːtɪd/ adj pusilánime, cobarde. **~ly** adv (weakly) débilmente; (indistinctly) indistintamente; (slightly) ligeramente

fair /feə(r)/ adj (-er, -est) (just) justo; (weather) bueno; (amount) razonable; (hair) rubio, güero (Mex fam); (skin)

blanco. ● adv limpio. ● n feria f. **~-haired** /-ˈheəd/ adj rubio, güero (Mex fam). **~ly** adv (justly) justamente; (rather) bastante. **~ness** n justicia f. **in all ~ness** sinceramente. **~ play** n juego m limpio

fairy /ˈfeərɪ/ n hada f. **~ story, ~ tale** n cuento m de hadas

faith /feɪθ/ n (trust) confianza f; (Relig) fe f. **~ful** adj fiel. **~fully** adv fielmente. **yours ~fully** (in letters) (le saluda) atentamente

fake /feɪk/ n falsificación f; (person) farsante m. ● adj falso. ● vt falsificar

falcon /ˈfɔːlkən/ n halcón m

Falkland Islands /ˈfɔːklklənd/ npl. **the Falkland Islands, the Falklands** las (Islas) Malvinas

fall /fɔːl/ vi (pt fell, pp fallen) caer; (decrease) bajar. ● n caída f; (Amer, autumn) otoño m; (in price) bajada f. ■ **~ apart** vi deshacerse. ■ **~ back on** vt recurrir a. ■ **~ down** vi (fall) caerse. ■ **~ for** vt 🄵 enamorarse de (person); dejarse engañar por (trick). ■ **~ in** vi (Mil) formar filas. ■ **~ off** vi caerse; (diminish) disminuir. ■ **~ out** vi (quarrel) reñir (**with** con); (drop out) caerse; (Mil) romper filas. ■ **~ over** vi caerse. vt tropezar con. ■ **~ through** vi no salir adelante

fallacy /ˈfæləsɪ/ n falacia f

fallible /ˈfælɪbl/ adj falible

fallout /ˈfɔːlaʊt/ n lluvia f radiactiva. **~ shelter** n refugio m antinuclear

fallow /ˈfæləʊ/ adj en barbecho

false /fɔːls/ adj falso. **~ alarm** n falsa alarma. **~hood** n mentira f. **~ly** adv falsamente. **~ teeth** npl dentadura f postiza

falsify /ˈfɔːlsɪfaɪ/ vt falsificar

falter /ˈfɔːltə(r)/ vi vacilar

fame /feɪm/ n fama f. **~d** adj famoso

familiar /fəˈmɪlɪə(r)/ adj familiar. **the name sounds ~** el nombre me suena. **be ~ with** conocer. **~ity** /-'ærətɪ/ n familiaridad f. **~ize** vt familiarizar

family /'fæməlɪ/ n familia f. •adj de (la) familia, familiar. **~ tree** n árbol m genealógico

famine /'fæmɪn/ n hambre f, hambruna f

famished /'fæmɪʃt/ adj hambriento

famous /'feɪməs/ adj famoso

fan /fæn/ n abanico m; (Mec) ventilador m; (enthusiast) aficionado m; (of group, actor) **fan** m & f; (of sport, team) hincha m & f. •vt (pt **fanned**) abanicar; avivar (interest). ■ **~ out** vi desparramarse en forma de abanico

fanatic /fə'nætɪk/ n fanático m. **~al** adj fanático. **~ism** /-sɪzəm/ n fanatismo m

fan belt n correa f de ventilador, banda f de ventilador (Mex)

fanciful /'fænsɪfl/ adj (imaginative) imaginativo; (impractical) extravagante

fancy /'fænsɪ/ n imaginación f; (liking) gusto m. **take a ~ to** tomar cariño a (person); aficionarse a (thing). •adj de lujo. •vt (imagine) imaginar; (believe) creer; (fam, want) apetecer a. **~ dress** n disfraz m

fanfare /'fænfeə(r)/ n fanfarria f

fang /fæŋ/ n (of animal) colmillo m; (of snake) diente m

fantasize /'fæntəsaɪz/ vi fantasear

fantastic /fæn'tæstɪk/ adj fantástico

fantasy /'fæntəsɪ/ n fantasía f

far /fɑː(r)/ adv lejos; (much) mucho. **as ~ as** hasta. **as ~ as I know** que yo sepa. **by ~** con mucho. •adj (**further**, **furthest** or **farther**, **farthest**) lejano. **~ away** lejano

farc|e /fɑːs/ n farsa f. **~ical** adj ridículo

fare /feə(r)/ n (on bus) precio m del billete, precio m del boleto (LAm); (on train, plane) precio m del billete,

precio m del pasaje (LAm); (food) comida f

Far East /fɑːr'iːst/ n Extremo or Lejano Oriente m

farewell /feə'wel/ int & n adiós (m)

far-fetched /fɑː'fetʃt/ adj improbable

farm /fɑːm/ n granja f. •vt cultivar. ■ **~ out** vt encargar (a terceros). •vi ser agricultor. **~er** n agricultor m, granjero m. **~house** n granja f. **~ing** n agricultura f. **~yard** n corral m

far: **~-off** adj lejano. **~-reaching** /fɑː'riːtʃɪŋ/ adj trascendental. **~-sighted** /fɑː'saɪtɪd/ adj con visión del futuro; (Med, Amer) hipermétrope

farther, farthest /'fɑːðə(r), 'fɑːðəst/ see **FAR**

fascinat|e /'fæsɪneɪt/ vt fascinar. **~ed** adj fascinado. **~ing** adj fascinante. **~ion** /-'neɪʃn/ n fascinación f

fascis|m /'fæʃɪzəm/ n fascismo m. **~t** adj & n fascista (m & f)

fashion /'fæʃn/ n (manner) manera f; (vogue) moda f. **be in/out of ~** estar de moda/estar pasado de moda. **~able** adj de moda

fast /fɑːst/ adj (**-er, -est**) rápido; (clock) adelantado; (secure) fijo; (colours) sólido. •adv rápidamente; (securely) firmemente. **~ asleep** profundamente dormido. •vi ayunar. •n ayuno m

fasten /'fɑːsn/ vt sujetar; cerrar (case); abrochar (belt etc). •vi (case) cerrar; (belt etc) cerrarse. **~er,** **~ing** n (on box, window) cierre m; (on door) cerrojo m

fat /fæt/ n grasa f. •adj (**fatter, fattest**) gordo; (meat) que tiene mucha grasa; (thick) grueso. **get ~** engordar

fatal /'feɪtl/ adj mortal; (fateful) fatídico. **~ity** /fə'tælətɪ/ n muerto m. **~ly** adv mortalmente

fate /feɪt/ n destino m; (one's lot)

suerte f. **~d** adj predestinado.
~ful adj fatídico

father /'fɑːðə(r)/ n padre m. **~hood**
m paternidad f. **~-in-law** m (pl
~s-in-law) m suegro m. **~ly** adj
paternal

fathom /'fæðəm/ n braza f. •vt. **~
(out)** comprender

fatigue /fə'tiːg/ n fatiga f. •vt
fatigar

fat|ten vt. **~ten (up)** cebar
(animal). **~tening** adj que engorda.
~ty adj graso, grasoso (LAm). •n 🄵
gordinflón m

fatuous /'fætjʊəs/ adj fatuo

faucet /'fɔːsɪt/ n (Amer) grifo m,
llave f (LAm)

fault /fɔːlt/ n defecto m; (blame)
culpa f; (tennis) falta f; (in geology)
falla f. **at ~** culpable. •vt
encontrarle defectos a. **~less** adj
impecable. **~y** adj defectuoso

favour /'feɪvə(r)/ n favor m. •vt
favorecer; (support) estar a favor
de; (prefer) preferir. **~able** adj
favorable. **~ably** adv
favorablemente. **~ite** adj & n
preferido (m). **~itism** n
favoritismo m

fawn /fɔːn/ n cervato m. •adj beige,
beis. •vi. **~ on** adular

fax /fæks/ n fax m. •vt faxear

fear /fɪə(r)/ n miedo m. •vt temer.
~ful adj (frightening) espantoso;
(frightened) temeroso. **~less** adj
intrépido. **~some** /-səm/ adj
espantoso

feasib|ility /fiːzə'bɪlɪti/ n
viabilidad f. **~le** /'fiːzəbl/ adj
factible; (likely) posible

feast /fiːst/ n (Relig) fiesta f; (meal)
banquete m

feat /fiːt/ n hazaña f

feather /'feðə(r)/ n pluma f.
~weight n peso m pluma

feature /'fiːtʃə(r)/ n (on face) rasgo
m; (characteristic) característica f; (in
newspaper) artículo m; **~ (film)**
película f principal, largometraje

m. •vt presentar; (give prominence to)
destacar

February /'februəri/ n febrero m

fed /fed/ see FEED

feder|al /'fedərəl/ adj federal.
~ation /fedə'reɪʃn/ n federación f

fed up adj 🄵 harto (**with** de)

fee /fiː/ n (professional) honorarios
mpl; (enrolment) derechos mpl; (club)
cuota f

feeble /'fiːbl/ adj (**-er, -est**) débil

feed /fiːd/ vt (pt fed) dar de comer
a; (supply) alimentar. •vi comer. •n
(for animals) pienso m; (for babies)
comida f. **~back** n reacción f

feel /fiːl/ vt (pt felt) sentir; (touch)
tocar; (think) considerar. **do you ~
it's a good idea?** ¿te parece
buena idea? **~ as if** tener la
impresión de que. **~ hot/hungry**
tener calor/hambre. **~ like** (fam,
want) tener ganas de. •n sensación
f. **get the ~ of sth**
acostumbrarse a algo. **~er** n (of
insect) antena f. **~ing** n
sentimiento m; (physical) sensación f

feet /fiːt/ see FOOT

feign /feɪn/ vt fingir

feint /feɪnt/ n finta f

fell /fel/ see FALL. •vt derribar; talar
(tree)

fellow /'feləʊ/ n 🄵 tipo m; (comrade)
compañero m; (of society) socio m. **~
countryman** n compatriota m. **~
passenger/traveller** n
compañero m de viaje

felony /'feləni/ n delito m grave

felt /felt/ see FEEL. •n fieltro m

female /'fiːmeɪl/ adj hembra; (voice,
sex etc) femenino. •n mujer f;
(animal) hembra f

femini|ne /'femənɪn/ adj & n
femenino (m). **~nity** /-'nɪnəti/ n
feminidad f. **~st** adj & n feminista
m & f

fenc|e /fens/ n cerca f, cerco m
(LAm). •vt. **~e (in)** encerrar,
cercar. •vi (Sport) practicar la

esgrima. **~er** n esgrimidor m.
~ing n (Sport) esgrima f

fend /fend/ vi. **~ for o.s.** valerse
por sí mismo. ■ **~ off** vt
defenderse de

fender /'fendə(r)/ n rejilla f; (Amer,
Auto) guardabarros m, salpicadera f
(Mex)

ferment /fə'ment/ vt/i fermentar.
~ation /-'teɪʃn/ n fermentación f

fern /fɜːn/ n helecho m

feroci|ous /fə'rəʊʃəs/ adj feroz.
~ty /fə'rɒsəti/ n ferocidad f

ferret /'ferɪt/ n hurón m. ●vi (pt
ferreted) **~ about** husmear. ●vt.
~ out descubrir

ferry /'ferɪ/ n ferry m. ●vt
transportar

fertil|e /'fɜːtaɪl/ adj fértil. **~ity**
/-'tɪlətɪ/ n fertilidad f. **~ize**
/'fɜːtəlaɪz/ vt fecundar, abonar (soil).
~izer n fertilizante m

ferv|ent /'fɜːvənt/ adj ferviente.
~our /-və(r)/ n fervor m

fester /'festə(r)/ vi enconarse

festival /'festəvl/ n fiesta f; (of arts)
festival m

festiv|e /'festɪv/ adj festivo. **the ~e
season** n las Navidades. **~ity**
/fe'strvətɪ/ n festividad f

fetch /fetʃ/ vt (go for) ir a buscar;
(bring) traer; (be sold for) venderse
en. **~ing** adj atractivo

fête /feɪt/ n fiesta f. ●vt festejar

fetish /'fetɪʃ/ n fetiche m

fetter /'fetə(r)/ vt encadenar

feud /fjuːd/ n contienda f

feudal /'fjuːdl/ adj feudal. **~ism** n
feudalismo m

fever /'fiːvə(r)/ n fiebre f. **~ish** adj
febril

few /fjuː/ adj pocos. **a ~ houses**
algunas casas. ●n pocos mpl. **a ~**
unos (pocos). **a good ~, quite a
~** 🛈 muchos. **~er** adj & n menos.
~est adj el menor número de

fiancé /fɪ'ɒnseɪ/ n novio m. **~e**
/fɪ'ɒnseɪ/ n novia f

fiasco /fɪ'æskəʊ/ n (pl **-os**) fiasco m

fib /fɪb/ n 🛈 mentirilla f. ●vi 🛈
mentir, decir mentirillas

fibre /'faɪbə(r)/ n fibra f. **~glass** n
fibra f de vidrio

fickle /'fɪkl/ adj inconstante

ficti|on /'fɪkʃn/ n ficción f. **(works
of) ~** novelas fpl. **~onal** adj
novelesco. **~tious** /fɪk'tɪʃəs/ adj
ficticio

fiddle /'fɪdl/ n 🛈 violín m; (fam,
swindle) trampa f. ●vt 🛈 falsificar.
~ with juguetear con

fidget /'fɪdʒɪt/ vi (pt **fidgeted**)
moverse, ponerse nervioso. **~
with** juguetear con. ●n persona f
inquieta. **~y** adj inquieto

field /fiːld/ n campo m. **~ day** n.
have a ~ day hacer su agosto. **~
glasses** npl gemelos mpl. **F~
Marshal** n mariscal m de campo.
~ trip n viaje m de estudio.
~work n investigaciones fpl en el
terreno

fiend /fiːnd/ n demonio m. **~ish** adj
diabólico

fierce /fɪəs/ adj (**-er, -est**) feroz;
(attack) violento. **~ly** adv (growl)
con ferocidad; (fight) con fiereza

fiery /'faɪərɪ/ adj (**-ier, -iest**)
ardiente; (temper) exaltado

fifteen /fɪf'tiːn/ adj & n quince (m).
~th adj decimoquinto. ●n
quinceavo m

fifth /fɪfθ/ adj & n quinto (m)

fift|ieth /'fɪftɪəθ/ adj
quincuagésimo. ●n cincuentavo m.
~y adj & n cincuenta (m). **~y-~y**
adv mitad y mitad, a medias. ●adj.
a ~y-~y chance una posibilidad
de cada dos

fig /fɪg/ n higo m

fight /faɪt/ vi (pt **fought**) luchar;
(quarrel) disputar. ●vt luchar contra.
●n pelea m; (struggle) lucha f;
(quarrel) disputa f; (Mil) combate m.
■ **~ back** vi defenderse. ■ **~ off** vt

rechazar (attack); luchar contra (illness). **~er** n luchador m; (aircraft) avión m de caza. **~ing** n luchas fpl

figment /'fɪgmənt/ n. **~ of the imagination** producto m de la imaginación

figurative /'fɪɡjʊrətɪv/ adj figurado

figure /'fɪɡə(r)/ n (number) cifra f; (person) figura f; (shape) forma f; (of woman) tipo m. ●vt imaginar; (Amer fam, reckon) calcular. ●vi figurar. **that ~s** (fam) es lógico. ■ **~ out** vt entender. **~head** n testaferro m, mascarón de proa. **~ of speech** n figura f retórica

filch /fɪltʃ/ vt 🄣 hurtar

file /faɪl/ n (tool, for nails) lima f; (folder) carpeta f; (set of papers) expediente m; (Comp) archivo m; (row) fila f. **in single ~** en fila india. ●vt archivar (papers); limar (metal, nails). ●**~ in** vi entrar en fila. **~ past** vt desfilar ante

filing cabinet /'faɪlɪŋ/ n archivador m

fill /fɪl/ vt llenar. ●vi llenarse. ●n. **eat one's ~** hartarse de comer. **have had one's ~ of** estar harto de ■ **~ in** vt rellenar (form, hole), ■ **~ out** vt rellenar (form). vi (get fatter) engordar. ■ **~ up** vt llenar. vi llenarse

fillet /'fɪlɪt/ n filete m. ●vt (pt **filleted**) cortar en filetes (meat); quitar la espina a (fish)

filling /'fɪlɪŋ/ n (in tooth) empaste m, tapadura f (Mex). **~ station** n gasolinera f

film /fɪlm/ n película f. ●vt filmar. **~ star** n estrella f de cine

filter /'fɪltə(r)/ n filtro m. ●vt filtrar. ●vi filtrarse. **~-tipped** adj con filtro

filth /fɪlθ/ n mugre f. **~y** adj mugriento

fin /fɪn/ n aleta f

final /'faɪnl/ adj último; (conclusive) decisivo. ●n (Sport) final f. **~s** npl (Schol) exámenes mpl de fin de curso

finale /fɪ'nɑːlɪ/ n final m

finallist n finalista m & f. **~ize** vt ultimar. **~ly** adv (lastly) finalmente, por fin

financle /'faɪnæns/ n finanzas fpl. ●vt financiar. **~ial** /faɪ'nænʃl/ adj financiero; (difficulties) económico

find /faɪnd/ vt (pt **found**) encontrar. **~ out** vt descubrir. ●vi (learn) enterarse. **~ings** npl conclusiones fpl

fine /faɪn/ adj (-er, -est) (delicate) fino; (excellent) excelente. ●adv muy bien. ●n multa f. ●vt multar. **~ arts** npl bellas artes fpl. **~ly** adv (cut) en trozos pequeños; (adjust) con precisión

finger /'fɪŋɡə(r)/ n dedo m. ●vt tocar. **~nail** n uña f. **~print** n huella f digital. **~tip** n punta f del dedo

finish /'fɪnɪʃ/ vt/i terminar, acabar. **~ doing** terminar de hacer. ●n fin m; (of race) llegada f

finite /'faɪnaɪt/ adj finito

Fin|land /'fɪnlənd/ n Finlandia f. **~n** n finlandés m. **~nish** adj & n finlandés (m)

fiord /fjɔːd/ n fiordo m

fir /fɜː(r)/ n abeto m

fire /faɪə(r)/ n fuego m; (conflagration) incendio m. ●vt disparar (gun); (dismiss) despedir; avivar (imagination). ●vi disparar. **~ alarm** n alarma f contra incendios. **~arm** n arma f de fuego. **~ brigade, ~ department** (Amer) n cuerpo m de bomberos. **~ engine** n coche m de bomberos, carro m de bomberos (Mex). **~escape** n escalera f de incendios. **~ extinguisher** n extintor m, extinguidor m (LAm). **~fighter** n bombero m. **~man** /-mən/ n bombero m. **~place** n chimenea f. **~side** n hogar m. **~ truck** n (Amer) see → ENGINE. **~wood** n leña f. **~work** n fuego m artificial

firm /fɜːm/ n empresa f. ●adj (-er, -est) firme. **~ly** adv firmemente

first /fɜːst/ adj primero, (before masculine singular noun) primer. **at ~ hand** directamente. ●n primero m. ●adv primero; (first time) por primera vez. **~ of all** primero. **~ aid** n primeros auxilios mpl. **~ aid kit** n botiquín m. **~ class** /-'klɑːs/ adv (travel) en primera clase. **~-class** adj de primera clase. **~ floor** n primer piso m; (Amer) planta f baja. **F~ Lady** n (Amer) Primera Dama f. **~ly** adv en primer lugar. **~ name** n nombre m de pila. **~-rate** /-'reɪt/ adj excelente

fish /fɪʃ/ n (pl invar or **-es**) pez m; (as food) pescado m. ●vi pescar. **go ~ing** ir de pesca. ■ **~ out** vt sacar. **~erman** n pescador m. **~ing** n pesca f. **~ing pole** (Amer), **~ing rod** n caña f de pesca. **~monger** n pescadero m. **~ shop** n pescadería f. **~y** adj (smell) a pescado; (fam, questionable) sospechoso

fission /'fɪʃn/ n fisión f

fist /fɪst/ n puño m

fit /fɪt/ adj (**fitter, fittest**) (healthy) en forma; (good enough) adecuado; (able) capaz. ●n (attack) ataque m; (of clothes) corte m. ●vt (pt **fitted**) (adapt) adaptar; (be the right size for) quedarle bien a; (install) colocar. ●vi encajar; (in certain space) caber. (clothes) quedarle bien a uno. ■ **~ in** vi caber. **~ful** adj irregular. **~ness** n salud f; (Sport) (buena) forma f física. **~ting** adj apropiado. ●n (of clothes) prueba f. **~ting room** n probador m

five /faɪv/ adj & n cinco (m)

fix /fɪks/ vt fijar; (mend, deal with) arreglar. ●n. **in a ~** en un aprieto. **~ed** adj fijo. **~ture** /'fɪkstʃə(r)/ n (Sport) partido m

fizz /fɪz/ vi burbujear. ●n efervescencia f. **~le** /fɪzl/ vi. **~le out** fracasar. **~y** adj efervescente; (water) con gas

fjord /fjɔːd/ n fiordo m

flabbergasted /'flæbəgɑːstɪd/ adj estupefacto

flabby /'flæbɪ/ adj flojo

flag /flæg/ n bandera f. ●vi (pt **flagged**) (weaken) flaquear; (conversation) languidecer

flagon /'flægən/ n botella f grande, jarro m

flagpole /'flægpəʊl/ n asta f de bandera

flagrant /'fleɪgrənt/ adj flagrante

flair /fleə(r)/ n don m (**for** de)

flak|e /fleɪk/ n copo m; (of paint, metal) escama f. ●vi desconcharse. **~y** adj escamoso

flamboyant /flæm'bɔɪənt/ adj (clothes) vistoso; (manner) extravagante

flame /fleɪm/ n llama f. **go up in ~s** incendiarse

flamingo /flə'mɪŋgəʊ/ n (pl **-o(e)s** flamenco m

flammable /'flæməbl/ adj inflamable

flan /flæn/ n tartaleta f

flank /flæŋk/ n (of animal) ijada f; (of person) costado m; (Mil, Sport) flanco m

flannel /'flænl/ n franela f; (for face) paño m (para lavarse la cara).

flap /flæp/ vi (pt **flapped**) ondear; (wings) aletear. ●vt batir (wings); agitar (arms). ●n (cover) tapa f; (of pocket) cartera f; (of table) ala f. **get into a ~** 🄓 ponerse nervioso

flare /fleə(r)/ ●n llamarada f; (Mil) bengala f; (in skirt) vuelo m. ■ **~ up** vi llamear; (fighting) estallar; (person) encolerizarse

flash /flæʃ/ ●vi destellar. ●vt (aim torch) dirigir; (flaunt) hacer ostentación de. **~ past** pasar como un rayo. ●n destello m; (Photo) flash m. **~back** n escena f retrospectiva. **~light** n (Amer, torch) linterna f. **~y** adj ostentoso

flask /flɑːsk/ n frasco m; (vacuum flask) termo m

flat /flæt/ adj (**flatter, flattest**) plano; (tyre) desinflado; (refusal) categórico; (fare, rate) fijo; (Mus) bemol. ●adv (Mus) demasiado bajo. **~ out** (at top speed) a toda velocidad. ●n (rooms) apartamento m, piso m; Ⓣ pinchazo m; (Mus) (Auto, esp Amer) bemol m. **~ly** adv categóricamente. **~ten** vt allanar, aplanar

flatter /ˈflætə(r)/ vt adular. **~ing** adj (person) lisonjero; (clothes) favorecedor. **~y** n adulación f

flaunt /flɔːnt/ vt hacer ostentación de

flavour /ˈfleɪvə(r)/ n sabor m. ●vt sazonar. **~ing** n condimento m

flaw /flɔː/ n defecto m. **~less** adj perfecto

flea /fliː/ n pulga f

fleck /flek/ n mancha f, pinta f

fled /fled/ see FLEE

flee /fliː/ vi (pt **fled**) huir. ●vt huir de

fleece /fliːs/ n vellón m. ●vt Ⓣ desplumar

fleet /fliːt/ n flota f; (of cars) parque m móvil

fleeting /ˈfliːtɪŋ/ adj fugaz

Flemish /ˈflemɪʃ/ adj & n flamenco (m)

flesh /fleʃ/ n carne f. **in the ~** en persona

flew /fluː/ see FLY

flex /fleks/ vt doblar; flexionar (muscle). ●n (Elec) cable m

flexib|ility /fleksəˈbɪlətɪ/ n flexibilidad f. **~le** /ˈfleksəbl/ adj flexible

flexitime/ˈfleksɪtaɪm/, (Amer) **flextime** /ˈflekstaɪm/n horario m flexible

flick /flɪk/ n golpecito m. ●vt dar un golpecito a. ■ **~ through** vt hojear

flicker /ˈflɪkə(r)/ vi parpadear. ●n

parpadeo m; (of hope) resquicio m

flies /flaɪz/ npl (on trousers) bragueta f

flight /flaɪt/ n vuelo m; (fleeing) huida f, fuga f. **~ of stairs** tramo m de escalera f. **take (to) ~** darse a la fuga. **~ attendant** n (male) sobrecargo m, aeromozo m (LAm); (female) azafata f, aeromoza f (LAm). **~-deck** n cubierta f de vuelo

flimsy /ˈflɪmzɪ/ adj (**-ier, -iest**) flojo, débil, poco sólido

flinch /flɪntʃ/ vi retroceder (**from** ante)

fling /flɪŋ/ vt (pt **flung**) arrojar. ●n (love affair) aventura f; (wild time) juerga f

flint /flɪnt/ n pedernal m; (for lighter) piedra f

flip /flɪp/ vt (pt **flipped**) dar un golpecito a. ●n golpecito m. ■ **~ through** vt hojear.

flippant /ˈflɪpənt/ adj poco serio

flipper /ˈflɪpə(r)/ n aleta f

flirt /flɜːt/ vi coquetear. ●n (woman) coqueta f; (man) coqueto m

flit /flɪt/ vi (pt **flitted**) revolotear

float /fləʊt/ vi flotar. ●vt hacer flotar; introducir en Bolsa (company). ●n flotador m; (cash) caja f chica

flock /flɒk/ n (of birds) bandada f; (of sheep) rebaño m. ●vi congregarse

flog /flɒg/ vt (pt **flogged**) (beat) azotar; (fam, sell) vender

flood /flʌd/ n inundación f; (fig) avalancha f. ●vt inundar. ●vi (building etc) inundarse; (river) desbordar. **~light** n foco m. ●vt (pt **~lit**) iluminar (con focos)

floor /flɔː(r)/ n suelo m; (storey) piso m; (for dancing) pista f. ●vt derribar; (baffle) confundir

flop /flɒp/ vi (pt **flopped**) dejarse caer pesadamente; (fam, fail) fracasar. ●n Ⓣ fracaso m. **~py** adj flojo. ●**~py disk** n disquete m, floppy (disk) m

floral /ˈflɔːrəl/ adj floral

florid /ˈflɒrɪd/ adj florido

florist /ˈflɒrɪst/ n florista m & f

flounder /ˈflaʊndə(r)/ vi (in water) luchar para mantenerse a flote; (speaker) quedar sin saber qué decir

flour /flaʊə(r)/ n harina f

flourish /ˈflʌrɪʃ/ vi florecer; (business) prosperar. •vt blandir. •n ademán m elegante; (in handwriting) rasgo m. ∼ing adj próspero

flout /flaʊt/ vt burlarse de

flow /fləʊ/ vi fluir; (blood) correr; (hang loosely) caer. •n flujo m; (stream) corriente f; (of traffic, information) circulación f. ∼ **chart** n organigrama m

flower /ˈflaʊə(r)/ n flor f. •vi florecer, florear (Mex). ∼ **bed** n macizo m de flores. ∼y adj florido

flown /fləʊn/ see FLY

flu /fluː/ n gripe f

fluctuat|e /ˈflʌktjʊeɪt/ vi fluctuar. ∼ion /-ˈeɪʃn/ n fluctuación f

flue /fluː/ n tiro m

fluen|cy /ˈfluːənsɪ/ n fluidez f. ∼t adj (style) fluido; (speaker) elocuente. **be** ∼t **in a language** hablar un idioma con fluidez. ∼tly adv con fluidez

fluff /flʌf/ n pelusa f. ∼y adj (-ier, -iest) velloso

fluid /ˈfluːɪd/ adj & n fluido (m)

flung /flʌŋ/ see FLING

fluorescent /flʊəˈresnt/ adj fluorescente

flush /flʌʃ/ vi ruborizarse. •vt. ∼ **the toilet** tirar de la cadena, jalarle a la cadena (LAm). •n (blush) rubor m

fluster /ˈflʌstə(r)/ vt poner nervioso

flute /fluːt/ n flauta f

flutter /ˈflʌtə(r)/ vi ondear; (bird) revolotear. •n (of wings) revoloteo m; (fig) agitación f

flux /flʌks/ n flujo m. **be in a state of** ∼ estar siempre cambiando

fly /flaɪ/ vi (pt flew, pp flown) volar; (passenger) ir en avión; (flag) flotar; (rush) correr. •vt pilotar, pilotear (LAm) (aircraft); transportar en avión (passengers, goods); izar (flag). •n mosca f; (of trousers) see FLIES. ∼ing adj volante. ∼ing visit visita f relámpago. •n (activity) aviación f. ∼leaf n guarda f. ∼over n paso m elevado

foal /fəʊl/ n potro m

foam /fəʊm/ n espuma f. •vi espumar. ∼ **rubber** n goma f espuma, hule m espuma (Mex)

fob /fɒb/ vt (pt fobbed). ∼ **sth off onto s.o.** (palm off) encajarle algo a uno

focal /ˈfəʊkl/ adj focal

focus /ˈfəʊkəs/ n (pl -cuses or -ci /-saɪ/) foco m; (fig) centro m. **in** ∼ enfocado. **out of** ∼ desenfocado. •vt (pt focused) enfocar; (fig) concentrar. •vi enfocar; (fig) concentrarse (**on** en)

fodder /ˈfɒdə(r)/ n forraje m

foe /fəʊ/ n enemigo m

foetus /ˈfiːtəs/ n (pl -tuses) feto m

fog /fɒg/ n niebla f

fog|gy adj (-ier, -iest) nebuloso. **it is** ∼**gy** hay niebla. ∼**horn** n sirena f de niebla

foible /ˈfɔɪbl/ n punto m débil

foil /fɔɪl/ vt (thwart) frustrar. •n papel m de plata

foist /fɔɪst/ vt encajar (**on** a)

fold /fəʊld/ vt doblar; cruzar (arms). •vi doblarse; (fail) fracasar. •n pliegue m. (for sheep) redil m. ∼**er** n carpeta f. ∼**ing** adj plegable

foliage /ˈfəʊlɪɪdʒ/ n follaje m

folk /fəʊk/ n gente f. ●adj popular. **~lore** /-lɔː(r)/ n folklore m. **~ music** n música f folklórica; (modern) música f folk. **~s** npl (one's relatives) familia f

follow /ˈfɒləʊ/ vt/i seguir. ■ **~ up** vt seguir. **~er** n seguidor m. **~ing** n partidarios mpl. ●adj siguiente. ●prep después de

folly /ˈfɒlɪ/ n locura f

fond /fɒnd/ adj (-er, -est) (loving) cariñoso; (hope) vivo. **be ~ of s.o.** tener(le) cariño a uno. **be ~ of sth** ser aficionado a algo

fondle /ˈfɒndl/ vt acariciar

fondness /ˈfɒndnɪs/ n cariño m; (for things) afición f

font /fɒnt/ n pila f bautismal

food /fuːd/ n comida f. **~ processor** n robot m de cocina

fool /fuːl/ n idiota m & f ●vt engañar. ■ **~ about** vi hacer payasadas. **~hardy** adj temerario. **~ish** adj tonto. **~ishly** adv tontamente. **~ishness** n tontería f. **~proof** adj infalible

foot /fʊt/ n (pl **feet**) pie m; (measure) pie m (= 30,48cm); (of animal, furniture) pata f. **get under s.o 's feet** estorbar a uno. **on ~** a pie. **on/to one's feet** de pie. **put one's ~ in it** meter la pata. ●vt pagar (bill). **~age** /-ɪdʒ/ n (of film) secuencia f. **~-and-mouth disease** n fiebre f aftosa. **~ball** n (ball) balón m; (game) fútbol m; (American ~ball) fútbol m americano. **~baller** n futbolista m & f. **~bridge** n puente m para peatones. **~hills** npl estribaciones fpl. **~hold** n punto m de apoyo. **~ing** n pie m. **on an equal ~ing** en igualdad de condiciones. **~lights** npl candilejas fpl. **~man** /-mən/ n lacayo m. **~note** n nota f (al pie de la página). **~path** n (in country) senda f; (in town) acera f, banqueta f (Mex). **~print** n huella f. **~step** n paso m. **~wear** n calzado m

for /fɔː(r)//fə(r)/
●preposition

┈┈▸ (intended for) para. **it's ~ my mother** es para mi madre. **she works ~ a multinational** trabaja para una multinacional

┈┈▸ (on behalf of) por. **I did it ~ you** lo hice por ti

▶ See entries **para** and **por** for further information

┈┈▸ (expressing purpose) para. **I use it ~ washing the car** lo uso para limpiar el coche. **what ~?** ¿para qué?. **to go out ~ a meal** salir a comer fuera

┈┈▸ (in favour of) a favor de. **are you ~ or against the idea?** ¿estás a favor o en contra de la idea?

┈┈▸ (indicating cost, in exchage for) por. **I bought it ~ 30 pounds** lo compré por 30 libras. **she left him ~ another man** lo dejó por otro. **thanks ~ everything** gracias por todo. **what's the Spanish ~ toad'?** ¿cómo se dice toad' en español?

┈┈▸ (expressing duration) **he read ~ two hours** leyó durante dos horas. **how long are you going ~?** ¿por cuánto tiempo vas? **I've been waiting ~ three hours** hace tres horas que estoy esperando, llevo tres horas esperando

┈┈▸ (in the direction of) para. **the train ~ Santiago** el tren para Santiago

●conjunction (because) porque, pues (literary usage). **she left at once, ~ it was getting late** se fue en seguida, porque or pues se hacía tarde

forage /ˈfɒrɪdʒ/ vi forrajear. ●n forraje m

forbade /fəˈbæd/ see **FORBID**

forbearance /fɔːˈbeərəns/ n paciencia f

forbid /fəˈbɪd/ vt (pt **forbade**, pp **forbidden**) prohibir (**s.o. to do a**

uno hacer). **~ s.o. sth** prohibir algo a uno. **~ding** adj imponente

force /fɔːs/ n fuerza f. **by ~** a la fuerza. **come into ~** entrar en vigor. **the ~s** las fuerzas fpl armadas. •vt forzar; (compel) obligar (**s.o. to do sth** a uno a hacer algo). **~ on** imponer a. **~ open** forzar. **~d** adj forzado. **~-feed** vt alimentar a la fuerza. **~ful** adj enérgico

forceps /'fɔːseps/ n fórceps m

forcibl|e /'fɔːsəbl/ adj a la fuerza. **~y** adv a la fuerza

ford /fɔːd/ n vado m •vt vadear

fore /fɔː(r)/ adj anterior. •n. **come to the ~** hacerse evidente

forearm /'fɔːrɑːm/ n antebrazo m

foreboding /fɔː'bəʊdɪŋ/ n presentimiento m

forecast /'fɔːkɑːst/ vt (pt **forecast**) pronosticar (weather); prever (result). •n pronóstico m. **weather ~** pronóstico m del tiempo

forecourt /'fɔːkɔːt/ n patio m delantero

forefinger /'fɔːfɪŋgə(r)/ n (dedo m) índice m

forefront /'fɔːfrʌnt/ n vanguardia f. **in the ~** a la vanguardia

forego /fɔː'gəʊ/ vt (pt **forewent**, pp **foregone**) see FORGO

foregone /'fɔːgɒn/ adj. **~ conclusion** resultado m previsto

foreground /'fɔːgraʊnd/ n. **in the ~** en primer plano

forehead /'fɒrɪd/ n frente f

foreign /'fɒrən/ adj extranjero; (trade) exterior; (travel) al extranjero, en el extranjero. **~er** n extranjero m

foreman /'fɔːmən/ n (pl **-men** /-mən/) n capataz m

foremost /'fɔːməʊst/ adj primero. •adv. **first and ~** ante todo

forerunner /'fɔːrʌnə(r)/ n precursor m

foresee /fɔː'siː/ vt (pt **-saw**, pp **-seen**) prever. **~able** adj previsible

foresight /'fɔːsaɪt/ n previsión f

forest /'fɒrɪst/ n bosque m

forestall /fɔː'stɔːl/ vt (prevent) prevenir; (preempt) anticiparse a

forestry /'fɒrɪstrɪ/ n silvicultura f

foretaste /'fɔːteɪst/ n anticipo m

foretell /fɔː'tel/ vt (pt **foretold**) predecir

forever /fə'revə(r)/ adv para siempre; (always) siempre

forewarn /fɔː'wɔːn/ vt advertir

forewent /fɔː'went/ see FOREGO

foreword /'fɔːwɜːd/ n prefacio m

forfeit /'fɔːfɪt/ n (penalty) pena f; (in game) prenda f. •vt perder; perder el derecho a (property)

forgave /fə'geɪv/ see FORGIVE

forge /fɔːdʒ/ n fragua f. •vt fraguar; (copy) falsificar. ■ **~ ahead** vi adelantarse rápidamente. **~r** n falsificador m. **~ry** n falsificación f

forget /fə'get/ vt (pt **forgot**, pp **forgotten**) olvidar, olvidarse de. •vi olvidarse (**about** de). **I forgot** se me olvidó. **~ful** adj olvidadizo

forgive /fə'gɪv/ vt (pt **forgave**, pp **forgiven**) perdonar. **~ s.o. for sth** perdonar algo a uno. **~ness** n perdón m

forgo /fɔː'gəʊ/ vt (pt **forwent**, pp **forgone**) renunciar a

fork /fɔːk/ n tenedor m; (for digging) horca f; (in road) bifurcación f. •vi (road) bifurcarse. ■ **~ out** vt 🔲 desembolsar, aflojar 🔲. **~-lift truck** n carretilla f elevadora

forlorn /fə'lɔːn/ adj (hope, attempt) desesperado; (smile) triste

form /fɔːm/ n forma f; (document) formulario m; (Schol) clase f. •vt formar. •vi formarse

formal /'fɔːml/ adj formal; (person) formalista; (dress) de etiqueta. **~ity** n /-'mælətɪ/ n formalidad f. **~ly** adv oficialmente

format /'fɔːmæt/ n formato m. • vt
(pt **formatted**) (Comp) formatear

formation /fɔː'meɪʃn/ n
formación f

former /'fɔːmə(r)/ adj anterior; (first
of two) primero. • n. **the ~** el
primero m, la primera f, los
primeros mpl, las primeras fpl. **~ly**
adv antes

formidable /'fɔːmɪdəbl/ adj
formidable

formula /'fɔːmjʊlə/ n (pl **-ae** /-iː/ or
-as) fórmula f. **~te** /-leɪt/ vt
formular

forsake /fə'seɪk/ vt (pt **forsook**, pp
forsaken) abandonar

fort /fɔːt/ n fuerte m

forth /fɔːθ/ adv. **and so ~** y así
sucesivamente. **~coming**
/-'kʌmɪŋ/ adj próximo, venidero;
(sociable) comunicativo. **~right** adj
directo. **~with** /-'wɪθ/ adv
inmediatamente

fortieth /'fɔːtɪɪθ/ adj cuadragésimo.
• n cuadragésima parte f

fortnight /'fɔːtnaɪt/ n quince días
mpl, quincena f. **~ly** adj bimensual.
• adv cada quince días

fortress /'fɔːtrɪs/ n fortaleza f

fortunate /'fɔːtʃənət/ adj
afortunado. **be ~** tener suerte.
~ly adv afortunadamente

fortune /'fɔːtʃuːn/ n fortuna f.
~-teller n adivino m

forty /'fɔːtɪ/ adj & n cuarenta (m). **~
winks** un sueñecito

forum /'fɔːrəm/ n foro m

forward /'fɔːwəd/ adj (movement)
hacia adelante; (advanced) precoz;
(pert) impertinente. • n (Sport)
delantero m. • adv adelante. **go ~**
avanzar. • vt hacer seguir (letter);
enviar (goods). **~s** adv adelante

forwent /fɔː'went/ see **FORGO**

fossil /'fɒsl/ adj & n fósil (m)

foster /'fɒstə(r)/ vt (promote)
fomentar; criar (child). **~ child** n
hijo m adoptivo

fought /fɔːt/ see **FIGHT**

foul /faʊl/ adj (**-er, -est**) (smell)
nauseabundo; (weather) pésimo;
(person) asqueroso; (dirty) sucio;
(language) obsceno. • n (Sport) falta f.
• vt contaminar; (entangle) enredar.
~ play n (Sport) jugada f sucia;
(crime) delito m

found /faʊnd/ see **FIND**. • vt fundar.

foundation /faʊn'deɪʃn/ n
fundación f; (basis) fundamento.
(cosmetic) base f (de maquillaje).
~s npl (of building) cimientos mpl

founder /'faʊndə(r)/ n fundador m.
• vi (ship) hundirse

fountain /'faʊntɪn/ n fuente f. **~
pen** n pluma f (estilográfica) f,
estilográfica f

four /fɔː(r)/ adj & n cuatro (m).
~fold adj cuádruple. • adv cuatro
veces. **~some** /-səm/ n grupo m de
cuatro personas **~teen** /'fɔːtiːn/ adj
& n catorce (m). **~teenth** adj & n
decimocuarto (m). **~th** /-fɔːθ/ adj &
n cuarto (m). **~wheel drive** n
tracción f integral

fowl /faʊl/ n ave f

fox /fɒks/ n zorro m, zorra f. • vt ▣
confundir

foyer /'fɔɪeɪ/ n (of theatre) foyer m;
(of hotel) vestíbulo m

fraction /'frækʃn/ n fracción f

fracture /'fræktʃə(r)/ n fractura f.
• vt fracturar. • vi fracturarse

fragile /'frædʒaɪl/ adj frágil

fragment /'frægmənt/ n fragmento
m. **~ary** /-ərɪ/ adj fragmentario

fragran|ce /'freɪgrəns/ n fragancia
f. **~t** adj fragante

frail /freɪl/ adj (**-er, -est**) frágil

frame /freɪm/ n (of picture, door,
window) marco m; (of spectacles)
montura f; (fig, structure) estructura
f. • vt enmarcar (picture); formular
(plan, question); (fam, incriminate unjustly)
incriminar falsamente. **~work** n
estructura f; (context) marco m

France /frɑːns/ n Francia f

frank /fræŋk/ adj franco. • vt
franquear. ~**ly** adv francamente

frantic /'fræntɪk/ adj frenético. ~
with loco de

fratern|al /frə'tɜːnl/ adj fraternal.
~**ity** /frə'tɜːnɪtɪ/ n fraternidad f;
(club) asociación f. ~**ize**
/'frætənaɪz/ vi fraternizar

fraud /frɔːd/ n fraude m; (person)
impostor m. ~**ulent** /-jʊlənt/adj
fraudulento

fraught /frɔːt/ adj (tense) tenso. ~
with cargado de

fray /freɪ/ n riña f

freak /friːk/ n fenómeno m; (monster)
monstruo m. • adj anormal. ~**ish**
adj anormal

freckle /'frekl/ n peca f. ~**d** adj
pecoso

free /friː/ adj (**freer** /'friːə(r)/, **freest**
/'friːɪst/) libre; (gratis) gratuito. ~
of charge gratis. • vt (pt **freed**) (set
at liberty) poner en libertad; (relieve
from) liberar (**from/of** de);
(untangle) desenredar. ~**dom** n
libertad f. ~**hold** n propiedad f
absoluta. ~ **kick** n tiro m libre.
~**lance** adj & adv por cuenta
propia. ~**ly** adv libremente.
~**mason** n masón m. ~**-range** adj
(eggs) de granja. ~ **speech** n
libertad f de expresión. ~**style** n
estilo m libre. ~**way** n (Amer)
autopista f

freez|e /friːz/ vt (pt **froze**, pp
frozen) helar; congelar (food,
wages). • vi helarse; (become
motionless) quedarse inmóvil. • n (on
wages, prices) congelación f. ~**er** n
congelador m. ~**ing** adj glacial. • n.
~**ing (point)** punto m de
congelación f. **below** ~**ing** bajo
cero

freight /freɪt/ n (goods) mercancías
fpl. ~**er** n buque m de carga

French /frentʃ/ adj francés. • n
(language) francés m. • npl. **the** ~
(people) los franceses. ~ **fries** npl
patatas fpl fritas, papas fpl fritas
(LAm). ~**man** /-mən/ n francés m.
~ **window** n puerta f ventana.

~**woman** f francesa f

frenz|ied /'frenzɪd/ adj frenético.
~**y** n frenesí m

frequency /'friːkwənsɪ/ n
frecuencia f

frequent /frɪ'kwent/ vt frecuentar.
• /'friːkwənt/ adj frecuente. ~**ly** adv
frecuentemente

fresh /freʃ/ adj (**-er, -est**) fresco;
(different, additional) nuevo; (water)
dulce. ~**en** vi refrescar. ■ ~**en up**
vi (person) refrescarse. ~**er** n ① see
~MAN. ~**ly** adv recientemente.
~**man** n /-mən/ estudiante m de
primer año. ~**ness** n frescura f

fret /fret/ vi (pt **fretted**)
preocuparse. ~**ful** adj (discontented)
quejoso; (irritable) irritable

friction /'frɪkʃn/ n fricción f

Friday /'fraɪdeɪ/ n viernes m

fridge /frɪdʒ/ n ① frigorífico m,
nevera f, refrigerador m (LAm)

fried /fraɪd/ see FRY. • adj frito

friend /frend/ n amigo m. ~**liness**
n simpatía f. ~**ly** adj (**-ier, -iest**)
simpático. ~**ship** n amistad f

fries /fraɪz/ npl see FRENCH FRIES.

frieze /friːz/ n friso m

frigate /'frɪgət/ n fragata f

fright /fraɪt/ n miedo m; (shock)
susto m. ~**en** vt asustar. ■ ~ **off** vt
ahuyentar. ~**ened** adj asustado.
be ~**ened** tener miedo (**of** de.)
~**ful** adj espantoso, horrible.
~**fully** adv terriblemente

frigid /'frɪdʒɪd/ adj frígido

frill /frɪl/ n volante m, olán m (Mex).
~**s** npl (fig) adornos mpl. **with no**
~**s** sencillo

fringe /frɪndʒ/ n (sewing) fleco m;
(ornamental border) franja f; (of hair)
flequillo m, cerquillo m (LAm), fleco
m (Mex); (of area) periferia f; (of
society) margen m

fritter /'frɪtə(r)/ vt. ■ ~ **away** vt
desperdiciar (time); malgastar
(money)

frivol|ity /frɪ'vɒlətɪ/ n frivolidad f.

~ous /'frɪvələs/ adj frívolo

fro /frəʊ/ see TO AND FRO

frock /frɒk/ n vestido m

frog /frɒg/ n rana f. **have a ~ in one's throat** tener carraspera. **~man** /-mən/ n hombre m rana. **~spawn** n huevos mpl de rana

frolic /'frɒlɪk/ vi (pt **frolicked**) retozar

from /frɒm//frəm/ prep de; (indicating starting point) desde; (habit, conviction) por; ~ **then on** a partir de ahí

front /frʌnt/ n parte f delantera; (of building) fachada f; (of clothes) delantera f; (Mil, Pol) frente f; (of book) principio m; (fig, appearance) apariencia f; (seafront) paseo m marítimo, malecón m (LAm). **in ~ of** delante de. ● adj delantero; (first) primero. **~al** adj frontal; (attack) de frente. ~ **door** n puerta f principal

frontier /'frʌntɪə(r)/ n frontera f

front page n (of newspaper) primera plana f

frost /frɒst/ n (freezing) helada f; (frozen dew) escarcha f. **~bite** n congelación f. **~bitten** adj congelado. **~ed** adj (glass) esmerilado. **~ing** n (Amer) glaseado m. **~y** adj (weather) helado; (night) de helada, (fig) glacial

froth /frɒθ/ n espuma f. ● vi espumar. **~y** adj espumoso

frown /fraʊn/ vi fruncir el entrecejo ● n ceño m. ■ **~ on** vt desaprobar

froze /frəʊz/ see FREEZE. **~n** /'frəʊzn/ see FREEZE. ● adj congelado; (region) helado

frugal /'fru:gl/ adj frugal

fruit /fru:t/ n (in botany) fruto m; (as food) fruta f. **~ful** /'fru:tfl/ adj fértil; (fig) fructífero. **~ion** /fru:'ɪʃn/ n. **come to ~ion** realizarse. **~less** adj infructuoso. ~ **salad** n macedonia f de frutas. **~y** adj que sabe a fruta

frustrat|e /frʌ'streɪt/ vt frustrar.

~ion /-ʃn/ n frustración f. **~ed** adj frustrado. **~ing** adj frustrante

fry /fraɪ/ vt (pt **fried**) freír. ● vi freírse. **~ing pan** n sártén f, sartén m (LAm)

fudge /fʌdʒ/ n dulce m de azúcar

fuel /'fju:əl/ n combustible m

fugitive /'fju:dʒɪtɪv/ adj & n fugitivo (m)

fulfil /fʊl'fɪl/ vt (pt **fulfilled**) cumplir (con) (promise, obligation); satisfacer (condition); hacer realidad (ambition). **~ment** n (of promise, obligation) cumplimiento m; (of conditions) satisfacción f; (of hopes, plans) realización f

full /fʊl/ adj (**-er, -est**) lleno; (bus, hotel) completo; (account) detallado. **at ~ speed** a máxima velocidad. **be ~ (up)** (with food) no poder más. ● n. **in ~** sin quitar nada. **to the ~** completamente. **write in ~** escribir con todas las letras. **~back** n (Sport) defensa m & f. **~-blown** /-'bləʊn/ adj verdadero. **~-fledged** /-'fledʒd/ adj (Amer) see FULLY-FLEDGED. **~ moon** n luna f llena. **~-scale** /-'skeɪl/ adj (drawing) de tamaño natural; (fig) amplio. ~ **stop** n punto m. **~-time** adj (employment) de jornada completa. ● /-'taɪm/ adv a tiempo completo. **~y** adv completamente. **~-fledged** /-'fledʒd/ adj (chick) capaz de volar; (lawyer, nurse) hecho y derecho

fulsome /'fʊlsəm/ adj excesivo

fumble /'fʌmbl/ vi buscar (a tientas)

fume /fju:m/ vi despedir gases; (fig, be furious) estar furioso. **~s** npl gases mpl

fumigate /'fju:mɪgeɪt/ vt fumigar

fun /fʌn/ n (amusement) diversión f; (merriment) alegría f. **for ~** en broma. **have ~** divertirse. **make ~ of** burlarse de

function /'fʌŋkʃn/ n (purpose, duty) función f; (reception) recepción f. ● vi funcionar. **~al** adj funcional

fund /fʌnd/ n fondo m. • vt financiar

fundamental /fʌndəˈmentl/ adj fundamental. **~ist** adj & n fundamentalista (m & f)

funeral /ˈfjuːnərəl/ n entierro m, funerales mpl. **~ director** n director m de pompas fúnebres

funfair /ˈfʌnfeə(r)/ n feria f; (permanent) parque m de atracciones, parque m de diversiones (LAm)

fungus /ˈfʌŋgəs/ n (pl **-gi** /-gaɪ/) hongo m

funnel /ˈfʌnl/ n (for pouring) embudo m; (of ship) chimenea f

funn|ily /ˈfʌnɪlɪ/ adv (oddly) curiosamente. **~y** adj (**-ier, -iest**) divertido, gracioso; (odd) curioso, raro

fur /fɜː(r)/ n pelo m; (pelt) piel f

furious /ˈfjʊərɪəs/ adj furioso. **~ly** adv furiosamente

furlough /ˈfɜːləʊ/ n (Amer) permiso m. **on ~** de permiso

furnace /ˈfɜːnɪs/ n horno m

furnish /ˈfɜːnɪʃ/ vt amueblar, amoblar (LAm); (supply) proveer. **~ings** npl muebles mpl, mobiliario m

furniture /ˈfɜːnɪtʃə(r)/ n muebles mpl, mobiliario m. **a piece of ~** un mueble

furrow /ˈfʌrəʊ/ n surco m

furry /ˈfɜːrɪ/ adj peludo

furthe|r /ˈfɜːðə(r)/ adj más lejano; (additional) nuevo. • adv más lejos; (more) además. • vt fomentar. **~rmore** adv además. **~st** adj más lejano. • adv más lejos

furtive /ˈfɜːtɪv/ adj furtivo

fury /ˈfjʊərɪ/ n furia f

fuse /fjuːz/ vt (melt) fundir; (fig, unite) fusionar. **~ the lights** fundir los plomos. • vi fundirse; (fig) fusionarse. • n fusible m, plomo m; (of bomb) mecha f. **~box** n caja f de fusibles

fuselage /ˈfjuːzəlɑːʒ/ n fuselaje m

fusion /ˈfjuːʒn/ n fusión f

fuss /fʌs/ n (commotion) jaleo m. **kick up a ~** armar un lío, armar una bronca. **make a ~ of** tratar con mucha atención. • vi preocuparse. **~y** adj (**-ier, -iest**) (finicky) remilgado; (demanding) exigente

futil|e /ˈfjuːtaɪl/ adj inútil, vano. **~ity** /fjuːˈtɪlətɪ/ n inutilidad f

futur|e /ˈfjuːtʃə(r)/ adj futuro. • n futuro m. **in ~e** de ahora en adelante. **~istic** /fjuːtʃəˈrɪstɪk/ adj futurista

fuzz /fʌz/ n pelusa f. **~y** adj (hair) crespo; (photograph) borroso

Gg

gab /gæb/ n. **have the gift of the ~** tener un pico de oro

gabardine /gæbəˈdiːn/ n gabardina f

gabble /ˈgæbl/ vi hablar atropelladamente

gable /ˈgeɪbl/ n aguilón m

gad /gæd/ vi (pt **gadded**). **~ about** callejear

gadget /ˈgædʒɪt/ n chisme m

Gaelic /ˈgeɪlɪk/ adj & n gaélico (m)

gaffe /gæf/ n plancha f, metedura f de pata, metida f de pata (LAm)

gag /gæg/ n mordaza f; (joke) chiste

m. ●vt (pt **gagged**) amordazar. ●vi hacer arcadas

gaiety /'geɪətɪ/ n alegría f

gaily /'geɪlɪ/ adv alegremente

gain /geɪn/ vt ganar; (acquire) adquirir; (obtain) conseguir. ●vi (clock) adelantar. ●n ganancia f; (increase) aumento m

gait /geɪt/ n modo m de andar

gala /'gɑːlə/ n fiesta f. ~ **performance** (función f de) gala f

galaxy /'gæləksɪ/ n galaxia f

gale /geɪl/ n vendaval m

gall /gɔːl/ n bilis f; (fig) hiel f; (impudence) descaro m

gallant /'gælənt/ adj (brave) valiente; (chivalrous) galante. ~**ry** n valor m

gall bladder /'gɔːlblædə(r)/ n vesícula f biliar

gallery /'gælərɪ/ n galería f

galley /'gælɪ/ n (ship) galera f; (ship's kitchen) cocina f. ~ **(proof)** n galerada f

gallivant /'gælɪvænt/ vi ▣ callejear

gallon /'gælən/ n galón m (imperial = 4,546l; Amer = 3,785l)

gallop /'gæləp/ n galope m. ●vi (pt **galloped**) galopar

gallows /'gæləʊz/ n horca f

galore /gə'lɔː(r)/ adj en abundancia

galvanize /'gælvənaɪz/ vt galvanizar

gambl|e /'gæmbl/ vi jugar. ~**e on** contar con. ●vt jugarse. ●n (venture) empresa f arriesgada; (bet) apuesta f; (risk) riesgo m. ~**er** n jugador m. ~**ing** n juego m

game /geɪm/ n juego m; (match) partido m; (animals, birds) caza f. ●adj valiente. ~ **for** listo para. ~**keeper** n guardabosque m. ~**s** n (in school) deportes mpl

gammon /'gæmən/ n jamón m fresco

gamut /'gæmət/ n gama f

gander /'gændə(r)/ n ganso m

gang /gæŋ/ n pandilla f; (of workmen) equipo m. ~**master** n contratista de mano de obra indocumentada. ■ ~ **up** vi unirse (**on** contra)

gangling /'gæŋglɪŋ/ adj larguirucho

gangrene /'gæŋgriːn/ n gangrena f

gangster /'gæŋstə(r)/ n bandido m, gángster m & f

gangway /'gæŋweɪ/ n pasillo m; (of ship) pasarela f

gaol /dʒeɪl/ n cárcel f. ~**er** n carcelero m

gap /gæp/ n espacio m; (in fence, hedge) hueco m; (in time) intervalo m; (in knowledge) laguna f; (difference) diferencia f

gap|e /geɪp/ vi quedarse boquiabierto; (be wide open) estar muy abierto. ~**ing** adj abierto; (person) boquiabierto

garage /'gærɑːʒ/ n garaje m, garage m (LAm), cochera f (Mex); (petrol station) gasolinera f; (for repairs, sales) taller m, garage m (LAm)

garbage /'gɑːbɪdʒ/ n basura f. ~ **can** n (Amer) cubo m de la basura, bote m de la basura (Mex). ~ **collector**, ~ **man** n (Amer) basurero m

garble /'gɑːbl/ vt tergiversar, embrollar

garden /'gɑːdn/ n (of flowers) jardín m; (of vegetables/fruit) huerto m. ●vi trabajar en el jardín. ~**er** /'gɑːdnə(r)/ n jardinero m. ~**ing** n jardinería f; (vegetable growing) horticultura f

gargle /'gɑːgl/ vi hacer gárgaras

gargoyle /'gɑːgɔɪl/ n gárgola f

garish /'geərɪʃ/ adj chillón

garland /'gɑːlənd/ n guirnalda f

garlic /'gɑːlɪk/ n ajo m

garment /'gɑːmənt/ n prenda f (de vestir)

garnish /'gɑːnɪʃ/ vt adornar,

decorar. •n adorno m

garret /'gærət/ n buhardilla f

garrison /'gærɪsn/ n guarnición f

garrulous /'gærələs/ adj hablador

garter /'ɡɑːtə(r)/ n liga f

gas /ɡæs/ n (pl **gases**) gas m; (anaesthetic) anestésico m; (Amer, petrol) gasolina f. •vt (pt **gassed**) asfixiar con gas

gash /ɡæʃ/ n tajo m. •vt hacer un tajo de

gasket /'ɡæskɪt/ n junta f

gas: ~ **mask** n careta f antigás. ~ **meter** n contador m de gas

gasoline /'ɡæsəliːn/ n (Amer) gasolina f

gasp /ɡɑːsp/ vi jadear; (with surprise) dar un grito ahogado. •n exclamación f, grito m

gas: ~ **ring** n hornillo m de gas. ~ **station** n (Amer) gasolinera f

gastric /'ɡæstrɪk/ adj gástrico

gate /ɡeɪt/ n puerta f; (of metal) verja f; (barrier) barrera f

gate: ~**crash** vt colarse en. ~**crasher** n intruso m (que ha entrado sin ser invitado). ~**way** n puerta f

gather /'ɡæðə(r)/ vt reunir (people, things); (accumulate) acumular; (pick up) recoger; recoger (flowers); (fig, infer) deducir; (sewing) fruncir. ~ **speed** acelerar. •vi (people) reunirse; (things) acumularse. ~**ing** n reunión f

gaudy /'ɡɔːdɪ/ adj (-ier, -iest) chillón

gauge /ɡeɪdʒ/ n (measurement) medida f; (Rail) entrevía f; (instrument) indicador m. •vt medir; (fig) estimar

gaunt /ɡɔːnt/ adj descarnado; (from illness) demacrado

gauntlet /'ɡɔːntlɪt/ n. **run the ~ of** aguantar el acoso de

gauze /ɡɔːz/ n gasa f

gave /ɡeɪv/ see GIVE

gawky /'ɡɔːkɪ/ adj (-ier, -iest) torpe

gawp /ɡɔːp/ vi. ~ **at** mirar como un tonto

gay /ɡeɪ/ adj (-er, -est) (fam, homosexual) homosexual, gay 𝕋; (dated, joyful) alegre

gaze /ɡeɪz/ vi. ~ (**at**) mirar (fijamente). •n mirada f (fija)

gazelle /ɡə'zel/ n (pl invar or -s) gacela f

GB abbr see GREAT BRITAIN

gear /ɡɪə(r)/ n equipo m; (Tec) engranaje m; (Auto) marcha f, cambio m. **in ~** engranado. **out of ~** desengranado. **change ~, shift ~** (Amer) cambiar de marcha. •vt adaptar. ~**box** n (Auto) caja f de cambios

geese /ɡiːs/ see GOOSE

gel /dʒel/ n gel m

gelatine /'dʒelətiːn/ n gelatina f

gelignite /'dʒelɪɡnaɪt/ n gelignita f

gem /dʒem/ n piedra f preciosa

Gemini /'dʒemɪnaɪ/ n Géminis mpl

gender /'dʒendə(r)/ n género m

gene /dʒiːn/ n gen m, gene m

genealogy /dʒiːnɪ'ælədʒɪ/ n genealogía f

general /'dʒenərəl/ adj general. •n general m. **in ~** en general. ~ **election** n elecciones fpl generales. ~**ization** /-'zeɪʃn/ n generalización f. ~**ize** vt/i generalizar. ~ **knowledge** n cultura f general. ~**ly** adv generalmente. ~ **practitioner** n médico m de cabecera

generat|e /'dʒenəreɪt/ vt generar. ~**ion** /-'reɪʃn/ n generación f. ~**ion gap** n brecha f generacional. ~**or** n generador m

genero|sity /dʒenə'rɒsətɪ/ n generosidad f. ~**us** /'dʒenərəs/ adj generoso; (plentiful) abundante

genetic /dʒɪ'netɪk/ adj genético. ~**s** n genética f

Geneva /dʒɪ'niːvə/ n Ginebra f

genial /'dʒiːnɪəl/ adj simpático, afable

genital /'dʒenɪtl/ adj genital. ~s npl genitales mpl

genitive /'dʒenɪtɪv/ adj & n genitivo (m)

genius /'dʒiːnɪəs/ n (pl **-uses**) genio m

genocide /'dʒenəsaɪd/ n genocidio m

genome /'dʒiːnəʊm/ n genoma m

genre /ʒɑːŋr/ n género m

gent /dʒent/ n 🔢 señor m. ~s n aseo m de caballeros

genteel /dʒen'tiːl/ adj distinguido

gentl|e /'dʒentl/ adj (**-er, -est**) (person) dulce; (murmur, breeze) suave; (hint) discreto. ~**eman** n señor m; (well-bred) caballero m. ~**eness** n amabilidad f

genuine /'dʒenjʊɪn/ adj verdadero; (person) sincero

geograph|er /dʒɪ'ɒgrəfə(r)/ n geógrafo m. ~**ical** /dʒɪə'græfɪkl/ adj geográfico. ~**y** /dʒɪ'ɒgrəfɪ/ n geografía f

geolog|ical /dʒɪə'lɒdʒɪkl/ adj geológico. ~**ist** /dʒɪ'ɒlədʒɪst/ n geólogo m. ~**y** /dʒɪ'ɒlədʒɪ/ n geología f

geometr|ic(al) /dʒɪə'metrɪk(l)/ adj geométrico. ~**y** /dʒɪ'ɒmətrɪ/ n geometría f

geranium /dʒə'reɪnɪəm/ n geranio m

geriatric /dʒerɪ'ætrɪk/ adj (patient) anciano; (ward) de geriatría. ~**s** n geriatría f

germ /dʒɜːm/ n microbio m, germen m

German /'dʒɜːmən/ adj & n alemán (m). ~**ic** /dʒɜː'mænɪk/ adj germánico. ~ **measles** n rubéola f. ~**y** n Alemania f

germinate /'dʒɜːmɪneɪt/ vi germinar

gesticulate /dʒe'stɪkjʊleɪt/ vi hacer ademanes, gesticular

gesture /'dʒestʃə(r)/ n gesto m, ademán m; (fig) gesto m. ●vi hacer gestos

---

get /get/

past **got**; past participle **got, gotten** (Amer); present participle **getting**

● transitive verb

····▸ (obtain) conseguir, obtener. **did you get the job?** ¿conseguiste el trabajo?

····▸ (buy) comprar. **I got it in the sales** lo compré en las rebajas

····▸ (achieve, win) sacar. **she got very good marks** sacó muy buenas notas

····▸ (receive) recibir. **I got a letter from Alex** recibí una carta de Alex

····▸ (fetch) ir a buscar. ~ **your coat** vete a buscar tu abrigo

····▸ (experience) llevarse. **I got a terrible shock** me llevé un shock espantoso

····▸ (fam, understand) entender. **I don't ~ what you mean** no entiendo lo que quieres decir

····▸ (ask or persuade) **to ~ s.o. to do sth** hacer que uno haga algo

Note that *hacer que* is followed by the subjunctive form of the verb

····▸ (cause to be done or happen) **I must ~ this watch fixed** tengo que llevar a arreglar este reloj. **they got the roof mended** hicieron arreglar el techo

● intransitive verb

····▸ (arrive, reach) llegar. **I got there late** llegué tarde. **how do you ~ to Paddington?** ¿cómo se llega a Paddington?

····▸ (become) **to ~ tired** cansarse. **she got very angry** se puso furiosa. **it's ~ting late** se está haciendo tarde

▶ For translations of expressions such as **get better**, **get old** see entries **better**, **old** etc. See also **got**

·····▶ **to get to do sth** (manage to) llegar a. **did you get to see him?** ¿llegaste a verlo? ■**get along** vi (manage) arreglárselas; (progress) hacer progresos. ■**get along with** vt llevarse bien con. ■**get at** vt (reach) llegar a; (imply) querer decir. ■**get away** vi salir; (escape) escaparse. ■**get back** vi volver. vt (recover) recobrar. ■**get by** vi (manage) arreglárselas; (pass) pasar. ■**get down** vi bajar. vt (make depressed) deprimir. ■**get in** vi entrar. ■**get into** vt entrar en; subir a (car) ■**get off** vt bajar(se) de (train etc). vi (from train etc) bajarse; (Jurid) salir absuelto. ■**get on** vi (progress) hacer progresos; (succeed) tener éxito. vt subirse a (train etc). ■**get on with** vt (be on good terms with) llevarse bien con; (continue) seguir con. ■**get out** vi salir. vt (take out) sacar. ■**get out of** vt (fig) librarse de. ■**get over** vt reponerse de (illness). ■**get round** vt soslayar (difficulty etc); engatusar (person). ■**get through** vi pasar; (on phone) comunicarse (**to** con). ■**get together** vi (meet up) reunirse. vt (assemble) reunir. ■**get up** vi levantarse; (climb) subir

geyser /'gi:zə(r)/ n géiser m

ghastly /'ɡɑːstlɪ/ adj (**-ier**, **-iest**) horrible

gherkin /'gɜːkɪn/ n pepinillo m

ghetto /'ɡetəʊ/ n (pl **-os**) gueto m

ghost /ɡəʊst/ n fantasma m. ∼**ly** adj espectral

giant /'dʒaɪənt/ n gigante m. ● adj gigantesco

gibberish /'dʒɪbərɪʃ/ n jerigonza f

gibe /dʒaɪb/ n pulla f

giblets /'dʒɪblɪts/ npl menudillos mpl

gidd|iness /'gɪdɪnɪs/ n vértigo m. ∼**y** adj (**-ier**, **-iest**) mareado. **be/feel** ∼**y** estar/sentirse mareado

gift /gɪft/ n regalo m; (ability) don m. ∼**ed** adj dotado de talento. ∼**-wrap** vt envolver para regalo

gigantic /dʒaɪˈgæntɪk/ adj gigantesco

giggle /'gɪgl/ vi reírse tontamente. ● n risita f

gild /gɪld/ vt dorar

gills /gɪlz/ npl agallas fpl

gilt /gɪlt/ n dorado m. ● adj dorado

gimmick /'gɪmɪk/ n truco m

gin / dʒɪn/ n ginebra f

ginger /'dʒɪndʒə(r)/ n jengibre m. ● adj rojizo. **he has** ∼ **hair** es pelirrojo. ∼**bread** n pan m de jengibre

gipsy /'dʒɪpsɪ/ n gitano m

giraffe /dʒɪˈrɑːf/ n jirafa f

girder /'gɜːdə(r)/ n viga f

girdle /'gɜːdl/ n (belt) cinturón m; (corset) corsé n

girl /gɜːl/ n chica f, muchacha f; (child) niña f. ∼ **band** n grupo m pop de chicas. ∼**friend** n amiga f; (of boy) novia f. ∼**ish** adj de niña; (boy) afeminado. ∼ **scout** n (Amer) exploradora f, guía f

giro /'dʒaɪrəʊ/ n (pl **-os**) giro m (bancario)

girth /gɜːθ/ n circunferencia f

gist /dʒɪst/ n lo esencial

give /gɪv/ vt (pt **gave**, pp **given**) dar; (deliver) entregar; regalar (present); prestar (aid, attention). ∼ **o.s. to** darse a. ● vi dar; (yield) ceder; (stretch) dar de sí. ● n elasticidad f. ■∼ **away** vt regalar; revelar (secret). ■∼ **back** vt devolver. ■∼ **in** vi ceder. ■∼ **off** vt emitir. ■∼ **out** vt distribuir. (become used up) agotarse. ■∼ **up** vt renunciar a;

(yield) ceder. ~ **up doing sth**
dejar de hacer algo. ~ **o.s. up**
entregarse (**to** a). vi rendirse. ~n
/'gɪvn/ see GIVE. ●adj dado. ~n
name n nombre m de pila

glacier /'glæsɪə(r)/ n glaciar m

glad /glæd/ adj contento. **be** ~
alegrarse (**about** de). ~**den** vt
alegrar

gladly /'glædlɪ/ adv alegremente;
(willingly) con mucho gusto

glamo|rous /'glæmərəs/ adj
glamoroso. ~**ur** /'glæmə(r)/ n
glamour m

glance /glɑːns/ n ojeada f. ●vi. ~ **at**
dar un vistazo a

gland /glænd/ n glándula f

glar|e /gleə(r)/ vi (light) deslumbrar;
(stare angrily) mirar airadamente. ●n
resplandor m; (stare) mirada f
airada. ~**ing** adj deslumbrante;
(obvious) manifiesto

glass /glɑːs/ n (material) cristal m,
vidrio m; (without stem or for wine)
vaso m; (with stem) copa f; (for beer)
caña f; (mirror) espejo m. ~**es** npl
(spectacles) gafas fpl, lentes fpl (LAm),
anteojos mpl (LAm). ~**y** adj vítreo

glaze /gleɪz/ vt poner cristal(es) or
vidrio(s) a (windows, doors); vidriar
(pottery). ●vi. ~ (**over**) (eyes)
vidriarse. ●n barniz m; (for pottery)
esmalte m

gleam /gliːm/ n destello m. ●vi
destellar

glean /gliːn/ vt espigar; recoger
(information)

glee /gliː/ n regocijo m

glib /glɪb/ adj de mucha labia; (reply)
fácil

glid|e /glaɪd/ vi deslizarse; (plane)
planear. ~**er** n planeador m. ~**ing**
n planeo m

glimmer /'glɪmə(r)/ n destello m.
●vi destellar

glimpse /glɪmps/ n. **catch a** ~ **of**

vislumbrar, ver brevemente. ●vt
vislumbrar

glint /glɪnt/ n destello m. ●vi
destellar

glisten /'glɪsn/ vi brillar

glitter /'glɪtə(r)/ vi brillar. ●n
brillo m

gloat /gləʊt/ vi. ~ **on**/**over**
regodearse sobre

glob|al /'gləʊbl/ adj (worldwide)
mundial; (all-embracing) global. ~**al
warming** n calentamiento m
global. ~**e** /gləʊb/ n globo m

gloom /gluːm/ n oscuridad f;
(sadness, fig) tristeza f. ~**y** adj (-**ier**,
-**iest**) triste; (pessimistic) pesimista

glor|ify /'glɔːrɪfaɪ/ vt glorificar.
~**ious** /'glɔːrɪəs/ adj espléndido;
(deed, hero etc) glorioso. ~**y** /'glɔːrɪ/
n gloria f

gloss /glɒs/ n lustre m. ~ (**paint**)
(pintura f al or de) esmalte m. ■ ~
over vt (make light of) minimizar;
(cover up) encubrir

glossary /'glɒsərɪ/ n glosario m

glossy /'glɒsɪ/ adj brillante

glove /glʌv/ n guante m. ~
compartment n (Auto) guantera f,
gaveta f

glow /gləʊ/ vi brillar. ●n brillo m.
~**ing** /'gləʊɪŋ/ adj incandescente;
(account) entusiasta; (complexion) rojo

glucose /'gluːkəʊs/ n glucosa f

glue /gluː/ n cola f, goma f de pegar.
●vt (pres p **gluing**) pegar

glum /glʌm/ adj (**glummer,
glummest**) triste

glutton /'glʌtn/ n glotón m

gnarled /nɑːld/ adj nudoso

gnash /næʃ/ vt. ~ **one's teeth**
rechinar los dientes

gnat /næt/ n jején m, mosquito m

gnaw /nɔː/ vt roer. ●vi. ~ **at** roer

gnome /nəʊm/ n gnomo m

go /gəʊ/

3rd pers sing present **goes**; past **went**; past participle **gone**

● intransitive verb

····► ir. **I'm going to France** voy a Francia. **to go shopping** ir de compras. **to go swimming** ir a nadar

····► (*leave*) irse. **we're going on Friday** nos vamos el viernes

····► (*work, function*) (engine, clock) funcionar

····► (*become*) **to go deaf** quedarse sordo. **to go mad** volverse loco. **his face went red** se puso colorado

····► (*stop*) (headache, pain) irse (+ me/te/le). **the pain's gone** se me ha ido el dolor

····► (*turn out, progress*) ir. **everything's going very well** todo va muy bien. **how did the exam go?** ¿qué tal te fue en el examen?

····► (*match, suit*) combinar. **the jacket and the trousers go well together** la chaqueta y los pantalones combinan bien.

····► (*cease to function*) (bulb, fuse) fundirse. **the brakes have gone** los frenos no funcionan

● auxiliary verb **to be going to** + infinitive **ir a** + infinitivo. **it's going to rain** va a llover. **she's going to win!** ¡va a ganar!

● noun (pl **goes**)

····► (*turn*) turno m. **you have three goes** tienes tres turnos. **it's your go** te toca a ti

····► (*attempt*) **to have a go at doing sth** intentar hacer algo. **have another go** inténtalo de nuevo

····► (*energy, drive*) empuje m. **she has a lot of go** tiene mucho empuje

····► (*in phrases*) **I've been on the go all day** no he parado en todo el día. **to make a go of sth** sacar algo adelante ■ **go across** vt/vi cruzar. ■ **go after** vi

perseguir. ■ **go away** vt irse. ■ **go back** vi volver. ■ **go back on** vt faltar a (promise etc). ■ **go by** vi pasar. ■ **go down** vi bajar; (sun) ponerse. ■ **go for** vt (fam, attack) atacar. ■ **go in** vi entrar. ■ **go in for** vt presentarse para (exam); participar en (competition). ■ **go off** vi (leave) irse; (go bad) pasarse; (explode) estallar; (lights) apagarse. ■ **go on** vi seguir; (happen) pasar; (be switched on) encenderse, prenderse (LAm). ■ **go out** vi salir; (fire, light) apagarse. ■ **go over** vt (check) revisar; (revise) repasar. ■ **go through** vt pasar por; (search) registrar; (check) examinar. ■ **go up** vi/vt subir. ■ **go without** vt pasar sin

goad /gəʊd/ vt aguijonear

go-ahead /'gəʊəhed/ n luz f verde. ● adj dinámico

goal /gəʊl/ n (Sport) gol m; (objective) meta f. ~**ie** /'gəʊlɪ/ n 🔢, ~**keeper** n portero m, arquero m (LAm). ~**post** n poste m de la portería, poste m del arco (LAm)

goat /gəʊt/ n cabra f

gobble /'gɒbl/ vt engullir

goblin /'gɒblɪn/ n duende m

god /gɒd/ n dios m. **G**~ n Dios m. ~**child** n ahijado m. ~**daughter** n ahijada f. ~**dess** /'gɒdes/ n diosa f. ~**father** n padrino m. ~**forsaken** adj olvidado de Dios. ~**mother** n madrina f. ~**send** n beneficio m inesperado. ~**son** n ahijado m

going /'gəʊɪŋ/ n camino m; (racing) (estado m del) terreno m. **it is slow/hard** ~ es lento/difícil. ● adj (price) actual; (concern) en funcionamiento

gold /gəʊld/ n oro m. ● adj de oro. ~**en** adj de oro; (in colour) dorado; (opportunity) único. ~**en wedding** n bodas fpl de oro. ~**fish** n invar pez m de colores. ~**mine** n mina f de oro; (fig) fuente f de gran riqueza. ~**-plated** /-'pleɪtɪd/ adj chapado en oro. ~**smith** n orfebre m

golf /gɒlf/ n golf m. **~ ball** n pelota f de golf. **~ club** n palo m de golf; (place) club m de golf. **~course** n campo m de golf. **~er** n jugador m de golf

gondola /'gɒndələ/ n góndola f

gone /gɒn/ see GO. ●adj pasado. **~ six o'clock** después de las seis

gong /gɒŋ/ n gong(o) m

good /gʊd/ adj (**better**, **best**) bueno, (before masculine singular noun) buen. **~ afternoon** buenas tardes. **~ evening** (before dark) buenas tardes; (after dark) buenas noches. **~ morning** buenos días. **~ night** buenas noches. **as ~ as** (almost) casi. **feel ~** sentirse bien. **have a ~ time** divertirse. ●n bien m. **for ~** para siempre. **it is no ~ shouting** es inútil gritar etc. **~bye** /-'baɪ/ int ¡adiós! ●n adiós m. **say ~bye to** despedirse de. **~-for-nothing** /-fənʌθɪŋ/ adj & n inútil (m). **G~ Friday** n Viernes m Santo. **~-looking** /-'lʊkɪŋ/ adj guapo, buen mozo m (LAm), buena moza f (LAm). **~ness** n bondad f. **~ness!**, **~ness gracious!**, **~ness me!**, **my ~ness!** ¡Dios mío! **~s** npl mercancías fpl. **~will** /-'wɪl/ n buena voluntad f. **~y** n (Culin, fam) golosina f; (in film) bueno m

gooey /'guːɪ/ adj (**gooier**, **gooiest**) 🄸 pegajoso; (fig) sentimental

goofy /'guːfɪ/ adj (Amer) necio

google (®) /'guːgl/ vt, vi 🄸 googlear 🄸

goose /guːs/ n (pl **geese**) oca f, ganso m. **~berry** /'gʊzbərɪ/ n uva f espina, grosella f espinosa. **~flesh** n, **~-pimples** npl carne f de gallina

gore /gɔː(r)/ n sangre f. ●vt cornear

gorge /gɔːdʒ/ n (of river) garganta f. ●vt. **~ o.s.** hartarse (**on** de)

gorgeous /'gɔːdʒəs/ adj precioso; (splendid) magnífico

gorilla /gə'rɪlə/ n gorila m

gorse /gɔːs/ n aulaga f

gory /'gɔːrɪ/ adj (**-ier**, **-iest**) 🄸 sangriento

gosh /gɒʃ/ int ¡caramba!

go-slow /gəʊ'sləʊ/ n huelga f de celo, huelga f pasiva

gospel /'gɒspl/ n evangelio m

gossip /'gɒsɪp/ n (chatter) chismorreo m; (person) chismoso m. ●vi (pt **gossiped**) (chatter) chismorrear; (repeat scandal) contar chismes

got /gɒt/ see GET. **have ~** tener. **I've ~ to do it** tengo que hacerlo.

gotten /'gɒtn/ see GET

gouge /gaʊdʒ/ vt abrir (hole). ■ **~ out** vt sacar

gourmet /'gʊəmeɪ/ n gastrónomo m

govern /'gʌvən/ vt/i gobernar. **~ess** n institutriz f. **~ment** n gobierno m. **~or** n gobernador m

gown /gaʊn/ n vestido m; (of judge, teacher) toga f

GP abbr see GENERAL PRACTITIONER

GPS abbrev **Global Positioning System** GPS m

grab /græb/ vt (pt **grabbed**) agarrar

grace /greɪs/ n gracia f. **~ful** adj elegante

gracious /'greɪʃəs/ adj (kind) amable; (elegant) elegante

grade /greɪd/ n clase f, categoría f; (of goods) clase f, calidad f; (on scale) grado m; (school mark) nota f; (Amer, class) curso m, año m

gradient /'greɪdɪənt/ n pendiente f, gradiente f (LAm)

gradual /'grædʒʊəl/ adj gradual. **~ly** adv gradualmente, poco a poco

graduat|e /'grædʒʊət/ n (Univ) licenciado. ●/'grædʒʊeɪt/ vi licenciarse. **~ion** /-'eɪʃn/ n graduación f

graffiti /grə'fiːtɪ/ npl graffiti mpl, pintadas fpl

graft /grɑːft/ n (Med, Bot) injerto m; (Amer fam, bribery) chanchullos mpl. • vt injertar

grain /greɪn/ n grano m

gram /græm/ n gramo m

gramma|r /'græmə(r)/ n gramática f. ~**tical** /grə'mætɪkl/ adj gramatical

gramme /græm/ n gramo m

grand /grænd/ adj (**-er, -est**) magnífico; (fam, excellent) estupendo. ~**child** n nieto m. ~**daughter** n nieta f. ~**eur** /'grændʒə(r)/ n grandiosidad f. ~**father** n abuelo m. ~**father clock** n reloj m de caja. ~**iose** /'grændɪəʊs/ adj grandioso. ~**mother** n abuela f. ~**parents** npl abuelos mpl. ~ **piano** n piano m de cola. ~**son** n nieto m. ~**stand** /'grænstænd/ n tribuna f

granite /'grænɪt/ n granito m

granny /'grænɪ/ n Ⓘ abuela f

grant /grɑːnt/ vt conceder; (give) donar; (admit) admitir (**that** que). **take for** ~**ed** dar por sentado. • n concesión f; (Univ) beca f

granule /'grænuːl/ n gránulo m

grape /greɪp/ n uva f. ~**fruit** n invar pomelo m, toronja f (LAm)

graph /grɑːf/ n gráfica f

graphic /'græfɪk/ adj gráfico. ~**s** npl diseño m gráfico; (Comp) gráficos mpl

grapple /'græpl/ vi. ~ **with** forcejear con; (mentally) lidiar con

grasp /grɑːsp/ vt agarrar. • n (hold) agarro m; (fig) comprensión f. ~**ing** adj avaro

grass /grɑːs/ n hierba f. ~**hopper** n saltamontes m. ~ **roots** npl base f popular. • adj de las bases. ~**y** adj cubierto de hierba

grate /greɪt/ n rejilla f; (fireplace) chimenea f. • vt rallar. • vi rechinar; (be irritating) ser crispante

grateful /'greɪtfl/ adj agradecido. ~**ly** adv con gratitud

grater /'greɪtə(r)/ n rallador m

gratif|ied /'grætɪfaɪd/ adj contento. ~**y** /'grætɪfaɪ/ vt satisfacer; (please) agradar a. ~**ying** adj agradable

grating /'greɪtɪŋ/ n reja f

gratitude /'grætɪtjuːd/ n gratitud f

gratuitous /grə'tjuːɪtəs/ adj gratuito

gratuity /grə'tjuːətɪ/ n (tip) propina f

grave /greɪv/ n sepultura f. • adj (**-er, -est**) (serious) grave

gravel /'grævl/ n grava f

gravely /'greɪvlɪ/ adv (seriously) seriamente; (solemnly) con gravedad

grave: ~**stone** n lápida f. ~**yard** n cementerio m

gravitate /'grævɪteɪt/ vi gravitar

gravity /'grævətɪ/ n gravedad f

gravy /'greɪvɪ/ n salsa f

gray /greɪ/ adj & n (Amer) see GREY

graze /greɪz/ vi (eat) pacer. • vt (touch) rozar; (scrape) raspar. • n rasguño m

greas|e /griːs/ n grasa f. • vt engrasar. ~**eproof paper** n papel m encerado or de cera. ~**y** adj (hands) grasiento; (food) graso; (hair, skin) graso, grasoso (LAm)

great /greɪt/ adj (**-er, -est**) grande, (before singular noun) gran; (fam, very good) estupendo. G~ **Britain** n Gran Bretaña f. ~**-grandfather** /-'grænfɑːðə(r)/ n bisabuelo m. ~**-grandmother** /-'grænmʌðə(r)/ n bisabuela f. ~**ly** adv (very) muy; (much) mucho

Greece /griːs/ n Grecia f

greed /griːd/ n avaricia f; (for food) glotonería f. ~**y** adj avaro; (for food) glotón

Greek /griːk/ adj & n griego (m)

green /griːn/ adj (**-er, -est**) verde. • n verde m; (grass) césped m. ~ **belt** n zona f verde. ~ **card** n (Amer) permiso m de residencia y trabajo. ~**ery** n verdor m. ~**gage**

/-geɪdʒ/ n claudia f. **~grocer** n
verdulero m. **~house** n
invernadero m. **the ~house
effect** el efecto invernadero. **~
light** n luz f verde. **~s** npl
verduras fpl

greet /griːt/ vt saludar; (receive)
recibir. **~ing** n saludo m

gregarious /grɪˈgeərɪəs/ adj
gregario; (person) sociable

grenade /grɪˈneɪd/ n granada f

grew /gruː/ see GROW

grey /greɪ/ adj (-er, -est) gris. **have
~ hair** ser canoso. ● n gris m.
~hound n galgo m

grid /grɪd/ n reja f; (Elec, network) red
f; (on map) cuadriculada m

grief /griːf/ n dolor m. **come to ~**
(person) acabar mal; (fail) fracasar

grievance /ˈgriːvns/ n queja f
formal

grieve /griːv/ vt apenar. ● vi
afligirse. **~ for** llorar

grievous /ˈgriːvəs/ adj doloroso;
(serious) grave. **~ bodily harm**
(Jurid) lesiones fpl (corporales)
graves

grill /grɪl/ n parrilla f. ● vt asar a la
parrilla; (⯐, interrogate) interrogar

grille /grɪl/ n rejilla f

grim /grɪm/ adj (**grimmer,
grimmest**) severo

grimace /ˈgrɪməs/ n mueca f. ● vi
hacer muecas

grim|e /graɪm/ n mugre f. **~y** adj
mugriento

grin /grɪn/ vt (pt **grinned**) sonreír.
● n sonrisa f (abierta)

grind /graɪnd/ vt (pt **ground**) moler
(coffee, corn etc); (pulverize) pulverizar;
(sharpen) afilar; (Amer) picar, moler
(meat)

grip /grɪp/ vt (pt **gripped**) agarrar;
(interest) captar. ● n (hold) agarro m;
(strength of hand) apretón m; (hairgrip)
horquilla f, pasador m (Mex). **come
to ~s with** entender (subject)

grisly /ˈgrɪzlɪ/ adj (-ier, -iest)
horrible

gristle /ˈgrɪsl/ n cartílago m

grit /grɪt/ n arenilla f; (fig) agallas
fpl. ● vt (pt **gritted**) echar arena en
(road). **~ one's teeth** (fig)
acorazarse

groan /grəʊn/ vi gemir. ● n
gemido m

grocer /ˈgrəʊsə(r)/ n tendero m,
abarrotero m (Mex). **~ies** npl
comestibles mpl. **~y** n tienda f de
comestibles, tienda f de abarrotes
(Mex)

groggy /ˈgrɒgɪ/ adj (weak) débil;
(unsteady) inseguro; (ill) malucho

groin /grɔɪn/ n ingle f

groom /gruːm/ n mozo m de
caballos; (bridegroom) novio m. ● vt
almohazar (horses); (fig) preparar

groove /gruːv/ n ranura f; (in record)
surco m

grope /grəʊp/ vi (find one's way)
moverse a tientas. **~ for** buscar a
tientas

gross /grəʊs/ adj (-er, -est) (coarse)
grosero; (Com) bruto; (fat) grueso;
(flagrant) flagrante. ● n invar gruesa f.
~ly adv (very) enormemente

grotesque /grəʊˈtesk/ adj grotesco

ground /graʊnd/ see GRIND. ● n
suelo m; (area) terreno m; (reason)
razón f; (Amer, Elec) toma f de tierra.
● vt fundar (theory); retirar del
servicio (aircraft). **~s** npl jardines
mpl; (sediment) poso m. **~ beef** n
(Amer) carne f picada, carne f
molida. **~ cloth** n (Amer) see
~SHEET. ~ floor n planta f baja.
~ing n base f, conocimientos mpl
(**in** de). **~less** adj infundado.
~sheet n suelo m impermeable
(de una tienda de campaña).
~work n trabajo m preparatorio

group /gruːp/ n grupo m. ● vt
agrupar. ● vi agruparse

grouse /graʊs/ n invar (bird) urogallo
m. ● vi ⯐ rezongar

grovel /ˈgrɒvl/ vi (pt **grovelled**)

postrarse; (fig) arrastrarse

grow /grəʊ/ vi (pt **grew**, pp **grown**) crecer; (become) volverse, ponerse. •vt cultivar. ~ **a beard** dejarse (crecer) la barba. ∎ ~ **up** vi hacerse mayor. ~**ing** adj (quantity) cada vez mayor; (influence) creciente

growl /graʊl/ vi gruñir. •n gruñido m

grown /grəʊn/ see **GROW**. •adj adulto. ~**-up** adj & n adulto (m)

growth /grəʊθ/ n crecimiento m; (increase) aumento m; (development) desarrollo m; (Med) bulto m, tumor m

grub /grʌb/ n (larva) larva f; (fam, food) comida f

grubby /'grʌbɪ/ adj (**-ier, -iest**) mugriento

grudg|e /grʌdʒ/ vt see **BEGRUDGE**. •n rencilla f. **bear/have a ~e against s.o.** guardarle rencor a uno. ~**ingly** adv de mala gana

gruelling /'gruːəlɪŋ/ adj agotador

gruesome /'gruːsəm/ adj horrible

gruff /grʌf/ adj (**-er, -est**) (manners) brusco; (voice) ronco

grumble /'grʌmbl/ vi rezongar

grumpy /'grʌmpɪ/ adj (**-ier, -iest**) malhumorado

grunt /grʌnt/ vi gruñir. •n gruñido m

guarant|ee /gærən'tiː/ n garantía f. •vt garantizar. ~**or** n garante m & f

guard /gɑːd/ vt proteger; (watch) vigilar. •n (vigilance, Mil group) guardia f; (person) guardia m; (on train) jefe m de tren. ∎ ~ **against** vt evitar; protegerse contra (risk). ~**ed** adj cauteloso. ~**ian** /-ɪən/ n guardián m; (of orphan) tutor m

Guatemala /gwɑːtə'mɑːlə/ n Guatemala f. ~**n** adj & n guatemalteco (m)

guer(r)illa /gə'rɪlə/ n guerrillero m. ~ **warfare** n guerrilla f

guess /ges/ vt adivinar; (Amer,

suppose) suponer. •n conjetura f. ~**work** n conjeturas fpl

guest /gest/ n invitado m; (in hotel) huésped m. ~**house** n casa f de huéspedes

guffaw /gʌ'fɔː/ n carcajada f. •vi reírse a carcajadas

guidance /'gaɪdəns/ n (advice) consejos mpl; (information) información f

guide /gaɪd/ n (person) guía m & f; (book) guía f. **Girl G~** exploradora f, guía f. •vt guiar. ~**book** n guía f. ~ **dog** n perro m guía, perro m lazarillo. ~**d missile** n proyectil m teledirigido. ~**lines** npl pauta f

guild /gɪld/ n gremio m

guile /gaɪl/ n astucia f

guillotine /'gɪləti:n/ n guillotina f

guilt /gɪlt/ n culpa f; (Jurid) culpabilidad f. ~**y** adj culpable

guinea pig /'gɪnɪ/ n conejillo m de Indias, cobaya f

guitar /gɪ'tɑ:(r)/ n guitarra f. ~**ist** n guitarrista m & f

gulf /gʌlf/ n (part of sea) golfo m; (gap) abismo m

gull /gʌl/ n gaviota f

gullet /'gʌlɪt/ n garganta f, gaznate m ⓘ

gullible /'gʌləbl/ adj crédulo

gully /'gʌlɪ/ n (ravine) barranco m

gulp /gʌlp/ vt. ∎ ~ **(down)** tragarse de prisa. •vi tragar saliva. •n trago m

gum /gʌm/ n (in mouth) encía f; (glue) goma f de pegar; (for chewing) chicle m. •vt (pt **gummed**) engomar

gun /gʌn/ n (pistol) pistola f; (rifle) fusil m, escopeta f; (artillery piece) cañón m. •vt (pt **gunned**). ∎ ~ **down** vt abatir a tiros. ~**fire** n tiros mpl

gun: ~**man** /-mən/ n pistolero m, gatillero m (Mex). ~**powder** n pólvora f. ~**shot** n disparo m

gurgle /'gɜːgl/ vi (liquid) gorgotear; (baby) gorjear

gush /gʌʃ/ vi. ~ **(out)** salir a borbotones. ●n (of liquid) chorro m; (fig) torrente m

gusset /'gʌsɪt/ n entretela f

gust /gʌst/ n ráfaga f

gusto /'gʌstəʊ/ n entusiasmo m

gusty /'gʌstɪ/ adj borrascoso

gut /gʌt/ n intestino m. ●vt (pt **gutted**) destripar; (fire) destruir. ~s npl tripas fpl; (fam, courage) agallas fpl

gutter /'gʌtə(r)/ n (on roof) canalón m, canaleta f; (in street) cuneta f; (fig, slum) arroyo m

guttural /'gʌtərəl/ adj gutural

guy /gaɪ/ n (fam, man) tipo m 🔲, tío m 🔲

guzzle /'gʌzl/ vt (drink) chupar 🔲; (eat) tragarse

gym /dʒɪm/ n 🔲 (gymnasium) gimnasio m; (gymnastics) gimnasia f

gymnasium /dʒɪm'neɪzɪəm/ n gimnasio m

gymnast /'dʒɪmnæst/ n gimnasta m & f. ~ics /dʒɪm'næstɪks/ npl gimnasia f

gymslip /'dʒɪmslɪp/ n túnica f (de gimnasia)

gynaecolog|ist /gaɪnɪ'kɒlədʒɪst/ n ginecólogo m. ~y n ginecología f

gypsy /'dʒɪpsɪ/ n gitano m

gyrate /dʒaɪə'reɪt/ vi girar

g
h

Hh

haberdashery /'hæbədæʃərɪ/ n mercería f; (Amer, clothes) ropa f y accesorios mpl para caballeros

habit /'hæbɪt/ n costumbre f; (Relig, costume) hábito m. **be in the** ~ **of** (+ gerund) tener la costumbre de (+ infinitivo), soler (+ infinitivo). **get into the** ~ **of** (+ gerund) acostumbrarse a (+ infinitivo)

habitable /'hæbɪtəbl/ adj habitable

habitat /'hæbɪtæt/ n hábitat m

habitation /hæbɪ'teɪʃn/ n habitación f

habitual /hə'bɪtjʊəl/ adj habitual; (liar) inveterado. ~ly adv de costumbre

hack /hæk/ n (old horse) jamelgo m; (writer) escritorzuelo m. ●vt cortar. ~er n (Comp) pirata m informático

hackneyed /'hæknɪd/ adj manido

had /hæd/ see **HAVE**

haddock /'hædək/ n invar eglefino m

haemorrhage /'hemərɪdʒ/ n hemorragia f

haemorrhoids /'hemərɔɪdz/ npl hemorroides fpl

hag /hæg/ n bruja f

haggard /'hægəd/ adj demacrado

hail /heɪl/ n granizo m. ●vi granizar. ●vt (greet) saludar; llamar (taxi). ■ ~ **from** vt venir de. ~**stone** n grano m de granizo

hair /heə(r)/ n pelo m. ~**band** n cinta f, banda f (Mex). ~**brush** n cepillo m (para el pelo). ~**cut** n corte m de pelo. **have a** ~**cut** cortarse el pelo. ~**do** n 🔲 peinado m. ~**dresser** n peluquero m. ~**dresser's (shop)** n peluquería f. ~**dryer** n secador m, secadora f (Mex). ~**grip** n horquilla f, pasador m (Mex). ~**pin** n horquilla f. ~**pin bend** n curva f cerrada. ~**raising** adj espeluznante. ~**spray** n laca f, fijador m (para el pelo). ~**style** n peinado m. ~**y** adj (**-ier, -iest**) peludo

half /hɑːf/ n (pl **halves**) mitad f. ●adj medio. ~ **a dozen** media docena f. ~ **an hour** media hora f. ●adv medio, a medias. **a medias.** ~**-hearted** /-'hɑːtɪd/ adj poco entusiasta. ~**-mast** /-'mɑːst/ n. **at** ~**-mast** a media asta. ~ **term** n vacaciones fpl de medio trimestre. ~**-time** n (Sport) descanso m, medio tiempo m (LAm). ~**way** adj medio. ●adv a medio camino

hall /hɔːl/ n (entrance) vestíbulo m; (for public events) sala f, salón m. ~ **of residence** residencia f universitaria, colegio m mayor. ~**mark** /-mɑːk/ n (on gold, silver) contraste m; (fig) sello m (distintivo)

hallo /hə'ləʊ/ int see HELLO

Hallowe'en /ˌhæləʊ'iːn/ n víspera f de Todos los Santos

hallucination /həluːsɪ'neɪʃn/ n alucinación f

halo /'heɪləʊ/ n (pl **-oes**) aureola f

halt /hɔːlt/ n. **come to a** ~ pararse. ●vt parar. ●vi pararse

halve /hɑːv/ vt reducir a la mitad; (divide into halves) partir por la mitad

halves /hɑːvz/ see HALF

ham /hæm/ n jamón m

hamburger /'hæmbɜːgə(r)/ n hamburguesa f

hammer /'hæmə(r)/ n martillo m. ●vt martill(e)ar

hammock /'hæmək/ n hamaca f

hamper /'hæmpə(r)/ n cesta f. ●vt estorbar

hamster /'hæmstə(r)/ n hámster m

hand /hænd/ n mano f; (of clock, watch) manecilla f; (worker) obrero m. **by** ~ a mano. **lend a** ~ echar una mano. **on** ~ a mano. **on the one** ~... **on the other** ~ por un lado... por otro. **out of** ~ fuera de control. **to** ~ a mano. ●vt pasar. ■ ~ **down** vt pasar. ■ ~ **in** vt

entregar. ■ ~ **over** vt entregar. ■ ~ **out** vt distribuir. ~**bag** n bolso m, cartera f (LAm), bolsa f (Mex). ~**brake** n (in car) freno m de mano. ~**cuffs** npl esposas fpl. ~**ful** n puñado m; (fam, person) persona f difícil

handicap /'hændɪkæp/ n desventaja f; (Sport) hándicap m. ~**ped** adj minusválido

handicraft /'hændɪkrɑːft/ n artesanía f

handkerchief /'hæŋkətʃɪf/ n (pl **-fs** or **-chieves** /-'tʃiːvz/) pañuelo m

handle /'hændl/ n (of door) picaporte m; (of drawer) tirador m; (of implement) mango m; (of cup, bag, jug) asa f. ●vt manejar; (touch) tocar. ~**bars** npl manillar m, manubrio m (LAm).

hand: ~**out** n folleto m; (of money, food) dádiva f. ~**shake** n apretón m de manos

handsome /'hænsəm/ adj (good-looking) guapo, buen mozo, buena moza (LAm); (generous) generoso

handwriting /'hændraɪtɪŋ/ n letra f

handy /'hændɪ/ adj (**-ier, -iest**) (useful) práctico; (person) diestro; (near) a mano. **come in** ~ venir muy bien. ~**man** n hombre m habilidoso

hang /hæŋ/ vt (pt **hung**) colgar; (pt **hanged**) (capital punishment) ahorcar. ●vi colgar; (clothing) caer. ●n. **get the** ~ **of sth** coger el truco de algo. ■ ~ **about, around** vi holgazanear. ■ ~ **on** vi (wait) esperar. ■ ~ **out** vt tender (washing). ■ ~ **up** vi (also telephone) colgar

hangar /'hæŋə(r)/ n hangar m

hang: ~**er** n (for clothes) percha f. ~**-glider** n ala f delta, deslizador m (Mex). ~**over** (after drinking) resaca f. ~**-up** n 🔢 complejo m

hankie, hanky /'hæŋkɪ/ n 🆒 pañuelo m

haphazard /hæp'hæzəd/ adj fortuito. ~ly adv al azar

happen /'hæpən/ vi pasar, suceder, ocurrir. **if he ~s to come** si acaso viene. ~ing n acontecimiento m

happ|ily /'hæpɪlɪ/ adv alegremente; (fortunately) afortunadamente. ~iness n felicidad f. ~y adj (-ier, -iest) feliz; (satisfied) contento

harass /'hærəs/ vt acosar. ~ment n acoso m

harbour /'hɑːbə(r)/ n puerto m

hard /hɑːd/ adj (-er, -est) duro; (difficult) difícil. ● adv (work) mucho; (pull) con fuerza. ~ **done by** tratado injustamente. ~-**boiled egg** /-'bɔɪld/ n huevo m duro. ~ **disk** n disco m duro. ~**en** vt endurecer. ● vi endurecerse. ~-**headed** /-'hedɪd/ adj realista

hardly /'hɑːdlɪ/ adv apenas. ~ **ever** casi nunca

hard: ~**ness** n dureza f. ~**ship** n apuro m. ~ **shoulder** n arcén m, acotamiento m (Mex). ~**ware** /-weə(r)/ n ferretería f; (Comp) hardware m. ~**ware store** n (Amer) ferretería f. ~**working** /-'wɜːkɪŋ/ adj trabajador

hardy /'hɑːdɪ/ adj (-ier, -iest) fuerte; (plants) resistente

hare /heə(r)/ n liebre f

hark /hɑːk/ vi escuchar. ■ ~ **back to** vt volver a

harm /hɑːm/ n daño m. **there is no ~ in asking** con preguntar no se pierde nada. ● vt hacer daño a (person); dañar (thing); perjudicar (interests). ~**ful** adj perjudicial. ~**less** adj inofensivo

harmonica /hɑː'mɒnɪkə/ n armónica f

harmon|ious /hɑː'məʊnɪəs/ adj armonioso. ~**y** /'hɑːmənɪ/ n armonía f

harness /'hɑːnɪs/ n arnés m. ● vt poner el arnés a (horse); (fig) aprovechar

harp /hɑːp/ n arpa f. ● vi. ~ **on (about)** machacar (con)

harpoon /hɑː'puːn/ n arpón m

harpsichord /'hɑːpsɪkɔːd/ n clavicémbalo m, clave m

harrowing /'hærəʊɪŋ/ adj desgarrador

harsh /hɑːʃ/ adj (-er, -est) duro, severo; (light) fuerte; (climate) riguroso. ~**ly** adv severamente. ~**ness** n severidad f

harvest /'hɑːvɪst/ n cosecha f. ● vt cosechar

has /hæz/ see HAVE

hassle /'hæsl/ n 🆒 lío m 🆒, rollo m 🆒. ● vt (harass) fastidiar

hast|e /heɪst/ n prisa f, apuro m (LAm). **make ~e** darse prisa. ~**ily** /'heɪstɪlɪ/ adv de prisa. ~**y** /'heɪstɪ/ adj (-ier, -iest) rápido; (rash) precipitado

hat /hæt/ n sombrero m

hatch /hætʃ/ n (for food) ventanilla f; (Naut) escotilla f. ● vt empollar (eggs), tramar (plot). ● vi salir del cascarón. ~**back** n coche m con tres/cinco puertas; (door) puerta f trasera

hatchet /'hætʃɪt/ n hacha f

hat|e /heɪt/ n odio m. ● vt odiar. ~**eful** adj odioso. ~**red** /'heɪtrɪd/ n odio m

haughty /'hɔːtɪ/ adj (-ier, -iest) altivo

haul /hɔːl/ vt arrastrar; transportar (goods). ● n (catch) redada f; (stolen goods) botín m; (journey) recorrido m. ~**age** /-ɪdʒ/ n transporte m. ~**er** (Amer), ~**ier** n transportista m & f

haunt /hɔːnt/ vt frecuentar; (ghost) rondar. ● n sitio m preferido. ~**ed** adj (house) embrujado; (look) angustiado

h

have /hæv//həv, əv/

3rd person singular present **has**, past **had**

● transitive verb

····▶ tener. **I ~ three sisters** tengo tres hermanas. **do you ~ a credit card?** ¿tiene una tarjeta de crédito?

····▶ (in requests) **can I ~ a kilo of apples, please?** ¿me da un kilo de manzanas, por favor?

····▶ (eat) comer. **I had a pizza** comí una pizza

····▶ (drink) tomar. **come and ~ a drink** ven a tomar una copa

····▶ (smoke) fumar. (cigarette)

····▶ (hold, organize) hacer. (party, meeting)

····▶ (get, receive) **I had a letter from Tony yesterday** recibí una carta de Tony ayer. **we've had no news of her** no hemos tenido noticias suyas

····▶ (illness) tener. (flu, headache). **to ~ a cold** estar resfriado, tener catarro

····▶ **to have sth done: we had it painted** lo hicimos pintar. **I had my hair cut** me corté el pelo

····▶ **to have it in for s.o.** tenerle manía a uno

● auxiliary verb

····▶ haber. **I've seen her already** ya la he visto, ya la vi (LAm)

····▶ **to have just done sth** acabar de hacer algo. **I've just seen her** acabo de verla

····▶ **to have to do sth** tener que hacer algo. **I ~ to** or **I've got to go to the bank** tengo que ir al banco

····▶ (in tag questions) **you've met her, ~n't you?** ya la conoces, ¿no? or ¿verdad? or ¿no es cierto?

····▶ (in short answers) **you've forgotten something - have I?** has olvidado algo - ¿sí?

haven /'heɪvn/ n puerto m; (refuge) refugio m

haversack /'hævəsæk/ n mochila f

havoc /'hævək/ n estragos mpl

hawk /hɔːk/ n halcón m

hawthorn /'hɔːθɔːn/ n espino m

hay /heɪ/ n heno m. **~ fever** n fiebre f del heno. **~stack** n almiar m. **~wire** adj. **go ~wire** (plans) desorganizarse; (machine) estropearse

hazard /'hæzəd/ n riesgo m. **~ous** adj arriesgado

haze /heɪz/ n neblina f

hazel /'heɪzl/ n avellano m. **~nut** n avellana f

hazy /'heɪzɪ/ adj (-ier, -iest) nebuloso

he /hiː/ pron él

head /hed/ n cabeza f; (of family, government) jefe m; (of organization) director m; (of beer) espuma f. **~s or tails** cara o cruz. ● adj principal. ● vt encabezar, cabecear (ball). ■ **~ for** vt dirigirse a. **~ache** n dolor m de cabeza. **~er** n (football) cabezazo m. **~first** /-'fɜːst/ adv de cabeza. **~ing** n título m, encabezamiento m. **~lamp** n faro m, foco m (LAm). **~land** /-lənd/ n promontorio m. **~line** n titular m. **the news ~lines** el resumen informativo. **~long** adv de cabeza; (precipitately) precipitadamente. **~master** n director m. **~mistress** n directora f. **~-on** /-'ɒn/ adj & adv de frente. **~phones** npl auriculares mpl, cascos mpl. **~quarters** /-'kwɔːtəz/ n (of business) oficina f central; (Mil) cuartel m general. **~strong** adj testarudo. **~teacher** /-'tiːtʃə(r)/ n director m. **~y** adj (-ier, -iest) (scent) embriagador

heal /hiːl/ vt curar. ● vi cicatrizarse

health /helθ/ n salud f. **~y** adj sano

heap /hiːp/ n montón m. ● vt amontonar.

hear /hɪə(r)/ vt/i (pt **heard** /hɜːd/) oír. **~, ~!** ¡bravo! **~ about** oír hablar de. **~ from** recibir noticias de. **~ing** n oído m; (Jurid) vista f.

~**ing-aid** n audífono m. ~**say** n rumores mpl

hearse /hɜːs/ n coche m fúnebre

heart /hɑːt/ n corazón m. **at ~** en el fondo. **by ~** de memoria. **lose ~** descorazonarse. ~**ache** n congoja f. ~ **attack** n ataque m al corazón, infarto m. ~**break** n congoja f. ~**breaking** adj desgarrador. ~**burn** n ardor m de estómago. ~**felt** adj sincero

hearth /hɑːθ/ n hogar m

heart: ~**ily** adv de buena gana. ~**less** adj cruel. ~**y** adj (welcome) caluroso; (meal) abundante

heat /hiːt/ n calor m; (contest) (prueba f) eliminatoria f. ●vt calentar. ●vi calentarse. ~**ed** adj (fig) acalorado. ~**er** n calentador m

heath /hiːθ/ n brezal m, monte m

heathen /ˈhiːðn/ adj & n pagano (m)

heather /ˈheðə(r)/ n brezo m

heat: ~**ing** n calefacción f. ~**stroke** n insolación f. ~**wave** n ola f de calor

heave /hiːv/ vt (lift) levantar; exhalar (sigh); (fam, throw) tirar. ●vi (pull) tirar, jalar (LAm); (🔲, retch) dar arcadas

heaven /ˈhevn/ n cielo m. ~**ly** adj celestial; (astronomy) celeste; (fam, excellent) divino

heav|ily /ˈhevɪlɪ/ adv pesadamente; (smoke, drink) mucho. ~**y** adj (**-ier**, **-iest**) pesado; (rain) fuerte; (traffic) denso. ~**yweight** n peso m pesado

heckle /ˈhekl/ vt interrumpir

hectic /ˈhektɪk/ adj febril

he'd /hiːd/ = **he had**, **he would**

hedge /hedʒ/ n seto m (vivo). ●vi escaparse por la tangente. ~**hog** n erizo m

heed /hiːd/ vt hacer caso de. ●n. **take ~** tener cuidado

heel /hiːl/ n talón m; (of shoe) tacón m

hefty /ˈheftɪ/ adj (**-ier**, **-iest**) (sturdy) fuerte; (heavy) pesado

heifer /ˈhefə(r)/ n novilla f

height /haɪt/ n altura f; (of person) estatura f; (of fame, glory) cumbre f. ~**en** vt elevar; (fig) aumentar

heir /eə(r)/ n heredero m. ~**ess** n heredera f. ~**loom** n reliquia f heredada

held /held/ see **HOLD**

helicopter /ˈhelɪkɒptə(r)/ n helicóptero m

hell /hel/ n infierno m

he'll /hiːl/ = **he will**

hello /həˈləʊ/ int ¡hola!; (Telephone, caller) ¡oiga!, ¡bueno! (Mex); (Telephone, person answering) ¡diga!, ¡bueno! (Mex). **say ~ to** saludar

helm /helm/ n (Naut) timón m

helmet /ˈhelmɪt/ n casco m

help /help/ vt/i ayudar. **he cannot ~ laughing** no puede menos de reír. **~ o.s. to** servirse. **it cannot be ~ed** no hay más remedio. ●n ayuda f. ●int ¡socorro! ~**er** n ayudante m. ~**ful** adj útil; (person) amable. ~**ing** n porción f. ~**less** adj (unable to manage) incapaz; (defenceless) indefenso

hem /hem/ n dobladillo m

hemisphere /ˈhemɪsfɪə(r)/ n hemisferio m

hen /hen/ n (chicken) gallina f; (female bird) hembra f

hence /hens/ adv de aquí. ~**forth** adv de ahora en adelante

henpecked /ˈhenpekt/ adj dominado por su mujer

her /hɜː(r)/ pron (direct object) la; (indirect object) le; (after prep) ella. **I know ~** la conozco. ●adj su, sus pl

herb /hɜːb/ n hierba f. ~**al** adj de hierbas

herd /hɜːd/ n (of cattle, pigs) manada f; (of goats) rebaño m. ●vt arrear. **~ together** reunir

here /hɪə(r)/ adv aquí, acá (esp LAm). **~!** (take this) ¡tenga! ~**abouts**

h

hereditary | hill

/-ə'baʊts/ adv por aquí. ~after /-'ɑːftə(r)/ adv en el futuro. ~by /-'baɪ/ adv por este medio

heredit|ary /hɪ'redɪtərɪ/ adj hereditario

here|sy /'herəsɪ/ n herejía f. ~**tic** n hereje m & f

herewith /hɪə'wɪð/ adv adjunto

heritage /'herɪtɪdʒ/ n herencia f; (fig) patrimonio m. ~ **tourism** n turismo m cultural, turismo m patrimonial (LAm)

hermetically /hɜː'metɪklɪ/ adv. ~ **sealed** herméticamente cerrado

hermit /'hɜːmɪt/ n ermitaño m, eremita m

hernia /'hɜːnɪə/ n hernia f

hero /'hɪərəʊ/ n (pl -**oes**) héroe m. ~**ic** /hɪ'rəʊɪk/ adj heroico

heroin /'herəʊɪn/ n heroína f

hero: ~ine /'herəʊɪn/ n heroína f. ~**ism** /'herəʊɪzm/ n heroismo m

heron /'herən/ n garza f (real)

herring /'herɪŋ/ n arenque m

hers /hɜːz/ poss pron (el) suyo m, (la) suya f, (los) suyos mpl, (las) suyas fpl

herself /hɜː'self/ pron ella misma; (reflexive) se; (after prep) sí misma

he's /hiːz/ = he is, he has

hesit|ant /'hezɪtənt/ adj vacilante. ~**ate** /-teɪt/ vi vacilar. ~**ation** /-'teɪʃn/ n vacilación f

heterosexual /hetərəʊ'seksjʊəl/ adj & n heterosexual (m & f)

het up /het'ʌp/ adj 🄵 nervioso

hew /hjuː/ vt (pp **hewed** or **hewn**) cortar; (cut into shape) tallar

hexagon /'heksəgən/ n hexágono m. ~**al** /-'ægənl/ adj hexagonal

hey /heɪ/ int ¡eh!; (expressing dismay, protest) ¡oye!

heyday /'heɪdeɪ/ n apogeo m

hi /haɪ/ int 🄵 ¡hola!

hibernat|e /'haɪbəneɪt/ vi hibernar. ~**ion** /-'neɪʃn/ n hibernación f

hiccough, hiccup /'hɪkʌp/ n hipo m. **have (the) ~s** tener hipo. •vi hipar

hide /haɪd/ vt (pt **hid**, pp **hidden**) esconder. •vi esconderse. •n piel f; (tanned) cuero m. ~**-and-seek** /'haɪdnsiːk/ n. **play ~-and-seek** jugar al escondite, jugar a las escondidas (LAm)

hideous /'hɪdɪəs/ adj (dreadful) horrible; (ugly) feo

hideout /'haɪdaʊt/ n escondrijo m

hiding /'haɪdɪŋ/ n (🄵, thrashing) paliza f. **go into ~** esconderse. ~ **place** n escondite m, escondrijo m

hierarchy /'haɪərɑːkɪ/ n jerarquía f

hieroglyphics /haɪərə'glɪfɪks/ n jeroglíficos mpl

hi-fi /'haɪfaɪ/ adj de alta fidelidad. •n equipo m de alta fidelidad, hi-fi m

high /haɪ/ adj (-**er**, -**est**) alto; (ideals) elevado; (wind) fuerte; (fam, drugged) drogado, colocado 🄵; (voice) agudo; (meat) pasado. •n alto nivel m. **a (new) ~** un récord. • adv alto. ~**er education** n enseñanza f superior. ~**-handed** /-'hændɪd/ adj prepotente. ~ **heels** npl zapatos mpl de tacón alto. ~**lands** /-ləndz/ npl tierras fpl altas. ~**-level** adj de alto nivel. ~**light** n punto m culminante. •vt destacar; (Art) realzar. ~**ly** adv muy; (paid) muy bien. ~**ly strung** adj nervioso. **H~ness** n (title) alteza f. ~**-rise** adj (building) alto. ~ **school** n (Amer) instituto m, colegio m secundario. ~ **street** n calle f principal. ~**-strung** adj (Amer) nervioso. ~**way** n carretera f

hijack /'haɪdʒæk/ vt secuestrar. •n secuestro m. ~**er** n secuestrador

hike /haɪk/ n caminata f. •vi ir de caminata. ~**r** n excursionista m & f

hilarious /hɪ'leərɪəs/ adj muy divertido

hill /hɪl/ n colina f; (slope) cuesta f.

~side n ladera f. ~y adj accidentado

hilt /hɪlt/ n (of sword) puño m. **to the ~** (fig) totalmente

him /hɪm/ pron (direct object) lo, le (only Spain); (indirect object) le; (after prep) él. **I know ~** lo/le conozco. ~self pron él mismo; (reflexive) se; (after prep) sí mismo

hind|er /ˈhɪndə(r)/ vt estorbar. ~rance /ˈhɪndrəns/ n obstáculo m

hindsight /ˈhaɪnsaɪt/ n. **with ~** retrospectivamente

Hindu /ˈhɪnduː/ adj & n hindú (m & f). ~ism n hinduismo m

hinge /hɪndʒ/ n bisagra f

hint /hɪnt/ n indirecta f; (advice) consejo m. • vi soltar una indirecta. **~ at** dar a entender

hip /hɪp/ n cadera f

hippie /ˈhɪpɪ/ n hippy m & f

hippopotamus /hɪpəˈpɒtəməs/ n (pl -muses or -mi /-maɪ/) hipopótamo m

hire /ˈhaɪə(r)/ vt alquilar (thing); contratar (person). • n alquiler m. **car ~** alquiler m de coches. **~ purchase** n compra f a plazos

his /hɪz/ adj su, sus pl. • poss pron (el) suyo m, (la) suya f, (los) suyos mpl, (las) suyas fpl

Hispan|ic /hɪˈspænɪk/ adj hispánico. • n (Amer) hispano m. ~ist /ˈhɪspənɪst/ n hispanista m & f

hiss /hɪs/ n silbido. • vt/i silbar

histor|ian /hɪˈstɔːrɪən/ n historiador m. ~ic(al) /hɪˈstɒrɪk(l)/ adj histórico. ~y /ˈhɪstərɪ/ n historia f.

hit /hɪt/ vt (pt hit, pres p hitting) golpear (object); pegarle a (person); (collide with) chocar con; (affect) afectar. **~ it off with** hacer buenas migas con. ∎**~ on** vt dar con. • n (blow) golpe m; (success) éxito m. (Internet) visita f

hitch /hɪtʃ/ vt (fasten) enganchar. • n (snag) problema m. **~ a lift, ~ a**

ride (Amer) see ~HIKE. ~hike vi hacer autostop, hacer dedo, ir de aventón (Mex). ~hiker n autoestopista m & f

hither /ˈhɪðə(r)/ adv aquí, acá. **~ and thither** acá y allá. ~to adv hasta ahora

hit-or-miss /hɪtɔːˈmɪs/ adj (approach) poco científico

hive /haɪv/ n colmena f

hoard /hɔːd/ vt acumular. • n provisión f; (of money) tesoro m

hoarding /ˈhɔːdɪŋ/ n valla f publicitaria

hoarse /hɔːs/ adj (-er, -est) ronco. ~ly adv con voz ronca

hoax /həʊks/ n engaño m. • vt engañar

hob /hɒb/ n (of cooker) hornillos mpl, hornillas fpl (LAm)

hobble /ˈhɒbl/ vi cojear, renguear (LAm)

hobby /ˈhɒbɪ/ n pasatiempo m. ~horse n (toy) caballito m (de niño); (fixation) caballo m de batalla

hockey /ˈhɒkɪ/ n hockey m; (Amer) hockey m sobre hielo

hoe /həʊ/ n azada f. • vt (pres p hoeing) azadonar

hog /hɒg/ n (Amer) cerdo m. • vt (pt hogged) 🅴 acaparar

hoist /hɔɪst/ vt levantar; izar (flag). • n montacargas m

hold /həʊld/ vt (pt held) tener; (grasp) coger (esp Spain), agarrar; (contain) contener; mantener (interest); (believe) creer. • vi mantenerse. • n (influence) influencia f; (Naut, Aviat) bodega f. **get ~ of** agarrar; (fig, acquire) adquirir. ∎**~ back** vt (contain) contener. ∎**~ on** vi (stand firm) resistir; (wait) esperar. ∎**~ on to** vt (keep) guardar; (cling to) agarrarse a. ∎**~ out** vt (offer) ofrecer. vi (resist) resistir. ∎**~ up** vt (raise) levantar; (support) sostener; (delay) retrasar; (rob) atracar. ~all n bolsa f (de viaje). ~er n tenedor m; (of post) titular m; (wallet) funda f. **~up** atraco m

hole /həʊl/ n agujero m; (in ground) hoyo m; (in road) bache m. ● vt agujerear

holiday /'hɒlɪdeɪ/ n vacaciones fpl; (public) fiesta f. **go on ~** ir de vacaciones. **~maker** n veraneante m & f

holiness /'həʊlɪnɪs/ n santidad f

Holland /'hɒlənd/ n Holanda f

hollow /'hɒləʊ/ adj & n hueco (m)

holly /'hɒlɪ/ n acebo m

holocaust /'hɒləkɔːst/ n holocausto m

holster /'həʊlstə(r)/ n pistolera f

holy /'həʊlɪ/ adj (**-ier, -iest**) santo, sagrado. **H~ Ghost** n, **H~ Spirit** n Espíritu m Santo. **~ water** n agua f bendita

homage /'hɒmɪdʒ/ n homenaje m. **pay ~ to** rendir homenaje a

home /həʊm/ n casa f; (for old people) residencia f de ancianos; (native land) patria f. ● adj (cooking) casero; (address) particular; (background) familiar; (Pol) interior; (match) de casa. ● adv. **(at) ~** en casa. **~land** n patria f. **~land security** seguridad f nacional. **~less** adj sin hogar. **~ly** adj (**-ier, -iest**) casero; (Amer, ugly) feo. **~-made** adj hecho en casa. **~ page** n (Comp) página f frontal. **~sick** adj. **be ~sick** echar de menos a su familia/su país, extrañar a su familia/su país (LAm). **~ town** n ciudad f natal. **~work** n deberes mpl

homicide /'hɒmɪsaɪd/ n homicidio m

homoeopathic /ˌhəʊmɪəʊ'pæθɪk/ adj homeopático

homogeneous /ˌhɒməʊ'dʒiːnɪəs/ adj homogéneo

homosexual /ˌhəʊməʊ'seksjʊəl/ adj & n homosexual (m)

honest /'ɒnɪst/ adj honrado; (frank) sincero. **~ly** adv honradamente. **~y** n honradez f

honey /'hʌnɪ/ n miel f. **~comb** n panal m. **~moon** n luna f de miel. **~suckle** n madreselva f

honorary /'ɒnərərɪ/ adj honorario

honour /'ɒnə(r)/ n honor m. ● vt honrar; cumplir (con) (promise). **~able** adj honorable

hood /hʊd/ n capucha f; (car roof) capota f; (Amer, car bonnet) capó m, capote m (Mex)

hoodwink /'hʊdwɪŋk/ vt engañar

hoof /huːf/ n (pl **hoofs** or **hooves**) (of horse) casco m, pezuna f (Mex); (of cow) pezuña f

hook /hʊk/ n gancho m; (on garment) corchete m; (for fishing) anzuelo m. **let s.o. off the ~** dejar salir a uno del atolladero. **off the ~** (telephone) descolgado. ● vt. **~ed on** 🅴 adicto a. ■ **~ up** vt enganchar. **~ed** adj (tool) en forma de gancho; (nose) aguileño

hookey /'hʊkɪ/ n. **play ~** (Amer fam) faltar a clase, hacer novillos

hooligan /'huːlɪgən/ n vándalo m, gamberro m

hoop /huːp/ n aro m

hooray /hʊ'reɪ/ int & n ¡viva! (m)

hoot /huːt/ n (of horn) bocinazo m; (of owl) ululato m. ● vi tocar la bocina; (owl) ulular

Hoover /'huːvə(r)/ n (®) aspiradora f. ● vt pasar la aspiradora por, aspirar (LAm)

hooves /huːvz/ see HOOF

hop /hɒp/ vi (pt **hopped**) saltar a la pata coja; (frog, rabbit) brincar, saltar; (bird) dar saltitos. ● n salto m; (flight) etapa f. **~(s)** (plant) lúpulo m

hope /həʊp/ n esperanza f. ● vt/i esperar. **~ for** esperar. **~ful** adj (optimistic) esperanzado; (promising) esperanzador. **~fully** adv con optimismo; (it is hoped) se espera. **~less** adj desesperado

horde /hɔːd/ n horda f

horizon /hə'raɪzn/ n horizonte m

horizontal /ˌhɒrɪˈzɒntl/ adj
horizontal. **~ly** adv
horizontalmente

hormone /ˈhɔːməʊn/ n hormona f

horn /hɔːn/ n cuerno m, asta f,
cacho m (LAm); (of car) bocina f;
(Mus) trompa f. **~ed** adj con
cuernos

hornet /ˈhɔːnɪt/ n avispón m

horoscope /ˈhɒrəskəʊp/ n
horóscopo m

horrible /ˈhɒrəbl/ adj horrible

horrid /ˈhɒrɪd/ adj horrible

horrific /həˈrɪfɪk/ adj horroroso

horrify /ˈhɒrɪfaɪ/ vt horrorizar

horror /ˈhɒrə(r)/ n horror m

hors-d'oeuvre /ɔːˈdɜːvr/ n (pl **-s**
/-ˈdɜːvr/ entremés m, botana f (Mex)

horse /hɔːs/ n caballo m. **~back** n.
on ~back a caballo. **~power** n
(unit) caballo m (de fuerza).
~racing n carreras fpl de caballos.
~shoe n herradura f

horticultur|al /ˌhɔːtɪˈkʌltʃərəl/ adj
horticola. **~e** /ˈhɔːtɪkʌltʃə(r)/ n
horticultura f

hose /həʊz/ n manguera f, manga f.
● vt. **~ down** lavar (con
manguera). **~pipe** n manga f

hosiery /ˈhəʊzɪərɪ/ n calcetería f

hospice /ˈhɒspɪs/ n residencia f
para enfermos desahuciados

hospitable /hɒˈspɪtəbl/ adj
hospitalario

hospital /ˈhɒspɪtl/ n hospital m

hospitality /ˌhɒspɪˈtælətɪ/ n
hospitalidad f

host /həʊst/ n (master of house)
anfitrión m; (Radio, TV) presentador
m; (multitude) gran cantidad f; (Relig)
hostia f

hostage /ˈhɒstɪdʒ/ n rehén m

hostel /ˈhɒstl/ n (for students)
residencia f; (for homeless people)
hogar m

hostess /ˈhəʊstɪs/ n anfitriona f

hostil|e /ˈhɒstaɪl/ adj hostil. **~ity**
/-ˈtɪlətɪ/ n hostilidad f

hot /hɒt/ adj (**hotter, hottest**)
caliente; (weather, day) caluroso;
(climate) cálido; (Culin) picante;
(news) de última hora. **be/feel ~**
tener calor. **get ~** calentarse. **it is
~** hace calor. **~bed** n (fig)
semillero m

hotchpotch /ˈhɒtʃpɒtʃ/ n
mezcolanza f

hot dog n perrito m caliente

hotel /həʊˈtel/ n hotel m. **~ier**
/-ɪeɪ/ n hotelero m

hot: ~house n invernadero m.
~plate n placa f, hornilla f (LAm).
~-water bottle /-ˈwɔːtə(r)/ n
bolsa f de agua caliente

hound /haʊnd/ n perro m de caza.
● vt perseguir

hour /aʊə(r)/ n hora f. **~ly** adj (rate)
por hora. ● adv (every hour) cada
hora; (by the hour) por hora

house /haʊs/ n (pl **-s** /ˈhaʊzɪz/) casa
f; (Pol) cámara f. ● /haʊz/ vt alojar;
(keep) guardar. **~hold** n casa f.
~holder n dueño m de una casa.
~keeper n ama f de llaves.
~maid n criada f, mucama f (LAm).
~proud adj meticuloso.
~warming (party) n fiesta de
inauguración de una casa. **~wife**
n ama f de casa. **~work** n tareas fpl
domésticas

housing /ˈhaʊzɪŋ/ n alojamiento m.
~ development (Amer), **~ estate**
n complejo m habitacional,
urbanización f

hovel /ˈhɒvl/ n casucha f

hover /ˈhɒvə(r)/ vi (bird, threat etc)
cernerse; (loiter) rondar. **~craft** n
(pl invar or **-crafts**) aerodeslizador m

how /haʊ/ adv cómo. **~ about a
walk?** ¿qué te parece si damos un
paseo? **~ are you?** ¿cómo está
Vd? **~ do you do?** (in introduction)
mucho gusto. **~ long?** (in time)
¿cuánto tiempo? **~ long is the
room?** ¿cuánto mide de largo el
cuarto? **~ often?** ¿cuántas veces?

however /haʊˈevə(r)/ adv (nevertheless) no obstante, sin embargo; (with verb) de cualquier manera que (+ subjunctive); (with adjective or adverb) por... que (+ subjunctive). **~ much it rains** por mucho que llueva

howl /haʊl/ n aullido. • vi aullar

hp abbr see **HORSEPOWER**

HP abbr see **HIRE-PURCHASE**

hub /hʌb/ n (of wheel) cubo m; (fig) centro m

hubcap /ˈhʌbkæp/ n tapacubos m

huddle /ˈhʌdl/ vi apiñarse

hue /hjuː/ n (colour) color m

huff /hʌf/ n. **be in a ~** estar enfurruñado

hug /hʌɡ/ vt (pt **hugged**) abrazar. • n abrazo m

huge /hjuːdʒ/ adj enorme. **~ly** adv enormemente

hulk /hʌlk/ n (of ship) barco m viejo

hull /hʌl/ n (of ship) casco m

hullo /həˈləʊ/ int see **HELLO**

hum /hʌm/ vt/i (pt **hummed**) (person) canturrear; (insect, engine) zumbar. • n zumbido m

human /ˈhjuːmən/ adj & n humano (m). **~ being** n ser m humano. **~e** /hjuːˈmeɪn/ adj humano. **~itarian** /hjuːmænɪˈteərɪən/ adj humanitario. **~ity** /hjuːˈmænəti/ n humanidad f

humbl|e /ˈhʌmbl/ adj (**-er, -est**) humilde. • vt humillar. **~y** adv humildemente

humdrum /ˈhʌmdrʌm/ adj monótono

humid /ˈhjuːmɪd/ adj húmedo. **~ity** /hjuːˈmɪdəti/ n humedad f

humiliat|e /hjuːˈmɪlɪeɪt/ vt humillar. **~ion** /-ˈeɪʃn/ n humillación f

humility /hjuːˈmɪləti/ n humildad f

humongous /hjuːˈmʌŋɡəs/ adj Ⓘ de primera

humo|rist /ˈhjuːmərɪst/ n

humorista m & f. **~rous** /-rəs/ adj humorístico. **~rously** adv con gracia. **~ur** /ˈhjuːmə(r)/ n humor m. **sense of ~ur** sentido m del humor

hump /hʌmp/ n (of person, camel) joroba f; (in ground) montículo m

hunch /hʌntʃ/ vt encorvar. • n presentimiento m; (lump) joroba f. **~back** n jorobado m

hundred /ˈhʌndrəd/ adj ciento, (before noun) cien. **one ~ and ninety-eight** ciento noventa y ocho. **two ~** doscientos. **three ~ pages** trescientas páginas. **four ~** cuatrocientos. **five ~** quinientos. • n ciento m. **~s of** centenares de. **~th** adj & n centésimo (m). **~weight** n 50,8kg; (Amer) 45,36kg

hung /hʌŋ/ see **HANG**

Hungar|ian /hʌŋˈɡeərɪən/ adj & n húngaro (m). **~y** /ˈhʌŋɡəri/ n Hungría f

hung|er /ˈhʌŋɡə(r)/ n hambre f. • vi. **~er for** tener hambre de. **~rily** /ˈhʌŋɡrəli/ adv ávidamente. **~ry** adj (**-ier, -iest**) hambriento. **be ~ry** tener hambre

hunk /hʌŋk/ n (buen) pedazo m

hunt /hʌnt/ vt cazar. • vi cazar. **~ for** buscar. • n caza f. **~er** n cazador m. **~ing** n caza f. **go ~ing** ir de caza

hurl /hɜːl/ vt lanzar

hurrah /hʊˈrɑː/, **hurray** /hʊˈreɪ/ int & n ¡viva! (m)

hurricane /ˈhʌrɪkən/ n huracán m

hurr|ied /ˈhʌrɪd/ adj apresurado. **~iedly** adv apresuradamente. **~y** vi darse prisa, apurarse (LAm). • vt meter prisa a, apurar (LAm). • n prisa f. **be in a ~y** tener prisa, estar apurado (LAm)

hurt /hɜːt/ vt (pt **hurt**) hacer daño a, lastimar (LAm). **~ s.o.'s feelings** ofender a uno. • vi doler. **my head ~s** me duele la cabeza. **~ful** adj hiriente

hurtle /ˈhɜːtl/ vt ir volando. • vi. **~**

along mover rápidamente

husband /'hʌzbənd/ n marido m, esposo m

hush /hʌʃ/ vt acallar. •n silencio m. ■ ~ **up** vt acallar (affair). ~**hush** adj 🄸 super secreto

husk /hʌsk/ n cáscara f

husky /'hʌskɪ/ adj (**-ier, -iest**) (hoarse) ronco

hustle /'hʌsl/ vt (jostle) empujar. •vi (hurry) darse prisa, apurarse (LAm). •n empuje m

hut /hʌt/ n cabaña f

hutch /hʌtʃ/ n conejera f

hybrid /'haɪbrɪd/ adj & n híbrido (m)

hydrangea /haɪ'dreɪndʒə/ n hortensia f

hydrant /'haɪdrənt/ n. (**fire**) ~ n boca f de riego, boca f de incendios (LAm)

hydraulic /haɪ'drɔːlɪk/ adj hidráulico

hydroelectric /haɪdrəʊ'lektrɪk/ adj hidroeléctrico

hydrofoil /'haɪdrəfɔɪl/ n hidrodeslizador m

hydrogen /'haɪdrədʒən/ n hidrógeno m

hyena /haɪ'iːnə/ n hiena f

hygien|e /'haɪdʒiːn/ n higiene f. ~**ic** /haɪ'dʒiːnɪk/ adj higiénico

hymn /hɪm/ n himno m

hyper... /'haɪpə(r)/ pref hiper...

hyphen /'haɪfn/ n guión m. ~**ate** /-eɪt/ vt escribir con guión

hypno|sis /hɪp'nəʊsɪs/ n hipnosis f. ~**tic** /-'nɒtɪk/ adj hipnótico. ~**tism** /'hɪpnətɪzəm/ n hipnotismo m. ~**tist** /'hɪpnətɪst/ n hipnotista m & f. ~**tize** /'hɪpnətaɪz/ vt hipnotizar

hypochondriac /haɪpə'kɒndrɪæk/ n hipocondríaco m

hypocri|sy /hɪ'pɒkrəsɪ/ n hipocresía f. ~**te** /'hɪpəkrɪt/ n hipócrita m & f. ~**tical** /hɪpə'krɪtɪkl/ adj hipócrita

hypodermic /haɪpə'dɜːmɪk/ adj hipodérmico. •n hipodérmica f

hypothe|sis /haɪ'pɒθəsɪs/ n (pl **-theses** /-siːz/) hipótesis f. ~**tical** /-ə'θetɪkl/ adj hipotético

hysteri|a /hɪ'stɪərɪə/ n histerismo m. ~**cal** /-'terɪkl/ adj histérico. ~**cs** /hɪ'sterɪks/ npl histerismo m. **have** ~**cs** ponerse histérico; (laugh) morir de risa

Ii

I /aɪ/ pron yo

ice /aɪs/ n hielo m. •vt helar; glasear (cake). •vi. ~ (**up**) helarse, congelarse. ~**berg** /-bɜːg/ n iceberg m. ~ **box** n (compartment) congelador; (Amer fam, refrigerator) frigorífico m, refrigerador m (LAm). ~**cream** n helado m. ~ **cube** n cubito m de hielo

Iceland /'aɪslənd/ n Islandia f

ice: ~ **lolly** polo m, paleta f helada (LAm). ~ **rink** n pista f de hielo.

~ **skating** n patinaje m sobre hielo

icicle /'aɪsɪkl/ n carámbano m

icing /'aɪsɪŋ/ n glaseado m

icon /'aɪkɒn/ n icono m

icy /'aɪsɪ/ adj (**-ier, -iest**) helado; (fig) glacial

I'd /aɪd/ = **I had, I would**

idea /aɪ'dɪə/ n idea f

ideal /aɪ'dɪəl/ adj & n ideal (m).

~**ism** n idealismo m. ~**ist** n idealista m & f. ~**istic** /-'lɪstɪk/ adj idealista. ~**ize** vt idealizar. ~**ly** adv idealmente

identical /aɪ'dentɪkl/ adj idéntico. ~ **twins** npl gemelos mpl idénticos, gemelos mpl (LAm)

identif|ication /aɪdentɪfɪ'keɪʃn/ n identificación f. ~**y** /aɪ'dentɪfaɪ/ vt identificar. ●vi. ~**y with** identificarse con

identity /aɪ'dentɪtɪ/ n identidad f. ~ **card** n carné m de identidad. ~ **theft** n robo m de identidad

ideolog|ical /aɪdɪə'lɒdʒɪkl/ adj ideológico. ~**y** /aɪdɪ'ɒlədʒɪ/ n ideología f

idiocy /'ɪdɪəsɪ/ n idiotez f

idiom /'ɪdɪəm/ n locución f. ~**atic** /-'mætɪk/ adj idiomático

idiot /'ɪdɪət/ n idiota m & f. ~**ic** /-'ɒtɪk/ adj idiota

idle /'aɪdl/ adj (-er, -est) ocioso; (lazy) holgazán; (out of work) desocupado; (machine) parado. ●vi (engine) andar al ralentí. ~**ness** n ociosidad f; (laziness) holgazanería f

idol /'aɪdl/ n ídolo m. ~**ize** vt idolatrar

idyllic /ɪ'dɪlɪk/ adj idílico

i.e. abbr (= id est) es decir

if /ɪf/ conj si

igloo /'ɪglu:/ n iglú m

ignit|e /ɪg'naɪt/ vt encender. ●vi encenderse. ~**ion** /-'nɪʃn/ n ignición f; (Auto) encendido m. ~**ion key** n llave f de contacto

ignoramus /ɪgnə'reɪməs/ n (pl-muses) ignorante

ignoran|ce /'ɪgnərəns/ n ignorancia f. ~**t** adj ignorante

ignore /ɪg'nɔ:(r)/ vt no hacer caso de; hacer caso omiso de (warning)

ill /ɪl/ adj enfermo. ●adv mal. ●n mal m

I'll /aɪl/ = **I will**

ill: ~-advised /-əd'vaɪzd/ adj imprudente. ~ **at ease** /-ət'i:z/ adj incómodo. ~**-bred** /-'bred/ adj mal educado

illegal /ɪ'li:gl/ adj ilegal

illegible /ɪ'ledʒəbl/ adj ilegible

illegitima|cy /ɪlɪ'dʒɪtɪməsɪ/ n ilegitimidad f. ~**te** /-ət/ adj ilegítimo

illitera|cy /ɪ'lɪtərəsɪ/ n analfabetismo m. ~**te** /-ət/ adj analfabeto

illness /'ɪlnɪs/ n enfermedad f

illogical /ɪ'lɒdʒɪkl/ adj ilógico

illuminat|e /ɪ'lu:mɪneɪt/ vt iluminar. ~**ion** /-'neɪʃn/ n iluminación f

illus|ion /ɪ'lu:ʒn/ n ilusión f. ~**sory** /-serɪ/ adj ilusorio

illustrat|e /'ɪləstreɪt/ vt ilustrar. ~**ion** /-'streɪʃn/ n ilustración f; (example) ejemplo m

illustrious /ɪ'lʌstrɪəs/ adj ilustre

ill will /ɪl'wɪl/ n mala voluntad f

I'm /aɪm/ = **I am**

image /'ɪmɪdʒ/ n imagen f. ~**ry** n imágenes fpl

imagin|able /ɪ'mædʒɪnəbl/ adj imaginable. ~**ary** adj imaginario. ~**ation** /-'neɪʃn/ n imaginación f. ~**ative** adj imaginativo. ~**e** /ɪ'mædʒɪn/ vt imaginar(se)

imbalance /ɪm'bæləns/ n desequilibrio m

imbecile /'ɪmbəsi:l/ n imbécil m & f

imitat|e /'ɪmɪteɪt/ vt imitar. ~**ion** /-'teɪʃn/ n imitación f. ●adj de imitación. ~**or** n imitador m

immaculate /ɪ'mækjʊlət/ adj inmaculado

immatur|e /ɪmə'tjʊə(r)/ adj inmaduro. ~**ity** n inmadurez f

immediate /ɪ'mi:dɪət/ adj inmediato. ~**ly** adv inmediatamente. ●conj en cuanto (+ subjunctive)

immens|e /ɪ'mens/ adj inmenso.

~**ely** adv inmensamente; (fam, very much) muchísimo

immers|e /ɪ'mɜːs/ vt sumergir. ~**ion** /-ʃn/ n inmersión f. ~**ion heater** n calentador m de inmersión

immigra|nt /'ɪmɪgrənt/ adj & n inmigrante (m & f). ~**tion** /-'greɪʃn/ n inmigración f

imminent /'ɪmɪnənt/ adj inminente

immobil|e /ɪ'məʊbaɪl/ adj inmóvil. ~**ize** /-bɪlaɪz/ vt inmovilizar. ~**izer** /-bɪlaɪzə(r)/ n inmovilizador m

immoderate /ɪ'mɒdərət/ adj inmoderado

immodest /ɪ'mɒdɪst/ adj inmodesto

immoral /ɪ'mɒrəl/ adj inmoral. ~**ity** /ɪmə'rælətɪ/ n inmoralidad f

immortal /ɪ'mɔːtl/ adj inmortal. ~**ity** /-'tælətɪ/ n inmortalidad f. ~**ize** vt inmortalizar

immun|e /ɪ'mjuːn/ adj inmune (**to** a). ~**ity** n inmunidad f. ~**ization** /ɪmjʊnaɪ'zeɪʃn/ n inmunización f. ~**ize** /'ɪmjʊnaɪz/ vt inmunizar

imp /ɪmp/ n diablillo m

impact /'ɪmpækt/ n impacto m

impair /ɪm'peə(r)/ vt perjudicar

impale /ɪm'peɪl/ vt atravesar (**on** con)

impart /ɪm'pɑːt/ vt comunicar (news); impartir (knowledge)

impartial /ɪm'pɑːʃl/ adj imparcial. ~**ity** /-ɪ'ælətɪ/ n imparcialidad f

impassable /ɪm'pɑːsəbl/ adj (road) intransitable

impassive /ɪm'pæsɪv/ adj impasible

impatien|ce /ɪm'peɪʃəns/ n impaciencia f. ~**t** adj impaciente. **get** ~**t** impacientarse. ~**tly** adv con impaciencia

impeccable /ɪm'pekəbl/ adj impecable

impede /ɪm'piːd/ vt estorbar

impediment /ɪm'pedɪmənt/

obstáculo m. (**speech**) ~ n defecto m del habla

impending /ɪm'pendɪŋ/ adj inminente

impenetrable /ɪm'penɪtrəbl/ adj impenetrable

imperative /ɪm'perətɪv/ adj imprescindible. •n (Gram) imperativo m

imperceptible /ɪmpə'septəbl/ adj imperceptible

imperfect /ɪm'pɜːfɪkt/ adj imperfecto. ~**ion** /ɪmpə'fekʃn/ n imperfección f

imperial /ɪm'pɪərɪəl/ adj imperial. ~**ism** n imperialismo m

impersonal /ɪm'pɜːsənl/ adj impersonal

impersonat|e /ɪm'pɜːsəneɪt/ vt hacerse pasar por; (mimic) imitar. ~**ion** /-'neɪʃn/ n imitación f. ~**or** n imitador m

impertinen|ce /ɪm'pɜːtɪnəns/ n impertinencia f. ~**t** adj impertinente

impervious /ɪm'pɜːvɪəs/ adj. ~ **to** impermeable a

impetuous /ɪm'petjʊəs/ adj impetuoso

impetus /'ɪmpɪtəs/ n ímpetu m

implacable /ɪm'plækəbl/ adj implacable

implant /ɪm'plɑːnt/ vt implantar

implement /'ɪmplɪmənt/ n instrumento m, implemento m (LAm). •/'ɪmplɪment/ vt implementar

implementation /ɪmplɪmen'teɪʃn/ n implementación f

implicat|e /'ɪmplɪkeɪt/ vt implicar. ~**ion** /-'keɪʃn/ n implicación f

implicit /ɪm'plɪsɪt/ adj (implied) implícito; (unquestioning) absoluto

implore /ɪm'plɔː(r)/ vt implorar

imply /ɪm'plaɪ/ vt (involve) implicar; (insinuate) dar a entender, insinuar

impolite | inappropriate

impolite /ɪmpəˈlaɪt/ adj mal educado

import /ɪmˈpɔːt/ vt importar. •/ˈɪmpɔːt/ n importación f; (item) artículo m de importación; (meaning) significación f

importan|ce /ɪmˈpɔːtəns/ n importancia f. ~**t** adj importante

importer /ɪmˈpɔːtə(r)/ n importador m

impos|e /ɪmˈpəʊz/ vt imponer. •vi. ~**e on** abusar de la amabilidad de. ~**ing** adj imponente. ~**ition** /ɪmpəˈzɪʃn/ n imposición f; (fig) abuso m

impossib|ility /ɪmpɒsəˈbɪləti/ n imposibilidad f. ~**le** /ɪmˈpɒsəbl/ adj imposible

impostor /ɪmˈpɒstə(r)/ n impostor m

impoten|ce /ˈɪmpətəns/ n impotencia f. ~**t** adj impotente

impound /ɪmˈpaʊnd/ vt confiscar

impoverished /ɪmˈpɒvərɪʃt/ adj empobrecido

impractical /ɪmˈpræktɪkl/ adj poco práctico

impregnable /ɪmˈpregnəbl/ adj inexpugnable

impregnate /ˈɪmpregneɪt/ vt impregnar (**with** con, de)

impress /ɪmˈpres/ vt impresionar; (make good impression) causar una buena impresión a. •vi impresionar

impression /ɪmˈpreʃn/ n impresión f. ~**able** adj impresionable. ~**ism** n impresionismo m

impressive /ɪmˈpresɪv/ adj impresionante

imprint /ˈɪmprɪnt/ n impresión f. •/ɪmˈprɪnt/ vt imprimir

imprison /ɪmˈprɪzn/ vt encarcelar. ~**ment** n encarcelamiento m

improbab|ility /ɪmprɒbəˈbɪləti/ n improbabilidad f. ~**le** /ɪmˈprɒbəbl/ adj improbable

impromptu /ɪmˈprɒmptjuː/ adj improvisado. •adv de improviso

improper /ɪmˈprɒpə(r)/ adj impropio; (incorrect) incorrecto

improve /ɪmˈpruːv/ vt mejorar. •vi mejorar. ~**ment** n mejora f

improvis|ation /ɪmprəvaɪˈzeɪʃn/ n improvisación f. ~**e** /ˈɪmprəvaɪz/ vt/i improvisar

impuden|ce /ˈɪmpjʊdəns/ n insolencia f. ~**t** adj insolente

impuls|e /ˈɪmpʌls/ n impulso m. **on** ~**e** sin reflexionar. ~**ive** adj irreflexivo

impur|e /ɪmˈpjʊə(r)/ adj impuro. ~**ity** n impureza f

in /ɪn/ prep en; (within) dentro de. ~ **a firm manner** de una manera terminante. ~ **an hour('s time)** dentro de una hora. ~ **doing** al hacer. ~ **so far as** en la medida en que. ~ **the evening** por la tarde. ~ **the rain** bajo la lluvia. ~ **the sun** al sol. **one** ~ **ten** uno de cada diez. **the best** ~ **the world** el mejor del mundo. •adv (inside) dentro; (at home) en casa. **come** ~ entrar. •n. **the** ~**s and outs of** los detalles de

inability /ɪnəˈbɪləti/ n incapacidad f

inaccessible /ɪnækˈsesəbl/ adj inaccesible

inaccura|cy /ɪnˈækjʊrəsi/ n inexactitud f. ~**te** /-ət/ adj inexacto

inactiv|e /ɪnˈæktɪv/ adj inactivo. ~**ity** /-ˈtɪvəti/ n inactividad f

inadequa|cy /ɪnˈædɪkwəsi/ adj insuficiencia f. ~**te** /-ət/ adj insuficiente

inadvertently /ɪnədˈvɜːtəntli/ adv sin querer

inadvisable /ɪnədˈvaɪzəbl/ adj desaconsejable

inane /ɪˈneɪn/ adj estúpido

inanimate /ɪnˈænɪmət/ adj inanimado

inappropriate /ɪnəˈprəʊprɪət/ adj inoportuno

inarticulate /ɪnɑːˈtɪkjʊlət/ adj incapaz de expresarse claramente

inattentive /ɪnəˈtentɪv/ adj desatento

inaudible /ɪnˈɔːdəbl/ adj inaudible

inaugurate /ɪˈnɔːgjʊreɪt/ vt inaugurar

inborn /ˈɪnbɔːn/ adj innato

inbred /ɪnˈbred/ adj (inborn) innato; (social group) endogámico

Inc /ɪŋk/ abbr (Amer) (= **Incorporated**) S.A., Sociedad Anónima

incalculable /ɪnˈkælkjʊləbl/ adj incalculable

incapable /ɪnˈkeɪpəbl/ adj incapaz

incapacit|ate /ɪnkəˈpæsɪteɪt/ vt incapacitar. ~y n incapacidad f

incarcerate /ɪnˈkɑːsəreɪt/ vt encarcelar

incarnat|e /ɪnˈkɑːnət/ adj encarnado. ~ion /-ˈneɪʃn/ n encarnación f

incendiary /ɪnˈsendɪərɪ/ adj incendiario. ~ **bomb** bomba f incendiaria

incense /ˈɪnsens/ n incienso m. • /ɪnˈsens/ vt enfurecer

incentive /ɪnˈsentɪv/ n incentivo m

incessant /ɪnˈsesnt/ adj incesante. ~ly adv sin cesar

incest /ˈɪnsest/ n incesto m. ~uous /ɪnˈsestjʊəs/ adj incestuoso

inch /ɪntʃ/ n pulgada f; (= 2,54cm). • vi. ~ **forward** avanzar lentamente

incidence /ˈɪnsɪdəns/ n frecuencia f

incident /ˈɪnsɪdənt/ n incidente m

incidental /ɪnsɪˈdentl/ adj (effect) secundario; (minor) incidental. ~ly adv a propósito

incinerat|e /ɪnˈsɪnəreɪt/ vt incinerar. ~or n incinerador m

incision /ɪnˈsɪʒn/ n incisión f

incite /ɪnˈsaɪt/ vt incitar. ~ment n incitación f

inclination /ɪnklɪˈneɪʃn/ n inclinación f. **have no ~ to** no tener deseos de

incline /ɪnˈklaɪn/ vt inclinar. **be ~d to** tener tendencia a. • vi inclinarse. • /ˈɪnklaɪn/ n pendiente f

inclu|de /ɪnˈkluːd/ vt incluir. ~**ding** prep incluso. ~**sion** /-ʒn/ n inclusión f. ~**sive** /-sɪv/ adj inclusivo

incognito /ɪnkɒgˈniːtəʊ/ adv de incógnito

incoherent /ɪnkəʊˈhɪərənt/ adj incoherente

incom|e /ˈɪnkʌm/ n ingresos mpl. ~**e tax** n impuesto m sobre la renta. ~**ing** adj (tide) ascendente

incomparable /ɪnˈkɒmpərəbl/ adj incomparable

incompatible /ɪnkəmˈpætəbl/ adj incompatible

incompeten|ce /ɪnˈkɒmpɪtəns/ n incompetencia f. ~t adj incompetente

incomplete /ɪnkəmˈpliːt/ adj incompleto

incomprehensible /ɪnkɒmprɪˈhensəbl/ adj incomprensible

inconceivable /ɪnkənˈsiːvəbl/ adj inconcebible

inconclusive /ɪnkənˈkluːsɪv/ adj no concluyente

incongruous /ɪnˈkɒŋgrʊəs/ adj incongruente

inconsiderate /ɪnkənˈsɪdərət/ adj desconsiderado

inconsisten|cy /ɪnkənˈsɪstənsɪ/ n inconsecuencia f. ~t adj inconsecuente. **be ~t with** no concordar con

inconspicuous /ɪnkənˈspɪkjʊəs/ adj que no llama la atención. ~ly adv sin llamar la atención

incontinent /ɪnˈkɒntɪnənt/ adj incontinente

inconvenien|ce /ɪnkənˈviːnɪəns/

i

adj inconveniencia f; (drawback) inconveniente m. ~t adj inconveniente

incorporate /ɪn'kɔ:pəreɪt/ vt incorporar; (include) incluir; (Com) constituir (en sociedad)

incorrect /ɪnkə'rekt/ adj incorrecto

increas|e /'ɪnkri:s/ n aumento m (**in** de). ● /ɪn'kri:s/ vt/i aumentar. ~**ing** /ɪn'kri:sɪŋ/ adj creciente. ~**ingly** adv cada vez más

incredible /ɪn'kredəbl/ adj increíble

incredulous /ɪn'kredjʊləs/ adj incrédulo

incriminat|e /ɪn'krɪmɪneɪt/ vt incriminar. ~**ing** adj comprometedor

incubat|e /'ɪŋkjʊbeɪt/ vt incubar. ~**ion** /-'beɪʃn/ n incubación f. ~**or** n incubadora f

incur /ɪn'kɜ:(r)/ vt (pt **incurred**) incurrir en; contraer (debts)

incurable /ɪn'kjʊərəbl/ adj (disease) incurable; (romantic) empedernido

indebted /ɪn'detɪd/ adj. **be ~ to s.o.** estar en deuda con uno

indecen|cy /ɪn'di:snsɪ/ n indecencia f. ~**t** adj indecente

indecisi|on /ɪndɪ'sɪʒn/ n indecisión f. ~**ve** /-'saɪsɪv/ adj indeciso

indeed /ɪn'di:d/ adv en efecto; (really?) ¿de veras?

indefinable /ɪndɪ'faɪnəbl/ adj indefinible

indefinite /ɪn'defɪnət/ adj indefinido. ~**ly** adv indefinidamente

indelible /ɪn'delɪbl/ adj indeleble

indemni|fy /ɪn'demnɪfaɪ/ vt (insure) asegurar; (compensate) indemnizar. ~**ty** /-ətɪ/ n (insurance) indemnidad f; (payment) indemnización f

indent /ɪn'dent/ vt sangrar (text). ~**ation** /-'teɪʃn/ n mella f

independen|ce /ɪndɪ'pendəns/ n independencia f. ~**t** adj

independiente. ~**tly** adv independientemente

in-depth /ɪn'depθ/ adj a fondo

indescribable /ɪndɪ'skraɪbəbl/ adj indescriptible

indestructible /ɪndɪ'strʌktəbl/ adj indestructible

indeterminate /ɪndɪ'tɜ:mɪnət/ adj indeterminado

index /'ɪndeks/ n (pl **indexes**) (in book) índice m; (pl **indexes** or **indices**) (Com, Math) índice m. ● vt poner índice a; (enter in index) poner en un índice. ~ **finger** n (dedo m) índice m. ~**-linked** /-'lɪŋkt/ adj indexado

India /'ɪndɪə/ n la India. ~**n** adj & n indio (m)

indicat|e /'ɪndɪkeɪt/ vt indicar. ~**ion** /-'keɪʃn/ n indicación f. ~**ive** /ɪn'dɪkətɪv/ adj & n indicativo (m). ~**or** /'ɪndɪkeɪtə(r)/ n indicador m; (Auto) intermitente m

indices /'ɪndɪsi:z/ see **INDEX**

indict /ɪn'daɪt/ vt acusar. ~**ment** n acusación f

indifferen|ce /ɪn'dɪfrəns/ n indiferencia f. ~**t** adj indiferente; (not good) mediocre

indigesti|ble /ɪndɪ'dʒestəbl/ adj indigesto. ~**on** /-tʃən/ n indigestión f

indigna|nt /ɪn'dɪgnənt/ adj indignado. ~**tion** /-'neɪʃn/ n indignación f

indirect /ɪndɪ'rekt/ adj indirecto. ~**ly** adv indirectamente

indiscre|et /ɪndɪ'skri:t/ adj indiscreto. ~**tion** /-'kreʃn/ n indiscreción f

indiscriminate /ɪndɪ'skrɪmɪnət/ adj indistinto. ~**ly** adv indistintamente

indispensable /ɪndɪ'spensəbl/ adj indispensable, imprescindible

indisposed /ɪndɪ'spəʊzd/ adj indispuesto

indisputable /ɪndɪˈspjuːtəbl/ adj
indiscutible

indistinguishable
/ɪndɪˈstɪŋgwɪʃəbl/ adj indistinguible
(**from** de)

individual /ɪndɪˈvɪdjʊəl/ adj
individual. ● n individuo m. ~ly
adv individualmente

indoctrinat|e /ɪnˈdɒktrɪneɪt/ vt
adoctrinar. ~ion /-ˈneɪʃn/ n
adoctrinamiento m

indolen|ce /ˈɪndələns/ n indolencia
f. ~t adj indolente

indomitable /ɪnˈdɒmɪtəbl/ adj
indómito

indoor /ˈɪndɔː(r)/ adj interior;
(clothes etc) de casa; (covered)
cubierto. ~s adv dentro, adentro
(LAm)

induc|e /ɪnˈdjuːs/ vt inducir.
~ement n incentivo m

indulge /ɪnˈdʌldʒ/ vt satisfacer
(desires); complacer (person). ● vi. ~
in permitirse. ~nce /-əns/ n (of
desires) satisfacción f; (extravagance)
lujo m. ~nt adj indulgente

industrial /ɪnˈdʌstrɪəl/ adj
industrial; (unrest) laboral. ~ist n
industrial m & f. ~ized adj
industrializado

industrious /ɪnˈdʌstrɪəs/ adj
trabajador

industry /ˈɪndəstrɪ/ n industria f;
(zeal) aplicación f

inebriated /ɪˈniːbrɪeɪtɪd/ adj beodo,
ebrio

inedible /ɪnˈedɪbl/ adj incomible

ineffective /ɪnɪˈfektɪv/ adj ineficaz;
(person) incompetente

ineffectual /ɪnɪˈfektjʊəl/ adj
ineficaz

inefficien|cy /ɪnɪˈfɪʃnsɪ/ n
ineficacia f; (of person)
incompetencia f. ~t adj ineficaz;
(person) incompetente

ineligible /ɪnˈelɪdʒəbl/ adj
inelegible. **be ~ for** no tener
derecho a

inept /ɪˈnept/ adj inepto

inequality /ɪnɪˈkwɒlətɪ/ n
desigualdad f

inert /ɪˈnɜːt/ adj inerte. ~ia /ɪˈnɜːʃə/
n inercia f

inescapable /ɪnɪˈskeɪpəbl/ adj
ineludible

inevitabl|e /ɪnˈevɪtəbl/ adj
inevitable. ● n. **the ~e** lo
inevitable. ~y adv
inevitablemente

inexact /ɪnɪgˈzækt/ adj inexacto

inexcusable /ɪnɪkˈskjuːsəbl/ adj
imperdonable

inexpensive /ɪnɪkˈspensɪv/ adj
económico, barato

inexperience /ɪnɪkˈspɪərɪəns/ n
falta f de experiencia. ~d adj
inexperto

inexplicable /ɪnɪkˈsplɪkəbl/ adj
inexplicable

infallib|ility /ɪnfæləˈbɪlətɪ/ n
infalibilidad f. ~le /ɪnˈfæləbl/ adj
infalible

infam|ous /ˈɪnfəməs/ adj infame
~y n infamia f

infan|cy /ˈɪnfənsɪ/ n infancia f. ~t n
niño m. ~tile /ˈɪnfəntaɪl/ adj
infantil

infantry /ˈɪnfəntrɪ/ n infantería f

infatuat|ed /ɪnˈfætjʊeɪtɪd/ adj. **be
~ed with** estar encaprichado
con. ~ion /-ˈeɪʃn/ n
encaprichamiento m

infect /ɪnˈfekt/ vt infectar; (fig)
contagiar. ~ **s.o. with sth**
contagiarle algo a uno. ~ion /-ʃn/
n infección f. ~ious /-ʃəs/ adj
contagioso

infer /ɪnˈfɜː(r)/ vt (pt **inferred**)
deducir

inferior /ɪnˈfɪərɪə(r)/ adj & n
inferior (m & f). ~ity /-ˈɒrətɪ/ n
inferioridad f

inferno /ɪnˈfɜːnəʊ/ n (pl **-os**)
infierno m

infertil|e /ɪnˈfɜːtaɪl/ adj estéril.

i

~ity /-'tɪlətɪ/ n esterilidad f

infest /ɪn'fest/ vt infestar

infidelity /ɪnfɪ'delətɪ/ n infidelidad f

infiltrat|e /'ɪnfɪltreɪt/ vt infiltrarse en. •vi infiltrarse. ~or n infiltrado m

infinite /'ɪnfɪnət/ adj infinito. ~ly adv infinitamente

infinitesimal /ɪnfɪnɪ'tesɪml/ adj infinitesimal

infinitive /ɪn'fɪnətɪv/ n infinitivo m

infinity /ɪn'fɪnətɪ/ n (infinite distance) infinito m; (infinite quantity) infinidad f

infirm /ɪn'fɜːm/ adj enfermizo. ~ity n enfermedad f

inflam|e /ɪn'fleɪm/ vt inflamar. ~mable /ɪn'flæməbl/ adj inflamable. ~mation /-ə'meɪʃn/ n inflamación f

inflat|e /ɪn'fleɪt/ vt inflar. ~ion /-ʃn/ n inflación f. ~ionary adj inflacionario

inflection /ɪn'flekʃn/ n inflexión f

inflexible /ɪn'fleksəbl/ adj inflexible

inflict /ɪn'flɪkt/ vt infligir (on a)

influen|ce /'ɪnfluəns/ n influencia f. under the ~ce (fam, drunk) borracho. •vt influir (en). ~tial /-'enʃl/ adj influyente

influenza /ɪnflʊ'enzə/ n gripe f

influx /'ɪnflʌks/ n afluencia f

inform /ɪn'fɔːm/ vt informar. keep ~ed tener al corriente. •vi. ~ on s.o. delatar a uno

informal /ɪn'fɔːml/ adj informal; (language) familiar. ~ity /-'mælətɪ/ n falta f de ceremonia. ~ly adv (casually) de manera informal; (unofficially) informalmente

inform|ation /ɪnfə'meɪʃn/ n información f. ~ation technology n informática f. ~ative adj /ɪn'fɔːmətɪv/ informativo. ~er /ɪb'fɔːmə(r)/ n informante m & f

infrared /ɪnfrə'red/ adj infrarrojo

infrequent /ɪn'friːkwənt/ adj poco frecuente. ~ly adv raramente

infringe /ɪn'frɪndʒ/ vt infringir. ~ on violar. ~ment n violación f

infuriat|e /ɪn'fjʊərɪeɪt/ vt enfurecer. ~ing adj exasperante

ingen|ious /ɪn'dʒiːnɪəs/ adj ingenioso. ~uity /ɪndʒɪ'njuːətɪ/ n ingeniosidad f

ingot /'ɪŋgət/ n lingote m

ingrained /ɪn'greɪnd/ adj (belief) arraigado

ingratiate /ɪn'greɪʃɪeɪt/ vt. ~ o.s. with congraciarse con

ingratitude /ɪn'grætɪtjuːd/ n ingratitud f

ingredient /ɪn'griːdɪənt/ n ingrediente m

ingrowing /'ɪngrəʊɪŋ/, ingrown /'ɪngrəʊn/ adj. ~ nail n uñero m, uña f encarnada

inhabit /ɪn'hæbɪt/ vt habitar. ~able adj habitable. ~ant n habitante m

inhale /ɪn'heɪl/ vt aspirar. •vi (when smoking) aspirar el humo. ~r n inhalador m

inherent /ɪn'hɪərənt/ adj inherente. ~ly adv intrínsecamente

inherit /ɪn'herɪt/ vt heredar. ~ance /-əns/ n herencia f

inhibit /ɪn'hɪbɪt/ vt inhibir. ~ed adj inhibido. ~ion /-'bɪʃn/ n inhibición f

inhospitable /ɪnhə'spɪtəbl/ adj (place) inhóspito; (person) inhospitalario

inhuman /ɪn'hjuːmən/ adj inhumano. ~e /ɪnhjuː'meɪn/ adj inhumano. ~ity /ɪnhjuː'mænətɪ/ n inhumanidad f

initial /ɪ'nɪʃl/ n inicial f. •vt (pt initialled) firmar con iniciales. •adj inicial. ~ly adv al principio

initiat|e /ɪ'nɪʃɪeɪt/ vt iniciar; promover (scheme etc). ~ion /-'eɪʃn/ n iniciación f

initiative /ɪˈnɪʃətɪv/ n iniciativa f.
on one's own ~ por iniciativa
propia. **take the ~** tomar la
iniciativa

inject /ɪnˈdʒekt/ vt inyectar. **~ion**
/-ʃn/ n inyección f

injur|e /ˈɪndʒə(r)/ vt herir. **~y** n
herida f

injustice /ɪnˈdʒʌstɪs/ n injusticia f

ink /ɪŋk/ n tinta f. **~well** n tintero
m. **~y** adj manchado de tinta

inland /ˈɪnlənd/ adj interior.
●/ɪnˈlænd/ adv tierra adentro. **I~
Revenue** /ɪnlənd/ n Hacienda f

in-laws /ˈɪnlɔːz/ npl parientes mpl
políticos

inlay /ɪnˈleɪ/ vt (pt **inlaid**) taracear,
incrustar. ●/ˈɪnleɪ/ n taracea f,
incrustación f

inlet /ˈɪnlet/ n (in coastline) ensenada
f; (of river, sea) brazo m

inmate /ˈɪnmeɪt/ n (of asylum)
interno m; (of prison) preso m

inn /ɪn/ n posada f

innate /ɪˈneɪt/ adj innato

inner /ˈɪnə(r)/ adj interior; (fig)
íntimo. **~most** adj más íntimo. **~
tube** n cámara f

innocen|ce /ˈɪnəsns/ n inocencia f.
~t adj & n inocente (m & f)

innocuous /ɪˈnɒkjʊəs/ adj inocuo

innovat|e /ˈɪnəveɪt/ vi innovar.
~ion /-ˈveɪʃn/ n innovación f.
~ive /ˈɪnəvɪtɪv/ adj innovador.
~or n innovador m

innuendo /ɪnjuːˈendəʊ/ n (pl **-oes**)
insinuación f

innumerable /ɪˈnjuːmərəbl/ adj
innumerable

inoculat|e /ɪˈnɒkjʊleɪt/ vt inocular.
~ion /-ˈleɪʃn/ n inoculación f

inoffensive /ɪnəˈfensɪv/ adj
inofensivo

inopportune /ɪnˈɒpətjuːn/ adj
inoportuno

input /ˈɪnpʊt/ n aportación f, aporte
m (LAm); (Comp) entrada f. ●vt (pt
input, pres p **inputting**) entrar
(data)

inquest /ˈɪnkwest/ n investigación f
judicial

inquir|e /ɪnˈkwaɪə(r)/ vt/i
preguntar. **~e about** informarse
de. **~y** n pregunta f; (investigation)
investigación f

inquisition /ɪnkwɪˈzɪʃn/ n
inquisición f

inquisitive /ɪnˈkwɪzətɪv/ adj
inquisitivo

insan|e /ɪnˈseɪn/ adj loco. **~ity**
/ɪnˈsænətɪ/ n locura f

insatiable /ɪnˈseɪʃəbl/ adj
insaciable

inscri|be /ɪnˈskraɪb/ vt inscribir
(letters); grabar (design). **~ption**
/-ɪpʃn/ n inscripción f

inscrutable /ɪnˈskruːtəbl/ adj
inescrutable

insect /ˈɪnsekt/ n insecto m. **~icide**
/ɪnˈsektɪsaɪd/ n insecticida f

insecur|e /ɪnsɪˈkjʊə(r)/ adj
inseguro. **~ity** n inseguridad f

insensitive /ɪnˈsensətɪv/ adj
insensible

inseparable /ɪnˈsepərəbl/ adj
inseparable

insert /ˈɪnsɜːt/ n materia f
insertada. ●/ɪnˈsɜːt/ vt insertar.
~ion /ɪnˈsɜːʃn/ n inserción f

inside /ɪnˈsaɪd/ n interior m. **~ out**
al revés; (thoroughly) a fondo. ●adj
interior. ●adv dentro, adentro
(LAm). ●prep dentro de. **~s** npl
tripas fpl

insight /ˈɪnsaɪt/ n perspicacia f.
gain an ~ into llegar a
comprender bien

insignificant /ɪnsɪɡˈnɪfɪkənt/ adj
insignificante

insincer|e /ɪnsɪnˈsɪə(r)/ adj poco
sincero. **~ity** /-ˈserətɪ/ n falta f de
sinceridad

insinuat|e /ɪnˈsɪnjʊeɪt/ vt insinuar.
~ion /-ˈeɪʃn/ n insinuación f

insipid /ɪnˈsɪpɪd/ adj insípido

insist /ɪnˈsɪst/ vt insistir (**that** en que). • vi insistir. **~ on** insistir en. **~ence** /-əns/ n insistencia f. **~ent** adj insistente. **~ently** adv con insistencia

insolen|ce /ˈɪnsələns/ n insolencia f. **~t** adj insolente

insoluble /ɪnˈsɒljʊbl/ adj insoluble

insolvent /ɪnˈsɒlvənt/ adj insolvente

insomnia /ɪnˈsɒmnɪə/ n insomnio m. **~c** /-ɪæk/ n insomne m & f

inspect /ɪnˈspekt/ vt (officially) inspeccionar; (look at closely) revisar, examinar. **~ion** /-ʃn/ n inspección f. **~or** n inspector m; (on train, bus) revisor m, inspector m (LAm)

inspir|ation /ɪnspəˈreɪʃn/ n inspiración f. **~e** /ɪnˈspaɪə(r)/ vt inspirar. **~ing** adj inspirador

instability /ɪnstəˈbɪlətɪ/ n inestabilidad f

install /ɪnˈstɔːl/ vt instalar. **~ation** /-əˈleɪʃn/ n instalación f

instalment /ɪnˈstɔːlmənt/ n (payment) plazo m; (of publication) entrega f; (of radio, TV serial) episodio m

instance /ˈɪnstəns/ n ejemplo m; (case) caso m. **for ~** por ejemplo. **in the first ~** en primer lugar

instant /ˈɪnstənt/ adj instantáneo. • n instante m. **~aneous** /ɪnstənˈteɪnɪəs/ adj instantáneo

instead /ɪnˈsted/ adv en cambio. **~ of** en vez de, en lugar de

instigat|e /ˈɪnstɪɡeɪt/ vt instigar. **~ion** /-ˈɡeɪʃn/ n instigación f

instinct /ˈɪnstɪŋkt/ n instinto m. **~ive** adj instintivo

institut|e /ˈɪnstɪtjuːt/ n instituto m. • vt instituir; iniciar (enquiry etc). **~ion** /-ˈtjuːʃn/ n institución f. **~ional** adj institucional

instruct /ɪnˈstrʌkt/ vt instruir; (order) mandar. **~ s.o. in sth** enseñar algo a uno. **~ion** /-ʃn/ n instrucción f. **~ions** npl (for use) modo m de empleo. **~ive** adj instructivo. **~or** n instructor m

instrument /ˈɪnstrəmənt/ n instrumento m. **~al** /ɪnstrəˈmentl/ adj instrumental. **be ~al in** jugar un papel decisivo en

insubordinat|e /ɪnsəˈbɔːdɪnət/ adj insubordinado. **~ion** /-ˈneɪʃn/ n insubordinación f

insufferable /ɪnˈsʌfərəbl/ adj (person) insufrible; (heat) insoportable

insufficient /ɪnsəˈfɪʃnt/ adj insuficiente

insular /ˈɪnsjʊlə(r)/ adj insular; (narrow-minded) estrecho de miras

insulat|e /ˈɪnsjʊleɪt/ vt aislar. **~ion** /-ˈleɪʃn/ n aislamiento m

insulin /ˈɪnsjʊlɪn/ n insulina f

insult /ɪnˈsʌlt/ vt insultar. • /ˈɪnsʌlt/ n insulto m. **~ing** /ɪnˈsʌltɪŋ/ adj insultante

insur|ance /ɪnˈʃʊərəns/ n seguro m. **~e** /ɪnˈʃʊə(r)/ vt (Com) asegurar; (Amer) see ENSURE

insurmountable /ɪnsəˈmaʊntəbl/ adj insuperable

intact /ɪnˈtækt/ adj intacto

integral /ˈɪntɪɡrəl/ adj integral

integrat|e /ˈɪntɪɡreɪt/ vt integrar. • vi integrarse. **~ion** /-ˈɡreɪʃn/ n integración f

integrity /ɪnˈteɡrətɪ/ n integridad f

intellect /ˈɪntəlekt/ n intelecto m. **~ual** /ɪntəˈlektʃʊəl/ adj & n intelectual (m & f)

intelligen|ce /ɪnˈtelɪdʒəns/ n inteligencia f. **~t** adj inteligente. **~tly** adv inteligentemente

intelligible /ɪnˈtelɪdʒəbl/ adj inteligible

intend /ɪnˈtend/ vt. **~ to do** pensar hacer

intens|e /ɪnˈtens/ adj intenso; (person) apasionado. **~ely** adv intensamente; (very) sumamente. **~ify** /-ɪfaɪ/ vt intensificar. • vi intensificarse. **~ity** /-ɪtɪ/ n intensidad f

intensive /ɪn'tensɪv/ adj intensivo. ~ **care** n cuidados mpl intensivos

intent /ɪn'tent/ n propósito m. ●adj atento. ~ **on** absorto en. ~ **on doing** resuelto a hacer

intention /ɪn'tenʃn/ n intención f. ~**al** adj intencional

intently /ɪn'tentlɪ/ adv atentamente

interact /ɪntər'ækt/ vi relacionarse. ~**ion** /-ʃn/ n interacción f

intercept /ɪntə'sept/ vt interceptar. ~**ion** /-ʃn/ n interceptación f

interchange /ɪntə'tʃeɪndʒ/ vt intercambiar. ●/'ɪntətʃeɪndʒ/ n intercambio m; (road junction) cruce m. ~**able** /-'tʃeɪndʒəbl/ adj intercambiable

intercity /ɪntə'sɪtɪ/ adj rápido interurbano m

intercourse /'ɪntəkɔːs/ n trato m; (sexual) acto m sexual

interest /'ɪntrəst/ n interés m. ●vt interesar. ~**ed** adj interesado. **be** ~**ed in** interesarse por. ~**ing** adj interesante

interface /'ɪntəfeɪs/ interfaz m & f; (interaction) interrelación f

interfere /ɪntə'fɪə(r)/ vi entrometerse. ~ **in** entrometerse en. ~ **with** afectar (a); interferir (radio). ~**nce** /-rəns/ n intromisión f; (Radio) interferencia f

interior /ɪn'tɪərɪə(r)/ adj & n interior (m)

interjection /ɪntə'dʒekʃn/ n interjección f

interlude /'ɪntəluːd/ n intervalo m; (theatre, music) interludio m

intermediary /ɪntə'miːdɪərɪ/ adj & n intermediario (m)

interminable /ɪn'tɜːmɪnəbl/ adj interminable

intermittent /ɪntə'mɪtnt/ adj intermitente. ~**ly** adv con discontinuidad

intern /ɪn'tɜːn/ vt internar. ●/'ɪntɜːn/ n (Amer, doctor) interno m

internal /ɪn'tɜːnl/ adj interno. ~**ly** adv internamente. **I~ Revenue Service** n (Amer) Hacienda f

international /ɪntə'næʃənl/ adj internacional

Internet /'ɪntənet/ n. **the ~** el Internet

interpret /ɪn'tɜːprɪt/ vt/i interpretar. ~**ation** /-'teɪʃn/ n interpretación f. ~**er** n intérprete m & f

interrogat|e /ɪn'terəgeɪt/ vt interrogar. ~**ion** /-'geɪʃn/ n interrogatorio m. ~**ive** /-'rɒgətɪv/ adj interrogativo

interrupt /ɪntə'rʌpt/ vt/i interrumpir. ~**ion** /-ʃn/ n interrupción f

intersect /ɪntə'sekt/ vt cruzar. ●vi (roads) cruzarse; (geometry) intersecarse. ~**ion** /-ʃn/ n (roads) cruce m; (geometry) intersección f

intersperse /ɪntə'spɜːs/ vt intercalar

interstate (highway) /'ɪntəsteɪt/ n (Amer) carretera f interestal

intertwine /ɪntə'twaɪn/ vt entrelazar. ●vi entrelazarse

interval /'ɪntəvl/ n intervalo m; (theatre) descanso m. **at ~s** a intervalos

interven|e /ɪntə'viːn/ vi intervenir. ~**tion** /-'venʃn/ n intervención f

interview /'ɪntəvjuː/ n entrevista f. ●vt entrevistar. ~**ee** /-'iː/ n entrevistado m. ~**er** n entrevistador m

intestine /ɪn'testɪn/ n intestino m

intimacy /'ɪntɪməsɪ/ n intimidad f

intimate /'ɪntɪmət/ adj íntimo. ●/'ɪntɪmeɪt/ vt (state) anunciar; (imply) dar a entender. ~**ly** /'ɪntɪmətlɪ/ adv íntimamente

intimidat|e /ɪn'tɪmɪdeɪt/ vt intimidar. ~**ion** /-'deɪʃn/ n intimidación f

into /'ɪntuː//'ɪntə/ prep en; (translate) a

intolerable /ɪn'tɒlərəbl/ adj
intolerable

intoleran|ce /ɪn'tɒlərəns/ n
intolerancia f. **~t** adj intolerante

intoxicat|e /ɪn'tɒksɪkeɪt/ vt
embriagar; (Med) intoxicar. **~ed**
adj ebrio; **~ing** adj (substance)
estupefaciente. **~ion** /-'keɪʃn/ n
embriaguez f; (Med) intoxicación f

intransitive /ɪn'trænsɪtɪv/ adj
intransitivo

intravenous /ɪntrə'viːnəs/ adj
intravenoso

intrepid /ɪn'trepɪd/ adj intrépido

intrica|cy /'ɪntrɪkəsɪ/ n
complejidad f. **~te** /-ət/ adj
complejo

intrigu|e /ɪn'triːg/ vt/i intrigar.
● /'ɪntriːg/ n intriga f. **~ing**
/ɪn'triːgɪŋ/ adj intrigante

intrinsic /ɪn'trɪnsɪk/ adj intrínseco.
~ally adv intrínsecamente

introduc|e /ɪntrə'djuːs/ vt
introducir; presentar (person).
~tion /ɪntrə'dʌkʃn/ n
introducción f; (to person)
presentación f. **~tory**
/ɪntrə'dʌktərɪ/ adj preliminar;
(course) de introducción

introvert /'ɪntrəvɜːt/ n
introvertido m

intru|de /ɪn'truːd/ vi entrometerse;
(disturb) importunar. **~der** n
intruso m. **~sion** /-ʒn/ n intrusión
f. **~sive** /-sɪv/ adj impertinente

intuiti|on /ɪntjuː'ɪʃn/ n intuición f.
~ve /ɪn'tjuːɪtɪv/ adj intuitivo

inundat|e /'ɪnʌndeɪt/ vt inundar.
~ion /-'deɪʃn/ n inundación f

invade /ɪn'veɪd/ vt invadir. **~r** n
invasor m

invalid /'ɪnvəlɪd/ n inválido m.
● /ɪn'vælɪd/ adj inválido. **~ate**
/ɪn'vælɪdeɪt/ vt invalidar

invaluable /ɪn'væljʊəbl/ adj
inestimable, invalorable (LAm)

invariabl|e /ɪn'veərɪəbl/ adj
invariable. **~y** adv
invariablemente

invasion /ɪn'veɪʒn/ n invasión f

invent /ɪn'vent/ vt inventar. **~ion**
/-'venʃn/ n invención f. **~ive** adj
inventivo. **~or** n inventor m

inventory /'ɪnvəntrɪ/ n
inventario m

invertebrate /ɪn'vɜːtɪbrət/ n
invertebrado m

inverted commas
/ɪnvɜːtɪd'kɒməz/npl comillas fpl

invest /ɪn'vest/ vt invertir. ●vi. **~ in**
invertir en

investigat|e /ɪn'vestɪgeɪt/ vt
investigar. **~ion** /-'geɪʃn/ n
investigación f. **under ~ion**
sometido a examen. **~or** n
investigador m

investment /ɪn'vestmənt/
inversión f

investor /ɪn'vestə(r)/ inversionista
m & f

inveterate /ɪn'vetərət/ adj
inveterado

invidious /ɪn'vɪdɪəs/ adj (hateful)
odioso; (unfair) injusto

invigorating /ɪn'vɪgəreɪtɪŋ/ adj
vigorizante; (stimulating)
estimulante

invincible /ɪn'vɪnsɪbl/ adj
invencible

invisible /ɪn'vɪzəbl/ adj invisible

invit|ation /ɪnvɪ'teɪʃn/ n invitación
f. **~e** /ɪn'vaɪt/ vt invitar; (ask for)
pedir. ● /'ɪnvaɪt/ n 🄸 invitación f.
~ing /ɪn'vaɪtɪŋ/ adj atrayente

invoice /'ɪnvɔɪs/ n factura f. ●vt. **~
s.o. (for sth)** pasarle a uno
factura (por algo)

involuntary /ɪn'vɒləntərɪ/ adj
involuntario

involve /ɪn'vɒlv/ vt (entail) suponer;
(implicate) implicar. **~d in** envuelto

en. ~d adj (complex) complicado. ~ment n participación f; (relationship) enredo m

inward /'ɪnwəd/ adj interior. •adv hacia adentro. ~s adv hacia dentro

iodine /'aɪədiːn/ n yodo m

ion /'aɪən/ n ion m

iota /aɪˈəʊtə/ n (amount) pizca f

IOU /aɪəʊˈjuː/ abbr (= I owe you) pagaré m

IQ abbr (= intelligence quotient) CI m, cociente m intelectual

Iran /ɪˈrɑːn/ n Irán m. ~ian /ɪˈreɪnɪən/ adj & n iraní (m & f)

Iraq /ɪˈrɑːk/ n Irak m. ~i adj & n iraquí (m & f)

irate /aɪˈreɪt/ adj colérico

Ireland /'aɪələnd/ n Irlanda f

iris /'aɪərɪs/ n (of eye) iris m; (flower) lirio m

Irish /'aɪərɪʃ/ adj irlandés. •n (language) irlandés m. npl. **the ~** (people) los irlandeses. ~man /-mən/ n irlandés m. ~woman n irlandesa f

iron /'aɪən/ n hierro m; (appliance) plancha f. •adj de hierro. •vt planchar. ■ ~ out vt allanar

ironic /aɪˈrɒnɪk/ adj irónico. ~ally adv irónicamente

ironing board /'aɪənɪŋ/ n tabla f de planchar, burro m de planchar (Mex)

iron: ~monger /-mʌŋɡə(r)/ n ferretero m. ~monger's n ferretería f

irony /'aɪərənɪ/ n ironía f

irrational /ɪˈræʃənl/ adj irracional

irrefutable /ɪrɪˈfjuːtəbl/ adj irrefutable

irregular /ɪˈreɡjʊlə(r)/ adj irregular. ~ity /-ˈlærətɪ/ n irregularidad f

irrelevan|ce /ɪˈreləvəns/ n

irrelevancia f. ~t adj irrelevante

irreparable /ɪˈrepərəbl/ adj irreparable

irreplaceable /ɪrɪˈpleɪsəbl/ adj irreemplazable

irresistible /ɪrɪˈzɪstəbl/ adj irresistible

irrespective /ɪrɪˈspektɪv/ adj. ~ of sin tomar en cuenta

irresponsible /ɪrɪˈspɒnsəbl/ adj irresponsable

irretrievable /ɪrɪˈtriːvəbl/ adj irrecuperable

irreverent /ɪˈrevərənt/ adj irreverente

irrevocable /ɪˈrevəkəbl/ adj irrevocable

irrigat|e /'ɪrɪɡeɪt/ vt regar, irrigar. ~ion /-ˈɡeɪʃn/ n riego m, irrigación f

irritable /'ɪrɪtəbl/ adj irritable

irritat|e /'ɪrɪteɪt/ vt irritar. ~ed adj irritado. ~ing adj irritante. ~ion /-ˈteɪʃn/ n irritación f

IRS abbr (Amer) see **INTERNAL REVENUE SERVICE**

is /ɪz/ see **BE**

ISDN abbr (**Integrated Services Digital Network**) RDSI

Islam /'ɪzlɑːm/ n el Islam. ~ic /ɪzˈlæmɪk/ adj islámico

island /'aɪlənd/ n isla f. ~er n isleño m

isolat|e /'aɪsəleɪt/ vt aislar. ~ion /-ˈleɪʃn/ n aislamiento m

Israel /'ɪzreɪl/ n Israel m. ~i /ɪzˈreɪlɪ/ adj & n israelí (m)

issue /'ɪʃuː/ n tema m, asunto m; (of magazine etc) número m; (of stamps, bank notes) emisión f; (of documents) expedición f. **take ~ with** discrepar de. •vt hacer público (statement); expedir (documents); emitir (stamps etc); prestar (library book)

it /ɪt/ pronoun

····➤ (*as subject*) generally not translated. **it's huge** es enorme. **where is it?** ¿dónde está?. **it's all lies** son todas mentiras

····➤ (*as direct object*) lo (m), la (f). **he read it to me** me lo/la leyó. **give it to me** dámelo/dámela

····➤ (*as indirect object*) le. **I gave it another coat of paint** le di otra mano de pintura

····➤ (*after a preposition*) generally not translated. **there's nothing behind it** no hay nada detrás

! Note, however, that in some cases *él* or *ella* must be used e.g. **he picked up the spoon and hit me with it** *agarró la cuchara y me golpeó con ella*

····➤ (*at door*) **who is it?** ¿quién es?. **it's me** soy yo; (*on telephone*) **who is it, please?** ¿quién habla, por favor?; (*before passing on to sb else*) ¿de parte de quién, por favor? **it's Carol** soy Carol (Spain), habla Carol

····➤ (*in impersonal constructions*) **it is well known that ...** bien se sabe que ... **it's five o'clock** son las cinco. **so it seems** así parece

····➤ **that's it** (*that's right*) eso es; (*that's enough, that's finished*) ya está

Italian /ɪ'tæljən/ adj & n italiano (m)

italics /ɪ'tælɪks/ npl (letra f) cursiva f

Italy /'ɪtəlɪ/ n Italia f

itch /ɪtʃ/ n picazón f. •vi picar. **I'm ~ing to** estoy que me muero por. **my arm ~es** me pica el brazo. **~y** adj que pica. **I've got an ~y nose** me pica la nariz

it'd /ɪtəd/ = **it had**, **it would**

item /'aɪtəm/ n artículo m; (on agenda) punto m. **news ~** n noticia f. **~ize** vt detallar

itinerary /aɪ'tɪnərərɪ/ n itinerario m

it'll /'ɪtl/ = **it will**

its /ɪts/ adj su, sus (pl). •pron (el) suyo m, (la) suya f, (los) suyos mpl, (las) suyas fpl

it's /ɪts/ = **it is**, **it has**

itself /ɪt'self/ pron él mismo, ella misma, ello mismo; (reflexive) se; (after prep) sí mismo, sí misma

I've /aɪv/ = **I have**

ivory /'aɪvərɪ/ n marfil m. **~ tower** n torre f de marfil

ivy /'aɪvɪ/ n hiedra f

Jj

jab /dʒæb/ vt (pt **jabbed**) pinchar; (thrust) hurgonear. •n pinchazo m

jack /dʒæk/ n (Mec) gato m; (socket) enchufe m hembra; (Cards) sota f. ▪ **~ up** vt alzar con gato

jackal /'dʒækl/ n chacal m

jackdaw /'dʒækdɔː/ n grajilla f

jacket /'dʒækɪt/ n chaqueta f; (casual) americana f, saco m (LAm); (Amer, of book) sobrecubierta f; (of record) funda f, carátula f

jack: ~ knife vi (lorry) plegarse. **~pot** n premio m gordo. **hit the ~pot** sacar el premio gordo

jade /dʒeɪd/ n (stone) jade m

jagged /'dʒægɪd/ adj (edge, cut) irregular; (rock) recortado

jaguar /'dʒægjʊə(r)/ n jaguar m

jail /dʒeɪl/ n cárcel m, prisión f. •vt encarcelar. **~er** n carcelero m. **~house** n (Amer) cárcel f

jam /dʒæm/ vt (pt **jammed**) interferir con (radio); atestar (road). **~ sth into sth** meter algo a la fuerza en algo. •vi (brakes) bloquearse; (machine) trancarse. •n mermelada f; (fam, situation) apuro m

jangle /'dʒæŋgl/ n sonido m metálico (y áspero). •vi hacer ruido (metálico)

janitor /'dʒænɪtə(r)/ n portero m

January /'dʒænjʊərɪ/ n enero m

Japan /dʒə'pæn/ n (el) Japón m. **~ese** /dʒæpə'niːz/ adj & n invar japonés (m)

jar /dʒɑː(r)/ n tarro m, bote m. •vi (pt **jarred**) (clash) desentonar. •vt sacudir

jargon /'dʒɑːgən/ n jerga f

jaundice /'dʒɔːndɪs/ n icterica f

jaunt /dʒɔːnt/ n excursión f

jaunty /'dʒɔːntɪ/ adj (**-ier, -iest**) garboso

jaw /dʒɔː/ n mandíbula f. **~s** npl fauces fpl. **~bone** n mandíbula f, maxilar m; (of animal) quijada f

jay /dʒeɪ/ n arrendajo m. **~walk** vi cruzar la calle descuidadamente. **~walker** n peatón m imprudente

jazz /dʒæz/ n jazz m. ■ **~ up** vt animar. **~y** adj chillón

jealous /dʒeləs/ adj celoso; (envious) envidioso. **~y** n celos mpl

jeans /dʒiːnz/ npl vaqueros mpl, jeans mpl, tejanos mpl, pantalones mpl de mezclilla (Mex)

Jeep ®, **jeep** /dʒiːp/ n Jeep m ®

jeer /dʒɪə(r)/ vi. **~ at** mofarse de; (boo) abuchear. •n burla f; (boo) abucheo m

Jell-O /'dʒeləʊ/ n ® (Amer) gelatina f (con sabor a frutas)

jelly /'dʒelɪ/ n (clear jam) jalea f; (pudding) see JELL-O; (substance) gelatina f. **~fish** n (pl invar or **-es**) medusa f

jeopardize /'dʒepədaɪz/ vt arriesgar

jerk /dʒɜːk/ n sacudida f; (sl, fool) idiota m & f. •vt sacudir

jersey /'dʒɜːzɪ/ n (pl **-eys**) jersey m, suéter m, pulóver m

jest /dʒest/ n broma f. •vi bromear

Jesus /'dʒiːzəs/ n Jesús m

jet /dʒet/ n (stream) chorro m; (plane) avión m (con motor a reacción); (mineral) azabache m. **~-black** /-'blæk/ adj azabache negro a invar. **~ lag** n jet lag m, desfase f horario. **have ~ lag** estar desfasado. **~-propelled** /-prə'peld/ adj (de propulsión) a reacción

jettison /'dʒetɪsn/ vt echar al mar; (fig, discard) deshacerse de

jetty /'dʒetɪ/ n muelle m

Jew /dʒuː/ n judío m

jewel /'dʒuːəl/ n joya f. **~ler** n joyero m. **~lery** n joyas fpl

Jewish /'dʒuːɪʃ/ adj judío

jiffy /'dʒɪfɪ/ n momentito m. **do sth in a ~** hacer algo en un santiamén

jig /dʒɪg/ n (dance) giga f

jigsaw /'dʒɪgsɔː/ n. **~ (puzzle)** rompecabezas m

jilt /dʒɪlt/ vt dejar plantado

jingle /'dʒɪŋgl/ vt hacer sonar. •vi tintinear. •n tintineo m; (advert) jingle m (publicitario)

job /dʒɒb/ n empleo m, trabajo m; (piece of work) trabajo m. **it is a good ~ that** menos mal que. **~less** adj desempleado

jockey /'dʒɒkɪ/ n jockey m

jocular /'dʒɒkjʊlə(r)/ adj jocoso

jog /dʒɒg/ vt (pt **jogged**) empujar; refrescar (memory). •vi hacer footing, hacer jogging. **~er** n persona f que hace footing. **~ging** n footing m, jogging m. **go ~ging** salir a hacer footing or jogging

join /dʒɔɪn/ vt (link) unir; hacerse socio de (club); hacerse miembro de (political group); alistarse en (army); reunirse con (another person). • n juntura. • vi. **~ together** unirse; (roads etc) empalmar; (rivers) confluir. **■ ~ in** vi participar (en). **■ ~ up** vi (Mil) alistarse. **~er** n carpintero m

joint /dʒɔɪnt/ adj conjunto. • n (join) unión f, junta f; (in limbs) articulación f. (Culin) trozo m de carne (para asar). **out of ~** descoyuntado. **~ account** n cuenta f conjunta. **~ly** adv conjuntamente. **~ owner** n copropietario m.

joist /dʒɔɪst/ n viga f

jok|e /dʒəʊk/ n (story) chiste m; (practical joke) broma f. • vi bromear. **~er** n bromista m & f; (Cards) comodín m. **~y** adj jocoso

jolly /dʒɒlɪ/ adj (-ier, -iest) alegre. • adv 🇬🇧 muy

jolt /dʒɒlt/ vt sacudir. • vi (vehicle) dar una sacudida. • n sacudida f

jostle /dʒɒsl/ vt empujar. • vi empujarse

jot /dʒɒt/ n pizca f. • vt (pt jotted). **■ ~ down** vt apuntar (rápidamente). **~ter** n bloc m

journal /dʒɜːnl/ n (diary) diario m; (newspaper) periódico m; (magazine) revista f. **~ism** n periodismo m. **~ist** n periodista m & f

journey /dʒɜːnɪ/ n viaje m. **go on a ~** hacer un viaje. • vi viajar

jovial /dʒəʊvɪəl/ adj jovial

joy /dʒɔɪ/ n alegría f. **~ful** adj feliz. **~ous** adj feliz. **~rider** n joven m que roba un coche para dar una vuelta. **~stick** n (in aircraft) palanca f de mando; (Comp) mando m, joystick m

jubila|nt /dʒuːbɪlənt/ adj jubiloso. **~tion** /-ˈleɪʃn/ n júbilo m

jubilee /dʒuːbɪliː/ n aniversario m especial

Judaism /dʒuːdeɪɪzəm/ n judaísmo m

judge /dʒʌdʒ/ n juez m. • vt juzgar. **~ment** n juicio m

judicia|l /dʒuːˈdɪʃl/ adj judicial. **~ry** /-ərɪ/ n judicatura f

judo /dʒuːdəʊ/ n judo m

jug /dʒʌg/ n jarra f

juggernaut /dʒʌɡənɔːt/ n camión m grande

juggle /dʒʌɡl/ vi hacer malabarismos. • vt hacer malabarismos con. **~r** n malabarista m & f

juic|e /dʒuːs/ n jugo m, zumo m. **~y** adj jugoso, zumoso; (story etc) 🇬🇧 picante

jukebox /dʒuːkbɒks/ n máquina f de discos, rocola f (LAm)

July /dʒuːˈlaɪ/ n julio m

jumble /dʒʌmbl/ vt. **~ (up)** mezclar. • n (muddle) revoltijo m. **~ sale** n venta f de objetos usados m

jumbo /dʒʌmbəʊ/ adj gigante. **~ jet** n jumbo m

jump /dʒʌmp/ vt saltar. **~ rope** (Amer) saltar a la comba, saltar a la cuerda. **~ the gun** obrar prematuramente. **~ the queue** colarse. • vi saltar; (start) sobresaltarse; (prices) alzarse. **~ at an opportunity** apresurarse a aprovechar una oportunidad. • n salto m; (start) susto m; (increase) aumento m. **~er** n jersey m, suéter m, pulóver m, (Amer, dress) pichi m, jumper m & f (LAm). **~er cables** (Amer), **~ leads** npl cables mpl de arranque. **~ rope** (Amer) comba f, cuerda f, reata f (Mex). **~suit** n mono m. **~y** adj nervioso

junction /dʒʌŋkʃn/ n (of roads, rails) cruce m; (Elec) empalme m

June /dʒuːn/ n junio m

jungle /dʒʌŋgl/ n selva f, jungla f

junior /dʒuːnɪə(r)/ adj (in age) más joven (**to que**); (in rank) subalterno. • n menor m

junk /dʒʌŋk/ n trastos mpl viejos; (worthless stuff) basura f. • vt 🇬🇧 tirar. **~ food** n comida f basura,

alimento m chatarra (Mex). **~ie**
/'dʒʌŋki/ n 🗓 drogadicto m, yonqui
m & f 🗓. **~ mail** n propaganda f
que se recibe por correo. **~ shop**
n tienda f de trastos viejos

junta /'dʒʌntə/ n junta f militar

Jupiter /'dʒuːpɪtə(r)/ n Júpiter m

jurisdiction /dʒʊərɪs'dɪkʃn/ n
jurisdicción f

jur|or /'dʒʊərə(r)/ n (miembro m de
un) jurado m. **~y** n jurado m

just /dʒʌst/ adj (fair) justo. •adv
exactamente, justo; (barely) justo;
(only) sólo, solamente. **~ as tall**

tan alto (**as** como). **~ listen!**
¡escucha! **he has ~ arrived** acaba
de llegar, recién llegó (LAm)

justice /'dʒʌstɪs/ n justicia f. **J~ of
the Peace** juez m de paz

justif|iable /dʒʌstɪ'faɪəbl/ adj
justificable. **~iably** adv con razón.
~ication /dʒʌstɪfɪ'keɪʃn/ n
justificación f. **~y** /'dʒʌstɪfaɪ/ vt
justificar

jut /dʒʌt/ vi (pt **jutted**). **~ (out)**
sobresalir

juvenile /'dʒuːvənaɪl/ adj juvenil;
(childish) infantil. •n (Jurid) menor m
& f

Kk

kaleidoscope /kə'laɪdəskəʊp/ n
caleidoscopio m

kangaroo /kæŋgə'ruː/ n canguro m

karate /kə'rɑːtɪ/ n kárate m, karate
m (LAm)

keel /kiːl/ n (of ship) quilla f. ■ **~
over** vi volcar(se)

keen /kiːn/ adj (-er, -est) (interest,
feeling) vivo; (wind, mind, analysis)
penetrante; (eyesight) agudo; (eager)
entusiasta. **I'm ~ on golf** me
encanta el golf. **he's ~ on
Shostakovich** le gusta
Shostakovich. **~ly** adv vivamente;
(enthusiastically) con entusiasmo.
~ness n intensidad f; (enthusiasm)
entusiasmo m.

keep /kiːp/ vt (pt **kept**) guardar;
cumplir (promise); tener (shop,
animals); mantener (family); observar
(rule); (celebrate) celebrar; (delay)
detener; (prevent) impedir. •vi (food)
conservarse; (remain) quedarse;
(continue) seguir. **~ doing** seguir
haciendo. •n subsistencia f; (of
castle) torreón m. **for ~s** 🗓 para
siempre. ■ **~ back** vt retener. •vi

no acercarse. ■ **~ in** vt no dejar
salir. ■ **~ off** vt mantenerse
alejado de (land). '**~ off the
grass**' 'prohibido pisar el césped'.
■ **~ on** vi seguir. **~ on doing sth**
seguir haciendo. ■ **~ out** vt no
dejar entrar. ■ **~ up** vt mantener.
■ **~ up with** vt estar al día en

kennel /'kenl/ n casa f del perro;
(Amer, for boarding) residencia f
canina. **~s** n invar residencia f
canina

kept /kept/ see **KEEP**

kerb /kɜːb/ n bordillo m (de la
acera), borde m de la banqueta
(Mex)

kerosene /'kerəsiːn/ n queroseno m

ketchup /'ketʃʌp/ n salsa f de
tomate

kettle /'ketl/ n pava f, tetera f (para
calentar agua)

key /kiː/ n llave f; (of computer, piano)
tecla f; (Mus) tono m. **be off ~** no
estar en el tono. •adj clave. ■ **~ in**
vt teclear. **~board** n teclado m.
~hole n ojo m de la cerradura.
~ring n llavero m

khaki /'kɑːkɪ/ adj caqui

kick /kɪk/ vt dar una patada a (person); patear (ball). • vi dar patadas; (horse) cocear. • n patada f; (of horse) coz f; (fam, thrill) placer m. ■ ~ **out** vt 🔲 echar. ■ ~ **up** vt armar (fuss etc). **~off** n (Sport) saque m inicial. ~ **start** vt arrancar (con el pedal de arranque) (engine)

kid /kɪd/ n (young goat) cabrito m; (fam, child) niño m, chaval m, escuincle m (Mex). • vt (pt **kidded**) tomar el pelo a. • vi bromear

kidnap /'kɪdnæp/ vt (pt **kidnapped**) secuestrar. ~**per** n secuestrador m. ~**ping** n secuestro m

kidney /'kɪdnɪ/ n riñón m

kill /kɪl/ vt matar; (fig) acabar con. • n matanza f. ■ ~ **off** vt matar. ~**er** n asesino m. ~**ing** n matanza f; (murder) asesinato m. **make a ~ing** (fig) hacer un gran negocio

kiln /kɪln/ n horno m

kilo /'kiːləʊ/ n (pl -os) kilo m. ~**gram(me)** /'kɪləgræm/ n kilogramo m. ~**metre** /'kɪləmiːtə(r)/, /kɪ'lɒmɪtə(r)/ n kilómetro m. ~**watt** /'kɪləwɒt/ n kilovatio m

kilt /kɪlt/ n falda f escocesa

kin /kɪn/ n familiares mpl

kind /kaɪnd/ n tipo m, clase f. ~ **of** (fam, somewhat) un poco. **in ~** en especie. **be two of a ~** ser tal para cual. • adj amable

kindergarten /'kɪndəgɑːtn/ n jardín m de infancia

kind-hearted /kaɪnd'hɑːtɪd/ adj bondadoso

kindle /'kɪndl/ vt encender

kind|ly adj (-ier, -iest) bondadoso. • adv amablemente; (please) haga el favor de. ~**ness** n bondad f; (act) favor m

king /kɪŋ/ n rey m. ~**dom** n reino m. ~**fisher** n martín m pescador. ~**-size(d)** adj extragrande

kink /kɪŋk/ n (in rope) vuelta f, curva

f; (in hair) onda f. ~**y** adj 🔲 pervertido

kiosk /'kiːɒsk/ n quiosco m

kipper /'kɪpə(r)/ n arenque m ahumado

kiss /kɪs/ n beso m. • vt besar. • vi besarse

kit /kɪt/ n avíos mpl. **tool ~** caja f de herramientas. ■ ~ **out** vt (pt **kitted**) equipar

kitchen /'kɪtʃɪn/ n cocina f

kite /kaɪt/ n cometa f, papalote m (Mex)

kitten /'kɪtn/ n gatito m

knack /næk/ n truco m

knapsack /'næpsæk/ n mochila f

knead /niːd/ vt amasar

knee /niː/ n rodilla f. ~**cap** n rótula f

kneel /niːl/ vi (pt **kneeled** or **knelt**). ~ **(down)** arrodillarse; (be on one's knees) estar arrodillado

knelt /nelt/ see KNEEL

knew /njuː/ see KNOW

knickers /'nɪkəz/ npl bragas fpl, calzones mpl (LAm), pantaletas fpl (Mex)

knife /naɪf/ n (pl **knives**) cuchillo m. • vt acuchillar

knight /naɪt/ n caballero m; (Chess) caballo m. • vt conceder el título de Sir a. ~**hood** n título m de Sir

knit /nɪt/ vt (pt **knitted** or **knit**) hacer, tejer (LAm). • vi tejer, hacer punto. ~ **one's brow** fruncir el ceño. ~**ting** n tejido m, punto m. ~**ting needle** n aguja f de hacer punto, aguja f de tejer

knives /naɪvz/ see KNIFE

knob /nɒb/ n botón m; (of door, drawer etc) tirador m. ~**bly** adj nudoso

knock /nɒk/ vt golpear; (criticize) criticar. • vi golpear; (at door) llamar, golpear (LAm). • n golpe m. ■ ~ **about** vt maltratar. ■ ~ **down** vt derribar; atropellar (person). ■ ~ **off** vt hacer caer. • vi (fam, finish work) terminar, salir del trabajo. ■~ **out** vt (by blow) dejar sin sentido; (eliminate) eliminar. ■~ **over** vt tirar; atropellar (person). ~**er** n aldaba f. ~**-kneed** /-'niːd/ adj patizambo. ~**out** n (Boxing) nocaut m

knot /nɒt/ n nudo m. ●vt (pt **knotted**) anudar

know /nəʊ/ vt (pt **knew**) saber; (be acquainted with) conocer. **let s.o. ~ sth** decirle algo a uno; (warn) avisarle algo a uno. ●vi saber. ~ **how to do sth** saber hacer algo. ~ **about** entender de (cars etc). ~ **of** saber de. ●n. **be in the ~** estar enterado. ~**-all** n n sabelotodo m &

f. ~**-how** n know-how m, conocimientos mpl y experiencia. ~**ingly** adv a sabiendas. ~**-it-all** n (Amer) see ~**-ALL**

knowledge /'nɒlɪdʒ/ n saber m; (awareness) conocimiento m; (learning) conocimientos mpl. ~**able** adj informado

known /nəʊn/ see KNOW. ●adj conocido

knuckle /'nʌkl/ n nudillo m. ■~ **under** vi someterse

Korea /kə'rɪə/ n Corea f. ~**n** adj & n coreano m

kudos /'kjuːdɒs/ n prestigio m

Ll

lab /læb/ n ⊞ laboratorio m

label /'leɪbl/ n etiqueta f. ●vt (pt **labelled**) poner etiqueta a; (fig, describe as) tachar de

laboratory /lə'bɒrətərɪ/ n laboratorio m

laborious /lə'bɔːrɪəs/ adj penoso

labour /'leɪbə(r)/ n trabajo m; (workers) mano f de obra; (Med) parto m. **in ~** de parto. ●vi trabajar. ●vt insistir en. **L~** n el partido m laborista. ●adj laborista. ~**er** n peón m

lace /leɪs/ n encaje m; (of shoe) cordón m, agujeta f (Mex). ●vt (fasten) atar

lacerate /'læsəreɪt/ vt lacerar

lack /læk/ n falta f. **for ~ of** por falta de. ●vt faltarle a uno. **he ~s confidence** le falta confianza en sí mismo. ~**ing** adj. **be ~ing** faltar. **be ~ing in** no tener

lad /læd/ n muchacho m

ladder /'lædə(r)/ n escalera f (de mano); (in stocking) carrera f. ●vt

hacerse una carrera en. ●vi hacérsele una carrera a

laden /'leɪdn/ adj cargado (**with** de)

ladle /'leɪdl/ n cucharón m

lady /'leɪdɪ/ n señora f. **young ~** señorita f. ~**bird** n, ~**bug** n (Amer) mariquita f, catarina f (Mex). ~**in-waiting** n dama f de honor. ~**like** adj fino

lag /læg/ vi (pt **lagged**). ~ **(behind)** retrasarse. ●vt revestir (pipes). ●n (interval) intervalo m

lager /'lɑːgə(r)/ n cerveza f (rubia)

lagging /'lægɪŋ/ n revestimiento m

lagoon /lə'guːn/ n laguna f

laid /leɪd/ see LAY

lain /leɪn/ see LIE¹

lair /leə(r)/ n guarida f

lake /leɪk/ n lago m

lamb /læm/ n cordero m

lame /leɪm/ adj (**-er, -est**) cojo, rengo (LAm); (excuse) pobre, malo

lament /lə'ment/ n lamento m. ●vt

lamentar. ~able /'læməntəbl/ adj lamentable

lamp /læmp/ n lámpara f. **lamp~post** n farol m. **~shade** n pantalla f

lance /lɑːns/ n lanza f

land /lænd/ n tierra f; (country) país m; (plot) terreno m. ● vt desembarcar; (obtain) conseguir; dar (blow). ● vi (from ship) desembarcar; (aircraft) aterrizar. ■~ **up** vi ir a parar. ~**ing** n desembarque m; (by aircraft) aterrizaje m; (top of stairs) descanso m. ~**lady** n casera f; (of inn) dueña f. ~**lord** n casero m, dueño m; (of inn) dueño m. ~**mark** n punto m destacado. ~**scape** /-skeɪp/ n paisaje m. ~**slide** n desprendimiento m de tierras; (Pol) victoria f arrolladora

lane /leɪn/ n (path, road) camino m, sendero m; (strip of road) carril m

language /'læŋgwɪdʒ/ n idioma m; (speech, style) lenguaje m

lank /læŋk/ adj (hair) lacio. ~**y** adj (-**ier**, -**iest**) larguirucho

lantern /'læntən/ n linterna f

lap /læp/ n (of body) rodillas fpl; (Sport) vuelta f. ■~ **up** vt (pt **lapped**) beber a lengüetazos; (fig) aceptar con entusiasmo. ● vi (waves) chapotear

lapel /lə'pel/ n solapa f

lapse /læps/ vi (decline) degradarse; (expire) caducar; (time) transcurrir. ~ **into silence** callarse. ● n error m; (of time) intervalo m

laptop /'læptɒp/ n. ~ (**computer**) laptop m, portátil m

lard /lɑːd/ n manteca f de cerdo

larder /'lɑːdə(r)/ n despensa f

large /lɑːdʒ/ adj (-**er**, -**est**) grande, (before singular noun) gran. ● n. **at** ~ en libertad. ~**ly** adv en gran parte

lark /lɑːk/ n (bird) alondra f; (joke) broma f; (bit of fun) travesura f. ■~ **about** vt hacer el tonto 🔟

larva /'lɑːvə/ n (pl **-vae**/-viː/) larva f

laser /'leɪzə(r)/ n láser m. ~ **beam** n rayo m láser. ~ **printer** n impresora f láser

lash /læʃ/ vt azotar. ■~ **out** vi atacar. ~ **out against** vt atacar. ● n latigazo m; (eyelash) pestaña f; (whip) látigo m

lashings /'læʃɪŋz/ npl. ~ **of** (fam, cream etc) montones de

lass /læs/ n muchacha f

lasso /læ'suː/ n (pl **-os**) lazo m

last /lɑːst/ adj último; (week etc) pasado. ~ **Monday** el lunes pasado. ~ **night** anoche. ● adv último; (most recently) la última vez. **he came** ~ llegó el último. ● n último m; (remainder) lo que queda. ~ **but one** penúltimo. **at (long)** ~ por fin. ● vi/t durar. ■~ **out** vi sobrevivir. ~**ing** adj duradero. ~**ly** adv por último

latch /lætʃ/ n pestillo m

late /leɪt/ adj (-**er**, -**est**) (not on time) tarde; (recent) reciente; (former) antiguo, ex. **be** ~ llegar tarde. **in** ~ **July** a fines de julio. **the** ~ **Dr Phillips** el difunto Dr. Phillips. ● adv tarde. ~**ly** adv últimamente

latent /'leɪtnt/ adj latente

later /'leɪtə(r)/ adv más tarde

lateral /'lætərəl/ adj lateral

latest /'leɪtɪst/ adj último. ● n. **at the** ~ a más tardar

lathe /leɪð/ n torno m

lather /'lɑːðə(r)/ n espuma f

Latin /'lætɪn/ n (language) latín m. ● adj latino. ~ **America** n América f Latina, Latinoamérica f. ~ **American** adj & n latinoamericano (m)

latitude /'lætɪtjuːd/ n latitud m

latter /'lætə(r)/ adj último; (of two) segundo. ● n. **the** ~ éste m, ésta f, éstos mpl, éstas fpl

laugh /lɑːf/ vi reír(se). ~ **at** reírse de. ● n risa f. ~**able** adj ridículo. ~**ing stock** n hazmerreír m. ~**ter** n risas fpl

launch /lɔːntʃ/ vt lanzar; botar (new vessel). • n lanzamiento m; (of new vessel) botadura; (boat) lancha f (a motor). ∼**ing pad**, ∼ **pad** n plataforma f de lanzamiento

laund|er /ˈlɔːndə(r)/ vt lavar (y planchar). ∼**erette** /-et/, **L**∼**romat** /ˈlɔːndrəmæt/ (Amer) ® n lavandería f automática. ∼**ry** n (place) lavandería f; (dirty clothes) ropa f sucia; (clean clothes) ropa f limpia

lava /ˈlɑːvə/ n lava f

lavatory /ˈlævətərɪ/ n (cuarto m de) baño m. **public** ∼ servicios mpl, baños mpl (LAm)

lavish /ˈlævɪʃ/ adj (lifestyle) de derroche; (meal) espléndido; (production) fastuoso. • vt prodigar (**on** a)

law /lɔː/ n ley f; (profession, subject of study) derecho m. ∼ **and order** n orden m público. ∼ **court** n tribunal m

lawn /lɔːn/ n césped m, pasto m (LAm). ∼**mower** n cortacésped f, cortadora f de pasto (LAm)

lawsuit /ˈlɔːsuːt/ n juicio m

lawyer /ˈlɔːjə(r)/ n abogado m

lax /læks/ adj descuidado; (morals etc) laxo

laxative /ˈlæksətɪv/ n laxante m

lay /leɪ/ see **LIE**. • vt (pt **laid**) poner (also table, eggs); tender (trap); formar (plan). ∼ **hands on** echar mano a. ∼ **hold of** agarrar. • adj (non-clerical) laico; (opinion etc) profano. ∎∼ **down** vt dejar a un lado; imponer (condition). ∎∼ **into** vt 🅿 dar una paliza a. ∎∼ **off** vt despedir (worker). vi 🅸 terminar. ∎∼ **on** vt (provide) proveer. ∎∼ **out** vt (design) disponer; (display) exponer; gastar (money). ∼**about** n holgazán m. ∼**by** n área f de reposo

layer /ˈleɪə(r)/ n capa f

layette /leɪˈet/ n canastilla f

layman /ˈleɪmən/ n (pl **-men**) lego m

layout /ˈleɪaʊt/ n disposición f

laz|e /leɪz/ vi holgazanear; (relax) descansar. ∼**iness** n pereza f. ∼**y** adj perezoso. ∼**ybones** n holgazán m

lead[1] /liːd/ vt (pt **led**) conducir; dirigir (team); llevar (life); encabezar (parade, attack). **I was led to believe that ...** me dieron a entender que .... • vi (go first) ir delante; (in race) aventajar. • n mando m; (clue) pista f; (leash) correa f; (wire) cable m. **be in the** ∼ llevar la delantera

lead[2] /led/ n plomo m; (of pencil) mina f. ∼**ed** adj (fuel) con plomo

lead /liːd/ ∼**er** n jefe m; (Pol) líder m & f; (of group) cabecilla m. ∼**ership** n dirección f. ∼**ing** adj principal; (in front) delantero

leaf /liːf/ n (pl **leaves**) hoja f. ∎∼ **through** vi hojear ∼**let** /ˈliːflɪt/ n folleto m. ∼**y** adj frondoso

league /liːg/ n liga f. **be in** ∼ **with** estar aliado con

leak /liːk/ n (hole) agujero m; (of gas, liquid) escape m; (of information) filtración f; (in roof) gotera f; (in boat) vía f de agua. • vi gotear; (liquid) salirse; (boat) hacer agua. • vt perder; filtrar (information). ∼**y** adj (receptacle) agujereado; (roof) que tiene goteras

lean /liːn/ (pt **leaned** or **leant** /lent/) vt apoyar. • vi inclinarse. ∎∼ **against** vt apoyarse en. ∎∼ **on** vt apoyarse en. ∎∼ **out** vt asomarse (**of** a). ∎∼ **over** vi inclinarse • adj (**-er**, **-est**) (person) delgado; (animal) flaco; (meat) magro. ∼**ing** adj inclinado. ∼**-to** n colgadizo m

leap /liːp/ vi (pt **leaped** or **leapt** /lept/) saltar. • n salto m. ∼**frog** n. **play** ∼**frog** saltar al potro, jugar a la pídola, brincar al burro (Mex). • vi (pt **-frogged**) saltar. ∼ **year** n año m bisiesto

learn /lɜːn/ vt/i (pt **learned** or **learnt**) aprender (**to do** a hacer). ∼**ed** /-ɪd/ adj culto. ∼**er** n principiante m & f; (apprentice) aprendiz m. ∼**ing** n saber m. **~ing curve** n curva f del aprendizaje

lease /liːs/ n arriendo m. ●vt arrendar

leash /liːʃ/ n correa f

least /liːst/ adj (smallest amount of) mínimo; (slightest) menor; (smallest) más pequeño. ●n. **the ~** lo menos. **at ~** por lo menos. **not in the ~** en absoluto. ●adv menos

leather /ˈleðə(r)/ n piel f, cuero m

leave /liːv/ vt (pt **left**) dejar; (depart from) salir de. **~ alone** dejar de tocar (thing); dejar en paz (person). ●vi marcharse; (train) salir. ●n permiso m. ■**~ behind** vt dejar. ■**~ out** vt omitir. ■**~ over** vt. **be left over** quedar. **on ~** (Mil) de permiso

leaves /liːvz/ see LEAF

lecture /ˈlektʃə(r)/ n conferencia f; (Univ) clase f; (rebuke) sermón m. ●vi dar clase. ●vt (scold) sermonear. **~r** n conferenciante m & f, conferencista m & f (LAm); (Univ) profesor m universitario

led /led/ see LEAD¹

ledge /ledʒ/ n cornisa f; (of window) alféizar m

leek /liːk/ n puerro m

leer /ˈlɪə(r)/ vi. **~ at** mirar impúdicamente. ●n mirada f impúdica f

left /left/ see LEAVE. adj izquierdo. ●adv a la izquierda. ●n izquierda f. **~-handed** /-ˈhændɪd/ adj zurdo. **~ luggage** n consigna f. **~overs** npl restos mpl. **~-wing** /-ˈwɪŋ/ adj izquierdista

leg /leg/ n pierna f; (of animal, furniture) pata f; (of pork) pernil m; (of lamb) pierna f; (of journey) etapa f. **on its last ~s** en las últimas. **pull s.o.'s ~** 🄸 tomarle el pelo a uno

legacy /ˈlegəsɪ/ n herencia f

legal /ˈliːgl/ adj (permitted by law) lícito; (recognized by law) legítimo; (system etc) jurídico. **~ity** /liːˈgælətɪ/ n legalidad f. **~ize** vt legalizar. **~ly** adv legalmente

legend /ˈledʒənd/ n leyenda f. **~ary** adj legendario

legible /ˈledʒəbl/ adj legible

legislat|e /ˈledʒɪsleɪt/ vi legislar. **~ion** /-ˈleɪʃn/ n legislación f

legitimate /lɪˈdʒɪtɪmət/ adj legítimo

leisure /ˈleʒə(r)/ n ocio m. **at your ~** cuando le venga bien. **~ly** adj lento, pausado

lemon /ˈlemən/ n limón m. **~ade** /-ˈneɪd/ n (fizzy) gaseosa f (de limón); (still) limonada f

lend /lend/ vt (pt **lent**) prestar. **~ing** n préstamo m

length /leŋθ/ n largo m; (of time) duración f; (of cloth) largo m. **at ~** (at last) por fin. **at (great) ~** detalladamente. **~en** /ˈleŋθən/ vt alargar. ●vi alargarse. **~ways** adv a lo largo. **~y** adj largo

lenient /ˈliːnɪənt/ adj indulgente

lens /lenz/ n lente f; (of camera) objetivo m. **(contact) ~es** npl (optics) lentillas fpl, lentes mpl de contacto (LAm)

lent /lent/ see LEND

Lent /lent/ n cuaresma f

Leo /ˈliːəʊ/ n Leo m

leopard /ˈlepəd/ n leopardo m

leotard /ˈliːətɑːd/ n malla f

lesbian /ˈlezbɪən/ n lesbiana f. ●adj lesbiano

less /les/ adj, n & adv & prep menos. **~ than** menos que; (with numbers) menos de. **~ and ~** cada vez menos. **none the ~** sin embargo. **~en** vt/i disminuir

lesson /ˈlesn/ n clase f

lest /lest/ conj no sea que (+ subjunctive)

let /let/ vt (pt **let**, pres p **letting**) dejar; (lease) alquilar. **~ me do it** déjame hacerlo. ●modal verb. **~'s go!** ¡vamos!, ¡vámonos! **~'s see**

(vamos) a ver. ~'s **talk/drink** hablemos/bebamos. ∎~ **down** vt bajar; (deflate) desinflar; (fig) defraudar. ∎~ **go** vt soltar. ∎~ **in** vt dejar entrar. ∎~ **off** vt disparar (gun); (cause to explode) hacer explotar; hacer estallar (firework); (excuse) perdonar. ∎~ **on** vt dejar salir. ∎~ **out** vt dejar salir. ∎~ **through** vt dejar pasar. ∎~ **up** vi disminuir. ~**down** n desilusión f

lethal /'li:θl/ adj (dose, wound) mortal; (weapon) mortífero

letharg|ic /lɪ'θɑːdʒɪk/ adj letárgico. ~**y** /'leθədʒɪ/ n letargo m

letter /'letə(r)/ n (of alphabet) letra f; (written message) carta f. ~ **bomb** n carta f bomba. ~**box** n buzón m. ~**ing** n letras fpl

lettuce /'letɪs/ n lechuga f

let-up /'letʌp/ n interrupción f

leukaemia /luː'kiːmɪə/ n leucemia f

level /'levl/ adj (flat, even) plano, parejo (LAm); (spoonful) raso. ~ **with** (at same height) al nivel de. ●n nivel m. ●vt (pt **levelled**) nivelar; (aim) apuntar. ~ **crossing** n paso m a nivel, crucero m (Mex)

lever /'liːvə(r)/ n palanca f. ●vt apalancar. ~ **open** abrir haciendo palanca. ~**age** /-ɪdʒ/ n apalancamiento m

levy /'levɪ/ vt imponer (tax). ●n impuesto m

lewd /luːd/ adj (-er, -est) lascivo

liab|ility /laɪə'bɪlətɪ/ n responsabilidad f; (fam, disadvantage) lastre m. ~**ilities** npl (debts) deudas fpl. ~**le** /'laɪəbl/ adj. **be** ~**le to do** tener tendencia a hacer. ~**le for** responsable de. ~**le to** susceptible de; expuesto a (fine)

liais|e /lɪ'eɪz/ vi actuar de enlace (**with** con). ~**on** /-ɒn/ n enlace m

liar /'laɪə(r)/ n mentiroso m

libel /'laɪbl/ n difamación f. ●vt (pt **libelled**) difamar (por escrito)

liberal /'lɪbərəl/ adj liberal; (generous) generoso. **L~** (Pol) del Partido Liberal. ●n liberal m & f. ~**ly** adv liberalmente; (generously) generosamente

liberat|e /'lɪbəreɪt/ vt liberar. ~**ion** /-'reɪʃn/ n liberación f

liberty /'lɪbətɪ/ n libertad f. **take liberties** tomarse libertades. **take the** ~ **of** tomarse la libertad de

Libra /'liːbrə/ n Libra f

librar|ian /laɪ'breərɪən/ n bibliotecario m. ~**y** /'laɪbrərɪ/ n biblioteca f

lice /laɪs/ see LOUSE

licence /'laɪsns/ n licencia f, permiso m

license /'laɪsns/ vt autorizar. ●n (Amer) see LICENCE. ~ **number** n (Amer) (número m de) matrícula f. ~ **plate** n (Amer) matrícula f, placa f (LAm)

lick /lɪk/ vt lamer; (sl, defeat) dar una paliza a. ●n lametón m

licorice /'lɪkərɪs/ n (Amer) regaliz m

lid /lɪd/ n tapa f; (eyelid) párpado m

lie¹ /laɪ/ vi (pt **lay**, pp **lain**, pres p **lying**) echarse, tenderse; (be in lying position) estar tendido; (be) estar, encontrarse. ~ **low** quedarse escondido. ∎~ **down** vi echarse, tenderse

lie² /laɪ/ n mentira f. ●vi (pt **lied**, pres p **lying**) mentir

lie-in /laɪ'ɪn/ n. **have a** ~ quedarse en la cama

lieutenant /lef'tenənt/ n (Mil) teniente m

life /laɪf/ n (pl **lives**) vida f. ~ **belt** n salvavidas m. ~**boat** n lancha f de salvamento; (on ship) bote m salvavidas. ~**buoy** n boya f salvavidas. ~ **coach** n coach m & f personal. ~**guard** n salvavidas m & f, socorrista m & f. ~ **jacket** n chaleco m salvavidas. ~**less** adj sin vida. ~**like** adj verosímil. ~**line** n cuerda f de salvamento; (fig) tabla f de salvación. ~**long** adj de toda la vida. ~ **preserver** n (Amer, buoy) see ~**BUOY**; (jacket) see ~ **JACKET**. ~**ring** n (Amer) see ~ **BELT**. ~**saver** n (person) salvavidas m & f; (fig) salvación f. ~**size(d)** adj (de) tamaño natural. ~**time** n vida f. ~**vest** n (Amer) see ~ **JACKET**

lift /lɪft/ vt levantar. •vi (fog) disiparse. •n ascensor m. **give a ~ to s.o.** llevar a uno en su coche, dar aventón a uno (Mex). ■ ~ **up** vt levantar. ~**off** n despegue m

light /laɪt/ n luz f; (lamp) lámpara f, luz f; (flame) fuego m. **come to ~** salir a la luz. **have you got a ~?** ¿tienes fuego? **the ~s** npl (traffic signals) el semáforo; (on vehicle) las luces. •adj (-er, -est) (in colour) claro; (not heavy) ligero. •vt (pt **lit** or **lighted**) encender, prender (LAm); (illuminate) iluminar. •vi encenderse, prenderse (LAm). ~ **up** vt iluminar. •vi iluminarse. ~**bulb** n bombilla f, foco m (Mex). ~**en** vt (make less heavy) aligerar, aliviar (LAm); (give light to) iluminar; (make brighter) aclarar. ~**er** n (for cigarettes) mechero m, encendedor m. ~**-hearted** /-'hɑːtɪd/ adj alegre. ~**house** n faro m. ~**ly** adv ligeramente

lightning /'laɪtnɪŋ/ n. **flash of ~** relámpago m. •adj relámpago

lightweight adj ligero, liviano (LAm)

like /laɪk/ adj parecido. •prep como. •conj 🔲 como. •vt. **I ~ chocolate** me gusta el chocolate. **they ~ swimming** (a ellos) les gusta nadar. **would you ~ a coffee?** ¿quieres un café?. ~**able** adj simpático.

like|lihood /'laɪklɪhʊd/ n probabilidad f. ~**ly** adj (-ier, -iest) probable. **he is ~ly to come** es probable que venga. •adv probablemente. **not ~ly!** ¡ni hablar! ~**n** vt comparar (**to** con, a). ~**ness** n parecido m. **be a good ~ness** parecerse mucho. ~**wise** adv (also) también; (the same way) lo mismo

liking /'laɪkɪŋ/ n (for thing) afición f;

(for person) simpatía f

lilac /'laɪlək/ adj lila. •n lila f; (colour) lila m

lily /'lɪlɪ/ n lirio m; (white) azucena f

limb /lɪm/ n miembro m. **out on a ~** aislado

lime /laɪm/ n (white substance) cal f; (fruit) lima f. ~**light** n. **be in the ~light** ser el centro de atención

limerick /'lɪmərɪk/ n quintilla f humorística

limit /'lɪmɪt/ n límite m. •vt limitar. ~**ation** /-'teɪʃn/ n limitación f. ~**ed** adj limitado. ~**ed company** n sociedad f anónima

limousine /'lɪməziːn/ n limusina f

limp /lɪmp/ vi cojear, renguear (LAm). •n cojera f, renguera f (LAm). **have a ~** cojear. •adj (-er, -est) flojo

linden /'lɪndn/ n (Amer) tilo m

line /laɪn/ n línea f; (track) vía f; (wrinkle) arruga f; (row) fila f; (of poem) verso m; (rope) cuerda f; (of goods) surtido m; (Amer, queue) cola f. **stand in ~** (Amer) hacer cola. **get in ~** (Amer) ponerse en la cola.. **cut in ~** (Amer) colarse. **in ~ with** de acuerdo con. •vt forrar (skirt, box); bordear (streets etc). ■ ~ **up** vi alinearse; (in queue) hacer cola. vt (form into line) poner en fila; (align) alinear. ~**d** adj (paper) con renglones; (with fabric) forrado

linen /'lɪnɪn/ n (sheets etc) ropa f blanca; (material) lino m

liner /'laɪnə(r)/ n (ship) transatlántico m

linger /'lɪŋɡə(r)/ vi tardar en marcharse. ~ **(on)** (smells etc) persistir. ■ ~ **over** vt dilatarse en

lingerie /'lænʒərɪ/ n lencería f

linguist /'lɪŋɡwɪst/ n políglota m & f; lingüista m & f. ~**ic** /lɪŋ'ɡwɪstɪk/ adj lingüístico. ~**ics** n lingüística f

lining /'laɪnɪŋ/ n forro m

link /lɪŋk/ n (of chain) eslabón m; (connection) conexión f; (bond)

vínculo m; (transport, telecommunications) conexión f, enlace m. ● vt conectar; relacionar (facts, events). ■ ~ **up** vt/i conectar

lino /'laɪnəʊ/ n (pl **-os**) linóleo m

lint /lɪnt/ n (Med) hilas fpl

lion /'laɪən/ n león m. ~**ess** /-nɪs/ n leona f

lip /lɪp/ n labio m; (edge) borde m. ~**read** vi leer los labios. ~**salve** n crema f para los labios. ~ **service** n. **pay ~ service to** aprobar de boquilla, aprobar de los dientes para fuera (Mex). ~**stick** n lápiz m de labios

liqueur /lɪ'kjʊə(r)/ n licor m

liquid /'lɪkwɪd/ adj & n líquido (m)

liquidate /'lɪkwɪdeɪt/ vt liquidar

liquidize /'lɪkwɪdaɪz/ vt licuar. ~**r** n licuadora f

liquor /'lɪkə(r)/ n bebidas fpl alcohólicas

liquorice /'lɪkərɪs/ n regaliz m

liquor store n (Amer) tienda f de bebidas alcohólicas

lisp /lɪsp/ n ceceo m. **speak with a ~** cecear. ● vi cecear

list /lɪst/ n lista f. ● vt hacer una lista de; (enter in a list) inscribir. ● vi (ship) escorar

listen /'lɪsn/ vi escuchar. ~ **in (to)** escuchar. ~ **to** escuchar. ~**er** n oyente m & f

listless /'lɪstlɪs/ adj apático

lit /lɪt/ see LIGHT

literacy /'lɪtərəsɪ/ n alfabetismo m

literal /'lɪtərəl/ adj literal. ~**ly** adv literalmente

literary /'lɪtərərɪ/ adj literario

literate /'lɪtərət/ adj alfabetizado

literature /'lɪtərətʃə(r)/ n literatura f; (fig) folletos mpl

lithe /laɪð/ adj ágil

litre /'liːtə(r)/ n litro m

litter /'lɪtə(r)/ n basura f; (of animals)

camada f. ● vt ensuciar; (scatter) esparcir. ~**ed with** lleno de. ~**bin** n papelera f. ~**bug**, ~ **lout** n persona f que tira basura en lugares públicos

little /'lɪtl/ adj pequeño; (not much) poco. **a ~ water** un poco de agua. ● pron poco, poca. **a ~** un poco. ● adv poco. ~ **by** ~ poco a poco. ~ **finger** n (dedo m) meñique m

live /lɪv/ vt/i vivir. ■ ~ **down** vt lograr borrar. ■ ~ **off** vt vivir a costa de (family, friends); (feed on) alimentarse de. ■ ~ **on** vt (feed o.s. on) vivir de. vi (memory) seguir presente; (tradition) seguir existiendo. ■ ~ **up** vt. ~ **it up** 🔲 darse la gran vida. ■ ~ **up to** vt vivir de acuerdo con; cumplir (promise). ● /laɪv/ adj vivo; (wire) con corriente; (broadcast) en directo

livelihood /'laɪvlɪhʊd/ n sustento m

lively /'laɪvlɪ/ adj (**-ier**, **-iest**) vivo

liven up /'laɪvn/ vt animar. ● vi animar(se)

liver /'lɪvə(r)/ n hígado m

lives /laɪvz/ see LIFE

livestock /'laɪvstɒk/ n animales mpl (de cría); (cattle) ganado m

livid /'lɪvɪd/ adj lívido; (fam, angry) furioso

living /'lɪvɪŋ/ adj vivo. ● n vida f. **make a ~** ganarse la vida. ~ **room** n salón m, sala f (de estar), living m (LAm)

lizard /'lɪzəd/ n lagartija f; (big) lagarto m

load /ləʊd/ n (also Elec) carga f; (quantity) cantidad f; (weight, strain) peso m. ~**s of** 🔲 montones de. ● vt cargar. ~**ed** adj cargado

loaf /ləʊf/ n (pl **loaves**) pan m; (stick of bread) barra f de pan. ● vi. ~ **(about)** holgazanear

loan /ləʊn/ n préstamo m. **on ~** prestado. ● vt prestar

loathe /ləʊð/ vt odiar. ~**ing** n odio

m (**of** a). ~**esome** /-səm/ adj
repugnante

lobby /'lɒbɪ/ n vestíbulo m; (Pol)
grupo m de presión. ●vt ejercer
presión sobre. ●vi. ~ **for sth**
ejercer presión para obtener algo

lobe /ləʊb/ n lóbulo m

lobster /'lɒbstə(r)/ n langosta f,
bogavante m

local /'ləʊkl/ adj local. ~ **(phone)
call** llamada f urbana. ●n (fam, pub)
bar m. **the** ~**s** los vecinos mpl. ~
government n administración f
municipal. ~**ity** /-'kælətɪ/ n
localidad f. ~**ization** n
localización f. ~**ly** adv (live, work) en
la zona

locat|e /ləʊ'keɪt/ vt (situate) situar,
ubicar (LAm); (find) localizar, ubicar
(LAm). ~**ion** /-ʃn/ n situación f,
ubicación f (LAm). **on** ~**ion** fuera
del estudio. **to film on** ~**ion in
Andalusia** rodar en Andalucía

lock /lɒk/ n (of door etc) cerradura f;
(on canal) esclusa f; (of hair) mechón
m. ●vt cerrar con llave. ●vi cerrarse
con llave. ■ ~ **in** vt encerrar. ■ ~
out vt cerrar la puerta a. ■ ~ **up** vt
encerrar (person); cerrar con llave
(building)

locker /'lɒkə(r)/ n armario m, locker
m (LAm). ~ **room** n (Amer)
vestuario m, vestidor m (Mex)

locket /'lɒkɪt/ n medallón m

lock: ~**out** /'lɒkaʊt/ n cierre m
patronal, paro m patronal (LAm).
~**smith** n cerrajero m

locomotive /ləʊkə'məʊtɪv/ n
locomotora f

lodg|e /lɒdʒ/ n (of porter) portería f.
●vt alojar; presentar (complaint).
~**er** n huésped m. ~**ings** n
alojamiento m; (room) habitación f
alquilada

loft /lɒft/ n desván m, altillo m (LAm)

lofty /'lɒftɪ/ adj (-ier, -iest) elevado;
(haughty) altanero

log /lɒg/ n (of wood) tronco m; (as
fuel) leño m; (record) diario m. **sleep
like a** ~ dormir como un tronco.

●vt (pt **logged**) registrar. ■ ~ **in**,
~ **on** vi (Comp) entrar (al sistema).
■ ~ **off**, ~ **out** vi (Comp) salir (del
sistema)

logarithm /'lɒgərɪðəm/ n
logaritmo m

loggerheads /'lɒgəhedz/ npl. **be at
~ with** estar a matar con

logic /'lɒdʒɪk/ adj lógica f. ~**al** adj
lógico. ~**ally** adv lógicamente

logistics /lə'dʒɪstɪks/ n logística f.
●npl (practicalities) problemas mpl
logísticos

logo /'ləʊgəʊ/ n (pl -**os**) logo m

loin /lɔɪn/ n (Culin) lomo m. ~**s** npl
entrañas fpl

loiter /'lɔɪtə(r)/ vi perder el tiempo

loll /lɒl/ vi repantigarse

loll|ipop /'lɒlɪpɒp/ n pirulí m. ~**y** n
polo m, paleta f (helada) (LAm)

London /'lʌndən/ n Londres m. ●adj
londinense. ~**er** n londinense m
& f

lone /ləʊn/ adj solitario. ~**ly** adj
(-ier, -iest) solitario. **feel** ~**ly**
sentirse muy solo. ~**r** n solitario
m. ~**some** /-səm/ adj solitario

long /lɒŋ/ adj (-**er**, -**est**) largo. **a** ~
time mucho tiempo. **how** ~ **is
it?** ¿cuánto tiene de largo? ●adv
largo/mucho tiempo. **as** ~ **as**
(while) mientras; (provided that) con
tal que (+ subjunctive). **before** ~
dentro de poco. **so** ~! ¡hasta
luego! **so** ~ **as** (provided that) con
tal que (+ subjunctive). ■ ~ **for** vi
anhelar. ~ **to do** estar deseando
hacer. ~**-distance** /-'dɪstəns/ adj de
larga distancia. ~**-distance
phone call** llamada f de larga
distancia, conferencia f. ~**er** adv.
no ~**er** ya no. ~**-haul** /-'hɔːl/ adj
de larga distancia. ~**ing** n anhelo
m, ansia f

longitude /'lɒŋgɪtjuːd/ n longitud f

long: ~ **jump** n salto m de
longitud. ~**-playing record** n
elepé m. ~**-range** adj de largo
alcance. ~**-sighted** /-'saɪtɪd/ adj
hipermétrope. ~**-term** adj a largo

plazo. **~-winded** /-'wɪndɪd/ adj
prolijo

loo /lu:/ n 🔲 váter m, baño m (LAm)

look /lʊk/ vt mirar; representar
(age). •vi mirar; (seem) parecer;
(search) buscar. •n mirada f;
(appearance) aspecto m. **good ~s**
belleza f. ■ **~ after** vt cuidar
(person); (be responsible for)
encargarse de. ■ **~ at** vt mirar;
(consider) considerar. ■ **~ down on**
vt despreciar. ■ **~ for** vt buscar.
■ **~ forward to** vt esperar con
ansia. ■ **~ into** vt investigar. ■ **~
like** vt parecerse a. ■ **~ on** vi
mirar. ■ **~ out** vi tener cuidado.
■ **~ out for** vt buscar; (watch)
tener cuidado con. ■ **~ round** vi
volver la cabeza. ■ **~ through** vt
hojear. ■ **~ up** vt buscar (word);
(visit) ir a ver. ■ **~ up to** vt
admirar. **~alike** n 🔲 doble m & f.
~out n (Mil, person) vigía m. **be on
the ~out for** andar a la caza de.
~s npl belleza f

loom /lu:m/ n telar m. •vi
aparecerse

looney, loony /'lu:nɪ/ adj & n 🔳
chiflado (m), loco (m)

loop /lu:p/ n (shape) curva f ; (in
string) lazada f. •vt hacer una
lazada con. **~hole** n (in rule)
escapatoria f

loose /lu:s/ adj (-er, -est) suelto;
(garment, thread, hair) flojo; (inexact)
vago; (not packed) suelto. **be at a ~
end** no tener nada que hacer. **~ly**
adv sueltamente; (roughly)
aproximadamente. **~n** vt aflojar

loot /lu:t/ n botín m. •vt/i saquear.
~er n saqueador m

lop /lɒp/ vt (pt lopped). **~ off**
cortar

lop-sided /-'saɪdɪd/ adj ladeado

lord /lɔːd/ n señor m; (British title) lord
m. **(good) L~!** 🔲 ¡Dios mío! **the L~**
el Señor. **the (House of) L~s** la
Cámara de los Lores

lorry /'lɒrɪ/ n camión m. **~ driver** n
camionero m

lose /lu:z/ vt/i (pt lost) perder. **~r** n
perdedor m

loss /lɒs/ n pérdida f. **be at a ~**
estar perplejo. **be at a ~ for
words** no encontrar palabras

lost /lɒst/ see LOSE. •adj perdido.
get ~ perderse. **~ property** n, **~
and found** (Amer) oficina f de
objetos perdidos

lot /lɒt/ n (fate) suerte f; (at auction)
lote m; (land) solar m. **a ~ (of)**
muchos. **quite a ~ of** 🔲
bastante. **~s (of)** 🔲 muchos.
they ate the ~ se lo comieron
todo

lotion /'ləʊʃn/ n loción f

lottery /'lɒtərɪ/ n lotería f

loud /laʊd/ adj (-er, -est) fuerte;
(noisy) ruidoso; (gaudy) chillón. **out
~** en voz alta. **~hailer** /-'heɪlə(r)/
n megáfono m. **~ly** adv (speak) en
voz alta; (shout) fuerte; (complain) a
voz en grito. **~speaker**
/-'spiːkə(r)/ n altavoz m,
altoparlante m (LAm)

lounge /laʊndʒ/ vi repantigarse. •n
salón m, sala f (de estar), living m
(LAm)

lous|e /laʊs/ n (pl lice) piojo m. **~y**
/'laʊzɪ/ adj (-ier, -iest) (sl, bad)
malísimo

lout /laʊt/ n patán m

lov|able /'lʌvəbl/ adj adorable. **~e**
/lʌv/ n amor m; (tennis) cero m. **be
in ~e (with)** estar enamorado
(de). **fall in ~e (with)**
enamorarse (de). •vt querer, amar
(person). **I ~e milk** me encanta la
leche. **~e affair** n aventura f,
amorío m

lovely /'lʌvlɪ/ adj (-ier, -iest)
(appearance) precioso, lindo (LAm);
(person) encantador, amoroso (LAm)

lover /'lʌvə(r)/ n amante m & f

loving /'lʌvɪŋ/ adj cariñoso

low /ləʊ/ adj & adv (-er, -est) bajo.
•vi (cattle) mugir. **~er** vt bajar. **~er**

o.s. envilecerse. **~-level** adj a bajo nivel. **~ly** adj (**-ier, -iest**) humilde

loyal /'lɔɪəl/ adj leal, fiel. **~ty** n lealtad f. **~ty card** tarjeta f de fidelidad

lozenge /'lɒzɪndʒ/ n (shape) rombo m; (tablet) pastilla f

LP abbr (= **long-playing record**) elepé m

Ltd /'lɪmɪtɪd/ abbr (= **Limited**) S.A., Sociedad Anónima

lubricate /'lu:brɪkeɪt/ vt lubricar

lucid /'lu:sɪd/ adj lúcido

luck /lʌk/ n suerte f. **good ~!** ¡(buena) suerte! **~ily** adv por suerte. **~y** adj (**-ier, -iest**) (person) con suerte. **be ~y** tener suerte. **~y number** número m de la suerte

lucrative /'lu:krətɪv/ adj lucrativo

ludicrous /'lu:dɪkrəs/ adj ridículo

lug /lʌg/ vt (pt **lugged**) 🔢 arrastrar

luggage /'lʌgɪdʒ/ n equipaje m. **~ rack** n rejilla f

lukewarm /'lu:kwɔːm/ adj tibio; (fig) poco entusiasta

lull /lʌl/ vt (soothe, send to sleep) adormecer; (calm) calmar. ●n periodo m de calma

lullaby /'lʌləbaɪ/ n canción f de cuna

lumber /'lʌmbə(r)/ n trastos mpl viejos; (wood) maderos mpl. ●vt. **~ s.o. with sth** 🔢 endilgar algo a uno. **~jack** n leñador m

luminous /'lu:mɪnəs/ adj luminoso

lump /lʌmp/ n (swelling) bulto m; (as result of knock) chichón m; (in liquid) grumo m; (of sugar) terrón m. ●vt. **~ together** agrupar. **~ it** 🔢

aguantarse. **~ sum** n suma f global. **~y** adj (sauce) grumoso; (mattress, cushions) lleno de protuberancias

lunacy /'lu:nəsɪ/ n locura f

lunar /'lu:nə(r)/ adj lunar

lunatic /'lu:nətɪk/ n loco m

lunch /lʌntʃ/ n comida f, almuerzo m. **have ~** comer, almorzar

luncheon /'lʌntʃən/ n comida f, almuerzo m. **~ voucher** n vale m de comida

lung /lʌŋ/ n pulmón m

lunge /lʌndʒ/ n arremetida f. ●vi. **~ at** arremeter contra

lurch /lɜːtʃ/ vi tambalearse. ●n. **leave in the ~** dejar plantado

lure /ljʊə(r)/ vt atraer

lurid /'ljʊərɪd/ adj (colour) chillón; (shocking) morboso

lurk /lɜːk/ vi merodear; (in ambush) estar al acecho

luscious /'lʌʃəs/ adj delicioso

lush /lʌʃ/ adj exuberante

lust /lʌst/ n lujuria f; (craving) deseo m. ●vi. **~ after** codiciar

lute /lu:t/ n laúd m

Luxembourg, Luxemburg /'lʌksəmbɜːg/ n Luxemburgo m

luxuriant /lʌg'zjʊərɪənt/ adj exuberante

luxur|ious /lʌg'zjʊərɪəs/ adj lujoso. **~y** /'lʌkʃərɪ/ n lujo m. ●adj de lujo

lying /'laɪɪŋ/ see LIE¹, LIE². ●n mentiras fpl. ●adj mentiroso

lynch /lɪntʃ/ vt linchar

lyric /'lɪrɪk/ adj lírico. **~al** adj lírico. **~s** npl letra f

Mm

MA /em'eɪ/ abbr see **MASTER**

mac /mæk/ n ⓘ impermeable m

macabre /mə'kɑːbrə/ adj macabro

macaroni /mækə'rəʊnɪ/ n macarrones mpl

mace /meɪs/ n (staff) maza f; (spice) macis f. **M~** ® (Amer) gas m para defensa personal

machine /mə'ʃiːn/ n máquina f. **~ gun** n ametralladora f. **~ry** n maquinaria f; (working parts, fig) mecanismo m

mackintosh /'mækɪntɒʃ/ n impermeable m

macro /'mækrəʊ/ n (pl **-os**) (Comp) macro m

macrobiotic /mækrəʊbaɪ'ɒtɪk/ adj macrobiótico

mad /mæd/ adj (**madder, maddest**) loco; (fam, angry) furioso. **be ~ about** estar loco por

madam /'mædəm/ n señora f

mad: ~cap adj atolondrado. **~ cow disease** f enfermedad † de las vacas locas. **~den** vt (make mad) enloquecer; (make angry) enfurecer

made /meɪd/ see **MAKE**. **~-to-measure** hecho a (la) medida

mad: ~house n manicomio m. **~ly** adv (interested, in love etc) locamente; (frantically) como un loco. **~man** /-mən/ n loco m. **~ness** n locura f

Madonna /mə'dɒnə/ n. **the ~** (Relig) la Virgen

maestro /'maɪstrəʊ/ n (pl **maestri** /-striː/ or **-os**) maestro m

Mafia /'mæfɪə/ n mafia f

magazine /mægə'ziːn/ n revista f;

(of gun) recámara f

magenta /mə'dʒentə/ adj magenta, morado

maggot /'mægət/ n gusano m

magic /'mædʒɪk/ n magia f. ● adj mágico. **~al** adj mágico. **~ian** /mə'dʒɪʃn/ n mago m

magistrate /'mædʒɪstreɪt/ n juez m que conoce de faltas y asuntos civiles de menor importancia

magnet /'mægnɪt/ n imán m. **~ic** /-'netɪk/ adj magnético; (fig) lleno de magnetismo. **~ism** n magnetismo m. **~ize** vt imantar, magnetizar

magnif|ication /mægnɪfɪ'keɪʃn/ n aumento m. **~y** /'mægnɪfaɪ/ vt aumentar. **~ying glass** n lupa f

magnificen|ce /mæg'nɪfɪsns/ adj magnificencia f. **~t** adj magnífico

magnitude /'mægnɪtjuːd/ n magnitud f

magpie /'mægpaɪ/ n urraca †

mahogany /mə'hɒgənɪ/ n caoba f

maid /meɪd/ n (servant) criada f, sirvienta f; (girl, old use) doncella f. **old ~** solterona f

maiden /'meɪdn/ n doncella f. ● adj (voyage) inaugural. **~ name** n apellido m de soltera

mail /meɪl/ n correo m; (armour) (cota f de) malla f. ● adj correo. ● vt echar al correo (letter); (send) enviar por correo. **~box** n (Amer) buzón m. **~ing list** n lista f de direcciones. **~man** /-mən/ n (Amer) cartero m. **~ order** n venta f por correo

maim /meɪm/ vt mutilar

main /meɪn/ n. (water/gas) **~** cañería f principal. **in the ~** en su mayor parte. **the ~s** npl (Elec) la red f de suministro. ●adj principal. **~ course** n plato m principal, plato m fuerte. **~ frame** n (Comp) unidad f central. **~land** n. **the ~land** la masa territorial de un país excluyendo sus islas. ●adj. **~land China** (la) China continental. **~ly** adv principalmente. **~ road** n carretera f principal. **~stream** adj (culture) establecido. **~ street** n calle f principal

maint|ain /meɪnˈteɪn/ vt mantener. **~enance** /ˈmeɪntənəns/ n mantenimiento m

maisonette /meɪzəˈnet/ n (small house) casita f; (part of house) dúplex m

maize /meɪz/ n maíz m

majestic /məˈdʒestɪk/ adj majestuoso

majesty /ˈmædʒəstɪ/ n majestad f

major /ˈmeɪdʒə(r)/ adj (important) muy importante; (Mus) mayor. **a ~ road** una calle prioritaria. ●n comandante m & f, mayor m & f (LAm). ●vi. **~ in** (Amer, Univ) especializarse en

Majorca /məˈjɔːkə/ n Mallorca f

majority /məˈdʒɒrətɪ/ n mayoría f. ●adj mayoritario

make /meɪk/ vt (pt **made**) hacer; (manufacture) fabricar; ganar (money); tomar (decision); llegar a (destination). **~ s.o. do sth** obligar a uno a hacer algo. **be made of** estar hecho de. **I ~ it two o'clock** yo tengo las dos. **~ believe** fingir. **~ do** (manage) arreglarse. **~ do with** (content o.s.) contentarse con. **~ it** llegar; (succeed) tener éxito. ●n marca f. **~ for** vt dirigirse a. **~ good** vt compensar; (repair) reparar. ■**~ off** vi escaparse (**with** con). ■**~ out** vt distinguir; (understand) entender; (write out) hacer; (assert) dar a entender. vi (cope) arreglárselas. ■**~ up** vt (constitute) formar; (prepare) preparar; inventar (story); **~ it up**

(become reconciled) hacer las paces. **~ up** (one's face) maquillarse. ■**~ up for** vt compensar. **~-believe** adj fingido, simulado. n ficción f. **~over** n (Amer) maquillaje m. **~r** n fabricante m & f. **~shift** adj (temporary) provisional, provisorio (LAm); (improvised) improvisado. **~up** n maquillaje m. **put on ~up** maquillarse.

making /ˈmeɪkɪŋ/ n. **he has the ~s of** tiene madera de. **in the ~** en vías de formación

maladjusted /mælæˈdʒʌstɪd/ adj inadaptado

malaria /məˈleərɪə/ n malaria f, paludismo m

Malaysia /məˈleɪzɪə/ n Malasia f. **~n** adj & n malaisio (m)

male /meɪl/ adj macho; (voice, attitude) masculino. ●n macho m; (man) varón m

malevolent /məˈlevələnt/ adj malévolo

malfunction /mælˈfʌŋkʃn/ vi fallar, funcionar mal

malic|e /ˈmælɪs/ n mala intención f, maldad f. **bear s.o. ~e** guardar rencor a uno. **~ious** /məˈlɪʃəs/ adj malintencionado. **~iously** adv con malevolencia

malignant /məˈlɪgnənt/ adj maligno

mallet /ˈmælɪt/ n mazo m

malnutrition /mælnjuːˈtrɪʃn/ n desnutrición f

malpractice /mælˈpræktɪs/ n mala práctica f (en el ejercicio de una profesión)

malt /mɔːlt/ n malta f

Malt|a /ˈmɔːltə/ n Malta f. **~ese** /-ˈtiːz/ adj & n maltés (m)

mammal /ˈmæml/ n mamífero m

mammoth /ˈmæməθ/ n mamut m. ●adj gigantesco

man /mæn/ n (pl **men** /men/) hombre m; (Chess) pieza f. **~ in the street** hombre m de la calle. ●vt (pt **manned**) encargarse de (switchboard); tripular (ship); servir (guns)

manacles /'mænəklz/ n (for wrists) esposas fpl; (for legs) grillos mpl

manag|e /'mænɪdʒ/ vt dirigir; administrar (land, finances); (handle) manejar. •vi (Com) dirigir; (cope) arreglárselas. **~e to do** lograr hacer. **~eable** adj (task) posible de alcanzar; (size) razonable. **~ement** n dirección f. **~er** n director m; (of shop) encargado m; (of soccer team) entrenador m, director m técnico (LAm). **~eress** /-'res/ n encargada f. **~erial** /-'dʒɪərɪəl/ adj directivo, gerencial (LAm). **~ing director** n director m ejecutivo

mandate /'mændeɪt/ n mandato m

mandatory /'mændətərɪ/ adj obligatorio

mane /meɪn/ n (of horse) crin(es) f(pl); (of lion) melena f

mangle /'mæŋgl/ n rodillo m (escurridor). •vt destrozar

man: **~handle** vt mover a pulso; (treat roughly) maltratar. **~hole** n registro m. **~hood** n madurez f; (quality) virilidad f. **~-hour** n hora f hombre. **~hunt** n persecución f

mania /'meɪnɪə/ n manía f. **~c** /-ræk/ n maníaco m

manicure /'mænɪkjʊə(r)/ n manicura f, manicure f (LAm)

manifest /'mænɪfest/ adj manifiesto. •vt manifestar. **~ation** /-'steɪʃn/ n manifestación f

manifesto /mænɪ'festəʊ/ n (pl **-os**) manifiesto m

manipulat|e /mə'nɪpjʊleɪt/ vt manipular. **~ion** /-'leɪʃn/ n manipulación f. **~ive** /-lətɪv/ adj manipulador

man: **~kind** n humanidad f. **~ly** adj viril. **~-made** adj artificial

manner /'mænə(r)/ n manera f; (demeanour) actitud f; (kind) clase f. **~ed** adj amanerado. **~s** npl

modales mpl, educación f. **bad ~s** mala educación

manoeuvre /mə'nu:və(r)/ n maniobra f. •vt/i maniobrar

manor /'mænə(r)/ n. **~ house** casa f solariega

manpower n mano f de obra

mansion /'mænʃn/ n mansión f

man: **~-size(d)** adj grande. **~slaughter** n homicidio m sin premeditación

mantelpiece /'mæntlpi:s/ n repisa f de la chimenea

manual /'mænjʊəl/ adj manual. •n (handbook) manual m

manufacture /mænjʊ'fæktʃə(r)/ vt fabricar. •n fabricación f. **~r** n fabricante m & f

manure /mə'njʊə(r)/ n estiércol m

manuscript /'mænjʊskrɪpt/ n manuscrito m

many /'menɪ/ adj & pron muchos, muchas. **~ people** mucha gente. **a great/good ~** muchísimos. **how ~?** ¿cuántos? **so ~** tantos. **too ~** demasiados

map /mæp/ n mapa m; (of streets etc) plano m

mar /mɑ:(r)/ vt (pt **marred**) estropear

marathon /'mærəθən/ n maratón m & f

marble /'mɑ:bl/ n mármol m; (for game) canica f

march /mɑ:tʃ/ vi (Mil) marchar. **~ off** vi irse. •n marcha f

March /mɑ:tʃ/ n marzo m

march-past /'mɑ:tʃpɑ:st/ n desfile m

mare /meə(r)/ n yegua f

margarine /mɑ:dʒə'ri:n/ n margarina f

margin /'mɑ:dʒɪn/ n margen f. **~al** adj marginal

marijuana /mærɪ'hwɑ:nə/ n marihuana f

marina /məˈriːnə/ n puerto m deportivo

marine /məˈriːn/ adj marino. ●n (sailor) infante m de marina

marionette /ˌmærɪəˈnet/ n marioneta f

marital status /ˌmærɪtl ˈsteɪtəs/ n estado m civil

mark /mɑːk/ n marca f; (stain) mancha f; (Schol) nota f; (target) blanco m. ●vt (indicate) señalar, marcar; (stain) manchar; corregir (exam). ~ **time** marcar el paso. ■~ **out** vt (select) señalar; (distinguish) distinguir. ~**ed** adj marcado. ~**edly** /-kɪdlɪ/ adv marcadamente. ~**er** n marcador m. ~**er (pen)** n rotulador m, marcador m (LAm)

market /ˈmɑːkɪt/ n mercado m. **on the** ~ en venta. ●vt comercializar. ~ **garden** n huerta f. ~**ing** n marketing m

marking /ˈmɑːkɪŋ/ n marcas fpl; (on animal, plant) mancha f

marksman /ˈmɑːksmən/ n (pl -**men**) tirador m. ~**ship** n puntería f

marmalade /ˈmɑːməleɪd/ n mermelada f (de cítricos)

maroon /məˈruːn/ adj & n granate (m). ●vt abandonar (en una isla desierta)

marquee /mɑːˈkiː/ n toldo m, entoldado m; (Amer, awning) marquesina f

marriage /ˈmærɪdʒ/ n matrimonio m; (ceremony) casamiento m

married /ˈmærɪd/ adj casado; (life) conyugal

marrow /ˈmærəʊ/ n (of bone) tuétano m; (vegetable) calabaza f verde alargada. ~ **squash** n (Amer) calabaza f verde alargada

marry /ˈmærɪ/ vt casarse con; (give or unite in marriage) casar. ●vi casarse. **get married** casarse (**to** con)

Mars /mɑːz/ n Marte m

marsh /mɑːʃ/ n pantano m

marshal /ˈmɑːʃl/ n (Mil) mariscal m; (Amer, police chief) jefe m de policía. ●vt (pt **marshalled**) reunir; poner en orden (thoughts)

marsh: ~**mallow** /-ˈmæləʊ/ n malvavisco m, bombón m (LAm). ~**y** adj pantanoso

martial /ˈmɑːʃl/ adj marcial. ~ **arts** npl artes fpl marciales. ~ **law** n ley f marcial

martyr /ˈmɑːtə(r)/ n mártir m & f

marvel /ˈmɑːvl/ n maravilla f. ●vi (pt **marvelled**) maravillarse (**at** de). ~**lous** adj maravilloso

Marxis|m /ˈmɑːksɪzəm/ n marxismo m. ~**t** adj & n marxista (m & f)

marzipan /ˈmɑːzɪpæn/ n mazapán m

mascara /mæˈskɑːrə/ n rímel ® m

mascot /ˈmæskɒt/ n mascota f

masculin|e /ˈmæskjʊlɪn/ adj & n masculino (m). ~**ity** /-ˈlɪnətɪ/ n masculinidad f

mash /mæʃ/ n (Brit 🔲, potatoes) puré m de patatas, puré m de papas (LAm). ●vt hacer puré de, moler (Mex). ~**ed potatoes** n puré m de patatas, puré m de papas (LAm)

mask /mɑːsk/ n máscara f; (Sport) careta f. ●vt ocultar

masochis|m /ˈmæsəkɪzəm/ n masoquismo m. ~**t** n masoquista m & f. ~**tic** /-ˈkɪstɪk/ adj masoquista

mason /ˈmeɪsn/ n (stone ~) mampostero m. **M~** (freemason) masón m. ~**ry** /ˈmeɪsnrɪ/ n albañilería f

masquerade /ˌmɑːskəˈreɪd/ n mascarada f. ●vi. ~ **as** hacerse pasar por

mass /mæs/ n masa f; (Relig) misa f; (large quantity) montón m. **the** ~**es** las masas. ●vi concentrarse

massacre /ˈmæsəkə(r)/ n masacre f, matanza f. ●vt masacrar

mass|age /ˈmæsɑːʒ/ n masaje m. ●vt masajear. ~**eur** /mæˈsɜː(r)/ n masajista m. ~**euse** /mæˈsɜːz/ n masajista f

m

massive /'mæsɪv/ adj masivo; (heavy) macizo; (huge) enorme

mass: ∼ **media** n medios mpl de comunicación. ∼**-produce** /-prə'dju:s/ vt fabricar en serie

mast /mɑːst/ n mástil m; (for radio, TV) antena f repetidora

master /'mɑːstə(r)/ n amo m; (expert) maestro m; (in secondary school) profesor m; (of ship) capitán m; (master copy) original m. ∼**'s degree** n master m, maestría f. **M∼ of Arts (MA)** poseedor m de una maestría en folosofía y letras. **M∼ of Science (MSc)** poseedor m de una maestría en ciencias. ●vt llegar a dominar. ∼ **key** n llave f maestra. ∼**mind** n cerebro m. ●vt dirigir. ∼**piece** n obra f maestra. ∼**stroke** n golpe m de maestro. ∼**y** n dominio m; (skill) maestría f

masturbat|e /'mæstəbeɪt/ vi masturbarse. ∼**ion** /-'beɪʃn/ n masturbación f

mat /mæt/ n estera f; (at door) felpudo m. ●adj (Amer) see **MATT**

match /mætʃ/ n (Sport) partido m; (for fire) cerilla f, fósforo m (LAm), cerillo m (Mex); (equal) igual m. ●vt emparejar; (equal) igualar; (clothes, colours) hacer juego con. ●vi hacer juego. ∼**box** n caja f de cerillas, caja f de fósforos (LAm), caja f de cerillos (Mex). ∼**ing** adj que hace juego. ∼**stick** n cerilla f, fósforo m (LAm), cerillo m (Mex)

mate /meɪt/ n (of person) pareja f; (of animals, male) macho m; (of animals, female) hembra f; (assistant) ayudante m; (▣, friend) amigo m, cuate m (Mex); (Chess) (jaque m) mate m. ●vi aparearse

material /mə'tɪərɪəl/ n material m; (cloth) tela f. ●adj material. ∼**istic** /-'lɪstɪk/ adj materialista. ∼**ize** vi materializarse. ∼**s** npl materiales mpl

matern|al /mə'tɜːnl/ adj maternal. ∼**ity** /-ətɪ/ n maternidad f. ●adj (ward) de obstetricia; (clothes) premamá, de embarazada

math /mæθ/ n (Amer) see **MATHS**

mathematic|ian /mæθəmə'tɪʃn/ n matemático m. ∼**al** /-'mætɪkl/ adj matemático. ∼**s** /-'mætɪks/ n matemática(s) f(pl)

maths /mæθs/ n matemática(s) f(pl)

matinée, matinee /'mætɪneɪ/ n (Theatre) función f de tarde; (Cinema) primera sesión f (de la tarde)

matrices /'meɪtrɪsiːz/ see **MATRIX**

matriculat|e /mə'trɪkjʊleɪt/ vi matricularse. ∼**ion** /-'leɪʃn/ n matrícula f

matrimon|ial /mætrɪ'məʊnɪəl/ adj matrimonial. ∼**y** /'mætrɪmənɪ/ n matrimonio m

matrix /'meɪtrɪks/ n (pl **matrices**) matriz f

matron /'meɪtrən/ n (married, elderly) matrona f; (in school) ama f de llaves; (former use, in hospital) enfermera f jefe

matt, matte (Amer) /mæt/ adj mate

matted /'mætɪd/ adj enmarañado y apelmazado

matter /'mætə(r)/ n (substance) materia f; (affair) asunto m; (pus) pus m. **as a ∼ of fact** en realidad. **no ∼** no importa. **what is the ∼?** ¿qué pasa? **to make ∼s worse** para colmo (de males). ●vi importar. **it doesn't** ∼ no importa. ∼**-of-fact** /-əv'fækt/ adj (person) práctico

mattress /'mætrɪs/ n colchón m

matur|e /mə'tjʊə(r)/ adj maduro. ●vi madurar. ∼**ity** n madurez f

maudlin /'mɔːdlɪn/ adj llorón

maul /mɔːl/ vt atacar (y herir)

mauve /məʊv/ adj & n malva (m)

maverick /'mævərɪk/ n inconformista m & f

maxim /'mæksɪm/ n máxima f

maxim|ize /'mæksɪmaɪz/ vt maximizar. ∼**um** /-əm/ adj & n máximo (m)

may /meɪ/,

past **might**

auxiliary verb

····▸ (expressing possibility) **he ~ come** puede que venga, es posible que venga. **it ~ be true** puede ser verdad. **she ~ not have seen him** es posible que or puede que no lo haya visto

····▸ (asking for or giving permission) **~ I smoke?** ¿puedo fumar?, ¿se puede fumar? **~ I have your name and address, please?** ¿quiere darme su nombre y dirección, por favor?

····▸ (expressing a wish) **~ he be happy** que sea feliz

····▸ (conceding) **he ~ not have much experience, but he's very hardworking** no tendrá mucha experiencia, pero es muy trabajador. **that's as ~ be** puede ser

····▸ **I ~ as well stay** más vale quedarme

May /meɪ/ n mayo m

maybe /'meɪbɪ/ adv quizá(s), tal vez, a lo mejor

May Day n el primero de mayo

mayhem /'meɪhem/ n caos m

mayonnaise /meɪə'neɪz/ n mayonesa f, mahonesa f

mayor /meə(r)/ n alcalde m, alcaldesa f. **~ess** /-ɪs/ n alcaldesa f

maze /meɪz/ n laberinto m

me /miː/ pron me; (after prep) mí. **he knows ~ me conoce. it's ~** soy yo

meadow /'medəʊ/ n prado m, pradera f

meagre /'miːgə(r)/ adj escaso

meal /miːl/ n comida f. **~time** n hora f de comer

mean /miːn/ vt (pt **meant**) (intend) tener la intención de, querer; (signify) querer decir, significar. **~ to do** tener la intención de hacer. **~ well** tener buenas intenciones.

be meant for estar destinado a. • adj (**-er, -est**) (miserly) tacaño; (unkind) malo; (Math) medio. • n media f; (average) promedio m

meander /mɪ'ændə(r)/ vi (river) serpentear

meaning /'miːnɪŋ/ n sentido m. **~ful** adj significativo. **~less** adj sin sentido

meanness /'miːnnɪs/ n (miserliness) tacañería f; (unkindness) maldad f

means /miːnz/ n medio m. **by ~ of** por medio de, mediante. **by all ~** por supuesto. **by no ~** de ninguna manera. • npl (wealth) medios mpl, recursos mpl. **~ test** n investigación f de ingresos

meant /ment/ see MEAN

meantime /'miːntaɪm/ adv mientras tanto, entretanto. • n. **in the ~** mientras tanto, entretanto

meanwhile /'miːnwaɪl/ adv mientras tanto, entretanto

measl|es /'miːzlz/ n sarampión m. **~y** /'miːzlɪ/ adj 🔟 miserable

measure /'meʒə(r)/ n medida f; (ruler) regla f. • vt/i medir. ■ **~ up to** vt estar a la altura de. **~ment** n medida f

meat /miːt/ n carne f. **~ball** n albóndiga f. **~y** adj (taste, smell) a carne; (soup, stew) con mucha carne

mechan|ic /mɪ'kænɪk/ n mecánico m. **~ical** adj mecánico. **~ics** n mecánica f. **~ism** /'mekənɪzəm/ n mecanismo m. **~ize** /'mekənaɪz/ vt mecanizar

medal /'medl/ n medalla f. **~list** /'medəlɪst/ n medallista m & f. **be a gold ~list** ganar una medalla de oro

meddle /'medl/ vi meterse, entrometerse (**in** en). **~ with** (tinker) toquetear

media /'miːdɪə/ see MEDIUM. • npl **the ~** los medios de comunicación

mediat|e /'miːdɪeɪt/ vi mediar.

~**ion** /-'eɪʃn/ n mediación f. ~**or** n mediador m

medical /'medɪkl/ adj médico; (student) de medicina. ●n revisión m médica

medicat|ed /'medɪkeɪtɪd/ adj medicinal. ~**ion** /-'keɪʃn/ n medicación f

medicin|al /mɪ'dɪsɪnl/ adj medicinal. ~**e** /'medsɪn/ n medicina f

medieval /medɪ'i:vl/ adj medieval

mediocre /mi:dɪ'əʊkə(r)/ adj mediocre

meditat|e /'medɪteɪt/ vi meditar. ~**ion** /-'teɪʃn/ n meditación f

Mediterranean /medɪtə'reɪnɪən/ adj mediterráneo. ●n. **the ~** el Mediterráneo

medium /'mi:dɪəm/ n (pl **media**) medio m. **happy ~** término m medio. ●adj mediano. ~-**size(d)** /-saɪz(d)/ adj de tamaño mediano

medley /'medlɪ/ n (Mus) popurrí m; (mixture) mezcla f

meek /mi:k/ adj (-**er**, -**est**) dócil

meet /mi:t/ vt (pt **met**) encontrar; (bump into s.o.) encontrarse con; (fetch) ir a buscar; (get to know, be introduced to) conocer. ●vi encontrarse; (get to know) conocerse; (have meeting) reunirse. ~ **up** vi encontrarse (**with** con). ■ ~ **with** vt ser recibido con; (Amer, meet) encontrarse con. ~**ing** n reunión f; (accidental between two people) encuentro m

megabyte /'megəbaɪt/ n (Comp) megabyte m, megaocteto m

megaphone /'megəfəʊn/ n megáfono m

melanchol|ic /melən'kɒlɪk/ adj melancólico. ~**y** /'melənkɒlɪ/ n melancolía f. ●adj melancólico

mellow /'meləʊ/ adj (-**er**, -**est**) (fruit) maduro; (sound) dulce; (colour) tenue; (person) apacible

melodrama /'melədrɑːmə/ n melodrama m. ~**tic**

/melədrə'mætɪk/ adj melodramático

melody /'melədɪ/ n melodía f

melon /'melən/ n melón m

melt /melt/ vt (make liquid) derretir; fundir (metals). ●vi (become liquid) derretirse; (metals) fundirse. ■ ~ **down** vt fundir

member /'membə(r)/ n miembro m & f; (of club) socio m. ~ **of staff** empleado m. **M~ of Congress** n (Amer) miembro m & f del Congreso. **M~ of Parliament** n diputado m. ~**ship** n calidad f de socio; (members) socios mpl, membresía f (LAm)

membrane /'membreɪn/ n membrana f

memento /mɪ'mentəʊ/ n (pl -**os** or -**oes**) recuerdo m

memo /'meməʊ/ n (pl -**os**) memorándum m, memo m

memoir /'memwɑː(r)/ n memoria f

memorable /'memərəbl/ adj memorable

memorandum /memə'rændəm/ n (pl -**ums** or -**da** /-də/') memorándum m

memorial /mɪ'mɔːrɪəl/ n monumento m. ●adj conmemorativo

memor|ize /'meməraɪz/ vt aprender de memoria. ~**y** /'memərɪ/ n (faculty) memoria f; (thing remembered) recuerdo m. **from ~y** de memoria. **in ~y of** a la memoria de

men /men/ see MAN

menac|e /'menəs/ n amenaza f; (fam, nuisance) peligro m público. ●vt amenazar. ~**ing** adj amenazador

mend /mend/ vt reparar; arreglar (garment). ~ **one's ways** enmendarse. ●n remiendo m. **be on the ~** ir mejorando

menfolk /'menfəʊk/ n hombres mpl

menial /'mi:nɪəl/ adj servil

meningitis /menɪn'dʒaɪtɪs/ n meningitis f

menopause /'menəpɔːz/ n
menopausia f

menstruat|e /'menstrʊeɪt/ vi
menstruar. **~ion** /-'eɪʃn/ n
menstruación f

mental /'mentl/ adj mental;
(hospital) psiquiátrico. **~ity**
/-'tælətɪ/ n mentalidad f. **~ly** adv
mentalmente. **be ~ly ill** ser un
enfermo mental

mention /'menʃn/ vt mencionar.
don't ~ it! ¡no hay de qué! ● n
mención f

mentor /'mentɔː(r)/ n mentor m

menu /'menjuː/ n menú m

meow /mɪ'aʊ/ n & vi see MEW

mercenary /'mɜːsɪnərɪ/ adj & n
mercenario (m)

merchandise /'mɜːtʃəndaɪz/ n
mercancías fpl, mercadería f (LAm)

merchant /'mɜːtʃənt/ n
comerciante m. ● adj (ship, navy)
mercante. **~ bank** n banco m
mercantil

merci|ful /'mɜːsɪfl/ adj
misericordioso. **~less** adj
despiadado

mercury /'mɜːkjʊrɪ/ n mercurio m.
M~ (planet) Mercurio m

mercy /'mɜːsɪ/ n compasión f. **at
the ~ of** a merced de

mere /mɪə(r)/ adj simple. **~ly** adv
simplemente

merge /mɜːdʒ/ vt unir; fusionar
(companies). ● vi unirse; (companies)
fusionarse. **~r** n fusión f

meridian /mə'rɪdɪən/ n
meridiano m

meringue /mə'ræŋ/ n merengue m

merit /'merɪt/ n mérito m. ● vt (pt
merited) merecer

mermaid /'mɜːmeɪd/ n sirena f

merr|ily /'merəlɪ/ adv alegremente.
~iment /'merɪmənt/ n alegría f.
~y /'merɪ/ adj (**-ier, -iest**) alegre.
make ~ divertirse. **~y-go-round**
n tiovivo m, carrusel m (LAm).

~y-making n jolgorio m

mesh /meʃ/ n malla f

mesmerize /'mezməraɪz/ vt
hipnotizar; (fascinate) cautivar

mess /mes/ n desorden m; (dirt)
suciedad f; (Mil) rancho m. **make a
~ of** estropear. ■ **~ up** vt
desordenar; (dirty) ensuciar;
estropear (plans). ■ **~ about** vi
tontear. ■ **~ with** vt (tinker with)
manosear

mess|age /'mesɪdʒ/ n mensaje m;
(when phoning) recado m. **~enger**
/'mesɪndʒə(r)/ n mensajero m

Messiah /mɪ'saɪə/ n Mesías m

Messrs /'mesəz/ npl. **~ Smith** los
señores Smith, los Sres. Smith

messy /'mesɪ/ adj (**-ier, -iest**) en
desorden; (dirty) sucio

met /met/ see MEET

metabolism /mɪ'tæbəlɪzəm/ n
metabolismo m

metal /'metl/ n metal. ● adj de
metal. **~lic** /mə'tælɪk/ adj metálico

metaphor /'metəfə(r)/ n metáfora
f. **~ical** /-'fɒrɪkl/ adj metafórico

mete /miːt/ vt. **~ out** repartir; dar
(punishment)

meteor /'miːtɪə(r)/ n meteoro m.
~ic /-'ɒrɪk/ adj meteórico. **~ite**
/'miːtɪəraɪt/ n meteorito m

meteorolog|ical /miːtɪərə'lɒdʒɪkl/
adj meteorológico. **~ist**
/-'rɒlədʒɪst/ n meteorólogo m. **~y**
/-'rɒlədʒɪ/ n meteorología f

meter /'miːtə(r)/ n contador m,
medidor m (LAm); (Amer) see METRE

method /'meθəd/ n método m.
~ical /mɪ'θɒdɪkl/ adj metódico.
M~ist /'meθədɪst/ adj & n
metodista (m & f)

methylated /'meθɪleɪtɪd/ adj. **~
spirit(s)** n alcohol m
desnaturalizado

meticulous /mɪ'tɪkjʊləs/ adj
meticuloso

metre /'miːtə(r)/ n metro m

metric /'metrɪk/ adj métrico

metropoli|s /mɪ'trɒpəlɪs/ n metrópoli(s) f

mettle /'metl/ n. **be on one's ~** (fig) estar dispuesto a dar lo mejor de sí

mew /mju:/ n maullido m. • vi maullar

Mexic|an /'meksɪkən/ adj & n mejicano (m), mexicano (m). **~o** /-kəʊ/ n Méjico m, México m

miaow /miːˈaʊ/ n & vi see **MEW**

mice /maɪs/ see **MOUSE**

mickey /'mɪkɪ/ n. **take the ~ out of** 🇬🇧 tomar el pelo a

micro... /'maɪkrəʊ/ pref micro...

microbe /'maɪkrəʊb/ n microbio m

micro: ~chip n pastilla f. **~film** n microfilme m. **~light** n aeroligero m. **~phone** n micrófono m. **~processor** /-'prəʊsesə(r)/ n microprocesador m. **~scope** n microscopio m. **~scopic** /-'skɒpɪk/ adj microscópico. **~wave** n microonda f. **~wave oven** n horno m de microondas

mid- /mɪd/ pref. **in ~ air** en pleno aire. **in ~ March** a mediados de marzo

midday /mɪd'deɪ/ n mediodía m

middl|e /'mɪdl/ adj de en medio. • n medio m. **in the ~e of** en medio de. **~e-aged** /-'eɪdʒd/ adj de mediana edad. **M~e Ages** npl Edad f Media. **~e class** n clase f media. **~e-class** adj de la clase media. **M~e East** n Oriente m Medio. **~eman** n intermediario m. **~e name** n segundo nombre m. **~ing** adj regular

midge /mɪdʒ/ n mosquito m

midget /'mɪdʒɪt/ n enano m. • adj minúsculo

Midlands /'mɪdləndz/ npl región f central de Inglaterra

midnight /'mɪdnaɪt/ n medianoche f

midriff /'mɪdrɪf/ n diafragma m

midst /mɪdst/ n. **in our ~** entre nosotros. **in the ~ of** en medio de

midsummer /mɪd'sʌmə(r)/ n pleno verano m; (solstice) solsticio m de verano

midway /mɪd'weɪ/ adv a mitad de camino

Midwest /mɪd'west/ región f central de los EE.UU.

midwife /'mɪdwaɪf/ n comadrona f, partera f

midwinter /mɪd'wɪntə(r)/ n pleno invierno m

might /maɪt/ see **MAY**. • n (strength) fuerza f; (power) poder m. **~y** adj (strong) fuerte; (powerful) poderoso. • adv 🇬🇧 muy

migraine /'miːgreɪn/ n jaqueca f

migra|nt /'maɪgrənt/ adj migratorio. • n (person) emigrante m & f. **~te** /maɪ'greɪt/ vi emigrar. **~tion** /-'greɪʃn/ n migración f

mild /maɪld/ adj (**-er, -est**) (person) afable; (climate) templado; (slight) ligero; (taste, manner) suave

mildew /'mɪldjuː/ n moho m; (on plants) mildeu m, mildiu m

mildly /'maɪldlɪ/ adv (gently) suavemente; (slightly) ligeramente

mile /maɪl/ n milla f. **~s better** 🇬🇧 mucho mejor. **~s too big** 🇬🇧 demasiado grande. **~age** /-ɪdʒ/ n (loosely) kilometraje m. **~ometer** /maɪ'lɒmɪtə(r)/ n (loosely) cuentakilómetros m. **~stone** n mojón m; (event, stage, fig) hito m

militant /'mɪlɪtənt/ adj & n militante (m & f)

military /'mɪlɪtərɪ/ adj militar

militia /mɪ'lɪʃə/ n milicia f

milk /mɪlk/ n leche f. • adj (product) lácteo; (chocolate) con leche. • vt ordeñar (cow). **~man** /-mən/ n lechero m. **~ shake** n batido m, (leche f) malteada f (LAm), licuado m con leche (LAm). **~y** adj lechoso.

M~y Way n Vía f Láctea

mill /mɪl/ n molino m; (for coffee, pepper) molinillo m; (factory) fábrica f de tejidos de algodón. ●vt moler. ■ ~ **about, mill around** vi dar vueltas

millennium /mɪˈlenɪəm/ n (pl -ia /-ɪə/ or -iums) milenio m

miller /ˈmɪlə(r)/ n molinero m

milli... /ˈmɪlɪ/ pref mili...
~gram(me) n miligramo m.
~metre n milímetro m

milliner /ˈmɪlɪnə(r)/ n sombrerero m

million /ˈmɪljən/ n millón m. **a ~ pounds** un millón de libras.
~aire /-ˈeə(r)/ n millonario m

millstone /ˈmɪlstəʊn/ n muela f (de molino); (fig, burden) carga f

mime /maɪm/ n mímica f. ●vt imitar, hacer la mímica de. ●vi hacer la mímica

mimic /ˈmɪmɪk/ vt (pt **mimicked**) imitar. ●n imitador m. **~ry** n imitación f

mince /mɪns/ vt picar, moler (LAm) (meat). **not to ~ matters/words** no andar(se) con rodeos. ●n carne f picada, carne f molida (LAm). **~ pie** n pastelito m de Navidad (pastelito relleno de picadillo de frutos secos). **~r** n máquina f de picar carne, máquina f de moler carne (LAm)

mind /maɪnd/ n mente f; (sanity) juicio m. **to my ~** a mi parecer. **be on one's mind** preocuparle a uno. **make up one's ~** decidirse.●vt (look after) cuidar (de); atender (shop). **~ the steps!** ¡cuidado con las escaleras! **never ~ him** no le hagas caso. **I don't ~ the noise** no me molesta el ruido. **would you ~ closing the door?** ¿le importaría cerrar la puerta? ●vi. **never ~** no importa, no te preocupes. **I don't ~** (don't object) me da igual. **do you ~ if I smoke?** ¿le importa si fumo? **~ful** adj atento (**of** a). **~less** adj (activity) mecánico; (violence) ciego

mine¹ /maɪn/ poss pron (sing) mío, mía; (pl) míos, mías. **it is ~** es mío. **~ are blue** los míos/las mías son azules. **a friend of ~** un amigo mío/una amiga mía

mine² /maɪn/ n mina f; (Mil) mina f. ●vt extraer. **~field** n campo m de minas. **~r** n minero m

mineral /ˈmɪnərəl/ adj & n mineral (m). **~ water** n agua f mineral

mingle /ˈmɪŋɡl/ vi mezclarse

mini... /ˈmɪnɪ/ pref mini...

miniature /ˈmɪnɪtʃə(r)/ n miniatura f. ●adj en miniatura

mini: ~bus n microbús m. **~cab** n taxi m (que se pide por teléfono)

minim|al /ˈmɪnɪml/ adj mínimo.
~ize vt reducir al mínimo. **~um** /-məm/ adj & n (pl -ima /-mə/) mínimo (m)

mining /ˈmaɪnɪŋ/ n minería f. ●adj minero

miniskirt /ˈmɪnɪskɜːt/ n minifalda f

minist|er /ˈmɪnɪstə(r)/ n ministro m, secretario m (Mex); (Relig) pastor m. **~erial** /-ˈstɪərɪəl/ adj ministerial. **~ry** n ministerio m, secretaría f (Mex)

mink /mɪŋk/ n visón m

minor /ˈmaɪnə(r)/ adj (also Mus) menor; (injury) leve; (change) pequeño; (operation) de poca importancia. ●n menor m & f de edad. **~ity** /maɪˈnɒrətɪ/ n minoría f. ●adj minoritario

minstrel /ˈmɪnstrəl/ n juglar m

mint /mɪnt/ n (plant) menta f; (sweet) pastilla f de menta; (Finance) casa f de la moneda. **in ~ condition** como nuevo. ●vt acuñar

minus /ˈmaɪnəs/ prep menos; (fam, without) sin. ●n (sign) menos m. **five ~ three is two** cinco menos tres is igual a dos. **~ sign** n (signo m de) menos m

minute¹ /ˈmɪnɪt/ n minuto m. **the ~s** npl (of meeting) el acta f

minute² /maɪˈnjuːt/ adj diminuto;

(detailed) minucioso

mirac|le /'mɪrəkl/ n milagro m.
~ulous /mɪ'rækjʊləs/ adj
milagroso

mirage /'mɪrɑːʒ/ n espejismo m

mirror /'mɪrə(r)/ n espejo m; (driving
~) (espejo m) retrovisor m. ●vt
reflejar

mirth /mɜːθ/ n regocijo m; (laughter)
risas fpl

misapprehension
/ˌmɪsæprɪ'henʃn/ n malentendido m

misbehav|e /ˌmɪsbɪ'heɪv/ vi
portarse mal. **~iour** n mala
conducta

miscalculat|e /ˌmɪs'kælkjʊleɪt/ vt/i
calcular mal. **~ion** /-'leɪʃn/ n error
m de cálculo

miscarr|iage /'mɪskærɪdʒ/ n
aborto m espontáneo. **~iage of
justice** n injusticia f. **~y** vi abortar

miscellaneous /ˌmɪsə'leɪnɪəs/ adj
heterogéneo

mischie|f /'mɪstʃɪf/ n (foolish conduct)
travesura f; (harm) daño m. **get
into ~** hacer travesuras. **make
~f** causar daños. **~vous**
/'mɪstʃɪvəs/ adj travieso; (grin)
pícaro

misconception /ˌmɪskən'sepʃn/ n
equivocación f

misconduct /mɪs'kɒndʌkt/ n mala
conducta f

misdeed /mɪs'diːd/ n fechoría f

misdemeanour /ˌmɪsdɪ'miːnə(r)/ n
delito m menor, falta f

miser /'maɪzə(r)/ n avaro m

miserable /'mɪzərəbl/ adj (sad)
triste; (in low spirits) abatido;
(wretched, poor) mísero; (weather)
pésimo

miserly /'maɪzəlɪ/ adj avariento

misery /'mɪzərɪ/ n (unhappiness)
tristeza f; (pain) sufrimiento m

misfire /mɪs'faɪə(r)/ vi fallar

misfit /'mɪsfɪt/ n inadaptado m

misfortune /mɪs'fɔːtʃuːn/ n
desgracia f

misgiving /mɪs'gɪvɪŋ/ n recelo m

misguided /mɪs'gaɪdɪd/ adj
equivocado

mishap /'mɪshæp/ n percance m

misinform /ˌmɪsɪn'fɔːm/ vt
informar mal

misinterpret /ˌmɪsɪn'tɜːprɪt/ vt
interpretar mal

misjudge /mɪs'dʒʌdʒ/ vt juzgar
mal; (miscalculate) calcular mal

mislay /mɪs'leɪ/ vt (pt **mislaid**)
extraviar, perder

mislead /mɪs'liːd/ vt (pt **misled**
/mɪs'led/) engañar. **~ing** adj
engañoso

mismanage /mɪs'mænɪdʒ/ vt
administrar mal. **~ment** n mala
administración f

misplace /mɪs'pleɪs/ vt (lose)
extraviar, perder

misprint /'mɪsprɪnt/ n errata f

miss /mɪs/ vt (fail to hit) no dar en;
(regret absence of) echar de menos,
extrañar (LAm); perder (train, party);
perder (chance). **~ the point** no
comprender. ●vi errar el tiro,
fallar; (bullet) no dar en el blanco.
●n fallo m, falla f (LAm); (title)
señorita f. ■**~ out** vt saltarse
(line). **~out on sth** perderse algo

misshapen /mɪs'ʃeɪpən/ adj
deforme

missile /'mɪsaɪl/ n (Mil) misil m

missing /'mɪsɪŋ/ adj (lost) perdido.
be ~ faltar. **go ~** desaparecer. **~
person** desaparecido m

mission /'mɪʃn/ n misión f. **~ary**
/'mɪʃənərɪ/ n misionero m

mist /mɪst/ n neblina f; (at sea)
bruma f. ■**~ up** vi empañarse

mistake /mɪ'steɪk/ n error m. **make
a ~** cometer un error. **by ~** por
error. ●vt (pt **mistook**, pp **mistaken**)
confundir. **~ for** confundir con.
~n /-ən/ adj equivocado. **be ~n**
equivocarse

mistletoe /'mɪsltəʊ/ n muérdago m

mistreat /mɪs'triːt/ vt maltratar

mistress /'mɪstrɪs/ n (of house) señora f; (lover) amante f

mistrust /mɪs'trʌst/ vt desconfiar de. ●n desconfianza f. **~ful** adj desconfiado

misty /'mɪstɪ/ adj (**-ier, -iest**) neblinoso; (day) de neblina. **it's ~** hay neblina

misunderstand /mɪsʌndə'stænd/ vt (pt **-stood**) entender mal. **~ing** n malentendido m

misuse /mɪs'juːz/ vt emplear mal; malversar (funds). ●/mɪs'juːs/ n mal uso m; (unfair use) abuso m; (of funds) malversación f

mite /maɪt/ n (insect) ácaro m

mitten /'mɪtn/ n mitón m

mix /mɪks/ vt mezclar. ●vi mezclarse; (go together) combinar. **~ with** tratarse con (people). ●n mezcla f. ■ **~ up** vt mezclar; (confuse) confundir. **~ed** adj (school etc) mixto; (assorted) mezclado. **be ~ed up** estar confuso. **~er** n (Culin) batidora f; (TV, machine) mezcladora f. **~ture** /'mɪkstʃə(r)/ n mezcla f. **~-up** n lío m

moan /məʊn/ n gemido m. ●vi gemir; (complain) quejarse (**about** de)

moat /məʊt/ n foso m

mob /mɒb/ n turba f. ●vt (pt **mobbed**) acosar

mobil|e /'məʊbaɪl/ adj móvil. **~e home** n caravana f fija, trailer m (LAm). **~e (phone)** n (teléfono m) móvil m, (teléfono m) celular m (LAm). ●n móvil m. **~ize** /'məʊbɪlaɪz/ vt movilizar. ●vi movilizarse

mock /mɒk/ vt burlarse de. ●adj (anger) fingido; (exam) de práctica. **~ery** /'mɒkərɪ/ n burla f. **make a ~ery of sth** ridiculizar algo

model /'mɒdl/ n (example) modelo m; (mock-up) maqueta f; (person) modelo m. ●adj (exemplary) modelo;

(car etc) en miniatura. ●vt (pt **modelled**) modelar. **~ s.o. on s.o.** tomar a uno como modelo

modem /'məʊdem/ n (Comp) módem m

moderat|e /'mɒdərət/ adj & n moderado (m). ●/'mɒdəreɪt/ vt moderar. **~ely** /'mɒdərətlɪ/ adv (fairly) medianamente. **~ion** /-'reɪʃn/ n moderación f. **in ~ion** con moderación

modern /'mɒdn/ adj moderno. **~ize** vt modernizar

modest /'mɒdɪst/ adj modesto. **~y** n modestia f

modif|ication /mɒdɪfɪ'keɪʃn/ n modificación f. **~y** /-faɪ/ vt modificar

module /'mɒdjuːl/ n módulo m

moist /mɔɪst/ adj (**-er, -est**) húmedo. **~en** /'mɔɪsn/ vt humedecer

moistur|e /'mɔɪstʃə(r)/ n humedad f. **~ize** vt hidratar. **~izer**, **~izing cream** n crema f hidratante

mole /məʊl/ n (animal) topo m; (on skin) lunar m

molecule /'mɒlɪkjuːl/ n molécula f

molest /mə'lest/ vt abusar (sexualmente) de

mollify /'mɒlɪfaɪ/ vt aplacar

mollusc /'mɒləsk/ n molusco m

mollycoddle /'mɒlɪkɒdl/ vt mimar

molten /'məʊltən/ adj fundido; (lava) líquido

mom /mɒm/ n (Amer, 🔲) mamá f 🔲

moment /'məʊmənt/ n momento m. **at the ~** en este momento. **for the ~** de momento. **~ary** /'məʊməntərɪ/ adj momentáneo

momentous /mə'mentəs/ adj trascendental

momentum /mə'mentəm/ n momento m; (speed) velocidad f

mommy /'mɒmɪ/ n (Amer, fam) mamá m 🔲

monarch /'mɒnək/ n monarca m.

~y n monarquía f

monastery /'mɒnəstərɪ/ n
monasterio m

Monday /'mʌndeɪ/ n lunes m

money /'mʌnɪ/ n dinero m, plata f
(LAm). ~**box** n hucha f, alcancía f
(LAm). ~ **order** n giro m postal

mongrel /'mʌŋɡrəl/ n perro m
mestizo, chucho m 🔲

monitor /'mɒnɪtə(r)/ n (Tec)
monitor m. •vt observar (elections);
seguir (progress); (electronically)
monitorizar, escuchar

monk /mʌŋk/ n monje m. ~**fish** n
rape m

monkey /'mʌŋkɪ/ n mono m.
~-**nut** n cacahuete m, cacahuate m
(Mex), maní m (LAm). ~**wrench** n
llave f inglesa

mono /'mɒnəʊ/ n monofonía f

monologue /'mɒnəlɒɡ/ n
monólogo m

monopol|ize /mə'nɒpəlaɪz/ vt
monopolizar; acaparar (conversation).
~y n monopolio m

monoton|e /'mɒnətəʊn/ n tono m
monocorde. ~**ous** /mə'nɒtənəs/ adj
monótono. ~y n monotonía f

monsoon /mɒn'suːn/ n monzón m

monst|er /'mɒnstə(r)/ n monstruo
m. ~**rous** /-strəs/ adj monstruoso

month /mʌnθ/ n mes m. **£200 a** ~
200 libras mensuales or al mes.
~**ly** adj mensual. ~**ly payment**
mensualidad f, cuota f mensual
(LAm). •adv mensualmente

monument /'mɒnjʊmənt/ n
monumento m. ~**al** /-'mentl/ adj
monumental

moo /muː/ n mugido m. •vi mugir

mood /muːd/ n humor m. **be in a
good/bad** ~ estar de buen/mal
humor. ~y adj (-**ier, -iest**)
temperamental; (bad-tempered)
malhumorado

moon /muːn/ n luna f. ~**light** n luz
f de la luna. ~**lighting** n
pluriempleo m. ~**lit** adj iluminado
por la luna; (night) de luna

moor /mʊə(r)/ n páramo m; (of
heather) brezal m. •vt amarrar.
~**ing** n (place) amarradero m.
~**ings** npl (ropes) amarras fpl

moose /muːs/ n invar alce m
americano

mop /mɒp/ n fregona f, trapeador m
(LAm). ~ **of hair** pelambrera f. •vt
(pt **mopped**). ~ (**up**) limpiar

mope /məʊp/ vi estar abatido

moped /'məʊped/ n ciclomotor m

moral /'mɒrəl/ adj moral. •n (of tale)
moraleja f

morale /mə'rɑːl/ n moral f

moral|ity /mə'rælətɪ/ n moralidad
f. ~**ly** adv moralmente. ~**s** npl
moralidad f

morbid /'mɔːbɪd/ adj morboso

more /mɔː(r)/ adj más. **two** ~
bottles dos botellas más. •pron
más. **you ate** ~ **than me** comiste
más que yo. **some** ~ más. ~
than six más de seis. **the** ~ **he
has, the** ~ **he wants** cuánto más
tiene, más quiere. • adv más. ~
and ~ cada vez más. ~ **or less**
más o menos. **once** ~ una vez
más. **she doesn't live here any**
~ ya no vive aquí. ~**over**
/mɔː'rəʊvə(r)/ adv además

morgue /mɔːɡ/ n depósito m de
cadáveres, morgue f (LAm)

morning /'mɔːnɪŋ/ n mañana f;
(early hours) madrugada f. **at 11
o'clock in the** ~ a las once de la
mañana. **in the** ~ por la mañana,
en la mañana (LAm). **tomorrow/
yesterday** ~ mañana/ayer por la
mañana or (LAm) en la mañana.
(**good**) ~! ¡buenos días!

Morocc|an /mə'rɒkən/ adj & n
marroquí (m & f). ~**o** /-kəʊ/ n
Marruecos m

moron /'mɔːrɒn/ n imbécil m & f

morose /mə'rəʊs/ adj taciturno

Morse /mɔːs/ n Morse m. **in** ~
(**code**) n en (código) morse

morsel /'mɔːsl/ n bocado m

mortal /'mɔːtl/ adj & n mortal (m). ~ity /-'tælətɪ/ n mortalidad f

mortar /'mɔːtə(r)/ n (all senses) mortero m

mortgage /'mɔːgɪdʒ/ n hipoteca f. • vt hipotecar

mortify /'mɔːtɪfaɪ/ vt darle mucha vergüenza a

mortuary /'mɔːtjʊərɪ/ n depósito m de cadáveres, morgue f (LAm)

mosaic /məʊ'zeɪk/ n mosaico m

mosque /mɒsk/ n mezquita f

mosquito /mɒs'kiːtəʊ/ n (pl -oes) mosquito m, zancudo m (LAm)

moss /mɒs/ n musgo m

most /məʊst/ adj la mayoría de, la mayor parte de. ~ **days** casi todos los días. • pron la mayoría, la mayor parte. **at** ~ como máximo. **make the** ~ **of** aprovechar al máximo. • adv más; (very) muy; (Amer, almost) casi. ~**ly** adv principalmente

MOT n. ~ **(test)** ITV f, inspección f técnica de vehículos

motel /məʊ'tel/ n motel m

moth /mɒθ/ n mariposa f de la luz, palomilla f; (in clothes) polilla f

mother /'mʌðə(r)/ n madre f. • vt mimar. ~-**in-law** n (pl ~**s-in-law**) suegra f. ~**land** n patria f. ~**ly** adj maternal. ~-**of-pearl** n nácar m, madreperla f. **M**~**'s Day** n el día m de la Madre. ~-**to-be** n futura madre f. ~ **tongue** n lengua f materna

motif /məʊ'tiːf/ n motivo m

motion /'məʊʃn/ n movimiento m; (proposal) moción f. **put** or **set in** ~ poner algo en marcha. • vt/i. ~ **(to) s.o. to** hacerle señas a uno para que. ~**less** adj inmóvil

motiv|ate /'məʊtɪveɪt/ vt motivar. ~**ation** /-'veɪʃn/ n motivación f. ~**e** /'məʊtɪv/ n motivo m

motley /'mɒtlɪ/ adj variopinto

motor /'məʊtə(r)/ n motor m. • adj motor; (fem) motora, motriz. ~

bike n 🅃 motocicleta f, moto f 🅃. ~ **boat** n lancha f a motor. ~ **car** n automóvil m. ~ **cycle** n motocicleta f. ~**cyclist** n motociclista m & f. ~**ing** n automovilismo m. ~**ist** n automovilista m & f. ~**way** n autopista f

motto /'mɒtəʊ/ n (pl -oes) lema m

mould /məʊld/ n molde m; (fungus) moho m. • vt moldear; formar (character). ~**ing** n (on wall etc) moldura f. ~**y** adj mohoso

moult /məʊlt/ vi mudar de pelo/ piel/plumas

mound /maʊnd/ n montículo m; (pile, fig) montón m

mount /maʊnt/ vt montar (horse); engarzar (gem); preparar (attack). • vi subir, crecer. • n. montura f; (mountain) monte m. ■ ~ **up** vi irse acumulando

mountain /'maʊntɪn/ n montaña f. ~**eer** /maʊntɪ'nɪə(r)/ n alpinista m & f. ~**eering** n alpinismo m. ~**ous** adj montañoso

mourn /mɔːn/ vt llorar. • vi lamentarse. ~ **for s.o.** llorar a uno. ~**er** n doliente m & f. ~**ful** adj triste. ~**ing** n duelo m, luto m. **be in** ~**Ing** estar de duelo

mouse /maʊs/ n (pl **mice**) ratón m. ~**trap** n ratonera f

mousse /muːs/ n (Culin) mousse f or m; (for hair) mousse f

moustache /mə'stɑːʃ/ n bigote m

mouth /maʊθ/ n boca f; (of cave) entrada f; (of river) desembocadura f. ~**ful** n bocado m. ~**organ** n armónica f. ~**wash** n enjuague m bucal

move /muːv/ vt mover; (relocate) trasladar; (with emotion) conmover; (propose) proponer. ~ **the television** cambiar de lugar la televisión. ~ **house** mudarse de casa. • vi moverse; (be in motion) estar en movimiento; (take action) tomar medidas. • n movimiento m; (in game) jugada f; (player's turn)

turno m; (removal) mudanza f. ■ ~
away vi alejarse. ■ ~ **in** vi
instalarse. ~ **in with s.o.** irse a
vivir con uno. ■ ~ **over** vi
correrse. ~**ment** n movimiento m

movie /'mu:vɪ/ n (Amer) película f.
the ~s npl el cine. ~ **camera** n
(Amer) tomavistas m, filmadora f
(LAm)

moving /'mu:vɪŋ/ adj en
movimiento; (touching) conmovedor

mow /məʊ/ vt (pt mowed or mown
/məʊn/) cortar (lawn); segar (hay).
■ ~ **down** vt acribillar. ~**er** n (for
lawn) cortacésped m

MP abbr see **MEMBER OF PARLIAMENT**

Mr /'mɪstə(r)/ abbr (pl Messrs) (=
Mister) Sr. ~ **Coldbeck** Sr.
Coldbeck

Mrs /'mɪsɪz/ abbr (pl Mrs) (= Missis)
Sra. ~ **Andrews** Sra. Andrews

Ms /mɪz/ abbr (title of married or
unmarried woman)

MSc abbr see **MASTER**

much /mʌtʃ/ adj & pron mucho,
mucha ● adv mucho; (before pp)
muy. ● ~ **as** por mucho que. **the
same** más o menos lo mismo.
how ~? ¿cuánto?. **so ~** tanto.
too ~ demasiado

muck /mʌk/ n estiércol m; (fam, dirt)
mugre f. ■ ~ **about** vi 🇬🇧 tontear

mud /mʌd/ n barro m, lodo m

muddle /'mʌdl/ vt embrollar. ● n
desorden m; (mix-up) lío m. ■ ~
through vi salir del paso

muddy adj lodoso; (hands etc)
cubierto de lodo. ~**guard** n
guardabarros m, salpicadera f (Mex)

muffle /'mʌfl/ vt amortiguar
(sound). ~**r** n (scarf) bufanda f;
(Amer, Auto) silenciador m

mug /mʌg/ n taza f (alta y sin platillo),
tarro m (Mex); (for beer) jarra f; (fam,
face) cara f, jeta f 🇬🇧; (fam, fool)
idiota m & f. ● vt (pt mugged)
asaltar. ~**ger** n asaltante m & f.
~**ging** n asalto m

muggy /'mʌgɪ/ adj bochornoso

mule /mju:l/ n mula f

mull /mʌl/ (Amer), ~ **over** vt
reflexionar sobre

multi|coloured /mʌltɪ'kʌləd/ adj
multicolor. ~**national** /-'næʃənl/
adj & n multinacional (f)

multipl|e /'mʌltɪpl/ adj múltiple. ● n
múltiplo m. ~**ication**
/mʌltɪplɪ'keɪʃn/ n multiplicación f.
~**y** /'mʌltɪplaɪ/ vt multiplicar. ● vi
(Math) multiplicar; (increase)
multiplicarse

multitude /'mʌltɪtjuːd/ n **a ~ of
problems** múltiples problemas

mum /mʌm/ n 🇬🇧 mamá f 🇬🇧

mumble /'mʌmbl/ vt mascullar. ● vi
hablar entre dientes

mummy /'mʌmɪ/ n (fam, mother)
mamá f 🇬🇧; (archaeology) momia f

mumps /mʌmps/ n paperas fpl

munch /mʌntʃ/ vt/i mascar

mundane /mʌn'deɪn/ adj mundano

municipal /mju:'nɪsɪpl/ adj
municipal

mural /'mjʊərəl/ adj & n mural (f)

murder /'mɜːdə(r)/ n asesinato m.
● vt asesinar. ~**er** n asesino m

murky /'mɜːkɪ/ adj (-ier, -iest)
turbio

murmur /'mɜːmə(r)/ n murmullo m.
● vt/i murmurar

musc|le /'mʌsl/ n músculo m.
~**ular** /'mʌskjʊlə(r)/ adj muscular;
(arm, body) musculoso

muse /mju:z/ vi meditar (**on** sobre)

museum /mju:'zɪəm/ n museo m

mush /mʌʃ/ n papilla f

mushroom /'mʌʃrʊm/ n
champiñón m; (in botany) seta f. ● vi
aparecer como hongos

mushy /'mʌʃɪ/ adj blando

music /'mju:zɪk/ n música f. ~**al** adj
musical. **be ~** tener sentido
musical. ● n musical m. ~**ian**
/mju:'zɪʃn/ n músico m

Muslim /'mʊzlɪm/ adj & n
musulmán (m)

m

mussel /'mʌsl/ n mejillón m

must /mʌst/ modal verb deber, tener que; (expressing supposition) deber (de). **he ~ be old** debe (de) ser viejo. **I ~ have done it** debo (de) haberlo hecho. ●n. **be a ~** ser imprescindible

mustache /mʌstæʃ/ n (Amer) bigote m

mustard /'mʌstəd/ n mostaza f

muster /'mʌstə(r)/ vt reunir

musty /'mʌsti/ adj (-ier, -iest) que huele a humedad

mutation /mju:'teɪʃn/ n mutación f

mute /mju:t/ adj mudo

mutilate /'mju:tɪleɪt/ vt mutilar

mutiny /'mju:tɪnɪ/ n motín m. ●vi amotinarse

mutter /'mʌtə(r)/ vt/i murmurar

mutton /'mʌtn/ n carne f de ovino

mutual /'mju:tʃʊəl/ adj mutuo; (fam, common) común

muzzle /'mʌzl/ n (snout) hocico m; (device) bozal m

my /maɪ/ adj (sing) mi; (pl) mis

myself /maɪ'self/ pron (reflexive) me; (used for emphasis) yo mismo m, yo misma f. **I cut ~** me corté. **I made it ~** lo hice yo mismo/misma. **I was by ~** estaba solo/sola

myster|ious /mɪ'stɪərɪəs/ adj misterioso. **~y** /'mɪstərɪ/ n misterio m

mystical /'mɪstɪkl/ adj místico

mystify /'mɪstɪfaɪ/ vt dejar perplejo

mystique /mɪ'sti:k/ n mística f

myth /mɪθ/ n mito m. **~ical** adj mítico. **~ology** /mɪ'θɒlədʒɪ/ n mitología f

Nn

N abbr (= **north**) N

nab /næb/ vt (pt **nabbed**) (sl, arrest) pescar; (snatch) agarrar

nag /næg/ vt (pt **nagged**) fastidiar; (scold) estarle encima a. ●vi criticar

nail /neɪl/ n clavo m; (of finger, toe) uña f. **~ polish** esmalte m para las uñas. ●vt. **~ (down)** clavar

naive /naɪ'i:v/ adj ingenuo

naked /'neɪkɪd/ adj desnudo. **to the ~ eye** a simple vista

name /neɪm/ n nombre m; (of book, film) título m; (fig) fama f. **my ~ is Chris** me llamo Chris. **good ~** buena reputación. ●vt ponerle nombre a; (appoint) nombrar. **a man ~d Jones** un hombre llamado Jones. **she was ~d after** or (Amer) **for her grandmother** le pusieron el nombre de su abuela.

~less adj anónimo. **~ly** adv a saber. **~sake** n (person) tocayo m

nanny /'nænɪ/ n niñera f

nap /næp/ n (sleep) sueñecito m; (after lunch) siesta f. **have a ~** echarse un sueño

napkin /'næpkɪn/ n servilleta f

nappy /'næpɪ/ n pañal m

narcotic /nɑ:'kɒtɪk/ adj & n narcótico (m)

narrat|e /nə'reɪt/ vt narrar. **~ive** /'nærətɪv/ n narración f. **~or** /nə'reɪtə(r)/ n narrador m

narrow /'nærəʊ/ adj (-er, -est) estrecho, angosto (LAm). **have a ~ escape** salvarse de milagro. ●vt estrechar; (limit) limitar. ●vi estrecharse. **~ly** adv (just) por poco. ~-minded /-'maɪndɪd/ adj de miras estrechas

nasal /'neɪzl/ adj nasal; (voice) gangoso

nasty /'nɑːstɪ/ adj (**-ier, -iest**) desagradable; (spiteful) malo (**to** con); (taste, smell) asqueroso; (cut) feo

nation /'neɪʃn/ n nación f

national /'næʃənl/ adj nacional. ●n ciudadano m. ~ **anthem** n himno m nacional. ~**ism** n nacionalismo m. ~**ity** /næʃə'nælətɪ/ n nacionalidad f. ~**ize** vt nacionalizar. ~**ly** adv a escala nacional

nationwide /'neɪʃnwaɪd/ adj & adv a escala nacional

native /'neɪtɪv/ n natural m & f. **be a ~ of** ser natural de. ●adj nativo; (country, town) natal; (language) materno; (plant, animal) autóctono. **N~ American** indio m americano

nativity /nə'tɪvətɪ/ n. **the N~** la Natividad f

NATO /'neɪtəʊ/ abbr (= **North Atlantic Treaty Organization**) OTAN f

natter /'nætə(r)/ 🔲 vi charlar. ●n charla f

natural /'nætʃərəl/ adj natural. ~ **history** n historia f natural. ~**ist** n naturalista m & f. ~**ized** adj (citizen) naturalizado. ~**ly** adv (of course) naturalmente; (by nature) por naturaleza

nature /'neɪtʃə(r)/ n naturaleza f; (of person) carácter m; (of things) naturaleza f

naught /nɔːt/ n cero m

naughty /'nɔːtɪ/ adj (**-ier, -iest**) malo, travieso

nausea|a /'nɔːzɪə/ n náuseas fpl. ~**ous** /-ɪəs/ adj nauseabundo

nautical /'nɔːtɪkl/ adj náutico. ~ **mile** n milla f marina

naval /'neɪvl/ adj naval; (officer) de marina

nave /neɪv/ n nave f

navel /'neɪvl/ n ombligo m

naviga|ble /'nævɪgəbl/ adj navegable. ~**te** /'nævɪgeɪt/ vt navegar por (sea etc); gobernar (ship). ●vi navegar. ~**tion** /-'geɪʃn/ n navegación f. ~**tor** n oficial m & f de derrota

navy /'neɪvɪ/ n marina f de guerra. ~ **(blue)** adj & n azul (m) marino

NE abbr (= **north-east**) NE

near /'nɪə(r)/ adv cerca. **draw ~** acercarse. ●prep. ~ **(to)** cerca de. **go ~ (to) sth** acercarse a algo. ●adj cercano. ●vt acercarse a. ~**by** adj cercano. ~**ly** adv casi. **he ~ly died** por poco se muere, casi se muere. **not ~ly** ni con mucho. ~**sighted** /-'saɪtɪd/ adj miope, corto de vista

neat /niːt/ adj (**-er, -est**) (person) pulcro; (room etc) bien arreglado; (ingenious) hábil; (whisky, gin) solo; ; (Amer fam, great) fantástico 🔲. ~**ly** adv pulcramente; (organized) cuidadosamente

necessar|ily /nesə'serɪlɪ/ adv necesariamente. ~**y** /'nesəserɪ/ adj necesario

necessit|ate /nə'sesɪteɪt/ vt exigir. ~**y** /nɪ'sesətɪ/ n necesidad f. **the bare ~ies** lo indispensable

neck /nek/ n (of person, bottle, dress) cuello m; (of animal) pescuezo m. ~ **and ~** a la par, parejos (LAm). ~**lace** /'nekləs/ n collar m. ~**line** n escote m

nectar /'nektə(r)/ n néctar m

nectarine /'nektərɪn/ n nectarina f

née /neɪ/ adj de soltera

need /niːd/ n necesidad f (**for** de). ●vt necesitar; (demand) exigir. **you ~ not speak** no tienes que hablar

needle /'niːdl/ n aguja f. ●vt (fam, annoy) pinchar

needless /'niːdlɪs/ adj innecesario

needlework /'niːdlwɜːk/ n labores fpl de aguja; (embroidery) bordado m

needy /'ni:dɪ/ adj (-ier, -iest) necesitado

negative /'negatɪv/ adj negativo. •n (of photograph) negativo m; (no) negativa f

neglect /nɪ'glekt/ vt descuidar (house); desatender (children); no cumplir con (duty). •n negligencia f. **(state of)** ~ abandono m. ~**ful** adj negligente

neglig|ence /'neglɪdʒəns/ n negligencia f, descuido m. ~**ent** adj negligente. ~**ible** /'neglɪdʒəbl/ adj insignificante

negotia|ble /nɪ'gəʊʃəbl/ adj negociable. ~**te** /nɪ'gəʊʃɪeɪt/ vt/i negociar. ~**tion** /-'eɪʃn/ n negociación f. ~**tor** n negociador m

neigh /neɪ/ vi relinchar

neighbour /'neɪbə(r)/ n vecino m. ~**hood** n vecindad f, barrio m. **in the** ~**hood of** alrededor de. ~**ing** adj vecino

neither /'naɪðə(r)/ adj. ~ **book** ninguno de los libros. •pron ninguno, -na. •conj. **neither...nor** ni...ni. ~ **do I** yo tampoco

neon /'ni:ɒn/ n neón m. •adj (lamp etc) de neón

nephew /'nevju:/ n sobrino m

Neptune /'neptju:n/ n Neptuno m

nerv|e /nɜ:v/ n nervio m; (courage) valor m; (calm) sangre f fría; (fam, impudence) descaro m. ~**es** npl (before exams etc) nervios mpl. **get on s.o.'s** ~**es** ponerle los nervios de punta a uno. ~**e-racking** adj exasperante. ~**ous** /'nɜ:vəs/ adj nervioso. **be/feel** ~**ous** estar nervioso. ~**ousness** n nerviosismo m. ~**y** /'nɜ:vɪ/ adj nervioso; (Amer fam) descarado

nest /nest/ n nido m. •vi anidar

nestle /'nesl/ vi acurrucarse

net /net/ n red f. **the N**~ (Comp) la Red. •vt (pt **netted**) pescar (con red) (fish). •adj neto. ~**ball** n especie de baloncesto

Netherlands /'neðələndz/ npl. **the** ~ los Países Bajos

netting /'netɪŋ/ n redes fpl. **wire** ~ tela f metálica

nettle /'netl/ n ortiga f

network /'netwɜ:k/ n red f; (TV) cadena f

neuro|sis /njʊə'rəʊsɪs/ n (pl **-oses** /-si:z/) neurosis f. ~**tic** /-'rɒtɪk/ adj & n neurótico (m)

neuter /'nju:tə(r)/ adj & n neutro (m). •vt castrar (animals)

neutral /'nju:trəl/ adj neutral; (colour) neutro; (Elec) neutro. ~ **(gear)** (Auto) punto m muerto. ~**ize** vt neutralizar

neutron /'nju:trɒn/ n neutrón m

never /'nevə(r)/ adv nunca; (more emphatic) jamás; (fam, not) no. ~ **again** nunca más. **he** ~ **smiles** no sonríe nunca, nunca sonríe. **I** ~ **saw him** 🛈 no lo vi. ~**-ending** adj interminable. ~**theless** /-ðə'les/ adv sin embargo, no obstante

new /nju:/ adj (-er, -est) nuevo. ~**born** adj recién nacido. ~**comer** n recién llegado m. ~**fangled** /-'fæŋgld/ adj (pej) moderno. ~**ly** adv recién. ~**ly-weds** npl recién casados mpl

news /nju:z/ n. **a piece of** ~ una noticia. **good/bad** ~ buenas/malas noticias. **the** ~ (TV, Radio) las noticias. ~**agent** n vendedor m de periódicos. ~**caster** n locutor m. ~**dealer** n (Amer) see ~**AGENT**. ~**flash** n información f de última hora. ~**letter** n boletín m, informativo m. ~**paper** n periódico m, diario m. ~**reader** n locutor m

newt /nju:t/ n tritón m

New Year /nju:'jɪə(r)/ n Año m Nuevo. **N**~**'s Day** n día m de Año Nuevo. **N**~**'s Eve** n noche f vieja, noche f de fin de Año

New Zealand /nju:'zi:lənd/ n Nueva Zeland(i)a f

next /nekst/ adj próximo; (week,

month etc) que viene, próximo;
(adjoining) vecino; (following)
siguiente. ● adv luego, después. ~
to al lado de. **when you see me
~** la próxima vez que me veas. ~
to nothing casi nada. ~ **door** al
lado (**to** de). ~**-door** adj de al
lado. ~ **of kin** n familiar(es) m(pl)
más cercano(s)

nib /nɪb/ n plumilla f

nibble /ˈnɪbl/ vt/i mordisquear. ● n
mordisco m

Nicaragua /nɪkəˈræɡjʊə/ n
Nicaragua f. ~**n** adj & n
nicaragüense (m & f)

nice /naɪs/ adj (-er, -est) agradable;
(likeable) simpático; (kind) amable;
(weather, food) bueno. **we had a ~
time** lo pasamos bien. ~**ly** adv
(kindly) amablemente; (politely) con
buenos modales

niche /nɪtʃ, niːʃ/ n nicho m

nick /nɪk/ n corte m pequeño. **in
the ~ of time** justo a tiempo. ● vt
(sl, steal) afanar 🇬🇧

nickel /ˈnɪkl/ n (metal) níquel m;
(Amer) moneda f de cinco centavos

nickname /ˈnɪkneɪm/ n apodo m.
● vt apodar

nicotine /ˈnɪkətiːn/ n nicotina f

niece /niːs/ n sobrina f

niggling /ˈnɪɡlɪŋ/ adj (doubt)
constante

night /naɪt/ n noche f; (evening)
tarde f. **at ~** por la noche, de
noche. **good ~** ¡buenas noches!
● adj nocturno, de noche. ~**cap** n
(drink) bebida f (tomada antes de
acostarse). ~**club** n club m
nocturno. ~**dress** n camisón m.
~**fall** n anochecer m. ~**gown**,
~**ie** /ˈnaɪtɪ/ 🇬🇧 n camisón m. ~**life**
n vida f nocturna. ~**ly** adj de todas
las noches. ~**mare** n pesadilla f. ~
school n escuela f nocturna.
~**-time** n noche f. ~**watchman** n
sereno m

nil /nɪl/ n nada f; (Sport) cero m

nimble /ˈnɪmbl/ adj (-er, -est) ágil

nine /naɪn/ adj & n nueve (m).
~**teen** /naɪnˈtiːn/ adj & n
diecinueve (m). ~**teenth** adj
decimonoveno. ● n diecinueveavo
m. ~**tieth** /ˈnaɪntɪəθ/ adj
nonagésimo. ● n noventavo m. ~**ty**
adj & n noventa (m)

ninth /ˈnaɪnθ/ adj & n noveno (m)

nip /nɪp/ vt (pt **nipped**) (pinch)
pellizcar; (bite) mordisquear. ● vi
(fam, rush) correr

nipple /ˈnɪpl/ n (of woman) pezón m;
(of man) tetilla f; (of baby's bottle)
tetina f, chupón m (Mex)

nippy /ˈnɪpɪ/ adj (-ier, -iest) (fam,
chilly) fresquito

nitrogen /ˈnaɪtrədʒən/ n
nitrógeno m

no /nəʊ/ adj ninguno, (before masculine
singular noun) ningún. **I have ~
money** no tengo dinero. **there's
~ food left** no queda nada de
comida. **it has ~ windows** no
tiene ventanas. **I'm ~ expert** no
soy ningún experto. ~ **smoking**
prohibido fumar. ~ **way!** 🇺🇸 ¡ni
hablar! ● adv & int no. ● n (pl **noes**)
no m

noble /ˈnəʊbl/ adj (-er, -est) noble.
~**man** /-mən/ n noble m

nobody /ˈnəʊbədɪ/ pron nadie.
there's ~ there no hay nadie

nocturnal /nɒkˈtɜːnl/ adj nocturno

nod /nɒd/ vt (pt **nodded**). ~ **one's
head** asentir con la cabeza. ● vi (in
agreement) asentir con la cabeza; (in
greeting) saludar con la cabeza. ■ ~
off vi dormirse

nois|e /nɔɪz/ n ruido m. ~**ily** adv
ruidosamente. ~**y** adj (-ier, -iest)
ruidoso. **it's too ~y here** hay
demasiado ruido aquí

nomad /ˈnəʊmæd/ n nómada m & f.
~**ic** /-ˈmædɪk/ adj nómada

no man's land n tierra f de nadie

nominat|e /ˈnɒmɪneɪt/ vt (put
forward) proponer; postular (LAm);
(appoint) nombrar. ~**ion** /-ˈneɪʃn/ n
nombramiento m; (Amer, Pol)
proclamación f

non-... | notable

476

non-... /nɒn/ pref no ...

nonchalant /ˈnɒnʃələnt/ adj despreocupado

non-committal /nɒnkəˈmɪtl/ adj evasivo

nondescript /ˈnɒndɪskrɪpt/ adj anodino

none /nʌn/ pron ninguno, ninguna. **there were ~ left** no quedaba ninguno/ninguna. **~ of us** ninguno de nosotros. ● adv no, de ninguna manera. **he is ~ the happier** no está más contento

nonentity /nɒˈnentətɪ/ n persona f insignificante

non-existent /nɒnɪgˈzɪstənt/ adj inexistente

nonplussed /nɒnˈplʌst/ adj perplejo

nonsens|e /ˈnɒnsns/ n tonterías fpl, disparates mpl. **~ical** /-ˈsensɪkl/ adj disparatado

non-smoker /nɒnˈsməʊkə(r)/ n no fumador m. **I'm a ~** no fumo

non-stop /nɒnˈstɒp/ adj (train) directo; (flight) sin escalas. ● adv sin parar; (by train) directamente; (by air) sin escalas

noodles /ˈnuːdlz/ npl fideos mpl

nook /nʊk/ n rincón m

noon /nuːn/ n mediodía m

no-one /ˈnəʊwʌn/ pron nadie

noose /nuːs/ n soga f

nor /nɔː(r)/ conj ni, tampoco. **neither blue ~ red** ni azul ni rojo. **he doesn't play the piano, ~ do I** no sabe tocar el piano, ni yo tampoco

norm /nɔːm/ n norma f

normal /ˈnɔːml/ adj normal. **~cy** (Amer) normalidad f. **~ity** /-ˈmælətɪ/ n normalidad f. **~ly** adv normalmente

north /nɔːθ/ n norte m. ● adj norte. ● adv hacia el norte. **N~ America** n América f del Norte, Norteamérica f. **N~ American** adj

& n norteamericano (m). **~east** n nor(d)este m. ● adj nor(d)este. ● adv (go) hacia el nor(d)este. **it's ~east of Leeds** está al nor(d)este de Leeds. **~erly** /ˈnɔːðəlɪ/ adj (wind) del norte. **~ern** /ˈnɔːðən/ adj del norte. **~erner** n norteño m. **N~ern Ireland** n Irlanda f del Norte. **N~ Sea** n mar m del Norte. **~ward** /ˈnɔːθwəd/, **~wards** adv hacia el norte. **~west** n noroeste m. ● adj noroeste. ● adv hacia el noroeste

Norw|ay /ˈnɔːweɪ/ n Noruega f. **~egian** /-ˈwiːdʒən/ adj & n noruego (m)

nose /nəʊz/ n nariz f. **~bleed** n hemorragia f nasal. **~dive** vi descender en picado, descender en picada (LAm)

nostalgi|a /nɒˈstældʒə/ n nostalgia f. **~c** adj nostálgico

nostril /ˈnɒstrɪl/ n ventana f de la nariz f

nosy /ˈnəʊzɪ/ adj (-ier, -iest) 🔁 entrometido, metiche (LAm)

---

not /nɒt/

Cuando **not** va precedido del verbo auxiliar **do** or **have** o de un verbo modal como **should** etc, se suele emplear la forma contraída **don't, haven't, shouldn't** etc

adverb

····▸ no. **I don't know** no sé. **~ yet** todavía no. **~ me** yo no

····▸ (replacing a clause) **I suppose ~** supongo que no. **of course ~** por supuesto que no. **are you going to help me or ~?** ¿me vas a ayudar o no?

····▸ (emphatic) ni. **~ a penny more!** ¡ni un penique más!

····▸ (in phrases) **certainly ~** de ninguna manera . **~ you again!** ¡tú otra vez!

notab|le /ˈnəʊtəbl/ adj notable; (author) distinguido. **~y** /ˈnəʊtəblɪ/ adv notablemente; (in particular) particularmente

notch /nɒtʃ/ n muesca f. ■ **~ up** vt apuntarse

note /nəʊt/ n (incl Mus) nota f; (banknote) billete m. **take ~s** tomar apuntes. ●vt (notice) observar; (record) anotar. ■ **~ down** vt apuntar. **~book** n cuaderno m. **~d** adj célebre. **~paper** n papel m de carta(s)

nothing /'nʌθɪŋ/ pron nada. **he eats ~** no come nada. **for ~** (free) gratis; (in vain) en vano. **~ else** nada más. **~ much happened** no pasó gran cosa. **he does ~ but complain** no hace más que quejarse

notice /'nəʊtɪs/ n (sign) letrero m; (item of information) anuncio m; (notification) aviso m; (of termination of employment) preaviso m; **~ (of dismissal)** despido m. **take ~ of** hacer caso a (person). ●vt notar. ●vi darse cuenta. **~able** adj perceptible. **~ably** adv perceptiblemente. **~board** n tablón m de anuncios, tablero m de anuncios (LAm)

notif|ication /nəʊtɪfɪ'keɪʃn/ n notificación f. **~y** /'nəʊtɪfaɪ/ vt informar; (in writing) notificar. **~y s.o. of sth** comunicarle algo a uno

notion /'nəʊʃn/ n (concept) concepto m; (idea) idea f

notorious /nəʊ'tɔːrɪəs/ adj notorio

notwithstanding /nɒtwɪθ'stændɪŋ/ prep a pesar de. ●adv no obstante

nougat /'nuːgɑː/ n turrón m

nought /nɔːt/ n cero m

noun /naʊn/ n sustantivo m, nombre m

nourish /'nʌrɪʃ/ vt alimentar. **~ment** n alimento m

novel /'nɒvl/ n novela f. ●adj original, novedoso. **~ist** n novelista m & f. **~ty** n novedad f

November /nəʊ'vembə(r)/ n noviembre m

novice /'nɒvɪs/ n principiante m & f

now /naʊ/ adv ahora. **~ and again, ~ and then** de vez en cuando. **right ~** ahora mismo. **from ~ on** a partir de ahora. ●conj. **~ (that)** ahora que. **~adays** /'naʊədeɪz/ adv hoy (en) día

nowhere /'nəʊweə(r)/ adv por ninguna parte, por ningún lado; (after motion towards) a ninguna parte, a ningún lado

nozzle /'nɒzl/ n (on hose) boca f; (on fire extinguisher) boquilla f

nuance /'njuːɑːns/ n matiz m

nuclear /'njuːklɪə(r)/ adj nuclear

nucleus /'njuːklɪəs/ n (pl **-lei** /-lɪaɪ/) núcleo m

nude /njuːd/ adj & n desnudo (m). **in the ~** desnudo

nudge /nʌdʒ/ vt codear (ligeramente). ●n golpe m (suave) con el codo

nudi|st /'njuːdɪst/ n nudista m & f. **~ty** /'njuːdətɪ/ n desnudez f

nuisance /'njuːsns/ n (thing, event) molestia f, fastidio m; (person) pesado m

null /nʌl/ adj nulo

numb /nʌm/ adj entumecido. **go ~** entumecerse ●vt entumecer

number /'nʌmbə(r)/ n número m; (telephone number) número m de teléfono. **a ~ of people** varias personas. ●vt numerar; (count, include) contar. **~plate** n matrícula f, placa f (LAm)

numer|al /'njuːmərəl/ n número m. **~ical** /njuːˈmerɪkl/ adj numérico. **~ous** /'njuːmərəs/ adj numeroso

nun /nʌn/ n monja f

nurse /nɜːs/ n enfermero m, enfermera f; (nanny) niñera f. ●vt cuidar; abrigar (hope etc)

nursery /'nɜːsərɪ/ n (for plants) vivero m; (day **~**) guardería f. **~ rhyme** n canción f infantil. **~ school** n jardín m de infancia, jardín m infantil (LAm)

nursing home /'nɜːsɪŋ/ n (for older people) residencia f de ancianos

n

(con mayor nivel de asistencia médica)

nut /nʌt/ n fruto m seco (nuez, almendra, avellana etc); (Tec) tuerca f. ~**case** n Ⓣ chiflado m. ~**crackers** npl cascanueces m. ~**meg** /-meg/ n nuez f moscada

nutri|ent /'nju:trɪənt/ n nutriente m. ~**tion** /nju:'trɪʃn/ n nutrición f. ~**tious** /nju:'trɪʃəs/ adj nutritivo

nuts /nʌts/ adj (fam, crazy) chiflado

nutshell /'nʌtʃel/ n cáscara f de nuez. **in a** ~ en pocas palabras

NW abbr (= **north-west**) NO

nylon /'naɪlɒn/ n nylon m

Oo

oaf /əuf/ n zoquete m

oak /əuk/ n roble m

OAP /əuer'pi:/ abbr (= **old-age pensioner**) n pensionista m & f, pensionado m

oar /ɔ:(r)/ n remo m

oasis /əu'eɪsɪs/ n (pl **oases** /-si:z/) oasis m

oath /əuθ/ n juramento m

oat|meal /'əutmi:l/ n harina f de avena; (Amer, flakes) avena f (en copos). ~**s** /əuts/ npl avena f

obedien|ce /əu'bi:dɪəns/ n obediencia f. ~**t** adj obediente. ~**tly** adv obedientemente

obes|e /əu'bi:s/ adj obeso. ~**ity** n obesidad f

obey /əu'beɪ/ vt/i obedecer

obituary /ə'bɪtʃuərɪ/ n nota f necrológica, obituario m

object /'ɒbdʒɪkt/ n objeto m; (aim) objetivo m. •/əb'dʒekt/ vi oponerse (**to** a). ~**ion** /əb'dʒekʃn/ n objeción f. ~**ionable** adj censurable; (unpleasant) desagradable. ~**ive** /əb'dʒektɪv/ adj & n objetivo (m)

oblig|ation /ɒblɪ'geɪʃn/ n obligación f. **be under an** ~**ation to** estar obligado a. ~**atory** /ə'blɪgətrɪ/ adj obligatorio. ~**e** /ə'blaɪdʒ/ vt obligar. **I'd be much** ~**ed if you could help me** le

quedaría muy agradecido si pudiera ayudarme. ~**ing** adj atento

oblique /ə'bli:k/ adj oblicuo

obliterate /ə'blɪtəreɪt/ vt arrasar; (erase) borrar

oblivio|n /ə'blɪvɪən/ n olvido m. ~**us** /-vɪəs/ adj (unaware) inconsciente (**to, of** de)

oblong /'ɒblɒŋ/ adj oblongo. •n rectángulo m

obnoxious /əb'nɒkʃəs/ adj odioso

oboe /'əubəu/ n oboe m

obscen|e /əb'si:n/ adj obsceno. ~**ity** /əb'senətɪ/ n obscenidad f

obscur|e /əb'skjuə(r)/ adj oscuro. •vt ocultar; impedir ver claramente (issue). ~**ity** n oscuridad f

obsequious /əb'si:kwɪəs/ adj servil

observ|ant /əb'zɜ:vənt/ adj observador. ~**ation** /ɒbzə'veɪʃn/ n observación f. ~**atory** /əb'zɜ:vətrɪ/ n observatorio m. ~**e** /əb'zɜ:v/ vt observar. ~**er** n observador m

obsess /əb'ses/ vt obsesionar. ~**ed** /əb'sest/ adj obsesionado. ~**ion** /-ʃn/ n obsesión f. ~**ive** adj obsesivo

obsolete /'ɒbsəli:t/ adj obsoleto

obstacle /'ɒbstəkl/ n obstáculo m

obstina|cy /'ɒbstɪnəsɪ/ n

obstinación f. ~**te** /-ət/ adj
obstinado. ~**tely** adv
obstinadamente

obstruct /əb'strʌkt/ vt obstruir;
bloquear (traffic). ~**ion** /-ʃn/ n
obstrucción f

obtain /əb'teɪn/ vt conseguir,
obtener. ~**able** adj asequible

obtrusive /əb'truːsɪv/ adj (presence)
demasiado prominente; (noise)
molesto

obtuse /əb'tjuːs/ adj obtuso

obvious /'ɒbvɪəs/ adj obvio. ~**ly** adv
obviamente

occasion /ə'keɪʒn/ n ocasión f. ~**al**
adj esporádico. ~**ally** adv de vez en
cuando

occult /ɒ'kʌlt/ adj oculto

occup|ant /'ɒkjʊpənt/ n ocupante
m & f. ~**ation** /ɒkjʊ'peɪʃn/ n
ocupación f. ~**ier** /'ɒkjʊpaɪə(r)/ n
ocupante m & f. ~**y** /'ɒkjʊpaɪ/ vt
ocupar. **keep o.s.** ~**ied**
entretenerse

occur /ə'kɜː(r)/ vi (pt **occurred**)
tener lugar, ocurrir; (change)
producirse; (exist) encontrarse. **it**
~**red to me that** se me ocurrió
que. ~**rence** /ə'kʌrəns/ n (incidence)
incidencia f. **it is a rare** ~**rence**
no es algo frecuente

ocean /'əʊʃn/ n océano m

o'clock /ə'klɒk/ adv. **it is 7** ~ son
las siete. **it's one** ~ es la una

octagon /'ɒktəgən/ n octágono m

octave /'ɒktɪv/ n octava f

October /ɒk'təʊbə(r)/ n octubre m

octopus /'ɒktəpəs/ n (pl -**puses**)
pulpo m

odd /ɒd/ adj (-**er**, -**est**) extraño, raro;
(number) impar; (one of pair)
desparejado. **smoke the** ~
cigarette fumarse algún que otro
cigarillo. **fifty-**~ unos cincuenta,
cincuenta y pico. **the** ~ **one out**
la excepción. ~**ity** n (thing) rareza
f; (person) bicho m raro. ~**ly** adv de
una manera extraña. ~**ly enough**
por extraño que parezca. ~**ment**

n retazo m. ~**s** npl probabilidades
fpl; (in betting) apuesta f. **be at** ~**s**
estar en desacuerdo. ~**s and
ends** mpl 🎁 cosas fpl sueltas

odious /'əʊdɪəs/ adj odioso

odometer /ɒ'dɒmətə(r)/ n (Amer)
cuentakilómetros m

odour /'əʊdə(r)/ n olor m

---

of /ɒv//əv/ preposition

····▶ de. **a pound of cheese** una
libra de queso. **it's made of
wood** es de madera. **a girl of
ten** una niña de diez años

····▶ (in dates) de. **the fifth of
November** el cinco de
noviembre

····▶ (Amer, when telling the time)
it's ten (minutes) of five son las
cinco menos diez, son diez para
las cinco (LAm)

❗ **of** is not translated in cases
such as the following: **a
colleague of mine** un colega
mío; **there were six of us** éramos
seis; **that's very kind of you** es
Ud muy amable

---

off /ɒf/ prep (from) de. **he picked it
up** ~ **the floor** lo recogió del
suelo; (distant from) **just** ~ **the
coast of Texas** a poca distancia
de la costa de Tejas. **2 ft** ~ **the
ground** a dos pies del suelo;
(absent from) **I've been** ~ **work
for a week** hace una semana que
no voy a trabajar. ● adv (removed)
the lid was ~ la tapa no estaba
puesta; (distant) **some way** ~ a
cierta distancia; (leaving) **I'm** ~ me
voy; (switched off) (light, TV) apagado;
(water) cortado; (cancelled) (match)
cancelado; (not on duty) (day) libre.
● adj. **be** ~ (meat) estar malo, estar
pasado; (milk) estar cortado.
~-**beat** adj poco convencional. ~
chance n. **on the** ~ **chance** por
si acaso

offen|ce /ə'fens/ n (breach of law)
infracción f; (criminal ~ce) delito m;
(cause of outrage) atentado m; (Amer,
attack) ataque m. **take** ~**ce**

O

ofenderse. ~**d** vt ofender. ~**der** n
delincuente m & f. ~**sive** /-sɪv/ adj
ofensivo; (disgusting) desagradable

offer /'ɒfə(r)/ vt ofrecer. ~ **to do
sth** ofrecerse a hacer algo. ●n
oferta f. **on** ~ de oferta

offhand /ɒf'hænd/ adj (brusque)
brusco. **say sth in an** ~ **way**
decir algo a la ligera. ●adv de
improviso

office /'ɒfɪs/ n oficina f; (post) cargo
m. **doctor's** ~ (Amer) consultorio
m, consulta m. ~ **block** n edificio
m de oficinas ~**r** n oficial m & f;
(police ~**r**) policía m & f; (as form of
address) agente

offici|al /ə'fɪʃl/ adj oficial. ●n
funcionario m del Estado; (of party,
union) dirigente m & f. ~**ally** adv
oficialmente. ~**ous** /ə'fɪʃəs/ adj
oficioso

offing /'ɒfɪŋ/ n. **in the** ~ en
perspectiva

off: ~**-licence** n tienda f de vinos
y licores. ~**-putting** adj
(disconcerting) desconcertante;
(disagreeable) desagradable. ~**set** vt
(pt **-set**, pres p **-setting**) compensar.
~**shore** adj (breeze) que sopla
desde la tierra; (drilling) offshore;
(well) submarino. ●adv a un lugar
de mano de obra barata. ~**side**
/ɒf'saɪd/ adj (Sport) fuera de juego.
~**spring** n invar prole f. ~**-stage**
/-'steɪdʒ/ adv fuera del escenario.
~**-white** adj color hueso

often /'ɒfn/ adv a menudo, con
frecuencia. **how** ~? ¿con qué
frecuencia? **more** ~ con más
frecuencia

ogle /'əʊgl/ vt comerse con los ojos

ogre /'əʊgə(r)/ n ogro m

oh /əʊ/ int ¡ah!; (expressing dismay) ¡ay!

oil /ɔɪl/ n aceite m; (petroleum)
petróleo m. ●vt lubricar. ~**field** n
yacimiento m petrolífero. ~
painting n pintura f al óleo;
(picture) óleo m. ~ **rig** n plataforma
f petrolífera. ~**y** adj (substance)
oleaginoso; (food) aceitoso

ointment /'ɔɪntmənt/ n
ungüento m

OK /əʊ'keɪ/ int ¡vale!, ¡de acuerdo!,
¡bueno! (LAm). ●adj ~, **thanks**
bien, gracias. **the job's** ~ el
trabajo no está mal

old /əʊld/ adj (-er, -est) viejo; (not
modern) antiguo; (former) antiguo;
an ~ **friend** un viejo amigo. **how**
~ **is she?** ¿cuántos años tiene?
she is ten years ~ tiene diez
años. **his** ~**er sister** su hermana
mayor. ~ **age** n vejez f.
~**-fashioned** /-'fæʃənd/ adj
anticuado

olive /'ɒlɪv/ n aceituna f.

Olympic /ə'lɪmpɪk/ adj olímpico.
the ~**s** npl, **the** ~ **Games** npl los
Juegos Olímpicos

omelette /'ɒmlɪt/ n tortilla f
francesa, omelette m (LAm)

omen /'əʊmen/ n agüero m

omi|ssion /ə'mɪʃn/ n omisión f. ~**t**
/əʊ'mɪt/ vt (pt **omitted**) omitir

on /ɒn/ prep en, sobre; (about) sobre.
~ **foot** a pie. ~ **Monday** el
lunes. ~ **seeing** al ver. **I heard it**
~ **the radio** lo oí por la radio.
●adv (light etc) encendido, prendido
(LAm); (machine) en marcha; (tap)
abierto. ~ **and** ~ sin cesar. **and
so** ~ y así sucesivamente. **have a
hat** ~ llevar (puesto) un
sombrero. **further** ~ un poco más
allá. **what's** ~ **at the Odeon?**
¿qué dan en el Odeon? **go** ~
continuar. **later** ~ más tarde

once /wʌns/ adv una vez; (formerly)
antes. **at** ~ inmediatamente. ~
upon a time there was... érase
una vez.... ~ **and for all** de una
vez por todas. ●conj una vez que

one /wʌn/ adj uno, (before masculine
singular noun) un. **the** ~ **person I
trusted** la única persona en la
que confiaba. ●n uno m. ~ **by** ~
uno a uno.. ●pron uno (m), una (f).
the blue ~ el/la azul. **this** ~
éste/ésta. ~ **another** el uno al
otro

onerous /'ɒnərəs/ adj (task) pesado

one: ~**self** /-'self/ pron (reflexive) se; (after prep) sí (mismo); (emphatic use) uno mismo, una misma. **by** ~**self** solo. ~**-way** adj (street) de sentido único; (ticket) de ida, sencillo

onion /'ʌnɪən/ n cebolla f

onlooker /'ɒnlʊkə(r)/ n espectador m

only /'əʊnlɪ/ adj único. **she's an** ~ **child** es hija única. ● adv sólo, solamente. ~ **just** (barely) apenas. **I've** ~ **just arrived** acabo de llegar. ● conj pero, sólo que

onset /'ɒnset/ n comienzo m; (of disease) aparición f

onshore /'ɒnʃɔ:(r)/ adj (breeze) que sopla desde el mar; (oil field) en tierra

onslaught /'ɒnslɔːt/ n ataque m

onus /'əʊnəs/ n responsabilidad f

onward(s) /'ɒnwəd(z)/ adj & adv hacia adelante

ooze /uːz/ vt/i rezumar

opaque /əʊ'peɪk/ adj opaco

open /'əʊpən/ adj abierto; (question) discutible. ● n. **in the** ~ al aire libre. ● vt/i abrir. ~**ing** n abertura f; (beginning) principio m. ~**ly** adv abiertamente. ~**-minded** /-'maɪndɪd/ adj de actitud abierta

opera /'ɒprə/ n ópera f

operate /'ɒpəreɪt/ vt manejar, operar (Mex) (machine). ● vi funcionar; (company) operar. ~ **(on)** (Med) operar (a)

operatic /ɒpə'rætɪk/ adj operístico

operation /ɒpə'reɪʃn/ n operación f; (Mec) funcionamiento m; (using of machine) manejo m. **he had an** ~ lo operaron. **in** ~ en vigor. ~**al** adj operacional

operative /'ɒpərətɪv/ adj. **be** ~ estar en vigor

operator n operador m

opinion /ə'pɪnɪən/ n opinión f. **in my** ~ en mi opinión, a mi parecer

opponent /ə'pəʊnənt/ n adversario

m; (in sport) contrincante m & f

opportun|e /'ɒpətju:n/ adj oportuno. ~**ist** /ɒpə'tju:nɪst/ n oportunista m & f. ~**ity** /ɒpə'tju:nətɪ/ n oportunidad f

oppos|e /ə'pəʊz/ vt oponerse a. **be** ~**ed to** oponerse a, estar en contra de. ~**ing** adj opuesto. ~**ite** /'ɒpəzɪt/ adj (contrary) opuesto; (facing) de enfrente. ● n. **the** ~**ite** lo contrario. **quite the** ~**ite** al contrario. ● adv enfrente. ● prep enfrente de. ~**ite number** n homólogo m. ~**ition** /ɒpə'zɪʃn/ n oposición f; (resistance) resistencia f

oppress /ə'pres/ vt oprimir. ~**ion** /-ʃn/ n opresión f. ~**ive** adj (cruel) opresivo; (heat) sofocante

opt /ɒpt/ vi. ~ **to** optar por. ■ ~ **out** vi decidir no tomar parte

optic|al /'ɒptɪkl/ adj óptico. ~**ian** /ɒp'tɪʃn/ n óptico m

optimis|m /'ɒptɪmɪzəm/ n optimismo m. ~**t** n optimista m & f. ~**tic** /-'mɪstɪk/ adj optimista

option /'ɒpʃn/ n opción f ~**al** adj facultativo

or /ɔ:(r)/ conj o; (before **o-** and **ho-**) u; (after negative) ni. ~ **else** si no, o bien

oral /'ɔːrəl/ adj oral. ● n 🔲 examen m oral

orange /'ɒrɪndʒ/ n naranja f; (colour) naranja m. ● adj naranja. ~**ade** /-'eɪd/ n naranjada f

orbit /'ɔːbɪt/ n órbita f. ● vt orbitar

orchard /'ɔːtʃəd/ n huerto m

orchestra /'ɔːkɪstrə/ n orquesta f; (Amer, in theatre) platea f. ~**l** /-'kestrəl/ adj orquestal. ~**te** /-eɪt/ vt orquestar

orchid /'ɔːkɪd/ n orquídea f

ordain /ɔː'deɪn/ vt (Relig) ordenar; (decree) decretar

ordeal /ɔː'diːl/ n dura prueba f

order /'ɔːdə(r)/ n orden m; (Com) pedido m; (command) orden f. **in** ~ **that** para que. **in** ~ **to** para. ● vt

O

(command) ordenar, mandar; (Com) pedir; (in restaurant) pedir, ordenar (LAm); encargar (book); llamar, ordenar (LAm) (taxi). ~ly adj ordenado. • n camillero m

ordinary /'ɔːdɪnrɪ/ adj corriente; (average) medio; (mediocre) ordinario

ore /ɔː(r)/ n mena f

organ /'ɔːɡən/ n órgano m

organ|ic /ɔːˈɡænɪk/ adj orgánico. ~**ism** /'ɔːɡənɪzəm/ n organismo m. ~**ist** /'ɔːɡənɪst/ n organista m & f. ~**ization** /ɔːɡənaɪˈzeɪʃn/ n organización f. ~**ize** /'ɔːɡənaɪz/ vt organizar. ~**izer** n organizador m

orgasm /'ɔːɡæzəm/ n orgasmo m

orgy /'ɔːdʒɪ/ n orgía f

Orient /'ɔːrɪənt/ n Oriente m. ~**al** /-'entl/ adj oriental

orientat|e /'ɔːrɪənteɪt/ vt orientar. ~**ion** /-'teɪʃn/ n orientación f

origin /'ɒrɪdʒɪn/ n origen m. ~**al** /əˈrɪdʒənl/ adj original. ~**ally** adv originariamente. ~**ate** /əˈrɪdʒmeɪt/ vi. ~**ate from** provenir de

ornament /'ɔːnəmənt/ n adorno m. ~**al** /-'mentl/ adj de adorno

ornate /ɔːˈneɪt/ adj ornamentado; (style) recargado

ornithology /ɔːnɪˈθɒlədʒɪ/ n ornitología f

orphan /'ɔːfn/ n huérfano m. •vt. **be ~ed** quedar huérfano. ~**age** /-ɪdʒ/ n orfanato m

orthodox /'ɔːθədɒks/ adj ortodoxo

oscillate /'ɒsɪleɪt/ vi oscilar

ostentatious /ɒstenˈteɪʃəs/ adj ostentoso

osteopath /'ɒstɪəpæθ/ n osteópata m & f

ostracize /'ɒstrəsaɪz/ vt hacerle vacío a

ostrich /'ɒstrɪtʃ/ n avestruz m

other /'ʌðə(r)/ adj & pron otro. ~ **than** aparte de. **the ~ one** el otro. ~**wise** adv de lo contrario, si no

otter /'ɒtə(r)/ n nutria f

ouch /aʊtʃ/ int ¡ay!

ought /ɔːt/ modal verb. **I ~ to see it** debería verlo. **he ~ to have done it** debería haberlo hecho

ounce /aʊns/ n onza f (= 28.35 gr.)

our /'aʊə(r)/ adj (sing) nuestro, nuestra, (pl) nuestros, nuestras. ~**s** /'aʊəz/ poss pron (sing) nuestro, nuestra, (pl) nuestros, nuestras. ~**s is red** el nuestro es rojo. **a friend of ~s** un amigo nuestro. ~**selves** /-'selvz/ pron (reflexive) nos; (used for emphasis and after prepositions) nosotros mismos, nosotras mismas. **we behaved ~selves** nos portamos bien. **we did it ~selves** lo hicimos nosotros mismos/nosotras mismas

oust /aʊst/ vt desbancar; derrocar (government)

out /aʊt/ adv (outside) fuera, afuera (LAm); (not lighted, not on) apagado; (in blossom) en flor; (in error) equivocado. **he's ~** (not at home) no está; (to be) estar resuelto a. ~ **of** prep (from inside) de; (outside) fuera, afuera (LAm). **five ~ of six** cinco de cada seis. **made ~ of** hecho de. **we're ~ of bread** nos hemos quedado sin pan. ~**break** n (of war) estallido m; (of disease) brote m. ~**burst** n arrebato m. ~**cast** n paria m & f. ~**come** n resultado m. ~**cry** n protesta f. ~**dated** /-'deɪtɪd/ adj anticuado. ~**do** /-'duː/ vt (pt **-did**, pp **-done**) superar. ~**door** adj (clothes) de calle; (pool) descubierto. ~**doors** /-'dɔːz/ adv al aire libre

outer /'aʊtə(r)/ adj exterior

out: ~**fit** n equipo m; (clothes) conjunto m. ~**going** adj (minister etc) saliente; (sociable) abierto. ~**goings** npl gastos mpl. ~**grow** /-'ɡrəʊ/ vt (pt **-grew**, pp **-grown**) crecer más que (person). **he's ~grown his new shoes** le han quedado pequeños los zapatos nuevos. ~**ing** n excursión f

outlandish /aʊtˈlændɪʃ/ adj
extravagante

out: ~**law** n forajido m. •vt
proscribir. ~**lay** n gastos mpl.
~**let** n salida f; (Com) punto m de
venta; (Amer, Elec) toma f de
corriente. ~**line** n contorno m;
(summary) resumen m; (plan of project)
esquema m.•vt trazar; (summarize)
esbozar. ~**live** /-ˈlɪv/ vt sobrevivir
a. ~**look** n perspectivas fpl;
(attitude) punto m de vista. ~**lying**
adj alejado. •/-ˈlaɪ/ vt
/-ˈnʌmbə(r)/ vt superar en número.
~**-of-date** adj (ideas) desfasado;
(clothes) pasado de moda.
~**patient** n paciente m externo.
~**post** n avanzada f. ~**put** n
producción f; (of machine, worker)
rendimiento m. ~**right** adv
completamente; (frankly)
abiertamente; (kill) en el acto. •adj
completo; (refusal) rotundo. ~**set**
n principio m. •at the ~ al
principio m. al principio. ~**side** adj & n
exterior (m). **at the ~** como
máximo. •/-ˈsaɪd/ adv fuera, afuera
(LAm). •prep fuera de. ~**size** adj de
talla gigante. ~**skirts** npl afueras
fpl. ~**spoken** /-ˈspəʊkn/ adj
directo, franco. ~**standing**
/-ˈstændɪŋ/ adj excepcional; (debt)
pendiente. ~**stretched**
/aʊtˈstretʃt/ adj extendido. ~**strip**
/-ˈstrɪp/ vt (pt **-stripped**) (run faster
than) tomarle la delantera a;
(exceed) sobrepasar. ~**ward**
/-wəd/ adj (appearance) exterior; (sign)
externo; (journey) de ida. ~**wardly**
adv por fuera, exteriormente. ~**(s)**
adv hacia afuera. ~**weigh** /-ˈweɪ/
vt ser mayor que. ~**wit** /-ˈwɪt/ vt
(pt **-witted**) burlar

oval /ˈəʊvl/ adj ovalado, oval. •n
óvalo m

ovary /ˈəʊvərɪ/ n ovario m

ovation /əʊˈveɪʃn/ n ovación f

oven /ˈʌvn/ n horno m

over /ˈəʊvə(r)/ prep por encima de;
(across) al otro lado de; (during)
durante; (more than) más de. ~ **and
above** por encima de. •adv por
encima; (ended) terminado; (more)
más; (in excess) de sobra. ~ **again**
otra vez. ~ **and** una y otra vez.
~ **here** por aquí. ~ **there** por
allí. **all** ~ (finished) acabado;
(everywhere) por todas partes

over... /ˈəʊvə(r)/ pref excesivamente,
demasiado

over: ~**all** /-ˈɔːl/ adj global; (length,
cost) total. •adv en conjunto.
•/ˈəʊvərɔːl/ n, ~**alls** npl mono m,
overol m (LAm); (Amer, dungarees)
peto m, overol m. ~**awe** /-ˈɔː/ vt
intimidar. ~**balance** /-ˈbæləns/ vi
perder el equilibrio. ~**bearing**
/-ˈbeərɪŋ/ adj dominante. ~**board**
adv (throw) por la borda. ~**cast**
/-ˈkɑːst/ adj (day) nublado; (sky)
cubierto. ~**charge** /-ˈtʃɑːdʒ/ vt
cobrarle de más a. ~**coat** n
abrigo m. ~**come** /-ˈkʌm/ vt (pt
-came, pp **-come**) superar, vencer.
~**crowded** /-ˈkraʊdɪd/ adj
abarrotado (de gente). ~**do**
/-ˈduː/ vt (pt **-did**, pp **-done**)
exagerar; (Culin) recocer. ~**dose**
n sobredosis f. ~**draft** n
descubierto m. ~**draw** /-ˈdrɔː/ vt
(pt **-drew**, pp **-drawn**) girar en
descubierto. **be ~drawn** tener
un descubierto. ~**due** /-ˈdjuː/ adj.
the book is a month ~due el
plazo de devolución del libro
venció hace un mes. ~**estimate**
/-ˈestɪmeɪt/ vt sobreestimar.
~**flow** /-ˈfləʊ/ vi desbordarse. •n
/-ˈfləʊ/ (excess) exceso m; (outlet)
rebosadero m. ~**flow car park**
n estacionamiento m extra (LAm),
aparcamiento m extra (Esp).
~**grown** /-ˈɡrəʊn/ adj demasiado
grande; (garden) lleno de maleza.
~**haul** /-ˈhɔːl/ vt revisar. •/-ˈhɔːl/
revisión f. ~**head** /-ˈhed/ adv por
encima. •/-ˈhed/ adj de arriba.
~**heads** /-ˈhedz/ npl, ~**head** n
(Amer) gastos mpl indirectos.
~**hear** /-ˈhɪə(r)/ vt (pt **-heard**) oír
por casualidad. ~**joyed** /-ˈdʒɔɪd/
adj encantado. ~**land** a/adv por
tierra. ~**lap** /-ˈlæp/ vi (pt **-lapped**)
traslaparse. ~**leaf** /-ˈliːf/ adv al
dorso. ~**load** /-ˈləʊd/ vt
sobrecargar. ~**look** /-ˈlʊk/ vt
(room) dar a; (not notice) pasar por

alto; (disregard) disculpar. ~night /-'naɪt/ adv durante la noche. **stay ~night** quedarse a pasar la noche. •adj (journey) de noche; (stay) de una noche. ~pass n paso m elevado, paso m a desnivel (Mex). ~pay /-'peɪ/ vt (pt -paid) pagar demasiado. ~power /-'paʊə(r)/ vt dominar (opponent); (emotion) abrumar. ~powering /-'paʊərɪŋ/ adj (smell) muy fuerte; (desire) irresistible. ~priced /-'praɪst/ adj demasiado caro. ~rated /-'reɪtɪd/ adj sobrevalorado. ~react /-rɪˈækt/ vi reaccionar en forma exagerada. ~ride /-'raɪd/ vt (pt -rode, pp -ridden) invalidar. ~riding /-'raɪdɪŋ/ adj dominante. ~rule /-'ru:l/ vt anular; rechazar (objection). ~run /-'rʌn/ vt (pt -ran, pp -run, pres p -running) invadir; exceder (limit). ~seas /-'si:z/ adj (trade) exterior; (investments) en el exterior; (visitor) extranjero. •adv al extranjero. ~see /-'si:/ vt (pt -saw, pp -seen) supervisar. ~seer /-sɪə(r)/ n capataz m & f, supervisor m. ~shadow /-'ʃædəʊ/ vt eclipsar. ~shoot /-'ʃu:t/ vt (pt -shot) excederse. ~sight n descuido m. ~sleep /-'sli:p/ vi (pt -slept) quedarse dormido. ~step /-'step/ vt (pt -stepped) sobrepasar. ~step the mark pasarse de la raya

overt /'əʊvɜ:t/ adj manifiesto

over:: ~take /-'teɪk/ vt/i (pt -took, pp -taken) sobrepasar; (Auto) adelantar, rebasar (Mex). ~throw /-'θrəʊ/ vt (pt -threw, pp -thrown) derrocar. ~time n horas fpl extra

overture /'əʊvətjʊə(r)/ n obertura f

over:: ~turn /-'tɜ:n/ vt darle la vuelta a. •vi volcar. ~weight /-'weɪt/ adj demasiado gordo. **be ~weight** pesar demasiado. ~whelm /-'welm/ vt aplastar; (with emotion) abrumar. ~whelming adj aplastante; (fig) abrumador. ~work /-'wɜ:k/ vt hacer trabajar demasiado. •vi trabajar demasiado. •n agotamiento m

ow|e /əʊ/ vt deber. ~ing to debido a

owl /aʊl/ n búho m

own /əʊn/ adj propio. **my ~ house** mi propia casa. •pron. **it's my ~** es mío (propio)/mía (propia). **on one's ~** solo. **get one's ~ back** 🄵 desquitarse. •vt tener. ∎ **~ up** vi. 🄵 confesarse culpable. ~er n propietario m, dueño m. ~ership n propiedad f

oxygen /'ɒksɪdʒən/ n oxígeno m

oyster /'ɔɪstə(r)/ n ostra f

Pp

p abbr (= **pence, penny**) penique(s) (m(pl))

p. (pl **pp.**) (= **page**) pág., p.

pace /peɪs/ n paso m. **keep ~ with s.o.** seguirle el ritmo a uno. •vi. **~ up and down** andar de un lado para otro. ~maker n (runner) liebre f; (Med) marcapasos m

Pacific /pə'sɪfɪk/ n. **the ~ (Ocean)** el (Océano) Pacífico m

pacif|ist /'pæsɪfɪst/ n pacifista m & f. ~y /'pæsɪfaɪ/ vt apaciguar

pack /pæk/ n fardo m; (of cigarettes) paquete m, cajetilla f; (of cards) baraja f; (of hounds) jauría f; (of wolves) manada f. **a ~ of lies** una sarta de mentiras. •vt empaquetar; hacer (suitcase); (press down) apisonar. •vi hacer la maleta, empacar (LAm). **~age** /-ɪdʒ/ n paquete m. **~age holiday** n vacaciones fpl organizadas. **~ed** /pækt/ adj lleno (de gente). **~et** /'pækɪt/ n paquete m

pact /pækt/ n pacto m, acuerdo m

pad /pæd/ n (for writing) bloc m. **shoulder ~s** hombreras fpl. ●vt (pt **padded**) rellenar

paddle /'pædl/ n pala f. ●vi mojarse los pies; (in canoe) remar (con pala)

paddock /'pædək/ n prado m

padlock /'pædlɒk/ n candado m. ●vt cerrar con candado

paed|iatrician /ˌpiːdɪə'trɪʃn/ n pediatra m & f. **~ophile** /'piːdəfaɪl/ n pedófilo m

pagan /'peɪgən/ adj & n pagano (m)

page /peɪdʒ/ n página f; (attendant) paje m; (in hotel) botones m. ●vt llamar por megafonía/por buscapersonas, vocear (LAm)

paid /peɪd/ see PAY. ●adj. **put ~ to** ⓘ acabar con

pail /peɪl/ n balde m, cubo m

pain /peɪn/ n dolor m. **I have a ~ in my back** me duele la espalda. m. **be in ~** tener dolores. **be a ~ in the neck** ⓘ ser un pesado; (thing) ser una lata. ●vt doler. **~ful** adj doloroso. **it's very ~ful** duele mucho. **~-killer** n analgésico m. **~less** adj indoloro. **~staking** /'peɪnzteɪkɪŋ/ adj concienzudo

paint /peɪnt/ n pintura f. ●vt/i pintar. **~er** n pintor m. **~ing** n (medium) pintura f; (picture) cuadro m

pair /peə(r)/ n par m; (of people) pareja f. **a ~ of trousers** unos pantalones. ■ **~off**, **~ up** vi formar parejas

pajamas /pə'dʒɑːməz/ npl (Amer) pijama m

Pakistan /pɑːkɪ'stɑːn/ n Pakistán m. **~i** adj & n paquistaní (m & f)

pal /pæl/ n ⓘ amigo m

palace /'pælɪs/ n palacio m

palat|able /'pælətəbl/ adj agradable. **~e** /'pælət/ n paladar m

pale /peɪl/ adj (**-er, -est**) pálido. **go ~, turn ~** palidecer. **~ness** n palidez f

Palestin|e /'pælɪstaɪn/ n Palestina f. **~ian** /-'stɪnɪən/ adj & n palestino (m)

palette /'pælɪt/ n paleta f

palm /pɑːm/ n palma f. ■ **~ off** vt encajar (**on** a). **P~ Sunday** n Domingo m de Ramos

palpable /'pælpəbl/ adj palpable

palpitat|e /'pælpɪteɪt/ vi palpitar. **~ion** /-'teɪʃn/ n palpitación f

pamper /'pæmpə(r)/ vt mimar

pamphlet /'pæmflɪt/ n folleto m

pan /pæn/ n cacerola f; (for frying) sartén f

panacea /pænə'sɪə/ n panacea f

Panama /'pænəmɑː/ n Panamá m. **~nian** /-'meɪnɪən/ adj & n panameño (m)

pancake /'pænkeɪk/ n crep(e) m, panqueque m (LAm)

panda /'pændə/ n panda m

pandemonium /pændɪ'məʊnɪəm/ n pandemonio m

pander /'pændə(r)/ vi. **~ to s.o.** consentirle los caprichos a uno

pane /peɪn/ n vidrio m, cristal m

panel /'pænl/ n panel m; (group of people) jurado m. **~ling** n paneles mpl

pang /pæŋ/ n punzada f

panic /'pænɪk/ n pánico m. ●vi (pt **panicked**) dejarse llevar por el pánico. **~-stricken** adj aterrorizado

panoram|a /pænə'rɑːmə/ n panorama m. **~ic** /-'ræmɪk/ adj panorámico

pansy /'pænzɪ/ n (flower) pensamiento m

pant /pænt/ vi jadear

panther /'pænθə(r)/ n pantera f

P

panties /'pæntɪz/ npl bragas fpl, calzones mpl (LAm), pantaletas fpl (Mex)

pantihose /'pæntɪhəuz/ npl see **PANTYHOSE**

pantomime /'pæntəmaɪm/ n pantomima f

pantry /'pæntrɪ/ n despensa f

pants /pænts/ npl (man's) calzoncillos mpl; (woman's) bragas fpl, calzones mpl (LAm), pantaletas fpl (Mex); (Amer, trousers) pantalones mpl

pantyhose /'pæntɪhəuz/ npl (Amer) panty m, medias fpl, pantimedias fpl (Mex)

paper /'peɪpə(r)/ n papel m; (newspaper) diario m, periódico m; (exam) examen m; (document) documento m. ● vt empapelar, tapizar (Mex). ~**back** n libro m en rústica. ~ **clip** n sujetapapeles m, clip m. ~**weight** n pisapapeles m. ~**work** n papeleo m, trabajo m administrativo

parable /'pærəbl/ n parábola f

parachut|e /'pærəʃu:t/ n paracaídas m. ● vi saltar en paracaídas. ~**ist** n paracaidista m & f

parade /pə'reɪd/ n desfile m; (Mil) formación f. ● vi desfilar. ● vt hacer alarde de

paradise /'pærədaɪs/ n paraíso m

paraffin /'pærəfɪn/ n queroseno m

paragraph /'pærəgrɑ:f/ n párrafo m

Paraguay /'pærəgwaɪ/ n Paraguay m. ~**an** adj & n paraguayo (m)

parallel /'pærəlel/ adj paralelo. ● n paralelo m; (line) paralela f

paraly|se /'pærəlaɪz/ vt paralizar. ~**sis** /pə'ræləsɪs/ n (pl -**ses** /-si:z/) parálisis f

parameter /pə'ræmɪtə(r)/ n parámetro m

paranoia /pærə'nɔɪə/ n paranoia f

parapet /'pærəpɪt/ n parapeto m

paraphernalia /pærəfə'neɪlɪə/ n trastos mpl

parasite /'pærəsaɪt/ n parásito m

paratrooper /'pærətru:pə(r)/ n paracaidista m (del ejército)

parcel /'pɑ:sl/ n paquete m

parch /pɑ:tʃ/ vt resecar. **be ~ed** 🗓 estar muerto de sed

parchment /'pɑ:tʃmənt/ n pergamino m

pardon /'pɑ:dn/ n perdón m; (Jurid) indulto m. **I beg your ~** perdón. **(I beg your) ~?** ¿cómo?, ¿mande? (Mex). ● vt perdonar; (Jurid) indultar. **~ me?** (Amer) ¿cómo?

parent /'peərənt/ n (father) padre m; (mother) madre f. **my ~s** mis padres. ~**al** /pə'rentl/ adj de los padres

parenthesis /pə'renθəsɪs/ n (pl -**theses** /-si:z/) paréntesis m

parenthood /'peərənthʊd/ n el ser padre/madre

Paris /'pærɪs/ n París m

parish /'pærɪʃ/ n parroquia f; (municipal) distrito m. ~**ioner** /pə'rɪʃənə(r)/ n feligrés m

park /pɑ:k/ n parque m. ~**-and-ride** estacionamiento m disuasorio (LAm), aparcamiento m disuasorio (Esp). ● vt/i aparcar, estacionar (LAm)

parking /'pɑ:kɪŋ/ n ~ **lot** n (Amer) aparcamiento m, estacionamiento m (LAm). ~ **meter** n parquímetro m

parkway /'pɑ:kweɪ/ n (Amer) carretera f ajardinada

parliament /'pɑ:ləmənt/ n parlamento m. ~**ary** /-'mentrɪ/ adj parlamentario

parlour /'pɑ:lə(r)/ n salón m

parochial /pə'rəʊkɪəl/ adj (fig) provinciano

parody /'pærədɪ/ n parodia f. ● vt parodiar

parole /pə'rəʊl/ n libertad f condicional

parrot /'pærət/ n loro m, papagayo m

parsley /'pɑːslɪ/ n perejil m

parsnip /'pɑːsnɪp/ n pastinaca f

part /pɑːt/ n parte f; (of machine) pieza f; (of serial) episodio m; (in play) papel m; (Amer, in hair) raya f. **take ∼ in** tomar parte en, participar en. **for the most ∼** en su mayor parte. ●adv en parte. ●vt separar. ●vi separarse. ■ **∼ with** vt desprenderse de

partial /'pɑːʃl/ adj parcial. **be ∼ to** tener debilidad por. **∼ly** adv parcialmente

participa|nt /pɑːˈtɪsɪpənt/ n participante m & f. **∼te** /-peɪt/ vi participar. **∼tion** /-'peɪʃn/ n participación f

particle /'pɑːtɪkl/ n partícula f

particular /pəˈtɪkjʊlə(r)/ adj particular; (precise) meticuloso; (fastidious) quisquilloso. **in ∼** en particular. ●n detalle m. **∼ly** adv particularmente; (specifically) específicamente

parting /'pɑːtɪŋ/ n despedida f; (in hair) raya f. ●adj de despedida

partition /pɑːˈtɪʃn/ n partición f; (wall) tabique m. ●vt dividir

partly /'pɑːtlɪ/ adv en parte

partner /'pɑːtnə(r)/ n socio m; (Sport) pareja f. **∼ship** n asociación f; (Com) sociedad f

partridge /'pɑːtrɪdʒ/ n perdiz f

part-time /pɑːt'taɪm/ adj & adv a tiempo parcial, de medio tiempo (LAm)

party /'pɑːtɪ/ n reunión f, fiesta f; (group) grupo m; (Pol) partido m; (Jurid) parte f

pass /pɑːs/ vt (hand, convey) pasar; (go past) pasar por delante de; (overtake) adelantar, rebasar (Mex); (approve) aprobar (exam, bill, law); pronunciar (judgement). ●vi pasar; (pain) pasarse; (Sport) pasar la pelota. ■ **∼ away** vi fallecer. ■ **∼ down** vt transmitir. ■ **∼ out** vi desmayarse. ■ **∼round**

vt distribuir. ■ **∼ up** vt 🔲 dejar pasar. ●n (permit) pase m; (ticket) abono m; (in mountains) puerto m, desfiladero m; (Sport) pase m; (in exam) aprobado m. **make a ∼ at** 🔲 intentar besar. **∼able** adj pasable; (road) transitable

passage /'pæsɪdʒ/ n (voyage) travesía f; (corridor) pasillo m; (alleyway) pasaje m; (in book) pasaje m

passenger /'pæsɪndʒə(r)/ n pasajero m

passer-by /pɑːsə'baɪ/ n (pl **passers-by**) transeúnte m & f

passion /'pæʃn/ n pasión f. **∼ate** /-ət/ adj apasionado. **∼ately** adv apasionadamente

passive /'pæsɪv/ adj pasivo

Passover /'pɑːsəʊvə(r)/ n Pascua f de los hebreos

pass: ∼port n pasaporte m. **∼word** n contraseña f

past /pɑːst/ adj anterior; (life) pasado; (week, year) último. **in times ∼** en tiempos pasados. ●n pasado m. **in the ∼** (formerly) antes, antiguamente. ●prep por delante de; (beyond) más allá de. **it's twenty ∼ four** son las cuatro y veinte. ●adv. **drive ∼** pasar en coche. **go ∼** pasar

paste /peɪst/ n pasta f; (glue) engrudo m; (wallpaper **∼**) pegamento m; (jewellery) estrás m

pastel /'pæstl/ adj & n pastel (m)

pasteurize /'pɑːstʃəraɪz/ vt pasteurizar

pastime /'pɑːstaɪm/ n pasatiempo m

pastry /'peɪstrɪ/ n masa f; (cake) pastelito m

pasture /'pɑːstʃə(r)/ n pasto(s) mpl

pasty /'pæstɪ/ n empanadilla f, empanada f (LAm)

pat /pæt/ vt (pt **patted**) darle palmaditas. ●n palmadita f; (of butter) porción f

patch /pætʃ/ n (on clothes) remiendo

m, parche m; (over eye) parche m. **a bad ~** una mala racha. •vt remendar. ■**~ up** vt hacerle un arreglo a

patent /'pertnt/ adj patente. •n patente f. •vt patentar. **~ leather** n charol m. **~ly** adv. **it's ~ly obvious that...** está clarísimo que...

patern|al /pə'tɜːnl/ adj paterno. **~ity** /-ətɪ/ n paternidad f

path /pɑːθ/ n (pl **-s**/pɑːðz/) sendero m; (Sport) pista f; (of rocket) trayectoria f; (fig) camino m

pathetic /pə'θetɪk/ adj (pitiful) patético; (excuse) pobre. **don't be so ~** no seas tan pusilánime

patien|ce /'peɪ∫ns/ n paciencia f. **~t** adj & n paciente (m & f). **be ~t with s.o.** tener paciencia con uno. **~tly** adv pacientemente

patio /'pætɪəʊ/ n (pl **-os**) patio m

patriot /'pætrɪət/ n patriota m & f. **~ic** /-'ɒtɪk/ adj patriótico. **~ism** n patriotismo m

patrol /pə'trəʊl/ n patrulla f. •vt/i patrullar

patron /'peɪtrən/ n (of the arts) mecenas m & f; (of charity) patrocinador m; (customer) cliente m & f. **~age** /'pætrənɪdʒ/ n (sponsorship) patrocinio m; (of the arts) mecenazgo m. **~ize** /'pætrənaɪz/ vt ser cliente de; (fig) tratar con condescendencia. **~izing** adj condescendiente

pattern /'pætn/ n diseño m; (sample) muestra f; (in dressmaking) patrón m

paunch /pɔːnt∫/ n panza f

pause /pɔːz/ n pausa f. •vi hacer una pausa

pave /peɪv/ vt pavimentar; (with flagstones) enlosar. **~ment** n pavimento m; (at side of road) acera f, banqueta f (Mex)

paving stone /'peɪvɪŋstəʊn/ n losa f

paw /pɔː/ n pata f

pawn /pɔːn/ n (Chess) peón m; (fig) títere m. •vt empeñar. **~broker** n prestamista m & f

pay /peɪ/ vt (pt **paid**) pagar; prestar (attention); hacer (compliment, visit). **~ cash** pagar al contado. **~** (be profitable) rendir. •n paga f. **in the ~ of** al servicio de. ■**~ back** vt devolver; pagar (loan). ■**~ in** vt ingresar, depositar (LAm). ■**~ off** vt cancelar, saldar (debt). vi valer la pena. ■**~ up** vi pagar. **~able** adj pagadero. **~ment** n pago m. **~roll** n nómina f

pea /piː/ n guisante m, arveja f (LAm), chícharo m (Mex)

peace /piːs/ n paz f. **~ of mind** tranquilidad f. **~ful** adj tranquilo. **~maker** n conciliador m

peach /piːt∫/ n melocotón m, durazno m (LAm)

peacock /'piːkɒk/ n pavo m real

peak /piːk/ n cumbre f; (of career) apogeo m; (maximum) máximo m. **~ hours** npl horas fpl de mayor demanda (o consumo etc)

peal /piːl/ n repique m. **~s of laughter** risotadas fpl

peanut /'piːnʌt/ n cacahuete m, maní m (LAm), cacahuate m (Mex)

pear /peə(r)/ n pera f. **~ (tree)** peral m

pearl /pɜːl/ n perla f

peasant /'peznt/ n campesino m

peat /piːt/ n turba f

pebble /'pebl/ n guijarro m

peck /pek/ vt picotear. •n picotazo m; (kiss) besito m

peculiar /pɪ'kjuːlɪə(r)/ adj raro; (special) especial. **~ity** /-'ærətɪ/ n rareza f; (feature) particularidad f

pedal /'pedl/ n pedal m. •vi pedalear

pedantic /pɪ'dæntɪk/ adj pedante

peddle /'pedl/ vt vender por las calles

pedestal /'pedɪstl/ n pedestal m

pedestrian /pɪ'destrɪən/ n peatón m. **~ crossing** paso m de peatones. ● adj pedestre; (dull) prosaico

pedigree /'pedɪgri:/ linaje m; (of animal) pedigrí m. ● adj (animal) de raza

peek /pi:k/ vi mirar a hurtadillas

peel /pi:l/ n piel f, cáscara f. ● vt pelar (fruit, vegetables). ● vi pelarse

peep /pi:p/ vi. ~ **at** echarle un vistazo a. ● n (look) vistazo m; (bird sound) pío m

peer /pɪə(r)/ vi mirar. ~ **at** escudriñar. ● n (equal) par m & f; (contemporary) coetáneo m; (lord) par m. ~**age** /-ɪdʒ/ n nobleza f

peg /peg/ n (in ground) estaca f; (on violin) clavija f; (for washing) pinza f; (hook) gancho m; (for tent) estaquilla f. **off the** ~ de confección. ● vt (pt **pegged**) sujetar (con estacas, etc); fijar (precios)

pejorative /pɪ'dʒɒrətɪv/ adj peyorativo, despectivo

pelican /'pelɪkən/ n pelícano m

pellet /'pelɪt/ n bolita f; (for gun) perdigón m

pelt /pelt/ n pellejo m. ● vt. ~ **s.o. with sth** lanzarle algo a uno. ● vi. ~ **with rain**, ~ **down** llover a cántaros

pelvis /'pelvɪs/ n pelvis f

pen /pen/ n (for writing) pluma f; (ballpoint) bolígrafo m; (sheep ~) redil m; (cattle ~) corral m

penal /'pi:nl/ adj penal. ~**ize** vt sancionar. ~**ty** /'penltɪ/ n pena f; (fine) multa f; (in soccer) penalty m; (in US football) castigo m. ~**ty kick** n (in soccer) penalty m

penance /'penəns/ n penitencia f

pence /pens/ see PENNY

pencil /'pensl/ n lápiz m. ● vt (pt **pencilled**) escribir con lápiz. ~**-sharpener** n sacapuntas m

pendulum /'pendjʊləm/ n péndulo m

penetrat|e /'penɪtreɪt/ vt/i penetrar. ~**ing** adj penetrante.

~**ion** /-'treɪʃn/ n penetración f

penguin /'peŋgwɪn/ n pingüino m

penicillin /penɪ'sɪlɪn/ n penicilina f

peninsula /pə'nɪnsjʊlə/ n península f

penis /'pi:nɪs/ n pene m

pen: ~**knife** /'pennaɪf/ n (pl pen-**knives**) navaja f. ~**-name** n seudónimo m

penn|iless /'penɪlɪs/ adj sin un céntimo. ~**y** /'penɪ/ n (pl **pennies** or **pence**) penique m

pension /'penʃn/ n pensión f; (for retirement) pensión f de jubilación. ~**er** n jubilado m

pensive /'pensɪv/ adj pensativo

Pentecost /'pentɪkɒst/ n Pentecostés m

penthouse /'penthaʊs/ n penthouse m

pent-up /pent'ʌp/ adj reprimido; (confined) encerrado

penultimate /pen'ʌltɪmət/ adj penúltimo

people /'pi:pl/ npl gente f; (citizens) pueblo m. ~ **say (that)** se dice que, dicen que. **English** ~ los ingleses. **young** ~ los jóvenes. **the** ~ (nation) el pueblo. ● vt poblar

pepper /'pepə(r)/ n pimienta f; (vegetable) pimiento m. ● vt (interspersé) salpicar (**with** de). ~**box** n (Amer) pimentero m. ~**corn** n grano m de pimienta. ~**mint** n menta f; (sweet) caramelo m de menta. ~**pot** n pimentero m

per /pɜ:(r)/ prep por. ~ **annum** al año. ~ **cent** see PERCENT. ~ **head** por cabeza, por persona. **ten miles** ~ **hour** diez millas por hora

perceive /pə'si:v/ vt percibir; (notice) darse cuenta de

percent, per cent /pə'sent/ n (no pl) porcentaje m. ● adv por ciento. ~**age** /-ɪdʒ/ n porcentaje m

percepti|ble /pə'septəbl/ adj perceptible. ~**on** /-ʃn/ n

p

percepción f. ~ve /-tɪv/ adj perspicaz

perch /pɜːtʃ/ n (of bird) percha f; (fish) perca f. • vi (bird) posarse. ~ on (person) sentarse en el borde de

percolat|e /'pɜːkəleɪt/ vi filtrarse. ~or n cafetera f eléctrica

percussion /pə'kʌʃn/ n percusión f

perfect /'pɜːfɪkt/ adj perfecto; (place, day) ideal. • /pə'fekt/ vt perfeccionar. ~ion /pə'fekʃn/ n perfección f. to ~ion a la perfección. ~ly /'pɜːfɪktlɪ/ adv perfectamente

perform /pə'fɔːm/ vt desempeñar (function, role); ejecutar (task); realizar (experiment); representar (play); (Mus) interpretar. ~ an operation (Med) operar. • vi (actor) actuar; (musician) tocar; (produce results) (vehicle) responder; (company) rendir. ~ance /-əns/ n ejecución f; (of play) representación f; (of actor, musician) interpretación f; (of team) actuación f; (of car) rendimiento m. ~er n (actor) actor m; (entertainer) artista m & f

perfume /'pɜːfjuːm/ n perfume m

perhaps /pə'hæps/ adv quizá(s), tal vez, a lo mejor

peril /'perəl/ n peligro m. ~ous adj arriesgado, peligroso

perimeter /pə'rɪmɪtə(r)/ n perímetro m

period /'pɪərɪəd/ n período m; (in history) época f; (lesson) clase f; (Amer, Gram) punto m; (menstruation) período m, regla f. • adj de (la) época. ~ic /-'ɒdɪk/ adj periódico. ~ical /pɪərɪ'ɒdɪkl/ n revista f. ~ically adv periódico

peripher|al /pə'rɪfərəl/ adj secundario; (Comp) periférico. ~y /pə'rɪfərɪ/ n periferia f

perish /'perɪʃ/ vi perecer; (rot) deteriorarse. ~able adj perecedero. ~ing adj 🅸 glacial

perjur|e /'pɜːdʒə(r)/ vr. ~e o.s. perjurarse. ~y n perjurio m

perk /pɜːk/ n gaje m. ■ ~ up vt

reanimar. vi reanimarse

perm /pɜːm/ n permanente f. • vt. have one's hair ~ed hacerse la permanente

permanen|ce /'pɜːmənəns/ n permanencia f. ~t adj permanente. ~tly adv permanentemente

permissible /pə'mɪsəbl/ adj permisible

permission /pə'mɪʃn/ n permiso m

permit /pə'mɪt/ vt (pt permitted) permitir. • /'pɜːmɪt/ n permiso m

peroxide /pə'rɒksaɪd/ n peróxido m

perpendicular /pɜːpən'dɪkjʊlə(r)/ adj & n perpendicular (f)

perpetrat|e /'pɜːpɪtreɪt/ vt cometer. ~or n autor m

perpetua|l /pə'petʃʊəl/ adj perpetuo. ~te /pə'petʃʊeɪt/ vt perpetuar

perplex /pə'pleks/ vt dejar perplejo. ~ed adj perplejo

persecut|e /'pɜːsɪkjuːt/ vt perseguir. ~ion /-'kjuːʃn/ n persecución f

persever|ance /pɜːsɪ'vɪərəns/ n perseverancia f. ~e /pɜːsɪ'vɪə(r)/ vi perseverar, persistir

Persian /'pɜːʃn/ adj persa. the ~ Gulf n el golfo Pérsico

persist /pə'sɪst/ vi persistir. ~ence /-əns/ n persistencia f. ~ent adj persistente; (continual) continuo

person /'pɜːsn/ n persona f. in ~ en persona. ~al adj personal; (call) particular; (property) privado. ~al assistant n secretario m personal. ~ality /-'nælətɪ/ n personalidad f. ~ally adv personalmente. ~nel /pɜːsə'nel/ n personal m. P~nel (department) sección f de personal

perspective /pə'spektɪv/ n perspectiva f

perspir|ation /pɜːspə'reɪʃn/ n transpiración f. ~e /pəs'paɪə(r)/ vi transpirar

persua|de /pə'sweɪd/ vt convencer, persuadir. ~e s.o. to do sth convencer a uno para que haga algo. **~sion** n /-ʃn/ persuasión f. **~sive** /-sɪv/ adj persuasivo

pertinent /'pɜːtɪnənt/ adj pertinente. **~ly** adv pertinentemente

perturb /pə'tɜːb/ vt perturbar

Peru /pə'ruː/ n el Perú m

peruse /pə'ruːz/ vt leer cuidadosamente

Peruvian /pə'ruːvɪən/ adj & n peruano (m)

perver|se /pə'vɜːs/ adj retorcido; (stubborn) obstinado. **~sion** n perversión f. **~t** /pə'vɜːt/ vt pervertir. ● /'pɜːvɜːt/ n pervertido m

pessimis|m /'pesɪmɪzəm/ n pesimismo m. **~t** n pesimista m & f. **~tic** /-'mɪstɪk/ adj pesimista

pest /pest/ n plaga f; (🅸, person, thing) peste f

pester /'pestə(r)/ vt importunar

pesticide /'pestɪsaɪd/ n pesticida f

pet /pet/ n animal m doméstico; (favourite) favorito m. ● adj preferido. **my ~ hate** lo que más odio. ● vt (pt **petted**) acariciar

petal /'petl/ n pétalo m

petition /pɪ'tɪʃn/ n petición f

pet name n apodo m

petrified /'petrɪfaɪd/ adj (terrified) muerto de miedo; (rock) petrificado

petrol /'petrəl/ n gasolina f. **~ pump** n surtidor m. **~ station** n gasolinera f. **~ tank** n depósito m de gasolina. **~eum** /pɪ'trəʊlɪəm/ petróleo m.

petticoat /'petɪkəʊt/ n enagua f; (slip) combinación f

petty /'petɪ/ adj (**-ier, -iest**) insignificante; (mean) mezquino. **~ cash** n dinero m para gastos menores

petulant /'petjʊlənt/ adj irritable

pew /pjuː/ n banco m (de iglesia)

phantom /'fæntəm/ n fantasma m

pharma|ceutical /fɑːmə'sjuːtɪkl/ adj farmacéutico. **~cist** /'fɑːməsɪst/ n farmacéutico m. **~cy** /'fɑːməsɪ/ n farmacia f

phase /feɪz/ n etapa f. ■ **~ out** vt retirar progresivamente

PhD abbr (= **Doctor of Philosophy**) n doctorado m; (person) Dr., Dra.

pheasant /'feznt/ n faisán m

phenomen|al /fɪ'nɒmɪnl/ adj fenomenal. **~on** /-ɪnən/ n (pl **-ena** /-ɪnə/) fenómeno m

philistine /'fɪlɪstaɪn/ adj & n filisteo (m)

philosoph|er /fɪ'lɒsəfə(r)/ n filósofo m. **~ical** /-ə'sɒfɪkl/ adj filosófico. **~y** /fɪ'lɒsəfɪ/ n filosofía f

phlegm /flem/ n flema f. **~atic** /fleg'mætɪk/ adj flemático

phobia /'fəʊbɪə/ n fobia f

phone /fəʊn/ n 🅸 teléfono m. ● vt/i llamar (por teléfono). **~ back** (call again) volver a llamar; (return call) llamar (más tarde). **~ book** n guía f telefónica, directorio m (LAm). **~ booth**, **~ box** n cabina f telefónica. **~ call** n llamada f (telefónica). **~ card** n tarjeta f telefónica. **~ number** n número m de teléfono

phonetic /fə'netɪk/ adj fonético. **~s** n fonética f

phoney /'fəʊnɪ/ adj (**-ier, -iest**) 🅸 falso

phosph|ate /'fɒsfeɪt/ n fosfato m. **~orus** /'fɒsfərəs/ n fósforo m

photo /'fəʊtəʊ/ n (pl **-os**) 🅸 foto f. **take a ~** sacar una foto. **~copier** /-kɒpɪə(r)/ n fotocopiadora f. **~copy** n fotocopia f. ● vt fotocopiar. **~genic** /-'dʒenɪk/ adj fotogénico. **~graph** /-grɑːf/ n fotografía f. ● vt fotografiar, sacarle una fotografía a. **~grapher** /fə'tɒgrəfə(r)/ n fotógrafo m. **~graphic** /-'græfɪk/ adj fotográfico. **~graphy** /fə'tɒgrəfɪ/ n fotografía f

phrase /freɪz/ n frase f. ● vt

expresar. ~ **book** n manual m de
conversación

physi|cal /'fızıkl/ adj físico. ~**cian**
/fı'zıʃn/ n médico m. ~**cist**
/'fızısıst/ n físico m. ~**cs** /'fızıks/ n
física f. ~**ology** /fızı'ɒlədʒı/ n
fisiología f. ~**otherapist**
/fızıəʊ'θerəpıst/ n fisioterapeuta m
& f. ~**otherapy** /fızıəʊ'θerəpı/ n
fisioterapia f. ~**que** /fı'ziːk/ n
físico m

pian|ist /'pıənıst/ n pianista m & f.
~**o** /pı'ænəʊ/ n (pl -**os**) piano m

pick /pık/ (tool) pico m. •vt escoger;
cortar (flowers); recoger (fruit, cotton);
abrir con una ganzúa (lock). ~ **a
quarrel** buscar camorra. ~ **holes
in** criticar. ∎~ **on** vt meterse con.
∎~ **out** vt escoger; (identify)
reconocer. ∎~ **up** vt recoger; (lift)
levantar; (learn) aprender; adquirir
(habit, etc); contagiarse de (illness).
•vi mejorar; (sales) subir. ~**axe** n
pico m

picket /'pıkıt/ n (group) piquete m.
~ **line** n piquete m. •vt formar un
piquete frente a

pickle /'pıkl/ n (in vinegar) encurtido
m; (Amer, gherkin) pepinillo m; (relish)
salsa f (a base de encurtidos). •vt
encurtir

pick: ~pocket n carterista m & f.
~**-up** n (truck) camioneta f

picnic /'pıknık/ n picnic m

picture /'pıktʃə(r)/ n (painting)
cuadro m; (photo) foto f; (drawing)
dibujo m; (illustration) ilustración f;
(film) película f; (fig) descripción f.
•vt imaginarse. ~**sque** /-'resk/ adj
pintoresco

pie /paı/ n empanada f; (sweet)
pastel m, tarta f

piece /piːs/ n pedazo m, trozo m;
(part of machine) pieza f; (coin)
moneda f; (in chess) figura f. **a ~ of
advice** un consejo. **a ~ of
furniture** un mueble. **a ~ of
news** una noticia. **take to ~s**
desmontar. ∎~ **together** vt
juntar. ~**meal** adj gradual;

(unsystematic) poco sistemático. •adv
poco a poco

pier /pıə(r)/ n muelle m; (with
amusements) paseo con atracciones
sobre un muelle

pierc|e /pıəs/ vt perforar. ~**ing** adj
penetrante

piety /'paıətı/ n piedad f

pig /pıg/ n cerdo m, chancho m (LAm)

pigeon /'pıdʒın/ n paloma f; (Culin)
pichón m. ~**hole** n casillero m;
(fig) casilla f

piggy /'pıgı/ n cerdito m. ~**back** n.
give s.o. a ~back llevar a uno a
cuestas. ~ **bank** n hucha f

pig-headed /-'hedıd/ adj terco

pigment /'pıgmənt/ n pigmento m

pig|sty /'pıgstaı/ n pocilga f. ~**tail**
n (plait) trenza f; (bunch) coleta f

pike /paık/ n invar (fish) lucio m

pilchard /'pıltʃəd/ n sardina f

pile /paıl/ n (heap) montón m; (of
fabric) pelo m. •vt amontonar. ~ **it
on** exagerar. •vi amontonarse. ∎~
up vt amontonar. •vi amontonarse. ~**s** /paılz/ npl (Med) almorranas fpl.
~**-up** n choque m múltiple

pilgrim /'pılgrım/ n peregrino.
~**age** /-ıdʒ/ n peregrinación f

pill /pıl/ n pastilla f

pillar /'pılə(r)/ n columna f. ~ **box**
n buzón m

pillow /'pıləʊ/ n almohada f. ~**case**
n funda f de almohada

pilot /'paılət/ n piloto m. •vt pilotar.
~ **light** n fuego m piloto

pimple /'pımpl/ n grano m,
espinilla f (LAm)

pin /pın/ n alfiler m; (Mec) perno m.
~**s and needles** hormigueo m. •vt
(pt **pinned**) prender con alfileres;
(fix) sujetar

PIN /pın/ n (= **personal
identification number**) NIP m

pinafore /'pınəfɔː(r)/ n delantal m.
~ **dress** n pichi m, jumper m & f
(LAm)

pincers /'pɪnsəz/ npl tenazas fpl

pinch /pɪntʃ/ vt pellizcar; (fam, steal) hurtar. ●vi (shoe) apretar. ●n pellizco m; (small amount) pizca f. **at a ~** si fuera necesario

pine /paɪn/ n pino m. ●vi. **~ for sth** suspirar por algo. ■ **~ away** vi languidecer de añoranza. **~apple** /'paɪnæpl/ n piña f

ping-pong /'pɪŋpɒŋ/ n ping-pong m

pink /pɪŋk/ adj & n rosa (m), rosado (m)

pinnacle /'pɪnəkl/ n pináculo m

pin: **~point** vt determinar con precisión f. **~stripe** n raya f fina

pint /paɪnt/ n pinta f (= 0.57 litros)

pioneer /paɪə'nɪə(r)/ n pionero m

pious /'paɪəs/ adj piadoso

pip /pɪp/ n (seed) pepita f; (time signal) señal f

pipe /paɪp/ n tubo m; (Mus) caramillo m; (for smoking) pipa f. ●vt llevar por tuberías. **~-dream** n ilusión f. **~line** n conducto m; (for oil) oleoducto m. **in the ~line** en preparación f

piping /'paɪpɪŋ/ n tubería f. ●adv. **~ hot** muy caliente, hirviendo

pira|cy /'paɪərəsɪ/ n piratería f. **~te** /'paɪərət/ n pirata m

Pisces /'paɪsiːz/ n Piscis m

piss /pɪs/ vi ☒ mear. ■ **~ off** vi ☒. **~ off!** ¡vete a la mierda! **~ed** /pɪst/ adj (☒, drunk) como una cuba; (Amer, fed up) cabreado

pistol /'pɪstl/ n pistola f

piston /'pɪstən/ n pistón m

pit /pɪt/ n hoyo m; (mine) mina f; (Amer, in fruit) hueso m

pitch /pɪtʃ/ n (substance) brea f; (degree) grado m; (Mus) tono m; (Sport) campo m. ●vt (throw) lanzar; armar (tent). ●vi (ship) cabecear. **~-black** /-'blæk/ adj oscuro como boca de lobo. **~er** n jarra f

pitfall /'pɪtfɔːl/ n trampa f

pith /pɪθ/ n (of orange, lemon) médula f; (fig) meollo m

pitiful /'pɪtɪfl/ adj lastimoso

pittance /'pɪtns/ n miseria f

pity /'pɪtɪ/ n lástima f, pena f; (compassion) piedad f. **it's a ~ you can't come** es una lástima que no puedas venir. ●vt tenerle lástima a

pivot /'pɪvət/ n pivote m. ●vi pivotar; (fig) depender (**on** de)

placard /'plækɑːd/ n pancarta f; (sign) letrero m

placate /plə'keɪt/ vt apaciguar

place /pleɪs/ n lugar m; (seat) asiento m; (in firm, team) puesto m; (fam, house) casa f. **feel out of ~** sentirse fuera de lugar. **take ~** tener lugar. ●vt poner, colocar; (identify) identificar. **be ~d** (in race) colocarse. **~mat** n mantel m individual

placid /'plæsɪd/ adj plácido

plague /pleɪg/ n peste f; (fig) plaga f. ●vt atormentar

plaice /pleɪs/ n invar platija f

plain /pleɪn/ adj (**-er, -est**) (clear) claro; (simple) sencillo; (candid) franco; (ugly) feo. **in ~ clothes** de civil. ●adv totalmente. ●n llanura f. **~ly** adv claramente; (frankly) francamente; (simply) con sencillez

plaintiff /'pleɪntɪf/ n demandante m & f

plait /plæt/ vt trenzar. ●n trenza f

plan /plæn/ n plan m; (map) plano m; (of book, essay) esquema f. ●vt (pt **planned**) planear; planificar (strategies). **I'm ~ning to go to Greece** pienso ir a Grecia

plane /pleɪn/ n (tree) plátano m; (level) nivel m; (aircraft) avión m; (tool) cepillo m. ●vt cepillar

planet /'plænɪt/ n planeta m. **~ary** adj planetario

plank /plæŋk/ n tabla f

planning /'plænɪŋ/ n planificación f. **family ~** planificación familiar. **town ~** urbanismo m

P

plant /plɑːnt/ n planta f; (Mec) maquinaria f; (factory) fábrica f. •vt plantar; (place in position) colocar. ~**ation** /plænˈteɪʃn/ n plantación f

plaque /plæk/ n placa f

plasma /ˈplæzmə/ n plasma m

plaster /ˈplɑːstə(r)/ n yeso m; (on walls) revoque m; (sticking plaster) tirita f (®), curita f (®) (LAm); (for setting bones) yeso m, escayola f. •vt revocar; rellenar con yeso (cracks)

plastic /ˈplæstɪk/ adj & n plástico (m)

Plasticine /ˈplæstɪsiːn/ n (®) plastilina f (®)

plastic surgery /plæstɪkˈsɜːdʒərɪ/ n cirugía f estética

plate /pleɪt/ n plato m; (of metal) chapa f; (silverware) vajilla f de plata; (in book) lámina f. •vt recubrir (**with** de)

platform /ˈplætfɔːm/ n plataforma f; (Rail) andén m

platinum /ˈplætɪnəm/ n platino m

platitude /ˈplætɪtjuːd/ n lugar m común

platonic /pləˈtɒnɪk/ adj platónico

plausible /ˈplɔːzəbl/ adj verosímil; (person) convincente

play /pleɪ/ vt jugar a (game, cards); jugar a, jugar (LAm) (football, chess); tocar (instrument); (act role) representar el papel de. •vi jugar. •n juego m; (drama) obra f de teatro. ■ ~ **down** vt minimizar. ■ ~ **up** vi 🔢 (child) dar guerra; (car, TV) no funcionar bien. ~**er** n jugador m; (Mus) músico m. ~**ful** adj juguetón. ~**ground** n parque m de juegos infantiles; (in school) patio m de recreo. ~**group** n jardín m de la infancia. ~**ing card** n naipe m. ~**ing field** n campo m de deportes. ~**pen** n corralito m. ~**wright** /-raɪt/ n dramaturgo m

plc abbr (= **public limited company**) S.A.

plea /pliː/ n súplica f; (excuse) excusa f; (Jurid) defensa f

plead /pliːd/ vt (Jurid) alegar; (as excuse) pretextar. •vi suplicar. ~ **with** suplicarle a. ~ **guilty** declararse culpable

pleasant /ˈpleznt/ adj agradable

pleas|e /pliːz/ int por favor. •vt complacer; (satisfy) contentar. •vi agradar; (wish) querer. ~**ed** adj (satisfied) satisfecho; (happy) contento. ~**ed with** satisfecho de. ~**ing** adj agradable; (news) grato. ~**ure** /ˈpleʒə(r)/ n placer m

pleat /pliːt/ n pliegue m

pledge /pledʒ/ n cantidad f prometida

plent|iful /ˈplentɪfl/ adj abundante. ~**y** /ˈplentɪ/ n abundancia f. •pron. ~**y of** muchos, -chas; (of sth uncountable) mucho, -cha

pliable /ˈplaɪəbl/ adj flexible

pliers /ˈplaɪəz/ npl alicates mpl

plight /plaɪt/ n situación f difícil

plimsolls /ˈplɪmsəlz/ npl zapatillas fpl de lona

plod /plɒd/ vi (pt **plodded**) caminar con paso pesado

plot /plɒt/ n complot m; (of novel etc) argumento m; (piece of land) parcela f. •vt (pt **plotted**) tramar; (mark out) trazar. •vi conspirar

plough /plaʊ/ n arado m. •vt/i arar. ■ ~ **into** vt estrellarse contra. ■ ~ **through** vt avanzar laboriosamente por

ploy /plɔɪ/ n treta f

pluck /plʌk/ vt arrancar; depilarse (eyebrows); desplumar (bird). ~ **up courage to** armarse de valor para. •n valor m. ~**y** adj (**-ier, -iest**) valiente

plug /plʌg/ n (in bath) tapón m; (Elec) enchufe m; (spark ~) bujía f. •vt (pt **plugged**) tapar; (fam, advertise) hacerle propaganda a. ■ ~ **in** vt (Elec) enchufar. ~**hole** n desagüe m

plum /plʌm/ n ciruela f

plumage /ˈpluːmɪdʒ/ n plumaje m

plumb|er /'plʌmə(r)/ n fontanero m, plomero m (LAm). **~ing** n instalación f sanitaria, instalación f de cañerías

plume /pluːm/ n pluma f

plump /plʌmp/ adj (-er, -est) rechoncho

plunge /plʌndʒ/ vt hundir (knife); (in water) sumergir; (into state, condition) sumir. ●vi zambullirse; (fall) caer. ●n zambullida f

plural /'plʊərəl/ n plural m. ●adj en plural

plus /plʌs/ prep más. ●adj positivo. ●n signo m de más; (fig) ventaja f

plush /plʌʃ/ adj lujoso

Pluto /'pluːtəʊ/ n Plutón m

plutonium /pluː'təʊnɪəm/ n plutonio m

ply /plaɪ/ vt manejar (tool); ejercer (trade). **~ s.o. with drink** dar continuamente de beber a uno. **~wood** n contrachapado m

p.m. abbr (= **post meridiem**) de la tarde

pneumatic drill /njuː'mætɪk/ adj martillo m neumático

pneumonia /njuː'məʊnjə/ n pulmonía f

poach /pəʊtʃ/ vt escalfar (egg); cocer (fish etc); (steal) cazar furtivamente. **~er** n cazador m furtivo

PO box /piː'əʊ/ n Apdo. postal

pocket /'pɒkɪt/ n bolsillo m; (of air, resistance) bolsa f. ●vt poner en el bolsillo. **~book** n (notebook) libro m de bolsillo; (Amer, wallet) cartera f; (Amer, handbag) bolso m, cartera f (LAm), bolsa f (Mex). **~ money** n dinero m de bolsillo, mesada f (LAm)

pod /pɒd/ n vaina f

poem /'pəʊɪm/ n poema m

poet /'pəʊɪt/ n poeta m. **~ic** /-'etɪk/ adj poético. **~ry** /'pəʊɪtrɪ/ n poesía f

poignant /'pɔɪnjənt/ adj conmovedor

point /pɔɪnt/ n (dot, on scale) punto m; (sharp end) punta f; (in time) momento m; (statement) observación; (on agenda, in discussion) punto m; (Elec) toma f de corriente. **to the ~** pertinente. **up to a ~** hasta cierto punto. **be on the ~ of** estar a punto de. **get to the ~** ir al grano. **there's no ~ (in) arguing** no sirve de nada discutir. ●vt (aim) apuntar; (show) indicar. ●vi señalar. **~ at/to sth** señalar algo. **~ out** vt señalar. **~-blank** adj & adv a quemarropa. **~ed** adj (chin, nose) puntiagudo; (fig) mordaz. **~less** adj inútil

poise /pɔɪz/ n porte m; (composure) desenvoltura f

poison /'pɔɪzn/ n veneno m. ●vt envenenar. **~ous** adj venenoso; (chemical etc) tóxico

poke /pəʊk/ vt empujar; atizar (fire). ●vi hurgar; (pry) meterse. ●n golpe m. ■ **~ about** vi fisgonear. **~r** /'pəʊkə(r)/ n atizador m; (Cards) póquer m

poky /'pəʊkɪ/ adj (-ier, -iest) diminuto

Poland /'pəʊlənd/ n Polonia f

polar /'pəʊlə(r)/ adj polar. **~ bear** n oso m blanco

pole /pəʊl/ n palo m; (fixed) poste m; (for flag) mástil m; (in geography) polo m

police /pə'liːs/ n policía f. **~man** /-mən/ n policía m, agente m. **~ station** n comisaría f. **~woman** n policía f, agente f

policy /'pɒlɪsɪ/ n política f; (insurance) póliza f (de seguros)

polish /'pɒlɪʃ/ n (for shoes) betún m; (furniture ~) cera f para muebles; (floor ~) abrillantador m de suelos; (shine) brillo m; (fig) finura f. ●vt darle brillo a; limpiar (shoes); (refine) pulir. ■ **~ off** vt despachar. **~ed** adj pulido

Polish /'pəʊlɪʃ/ adj & n polaco (m)

polite /pə'laɪt/ adj cortés. **~ly** adv cortésmente. **~ness** n cortesía f

politic|al /pəˈlɪtɪkl/ adj político. **∼ian** /pɒlɪˈtɪʃn/ n político m. **∼s** /ˈpɒlətɪks/ n política f

poll /pəʊl/ n elección f; (survey) encuesta f. ●vt obtener (votes)

pollack /ˈpɒlæk/ n abadejo m

pollen /ˈpɒlən/ n polen m

polling booth n cabina f de votar

pollut|e /pəˈluːt/ vt contaminar. **∼ion** /-ʃn/ n contaminación f

polo /ˈpəʊləʊ/ n polo m. **∼ neck** n cuello m vuelto

poly|styrene /pɒlɪˈstaɪriːn/ n poliestireno m. **∼thene** /ˈpɒlɪθiːn/ n plástico, polietileno m

pomp /pɒmp/ n pompa f. **∼ous** adj pomposa

pond /pɒnd/ n (natural) laguna f; (artificial) estanque m

ponder /ˈpɒndə(r)/ vt considerar. **∼ous** adj pesado

pony /ˈpəʊnɪ/ n poni m. **∼-tail** n cola f de caballo

poodle /ˈpuːdl/ n caniche m

pool /puːl/ n charca f; (artificial) estanque m; (puddle) charco m. (common fund) fondos mpl comunes; (snooker) billar m americano. **(swimming)** ∼ n piscina f, alberca f (Mex). **∼s** npl quinielas fpl. ●vt aunar

poor /pʊə(r)/ adj (-er, -est) pobre; (quality, diet) malo. **be in ∼ health** estar mal de salud. **∼ly** adj 🔲 malito. ●adv mal

pop /pɒp/ n (Mus) música f pop; (Amer fam, father) papá m. ●vt (pt **popped**) hacer reventar; (put) poner. ■∼ **in** vi (visit) pasar por. ■∼ **out** vi saltar; (person) salir un rato. ■∼ **up** vi surgir, aparecer

popcorn /ˈpɒpkɔːn/ n palomitas fpl

pope /pəʊp/ n papa m

poplar /ˈpɒplə(r)/ n álamo m (blanco)

poppy /ˈpɒpɪ/ n amapola f

popular /ˈpɒpjʊlə(r)/ adj popular.

∼ity /-ˈlærətɪ/ n popularidad f. **∼ize** vt popularizar

populat|e /ˈpɒpjʊleɪt/ vt poblar. **∼ion** /-ˈleɪʃn/ n población f

pop-up /ˈpɒpʌp/ n ventana f emergente, pop-up m

porcelain /ˈpɔːsəlɪn/ n porcelana f

porch /pɔːtʃ/ n porche m

porcupine /ˈpɔːkjʊpaɪn/ n puerco m espín

pore /pɔː(r)/ n poro m

pork /pɔːk/ n carne f de cerdo m, carne f de puerco m (Mex)

porn /pɔːn/ n 🔲 pornografía f. **∼ographic** /-əˈgræfɪk/ adj pornográfico. **∼ography** /pɔːˈnɒɡrəfɪ/ n pornografía f

porpoise /ˈpɔːpəs/ n marsopa f

porridge /ˈpɒrɪdʒ/ n avena f (cocida)

port /pɔːt/ n puerto m; (Naut) babor m; (Comp) puerto m; (Culin) oporto m

portable /ˈpɔːtəbl/ adj portátil

porter /ˈpɔːtə(r)/ n (for luggage) maletero m; (concierge) portero m

porthole /ˈpɔːthəʊl/ n portilla f

portion /ˈpɔːʃn/ n porción f; (part) parte f

portrait /ˈpɔːtrɪt/ n retrato m

portray /pɔːˈtreɪ/ vt representar. **∼al** n representación f

Portug|al /ˈpɔːtjʊgl/ n Portugal m. **∼uese** /-ˈgiːz/ adj & n portugués (m)

pose /pəʊz/ n pose f, postura f. ●vt representar (threat); plantear (problem, question). ●vi posar. ∼ **as** hacerse pasar por

posh /pɒʃ/ adj 🔲 elegante

position /pəˈzɪʃn/ n posición f; (job) puesto m; (situation) situación f. ●vt colocar

positive /ˈpɒzətɪv/ adj positivo; (real) auténtico; (certain) seguro. ●n (Photo) positiva f. **∼ly** adv positivamente

possess /pəˈzes/ vt poseer. **∼ion**

/-ʃn/ n posesión f; (Jurid) bien m. ~**ive** adj posesivo

possib|ility /pɒsə'bɪlətɪ/ n posibilidad f. ~**le** /'pɒsəbl/ adj posible. ~**ly** adv posiblemente

post /pəʊst/ n (pole) poste m; (job) puesto m; (mail) correo m. ● vt echar al correo (letter); (send) enviar por correo. **keep s.o.** ~**ed** mantener a uno al corriente

post... /pəʊst/ pref post, pos

post: ~**age** /-ɪdʒ/ /-ɪdʒ/ n franqueo m. ~**al** adj postal. ~**al order** n giro m postal. ~ **box** n buzón m. ~**card** n (tarjeta f) postal f. ~**code** n código m postal

poster /'pəʊstə(r)/ n cartel m, póster m

posterity /pɒs'terətɪ/ n posteridad f

posthumous /'pɒstjʊməs/ adj póstumo

post: ~**man** /-mən/ n cartero m. ~**mark** n matasellos m

post mortem /pəʊst'mɔːtəm/ n autopsia f

post office n oficina f de correos, correos mpl, correo m (LAm)

postpone /pəʊst'pəʊn/ vt aplazar, posponer. ~**ment** n aplazamiento m

postscript /'pəʊstskrɪpt/ n posdata f

posture /'pɒstʃə(r)/ n postura f

posy /'pəʊzɪ/ n ramillete m

pot /pɒt/ n (for cooking) olla f; (for jam, honey) tarro m; (for flowers) tiesto m; (in pottery) vasija f. ~**s and pans** cacharros mpl

potato /pə'teɪtəʊ/ n (pl -**oes**) patata f, papa f (LAm)

potent /'pəʊtnt/ adj potente; (drink) fuerte

potential /pəʊ'tenʃl/ adj & n potencial (m). ~**ly** adv potencialmente

pot: ~**hole** n cueva f subterránea;

(in road) bache m. ~**holing** n espeleología f

potion /'pəʊʃn/ n poción f

pot-shot n tiro m al azar

potter /'pɒtə(r)/ n alfarero m. ● vi hacer pequeños trabajos agradables. ~**y** n (pots) cerámica f; (workshop, craft) alfarería f

potty /'pɒtɪ/ adj (-**ier, -iest**) 🔟 chiflado. ● n orinal m

pouch /paʊtʃ/ n bolsa f pequeña; (for correspondence) valija f

poultry /'pəʊltrɪ/ n aves fpl de corral

pounce /paʊns/ vi saltar. ~ **on** abalanzarse sobre

pound /paʊnd/ n (weight) libra f (= 454g); (money) libra f (esterlina); (for cars) depósito m. ● vt (crush) machacar. ● vi (heart) palpitar; (sound) retumbar

pour /pɔː(r)/ vt verter; echar (salt). ~ (**out**) servir (drink). ● vi (blood) manar; (water) salir; (rain) llover a cántaros. ■ ~ **out** vi (people) salir en tropel. ~**ing** adj. ~**ing rain** lluvia f torrencial

pout /paʊt/ vi hacer pucheros

poverty /'pɒvətɪ/ n pobreza f

powder /'paʊdə(r)/ n polvo m; (cosmetic) polvos mpl. ● vt empolvar. ~ **one's face** ponerse polvos en la cara. ~**y** adj como polvo

power /'paʊə(r)/ n poder m; (energy) energía f; (electricity) electricidad f; (nation) potencia f. ● vt. ~**ed by** impulsado por. ~ **cut** n apagón m. ~**ed** adj con motor. ~**ful** adj poderoso. ~**less** adj impotente. ~ **plant**, ~**-station** n central f eléctrica

PR = **public relations**

practicable /'præktɪkəbl/ adj practicable

practical /'præktɪkl/ adj práctico. ~ **joke** n broma f. ~**ly** adv prácticamente

practi|ce /'præktɪs/ n práctica f;

p

(custom) costumbre f; (exercise) ejercicio m; (Sport) entrenamiento m; (clients) clientela f. **he's out of ∼ce** le falta práctica. **in ∼ce** (in fact) en la práctica. **∼se** /'præktɪs/ vt practicar; ensayar (act); ejercer (profession). ● vi practicar; (professional) ejercer. **∼tioner** /-'tɪʃənə(r)/ n médico m

prairie /'preərɪ/ n pradera f

praise /preɪz/ vt (Relig) alabar; (compliment) elogiar. ● n (credit) elogios mpl. **∼worthy** adj loable

pram /præm/ n cochecito m

prank /præŋk/ n travesura f

prawn /prɔːn/ n gamba f, camarón m (LAm)

pray /preɪ/ vi rezar (**for** por). **∼er** /preə(r)/ n oración f

pre.. /priː/ pref pre...

preach /priːtʃ/ vt/i predicar. **∼er** n predicador m; (Amer, minister) pastor m

pre-arrange /priːə'reɪndʒ/ vt concertar de antemano

precarious /prɪ'keərɪəs/ adj precario. **∼ly** adv precariamente

precaution /prɪ'kɔːʃn/ n precaución f

precede /prɪ'siːd/ vt preceder. **∼nce** /'presədəns/ n precedencia f. **∼nt** /'presədənt/ n precedente m

preceding /prɪ'siːdɪŋ/ adj anterior

precept /'priːsept/ n precepto m

precinct /'priːsɪŋkt/ n recinto m; (Amer, police district) distrito m policial; (Amer, voting district) circunscripción f. **pedestrian ∼** zona f peatonal. **∼s** (of city) límites mpl

precious /'preʃəs/ adj precioso. ● adv 🄼 muy

precipice /'presɪpɪs/ n precipicio m

precipitate /prɪ'sɪpɪteɪt/ vt precipitar. ● /prɪ'sɪpɪtət/ n precipitado m. ● /prɪ'sɪpɪtət/ adj precipitado

precis|e /prɪ'saɪs/ adj (accurate)

exacto; (specific) preciso; (meticulous) minucioso. **∼ely** adv con precisión. **∼!** ¡exacto! **∼ion** /-'sɪʒn/ n precisión f

preclude /prɪ'kluːd/ vt excluir

precocious /prɪ'kəʊʃəs/ adj precoz. **∼ly** adv precozmente

preconce|ived /priːkən'siːvd/ adj preconcebido. **∼ption** /-'sepʃn/ n preconcepción f

precursor /priː'kɜːsə(r)/ n precursor m

predator /'predətə(r)/ n depredador m. **∼y** adj predador

predecessor /'priːdɪsesə(r)/ n predecesor m, antecesor m

predicament /prɪ'dɪkəmənt/ n aprieto m

predict /prɪ'dɪkt/ vt predecir. **∼ion** /-ʃn/ n predicción f

preen /priːn/ vt arreglar. **∼ o.s.** atildarse

prefab /'priːfæb/ n 🄼 casa f prefabricada. **∼ricated** /-'fæbrɪkeɪtɪd/ adj prefabricado

preface /'prefəs/ n prefacio m; (to event) prólogo m

prefect /'priːfekt/ n (Schol) monitor m; (official) prefecto m

prefer /prɪ'fɜː(r)/ vt (pt **preferred**) preferir. **∼ sth to sth** preferir algo a algo. **∼able** /'prefrəbl/ adj preferible. **∼ence** /'prefrəns/ n preferencia f. **∼ential** /-ə'renʃl/ adj preferente

pregnan|cy /'pregnənsɪ/ n embarazo m. **∼t** adj embarazada

prehistoric /priːhɪ'stɒrɪk/ adj prehistórico

prejudge /priː'dʒʌdʒ/ vt prejuzgar

prejudice /'predʒʊdɪs/ n prejuicio m. ● vt predisponer; (harm) perjudicar. **∼d** adj lleno de prejuicios

preliminary /prɪ'lɪmɪnərɪ/ adj preliminar

prelude /'preljuːd/ n preludio m

premature /ˈprematjʊə(r)/ adj prematuro

premeditated /priːˈmedɪteɪtɪd/ adj premeditado

premier /ˈpremɪə(r)/ n (Pol) primer ministro m

première /ˈpremɪeə(r)/ n estreno m

premise /ˈpremɪs/ n premisa f. ~s /ˈpremɪsɪz/ npl local m. **on the ~s** en el local

premium /ˈpriːmɪəm/ n (insurance ~) prima f de seguro. **be at a ~** escasear

premonition /priːməˈnɪʃn/ n premonición f, presentimiento m

preoccup|ation /priːɒkjʊˈpeɪʃn/ n (obsession) obsesión f; (concern) preocupación f. ~ied /-ˈɒkjʊpaɪd/ adj absorto; (worried) preocupado

preparat|ion /prepəˈreɪʃn/ n preparación f. ~ions npl preparativos mpl. ~ory /prɪˈpærətrɪ/ adj preparatorio

prepare /prɪˈpeə(r)/ vt preparar. ● vi prepararse. ● adj preparado (willing). **be ~d to** estar dispuesto a

preposition /prepəˈzɪʃn/ n preposición f

preposterous /prɪˈpɒstərəs/ adj absurdo

prerequisite /priːˈrekwɪzɪt/ n requisito m esencial

prerogative /prɪˈrɒgətɪv/ n prerrogativa f

Presbyterian /prezbɪˈtɪərɪən/ adj & n presbiteriano (m)

prescri|be /prɪˈskraɪb/ vt prescribir; (Med) recetar. ~ption /-ˈɪpʃn/ n (Med) receta f

presence /ˈprezns/ n presencia f. ~ **of mind** presencia f de ánimo

present /ˈpreznt/ n (gift) regalo m; (current time) presente m. **at ~** actualmente. **for the ~** por ahora. ● adj presente. ● /prɪˈzent/ vt presentar; (give) obsequiar. ~ **s.o. with** obsequiar a uno con. ~able /prɪˈzentəbl/ adj presentable.

~ation /prezn̩ˈteɪʃn/ n presentación f; (ceremony) ceremonia f de entrega. ~er /prɪˈzentə(r)/ n presentador m. ~ly /ˈprezntlɪ/ adv dentro de poco

preserv|ation /prezəˈveɪʃn/ n conservación f. ~ative /prɪˈzɜːvətɪv/ n conservante m. ~e /prɪˈzɜːv/ vt conservar; (maintain) mantener; (Culin) hacer conserva de. ● n coto m; (jam) confitura f. **wildlife ~e** (Amer) reserva f de animales

preside /prɪˈzaɪd/ vi presidir. ~ **over** presidir

presiden|cy /ˈprezɪdənsɪ/ n presidencia f. ~t n presidente m. ~tial /-ˈdenʃl/ adj presidencial

press /pres/ vt apretar; prensar (grapes); (put pressure on) presionar; (iron) planchar. **be ~ed for time** andar escaso de tiempo. ● vi apretar; (time) apremiar; (fig) urgir. ● n (Mec, newspapers) prensa f; (printing) imprenta f. ■ ~ **on** vi seguir adelante (**with** con). ~ **conference** n rueda f de prensa. ~ **cutting** n recorte m de periódico. ~ing adj urgente. ~-up n flexión f, fondo m

pressur|e /ˈpreʃə(r)/ n presión f. ● vt presionar. ~**e-cooker** n olla f a presión. ~ize vt presionar

prestig|e /preˈstiːʒ/ n prestigio m. ~ious /-ˈstɪdʒəs/ adj prestigioso

presum|ably /prɪˈzjuːməblɪ/ adv. ~... supongo que..., me imagino que... ~e /prɪˈzjuːm/ vt suponer. ~ptuous /prɪˈzʌmptʃʊəs/ adj impertinente

presuppose /priːsəˈpəʊz/ vt presuponer

preten|ce /prɪˈtens/ n fingimiento m; (claim) pretensión f; (pretext) pretexto m. ~d /-ˈtend/ vt/i fingir. ~sion /-ˈtenʃən/ n pretensión f. ~tious /-ˈtenʃəs/ adj pretencioso

pretext /ˈpriːtekst/ n pretexto m

pretty /ˈprɪtɪ/ adj (-ier, -iest) adv bonito, lindo (esp LAm)

prevail /prɪ'veɪl/ vi predominar; (win) prevalecer. ■ ~ **on** vt persuadir

prevalen|ce /'prevələns/ n (occurrence) preponderancia f; (predominance) predominio m. ~**t** adj extendido

prevent /prɪ'vent/ vt (hinder) impedir; (forestall) prevenir, evitar. ~**ion** /-ʃn/ n prevención f. ~**ive** adj preventivo

preview /'pri:vju:/ n preestreno m; (trailer) avance m

previous /'pri:vɪəs/ adj anterior. ~ **to** antes de. ~**ly** adv antes

prey /preɪ/ n presa f. **bird of** ~ ave f de rapiña

price /praɪs/ n precio m. •vt fijar el precio de. ~**less** adj inestimable; (fam, amusing) muy divertido. ~**y** adj 🅘 carito

prick /prɪk/ vt/i pinchar. •n pinchazo m

prickl|e /'prɪkl/ n (thorn) espina f; (of animal) púa f; (sensation) picor m. ~**y** adj espinoso; (animal) con púas; (touchy) quisquilloso

pride /praɪd/ n orgullo m. •vr. ~ **o.s. on** enorgullecerse de

priest /pri:st/ n sacerdote m. ~**hood** n sacerdocio m

prim /prɪm/ adj (**primmer, primmest**) mojigato; (affected) remilgado

primar|ily /'praɪmərɪli/ adv en primer lugar. ~**y** /'praɪmərɪ/ adj (principal) primordial; (first, basic) primario. ~ **school** n escuela f primaria

prime /praɪm/ vt cebar (gun); (prepare) preparar; aprestar (surface). •adj principal; (first rate) excelente. ~ **minister** n primer ministro m. •n. **be in one's** ~ estar en la flor de la vida. ~**r** n (paint) imprimación f

primeval /praɪ'mi:vl/ adj primigenio

primitive /'prɪmɪtɪv/ adj primitivo

primrose /'prɪmrəʊz/ n primavera f

prince /prɪns/ n príncipe m. ~**ss** /prɪn'ses/ n princesa f

principal /'prɪnsəpl/ adj principal. •n (of school) director m; (of university) rector m. ~**ly** /'prɪnsɪpəli/ adv principalmente

principle /'prɪnsəpl/ n principio m. **in** ~ en principio. **on** ~ por principio

print /prɪnt/ vt imprimir; (write in capitals) escribir con letras de molde. ~**ed matter** impresos mpl. •n (characters) letra f; (picture) grabado m; (Photo) copia f; (fabric) estampado m. **in** ~ (published) publicado; (available) a la venta. **out of** ~ agotado. ~**er** /'prɪntə(r)/ n impresor m; (machine) impresora f. ~**ing** n impresión f; (trade) imprenta f. ~**out** n listado m

prion /'praɪɒn/ n prión m

prior /'praɪə(r)/ n prior m. •adj previo. ~ **to** antes de. ~**ity** /praɪ'ɒrətɪ/ n prioridad f. ~**y** n priorato m

prise /praɪz/ vt. ~ **open** abrir haciendo palanca

prison /'prɪzn/ n cárcel m. ~**er** n prisionero m; (in prison) preso m; (under arrest) detenido m. ~ **officer** n funcionario m de prisiones

priva|cy /'prɪvəsɪ/ n privacidad f. ~**te** /'praɪvɪt/ adj privado; (confidential) personal; (lessons, house) particular. **in** ~**te** en privado; (secretly) en secreto. •n soldado m raso. ~**te detective** n detective m & f privado. ~**tely** adv en privado. ~**tion** /praɪ'veɪʃn/ n privación f

privilege /'prɪvɪlɪdʒ/ n privilegio m. ~**d** adj privilegiado. **be** ~**d to** tener el privilegio de

prize /praɪz/ n premio m. •adj (idiot etc) de remate. •vt estimar

pro /prəʊ/ n. ~**s and cons** los pros y los contras

probab|ility /prɒbə'bɪlətɪ/ n probabilidad f. ~**le** /'prɒbəbl/ adj probable. ~**ly** adv probablemente

probation /prə'beɪʃn/ n período m de prueba; (Jurid) libertad f condicional

probe /prəʊb/ n sonda f; (fig) investigación f. ●vt sondar. ●vi. ~ **into** investigar

problem /'prɒbləm/ n problema m. ●adj difícil. ~**atic** /-'mætɪk/ adj problemático

procedure /prə'si:dʒə(r)/ n procedimiento m

proceed /prə'si:d/ vi proceder; (move forward) avanzar. ~**ings** npl (report) actas fpl; (Jurid) proceso m. ~**s** /'prəʊsi:dz/ npl. **the** ~**s** lo recaudado

process /'prəʊses/ n proceso m. **in the** ~ **of** en vías de. ●vt tratar; revelar (photo); tramitar (order). ~**ion** /prə'seʃn/ n desfile m; (Relig) procesión f. ~**or** n procesador m. **food** ~ procesador m de alimentos

procla|im /prə'kleɪm/ vt proclamar. ~**mation** /prɒklə'meɪʃn/ n proclamación f

procure /prə'kjʊə(r)/ vt obtener

prod /prɒd/ vt (pt **prodded**) (with sth sharp) pinchar; (with elbow) darle un codazo a. ●n (with sth sharp) pinchazo m; (with elbow) codazo m

produce /prə'dju:s/ vt producir; surtir (effect); sacar (gun); producir (film); poner en escena (play). ●/'prɒdju:s/ n productos mpl. ~**er** /prə'dju:sə(r)/ n (TV, Cinema) productor m; (in theatre) director m; (manufacturer) fabricante m & f. ~**t** /'prɒdʌkt/ n producto m. ~**tion** /prə'dʌkʃn/ n (manufacture) fabricación f; (output) producción f; (of play) producción f. ~**tive** /prə'dʌktɪv/ adj productivo. ~**tivity** /prɒdʌk'tɪvətɪ/ n productividad f

profess /prə'fes/ vt profesar; (pretend) pretender. ~**ion** /-'feʃn/ n profesión f. ~**ional** adj & n profesional (m & f). ~**or** /-'fesə(r)/ n catedrático m; (Amer) profesor m

proficien|cy /prə'fɪʃənsɪ/ n

competencia f. ~**t** adj competente

profile /'prəʊfaɪl/ n perfil m

profit /'prɒfɪt/ n (Com) ganancia f; (fig) provecho m. ●vi. ~ **from** sacar provecho de. ~**able** adj provechoso

profound /prə'faʊnd/ adj profundo. ~**ly** adv profundamente

profus|e /prə'fju:s/ adj profuso. ~**ely** adv profusamente

prognosis /prɒg'nəʊsɪs/ n (pl **-oses**) pronóstico m

program /'prəʊgræm/ n (Comp) programa m; (Amer, course) curso m. ~**me** /'prəʊgræm/ n programa m. ●vt (pt **-med**) programar. ~**mer** n programador m

progress /'prəʊgres/ n progreso m; (development) desarrollo m. **make** ~ hacer progresos. **in** ~ en curso. ●/prə'gres/ vi hacer progresos; (develop) desarrollarse. ~**ion** /prə'greʃn/ n progresión f; (advance) evolución f. ~**ive** /prə'gresɪv/ adj progresivo; (reforming) progresista. ~**ively** adv progresivamente

prohibit /prə'hɪbɪt/ vt prohibir; (prevent) impedir. ~**ive** adj prohibitivo

project /prə'dʒekt/ vt proyectar. ●vi (stick out) sobresalir. ●/'prɒdʒekt/ n proyecto m; (Schol) trabajo m; (Amer, housing ~) complejo m de viviendas subvencionadas. ~**or** /prə'dʒektə(r)/ n proyector m

prolific /prə'lɪfɪk/ adj prolífico

prologue /'prəʊlɒg/ n prólogo m

prolong /prə'lɒŋ/ vt prolongar

prom /prɒm/ n (Amer) baile m del colegio. ~**enade** /prɒmə'nɑːd/ n paseo m marítimo. ●vi pasearse.

prominen|ce /'prɒmɪnəns/ n prominencia f; (fig) importancia f. ~**t** adj prominente; (important) importante; (conspicuous) destacado

promiscu|ity /prɒmɪ'skju:ətɪ/ n promiscuidad f. ~**ous** /prə'mɪskjʊəs/ adj promiscuo

promis|e /'prɒmɪs/ n promesa f.

•vt/i prometer. **~ing** adj prometedor; (future) halagüeño

promot|e /prə'məʊt/ vt promover; promocionar (product); (in rank) ascender. **~ion** /-'məʊʃn/ n promoción f; (in rank) ascenso m

prompt /prɒmpt/ adj rápido; (punctual) puntual. •adv en punto. •n (Comp) presto m. •vt incitar; apuntar (actor). **~ly** adv puntualmente

prone /prəʊn/ adj (tendido) boca abajo. **be ~ to** ser propenso a

pronoun /'prəʊnaʊn/ n pronombre m

pronounc|e /prə'naʊns/ vt pronunciar; (declare) declarar. **~ement** n declaración f. **~ed** adj pronunciado; (noticeable) marcado

pronunciation /prənʌnsɪ'eɪʃn/ n pronunciación f

proof /pruːf/ n prueba f, pruebas fpl; (of alcohol) graduación f normal. •adj. **~ against** a prueba de. **~-reading** n corrección f de pruebas

propaganda /prɒpə'gændə/ n propaganda f

propagate /'prɒpəgeɪt/ vt propagar. •vi propagarse

propel /prə'pel/ vt (pt **propelled**) propulsar. **~ler** n hélice f

proper /'prɒpə(r)/ adj correcto; (suitable) apropiado; (Gram) propio; (fam, real) verdadero. **~ly** adv correctamente; (eat, work) bien

property /'prɒpətɪ/ n propiedad f; (things owned) bienes mpl. •adj inmobiliario

prophe|cy /'prɒfəsɪ/ n profecía f. **~sy** /'prɒfɪsaɪ/ vt/i profetizar. **~t** /'prɒfɪt/ n profeta m. **~tic** /prə'fetɪk/ adj profético

proportion /prə'pɔːʃn/ n proporción f. **~al** adj, **~ate** /-ət/ adj proporcional

propos|al /prə'pəʊzl/ n propuesta f; (of marriage) proposición f matrimonial. **~e** /prə'pəʊz/ vt

proponer. •vi. **~e to s.o.** hacerle una oferta de matrimonio a una. **~ition** /prɒpə'zɪʃn/ n propuesta f; (offer) oferta f

proprietor /prə'praɪətə(r)/ n propietario m

pro rata /prəʊ'rɑːtə/ adv a prorrata

prose /prəʊz/ n prosa f

prosecut|e /'prɒsɪkjuːt/ vt procesar (**for** por); (carry on) proseguir. **~ion** /-'kjuːʃn/ n proceso m. **the ~** (side) la acusación. **~or** n fiscal m & f; (in private prosecutions) abogado m de la acusación

prospect /'prɒspekt/ n (possibility) posibilidad f (**of** de); (situation envisaged) perspectiva f. **~s** (chances) perspectivas fpl. **~ive** /prə'spektɪv/ adj posible; (future) futuro. **~or** /prə'spektə(r)/ n prospector m. **~us** /prə'spektəs/ n folleto m informativo

prosper /'prɒspə(r)/ vi prosperar. **~ity** /-'sperətɪ/ n prosperidad f. **~ous** adj próspero

prostitut|e /'prɒstɪtjuːt/ n prostituta f. **~ion** /-'tjuːʃn/ n prostitución f

prostrate /'prɒstreɪt/ adj postrado

protagonist /prə'tægənɪst/ n protagonista m & f

protect /prə'tekt/ vt proteger. **~ion** /-ʃn/ n protección f. **~ive** adj protector. **~or** n protector m

protein /'prəʊtiːn/ n proteína f

protest /'prəʊtest/ n protesta f. **in ~ (against)** en señal de protesta (contra). **under ~** bajo protesta. •/prə'test/ vt/i protestar

Protestant /'prɒtɪstənt/ adj & n protestante (m & f)

protester /prə'testə(r)/ n manifestante m & f

protocol /'prəʊtəkɒl/ n protocolo m

protrud|e /prə'truːd/ vi sobresalir. **~ing** adj (chin) prominente. **~ing eyes** ojos saltones

proud /praʊd/ adj orgulloso. **~ly**

adv con orgullo; (arrogantly)
orgullosamente

prove /pruːv/ vt probar; demostrar
(loyalty). • vi resultar. ~n adj
probado

proverb /'prɒvɜːb/ n refrán m,
proverbio m

provide /prə'vaɪd/ vt proporcionar;
dar (accommodation). ~ **s.o. with
sth** proveer a uno de algo. • vi. ~
for (allow for) prever; mantener
(person). ~d conj. ~d (that) con tal
de que, siempre que

providen|ce /'prɒvɪdəns/ n
providencia f. ~tial /-'denʃl/ adj
providencial

providing /prə'vaɪdɪŋ/ conj. ~ that
con tal de que, siempre que

provinc|e /'prɒvɪns/ n provincia f;
(fig) competencia f. ~ial /prə'vɪnʃl/
adj provincial

provision /prə'vɪʒn/ n provisión f;
(supply) suministro m; (stipulation)
disposición f. ~s npl provisiones
fpl, víveres mpl. ~al adj provisional

provo|cation /prɒvə'keɪʃn/ n
provocación f. ~cative /-'vɒkətɪv/
adj provocador. ~ke /prə'vəʊk/ vt
provocar

prow /praʊ/ n proa f

prowess /'praʊɪs/ n destreza †;
(valour) valor m

prowl /praʊl/ vi merodear. ~er n
merodeador m

proximity /prɒk'sɪmətɪ/ n
proximidad f

prude /pruːd/ n mojigato m

pruden|ce /'pruːdəns/ n prudencia
f. ~t adj prudente. ~tly adv
prudentemente

prudish /'pruːdɪʃ/ adj mojigato

prune /pruːn/ n ciruela f pasa. • vt
podar

pry /praɪ/ vi curiosear. ~ **into sth**
entrometerse en algo. vt (Amer) see
PRISE

PS n (postscript) P.D.

psalm /sɑːm/ n salmo m

psychiatr|ic /saɪkɪ'ætrɪk/ adj
psiquiátrico. ~ist /saɪ'kaɪətrɪst/ n
psiquiatra m & f. ~y /saɪ'kaɪətrɪ/ n
psiquiatría f

psychic /'saɪkɪk/ adj
para(p)sicológico

psycho|analysis /saɪkəʊə'næləsɪs/
n (p)sicoanálisis m. ~logical
/saɪkə'lɒdʒɪkl/ adj (p)sicológico.
~logist /saɪ'kɒlədʒɪst/ n
(p)sicólogo m. ~logy /saɪ'kɒlədʒɪ/
n (p)sicología f. ~therapy
/-'θerəpɪ/ n (p)sicoterapia f

pub /pʌb/ n bar m

puberty /'pjuːbətɪ/ n pubertad f

pubic /'pjuːbɪk/ adj pubiano, púbico

public /'pʌblɪk/ adj público. ~an n
tabernero m. ~ation /-'keɪʃn/ n
publicación f. ~ **holiday** n día m
festivo, día m feriado (LAm). ~
house n bar m. ~ity /pʌb'lɪsətɪ/ n
publicidad f. ~ize /'pʌblɪsaɪz/ vt
hacer público. ~ly adv
públicamente. ~ **school** n colegio
m privado; (Amer) instituto m,
escuela f pública

publish /'pʌblɪʃ/ vt publicar. ~er n
editor m. ~ing n publicación f.
~ing **house** editorial f

pudding /'pʊdɪŋ/ n postre m;
(steamed) budín m

puddle /'pʌdl/ n charco m

Puerto Ric|an /pwɜːtəʊ'riːkən/ adj
& n portorriqueño (m),
puertorriqueño (m). ~o /-əʊ/ n
Puerto Rico m

puff /pʌf/ n (of wind) ráfaga f; (of
smoke) nube f; (action) soplo m; (on
cigarette) chupada f, calada f. • vt/i
soplar. ~ **at** dar chupadas a (pipe).
~ **out** (swell up) inflar, hinchar.
~ed adj (out of breath) sin aliento.
~ **paste** (Amer), ~ **pastry** n
hojaldre m. ~y adj hinchado

pull /pʊl/ vt tirar de, jalar (LAm);
desgarrarse (muscle). ~ **a face**
hacer una mueca. ~ **a fast one**
hacer una mala jugada. • vi tirar,
jalar (LAm). ~ **at** tirar de, jalar
(LAm). • n tirón m, jalón m (LAm);

p

(pulling force) fuerza f; (influence) influencia f. ∎~ **away** vi (Auto) alejarse. ∎~ **back** vi retirarse. ∎~ **down** vt echar abajo (building); (lower) bajar. ∎~ **in** vi (Auto) parar. ∎~ **off** vt (remove) quitar; (achieve) conseguir. ∎~ **out** vt sacar; retirar (team). vi (Auto) salirse. ∎~ **through** vi recobrar la salud. ∎~ **up** vi (Auto) parar. vt (uproot) arrancar; (reprimand) regañar

pullover /ˈpʊləʊvə(r)/ n suéter m, pulóver m, jersey m

pulp /pʌlp/ n pulpa f; (for paper) pasta f

pulpit /ˈpʊlpɪt/ n púlpito m

pulse /pʌls/ n (Med) pulso m; (Culin) legumbre f

pummel /ˈpʌml/ vt (pt **pummelled**) aporrear

pump /pʌmp/ n bomba f; (for petrol) surtidor m. ●vt sacar con una bomba. ∎~ **up** vt inflar

pumpkin /ˈpʌmpkɪn/ n calabaza f

pun /pʌn/ n juego m de palabras

punch /pʌntʃ/ vt darle un puñetazo a; (perforate) perforar; hacer (hole). ●n puñetazo m; (vigour) fuerza f; (device) perforadora f; (drink) ponche m. ~ **in** vi (Amer) fichar (al entrar al trabajo). ~ **out** vi (Amer) fichar (al salir del trabajo)

punctual /ˈpʌŋktʃʊəl/ adj puntual. ~**ity** /-ˈælətɪ/ n puntualidad f. ~**ly** adv puntualmente

punctuat|e /ˈpʌŋktʃʊeɪt/ vt puntuar. ~**ion** /-ˈeɪʃn/ n puntuación f

puncture /ˈpʌŋktʃə(r)/ n (in tyre) pinchazo m. **have a** ~ pinchar. ●vt pinchar. ●vi pincharse

punish /ˈpʌnɪʃ/ vt castigar. ~**ment** n castigo m

punk /pʌŋk/ n punk m & f, punki m & f; (Music) punk m; (Amer, hoodlum) vándalo m

punt /pʌnt/ n (boat) batea f. ~**er** n apostante m & f

puny /ˈpjuːnɪ/ adj (**-ier, -iest**) enclenque

pup /pʌp/ n cachorro m

pupil /ˈpjuːpl/ n alumno m; (of eye) pupila f

puppet /ˈpʌpɪt/ n marioneta f, títere m; (glove ~) títere m

puppy /ˈpʌpɪ/ n cachorro m

purchase /ˈpɜːtʃəs/ vt adquirir. ●n adquisición f. ~**r** n comprador m

pur|e /ˈpjʊə(r)/ adj (**-er, -est**) puro. ~**ity** n pureza f

purgatory /ˈpɜːgətrɪ/ n purgatorio m

purge /pɜːdʒ/ vt purgar. ●n purga f

purif|ication /pjʊərɪfɪˈkeɪʃn/ n purificación f. ~**y** /ˈpjʊərɪfaɪ/ vt purificar

purist /ˈpjʊərɪst/ n purista m & f

puritan /ˈpjʊərɪtən/ n puritano m. ~**ical** /-ˈtænɪkl/ adj puritano

purple /ˈpɜːpl/ adj morado. ●n morado m, púrpura f

purport /pəˈpɔːt/ vt. ~ **to be** pretender ser

purpose /ˈpɜːpəs/ n propósito m; (determination) resolución f. **on** ~ a propósito. **serve a** ~ servir de algo. ~**ful** adj (resolute) resuelto. ~**ly** adv a propósito

purr /pɜː(r)/ vi ronronear

purse /pɜːs/ n monedero m; (Amer) bolso m, cartera f (LAm), bolsa f (Mex)

pursu|e /pəˈsjuː/ vt perseguir, continuar con (course of action). ~**it** /pəˈsjuːt/ n persecución f; (pastime) actividad f

pus /pʌs/ n pus m

push /pʊʃ/ vt empujar; apretar (button). ●vi empujar. ●n empujón m; (effort) esfuerzo m. ∎~ **back** vt hacer retroceder. ∎~ **off** vi 🅧 largarse. ~**chair** n sillita f de paseo, carreola f (Mex). **~y** adj (pej) ambicioso

pussy /pʊsɪ/ (pl **-sies**), **pussycat** /'pʊsɪkæt/ n 🔲 minino m

put /pʊt/ vt (pt **put**, pres p **putting**) poner; (with care, precision) colocar; (inside sth) meter; (express) decir. ∎ **~ across** vt comunicar. ∎ **~ away** vt guardar. ∎ **~ back** vt volver a poner; retrasar (clock). ∎ **~ by** vt guardar; ahorrar (money). ∎ **~ down** vt (on a surface) dejar; colgar (phone); (suppress) sofocar; (write) apuntar; (kill) sacrificar. ∎ **~ forward** vt presentar (plan); proponer (candidate); adelantar (clocks); adelantar (meeting). ∎ **~ in** vt (instal) poner; presentar (claim). ∎ **~ in for** vt solicitar. ∎ **~ off** vt aplazar, posponer; (disconcert) desconcertar. ∎ **~ on** vt (wear) ponerse; poner (CD, music); encender (light). ∎ **~ out** vt (extinguish) apagar; (inconvenience)

incomodar; extender (hand); (disconcert) desconcertar. ∎ **~ through** vt (phone) poner, pasar (**to** con). ∎ **~ up** vt levantar; aumentar (rent); subir (price); poner (sign); alojar (guest). ∎ **~ up with** vt aguantar, soportar

putrid /'pjuːtrɪd/ adj putrefacto

putt /pʌt/ n (golf) golpe m suave

puzzle /'pʌzl/ n misterio m; (game) rompecabezas m. ●vt dejar perplejo. **~ed** adj (expression) de desconcierto. **I'm ~ed about it** me tiene perplejo. **~ing** adj incomprensible; (odd) curioso

pygmy /'pɪgmɪ/ n pigmeo m

pyjamas /pə'dʒɑːməz/ npl pijama m, piyama m or f (LAm)

pylon /'paɪlɒn/ n pilón m

pyramid /'pɪrəmɪd/ n pirámide f

python /'paɪθn/ n pitón m

Qq

quack /kwæk/ n (of duck) graznido m; (person) charlatán m. **~ doctor** n curandero m

quadrangle /'kwɒdræŋgl/ n cuadrilátero m

quadruped /'kwɒdrʊped/ n cuadrúpedo m

quadruple /'kwɒdrʊpl/ adj & n cuádruplo (m). ●vt cuadruplicar

quagmire /'kwægmaɪə(r)/ n lodazal m

quaint /kweɪnt/ adj (**-er, -est**) pintoresco; (odd) curioso

quake /kweɪk/ vi temblar. ●n 🔲 terremoto m

qualif|ication /kwɒlɪfɪ'keɪʃn/ n título m; (requirement) requisito m; (ability) capacidad f; (Sport)

clasificación f; (fig) reserva f. **~ied** /'kwɒlɪfaɪd/ adj cualificado; (with degree, diploma) titulado; (competent) capacitado. **~y** /'kwɒlɪfaɪ/ vt calificar; (limit) limitar. ●vi titularse; (Sport) clasificarse. **~y for sth** (be entitled to) tener derecho a algo

qualit|ative /'kwɒlɪtətɪv/ adj cualitativo. **~y** /'kwɒlɪtɪ/ n calidad f; (attribute) cualidad f

qualm /kwɑːm/ n reparo m

quandary /'kwɒndrɪ/ n dilema m

quanti|fy /'kwɒntɪfaɪ/ vt cuantificar. **~ty** /-tɪ/ n cantidad f

quarantine /'kwɒrəntiːn/ n cuarentena f. ●vt poner en cuarentena

quarrel /'kwɒrəl/ n pelea f. ●vi (pt

quarrelled) pelearse, discutir. **~some** /-səm/ adj pendenciero

quarry /'kwɒrɪ/ n (excavation) cantera f; (prey) presa f

quart /kwɔ:t/ n cuarto m de galón

quarter /'kwɔ:tə(r)/ n cuarto m; (of year) trimestre m; (district) barrio m. **a ~ of an hour** un cuarto de hora. ●vt dividir en cuartos; (Mil) acuartelar. **~final** n cuarto m de final. **~ly** adj trimestral. ● adv trimestralmente

quartz /kwɔ:ts/ n cuarzo m

quay /ki:/ n muelle m

queasy /'kwi:zɪ/ adj mareado

queen /kwi:n/ n reina f. **~ mother** n reina f madre

queer /kwɪə(r)/ adj (-er, -est) extraño

quench /kwentʃ/ vt quitar (thirst); sofocar (desire)

query /'kwɪərɪ/ n pregunta f. ●vt preguntar; (doubt) poner en duda

quest /kwest/ n busca f

question /'kwestʃən/ n pregunta f; (for discussion) cuestión f. **in ~** en cuestión. **out of the ~** imposible. **without ~** sin duda. ●vt hacer preguntas a; (police etc) interrogar; (doubt) poner en duda. **~able** adj discutible. **~ mark** n signo m de interrogación. **~naire** /-'neə(r)/ n cuestionario m

queue /kju:/ n cola f. ●vi (pres p **queuing**) hacer cola

quibble /'kwɪbl/ vi discutir; (split hairs) sutilizar

quick /kwɪk/ adj (-er, -est) rápido. **be ~!** ¡date prisa! ●adv rápido. **~en** vt acelerar. ●vi acelerarse.

~ly adv rápido. **~sand** n arena f movediza. **~-tempered** /-'tempəd/ adj irascible

quid /kwɪd/ n invar 🇬🇧 libra f (esterlina)

quiet /'kwaɪət/ adj (-er, -est) tranquilo; (silent) callado; (discreet) discreto. ●n tranquilidad f. ●vt/i (Amer) see **QUIETEN**. **~en** vt calmar. ●n calmarse. **~ly** adv tranquilamente; (silently) silenciosamente; (discreetly) discretamente. **~ness** n tranquilidad f

quilt /kwɪlt/ n edredón m. **~ed** adj acolchado

quintet /kwɪn'tet/ n quinteto m

quirk /kwɜ:k/ n peculiaridad f

quit /kwɪt/ vt (pt **quitted**) dejar. **~ doing** (Amer, cease) dejar de hacer. ●vi (give in) abandonar; (stop) parar; (resign) dimitir

quite /kwaɪt/ adv bastante; (completely) totalmente; (really) verdaderamente. **~ (so!)** ¡claro! **~ a few** bastante

quits /kwɪts/ adj. **be ~** estar en paz. **call it ~** darlo por terminado

quiver /'kwɪvə(r)/ vi temblar

quiz /kwɪz/ n (pl **quizzes**) serie f de preguntas; (game) concurso m. ●vt (pt **quizzed**) interrogar. **~zical** adj burlón

quota /'kwəʊtə/ n cuota f

quot|ation /kwəʊ'teɪʃn/ n cita f; (price) presupuesto m. **~ation marks** npl comillas fpl. **~e** /kwəʊt/ vt citar; (Com) cotizar. ●n 🇬🇧 cita f; (price) presupuesto m. **in ~es** npl entre comillas

Rr

rabbi /'ræbaɪ/ n rabino m

rabbit /'ræbɪt/ n conejo m

rabi|d /'ræbɪd/ adj feroz; (dog) rabioso. ~**es** /'reɪbiːz/ n rabia f

race /reɪs/ n (in sport) carrera f; (ethnic group) raza f. • vt hacer correr (horse). • vi (run) correr, ir corriendo; (rush) ir de prisa. ~**course** n hipódromo m. ~**horse** n caballo m de carreras. ~ **relations** npl relaciones fpl raciales. ~**track** n hipódromo m

racial /'reɪʃl/ adj racial

racing /'reɪsɪŋ/ n carreras fpl. ~ **car** n coche m de carreras

racis|m /'reɪsɪzəm/ n racismo m. ~**t** adj & n racista (m & f)

rack¹ /ræk/ n (shelf) estante m; (for luggage) rejilla f; (for plates) escurreplatos m. • vt. ~ **one's brains** devanarse los sesos

rack² /ræk/ n. **go to ~ and ruin** quedarse en la ruina

racket /'rækɪt/ n (for sports) raqueta f; (din) alboroto m; (swindle) estafa f. ~**eer** /-ə'tɪə(r)/ n estafador m

racy /'reɪsɪ/ adj (**-ier, -iest**) vivo

radar /'reɪdɑː(r)/ n radar m

radian|ce /'reɪdɪəns/ n resplandor m. ~**t** adj radiante

radiat|e /'reɪdɪeɪt/ vt irradiar. • vi divergir. ~**ion** /-'eɪʃn/ n radiación f. ~**or** n radiador m

radical /'rædɪkl/ adj & n radical (m)

radio /'reɪdɪəʊ/ n (pl **-os**) radio f or m. • vt transmitir por radio. ~**active** /reɪdɪəʊ'æktɪv/ adj radiactivo. ~**activity** /-'tɪvɪtɪ/ n radiactividad f

radish /'rædɪʃ/ n rábano m

radius /'reɪdɪəs/ n (pl **-dii** /-dɪaɪ/) radio m

raffle /'ræfl/ n rifa f

raft /rɑːft/ n balsa f

rafter /'rɑːftə(r)/ n cabrio m

rag /ræg/ n andrajo m; (for wiping) trapo m. **in ~s** (person) andrajoso

rage /reɪdʒ/ n rabia f; (fashion) moda f. • vi estar furioso; (storm) bramar

ragged /'rægɪd/ adj (person) andrajoso; (clothes) hecho jirones

raid /reɪd/ n (Mil) incursión f; (by police etc) redada f; (by thieves) asalto m. • vt (Mil) atacar; (police) hacer una redada en; (thieves) asaltar. ~**er** n invasor m; (thief) ladrón m

rail /reɪl/ n barandilla f; (for train) riel m; (rod) barra f. **by ~** por ferrocarril. ~**ing** n barandilla f; (fence) verja f. ~**road** n (Amer), ~**way** n ferrocarril m. ~**way station** n estación f de ferrocarril

rain /reɪn/ n lluvia f. • vi llover. ~**bow** /-bəʊ/ n arco m iris. ~**coat** n impermeable m. ~**fall** n precipitación f. ~**y** adj (**-ier, -iest**) lluvioso

raise /reɪz/ vt levantar; (breed) criar; obtener (money etc); formular (question); plantear (problem); subir (price). • n (Amer) aumento m

raisin /'reɪzn/ n (uva f) pasa f

rake /reɪk/ n rastrillo m. • vt rastrillar; (search) buscar en. ■ ~ **up** vt remover

rally /'rælɪ/ vt reunir; (revive) reanimar. • n reunión f; (Auto) rally m

ram /ræm/ n carnero m. • vt (pt **rammed**) (thrust) meter por la fuerza; (crash into) chocar con

RAM /ræm/ n (= random access memory) (Comp) RAM f

ramble /'ræmbl/ n excursión f a pie. ●vi ir de paseo; (in speech) divagar. ■~e on vi divagar. ~er n excursionista m & f. ~ing adj (speech) divagador

ramp /ræmp/ n rampa f

rampage /ræm'peɪdʒ/ vi alborotarse. ●/'ræmpeɪdʒ/ n. **go on the ~** alborotarse

ramshackle /'ræmʃækl/ adj desvencijado

ran /ræn/ see **RUN**

ranch /rɑːntʃ/ n hacienda f

random /'rændəm/ adj hecho al azar; (chance) fortuito. ●n. **at ~** al azar

rang /ræŋ/ see **RING²**

range /reɪndʒ/ n alcance m; (distance) distancia f; (series) serie f; (of mountains) cordillera f; (extent) extensión f; (Com) surtido m; (stove) cocina f económica. ●vi extenderse; (vary) variar. ~r n guardabosque m

rank /ræŋk/ n posición f, categoría f; (row) fila f; (for taxis) parada f. **the ~ and file** la masa f. ~s npl soldados mpl rasos. ●adj (-er, -est) (smell) fétido; (fig) completo. ●vt clasificar. ●vi clasificarse

ransack /'rænsæk/ vt registrar; (pillage) saquear

ransom /'rænsəm/ n rescate m. **hold s.o. to ~** exigir rescate por uno. ●vt rescatar; (redeem) redimir

rant /rænt/ vi despotricar

rap /ræp/ n golpe m seco. ●vt/i (pt **rapped**) golpear

rape /reɪp/ vt violar. ●n violación f

rapid /'ræpɪd/ adj rápido. ~s npl rápidos mpl

rapist /'reɪpɪst/ n violador m

rapture /'ræptʃə(r)/ n éxtasis m. ~ous /-rəs/ adj extático

rare /reə(r)/ adj (-er, -est) raro;

(Culin) poco hecho. ~fied /'reərɪfaɪd/ adj enrarecido. ~ly adv raramente

raring /'reərɪŋ/ adj 🄵. ~ **to** impaciente por

rarity /'reərətɪ/ n rareza f

rascal /'rɑːskl/ n granuja m & f

rash /ræʃ/ adj (-er, -est) precipitado, imprudente. ●n erupción f

rasher /'ræʃə(r)/ n loncha f

rashly /'ræʃlɪ/ adv precipitadamente, imprudentemente

rasp /rɑːsp/ n (file) escofina f

raspberry /'rɑːzbrɪ/ n frambuesa f

rat /ræt/ n rata f

rate /reɪt/ n (ratio) proporción f; (speed) velocidad f; (price) precio m; (of interest) tipo m. **at any ~** de todas formas. **at this ~** así. ~s npl (taxes) impuestos mpl municipales. ●vt valorar; (consider) considerar; (Amer, deserve) merecer. ●vi ser considerado

rather /'rɑːðə(r)/ adv mejor dicho; (fairly) bastante; (a little) un poco. ●int claro. **I would ~ not** prefiero no

rating /'reɪtɪŋ/ n clasificación f; (sailor) marinero m; (number, TV) índice m

ratio /'reɪʃɪəʊ/ n (pl **-os**) proporción f

ration /'ræʃn/ n ración f. ~s npl (provisions) víveres mpl. ●vt racionar

rational /'ræʃənəl/ adj racional. ~ize vt racionalizar

rattle /'rætl/ vi traquetear. ●vt (shake) agitar; 🄵 desconcertar. ●n traqueteo m; (toy) sonajero m. ■~ off vt (fig) decir de corrida

raucous /'rɔːkəs/ adj estridente

ravage /'rævɪdʒ/ vt estragar

rave /reɪv/ vi delirar; (in anger) despotricar. ~ **about sth** poner a algo por las nubes

raven /'reɪvn/ n cuervo m

ravenous /ˈrævənəs/ adj voraz; (person) hambriento. **be** ~ morirse de hambre

ravine /rəˈviːn/ n barranco m

raving /ˈreɪvɪŋ/ adj. ~ **mad** loco de atar

ravishing /ˈrævɪʃɪŋ/ adj (enchanting) encantador

raw /rɔː/ adj (-er, -est) crudo; (sugar) sin refinar; (inexperienced) inexperto. ~ **deal** n tratamiento m injusto, injusticia f. ~ **materials** npl materias fpl primas

ray /reɪ/ n rayo m

raze /reɪz/ vt arrasar

razor /ˈreɪzə(r)/ n navaja f de afeitar; (electric) maquinilla f de afeitar

Rd /rəʊd/ abbr (= Road) C/, Calle f

re /riː/ prep con referencia a. ●pref re.

reach /riːtʃ/ vt alcanzar; (extend) extender; (arrive at) llegar a; (achieve) lograr; (hand over) pasar, dar. ●vi extenderse. ●n alcance m. **within** ~ **of** al alcance de; (close to) a corta distancia de. ■ ~ **out** vi alargar la mano

react /rɪˈækt/ vi reaccionar. ~**ion** /rɪˈækʃn/ n reacción f. ~ **ionary** adj & n reaccionario (m). ~**or** /rɪˈæktə(r)/ n reactor m

read /riːd/ vt (pt read /red/) leer; (study) estudiar; (interpret) interpretar. ●vi leer; (instrument) indicar. ■ ~ **out** vt leer en voz alta. ~**able** adj (clear) legible. ~**er** n lector m

readily /ˈredɪlɪ/ adv (willingly) de buena gana; (easily) fácilmente

reading /ˈriːdɪŋ/ n lectura f

readjust /riːəˈdʒʌst/ vt reajustar. ●vi readaptarse (**to** a)

ready /ˈredɪ/ adj (-ier, -iest) listo, preparado. **get** ~ prepararse. ~**-made** adj confeccionado

real /rɪəl/ adj verdadero. ●adv (Amer fam) verdaderamente. ~ **estate** n

bienes mpl raíces, propiedad f inmobiliaria. ~ **estate agent** see REALTOR. ~**ism** n realismo m. ~**ist** n realista m & f. ~**istic** /-ˈlɪstɪk/ adj realista. ~**ization** /rɪəlaɪˈzeɪʃn/ n realidad f. comprensión f. ~**ize** /ˈrɪəlaɪz/ vt darse cuenta de; (fulfil, Com) realizar. ~**ly** /ˈrɪəlɪ/ adv verdaderamente

realm /relm/ n reino m

realtor /ˈriːəltə(r)/ n (Amer) agente m inmobiliario

reap /riːp/ vt segar; (fig) cosechar

reappear /riːəˈpɪə(r)/ vi reaparecer

rear /rɪə(r)/ n parte f de atrás. ●adj posterior, trasero. ●vt (bring up, breed) criar. ●vi ~ **(up)** (horse) encabritarse

rearguard /ˈrɪəgɑːd/ n retaguardia f

rearrange /riːəˈreɪndʒ/ vt arreglar de otra manera

reason /ˈriːzn/ n razón f, motivo m. **within** ~ dentro de lo razonable. ●vi razonar. ~**able** adj razonable. ~**ing** n razonamiento m

reassur|ance /riːəˈʃʊərəns/ n promesa f tranquilizadora; (guarantee) garantía f. ~**e** /riːəˈʃʊə(r)/ vt tranquilizar

rebate /ˈriːbeɪt/ n (discount) rebaja f

rebel /ˈrebl/ n rebelde m & f. ●/rɪˈbel/ vi (pt rebelled) rebelarse. ~**lion** /rɪˈbelɪən/ n rebelión f. ~**lious** adj rebelde

rebound /rɪˈbaʊnd/ vi rebotar; (fig) recaer. ●/ˈriːbaʊnd/ n rebote m

rebuff /rɪˈbʌf/ vt rechazar. ●n desaire m

rebuild /riːˈbɪld/ vt (pt rebuilt) reconstruir

rebuke /rɪˈbjuːk/ vt reprender. ●n reprimenda f

recall /rɪˈkɔːl/ vt (call s.o. back) llamar; (remember) recordar. ●n /ˈriːkɔːl/ (of goods, ambassador) retirada f; (memory) memoria f

r

recap /ˈriːkæp/ vt/i (pt **recapped**) 🔲 resumir

recapitulate /riːkəˈpɪtʃʊleɪt/ vt/i resumir

recapture /riːˈkæptʃə(r)/ vt recobrar; (recall) hacer revivir

recede /rɪˈsiːd/ vi retroceder

receipt /rɪˈsiːt/ n recibo m. **~s** npl (Com) ingresos mpl

receive /rɪˈsiːv/ vt recibir. **~r** n (of stolen goods) perista m & f; (part of phone) auricular m

recent /ˈriːsnt/ adj reciente. **~ly** adv recientemente

recept|ion /rɪˈsepʃn/ n recepción f; (welcome) acogida f. **~ionist** n recepcionista m & f. **~ive** /-tɪv/ adj receptivo

recess /rɪˈses/ n hueco m; (holiday) vacaciones fpl. **~ion** /rɪˈseʃn/ n recesión f

recharge /riːˈtʃɑːdʒ/ vt cargar de nuevo, recargar

recipe /ˈresəpɪ/ n receta f. **~ book** n libro m de cocina

recipient /rɪˈsɪpɪənt/ n recipiente m & f; (of letter) destinatario m

recit|al /rɪˈsaɪtl/ n (Mus) recital m. **~e** /rɪˈsaɪt/ vt recitar; (list) enumerar

reckless /ˈreklɪs/ adj imprudente. **~ly** adv imprudentemente

reckon /ˈrekən/ vt/i calcular; (consider) considerar; (think) pensar. **■ ~ on** vt (rely) contar con

reclaim /rɪˈkleɪm/ vt reclamar; recuperar (land)

reclin|e /rɪˈklaɪn/ vi recostarse. **~ing** adj acostado; (seat) reclinable

recluse /rɪˈkluːs/ n ermitaño m

recogni|tion /rekəɡˈnɪʃn/ n reconocimiento m. **beyond ~tion** irreconocible. **~ze** /ˈrekəɡnaɪz/ vt reconocer

recoil /rɪˈkɔɪl/ vi retroceder. **●** /ˈriːkɔɪl/ n (of gun) culatazo m

recollect /rekəˈlekt/ vt recordar.

~ion /-ʃn/ n recuerdo m

recommend /rekəˈmend/ vt recomendar. **~ation** /-ˈdeɪʃn/ n recomendación f

reconcil|e /ˈrekənsaɪl/ vt reconciliar (people); conciliar (facts). **~e o.s.** resignarse (**to** a). **~iation** /-sɪlɪˈeɪʃn/ n reconciliación f

reconnaissance /rɪˈkɒnɪsns/ n reconocimiento m

reconnoitre /rekəˈnɔɪtə(r)/ vt (pres p **-tring**) (Mil) reconocer

re: **~consider** /riːkənˈsɪdə(r)/ vt volver a considerar. **~construct** /riːkənˈstrʌkt/ vt reconstruir

record /rɪˈkɔːd/ vt (in register) registrar; (in diary) apuntar; (Mus) grabar. **●** /ˈrekɔːd/ n (document) documento m; (of events) registro m; (Mus) disco m; (Sport) récord m. **off the ~** en confianza. **~er** /rɪˈkɔːdə(r)/ n registrador m; (Mus) flauta f dulce. **~ing** /rɪˈkɔːdɪŋ/ n grabación f. **~-player** /ˈrekɔːd-/ n tocadiscos m invar

recount /rɪˈkaʊnt/ vt contar, relatar

re-count /riːˈkaʊnt/ vt volver a contar; recontar (votes). **●** /ˈriːkaʊnt/ n (Pol) recuento m

recover /rɪˈkʌvə(r)/ vt recuperar. **●** vi reponerse. **~y** n recuperación f

recreation /rekrɪˈeɪʃn/ n recreo m. **~al** adj de recreo

recruit /rɪˈkruːt/ n recluta m. **●** vt reclutar; contratar (staff). **~ment** n reclutamiento m

rectang|le /ˈrektæŋɡl/ n rectángulo m. **~ular** /-ˈtæŋɡjʊlə(r)/ adj rectangular

rectify /ˈrektɪfaɪ/ vt rectificar

rector /ˈrektə(r)/ n párroco m; (of college) rector m. **~y** n rectoría f

recuperat|e /rɪˈkuːpəreɪt/ vt recuperar. **●** vi reponerse. **~ion** /-ˈreɪʃn/ n recuperación f

recur /rɪˈkɜː(r)/ vi (pt **recurred**) repetirse. **~rence** /rɪˈkʌrns/ n repetición f. **~rent** /rɪˈkʌrənt/ adj repetido

recycle /riːˈsaɪkl/ vt reciclar

red /red/ adj (**redder, reddest**) rojo. ●n rojo. **be in the ~** estar en números rojos. **~den** vi enrojecerse. **~dish** adj rojizo

redecorate /riːˈdekəreɪt/ vt pintar de nuevo

rede|em /rɪˈdiːm/ vt redimir. **~mption** /-ˈdempʃn/ n redención f

red: ~-handed /-ˈhændɪd/ adj. **catch s.o. ~handed** agarrar a uno con las manos en la masa. **~ herring** n (fig) pista f falsa. **~-hot** adj al rojo vivo. **~ light** n luz f roja

redo /riːˈduː/ vt (pt **redid**, pp **redone**) rehacer

redouble /rɪˈdʌbl/ vt redoblar

red tape /redˈteɪp/ n (fig) papeleo m

reduc|e /rɪˈdjuːs/ vt reducir; aliviar (pain). ●vi (Amer, slim) adelgazar. **~tion** /rɪˈdʌkʃn/ n reducción f

redundan|cy /rɪˈdʌndənsɪ/ n superfluidad f; (unemployment) despido m. **~t** superfluo. **she was made ~t** la despidieron por reducción de plantilla

reed /riːd/ n caña f; (Mus) lengüeta f

reef /riːf/ n arrecife m

reek /riːk/ n mal olor m. ●vi. **~ (of)** apestar a

reel /riːl/ n carrete m. ●vi dar vueltas; (stagger) tambalearse. ■**~ off** vt (fig) enumerar

refectory /rɪˈfektərɪ/ n refectorio m

refer /rɪˈfɜː(r)/ vt (pt **referred**) remitir. ●vi referirse. **~ to** referirse a; (consult) consultar. **~ee** /refəˈriː/ n árbitro m; (for job) referencia f. ●vi (pt **refereed**) arbitrar. **~ence** /ˈrefrəns/ n referencia f. **~ence book** n libro m de consulta. **in ~ to, with ~ to** con referencia a; (Com) respecto a. **~endum** /refəˈrendəm/ n (pl **-ums** or **-da**) referéndum m

refill /riːˈfɪl/ vt volver a llenar. ●/ˈriːfɪl/ n recambio m

refine /rɪˈfaɪn/ vt refinar. **~d** adj refinado. **~ry** /-ərɪ/ n refinería f

reflect /rɪˈflekt/ vt reflejar. ●vi reflejarse; (think) reflexionar. ■**~ badly upon** perjudicar. **~ion** /-ʃn/ n reflexión f; (image) reflejo m. **~or** n reflector m

reflex /ˈriːfleks/ adj & n reflejo (m). **~ive** /rɪˈfleksɪv/ adj (Gram) reflexivo

reform /rɪˈfɔːm/ vt reformar. ●vi reformarse. ●n reforma f

refrain /rɪˈfreɪn/ n estribillo m. ●vi abstenerse (**from** de)

refresh /rɪˈfreʃ/ vt refrescar. **~ing** adj refrescante. **~ments** npl (food and drink) refrigerio m

refrigerat|e /rɪˈfrɪdʒəreɪt/ vt refrigerar. **~or** n frigorífico m, refrigerador m (LAm)

refuel /riːˈfjuːəl/ vt/i (pt **refuelled**) repostar

refuge /ˈrefjuːdʒ/ n refugio m. **take ~** refugiarse. **~e** /refjʊˈdʒiː/ n refugiado m

refund /rɪˈfʌnd/ vt reembolsar. ●/ˈriːfʌnd/ n reembolso m

refusal /rɪˈfjuːzl/ n negativa f

refuse /rɪˈfjuːz/ vt rehusar. ●vi negarse. ●/ˈrefjuːs/ n residuos mpl

refute /rɪˈfjuːt/ vt refutar

regain /rɪˈgeɪn/ vt recobrar

regal /ˈriːgl/ adj real

regard /rɪˈgɑːd/ vt considerar; (look at) contemplar. **as ~s** en lo que se refiere a. ●n (consideration) consideración f; (esteem) estima f. **~s** npl saludos mpl. **kind ~s** recuerdos. **~ing** prep en lo que se refiere a. **~less** adv a pesar de todo. **~less of** sin tener en cuenta

regatta /rɪˈgætə/ n regata f

regime /reɪˈʒiːm/ n régimen m

regiment /ˈredʒɪmənt/ n regimiento m. **~al** /-ˈmentl/ adj del regimiento

region /ˈriːdʒən/ n región f. **in the**

r

~ **of** alrededor de. ~**al** adj
regional

register /'redʒɪstə(r)/ n registro m.
• vt registrar; matricular (vehicle);
declarar (birth); certificar (letter);
facturar (luggage). • vi (enrol)
inscribirse; (fig) producir
impresión

registrar /redʒɪ'strɑ:(r)/ n
secretario m del registro civil;
(Univ) secretario m general

registration /redʒɪ'streɪʃn/ n
registro m; (in register) inscripción f.
~ **number** n (Auto) (número de)
matrícula f

registry /'redʒɪstrɪ/ n. ~ **office** n
registro m civil

regret /rɪ'gret/ n pesar m; (remorse)
arrepentimiento m. • vt (pt
regretted) lamentar. **I** ~ **that**
siento (que). ~**table** adj
lamentable

regula|r /'regjʊlə(r)/ adj regular;
(usual) habitual. • n 🆃 cliente m
habitual. ~**rity** /-'lærətɪ/ n
regularidad f. ~**rly** adv con
regularidad. ~**te** /'regjʊleɪt/ vt
regular. ~**tion** /-'leɪʃn/ n
regulación f; (rule) regla f

rehears|al /rɪ'hɜ:sl/ n ensayo m.
~**e** /rɪ'hɜ:s/ vt ensayar

reign /reɪn/ n reinado m. • vi reinar

reindeer /'reɪndɪə(r)/ n invar reno m

reinforce /ri:ɪn'fɔ:s/ vt reforzar.
~**ment** n refuerzo m

reins /reɪnz/ npl riendas fpl

reiterate /ri:'ɪtəreɪt/ vt reiterar

reject /rɪ'dʒekt/ vt rechazar.
• /'ri:dʒekt/ n producto m
defectuoso. ~**ion** /rɪ'dʒekʃn/ n
rechazo m; (after job application)
respuesta f negativa

rejoice /rɪ'dʒɔɪs/ vi regocijarse

rejoin /rɪ'dʒɔɪn/ vt reunirse con

rejuvenate /rɪ'dʒu:vəneɪt/ vt
rejuvenecer

relapse /rɪ'læps/ n recaída f. • vi
recaer; (into crime) reincidir

relat|e /rɪ'leɪt/ vt contar; (connect)
relacionar. • vi relacionarse (**to**
con). ~**ed** adj emparentado; (ideas
etc) relacionado. ~**ion** /rɪ'leɪʃn/ n
relación f; (person) pariente m & f.
~**ionship** n relación f; (blood tie)
parentesco m; (affair) relaciones fpl.
~**ive** /'relətɪv/ n pariente m & f.
• adj relativo. ~**ively** adv
relativamente

relax /rɪ'læks/ vt relajar. • vi
relajarse. ~**ation** /-'seɪʃn/ n
relajación f; (rest) descanso m;
(recreation) recreo m. ~**ing** adj
relajante

relay /'ri:leɪ/ n relevo m. ~ **(race)** n
carrera f de relevos. • /rɪ'leɪ/ vt
transmitir

release /rɪ'li:s/ vt soltar; poner en
libertad (prisoner); estrenar (film);
(Mec) soltar; publicar (news). • n
liberación f; (of film) estreno m;
(record) disco m nuevo

relent /rɪ'lent/ vi ceder. ~**less** adj
implacable; (continuous) incesante

relevan|ce /'reləvəns/ n
pertinencia f. ~**t** adj pertinente

relia|bility /rɪlaɪə'bɪlətɪ/ n
fiabilidad f. ~**ble** /rɪ'laɪəbl/ adj
(person) de confianza; (car) fiable.
~**nce** /rɪ'laɪəns/ n dependencia f;
(trust) confianza f. ~**nt** /rɪ'laɪənt/
adj confiado

relic /'relɪk/ n reliquia f

relie|f /rɪ'li:f/ n alivio m; (assistance)
socorro m. **be on** ~**f** (Amer) recibir
prestaciones de la seguridad
social. ~**ve** /rɪ'li:v/ vt aliviar; (take
over from) relevar. ~**ved** adj
aliviado. **feel** ~**ved** sentir un
gran alivio

religio|n /rɪ'lɪdʒən/ n religión f.
~**us** /rɪ'lɪdʒəs/ adj religioso

relinquish /rɪ'lɪŋkwɪʃ/ vt
abandonar, renunciar

relish /'relɪʃ/ n gusto m; (Culin) salsa
f. • vt saborear

reluctan|ce /rɪ'lʌktəns/ n desgana
f. ~**t** adj mal dispuesto. **be** ~**t to**

no tener ganas de. **~tly** adv de mala gana

rely /rɪˈlaɪ/ vi. **~ on** contar con; (trust) fiarse de; (depend) depender

remain /rɪˈmeɪn/ vi (be left) quedar; (stay) quedarse; (continue to be) seguir. **~der** n resto m. **~s** npl restos mpl; (left-overs) sobras fpl

remand /rɪˈmɑːnd/ vt. **~ in custody** mantener bajo custodia. • n. **on ~** en prisión preventiva

remark /rɪˈmɑːk/ n observación f. • vt observar. **~able** adj notable

remarry /riːˈmærɪ/ vi volver a casarse

remedy /ˈremədɪ/ n remedio m. • vt remediar

remember /rɪˈmembə(r)/ vt acordarse de, recordar. • vi acordarse

remind /rɪˈmaɪnd/ vt recordar. **~er** n recordatorio m

reminisce /remɪˈnɪs/ vi rememorar los viejos tiempos. **~nces** /-ˈənsɪz/ npl recuerdos mpl. **~nt** /-ˈnɪsnt/ adj. **be ~nt of** recordar

remnant /ˈremnənt/ n resto m; (of cloth) retazo m; (trace) vestigio m

remorse /rɪˈmɔːs/ n remordimiento m. **~ful** adj arrepentido. **~less** adj implacable

remote /rɪˈməʊt/ adj remoto. **~ control** n mando m a distancia. **~ly** adv remotamente

removable /rɪˈmuːvəbl/ adj (detachable) de quita y pon; (handle) desmontable. **~al** n eliminación f; (from house) mudanza f. **~e** /rɪˈmuːv/ vt quitar; (dismiss) destituir; (get rid of) eliminar

render /ˈrendə(r)/ vt rendir (homage); prestar (help etc). **~ sth useless** hacer que algo resulte inútil

rendezvous /ˈrɒndɪvuː/ n (pl **-vous** /-vuːz/) cita f

renegade /ˈrenɪgeɪd/ n renegado

renew /rɪˈnjuː/ vt renovar; (resume)

reanudar. **~al** n renovación f

renounce /rɪˈnaʊns/ vt renunciar a

renovate /ˈrenəveɪt/ vt renovar. **~ion** /-ˈveɪʃn/ n renovación f

renown /rɪˈnaʊn/ n renombre m. **~ed** adj de renombre

rent /rent/ n alquiler m. • vt alquilar. **~al** n alquiler m. **car ~** (Amer) alquiler m de coche

renunciation /rɪnʌnsɪˈeɪʃn/ n renuncia f

reopen /riːˈəʊpən/ vt volver a abrir. • vi reabrirse

reorganize /riːˈɔːgənaɪz/ vt reorganizar

rep /rep/ n (Com) representante m & f

repair /rɪˈpeə(r)/ vt arreglar, reparar; arreglar (clothes, shoes). • n reparación f; (patch) remiendo m. **in good ~** en buen estado. **it's beyond ~** ya no tiene arreglo

repatriate /riːˈpætrɪeɪt/ vt repatriar

repay /riːˈpeɪ/ vt (pt **repaid**) reembolsar; pagar (debt); corresponder a (kindness). **~ment** n pago m

repeal /rɪˈpiːl/ vt revocar. • n revocación f

repeat /rɪˈpiːt/ vt repetir. • vi repetir(se). • n repetición f. **~edly** adv repetidas veces

repel /rɪˈpel/ vt (pt **repelled**) repeler. **~lent** adj repelente

repent /rɪˈpent/ vi arrepentirse. **~ant** adj arrepentido

repercussion /riːpəˈkʌʃn/ n repercusión f

repertoire /ˈrepətwɑː(r)/ n repertorio m

repetition /repɪˈtɪʃn/ n repetición f. **~ious** /-ˈtɪʃəs/ adj, **~ive** /rɪˈpetətɪv/ adj repetitivo

replace /rɪˈpleɪs/ vt reponer; cambiar (battery); (take the place of) sustituir. **~ment** n sustitución f;

r

(person) sustituto m

replay /'ri:pleɪ/ n (Sport) repetición f del partido; (recording) repetición f inmediata

replenish /rɪ'plenɪʃ/ vt reponer

replica /'replɪkə/ n réplica f

reply /rɪ'plaɪ/ vt/i responder, contestar. ~ **to sth** responder a algo, contestar algo. ●n respuesta f

report /rɪ'pɔːt/ vt (reporter) informar sobre; informar de (accident); (denounce) denunciar. ●vi informar; (present o.s.) presentarse. ●n informe m; (Schol) boletín m de notas; (rumour) rumor m; (in newspaper) reportaje m. ~ **card** (Amer) n boletín m de calificaciones. ~**edly** adv según se dice. ~**er** n periodista m & f, reportero m

reprehensible /reprɪ'hensəbl/ adj reprensible

represent /reprɪ'zent/ vt representar. ~**ation** /-'teɪʃn/ n representación f. ~**ative** adj representativo. ●n representante m & f; (Amer, in government) diputado m

repress /rɪ'pres/ vt reprimir. ~**ion** /-ʃn/ n represión f. ~**ive** adj represivo

reprieve /rɪ'priːv/ n indulto m; (fig) respiro m. ●vt indultar

reprimand /'reprɪmɑːnd/ vt reprender. ●n reprensión f

reprisal /rɪ'praɪzl/ n represalia f

reproach /rɪ'prəʊtʃ/ vt reprochar. ●n reproche m. ~**ful** adj de reproche

reproduc|e /ri:prə'djuːs/ vt reproducir. ●vi reproducirse. ~**tion** /-'dʌkʃn/ n reproducción f. ~**tive** /-'dʌktɪv/ adj reproductor

reprove /rɪ'pruːv/ vt reprender

reptile /'reptaɪl/ n reptil m

republic /rɪ'pʌblɪk/ n república f. ~**an** adj & n republicano (m). **R~** adj & n (in US) republicano (m)

repugnan|ce /rɪ'pʌgnəns/ n repugnancia f. ~**t** adj repugnante

repuls|e /rɪ'pʌls/ vt rechazar, repulsar. ~**ion** /-ʃn/ n repulsión f. ~**ive** adj repulsivo

reput|able /'repjʊtəbl/ adj acreditado, reputado. ~**ation** /repjʊ'teɪʃn/ n reputación f

request /rɪ'kwest/ n petición f. ●vt pedir

require /rɪ'kwaɪə(r)/ vt requerir; (need) necesitar; (demand) exigir. ~**d** adj necesario. ~**ment** n requisito m

rescue /'reskjuː/ vt rescatar, salvar. ●n rescate m. ~**r** n salvador m

research /rɪ'sɜːtʃ/ n investigación f. ●vt investigar. ~**er** n investigador m

resembl|ance /rɪ'zembləns/ n parecido m. ~**e** /rɪ'zembl/ vt parecerse a

resent /rɪ'zent/ vt guardarle rencor a (person). **she ~ed his success** le molestaba que él tuviera éxito. ~**ful** adj resentido. ~**ment** n resentimiento m

reserv|ation /rezə'veɪʃn/ n reserva f; (booking) reserva f. ~**e** /rɪ'zɜːv/ vt reservar. ●n reserva f; (in sports) suplente m & f. ~**ed** adj reservado. ~**oir** /'rezəvwɑː(r)/ n embalse m

reshuffle /riː'ʃʌfl/ n (Pol) reorganización f

residen|ce /'rezɪdəns/ n residencia f. ~**t** adj & n residente (m & f). ~**tial** /rezɪ'denʃl/ adj residencial

residue /'rezɪdjuː/ n residuo m

resign /rɪ'zaɪn/ vt/i dimitir. ~ **o.s. to** resignarse a. ~**ation** /rezɪg'neɪʃn/ n resignación f; (from job) dimisión f. ~**ed** adj resignado

resilien|ce /rɪ'zɪlɪəns/ n elasticidad f; (of person) resistencia f. ~**t** adj elástico; (person) resistente

resin /'rezɪn/ n resina f

resist /rɪ'zɪst/ vt resistir. ●vi resistirse. ~**ance** n resistencia f. ~**ant** adj resistente

resolut|e /'rezəluːt/ adj resuelto.

~ion /-'luːʃn/ n resolución f

resolve /rɪ'zɒlv/ vt resolver. **~ to do** resolver a hacer. ●n resolución f

resort /rɪ'zɔːt/ n recurso m; (place) lugar m turístico. **in the last ~** como último recurso. ■**~ to** vt recurrir a.

resource /rɪ'sɔːs/ n recurso m. **~ful** adj ingenioso

respect /rɪ'spekt/ n (esteem) respeto m; (aspect) respecto m. **with ~ to** con respecto a. ●vt respetar. **~able** adj respetable. **~ful** adj respetuoso. **~ive** adj respectivo. **~ively** adv respectivamente

respiration /respə'reɪʃn/ n respiración f

respite /'respaɪt/ n respiro m

respond /rɪ'spɒnd/ vi responder. **~se** /rɪ'spɒns/ n respuesta f; (reaction) reacción f

responsib|ility /rɪspɒnsə'bɪlətɪ/ n responsabilidad f. **~le** /rɪ'spɒnsəbl/ adj responsable; (job) de responsabilidad. **~ly** adv con formalidad

responsive /rɪ'spɒnsɪv/ adj que reacciona bien. **~ to** sensible a

rest /rest/ vt descansar; (lean) apoyar. ●vi descansar; (lean) apoyarse. ●n descanso m; (Mus) pausa f; (remainder) resto m, lo demás; (people) los demás, los otros mpl. **to have a ~** tomarse un descanso. ■**~ up** vi (Amer) descansar

restaurant /'restərɒnt/ n restaurante m

rest: ~ful adj sosegado. **~ive** adj impaciente. **~less** adj inquieto

restor|ation /restə'reɪʃn/ n restablecimiento m; (of building, monarch) restauración f. **~e** /rɪ'stɔː(r)/ vt restablecer; restaurar (building); devolver (confidence, health)

restrain /rɪ'streɪn/ vt contener. **~ o.s.** contenerse. **~ed** adj (moderate) moderado; (in control of self) comedido. **~t** n restricción f;

(moderation) compostura f

restrict /rɪ'strɪkt/ vt restringir. **~ion** /-ʃn/ n restricción f. **~ive** adj restrictivo

rest room n (Amer) baño m, servicio m

result /rɪ'zʌlt/ n resultado m. **as a ~ of** como consecuencia de. ●vi. **~ from** resultar de. **~ in** dar como resultado

resume /rɪ'zjuːm/ vt reanudar. ●vi reanudarse

résumé /'rezjʊmeɪ/ n resumen m, (Amer, CV) currículum m, historial m personal

resurrect /rezə'rekt/ vt resucitar. **~ion** /-ʃn/ n resurrección f

resuscitat|e /rɪ'sʌsɪteɪt/ vt resucitar. **~ion** /-'teɪʃn/ n resucitación f

retail /'riːteɪl/ n venta f al por menor. ●adj & adv al por menor. ●vt vender al por menor. ●vi venderse al por menor. **~er** n minorista m & f

retain /rɪ'teɪn/ vt retener; conservar (heat)

retaliat|e /rɪ'tælɪeɪt/ vi desquitarse; (Mil) tomar represalias. **~ion** /-'eɪʃn/ n represalias fpl

retarded /rɪ'tɑːdɪd/ adj retrasado

rethink /riː'θɪŋk/ vt (pt **rethought**) reconsiderar

reticen|ce /'retɪsns/ n reticencia f. **~t** adj reticente

retina /'retɪnə/ n retina f

retinue /'retɪnjuː/ n séquito m

retir|e /rɪ'taɪə(r)/ vi (from work) jubilarse; (withdraw) retirarse; (go to bed) acostarse. **~ed** adj jubilado. **~ement** n jubilación f. **~ing** adj retraído

retort /rɪ'tɔːt/ vt/i replicar. ●n réplica f

retrace /riː'treɪs/ vt. **~ one's steps** volver sobre sus pasos

retract /rɪ'trækt/ vt retirar

r

(statement). •vi retractarse

retrain /ri:'treɪn/ vi hacer un curso de reciclaje

retreat /rɪ'tri:t/ vi retirarse. •n retirada f; (place) refugio m

retrial /ri:'traɪəl/ n nuevo juicio m

retriev|al /rɪ'tri:vl/ n recuperación f. ~e /rɪ'tri:v/ vt recuperar. ~er n (dog) perro m cobrador

retro|grade /'retrəgreɪd/ adj retrógrado. ~spect /-spekt/ n. in ~ en retrospectiva. ~spective /-'spektɪv/ adj retrospectivo

return /rɪ'tɜ:n/ vi volver, regresar; (symptom) reaparecer. •vt devolver; corresponder a (affection). •n regreso m, vuelta f; (Com) rendimiento m; (to owner) devolución f. in ~ for a cambio de. **many happy ~s!** ¡feliz cumpleaños! ~ **ticket** n billete m or (LAm) boleto m de ida y vuelta, boleto m redondo (Mex). ~s npl (Com) ingresos mpl

reun|ion /ri:'ju:nɪən/ n reunión f. ~ite /ri:ju:'naɪt/ vt reunir

rev /rev/ n (Auto, fam) revolución f. •vt/i. ~ **(up)** (pt **revved**) (Auto, fam) acelerar(se)

reveal /rɪ'vi:l/ vt revelar. ~ing adj revelador

revel /'revl/ vi (pt **revelled**) tener un jolgorio. ~ **in** deleitarse en. ~ry n jolgorio m

revelation /revə'leɪʃn/ n revelación f

revenge /rɪ'vendʒ/ n venganza f. **take ~** vengarse. •vt vengar

revenue /'revənju:/ n ingresos mpl

revere /rɪ'vɪə(r)/ vt venerar. ~nce /'revərəns/ n reverencia f.

Reverend /'revərənd/ adj reverendo

reverent /'revərənt/ adj reverente

reverie /'revərɪ/ n ensueño m

revers|al /rɪ'vɜ:sl/ n inversión f. ~e /rɪ'vɜ:s/ adj inverso. •n contrario m; (back) revés m; (Auto)

marcha f atrás. •vt invertir; anular (decision); (Auto) dar marcha atrás a. •vi (Auto) dar marcha atrás

revert /rɪ'vɜ:t/ vi. ~ **to** volver a; (Jurid) revertir a

review /rɪ'vju:/ n revisión f; (Mil) revista f; (of book, play, etc) crítica f. •vt examinar (situation); reseñar (book, play, etc); (Amer, for exam) repasar

revis|e /rɪ'vaɪz/ vt revisar; (Schol) repasar. ~ion /rɪ'vɪʒn/ n revisión f; (Schol) repaso m

revive /rɪ'vaɪv/ vt resucitar (person)

revolt /rɪ'vəʊlt/ vi sublevarse. •n revuelta f. ~ing adj asqueroso

revolution /revə'lu:ʃn/ n revolución f. ~ary adj & n revolucionario (m). ~ize vt revolucionar

revolv|e /rɪ'vɒlv/ vi girar. ~er n revólver m. ~ing /rɪ'vɒlvɪŋ/ adj giratorio

revue /rɪ'vju:/ n revista f

revulsion /rɪ'vʌlʃn/ n asco m

reward /rɪ'wɔ:d/ n recompensa f. •vt recompensar. ~ing adj gratificante

rewrite /ri:'raɪt/ vt (pt **rewrote**, pp **rewritten**) volver a escribir or redactar; (copy out) escribir otra vez

rhetoric /'retərɪk/ n retórica f. ~al /rɪ'tɒrɪkl/ adj retórico

rheumatism /'ru:mətɪzəm/ n reumatismo m

rhinoceros /raɪ'nɒsərəs/ n (pl **-oses** or invar) rinoceronte m

rhubarb /'ru:bɑ:b/ n ruibarbo m

rhyme /raɪm/ n rima f; (poem) poesía f. •vt/i rimar

rhythm /'rɪðəm/ n ritmo m. ~ic(al) /'rɪðmɪk(l)/ adj rítmico

rib /rɪb/ n costilla f

ribbon /'rɪbən/ n cinta f

rice /raɪs/ n arroz m. ~ **pudding** n arroz con leche

rich /rɪtʃ/ adj (**-er, -est**) rico. •n ricos mpl. **~es** npl riquezas fpl

ricochet /ˈrɪkəʃeɪ/ vi rebotar

rid /rɪd/ vt (pt **rid**, pres p **ridding**) librar (**of** de). **get ~ of** deshacerse de. **~dance** /ˈrɪdns/ n. **good ~dance!** ¡adiós y buen viaje!

ridden /ˈrɪdn/ see RIDE

riddle /ˈrɪdl/ n acertijo m. •vt acribillar. **be ~d with** estar lleno de

ride /raɪd/ vi (pt **rode**, pp **ridden**) (on horseback) montar a caballo; (go) ir (en bicicleta, a caballo etc). •vt montar a (*horse*); ir en (*bicycle*); (*Amer*) ir en (*bus, train*); recorrer (*distance*). •n (on horse) cabalgata f; (in car) paseo m en coche. **take s.o. for a ~** 🔲 engañar a uno. **~r** (on horse) jinete m; (cyclist) ciclista m & f

ridge /rɪdʒ/ n (of hills) cadena f; (hilltop) cresta f

ridicule /ˈrɪdɪkjuːl/ n burlas fpl. •vt ridiculizar. **~ous** /rɪˈdɪkjʊləs/ adj ridículo

rife /raɪf/ adj difundido

rifle /ˈraɪfl/ n fusil m

rift /rɪft/ n grieta f; (fig) ruptura f

rig /rɪg/ vt (pt **rigged**) (pej) amañar. •n (at sea) plataforma f de perforación. ■ **~ up** vt improvisar

right /raɪt/ adj (answer) correcto; (morally) bueno; (not left) derecho; (suitable) adecuado. **be ~** (person) tener razón; (clock) estar bien. **it is ~** (just, moral) es justo. **put ~** rectificar. **the ~ person for the job** la persona indicada para el puesto. •n (entitlement) derecho m; (not left) derecha f; (not evil) bien m. **~ of way** (Auto) prioridad f. **be in the ~** tener razón. **on the ~** a la derecha. •vt enderezar; (fig) reparar. •adv a la derecha; (directly) derecho; (completely) completamente. **~ angle** n ángulo m recto. **~ away** adv inmediatamente. **~eous** /ˈraɪtʃəs/

adj recto; (cause) justo. **~ful** /ˈraɪtfl/ adj legítimo. **~-handed** /-ˈhændɪd/ adj diestro. **~-hand man** n brazo m derecho. **~ly** adv justamente. **~ wing** adj (Pol) derechista.

rigid /ˈrɪdʒɪd/ adj rígido

rig|orous /ˈrɪgərəs/ adj riguroso. **~our** /ˈrɪgə(r)/ n rigor m.

rim /rɪm/ n borde m; (of wheel) llanta f; (of glasses) montura f

rind /raɪnd/ n corteza f; (of fruit) cáscara f

ring[1] /rɪŋ/ n (circle) círculo m; (circle of metal etc) aro m; (on finger) anillo m; (on finger with stone) sortija f; (Boxing) cuadrilátero m; (bullring) ruedo m; (for circus) pista f; •vt cercar

ring[2] /rɪŋ/ n (of bell) toque m; (tinkle) tintineo m; (telephone call) llamada f. •vt (pt **rang**, pp **rung**) hacer sonar; (telephone) llamar por teléfono. **~ the bell** tocar el timbre. •vi sonar. **~ back** vt/i volver a llamar. ■ **~ up** vt llamar por teléfono. ■ **~ leader** /ˈrɪŋliːdə(r)/ n cabecilla m & f. **~ road** n carretera f de circunvalación

rink /rɪŋk/ n pista f

rinse /rɪns/ vt enjuagar. •n aclarado m; (of dishes) enjuague m; (for hair) tintura f (no permanente)

riot /ˈraɪət/ n disturbio m; (of colours) profusión f. **run ~** desenfrenarse. •vi causar disturbios

rip /rɪp/ vt (pt **ripped**) rasgar. •vi rasgarse. •n rasgón m. ■ **~ off** vt (pull off) arrancar; (🔲, cheat) robar

ripe /raɪp/ adj (**-er, -est**) maduro. **~n** /ˈraɪpn/ vt/i madurar

rip-off /ˈrɪpɒf/ n 🔲 timo m

ripple /ˈrɪpl/ n (on water) onda f

ris|e /raɪz/ vi (pt **rose**, pp **risen**) subir; (sun) salir; (river) crecer; (prices) subir; (land) elevarse; (get up) levantarse. •n subida f; (land) altura f; (increase) aumento m; (to power) ascenso m. **give ~e to**

r

ocasionar. **∼er** n. **early ∼er** n madrugador m. **∼ing** n. ● adj (sun) naciente; (number) creciente; (prices) en alza

risk /rɪsk/ n riesgo m. ●vt arriesgar. **∼y** adj (**-ier, -iest**) arriesgado

rite /raɪt/ n rito m.

ritual /ˈrɪtʃʊəl/ adj & n ritual (m)

rival /ˈraɪvl/ adj & n rival (m & f). **∼ry** n rivalidad f

river /ˈrɪvə(r)/ n río m

rivet /ˈrɪvɪt/ n remache m. **∼ing** adj fascinante

road /rəʊd/ n (in town) calle f; (between towns) carretera f; (route, way) camino m. **∼ map** n mapa m de carreteras. **∼side** n borde m de la carretera. **∼works** npl obras fpl. **∼worthy** adj (vehicle) apto para circular

roam /rəʊm/ vi vagar

roar /rɔː(r)/ n rugido m; (laughter) carcajada f. ●vt/i rugir. **∼ past** (vehicles) pasar con estruendo. **∼ with laughter** reírse a carcajadas. **∼ing** adj (trade etc) activo

roast /rəʊst/ vt asar; tostar (coffee). ● adj & n asado (m). **∼ beef** n rosbif m

rob /rɒb/ vt (pt **robbed**) atracar, asaltar (bank); robarle a (person). **∼ of** (deprive of) privar de. **∼ber** n ladrón m; (of bank) atracador m. **∼bery** n robo m; (of bank) atraco m

robe /rəʊb/ n bata f; (Univ etc) toga f

robin /ˈrɒbɪn/ n petirrojo m

robot /ˈrəʊbɒt/ n robot m

robust /rəʊˈbʌst/ adj robusto

rock /rɒk/ n roca f; (crag, cliff) peñasco m. ●vt mecer; (shake) sacudir. ●vi mecerse; (shake) sacudirse. ●n (Mus) música f rock. **∼-bottom** /-ˈbɒtəm/ adj 🄳 bajísimo

rocket /ˈrɒkɪt/ n cohete m

rock: **∼ing-chair** n mecedora f. **∼y** adj (**-ier, -iest**) rocoso; (fig,

shaky) bamboleante

rod /rɒd/ n vara f; (for fishing) caña f; (metal) barra f

rode /rəʊd/ see RIDE

rodent /ˈrəʊdnt/ n roedor m

rogue /rəʊg/ n pícaro m

role /rəʊl/ n papel m

roll /rəʊl/ vt hacer rodar; (roll up) enrollar; allanar (lawn); aplanar (pastry). ● vi rodar; (ship) balancearse; (on floor) revolcarse. **be ∼ing in money** 🄳 nadar en dinero ●n rollo m; (of ship) balanceo m; (of drum) redoble m; (of thunder) retumbo m; (bread) panecillo m, bolillo m (Mex). ■ **∼ over** vi (turn over) dar una vuelta. ■ **∼ up** vt enrollar; arremangar (sleeve). vi 🄳 llegar. **∼-call** n lista f

roller /ˈrəʊlə(r)/ n rodillo m; (wheel) rueda f; (for hair) rulo m. **R∼ blades** npl ® patines mpl en línea. **∼-coaster** n montaña f rusa. **∼-skate** n patín m de ruedas. **∼-skating** n patinaje m (sobre ruedas)

rolling /ˈrəʊlɪŋ/ adj ondulado. **∼-pin** n rodillo m

ROM /rɒm/ n (= read-only memory) ROM f

Roman /ˈrəʊmən/ adj & n romano (m). **∼ Catholic** adj & n católico (m) (romano)

romance /rəʊˈmæns/ n novela f romántica; (love) amor m; (affair) aventura f

Romania /ruːˈmeɪnɪə/ n Rumania f, Rumanía f. **∼n** adj & n rumano (m)

romantic /rəʊˈmæntɪk/ adj romántico

Rome /rəʊm/ n Roma f

romp /rɒmp/ vi retozar

roof /ruːf/ n techo m, tejado m; (of mouth) paladar m. ●vt techar. **∼rack** n baca f. **∼top** n tejado m

rook /rʊk/ n grajo m; (in chess) torre f

room /ruːm/ n cuarto m, habitación f; (bedroom) dormitorio m; (space) espacio m; (large hall) sala f. **~y** adj espacioso

roost /ruːst/ vi posarse. **~er** n gallo m

root /ruːt/ n raíz f. **take ~** echar raíces; (idea) arraigarse. ● vi echar raíces. **~ about** vi hurgar. **~ for** vt 🔲 alentar. ■ **~ out** vt extirpar

rope /rəʊp/ n cuerda f. **know the ~s** estar al corriente. ● vt atar; (Amer, lasso) enlazar. ■ **~ in** vt agarrar

rose¹ /rəʊz/ n rosa f; (nozzle) roseta f

rose² /rəʊz/ see RISE

rosé /ˈrəʊzeɪ/ n (vino m) rosado m

rot /rɒt/ vt (pt **rotted**) pudrir. ● vi pudrirse. ● n putrefacción f

rota /ˈrəʊtə/ n lista f (de turnos)

rotary /ˈrəʊtərɪ/ adj rotatorio

rotat|e /rəʊˈteɪt/ vt girar; (change round) alternar. ● vi girar; (change round) alternarse. **~ion** /-ʃn/ n rotación f

rote /rəʊt/ n. **by ~** de memoria

rotten /ˈrɒtn/ adj podrido; 🔲 pésimo 🔲; (weather) horrible

rough /rʌf/ adj (**-er, -est**) áspero, (person) tosco; (bad) malo; (ground) accidentado; (violent) brutal; (approximate) aproximado; (diamond) bruto. ● adv duro. **~ copy, ~ draft** borrador m. ● vt. **~ it** vivir sin comodidades. **~age** /ˈrʌfɪdʒ/ n fibra f. **~-and-ready** adj improvisado. **~ly** adv bruscamente; (more or less) aproximadamente

roulette /ruːˈlet/ n ruleta f

round /raʊnd/ adj (**-er, -est**) redondo. ● n círculo m; (of visits, drinks) ronda f; (of competition) vuelta f; (Boxing) asalto m. ● prep alrededor de. ● adv alrededor. **~ about** (approximately) aproximadamente. **come ~ to, go ~ to** (a friend etc) pasar por casa de. ● vt doblar (corner). ■ **~ off** vt terminar; redondear (number). ■ **~ up** vt rodear (cattle); hacer una redada

de (suspects). **~about** n tiovivo m, carrusel m (LAm); (for traffic) glorieta f, rotonda f. ● adj indirecto. **~ trip** n viaje m de ida y vuelta. **~-up** n resumen m; (of suspects) redada f

rous|e /raʊz/ vt despertar. **~ing** adj enardecedor

route /ruːt/ n ruta f; (Naut, Aviat) rumbo m; (of bus) línea f

routine /ruːˈtiːn/ n rutina f. ● adj rutinario

row¹ /rəʊ/ n fila f. ● vi remar

row² /raʊ/ n (fam, noise) bulla f 🔲; (quarrel) pelea f. ● vi 🔲 pelearse

rowboat /ˈrəʊbəʊt/ (Amer) n bote m de remos

rowdy /ˈraʊdɪ/ adj (**-ier, -iest**) n escandaloso, alborotador

rowing /ˈrəʊɪŋ/ n remo m. **~ boat** n bote m de remos

royal /ˈrɔɪəl/ adj real. **~ist** adj & n monárquico (m). **~ly** adv magníficamente. **~ty** n realeza f

rub /rʌb/ vt (pt **rubbed**) frotar. ■ **~ out** vt borrar

rubber /ˈrʌbə(r)/ n goma f, caucho m, hule m (Mex); (eraser) goma f (de borrar). **~ band** n goma f (elástica). **~-stamp** vt (fig) autorizar. **~y** adj parecido al caucho

rubbish /ˈrʌbɪʃ/ n basura f; (junk) trastos mpl; (fig) tonterías fpl. **~ bin** n cubo m de la basura, bote m de la basura (Mex). **~y** adj sin valor

rubble /ˈrʌbl/ n escombros mpl

ruby /ˈruːbɪ/ n rubí m

rucksack /ˈrʌksæk/ n mochila f

rudder /ˈrʌdə(r)/ n timón m

rude /ruːd/ adj (**-er, -est**) grosero, mal educado; (improper) indecente; (brusque) brusco. **~ly** adv groseramente. **~ness** n mala educación f

rudimentary /ruːdɪˈmentrɪ/ adj rudimentario

ruffian /ˈrʌfɪən/ n rufián m

r

ruffle | rye

ruffle /'rʌfl/ vt despeinar (hair); arrugar (clothes)

rug /rʌg/ n alfombra f, tapete m (Mex); (blanket) manta f de viaje

rugged /'rʌgɪd/ adj (coast) escarpado; (landscape) escabroso

ruin /'ru:ɪn/ n ruina f. ●vt arruinar; (spoil) estropear

rul|e /ru:l/ n regla f; (Pol) dominio m. **as a ~** por regla general. ●vt gobernar; (master) dominar; (Jurid) dictaminar. **~e out** vt descartar. **~ed paper** n papel m rayado. **~er** n (sovereign) soberano m; (leader) gobernante m & f; (measure) regla f. **~ing** adj (class) dirigente. ●n decisión f

rum /rʌm/ n ron m

rumble /'rʌmbl/ vi retumbar; (stomach) hacer ruidos

rummage /'rʌmɪdʒ/ vi hurgar

rumour /'ru:mə(r)/ n rumor m. ●vt. **it is ~ed that** se rumorea que

rump steak /rʌmpsteɪk/ n filete m de cadera

run /rʌn/ vi (pt **ran**, pp **run**, pres p **running**) correr; (water) correr; (function) funcionar; (melt) derretirse; (makeup) correrse; (colour) desteñir; (bus etc) circular; (in election) presentarse. ●vt correr (race); dirigir (business); correr (risk); (move, pass) pasar; tender (wire); preparar (bath). **~ a temperature** tener fiebre. ●n corrida f, carrera f; (outing) paseo m (en coche); (ski) pista f. **in the long ~** a la larga. **be on the ~** estar prófugo. ■ **~ away** vi huir, escaparse. ■ **~ down** vi bajar corriendo; (battery) descargarse. vt (Auto) atropellar; (belittle) denigrar. ■ **~ in** vi entrar corriendo. ■ **~ into** vt toparse con (friend); (hit) chocar con. ■ **~ off** vt sacar (copies). ■ **~ out** vi salir

corriendo; (liquid) salirse; (fig) agotarse. ■ **~ out of** vt quedarse sin. ■ **~ over** vt (Auto) atropellar. ■ **~ through** vt (review) ensayar; (rehearse) repasar. ■ **~ up** vt ir acumulando (bill). vi subir corriendo. **~away** n fugitivo m. **~ down** adj (person) agotado

rung¹ /rʌŋ/ n (of ladder) peldaño m

rung² /rʌŋ/ see RING

run: ~ner /'rʌnə(r)/ n corredor m; (on sledge) patín m. **~ner bean** n judía f escarlata. **~ner-up** n. **be ~er-up** quedar en segundo lugar. **~ning** n. **be in the ~ning** tener posibilidades de ganar. ●adj (water) corriente; (commentary) en directo. **four times ~ning** cuatro veces seguidas. **~ny** /'rʌnɪ/ adj líquido; (nose) que moquea. **~way** n pista f de aterrizaje

rupture /'rʌptʃə(r)/ n ruptura f. ●vt romper

rural /'rʊərəl/ adj rural

ruse /ru:z/ n ardid m

rush /rʌʃ/ n (haste) prisa f; (crush) bullicio m; (plant) junco m. ●vi precipitarse. ●vt apresurar; (Mil) asaltar. **~-hour** n hora f punta, hora f pico (LAm)

Russia /'rʌʃə/ n Rusia f. **~n** adj & n ruso (m)

rust /rʌst/ n orín m. ●vt oxidar. ●vi oxidarse

rustle /'rʌsl/ vt hacer susurrar; (Amer) robar. ●vi susurrar. ■ **~ up** vt 🄵 preparar.

rust: ~proof adj inoxidable. **~y** (**-ier, -iest**) oxidado

rut /rʌt/ n surco m. **be in a ~** estar anquilosado

ruthless /'ru:θlɪs/ adj despiadado

rye /raɪ/ n centeno m

Ss

S abbr (= **south**) S

sabot|age /ˈsæbətɑːʒ/ n sabotaje m. • vt sabotear. **~eur** /-ˈtɜː(r)/ n saboteador m

saccharin /ˈsækərɪn/ n sacarina f

sachet /ˈsæʃeɪ/ n bolsita f

sack /sæk/ n saco m. **get the ~** 🔲 ser despedido. • vt 🔲 despedir, echar

sacrament /ˈsækrəmənt/ n sacramento m

sacred /ˈseɪkrɪd/ adj sagrado

sacrifice /ˈsækrɪfaɪs/ n sacrificio m. • vt sacrificar

sacrileg|e /ˈsækrɪlɪdʒ/ n sacrilegio m. **~ious** /-ˈlɪdʒəs/ adj sacrílego

sad /sæd/ adj (**sadder, saddest**) triste. **~den** vt entristecer

saddle /ˈsædl/ n silla f de montar. • vt ensillar (horse). **~ s.o. with sth** (fig) endilgarle algo a uno

sadist /ˈseɪdɪst/ n sádico m. **~tic** /səˈdɪstɪk/ adj sádico

sadly /ˈsædlɪ/ adv tristemente; (fig) desgraciadamente. **~ness** n tristeza f

safe /seɪf/ adj (**-er, -est**) seguro; (out of danger) salvo; (cautious) prudente. **~ and sound** sano y salvo. • n caja f fuerte. **~ deposit** n caja f de seguridad. **~guard** n salvaguardia f. • vt salvaguardar. **~ly** adv sin peligro; (in safe place) en lugar seguro. **~ty** n seguridad f. **~ty belt** n cinturón m de seguridad. **~ty pin** n imperdible m

sag /sæg/ vi (pt **sagged**) (ceiling) combarse; (bed) hundirse

saga /ˈsɑːgə/ n saga f

Sagittarius /sædʒɪˈteərɪəs/ n Sagitario m

said /sed/ see SAY

sail /seɪl/ n vela f; (trip) paseo m (en barco). **set ~** zarpar. • vi navegar; (leave) partir; (Sport) practicar la vela; (fig) deslizarse. **go ~ing** salir a navegar. vt gobernar (boat). **~boat** n (Amer) barco m de vela. **~ing** n (Sport) vela f. **~ing boat** n, **~ing ship** n barco m de vela. **~or** n marinero m

saint /seɪnt/sənt/ n santo m. **~ly** adj santo

sake /seɪk/ n. **for the ~ of** por. **for God's ~** por el amor de Dios

salad /ˈsæləd/ n ensalada f. **~ bowl** n ensaladera f. **~ dressing** n aliño m

salary /ˈsælərɪ/ n sueldo m

sale /seɪl/ n venta f; (at reduced prices) liquidación f. **for ~** (sign) se vende. **be for ~** estar a la venta. **be on ~** (Amer, reduced) estar en liquidación. **~able** adj vendible. (for sale) estar a la venta. **~s clerk** n (Amer) dependiente m, dependienta f. **~sman** /mən/ n vendedor m; (in shop) dependiente m. **~swoman** n vendedora f; (in shop) dependienta f

saliva /səˈlaɪvə/ n saliva f

salmon /ˈsæmən/ n invar salmón m

saloon /səˈluːn/ n (on ship) salón m; (Amer, bar) bar m; (Auto) turismo m

salt /sɔːlt/ n sal f. • vt salar. **~ cellar** n salero m. **~y** adj salado

salute /səˈluːt/ n saludo m. • vt saludar. • vi hacer un saludo

Salvadorean, Salvadorian /sælvəˈdɔːrɪən/ adj & n salvadoreño (m)

salvage /ˈsælvɪdʒ/ vt salvar

salvation /sælˈveɪʃn/ n salvación f

same /seɪm/ adj igual (**as que**); (before noun) mismo (**as que**). **at the ~ time** al mismo tiempo. • pron. **the ~** lo mismo. **all the ~** de todas formas. • adv. **the ~** igual

sample /sɑːmpl/ n muestra f. • vt degustar (food)

sanct|ify /ˈsæŋktɪfaɪ/ vt santificar. **~ion** /~kʃn/ n sanción f. • vt sancionar. **~uary** /ˈsæŋktʃʊərɪ/ n (Relig) santuario m; (for wildlife) reserva f; (refuge) asilo m

sand /sænd/ n arena f. • vt pulir (floor). ■ **~ down** vt lijar (wood)

sandal /ˈsændl/ n sandalia f

sand: **~castle** n castillo m de arena. **~paper** n papel m de lija. • vt lijar. **~storm** n tormenta f de arena

sandwich /ˈsænwɪdʒ/ n bocadillo m, sandwich m. • vt. **be ~ed between** (person) estar apretujado entre

sandy /ˈsændɪ/ adj arenoso

sane /seɪn/ adj (**-er**, **-est**) (person) cuerdo; (sensible) sensato

sang /sæŋ/ see SING

sanitary /ˈsænɪtrɪ/ adj higiénico; (system etc) sanitario. **~ towel**, **~ napkin** n (Amer) compresa f (higiénica)

sanitation /sænɪˈteɪʃn/ n higiene f; (drainage) sistema m sanitario

sanity /ˈsænɪtɪ/ n cordura f

sank /sæŋk/ see SINK

Santa (Claus) /ˈsæntə(klɔːz)/ n Papá m Noel

sap /sæp/ n (in plants) savia f. • (pt **sapped**) minar

sapling /ˈsæplɪŋ/ n árbol m joven

sapphire /ˈsæfaɪə(r)/ n zafiro m

sarcas|m /ˈsɑːkæzəm/ n sarcasmo m. **~tic** /-ˈkæstɪk/ adj sarcástico

sardine /sɑːˈdiːn/ n sardina f

sash /sæʃ/ n (over shoulder) banda f; (round waist) fajín m.

sat /sæt/ see SIT

SAT abbr (Amer) (**Scholastic Aptitude Test**); (Brit) (**Standard Assessment Task**)

satchel /ˈsætʃl/ n cartera f

satellite /ˈsætəlaɪt/ adj & n satélite (m). **~ TV** n televisión f por satélite

satin /ˈsætɪn/ n raso m. • adj de raso

satir|e /ˈsætaɪə(r)/ n sátira f. **~ical** /səˈtɪrɪkl/ adj satírico. **~ize** /ˈsætəraɪz/ vt satirizar

satis|faction /sætɪsˈfækʃn/ n satisfacción f. **~factorily** /-ˈfæktərɪlɪ/ adv satisfactoriamente. **~factory** /-ˈfæktərɪ/ adj satisfactorio. **~fy** /ˈsætɪsfaɪ/ vt satisfacer; (convince) convencer. **~fying** adj satisfactorio

satphone /ˈsætfəʊn/ n teléfono m satélite

saturat|e /ˈsætʃəreɪt/ vt saturar. **~ed** adj saturado; (drenched) empapado

Saturday /ˈsætədeɪ/ n sábado m

Saturn /ˈsætən/ n Saturno m

sauce /sɔːs/ n salsa f; (cheek) descaro m. **~pan** /ˈsɔːspən/ n cazo m, cacerola f. **~r** /ˈsɔːsə(r)/ n platillo m

saucy /ˈsɔːsɪ/ adj (**-ier**, **-iest**) descarado

Saudi /ˈsaʊdɪ/ adj & n saudita (m & f). **~ Arabia** /-əˈreɪbɪə/ n Arabia f Saudí

sauna /ˈsɔːnə/ n sauna f

saunter /ˈsɔːntə(r)/ vi pasearse

sausage /ˈsɒsɪdʒ/ n salchicha f

savage /ˈsævɪdʒ/ adj salvaje; (fierce) feroz. • n salvaje m & f. • vt atacar. **~ry** n ferocidad f

sav|e /seɪv/ vt (rescue) salvar; ahorrar (money, time); (prevent) evitar; (Comp) guardar. • n (football) parada f. • prep salvo, excepto. ■ **~e up** vi/t ahorrar. **~er** n ahorrador m. **~ing** n ahorro m. **~ings** npl ahorros mpl

saviour /ˈseɪvɪə(r)/ n salvador m

savour /'seɪvə(r)/ vt saborear. ~**y**
adj (appetizing) sabroso; (not sweet) no
dulce

saw¹ /sɔ:/ see SEE¹

saw² /sɔ:/ n sierra f. ●vt (pt sawed,
pp **sawn**) serrar. ~**dust** n serrín m.
~**n** /sɔ:n/ see SAW²

saxophone /'sæksəfəʊn/ n saxofón
m, saxófono m

say /seɪ/ vt/i (pt **said** /sed/) decir;
rezar (prayer). ●n. **have a** ~
expresar una opinión; (in decision)
tener voz en capítulo. **have no** ~
no tener ni voz ni voto. ~**ing** n
refrán m

scab /skæb/ n costra f; (fam, blackleg)
esquirol m

scaffolding /'skæfəldɪŋ/ n
andamios mpl

scald /skɔ:ld/ vt escaldar

scale /skeɪl/ n (also Mus) escala f; (of
fish) escama f. ●vt (climb) escalar. ~
down vt reducir (a escala)
(drawing); recortar (operation). ~**s** npl
(for weighing) balanza f, peso m

scallion /'skæljən/ n (Amer)
cebolleta f

scalp /skælp/ vt quitar el cuero
cabelludo a

scamper /'skæmpə(r)/ vi. ~ **away**
irse correteando

scan /skæn/ vt (pt **scanned**)
escudriñar; (quickly) echar un
vistazo a; (radar) explorar

scandal /'skændl/ n escándalo m;
(gossip) chismorreo m. ~**ize** vt
escandalizar. ~**ous** adj
escandaloso

Scandinavia /skændɪ'neɪvɪə/ n
Escandinavia f. ~**n** adj & n
escandinavo (m)

scant /skænt/ adj escaso. ~**y** adj
(**-ier**, **-iest**) escaso

scapegoat /'skeɪpgəʊt/ n cabeza f
de turco

scar /skɑ:(r)/ n cicatriz f

scarce /skeəs/ adj (**-er**, **-est**) escaso.
be ~**e** escasear. **make o.s.** ~**e** 🅸

mantenerse lejos. ~**ely** adv
apenas. ~**ity** n escasez f

scare /skeə(r)/ vt asustar. **be** ~**d**
tener miedo. **be** ~**d of sth**
tenerle miedo a algo. ●n susto m.
~**crow** n espantapájaros m

scarf /skɑ:f/ n (pl **scarves**) bufanda
f; (over head) pañuelo m

scarlet /'skɑ:lət/ adj escarlata f. ~
fever n escarlatina f

scarves /skɑ:vz/ see SCARF

scary /'skeərɪ/ adj (**-ier**, **-iest**) que da
miedo

scathing /'skeɪðɪŋ/ adj mordaz

scatter /'skætə(r)/ vt (throw)
esparcir; (disperse) dispersar. ●vi
dispersarse. ~**ed** adj
disperso; (occasional) esporádico

scavenge /'skævɪndʒ/ vi escarbar
(en la basura)

scenario /sɪ'nɑ:rɪəʊ/ n (pl **-os**)
perspectiva f; (of film) guión m

scen|e /si:n/ n escena f; (sight) vista
f; (fuss) lío m. **behind the** ~**es**
entre bastidores. ~**ery** /'si:nərɪ/ n
paisaje m; (in theatre) decorado m.
~**ic** /-nɪk/ adj pintoresco

scent /sent/ n olor m; (perfume)
perfume m; (trail) pista f. ●vt intuir;
(make fragrant) perfumar

sceptic /'skeptɪk/ n escéptico m.
~**al** adj escéptico. ~**ism** /-sɪzəm/ n
escepticismo m

sceptre /'septə(r)/ n cetro m

schedule /'ʃedju:l, 'skedju:l/ n
programa f; (timetable) horario m.
behind ~ atrasado. **it's on** ~ va
de acuerdo a lo previsto. ●vt
proyectar. ~**d flight** n vuelo m
regular

scheme /ski:m/ n proyecto m; (plot)
intriga f. ●vi (pej) intrigar

schizophrenic /skɪtsə'frenɪk/ adj &
n esquizofrénico (m)

scholar /'skɒlə(r)/ n erudito m. ~**ly**
adj erudito. ~**ship** n erudición f;
(grant) beca f

school /sku:l/ n escuela f; (Univ)

facultad f. • adj (age, holidays, year) escolar. • vt instruir; (train) capacitar. ~boy n colegial m. ~girl n colegiala f. ~ing n instrucción f. ~master n (primary) maestro m; (secondary) profesor m. ~mistress n (primary) maestra f; (secondary) profesora f. ~teacher n (primary) maestro m; (secondary) profesor m

scien|ce /'saɪəns/ n ciencia f. **study ~ce** estudiar ciencias. ~ce **fiction** n ciencia f ficción. ~tific /-'tɪfɪk/ adj científico. ~tist /'saɪəntɪst/ n científico m

scissors /'sɪsəz/ npl tijeras fpl

scoff /skɒf/ vt 🔳 zamparse. • vi. ~ **at** mofarse de

scold /skəʊld/ vt regañar

scoop /skuːp/ n pala f; (news) primicia f. ■ ~ **out** vt sacar; excavar (hole)

scooter /'skuːtə(r)/ n escúter m; (for child) patinete m

scope /skəʊp/ n alcance m; (opportunity) oportunidad f

scorch /skɔːtʃ/ vt chamuscar. ~ing adj 🔳 de mucho calor

score /skɔː(r)/ n tanteo m; (Mus) partitura f; (twenty) veintena f. **on that ~** en cuanto a eso. **know the ~** 🔳 saber cómo son las cosas. • vt marcar (goal); anotarse (points); (cut, mark) rayar; conseguir (success). • vi marcar

scorn /skɔːn/ n desdén m. • vt desdeñar. ~ful adj desdeñoso

Scorpio /'skɔːpɪəʊ/ n Escorpio m, Escorpión m

scorpion /'skɔːpɪən/ n escorpión m

Scot /skɒt/ n escocés m. ~ch /skɒtʃ/ n whisky m, güisqui m

scotch /skɒtʃ/ vt frustrar; acallar (rumours)

Scotch tape n (Amer) celo m, cinta f Scotch

Scot: ~land /'skɒtlənd/ n Escocia f. ~s adj escocés. ~tish adj escocés

scoundrel /'skaʊndrəl/ n canalla f

scour /'skaʊə(r)/ vt fregar; (search) registrar. ~er n estropajo m

scourge /skɜːdʒ/ n azote m

scout /skaʊt/ n explorador m. **Boy S~** explorador m

scowl /skaʊl/ n ceño m fruncido. • vi fruncir el ceño

scram /skræm/ vi 🔳 largarse

scramble /'skræmbl/ vi (clamber) gatear. • n (difficult climb) subida f difícil; (struggle) rebatiña f. ~d **egg** n huevos mpl revueltos

scrap /skræp/ n pedacito m; (fam, fight) pelea f. • vt (pt **scrapped**) desechar. ~book n álbum m de recortes. ~s npl sobras fpl

scrape /skreɪp/ n (fig) apuro m. • vt raspar; (graze) rasparse; (rub) rascar. ■ ~ **through** vi/t aprobar por los pelos (exam). ■ ~ **together** vt reunir. ~r n rasqueta f

scrap: ~heap n montón m de deshechos. ~ **yard** n chatarrería f

scratch /skrætʃ/ vt rayar (furniture, record); (with nail etc) arañar; rascarse (itch). • vi arañar. • n rayón m; (from nail etc) arañazo m. **start from ~** empezar desde cero. **be up to ~** dar la talla

scrawl /skrɔːl/ n garabato m. • vt/i garabatear

scream /skriːm/ vt/i gritar. • n grito m

screech /skriːtʃ/ vi chillar; (brakes etc) chirriar. • n chillido m; (of brakes etc) chirrido m

screen /skriːn/ n pantalla f; (folding) biombo m. • vt (hide) ocultar; (protect) proteger; proyectar (film)

screw /skruː/ n tornillo m. • vt atornillar. ■ ~ **up** vt atornillar; entornar (eyes); torcer (face); (sl, ruin) fastidiar. ~driver n destornillador m

scribble /'skrɪbl/ vt/i garabatear. • n garabato m

script /skrɪpt/ n escritura f; (of film etc) guión m

scroll /skrəʊl/ n rollo m (de pergamino). ■ ~ **down** vi retroceder la pantalla. ■ ~ **up** vi avanzar la pantalla

scrounge /skraʊndʒ/ vt/i gorronear. ~**r** n gorrón m

scrub /skrʌb/ n (land) maleza f. ●vt/i (pt **scrubbed**) fregar

scruff /skrʌf/ n. **by the ~ of the neck** por el pescuezo. ~**y** adj (-**ier**, -**iest**) desaliñado

scrup|le /ˈskruːpl/ n escrúpulo m. ~**ulous** /-jʊləs/ adj escrupuloso

scrutin|ize /ˈskruːtɪnaɪz/ vt escudriñar; inspeccionar (document). ~**y** /ˈskruːtɪni/ n examen m minucioso

scuffle /ˈskʌfl/ n refriega f

sculpt /skʌlpt/ vt/i esculpir. ~**or** n escultor m. ~**ure** /-tʃə(r)/ n escultura f. ●vt/i esculpir

scum /skʌm/ n espuma f; (people, pej) escoria f

scupper /ˈskʌpə(r)/ vt echar por tierra (plans)

scurry /ˈskʌri/ vi corretear

scuttle /ˈskʌtl/ n cubo m del carbón. ●vt barrenar (ship). ●vi. ~ **away** escabullirse rápidamente

scythe /saɪð/ n guadaña f

SE abbr (= **south-east**) SE

sea /siː/ n mar m. **at ~** en el mar; (fig) confuso. **by ~** por mar. ~**food** n mariscos mpl. ~ **front** n paseo m marítimo, malecón m (LAm). ~**gull** n gaviota f. ~**horse** n caballito m de mar

seal /siːl/ n sello m; (animal) foca f. ●vt sellar

sea level n nivel m del mar

sea lion n león m marino

seam /siːm/ n costura f; (of coal) veta f

seaman /ˈsiːmən/ n (pl -**men**) marinero m

seamy /ˈsiːmi/ adj sórdido

seance /ˈseɪɑːns/ n sesión f de espiritismo

search /sɜːtʃ/ vt registrar; buscar en (records). ●vi buscar. ●n (for sth) búsqueda f; (of sth) registro m; (Comp) búsqueda f. **in ~ of** en busca de. ■ ~ **for** vt buscar. ~ **engine** n buscador m. ~**ing** adj penetrante. ~**light** n reflector m. ~ **party** n partida f de rescate

sea: ~**shore** n orilla f del mar. ~**sick** adj mareado. **be ~sick** marearse. ~**side** n playa f

season /ˈsiːzn/ n estación f; (period) temporada f. **high/low ~** temporada f alta/baja. ●vt (Culin) sazonar. ~**al** adj estacional; (demand) de estación. ~**ed** adj (fig) avezado. ~**ing** n condimento m. ~ **ticket** n abono m (de temporada)

seat /siːt/ n asiento m; (place) lugar m; (in cinema, theatre) localidad f; (of trousers) fondillos mpl. **take a ~** sentarse. ●vt sentar; (have seats for) (auditorium) tener capacidad para; (bus) tener asientos para. ~**belt** n cinturón m de seguridad

sea: ~ **trout** n reo m. ~**-urchin** n erizo m de mar. ~**weed** n alga f marina. ~**worthy** adj en condiciones de navegar

seclu|ded /sɪˈkluːdɪd/ adj aislado

second /ˈsekənd/ adj & n segundo (m). **on ~ thoughts** pensándolo bien. ●adv (in race etc) en segundo lugar. ●vt secundar. ~**s** npl (goods) artículos mpl de segunda calidad; (fam, more food) **have ~s** repetir. ●/sɪˈkɒnd/ vt (transfer) trasladar temporalmente. ~**ary** /ˈsekəndri/ adj secundario. ~**ary school** n instituto m (de enseñanza secundaria)

second: ~**-class** adj de segunda (clase). ~**-hand** adj de segunda mano. ~**ly** adv en segundo lugar. ~**-rate** adj mediocre

secre|cy /ˈsiːkrəsi/ n secreto m. ~**t** adj & n secreto (m). **in ~t** en secreto

secretar|ial /sekrəˈteərɪəl/ adj de

secretario; (course) de secretariado.
∼y /'sekrətrı/ n secretario m. **S∼y
of State** (in UK) ministro m: (in US)
secretario m de Estado

secretive /'si:krItIv/ adj reservado

sect /sekt/ n secta f. **∼arian**
/-'teərıən/ adj sectario

section /'sekʃn/ n sección f; (part)
parte f

sector /'sektə(r)/ n sector m

secular /'sekjʊlə(r)/ adj secular

secur|e /sI'kjʊə(r)/ adj seguro; (shelf)
firme. ●vt asegurar; (obtain)
obtener. **∼ely** adv seguramente.
∼ity n seguridad f; (for loan)
garantía f

sedat|e /sI'deIt/ adj reposado. ●vt
sedar. **∼ion** /sI'deIʃn/ n sedación f.
∼ive /'sedətIv/ adj & n sedante (m)

sediment /'sedImənt/ n
sedimento m

seduc|e /sI'dju:s/ vt seducir. **∼er** n
seductor m. **∼tion** /sI'dʌkʃn/ n
seducción f. **∼tive** /sI'dʌktIv/ adj
seductor

see /si:/ ●vt (pt saw, pp seen) ver;
(understand) comprender; (escort)
acompañar. **∼ing that** visto que.
∼ you later! ¡hasta luego! ●vi ver.
■ **∼ off** vt (say goodbye to)
despedirse de. ■ **∼ through** vt
llevar a cabo; calar (person). ■ **∼ to**
vt ocuparse de

seed /si:d/ n semilla f; (fig) germen
m; (Amer, pip) pepita f. **go to ∼**
granar; (fig) echarse a
perder.**∼ling** n planta f de
semillero. **∼y** adj (-ier, -iest)
sórdido

seek /si:k/ vt (pt sought) buscar;
pedir (approval). ■ **∼ out** vt buscar

seem /si:m/ vi parecer

seen /si:n/ see SEE

seep /si:p/ vi filtrarse

see-saw /'si:sɔ:/ n balancín m

seethe /si:ð/ vi (fig) estar furioso. **I
was seething with anger** me
hervía la sangre

see-through /'si:θru:/ adj
transparente

segment /'segmənt/ n segmento m;
(of orange) gajo m

segregat|e /'segrIgeIt/ vt segregar.
∼ion /-'geIʃn/ n segregación f

seiz|e /si:z/ vt agarrar; (Jurid)
incautar. **∼e on** vt aprovechar
(chance). ■ **∼e up** vi (Tec)
agarrotarse. **∼ure** /'si:ʒə(r)/ n
incautación f; (Med) ataque m

seldom /'seldəm/ adv rara vez

select /sI'lekt/ vt escoger; (Sport)
seleccionar. ●adj selecto; (exclusive)
exclusivo. **∼ion** /-ʃn/ n selección f.
∼ive adj selectivo

self /self/ n (pl selves). **he's his old
∼ again** vuelve a ser el de antes.
∼-addressed adj con el nombre y
la dirección del remitente.
∼-catering adj con facilidades
para cocinar. **∼-centred** adj
egocéntrico. **∼-confidence** n
confianza f en sí mismo.
∼-confident adj seguro de sí
mismo. **∼-conscious** adj cohibido.
∼-contained adj independiente.
∼-control n dominio m de sí
mismo. **∼-defence** n defensa f
propia. **∼-employed** adj que
trabaja por cuenta propia.
∼-evident adj evidente.
∼-important adj presumido.
∼-indulgent adj inmoderado.
∼-interest n interés m (personal).
∼ish adj egoísta. **∼ishness** n
egoísmo m. **∼-pity** n
autocompasión f. **∼-portrait** n
autorretrato m. **∼-respect** n amor
m propio. **∼-righteous** adj
santurrón. **∼-sacrifice** n
abnegación f. **∼-satisfied** adj
satisfecho de sí mismo. **∼-serve**
(Amer), **∼-service** adj & n
autoservicio (m). **∼-sufficient** adj
independiente

sell /sel/ vt (pt sold) vender. ●vi
venderse. ■ **∼ off** vt liquidar. **∼
out** vi. **we've sold out of gloves**
los guantes están agotados. **∼-by
date** n fecha f límite de venta.
∼er n vendedor m

S

Sellotape /'seləteɪp/ n (®) celo m, cinta f Scotch

sell-out /'selaʊt/ n (performance) éxito m de taquilla; (fam, betrayal) capitulación f

semblance /'sembləns/ n apariencia f

semester /sɪ'mestə(r)/ n (Amer) semestre m

semi... /semɪ/ pref semi...

semi|breve /-bri:v/ n redonda f. ~circle n semicírculo m. ~colon /-'kəʊlən/ n punto m y coma. ~detached /-dɪ'tætʃt/ adj (house) adosado. ~final /-'faɪnl/ n semifinal f

seminar /'semɪnɑː(r)/ n seminario m

senat|e /'senɪt/ n senado m. **the S~e** (Amer) el Senado. ~or /-ətə(r)/ n senador m

send /send/ vt/i (pt **sent**) mandar, enviar. ■ ~ **away** vt despedir. ■ ~ **away for** vt pedir (por correo). ■ ~ **for** vt enviar a buscar. ■ ~ **off for** vt pedir (por correo). ■ ~ **up** vt 🔲 parodiar. ~**er** n remitente m. ~**off** n despedida f

senile /'si:naɪl/ adj senil

senior /'si:nɪə(r)/ adj mayor; (in rank) superior; (partner etc) principal. ●n mayor m & f. ~ **citizen** n jubilado m. ~ **high school** n (Amer) colegio m secundario. ~**ity** /-'ɒrəti/ n antigüedad f

sensation /sen'seɪʃn/ n sensación f. ~**al** adj sensacional

sens|e /sens/ n sentido m; (common sense) juicio m; (feeling) sensación f. **make ~e of sth** entender algo. ~**eless** adj sin sentido. ~**ible** /'sensəbl/ adj sensato; (clothing) práctico. ~**itive** /'sensɪtɪv/ adj sensible; (touchy) susceptible. ~**itivity** /-'tɪvəti/ n sensibilidad f. ~**ual** /'senʃʊəl/ adj sensual. ~**uous** /'sensʊəs/ adj sensual

sent /sent/ see SEND

sentence /'sentəns/ n frase f; (judgment) sentencia f; (punishment) condena f. ●vt. ~ **to** condenar a

sentiment /'sentɪmənt/ n sentimiento m; (opinion) opinión f. ~**al** /-'mentl/ adj sentimental. ~**ality** /-'tæləti/ n sentimentalismo m

sentry /'sentrɪ/ n centinela f

separa|ble /'sepərəbl/ adj separable. ~**te** /'sepərət/ adj separado; (independent) independiente. ●vt /'sepəreɪt/ separar. ●vi separarse. ~**tely** /'sepərətlɪ/ adv por separado. ~**tion** /-'reɪʃn/ n separación f. ~**tist** /'sepərətɪst/ n separatista m & f

September /sep'tembə(r)/ n se(p)tiembre m

septic /'septɪk/ adj séptico

sequel /'si:kwəl/ n continuación f; (later events) secuela f

sequence /'si:kwəns/ n sucesión f; (of film) secuencia f

Serb /sɜːb/ adj & n see SERBIAN. ~**ia** /'sɜːbɪə/ n Serbia f ~**ian** adj & n serbio (m)

serenade /serə'neɪd/ n serenata f. ●vt dar serenata a

serene /sɪ'riːn/ adj sereno

sergeant /'sɑːdʒənt/ n sargento m

serial /'sɪərɪəl/ n serie f. ~**ize** vt serializar

series /'sɪəriːz/ n serie f

serious /'sɪərɪəs/ adj serio. ~**ly** adv seriamente; (ill) gravemente. **take ~ly** tomar en serio

sermon /'sɜːmən/ n sermón m

serum /'sɪərəm/ n (pl **-a**) suero m

servant /'sɜːvənt/ n criado m

serve /sɜːv/ vt servir; servir a (country); cumplir (sentence). ~ **as** servir de. **it ~s you right** ¡bien te lo mereces! ●vi servir; (in tennis) sacar. ●n (in tennis) saque m. ~**r** n (Comp) servidor m

service /'sɜːvɪs/ n servicio m; (of car

etc) revisión f. •vt revisar (car etc).
~ **charge** n (in restaurant) servicio
m. ~**s** npl (Mil) fuerzas fpl armadas.
~ **station** n estación f de servicio

serviette /ˈsɜːvɪˈet/ n servilleta f

servile /ˈsɜːvaɪl/ adj servil

session /ˈseʃn/ n sesión f

set /set/ vt (pt **set**, pres p **setting**)
poner; poner en hora (clock etc);
fijar (limit etc); (typeset) componer.
~ **fire to** prender fuego a. ~
free vt poner en libertad. •vi (sun)
ponerse; (jelly) cuajarse. •n serie f;
(of cutlery etc) juego m; (tennis) set m;
(TV, Radio) aparato m; (in theatre)
decorado m; (of people) círculo m.
•adj fijo. **be ~ on** estar resuelto a.
■ ~ **back** vt (delay) retardar; (fam,
cost) costar. ■ ~ **off** vi salir. vt
hacer sonar (alarm); hacer explotar
(bomb). ■ ~ **out** vt exponer
(argument). vi (leave) salir. ■ ~ **up** vt
establecer. ~**back** n revés m

settee /seˈtiː/ n sofá m

setting /ˈsetɪŋ/ n (of dial, switch)
posición f

settle /ˈsetl/ vt (arrange) acordar;
arreglar (matter); resolver (dispute);
pagar (bill); saldar (debt). •vi (live)
establecerse. ■ ~ **down** vi
calmarse; (become more responsible)
sentar (la) cabeza. ■ ~ **for** vt
aceptar. ■ ~ **up** vi arreglar
cuentas. ~**ment** n
establecimiento m; (agreement)
acuerdo m; (of debt) liquidación f;
(colony) colonia f. ~**r** n colono m

set: ~**-to** n pelea f. ~**-up** n 🄣
sistema m; (con) tinglado m

seven /ˈsevn/ adj & n siete (m).
~**teen** /sevnˈtiːn/ adj & n diecisiete
(m). ~**teenth** adj decimoséptimo.
•n diecisietavo m. ~**th** adj & n
séptimo (m). ~**tieth** /ˈsevəntɪθ/ adj
septuagésimo. •n setentavo m.
~**ty** /ˈsevntɪ/ adj & n setenta (m)

sever /ˈsevə(r)/ vt cortar; (fig)
romper

several /ˈsevrəl/ adj & pron varios

sever|e /sɪˈvɪə(r)/ adj (**-er, -est**)

severo; (serious) grave; (weather)
riguroso. ~**ely** adv severamente.
~**ity** /sɪˈverətɪ/ n severidad f;
(seriousness) gravedad f

sew /səʊ/ vt/i (pt **sewed**, pp **sewn**, or
sewed) coser. ■ ~ **up** vt coser

sew|age /ˈsuːɪdʒ/ n aguas fpl
residuales. ~**er** /ˈsuːə(r)/ n cloaca f

sewing /ˈsəʊɪŋ/ n costura f.
~**-machine** n máquina f de coser

sewn /səʊn/ see SEW

sex /seks/ n sexo m. **have ~** tener
relaciones sexuales. •adj sexual.
~**ist** adj & n sexista (m & f). ~**ual**
/ˈsekʃʊəl/ adj sexual. ~**ual**
intercourse n relaciones fpl
sexuales. ~**uality** /-ˈælətɪ/ n
sexualidad f. ~**y** adj (**-ier, -iest**)
excitante, sexy, provocativo

shabby /ˈʃæbɪ/ adj (**-ier, -iest**)
(clothes) gastado; (person)
pobremente vestido

shack /ʃæk/ n choza f

shade /ʃeɪd/ n sombra f; (of colour)
tono m; (for lamp) pantalla f; (nuance)
matiz m; (Amer, over window)
persiana f

shadow /ˈʃædəʊ/ n sombra f. •vt
(follow) seguir de cerca a. ~**y** adj
(fig) vago

shady /ˈʃeɪdɪ/ adj (**-ier, -iest**)
sombreado; (fig) turbio; (character)
sospechoso

shaft /ʃɑːft/ n (of arrow) astil m;
(Mec) eje m; (of light) rayo m; (of lift,
mine) pozo m

shaggy /ˈʃægɪ/ adj (**-ier, -iest**)
peludo

shake /ʃeɪk/ vt (pt **shook**, pp
shaken) sacudir; agitar (bottle);
(shock) desconcertar. ~ **hands**
with estrechar la mano a. ~
one's head negar con la cabeza;
(Amer, meaning yes) asentir con la
cabeza. •vi temblar. ■ ~ **off** vi
deshacerse de. •n sacudida f

shaky /ˈʃeɪkɪ/ adj (**-ier, -iest**)
tembloroso; (table etc) inestable

shall /ʃæl/ modal verb. **we ~ see**

veremos. ~ **we go to the cinema?** ¿vamos al cine?

shallow /'ʃæləʊ/ adj (**-er, -est**) poco profundo; (fig) superficial

sham /ʃæm/ n farsa f. ● adj fingido

shambles /'ʃæmblz/ npl (fam, mess) caos m

shame /ʃeɪm/ n (feeling) vergüenza f. **what a ~!** ¡qué lástima! ● vt avergonzar. ~**ful** adj vergonzoso. ~**less** adj desvergonzado

shampoo /ʃæm'pu:/ n champú m. ● vt lavar

shan't /ʃɑ:nt/ = **shall not**

shape /ʃeɪp/ n forma f. ● vt formar; determinar (future). ● vi tomar forma. ~**less** adj informe

share /ʃeə(r)/ n porción f; (Com) acción f. ● vt compartir; (divide) dividir. ● vi compartir. ~ **in sth** participar en algo. ■ ~ **out** vt repartir. ~**holder** n accionista m & f. ~**-out** n reparto m

shark /ʃɑ:k/ n tiburón m

sharp /ʃɑ:p/ adj (**-er, -est**) (knife etc) afilado; (pin etc) puntiagudo; (pain, sound) agudo; (taste) ácido; (bend) cerrado; (contrast) marcado; (clever) listo; (Mus) sostenido. ● adv en punto. **at seven o'clock ~** a las siete en punto. ● n (Mus) sostenido m. ~**en** vt afilar; sacar punta a (pencil). ~**ener** n (Mec) afilador m; (for pencils) sacapuntas m. ~**ly** adv bruscamente

shatter /'ʃætə(r)/ vt hacer añicos. **he was ~ed by the news** la noticia lo dejó destrozado. ● vi hacerse añicos. ~**ed** /'ʃætəd/ adj (exhausted) agotado

shav|e /ʃeɪv/ vt afeitar, rasurar (Mex). ● vi afeitarse, rasurarse (Mex). ● n afeitada f, rasurada f (Mex). **have a ~** afeitarse. ~**er** n maquinilla f (de afeitar). ~**ing brush** n brocha f de afeitar. ~**ing cream** n crema f de afeitar

shawl /ʃɔ:l/ n chal m

she /ʃi:/ pron ella

sheaf /ʃi:f/ n (pl **sheaves** /ʃi:vz/) gavilla f

shear /ʃɪə(r)/ vt (pp **shorn** or **sheared**) esquilar. ~**s** /ʃɪəz/ npl tijeras fpl grandes

shed /ʃed/ n cobertizo m. ● vt (pt **shed**, pres p **shedding**) perder; derramar (tears); despojarse de (clothes). ~ **light on** arrojar luz sobre

she'd /ʃi:(ə)d/ = **she had**, **she would**

sheep /ʃi:p/ n invar oveja f. ~**dog** n perro m pastor. ~**ish** adj avergonzado

sheer /ʃɪə(r)/ adj (as intensifier) puro; (steep) perpendicular

sheet /ʃi:t/ n sábana f; (of paper) hoja f; (of glass) lámina f; (of ice) capa f

shelf /ʃelf/ n (pl **shelves**) estante m. **a set of shelves** unos estantes

shell /ʃel/ n concha f; (of egg) cáscara f; (of crab, snail, tortoise) caparazón m; (explosive) proyectil m, obús m. ● vt pelar (peas etc); (Mil) bombardear

she'll /'ʃi:(ə)l/ = **she had**, **she would**

shellfish /'ʃelfɪʃ/ n invar marisco m; (collectively) mariscos mpl

shelter /'ʃeltə(r)/ n refugio m. **take ~** refugiarse. ● vt darle cobijo a (fugitive); (protect from weather) resguardar. ● vi refugiarse. ~**ed** /'ʃeltəd/ adj (spot) abrigado; (life) protegido

shelv|e /ʃelv/ vt (fig) dar carpetazo a. ~**ing** n estantería f

shepherd /'ʃepəd/ n pastor m. ~**ess** /-'des/ n pastora f

sherbet /'ʃɜ:bət/ n (Amer, water ice) sorbete m

sheriff /'ʃerɪf/ n (in US) sheriff m

sherry /'ʃerɪ/ n (vino m de) jerez m

she's /ʃi:z/ = **she is**, **she has**

shield /ʃi:ld/ n escudo m. ● vt proteger

shift /ʃɪft/ vt cambiar; correr (furniture etc). •vi (wind) cambiar; (attention, opinion) pasar a; (Amer, change gear) cambiar de velocidad. •n cambio m; (work) turno m; (workers) tanda f. ~**y** adj (**-ier, -iest**) furtivo

shilling /ˈʃɪlɪŋ/ n chelín m

shimmer /ˈʃɪmə(r)/ vi rielar, relucir

shin /ʃɪn/ n espinilla f

shine /ʃaɪn/ vi (pt **shone**) brillar. •vt sacar brillo a. ~ **a light on sth** alumbrar algo con una luz. •n brillo m

shingle /ˈʃɪŋɡl/ n (pebbles) guijarros mpl

shin|ing /ˈʃaɪnɪŋ/ adj brillante. ~**y** /ˈʃaɪnɪ/ adj (**-ier, -iest**) brillante

ship /ʃɪp/ n barco m, buque m. •vt (pt **shipped**) transportar; (send) enviar; (load) embarcar. ~**building** n construcción f naval. ~**ment** n envío m. ~**ping** n transporte m; (ships) barcos mpl. ~**shape** adj limpio y ordenado. ~**wreck** n naufragio m. ~**wrecked** adj naufragado. **be** ~**wrecked** naufragar. ~**yard** n astillero m

shirk /ʃɜːk/ vt esquivar

shirt /ʃɜːt/ n camisa f. **in** ~**-sleeves** en mangas de camisa

shit /ʃɪt/ n & int (vulgar) mierda f. •vi (vulgar) (pt **shat**, pres p **shitting**) cagar

shiver /ˈʃɪvə(r)/ vi temblar. •n escalofrío m

shoal /ʃəʊl/ n banco m

shock /ʃɒk/ n (of impact) choque m; (of earthquake) sacudida f; (surprise) shock m; (scare) susto m; (Elec) descarga f; (Med) shock m. **get a** ~ llevarse un shock. •vt escandalizar; (apall) horrorizar. ~**ing** adj escandaloso; 🅵 espantoso

shod /ʃɒd/ see SHOE

shoddy /ˈʃɒdɪ/ adj (**-ier, -iest**) mal hecho, de pacotilla

shoe /ʃuː/ n zapato m; (of horse) herradura f. •vt (pt **shod**, pres p **shoeing**) herrar (horse). ~**horn** n calzador m. ~**lace** n cordón m (de zapato). ~ **polish** n betún m

shone /ʃɒn/ see SHINE

shoo /ʃuː/ vt ahuyentar

shook /ʃʊk/ see SHAKE

shoot /ʃuːt/ vt (pt **shot**) disparar; rodar (film). •vi (hunt) cazar. •n (of plant) retoño m. ■ ~ **down** vt derribar. ■ ~ **out** vi (rush) salir disparado. ■ ~ **up** vi (prices) dispararse; (grow) crecer mucho

shop /ʃɒp/ n tienda f. **go to the** ~**s** ir de compras. **talk** ~ hablar del trabajo. •vi (pt **shopping**) hacer compras. **go** ~**ping** ir de compras. ■ ~ **around** vi buscar el mejor precio. ~ **assistant** n dependiente m, dependienta f, empleado m, empleada f (LAm). ~**keeper** n comerciante m, tendero m. ~**lifter** n ladrón m (que roba en las tiendas). ~**lifting** n hurto m (en las tiendas). ~**per** n comprador m. ~**ping** n (purchases) compras fpl. **do the** ~**ping** hacer la compra, hacer el mandado (Mex). ~**ping bag** n bolsa f de la compra. ~**ping cart** n (Amer) carrito m (de la compra). ~**ping centre**, ~**ping mall** (Amer) n centro m comercial. ~**ping trolley** n carrito m de la compra. ~ **steward** n enlace m sindical. ~ **window** n escaparate m, vidriera f (LAm), aparador m (Mex)

shore /ʃɔː(r)/ n orilla f

shorn /ʃɔːn/ see SHEAR

short /ʃɔːt/ adj (**-er, -est**) corto; (not lasting) breve; (person) bajo; (curt) brusco. **a** ~ **time ago** hace poco. **be** ~ **of time/money** andar corto de tiempo/dinero. **Mick is** ~ **for Michael** Mick es el diminutivo de Michael. •adv (stop) en seco. **we never went** ~ **of food** nunca nos faltó comida. •n. **in** ~ en resumen. ~**age** /-ɪdʒ/ n escasez f, falta f. ~**bread** n galleta f (de mantequilla). ~ **circuit** n cortocircuito m. ~**coming** n defecto m. ~ **cut** n atajo m. ~**en** vt acortar. ~**hand** n taquigrafía f. ~**ly** adv (soon) dentro de poco. ~**ly before midnight** poco antes de la medianoche. ~**s** npl pantalones m cortos, shorts mpl; (Amer, underwear) calzoncillos mpl. ~**sighted** /-'saɪtɪd/adj miope

shot /ʃɒt/ see **SHOOT**. • n (from gun) disparo m; tiro m; (in soccer) tiro m, disparo m; (in other sports) tiro m; (Photo) foto f. **be a good/poor** ~ ser un buen/mal tirador. **be off like a** ~ salir disparado. ~**gun** n escopeta f

should /ʃʊd, ʃəd/ modal verb. **I** ~ **go** debería ir. **you** ~**n't have said that** no deberías haber dicho eso. **I** ~ **like to see her** me gustaría verla. **if he** ~ **come** si viniese

shoulder /'ʃəʊldə(r)/ n hombro m. • vt cargar con (responsibility); ponerse al hombro (burden). ~ **blade** n omóplato m

shout /ʃaʊt/ n grito m. • vt/i gritar. ~ **at s.o.** gritarle a uno

shove /ʃʌv/ n empujón m. • vt empujar. (fam, put) poner. • vi empujar. ■ ~ **off** vi 🄵 largarse

shovel /'ʃʌvl/ n pala f. • vt (pt **shovelled**) palear (coal); espalar (snow)

show /ʃəʊ/ vt (pt **showed**, pp **shown**) mostrar; (put on display) exponer; poner (film). **I'll** ~ **you to your room** le acompaño a su cuarto. • vi (be visible) verse. • n muestra f; (exhibition) exposición f; (in theatre) espectáculo m; (on TV, radio) programa m; (ostentation) pompa f. **be on** ~ estar expuesto. ■ ~ **off** vt (pej) lucir, presumir de. vi presumir, lucirse. ■ ~ **up** vi (be visible) notarse; (arrive) aparecer. vt (reveal) poner de manifiesto; (embarrass) hacer quedar mal. ~**case** n vitrina f. ~**down** n confrontación f

shower /'ʃaʊə(r)/ n (of rain) chaparrón m; (for washing) ducha f.

have a ~, take a ~ ducharse. • vi ducharse

showjumping n concursos mpl hípicos.

shown /ʃəʊn/ see **SHOW**

show: ~**-off** n fanfarrón m. ~**room** n sala f de exposición f. ~**y** adj (**-ier, -iest**) llamativo; (attractive) ostentoso

shrank /ʃræŋk/ see **SHRINK**

shred /ʃred/ n pedazo m; (fig) pizca f. • vt (pt **shredded**) hacer tiras; destruir, triturar (documents). ~**der** n (for paper) trituradora f; (for vegetables) cortadora f

shrewd /ʃru:d/ adj (**-er, -est**) astuto

shriek /ʃri:k/ n chillido m; (of pain) alarido m. • vt/i chillar

shrift /ʃrɪft/ n. **give s.o. short** ~ despachar a uno con brusquedad. **give sth short** ~ desestimar algo de plano

shrill /ʃrɪl/ adj agudo

shrimp /ʃrɪmp/ n gamba f, camarón m (LAm); (Amer, large) langostino m

shrine /ʃraɪn/ n (place) santuario m; (tomb) sepulcro m

shrink /ʃrɪŋk/ vt (pt **shrank**, pp **shrunk**) encoger. • vi encogerse; (amount) reducirse, retroceder (recoil)

shrivel /'ʃrɪvl/ vi (pt **shrivelled**). ~ **(up)** (plant) marchitarse; (fruit) resecarse y arrugarse

shroud /ʃraʊd/ n mortaja f; (fig) velo m. • vt envolver

Shrove /ʃrəʊv/ n. ~ **Tuesday** n martes m de carnaval

shrub /ʃrʌb/ n arbusto m

shrug /ʃrʌg/ vt (pt **shrugged**) encogerse de hombros

shrunk /ʃrʌŋk/ see **SHRINK**. ~**en** adj encogido

shudder /'ʃʌdə(r)/ vi estremecerse. • n estremecimiento m

shuffle /'ʃʌfl/ vi andar arrastrando los pies. • vt barajar (cards). ~

S

one's feet arrastrar los pies

shun /ʃʌn/ vt (pt **shunned**) evitar

shunt /ʃʌnt/ vt cambiar de vía

shush /ʃʊʃ/ int ¡chitón!

shut /ʃʌt/ vt (pt **shut**, pres p **shutting**) cerrar. ●vi cerrarse. ●adj. **be** ~ estar cerrado. ■~ **down** vt/i cerrar. ■~ **up** vt cerrar; 𝕀 hacer callar. vi callarse. ~**ter** n contraventana f; (Photo) obturador m

shuttle /'ʃʌtl/ n lanzadera f; (by air) puente m aéreo; (space ~) transbordador m espacial. ●vi. ~ **(back and forth)** ir y venir. ~**cock** n volante m. ~ **service** n servicio m de enlace

shy /ʃaɪ/ adj (**-er, -est**) tímido. ●vi (pt **shied**) asustarse. ~**ness** n timidez f

sick /sɪk/ adj enfermo; (humour) negro; (fam, fed up) harto. **be** ~ estar enfermo; (vomit) vomitar. **be** ~ **of** (fig) estar harto de. **feel** ~ sentir náuseas. **get** ~ (Amer) caer enfermo, enfermarse (LAm). ~ **leave** n permiso m por enfermedad, baja f por enfermedad. ~**ly** /'sɪklɪ/ adj (**-lier, -liest**) enfermizo; (taste, smell etc) nauseabundo. ~**ness** /'sɪknɪs/ n enfermedad f

side /saɪd/ n lado m; (of hill) ladera f; (of person) costado m; (team) equipo m; (fig) parte f. ~ **by** ~ uno al lado del otro. **take** ~**s** tomar partido. ●adj lateral. ■~ **with** vt ponerse de parte de. ~**board** n aparador m. ~**dish** n acompañamiento m. ~**effect** n efecto m secundario; (fig) consecuencia f indirecta. ~**line** n actividad f suplementaria. ~ **road** n calle f secundaria. ~**step** vt eludir. ~**track** vt desviar del tema. ~**walk** n (Amer) acera f, vereda f (LAm), banqueta f (Mex). ~**ways** adj & adv de lado

siding /'saɪdɪŋ/ n apartadero m

sidle /'saɪdl/ vi. ~ **up to s.o.** acercarse furtivamente a uno

siege /si:dʒ/ n sitio m

sieve /sɪv/ n tamiz m. ●vt tamizar, cernir

sift /sɪft/ vt tamizar, cernir. ●vi. ~ **through sth** pasar algo por el tamiz

sigh /saɪ/ n suspiro m. ●vi suspirar

sight /saɪt/ n vista f; (spectacle) espectáculo m; (on gun) mira f. **at first** ~ a primera vista. **catch** ~ **of** ver; (in distance) avistar. **lose** ~ **of** perder de vista. **see the** ~**s** visitar los lugares de interés. **within** ~ **of** (near) cerca de. ●vt ver; divisar (land). ~**seeing** n. **go** ~ ir a visitar los lugares de interés. ~**seer** /-si:ə(r)/ n turista m & f

sign /saɪn/ n (indication) señal f, indicio m; (gesture) señal f, seña f; (notice) letrero m; (astrological) signo m. ●vt firmar. ■~ **on** vi (for unemployment benefit) anotarse para recibir el seguro de desempleo

signal /'sɪɡnəl/ n señal f. ●vt (pt **signalled**) señalar. ●vi. ~ **(to s.o.)** hacer señas (a uno); (Auto) poner el intermitente, señalizar

signature /'sɪɡnətʃə(r)/ n firma f. ~ **tune** n sintonía f

significan|ce /sɪɡ'nɪfɪkəns/ n importancia f. ~**t** adj (important) importante; (fact, remark) significativo

signify /'sɪɡnɪfaɪ/ vt significar

signpost /'saɪnpəʊst/ n señal f, poste m indicador

silen|ce /'saɪləns/ n silencio m. ●vt hacer callar. ~**cer** n (on gun and on car) silenciador m. ~**t** adj silencioso; (film) mudo. **remain** ~**t** quedarse callado. ~**tly** adv silenciosamente

silhouette /sɪluː'et/ n silueta f. ●vt. **be** ~**d** perfilarse (**against** contra)

silicon /'sɪlɪkən/ n silicio m. ~ **chip** n pastilla f de silicio

silk /sɪlk/ n seda f. ~**y** adj (of silk) de seda; (like silk) sedoso

silly /'sɪlɪ/ adj (**-ier, -iest**) tonto

silt /sɪlt/ n cieno m

silver /'sɪlvə(r)/ n plata f. ●adj de plata. ~**-plated** adj bañado en plata, plateado. ~**ware** /-weə(r)/ n platería f

simil|ar /'sɪmɪlə(r)/ adj parecido, similar. ~**arity** /-'lærətɪ/ n parecido m. ~**arly** adv de igual manera. ~**e** /'sɪmɪlɪ/ n símil m

simmer /'sɪmə(r)/ vt/i hervir a fuego lento. ■ ~ **down** vi calmarse

simpl|e /'sɪmpl/ adj (**-er, -est**) sencillo, simple; (person) (humble) simple; (backward) simple. ~**e-minded** /-'maɪndɪd/ adj ingenuo. ~**icity** /-'plɪsətɪ/ n simplicidad f, sencillez f. ~**ify** /'sɪmplɪfaɪ/ vt simplificar. ~**y** adv sencillamente, simplemente; (absolutely) realmente

simulate /'sɪmjʊleɪt/ vt simular

simultaneous /sɪml'teɪnɪəs/ adj simultáneo. ~**ly** adv simultáneamente

sin /sɪn/ n pecado m. ●vi (pt **sinned**) pecar

since /sɪns/

● preposition desde. **he's been living here** ~ **1991** vive aquí desde 1991. ~ **Christmas** desde Navidad. ~ **then** desde entonces. **I haven't been feeling well** ~ **Sunday** desde el domingo que no me siento bien. **how long is it** ~ **your interview?** ¿cuánto (tiempo) hace de la entrevista?

● adverb desde entonces. **I haven't spoken to her** ~ **then** no he hablado con ella desde entonces

● conjunction

····▸ desde que. **I haven't seen her** ~ **she left** no la he visto desde que se fue. ~ **coming to Manchester** desde que vine (or vino etc) a Manchester. **it's ten years** ~ **he died** hace diez años que se murió

····▸ (because) como, ya que. ~ **it**

was quite late, I decided to stay como or ya que era bastante tarde, decidí quedarme

sincer|e /sɪn'sɪə(r)/ adj sincero. ~**ely** adv sinceramente. **yours** ~**ely, ~ely (yours)** (in letters) (saluda) a usted atentamente. ~**ity** /-'serətɪ/ n sinceridad f

sinful /'sɪnfl/ adj (person) pecador; (act) pecaminoso

sing /sɪŋ/ vt/i (pt **sang**, pp **sung**) cantar

singe /sɪndʒ/ vt (pres p **singeing**) chamuscar

singer /'sɪŋə(r)/ n cantante m & f

single /'sɪŋgl/ adj solo; (not double) sencillo; (unmarried) soltero; (bed, room) individual, de una plaza (LAm); (ticket) de ida, sencillo. **not a** ~ **house** ni una sola casa. **every** ~ **day** todos los días sin excepción. ●n (ticket) billete m sencillo, boleto m de ida (LAm). ■ ~ **out** vt escoger; (distinguish) distinguir. ~**-handed** /-'hændɪd/ adj & adv sin ayuda. ~**s** npl (Sport) individuales mpl

singular /'sɪŋgjʊlə(r)/ n singular f. ●adj singular; (unusual) raro; (noun) en singular

sinister /'sɪnɪstə(r)/ adj siniestro

sink /sɪŋk/ vt (pt **sank**, pp **sunk**) hundir. ●vi hundirse. ●n fregadero m (Amer, in bathroom) lavabo m, lavamanos m. ■ ~ **in** vi penetrar

sinner /'sɪnə(r)/ n pecador m

sip /sɪp/ n sorbo m. ●vt (pt **sipped**) sorber

siphon /'saɪfən/ n sifón m. ~ **(out)** sacar con sifón. ■ ~ **off** vt desviar (money).

sir /sɜː(r)/ n señor m. **S**~ n (title) sir m. **Dear S~,** (in letters) De mi mayor consideración:

siren /'saɪərən/ n sirena f

sister /'sɪstə(r)/ n hermana f; (nurse) enfermera f jefe. ~**-in-law** n (pl ~**s-in-law**) cuñada f

S

sit /sɪt/ vi (pt **sat**, pres p **sitting**) sentarse; (committee etc) reunirse en sesión. **be ~ting** estar sentado. ●vt sentar; hacer (exam). ■ **~ back** vi (fig) relajarse. ■ **~ down** vi sentarse. **be ~ting down** estar sentado. ■ **~ up** vi (from lying) incorporarse; (straighten back) ponerse derecho. **~-in** n (strike) encierro m, ocupación f

site /saɪt/ n emplazamiento m; (piece of land) terreno m; (archaeological) yacimiento m. **building ~** n solar m. ●vt situar

sit: ~ting n sesión f; (in restaurant) turno m. **~ting room** n sala f de estar, living m

situat|e /'sɪtjʊeɪt/ vt situar. **~ion** /-'eɪʃn/ n situación f

six /sɪks/ adj & n seis (m). **~teen** /sɪk'stiːn/ adj & n dieciséis (m). **~teenth** adj decimosexto. ●n dieciseisavo m. **~th** adj & n sexto (m). **~tieth** /'sɪkstɪɪθ/ adj sexagésimo. ●n sesentavo m. **~ty** /'sɪkstɪ/ adj & n sesenta (m)

size /saɪz/ n tamaño m; (of clothes) talla f; (of shoes) número m; (of problem, operation) magnitud f. **what ~ do you take?** (clothes) ¿qué talla tiene?; (shoes) ¿qué número calza?. ■ **~ up** vt Ⓘ evaluar (problem); calar (person)

sizzle /'sɪzl/ vi crepitar

skat|e /skeɪt/ n patín m.●vi patinar. **~eboard** n monopatín m, patineta f (Mex). **~er** n patinador m. **~ing** n patinaje m. **~ing-rink** n pista f de patinaje

skeleton /'skelɪtn/ n esqueleto m. **~ key** n llave f maestra

sketch /sketʃ/ n (drawing) dibujo m; (rougher) esbozo m; (TV, Theatre) sketch m. ●vt esbozar. ●vi dibujar. **~y** adj (-ier, -iest) incompleto

ski /skiː/ n (pl **skis**) esquí m. ●vi (pt **skied**, pres p **skiing**) esquiar. **go ~ing** ir a esquiar

skid /skɪd/ vi (pt **skidded**) patinar. ●n patinazo m

ski: ~er n esquiador m. **~ing** n esquí m

skilful /'skɪlfl/ adj diestro

ski-lift /'skiːlɪft/ n telesquí m

skill /skɪl/ n habilidad f; (technical) destreza f. **~ed** adj hábil; (worker) cualificado

skim /skɪm/ vt (pt **skimmed**) espumar (soup); desnatar, descremar (milk); (glide over) pasar casi rozando. **~ milk** (Amer), **~med milk** n leche f desnatada, leche f descremada. **~ through** vt leer por encima

skimp /skɪmp/ vi. **~ on sth** escatimar algo. **~y** adj (-ier, -iest) escaso; (skirt, dress) brevísimo

skin /skɪn/ n piel f. ●vt (pt **skinned**) despellejar. **~-deep** adj superficial. **~-diving** n submarinismo m. **~ny** adj (-ier, -iest) flaco

skip /skɪp/ vi (pt **skipped**) vi saltar; (with rope) saltar a la comba, saltar a la cuerda. ●vt saltarse (chapter); faltar a (class). ●n brinco m; (container) contenedor m (para escombros). **~per** n capitán m. **~ping-rope**, **~rope** (Amer) n comba f, cuerda f de saltar, reata f (Mex)

skirmish /'skɜːmɪʃ/ n escaramuza f

skirt /skɜːt/ n falda f. ●vt bordear; (go round) ladear. **~ing-board** n rodapié m, zócalo m

skittle /'skɪtl/ n bolo m

skive off /skaɪv/ (vi Ⓘ, disappear) escurrir el bulto; (stay away from work) no ir a trabajar

skulk /skʌlk/ vi (hide) esconderse. **~ around** vi merodear

skull /skʌl/ n cráneo m; (remains) calavera f

sky /skaɪ/ n cielo m. **~lark** n alondra f. **~light** n tragaluz m. **~ marshal** n guardia m armado a bordo. **~scraper** n rascacielos m

slab /slæb/ n (of concrete) bloque m; (of stone) losa f

slack | sling

slack /slæk/ adj (**-er, -est**) flojo; (person) poco aplicado; (period) de poca actividad. •vi flojear. **∼en** vt aflojar. •vi (person) descansar. ∎ **∼en off** vt/i aflojar

slain /sleɪn/ see SLAY

slake /sleɪk/ vt apagar

slam /slæm/ vt (pt **slammed**). **∼ the door** dar un portazo. **∼ the door shut** cerrar de un portazo. **∼ on the brakes** pegar un frenazo; (sl, criticize) atacar violentamente. •vi cerrarse de un portazo

slander /'slɑːndə(r)/ n calumnia f. •vt difamar

slang /slæŋ/ n argot m

slant /slɑːnt/ vt inclinar. •n inclinación f

slap /slæp/ vt (pt **slapped**) (on face) pegarle una bofetada a; (put) tirar. **∼ s.o. on the back** darle una palmada a uno en la espalda. •n bofetada f; (on back) palmada f. •adv de lleno. **∼dash** adj descuidado; (work) chapucero

slash /slæʃ/ vt acuchillar; (fig) rebajar drásticamente. •n cuchillada f

slat /slæt/ n tablilla f

slate /sleɪt/ n pizarra f. •vt 🆂 poner por los suelos

slaughter /'slɔːtə(r)/ vt matar salvajemente; matar (animal). •n carnicería f; (of animals) matanza f

slave /sleɪv/ n esclavo m. •vi **∼ (away)** trabajar como un negro. **∼-driver** n 🆂 negrero m. **∼ry** /-ərɪ/ n esclavitud f

slay /sleɪ/ vt (pt **slew**, pp **slain**) dar muerte a

sleazy /'sliːzɪ/ adj (**-ier, -iest**) 🆂 sórdido

sled /sled/ (Amer), **sledge** /sledʒ/ n trineo m

sledge-hammer n mazo m, almádena f

sleek /sliːk/ adj (**-er, -est**) liso, brillante

sleep /sliːp/ n sueño m. **go to ∼** dormirse. •vi (pt **slept**) dormir. •vt poder alojar. **∼er** n (on track) traviesa f, durmiente m. **be a light/heavy ∼er** tener el sueño ligero/pesado. **∼ing bag** n saco m de dormir. **∼ing pill** n somnífero m. **∼less** adj. **have a ∼less night** pasar la noche en blanco. **∼walk** vi caminar dormido. **∼y** adj (**-ier, -iest**) soñoliento. **be/feel ∼y** tener sueño

sleet /sliːt/ n aguanieve f

sleeve /sliːv/ n manga f; (for record) funda f, carátula f. **up one's ∼** en reserva. **∼less** adj sin mangas

sleigh /sleɪ/ n trineo m

slender /'slendə(r)/ adj delgado; (fig) escaso

slept /slept/ see SLEEP

slew /sluː/ see SLAY

slice /slaɪs/ n (of ham) lonja f; (of bread) rebanada f; (of meat) tajada f; (of cheese) trozo m; (of sth round) rodaja f. •vt cortar (en rebanadas, tajadas etc)

slick /slɪk/ adj (performance) muy pulido. •n. (oil) ∼ marea f negra

slide /slaɪd/ vt (pt **slid**) deslizar. •vi (intentionally) deslizarse; (unintentionally) resbalarse. •n resbalón m; (in playground) tobogán m, resbaladilla f (Mex); (for hair) pasador m, broche m (Mex); (Photo) diapositiva f. **∼ing scale** n escala f móvil

slight /slaɪt/ adj (**-er, -est**) ligero; (slender) delgado. •vt desairar. •n desaire m. **∼est** adj mínimo. **not in the ∼est** en absoluto. **∼ly** adv un poco, ligeramente

slim /slɪm/ adj (**slimmer, slimmest**) delgado. •vi (pt **slimmed**) (become slimmer) adelgazar; (diet) hacer régimen

slim|e /slaɪm/ n limo m; (of snail, slug) baba f. **∼y** adj viscoso; (fig) excesivamente obsequioso

sling /slɪŋ/ n (Med) cabestrillo m. •vt (pt **slung**) lanzar

slip /slɪp/ vt (pt **slipped**) deslizar. ~ **s.o.'s mind** olvidársele a uno. •vi resbalarse. **it ~ped out of my hands** se me resbaló de las manos. **he ~ped out the back door** se deslizó por la puerta trasera •n resbalón m; (mistake) error m; (petticoat) combinación f; (paper) trozo m. **give s.o. the ~** lograr zafarse de uno. ~ **of the tongue** n lapsus m linguae. ■ ~ **away** vi escabullirse. ■ ~ **up** vi 🔢 equivocarse

slipper /'slɪpə(r)/ n zapatilla f

slippery /'slɪpərɪ/ adj resbaladizo

slip: ~ road n rampa f de acceso. **~shod** /'slɪpʃɒd/ adj descuidado. **~-up** n 🔢 error m

slit /slɪt/ n raja f; (cut) corte m. •vt (pt **slit**, pres p **slitting**) rajar; (cut) cortar

slither /'slɪðə(r)/ vi deslizarse

slobber /'slɒbə(r)/ vi babear

slog /slɒɡ/ vt (pt **slogged**) golpear. •vi caminar trabajosamente. •n golpetazo m; (hard work) trabajo m penoso. ■ ~ **away** vi sudar tinta 🔢

slogan /'sləʊɡən/ n eslogan m

slop /slɒp/ vt (pt **slopped**) derramar. •vi derramarse

slop|e /sləʊp/ vi inclinarse. •vt inclinar. n declive m, pendiente f. **~ing** adj inclinado

sloppy /'slɒpɪ/ adj (**-ier, -iest**) (work) descuidado; (person) desaliñado

slosh /slɒʃ/ vi 🔢 chapotear

slot /slɒt/ n ranura f. •vt (pt **slotted**) encajar

slot-machine n distribuidor m automático; (for gambling) máquina f tragamonedas

slouch /slaʊtʃ/ vi andar cargado de espaldas; (in chair) repanchigarse

Slovak /'sləʊvæk/ adj & n eslovaco (m). **~ia** n Eslovaquia f

slovenly /'slʌvnlɪ/ adj (work) descuidado; (person) desaliñado

slow /sləʊ/ adj (**-er, -est**) lento. **be ~** (clock) estar atrasado. **in ~ motion** a cámara lenta. •adv despacio. •vt retardar. •vi ir más despacio. ■ ~ **down, ~ up** vt retardar. vi ir más despacio. **~ly** adv despacio, lentamente

sludge /slʌdʒ/ n fango m

slug /slʌɡ/ n babosa f. **~gish** adj lento

slum /slʌm/ n barrio m bajo

slumber /'slʌmbə(r)/ vi dormir

slump /slʌmp/ n baja f repentina; (in business) depresión f. •vi desplomarse

slung /slʌŋ/ see **SLING**

slur /slɜː(r)/ vt (pt **slurred**). ~ **one's words** arrastrar las palabras. •n. **a racist ~** un comentario racista

slush /slʌʃ/ n nieve f medio derretida. ~ **fund** n fondo m de reptiles

sly /slaɪ/ adj (**slyer, slyest**) (crafty) astuto. •n. **on the ~** a hurtadillas. **~ly** adv astutamente

smack /smæk/ n manotazo m. •adv 🔢 ~ **in the middle** justo en el medio. **he went ~ into a tree** se dio contra un árbol. •vt pegarle a (con la mano)

small /smɔːl/ adj (**-er, -est**) pequeño, chico (LAm). •n. **the ~ of the back** la región lumbar. ~ **ads** npl anuncios mpl (clasificados), avisos mpl (clasificados) (LAm). ~ **change** n suelto m. **~pox** /-pɒks/ n viruela f. ~ **talk** n charla f sobre temas triviales

smart /smɑːt/ adj (**-er, -est**) elegante; (clever) listo; (brisk) rápido. •vi escocer. ■ **~en up** vt arreglar. vi (person) mejorar su aspecto, arreglarse. **~ly** adv elegantemente; (quickly) rápidamente

smash /smæʃ/ vt romper; (into little pieces) hacer pedazos; batir (record). •vi romperse; (collide) chocar (**into** con). •n (noise) estrépito m; (collision) choque m; (in sport) smash

m. ■ ~ **up** vt destrozar. ~**ing** adj 🔲 estupendo

smattering /'smætərɪŋ/ n nociones fpl

smear /smɪə(r)/ vt untar (**with** de); (stain) manchar (**with** de); (fig) difamar.● n mancha f

smell /smel/ n olor m; (sense) olfato m. ● vt (pt **smelt**) oler; (animal) olfatear. ● vi oler. ~ **of sth** oler a algo. ~**y** adj maloliente. **be ~y** oler mal

smelt /smelt/ see **SMELL**. ● vt fundir

smile /smaɪl/ n sonrisa f. ● vi sonreír. ~ **at s.o.** sonreírle a uno

smirk /smɜːk/ n sonrisita f (de suficiencia etc)

smith /smɪθ/ n herrero m

smithereens /smɪðə'riːnz/ npl. **smash sth to ~** hacer algo añicos

smock /smɒk/ n blusa f, bata f

smog /smɒg/ n smog m

smok|e /sməʊk/ n humo m. ● vt fumar (tobacco); ahumar (food). ● vi fumar. ~**eless** adj que arde sin humo. ~**er** n fumador m. ~**y** adj (room) lleno de humo

smooth /smuːð/ adj (-**er**, -**est**) (texture/stone) liso; (skin) suave; (movement) suave; (sea) tranquilo. ● vt alisar. ■ ~ **out** vt allanar (problems). ~**ly** adv suavemente; (without problems) sin problemas

smother /'smʌðə(r)/ vt asfixiar (person). ~ **s.o. with kisses** cubrir a uno de besos

smoulder /'sməʊldə(r)/ vi arder sin llama

smudge /smʌdʒ/ n borrón m. ● vi tiznarse

smug /smʌg/ adj (**smugger**, **smuggest**) pagado de sí mismo; (expression) de suficiencia

smuggl|e /'smʌgl/ vt pasar de contrabando. ~**er** n contrabandista m & f. ~**ing** n contrabando m

snack /snæk/ n tentempié m. ~ **bar** n cafetería f

snag /snæg/ n problema m

snail /sneɪl/ n caracol m. **at a ~'s pace** a paso de tortuga

snake /sneɪk/ n culebra f, serpiente f

snap /snæp/ vt (pt **snapped**) (break) romper. ~ **one's fingers** chasquear los dedos. ● vi romperse; (dog) intentar morder; (say) contestar bruscamente. ~ **at** (dog) intentar morder; (say) contestar bruscamente. ● n chasquido m; (Photo) foto f. ● adj instantáneo. ■ ~ **up** vt no dejar escapar (offer). ~**py** adj (-**ier**, -**iest**) 🔲 rápido. **make it ~py!** ¡date prisa! ~**shot** n foto f

snare /sneə(r)/ n trampa f

snarl /snɑːl/ vi gruñir

snatch /snætʃ/ vt. ~ **sth from s.o.** arrebatarle algo a uno; (steal) robar. ● n (short part) fragmento m

sneak /sniːk/ n soplón m. ● vi (past & pp **sneaked** or 🔲 **snuck**) entrar a hurtadillas. ~ **off** escabullirse. ~**ers** /'sniːkəz/ npl zapatillas fpl de deporte. ~**y** adj artero

sneer /snɪə(r)/ n expresión f desdeñosa. ● vi hacer una mueca de desprecio. ~ **at** hablar con desprecio a

sneeze /sniːz/ n estornudo m. ● vi estornudar

snide /snaɪd/ adj insidioso

sniff /snɪf/ vt oler. ● vi sorberse la nariz

snigger /'snɪgə(r)/ n risilla f. ● vi reírse (por lo bajo)

snip /snɪp/ vt (pt **snipped**) dar un tijeretazo a. ● n tijeretazo m

sniper /'snaɪpə(r)/ n francotirador m

snippet /'snɪpɪt/ n (of conversation) trozo m. ~**s of information** datos mpl aislados

snivel /'snɪvl/ vi (pt **snivelled**) lloriquear

snob /snɒb/ n esnob m & f. ~**bery** n esnobismo m. ~**bish** adj esnob

snooker /'snuːkə(r)/ n snooker m

snoop /snuːp/ vi 🔢 husmear

snooze /snuːz/ n sueñecito m. •vi dormitar

snore /snɔː(r)/ n ronquido m. •vi roncar

snorkel /'snɔːkl/ n esnórkel m

snort /snɔːt/ n bufido m. •vi bufar

snout /snaʊt/ n hocico m

snow /snəʊ/ n nieve f. •vi nevar. **be ~ed in** estar aislado por la nieve. **be ~ed under with work** estar agobiado de trabajo. ~**ball** n bola f de nieve. ~**drift** n nieve f amontonada. ~**fall** n nevada f. ~**flake** n copo m de nieve. ~**man** n muñeco m de nieve. ~**plough** n quitanieves m. ~**storm** n tormenta f de nieve. ~**y** adj (day, weather) nevoso; (landscape) nevado

snub /snʌb/ vt (pt **snubbed**) desairar. •n desaire m. ~**-nosed** adj chato

snuck /snʌk/ see SNEAK

snuff out /snʌf/ vt apagar (candle)

snug /snʌg/ adj (**snugger, snuggest**) cómodo; (tight) ajustado

snuggle (up) /'snʌgl/ vi acurrucarse

so /səʊ/ adv (before adj or adv) tan; (thus) así; **and ~ on, and ~ forth** etcétera (etcétera). **I think ~** creo que sí. **or ~** más o menos. ~ **long!** ¡hasta luego! •conj (therefore) así que. ~ **am I** yo también. ~ **as to** para. ~ **far** adv (time) hasta ahora. ~ **far as I know** que yo sepa. ~ **that** conj para que.

soak /səʊk/ vt remojar. •vi remojarse. ■ ~ **in** vi penetrar. ■ ~ **up** vt absorber. ~**ing** adj empapado

so-and-so /'səʊənsəʊ/ n fulano m

soap /səʊp/ n jabón m. •vt enjabonar. ~ **opera** n telenovela f, culebrón m. ~ **powder** n jabón m

en polvo. ~**y** adj jabonoso

soar /sɔː(r)/ vi (bird/plane) planear; (rise) elevarse; (price) dispararse. ~**ing** adj (inflation) galopante

sob /sɒb/ n sollozo m. •vi (pt **sobbed**) sollozar

sober /'səʊbə(r)/ adj (not drunk) sobrio

so-called /'səʊkɔːld/ adj denominado; (expert) supuesto

soccer /'sɒkə(r)/ n fútbol m, futbol m (Mex)

sociable /'səʊʃəbl/ adj sociable

social /'səʊʃl/ adj social; (sociable) sociable. ~**ism** n socialismo m. ~**ist** adj & n socialista (m & f). ~**ize** vt socializar. ~ **security** n seguridad f social. ~ **worker** n asistente m social

society /sə'saɪətɪ/ n sociedad f

sociolog|ical /səʊsɪə'lɒdʒɪkl/ adj sociológico. ~**ist** /-'ɒlədʒɪst/ n sociólogo m. ~**y** /-'ɒlədʒɪ/ n sociología f

sock /sɒk/ n calcetín m

socket /'sɒkɪt/ n (of joint) hueco m; (of eye) cuenca f; (wall plug) enchufe m; (for bulb) portalámparas m

soda /'səʊdə/ n soda f. ~**-water** n soda f

sodium /'səʊdɪəm/ n sodio m

sofa /'səʊfə/ n sofá m

soft /sɒft/ adj (-er, -est) blando; (light, colour) suave; (gentle) dulce, tierno; (not strict) blando. ~ **drink** n refresco m. ~**en** /'sɒfn/ vt ablandar; suavizar (skin). •vi ablandarse. ~**ly** adv dulcemente; (speak) bajito. ~**ware** n -weə(r)/ n software m

soggy /'sɒgɪ/ adj (-ier, -iest) empapado

soil /sɔɪl/ n tierra f; (Amer, dirt) suciedad f. •vt ensuciar

solar /'səʊlə(r)/ adj solar

sold /səʊld/ see SELL

solder /'sɒldə(r)/ vt soldar

soldier /'səʊldʒə(r)/ n soldado m. ∎ **~ on** vi ① seguir al pie del cañon

sole /səʊl/ n (of foot) planta f; (of shoe) suela f. ●adj único, solo. **~ly** adv únicamente

solemn /'sɒləm/ adj solemne

solicitor /sə'lɪsɪtə(r)/ n abogado m; (notary) notario m

solid /'sɒlɪd/ adj sólido; (gold etc) macizo; (unanimous) unánime; (meal) sustancioso. ●n sólido m. **~s** npl alimentos mpl sólidos. **~arity** /sɒlɪ'dærətɪ/ n solidaridad f. **~ify** /sə'lɪdɪfaɪ/ vi solidificarse

solitary /'sɒlɪtrɪ/ adj solitario

solitude /'sɒlɪtju:d/ n soledad f

solo /'səʊləʊ/ n (pl **-os**) (Mus) solo m. **~ist** n solista m & f

solstice /'sɒlstɪs/ n solsticio m

solu|ble /'sɒljʊbl/ adj soluble. **~tion** /sə'lu:ʃn/ n solución f

solve /sɒlv/ vt solucionar (problem); resolver (mystery). **~nt** /-vənt/ adj & n solvente (m)

sombre /'sɒmbə(r)/ adj sombrío

---

some /sʌm//səm/
● adjective
····▶ (unspecified number) unos, unas. he ate **~** olives comió unas aceitunas
····▶ (unspecified amount) not translated. I have to buy **~** bread tengo que comprar pan. would you like **~** coffee? ¿quieres café?
····▶ (certain, not all) algunos, -nas. I like **~** modern writers algunos escritores modernos me gustan
····▶ (a little) algo de. I eat **~** meat, but not much como algo de carne, pero no mucho
····▶ (considerable amount of) we've known each other for **~** time ya hace tiempo que nos conocemos
····▶ (expressing admiration) that's

~ car you've got! ¡vaya coche que tienes!
● pronoun
····▶ (a number of things or people) algunos, -nas, unos, unas. **~** are mine and **~** aren't algunos or unos son míos y otros no. aren't there any apples? we bought **~** yesterday ¿no hay manzanas? compramos algunas ayer
····▶ (part of an amount) he wants **~** quiere un poco. **~** of what he said parte or algo de lo que dijo
····▶ (certain people) algunos, -nas . **~** say that... algunos dicen que...
● adverb
····▶ (approximately) unos, unas, alrededor de. there were **~** fifty people there había unas cincuenta personas, había alrededor de cincuenta personas

some: **~body** /-bədɪ/ pron alguien. **~how** adv de algún modo. **~how or other** de una manera u otra. **~one** pron alguien

somersault /'sʌməsɔ:lt/ n salto m mortal. ●vi dar un salto mortal

some: **~thing** pron algo m. **~thing like** (approximately) alrededor de. **~time** adj ex. ●adv algún día. **~time next week** un día de la semana que viene. **~times** adv a veces. **~what** adv un tanto. **~where** adv en alguna parte, en algún lado

son /sʌn/ n hijo m

sonata /sə'nɑ:tə/ n sonata f

song /sɒŋ/ n canción f

sonic /'sɒnɪk/ adj sónico

son-in-law /'sʌnɪnlɔ:/ n (pl **sons-in-law**) yerno m

sonnet /'sɒnɪt/ n soneto m

son of a bitch n (pl **sons of bitches**) (esp Amer sl) hijo m de puta

soon /su:n/ adv (**-er, -est**) pronto; (in a short time) dentro de poco. **~**

after poco después. **∼er or later** tarde o temprano. **as ∼ as** en cuanto; **as ∼ as possible** lo antes posible. **the ∼er the better** cuanto antes mejor

soot /sʊt/ n hollín m

sooth|e /suːð/ vt calmar; aliviar (pain). **∼ing** adj (medicine) calmante; (words) tranquilizador

sooty /'sʊtɪ/ adj cubierto de hollín

sophisticated /sə'fɪstɪkeɪtɪd/ adj sofisticado; (complex) complejo

sophomore /'sɒfəmɔː(r)/ n (Amer) estudiante m & f de segundo curso (en la universidad)

sopping /'sɒpɪŋ/ adj. **∼ (wet)** empapado

soppy /'sɒpɪ/ adj (**-ier, -iest**) 🄸 sentimental

soprano /sə'prɑːnəʊ/ n (pl **-os**) soprano f

sordid /'sɔːdɪd/ adj sórdido

sore /sɔː(r)/ adj (**-er, -est**) dolorido; (Amer fam, angry) **be ∼ at s.o.** estar picado con uno. **∼ throat** n dolor m de garganta. **I've got a ∼ throat** me duele la garganta. •n llaga f.

sorrow /'sɒrəʊ/ n pena f, pesar m

sorry /'sɒrɪ/ adj (**-ier, -ier**) arrepentido; (wretched) lamentable. **I'm ∼** lo siento. **be ∼ for s.o.** (pity) compadecer a uno. **I'm ∼ you can't come** siento que no puedas venir. **say ∼** pedir perdón. **∼!** (apologizing) ¡lo siento! ¡perdón!. **∼?** (asking s.o. to repeat) ¿cómo?

sort /sɔːt/ n tipo m, clase f; (fam, person) tipo m. **a ∼ of** una especie de. •vt clasificar. ■ **∼ out** vt (organize) ordenar; organizar (finances); (separate out) separar; solucionar (problem)

so-so /'səʊsəʊ/ adj regular

soufflé /'suːfleɪ/ n suflé m

sought /sɔːt/ see SEEK

soul /səʊl/ n alma f

sound /saʊnd/ n sonido m; (noise) ruido m. •vt tocar. •vi sonar; (seem) parecer (**as if** que). **it ∼s interesting** suena interesante.. •adj (**-er, -est**) sano; (argument) lógico; (secure) seguro. •adv. **∼ asleep** profundamente dormido. **∼ barrier** n barrera f del sonido. **∼ly** adv sólidamente; (asleep) profundamente. **∼proof** adj insonorizado. **∼track** n banda f sonora

soup /suːp/ n sopa f

sour /'saʊə(r)/ adj (**-er, -est**) agrio; (milk) cortado

source /sɔːs/ n fuente f

south /saʊθ/ n sur m. •adj sur a invar; (wind) del sur. •adv (go) hacia el sur. **it's ∼ of** está al sur de. **S∼ Africa** n Sudáfrica f. **S∼ America** n América f (del Sur), Sudamérica f. **S∼ American** adj & n sudamericano (m). **∼-east** n sudeste m, sureste m. **∼erly** /'sʌðəlɪ/ (wind) del sur. **∼ern** /'sʌðən/ adj del sur, meridional. **∼erner** n sureño m. **∼ward** /-wəd/, **∼wards** adv hacia el sur. **∼-west** n sudoeste m, suroeste m

souvenir /suːvə'nɪə(r)/ n recuerdo m

sovereign /'sɒvrɪn/ adj & n soberano (m)

Soviet /'səʊvɪət/ adj (History) soviético. **the ∼ Union** n la Unión f Soviética

sow[1] /səʊ/ vt (pt **sowed**, pp **sowed** or **sown** /səʊn/) sembrar

sow[2] /saʊ/ n cerda f

soy (esp Amer), **soya** /'sɔɪə/ n. **∼ bean** n soja f

spa /spɑː/ n balneario m

space /speɪs/ n espacio m; (room) espacio m, lugar m. •adj (research etc) espacial. •vt espaciar. ■ **∼ out** vt espaciar. **∼craft, ∼ship** n nave f espacial

spade /speɪd/ n pala f. **∼s** npl (Cards) picas fpl

spaghetti /spə'geti/ n espaguetis mpl

Spain /spein/ n España f

spam /spæm/ n (Comp) correo m basura

span /spæn/ n (of arch) luz f; (of time) espacio m; (of wings) envergadura f. ●vt (pt **spanned**) extenderse sobre. ●adj see SPICK

Spaniard /'spænjəd/ n español m

spaniel /'spænjəl/ n spaniel m

Spanish /'spænɪʃ/ adj español; (language) castellano, español. ●n (language) castellano m, español m. npl. **the ~** (people) los españoles

spank /spæŋk/ vt pegarle a (en las nalgas)

spanner /'spænə(r)/ n llave f

spare /speə(r)/ vt. **if you can ~ the time** si tienes tiempo. **can you ~ me a pound?** ¿tienes una libra que me des? **~ no effort** no escatimar esfuerzos. **have money to ~** tener dinero de sobra. ●adj (not in use) de más; (replacement) de repuesto; (free) libre. **~ (part)** n repuesto m. **~ room** n cuarto m de huéspedes. **~ time** n tiempo m libre. **~ tyre** n neumático m de repuesto

sparingly /'speərɪŋli/ adv (use) con moderación

spark /spɑːk/ n chispa f. ●vt provocar (criticism); suscitar (interest). **~ing plug** n (Auto) bujía f

sparkle /'spɑːkl/ vi centellear. ●n destello m. **~ing** adj centelleante; (wine) espumoso

spark plug n (Auto) bujía f

sparrow /'spærəʊ/ n gorrión m

sparse /spɑːs/ adj escaso. **~ly** adv escasamente

spasm /'spæzəm/ n espasmo m; (of cough) acceso m. **~odic** /-'mɒdɪk/ adj espasmódico; (Med) irregular

spat /spæt/ see SPIT

spate /speit/ n racha f

spatial /'speɪʃl/ adj espacial

spatter /'spætə(r)/ vt salpicar (with de)

spawn /spɔːn/ n huevas fpl. ●vt generar. ●vi desovar

speak /spiːk/ vt/i (pt **spoke**, pp **spoken**) hablar. **~ for s.o.** hablar en nombre de uno. ■ **~ up** vi hablar más fuerte. **~er** n (in public) orador m; (loudspeaker) altavoz m; (of language) hablante m & f

spear /spɪə(r)/ n lanza f. **~head** vt (lead) encabezar

special /'speʃl/ adj especial. **~ist** /'speʃəlɪst/ n especialista m & f. **~ity** /-ɪ'ælətɪ/ n especialidad f. **~ization** /-əlaɪ'zeɪʃn/ n especialización f. **~ize** /-əlaɪz/ vi especializarse. **~ized** adj especializado. **~ly** adv especialmente. **~ty** n (Amer) especialidad f

species /'spiːʃiːz/ n especie f

specific /spə'sɪfɪk/ adj específico. **~ally** adv específicamente; (state) explícitamente. **~ation** /-ɪ'keɪʃn/ n especificación f. **~y** /'spesɪfaɪ/ vt especificar

specimen /'spesɪmɪn/ n muestra f

speck /spek/ n (of dust) mota f; (in distance) punto m

specs /speks/ npl 🔲 see SPECTACLES

spectacle /'spektəkl/ n espectáculo m. **~les** npl gafas fpl, lentes fpl (LAm), anteojos mpl (LAm). **~ular** /-'tækjʊlə(r)/ adj espectacular

spectator /spek'teɪtə(r)/ n espectador m

spectre /'spektə(r)/ n espectro m. **~um** /'spektrəm/ n (pl **-tra** /-trə/) espectro m; (of views) gama f

speculate /'spekjʊleɪt/ vi especular. **~ion** /-'leɪʃn/ n especulación f. **~or** n especulador m

sped /sped/ see SPEED

speech /spiːtʃ/ n (faculty) habla f; (address) discurso m. **~less** adj mudo

speed /spiːd/ n velocidad f; (rapidity) rapidez f. • vi (pt **speeded**) (drive too fast) ir a exceso de velocidad. ∎~ **off**, ~ **away** (pt **sped**) vi alejarse a toda velocidad. ∎~ **by** (pt **sped**) vi (time) pasar volando. ∎~ **up** (pt **speeded**) vt acelerar. vi acelerarse. **~boat** n lancha f motora. **~ camera** n cámara f de control de velocidad. ~ **dating** n cita f flash, speed dating m. ~ **limit** n velocidad f máxima. **~ometer** /spiˈdɒmɪtə(r)/ n velocímetro m. **~way** n (Amer) autopista f. **~y** adj (**-ier**, **-iest**) rápido

spell /spel/ n (magic) hechizo m; (of weather, activity) período m. **go through a bad ~** pasar por una mala racha. • vt/i (pt **spelled** or **spelt**) escribir. ∎~ **out** vt deletrear; (fig) explicar. ~ **checker** n corrector m ortográfico. **~ing** n ortografía f

spellbound /ˈspelbaʊnd/ adj embelesado

spelt /spelt/ see SPELL

spend /spend/ vt (pt **spent** /spent/) gastar (money); pasar (time); dedicar (care). • vi gastar dinero

sperm /spɜːm/ n (pl **sperms** or **sperm**) esperma f; (individual) espermatozoide m

spew /spjuː/ vt/i vomitar

spher|e /sfɪə(r)/ n esfera f. **~ical** /ˈsferɪkl/ adj esférico

spice /spaɪs/ n especia f

spick /spɪk/ adj. ~ **and span** limpio y ordenado

spicy /ˈspaɪsɪ/ adj picante

spider /ˈspaɪdə(r)/ n araña f

spik|e /spaɪk/ n (of metal etc) punta f. **~y** adj puntiagudo

spill /spɪl/ vt (pt **spilled** or **spilt**) derramar. • vi derramarse. ~ **over** vi (container) desbordarse; (liquid) rebosar

spin /spɪn/ vt (pt **spun**, pres p **spinning**) hacer girar; hilar (wool); centrifugar (washing). • vi girar. • n. **give sth a ~** hacer girar algo. **go**

for a ~ (Auto) ir a dar un paseo en coche

spinach /ˈspɪnɪdʒ/ n espinacas fpl

spindly /ˈspɪndlɪ/ adj larguirucho

spin-drier /spɪnˈdraɪə(r)/ n centrifugadora f (de ropa)

spine /spaɪn/ n columna f vertebral; (of book) lomo m; (on animal) púa f. **~less** adj (fig) sin carácter

spinning wheel /ˈspɪnɪŋ/ n rueca f

spin-off /ˈspɪnɒf/ n resultado m indirecto; (by-product) producto m derivado

spinster /ˈspɪnstə(r)/ n soltera f

spiral /ˈspaɪərəl/ adj espiral; (shape) de espiral. • n espiral f. • vi (pt **spiralled**) (unemployment) escalar; (prices) dispararse. ~ **staircase** n escalera f de caracol

spire /ˈspaɪə(r)/ n aguja f

spirit /ˈspɪrɪt/ n espíritu m. **be in good ~s** estar animado. **in low ~s** abatido. **~ed** adj animado, fogoso. **~s** npl (drinks) bebidas fpl alcohólicas (de alta graduación). **~ual** /ˈspɪrɪtjʊəl/ adj espiritual

spit /spɪt/ vt (pt **spat** or (Amer) **spit**, pres p **spitting**) escupir. • vi escupir. **it's ~ting** caen algunas gotas. • n saliva f; (for roasting) asador m

spite /spaɪt/ n rencor m. **in ~ of** a pesar de. • vt fastidiar. **~ful** adj rencoroso

spittle /ˈspɪtl/ n baba f

splash /splæʃ/ vt salpicar. • vi (person) chapotear. • n salpicadura f. **a ~ of paint** un poco de pintura. ∎~ **about** vi chapotear. ∎~ **down** vi (spacecraft) amerizar. ∎~ **out** vi gastarse un dineral (**on** en)

splend|id /ˈsplendɪd/ adj espléndido. **~our** /-ə(r)/ n esplendor m

splint /splɪnt/ n tablilla f

splinter /ˈsplɪntə(r)/ n astilla f. • vi astillarse

split /splɪt/ vt (pt **split**, pres p

splitting) partir; fisionar (atom); reventar (trousers); (divide) dividir. • vi partirse; (divide) dividirse. **a ~ting headache** un dolor de cabeza espantoso. ∎ n (in garment) descosido m; (in wood, glass) rajadura f. ∎ **~ up** vi separarse. **~ second** n fracción f de segundo

splutter /'splʌtə(r)/ vi chisporrotear; (person) farfullar

spoil /spɔɪl/ vt (pt **spoilt** or **spoiled**) estropear, echar a perder; (indulge) consentir, malcriar. **~s** npl botín m. **~-sport** n aguafiestas m & f

spoke[1] /spəʊk/ see SPEAK

spoke[2] /spəʊk/ n (of wheel) rayo m

spoken /spəʊkən/ see SPEAK

spokesman /'spəʊksmən/ n (pl **-men**) portavoz m

sponge /spʌndʒ/ n esponja f. • vt limpiar con una esponja. **~ off, ~ on** vt vivir a costillas de. • **~ cake** n bizcocho m

sponsor /'spɒnsə(r)/ n patrocinador m; (of the arts) mecenas m & f; (surety) garante m. • vt patrocinar. **~ship** n patrocinio m; (of the arts) mecenazgo m

spontaneous /spɒn'teɪnɪəs/ adj espontáneo. **~ously** adv espontáneamente

spoof /spu:f/ n 🔲 parodia f

spooky /'spu:kɪ/ adj (**-ier, -iest**) 🔲 espeluznante

spool /spu:l/ n carrete m

spoon /spu:n/ n cuchara f. **~ful** n cucharada f

sporadic /spə'rædɪk/ adj esporádico

sport /spɔ:t/ n deporte m. **~s car** n coche m deportivo. **~s centre** n centro m deportivo. **~sman** /-mən/ n, (pl **-men**), **~swoman** n deportista m & f

spot /spɒt/ n mancha f; (pimple) grano m; (place) lugar m; (in pattern) lunar m. **be in a ~** 🔲 estar en apuros. **on the ~** allí mismo; (decide) en ese mismo momento. • vt (pt **spotted**) manchar; (fam,

notice) ver, divisar; descubrir (mistake). **~ check** n control m hecho al azar. **~less** adj (clothes) impecable; (house) limpísimo. **~light** n reflector m; (in theatre) foco m. **~ted** adj moteado; (material) de lunares. **~ty** adj (**-ier, -iest**) (skin) lleno de granos; (youth) con la cara llena de granos

spouse /spaʊz/ n cónyuge m & f

spout /spaʊt/ n pico m; (jet) chorro m

sprain /spreɪn/ vt hacerse un esguince en. • n esguince m

sprang /spræŋ/ see SPRING

spray /spreɪ/ n (of flowers) ramillete m; (from sea) espuma f; (liquid in spray form) espray m; (device) rociador m. • vt rociar

spread /spred/ vt (pt **spread**) (stretch, extend) extender; desplegar (wings); difundir (idea, news). **~ butter on a piece of toast** untar una tostada con mantequilla. • vi extenderse; (disease) propagarse; (idea, news) difundirse. ∎ n (of ideas) difusión f; (of disease, fire) propagación f; (fam, feast) festín m. ∎ **~ out** vi (move apart) desplegarse

spree /spri:/ n. **go on a shopping ~** ir de expedición a las tiendas

sprightly /'spraɪtlɪ/ adj (**-ier, -iest**) vivo

spring /sprɪŋ/ n (season) primavera f; (device) resorte m; (in mattress) muelle m, resorte m (LAm); (elasticity) elasticidad f; (water) manantial m. • adj primaveral. • vi (pt **sprang**, pp **sprung**) saltar; (issue) brotar. **~ from sth** (problem) provenir de algo. ∎ **~ up** vi surgir. **~board** n trampolín m. **~-clean** /-'kli:n/ vi hacer una limpieza general. **~ onion** n cebolleta f. **~time** n primavera f. **~y** adj (**-ier, -iest**) (mattress, grass) mullido

sprinkle /'sprɪŋkl/ vt salpicar; (with liquid) rociar. • n salpicadura f; (of liquid) rociada f. **~r** n regadera f

sprint /sprɪnt/ n carrera f corta. • vi

(Sport) esprintar; (run fast) correr. **~er** n corredor m

sprout /spraʊt/ vi brotar. ●n brote m. **(Brussels) ~s** npl coles fpl de Bruselas

sprung /sprʌŋ/ see **SPRING**

spud /spʌd/ n 🄵 patata f, papa f (LAm)

spun /spʌn/ see **SPIN**

spur /spɜ:(r)/ n espuela f; (stimulus) acicate m. **on the ~ of the moment** sin pensarlo. ●vt (pt **spurred**). **~ (on)** espolear; (fig) estimular

spurn /spɜ:n/ vt desdeñar; (reject) rechazar

spurt /spɜ:t/ vi (liquid) salir a chorros. ●n chorro m; (of activity) racha f

spy /spaɪ/ n espía m & f. ●vt descubrir, ver. ●vi espiar. **~ on s.o.** espiar a uno

squabble /ˈskwɒbl/ vi reñir

squad /skwɒd/ n (Mil) pelotón m; (of police) brigada f; (Sport) equipo m. **~ car** n coche m patrulla. **~ron** /ˈskwɒdrən/ n (Mil, Aviat) escuadrón m; (Naut) escuadra f

squalid /ˈskwɒlɪd/ adj miserable

squall /skwɔ:l/ n turbión m

squalor /ˈskwɒlə(r)/ n miseria f

squander /ˈskwɒndə(r)/ vt derrochar; desaprovechar (opportunity)

square /skweə(r)/ n cuadrado m; (in town) plaza f. ●adj cuadrado; (meal) decente; (fam, old-fashioned) chapado a la antigua. ●vt (settle) arreglar; (Math) elevar al cuadrado. ●vi (agree) cuadrar. ■**~ up** vi arreglar cuentas (**with** con). **~ly** adv directamente

squash /skwɒʃ/ vt aplastar; (suppress) acallar. ●n. **it was a terrible ~** íbamos (or iban) terriblemente apretujados; (drink) **orange ~** naranjada f; (Sport) squash m; (vegetable) calabaza f. **~y** adj blando

squat /skwɒt/ vi (pt **squatted**) ponerse en cuclillas; (occupy illegally) ocupar sin autorización. ●adj rechoncho y bajo. **~ter** n ocupante m & f ilegal, okupa m & f

squawk /skwɔ:k/ n graznido m. ●vi graznar

squeak /skwi:k/ n chillido m; (of door) chirrido m. ●vi chillar; (door) chirriar; (shoes) crujir. **~y** adj chirriante

squeal /skwi:l/ n chillido m ●vi chillar

squeamish /ˈskwi:mɪʃ/ adj impresionable, delicado

squeeze /skwi:z/ vt apretar; exprimir (lemon etc). ●vi. **~ in** meterse. ●n estrujón m; (of hand) apretón m

squid /skwɪd/ n calamar m

squiggle /ˈskwɪgl/ n garabato m

squint /skwɪnt/ vi bizquear; (trying to see) entrecerrar los ojos. ●n estrabismo m

squirm /skwɜ:m/ vi retorcerse

squirrel /ˈskwɪrəl/ n ardilla f

squirt /skwɜ:t/ vt (liquid) echar un chorro de. ●vi salir a chorros. ●n chorrito m

St /sənt/ abbr (= saint) /sənt/ S, San(to); (= street) C/, Calle f

stab /stæb/ vt (pt **stabbed**) apuñalar. ●n puñalada f; (pain) punzada f. **have a ~ at sth** intentar algo

stabili|ty /stəˈbɪlətɪ/ n estabilidad f. **~ze** /ˈsteɪbɪlaɪz/ vt/i estabilizar

stable /ˈsteɪbl/ adj (**-er, -est**) estable. ●n caballeriza f, cuadra f

stack /stæk/ n montón m. ●vt. **~ (up)** amontonar

stadium /ˈsteɪdɪəm/ n (pl **-diums** or **-dia** /-dɪə/) estadio m

staff /stɑ:f/ n (stick) palo m; (employees) personal m. **teaching ~** personal m docente. **a member of ~** un empleado

stag /stæg/ n ciervo m. **~-night**,

~**-party** n (before wedding) fiesta f de despedida de soltero; (men-only party) fiesta f para hombres

stage /steɪdʒ/ n (in theatre) escenario f; (platform) plataforma f; (phase) etapa f. **the ~** (profession, medium) el teatro. • vt poner en escena (play); (arrange) organizar; (pej) orquestar. ~**coach** n diligencia f

stagger /'stægə(r)/ vi tambalearse. • vt dejar estupefacto; escalonar (holidays etc). ~**ing** adj asombroso

stagna|nt /'stægnənt/ adj estancado. ~**te** /stæg'neɪt/ vi estancarse

staid /steɪd/ adj serio, formal

stain /steɪn/ vt manchar; (colour) teñir. • n mancha f; (dye) tintura f. ~**ed glass window** n vidriera f de colores. ~**less steel** n acero m inoxidable. ~ **remover** n quitamanchas f

stair /steə(r)/ n escalón m. ~**s** npl escalera f. ~**case**, ~**way** n escalera f

stake /steɪk/ n estaca f, (wager) apuesta f; (Com) intereses mpl. **be at** ~ estar en juego. • vt estacar; jugarse (reputation). ~ **a claim** reclamar

stala|ctite /'stæləktaɪt/ n estalactita f. ~**gmite** /'stæləgmaɪt/ n estalagmita f

stale /steɪl/ adj (**-er, -est**) no fresco; (bread) duro; (smell) viciado. ~**mate** n (Chess) ahogado m; (deadlock) punto m muerto

stalk /stɔːk/ n tallo m. • vt acechar. • vi irse indignado

stall /stɔːl/ n (in stable) compartimiento m; (in market) puesto m. ~**s** npl (in theatre) platea f, patio m de butacas. • vt parar (engine). • vi (engine) pararse; (fig) andar con rodeos

stallion /'stæljən/ n semental m

stalwart /'stɔːlwət/ adj (supporter) leal, incondicional

stamina /'stæmɪnə/ n resistencia f

stammer /'stæmə(r)/ vi tartamudear. • n tartamudeo m

stamp /stæmp/ vt (with feet) patear; (press) estampar; (with rubber stamp) sellar; (fig) señalar. • vi dar patadas en el suelo. • n sello m, estampilla f (LAm), timbre m (Mex); (on passport) sello m; (with foot) patada f; (mark) marca f, señal f. ■~ **out** vt (fig) erradicar. ~**ed addressed envelope** n sobre m franqueado con su dirección

stampede /stæm'piːd/ n estampida f. • vi salir en estampida

stance /stɑːns/ n postura f

stand /stænd/ vi (pt **stood**) estar de pie, estar parado (LAm); (rise) ponerse de pie, pararse; (be) encontrarse; (Pol) presentarse como candidato (**for** en). **the offer ~s** la oferta sigue en pie. ~ **to reason** ser lógico. • vt (endure) soportar; (place) colocar. ~ **a chance** tener una posibilidad. • n posición f, postura f; (for lamp etc) pie m, sostén m; (at market) puesto m; (booth) quiosco m; (Sport) tribuna f. **make a ~ against sth** oponer resistencia a algo. ■~ **back** vi apartarse. ■~ **by** vi estar preparado. vt (support) apoyar. ■~ **down** vi retirarse. ■~ **for** vt significar. ■~ **in for** vt suplir a ■~ **out** vi destacarse. ■~ **up** vi ponerse de pie, pararse (LAm). ■~ **up for** vt defender. ~ **up for oneself** defenderse. ■~ **up to** vt resistir a

standard /'stændəd/ n norma f; (level) nivel m; (flag) estandarte m. • adj estándar a invar, normal. ~**ize** vt estandarizar. ~ **lamp** n lámpara f de pie. ~**s** npl principios mpl

stand: ~**-by** n (at airport) stand-by m. **be on** ~**-by** (police) estar en estado de alerta. ~**-in** n suplente m & f. ~**ing** adj de pie, parado (LAm); (permanent) permanente f. • n posición f; (prestige) prestigio m. ~**off** n (Amer, draw) empate m; (deadlock) callejón m sin salida. ~**point** n punto m de vista.

s

~still n. be at a ~still estar
paralizado. come to a ~still
(vehicle) parar; (city) quedar
paralizado

stank /stæŋk/ see STINK

staple /'steɪpl/ adj principal. • n
grapa f. • vt sujetar con una grapa.
~r n grapadora f

star /stɑː(r)/ n (incl Cinema, Theatre)
estrella f; (asterisk) asterisco m. • vi
(pt starred). ~ in a film
protagonizar una película.
~board n estribor m.

starch /stɑːtʃ/ n almidón m; (in food)
fécula f. • vt almidonar. ~y (food)
adj a base de féculas

stardom /'stɑːdəm/ n estrellato m

stare /steə(r)/ n mirada f fija. • vi. ~
(at) mirar fijamente

starfish /'stɑːfɪʃ/ n estrella f de
mar

stark /stɑːk/ adj (-er, -est) escueto.
• adv completamente

starling /'stɑːlɪŋ/ n estornino m

starry /'stɑːrɪ/ adj estrellado

start /stɑːt/ vt empezar, comenzar;
encender (engine); arrancar (car);
(cause) provocar; abrir (business). • vi
empezar; (car etc) arrancar; (jump)
dar un respingo. to ~ with (as
linker) para empezar. ~ off by
doing sth empezar por hacer
algo. • n principio m; (Sport) ventaja
f; (jump) susto m. make an early
~ (on journey) salir temprano. ~er
n (Auto) motor m de arranque;
(Culin) primer plato m. ~ing-point
n punto m de partida

startle /'stɑːtl/ vt asustar

starv|ation /stɑː'veɪʃn/ n hambre f,
inanición f. ~e /stɑːv/ vt hacer
morir de hambre. • vi morirse de
hambre. I'm ~ing me muero de
hambre

state /steɪt/ n estado m. be in a ~
estar agitado. the S~ los Estados
mpl Unidos. • vt declarar; expresar
(views); (fix) fijar. • adj del Estado;
(Schol) público; (with ceremony) de
gala. ~ly adj (-ier, -iest)

majestuoso. ~ly home n casa f
solariega. ~ment n declaración f;
(account) informe m. ~sman /-mən/
n estadista m

static /'stætɪk/ adj estacionario. • n
(interference) estática f

station /'steɪʃn/ n estación f; (on
radio) emisora f; (TV) canal m. • vt
colocar; (Mil) estacionar. ~ary adj
estacionario. ~er's (shop) n
papelería f. ~ery n artículos mpl
de papelería. ~ wagon n (Amer)
ranchera f, (coche m) familiar m,
camioneta f (LAm)

statistic /stə'tɪstɪk/ n estadística f.
~al adj estadístico. ~s n (science)
estadística f

statue /'stætʃuː/ n estatua f

stature /'stætʃə(r)/ n talla f,
estatura f

status /'steɪtəs/ n posición f social;
(prestige) categoría f; (Jurid)
estado m

statut|e /'stætʃuːt/ n estatuto m.
~ory /-ʊtrɪ/ adj estatutario

staunch /stɔːnʃ/ adj (-er, -est) leal

stave /steɪv/ n (Mus) pentagrama m.
■ ~ off vt evitar

stay /steɪ/ n (of time) estancia f,
estadía f (LAm); (Jurid) suspensión f.
• vi quedarse; (reside) alojarse. I'm
~ing in a hotel estoy en un
hotel. ■ ~ in vi quedarse en casa.
■ ~ up vi quedarse levantado

stead /sted/ n. in s.o.'s ~ en lugar
de uno. stand s.o. in good ~
resultarle muy útil a uno. ~ily adv
firmemente; (regularly)
regularmente. ~y adj (-ier, -iest)
firme; (regular) regular; (flow)
continuo; (worker) serio

steak /steɪk/ n. a ~ un filete.
some ~ carne para guisar

steal /stiːl/ vt (pt stole, pp stolen)
robar. ~ in vi entrar a hurtadillas

stealth /stelθ/ n. by ~
sigilosamente. ~y adj sigiloso

steam /stiːm/ n vapor m. let off ~
(fig) desahogarse. • vt (cook) cocer

al vapor. ●vi echar vapor. ■~ **up** vi empañarse. ~ **engine** n máquina f de vapor. ~**er** n (ship) barco m de vapor. ~**roller** n apisonadora f. ~**y** adj lleno de vapor

steel /stiːl/ n acero m. ●vt. ~ **o.s.** armarse de valor. ~ **industry** n industria f siderúrgica

steep /stiːp/ ●adj (**-er, -est**) empinado; (increase) considerable; (price) 🔢 excesivo

steeple /ˈstiːpl/ n aguja f, campanario m

steeply /ˈstiːplɪ/ adv abruptamente; (increase) considerablemente

steer /stɪə(r)/ vt dirigir; gobernar (ship). ●vi (in ship) estar al timón. ~ **clear of** evitar. ~**ing** n (Auto) dirección f. ~**ing wheel** n volante m

stem /stem/ n (of plant) tallo m; (of glass) pie m; (of word) raíz f. ●vt (pt **stemmed**) contener (bleeding). ●vi. ~ **from** provenir de

stench /stentʃ/ n hedor m

stencil /ˈstensl/ n plantilla f

stenographer /steˈnɒɡrəfə(r)/ n estenógrafo m

step /step/ vi (pt **stepped**). ~ **in sth** pisar algo. ■~ **aside** vi hacerse a un lado. ■~ **down** vi retirarse. ■~ **in** vi (fig) intervenir.■~ **up** vt intensificar; redoblar (security). ●n paso m; (stair) escalón m; (fig) medida f. **take** ~**s** tomar medidas. **be in** ~ llevar el paso. **be out of** ~ no llevar el paso. ~**brother** n hermanastro m. ~**daughter** n hijastra f. ~**father** n padrastro m. ~**ladder** n escalera f de tijera. ~**mother** n madrastra f. ~**ping-stone** n peldaño m. ~**sister** n hermanastra f. ~**son** n hijastro m

stereo /ˈsterɪəʊ/ n (pl **-os** estéreo m. ●adj estéreo a invar. ~**type** n estereotipo m

steril|e /ˈsteraɪl/ adj estéril. ~**ize** /ˈsterɪlaɪz/ vt esterilizar

sterling /ˈstɜːlɪŋ/ n libras fpl esterlinas. ●adj (pound) esterlina

stern /stɜːn/ n (of boat) popa f. ●adj (**-er, -est**) severo

stethoscope /ˈsteθəskəʊp/ n estetoscopio m

stew /stjuː/ vt/i guisar. ●n estofado m, guiso m

steward /ˈstjuːəd/ n administrador m; (on ship) camarero m; (air steward) sobrecargo m, aeromozo m (LAm). ~**ess** /-ˈdes/ n camarera f; (on aircraft) auxiliar f de vuelo, azafata f

stick /stɪk/ n palo m; (for walking) bastón m; (of celery etc) tallo m. ●vt (pt **stuck**) (glue) pegar; (fam, put) poner; (thrust) clavar; (fam, endure) soportar. ●vi pegarse; (jam) atascarse. ■~ **out** vi sobresalir. ■~ **to** vt ceñirse a. ■~ **up for** vt 🔢 defender. ~**er** n pegatina f. ~**ing plaster** n esparadrapo m; (individual) tirita f, curita f (LAm). ~**ler** /ˈstɪklə(r)/ n. **be a ~ler for** insistir en. ~**y** /ˈstɪkɪ/ adj (**-ier, -iest**) (surface) pegajoso; (label) engomado

stiff /stɪf/ adj (**-er, -est**) rígido; (joint, fabric) tieso; (muscle) entumecido; (difficult) difícil; (manner) estirado; (drink) fuerte. **have a** ~ **neck** tener tortícolis. ~**en** vi (become rigid) agarrotarse; (become firm) endurecerse. ~**ly** adv rígidamente

stifl|e /ˈstaɪfl/ vt sofocar. ~**ing** adj sofocante

stiletto (heel) /stɪˈletəʊ/ n (pl **-os**) tacón m de aguja

still /stɪl/ adj inmóvil; (peaceful) tranquilo; (drink) sin gas. **sit ~, stand** ~ quedarse tranquilo. ●adv todavía, aún; (nevertheless) sin embargo. ~**born** adj nacido muerto. ~ **life** n (pl **-s**) bodegón m. ~**ness** n tranquilidad f

stilted /ˈstɪltɪd/ adj rebuscado; (conversation) forzado

stilts /stɪlts/ npl zancos mpl

stimul|ant /ˈstɪmjʊlənt/ n estimulante m. ~**ate** /-leɪt/ vt estimular. ~**ation** /-ˈleɪʃn/ n

S

estímulo m. ~us /-əs/ n (pl -li /-laɪ/)
estímulo m

sting /stɪŋ/ n picadura f; (organ)
aguijón m. •vt/i (pt **stung**) picar

stingy /'stɪndʒɪ/ adj (-ier, -iest)
tacaño

stink /stɪŋk/ n hedor m. •vi (pt **stank**
or **stunk**, pp **stunk**) apestar, oler
mal

stipulat|e /'stɪpjʊleɪt/ vt/i estipular.
~**ion** /-'leɪʃn/ n estipulación f

stir /stɜː(r)/ vt (pt **stirred**) remover,
revolver; (move) agitar; estimular
(imagination). •vi moverse. ~ **up
trouble** armar lío 🔲. •n revuelo
m, conmoción f

stirrup /'stɪrəp/ n estribo m

stitch /stɪtʃ/ n (in sewing) puntada f;
(in knitting) punto m; (pain) dolor m
costado. **be in ~es** 🔲
desternillarse de risa. •vt coser

stock /stɒk/ n (Com, supplies)
existencias fpl; (Com, variety) surtido
m; (livestock) ganado m; (Culin) caldo
m. ~**s and shares**, ~**s and
bonds** (Amer) acciones fpl. **out of
~** agotado. **take ~ of sth** (fig)
hacer un balance de algo. •adj
estándar a invar; (fig) trillado. •vt
surtir, abastecer (**with** de). ■ ~
up vi abastecerse (**with** de).
~**broker** /-brəʊkə(r)/ n corredor m
de bolsa. **S~ Exchange** n bolsa f.
~**ing** n media f. ~**pile** n reservas
fpl. •vt almacenar. ~**still** adj
inmóvil. ~**taking** n (Com)
inventario m. ~**y** adj (-ier, -iest)
bajo y fornido

stodgy /'stɒdʒɪ/ (-dgier, -dgiest) adj
pesado

stoke /stəʊk/ vt echarle carbón (or
leña) a

stole /stəʊl/ see STEAL

stolen /'stəʊlən/ see STEAL

stomach /'stʌmək/ n estómago m.
•vt soportar. ~**ache** n dolor m de
estómago

ston|e /stəʊn/ n piedra f; (in fruit)
hueso m; (weight, pl **stone**) unidad
de peso equivalente a 14 libras o

6,35 kg. •adj de piedra. •vt
apedrear. ~**e-deaf** adj sordo como
una tapia. ~**y** adj (silence) sepulcral

stood /stʊd/ see STAND

stool /stuːl/ n taburete m

stoop /stuːp/ vi agacharse; (fig)
rebajarse. •n. **have a ~** ser
cargado de espaldas

stop /stɒp/ vt (pt **stopped**) (halt,
switch off) parar; (cease) terminar;
(prevent) impedir; (interrupt)
interrumpir. ~ **doing sth** dejar
de hacer algo. ~ **it!** ¡basta ya! •vi
(bus) parar, detenerse; (clock)
pararse. **it's ~ped raining** ha
dejado de llover. •n (bus etc)
parada f; (break on journey) parada f.
put a ~ to sth poner fin a algo.
come to a ~ detenerse. ~**gap** n
remedio m provisional. ~**over** n
escala f. ~**page** /'stɒpɪdʒ/ n
suspensión f, paradero m (LAm); (of
work) huelga f, paro m (LAm);
(interruption) interrupción f. ~**per** n
tapón m. ~**watch** n cronómetro m

storage /'stɔːrɪdʒ/ n
almacenamiento m

store /stɔː(r)/ n provisión f; (depot)
almacén m; (Amer, shop) tienda f;
(fig) reserva f. **in ~** en reserva. •vt
(for future) poner en reserva; (in
warehouse) almacenar. ■ ~ **up** vt
(fig) ir acumulando. ~**keeper** n
(Amer) tendero m, comerciante m &
f. ~**room** n almacén m; (for food)
despensa f

storey /'stɔːrɪ/ n (pl **-eys**) piso m,
planta f

stork /stɔːk/ n cigüeña f

storm /stɔːm/ n tempestad f. •vi
rabiar. •vt (Mil) asaltar. ~**y** adj
tormentoso; (sea, relationship)
tempestuoso

story /'stɔːrɪ/ n historia f; (in
newspaper) artículo m; (rumour)
rumor m; (🔲, lie) mentira f, cuento
m. ~**teller** n cuentista m & f

stout /staʊt/ adj (-er, -est) robusto,
corpulento. •n cerveza f negra

stove /stəʊv/ n estufa f

stow /stəʊ/ vt guardar; (hide) esconder. ■ **~ away** vi viajar de polizón. **~away** n polizón m & f

straggl|e /'stræɡl/ vi rezagarse. **~y** adj desordenado

straight /streɪt/ adj (**-er, -est**) (tidy) en orden; (frank) franco; (hair) lacio; (🅣, conventional) convencional. **be ~** estar derecho. ● adv (sit up) derecho; (direct) directamente; (without delay) inmediatamente. **~ away** en seguida, inmediatamente. **~ on** todo recto. **~ out** sin rodeos. ● n recta f. **~en** vt enderezar. ■ **~en up** vt ordenar. **~forward** /-'fɔːwəd/ adj franco; (easy) sencillo

strain /streɪn/ n (tension) tensión f; (injury) torcedura f. ● vt forzar (voice, eyesight); someter a demasiada tensión (relations); (sieve) colar. **~ one's back** hacerse daño en la espalda. **~ a muscle** hacerse un esguince. **~ed** adj forzado; (relations) tirante. **~er** n colador m. **~s** npl (Mus) acordes mpl

strait /streɪt/ n estrecho m. **be in dire ~s** estar en grandes apuros. **~jacket** n camisa f de fuerza

strand /strænd/ n (thread) hebra f. **a ~ of hair** un pelo. ● vt. **be ~ed** (ship) quedar encallado. **I was left ~ed** me abandonaron a mi suerte

strange /streɪndʒ/ adj (**-er, -est**) raro, extraño; (not known) desconocido. **~ly** adv de una manera rara. **~ly enough** aunque parezca mentira. **~r** n desconocido m; (from another place) forastero m

strangle /'stræŋɡl/ vt estrangular

strap /stræp/ n correa f; (of garment) tirante m. ● vt (pt **strapped**) atar con una correa

strat|egic /strə'tiːdʒɪk/ adj estratégico. **~egy** /'strætədʒɪ/ n estrategia f

straw /strɔː/ n paja f; (drinking ~) pajita f, paja f, popote m (Mex). **the last ~** el colmo. **~berry** /-bərɪ/ n fresa f; (large) fresón m

stray /streɪ/ vi (wander away) apartarse; (get lost) extraviarse; (deviate) desviarse (**from** de). ● adj (animal) (without owner) callejero; (lost) perdido. ● n (without owner) perro m/gato m callejero; (lost) perro m/gato m perdido

streak /striːk/ n lista f, raya f; (in hair) reflejo m; (in personality) veta f

stream /striːm/ n arroyo m; (current) corriente f. **a ~ of abuse** una sarta de insultos. ● vi correr. ■ **~ out** vi (people) salir en tropel. **~er** n (paper) serpentina f; (banner) banderín m. **~line** vt dar línea aerodinámica a; (simplify) racionalizar. **~lined** adj aerodinámico

street /striːt/ n calle f. **~car** n (Amer) tranvía m. **~ lamp** n farol m. **~ map, ~ plan** n plano m

strength /streŋθ/ n fuerza f; (of wall etc) solidez f. **~en** vt reforzar (wall); fortalecer (muscle)

strenuous /'strenjʊəs/ adj enérgico; (arduous) arduo; (tiring) fatigoso

stress /stres/ n énfasis f; (Gram) acento m; (Mec, Med, tension) tensión f. ● vt insistir en

stretch /stretʃ/ vt estirar; (extend) extender; forzar (truth); estirar (resources). ● vi estirarse; (when sleepy) desperezarse; (extend) extenderse; (be elastic) estirarse. ● n (period) período m; (of road) tramo m. **at a ~** sin parar. ■ **~ out** vi (person) tenderse. **~er** n camilla f

strict /strɪkt/ adj (**-er, -est**) estricto; (secrecy) absoluto. **~ly** adv con severidad; (rigorously) terminantemente. **~ly speaking** en rigor

stridden /strɪdn/ see **STRIDE**

stride /straɪd/ vi (pt **strode**, pp **stridden**) andar a zancadas. ● n zancada f. **take sth in one's ~** tomarse algo con calma. **~nt** /'straɪdnt/ adj estridente

strife /straɪf/ n conflicto m

strike /straɪk/ vt (pt **struck**) golpear; encender (match); encontrar (gold, oil); (clock) dar. **it ~s me as odd** me parece raro. ●vi golpear; (go on strike) declararse en huelga; (be on strike) estar en huelga; (attack) atacar; (clock) dar la hora. ●n (of workers) huelga f, paro m; (attack) ataque m. **come out on ~** ir a la huelga. ■ **~ off**, **~ out** vt tachar. **~ up a friendship** trabar amistad. **~r** n huelguista m & f; (Sport) artillero m

striking /ˈstraɪkɪŋ/ adj (resemblance) sorprendente; (colour) llamativo

string /strɪŋ/ n cordel m, mecate m (Mex); (Mus) cuerda f; (of lies, pearls) sarta f; (of people) sucesión f. ■ **~ along** vt 🔢 engañar

stringent /ˈstrɪndʒənt/ adj riguroso

strip /strɪp/ vt (pt **stripped**) desnudar (person); deshacer (bed). ●vi desnudarse. ●n tira f; (of land) franja f. **~ cartoon** n historieta f

stripe /straɪp/ n raya f. **~d** adj a rayas, rayado

strip lighting n luz f fluorescente

strive /straɪv/ vi (pt **strove**, pp **striven**). **~ to** esforzarse por

strode /strəʊd/ see STRIDE

stroke /strəʊk/ n golpe m; (in swimming) brazada f; (Med) ataque m de apoplejía; (of pen etc) trazo m; (of clock) campanada f; (caress) caricia f. **a ~ of luck** un golpe de suerte. ●vt acariciar

stroll /strəʊl/ vi pasearse. ●n paseo m. **~er** n (Amer) sillita f de paseo, cochecito m

strong /strɒŋ/ adj (**-er**, **-est**) fuerte. **~hold** n fortaleza f; (fig) baluarte m. **~ly** adv (greatly) fuertemente; (protest) enérgicamente; (deeply) profundamente. **~room** n cámara f acorazada

strove /strəʊv/ see STRIVE

struck /strʌk/ see STRIKE

structur|al /ˈstrʌktʃərəl/ adj estructural. **~e** /ˈstrʌktʃə(r)/ n estructura f

struggle /ˈstrʌɡl/ vi luchar; (thrash around) forcejear. ●n lucha f

strum /strʌm/ vt (pt **strummed**) rasguear

strung /strʌŋ/ see STRING

strut /strʌt/ n (in building) puntal m. ●vi (pt **strutted**) pavonearse

stub /stʌb/ n (of pencil, candle) cabo m; (counterfoil) talón m; (of cigarette) colilla. ■ **~ out** (pt **stubbed**) vt apagar

stubble /ˈstʌbl/ n rastrojo m; (beard) barba f de varios días

stubborn /ˈstʌbən/ adj terco

stuck /stʌk/ see STICK. ●adj. **the drawer is ~** el cajón se ha atascado. **the door is ~** la puerta se ha atrancado. **~-up** adj 🔢 estirado

stud /stʌd/ n tachuela f; (for collar) gemelo m.

student /ˈstjuːdənt/ n estudiante m & f; (at school) alumno m. **~ driver** n (Amer) persona que está aprendiendo a conducir

studio /ˈstjuːdɪəʊ/ n (pl **-os**) estudio m. **~ apartment**, **~ flat** n estudio m

studious /ˈstjuːdɪəs/ adj estudioso

study /ˈstʌdɪ/ n estudio m. ●vt/i estudiar

stuff /stʌf/ n 🔢 cosas fpl. **what's this ~ called?** ¿cómo se llama esta cosa?. ●vt rellenar; disecar (animal); (cram) atiborrar; (put) meter de prisa. **~ o.s.** 🔢 darse un atracón. **~ing** n relleno m. **~y** adj (**-ier**, **-iest**) mal ventilado; (old-fashioned) acartonado. **it's ~y in here** está muy cargado el ambiente

stumbl|e /ˈstʌmbl/ vi tropezar. **~e across**, **~e on** vt dar con. **~ing-block** n tropiezo m, impedimento m

stump /stʌmp/ n (of limb) muñón m; (of tree) tocón m

stun /stʌn/ vt (pt **stunned**) (daze) aturdir; (bewilder) dejar atónito.

~**ning** adj sensacional

stung /stʌŋ/ see **STING**

stunk /stʌŋk/ see **STINK**

stunt /stʌnt/ n 🖬 ardid m publicitario. ●vt detener, atrofiar. ~**ed** adj (growth) atrofiado; (body) raquítico. ~**man** n especialista m. ~**woman** n especialista f

stupendous /stjuːˈpendəs/ adj estupendo

stupid /ˈstjuːpɪd/ adj (foolish) tonto; (unintelligent) estúpido. ~**ity** /-ˈpɪdəti/ n estupidez f. ~**ly** adv estúpidamente

stupor /ˈstjuːpə(r)/ n estupor m

sturdy /ˈstɜːdɪ/ adj (**-ier, -iest**) robusto

stutter /ˈstʌtə(r)/ vi tartamudear. ●n tartamudeo m

sty /staɪ/ n (pl **sties**) pocilga f; (Med) orzuelo m

styl|e /staɪl/ n estilo m; (fashion) moda f; (design, type) diseño m. **in** ~ a lo grande. ●vt diseñar. ~**ish** adj elegante. ~**ist** n estilista m & f. **hair** ~**ist** estilista m & f

stylus /ˈstaɪləs/ n (pl **-uses**) aguja f (de tocadiscos)

suave /swɑːv/ adj elegante y desenvuelto

subconscious /sʌbˈkɒnʃəs/ adj & n subconsciente (m)

subdivide /sʌbdɪˈvaɪd/ vt subdividir

subdued /səbˈdjuːd/ adj apagado

subject /ˈsʌbdʒɪkt/ adj sometido. ~ **to** sujeto a. ●n (theme) tema m; (Schol) asignatura f, materia f (LAm); (Gram) sujeto m; (Pol) súbdito m. ●/səbˈdʒekt/ vt someter. ~**ive** /səbˈdʒektɪv/ adj subjetivo

subjunctive /səbˈdʒʌŋktɪv/ adj & n subjuntivo (m)

sublime /səˈblaɪm/ adj sublime

submarine /sʌbməˈriːn/ n submarino m

submerge /səbˈmɜːdʒ/ vt sumergir. ●vi sumergirse

submi|ssion /səbˈmɪʃn/ n sumisión f. ~**t** /səbˈmɪt/ vt (pt **submitted**) (subject) someter; presentar (application). ●vi rendirse

subordinate /səˈbɔːdɪnət/ adj & n subordinado (m). ●/səˈbɔːdɪneɪt/ vt subordinar

subscri|be /səbˈskraɪb/ vi suscribir. ~**be to** suscribirse a (magazine). ~**ber** n suscriptor m. ~**ption** /-rɪpʃn/ n (to magazine) suscripción f

subsequent /ˈsʌbsɪkwənt/ adj posterior, subsiguiente. ~**ly** adv posteriormente

subside /səbˈsaɪd/ vi (land) hundirse; (flood) bajar; (storm, wind) amainar. ~**nce** /ˈsʌbsɪdəns/ n hundimiento m

subsidiary /səbˈsɪdɪərɪ/ adj secundario; (subject) complementario. ●n (Com) filial

subsid|ize /ˈsʌbsɪdaɪz/ vt subvencionar, subsidiar (LAm). ~**y** /ˈsʌbsədɪ/ n subvención f, subsidio m

substance /ˈsʌbstəns/ n sustancia f

substandard /sʌbˈstændəd/ adj de calidad inferior

substantial /səbˈstænʃl/ adj (sturdy) sólido; (meal) sustancioso; (considerable) considerable

substitut|e /ˈsʌbstɪtjuːt/ n (person) substituto m; (thing) sucedáneo m. ●vt/i sustituir. ~**ion** /-ˈtjuːʃn/ n sustitución f

subterranean /sʌbtəˈreɪnjən/ adj subterráneo

subtitle /ˈsʌbtaɪtl/ n subtítulo m

subtle /ˈsʌtl/ adj (**-er, -est**) sutil; (tactful) discreto. ~**ty** n sutileza f

subtract /səbˈtrækt/ vt restar. ~**ion** /-ʃn/ n resta f

suburb /ˈsʌbɜːb/ n barrio m residencial de las afueras, colonia f. **the** ~**s** las afueras fpl. ~**an** /səˈbɜːbən/ adj suburbano. ~**ia** /səˈbɜːbɪə/ n zonas residenciales de las afueras de una ciudad

S

subversive /səb'vɜːsɪv/ adj subversivo

subway /'sʌbweɪ/ n paso m subterráneo; (Amer) metro m

succeed /sək'siːd/ vi (plan) dar resultado; (person) tener éxito. ~ **in doing** lograr hacer. ●vt suceder

success /sək'ses/ n éxito m. ~**ful** adj (person) de éxito, exitoso (LAm). **the ~ful applicant** el candidato que obtenga el puesto. ~**fully** adv satisfactoriamente. ~**ion** /-ʃn/ n sucesión f. **for 3 years in ~ion** durante tres años consecutivos. **in rapid ~ion** uno tras otro. ~**ive** adj sucesivo. ~**or** n sucesor m

succulent /'sʌkjʊlənt/ adj suculento

succumb /sə'kʌm/ vi sucumbir

such /sʌtʃ/ adj tal (+ noun), tan (+ adj). ~ **a big house** una casa tan grande. ●pron tal. ~ **and** ~ tal o cual. ~ **as** como. ~ **as it is** tal como es

suck /sʌk/ vt chupar (sweet, thumb); sorber (liquid). ■ ~ **up** vt (vacuum cleaner) aspirar; (pump) succionar. ■ ~ **up to** vt 🔲 dar coba a. ~**er** n (plant) chupón m; (fam, person) imbécil m

suckle /'sʌkl/ vt amamantar

suction /'sʌkʃn/ n succión f

sudden /'sʌdn/ adj repentino. **all of a ~** de repente. ~**ly** adv de repente

suds /sʌds/ npl espuma f de jabón

sue /suː/ vt (pres p **suing**) demandar (**for** por)

suede /sweɪd/ n ante m

suet /'suːɪt/ n sebo m

suffer /'sʌfə(r)/ vt sufrir; (tolerate) aguantar. ●vi sufrir; (be affected) resentirse

suffic|e /sə'faɪs/ vi bastar. ~**ient** /sə'fɪʃnt/ adj suficiente, bastante. ~**iently** adv (lo) suficientemente

suffix /'sʌfɪks/ n (pl -**ixes**) sufijo m

suffocat|e /'sʌfəkeɪt/ vt asfixiar. ●vi asfixiarse. ~**ion** /-'keɪʃn/ n asfixia f

sugar /'ʃʊɡə(r)/ n azúcar m & f. ~ **bowl** n azucarero m. ~**y** adj azucarado.

suggest /sə'dʒest/ vt sugerir. ~**ion** /-tʃən/ n sugerencia f

suicid|al /suː'saɪdl/ adj suicida. ~**e** /'suːɪsaɪd/ n suicidio m. **commit ~e** suicidarse

suit /suːt/ n traje m; (woman's) traje m de chaqueta; (Cards) palo m; (Jurid) pleito m. ●vt venirle bien a, convenirle a; (clothes) quedarle bien a; (adapt) adaptar. **be ~ed to** (thing) ser apropiado para. **I'm not ~ed to this kind of work** no sirvo para este tipo de trabajo. ~**able** adj apropiado, adecuado. ~**ably** adv (dressed) apropiadamente; (qualified) adecuadamente. ~**case** n maleta f, valija f (LAm)

suite /swiːt/ n (of furniture) juego m; (of rooms) suite f

sulk /sʌlk/ vi enfurruñarse

sullen /'sʌlən/ adj hosco

sulphur /'sʌlfə(r)/ n azufre m. ~**ic acid** /sʌl'fjʊərɪk/ n ácido m sulfúrico

sultan /'sʌltən/ n sultán m

sultana /sʌl'tɑːnə/ n pasa f de Esmirna

sultry /'sʌltrɪ/ adj (-ier, -iest) (weather) bochornoso; (fig) sensual

sum /sʌm/ n (of money) suma f, cantidad f; (Math) suma f. ■ ■ ~ **up** (pt **summed**) vt resumir. ●vi recapitular .

summar|ily /'sʌmərɪlɪ/ adv sumariamente. ~**ize** vt resumir. ~**y** n resumen m

summer /'sʌmə(r)/ n verano m. ~ **camp** n (in US) colonia f de vacaciones. ~**time** n verano m. ~**y** adj veraniego

summit /'sʌmɪt/ n (of mountain) cumbre f. ~ **conference** n conferencia f cumbre

summon /'sʌmən/ vt llamar;

convocar (meeting, s.o. to meeting);
(Jurid) citar. ■ ~ **up** vt armarse de.
~**s** n (Jurid) citación f. ●vt citar

sumptuous /'sʌmptjʊəs/ adj
suntuoso

sun /sʌn/ n sol m. ~**bathe** vi tomar
el sol, asolearse (LAm). ~**beam** n
rayo m de sol. ~**burn** n
quemadura f de sol. ~**burnt** adj
quemado por el sol

Sunday /'sʌndeɪ/ n domingo m

sunflower /'sʌnflaʊə(r)/ n
girasol m

sung /sʌŋ/ see SING

sunglasses /'sʌnglɑːsɪz/ npl gafas
fpl de sol, lentes mpl de sol (LAm)

sunk /sʌŋk/ see SINK. ~**en** /'sʌŋkən/
●adj hundido

sun: ~**light** n luz f del sol. ~**ny**
adj (-ier, -iest) (day) de sol; (place)
soleado. **it is** ~**ny** hace sol.
~**rise** n. **at** ~**rise** al amanecer.
salida f del sol. ~**roof** n techo m
corredizo. ~**set** n puesta f del sol.
~**shine** n sol m. ~**stroke** n
insolación f. ~**tan** n bronceado m.
get a ~**tan** broncearse. ~**tan
lotion** n bronceador m

super /'suːpə(r)/ adj 🄸 genial, super
adj invar

superb /suːˈpɜːb/ adj espléndido

supercilious /suːpəˈsɪlɪəs/ adj
desdeñoso

superficial /suːpəˈfɪʃl/ adj
superficial

superfluous /suːˈpɜːfluəs/ adj
superfluo

superhighway /'suːpəhaɪweɪ/ n
(Amer, Auto) autopista f; (Comp)
information ~ autopista f de la
comunicación

superhuman /suːpəˈhjuːmən/ adj
sobrehumano

superintendent
/suːpərɪnˈtendənt/ n director m;
(Amer, of building) portero m; (of
police) comisario m; (in US)
superintendente m & f

superior /suːˈpɪərɪə(r)/ adj & n

superior (m). ~**ity** /-ˈɒrətɪ/ n
superioridad f

superlative /suːˈpɜːlətɪv/ adj
inigualable. ●n superlativo m

supermarket /'suːpəmɑːkɪt/ n
supermercado m

supernatural /suːpəˈnætʃrəl/ adj
sobrenatural

superpower /'suːpəpaʊə(r)/ n
superpotencia f

supersede /suːpəˈsiːd/ vt
reemplazar, sustituir

supersonic /suːpəˈsɒnɪk/ adj
supersónico

superstitio|n /suːpəˈstɪʃn/ n
superstición f. ~**us** adj /-əs/
supersticioso

supervis|e /'suːpəvaɪz/ vt
supervisar. ~**ion** /-ˈvɪʒn/ n
supervisión f. ~**or** n supervisor m

supper /'sʌpə(r)/ n cena f (ligera),
comida f (ligera) (LAm)

supple /sʌpl/ adj flexible

supplement /'sʌplɪmənt/ n
suplemento m; (to diet, income)
complemento m. ●vt
complementar (diet, income). ~**ary**
/-ˈmentərɪ/ adj suplementario

suppl|ier /səˈplaɪə(r)/ n (Com)
proveedor m. ~**y** /səˈplaɪ/ vt
suministrar; proporcionar
(information). ~**y s.o. with sth**
(equipment) proveer a uno de algo;
(in business) abastecer a uno de
algo. ●n suministro m. ~**y and
demand** oferta f y demanda.
~**ies** npl provisiones mpl, víveres
mpl; (Mil) pertrechos mpl. **office**
~**ies** artículos mpl de oficina

support /səˈpɔːt/ vt (hold up)
sostener; (back) apoyar; mantener
(family). ●n apoyo m; (Tec) soporte
m. ~**er** n partidario m; (Sport)
hincha m & f

suppos|e /səˈpəʊz/ vt suponer,
imaginarse; (think) creer. **I'm** ~**ed
to start work at nine** se supone
que tengo que empezar a trabajar
a las nueve. ~**edly** adv

supuestamente. **~ition** /sʌpə'zɪʃn/ n suposición f

suppress /sə'pres/ vt reprimir (feelings); sofocar (rebellion). **~ion** /-ʃn/ n represión f

suprem|acy /su:'preməsɪ/ n supremacía f. **~e** /su:'pri:m/ adj supremo

sure /ʃʊə(r)/ adj (**-er, -est**) seguro. **make ~ that** asegurarse de que. ●adv ¡claro!. **~ly** adv (undoubtedly) seguramente; (gladly) desde luego. **~ly you don't believe that!** ¡no te creerás eso! **~ty** /-ətɪ/ n garantía f

surf /sɜ:f/ n oleaje m; (foam) espuma f. ●vi hacer surf. ●vt (Comp) surfear, navegar

surface /'sɜ:fɪs/ n superficie f. ●adj superficial. ●vt recubrir (**with** de). ●vi salir a la superficie; (problems) aflorar

surfboard /'sɜ:fbɔ:d/ n tabla f de surf

surfeit /'sɜ:fɪt/ n exceso m

surf: ~er n surfista m & f; (Internet) navegador m. **~ing** n surf m

surge /sɜ:dʒ/ vi (crowd) moverse en tropel; (sea) hincharse. ●n oleada f; (in demand, sales) aumento m

surg|eon /'sɜ:dʒən/ n cirujano m. **~ery** n cirugía f; (consulting room) consultorio m; (consulting hours) consulta f. **~ical** adj quirúrgico

surly /'sɜ:lɪ/ adj (**-ier, -iest**) hosco

surmise /sə'maɪz/ vt conjeturar

surmount /sə'maʊnt/ vt superar

surname /'sɜ:neɪm/ n apellido m

surpass /sə'pɑ:s/ vt superar

surplus /'sɜ:pləs/ adj & n excedente (m)

surpris|e /sə'praɪz/ n sorpresa f. ●vt sorprender. **~ed** adj sorprendido. **~ing** adj sorprendente. **~ingly** adv sorprendentemente

surrender /sə'rendə(r)/ vt entregar. ●vi rendirse. ●n rendición f

surreptitious /sʌrəp'tɪʃəs/ adj furtivo

surround /sə'raʊnd/ vt rodear; (Mil) rodear, cercar. **~ing** adj circundante. **~ings** npl alrededores mpl; (environment) ambiente m

surveillance /sɜ:'veɪləns/ n vigilancia f

survey /'sɜ:veɪ/ n inspección f; (report) informe m; (general view) vista f general. ●/sə'veɪ/ vt inspeccionar; (measure) medir; (look at) contemplar. **~or** n topógrafo m, agrimensor m; (of building) perito m

surviv|al /sə'vaɪvl/ n supervivencia f. **~e** /sə'vaɪv/ vt/i sobrevivir. **~or** n superviviente m & f

susceptible /sə'septəbl/ adj. **~ to** propenso a

suspect /sə'spekt/ vt sospechar; sospechar de (person). ●/'sʌspekt/ adj & n sospechoso (m)

suspen|d /sə'spend/ vt suspender. **~ders** npl (Amer, braces) tirantes mpl. **~se** /-s/ n (in film etc) suspense m, suspenso m (LAm). **keep s.o. in ~se** mantener a uno sobre ascuas. **~sion** /-ʃn/ n suspensión f. **~sion bridge** n puente m colgante

suspici|on /sə'spɪʃn/ n (belief) sospecha f; (mistrust) desconfianza f. **~ous** /-ʃəs/ adj desconfiado; (causing suspicion) sospechoso

sustain /sə'steɪn/ vt sostener; mantener (conversation, interest); (suffer) sufrir

SW abbr (= **south-west**) SO

swab /swɒb/ n (specimen) muestra f, frotis m

swagger /'swægə(r)/ vi pavonearse

swallow /'swɒləʊ/ vt/i tragar. ●n trago m; (bird) golondrina f

swam /swæm/ see SWIM

swamp /swɒmp/ n pantano m, ciénaga f. ●vt inundar. **~y** adj pantanoso

swan /swɒn/ n cisne m

swap /swɒp/ vt/i (pt **swapped**) intercambiar. **~ sth for sth** cambiar algo por algo. ●n cambio m

swarm /swɔːm/ n enjambre m. ●vi (bees) enjambrar; (fig) hormiguear

swarthy /ˈswɔːðɪ/ adj (**-ier**, **-iest**) moreno

swat /swɒt/ vt (pt **swatted**) matar (con matamoscas etc)

sway /sweɪ/ vi balancearse; (gently) mecerse. ●vt (influence) influir en

swear /sweə(r)/ vt/i (pt **swore**, pp **sworn**) jurar. **~word** n palabrota f

sweat /swet/ n sudor m, transpiración f. ●vi sudar

sweat|er /ˈswetə(r)/ n jersey m, suéter m. **~shirt** n sudadera f. **~suit** n (Amer) chándal m, equipo m de deportes

swede /swiːd/ n nabo m sueco

Swede /swiːd/ n sueco m. **~n** /ˈswiːdn/ n Suecia f. **~ish** adj sueco. ●n (language) sueco m. ●npl. **the ~** (people) los suecos

sweep /swiːp/ vt (pt **swept**) barrer; deshollinar (chimney). ●vi barrer. ●n barrido m. **~ away** vt (carry away) arrastrar; (abolish) erradicar. **~er** n barrendero m. **~ing** adj (gesture) amplio; (changes) radical; (statement) demasiado general

sweet /swiːt/ adj (**-er**, **-est**) dulce; (fragrant) fragante; (pleasant) agradable; (kind, gentle) dulce; (cute) rico. **have a ~ tooth** ser dulcero. ●n caramelo m, dulce m (Mex); (dish) postre m. **~en** vt endulzar. **~heart** n enamorado m; (as form of address) amor m. **~ly** adv dulcemente. **~ potato** n boniato m, batata f, camote m LAm

swell /swel/ vt (pt **swelled**, pp **swollen** or **swelled**) hinchar; (increase) aumentar. ●vi hincharse; (increase) aumentar. ●adj (Amer fam) fenomenal. ●n (of sea) oleaje m. **~ing** n hinchazón m

sweltering /ˈsweltərɪŋ/ vi sofocante

swept /swept/ see **SWEEP**

swerve /swɜːv/ vi virar bruscamente

swift /swɪft/ adj (**-er**, **-est**) veloz, rápido; (reply) rápido. ●n (bird) vencejo m. **~ly** adv rápidamente

swig /swɪɡ/ vt (pt **swigged**) 🔲 beber a grandes tragos. ●n 🔲 trago m

swim /swɪm/ vi (pt **swam**, pp **swum**) nadar. ●n baño m. **~mer** n nadador m. **~ming** n natación f. **~ming bath(s)** n(pl) piscina f cubierta, alberca f techada (Mex). **~ming pool** n piscina f, alberca f (Mex). **~ming trunks** npl bañador m, traje m de baño **~suit** n traje m de baño, bañador m

swindle /ˈswɪndl/ vt estafar. ●n estafa f. **~r** n estafador m

swine /swaɪn/ npl cerdos mpl. ●n (pl **swine**) (fam, person) canalla m & f. **~ fever** n fiebre f porcina

swing /swɪŋ/ vt (pt **swung**) balancear; (object on rope) hacer oscilar. ●vi (dangle) balancearse; (swing on a swing) columpiarse; (pendulum) oscilar. **~ open/shut** abrirse/cerrarse. ●n oscilación f, vaivén m; (seat) columpio m; (in opinion) cambio m. **in full ~** en plena actividad

swipe /swaɪp/ vt darle un golpe a; (fam, snatch) birlar. ●n golpe m

Swiss /swɪs/ adj suizo (m). ●npl. **the ~ los suizos**

switch /swɪtʃ/ n (Elec) interruptor m; (exchange) intercambio m; (Amer, Rail) agujas fpl.●vt cambiar; (deviate) desviar. ■ **~ off** vt (Elec) apagar (light, TV, heating); desconectar (electricity). ■ **~ on** vt encender, prender (LAm); arrancar (engine). **~board** n centralita f

Switzerland /ˈswɪtsələnd/ n Suiza f

swivel /ˈswɪvl/ vi (pt **swivelled**) girar. ●vt hacer girar

swollen /ˈswəʊlən/ see **SWELL**. ●adj hinchado

swoop /swuːp/ vi (bird) abatirse;

(police) llevar a cabo una redada.
• n (of bird) descenso m en picado or
(LAm) en picada; (by police) redada f

sword /sɔːd/ n espada f

swore /swɔː(r)/ see SWEAR

sworn /swɔːn/ see SWEAR. • adj
(enemy) declarado; (statement) jurado

swot /swɒt/ vt/i (pt **swotted**) (Schol,
fam) empollar, estudiar como loco.
• n (Schol, fam) empollón m, matado
m (Mex)

swum /swʌm/ see SWIM

swung /swʌŋ/ see SWING

syllable /ˈsɪləbl/ n sílaba f

syllabus /ˈsɪləbəs/ n (pl **-buses**)
plan m de estudios; (of a particular
subject) programa m

symbol /ˈsɪmbl/ n símbolo m.
~**ic(al)** /-ˈbɒlɪk(l)/ adj simbólico.
~**ism** n simbolismo m. ~**ize** vt
simbolizar

symmetr|ical /sɪˈmetrɪkl/ adj
simétrico. ~**y** /ˈsɪmətrɪ/ n
simetría f

sympath|etic /sɪmpəˈθetɪk/ adj
comprensivo; (showing pity)
compasivo. ~**ize** /ˈsɪmpəθaɪz/ vi
comprender; (commiserate) ~**ize
with s.o.** compadecer a uno. ~**y**
/ˈsɪmpəθɪ/ n comprensión f; (pity)

compasión f; (condolences) pésame m

symphony /ˈsɪmfənɪ/ n sinfonía f

symptom /ˈsɪmptəm/ n síntoma m.
~**atic** /-ˈmætɪk/ adj sintomático

synagogue /ˈsɪnəgɒg/ n sinagoga f

synchronize /ˈsɪŋkrənaɪz/ vt
sincronizar

syndicate /ˈsɪndɪkət/ n agrupación
f; (Amer, TV) agencia f de
distribución periodística

synonym /ˈsɪnənɪm/ n sinónimo m.
~**ous** /-ˈnɒnɪməs/ adj sinónimo

syntax /ˈsɪntæks/ n sintaxis f

synthesi|s /ˈsɪnθəsɪs/ n (pl **-theses**
/-siːz/) síntesis f. ~**ze** /-aɪz/ vt
sintetizar

synthetic /sɪnˈθetɪk/ adj sintético

syringe /ˈsɪrɪndʒ/ n jeringa f,
jeringuilla f

syrup /ˈsɪrəp/ n (sugar solution)
almíbar m; (with other ingredients)
jarabe m; (medicine) jarabe m

system /ˈsɪstəm/ n sistema m,
método m; (Tec, Mec, Comp) sistema
m. **the digestive ~** el aparato
digestivo. ~**atic** /-əˈmætɪk/ adj
sistemático. ~**atically** /-əˈmætɪklɪ/
adv sistemáticamente. ~**s analyst**
n analista m & f de sistemas

Tt

tab /tæb/ n (flap) lengüeta f; (label)
etiqueta f

table /ˈteɪbl/ n mesa f; (list) tabla f.
~**cloth** n mantel m. ~ **mat** n
salvamanteles m. ~**spoon** n
cuchara f grande; (measure)
cucharada f (grande)

tablet /ˈtæblɪt/ n pastilla f; (pill)
comprimido m

table tennis n tenis m de mesa,
ping-pong m

tabloid /ˈtæblɔɪd/ n tabloide m

taboo /təˈbuː/ adj & n tabú (m)

tacit /ˈtæsɪt/ adj tácito

taciturn /ˈtæsɪtɜːn/ adj taciturno

tack /tæk/ n tachuela f; (stitch)
hilván m. • vt clavar con tachuelas;
(sew) hilvanar. • vi (Naut) virar ■ ~
on vt añadir.

tackle /ˈtækl/ n (equipment) equipo
m; (soccer) entrada f fuerte; (US

football, Rugby) placaje m. **fishing ~** aparejo m de pesca. ●vt abordar (problem); (in soccer) entrarle a; (in US football, Rugby) placar

tacky /'tækɪ/ adj pegajoso

tact /tækt/ n tacto m. **~ful** adj diplomático

tactic|al /'tæktɪkl/ adj táctico. **~s** npl táctica f

tactless /'tæktləs/ adj indiscreto

tadpole /'tædpəʊl/ n renacuajo m

tag /tæg/ n (label) etiqueta f. ■**~ along** (pt **tagged**) vt 🆃 seguir

tail /teɪl/ n (of horse, fish, bird) cola f; (of dog, pig) rabo m. **~s** npl (tailcoat) frac m; (of coin) cruz f. ●vt seguir. ■**~ off** vi disminuir.

tailor /'teɪlə(r)/ n sastre m. **~ed** /'teɪləd/ adj entallado. **~-made** n hecho a (la) medida

taint /teɪnt/ vt contaminar

take /teɪk/ vt (pt **took**, pp **taken**) tomar, coger (esp Spain), agarrar (esp LAm); (capture) capturar; (endure) aguantar; (require) requerir; llevar (time); tomar (bath); tomar (medicine); (carry) llevar; aceptar (cheque). **I ~ a size 10** uso la talla 14. ■**~ after** vt parecerse a. ■**~ away** vt llevarse; (confiscate) quitar. ■**~ back** vt retirar (statement etc). ■**~ in** vt achicar (garment); (understand) asimilar; (deceive) engañar. ■**~ off** vt (remove) quitar, sacar; quitarse (shoes, jacket); (mimic) imitar. vi (aircraft) despegar. ■**~ on** vt contratar (employee). ■**~ out** vt sacar. ■**~ over** vt tomar posesión de; hacerse cargo de (job). vi (assume control) asumir el poder. ■**~ up** vt empezar a hacer (hobby); aceptar (challenge); subir (hem); llevar (time); ocupar (space). ●n (Cinema) toma f. **~-off** n despegue m. **~-over** n (Com) absorción f

takings /'teɪkɪŋz/ npl recaudación f; (at box office) taquilla f

talcum powder /'tælkəm/ n polvos mpl de talco, talco m (LAm)

tale /teɪl/ n cuento m

talent /'tælənt/ n talento m. **~ed** adj talentoso

talk /tɔːk/ vt/i hablar. **~ to s.o.** hablar con uno. **~ about** hablar de. ●n conversación f; (lecture) charla f. ■**~ over** vt discutir. **~ative** /-ətɪv/ adj hablador

tall /tɔːl/ adj (**-er**, **-est**) alto. **~ story** n 🆃 cuento m chino

tally /'tælɪ/ vi coincidir (**with** con)

talon /'tælən/ n garra f

tambourine /tæmbə'riːn/ n pandereta f

tame /teɪm/ adj (**-er**, **-est**) (animal) (by nature) manso; (tamed) domado. ●vt domar (wild animal)

tamper /'tæmpə(r)/ vi. **~ with** tocar; (alter) alterar, falsificar

tampon /'tæmpɒn/ n tampón m

tan /tæn/ vi (pt **tanned**) broncearse. ●n bronceado m. **get a ~** broncearse. ●adj habano

tang /tæŋ/ n sabor m fuerte

tangent /'tændʒənt/ n tangente f

tangerine /tændʒə'riːn/ n mandarina f

tangible /'tændʒəbl/ adj tangible

tangle /'tæŋgl/ vt enredar. **get ~d (up)** enredarse. ●n enredo m, maraña f

tango /'tæŋgəʊ/ n (pl **-os**) tango m

tank /tæŋk/ n depósito m; (Auto) tanque m; (Mil) tanque m

tanker /'tæŋkə(r)/ n (ship) buque m cisterna; (truck) camión m cisterna

tantrum /'tæntrəm/ n berrinche m, rabieta f

tap /tæp/ n grifo m, llave f (LAm); (knock) golpecito m. ●vt (pt **tapped**) (knock) dar un golpecito en; interceptar (phone). ●vi dar golpecitos (**on** en). **~ dancing** n claqué m

tape /teɪp/ n cinta f; (Med) esparadrapo m. ●vt (record) grabar. **~-measure** n cinta f métrica

taper /'teɪpə(r)/ vt afilar. ●vi

afilarse. ■~ **off** vi disminuir

tape recorder n magnetofón m, magnetófono m

tapestry /'tæpɪstrɪ/ n tapiz m

tar /tɑː(r)/ n alquitrán m. ● vt (pt **tarred**) alquitranar

target /'tɑːgɪt/ n blanco m; (fig) objetivo m

tarmac /'tɑːmæk/ n pista f. **T~** n (Amer, ®) asfalto m

tarnish /'tɑːnɪʃ/ vt deslustrar; empañar (reputation)

tart /tɑːt/ n pastel m; (individual) pastelillo m; (sl, woman) prostituta f, fulana f 🄸. ● vt. **~ o.s. up** 🄸 engalanarse. ● adj (**-er, -est**) ácido

tartan /'tɑːtn/ n tartán m, tela f escocesa

task /tɑːsk/ n tarea f. **take to ~** reprender

tassel /'tæsl/ n borla f

tast|e /teɪst/ n sabor m, gusto m; (liking) gusto m. ● vt probar. ● vi. **~e of** saber a. **~eful** adj de buen gusto. **~eless** adj soso; (fig) de mal gusto. **~y** adj (**-ier, -iest**) sabroso

tat /tæt/ see TIT FOR TAT

tatter|ed /'tætəd/ adj hecho jirones. **~s** /'tætəz/ npl andrajos mpl

tattoo /tæ'tuː/ n (on body) tatuaje m. ● vt tatuar

tatty /'tætɪ/ adj (**-ier, -iest**) gastado, estropeado

taught /tɔːt/ see TEACH

taunt /tɔːnt/ vt provocar mediante burlas. ● n pulla f

Taurus /'tɔːrəs/ n Tauro m

taut /tɔːt/ adj tenso

tavern /'tævən/ n taberna f

tax /tæks/ n impuesto m. ● vt imponer contribuciones a (person); gravar (thing); (strain) poner a prueba. **~able** adj imponible. **~ation** /-'seɪʃn/ n impuestos mpl; (system) sistema m tributario. **~ collector** n recaudador m de

impuestos. **~-free** adj libre de impuestos

taxi /'tæksɪ/ n (pl **-is**) taxi m. ● vi (pt **taxied**, pres p **taxiing**) (aircraft) rodar por la pista

taxpayer /'tækspeɪə(r)/ n contribuyente m & f

tea /tiː/ n té m; (afternoon tea) merienda f, té m. **~ bag** n bolsita f de té

teach /tiːtʃ/ vt (pt **taught**) dar clases de, enseñar (subject); dar clase a (person). **~ school** (Amer) dar clase(s) en un colegio. ● vi dar clase(s). **~er** n profesor m; (primary) maestro m; (secondary) profesor m. **~ing** n enseñanza f. ● adj docente

tea: **~cup** n taza f de té. **~ leaf** n hoja f de té

team /tiːm/ n equipo m. ■ ~ **up** vi asociarse (**with** con). **~ work** n trabajo m de equipo

teapot /'tiːpɒt/ n tetera f

tear¹ /teə(r)/ vt (pt **tore**, pp **torn**) romper, rasgar. ● vi romperse, rasgarse. ● n rotura f; (rip) desgarrón m. ■ ~ **along** vi ir a toda velocidad. ■ ~ **apart** vt desgarrar. ■ ~ **off**, ■ ~ **out** vt arrancar. ■ ~ **up** vt romper

tear² /tɪə(r)/ n lágrima f. **be in ~s** estar llorando. **~ful** adj lloroso (farewell) triste. **~ gas** n gas m lacrimógeno

tease /tiːz/ vt tomarle el pelo a

tea: **~ set** n juego m de té. **~spoon** n cucharita f, cucharilla f; (amount) cucharadita f

teat /tiːt/ n (of animal) tetilla f; (for bottle) tetina f

tea towel /'tiːtaʊəl/ n paño m de cocina

techni|cal /'teknɪkl/ adj técnico. **~cality** n /-'kælətɪ/ n detalle m técnico. **~cally** adv técnicamente. **~cian** /tek'nɪʃn/ n técnico m. **~que** /tek'niːk/ n técnica f

technolog|ical /teknə'lɒdʒɪkl/ adj

tecnológico. ~y /tek'nɒlədʒɪ/ n tecnología f

teddy bear /'tedɪ/ n osito m de peluche

tedi|ous /'tiːdɪəs/ adj tedioso. ~um /'tiːdɪəm/ n tedio m

teem /tiːm/ vi abundar (**with** en), estar repleto (**with** de)

teen|age /'tiːneɪdʒ/ adj adolescente; (for teenagers) para jóvenes. ~**ager** n adolescente m & f. ~s /tiːnz/ npl adolescencia f

teeny /'tiːnɪ/ adj (-ier, -iest) 🄸 chiquito

teeter /'tiːtə(r)/ vi balancearse

teeth /tiːθ/ see TOOTH. ~e /tiːð/ vi. **he's** ~**ing** le están saliendo los dientes. ~**ing troubles** npl (fig) problemas mpl iniciales

tele|communications /telɪkəmjuːnɪ'keɪʃnz/ npl telecomunicaciones fpl. ~**gram** /'telɪgræm/ n telegrama m. ~**pathic** /telɪ'pæθɪk/ adj telepático. ~**pathy** /tə'lepəθɪ/ n telepatía f

telephon|e /'telɪfəʊn/ n teléfono m. ● vt llamar por teléfono. ~**e booth**, ~**e box** n cabina f telefónica. ~**e call** n llamada f telefónica. ~**e card** n tarjeta f telefónica. ~**e directory** n guía f telefónica. ~**e exchange** n central f telefónica. ~**ist** /tɪ'lefənɪst/ n telefonista m & f

tele|sales /'telɪseɪlz/ npl televentas fpl. ~**scope** n telescopio m. ~**scopic** /-'skɒpɪk/ adj telescópico. ~**text** n teletex(to) m. ~**working** n teletrabajo m

televis|e /'telɪvaɪz/ vt televisar. ~**ion** /-'telɪvɪʒn/ n (medium) televisión f. ~**ion (set)** n televisor m

telex /'teleks/ n télex m

tell /tel/ vt (pt **told**) decir; contar (story, joke); (distinguish) distinguir. ~ **the difference** notar la diferencia. ~ **the time** decir la hora. ■ vi (produce an effect) tener efecto; (know) saber. ∎~ **off** vt

regañar. ~**ing** adj revelador. ~-**tale** n soplón m. ● adj revelador

telly /'telɪ/ n 🄸 tele f

temp /temp/ n empleado m eventual or temporal

temper /'tempə(r)/ n (mood) humor m; (disposition) carácter m; (fit of anger) cólera f. **be in a** ~ estar furioso. **lose one's** ~ perder los estribos. ~**ament** /'tempramənt/ n temperamento m. ~**amental** /-'mentl/ adj temperamental. ~**ate** /'tempərət/ adj templado. ~**ature** /'temprɪtʃə(r)/ n temperatura f. **have a** ~**ature** tener fiebre

tempestuous /tem'pestjʊəs/ adj tempestuoso

temple /'templ/ n templo m; (of head) sien f

tempo /'tempəʊ/ n (pl **-os** or **tempi**) ritmo m

temporar|ily /'tempərərəlɪ/ adv temporalmente, temporariamente (LAm). ~**y** /'tempərərɪ/ adj temporal, provisional; (job) eventual, temporal

tempt /tempt/ vt tentar. ~**ation** /-'teɪʃn/ n tentación f. ~**ing** adj tentador

ten /ten/ adj & n diez (m)

tenaci|ous /tɪ'neɪʃəs/ adj tenaz. ~**ty** /tɪ'næsətɪ/ n tenacidad f

tenan|cy /'tenənsɪ/ n inquilinato m. ~**t** n inquilino m, arrendatorio m

tend /tend/ vi. ~ **to** tender a. ● vt cuidar (de). ~**ency** /'tendənsɪ/ n tendencia f

tender /'tendə(r)/ adj tierno; (painful) sensible. ● n (Com) oferta f. **legal** ~ n moneda f de curso legal. ● vt ofrecer, presentar. ~**ly** adv tiernamente

tendon /'tendən/ n tendón m

tennis /'tenɪs/ n tenis m

tenor /'tenə(r)/ n tenor m

tens|e /tens/ adj (**-er**, **-est**) (taut) tenso, tirante; (person) tenso. ● n (Gram) tiempo m. ~**ion** /'tenʃn/ n tensión f; (between two parties) conflicto m

tent /tent/ n tienda f (de campaña), carpa f (LAm)

tentacle /'tentəkl/ n tentáculo m

tentative /'tentətɪv/ adj (plan) provisional; (offer) tentativo; (person) indeciso

tenterhooks /'tentəhʊks/ npl. **be on ~** estar en ascuas

tenth /tenθ/ adj & n décimo (m)

tenuous /'tenjʊəs/ adj (claim) poco fundado; (link) indirecto

tenure /'tenjʊə(r)/ n tenencia f; (period of office) ejercicio m

tepid /'tepɪd/ adj tibio

term /tɜːm/ n (of time) período m; (Schol) trimestre m; (word etc) término m. **~s** npl condiciones fpl; (Com) precio m. **on good/bad ~s** en buenas/malas relaciones. ●vt calificar de

termin|al /'tɜːmɪnl/ adj terminal. ●n (transport) terminal f; (Comp, Elec) terminal m. **~ate** /-eɪt/ vt poner fin a; poner término a (contract); (Amer, fire) despedir. ●vi terminarse. **~ology** /-'nɒlədʒɪ/ n terminología f

terrace /'terəs/ n terraza f; (houses) hilera f de casas

terrain /tə'reɪn/ n terreno m

terrestrial /tɪ'restrɪəl/ adj terrestre

terribl|e /'terəbl/ adj espantoso. **~y** adv terriblemente

terrif|ic /tə'rɪfɪk/ adj (fam, excellent) estupendo; (fam, huge) enorme. **~ied** /'terɪfaɪd/ adj aterrorizado. **~y** /'terɪfaɪ/ vt aterrorizar. **~ying** adj aterrador

territor|ial /terɪ'tɔːrɪəl/ adj territorial. **~y** /'terɪtrɪ/ n territorio m

terror /'terə(r)/ n terror m. **~ism** n terrorismo m. **~ist** n terrorista m & f. **~ize** vt aterrorizar

terse /tɜːs/ adj seco, lacónico

test /test/ n (of machine, drug) prueba f; (exam) prueba f, test m; (of blood) análisis m; (for eyes, hearing) examen m. ●vt probar, poner a prueba (product); hacerle una prueba a (student); evaluar (knowledge); examinar (sight)

testament /'testəmənt/ n (will) testamento m. **Old/New T~** Antiguo/Nuevo Testamento

testicle /'testɪkl/ n testículo m

testify /'testɪfaɪ/ vt atestiguar. ●vi declarar

testimon|ial /testɪ'məʊnɪəl/ n recomendación f. **~y** /'testɪmənɪ/ n testimonio m

test: ~ match n partido m internacional. **~ tube** n tubo m de ensayo, probeta f

tether /'teðə(r)/ vt atar. ●n. **be at the end of one's ~** no poder más

text /tekst/ n texto m. ●vt mandar un mensaje a. **~book** n libro m de texto

textile /'tekstaɪl/ adj & n textil (m)

texture /'tekstʃə(r)/ n textura f

Thames /temz/ n Támesis m

than /ðæn, ðən/ conj que; (with quantity) de

thank /θæŋk/ vt darle las gracias a, agradecer. **~ you** gracias. **~ful** adj agradecido. **~fully** adv (happily) gracias a Dios. **~less** adj ingrato. **~s** npl agradecimiento m. **~s!** 🅣 ¡gracias!. **~s to** gracias a

Thanksgiving (Day) /θæŋks'gɪvɪŋ/ n (in US) el día de Acción de Gracias

that /ðæt, ðət/ adj (pl **those**) ese, aquel, esa, aquella. ●pron (pl **those**) ése, aquél, ésa, aquélla. **~ is** es decir. **~'s not true** no es cierto. **~'s why** por eso. **is ~ you?** ¿eres tú? **like ~** así. ●adv tan. ●rel pron que; (with prep) el que, la que, el cual, la cual. ●conj que

thatched /θætʃt/ adj (roof) de paja; (cottage) con techo de paja

thaw /θɔː/ vt descongelar. ●vi

descongelarse; (snow) derretirse.
● n deshielo m

the definite article
····▸ el (m), la (f), los (mpl), las
(fpl). **~ building** el edificio. **~
windows** las ventanas

❗ Feminine singular nouns
beginning with a stressed or
accented a or ha take the article el
instead of la, e.g. **~ soul** el alma;
~ axe el hacha; **~ eagle** el
águila

Note that when el follows the
prepositions de and a, it combines
to form del and al, e.g. **of ~
group** del grupo. **I went to ~
bank** fui al banco

····▸ (before an ordinal number in
names, titles) not translated. **Henry
~ Eighth** Enrique Octavo.
Elizabeth ~ Second Isabel
Segunda

····▸ (in abstractions) lo. **~
impossible** lo imposible

theatr|e /'θɪətə(r)/ n teatro m; (Amer,
movie theater) cine m. **~ical** /-'ætrɪkl/
adj teatral

theft /θeft/ n hurto m

their /ðeə(r)/ adj su, sus pl. **~s**
/ðeəz/ poss pron (el) suyo m, (la)
suya f, (los) suyos mpl, (las) suyas
fpl

them /ðem, ðəm/ pron (accusative) los
m, las f; (dative) les; (after prep) ellos
m, ellas f

theme /θiːm/ n tema m. **~ park** n
parque m temático. **~ song** n
motivo m principal

themselves /ðəm'selvz/ pron ellos
mismos m, ellas mismas f; (reflexive)
se; (after prep) sí mismos m, sí
mismas f

then /ðen/ adv entonces; (next)
luego, después. **by ~** para
entonces. **now and ~** de vez en
cuando. **since ~** desde entonces.
● adj entonces

theology /θɪ'ɒlədʒɪ/ n teología f

theor|etical /θɪə'retɪkl/ adj teórico.
~y /'θɪərɪ/ n teoría f

therap|eutic /θerə'pjuːtɪk/ adj
terapéutico. **~ist** /'θerəpɪst/ n
terapeuta m & f. **~y** /θerəpɪ/ n
terapia f

there /ðeə(r)/ adv ahí; (further away)
allí, ahí; (less precise, further) allá. **~
is, ~ are** hay. **~ it is** ahí está.
down ~ ahí abajo. **up ~** ahí
arriba. ● int. **~! that's the last
box** ¡listo! ésa es la última caja.
~, ~, don't cry! vamos, no
llores. **~abouts** adv por ahí.
~fore /-fɔː(r)/ adv por lo tanto.

thermometer /θə'mɒmɪtə(r)/ n
termómetro m

Thermos /'θɜːməs/ n (®) termo m

thermostat /'θɜːməstæt/ n
termostato m

thesaurus /θɪ'sɔːrəs/ n (pl **-ri**/-raɪ/)
diccionario m de sinónimos

these /ðiːz/ adj estos, estas. ● pron
éstos, éstas

thesis /'θiːsɪs/ n (pl **theses**/-siːz/)
tesis f

they /ðeɪ/ pron ellos m, ellas f. **~
say that** dicen or se dice que

they'd /ðeɪ(ə)d/ = **they had, they
would**

they'll /ðeɪl/ = **they will**

they're /ðeɪə(r)/ = **they are**

they've /ðeɪv/ = **they have**

thick /θɪk/ adj (**-er, -est**) (layer,
sweater) grueso, gordo; (sauce)
espeso; (fog, smoke) espeso, denso;
(fur) tupido; (fam, stupid) burro. ● adv
espesamente, densamente. ● n. **in
the ~ of** en medio de. **~en** vt
espesar. ● vi espesarse. **~et** /-ɪt/ n
matorral m. **~ness** n (of fabric)
grosor m; (of paper, wood, wall)
espesor m

thief /θiːf/ n (pl **thieves** /θiːvz/)
ladrón m

thigh /θaɪ/ n muslo m

thimble /'θɪmbl/ n dedal m

thin /θɪn/ adj (**thinner, thinnest**)

(person) delgado, flaco; (layer, slice) fino; (hair) ralo

thing /θɪŋ/ n cosa f. **it's a good ~ (that)...** menos mal que.... **just the ~** exactamente lo que se necesita. **poor ~!** ¡pobrecito!

think /θɪŋk/ vt (pt **thought**) pensar, creer. • vi pensar (**about** en); (carefully) reflexionar; (imagine) imaginarse. **I ~ so** creo que sí. **~ of s.o.** pensar en uno. **I hadn't thought of that** eso no se me ha ocurrido. **~ over** vt pensar bien. **~ up** vt idear, inventar. **~er** n pensador m. **~-tank** n gabinete m estratégico

third /θɜːd/ adj tercero, (before masculine singular noun) tercer. • n tercio m, tercera parte f. **~ (gear)** n (Auto) tercera f. **~-rate** adj muy inferior. **T~ World** n Tercer Mundo m

thirst /θɜːst/ n sed f. **~y** adj sediento. **be ~y** tener sed

thirt|een /θɜːˈtiːn/ adj & n trece (m). **~teenth** adj decimotercero. • n treceavo m **~ieth** /ˈθɜːtɪəθ/ adj trigésimo. • n treintavo m. **~y** /ˈθɜːtɪ/ adj & n treinta (m)

this /ðɪs/ adj (pl **these**) este, esta. **~ one** éste, ésta. • pron (pl **these**) éste, ésta, esto. **like ~** así

thistle /ˈθɪsl/ n cardo m

thong /θɒŋ/ n correa f; (Amer, sandal) chancla f

thorn /θɔːn/ n espina f. **~y** adj espinoso

thorough /ˈθʌrə/ adj (investigation) riguroso; (cleaning etc) a fondo; (person) concienzudo. **~bred** /-bred/ adj de pura sangre. **~fare** n vía f pública; (street) calle f. **no ~fare** prohibido el paso. **~ly** adv (clean) a fondo; (examine) minuciosamente; (completely) perfectamente

those /ðəʊz/ adj esos, esas, aquellos, aquellas. • pron ésos, ésas, aquéllos, aquéllas

though /ðəʊ/ conj aunque. • adv sin

embargo. **as ~** como si

thought /θɔːt/ see THINK. • n pensamiento m; (idea) idea f. **~ful** adj pensativo; (considerate) atento. **~fully** adv pensativamente; (considerately) atentamente. **~less** adj desconsiderado

thousand /ˈθaʊznd/ adj & n mil (m). **~th** adj & n milésimo (m)

thrash /θræʃ/ vt azotar; (defeat) derrotar

thread /θred/ n hilo m; (of screw) rosca f. • vt enhebrar (needle); ensartar (beads). **~bare** adj gastado, raído

threat /θret/ n amenaza f. **~en** vt/i amenazar. **~ening** adj amenazador

three /θriː/ adj & n tres (m). **~fold** adj triple. • adv tres veces

threshold /ˈθreʃhəʊld/ n umbral m

threw /θruː/ see THROW

thrift /θrɪft/ n economía f, ahorro m. **~y** adj frugal

thrill /θrɪl/ n emoción f. • vt emocionar. **~ed** adj contentísimo (**with** con). **~er** n (book) libro m de suspense or (LAm) suspenso; (film) película f de suspense or (LAm) suspenso. **~ing** adj emocionante

thriv|e /θraɪv/ vi prosperar. **~ing** adj próspero

throat /θrəʊt/ n garganta f

throb /θrɒb/ vi (pt **throbbed**) palpitar; (with pain) dar punzadas; (engine) vibrar. **~bing** adj (pain) punzante

throes /θrəʊz/ npl. **be in one's death ~** estar agonizando

throne /θrəʊn/ n trono m

throng /θrɒŋ/ n multitud f

throttle /ˈθrɒtl/ n (Auto) acelerador m (que se acciona con la mano). • vt estrangular

through /θruː/ prep por, a través de; (during) durante; (by means of) a través de; (Amer, until and including)

Monday ~ Friday de lunes a viernes. • adv de parte a parte, de un lado a otro; (entirely) completamente; (to the end) hasta el final. **be ~** (finished) haber terminado. • adj (train etc) directo. **no ~ road** calle sin salida. **~out** /-'aʊt/ prep (push in todo); (time) por todo; (time) durante todo. **~out his career** a lo largo de su carrera

throve /θrəʊv/ see THRIVE

throw /θrəʊ/ vt (pt **threw**, pp **thrown**) tirar, aventar (Mex); lanzar (grenade, javelin); (disconcert) desconcertar; 🔲 hacer, dar (party). • n (of ball) tiro m; (of dice) tirada f. ■ **~ away** vt tirar. ■ **~ up** vi (vomit) vomitar.

thrush /θrʌʃ/ n tordo m

thrust /θrʌst/ vt (pt **thrust**) empujar; (push in) clavar. • n empujón m; (of sword) estocada f

thud /θʌd/ n ruido m sordo

thug /θʌg/ n matón m

thumb /θʌm/ n pulgar m. • vt. **~ a lift** ir a dedo. **~tack** n (Amer) chincheta f, tachuela f, chinche f (Mex)

thump /θʌmp/ vt golpear. • vi (heart) latir fuertemente. • n golpazo m

thunder /'θʌndə(r)/ n truenos mpl, (of traffic) estruendo m. • vi tronar. **~bolt** n rayo m. **~storm** n tormenta f eléctrica. **~y** adj con truenos

Thursday /'θɜːzdeɪ/ n jueves m

thus /ðʌs/ adv así

thwart /θwɔːt/ vt frustrar

tic /tɪk/ n tic m

tick /tɪk/ n (sound) tic m; (insect) garrapata f, (mark) marca f, visto m, palomita f (Mex); (fam, instant) momentito m. • vi hacer tictac. • vt. **~ (off)** marcar

ticket /'tɪkɪt/ n (for bus, train) billete m, boleto m (LAm); (for plane) pasaje m, billete m; (for theatre, museum) entrada f; (for baggage, coat) ticket m; (fine) multa f. **~ collector** n

revisor m. **~ office** n (transport) mostrador m de venta de billetes or (LAm) boletos; (in theatre) taquilla f, boletería f (LAm)

tickle /'tɪkl/ vt hacerle cosquillas a. • n cosquilleo m. **~ish** /'tɪklɪʃ/ adj. **be ~ish** tener cosquillas

tidal wave /'taɪdl/ n maremoto m

tide /taɪd/ n marea f. **high/low ~** marea alta/baja. ■ **~ over** vt ayudar a salir de un apuro

tid|ily /'taɪdɪlɪ/ adv ordenadamente. **~iness** n orden m. **~y** adj (**-ier, -iest**) ordenado. • vt/i **~y (up)** ordenar, arreglar

tie /taɪ/ vt (pres p **tying**) atar, amarrar (LAm); hacer (knot). • vi (Sport) empatar. • n (constraint) atadura f; (bond) lazo m; (necktie) corbata f; (Sport) empate m. **~ in with** vt concordar con. ■ **~ up** vt atar. **be ~d up** (busy) estar ocupado

tier /tɪə(r)/ n hilera f superpuesta; (in stadium etc) grada f; (of cake) piso m

tiger /'taɪɡə(r)/ n tigre m

tight /taɪt/ adj (**-er, -est**) (clothes) ajustado, ceñido; (taut) tieso; (control) estricto; (knot, nut) apretado; (fam, drunk) borracho. **~en** vt apretar. ■ **~en up** vt hacer más estricto. **~-fisted** /-'fɪstɪd/ adj tacaño. **~ly** adv bien, fuerte; (fastened) fuertemente. **~rope** n cuerda f floja. **~s** npl (for ballet etc) leotardo(s) m(pl); (pantyhose) medias fpl

tile /taɪl/ n (decorative) azulejo m; (on roof) teja f; (on floor) baldosa f. • vt azulejar; tejar (roof); embaldosar (floor)

till /tɪl/ prep hasta. • conj hasta que. • n caja f. • vt cultivar

tilt /tɪlt/ vt inclinar. • vi inclinarse. • n inclinación f

timber /'tɪmbə(r)/ n madera f (para construcción)

time /taɪm/ n tiempo m; (moment) momento m; (occasion) ocasión f; (by clock) hora f; (epoch) época f; (rhythm) compás m. **at ~s** a veces. **for the ~ being** por el momento. **from ~ to ~** de vez en cuando. **have a good ~** divertirse, pasarlo bien. **in a year's ~** dentro de un año. **in no ~** en un abrir y cerrar de ojos. **in ~ a** tiempo; (eventually) con el tiempo. **arrive on ~** llegar a tiempo. **it's ~ we left** es hora de irnos. ●vt elegir el momento; cronometrar (race). **~ bomb** f de tiempo. **~ly** adj oportuno. **~r** n cronómetro m; (Culin) avisador m; (with sand) reloj m de arena; (Elec) interruptor m de reloj. **~s** /taɪmz/ prep. **2 ~s 4 is 8** 2 (multiplicado) por 4 son 8. **~table** n horario m

timid /'tɪmɪd/ adj tímido; (fearful) miedoso

tin /tɪn/ n estaño m; (container) lata f. **~ foil** n papel m de estaño

tinge /tɪndʒ/ vt. **be ~d with sth** estar matizado de algo. ●n matiz m

tingle /'tɪŋɡl/ vi sentir un hormigueo

tinker /'tɪŋkə(r)/ vi. **~ with** juguetear con

tinkle /'tɪŋkl/ vi tintinear

tinned /tɪnd/ adj en lata, enlatado

tin opener n abrelatas m

tint /tɪnt/ n matiz m

tiny /'taɪnɪ/ adj (**-ier, -iest**) minúsculo, diminuto

tip /tɪp/ n punta f. ●vt (pt **tipped**) (tilt) inclinar; (overturn) volcar; (pour) verter; (give gratuity to) darle (una) propina a. ■ **~ off** vt avisar. ■ **~ out** vt verter. ■ **~ over** vi caerse. n propina f; (advice) consejo m (práctico); (for rubbish) vertedero m. **~ped** adj (cigarette) con filtro

tipsy /'tɪpsɪ/ adj achispado

tiptoe /'tɪptəʊ/ n. **on ~** de puntillas

tiptop /'tɪptɒp/ adj 🄵 de primera. **in ~ condition** en excelente estado

tire /'taɪə(r)/ n (Amer) see TYRE. ●vt cansar. ●vi cansarse. **~d** /'taɪəd/ adj cansado; (efforts) cansado. **get ~d** cansarse. **~d of** harto de. **~d out** agotado. **~less** adj incansable; (efforts) inagotable. **~some** /-səm/ adj (person) pesado; (task) tedioso

tiring /'taɪərɪŋ/ adj cansado, cansador (LAm)

tissue /'tɪʃu:/ n (of bones, plants) tejido m; (paper handkerchief) pañuelo m de papel. **~ paper** n papel m de seda

tit /tɪt/ n (bird) paro m; (🄳, breast) teta f

titbit /'tɪtbɪt/ n exquisitez f

tit for tat n **it was ~** fue ojo por ojo, diente por diente

title /'taɪtl/ n título m

to /tu:, tə/ prep a; (towards) hacia; (in order to) para; (as far as) hasta; (of) de. **give it ~ me** dámelo. **what did you say ~ him?** ¿qué le dijiste?; **I don't want ~** no quiero. **it's twenty ~ seven** (by clock) son las siete menos veinte, son veinte para las siete (LAm). ●adv. **pull ~** cerrar. **~ and fro** adv de un lado a otro

toad /təʊd/ n sapo m. **~stool** n hongo m (no comestible)

toast /təʊst/ n pan m tostado, tostadas fpl; (drink) brindis m. **a piece of ~** una tostada, un pan tostado (Mex). **drink a ~ to** brindar por. ●vt (Culin) tostar; (drink to) brindar por. **~er** n tostadora f (eléctrica), tostador m

tobacco /tə'bækəʊ/ n tabaco m. **~nist** /-ənɪst/ n estanquero m

toboggan /tə'bɒɡən/ n tobogán m

today /tə'deɪ/ n & adv hoy (m)

toddler /'tɒdlə(r)/ n niño m pequeño (entre un año y dos años y medio de edad)

toe /təʊ/ n dedo m (del pie); (of shoe) punta f. **big ~** dedo m gordo (del pie). **on one's ~s** (fig) alerta. ●vt. **~ the line** acatar la disciplina

toffee /'tɒfɪ/ n toffee m (golosina hecha con azúcar y mantequilla)

together /tə'geðə(r)/ adv juntos; (at same time) a la vez. ~ **with** junto con

toil /tɔɪl/ vi afanarse. ●n trabajo m duro

toilet /'tɔɪlɪt/ n servicio m, baño m (LAm). ~ **paper** n papel m higiénico. ~**ries** /'tɔɪlɪtrɪz/ npl artículos mpl de tocador. ~ **roll** n rollo m de papel higiénico

token /'təʊkən/ n muestra f; (voucher) vale m; (coin) ficha f. ●adj simbólico

told /təʊld/ see TELL

tolera|ble /'tɒlərəbl/ adj tolerable; (not bad) pasable. ~**nce** /'tɒlərəns/ n tolerancia f. ~**nt** adj tolerante. ~**te** /-reɪt/ vt tolerar. ~**tion** /'reɪʃən/ n tolerancia f

toll /təʊl/ n (on road) peaje m, cuota f (Mex). **death** ~ número m de muertos. ~ **call** n (Amer) llamada f interurbana, conferencia f. ●vi doblar, tocar a muerto

tomato /tə'mɑːtəʊ/ n (pl **-oes**) tomate m, jitomate m (Mex)

tomb /tuːm/ n tumba f, sepulcro m. ~**stone** n lápida f

tomorrow /tə'mɒrəʊ/ n & adv mañana (f). **see you** ~! ¡hasta mañana!

ton /tʌn/ n tonelada f (= 1,016kg). ~**s of** 🔲 montones de. **metric** ~ tonelada f (métrica) (= 1,000kg)

tone /təʊn/ n tono m. ■ ~ **down** vt atenuar; moderar (language). ~**-deaf** adj que no tiene oído (musical)

tongs /tɒŋz/ npl tenacillas fpl

tongue /tʌŋ/ n lengua f. **say sth** ~ **in cheek** decir algo medio burlándose. ~**-tied** adj cohibido. ~**-twister** n trabalenguas m

tonic /'tɒnɪk/ adj tónico. ●n (Med, fig) tónico m. ~ **(water)** n tónica f

tonight /tə'naɪt/ adv & n esta noche (f); (evening) esta tarde (f)

tonne /tʌn/ n tonelada f (métrica)

tonsil /'tɒnsl/ n amígdala f. ~**litis** /-'laɪtɪs/ n amigdalitis f

too /tuː/ adv (excessively) demasiado; (also) también. **I'm not** ~ **sure** no estoy muy seguro. ~ **many** demasiados. ~ **much** demasiado

took /tʊk/ see TAKE

tool /tuːl/ n herramienta f

tooth /tuːθ/ n (pl **teeth**) diente m; (molar) muela f. ~**ache** n dolor m de muelas. ~**brush** n cepillo m de dientes. ~**paste** n pasta f dentífrica, pasta f de dientes. ~**pick** n palillo m (de dientes)

top /tɒp/ n parte f superior, parte f de arriba; (of mountain) cima f; (of tree) copa f; (of page) parte f superior; (lid, of bottle) tapa f; (of pen) capuchón m; (spinning ~) trompo m, peonza f. **be** ~ **of the class** ser el primero de la clase. **from** ~ **to bottom** de arriba abajo. **on** ~ **of** encima de; (besides) además de. ●adj más alto; (shelf) superior; (speed) máximo; (in rank) superior; (leading) más destacado. ●vt (pt **topped**) cubrir; (exceed) exceder. ~ **floor** n último piso m. ■ ~ **up** vt llenar. ~ **hat** n chistera f. ~**-heavy** /-'hevɪ/ adj inestable (por ser más pesado en su parte superior)

topic /'tɒpɪk/ n tema m. ~**al** adj de actualidad

topless /'tɒples/ adj topless

topple /'tɒpl/ vi (Pol) derribar; (overturn) volcar. ●vi caerse

top secret /tɒp'siːkrɪt/ adj secreto, reservado

torch /tɔːtʃ/ n linterna f; (flaming) antorcha f

tore /tɔː(r)/ see TEAR¹

torment /'tɔːment/ n tormento m. ●/tɔː'ment/ vt atormentar

torn /tɔːn/ see TEAR¹

tornado /tɔː'neɪdəʊ/ n (pl **-oes**) tornado m

torpedo /tɔː'piːdəʊ/ n (pl **-oes**)

torpedo m. •vt torpedear

torrent /'tɒrənt/ n torrente m. ~**ial** /təˈrenʃl/ adj torrencial

torrid /'tɒrɪd/ adj tórrido; (affair) apasionado

tortoise /'tɔːtəs/ n tortuga f. ~**shell** n carey m

tortuous /'tɔːtjʊəs/ adj tortuoso

torture /'tɔːtʃə(r)/ n tortura f. •vt torturar

Tory /'tɔːrɪ/ adj & n tory m & f

toss /tɒs/ vt tirar, lanzar (ball); (shake) sacudir. •vi. ~ **and turn** (in bed) dar vueltas

tot /tɒt/ n pequeño m; (fam, of liquor) trago m. •vt (pt **totted**). ~ **up** 🅃 sumar

total /'təʊtl/ adj & n total (m). •vt (pt **totalled**) ascender a un total de; (add up) totalizar. ~**itarian** /təʊtælɪ'teəriən/ adj totalitario. ~**ly** adv totalmente

totter /'tɒtə(r)/ vi tambalearse

touch /tʌtʃ/ vt tocar; (move) conmover; (concern) afectar. •vi tocar; (wires) tocarse. •n toque m; (sense) tacto m; (contact) contacto m. **be/get/stay in ~ with** estar/ponerse/mantenerse en contacto con. ■ ~ **down** vi (aircraft) aterrizar. ■ ~ **up** vt retocar. ~**ing** adj enternecedor. ~**y** adj quisquilloso

tough /tʌf/ adj (**-er, -est**) duro; (strong) fuerte, resistente; (difficult) difícil; (severe) severo. ~**en.** ■ ~ **(up)** vt endurecer; hacer más fuerte (person)

tour /tʊə(r)/ n viaje m; (visit) visita f; (excursion) excursión f; (by team etc) gira f. **be on ~** estar de gira. •vt recorrer; (visit) visitar. ~ **guide** n guía de turismo

touris|m /'tʊərɪzəm/ n turismo m. ~**t** /'tʊərɪst/ n turista m & f. •adj turístico. ~**t office** n oficina f de turismo

tournament /'tɔːnəmənt/ n torneo m

tousle /'taʊzl/ vt despeinar

tout /taʊt/ vi. ~ **(for)** solicitar

tow /təʊ/ vt remolcar. •n remolque m

toward(s) /tə'wɔːd(z)/ prep hacia. **his attitude ~ her** su actitud para con ella

towel /'taʊəl/ n toalla f

tower /'taʊə(r)/ n torre f. •vi. ~ **above** (building) descollar sobre; (person) destacar sobre. ~ **block** n edificio m or bloque m de apartamentos. ~**ing** adj altísimo; (rage) violento

town /taʊn/ n ciudad f; (smaller) pueblo m. **go to ~** 🅃 no escatimar dinero. ~ **hall** n ayuntamiento m

toxic /'tɒksɪk/ adj tóxico

toy /tɔɪ/ n juguete m. ■ ~ **with** vt juguetear con (object); darle vueltas a (idea). ~**shop** n juguetería f

trac|e /treɪs/ n señal f, rastro m. •vt trazar; (draw) dibujar; (with tracing paper) calcar; (track down) localizar. ~**ing paper** n papel m de calcar

track /træk/ n pista f, huellas fpl; (path) sendero m; (Sport) pista f. **the ~(s)** la vía férrea; (Rail) vía f. **keep ~ of** seguirle la pista a (person). •vt seguirle la pista a. ■ ~ **down** vt localizar. ~ **suit** n equipo m (de deportes) chándal m

tract /trækt/ n (land) extensión f; (pamphlet) tratado m breve

traction /'trækʃn/ n tracción f

tractor /'træktə(r)/ n tractor m

trade /treɪd/ n comercio m; (occupation) oficio m; (exchange) cambio m; (industry) industria f. •vt. ~ **sth for sth** cambiar algo por algo. •vi comerciar. ■ ~ **in** (give in part-exchange) entregar como parte del pago. ~ **mark** n marca f (de fábrica). ~**r** n comerciante m & f. ~ **union** n sindicato m

tradition /trə'dɪʃn/ n tradición f. ~**al** adj tradicional

traffic /'træfɪk/ n tráfico m. • vi (pt **trafficked**) comerciar (**in** en). ~ **circle** n (Amer) glorieta f, rotonda f. ~ **island** n isla f peatonal. ~ **jam** n embotellamiento m, atasco m. ~ **lights** npl semáforo m. ~ **warden** n guardia m, controlador m de tráfico

trag|edy /'trædʒɪdɪ/ n tragedia f. ~**ic** /'trædʒɪk/ adj trágico

trail /treɪl/ vi arrastrarse; (lag) rezagarse. • vt (track) seguir la pista de. • n (left by animal, person) huellas fpl; (path) sendero m. **be on the ~ of s.o./sth** seguir la pista de uno/algo ~**er** n remolque m; (Amer, caravan) caravana f, rulot m; (film) avance m

train /treɪn/ n (Rail) tren m; (of events) serie f; (of dress) cola f. • vt capacitar (employee); adiestrar (soldier); (Sport) entrenar; educar (voice); guiar (plant); amaestrar (animal). • vi estudiar; (Sport) entrenarse. ~**ed** adj (skilled) cualificado, calificado; (doctor) diplomado. ~**ee** /treɪ'niː/ n aprendiz m, (Amer, Mil) recluta m & f. ~**er** n (Sport) entrenador m; (of animals) amaestrador m. ~**ers** mpl zapatillas fpl de deporte. ~**ing** n capacitación f; (Sport) entrenamiento m

trait /treɪ(t)/ n rasgo m

traitor /'treɪtə(r)/ n traidor m

tram /træm/ n tranvía m

tramp /træmp/ vi. ~ (**along**) caminar pesadamente. • n vagabundo m

trample /'træmpl/ vt pisotear. • vi. ~ **on** pisotear

trampoline /'træmpəliːn/ n trampolín m

trance /trɑːns/ n trance m

tranquil /'træŋkwɪl/ adj tranquilo. ~**lity** /-'kwɪlətɪ/ n tranquilidad f; (of person) serenidad f. ~**lize** /'træŋkwɪlaɪz/ vt sedar, dar un sedante a. ~**lizer** n sedante m, tranquilizante m

transaction /træn'zækʃən/ n transacción f, operación f

transatlantic /trænzət'læntɪk/ adj transatlántico

transcend /træn'send/ vt (go beyond) exceder

transcript /'trænskrɪpt/ n transcripción f

transfer /træns'fɜː(r)/ vt (pt **transferred**) trasladar; traspasar (player); transferir (funds, property); pasar (call). • vi trasladarse. • /'trænsfɜː(r)/ n traslado m; (of player) traspaso m; (of funds, property) transferencia †; (paper) calcomanía f

transform /træns'fɔːm/ vt transformar. ~**ation** /-ə'meɪʃn/ n transformación f. ~**er** n transformador m

transfusion /træns'fjuːʒn/ n transfusión f

transient /'trænzɪənt/ adj pasajero

transistor /træn'zɪstə(r)/ n transistor m

transit /'trænsɪt/ n tránsito m. ~**ion** /træn'zɪʒn/ n transición f. ~**ive** /'trænsɪtɪv/ adj transitivo

translat|e /trænz'leɪt/ vt traducir. ~**ion** /-ʃn/ n traducción f. ~**or** n traductor m

transmission /træns'mɪʃn/ n transmisión f

transmit /trænz'mɪt/ vt (pt **transmitted**) transmitir. ~**ter** n transmisor m

transparen|cy /træns'pærənsɪ/ n transparencia f; (Photo) diapositiva f. ~**t** adj transparente

transplant /træns'plɑːnt/ vt trasplantar. • /'trænsplɑːnt/ n trasplante m

transport /træn'spɔːt/ vt transportar. • /'trænspɔːt/ n transporte m. ~**ation** /-'teɪʃn/ n transporte m

trap /træp/ n trampa f. • vt (pt trapped) atrapar; (jam) atascar; (cut off) bloquear. ~**door** n trampilla f

t

trapeze /trəˈpiːz/ n trapecio m

trash /træʃ/ n basura f; (Amer, worthless people) escoria f. ~ **can** n (Amer) cubo m de la basura, bote m de la basura (Mex). ~**y** adj (souvenir) de porquería; (magazine) malo

travel /ˈtrævl/ vi (pt travelled) viajar; (vehicle) desplazarse. ●vt recorrer. ●n viajes mpl. ~ **agency** n agencia f de viajes. ~**ler** n viajero m. ~**ler's cheque** n cheque m de viaje or viajero. ~**ling expenses** npl gastos mpl de viaje

trawler /ˈtrɔːlə(r)/ n barca f pesquera

tray /treɪ/ n bandeja f

treacher|ous adj traidor; (deceptive) engañoso. ~**y** n traición f

treacle /ˈtriːkl/ n melaza f

tread /tred/ vi (pt trod, pp trodden) pisar. ~ **on sth** pisar algo. ~ **carefully** andarse con cuidado. ●n (step) paso m; (of tyre) banda f de rodamiento

treason /ˈtriːzn/ n traición f

treasur|e /ˈtreʒə(r)/ n tesoro m. ~**ed** /ˈtreʒəd/ adj (possession) preciado. ~**er** /ˈtreʒərə(r)/ n tesorero m. ~**y** n erario m, tesoro m. **the T~y** el fisco, la hacienda pública. **Department of the T~y** (in US) Departamento m del Tesoro

treat /triːt/ vt tratar; (Med) tratar. ~ **s.o.** (to meal etc) invitar a uno. ●n placer m; (present) regalo m

treatise /ˈtriːtɪz/ n tratado m

treatment /ˈtriːtmənt/ n tratamiento m

treaty /ˈtriːtɪ/ n tratado m

treble /ˈtrebl/ adj triple; (clef) de sol; (voice) de tiple. ●vt triplicar. ●vi triplicarse. ●n tiple m & f

tree /triː/ n árbol m

trek /trek/ n caminata f. ●vi (pt trekked) caminar

trellis /ˈtrelɪs/ n enrejado m

tremble /ˈtrembl/ vi temblar

tremendous /trɪˈmendəs/ adj formidable; (fam, huge) tremendo. ~**ly** adv tremendamente

tremor /ˈtremə(r)/ n temblor m

trench /trentʃ/ n zanja f; (Mil) trinchera f

trend /trend/ n tendencia f; (fashion) moda f. ~**y** adj (-ier, -iest) 🔲 moderno

trepidation /trepɪˈdeɪʃn/ n inquietud f

trespass /ˈtrespəs/ vi. ~ **on** entrar sin autorización (en propiedad ajena). ~**er** n intruso m

trial /ˈtraɪəl/ n prueba f; (Jurid) proceso m, juicio m; (ordeal) prueba f dura. **by ~ and error** por ensayo y error. **be on ~** estar a prueba; (Jurid) estar siendo procesado

triang|le /ˈtraɪæŋgl/ n triángulo m. ~**ular** /-ˈæŋgjʊlə(r)/ adj triangular

trib|al /ˈtraɪbl/ adj tribal. ~**e** /traɪb/ n tribu f

tribulation /trɪbjʊˈleɪʃn/ n tribulación f

tribunal /traɪˈbjuːnl/ n tribunal m

tributary /ˈtrɪbjʊtrɪ/ n (of river) afluente m

tribute /ˈtrɪbjuːt/ n tributo m; (acknowledgement) homenaje m. **pay ~ to** rendir homenaje a

trick /trɪk/ n trampa f, ardid m; (joke) broma f; (feat) truco m; (in card games) baza f. **play a ~ on** gastar una broma a. ●vt engañar. ~**ery** n engaño m

trickle /ˈtrɪkl/ vi gotear. ~ **in** (fig) entrar poco a poco

trickster /ˈtrɪkstə(r)/ n estafador m

tricky /ˈtrɪkɪ/ adj delicado, difícil

tricycle /ˈtraɪsɪkl/ n triciclo m

tried /traɪd/ see **TRY**

trifl|e /ˈtraɪfl/ n nimiedad f; (Culin) postre de bizcocho, jerez, frutas y nata. ●vi. ■ **e with** vt jugar con. ~**ing** adj insignificante

trigger /ˈtrɪgə(r)/ n (of gun) gatillo

m. ●vt. ~ **(off)** desencadenar

trim /trɪm/ adj (**trimmer, trimmest**)
(slim) esbelto; (neat) elegante. ●vt
(pt **trimmed**) (cut) recortar; (adorn)
adornar. ●n (cut) recorte m. **in ~**
en buen estado. ~**mings** npl
recortes mpl

trinity /'trɪnɪti/ n. **the (Holy) T~**
la (Santísima) Trinidad

trinket /'trɪŋkɪt/ n chuchería f

trio /'triːəʊ/ n (pl **-os**) trío m

trip /trɪp/ (pt **tripped**) vt ~ **(up)**
hacerle una zancadilla a, hacer
tropezar ●vi tropezar. ●n (journey)
viaje m; (outing) excursión f;
(stumble) traspié m

tripe /traɪp/ n callos mpl, mondongo
m (LAm), pancita f (Mex); (fam,
nonsense) paparruchas fpl

triple /'trɪpl/ adj triple. ●vt triplicar.
●vi triplicarse. ~**t** /'trɪplɪt/ n
trillizo m

triplicate /'trɪplɪkət/ adj triplicado.
in ~ por triplicado

tripod /'traɪpɒd/ n trípode m

trite /traɪt/ adj trillado

triumph /'traɪʌmf/ n triunfo m. ●vi
triunfar (**over sobre**). ~**al** /-'ʌmfl/
adj triunfal. ~**ant** /-'ʌmfnt/ adj
(troops) triunfador; (moment)
triunfal; (smile) de triunfo

trivial /'trɪvɪəl/ adj insignificante;
(concerns) trivial. ~**ity** /-'ælətɪ/ n
trivialidad f

trod, trodden /trɒd, trɒdn/ see
TREAD

trolley /'trɒlɪ/ n (pl **-eys**) carretón
m; (in supermarket, airport) carrito m;
(for food, drink) carrito m, mesa f
rodante. ~ **car** n (Amer) tranvía f

trombone /trɒm'bəʊn/ n
trombón m

troop /truːp/ n compañía f; (of
cavalry) escuadrón m. ●vi. ~ **in**
entrar en tropel. ~ **out** salir en
tropel. ~**er** n soldado m de
caballería; (Amer, state police officer)
agente m & f. ~**s** npl (Mil) tropas fpl

trophy /'trəʊfɪ/ n trofeo m

tropic /'trɒpɪk/ n trópico m. ~**al** adj
tropical. ~**s** npl trópicos mpl

trot /trɒt/ n trote m. ●vi (pt **trotted**)
trotar

trouble /'trʌbl/ n problemas mpl;
(awkward situation) apuro m;
(inconvenience) molestia f. **be in ~**
estar en apuros. **get into ~**
meterse en problemas. **look for**
~ buscar camorra. **take the ~ to**
do sth molestarse en hacer algo.
●vt (bother) molestar; (worry)
preocupar. ~**maker** n
alborotador m. ~**some** /-səm/ adj
problemático. ~ **spot** n punto m
conflictivo

trough /trɒf/ n (for drinking)
abrevadero m; (for feeding)
comedero m

troupe /truːp/ n compañía f teatral

trousers /'traʊzəz/ npl pantalón m,
pantalones mpl

trout /traʊt/ n (pl **trout**) trucha f

trowel /'traʊəl/ n (garden)
desplantador m; (for mortar) paleta f

truant /'truːənt/ n. **play ~** hacer
novillos

truce /truːs/ n tregua f

truck /trʌk/ n camión m; (Rail)
vagón m, furgón m; (Amer, vegetables,
fruit) productos mpl de la huerta. ~
driver, ~**er** (Amer) n camionero m.
~**ing** n transporte m por carretera

trudge /trʌdʒ/ vi andar
penosamente

true /truː/ adj (**-er, -est**) verdadero;
(story, account) verídico; (friend)
auténtico, de verdad. ~ **to sth/**
s.o. fiel a algo/uno. **be ~** ser
cierto. **come ~** hacerse realidad

truffle /'trʌfl/ n trufa f; (chocolate)
trufa f de chocolate

truly /'truːlɪ/ adv verdaderamente;
(sincerely) sinceramente. **yours ~**
(in letters) cordiales saludos

trump /trʌmp/ n (Cards) triunfo m;
(fig) baza f

trumpet /'trʌmpɪt/ n trompeta f.

~er n trompetista m & f, trompeta m & f

truncheon /'trʌntʃən/ n porra f

trunk /trʌŋk/ n (of tree) tronco m; (box) baúl m; (of elephant) trompa f; (Amer, Auto) maletero m, cajuela f (Mex). **~s** npl bañador m, traje m de baño

truss /trʌs/ vt. **truss (up)** vt atar

trust /trʌst/ n confianza f; (money, property) fondo m de inversiones; (institution) fundación f. **on ~** a ojos cerrados; (Com) al fiado. ●vi. **~ in s.o./sth** confiar en uno/algo. ●vt confiar en; (in negative sentences) fiarse; (hope) esperar. **~ed** adj leal. **~ee** /trʌs'tiː/ n fideicomisario m. **~ful** adj confiado. **~ing** adj confiado. **~worthy**, **~y** adj digno de confianza

truth /truːθ/ n (pl **-s** /truːðz/) verdad f; (of account, story) veracidad f. **~ful** adj veraz

try /traɪ/ vt (pt **tried**) intentar; probar (food, product); (be a strain on) poner a prueba; (Jurid) procesar. **~ to do sth** tratar de algo, intentar hacer algo. **~ not to forget** procura no olvidarte. ●n tentativa f, prueba f; (Rugby) ensayo m. ■ **~ on** vt probarse (garment). ■ **~ out** vt probar. **~ing** adj duro; (annoying) molesto

tsar /zɑː(r)/ n zar m

T-shirt /'tiːʃɜːt/ n camiseta f

tub /tʌb/ n cuba f; (for washing clothes) tina f; (bathtub) bañera f; (for ice cream) envase m, tarrina f

tuba /'tjuːbə/ n tuba f

tubby /'tʌbɪ/ adj (**-ier**, **-iest**) rechoncho

tube /tjuːb/ n tubo m; (fam, Rail) metro m; (Amer fam, television) tele f. **inner ~** n cámara f de aire

tuberculosis /tjuːbɜːkjuː'ləʊsɪs/ n tuberculosis f

tub|ing /'tjuːbɪŋ/ n tubería f. **~ular** /-jʊlə(r)/ adj tubular

tuck /tʌk/ n (fold) jareta f. ●vt

plegar; (put) meter. ■ **~ in(to)** vi (fam, eat) ponerse a comer. ■ **~ up** vt arropar (child)

Tuesday /'tjuːzdeɪ/ n martes m

tuft /tʌft/ n (of hair) mechón m; (of feathers) penacho m; (of grass) mata f

tug /tʌg/ vt (pt **tugged**) tirar de. ●vi. **~ at sth** tirar de algo. ●n tirón m; (Naut) remolcador m. **~-of-war** n juego de tira y afloja

tuition /tjuː'ɪʃn/ n clases fpl

tulip /'tjuːlɪp/ n tulipán m

tumble /'tʌmbl/ vi caerse. ●n caída f. **~down** adj en ruinas. **~drier** n secadora f. **~r** n (glass) vaso m (de lados rectos)

tummy /'tʌmɪ/ n 🅸 barriga f

tumour /'tjuːmə(r)/ n tumor m

tumult /'tjuːmʌlt/ n tumulto m. **~uous** /-'mʌltjʊəs/ adj (applause) apoteósico

tuna /'tjuːnə/ n (pl **tuna**) atún m

tune /tjuːn/ n melodía f; (piece) tonada f. **be in ~** estar afinado. **be out of ~** estar desafinado. ●vt afinar, sintonizar (radio, TV); (Mec) poner a punto. ●vi. **~ in (to)** sintonizar (con). ■ **~ up** vt/i afinar. **~ful** adj melodioso. **~r** n afinador m; (Radio) sintonizador m

tunic /'tjuːnɪk/ n túnica f

tunnel /'tʌnl/ n túnel m. ●vi (pt **tunnelled**) abrir un túnel

turban /'tɜːbən/ n turbante m

turbine /'tɜːbaɪn/ n turbina f

turbo /'tɜːbəʊ/ n (pl **-os**) turbo(compresor) m

turbulen|ce /'tɜːbjʊləns/ n turbulencia f. **~t** adj turbulento

turf /tɜːf/ n (pl **turfs** or **turves**) césped m; (segment of grass) tepe m. ■ **~ out** vt 🅸 echar

turgid /'tɜːdʒɪd/ adj (language) ampuloso

turkey /'tɜːkɪ/ n (pl **-eys**) pavo m

Turk|ey /'tɜːkɪ/ f Turquía f. **~ish** adj & n turco (m)

turmoil /'tɜːmɔɪl/ n confusión f

turn /tɜːn/ vt hacer girar; volver (head, page); doblar (corner); (change) cambiar; (deflect) desviar. ~ **sth into sth** convertir or transformar algo en algo. ●vi (handle) girar, dar vueltas; (person) volverse, darse la vuelta. ~ **right** girar or doblar or torcer a la derecha. ~ **red** ponerse rojo. ~ **into sth** convertirse en algo. ●n vuelta f; (in road) curva f; (change) giro m; (sequence) turno m; (fam, of illness) ataque m. **good** ~ favor m. **in** ~ a su vez. ■~ **down** vt (fold) doblar; (reduce) bajar; (reject) rechazar. ■~ **off** vt cerrar (tap); apagar (light, TV, etc). vi (from road) doblar. ■~ **on** vt abrir (tap); encender, prender (LAm) (light etc). ■~ **out** vt apagar (light etc). vi (result) resultar. ■~ **round** vi darse la vuelta. ■~ **up** vi aparecer. vt (find) encontrar; levantar (collar); subir (hem); acortar (trousers); poner más fuerte (gas). ~**ed-up** adj (nose) respingón. ~**ing** n (in town) bocacalle f. **we've missed the** ~**ing** nos hemos pasado la calle (or carretera). ~**ing-point** n momento m decisivo.

turnip /'tɜːnɪp/ n nabo m

turn: ~**over** n (Com) facturación f; (of staff) movimiento m. ~**pike** n (Amer) autopista f de peaje. ~**stile** n torniquete m. ~**table** n platina f. ~**up** n (of trousers) vuelta f, valenciana f (Mex)

turquoise /'tɜːkwɔɪz/ adj & n turquesa (f)

turret /'tʌrɪt/ n torrecilla f

turtle /'tɜːtl/ n tortuga f de mar; (Amer, tortoise) tortuga f

turves /tɜːvz/ see TURF

tusk /tʌsk/ n colmillo m

tussle /'tʌsl/ n lucha f

tutor /'tjuːtə(r)/ n profesor m particular

tuxedo /tʌk'siːdəʊ/ n (pl **-os**) (Amer) esmoquin m, smoking m

TV /tiː'viː/ n televisión f, tele f 🔲

twang /twæŋ/ n tañido m; (in voice) gangueo m

tweet /twiːt/ n piada f. ●vi piar

tweezers /'twiːzəz/ npl pinzas fpl

twel|fth /twelfθ/ adj duodécimo. ●n doceavo m. ~**ve** /twelv/ adj & n doce (m)

twent|ieth /'twentɪəθ/ adj vigésimo. ●n veinteavo m. ~**y** /'twentɪ/ adj & n veinte (m)

twice /twaɪs/ adv dos veces. ~ **as many people** el doble de gente

twiddle /'twɪdl/ vt (hacer) girar

twig /twɪg/ n ramita f. ●vi (pt **twigged**) 🔲 caer, darse cuenta

twilight /'twaɪlaɪt/ n crepúsculo m

twin /twɪn/ adj & n gemelo (m), mellizo (m) (LAm)

twine /twaɪn/ n cordel m, bramante m

twinge /twɪndʒ/ n punzada f; (of remorse) punzada f

twinkle /'twɪŋkl/ vi centellear. ●n centelleo m; (in eye) brillo m

twirl /twɜːl/ vt (hacer) girar. ●vi girar. ●n vuelta f

twist /twɪst/ vt retorcer; (roll) enrollar; girar (knob); tergiversar (words); (distort) retorcer. ~ **one's ankle** torcerse el tobillo. ●vi (rope, wire) enrollarse; (road, river) serpentear. ●n torsión f; (curve) vuelta f

twit /twɪt/ n 🔲 imbécil m

twitch /twɪtʃ/ vi moverse. ●n tic m

twitter /'twɪtə(r)/ vi gorjear

two /tuː/ adj & n dos (m). ~**-bit** adj (Amer) de tres al cuarto. ~**-faced** adj falso, insincero. ~**fold** adj doble. ●adv dos veces. ~**pence** /'tʌpəns/ n dos peniques mpl. ~**-piece** (suit) n traje m de dos piezas. ~**-way** adj (traffic) de doble sentido

tycoon /taɪ'kuːn/ n magnate m

t

tying /'taɪɪŋ/ see TIE

type /taɪp/ n tipo m. ●vt/i escribir a máquina. **~cast** adj (actor) encasillado. **~script** n texto m mecanografiado, manuscrito m (de una obra, novela etc). **~writer** n máquina f de escribir. **~written** adj escrito a máquina, mecanografiado

typhoon /taɪ'fu:n/ n tifón m

typical /'tɪpɪkl/ adj típico. **~ly** adv típicamente

typify /'tɪpɪfaɪ/ vt tipificar

typi|ng /'taɪpɪŋ/ n mecanografía f. **~st** n mecanógrafo m

tyran|nical /tɪ'rænɪkl/ adj tiránico. **~ny** /'tɪrəni/ n tiranía f. **~t** /'taɪərənt/ n tirano m

tyre /'taɪə(r)/ n neumático m, llanta f (LAm)

Uu

udder /'ʌdə(r)/ n ubre f

UFO /'ju:fəʊ/ abbr (= **unidentified flying object**) OVNI m (objeto volante no identificado)

ugly /'ʌglɪ/ adj (**-ier, -iest**) feo

UK /ju:'keɪ/ abbr (= **United Kingdom**) Reino m Unido

Ukraine /ju:'kreɪn/ n Ucrania f

ulcer /'ʌlsə(r)/ n úlcera f; (external) llaga f

ultimate /'ʌltɪmət/ adj (eventual) final; (utmost) máximo. **~ly** adv en última instancia; (in the long run) a la larga

ultimatum /ʌltɪ'meɪtəm/ n (pl **-ums**) ultimátum m

ultra... /'ʌltrə/ pref ultra... **~violet** /-'vaɪələt/ adj ultravioleta

umbilical cord /ʌm'bɪlɪkl/ n cordón m umbilical

umbrella /ʌm'brelə/ n paraguas m

umpire /'ʌmpaɪə(r)/ n árbitro m. ●vt arbitrar

umpteen /'ʌmpti:n/ adj 🔁 tropecientos 🔁. **~th** adj 🔁 enésimo

un... /ʌn/ pref in..., des..., no, poco, sin

UN /ju:'en/ abbr (= **United Nations**)

ONU f (Organización de las Naciones Unidas)

unable /ʌn'eɪbl/ adj. **be ~ to** no poder; (be incapable of) ser incapaz de

unacceptable /ʌnək'septəbl/ adj (behaviour) inaceptable; (terms) inadmisible

unaccompanied /ʌnə'kʌmpənɪd/ adj (luggage) no acompañado; (person, instrument) solo; (singing) sin acompañamiento

unaccustomed /ʌnə'kʌstəmd/ adj desacostumbrado. **be ~ to** adj no estar acostumbrado a

unaffected /ʌnə'fektɪd/ adj natural

unaided /ʌn'eɪdɪd/ adj sin ayuda

unanimous /ju:'nænɪməs/ adj unánime. **~ly** adv unánimemente; (elect) por unanimidad

unarmed /ʌn'ɑ:md/ adj desarmado

unattended /ʌnə'tendɪd/ adj sin vigilar

unattractive /ʌnə'træktɪv/ adj poco atractivo

unavoidabl|e /ʌnə'vɔɪdəbl/ adj inevitable. **~y** adv. **I was ~y delayed** no pude evitar llegar tarde

unaware /ʌnə'weə(r)/ adj. **be ~ of**

ignorar, no ser consciente de. ~**s** /-eəz/ adv desprevenido

unbearabl|e /ʌn'beərəbl/ adj insoportable, inaguantable. ~**y** adv inaguantablemente

unbeat|able /ʌn'biːtəbl/ adj (quality) insuperable; (team) invencible. ~**en** adj no vencido; (record) insuperado

unbelievabl|e /ʌnbɪ'liːvəbl/ adj increíble. ~**y** adv increíblemente

unbiased /ʌn'baɪəst/ adj imparcial

unblock /ʌn'blɒk/ vt desatascar

unbolt /ʌn'bəʊlt/ vt descorrer el pestillo de

unborn /ʌn'bɔːn/ adj que todavía no ha nacido

unbreakable /ʌn'breɪkəbl/ adj irrompible

unbroken /ʌn'brəʊkən/ adj (intact) intacto, (continuous) ininterrumpido

unbutton /ʌn'bʌtn/ vt desabotonar, desabrochar

uncalled-for /ʌn'kɔːldfɔː(r)/ adj fuera de lugar

uncanny /ʌn'kænɪ/ adj (-ier, -iest) raro, extraño

uncertain /ʌn'sɜːtn/ adj incierto; (hesitant) vacilante. **be ~ of/about sth** no estar seguro de algo. ~**ty** n incertidumbre f

uncharitable /ʌn'tʃærɪtəbl/ adj severo

uncivilized /ʌn'sɪvɪlaɪzd/ adj incivilizado

uncle /'ʌŋkl/ n tío m

unclean /ʌn'kliːn/ adj impuro

unclear /ʌn'klɪə(r)/ adj poco claro

uncomfortable /ʌn'kʌmfətəbl/ adj incómodo

uncommon /ʌn'kɒmən/ adj poco común

uncompromising /ʌn'kɒmprəmaɪzɪŋ/ adj intransigente

unconcerned /ʌnkən'sɜːnd/ adj indiferente

unconditional /ʌnkən'dɪʃənl/ adj incondicional

unconnected /ʌnkə'nektɪd/ adj (unrelated) sin conexión. **the events are ~** estos acontecimientos no guardan ninguna relación (entre sí)

unconscious /ʌn'kɒnʃəs/ adj (Med) inconsciente. ~**ly** adv inconscientemente

unconventional /ʌnkən'venʃənl/ adj poco convencional

uncork /ʌn'kɔːk/ vt descorchar

uncouth /ʌn'kuːθ/ adj zafio

uncover /ʌn'kʌvə(r)/ vt destapar; revelar (plot, scandal)

undaunted /ʌn'dɔːntɪd/ adj impertérrito

undecided /ʌndɪ'saɪdɪd/ adj indeciso

undeniabl|e /ʌndɪ'naɪəbl/ adj innegable. ~**y** adv sin lugar a dudas

under /'ʌndə(r)/ prep debajo de; (less than) menos de; (heading) bajo; (according to) según, (expressing movement) por debajo de. ●adv debajo, abajo

under... pref sub...

under: ~**carriage** n tren m de aterrizaje. ~**charge** vt /-'tʃɑːdʒ/ cobrarle de menos a. ~**clothes** npl ropa f interior. ~**coat**, ~**coating** (Amer) n (paint) pintura f base; (first coat) primera mano f de pintura. ~**cover** adj /-'kʌvə(r)/ secreto. ~**current** n corriente f submarina. ~**dog** n. **the ~dog** el que tiene menos posibilidades. **the ~dogs** npl los de abajo. ~**done** adj /-'dʌn/ (meat) poco hecho. ~**estimate** /-'estɪmeɪt/ vt (underrate) subestimar. ~**fed** /-'fed/ adj subalimentado. ~**foot** /-'fʊt/ adv debajo de los pies. ~**go** vt (pt -**went**, pp -**gone**) sufrir. ~**graduate** /-'grædjʊət/ n estudiante m universitario (no licenciado). ~**ground** /-'graʊnd/ adv bajo tierra; (in secret)

u

clandestinamente. •/-graʊnd/ adj
subterráneo; (secret) clandestino.
•n metro m. **~growth** n maleza
f. **~hand** /-'hænd/ adj (secret)
clandestino; (deceptive)
fraudulento. **~lie** /-'laɪ/ vt (pt **-lay**,
pp **-lain**, pres p **-lying**) subyacer a.
~line /-'laɪn/ vt subrayar.
~lying /-'laɪɪŋ/ adj subyacente.
~mine /-'maɪn/ vt socavar.
~neath /-'ni:θ/ prep debajo de,
abajo de (LAm). • adv por debajo.
~paid /-'peɪd/ adj mal pagado.
~pants npl calzoncillos mpl.
~pass n paso m subterráneo; (for
traffic) paso m inferior.
~privileged /-'prɪvəlɪdʒd/ adj
desfavorecido. **~rate** /-'reɪt/ vt
subestimar. **~rated** /-'reɪtɪd/ adj
no debidamente apreciado.
~shirt n (Amer) camiseta f
(interior).

understand /ʌndə'stænd/ vt (pt
-stood) entender; (empathize with)
comprender, entender. • vi
entender, comprender. **~able** adj
comprensible. **~ing** adj
comprensivo. •n (grasp)
entendimiento m; (sympathy)
comprensión f; (agreement)
acuerdo m

under: ~statement n
subestimación f. **~take** /-'teɪk/ (pt
-took, pp **-taken**) emprender (task);
asumir (responsibility). **~take to do
sth** comprometerse a hacer algo.
~taker n director m de pompas
fúnebres. **~taking** /-'teɪkɪŋ/ n
empresa f; (promise) promesa f.
~tone n. **in an ~tone** en voz
baja. **~value** /-'vælju:/ vt
subvalorar. **~water** /-'wɔ:tə(r)/
adj submarino. • adv debajo del
agua. **~wear** n ropa f interior.
~weight /-'weɪt/ adj de peso más
bajo que el normal. **~went**
/-'went/ see **UNDERGO. ~world** n
(criminals) hampa f. **~write** /-'raɪt/
vt (pt **-wrote**, pp **-written**) (Com)
asegurar; (guarantee financially)
financiar

undeserved /ʌndɪ'zɜ:vd/ adj
inmerecido

undesirable /ʌndɪ'zaɪərəbl/ adj
indeseable

undignified /ʌn'dɪgnɪfaɪd/ adj
indecoroso

undisputed /ʌndɪs'pju:tɪd/ adj
(champion) indiscutido; (facts)
innegable

undo /ʌn'du:/ vt (pt **-did**, pp **-done**)
desabrochar (button, jacket); abrir
(zip); desatar (knot, laces)

undoubted /ʌn'daʊtɪd/ adj
indudable. **~ly** adv
indudablemente, sin duda

undress /ʌn'dres/ vt desvestir,
desnudar. • vi desvestirse,
desnudarse

undue /ʌn'dju:/ adj excesivo

undulate /'ʌndjʊleɪt/ vi ondular

unduly /ʌn'dju:lɪ/ adv
excesivamente

unearth /ʌn'ɜ:θ/ vt desenterrar;
descubrir (document)

unearthly /ʌn'ɜ:θlɪ/ adj
sobrenatural. **at an ~ hour** a
estas horas intempestivas

uneasy /ʌn'i:zɪ/ adj incómodo

uneconomic /ʌni:kə'nɒmɪk/ adj
poco económico

uneducated /ʌn'edjʊkeɪtɪd/ adj sin
educación

unemploy|ed /ʌnɪm'plɔɪd/ adj
desempleado, parado. **~ment** n
desempleo m, paro m

unending /ʌn'endɪŋ/ adj
interminable, sin fin

unequal /ʌn'i:kwəl/ adj desigual

unequivocal /ʌnɪ'kwɪvəkl/ adj
inequívoco

unethical /ʌn'eθɪkl/ adj poco ético,
inmoral

uneven /ʌn'i:vn/ adj desigual

unexpected /ʌnɪk'spektɪd/ adj
inesperado; (result) imprevisto.
~ly adv (arrive) de improviso;
(happen) de forma imprevista

unfair /ʌn'feə(r)/ adj injusto;

improcedente (dismissal). **~ly** adv
injustamente

unfaithful /ʌnˈfeɪθfl/ adj infiel

unfamiliar /ʌnfəˈmɪlɪə(r)/ adj
desconocido. **be ~ with**
desconocer

unfasten /ʌnˈfɑːsn/ vt desabrochar
(clothes); (untie) desatar

unfavourable /ʌnˈfeɪvərəbl/ adj
desfavorable

unfeeling /ʌnˈfiːlɪŋ/ adj insensible

unfit /ʌnˈfɪt/ adj. **I'm ~** no estoy en
forma. **~ for human
consumption** no apto para el
consumo

unfold /ʌnˈfəʊld/ vt desdoblar;
desplegar (wings); (fig) revelar. • vi
(leaf) abrirse; (events) desarrollarse

unforeseen /ʌnfɔːˈsiːn/ adj
imprevisto

unforgettable /ʌnfəˈgetəbl/ adj
inolvidable

unforgivable /ʌnfəˈgɪvəbl/ adj
imperdonable

unfortunate /ʌnˈfɔːtʃənət/ adj
desafortunado; (regrettable)
lamentable. **~ly** adv
desafortunadamente; (stronger) por
desgracia, desgraciadamente

unfounded /ʌnˈfaʊndɪd/ adj
infundado

unfriendly /ʌnˈfrendlɪ/ adj poco
amistoso; (stronger) antipático

unfurl /ʌnˈfɜːl/ vt desplegar

ungainly /ʌnˈgeɪnlɪ/ adj desgarbado

ungrateful /ʌnˈgreɪtfl/ adj
desagradecido, ingrato

unhapp|iness /ʌnˈhæpɪnes/ n
infelicidad f, tristeza f. **~y** adj (**-ier,
-iest**) infeliz, triste; (unsuitable)
inoportuno. **be ~y about sth** no
estar contento con algo

unharmed /ʌnˈhɑːmd/ adj (person)
ileso

unhealthy /ʌnˈhelθɪ/ adj (**-ier,
-iest**) (person) de mala salud;
(complexion) enfermizo; (conditions)
poco saludable

unhurt /ʌnˈhɜːt/ adj ileso

unification /juːnɪfɪˈkeɪʃn/ n
unificación f

uniform /ˈjuːnɪfɔːm/ adj & n
uniforme (m). **~ity** /-ˈfɔːmətɪ/ n
uniformidad f

unify /ˈjuːnɪfaɪ/ vt unir

unilateral /juːnɪˈlætərəl/ adj
unilateral

unimaginable /ʌnɪˈmædʒɪnəbl/ adj
inimaginable

unimaginative /ʌnɪˈmædʒɪnətɪv/
adj (person) poco imaginativo

unimportant /ʌnɪmˈpɔːtnt/ adj sin
importancia

uninhabited /ʌnɪnˈhæbɪtɪd/ adj
deshabitado; (island) despoblado

unintelligible /ʌnɪnˈtelɪdʒəbl/ adj
ininteligible

unintentional /ʌnɪnˈtenʃənl/ adj
involuntario

union /ˈjuːnjən/ n unión f; (trade
union) sindicato m; (student ~)
asociación f de estudiantes. **U~
Jack** n bandera f del Reino Unido

unique /juːˈniːk/ adj único

unison /ˈjuːnɪsn/ n. **in ~** al
unísono

unit /ˈjuːnɪt/ n unidad f; (of furniture
etc) módulo m; (in course) módulo m

unite /juːˈnaɪt/ vt unir. • vi unirse.
U~d Kingdom n Reino m Unido.
U~d Nations n Organización f de
las Naciones Unidas (ONU). **U~d
States (of America)** n Estados mpl
Unidos (de América)

unity /ˈjuːnɪtɪ/ n unidad f

univers|al /juːnɪˈvɜːsl/ adj
universal. **~e** /ˈjuːnɪvɜːs/ n
universo m

university /juːnɪˈvɜːsətɪ/ n
universidad f. • adj universitario

unjust /ʌnˈdʒʌst/ adj injusto.
~ified /-ɪfaɪd/ adj injustificado

unkind /ʌnˈkaɪnd/ adj poco amable;
(cruel) cruel; (remark) hiriente

u

unknown /ʌnˈnəʊn/ adj desconocido

unlawful /ʌnˈlɔːfl/ adj ilegal

unleaded /ʌnˈledɪd/ adj (fuel) sin plomo

unleash /ʌnˈliːʃ/ vt soltar

unless /ʌnˈles, ənˈles/ conj a menos que, a no ser que

unlike /ʌnˈlaɪk/ prep diferente de. (in contrast to) a diferencia de. ~ly adj improbable

unlimited /ʌnˈlɪmɪtɪd/ adj ilimitado

unlisted /ʌnˈlɪstɪd/ adj (Amer) que no figura en la guía telefónica, privado (Mex)

unload /ʌnˈləʊd/ vt descargar

unlock /ʌnˈlɒk/ vt abrir (con llave)

unluck|ily /ʌnˈlʌkɪlɪ/ adv desgraciadamente. ~y adj (-ier, -iest) (person) sin suerte, desafortunado. **be ~y** tener mala suerte; (bring bad luck) traer mala suerte

unmarried /ʌnˈmærɪd/ adj soltero

unmask /ʌnˈmɑːsk/ vt desenmascarar

unmentionable /ʌnˈmenʃənəbl/ adj inmencionable

unmistakable /ʌnmɪˈsteɪkəbl/ adj inconfundible

unnatural /ʌnˈnætʃərəl/ adj poco natural; (not normal) anormal

unnecessar|ily /ʌnˈnesəsərɪlɪ/ adv innecesariamente. ~y adj innecesario

unnerve /ʌnˈnɜːv/ vt desconcertar

unnoticed /ʌnˈnəʊtɪst/ adj inadvertido

unobtainable /ʌnəbˈteɪnəbl/ adj imposible de conseguir

unobtrusive /ʌnəbˈtruːsɪv/ adj discreto

unofficial /ʌnəˈfɪʃl/ adj no oficial. ~ly adv extraoficialmente

unpack /ʌnˈpæk/ vt sacar las cosas de (bags); deshacer, desempacar (LAm) (suitcase). •vi deshacer las maletas, desempacar (LAm)

unpaid /ʌnˈpeɪd/ adj (work) no retribuido, no remunerado; (leave) sin sueldo

unperturbed /ʌnpəˈtɜːbd/ adj impasible. **he carried on ~** siguió sin inmutarse

unpleasant /ʌnˈpleznt/ adj desagradable

unplug /ʌnˈplʌg/ vt desenchufar

unpopular /ʌnˈpɒpjʊlə(r)/ adj impopular

unprecedented /ʌnˈpresɪdentɪd/ adj sin precedentes

unpredictable /ʌnprɪˈdɪktəbl/ adj imprevisible

unprepared /ʌnprɪˈpeəd/ adj no preparado; (unready) desprevenido

unprofessional /ʌnprəˈfeʃənəl/ adj poco profesional

unprofitable /ʌnˈprɒfɪtəbl/ adj no rentable

unprotected /ʌnprəˈtektɪd/ adj sin protección; (sex) sin el uso de preservativos

unqualified /ʌnˈkwɒlɪfaɪd/ adj sin título; (fig) absoluto

unquestion|able /ʌnˈkwestʃənəbl/ adj incuestionable, innegable. ~ing adj (obedience) ciego; (loyalty) incondicional

unravel /ʌnˈrævl/ vt (pt **unravelled**) desenredar; desentrañar (mystery)

unreal /ʌnˈrɪəl/ adj irreal. ~istic /-ˈlɪstɪk/ adj poco realista

unreasonable /ʌnˈriːzənəbl/ adj irrazonable

unrecognizable /ʌnrekəgˈnaɪzəbl/ adj irreconocible

unrelated /ʌnrɪˈleɪtɪd/ adj (facts) no relacionados (entre sí); (people) no emparentado

unreliable /ʌnrɪˈlaɪəbl/ adj (person) informal; (machine) poco fiable; (information) poco fidedigno

unrepentant /ʌnrɪ'pentənt/ adj impenitente

unrest /ʌn'rest/ n (discontent) descontento m; (disturbances) disturbios mpl

unrivalled /ʌn'raɪvld/ adj incomparable

unroll /ʌn'rəʊl/ vt desenrollar. •vi desenrollarse

unruffled /ʌn'rʌfld/ (person) sereno

unruly /ʌn'ruːlɪ/ adj (class) indisciplinado; (child) revoltoso

unsafe /ʌn'seɪf/ adj inseguro

unsatisfactory /ʌnsætɪs'fæktərɪ/ adj insatisfactorio

unsavoury /ʌn'seɪvərɪ/ adj desagradable

unscathed /ʌn'skeɪðd/ adj ileso

unscheduled /ʌn'ʃedjuːld/ adj no programado, no previsto

unscrew /ʌn'skruː/ vt destornillar; desenroscar (lid)

unscrupulous /ʌn'skruːpjʊləs/ adj inescrupuloso

unseemly /ʌn'siːmlɪ/ adj indecoroso

unseen /ʌn'siːn/ adj (danger) oculto; (unnoticed) sin ser visto

unselfish /ʌn'selfɪʃ/ adj (act) desinteresado; (person) nada egoísta

unsettle /ʌn'setl/ vt desestabilizar (situation); alterar (plans). **~d** adj agitado; (weather) inestable; (undecided) pendiente (de resolución)

unshakeable /ʌn'ʃeɪkəbl/ adj inquebrantable

unshaven /ʌn'ʃeɪvn/ adj sin afeitar, sin rasurar (Mex)

unsightly /ʌn'saɪtlɪ/ adj feo

unskilled /ʌn'skɪld/ adj (work) no especializado; (worker) no cualificado, no calificado

unsociable /ʌn'səʊʃəbl/ adj insociable

unsolved /ʌn'sɒlvd/ adj no resuelto; (murder) sin esclarecerse

unsophisticated /ʌnsə'fɪstɪkeɪtɪd/ adj sencillo

unsound /ʌn'saʊnd/ adj poco sólido

unspecified /ʌn'spesɪfaɪd/ adj no especificado

unstable /ʌn'steɪbl/ adj inestable

unsteady /ʌn'stedɪ/ adj inestable, poco firme

unstuck /ʌn'stʌk/ adj despegado. **come ~** despegarse; (fail) fracasar

unsuccessful /ʌnsək'sesfʊl/ adj (attempt) infructuoso. **be ~** no tener éxito, fracasar

unsuitable /ʌn'suːtəbl/ adj (clothing) poco apropiado, poco adecuado; (time) inconveniente. **she is ~ for the job** no es la persona indicada para el trabajo

unsure /ʌn'ʃʊə(r)/ adj inseguro

unthinkable /ʌn'θɪŋkəbl/ adj inconcebible

untidi|ness /ʌn'taɪdɪnəs/ n desorden m. **~y** adj (-ier, -iest) desordenado; (appearance, writing) descuidado

untie /ʌn'taɪ/ vt desatar, desamarrar (LAm)

until /ən'tɪl, ʌn'tɪl/ prep hasta. •conj hasta que

untold /ʌn'təʊld/ adj incalculable

untouched /ʌn'tʌtʃt/ adj intacto

untried /ʌn'traɪd/ adj no probado

untrue /ʌn'truː/ adj falso

unused /ʌn'juːzd/ adj nuevo. •/ʌn'juːst/ adj. **~ to** no acostumbrado a

unusual /ʌn'juːʒʊəl/ adj poco común, poco corriente. **it's ~ to see so many people** es raro ver a tanta gente. **~ly** adv excepcionalmente, inusitadamente

unveil /ʌn'veɪl/ vt descubrir

unwanted /ʌn'wɒntɪd/ adj superfluo; (child) no deseado

u

unwelcome /ʌn'welkəm/ adj (news) poco grato; (guest) inoportuno

unwell /ʌn'wel/ adj indispuesto

unwieldy /ʌn'wiːldɪ/ adj pesado y difícil de manejar

unwilling /ʌn'wɪlɪŋ/ adj mal dispuesto. **be ~** no querer

unwind /ʌn'waɪnd/ vt (pt **unwound**) desenrollar. ● vi (fam, relax) relajarse

unwise /ʌn'waɪz/ adj poco sensato

unworthy /ʌn'wɜːðɪ/ adj indigno

unwrap /ʌn'ræp/ vt (pt **unwrapped**) desenvolver

unwritten /ʌn'rɪtn/ adj no escrito; (agreement) verbal

up /ʌp/ adv arriba; (upwards) hacia arriba; (higher) más arriba. **~ here** aquí arriba. **~ there** allí arriba. **~ to** hasta. **he's not ~ yet** todavía no se ha levantado. **be ~ against** enfrentarse con. **come ~** subir. **go ~** subir. **he's not ~ to the job** no tiene las condiciones necesarias para el trabajo. **it's ~ to you** depende de ti. **what's ~?** ¿qué pasa? ● prep. **go ~ the stairs** subir la escalera. **it's just ~ the road** está un poco más allá. ● vt (pt **upped**) aumentar. ● n. **~s and downs** npl altibajos mpl; (of life) vicisitudes fpl. **~bringing** /'ʌpbrɪŋɪŋ/ n educación f. **~date** /ʌp'deɪt/ vt poner al día. **~grade** /ʌp'greɪd/ vt elevar de categoría (person); mejorar (equipment). **~heaval** /ʌp'hiːvl/ n trastorno m. **~hill** /ʌp'hɪl/ adv cuesta arriba. **~hold** /ʌp'həʊld/ vt (pt **upheld**) mantener (principle); confirmar (decision). **~holster** /ʌp'həʊlstə(r)/ vt tapizar. **~holstery** /ʌp'həʊlstərɪ/ n tapicería f. **~keep** n mantenimiento m. **~-market** /ʌp'mɑːkɪt/ adj de categoría

upon /ə'pɒn/ prep sobre. **once ~ a time** érase una vez

upper /'ʌpə(r)/ adj superior. **~ class** n clase f alta

up::~right adj vertical; (citizen)

recto. **place sth ~right** poner algo de pie. **~rising** /'ʌpraɪzɪŋ/ n levantamiento m. **~roar** n tumulto m

upset /ʌp'set/ vt (pt **upset**, pres p **upsetting**) (hurt) disgustar; (offend) ofender; (distress) alterar; desbaratar (plans). ● adj (hurt) disgustado; (distressed) alterado; (offended) ofendido; (disappointed) desilusionado. ● /'ʌpset/ n trastorno m. **have a stomach ~** estar mal del estómago

up: ~shot n resultado m. **~side down** /ʌpsaɪd'daʊn/ adv al revés (con la parte de arriba abajo); (in disorder) patas arriba. **turn sth ~side down** poner algo boca abajo. **~stairs** /ʌp'steəz/ adv arriba. **go ~stairs** subir. ● /'ʌpsteəz/ adj de arriba. **~start** n advenedizo m. **~state** adv (Amer). **I live ~state** vivo en el norte del estado. **~stream** /ʌp'striːm/ adv río arriba. **~take**. **be quick on the ~take** agarrar las cosas al vuelo. **~-to-date** /ʌptə'deɪt/ adj al día; (news) de última hora. **~turn** n repunte m, mejora f. **~ward** /'ʌpwəd/ adj (movement) ascendente; (direction) hacia arriba. ● adv hacia arriba. **~wards** adv hacia arriba

uranium /jʊ'reɪnɪəm/ n uranio m

Uranus /'jʊərənəs//jʊə'reɪnəs/ n Urano m

urban /'ɜːbən/ adj urbano

urchin /'ɜːtʃɪn/ n pilluelo m

urge /ɜːdʒ/ vt instar. **~ s.o. to do sth** instar a uno a que haga algo. ● n impulso m; (wish, whim) ganas fpl. ■ **~ on** vt animar

urgen|cy /'ɜːdʒənsɪ/ n urgencia f. **~t** adj urgente. **~tly** adv urgentemente, con urgencia

urin|ate /'jʊərɪneɪt/ vi orinar. **~e** /'jʊərɪn/ n orina f

Uruguay /jʊərəgwaɪ/ n Uruguay m. **~an** adj & n uruguayo (m)

us /ʌs, əs/ pron nos; (after prep) nosotros m, nosotras f

u

US(A) /juːes'eɪ/ abbr (= **United States (of America)**) EE.UU. (only written), Estados mpl Unidos

usage /'juːzɪdʒ/ n uso m

use /juːz/ vt usar; utilizar (service, facilities); consumir (fuel). • /juːs/ n uso m, empleo m. **be of ~** servir. **it is no ~** es inútil. ■ **~ up** vt agotar, consumir. **~d** /juːzd/ adj usado. • /juːst/ v mod **~ to. he ~d to say** decía, solía decir. **there ~d to be** (antes) había. • adj/ juːst/. **be ~d to** estar acostumbrado a. **~ful** /'juːsfl/ adj útil. **~fully** adv útilmente. **~less** adj inútil; (person) incompetente. **~r** /-zə(r)/ n usuario m. **drug ~** n consumidor m de drogas

usher /'ʌʃə(r)/ n (in theatre etc) acomodador m. ■ **~ in** vt hacer pasar; marcar el comienzo de (new era). **~ette** /-'ret/ n acomodadora f

USSR abbr (History) (= **Union of Soviet Socialist Republics**) URSS

usual /'juːʒəl/ adj usual; (habitual) acostumbrado, habitual; (place, route) de siempre. **as ~** como de costumbre, como siempre. **~ly** adv normalmente. **he ~ly wakes up early** suele despertarse temprano

utensil /juː'tensl/ n utensilio m

utilize /'juːtɪlaɪz/ vt utilizar

utmost /'ʌtməʊst/ adj sumo. • n. **do one's ~** hacer todo lo posible (**to** para)

utter /'ʌtə(r)/ adj completo. • vt pronunciar (word); dar (cry). **~ly** adv totalmente

U-turn /'juːtɜːn/ n cambio m de sentido

Vv

vacan|cy /'veɪkənsɪ/ n (job) vacante f; (room) habitación f libre. **~t** adj (building) desocupado, (seat) libre; (post) vacante; (look) ausente

vacate /və'keɪt/ vt dejar

vacation /və'keɪʃn/ n (Amer) vacaciones fpl. **go on ~** ir de vacaciones. **~er** n (Amer) veraneante m & f

vaccin|ate /'væksɪneɪt/ vt vacunar. **~ation** /-'neɪʃn/ n vacunación f. **~e** /'væksiːn/ n vacuna f

vacuum /'vækjʊəm/ n vacío m. **~ cleaner** n aspiradora f

vagina /və'dʒaɪnə/ n vagina f

vague /veɪɡ/ adj (**-er, -est**) vago; (outline) borroso; (person, expression) despistado. **~ly** adv vagamente

vain /veɪn/ adj (**-er, -est**) vanidoso; (useless) vano. **in ~** en vano

Valentine's Day /'væləntaɪmz/ n el día de San Valentín

valiant /'vælɪənt/ adj valeroso

valid /'vælɪd/ adj válido. **~ate** /-eɪt/ vt dar validez a; validar (contract). **~ity** /-'ɪdətɪ/ n validez f

valley /'vælɪ/ n (pl **-eys**) valle m

valour /'vælə(r)/ n valor m

valu|able /'væljʊəbl/ adj valioso. **~ables** npl objetos mpl de valor. **~ation** /-'eɪʃn/ n valoración f. **~e** /'vælju:/ n valor m. • vt valorar; tasar, valorar, avaluar (LAm) (property). **~e added tax** n impuesto m sobre el valor añadido

valve /vælv/ n válvula f

vampire /'væmpaɪə(r)/ n vampiro m

van /væn/ n furgoneta f, camioneta f; (Rail) furgón m

vandal /'vændl/ n vándalo m. **~ism** n vandalismo m. **~ize** vt destruir

vanilla /və'nɪlə/ n vainilla f

vanish /'vænɪʃ/ vi desaparecer

vanity /'vænɪtɪ/ n vanidad f. **~ case** n neceser m

vapour /'veɪpə(r)/ n vapor m

varia|ble /'veərɪəbl/ adj variable. **~nce** /-əns/ n. **at ~ce** en desacuerdo. **~nt** n variante f. **~tion** /-'eɪʃn/ n variación f

vari|ed /'veərɪd/ adj variado. **~ety** /və'raɪətɪ/ n variedad f. **~ety show** n espectáculo m de variedades. **~ous** /'veərɪəs/ adj (several) varios; (different) diversos

varnish /'vɑːnɪʃ/ n barniz m; (for nails) esmalte m. •vt barnizar; pintar (nails)

vary /'veərɪ/ vt/i variar

vase /vɑːz/, (Amer) /veɪs/ n (for flowers) florero m; (ornamental) jarrón m

vast /vɑːst/ adj vasto, extenso; (size) inmenso. **~ly** adv infinitamente

vat /væt/ n cuba f

VAT /viːeɪ'tiː/ abbr (= value added tax) IVA m

vault /vɔːlt/ n (roof) bóveda f; (in bank) cámara f acorazada; (tomb) cripta f. •vt/i saltar

VCR n = **videocassette recorder**

VDU n = **visual display unit**

veal /viːl/ n ternera f

veer /vɪə(r)/ vi dar un viraje, virar

vegeta|ble /'vedʒɪtəbl/ adj vegetal. •n verdura f. **~rian** /vedʒɪ'teərɪən/ adj & n vegetariano (m). **~tion** /vedʒɪ'teɪʃn/ n vegetación f

vehement /'viːəmənt/ adj vehemente. **~tly** adv con vehemencia

vehicle /'viːɪkl/ n vehículo m

veil /veɪl/ n velo m

vein /veɪn/ n vena f; (in marble) veta f

velocity /vɪ'lɒsɪtɪ/ n velocidad f

velvet /'velvɪt/ n terciopelo m

vendetta /ven'detə/ n vendetta f

vend|ing machine /'vendɪŋ/ n distribuidor m automático. **~or** /'vendə(r)/ n vendedor m

veneer /və'nɪə(r)/ n chapa f, enchapado m; (fig) barniz m, apariencia f

venerate /'venəreɪt/ vt venerar

venereal /və'nɪərɪəl/ adj venéreo

Venetian blind /və'niːʃn/ n persiana f veneciana

Venezuela /venə'zweɪlə/ n Venezuela f. **~n** adj & n venezolano (m)

vengeance /'vendʒəns/ n venganza f. **with a ~** (fig) con ganas

venom /'venəm/ n veneno m. **~ous** adj venenoso

vent /vent/ n (conducto m de) ventilación; (air ~) respiradero m. **give ~ to** dar rienda suelta a. •vt descargar

ventilat|e /'ventɪleɪt/ vt ventilar. **~ion** /-'eɪʃn/ n ventilación f

ventriloquist /ven'trɪləkwɪst/ n ventrílocuo m

venture /'ventʃə(r)/ n empresa f. •vt aventurar. •vi atreverse

venue /'venjuː/ n (for concert) lugar m de actuación

Venus /'viːnəs/ n Venus m

veranda /və'rændə/ n galería f

verb /vɜːb/ n verbo m. **~al** adj verbal

verdict /'vɜːdɪkt/ n veredicto m; (opinion) opinión f

verge /vɜːdʒ/ n borde m. ■ **~ on** vt rayar en

verify /'verɪfaɪ/ vt (confirm) confirmar; (check) verificar

vermin /'vɜːmɪn/ n alimañas fpl

versatil|e /'vɜːsətaɪl/ adj versátil. **~ity** /-'tɪlətɪ/ n versatilidad f

verse /vɜːs/ n estrofa f; (poetry) poesías fpl. **~d** /vɜːst/ adj. **be**

V

well-~ed in ser muy versado en. **~ion** /'vɜːʃn/ n versión f

versus /'vɜːsəs/ prep contra

vertebra /'vɜːtɪbrə/ n (pl **-brae** /-briː/) vértebra f. **~te** /-brət/ n vertebrado m

vertical /'vɜːtɪkl/ adj & n vertical (f). **~ly** adv verticalmente

vertigo /'vɜːtɪgəʊ/ n vértigo m

verve /vɜːv/ n brío m

very /'verɪ/ adv muy. **~ much** muchísimo. **~ well** muy bien. **the ~ first** el primero de todos. ●adj mismo. **the ~ thing** exactamente lo que hace falta

vessel /'vesl/ n (receptacle) recipiente m; (ship) navío m, nave f

vest /vest/ n camiseta f; (Amer) chaleco m.

vestige /'vestɪdʒ/ n vestigio m

vet /vet/ n veterinario m; (Amer fam, veteran) veterano m. ●vt (pt **vetted**) someter a investigación (applicant)

veteran /'vetərən/ n veterano m

veterinary /'vetərɪnərɪ/ adj veterinario. **~ surgeon** n veterinario m

veto /'viːtəʊ/ n (pl **-oes**) veto m. ●vt vetar

vex /veks/ vt fastidiar

via /'vaɪə/ prep por, por vía de

viable /'vaɪəbl/ adj viable

viaduct /'vaɪədʌkt/ n viaducto m

vibrat|e /vaɪ'breɪt/ vt/i vibrar. **~ion** /-ʃn/ n vibración f

vicar /'vɪkə(r)/ n párroco m. **~age** /-rɪdʒ/ n casa f del párroco

vice /vaɪs/ n vicio m; (Tec) torno m de banco

vice versa /vaɪsɪ'vɜːsə/ adv viceversa

vicinity /vɪ'sɪnɪtɪ/ n vecindad f. **in the ~ of** cerca de

vicious /'vɪʃəs/ adj (attack) feroz; (dog) fiero; (rumour) malicioso. **~ circle** n círculo m vicioso

victim /'vɪktɪm/ n víctima f. **~ize** vt victimizar

victor /'vɪktə(r)/ n vencedor m

Victorian /vɪk'tɔːrɪən/ adj victoriano

victor|ious /vɪk'tɔːrɪəs/ adj (army) victorioso; (team) vencedor. **~y** /'vɪktərɪ/ n victoria f

video /'vɪdɪəʊ/n (pl **-os**) vídeo m, video m (LAm). **~ camera** n videocámara f. **~(cassette) recorder** n magnetoscopio m. **~tape** n videocassette f

vie /vaɪ/ vi (pres p **vying**) rivalizar

Vietnam /vjet'næm/ n Vietnam m. **~ese** adj & n vietnamita (m & f)

view /vjuː/ n vista f; (mental survey) visión f de conjunto; (opinion) opinión f. **in my ~** a mi juicio. **in ~ of** en vista de. **on ~** expuesto. ●vt ver (scene, property); (consider) considerar. **~er** n (TV) televidente m & f. **~finder** n visor m. **~point** n punto m de vista

vigil|ance n vigilancia f. **~ant** adj vigilante

vigo|rous /'vɪgərəs/ adj enérgico; (growth) vigoroso. **~ur** /'vɪgə(r)/ n vigor m

vile /vaɪl/ adj (base) vil; (food) asqueroso; (weather, temper) horrible

village /'vɪlɪdʒ/ n pueblo m; (small) aldea f. **~r** n vecino m del pueblo; (of small village) aldeano m

villain /'vɪlən/ n maleante m & f; (in story etc) villano m

vindicate /'vɪndɪkeɪt/ vt justificar

vindictive /vɪn'dɪktɪv/ adj vengativo

vine /vaɪn/ n (on ground) vid f; (climbing) parra f

vinegar /'vɪnɪgə(r)/ n vinagre m

vineyard /'vɪnjəd/ n viña f

vintage /'vɪntɪdʒ/ n (year) cosecha f. ●adj (wine) añejo; (car) de época

vinyl /'vaɪnɪl/ n vinilo m

viola /vɪ'əʊlə/ n viola f

violat|e /'vaɪəleɪt/ vt violar. **~ion**
/-'leɪʃn/ n violación f

violen|ce /'vaɪələns/ n violencia f.
~t adj violento. **~tly** adv
violentamente

violet /'vaɪələt/ adj & n violeta (f);
(colour) violeta (m)

violin /vaɪə'lɪn/ n violín m. **~ist** n
violinista m & f

VIP /vi:aɪ'pi:/ abbr (= **very
important person**) VIP m

viper /'vaɪpə(r)/ n víbora f

virgin /'vɜːdʒɪn/ adj & n virgen (f)

Virgo /'vɜːgəʊ/ n Virgo f

virile /'vɪraɪl/ adj viril

virtual /'vɜːtʃʊəl/ adj. **traffic is at
a ~ standstill** el tráfico está
prácticamente paralizado. **~
reality** n realidad f virtual. **~ly**
adv prácticamente

virtue /'vɜːtʃu:/ n virtud f. **by ~ of**
en virtud de

virtuous /'vɜːtʃʊəs/ adj virtuoso

virulent /'vɪrʊlənt/ adj virulento

virus /'vaɪərəs/ n (pl **-uses**) virus m

visa /'vi:zə/ n visado m, visa f (LAm)

vise /vaɪs/ n (Amer) torno m de
banco

visib|ility /vɪzɪ'bɪlətɪ/ n visibilidad
f. **~le** /'vɪzɪbl/ adj visible; (sign,
improvement) evidente

vision /'vɪʒn/ n visión f; (sight)
vista f

visit /'vɪzɪt/ vt visitar; hacer una
visita a (a person). •vi hacer visitas.
~ with s.o. (Amer) ir a ver a uno.
•n visita f. **pay s.o. a ~** hacerle
una visita a uno. **~or** n visitante
m & f; (guest) visita f

visor /'vaɪzə(r)/ n visera f

visual /'vɪʒʊəl/ adj visual. **~ize** vt
imaginar(se); (foresee) prever

vital /'vaɪtl/ adj (essential) esencial;
(factor) de vital importancia; (organ)
vital. **~ity** /vaɪ'tælətɪ/ n vitalidad f

vitamin /'vɪtəmɪn/ n vitamina f.

vivacious /vɪ'veɪʃəs/ adj vivaz

vivid /'vɪvɪd/ adj vivo. **~ly** adv
intensamente; (describe)
gráficamente

vivisection /vɪvɪ'sekʃn/ n
vivisección f

vocabulary /və'kæbjʊlərɪ/ n
vocabulario m

vocal /'vəʊkl/ adj vocal. **~ist** n
cantante m & f

vocation /vəʊ'keɪʃn/ n vocación f.
~al adj profesional

vociferous /və'sɪfərəs/ adj
vociferador

vogue /vəʊg/ n moda f, boga f

voice /vɔɪs/ n voz f. •vt expresar

void /vɔɪd/ adj (not valid) nulo. •n
vacío m

volatile /'vɒlətaɪl/ adj volátil;
(person) imprevisible

volcan|ic /vɒl'kænɪk/ adj volcánico.
~o /vɒl'keɪnəʊ/ n (pl **-oes**)
volcán m

volley /'vɒlɪ/ n (pl **-eys**) (of gunfire)
descarga f cerrada; (sport) volea f.
~ball n vóleibol m

volt /vəʊlt/ n voltio m. **~age** /-ɪdʒ/
n voltaje m

volume /'vɒljuːm/ n volumen m;
(book) tomo m

voluntar|ily /'vɒləntərəlɪ/ adv
voluntariamente. **~y** adj
voluntario; (organization) de
beneficencia

volunteer /vɒlən'tɪə(r)/ n
voluntario m. •vt ofrecer. •vi. **~
(to)** ofrecerse (a)

vomit /'vɒmɪt/ vt/i vomitar. •n
vómito m

voracious /və'reɪʃəs/ adj voraz

vot|e /vəʊt/ n voto m; (right) derecho
m al voto; (act) votación f. •vi
votar. **~er** n votante m & f. **~ing** n
votación f

vouch /vaʊtʃ/ vi. **~ for s.o.**
responder por uno. **~er** /-ə(r)/ n
vale m

vow /vaʊ/ n voto m. •vi jurar

vowel /'vaʊəl/ n vocal f

voyage /'vɔɪɪdʒ/ n viaje m; (by sea) travesía f

vulgar /'vʌlɡə(r)/ adj (coarse) grosero, vulgar; (tasteless) de mal gusto. **~ity** /-'ɡærəti/ n vulgaridad f

vulnerable /'vʌlnərəbl/ adj vulnerable

vulture /'vʌltʃə(r)/ n buitre m

vying /'vaɪɪŋ/ see VIE

W abbr (= **West**) O

wad /wɒd/ n (of notes) fajo m; (tied together) lío m; (papers) montón m

waddle /'wɒdl/ vi contonearse

wade /weɪd/ vi caminar (por el agua etc)

wafer /'weɪfə(r)/ n galleta f de barquillo

waffle /'wɒfl/ n 🔧 palabrería f. •vi 🔧 divagar; (in essay, exam) meter paja 🔧. •n (Culin) gofre m, wafle m (LAm)

waft /wɒft/ vi flotar

wag /wæɡ/ vt (pt **wagged**) menear. •vi menearse

wage /weɪdʒ/ n sueldo m. **~s** npl salario m, sueldo m. **~r** n apuesta f

waggle /'wæɡl/ vt menear. •vi menearse

wagon /'wæɡən/ n carro m; (Rail) vagón m; (Amer, delivery truck) furgoneta f de reparto

wail /weɪl/ vi llorar

waist /weɪst/ n cintura f. **~coat** n chaleco m. **~line** n cintura f

wait /weɪt/ vi esperar; (at table) servir. **~ for** esperar. **~ on s.o.** atender a uno. •vt (await) esperar (chance, turn). **~ table** (Amer) servir a la mesa. **I can't ~ to see him** me muero de ganas de verlo. •n espera f. **lie in ~** acechar

waiter /'weɪtə(r)/ n camarero m, mesero m (LAm)

wait: **~ing-list** n lista f de espera. **~ing-room** n sala f de espera

waitress /'weɪtrɪs/ n camarera f, mesera f (LAm)

waive /weɪv/ vt renunciar a

wake /weɪk/ vt (pt **woke**, pp **woken**) despertar. •vi despertarse. •n (Naut) estela f. **In the ~ of** como resultado de. ■ **~ up** vt despertar. vi despertarse

Wales /weɪlz/ n (el país de) Gales

walk /wɔːk/ vi andar, caminar; (not ride) ir a pie; (stroll) pasear. •vt andar por (streets); llevar de paseo (dog). •n paseo m, (long) caminata f; (gait) manera f de andar. ■ **~ out** vi salir; (workers) declararse en huelga. ■ **~ out on** vt abandonar. **~er** n excursionista m & f

walkie-talkie /wɔːkɪ'tɔːkɪ/ n walkie-talkie m

walk: **~ing-stick** n bastón m. **W~man** /-mən/ n Walkman m ®. **~-out** n retirada en señal de protesta; (strike) abandono m del trabajo

wall /wɔːl/ n (interior) pared f; (exterior) muro m

wallet /'wɒlɪt/ n cartera f, billetera f

wallop /'wɒləp/ vt (pt **walloped**) 🔧 darle un golpazo a.

wallow /'wɒləʊ/ vi revolcarse

V

W

wallpaper /ˈwɔːlpeɪpə(r)/ n papel m pintado

walnut /ˈwɔːlnʌt/ n nuez f; (tree) nogal m

walrus /ˈwɔːlrəs/ n morsa f

waltz /wɔːls/ n vals m. ●vi valsar

wand /wɒnd/ n varita f (mágica)

wander /ˈwɒndə(r)/ vi vagar; (stroll) pasear; (digress) divagar. ●n vuelta f, paseo m. ~er n trotamundos m

wane /weɪn/ vi (moon) menguar; (interest) decaer. ●n. **be on the ~** (popularity) estar decayendo

wangle /wæŋgl/ vt 🔲 agenciarse

want /wɒnt/ vt querer; (need) necesitar. ●vi. ~ **for** carecer de. ●n necesidad f; (lack) falta f. ~ed adj (criminal) buscado

war /wɔː(r)/ n guerra f. **at ~** en guerra

warble /ˈwɔːbl/ vi trinar, gorjear

ward /wɔːd/ n (in hospital) sala f; (child) pupilo m. ■ ~ **off** vt conjurar (danger); rechazar (attack)

warden /ˈwɔːdn/ n guarda m

warder /ˈwɔːdə(r)/ n celador m (de una cárcel)

wardrobe /ˈwɔːdrəʊb/ n armario m; (clothes) guardarropa f, vestuario m

warehouse /ˈweəhaʊs/ n depósito m, almacén m

wares /weəz/ npl mercancía(s) f(pl)

war: ~fare n guerra f. ~**head** n cabeza f, ojiva f

warm /wɔːm/ adj (-er, -est) (water, day) tibio, templado; (room) caliente; (climate, wind) cálido; (clothes) de abrigo; (welcome) caluroso. **be ~** (person) tener calor. **it's ~ today** hoy hace calor. ●vt. ~ **(up)** calentar (room); recalentar (food); (fig) animar. ●vi. ~ **(up)** calentarse; (fig) animarse. ~-**blooded** /-ˈblʌdɪd/ adj de sangre caliente. ~**ly** adv (heartily) calurosamente. ~**th** n calor m; (of colour, atmosphere) calidez f

warn /wɔːn/ vt advertir. ~**ing** n

advertencia f; (notice) aviso m

warp /wɔːp/ vt alabear. ~**ed** /ˈwɔːpt/ adj (wood) alabeado; (mind) retorcido

warrant /ˈwɒrənt/ n orden f judicial; (search ~) orden f de registro; (for arrest) orden f de arresto. ●vt justificar. ~**y** n garantía f

warrior /ˈwɒrɪə(r)/ n guerrero m

warship /ˈwɔːʃɪp/ n buque m de guerra

wart /wɔːt/ n verruga f

wartime /ˈwɔːtaɪm/ n tiempo m de guerra

wary /ˈweərɪ/ adj (-ier, -iest) cauteloso. **be ~ of** recelar de

was /wəz, wɒz/ see BE

wash /wɒʃ/ vt lavar; fregar, lavar (LAm) (floor). ~ **one's face** lavarse la cara. ●vi lavarse. ●n (in washing machine) lavado m. **have a ~** lavarse. **I gave the car a ~** lavé el coche. ■ ~ **out** vt (clean) lavar; (rinse) enjuagar. ■ ~ **up** vi fregar los platos, lavar los trastes (Mex); (Amer, wash face and hands) lavarse. ~**able** adj lavable. ~**basin**, ~**bowl** (Amer) n lavabo m. ~**er** n arandela f. ~**ing** n lavado m; (dirty clothes) ropa f para lavar; (wet clothes) ropa f lavada. **do the ~ing** lavar la ropa, hacer la colada. ~**ing-machine** n máquina f de lavar, lavadora f. ~**ing-powder** n jabón m en polvo. ~**ing-up** n. **do the ~ing-up** lavar los platos, fregar (los platos). ~**ing-up liquid** n lavavajillas m. ~**out** n 🔲 desastre m. ~**room** n (Amer) baños mpl, servicios mpl

wasp /wɒsp/ n avispa f

waste /weɪst/ ●adj (matter) de desecho; (land) (barren) yermo; (uncultivated) baldío. ●n (of materials) desperdicio m; (of time) pérdida f; (refuse) residuos mpl. ●vt despilfarrar (electricity, money); desperdiciar (talent, effort); perder (time). ●vi. ~-**disposal unit** n trituradora f de desperdicios.

W

~ful adj poco económico; (person) despilfarrador. **~-paper basket** n papelera f

watch /wɒtʃ/ vt mirar; observar (person, expression); ver (TV); (keep an eye on) vigilar; (take heed) tener cuidado con. ●vi mirar. ●n (observation) vigilancia f; (period of duty) guardia f; (timepiece) reloj m. **~ out** vi (be careful) tener cuidado; (look carefully) estarse atento. **~dog** n perro m guardián. **~man** /-mən/ n (pl **-men**) vigilante m.

water /'wɔːtə(r)/ n agua f. ●vt regar (plants etc). ●vi (eyes) llorar. **make s.o.'s mouth ~** hacérsele la boca agua, hacérsele agua la boca (LAm). **~ down** vt diluir; aguar (wine). **~colour** n acuarela f. **~cress** n berro m. **~fall** n cascada f; (large) catarata f. **~ing-can** n regadera f. **~ lily** n nenúfar m. **~logged** /-lɒgd/ adj anegado; (shoes) empapado. **~proof** adj impermeable; (watch) sumergible. **~-skiing** n esquí m acuático. **~tight** adj hermético; (boat) estanco; (argument) irrebatible. **~way** n canal m navegable. **~y** adj acuoso; (eyes) lloroso

watt /wɒt/ n vatio m

wave /weɪv/ n onda f; (of hand) señal f; (fig) oleada f. ●vt agitar; (curl) ondular (hair). ●vi (signal) hacer señales con la mano; ondear (flag). **~band** n banda f de frecuencia. **~length** n longitud f de onda

waver /'weɪvə(r)/ vi (be indecisive) vacilar; (falter) flaquear

wavy /'weɪvɪ/ adj (-ier, -iest) ondulado

wax /wæks/ n cera f. ●vi (moon) crecer. **~work** n figura f de cera. **~works** npl museo m de cera

way /weɪ/ n (route) camino m; (manner) manera f, forma f, modo m; (direction) dirección f; (habit) costumbre f. **it's a long ~ from here** queda muy lejos de aquí. **be in the ~** estorbar. **by the ~** a propósito. **either ~** de cualquier

manera. **give ~** (collapse) ceder, romperse; (Auto) ceder el paso. **in a ~** en cierta manera. **in some ~s** en ciertos modos. **make ~** dejar paso a. **no ~!** ¡ni hablar! **on my ~ to** de camino a. **out of the ~** remoto; (extraordinary) fuera de lo común. **that ~** por allí. **this ~** por aquí. **~ in** n entrada f. **~lay** /weɪ'leɪ/ vt (pt **-laid**) abordar. **~ out** n salida f. **~-out** adj ultramoderno, original. **~s** npl costumbres fpl

we /wiː/ pron nosotros m, nosotras f

weak /wiːk/ adj (-er, -est) débil; (structure) poco sólido; (performance, student) flojo; (coffee) poco cargado; (solution) diluido; (beer) suave; (pej) aguado. **~en** vt debilitar. ●vi (resolve) flaquear. **~ling** n alfeñique m. **~ness** n debilidad f

wealth /welθ/ n riqueza f. **~y** adj (-ier, -iest) rico

weapon /'wepən/ n arma f. **~s of mass destruction** armas de destrucción masiva

wear /weə(r)/ vt (pt **wore**, pp **worn**) llevar; vestirse de (black, red, etc); (usually) usar. **I've got nothing to ~** no tengo nada que ponerme. ●vi (through use) gastarse; (last) durar. ●n en uso m; (damage) desgaste m; **~ and tear** desgaste m natural. ■ **~ out** vt gastar; (tire) agotar. vi gastarse

weary /'wɪərɪ/ adj (-ier, -iest) cansado. ●vt cansar. ●vi cansarse. **~ of** cansarse de

weather /'weðə(r)/ n tiempo m. **what's the ~ like?** ¿qué tiempo hace?. **the ~ was bad** hizo mal tiempo. **be under the ~** 🔲 no andar muy bien 🔲. ●vt (survive) sobrellevar. **~-beaten** adj curtido. **~ forecast** n pronóstico m del tiempo. **~vane** n veleta f

weave /wiːv/ vt (pt **wove**, pp **woven**) tejer; entretejer (threads). **~ one's way** abrirse paso. ●vi (person) zigzaguear; (road) serpentear. **~r** n tejedor m

W

web | we've

web /web/ n (of spider) telaraña f; (of intrigue) red f. ~ **page** n página web. ~ **site** n sitio web m

wed /wed/ vt (pt **wedded**) casarse con. ● vi casarse.

we'd /wi:d//wɪəd/ = **we had, we would**

wedding /'wedɪŋ/ n boda f, casamiento m. ~**-cake** n pastel m de boda. ~**-ring** n anillo m de boda

wedge /wedʒ/ n cuña f

Wednesday /'wenzdeɪ/ n miércoles m

wee /wi:/ adj 🄴 pequeñito. ● n. **have a** 🄴 hacer pis 🄴

weed /wi:d/ n mala hierba f. ● vt desherbar. ■ ~ **out** vt eliminar. ~**killer** n herbicida m. ~**y** adj (person) enclenque; (Amer, lanky) larguirucho 🄴

week /wi:k/ n semana f. ~**day** n día m de semana. ~**end** n fin m de semana. ~**ly** adj semanal. ● n semanario m. ● adv semanalmente

weep /wi:p/ vi (pt **wept**) llorar

weigh /weɪ/ vt/i pesar. ~ **anchor** levar anclas. ■ ~ **down** vt (fig) oprimir. ■ ~ **up** vt pesar; (fig) considerar

weight /weɪt/ n peso m; (sport) pesa f. **put on** ~ engordar. **lose** ~ adelgazar. ~**-lifting** n halterofilia f, levantamiento m de pesos

weir /wɪə(r)/ n presa f

weird /wɪəd/ adj (**-er, -est**) raro, extraño; (unearthly) misterioso

welcom|e /'welkəm/ adj bienvenido. **you're** ~**e!** (after thank you) ¡de nada! ● n bienvenida f; (reception) acogida f. ● vt dar la bienvenida a; (appreciate) alegrarse de. ~**ing** adj acogedor

weld /weld/ vt soldar. ● n soldadura f. ~**er** n soldador m

welfare /'welfeə(r)/ n bienestar m; (aid) asistencia f social. **W**~ **State** n estado m benefactor

well /wel/ adv (**better, best**) bien.

~ **done!** ¡muy bien!, ¡bravo! **as** ~ también. **as** ~ **as** además de. **we may as** ~ **go tomorrow** más vale que vayamos mañana. **do** ~ (succeed) tener éxito. **very** ~ muy bien. ● adj bien. **I'm very** ~ estoy muy bien. ● int (introducing, continuing sentence) bueno; (surprise) ¡vaya!; (indignation, resignation) bueno. ~ **I never!** ¡no me digas! ● n pozo m

we'll /wi:l//wɪəl/ = **we will**

well: ~**-behaved** /-bɪ'heɪvd/ adj que se porta bien, bueno. ~**-educated** /-'edjʊkeɪtɪd/ adj culto.

wellington (boot) /'welɪŋtən/ n bota f de goma or de agua; (Amer, short boot) botín m

well: ~**-known** /-'nəʊn/ adj conocido. ~ **off** adj adinerado. ~**-stocked** /-'stɒkt/ adj bien provisto. ~**-to-do** /-tə'du:/ adj adinerado

Welsh /welʃ/ adj & n galés (m). **the** ~ n los galeses

went /went/ see GO

wept /wept/ see WEEP

were /wɜ:(r), wə(r)/ see BE

we're /wɪə(r)/ = **we are**

west /west/ n oeste m. **the W**~ el Occidente m. ● adj oeste; (wind) del oeste. ● adv (go) hacia el oeste, al oeste. **it's** ~ **of York** está al oeste de York. ~**erly** /-əlɪ/ adj (wind) del oeste. ~**ern** /-ən/ adj occidental. ● n (film) película f del Oeste. ~**erner** n occidental m & f. **W**~ **Indian** adj & n antillano (m). **W**~ **Indies** npl Antillas fpl

wet /wet/ adj (**wetter, wettest**) mojado; (rainy) lluvioso; (fam, person) soso. '~ **paint**' 'pintura fresca'. **get** ~ mojarse. **he got his feet** ~ se mojó los pies. ● vt (pt **wetted**) mojar; (dampen) humedecer. ~ **o.s.** orinarse. ~**back** n espalda f mojada. ~ **blanket** n aguafiestas m & f. ~ **suit** n traje m de neopreno

we've /wi:v/ = **we have**

whack /wæk/ vt 🔊 golpear. ●n 🔊 golpe m.

whale /weɪl/ n ballena f. **we had a ~ of a time** 🔊 lo pasamos bomba 🔊

wham /wæm/ int ¡zas!

wharf /wɔːf/ n (pl **wharves** or **wharfs**) muelle m

what /wɒt/

●adjective

····▸ (in questions) qué. **~ perfume are you wearing?** ¿qué perfume llevas?. **~ colour are the walls?** ¿de qué color son las paredes?

····▸ (in exclamations) qué. **~ a beautiful house!** ¡qué casa más linda!. **~ a lot of people!** ¡cuánta gente!

····▸ (in indirect speech) qué. **I'll ask him ~ bus to take** le preguntaré qué autobús hay que tomar. **do you know ~ time it leaves?** ¿sabes a qué hora sale?

●pronoun

····▸ (in questions) qué. **~ is it?** ¿qué es? **~ for?** ¿para qué? **~'s the problem?** ¿cuál es el problema? **~'s he like?** ¿cómo es? **what?** (say that again) ¿cómo?, ¿qué?

····▸ (in indirect questions) qué. **I didn't know ~ to do** no sabía qué hacer

····▸ (relative) lo que. **I did ~ I could** hice lo que pude. **~ I need is a new car** lo que necesito es un coche nuevo

····▸ (in phrases) **~ about me?** ¿y yo qué? **~ if she doesn't come?** ¿y si no viene?

whatever /wɒt'evə(r)/ adj cualquiera. ●pron (todo) lo que, cualquier cosa que

whatsoever /wɒtsəʊ'evə(r)/ adj & pron = **whatever**

wheat /wiːt/ n trigo m

wheel /wiːl/ n rueda f. **at the ~** al volante. ●vt empujar (bicycle etc); llevar (en silla de ruedas etc) (person). **~barrow** n carretilla f. **~chair** n silla f de ruedas

wheeze /wiːz/ vi respirar con dificultad

when /wen/ adv cuándo. ●conj cuando. **~ever** /-'evə(r)/ adv (every time that) cada vez que, siempre que; (at whatever time) **we'll go ~ever you're ready** saldremos cuando estés listo

where /weə(r)/ adv & conj donde; (interrogative) dónde. **~ are you going?** ¿adónde vas? **~ are you from?** ¿de dónde eres?. **~abouts** /-əbaʊts/ adv en qué parte. ●n paradero m. **~as** /-'æz/ conj por cuanto; (in contrast) mientras (que). **~ver** /weər'evə(r)/ adv (in questions) dónde; (no matter where) en cualquier parte. ●conj donde (+ subjunctive), dondequiera (+ subjunctive)

whet /wet/ vt (pt **whetted**) abrir (appetite)

whether /'weðə(r)/ conj si. **I don't know ~ she will like it** no sé si le gustará. **~ you like it or not** te guste o no te guste

which /wɪtʃ/ adj (in questions) (sing) qué, cuál; (pl) qué, cuáles. **~ one** cuál. **~ one of you** cuál de ustedes. ●pron (in questions) (sing) cuál; (pl) cuáles; (relative) que; (object) el cual, la cual, lo cual, los cuales, las cuales. **~ever** /-'evə(r)/ adj cualquier. ●pron cualquiera que, el que, la que; (in questions) cuál; (pl) cuáles

while /waɪl/ n rato m. **a ~ ago** hace un rato. ●conj mientras; (although) aunque. ■**~ away** vt pasar (time)

whilst /waɪlst/ conj see **WHILE**

whim /wɪm/ n capricho m

whimper /'wɪmpə(r)/ vi gimotear. ●n quejido m

whine /waɪn/ vi (person) gemir; (child) lloriquear; (dog) aullar

whip /wɪp/ n látigo m; (for punishment) azote m. •vt (pt **whipped** /wɪpt/) fustigar, pegarle a (con la fusta) (horse); azotar (person); (Culin) batir

whirl /wɜ:l/ vi girar rápidamente. ~**pool** n remolino m. ~**wind** n torbellino m

whirr /wɜ:(r)/ n zumbido m. •vi zumbar

whisk /wɪsk/ vt (Culin) batir. •n (Culin) batidor m. ~ **away** llevarse

whisker /'wɪskə(r)/ n pelo m. ~s npl (of cat etc) bigotes mpl

whisky /'wɪskɪ/ n whisky m, güisqui m

whisper /'wɪspə(r)/ vt susurrar. •vi cuchichear. •n susurro m

whistle /'wɪsl/ n silbido m; (loud) chiflado m; (instrument) silbato m, pito m. •vt/i silbar; (loudly) chiflar

white /waɪt/ adj (-**er**, -**est**) blanco. **go** ~ ponerse pálido. •n blanco; (of egg) clara f. ~ **coffee** n café m con leche. ~-**collar worker** n empleado m de oficina. ~ **elephant** n objeto m inútil y costoso. ~-**hot** adj (metal) al rojo blanco. ~ **lie** n mentirijilla f. ~**n** vt/i blanquear. ~**wash** n cal f; (cover-up) tapadera f 🔲. •vt blanquear, encalar

Whitsun /'wɪtsn/ n Pentecostés m

whiz /wɪz/ vi (pt **whizzed**). ~ **by**, ~ **past** pasar zumbando. ~-**kid** n 🔲 lince m 🔲

who /hu:/ pron (in questions) quién; (pl) quiénes; (as relative) que; **the girl** ~ **lives there** la chica que vive allí. **those** ~ **can't come tomorrow** los que no puedan venir mañana. ~**ever** /hu:'evə(r)/ pron quienquiera que; (interrogative) quién

whole /həʊl/ adj. **the** ~ **country** todo el país. **there's a** ~ **bottle left** queda una botella entera. •n todo m, conjunto m; (total) total m. **on the** ~ en general. ~-**hearted** /-'hɑ:tɪd/ adj (support) incondicional; (approval) sin reservar. ~**meal** adj

integral. ~**sale** n venta f al por mayor. •adj & adv al por mayor. ~**some** /-səm/ adj sano

wholly /'həʊlɪ/ adv completamente

whom /hu:m/ pron que, a quien; (in questions) a quién

whooping cough /'hu:pɪŋ/ n tos f convulsa

whore /hɔ:(r)/ n puta f

whose /hu:z/ pron de quién; (pl) de quiénes. •adj (in questions) de quién; (pl) de quiénes; (relative) cuyo; (pl) cuyos

why /waɪ/ adv por qué. ~ **not?** ¿por qué no? **that's** ~ **I couldn't go** por eso no pude ir. •int ¡vaya!

wick /wɪk/ n mecha f

wicked /'wɪkɪd/ adj malo; (mischievous) travieso; (fam, very bad) malísimo

wicker /'wɪkə(r)/ n mimbre m. •adj de mimbre. ~**work** n artículos mpl de mimbre

wicket /'wɪkɪt/ n (cricket) rastrillo m

wide /waɪd/ adj (-**er**, -**est**) ancho; (range, experience) amplio; (off target) desviado. **it's four metres** ~ tiene cuatro metros de ancho. •adv. **open** ~! abra bien la boca. ~ **awake** adj completamente despierto; (fig) despabilado. **I left the door** ~ **open** dejé la puerta abierta de par en par. ~**ly** adv extensamente; (believed) generalmente; (different) muy. ~**n** vt ensanchar. •vi ensancharse. ~**spread** adj extendido; (fig) difundido

widow /'wɪdəʊ/ n viuda f. ~**er** n viudo m.

width /wɪdθ/ n anchura f. **in** ~ de ancho

wield /wi:ld/ vt manejar; ejercer (power)

wife /waɪf/ n (pl **wives**) mujer f, esposa f

wig /wɪg/ n peluca f

wiggle /'wɪgl/ vt menear. •vi menearse

W

wild /waɪld/ adj (-er, -est) (animal) salvaje; (flower) silvestre; (country) agreste; (enraged) furioso; (idea) extravagante; (with joy) loco. **a ~ guess** una conjetura hecha totalmente al azar. **I'm not ~ about the idea** la idea no me enloquece. ●adv en estado salvaje. **run ~** (children) criarse como salvajes. **~s** npl regiones fpl salvajes. **~erness** /ˈwɪldənɪs/ n páramo m. **~fire** n. **spread like ~fire** correr como un reguero de pólvora. **~-goose chase** n empresa f inútil. **~life** n fauna f. **~ly** adv violentamente; (fig) locamente

will /wɪl/
●auxiliary verb

past **would**; contracted forms **I'll, you'll**, etc = I will, you will, etc.; **won't** = will not

····▸ (talking about the future)

❗ The Spanish future tense is not always the first option for translating the English future tense. The present tense of ir a + a + verb is commonly used instead, particularly in Latin American countries. **he'll be here on Tuesday** estará el martes, va a estar el martes, **she won't agree** no va a aceptar, no aceptará

····▸ (in invitations and requests) **~ you have some wine?** ¿quieres (un poco de) vino? **you'll stay for dinner, won't you?** te quedas a cenar, ¿no?

····▸ (in tag questions) **you ~ be back soon, won't you?** vas a volver pronto, ¿no?

····▸ (in short answers) **will it be ready by Monday? - yes, it ~** ¿estará listo para el lunes? - sí

●noun

····▸ (mental power) voluntad f

····▸ (document) testamento m

willing /ˈwɪlɪŋ/ adj complaciente. **~**

to dispuesto a. **~ly** adv de buena gana

willow /ˈwɪləʊ/ n sauce m

will-power /ˈwɪlpaʊə(r)/ n fuerza f de voluntad

wilt /wɪlt/ vi marchitarse

win /wɪn/ vt (pt **won**, pres p **winning**) ganar; (achieve, obtain) conseguir. ●vi ganar. ●n victoria f. ■ **~ over** vt ganarse a

wince /wɪns/ vi hacer una mueca de dolor

winch /wɪntʃ/ n cabrestante m. ●vt levantar con un cabrestante

wind¹ /wɪnd/ n viento m; (in stomach) gases mpl. **~ instrument** instrumento m de viento. ●vt dejar sin aliento

wind² /waɪnd/ vt (pt **wound**) (wrap around) enrollar; dar cuerda a (clock etc). ●vi (road etc) serpentear. ■ **~ up** vt dar cuerda a (watch, clock); (fig) terminar, concluir

winding /ˈwaɪndɪŋ/ adj tortuoso

windmill /ˈwɪndmɪl/ n molino m (de viento)

window /ˈwɪndəʊ/ n ventana f; (in shop) escaparate m, vitrina f (LAm), vidriera f (LAm), aparador m (Mex); (of vehicle, booking-office) ventanilla f; (Comp) ventana f, window m. **~ box** n jardinera f. **~-shop** vi mirar los escaparates. **~sill** n alféizar m or repisa f de la ventana

wine /waɪn/ n vino m. **~-cellar** n bodega f. **~glass** n copa f de vino. **~-growing** n vinicultura f. ●adj vinícola. **~ list** n lista f de vinos. **~-tasting** n cata f de vinos

wing /wɪŋ/ n ala f; (Auto) aleta f. **under one's ~** bajo la protección de uno. **~er** n (Sport) ala m & f. **~s** npl (in theatre) bastidores m

wink /wɪŋk/ vi guiñar el ojo; (light etc) centellear. ●n guiño m. **not to sleep a ~** no pegar ojo

win: ~ner n ganador m. **~ning-post** n poste m de llegada. **~nings** npl ganancias fpl

W

wint|er /'wɪntə(r)/ n invierno m. •vi invernar. **~ry** adj invernal

wipe /waɪp/ vt limpiar, pasarle un trapo a; (dry) secar. **~ one's nose** limpiarse la nariz. •n. **give sth a ~** limpiar algo, pasarle un trapo a algo. ∎**~ out** vt (cancel) cancelar; (destroy) destruir; (obliterate) borrar. ∎**~ up** vt limpiar

wir|e /'waɪə(r)/ n alambre m; (Elec) cable m. **~ing** n instalación f eléctrica

wisdom /'wɪzdəm/ n sabiduría f. **~ tooth** n muela f del juicio

wise /waɪz/ adj (**-er, -est**) sabio; (sensible) prudente; (decision, choice) acertado. **~ly** adv sabiamente; (sensibly) prudentemente

wish /wɪʃ/ n deseo m; (greeting) saludo m. **make a ~** pedir un deseo. **best ~es, John** (in letters) saludos de John, un abrazo de John. •vt desear. **~ s.o. well** desear buena suerte a uno. **I ~ I were rich** ¡ojalá fuera rico! **he ~ed he hadn't told her** lamentó habérselo dicho. **~ful thinking** n ilusiones fpl

wistful /'wɪstfl/ adj melancólico

wit /wɪt/ n gracia f; (intelligence) ingenio m. **be at one's ~s' end** no saber más qué hacer

witch /wɪtʃ/ n bruja f. **~craft** n brujería f.

with /wɪð/ prep con; (cause, having) de. **come ~ me** ven conmigo. **take it ~ you** llévalo contigo; (formal) llévelo consigo. **the man ~ the beard** el hombre de la barba. **trembling ~ fear** temblando de miedo

withdraw /wɪð'drɔ:/ vt (pt **withdrew**, pp **withdrawn**) retirar. •vi apartarse. **~al** n retirada f. **~n** adj (person) retraído

wither /'wɪðə(r)/ vi marchitarse

withhold /wɪð'həʊld/ vt (pt **withheld**) retener; (conceal) ocultar (**from** a)

within /wɪð'ɪn/ prep dentro de. •adv dentro. **~ sight** a la vista

without /wɪð'aʊt/ prep sin. **~ paying** sin pagar

withstand /wɪð'stænd/ vt (pt **-stood**) resistir

witness /'wɪtnɪs/ n testigo m; (proof) testimonio m. •vt presenciar; atestiguar (signature). **~box** n tribuna f de los testigos

witt|icism /'wɪtɪsɪzəm/ n ocurrencia f. **~y** /'wɪtɪ/ adj (**-ier, -iest**) gracioso

wives /waɪvz/ see **WIFE**

wizard /'wɪzəd/ n hechicero m

wizened /'wɪznd/ adj arrugado

wobble /'wɒbl/ vi (chair) tambalearse; (bicycle) bambolearse; (voice, jelly, hand) temblar. **~y** adj (chair etc) cojo

woe /wəʊ/ n aflicción f

woke /wəʊk/, **woken** /'wəʊkən/ see **WAKE**

wolf /wʊlf/ n (pl **wolves** /wʊlvz/) lobo m

woman /'wʊmən/ n (pl **women**) mujer f

womb /wu:m/ n matriz f

women /'wɪmɪn/ npl see **WOMAN**

won /wʌn/ see **WIN**

wonder /'wʌndə(r)/ n maravilla f; (bewilderment) asombro m. **no ~** no es de extrañarse (**that** que). •vt (ask oneself) preguntarse. **I ~ whose book this is** me pregunto de quién será este libro; (in polite requests) **I ~ if you could help me?** ¿me podría ayudar? **~ful** adj maravilloso. **~fully** adv maravillosamente

won't /wəʊnt/ = **will not**

wood /wʊd/ n madera f; (for burning) leña f; (area) bosque m. **~ed** adj poblado de árboles, boscoso. **~en** adj de madera. **~land** n bosque m. **~wind** /-wɪnd/ n instrumentos mpl de viento de madera. **~work** n carpintería f; (in room etc) maderaje

W

m. ~**worm** n carcoma f. ~**y** adj
leñoso

wool /wʊl/ n lana f. **pull the ~
over s.o.'s eyes** engañar a uno.
~**len** adj de lana. ~**y** adj (**-ier,
-iest**) de lana; (unclear) vago. • n
jersey m

word /wɜːd/ n palabra f; (news)
noticia f. **by ~ of mouth** de
palabra. **I didn't say a ~** yo no
dije nada. **in other ~s** es decir.
• vt expresar. ~**ing** n redacción f;
(of question) formulación f. ~
processor n procesador m de
textos. ~**y** adj prolijo

wore /wɔː(r)/ see WEAR

work /wɜːk/ n trabajo m; (arts) obra
f. **be out of ~** estar sin trabajo,
estar desocupado. • vt hacer
trabajar; manejar (machine). • vi
trabajar; (machine) funcionar;
(student) estudiar; (drug etc) surtir
efecto. ■ ~ **off** vt desahogar. ■ ~
out vt resolver (problem); (calculate)
calcular; (understand) entender. • vi
(succeed) salir bien; (Sport)
entrenarse. ■ ~ **up** vt. **get ~ed
up** exaltarse. ~**able** adj (project,
solution) factible. ~**er** n trabajador
m; (manual) obrero m; (in office, bank)
empleado m. ~**ing** adj (day)
laborable; (clothes etc) de trabajo. **in
~ing order** en estado de
funcionamiento. ~**ing class** n
clase f obrera. ~**ing-class** adj de la
clase obrera. ~**man** /-mən/ n (pl
-men) obrero m. ~**manship** n
destreza f. ~**s** npl (building) fábrica
f; (Mec) mecanismo m. ~**shop** n
taller m

world /wɜːld/ n mundo m. **out of
this ~** maravilloso. • adj mundial.
W~ Cup n. **the W~ Cup** la Copa
del Mundo. ~**ly** adj mundano.
~**wide** adj universal. **W~ Wide
Web** n World Wide Web m

worm /wɜːm/ n gusano m, lombriz f

worn /wɔːn/ see WEAR. • adj gastado.
~**-out** adj gastado; (person) rendido

worr|ied /'wʌrɪd/ adj preocupado.
~**y** /'wʌrɪ/ vt preocupar; (annoy)
molestar. • vi preocuparse. • n

preocupación f. ~**ying** adj
inquietante

worse /wɜːs/ adj peor. **get ~**
empeorar. • adv peor; (more) más.
~**n** vt/i empeorar

worship /'wɜːʃɪp/ n culto m; (title)
Su Señoría. • vt (pt **worshipped**)
adorar

worst /wɜːst/ adj peor. **he's the ~
in the class** es el peor de la clase.
• adv peor. • n. **the ~** lo peor

worth /wɜːθ/ n valor m. • adj. **be ~**
valer. **it's ~ trying** vale la pena
probarlo. **it was ~ my while**
(me) valió la pena. ~**less** adj sin
valor. ~**while** /-'waɪl/ adj que vale
la pena. ~**y** /'wɜːðɪ/ adj meritorio;
(respectable) respetable; (laudable)
loable

would /wʊd/ modal verb. (in conditional
sentences) ~ **you go?** ¿irías tú? **he
~ come if he could** vendría si
pudiera; (in reported speech) **I
thought you'd forget** pensé que
te olvidarías; (in requests, invitations)
~ **you come here, please?**
¿quieres venir aquí? ~ **you
switch the television off?**
¿podrías apagar la televisión?; (be
prepared to) **he ~n't listen to me**
no me quería escuchar

wound¹ /wuːnd/ n herida f. • vt
herir

wound² /waʊnd/ see WIND²

wove, woven /wəʊv, 'wəʊvn/ see
WEAVE

wow /waʊ/ int ¡ah!

wrangle /'ræŋɡl/ vi reñir. • n riña f

wrap /ræp/ vt (pt **wrapped**)
envolver. • n bata f; (shawl) chal m.
~**per** n, ~**ping** n envoltura f

wrath /rɒθ/ n ira f

wreak /riːk/ vt sembrar. ~ **havoc**
causar estragos

wreath /riːθ/ n (pl **-ths** /-ðz/)
corona f

wreck /rek/ n (ship) restos mpl de
un naufragio; (vehicle) restos mpl de
un avión siniestrado. **be a**

W

nervous ~ tener los nervios destrozados. •vt provocar el naufragio de (ship); destrozar (car); (Amer, demolish) demoler; (fig) destrozar. **~age** /-ɪdʒ/ n restos mpl; (of building) ruinas fpl

wrench /rentʃ/ vt arrancar; (sprain) desgarrarse; dislocarse (joint). •n tirón m; (emotional) dolor m (causado por una separación); (tool) llave f inglesa

wrestl|e /'resl/ vi luchar. **~er** n luchador m. **~ing** n lucha f

wretch /retʃ/ n (despicable person) desgraciado m; (unfortunate person) desdichado m. **~ed** /-ɪd/ adj desdichado; (weather) horrible

wriggle /'rɪɡl/ vi retorcerse. ~ **out of** escaparse de

wring /rɪŋ/ vt (pt **wrung**) retorcer (neck). ~ **out of** (obtain from) arrancar. ■ ~ **out** vt retorcer

wrinkl|e /'rɪŋkl/ n arruga f. •vt arrugar. •vi arrugarse. **~y** adj arrugado

wrist /rɪst/ n muñeca f. **~watch** n reloj m de pulsera

writ /rɪt/ n orden m judicial

write /raɪt/ vt/i (pt **wrote**, pp **written**, pres p **writing**) escribir. ■ ~ **down** vt anotar. ■ ~ **off** vt cancelar (debt). **~-off** n. **the car**

was a ~-off el coche fue declarado un siniestro total. **~r** n escritor m

writhe /raɪð/ vi retorcerse

writing /'raɪtɪŋ/ n (script) escritura f; (handwriting) letra f. **in ~** por escrito. **~s** npl obra f, escritos mpl. ~ **desk** n escritorio m. ~ **pad** n bloc n. ~ **paper** n papel m de escribir

written /'rɪtn/ see WRITE

wrong /rɒŋ/ adj equivocado, incorrecto; (not just) injusto; (mistaken) equivocado. **be ~** no tener razón; (be mistaken) equivocarse. **what's ~?** ¿qué pasa? **it's ~ to steal** robar está mal. **what's ~ with that?** ¿qué hay de malo en eso?. •adv mal. **go ~** equivocarse; (plan) salir mal. •n injusticia f; (evil) mal m. **in the ~** equivocado. •vt ser injusto con. **~ful** adj injusto. **~ly** adv mal; (unfairly) injustamente

wrote /rəʊt/ see WRITE

wrought iron /rɔːt/ n hierro m forjado

wrung /rʌŋ/ see WRING

wry /raɪ/ adj (**wryer**, **wryest**) irónico. **make a ~ face** torcer el gesto

Xx, Yy, Zz

xerox /'zɪərɒks/ vt fotocopiar, xerografiar

Xmas /'krɪsməs/ n abbr (**Christmas**) Navidad f

X-ray /'eksreɪ/ n (ray) rayo m X; (photograph) radiografía f. **~s** npl rayos mpl. •vt hacer una radiografía de

xylophone /'zaɪləfəʊn/ n xilofón m, xilófono m

yacht /jɒt/ n yate m. **~ing** n

navegación f a vela

yank /jæŋk/ vt 🄴 tirar de (violentamente)

Yankee /'jæŋkɪ/ n 🄴 yanqui m & f

yap /jæp/ vi (pt **yapped**) (dog) ladrar (con ladridos agudos)

yard /jɑːd/ n patio m; (Amer, garden) jardín m; (measurement) yarda f (= 0.9144 metre)

yarn /jɑːn/ n hilo m; (fam, tale) cuento m

yawn /jɔːn/ vi bostezar. ● n bostezo m

yeah /jeə/ adv 🄸 sí

year /jɪə(r)/ n año m. **be three ~s old** tener tres años. **~ly** adj anual. ● adv cada año

yearn /ˈjɜːn/ vi. **~ to do sth** anhelar hacer algo. **~ for sth** añorar algo. **~ing** n anhelo m, ansia f

yeast /jiːst/ n levadura f

yell /jel/ vi gritar. ● n grito m

yellow /ˈjeləʊ/ adj & n amarillo (m)

yelp /jelp/ n gañido m. ● vi gañir

yes /jes/ int & n sí (m)

yesterday /ˈjestədeɪ/ adv & n ayer (m). **the day before ~** anteayer m. **~ morning** ayer por la mañana, ayer en la mañana (LAm)

yet /jet/ adv todavía, aún; (already) ya. **as ~** hasta ahora; (as a linker) sin embargo. ● conj pero

Yiddish /ˈjɪdɪʃ/ n yídish m

yield /jiːld/ vt (surrender) ceder; producir (crop/mineral); dar (results). ● vi ceder. **'yield'** (Amer, traffic sign) ceda el paso. ● n rendimiento m

yoga /ˈjəʊɡə/ n yoga m

yoghurt /ˈjɒɡət/ n yogur m

yoke /jəʊk/ n (fig also) yugo m

yokel /ˈjəʊkl/ n palurdo m

yolk /jəʊk/ n yema f (de huevo)

you /juː/ pronoun
····▶ (as the subject) (familiar form) (sing) tú, vos (River Plate and parts of Central America); (pl) vosotros, -tras (Spain), ustedes (LAm); (formal) (sing) usted; (pl) ustedes

❗ In Spanish the subject pronoun is usually only used to give emphasis or mark contrast.

····▶ (as the direct object) (familiar form) (sing) te; (pl) os (Spain), los, las (LAm); (formal) (sing) lo or (Spain) le, la; (pl) los or (Spain) les, las. **I love ~** te quiero

····▶ (as the indirect object) (familiar form) (sing) te; (pl) os (Spain), les (LAm); (formal) (sing) le; (pl) les. **I sent ~ the book yesterday** te mandé el libro ayer

❗ The pronoun se replaces the indirect object pronoun le or les when the latter is used with the direct object pronoun (lo, la etc), e.g. **I gave it to ~** se lo di

····▶ (when used after a preposition) (familiar form) (sing) ti, vos (River Plate and parts of Central America); (pl) vosotros, -tras (Spain), ustedes (LAm); (formal) (sing) usted; (pl) ustedes

····▶ (generalizing) uno, tú (esp Spain). **~ feel very proud** uno se siente muy orgulloso, te sientes muy orgulloso (esp Spain). **~ have to be patient** hay que tener paciencia

you'd /juːd/, /jʊəd/ = you had, you would

you'll /juːl/, /jʊəl/ = you will

young /jʌŋ/ adj (-er, -est) joven. **my ~er sister** mi hermana menor. **he's a year ~er than me** tiene un año menos que yo. **~ lady** n señorita f. **~ man** n joven m. **~ster** /-stə(r)/ n joven m

your /jɔː(r)/ adj (belonging to one person) (sing, familiar) tu; (pl, familiar) tus; (sing, formal) su; (pl, formal) sus; (belonging to more than one person) (sing, familiar) vuestro, -tra, su (LAm); (pl, familiar) vuestros, -tras, sus (LAm); (sing, formal) su; (pl, formal) sus

you're /jʊə(r)/, /jɔː(r)/ = you are

yours /jɔːz/ poss pron (belonging to one person) (sing, familiar) tuyo, -ya; (pl, familiar) tuyos, -yas; (sing, formal) suyo, -ya; (pl, formal) suyos, -yas. (belonging to more than one person) (sing, familiar) vuestro, -tra; (pl, familiar) vuestros, -tras, suyos, -yas (LAm); (sing, formal) suyo, -ya; (pl, formal)

y

suyos, -yas. **an aunt of** ~ una tía tuya/suya; ~ **is here** el tuyo/la tuya/el suyo/la suya está aquí

yoursel|f /jɔːˈself/ pron (reflexive). (emphatic use) 1 tú mismo, tú misma; (formal) usted mismo, usted misma. **describe** ~**f** descríbete; (Ud form) descríbase. **stop thinking about** ~**f** 1 deja de pensar en ti mismo; (formal) deje de pensar en sí mismo. **by** ~**f** solo, sola. ~**ves** /jɔːˈselvz/ pron vosotros mismos, vosotras mismas (familiar), ustedes mismos, ustedes mismas (LAm familiar), ustedes mismos, ustedes mismas (formal); (reflexive). **behave** ~**ves** ¡portaos bien! (familiar), ¡pórtense bien! (formal, LAm familiar). **by** ~**ves** solos, solas

youth /juːθ/ n (pl youths /juːðz/) (early life) juventud f; (boy) joven m; (young people) juventud f. ~**ful** adj joven, juvenil. ~ **hostel** n albergue m juvenil

you've /juːv/ = **you have**

Yugoslav /ˈjuːɡəslɑːv/ adj & n yugoslavo (m). ~**ia** /-ˈslɑːvɪə/ n Yugoslavia f

zeal /ziːl/ n fervor m, celo m

zeal|ot /ˈzelət/ n fanático m. ~**ous** /-əs/ adj ferviente; (worker) que pone gran celo en su trabajo

zebra /ˈzebrə/ n cebra f. ~ **crossing** n paso m de cebra

zenith /ˈzenɪθ/ n cenit m

zero /ˈzɪərəʊ/ n (pl **-os**) cero m

zest /zest/ n entusiasmo m; (peel) cáscara f

zigzag /ˈzɪɡzæɡ/ n zigzag m. ●vi (pt **zigzagged**) zigzaguear

zilch /zɪltʃ/ n ⊠ nada de nada

zinc /zɪŋk/ n cinc m

zip /zɪp/ n cremallera f, cierre m (LAm), zíper m (Mex). ●vt. ~ **(up)** cerrar (la cremallera). **Z**~ **code** n (Amer) código m postal. ~ **fastener** n cremallera f. ~**per** n/vt see **ZIP**

zodiac /ˈzəʊdɪæk/ n zodíaco m, zodiaco m

zombie /ˈzɒmbɪ/ n zombi m & f

zone /zəʊn/ n zona f. **time** ~ n huso m horario

zoo /zuː/ n zoo m, zoológico m. ~**logical** /zuːəˈlɒdʒɪkl/ adj zoológico. ~**logist** /zuːˈɒlədʒɪst/ n zoólogo m. ~**logy** /zuːˈɒlədʒɪ/ n zoología f

zoom /zuːm/. ■ ~ **in** vi (Photo) hacer un zoom in (**on** sobre). ■ ~ **past** vi/t pasar zumbando. ~ **lens** n teleobjetivo m, zoom m

zucchini /zʊˈkiːnɪ/ n (invar or ~**s**) (Amer) calabacín m

y
z

Summary of Spanish grammar

1 Nouns

All Spanish nouns are either masculine or feminine in gender, including nouns referring to objects or ideas. For this reason every Spanish noun mentioned in both sides of the dictionary is accompanied by gender information, shown in italics, *m* for masculine and *f* for feminine. Some nouns can be both masculine and feminine and this is indicated by the abbreviation *mf*, e.g. **belga** *mf* Belgian. Some nouns vary in gender according to region, e.g. **radio** (= radio) is masculine in most of Latin America and feminine in Spain. This information is also given in both sides of the dictionary. The following general rules will help to determine the gender of many nouns:

The following nouns are masculine:

- Male humans and male animals: **el hombre** *man*, **el muchacho** *boy*, **el toro** *bull*, **el león** *lion*, **el gallo** *cockerel*
- Nouns ending in **-o**: **el libro** *book*, **el rollo** *roll*, **el bolígrafo** *ballpoint pen*. Exceptions: **la mano** *hand*, **la foto** *photo*, **la moto** *motor-bike*
- Nouns ending in **-aje**: **el viaje** *journey*, **el equipaje** *luggage*
- Nouns ending in a stressed vowel (i.e. an accented vowel): **el tisú** *tissue*, **el menú** *menu*, **el sofá** *sofa*
- Days of the week and months: **el lunes** *Monday*, **los domingos** *Sundays*, **un diciembre frío** *a cold December*

The following nouns are feminine:

- Female humans and female animals: **la mujer** *woman*, **la actriz** *actress*, **la vaca** *cow*, **la gallina** *chicken*
- Nouns ending in **-a** (but see 'Gender problems' below for words ending in **-ma**): **la casa** *house*, **la comida** *meal*, **la camiseta** *tee-shirt*. Exceptions: **el día** *day*, **el mapa** *map*, **el planeta** *planet*, **el tranvía** *tramway*

- Nouns ending in **-ción**: **la nación** *nation*, **la calefacción** *heating*, **la elección** *election*

- Nouns ending in **-dad**, **-tad**, **-tud**, or **-is**; **la ciudad** *city*, **la libertad** *liberty*, **la actitud** *attitude*, **la crisis** *crisis*, **la apendicitis** *appendicitis*. Exceptions: **el análisis** *analysis*, **el tenis** *tennis*

Gender problems

- Some common nouns ending in **-ma** are masculine, e.g. **el programa** *programme*, **el diagrama** *diagram*, **el clima** *climate*, **el problema** *problem*

- Some nouns change their meaning according to their gender: **el corte** *cut*, but **la corte** *court* (i.e. the royal court), **el margen** *margin*, but **la margen** *river-bank*, **el orden** *order, sequence*, but **la orden** *order, command*

Plurals of nouns

The plural indicates more than one of a thing, and, as in English, it usually ends in **-s** in Spanish. The two most important ways of making Spanish plurals are:

- If a noun ends in a vowel (**a**, **e**, **i**, **o**, or **u**), add **-s**: **la casa-las casas** *house-houses*, **el hombre-los hombres** *man-men*, **el taxi-los taxis** *taxi-taxis*, **el tisú-los tisús** *tissue-tissues*.

- If a noun ends in a consonant (any letter except a vowel), add **-es**: **el corredor-los corredores** *runner-runners*, **el español-los españoles** *Spaniard-Spaniards*, **el inglés-los ingleses** *English person-English people*. Note: If the last consonant of a singular noun is **z**, the plural ends in **-ces**; **la voz-las voces** *voice-voices*.

   Exception: If the singular already ends in **-s** and the last vowel in the word does not have an accent, the plural is the same as the singular: **el martes-los martes** *Tuesday-Tuesdays*, **la crisis-las crisis** *crisis-crises*.

2 Adjectives

2.1 Simple adjectives

Spanish adjectives are different from English ones in two ways:

- They usually come after the noun: **un libro interesante** *an interesting book*, **el pan blanco** *white bread*, **las camisas azules** *blue shirts*. But some, like **grande** *big* or **pequeño** *small*, often come before the noun: **un gran escritor** *a great writer*, **un pequeño problema** *a small problem*.

- They agree with the noun or pronoun they describe. This means that if the noun is plural the adjective in Spanish must also be plural, and if the noun is feminine the adjective must also be feminine, if it has a variant feminine form

un hombre delgado	una mujer delgada	un coche nuevo	una camisa nueva
a thin man	*a thin woman*	*a new car*	*a new shirt*
hombres delgados	mujeres delgadas	tres coches nuevos	camisas nuevas
thin men	*thin women*	*three new cars*	*new shirts*

The following adjectives agree in both number and gender.

- Adjectives that end in **-o**. Add **-s** for the plural, change the **-o** to **-a** for the feminine: **el pañuelo blanco-los pañuelos blancos** *white handkerchief-white handkerchiefs*, **la bandera blanca-las banderas blancas** *white flag-white flags*.

- Adjectives that end in **-és**. Add **-a** for the feminine, and **-es** for the masculine plural. Note that the accent is no longer required, because the ending changes the stress pattern. **El vino francés-los vinos franceses** *French wine-French wines*, **la bebida francesa-las bebidas francesas** *French drink-French drinks*. Exceptions: **cortés** *polite* and **descortés** *impolite*. These have no separate feminine form, and the plural is **corteses/descorteses**.

- Most adjectives ending in **-n**. Add **-a** for the feminine, and **-es** for the masculine plural: **alemán-alemana-alemanes-alemanas** *German*. Exception: **marrón** (masculine and feminine) *brown*, plural **marrones** (masculine and feminine.)

■ **Español-española-españoles-españolas** *Spanish*, **andaluz-
andaluza-andaluces-andaluzas** *Andalusian*.

All adjectives ending in **-dor** add **-a** to show the feminine:
**tranquilizador-tranquilizadora-tranquilizadores-
tranquilizadoras** *soothing*.

The rest do not have a separate feminine form. Those ending in a
vowel (usually **-e**) simply add **-s** for the plural; those ending in anything
else add **-es**. If the singular ends in **-z**, the plural ends in **-ces**:

Singular masculine & fem.	Plural masculine & fem.	Meaning
grande	**grandes**	*big*
difícil	**difíciles**	*difficult*
superior	**superiores**	*superior/higher*
feroz	**feroces**	*ferocious*

2.2 Shortened adjectives

A few adjectives have a short form used immediately before a noun.
The most important are:

		Short form	When used
grande	*big*	**gran**	before all singular nouns
cualquiera	*any*	**cualquier**	before all singular nouns
bueno	*good*	**buen**	before singular masculine nouns
malo	*bad*	**mal**	before singular masculine nouns
primero	*first*	**primer**	before singular masculine nouns
tercero	*third*	**tercer**	before singular masculine nouns

Compare **un buen libro** *a good book* and **una buena respuesta** *a
good answer*.

2.3 Comparison of adjectives

The comparative form of the adjective (the -er form in English as in:
large, larger) is expressed in Spanish by putting **más** *more*, or **menos**
less in front of the adjective: **Luis es más/menos alto que ella** *Luis is
taller/less tall than her*.

To indicate the superlative form of the adjective (in English: *most…* or
least… of three or more things), put **el más/el menos** (or **la más/la
menos**, **los más/los menos**, **las más/las menos**, according to
gender) before the adjective:

pero ella es la más alta de todos *but she is the tallest of all.*

Note: the following two very common exceptions:

		singular	plural	
bueno/buen	*good*	**mejor**	**mejores**	*better/best*
malo/mal	*bad*	**peor**	**peores**	*worse/worst*

Example:

San Miguel es una de las mejores cervezas españolas
San Miguel is one of the best Spanish beers.

3 The definite and indefinite articles: el & la, un & una

These words vary in Spanish according to whether their noun is masculine or feminine, singular or plural:

	Singular	Plural	English equivalent
MASCULINE	**el**	**los**	the
FEMININE	**la**	**las**	

	Singular	Plural	
MASCULINE	**un**	**unos**	a *or* an
FEMININE	**una**	**unas**	

They are used in more or less the same way as their English equivalents:

el hombre compró una camisa y la mujer compró unos zapatos y un sombrero
the man bought a shirt, and the woman bought a pair of shoes and a hat.

Unos/unas means *some, a few* before plural nouns: **unos euros** *a few euros*, **unas muchachas** *some girls*. They mean *a pair of* before things that come in pairs like shoes or gloves (**unos guantes** = *a pair of gloves*).

But note the following points

■ Always use **el** and **un** before nouns that begin with **a-** or **ha-** when the **a** is stressed, even though these words may be feminine: **el agua** *water*, **el/un arma** *weapon*, **el hambre** *hunger*. These are all feminine nouns and their adjectives take feminine endings; their plurals are **las aguas**, **las armas**, etc.

- **De + el** (*of the*) is shortened to **del**: **el coche del profesor** *the teacher's car*. **A + el** (*to the*) is shortened to **al**: **doy el libro al profesor** *I give the book to the teacher*.

- Spanish uses the definite article for nouns that refer to things in general: *doctors say apples are good for children* means doctors, apples, and children in general. In Spanish this is: **los médicos dicen que las manzanas son buenas para los niños**. In the same way *el* **amor** = *love*, *la* **libertad** = *freedom*, *la* **justicia** = *justice*.

- The indefinite article **un/una** is not used in Spanish before professions or occupations: **es profesora** = *she is a teacher*, **soy estudiante** = *I am a student*.

---

4 Demonstratives

Demonstrative adjectives and pronouns are used to point out people and things. In Spanish the words for *this* and *that*, *this one* and *that one* must agree in number and gender with the following noun. Note that in Spanish there are two words for *that*, **ese/esa**, **aquel/aquella**. **aquel/aquella** refers to something distant or relatively distant from the speaker:

	Singular	Plural	
MASCULINE	**este**	**estos**	*this/these* or *this one/these ones*
FEMININE	**esta**	**estas**	
MASCULINE	**ese**	**esos**	*that/those* or *that one/those ones*
FEMININE	**esa**	**esas**	
MASCULINE	**aquel**	**aquellos**	*that/those over there* or *that one/*
FEMININE	**aquella**	**aquellas**	*those ones over there*

- When these words are used as pronouns, i.e. to mean *this one* or *that one*, they are usually written with an accent. **¿ves estos dos coches? éste es amarillo y ése es rojo** *do you see these two cars? this one is yellow and that one is red*. However, the Spanish *Real Academia de la Lengua* (Royal Academy of the (Spanish) Language) has ruled that these accents are no longer necessary, so follow your course book or your teacher's advice on this point.

- When these words do not refer to any noun in particular, a genderless form must be used, **esto**, **eso**, or **aquello**: **esto es**

terrible *this is terrible*, **no quiero hablar de eso** *I don't want to talk about that*. (**éste es terrible** means *this one is terrible* and would refer to something masculine. **no quiero hablar de ésa** means *I don't want to talk about that girl/woman* or some other feminine noun.)

5 Possessives

5.1 Possessive Adjectives

In Spanish the possessive adjectives (= my, your, his, her, our, their) agree in number with the thing possessed, not with the person that possesses it. Examples: **mi mano** *my hand* and **mis manos** *my hands*, **tu libro** *your book* and **tus libros** *your books*. Only **nuestro** and **vuestro** have special feminine forms: **nuestra casa** *our house*, **vuestras amigas** *your female friends*.

Note: Spanish has no separate words for *his*, *her*, or *their*: **su/sus** cover all these meanings:

Singular	Plural	
mi	mis	*my*
tu	tus	*your* (when speaking to a friend or relative)
su	sus	*his/her/their/your* (use **su** for *your* when using the **usted** form)
nuestro	nuestros	*our* (before masculine nouns)
nuestra	nuestras	*our* (before feminine nouns)
vuestro	vuestros	*your* (before masculine nouns)
vuestra	vuestras	*your* (before feminine nouns)

- **Vuestro** is used in Spain when speaking to more than one friend or relative. Latin Americans never use **vuestro** and always use **su** for *your* when speaking to more than one person.

- Spanish does not use these words with parts of the body or clothes.

 levanta la mano *put up your hand*
 ponte la camisa *put on your shirt*.

5.2 Possessive Pronouns

In Spanish the possessive pronouns (= mine, your, his, hers, ours, theirs) agree in gender and number with the noun that they refer to:

MASC.	**mío**	**míos**	*mine*
FEM.	**mía**	**mías**	
MASC.	**tuyo**	**tuyos**	*yours* (familiar form)
FEM.	**tuya**	**tuyas**	
MASC.	**suyo**	**suyos**	*his/hers/theirs/yours* (polite form)
FEM.	**suya**	**suyas**	
MASC.	**nuestro**	**nuestros**	*ours*
FEM.	**nuestra**	**nuestras**	
MASC.	**vuestro**	**vuestros**	*yours*
FEM.	**vuestra**	**vuestras**	

- **Vuestro** is used in Spain when speaking informally to more than one person. Latin Americans never use **vuestro** and always use **su** for *your* when speaking to more than one person.

- Examples: **este abrigo es mío/tuyo** *this coat is mine/yours*, **estas llaves son suyas** *these keys are his/hers/yours/theirs*, **esta dirección es nuestra** *this address is ours*. After a preposition (see page 1031) the article **el** or **la** must be used: **no vamos en tu coche**, **vamos en *el* mío** *we're not going in your car, we're going in mine*.

6 Personal pronouns

6.1 Me, you, it, us etc

Personal pronouns replace nouns, as in *'John saw Jill and John spoke to Jill'*. We normally say: *John saw Jill and he spoke to her. He* and *her* are the personal pronouns. The most important Spanish personal pronouns are the ones used to translate *me, him, her, us, them* in sentences like *John saw me, Anne bought it, Jenny met them*. These are the 'direct object pronouns' and they stand for the person or thing to whom something is done or happens:

me *me*
te *you* (familiar form)
lo *him, you* (male polite form), or *it*
la *her, you* (female polite form), or *it*

nos *us*
os *you* (familiar form)
los *them* (masculine), or *you* (male polite form)
las *them* (feminine), or *you* (female polite form)

- Note: in Spain, **le** is used for *him/you* (male) instead of **lo**, but **lo** must be used for *it* when it refers to a masculine thing like a book (**el libro**). Latin Americans use only **lo**. Both forms are considered correct, so follow your teacher or course book on this point.

- **Os** is not used in Latin America. Latin Americans say **los** for males, **las** for females.

- Personal pronouns come directly before verbs: **me ve** *he/she sees me*, **los veo** *I see them*. However, they are joined to the end of infinitives, gerunds, and imperatives (see below): **quiero verla** *I want to see her*, **estoy haciéndolo** *I'm doing it*, **cómpralo** *buy it*.

6.2 To me, to you, to him, etc

The same forms as above are used: **me da cien euros** *he gives 100 euros to me*, **te manda una carta** *he sends a letter to you*, **nos dicen todo** *they tell everything to us*. These forms are the 'indirect object pronouns'.

Note: There are two indirect object forms, **le** and **les**. **Le** means *to him, to her,* or *to you* (speaking formally). **Les** means *to them* and also *to you* when speaking formally: *le dije I said to him* or *to her or to you* (one person), **les dije** *I said to them* or *to you* (two or more people).

6.3 Order of pronouns

These pronouns can be combined, but the order is indirect object first, then direct object, i.e.

> **me** or **te** or **nos** or **os** first   then **lo**, **la**, **los**, or **las**

Examples: **me lo dan** *they give it to me*, **te lo dicen** *they say it to you*, **nos los mandan** *they send them to us*.

- The rule of two L's. It is an important rule of Spanish that when **le** or **les** is followed by **lo**, **la**, **los**, or **las**, the **le** or **les** becomes **se**. In other words, two pronouns beginning with L can never stand side-by-side: **se lo doy** *I give it to him/to her/to you*, not 'le lo doy'.

6.4 Subject pronouns

The equivalents of *I, you, he, she, we, they* exist in Spanish, but are not often used, because they are explicit in verb endings: **hablo** already means *I speak*, **vas** means *you go*, **compramos** means *we buy*. In nearly all situations the use of the personal pronouns as in, **yo hablo**,

tú vas, **nosotros compramos**, is to be avoided, because they are unnecessary. But they are needed sometimes, and their forms are as follows:

yo *I*	**nosotros** (males) *we*,
	nosotras (females) *we*
tú *you* (familiar form)	**vosotros** (to two or more males) *you*,
	vosotras (two or more females) *you*
usted *you* (formal form)	**ustedes** *you* (formal form)
él *he*	**ellos** *they* (males)
ella *she*	**ellas** *they* (females)

■ These words are used: (a) to contrast one person with another: **yo trabajo en casa y ella va a la oficina** *I work at home and she goes to the office*.
(b) when there is no following verb: —**¿quién lo hizo?** —**Yo** *'Who did it?' 'I did.'*

■ **Vosotros** and **vosotras** are not used in Latin America, where they always say **ustedes** to two or more persons.

■ **Tú** (note the accent) and **vosotros** or **vosotras** are the familiar forms used for people you know well (and anyone of your own age group if you are young), relatives, animals, and children. Nowadays Spaniards use them more and more even to complete strangers as a way of being friendly, but you must use **usted**, **ustedes** to people you do not know well, strangers, officials, policemen, etc.

■ **Usted** and **ustedes** are followed by third-person verb forms (i.e. the forms used for *he* and *they*): **usted habla** = *you speak*, **ustedes hablan** *you* (more than one) *speak*.

6.5 *mí* and *ti*

These are forms meaning *me* and *you* (familiar form) that are used after certain prepositions, e.g. after **de** *of/about*, **contra** *against*, **para** *for*, **por** *because of/on behalf of*, **sin** *without*: **hablamos de ti** *we're talking about you*, **esto es para mí** *this is for me*.

Note: When **con** + **mí** or **con** + **ti** are used together, the words **conmigo** *with me*, and **contigo** *with you* (familiar form) must be used: **Miguel va conmigo** *Miguel is going with me*.

7 Hay: There is; there are

There is and *there are* are both **hay** in Spanish: **hay lobos en España** *there are wolves in Spain*, **no hay pan** *there is no bread*.

There was and *there were* are **había** (never habían): **había lobos en Inglaterra** *there were* (or *there used to be*) *wolves in England*. For completed events in the past Spanish uses **hubo**: **hubo una explosión/un accidente** *there was an explosion/accident*. *There will be* is **habrá**.

8 Ser & estar: to be

Spanish has two important verbs for the English *to be*: **ser** and **estar**. Both are irregular and their forms are given on pages 1012 and 1006 respectively.

8.1 Ser

Generally **ser** is used to convey the idea of inherent qualities and is used in the following situations: When stating the origin of someone or something:

Es de California.	*He's* or *She's* or *It's from California.*
Es americano.	*He's American.*

When stating the material from which something is made:

Es de plata.	*It's made of silver.*

When stating ownership:

Son de Alfonso.	*They belong to Alfonso.*

When describing someone's characteristics:

Es un señor muy simpático.	*He's a very nice man.*
Es muy aburrido.	*He's very boring.*

When stating one's occupation:

Es abogada.	*She's a lawyer.*
Es aduanero.	*He's a customs officer.*

When expressing identity:

Soy Juan Muñoz.	*I'm Juan Muñoz.*
¿Es usted la Señora Sánchez?	*Are you Mrs Sánchez?*

8.2 Estar

As a general rule **estar** is used in the following circumstances:
To indicate location:

Está en la esquina.	*It's on the corner.*
Están en el jardín.	*They're in the garden.*
Está de viaje.	*She's away on a trip.*

To indicate the condition or state something or someone is in:

Las sábanas estaban sucias.	*The sheets were dirty.*
Estaba enferma.	*She was ill.*
Estoy aburrido.	*I'm bored.*
Está enamorado de ella.	*He's in love with her.*
Estaba furiosa.	*She was furious.*
Estoy de muy buen humor.	*I'm in a very good mood.*

8.3 Exceptions and anomalies

Ser is used with the following adjectives: **rico** *rich, wealthy*;
pobre *poor*; **feliz** *happy*; **desgraciado** *unfortunate*.

Son muy ricos.	*They are very wealthy.*
Somos felices.	*We are happy.*

Marital status. Both verbs can be used in this context. **Ser** is used in
formal contexts regarding marital status:

¿Es usted casado o soltero?	*Are you married or single?*
Está casado con mi prima.	*He's married to my cousin.*
Mis padres están divorciados.	*My parents are divorced.*

Ser is used when specifying where an event takes place:

¿Dónde es la fiesta?	*Where is the party?*
La reunión es a las diez.	*The meeting is at ten.*

Ser is used when telling the time:

Es la una.	*It's one o'clock.*
Son las tres.	*It's three o'clock.*

Estar is used with **muerto** *dead* and **vivo** *alive*:

Ya estaba muerta.	*She was already dead.*
Aún está vivo.	*He's still alive.*

9 Question words: how, what, which, when etc

These are written with an accent:

¿cómo? *how?*	**¿cuánto?** *how much?, how many?*	**¿qué?** *what?*
¿cuál? *which?*	**¿de quién?** *whose?*	**¿quién?** *who?*
¿cuándo? *when?*	**¿por qué?** *why?*	

¿Cuál? and **¿quién?** become **¿cuáles?** and **¿quiénes?** when they refer to more than one thing or person: **¿quiénes son?** *who are they?*, **¿cuáles quieres?** *which ones do you want?* **¿Cuánto?** agrees in number and gender with what it refers to: **¿cuánto dinero?** *how much money?*, **¿cuántos clavos?** *how many nails?*, **¿cuántas chicas?** *how many girls?*

■ Note: the accented form is used in indirect questions, i.e. when there is no question mark in the sentence: **no sé cuál prefiero** *I don't know which I prefer.*

■ Note: the meaning of these words changes when no accent is used: **como** = *as* or *like* (**habla como un niño** = *he talks like a little boy*), **porque** (one word) = *because*, **que** = *that* as in **dice que está enfermo** *he says that he is ill.*

10 Prepositions

These are words placed before nouns and pronouns to link them to the meaning of the rest of the sentence. In general they are used in more or less the same way as their English equivalents except that:

■ **a** basically means *to*, not *at*, which is usually **en** in Spanish: **en la estación** = *in the station* or *at the station*. *At the bus-stop* is **en la parada de autobús**, *at the traffic-lights* is **en el semáforo**. **A** means *at* only when movement is involved, as in **tiró una flecha al blanco** *he fired an arrow at the target.*

■ **personal a**: The use of **a** before personal objects of verbs is very important in Spanish. Note carefully the difference between these two sentences: **vi tu casa** *I saw your house*, and **vi a tu madre** *I* *saw your mother*. The **a** is necessary in the second example because the thing seen was a human being. So: **no conozco a María** *I don't know María* and **admiro al profesor** *I admire the teacher*, but **no conozco la ciudad** *I don't know the city*.

■ **para** and **por**: **para** means *for*, as in **este dinero es para ti** *this money is for you*. **Por** means, among other things, *because of*: **lo hago por amor, no por dinero** *I do it for love not for money* (it really means *because of love, because of money*), **lo hice para ti** = *I made it for you*, **lo hice por ti** = *I did it because of you*. **Para** and **por** have many shades of meaning, which are exemplified at their entries in the Spanish-English section of the dictionary.

---

11 Verbs

Transitive and intransitive verbs

Verbs may be transitive, i.e. they take a direct object, or they may be intransitive, i.e. they do not take a direct object. In the sentence: *he kicks the ball*, *kicks* is the transitive verb, and the direct object is *ball*. In the sentence: *he is sleeping,* the verb *is sleeping* is intransitive as there is no object. Spanish verbs are also transitive and intransitive and this information is shown by the abbreviations *vt* for 'verb transitive' and *vi* for 'verb intransitive'. It is important not to use transitive verbs intransitively and vice versa.

Reflexive verbs

These are verbs which have a personal pronoun object which is the same as the subject of the verb, e.g. *I shave myself*. Reflexive verbs are very common in Spanish and are listed in the dictionary with the infinitive followed by **se**, e.g. **lavarse** = *to wash oneself*. Note that in the third person, singular and plural, all genders, the reflexive pronoun is **se**. The following are the most important uses of reflexive verbs in Spanish.

■ If more than one human or animal is performing the action, it often shows that they are doing the action to one another: **se escriben mucho** *they write to one another a lot*.

■ Sometimes the reflexive form is the only form used, as in **me atrevo** *I dare*, or **te arrepientes** *you regret* (having done something).

Summary of Spanish grammar

■ If no human agent is involved, then the verb often has to be understood as a 'passive', as the translation shows: **este libro se publicó en Argentina** *this book was published in Argentina*, **se dijeron muchas cosas en la reunión** *many things were said in the meeting*.

■ The reflexive form of many verbs alters or intensifies the meaning of the basic verb: **ir** = *to go*, **irse** = *to go away*; **caer** = *to fall*, **caerse** = *to fall over*.

12 Tenses of verbs

12.1 The present tense

English has two ways of describing present actions: compare *I smoke*, which describes a habit, and *I'm smoking*, which shows that you are smoking right now. Spanish is very similar in this respect: **fumo** = *I smoke*, **estoy fumando** = *I am smoking* (right now). However, the second of these forms is used less than in English and the simple form, **fumo**, can be used for both meanings:

—¿Qué haces? —Fumo	*'What are you doing?' 'I'm smoking'*
Hablan mucho	*They talk a lot* or *They are talking a lot*
Vamos al cine	*We go to the movies* or *We're going to the movies*

See 12.6 for the use of the present tense with a future meaning.

12.2 The past tenses

In English there are several different verb forms that can be used to describe events that happened in the past. Compare *I did it*, *I have done it*, *I was doing it*, and *I had done it*. Spanish also has several ways of describing past events:

(a) The past simple tense (also referred to as the 'pretérito indefinido' in the verb tables): **hablé** *I spoke*, **llegaron** *they arrived*, **compraste** *you bought*.

(b) The imperfect tense (also referred to as the 'imperfecto' in the verb tables): **hablaba** *I was speaking* or *I used to speak*, **llegaban** *they were arriving* or *they used to arrive*, **comprabas** *you were buying* or *you used to buy*.

(c) The perfect tense: **he hablado** *I have spoken*, **han llegado** *they have arrived*, **has comprado** *you have bought*.

(d) The pluperfect tense: **había hablado** *I had spoken*, **habían llegado** *they had arrived*, **habías comprado** *you had bought*.

The two commonest past tenses in Spanish are the past simple and the imperfect.

12.3 The past simple and the imperfect tenses compared

The past simple is used to describe actions that took place *once* or a *specific number* of times in the past:

Ayer compré una nueva impresora	*Yesterday I bought a new printer*
Ganó la lotería	*He/She won the lottery*
Fue presidente durante tres años	*He was President for three years*
Estuve enfermo hace tres meses	*I was ill three months ago*

The imperfect is used to describe actions, events or processes that were not yet finished at the time we are talking about:

Miguel fumaba demasiado	*Miguel was smoking too much/ Miguel used to smoke too much*
Mi hermana iba mucho a la disco	*My sister used to go/was going to the disco a lot*
Roberto era alto y moreno	*Roberto was tall and dark*

If an event happened once or a specific number of times the past simple tense is used, regardless of how long it went on for: **los dinosaurios reinaron sobre la tierra durante millones de años** *dinosaurs reigned on earth for millions of years* (it only happened once), **ocurrió más de mil veces** *it happened more than a thousand times* (but it happened a specific number of times). The imperfect must be used when an event is described that was interrupted by another event: **yo dormía cuando empezó la tormenta** *I was sleeping when the storm started*.

12.4 The perfect tense

This tense is formed in Spanish with the present tense of **haber**, and the past participle of the verb, which in Spanish usually ends with **-ado**, **-ido**, or **-isto**, see verb tables pages 1003–1020. As a rule, whenever you say '*I have been*', '*she has done*', '*we have seen*', etc. in English, you use the parallel tense in Spanish: **he sido, ha hecho, hemos visto**.

Nunca he bebido vodka	*I have never drunk vodka*
He estado tres veces en Chicago	*I've been in Chicago three times*
¿Has visto La guerra de las galaxias?	*Have you seen Star Wars?*

Many Latin Americans replace this tense by the past simple tense described earlier: **nunca bebí vodka, estuve tres veces en Chicago, ¿viste La guerra de las galaxias?** If your teacher is Latin American, imitate him or her on this point.

Note: If you study Peninsular Spanish you will notice a big difference between English and Spanish: the latter often uses the perfect tense for any event that has happened since midnight: **esta mañana me he duchado, he desayunado, he cogido el metro y he llegado aquí a las nueve** *this morning I had a shower, I had breakfast, I took the metro, and I got here at nine o'clock.*

12.5 The pluperfect tense

This is almost exactly equivalent to the English tense formed with *had*: *I had seen, they had eaten,* **había visto, habían comido**. It is used in both languages to show that an event finished before another past event happened: **mamá ya se había ido cuando llegué a casa** *mother had already gone when I got home,* **yo iba a mandarles una tarjeta, pero mi hermano ya lo había hecho** *I was going to send them a card, but my brother had already done it.*

12.6 The future

There are several ways in English and Spanish of talking about future events:

(a) *We're going to arrive tomorrow*	**Vamos a llegar mañana** (ir + infinitive)
(b) *We are arriving tomorrow*	**Llegamos mañana** (present tense)
(c) *We will arrive tomorrow*	**Llegaremos mañana** (future tense)

The first two are more or less the same in both languages. Model (c) involves learning the forms of the future tense, see **hablar** [A1], **meter**

[E1] and **partir** [I1] in the verb tables, and is normally used where English uses *will*. It is used above all in promises and forecasts as in **te pagaré el dinero mañana** *I will pay you the money tomorrow*, and **el viernes hará buen tiempo** *the weather will be fine on Friday*.

12.7 The conditional tense

This tense, whose forms are given in the Spanish verb tables at **hablar** [A1], **meter** [E1] and **partir** [I1], is used to talk of an event that *would* happen: **estarías más guapa con el pelo recogido** *you would be more attractive with your hair up*, **en ese caso te costaría menos** *in that case it would cost you less*.

12.8 The imperative

The imperative is used to give orders or to ask someone to do something. The forms of the verb used vary:

- When addressing one person using the familiar form of *you*, the imperative is formed by dropping the **-s** from the **tú** form of the present tense: **das** = *you give*, so *give* is **da**; similarly **hablas** > **habla** *speak*, **comes** > **come** *eat*. There are eight important exceptions:

decir *to say* **di**	**poner** *to put* **pon**	**tener** *to have* **ten**
hacer *to make* **haz**	**salir** *to go out* **sal**	**venir** *to come* **ven**
ir *to go* **ve**	**ser** *to be* **sé**	

- When addressing one person formally the **usted** form is used, which is the same as the *present subjunctive* form for *he/she*. To speak formally to more than one person the **ustedes** form is used, which is the *they* form of the present subjunctive. These forms are given in the Spanish verb tables, beginning on page 1003. Examples: **¡venga!** *come!*, **¡conteste!** *answer!*, **¡vengan!** (plural) *come!*, **¡contesten!** *answer!* (plural)

- In Spain, when talking informally to more than one person, the **vosotros** form of the imperative is used. This is formed by replacing the **-r** of the infinitive form (the form by which verbs are listed in dictionaries) by **-d**. There are no important exceptions: **¡venid!** *come!*, **¡contestad!** *answer!*, **¡dad!** *give!* This form is never used in Latin America, where the formal **ustedes** form is used instead.

- To tell someone not to do something, the present subjunctive of the

verb is used: **¡no vengas!** (**tú**), **¡no venga!** (**usted**), **¡no vengan!**
(**ustedes**), **¡no vengáis!** (**vosotros**). These all mean *don't come!*,
but the form varies in Spanish according to whether you are
speaking to one or more people and whether you are using the
informal or formal options.

■ If we need to add pronouns, for example to translate *give it to her*,
sell me them, these are added to the end of the imperative. In these
examples **lo** and **los** refer to a masculine noun like **libro**, **libros**
book(s). Note the accents:

familiar to 1 person	formal to to 1 person	to 2 + people	to 2+ people: (familiar Spain)
dámelo *= give it to me*	**démelo**	**dénmelo**	**dádmelo**
mándanoslos *= send them to us*	**mándenoslos**	**mándennoslos**	**mandádnoslos**

But if the order is negative (i.e. it has **no** in front of it), the pronouns
come before the present subjunctive of the verb:

no me lo des *= don't give it to me*	**no me lo dé**	**no me lo den**	**no me lo deis**

---

13 The gerund (-ando, -iendo forms of verbs)

This form of the Spanish verb always ends in **-ando** or **-iendo** and it
never changes. It is used:

■ With the verb **estar** to stress the fact that an action is actually going
on right now, or was in the middle of happening: **estoy comiendo**
I'm eating (right now), **estabas durmiendo** *you were* (in the middle
of) *sleeping*. It is never used for actions in the future: **voy a Madrid
mañana** *I'm going to Madrid tomorrow*.

■ To show that another action happens at the same time as the main
action: **entré silbando** *I went in whistling*, **María salió llorando
de la clase** *María came out of the classroom crying*.

14 The subjunctive

The subjunctive is very important in Spanish. The forms of the present subjunctive are given in the Spanish verb tables, beginning on page 1003. The present subjunctive is used:

■ To give negative orders, i.e. to tell someone *not* to do something: see section 12.8 on the imperative.

■ In a sentence consisting of a present-tense *negative verb* + **que** + *another verb*, the second verb is in the subjunctive: compare **creo que está enferma** *I think that she is ill* and **no creo que esté enferma** *I don't think that she is ill*.

■ After the present tense of verbs **querer** *want* or **esperar** *hope* + **que**: **quiero que vengas a mi casa** *I want you to come to my house*, **espero que ganes** *I hope you win*. But if the person doing the wanting is the same person that is going to perform the action of the second verb, the infinitive (**-r** form) must be used for the second verb: **quiero ir a mi casa** *I want to go to my house*, **espero ganar** *I hope I'll win/I hope to win*.

■ After emotional reactions followed by **que**: **es una pena que no trabajes más** *it's a shame that you don't work more*, **estoy muy contento de que no haya llovido** *I'm very pleased that it hasn't rained* (**haya** is the present subjunctive of **haber**).

■ After certain words, when the action following them still has not happened. The most important of these are **cuando** *when*, **en cuanto** or **apenas** *as soon as*: **te daré el dinero cuando llegues** *I'll give you the money when you arrive*, **te llamaré apenas encuentre mi agenda** *I'll ring you as soon as I find my diary*.

■ Always after these words: **antes de que** *before*, **para que** *in order to*, **sin que** *without*, **con tal de que** *provided that*: **llegaremos antes de que salga el tren** *we'll arrive before the train leaves*, **te doy el dinero con tal de que me lo devuelvas** *I'll give you the money provided that you give it back to me*.

spanish verbs

Regular verbs:

in -ar (e.g. **comprar**)
Present: compr|o, ~as, ~a, ~amos, ~áis, ~an
Future: comprar|é, ~ás, ~á, ~emos, ~éis, ~án
Imperfect: compr|aba, ~abas, ~aba, ~ábamos, ~abais, ~aban
Preterite: compr|é, ~aste, ~ó, ~amos, ~asteis, ~aron
Present subjunctive: compr|e, ~es, ~e, ~emos, ~éis, ~en
Imperfect subjunctive:
compr|ara, ~aras ~ara, ~áramos, ~arais, ~aran
compr|ase, ~ases, ~ase, ~ásemos, ~aseis, ~asen
Conditional: comprar|ía, ~ías, ~ía, ~íamos, ~íais, ~ían
Present participle: comprando
Past participle: comprado
Imperative: compra, comprad

in -er (e.g. **beber**)
Present: beb|o, ~es, ~e, ~emos, ~éis, ~en
Future: beber|é, ~ás, ~á, ~emos, ~éis, ~án
Imperfect: beb|ía, ~ías, ~ía, ~íamos, ~íais, ~ían
Preterite: beb|í, ~iste, ~ió, ~imos, ~isteis, ~ieron
Present subjunctive: beb|a, ~as, ~a, ~amos, ~áis, ~an
Imperfect subjunctive:
beb|iera, ~ieras, ~iera, ~iéramos, ~ierais, ~ieran
beb|iese, ~ieses, ~iese, ~iésemos, ~ieseis, ~iesen
Conditional: beber|ía, ~ías, ~ía, ~íamos, ~íais, ~ían
Present participle: bebiendo
Past participle: bebido
Imperative: bebe, bebed

in -ir (e.g. **vivir**)
Present: viv|o, ~es, ~e, ~imos, ~ís, ~en
Future: vivir|é, ~ás, ~á, ~emos, ~éis, ~án
Imperfect: viv|ía, ~ías, ~ía, ~íamos, ~íais, ~ían
Preterite: viv|í, ~iste, ~ió, ~imos, ~isteis, ~ieron
Present subjunctive: viv|a, ~as, ~a, ~amos, ~áis, ~an
Imperfect subjunctive:
viv|iera, ~ieras, ~iera, ~iéramos, ~ierais, ~ieran
viv|iese, ~ieses, ~iese, ~iésemos, ~ieseis, ~iesen
Conditional: vivir|ía, ~ías, ~ía, ~íamos, ~íais, ~ían
Present participle: viviendo
Past participle: vivido
Imperative: vive, vivid

Irregular verbs:

[1] cerrar
Present: cierro, cierras, cierra, cerramos, cerráis, cierran
Present subjunctive: cierre, cierres, cierre, cerremos, cerréis, cierren
Imperative: cierra, cerrad

[2] contar, mover
Present: cuento, cuentas, cuenta, contamos, contáis, cuentan
muevo, mueves, mueve, movemos, movéis, mueven
Present subjunctive: cuente, cuentes, cuente, contemos, contéis, cuenten
mueva, muevas, mueva, movamos, mováis, muevan
Imperative: cuenta, contad mueve, moved

[3] jugar
Present: juego, juegas, juega, jugamos, jugáis, juegan
Preterite: jugué, jugaste, jugó, jugamos, jugasteis, jugaron
Present subjunctive: juegue, juegues, juegue, juguemos, juguéis, jueguen

[4] sentir
Present: siento, sientes, siente, sentimos, sentís, sienten
Preterite: sentí, sentiste, sintió, sentimos, sentisteis, sintieron
Present subjunctive: sienta, sientas, sienta, sintamos, sintáis, sientan
Imperfect subjunctive:
sint|iera, ~ieras, ~iera, ~iéramos, ~ierais, ~ieran
sint|iese, ~ieses, ~iese, ~iésemos, ~ieseis, ~iesen

Present participle: sintiendo
Imperative: siente, sentid

[5] pedir
Present: pido, pides, pide, pedimos, pedís, piden
Preterite: pedí, pediste, pidió, pedimos, pedisteis, pidieron
Present subjunctive: pid|a, ~as, ~a, ~amos, ~áis, ~an
Imperfect subjunctive:
pid|iera, ~ieras, ~iera, ~iéramos, ~ierais, ~ieran
pid|iese, ~ieses, ~iese, ~iésemos, ~ieseis, ~iesen
Present participle: pidiendo
Imperative: pide, pedid

[6] dormir
Present: duermo, duermes, duerme, dormimos, dormís, duermen
Preterite: dormí, dormiste, durmió, dormimos, dormisteis, durmieron
Present subjunctive: duerma, duermas, duerma, durmamos, durmáis, duerman
Imperfect subjunctive:
durm|iera, ~ieras, ~iera, ~iéramos, ~ierais, ~ieran
durm|iese, ~ieses, ~iese, ~iésemos, ~ieseis, ~iesen
Present participle: durmiendo
Imperative: duerme, dormid

[7] dedicar
Preterite: dediqué, dedicaste, dedicó, dedicamos, dedicasteis, dedicaron
Present subjunctive: dediqu|e, ~es, ~e, ~emos, ~éis, ~en

[8] delinquir
Present: delinco, delinques,

delinque, delinquimos, delinquís,
delinquen
Present subjunctive: delinc|a, ~as,
~a, ~amos, ~áis, ~an

[9] vencer, esparcir
Present: venzo, vences, vence,
vencemos, vencéis, vencen
esparzo, esparces, esparce,
esparcimos, esparcís, esparcen
Present subjunctive:
venz|a, ~as, ~a, ~amos, ~áis, ~an
esparz|a, ~as, ~a, ~amos, ~áis, ~an

[10] rechazar
Preterite: rechacé, rechazaste,
rechazó, rechazamos, rechazasteis,
rechazaron
Present subjunctive: rechac|e, ~es,
~e, ~emos, ~éis, ~en

[11] conocer, lucir
Present: conozco, conoces, conoce,
conocemos, conocéis, conocen
luzco, luces, luce, lucimos, lucís,
lucen
Present subjunctive:
conozc|a, ~as, ~a, ~amos, ~áis,
~an
luzc|a, ~as, ~a, ~amos, ~áis, ~an

[12] pagar
Preterite: pagué, pagaste, pagó,
pagamos, pagasteis, pagaron
Present subjunctive: pagu|e, ~es,
~e, ~emos, ~éis, ~en

[13] distinguir
Present: distingo, distingues,
distingue, distinguimos, distinguís,
distinguen

Present subjunctive: disting|a, ~as,
~a, ~amos, ~áis, ~an

[14] acoger, afligir
Present: acojo, acoges, acoge,
acogemos, acogéis, acogen
aflijo, afliges, aflige, afligimos,
afligís, afligen
Present subjunctive:
acoj|a, ~as, ~a, ~amos, ~áis, ~an
aflij|a, ~as, ~a, ~amos, ~áis, ~an

[15] averiguar
Preterite: averigüé, averiguaste,
averiguó, averiguamos,
averiguasteis, averiguaron
Present subjunctive: averigü|e, ~es,
~e, ~emos, ~éis, ~en

[16] agorar
Present: agüero, agüeras, agüera,
agoramos, agoráis, agüeran
Present subjunctive: agüere,
agüeres, agüere, agoremos,
agoréis, agüeren
Imperative: agüera, agorad

[17] huir
Present: huyo, huyes, huye, huimos,
huís, huyen
Preterite: huí, huiste, huyó, huimos,
huisteis, huyeron
Present subjunctive: huy|a, ~as, ~a,
~amos, ~áis, ~an
Imperfect subjunctive:
huy|era, ~eras, ~era, ~éramos,
~erais, ~eran
huy|ese, ~eses, ~ese, ~ésemos,
~eseis, ~esen
Present participle: huyendo
Imperative: huye, huid

[18] creer
Preterite: creí, creíste, creyó, creímos, creísteis, creyeron
Imperfect subjunctive:
crey|era, ~eras, ~era, ~éramos, ~erais, ~eran
crey|ese, ~eses, ~ese, ~ésemos, ~eseis, ~esen
Present participle: creyendo
Past participle: creído

[19] argüir
Present: arguyo, arguyes, arguye, argüimos, argüís, arguyen
Preterite: argüí, argüiste, arguyó, argüimos, argüisteis, arguyeron
Present subjunctive: arguy|a, ~as, ~a, ~amos, ~áis, ~an
Imperfect subjunctive:
arguy|era, ~eras, ~era, ~éramos, ~erais, ~eran
arguy|ese, ~eses, ~ese, ~ésemos, ~eseis, ~esen
Present participle: arguyendo
Imperative: arguye, argüid

[20] vaciar
Present: vacío, vacías, vacía, vaciamos, vaciáis, vacían
Present subjunctive: vacíe, vacíes, vacíe, vaciemos, vaciéis, vacíen
Imperative: vacía, vaciad

[21] acentuar
Present: acentúo, acentúas, acentúa, acentuamos, acentuáis, acentúan
Present subjunctive: acentúe, acentúes, acentúe, acentuemos, acentuéis, acentúen
Imperative: acentúa, acentuad

[22] atañer, engullir
Preterite:
atañ|í, ~iste, ~ó, ~imos, ~isteis, ~eron
engull|í ~iste, ~ó, ~imos, ~isteis, ~eron
Imperfect subjunctive:
atañ|era, ~eras, ~era, ~éramos, ~erais, ~eran
atañ|ese, ~eses, ~ese, ~ésemos, ~eseis, ~esen
engull|era, ~eras, ~era, ~éramos, ~erais, ~eran
engull|ese, ~eses, ~ese, ~ésemos, ~eseis, ~esen
Present participle: atañendo
engullendo

[23] aislar, aullar
Present: aíslo, aíslas, aísla, aislamos, aisláis, aíslan
aúllo, aúllas, aúlla, aullamos aulláis, aúllan
Present subjunctive: aísle, aísles, aísle, aislemos, aisléis, aíslen
aúlle, aúlles, aúlle, aullemos, aulléis, aúllen
Imperative: aísla, aislad
aúlla, aullad

[24] abolir
Present: abolimos, abolís
Present subjunctive: not used
Imperative: abolid

[25] andar
Preterite: anduv|e, ~iste, ~o, ~imos, ~isteis, ~ieron
Imperfect subjunctive:
anduv|iera, ~ieras, ~iera, ~iéramos, ~ierais, ~ieran
anduv|iese, ~ieses, ~iese, ~iésemos, ~ieseis, ~iesen

[26] dar
Present: doy, das, da, damos, dais, dan
Preterite: di, diste, dio, dimos, disteis, dieron
Present subjunctive: dé, des, dé, demos, deis, den
Imperfect subjunctive: diera, dieras, diera, diéramos, dierais, dieran
diese, dieses, diese, diésemos, dieseis, diesen

[27] estar
Present: estoy, estás, está, estamos, estáis, están
Preterite: estuv|e, ~iste, ~o, ~imos, ~isteis, ~leron
Present subjunctive: esté, estés, esté, estemos, estéis, estén
Imperfect subjunctive:
estuv|iera, ~ieras, ~iera, ~iéramos, ~ierais, ~ieran
estuv|iese, ~ieses, ~iese, ~iésemos, ~ieseis, ~iesen
Imperativo: está, estad

[28] caber
Present: quepo, cabes, cabe, cabemos, cabéis, caben
Future: cabr|é, ~ás, ~á, ~emos, ~éis, ~án
Preterite: cup|e, ~iste, ~o, ~imos, ~isteis, ~ieron
Present subjunctive: quep|a, ~as, ~a, ~amos, ~áis, ~an
Imperfect subjunctive:
cup|iera, ~ieras, ~iera, ~iéramos, ~ierais, ~ieran
cup|iese, ~ieses, ~iese, ~iésemos, ~ieseis, ~iesen
Conditional: cabr|ía, ~ías, ~ía, ~íamos, ~íais, ~ían

[29] caer
Present: caigo, caes, cae, caemos, caéis, caen
Preterite: caí, caiste, cayó, caímos, caísteis, cayeron
Present subjunctive: caig|a, ~as, ~a, ~amos, ~áis, ~an
Imperfect subjunctive:
cay|era, ~eras, ~era, ~éramos, ~erais, ~eran
cay|ese, ~eses, ~ese, ~ésemos, ~eseis, ~esen
Present participle: cayendo
Past participle: caido

[30] haber
Present: he, has, ha, hemos, habéis, han
Future: habr|é ~ás, ~á, ~emos, ~éis, ~án
Preterite: hub|e, ~iste, ~o, ~imos, ~isteis, ~ieron
Present subjunctive: hay|a, ~as, ~a, ~amos, ~áis, ~an
Imperfect subjunctive:
hub|iera, ~ieras, ~iera, ~iéramos, ~ierais, ~ieran
hub|iese, ~ieses, ~iese, ~iésemos, ~ieseis, ~iesen
Conditional: habr|ía, ~ías, ~ía, ~íamos, ~íais, ~ían
Imperative: he, habed

[31] hacer
Present: hago, haces, hace, hacemos, hacéis, hacen
Future: har|é, ~ás, ~á, ~emos, ~éis, ~án
Preterite: hice, hiciste, hizo, hicimos, hicisteis, hicieron
Present subjunctive: hag|a, ~as, ~a, ~amos, ~áis, ~an

Spanish verbs

Imperfect subjunctive:
hic|iera, ~ieras, ~iera, ~iéramos,
~ierais, ~ieran
hic|iese, ~ieses, ~iese, ~iésemos,
~ieseis, ~iesen
Conditional: har|ía, ~ías, ~ía,
~íamos, ~íais, ~ían
Past participle: hecho
Imperative: haz, haced

[32] placer

Present subjunctive: plazca
Imperfect subjunctive: placiera,
placiese

[33] poder

Present: puedo, puedes, puede,
podemos, podéis, pueden
Future: podr|é, ~ás, ~á, ~emos, ~éis,
~án
Preterite: pud|e, ~iste, ~o, ~imos,
~isteis, ~ieron
Present subjunctive: pueda,
puedas, pueda, podamos, podáis,
puedan
Imperfect subjunctive:
pud|iera, ~ieras, ~iera, ~iéramos,
~ierais, ~ieran
pud|iese, ~ieses, ~iese, ~iésemos,
~ieseis, ~iesen
Conditional: podr|ía, ~ías, ~ía,
~íamos, ~íais, ~ían
Past participle: pudiendo

[34] poner

Present: pongo, pones, pone,
ponemos, ponéis, ponen
Future: pondr|é, ~ás, ~á, ~emos,
~éis, ~án
Preterite: pus|e, ~iste, ~o, ~imos,
~isteis, ~ieron
Present subjunctive: pong|a, ~as,
~a, ~amos, ~áis, ~an

Imperfect subjunctive:
pus|iera, ~ieras, ~iera, ~iéramos,
~ierais, ~ieran
pus|iese, ~ieses, ~iese, ~iésemos,
~ieseis, ~iesen
Conditional: pondr|ía, ~ías, ~ía,
~íamos, ~íais, ~ían
Past participle: puesto
Imperative: pon, poned

[35] querer

Present: quiero, quieres, quiere,
queremos, queréis, quieren
Future: querr|é, ~ás, ~á, ~emos,
~éis, ~án
Preterite: quis|e, ~iste, ~o, ~imos,
~isteis, ~ieron
Present subjunctive: quiera, quieras,
quiera, queramos, queráis, quieran
Imperfect subjunctive:
quis|iera, ~ieras, ~iera, ~iéramos,
~ierais, ~ieran
quis|iese, ~ieses, ~iese, ~iésemos,
~ieseis, ~iesen
Conditional: querr|ía, ~ías, ~ía,
~íamos, ~íais, ~ían
Imperative: quiere, quered

[36] raer

Present: raigo/rayo, raes, rae,
raemos, raéis, raen
Preterite: raí, raíste, rayó, raímos,
raísteis, rayeron
Present subjunctive:
raig|a, ~as, ~a, ~amos, ~áis, ~an
ray|a, ~as, ~a, ~amos, ~áis, ~an
Imperfect subjunctive:
ray|era, ~eras, ~era, ~éramos,
~erais, ~eran
ray|ese, ~eses, ~ese, ~ésemos,
~eseis, ~esen
Present participle: rayendo
Past participle: raído

Spanish verbs

[37] roer
Present: roo, roes, roe, roemos, roéis, roen
Preterite: roí, roíste, royó, roímos, roísteis, royeron
Present subjunctive: ro|a, ~as, ~a, ~amos, ~áis, ~an
Imperfect subjunctive:
roy|era, ~eras, ~era, ~éramos, ~erais, ~eran
roy|ese, ~eses, ~ese, ~ésemos, ~eseis, ~esen
Present participle: royendo
Past participle: roído

[38] saber
Present: sé, sabes, sabe, sabemos, sabéis, saben
Future: sabr|é, ~ás, ~á, ~emos, ~éis, ~án
Preterite: sup|e, ~iste, ~o, ~imos, ~isteis, ~ieron
Present subjunctive: sep|a, ~as, ~a, ~amos, ~áis, ~an
Imperfect subjunctive:
sup|iera, ~ieras, ~iera, ~iéramos, ~ierais, ~ieran
sup|iese, ~ieses, ~iese, ~iésemos, ~ieseis, ~iesen
Conditional: sabr|ía, ~ías, ~ía, ~íamos, ~íais, ~ían

[39] ser
Present: soy, eres, es, somos, sois, son
Imperfect: era, eras, era, éramos, erais, eran
Preterite: fui, fuiste, fue, fuimos, fuisteis, fueron
Present subjunctive: se|a, ~as, ~a, ~amos, ~áis, ~an
Imperfect subjunctive:
fu|era, ~eras, ~era, ~éramos, ~erais, ~eran
fu|ese, ~eses, ~ese, ~ésemos, ~eseis, ~esen
Imperative: sé, sed

[40] tener
Present: tengo, tienes, tiene, tenemos, tenéis, tienen
Future: tendr|é, ~ás, ~á, ~emos, ~éis, ~án
Preterite: tuv|e, ~iste, ~o, ~imos, ~isteis, ~ieron
Present subjunctive: teng|a, ~as, ~a, ~amos, ~áis, ~an
Imperfect subjunctive:
tuv|iera, ~ieras, ~iera, ~iéramos, ~ierais, ~ieran
tuv|iese, ~ieses, ~iese, ~iésemos, ~ieseis, ~iesen
Conditional: tendr|ía, ~ías, ~ía, ~íamos, ~íais, ~ían
Imperative: ten, tened

[41] traer
Present: traigo, traes, trae, traemos, traéis, traen
Preterite: traj|e, ~iste, ~o, ~imos, ~isteis, ~eron
Present subjunctive: traig|a, ~as, ~a, ~amos, ~áis, ~an
Imperfect subjunctive:
traj|era, ~eras, ~era, ~éramos, ~erais, ~eran
traj|ese, ~eses, ~ese, ~ésemos, ~eseis, ~esen
Present participle: trayendo
Past participle: traído

[42] valer
Present: valgo, vales, vale, valemos, valéis, valen
Future: vald|ré, ~ás, ~á, ~emos, ~éis, ~án

Present subjunctive: valg|a, ~as, ~a, ~amos ~áis, ~an
Conditional: vald|ría, ~ías, ~ía, ~íamos, ~íais, ~ían
Imperative: vale, valed

[43] ver

Present: veo, ves, ve,vemos, veis, ven
Imperfect: ve|ía, ~ías, ~ía, ~íamos, ~íais, ~ían
Preterite: vi, viste, vio, vimos, visteis, vieron
Present subjunctive: ve|a, ~as, ~a, ~amos, ~áis, ~an
Past participle: visto

[44] yacer

Present: yazco, yaces, yace, yacemos, yacéis, yacen
Present subjunctive: yazc|a, ~as, ~a, ~amos, ~áis, ~an
Imperative: yace, yaced

[45] asir

Present: asgo, ases, ase, asimos, asís, asen
Present subjunctive: asg|a, ~as, ~a, ~amos, ~áis, ~an

[46] decir

Present: digo, dices, dice, decimos, decís, dicen
Future: dir|é, ~ás, ~á, ~emos, ~éis, ~án
Preterite: dij|e, ~iste, ~o, ~imos, ~isteis, ~eron
Present subjunctive: dig|a, ~as, ~a, ~amos, ~áis, ~an
Imperfect subjunctive:
  dij|era, ~eras, ~era, ~éramos, ~erais,~eran
  dij|ese, ~eses, ~ese, ~ésemos,

~eseis, ~esen
Conditional: dir|ía, ~ías, ~ía, ~íamos, ~íais, ~ían
Present participle: dicho
Imperative: di, decid

[47] reducir

Present: reduzco, reduces, reduce, reducimos, reducís, reducen
Preterite: reduj|e, ~iste, ~o, ~imos, ~isteis, ~eron
Present subjunctive: reduzc|a, ~as, ~a, ~amos, ~áis, ~an
Imperfect subjunctive:
  reduj|era, ~eras, ~era, ~éramos, ~erais, ~eran
  reduj|ese, ~eses, ~ese, ~ésemos, ~eseis, ~esen

[48] erguir

Present: yergo, yergues, yergue, erguimos, erguís, yerguen
Preterite: erguí, erguiste, irguió, erguimos, erguisteis, irguieron
Present subjunctive: yerg|a, ~as, ~a, ~amos, ~áis, ~an
Imperfect subjunctive:
  irgu|iera, ~ieras, ~iera, ~iéramos, ~ierais, ~ieran
  irgu|iese, ~ieses, ~iese, ~iésemos, ~ieseis, ~iesen
Present participle: irguiendo
Imperative: yergue, erguid

[49] ir

Present: voy, vas, va, vamos, vais, van
Imperfect: iba, ibas, iba, íbamos, ibais, iban
Preterite: fui, fuiste, fue, fuimos, fuisteis, fueron
Present subjunctive: vay|a, ~as, ~a, ~amos, ~áis, ~an

Spanish verbs

Imperfect subjunctive:
fu|era, ~eras, ~era, ~éramos,
~erais, ~eran
fu|ese, ~eses, ~ese, ~ésemos,
~eseis, ~esen
Present participle: yendo
Imperative: ve, id

[50] oír
Present. oigo, oyes, oye, oímos, oís,
oyen
Preterite: oí, oíste, oyó, oímos,
oísteis, oyeron
Present subjunctive: oig|a, ~as, ~a,
~amos, ~áis, ~an
Imperfect subjunctive:
oy|era, ~eras, ~era, ~éramos,
~erais, ~eran
oy|ese, ~eses, ~ese, ~ésemos,
~eseis, ~esen
Present participle: oyendo
Past participle: oído
Imperative: oye, oid

[51] reír
Present: rió, ríes, ríe, reímos, reís,
ríen
Preterite: reí, reíste, rió, reímos,
reísteis, rieron
Present subjunctive: ría, rías, ría,
riamos, riáis, rían
Present participle: riendo
Past participle: reído
Imperative: ríe, reíd

[52] salir
Present: salgo, sales, sale, salimos,
salís, salen
Future: saldr|é, ~ás, ~á, ~emos, ~éis,
~án
Present subjunctive: salg|a, ~as, ~a,
~amos, ~áis, ~an

Conditional: saldr|ía, ~ías, ~ía,
~íamos, ~íais, ~ían
Imperative: sal, salid

[53] venir
Present: vengo, vienes, viene,
venimos, venís, vienen
Future: vendr|é, ~ás, ~á, ~emos,
~éis, ~án
Preterite: vin|e, ~iste, ~o, ~imos,
~isteis, ~ieron
Present subjunctive: veng|a, ~as,
~a, ~amos, ~áis, ~an
Imperfect subjunctive:
vin|iera, ~ieras, ~iera, ~iéramos,
~ierais, ~ieran
vin|iese, ~ieses, ~iese, ~iésemos,
~ieseis, ~iesen
Conditional: vendr|ía, ~ías, ~ía,
~íamos, ~íais, ~ían
Present participle: viniendo
Imperative: ven, venid